Population

Also by WILLIAM PETERSEN

Some Factors Influencing Postwar Emigration from the Netherlands (1952)

Planned Migration: The Social Determinants of the Dutch-Canadian Movement (1955)

American Social Patterns (1956; editor)

A Critical Survey of Several Forecasts of the Population of Colorado (1957)

University Adult Education: A Guide to Policy (1960; with Renee Petersen)

Social Controversy (1963; co-editor with David Matza)

The Realities of World Communism (1963; editor and contributor)

Nevada's Changing Population (1963; with Lionel L. Lewis)

The Politics of Population (1964, 1970)

Japanese Americans: Oppression and Success (1971)

Readings in Population (1972; editor)

POPULATION

THIRD EDITION

William Petersen

ROBERT LAZARUS PROFESSOR OF SOCIAL DEMOGRAPHY
THE OHIO STATE UNIVERSITY

Macmillan Publishing Co., Inc.
NEW YORK
Collier Macmillan Publishers
LONDON

Macmillan Publishing Co., Inc.
866 Third Avenue, New York, New York 10022

Collier-Macmillan Canada, Ltd.

Library of Congress Cataloging in Publication Data

Petersen, William.
  Population.

  Includes bibliographical references.
  1.   Population.
HB851.P46   1975   301.32   73–18768
ISBN 0–02–394880–9

Printing: 1 2 3 4 5 6 7 8   Year: 5 6 7 8 9 0

Preface

This edition, like the other two, is intended mainly for undergraduate sociology courses. Most students who enroll in a first course in demography see it as part of their liberal education, and this work stresses the links between population phenomena and their sociological, economic, historical, and biological contexts. The book is not an almanac; many up-to-date figures are given, but primarily to illustrate theses with numerical examples. Nor is it a professional manual; the tools of the discipline are taught not to train the technician but to inform the layman or beginner. For although population data are generally the most accurate and complete of any in the social sciences, they are also far less so than is generally supposed; a person totally ignorant of how a census is taken, for example, or of the effect of age structure on crime rates, is bound to misunderstand much in the world around him.

Any author of a book in sociology with some pretense to generality faces a dilemma. To write, without close attention to culture-bound specifics, about other social systems, markets, family structures, and so on, could easily become an exercise in half-disguised ethnocentrism. But to analyze in full even some of the social–cultural data relevant to so broad a subject as population could swamp the reader in minutiae. A compromise is difficult to realize, especially so in a volume that assumes no prior knowledge of the field. Whether I have succeeded in maintaining a balance between broad theory and topical exemplification, using each to reinforce the other, the reader will judge better than I; but it may help to elucidate how I have tried to resolve this dilemma. The book is divided into two parts, the first on the general determinants of population processes and the second on how these operate in primitive, preindustrial, and modern societies. To some degree, the division is thus between the two main theories generally used to analyze population trends, the culture-free Malthusian opposition between people and resources and, on the other hand, the culture-bound theory of the demographic transition.

The most obvious revisions from the second edition, published in 1969, have been to bring numerical examples up to date, using in particular the 1970 censuses of the United States and the Soviet Union. But much has happened in the interim apart from new population counts. The shift of demography from an analytical to a policy orientation, well under way in the 1960s, has continued.

I have tried to include the main theses of the ongoing debate about such issues as the relation of numbers to food, space, pollution, and so on, but have avoided the more frenetic spokesmen as both too numerous and generally too alien to professional competence. Some of my personal experiences contributed to the revision. For several years I was a member, jointly with Sociology, of a Department of Preventive Medicine, and this closer acquaintance with epidemiology is reflected in a number of ways. In 1973 I participated in an interdisciplinary course designed to give archeologists a better background for some of the techniques they use, and my reading for the lectures was used in the chapter on the population of prehistoric peoples. This edition is somewhat longer than the second, for I have not balanced the additions with nearly as many cuts.

Professor Richard Pipes was kind enough to read the chapter on the Soviet population and to correct some errors; I thank him most gratefully but do not hold him responsible for the product. In the vast amount of detailed work that goes into so long a book, I was assisted by two graduate students, Linda Gordon and Sharon Bleda. Their conscientious competence and diligence contributed substantially to the book, which is better for their participation.

WILLIAM PETERSEN

Columbus, Ohio

Contents

Part II
The Population of
Various Societal Types

POPULATION AS A
FIELD OF STUDY

1

Demography, or the systematic analysis of population phenomena, denotes a subject matter that impinges on our everyday life in a variety of ways, but that most persons are ill equipped to understand. We read that in underdeveloped areas the increase in numbers is outstripping the food supply; is this a correct appraisal, and are there means available to cope with the problem? We are told that the "marriage rate" has gone up; what is a marriage rate, and how adequate a measure is it of the formation of new families? The United States is becoming increasingly "urban"; what size of population is defined as an urban settlement, and what difference does living in towns make in the way that people behave? Our insurance broker informs us that the cost of insuring our life is not the same as it would have been a year before; what is a "life table," which gives the probability that a person of one or another age will die during the next year? The decision of our church to erect a new building across town from our home was based on an expert's prognosis that the population of that presently barren area would grow very fast and would moreover include a large proportion of the social class from which our church membership is drawn; how accurate are such forecasts likely to be?

The first reason, then, for studying demography is to attain an appreciably better understanding of the world in which we live. This essential part of a liberal education can conveniently be attained by focusing one's attention on what are aptly termed the vital processes.

Supplementing this most general reason for studying population is a second, more specific one that applies to those particularly interested in the analysis of society. One cannot put a society under a microscope; one cannot take an institution into a laboratory; one cannot photograph a social class. Some of the important techniques that have made possible the rapid advance in physical and natural sciences[1] are largely ruled out of sociology, and many of the central issues in methodology relate to the dilemmas that this contrast poses. How is

---

[1] This statement does not imply that we in the social disciplines should accept a naive view of how natural sciences advance. For a fascinating analysis specifically aimed at hyper-positivist sociologists, see Thomas S. Kuhn, "The Function of Measurement in Modern Physical Science," in Harry Woolf, editor, *Quantification: A History of the Meaning of Measurement in the Natural and Social Sciences* (Indianapolis: Bobbs-Merrill, 1961).

it possible to structure social data so that the analyst can try to use the same procedures as other sciences; or, in a more specific version of this question, how can one quantify social findings without falsifying them?

In demography this dilemma is not so persistent a problem. Its data, unlike most that the sociologist analyzes, are assembled by the government, and at least in the Western world this means that they constitute the most complete and the longest series available on almost any subject. It also means that the collection of the data has the authority of the state behind it; and, although no questionnaire is ever answered completely accurately by all respondents, where vital statistics and the census have been in existence for a long time and have thus attained an almost automatic acceptance, this established legitimacy is as good a guarantee of reliability as one can hope for. Moreover, these excellent data pertain to the most significant happenings—literally life-and-death—and to events that often constitute natural units. It is not necessary to convert births or deaths into a form amenable to mathematical analysis; one begins by counting them and proceeds by comparing the fertility or mortality of various sectors of the population. On the other hand, the difficulties encountered in classifying a population by social class, urban–rural residence, or ethnic group are much closer to the usual methodological problems in the social sciences. There is no single entity that defines itself, as it were, to be "middle class," or a "city," or even "American Indians." Because all definitions of such categories are somewhat arbitrary, an analysis based on them varies according to how each is delimited. A beginning student in the field must thus learn to take full advantage of the unique quality of basic demographic data and to avoid a facile acceptance of any classificatory principle.

Demography, essentially a social science, in some respects borders on disciplines as diverse as biology, mathematics, and ethics. In order to demarcate this area of study, therefore, we must note its boundaries along several dimensions, and in doing so we will also indicate more fully than in the table of contents how the theme of the book is developed.

FORMAL DEMOGRAPHY VERSUS POPULATION ANALYSIS

Population growth can be analyzed with three different models:

1. It is a self-contained process; for example, a high (or low) fertility tends to generate an age structure with a large (or small) proportion of potential parents in the following generation.

2. Such self-propelled population processes, however, are controlled in their rate and especially in their ultimate limit by such other factors as natural resources, economic growth, social mobility, and family norms, all of which can be taken as independent variables that together determine the population.

3. On the other hand, population growth acts also as an independent variable, as a cause of change in the economy or in society—for instance, as a stimulus to business activity or as an impediment to development.

There is an important difference between the first model and the other two. Population growth as a self-contained process can be analyzed apart from the muddying influences of its social context and thus with greater precision and depth. The analysis of population trends in their total setting, on the other hand, involves every element of a culture or a social structure that may have a significant effect on population trends and, vice versa, every such element that may be influenced by a change in population size or composition. Thus, greater breadth is achieved by sacrificing narrow precision. It is convenient to label these two emphases in demography **formal demography**, i.e., the gathering, collating, statistical analysis, and technical presentation of population data, and **population analysis**, the systematic study of population trends and phenomena in relation to their social setting. The distinction relates in part to training. Formal demography demands mathematical skills, sometimes of a high order; population analysis is tied to the data and concepts of sociology, economics, or another of the social disciplines. The differentiation exists also in the fields for which these two types of training prepare one. Most of the professional practitioners of formal demography are employees of government bureaus or insurance companies, and the pressure (indeed, sometimes resisted) from such official or commercial positions is to avoid broad interpretations of the figures they compile. On the other hand, social scientists who recognize the importance of population trends and therefore include them among the social, economic, and historical processes they study typically do this without first acquiring the skills of an actuary. There is a legitimate division of labor here but also the necessity for communication. For example, a census director must be able to judge which of several possible questions would ultimately yield the most significant results in subsequent analyses, and a sociologist must know something of how population data are collected and compiled if he is to use them well.

This introduction to demography, it is hoped, will of itself make each person who uses it into an intelligent consumer of population analysis. This ability demands a limited competence, but a rare one; for just as a person barely able to read accepts as gospel anything in print, so the average product of the American school system, only just literate in mathematics, tends to be insufficiently critical of any numerical datum. A large portion of this book—all of Chapter 2 and sections of other chapters—is designed to instill both discrimination and appreciation of demographic statistics and techniques, the ability to see them for what they are, neither more nor less. Technical details and demographic tools are discussed when they are deemed useful in the skillful *interpretation* of population trends. For instance, the full description of the life table in Chapter 7 is designed to teach the minimum function of this indispensable tool, but anyone who wants to understand the full range of uses that actuaries make of it must seek guidance from other works. Or, as another example, the analysis of

Man's culture alters the biological balance with his environment. Land is reclaimed from the sea, in Holland (*Netherlands Information Service*), . . .

forecasts in Chapter 9, although it does not equip the reader to calculate projections himself, should enable him to understand better the meaning and probable accuracy of those prepared by others. In short, some of the techniques that a student would learn in a more advanced course are passed over in order to lay heavier stress on the significance of such techniques in the various social disciplines.

BIOLOGY VERSUS CULTURE

Man is born, he lives, and he dies. These are the natural dimensions of human life, as they are of all life. The immutable facts of birth and death designate man as part of nature, one animal species among the others. Like all other living things, man must meet certain physical needs to live, and he must reproduce his kind if the species is not to die out.

But while man is a part of the biological world, he is also set off from other species by a fundamental difference. The relation of all other living things to their physical environment is mainly passive. When it changes, they adapt to it principally at the ponderous rate of evolutionary change; once such an adaptation has been completed, the new body form that has evolved may prove to be overspecialized, leading to a limited life sphere or even to the extinction of the species, as of the great reptiles of an earlier geologic era. Man on the contrary takes a more active part than any other species in shaping his environment to suit his

... and from the desert, in Israel (*Jerry Cooke*).

needs. Instead of growing hooves for walking, he has made shoes of animal hides or of synthetics that did not exist in nature; instead of talons for grasping, he has iron pliers. Instead of the specialized parts of the body evolved by other animals for certain narrow functions, man has developed tools. In contradistinction to all other living beings, mankind has a full culture.

Defining the boundary between man as an animal and man as a member of a social group—that is to say, between the influence of biology and that of culture —has been a recurrent and vexatious problem in all of the social sciences. For example, psychologists who use the results of experiments on lower animals to increase our knowledge of "human nature" can be contrasted with social psychologists who study "personality" as it has developed in various specific cultural settings. Similarly, the sharpest split in anthropology, "the study of man and his works," has always been between the two terms of this definition, between the physical anthropologists, who study man as an animal, and the cultural or social anthropologists, who study him in the context of his works. Analysts of population have also had to cope with this distinction. The birth and death of an individual are biological events, but they take place in a social milieu. Population processes are the consequence of both natural laws and cultural conditions, but where does one leave off and the other begin?

Consider, for example, 19th-century birth rates, which in one Western country after another underwent a long-term decline. The many analysts who attempted to explain this new trend can be divided into two broad schools—those who held that the *physiological* ability of women to bear children was being impaired by the urban–industrial way of life, and those who held that this new *cultural* setting was creating the desire for smaller families and the means to satisfy it. This dispute has not really been settled to the full satisfaction of all demographers.

The two elements of population phenomena, factors general to all of mankind and those specific to one type of society, are analyzed respectively in the two parts of this work. The contrast is not always sharp, particularly when, as in many instances in the book, general theses are exemplified with data drawn from one or another particular culture. Yet without such a distinction to structure our thinking we can hardly escape the most common failing of social scientists— confusing the characteristic features of *our own* society with the necessary components of *every* society. All humans irrespective of their specific cultural setting are born both as a consequence of sexual intercourse and also into a family, a social unit of adults that cares for and protects the helpless infant and trains the child, but the norms by which families are formed vary greatly. All humans are subject to death from the same general causes—lack of food, disease, injury, and old age, but the average expectation of life differs over a considerable range from one societal type to another. Men are distinguished from women both by physiology and by cultural roles, which differ according to sex in various societies. Any population larger than a primitive band of food gatherers is structured into subpopulations according to some principle of internal classification, but how this differentiation is established depends very often on criteria specific to each culture.

The framework in which universal factors are usually assembled is "the" Malthusian theory that populations everywhere tend to grow faster than the resources on which they subsist.[2] The thesis would be more aptly formulated if for the ambiguous term *tend* one substituted *have the potential*. If any population were to breed up to its biological limit, it would indeed outpace its food supply. Sometimes this happens, and many die from starvation; sometimes, on the contrary, the level of fertility is kept well below the maximum possible. Which type of accommodation between man and his habitat predominates varies from one societal type to another. Part II of this book traces this demographic transition, the cultural evolution of mankind as it pertains to population trends.

As the very words "cultural evolution," however, still constitute almost an invitation to misunderstanding, it is important to distinguish the classical definition of this term from what it is intended to convey here. Anthropology in the middle of the 19th century was passing from an emphasis on the collection of data to their systematization. Partly as a result of the intellectual furor aroused by Darwin's *Origin of Species*, partly as a parallel expression of the zeitgeist of progress, this systematization usually took the form of a theory of cultural evolution. According to Edward B. Tylor, Lewis Henry Morgan, Herbert Spencer, and dozens of lesser figures, mankind evolved through a series of cultural stages, each one well defined by its technical culture, family type, social organization, religion, art, and so on. Morgan, for example, divided all of human history and prehistory into three main stages, which he termed Savagery, Barbarism, and Civilization (as we shall see, there is a partial parallel with the three stages of the demographic transition). The data he collated on peoples as widely separated as ancient Greeks and Romans, the natives of Australia and America, were structured largely in terms of the Iroquois, whom he knew by personal study. Thus, because the relatively advanced Polynesians lacked the bow and arrow, they were placed in the middle status of Savagery, or below the level of all North American tribes.[3] This example is typical of the egregious error of the 19th-century evolutionary theorists—their assumption that the level of technology determined directly and without exception all other cultural and social forms. The family, thus, was postulated to have begun with indiscriminate mating in a food-gathering horde, developed through matriarchy to polygyny in agricultural societies, and reached its moral apex in the monogamy of industrial Europe. Today no Western anthropologist would support either the substance or the ethical overtones of this "history" of the family, and as more and better ethnographic data were collected from various parts of the world, it became clear that the evolutionary schema was no more adequate in many of its other details.

---

[2] The ascription of this point of view to Malthus is correct but incomplete. As we shall see, he anticipated both Darwin's theory of natural selection and the Dumont–Banks model of social mobility (see pp. 528–530), so that in an important sense he is the progenitor both of the Malthusian theory as this is popularly understood and of the theory of the demographic transition.

[3] For a convenient summary and commentary, see Robert H. Lowie, *The History of Ethnological Theory* (New York: Rinehart, 1937), chap. 6.

By the beginning of the 20th century anthropologists were attacking the doctrine of cultural evolution itself. It was necessary to start fresh, to clean out all these fanciful theories and concentrate on building a solid empirical base. The most influential person in this movement, at least in the United States, was Franz Boas, who taught a whole generation of anthropologists and stamped them with his methodological and conceptual predilections.[4] Boas had important limitations, however, as well as great merit. The "Boas school," although performing a very necessary pruning job, ended by chopping at the very tree of the theory of culture change.

During the past several decades interest in the concept of cultural evolution has undergone a marked revival. The **unilinear** evolutionary scheme developed by Tylor, Morgan, and others was clearly wrong in many respects, but its essential outline is beyond question. The culture of the human species has indeed developed through a number of broad stages. No one doubts that hunting and gathering preceded the domestication of plants and animals, and that agriculture was a prerequisite to urban civilization wherever this developed. All of mankind, that is, has participated in **universal** evolution, but as a concept this is highly abstract and difficult to relate to actual cultures, rather than "culture." A third schema, **multilinear** evolution, is more empirical than deductive, and variation within societal types is no less emphasized than their general features.[5] By such an approach, an attempt is made to overcome the conceptual limitations both of unilinear evolutionists (culture stages relatively bare of empirical data) and of anti-evolutionists (a large number of ethnographic studies with no overall theory in which their interrelations can be indicated).

Multilinear evolution is a theoretical framework especially appropriate to a work on population. Whether the art or the religion or the language of advanced civilizations is "higher" than that of primitives is a moot, if not indeed a meaningless, question. That there is an enormous difference in population, however, is indisputable; and with respect to this variable, apart from short-term fluctuations, the change has been all in one direction. Even to term this consistent increase "progress" is not altogether ethnocentric, for the death control that has been attained by modern Western society, and to a lesser degree by other high civilizations, is a universal value.

THE THEORY OF THE DEMOGRAPHIC TRANSITION

As we can see from the rate of increase in the human species over the whole of the time that man has inhabited the earth, our present era is a demographic anomaly. The first higher primates evolved from an apelike predecessor some 2

[4] For a sympathetic appreciation of Boas, see Melville J. Herskovits, *Franz Boas: The Science of Man in the Making* (New York: Scribner, 1953).

[5] See Julian H. Steward, *Theory of Culture Change: The Methodology of Multilinear Evolution* (Urbana: University of Illinois Press, 1955), chap. 1.

or 2.5 million years ago, and the first specimens of *Homo sapiens* appeared about 100,000 years ago. Whether we discuss the human species in its present form or the human genus, which includes such extinct varieties as Neanderthal man, is of no importance here. In either case, we can postulate that the number started from a single pair and that it grew more or less steadily up to the date for which we have the earliest reliable estimate of the population of the world. That date is 1650, and at that time mankind totaled about 500 million. Three hundred years later, in 1950, the figure was more than 2,500 million, and in 1970 it was over 3,600 million. In the year 2000, according to a U.N. estimate, the world's population will be between a "low" of 5,300 million and a "high" of 6,800 million. These figures, enormous though they are, are based on an assumption that the world's present fertility will decline somewhat. If the birth rates of each age category remain constant, the world at the end of the century will have 7,400 million people, growing at an accelerating rate (United Nations 1966).

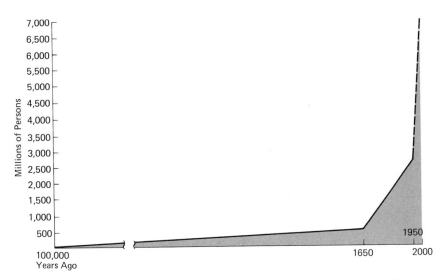

Figure 1-1.   A Schematic Representation of the Increase in the Human Species

The significance of these data can be seen more easily in Figure 1-1. It must be emphasized that this is a *schematic* representation; what little we know about the growth of particular areas before the modern era suggests an irregular alternation of periods of rapid increase with stagnation or decline. We have good reason to believe that the population of the world in 1650 was about 500 million and that it had never been larger than that at any earlier date, but there are no data to round out these statements. For well over 99 percent of the time since the human species first evolved, it grew slowly, fitfully. Then, during the remaining 1 percent, it increased fivefold; and the rate of increase in 1970 was about 2.0 percent per year, which would lead to another doubling in 35 years. In the physical sciences such a sudden acceleration is called an explosion, and demographers have adopted this metaphor to describe what is happening during our era—a population explosion.

The reason that the population of the world is increasing at an unprecedentedly high rate to unprecedented totals is no mystery; mortality has fallen sharply, and fertility has not. As originally formulated a generation ago, this demographic transition was conceived as taking place in three broad stages: (1) preindustrial societies, with high fertility and mortality and a consequent low natural increase; (2) societies in transition, with continuing high fertility but declining mortality and a consequent rapid natural increase; and (3) modern societies, with both fertility and mortality stabilized at a low level and a consequent more or less static population. Although some of its details have proved to be false and some of its implications misleading, in its simplest form the theory of the demographic transition is nevertheless one of the best documented generalizations in the social sciences. Duly amended and supplemented, it is one useful framework within which to organize an analysis of population.

Preindustrial Societies

In this type are included all cultures with little or no contact with modern Western technology and science, i.e., all cultures before that great transformation that we call the industrial revolution as well as those contemporary nonindustrial societies that have not been significantly influenced by the West. Seemingly, this is a catch-all category, with subclasses as diverse as prehistoric peoples, contemporary primitives, and twenty of the twenty-one civilizations that Arnold Toynbee demarcated in his *Study of History*. But, however varied in other respects, these cultures are similar at least in those features that shape their populations. In all of them people live no more than 35 or 40 years on the average, for as many, or almost as many, die in infancy and childhood as grow to maturity. Cultural values typically favor a high birth rate, without which the continuing existence of the society would be threatened.

In this book the population of preindustrial societies is analyzed in the two opening chapters of Part II, the first on primitive societies and the second on preindustrial civilizations.

Early Western Societies

The contrast between preindustrial and modern societies is one of the most familiar conceptual frameworks in sociology. It has become customary to use Ferdinand Tönnies's terms, **Gemeinschaft** and **Gesellschaft** (sometimes translated as Community and Society) to designate the two culture types not only as defined by him but also, more generally and approximately, as drawn by other social analysts. For, though the variety of terminology reflects some differences in meaning and especially in emphasis, there is also a large overlap among all the pairs,[6] as well as with the dichotomies rural versus urban and under-developed versus developed in their most general senses.

In a population analysis perhaps the most pertinent element of the polarity is that discussed in detail by Max Weber in his contrast between traditionalist and rational. In his words, **traditionalism** is "the belief in the everyday routine as an inviolable norm of conduct." "Domination that rests upon this basis, that is, upon piety for what actually, allegedly, or presumably has always existed," he termed "traditionalist authority." A **rational** pattern, on the other hand, denotes "the methodological attainment of a definitely given and practical end by means of an increasingly precise calculation of adequate means," or, on an abstract level, the "increasing theoretical mastery of reality by means of increasingly precise and abstract concepts."[7] The rational sector of culture, in short, includes any area of social life in which a realizable end is consciously sought by nonmystical means. The development of advanced civilizations from primitive societies has in large measure consisted in the extension of the area of rational action.[8] In the modern West in particular, the calculated choice between alternative acts on the basis of their probable consequences is a usual behavior pattern. In technology and commerce, two broad areas of life whose rational element is strong in many cultures, Western man has reached the ultimate point, scientific method and bookkeeping. And, what is more important in this context, rationality has spread from these to such other institutions as child-bearing, which in other cultures are typically regulated mainly by traditionalist norms.

Until a situation is seen in rational (i.e., instrumental) terms, no instrument is relevant, however effective it may be. The point can be illustrated by citing a health survey of an Iraqi village made by the inhabitants themselves. According to this self-estimate the state of health in the village was good: the incidence of many diseases was so high that they were not seen as abnormalities. All persons have two eyes, and most of them have trachoma; the difference was seen as one in degree, not in kind. Both two-eyedness and trachoma are part of "nature," and a person who knows this would not attempt either to create a third eye or to remove the inflammation from the two that are there. That such a community

[6] A list of only some of the most important examples in addition to Tönnies would include Henry Maine's society of status vs. society of contract, Weber's traditionalist vs. rational authority, Emile Durkheim's mechanical vs. organic solidarity, Robert MacIver's culture vs. civilization, Howard Becker's sacred vs. secular society, Robert Redfield's folk vs. urban society, David Riesman's tradition-directed vs. other-directed character.

[7] Max Weber, *Essays in Sociology*, edited and translated by H. H. Gerth and C. Wright Mills (New York: Oxford University Press, 1946), pp. 293–296.

[8] This is not meant to imply that there has been no change from more to less rational. In many preindustrial cultures marriages are arranged according to a careful reckoning of which potential mate would best serve family interests rather than by the more erratic dictates of romantic love, and a religious *quid pro quo* of so much sacrifice for so much benefit is less mystical than present-day Christianity.

lacks scientific medicine is obvious, but this cannot be supplied in the portable form of Western know-how. For, as the villagers define their situation, there is no problem to be solved, no sickness to be cured.

This distinction between the efficiency of an instrument and its relevance pertains more often to the control of fertility than of mortality. To analyze the causes of the secular decline in Western birth rates, it is necessary to consider not only the instrument (the invention of effective contraceptives) and the social environment (the conversion of an agrarian civilization into an urban–industrial one), but also the shift in typical attitudes that made these other factors operative. Children were no longer seen as facts of nature, as gifts of God, but rather as the consequence of acts that could be regulated, within limits, in order to bring about families of a larger or a smaller size. Once childbearing came to be so defined, in rational rather than natural terms, other circumstances could vary without affecting the fertility trend decisively.

In this book the principal analysis of the population transition is presented in two chapters, one mainly historical and the other mainly theoretical. The first concerns England in the late 18th and early 19th centuries, the birthplace of modern industry and the earliest and perhaps most thoroughly studied example of population change during such a social transformation. The second chapter, concerning the cities of industrial and underdeveloped societies, poses the question whether urbanization, a prime medium of modernization, has been essentially the same in the Western nations that achieved industrialization in the past as it is in the nations of Asia, Africa, and Latin America that have begun a somewhat similar process today.

When the theoretical reconstruction of history into three population types was first proposed, it was assumed that the demographic transition of the West would be followed in its essentials by the countries of the world currently undergoing industrialization. And indeed, one might ask, are not India and Egypt experiencing the same process that began in the English Midlands some two centuries ago? Is it not true that industrialism implies a high incidence of several important characteristics—not only nonagricultural employment but also, for instance, urban residence, literacy, and secularization—and that these will presumably also evolve in any developing society today? But social change is so much faster than in the past, and the contrast between the traditional style of life and the one that is replacing it is so much sharper, that it is misleading to perceive the process today as merely a continuation of 19th-century Western history. In Europe some of the features of modern society unfolded over a period of centuries. For example, the most specific element of industrialism, the introduction of technical innovations, is in part an expression of scientific method—that is, of a way of perceiving and understanding the world that was already well advanced at the time of the grand synthesis in Isaac Newton's *Principia* (1687). Because today's underdeveloped countries lack this long preparation for modernization, any attempt to predict the non-Western future from the Western past, as in the first statement of the demographic transition, is likely to be quite unsuccessful. Indeed, the shift in thinking from unilinear to multilinear evolution as a theoretical framework means precisely that to postulate a single type of transition, leading to a single type of modern society, is far too simple.

Modern Western Societies

Analysis of the original transitional type, designated as Early Western, is exemplified by the countries of Western Europe and some of its principal overseas extensions. They are mostly industrial; or, if their economies are based on agriculture, like those of Denmark or New Zealand, it is a rationalized agronomy rather than traditional peasant practice. They are mostly democratic or, at least, lack the full development of a totalitarian state. Rational—in Weber's sense of the word—death control was followed after a considerable interim by rational birth control, so that as a goal if not yet in actuality, babies are born only to parents who want them, and persons die, at least in peacetime, only of old age or accidents. These populations naturally comprise a major element of any general work on demography, because the countries are important and because the data available are excellent.

Underdeveloped Societies

To lump together countries as diverse as those in Latin America, Central Africa, the Near East, and Asia, passing over the great variety in historical and cultural background, is permissible only because of two overriding characteristics—the lack of modern industry and the endeavor to achieve parity with the Western nations. As the very designation "underdeveloped" suggests, today's nonindustrial societies take the "developed" countries as one of their standards. "Underdeveloped," like the analogous "underprivileged" as applied to individuals, implies an egalitarian norm; it includes both the fact of difference and the no less important fact that it is seen as unjust and remediable. It is generally not true of today's nonindustrial peoples, as it used to be true of their preindustrial partial counterparts, that most persons accept their lower level of life as their inevitable, immutable fate.

Whether the efforts to achieve parity with the industrial nations will succeed depends in part on the indigenous society and culture, but exactly what their influence is we do not know. Is it more relevant that India has an old and complex civilization, comparable in these respects with that of the West, or that one important element of this civilization is the pervasive caste system, which strongly impedes any shift in the social structure? Modernization means a greater transformation in Negro Africa than in India; but since the traditional society there, just because of the lower cultural level, is weaker, is it not therefore perhaps less resistant to change? Can underdeveloped areas that have acquired a European language and religion, as in Latin America, be regarded as halfway toward full modernization?

To all such questions we have no firm answers. Paradoxically, the more unprepared a country is, the more likely it is to be interested in rapid development; an area that has had least association with the West and thus perhaps the smallest benefit from its more efficient institutions may for that very reason be most strongly motivated to seek immediate and direct contact with industrial society. The relation then is in the form of a fantastic jump, with the most backward areas absorbing the most advanced elements of modern urban culture. Eskimos who have never seen a bicycle or automobile are quite familiar with airplanes. The potions of witchdoctors are replaced by the latest antibiotic. It is quite common to see Papuans walking along jungle trails listening to transistor radios. One of the largest steel plants in the world is in India. Countries like Russia and China, less developed economically and thus with a smaller proportion of industrial workers, have undergone the "proletarian" revolution that Marx predicted for the West. In short, the urban–industrial civilization, the most dynamic force in the world today, does not gradually seep into other societies but often splits their traditional forms asunder.

To analyze specifically the population trends that accompany modernization demands a certain simplification. But it is also true that population is a key question: the success of development programs depends on very many factors, but none is more crucial than whether the increased production leads to improved living or only to an increased number of persons existing at the same substandard level. Typically the measures to reduce mortality, introduced on a mass scale, resulted in precipitous falls in the death rates. But efforts to cut fertility, although partially successful in a few areas, have lagged far behind. The growth of numbers has been on a scale new in human history.

Totalitarian Societies

Just as it is useful to divide the transitional type into Early Western and Underdeveloped, so it adds considerably to our understanding if economically advanced societies are classified according to their style of government. In contrast to the laissez-faire West of the 19th century, states today intervene in various ways in trying to achieve demographic goals with respect to fertility (family subsidies, state birth-control or abortion centers); with respect to mortality (state support of medical and agricultural research, health insurance, genocide); and with respect to migration (immigration or emigration restrictions or subsidies; forced migration). Simply to relate population to the natural resources and unplanned economy is no longer adequate.

This is particularly so in totalitarian societies, where the processes of especially mortality and migration are significantly different from those typical in the West, because all institutions are essentially subordinated to the state and its ideological guide, the party. That such states constitute a different species of society is a commonplace among political scientists, but in most demographic analyses the differentiation is ignored. If totalitarian practices intrude too obviously on the demographer's consciousness, they sometimes define population phenomena so as to leave them out. For example, a high proportion of those who migrate today, especially within or from totalitarian countries, do so under one degree or another of coercion, but standard works usually omit all such migration from the concept. A generation that has witnessed the willful slaughter of millions of Jews is informed even in a work relating demography to politics that "the adoption of a policy to increase mortality, or to diminish efforts to increase longevity, is unthinkable" (Hauser 1960). Ethnocentrism, which used to create a view of the analysts' own society as supreme in all respects, now more often blinds them to those systematic differences that, in terms of our values, indicate the unique virtues of Western society.

In this book one chapter deals with the populations of totalitarian societies, the Soviet Union and Nazi Germany, as well as Communist China, which is an example of a combined underdeveloped–totalitarian type.

SUMMARY

Whether there are theories appropriate to demographic analysis is a moot question (Vance 1952; Gutman 1960). In fact, such conceptual models as exist are of two kinds. Some apply to populations anywhere, because of the transcultural qualities of the age structure, for instance, or of the interaction between humans and the plant and animal life on which they must subsist. Such theories are expounded and exemplified in Part I. But other population theories are specific to a particular time, place, and level of the economy. Part II of the book is arranged according to an amended version of the theory of the demographic transition, which is a useful framework in spite of the valid criticisms that can be made of the early formulations. The five societal types to be analyzed are summarized in Table 1-1.

Table 1-1.   Demographic and Social Characteristics of Five Types of Society

Type	Economy	Fertility	Mortality	Population Growth
I. Preindustrial	Primitive or agrarian	High	Fluctuating and high	Static to low
II. Early Western	Mixed	High	Falling	High
III. Modern Western	Urban-industrial	Controlled	Low	Indeterminate; often low
IV. Underdeveloped	Mixed	High	Falling rapidly to low	Very high
V. Totalitarian	Urban-industrial	Controlled	Controlled	Indeterminate; often fluctuates widely

The purpose of this text is to introduce students to the subject of demography. Some undoubtedly will go on with further study in the field, and a few may eventually become professional demographers. Even those who stop with this work will have been trained, it is hoped, as intelligent and discriminating consumers of population figures. The extended discussion of demographic concepts, data, and techniques is structured, first of all, to facilitate the correct *interpretation* of population trends, a quality useful both in itself and as preparation for more advanced work.

CITED REFERENCES AND SUGGESTIONS FOR FURTHER READING

There are two excellent short introductions to demography, by Wrong (1967) and Pressat (1970), either of which can be read almost at a sitting. A number of general works at more or less the introductory level are worth noting. Thompson and Lewis (1965) is the fifth edition of a standard text whose senior author was one of the most important demographers of the past generation. Thomlinson (1965) attempts more fully than Thompson–Lewis to assimilate demographic analysis with sociological themes. The works by Goldscheider (1971) and Matras (1973) are weighted toward their particular interests—respectively, the analysis of ethnicity and of ecological patterns; and they are worth consulting especially for these topics. Carr-Saunders (1964), an unchanged reprint of a work originally published in 1936, is obviously out of date in both its statistics and its obsessive concern with depopulation, but it remains a useful and interesting work. Of the three works on the population of the United States (Bogue 1959; Stockwell 1968; and Taeuber and Taeuber 1971), Stockwell is perhaps the most useful for the general reader, but Taeuber and Taeuber reflects the senior author's detailed and intimate acquaintance with the Bureau of the Census and its operations. Special note should be taken of Shryock and Siegel (1971), which in about 900 large pages covers the whole range of demography. It is both too detailed and in some respects too technical for the beginning student, but even he will find it useful as an occasional supplement to this text.

Among multi-authored works, *The Determinants and Consequences of Population Trends* of the United Nations (1953), though out of date (a new edition has been in process for several years), still represents a significant effort to bring together all that was known or surmised on the subject, with the virtues but also the faults of an anonymous work by an international agency. The two volumes edited by Spengler and Duncan (1956a and 1956b), though obviously also out of date, represent some of the best analyses of that time. The collection of articles edited by Hauser and Duncan (1959) suffers from undue repetition and certain gaps, yet constitutes one important inventory of demographic knowledge. That edited by Freedman (1964) is more popular but no less authoritative. Several recent anthologies (Nam 1968; Heer 1968; Kammeyer 1969) have been compiled with discernment. The book of readings edited by the author of this text (Petersen 1972) was designed specifically to supplement it.

Most of the books here listed include bibliographies of varying completeness and usefulness; an especially long list in several languages is given in United Nations (1953). The best annotated bibliography up to the date of its publication is Eldridge

(1959). Driver (1971) is a mammoth annotated guide to works on population policy, very broadly defined. These works can be usefully supplemented by *Population Index*, a bibliographic quarterly published by the Office of Population Research, Princeton University, and by Fuguitt (1964) for references to dissertations.

Sociological, economic, geographical, historical, and other journals often publish papers on population. There are three first-rate American journals more narrowly focused on the discipline, *Demography*, *Social Biology*, and the *Milbank Memorial Fund Quarterly* (now called *Health and Society*). These should be supplemented by *Population Studies*, published in London, and *Population*, a French-language journal published in Paris. At a more popular level one can recommend the *Population Bulletin*, issued by the Population Reference Bureau, Washington, D.C.

The list of works appended to each chapter includes all that were cited in the text. Books or articles especially recommended are marked with an asterisk.

BOGUE, DONALD J. 1959. *The Population of the United States.* New York: Free Press.

CARR-SAUNDERS, A. M. 1964. *World Population: Past Growth and Present Trends.* London: Cass.

DRIVER, EDWIN D. 1971. *World Population Policy: An Annotated Bibliography.* Lexington, Mass.: Lexington Books.

*ELDRIDGE, HOPE T. 1959. *The Materials of Demography: A Selected and Annotated Bibliography.* International Union for the Scientific Study of Population and Population Association of America. New York: Columbia University Press.

FREEDMAN, RONALD, editor. 1964. *Population: The Vital Revolution.* Garden City, N.Y.: Doubleday-Anchor.

FUGUITT, GLENN V. 1964. "Dissertations in Demography, 1933–1963." Madison: Department of Rural Sociology, University of Wisconsin. Mimeographed.

GOLDSCHEIDER, CALVIN. 1971. *Population, Modernization, and Social Structure.* Boston: Little, Brown.

GUTMAN, ROBERT. 1960. "In Defense of Population Theory," *American Sociological Review*, **25**, 325–333.

HAUSER, PHILIP M. 1960. "Demographic Dimensions of World Politics," *Science*, **131**, 1641–1647.

————, and OTIS DUDLEY DUNCAN, editors. 1959. *The Study of Population: An Inventory and Appraisal.* Chicago: University of Chicago Press.

HEER, DAVID M., editor. 1968. *Readings on Population.* Englewood Cliffs, N.J.: Prentice-Hall.

KAMMEYER, KENNETH C. W., editor. 1969. *Population Studies: Selected Essays and Research.* Chicago: Rand McNally.

MATRAS, JUDAH. 1973. *Populations and Societies.* Englewood Cliffs, N.J.: Prentice-Hall.

NAM, CHARLES B., editor. 1968. *Population and Society: A Textbook of Readings.* Boston: Houghton Mifflin.

*PETERSEN, WILLIAM, editor. 1972. *Readings in Population.* New York: Macmillan.

PRESSAT, ROLAND. 1970. *Population.* London: Watts.

*SHRYOCK, HENRY S., and JACOB S. SIEGEL. 1971. *The Methods and Materials of Demography*, 2 vol. Washington, D.C.: U.S. Bureau of the Census.

SPENGLER, JOSEPH J., and OTIS DUDLEY DUNCAN, editors. 1956a. *Demographic Analysis: Selected Readings.* New York: Free Press.

SPENGLER, JOSEPH J. and OTIS DUDLEY DUNCAN. 1956b. *Population Theory and Policy: Selected Readings*. New York: Free Press.

STOCKWELL, EDWARD G. 1968. *Population and People*. Chicago: Quadrangle.

TAEUBER, CONRAD, and IRENE B. TAEUBER. 1971. *People of the United States in the 20th Century*. Washington, D.C.: U.S. Government Printing Office.

THOMLINSON, RALPH. 1965. *Population Dynamics: Causes and Consequences of World Demographic Change*. New York: Random House.

THOMPSON, WARREN S., and DAVID T. LEWIS. 1965. *Population Problems*, 5th ed. New York: McGraw-Hill.

UNITED NATIONS. 1953. *The Determinants and Consequences of Population Trends*. Population Studies, no. 17. New York.

———. 1966. *World Population Prospects, as Assessed in 1963*. New York.

VANCE, RUPERT B. 1952. "Is Theory for Demographers?" *Social Forces*, 31, 9–13.

*WRONG, DENNIS H. 1967. *Population and Society*, 3rd ed. New York: Random House.

The Universal
Elements of
Population Analysis

BASIC DEMOGRAPHIC CONCEPTS AND DATA

2

Each of the societal types specified in the previous chapter differs in its range and quality of population data. Primitive societies, which by definition lack any written records of their own, begin to acquire accurate measurements only as they lose their isolation. And although virtually every civilization of the past compiled records on certain portions of its population, for demographic analysis such counts have two important flaws. (1) Because their usual purpose was to impose taxation, military duty, or some other onerous service upon those eligible, some—the proportion varied with the regime's efficiency—always succeeded in evading enumeration; thus, (2) once one has evaluated the accuracy of the figures themselves, one must still extrapolate from this part to the whole population.

Demographic statistics *per se* are a product of modern societies. The first count of a total population may have been in New France (present-day Quebec) in 1665, and sixteen counts in all were taken there over the next century. Like the several early censuses in England's American colonies, these may be viewed as an extension of mercantilist bookkeeping.[1] The earliest accurate counts that any country made of its own population were in Scandinavia,[2] largely for the same kind of reasons. Like the clergy elsewhere, the Lutheran ministers of Sweden had long been keeping records of their parishioners, and at five-year intervals from 1749 on the government required all clergy to submit data from which population totals could be calculated. The system applied also in Finland as long as it was joined to Sweden, and a similar gradual secularization of ecclesiastical records took place in Denmark and Iceland.

---

[1] The word *statistics* (brought into English from the French *statistique*, which derived from the German *Statistik*) is related to the word *state*, and the connotation from this etymology is that statistics constitute a kind of national accounting. The word *statist*, now rare in any sense, can mean either statesman or statistician.

[2] It may be, however, that a 17th-century census was taken in France. In 1694 a head count was ordered, a questionnaire was distributed, and returns from three districts are extant; but whether the forms were completed throughout the country and have since been lost is not clear. See Edmond Esmonin, *Etudes sur la France des XVIIe et XVIIIe siècles* (Paris: Presses Universitaires de France, 1964). The many partial and unreliable data for France of the 17th and 18th centuries generally do not afford more than a shaky base from which to estimate total population figures.

21

In the United States, the institution of the census was related to efforts to establish the national government. One of the principal impediments to a federal system was the jealousy between large states and small ones. Power was balanced between them by establishing a bicameral Congress: in the Senate, with equal representation from each member of the union, the less populous states had relatively greater power; and in the House, with representation proportionate to the population, the larger ones dominated. To maintain this balance, the number in the lower house had to be adjusted periodically to population growth; the Constitution itself provided for a decennial count. The first American census, in 1790, was thus not the first in the world, but because of this political context, it set an important precedent.

Until the 19th century the statistical data gathered by countries of continental Europe were usually treated as secrets of state. The modern census began in the United States in close association with democratic forms of government, and even at the start the results were immediately made public. . . . There can be no doubt that the periodic censuses of the United States have been pre-eminently responsible for introducing the practice into other countries [Willcox 1930].

From these various beginnings, a system for the regular collection of population statistics was gradually established. By modern standards most of the earliest data are quite poor. The total head count was not accurate, and consistent classification into even the most basic categories developed only slowly. Yet by the end of the 19th century the compilation of population statistics was well established in Western Europe and its overseas extensions, and more erratic, generally less satisfactory efforts had been made in some countries of Eastern Europe and Latin America. In the rest of the world, more or less adequate population statistics exist for the period before 1900 (or even 1945) only when a European power instituted them in a colony: thus, England in India and the British West Indies, France in Algeria and (as we have noted) Canada, the Netherlands in the Dutch East Indies. Before today's underdeveloped nations began to collect population data systematically, techniques had improved greatly from these beginnings in the West European nucleus.

INTERNATIONAL STATISTICS

The two main processes of data collection are differentiated in conventional terminology: **enumeration**, the periodic count of the whole population and its characteristics made in a census, is contrasted with **registration**, a continuous notation of vital events recorded usually right after their occurrence. Enumerating the inhabitants of a designated area and registering its vital events are such straightforward procedures that, in the early days of population statistics, no conceptual framework was deemed to be necessary. It became evident, however, that the understanding of "obvious" terms and "simple" procedures varied greatly from one person to another even within a single country. Each statistical office undertook to standardize its own terminology and to issue detailed instructions to those charged with the collection and presentation of its data, and this effort to establish professional norms started to become meaningful once the compilation of statistics was made the responsibility of a separate agency.

A great impetus toward standardization came with the development of international statistical organizations (United Nations 1955: 9–11). Even before the Statistical Society of London grew into the Royal Statistical Society, it was the cradle of international cooperation. Two men played an especially significant role: Adolphe Quetelet, the Belgian astronomer and social statistician (cf. Lazarsfeld 1961), and that indefatigable patron of all scientific progress, Prince Albert of Saxe-Coberg-Gotha, later the husband of Queen Victoria. In 1853, at an international statistical congress they helped to organize, representatives of twenty-six countries met in Brussels and recommended that all nations adopt uniform bases for their statistics, which only then would be internationally comparable. The permanent commission that eventually developed out of the congress often could get no more than partial and reluctant cooperation from the various national governments. Imperial Germany objected regularly even to the convention that proceedings were published in French, at the time still the standard language of diplomacy. The effective life of the commission came to an end after the Franco–Prussian War, and its successor, which met at irregular intervals between 1878 and 1912, almost foundered during World War I (Willcox 1949). As these dates suggest, the difficulties derived mainly from the basic contradiction of international statistics: the cold quantitative record of nations' achievements and failures—for scholars the neutral subject matter of their discipline—may not by some interpretations of national interest be fully divulged.

Nevertheless the International Institute of Statistics survived World War I, and three periodical publications gave population figures during the following years for the world and its major components: the Institute's *Aperçu de la démographie des divers pays du monde*; the *Statistical Year-Book*, published by the League of Nations; and the *International Year-Book of Agricultural Statistics*, published by the International Institute of Agriculture. In 1930 the highest and the lowest estimates of the world's population given in these three works differed by only 40 million, or less than 2 percent of the average of the three figures. The reason for this seeming agreement, however, was that the three estimates were in fact not wholly independent, particularly with respect to countries with the least reliable statistics.

These series have now been superseded by the various publications of the United Nations, which reflect both the continuing inherent difficulties of an international organization and the substantial improvement in professional demographic standards during the past half century or so. The Population Commission, established only two years after the founding of the United Nations itself with representatives from twelve (later eighteen) nations, guides the demographic activities of the organization's various units, especially but not exclusively through the Population Division. However, the Commission was long divided between a Catholic–Communist coalition, strangely allied on population matters, and what might be termed the "neo-Malthusians" or, more accurately, the professional demographers of Western nations, so that any work related to policy questions was seriously hampered. In 1969 the United Nations established a Fund for Population Acitivities, designed to assist underdeveloped countries in various demographic tasks. In eight heavily populated nations the Fund helped the governments set up family-planning services available to "all who wished to take advantage of them." The $6.7 million expended in 1970, the first year of the Fund's operations, was increased to an estimated $30.6 million in 1971 (Table 2-1). Measured against the size and the urgency of the problem, these amounts must be denoted as piddling, especially since so large a proportion was to be spent for otherwise unspecified "comprehensive projects" (cf. Symonds and Carder 1973).

Among the achievements of the U.N. Population Commission, perhaps the most important is its encouragement of data gathering. Censuses were initiated in countries or even whole regions where they hardly existed before. The prodigious difficulties encountered in such efforts, as earlier by the International

Table 2-1.   Projects Approved for Financing by the United Nations Fund for Population Activities, by Type of Activity and Geographic Region, 1970–71

Activity and Region	Millions of Dollars	
	1970	1971 (EST.)
Type of activity		
Education and training	1.3	2.2
Research and studies	0.6	1.0
Advisory and technical services	1.6	2.2
Meetings and seminars	0.4	0.7
Equipment and supplies	0.7	0.8
Comprehensive projects	1.2	21.9
Infrastructure	0.9	1.8
Geographic region		
Africa	0.6	4.4
Near and Middle East	0.6	4.4
Asia and Far East	2.4	12.1
Latin America	0.5	3.1
Interregional	2.6	6.6
TOTAL[a]	6.7	30.6

[a] The total under either "Type of activity" or "Geographic region," not both together.
SOURCE: United Nations, *Population Fund* (New York, n.d.).

Institute of Statistics and the League of Nations, have often been political rather than technical. During the 1960s so many of the new postcolonial nations were admitted to membership that as a bloc they could control the technical agencies' activities, and usually their representatives did not favor a full and accurate disclosure of these countries' poverty, illiteracy, and generally low status. In 1972, as an egregious example of the intrusion of politics into the technical work of the United Nations, it was announced that none of its statistical series would ever again include data from Taiwan "in any form whatsoever." This ruling, made at the insistence of Communist China, makes an uncountry of a nation with a larger population than two-thirds of the member states, a more robust economy than perhaps three-quarters of them. (Reality has again overtaken fiction: in George Orwell's *1984* individuals were converted into unpersons, but no nation of 13.5 million was made to disappear.) Working against such hindrances, the demographers at the United Nations have compiled a *Demographic Yearbook* from the statistics furnished by the countries

French-speaking team at the Census Training Center for Asia and the Far East, Tokyo. A peasant is watching the instructor point out a farm household near the city (*United Nations*).

themselves. With all their faults, these are the best data available on a world scale and each edition has a valuable introduction to a particular range of data. Several international population congresses under U.N. auspices have afforded excellent opportunities for the exchange of ideas across geographical and ideological lines. Another world congress took place in 1974, designated as World Population Year (cf. Bourgeois-Pichat 1972).

DEFINITION OF CONCEPTS

From the post-1945 efforts to develop population statistics in underdeveloped countries, it became even more apparent that, in demography no less than in other disciplines, before we start counting we must designate our units. It is now universally recognized that a precise definition of concepts is the prerequisite to the collection of data. Nothing can be taken for granted. The meanings that have been given to even the most basic terms—*family* or *live birth*, for example— have varied from one time or place to another, and such concepts as the *cause of death* or *international migration* can be delineated only by accepting one convention or another as a compromise. These terms will be discussed as we come to them in the following chapters; here we shall restrict ourselves to a general introduction to the problem they exemplify.

Take so simple a question, one so fundamental to population analysis, as "How many persons inhabited Country A on such and such a date?" This would seem to be so straightforward as to admit, apart from errors, of only one answer. In fact, neither *inhabitant* nor *country* is entirely unambiguous.

By the standards of the U.S. Department of State, the number of independent states in the world increased from 70 on the eve of World War II to 136 in 1969. (Of the total in 1969, only 123 were members of the United Nations, not including Byelorussia, Mongolia, and the Ukraine, which are component elements of the Soviet Union.) Eight areas were classified as quasi-independent, meaning usually that self-rule was combined with lack of control over foreign affairs, and almost as many were said to "defy classification." As any day's newspaper informs us, national independence has typically been realized by such protracted processes as war, revolution, and persistent nonviolent pressure. The moment when a state comes into being or ceases to exist must often be arbitrary. For instance, the forcible anschluss of Estonia, Latvia, and Lithuania into the Soviet Union has not been recognized by the United States, yet even a publication of the U.S. Department of State (1969) no longer defines them as independent.

The political boundaries of national states and their subdivisions, moreover, often define units quite inappropriate for social or economic analysis, and to set more suitable boundaries usually requires a more or less arbitrary judgment. What are the precise limits of "Western Europe," "Southeast Asia," "the Arab World," "Latin America," and all the other designations that we accept in the context of a historical or political analysis? Are the new African states the best units for a particular analysis, or rather the tribal areas that in many cases overlap their boundaries? If, in a country like the United States, counties and most states do not constitute meaningful social–economic units, how shall we fashion these?

Once the geographical boundaries of an area have been designated, it is necessary to define what is meant by an inhabitant. The United States uses a so-called *de jure* enumeration, meaning that persons are listed under their "usual place of residence." In Australia, as an example of a *de facto* enumeration, persons are classified according to where they happen to be on the day of the census count.[3] In England the two are combined: for persons enumerated elsewhere than at their usual place of residence, this is also given. The difference between *de facto* and *de jure* enumeration, moreover, is only the most important of the variations in how *inhabitant* is understood. Consider American students who leave their state of residence to spend a protracted, but presumably temporary, period at a college in another state; when the U. S. Census Bureau changed its definition of "usual place of residence" to include such institutions, the population of college towns and even of some states increased appreciably.

The approximate population of the United States on April 1, 1970, the date of the last census, was 201,064,000 or 203,235,000 or 204,335,000, depending on whether armed forces were included and, if so, whether also troops overseas. The usual census count is given as the second of these three figures or, more precisely, 203,235,298. In an extreme case, the population statistics of Finland provided four different totals for Finnish nationals, with a difference of some 8 percent between the maximum and the minimum at any one date (Kirk 1949). Of course, a person who uses the original documents or authoritative compilations and reads all the introductory definitions and the explanatory footnotes knows what is intended by each such figure; but that is the point: "What was the population of Country A in 19—?" is not so simple a question as it seems.

The **classification** of a population into categories and subcategories must also often seem arbitrary. Any population is what is known as a discontinuous variable; that is, it changes only by whole units. A hamlet with 100 inhabitants can increase to 101 or decrease to 99, but it cannot change to an intermediate figure. Many characteristics of a population, however, are continuous variables, changes in which cannot be measured precisely by even the smallest unit. The measurement of age, for instance, whether counted in years, as is usual, or by the smallest unit conceivable, say milliseconds, transforms the continuous process of aging into a more or less jerky counterpart. The classification of any population according to its characteristics, thus, often means that one must group variables more or less arbitrarily into precise class intervals.

[3] For a discussion of the relative advantages and disadvantages of *de jure* and *de facto* enumerations, see Spiegelman 1968: 9–13. In societies with cultures markedly different from those of Western countries, the classification of residences can be more complicated. Fischer (1958) gives some examples of the problems that one encounters in enumerating primitive peoples and offers some partial solutions.

Dividing a continuum into intervals can be exemplified in terms of age: (1) Women are physiologically able to reproduce between puberty and menopause or, roughly, between the ages of 15 and 45; and the general fertility rate, defined as the number of births per 1,000 females in the fecund period, varies widely according to where the age limits of fecundity are set (see p. 88). (2) The age at which Americans were deemed to enter the working population was raised twice, from 10 years to 14 and then to 16. Certainly the age at which persons ordinarily enter the labor force rose, and most jurisdictions have laws prohibiting the work of "children," variously defined. The new definitions reflected this trend, but not precisely. (3) The author of one work on aging set 60 years as the lower limit of future research, in spite of the fact that in the United States 65 is the usual point to mark retirement, social-security benefits (for males, but it is 62 for females), and so on. In short, there is usually no one correct decision on such dividing points, even at any particular time in a given culture. In most cases any of several more or less arbitrary classifications is equally acceptable.

The goal of complete formal international comparability in census statistics, to be achieved through standard international recommendations, is probably a false goal. . . . For a few simple biological items there are no important conceptual difficulties. . . . [But] a standard international definition for [other] characteristics can achieve comparable statistics only to the extent that the social and economic features of the countr[ies] are similar. In two dissimilar countries, it may be that greater comparability of meaning for a census item can be obtained if the census question is asked in distinctly different ways [Linder 1955].

In other words, "measurement presupposes a bounded network of shared meanings, i.e., a theory of culture" (Cicourel 1964: 14). This completely valid statement is unfortunately no truism. The naiveté of laymen has combined with the hyperpositivist stance of some demographers to obscure the fact that to some degree population data, like those in all other social disciplines, are culturally defined. Analytic rigor is sacrificed when we postulate a more universal base to the discipline than in fact exists.

POPULATION REGISTERS

Population data are available primarily from three sources: the census, which corresponds in business practice to a periodic inventory of stock; vital statistics, which are like a record of inputs and outputs; and migration statistics, which are comparable to domestic and foreign purchases and sales.

In the most advanced firms these three kinds of accounts are in fact part of a permanent inventory, which gives the businessman a precise overview of his stock on hand at any time and of the production and sales during a specified period. The counterpart in demography is a continuous **population register**, such as is maintained in the Netherlands, Belgium, Finland, and the three Scandinavian countries.[4] In each of these European nations, local registration bureaus maintain a separate card for each individual from the time of his birth (or immigration) to his death (or emigration), and on this are entered such changes in his civil status as marriage and divorce and other demographic data. With a population register, it is thus possible at any time to have the information ordinarily derived from both vital statistics and the census and, in addition, to know what part migration has played in bringing about population changes. Disadvantages are that it is quite expensive to set up and maintain, that to work properly it requires a high cultural level in the general population, and that conceivably so complete a record might constitute an infringement on individual liberty.

THE CENSUS

In the United Nations manual on the subject (1954: 1) a **census** is defined as "the simultaneous recording of demographic data by the government, at a particular time, pertaining to all the persons who live in a particular territory." Indeed, the term is often used to denote population counts of all kinds, and even other enumerations by a government (like the U.S. Census of Manufactures), but it is preferable to restrict its meaning to those that more or less comply with this United Nations definition, whose terms are elucidated in the following paragraphs:

1. A census is **made by the government**. No other institution can provide the legitimate authority and thus the presumption of objectivity, or the elaborate and expensive organization required to make a full and accurate enumeration.

2. A census is of the population of a **strictly defined territory**. One major difficulty in using the so-called censuses of ancient China, for example, is that "China" varied considerably from one period to another, depending on the military successes of the central government, and it is often not clear how much of the outlying regions was included in population counts.

3. The census enumeration is in principle **universal**, including every person in the designated area without omission or duplication. However, as we shall note shortly, this inclusion can be merely implicit, through the enumeration only of a properly drawn sample of the total population.

4. Ideally, a census consists of a **personal enumeration** of each individual in the area covered. In the usual practice of Western nations, enumerators try to reach at least one adult in each household or, if he proves to be repeatedly unavailable, a neighbor. In some population counts a personal enumeration is not attempted. Colonial censuses of Negro Africa, for example, often consisted of

[4] In the United States a population register is maintained of certain Indian tribes (cf. Johnston 1966: 11), and the establishment of an integrated Federal Statistical Data Center has been proposed (cf. Glaser *et al.* 1967; Dunn 1967). Thomas (1938) has given an interesting account of how the systems in Europe were set up.

Table 2-2. Subjects of Inquiries Included in the U.S. Population Censuses, 1790–1970

Topic	1790	1800	1810	1820	1830	1840	1850	1860	1870	1880	1890	1900	1910	1920	1930	1940[a]	1950[a]	1960[a]	1970[a]
Name	P	P	P	P	P	P	×	×	×	×	×	×	×	×	×	×	×	×	×
Address	×	×	×	×	×	×	×	×	×	×	×	×	×	×	×	×	×	×	×
Farm residence															×	×	×	25	20
Families, persons, per house											×								
Relationship to family head										×	×	×	×	×	×	×	×	×	×
Sex	P	P	P	P	P	P	×	×	×	×	×	×	×	×	×	×	×	×	×
Age	P	P	P	P	P	P	×	×	×	×	×	×	×	×	×	×	×	×	×
Marital status										×	×	×	×	×	×	×	×	×	×
Free whites	×	×	×	×	×	×													
Free nonwhites	P	P	P	P	P	P													
Slaves	×	×	×	×	×	×	S	S											
Color							P	P	×										
Race										×	×	×	×	×	×	×	×	×	×
Indians										S	S	×	S	×	×	×	S	×	×
Year of immigration											×	×	×	×	×				5
Unnaturalized aliens			×		×						×	×	×	×	×				
Naturalization papers taken out											×								
Year of naturalization													×						
Speak English											×	×	×	×	×				
Native language										×			×	×	×	5		25	15
Place of birth							×	×	×	×	×	×	×	×	×	×	×	25	20
Places of parents' birth									P	×	×	×	×	×	×	5	20	25	15
Parents' native languages													×						
Citizenship				×												×	×		5
Spanish descent																			5
Residence 1 (5) year(s) earlier																×	20	25	15
How long at present address																		25	15
Americans overseas																	S	S	S
Profession, occupation, or trade				×		×	×	×	×	×	×	×	×	×	×	5	×	25	20
Industry, occupation 5 years earlier																			5
Whether unemployed										×	×	×	×		S	S	×	25	20
How long unemployed																	20	25	20
Hours worked																×	×	25	20
Place of work																		25	15
Activity 5 years earlier																			20

Table 2-2.—*Continued*

Topic	1790	1800	1810	1820	1830	1840	1850	1860	1870	1880	1890	1900	1910	1920	1930	1940[a]	1950[a]	1960[a]	1970[a]
Means of transportation to work																		25	15
Income																×	20	25	20
Value of real (and personal) estate							×	×	×						×	×			
Home (farm) rented or owned, mortgaged											×	×	×	×	×	×			
Radio set															×	×			
Whether attending school						×	×	×	×	×		×	×	×	×	×	20	25	15
Public or private school																		25	15
Vocational training																			5
Educational attainment																×	20	25	20
Whether literate						×	×	×	×		×	×	×	×	×				
Deaf or dumb					×	×	×	×	×	S	S	S	S	S	S				
Blind					×	×	×	×	×	S	S	S	S	S	S				
Sick or disabled										×	×								
Insane, idiotic, or feeble-minded						×	×	×	×	S	S		S						
Acute or chronic disease										×	×								5
Military pensioner or veteran						×						P	P		×	5	20	25	15
Pauper or convict							S	S	S	S	×		S						
Social-security or retirement status																5			
Born within recent period											×	×			S	S			
Death within year							S	S	S	S	S								
Death in the family								×	×	×	×	×							
Age at first marriage															×	5			
When, how often, married							P	P	P	P	P	×				5	3.3	25	5
How long married													×					25	5
Whether first marriage ended by death																			5
How many (living) children											×	×	×			5	3.3	25	20
Persons in family										×									

P—partial data.
S—special report or details.
[a] Items marked × were asked of all persons, other items of the designated percentage of the population.

SOURCE: Henry S. Shryock and Jacob S. Siegel, *The Methods and Materials of Demography* (Washington, D.C.: U.S. Bureau of the Census, 1971), Table 2-3.

compilations of data furnished by village chieftains; and the so-called censuses of religious bodies in the United States, similarly, were based on information given by the various denominations.

5. The enumeration of the entire population should be **simultaneous**, made on a single day, and in the small nations of the Western world this ideal is approached. In so large a country as the United States the census ordinarily takes three or four weeks, and in more primitive areas it may take months or even years. One day is nevertheless set as the date of the census, and demographic events occurring after this are in principle excluded from the count.

6. Censuses furnish not only information about the population at a given time but, in combination, no less significant data about its development over a period. Censuses are most useful if a **regular interval** is maintained between them. The director of a census, moreover, must weigh the advantages to be derived from any new procedure that is proposed against the disadvantage that comparability with previous data will be lost.

A long period of preparatory work must precede the actual enumeration. The legal and financial foundations must be assured, the census organization instituted if it does not already exist, and the general program laid out. Geographers mark the census areas on large-scale maps; others design the questionnaire and preferably test it in a trial census. Particularly in countries without a census tradition, the bureau must try to allay possible suspicion of the enumerators by full and repeated publicity on the benefits to be derived from a formal count of the population. After enumeration, the data are checked for accuracy and consistency, compiled and tabulated, and published, often first in a preliminary version and then in final form. In some countries the questions raised by the data are regularly followed by special research, with consequent postcensal reports.

Even in their original form, **census schedules** (as the questionnaires are called) have generally included more questions than required for their stipulated purpose, and over the decades, in response to the needs of increasingly complex civilizations, and sometimes anticipating these needs, new questions were added to the various countries' schedules. In the United States, for instance, the regularity of the decennial count is in contrast with a great diversity in the information collected (Table 2-2). For the first six censuses the unit of enumeration was the family, and the data collected began with the name of each family head but only the characteristics of the other members. In 1850 the unit was changed to the individual. At no time, however, have statistics been released in a form that permits anyone to identify a particular person except for such a legitimate purpose as tracing one's own genealogy. The other items included, and then sometimes dropped, reflect the rise and fall of various public issues on which better information was needed. The effort to measure America's ethnic pattern, exerted in various ways, was boiled down eventually to four main questions: on race, native language, birthplace, and parents' birthplaces. The measurement of physical disabilities during the latter half of the 19th century was largely abandoned, though the item reappeared in 1970. Efforts to measure the trend in family size have increased. And so on, through the other classes of questions.

In England, as another instance, the large in-migration to the new industrial towns brought a question on birthplace in 1841 and more detailed ones on the job structure in 1851. From 1901 on, the effort to cope with Britain's housing problem was reflected in new queries. As in the United States, the number of questions designed to measure fertility has increased (cf. Benjamin 1970).

The items recommended by international agencies have also varied, though the minimum is fairly well established at something like those given in Table 2-3, which "have emerged after decades of census experience as of the greatest utility for both national and international purposes." Other recent ideas for the improvement of censuses can be typified by the discussion at the Second European Population Conference, held in Strasbourg in 1971. For this group of demographers, migration data were those most in need of basic revision, though short of maintaining a population register no recommendations were made for a substantial change in the presently inadequate system. It was noted that the jurisdictional units by which population statistics are invariably reported are usually inappropriate for social analysis but that, if the precise location of each household is recorded, computers make it possible to group the data in any combinations that are useful. (In the United States the 1970 statistics could be grouped by single blocks for all urbanized areas.) But the smallest social unit is now one of the most difficult to define. "The very concept of a household is becoming vaguer as more people have more than one household that could be called theirs, while the head of the household is almost an obsolete term in everyday life" (Hollingsworth 1971).

"The quality of the census results is wholly dependent on the enumeration, and no country can afford to have a poor enumeration in the hope that office work will subsequently improve it" (United Nations 1954: 21). For the United States census of 1960, for instance, some 160,000 enumerators were hired and trained, or approximately one per 1,100 persons to be counted (the world average was about one per 500 persons). Most of the enumerators were women, who are more often able and willing to take on a full-time job for two weeks or so. They were given nine hours of classroom training, designed to explain both the specific duties and the importance of taking an accurate census, and then had to pass an examination. Paid on a piece-work basis, they received about $13 a day (in many countries enumerators get only a token remuneration or even no payment at all), and about 2,000 were fired for inefficiency. Work in the field was directly controlled by about 10,000 crew leaders and, at a greater distance, by about 400 district supervisors. In 1970, persons residing in 145 of the larger metropolitan areas and some rural test counties (together about 60 percent of the total U.S. population) were sent a questionnaire through the post and asked to mail it back to the local field office. Enumerators visited those households only when there was no response or when it was necessary to

Table 2-3.   Recommended Items (marked with an asterisk) and "Other Useful Topics" for the 1970 Population Censuses

Topic in Census Schedule	Derived Topic
Geographic characteristics	
*Place where found at time of census	*Total population
*Place of usual residence	*Locality subdivision
*Place of birth	*Urban–rural division
Duration of residence	
Place of previous residence	
Place of work	
Personal and household characteristics	
*Sex	*Household composition
*Age	Family composition
*Relationship to head of household	
Relationship to head of family	
*Marital status	
Age at marriage	
Duration of marriage	
Marriage order	
*Children born alive	
*Children living	
Citizenship	
*Literacy	
*School attendance	
*Educational attainment	
Educational qualifications	
National and/or ethnic group	
Language	
Religion	
Economic characteristics	
*Type of activity	Social–economic status
*Occupation	Dependency
*Industry	
*Status as employer, employee, etc.	
Main source of livelihood	

SOURCE: United Nations, *Principles and Recommendations for the 1970 Population Censuses*, Statistical Papers, Series M, no. 44 (New York, 1967).

complete questionnaires not filled in correctly. Lists were obtained from commercial sources, then corrected in each postal district by the local letter carrier. Coverage was thus improved at a considerable reduction in cost (U.S. Bureau of the Census 1970b, vol. 1: 23–26).

The difficulties of enumeration in a country like the United States are as nothing compared to those in some territories. Each of the approximately 18,500 enumerators who counted Australia's population in 1966 took along not only the schedule but a guide to eight languages and instructions on how to communicate with the aborigines in sign language. They moved about Australia's vast spaces by plane and jeep, on horseback and skis, by motor launch. From Humbug Scrub to Boologooroo, census takers sought out opal gougers, oil drillers, boundary riders, and wandering rabbit hunters. A truck driver induced to help returned from No Tree Plain with 200 completed questionnaires and 5 tons of rabbits (*Time*, July 22, 1966).

Nor was it an easy task to administer the 1962 census of Nigeria, the first since that country's independence. The central government undertook a massive propaganda effort: radio singers gave daily census chants, schoolchildren marched for the census, placards covered the towns and villages. According to reports reaching the capital, enumerators were nonetheless beaten and kidnapped, for they were taken to be tax collectors in disguise. Census officials discovered whole areas—for example, a cluster of fishing villages with a total population of some 20,000—that had been overlooked in the 1952 count, the last taken under British auspices. On the other hand, administrators worked to inflate the count in their constituencies, in order to get a larger share of development and welfare funds (*New York Times*, May 27, 1962). In 1973, when the next count was made, all business in the nation's capital of Lagos stopped for three days, and road checks were set up to "deal firmly" with anyone who had not remained at home until he was counted. The census was taken by 130,000 enumerators, an equal number of unarmed soldiers, and all government clerks. It was hoped that with such emergency measures the count would be more accurate than the prior one (*New York Times*, December 2, 1973).

Afghanistan's first "census" ever was taken by ERTS (Earth Resources Technology Satellite), America's beginning attempt to explore the earth through space photography. (In the United States, ERTS will be used for such purposes as to distinguish sickly from healthy crops, to note the land use over some 30,000 square miles between New Jersey and Virginia, and to map the breeding areas of wild ducks.) Its cameras are powerful enough to record villages and cities, fields and wastelands, and even nomad encampments. These data were converted into population estimates for regions of Afghanistan with formulas giving the approximate densities of various types of settlements (*Wall Street Journal*, July 21, 1972).

The technical skill and equipment used in compiling the data collected have improved greatly. As long ago as 1890, American census results were entered on Hollerith punch cards, with which it is possible by a simple adjustment to sum up involved cross tabulations. In 1950, the last time the data were all transferred to punch cards, it took 200,000 operator-days, costing some $6 million, to punch the 240 million cards containing the characteristics of a population of 151 million. The information on the cards was then transferred to tapes that could be fed into the new UNIVAC computer, but by today's standards the process was slow and inefficient. By the time of the 1960 census the Bureau was using a new piece of equipment—FOSDIC, which stands for Film

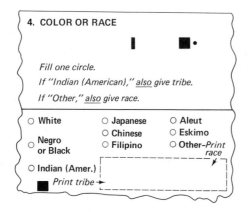

DATE OF BIRTH				
5. Month and year of birth and age last birthday *Print*	6. Month of birth *Fill one circle*	7. Year of birth *Fill one circle for first three numbers*	*Fill one circle for last number*	8. WHAT IS EACH PERSON'S MARITAL STATUS? *Fill one circle*
Month _____ Year _____ Age _____	○ Jan.–Mar. ○ Apr.–June ○ July–Sept. ○ Oct.–Dec. ■	○ 186– ○ 192– ○ 187– ○ 193– ○ 188– ○ 194– ○ 189– ○ 195– ○ 190– ○ 196– ○ 191– ○ 197–	○ 0 ○ 5 ○ 1 ○ 6 ○ 2 ○ 7 ○ 3 ○ 8 ○ 4 ○ 9 ■	○ Now married ○ Widowed ○ Divorced ○ Separated ○ Never married
Month _____ Year _____ Age _____	○ Jan.–Mar. ○ Apr.–June ○ July–Sept. ○ Oct.–Dec.	○ 186– ○ 192– ○ 187– ○ 193– ○ 188– ○ 194– ○ 189– ○ 195– ○ 190– ○ 196– ○ 191– ○ 197–	○ 0 ○ 5 ○ 1 ○ 6 ○ 2 ○ 7 ○ 3 ○ 8 ○ 4 ○ 9	○ Now married ○ Widowed ○ Separated ○ Divorced ○ Never married
Month _____	○ Jan.–Mar. ○ Apr.–June	○ 186– ○ 192– ○ 187– ○ 193– ○ 188– ○ 194–	○ 0 ○ 5 ○ 1 ○ 6 ○ 2 ○ 7	○ Now married ○ Widowed ○ Divorced

Figure 2-1.   Illustrative Portions of the FOSDIC Questionnaire, 1970 U.S. Census

Optical Sensing Device for Input to Computers. FOSDIC produced as much in one minute as a 1950 punch operator had in a day.

In 1970, forty cameras were used, each able to take fifty shots a minute. To make the conversion of data in this manner possible, special census forms had to be prepared: basic information, given by filling in a circle, was picked up by the camera and converted into figures. Complete-count data were transferred directly to microfilm. Partial-count data, which often permit too great a range of replies to be processed automatically, had first to be hand-coded and then were transferred to film. The partial-count data were then weighted with appropriate multipliers in order to give the estimated characteristics of the populations even of small areas. The resultant Basic Record Tapes were the source of both the printed census reports and the microfilms made for public use. The printing was done with a Linotron photocomposer, first used in 1970.

The image of a character is scanned by a TV-like "camera" from a grid of available characters. The character, after it has been electronically amplified to the appropriate point size, is produced on the face of a cathode-ray tube at a proper position. This image on the face of the cathode-ray tube exposes a sheet of photographic film or photosensitive paper, which can then be used for reproduction. . . . Characters are processed at the rate of 1,000 per second when the system is setting in 6-point type [Dalzell 1970].

In principle, as we have noted, a census is universal, but in practice this universality can be approximated by getting information only from a survey population, a fraction that is related to the aggregate population in a known and regular way. The ideal relation is what one author terms Epsem (equal probability of selection method) Sampling, by which each element in the population has the same chance of being represented in the sample (Kish 1965: 21). This results in the smallest **sampling error**, or the difference in the count that could result from using a sample rather than a full enumeration.

A sample can have a number of advantages over a complete census: (1) economy; (2) speed, and therefore timeliness; (3) quality and accuracy, since it is often difficult to obtain enough trained personnel for a full count; and (4) reduced bulk of completed records. Among the advantages of complete enumeration or registration, as opposed to a sample survey, are the following: (1) data are provided for small geographical units, small classes of the population, and, in particular, individuals; and (2) the public is less likely to understand the limitations of a sample survey and is thus more apt to misinterpret the data.[5]

In the United States sampling was first used in the 1940 census, when one person out of twenty was asked questions in addition to those on the regular schedule, and this procedure set a precedent for the subsequent censuses. A recurrent survey that the Works Progress Administration (WPA) had initiated during the 1930s to chart the trend in unemployment was later transferred to the Census Bureau, which converted in into a monthly *Current Population Survey* (U.S. Bureau of the Census 1963). In Britain a one-in-ten sample filled in a complete census schedule in 1966, thus reducing the period between censuses from ten to five years. The cost was less than half that of a census of the 1961 type, with basic information from the whole population and more elaborate data from a sample of 10 percent, and only a small fraction of one of the 1951 type, when all respondents answered all questions. In the introduction to the 1961

[5] Much of the journalistic commentary on unemployment statistics, for example, ignores the fact that most of the month-to-month change may be sampling error. Cf. Raymond T. Bowman and Margaret E. Martin, "Special Report on Unemployment Statistics: Meaning and Measurement," *American Statistician*, **16** (1962), 14–22.

Automatic page turners used to photograph the questionnaire pages during the microfilming of the 1970 census (*U.S. Bureau of the Census*).

British census it was noted, however, that the sample of 10 percent that had been asked some of the questions was seriously biased, with the more crowded households overrepresented and the less crowded ones underrepresented. One factor may have been that the agency responsible for the censuses, unlike the U.S. Bureau of the Census with its large permanent staff, is forced to go through a "traumatic redeployment" of forces for each one. "The General Register Office is therefore ill equipped for the careful planning that is a prerequisite of successful sampling" (Benjamin 1970: 11–19).

A census may be partly or even wholly based on a sample of the population, and a survey is so based by definition. Obviously the difference between the two need not be sharp. Surveys are likely to have a less formal foundation; for instance, the legal obligation in the United States to answer all questions in the census does not apply to the population survey. Preferably censuses are conducted at regular intervals; surveys may be regularly spaced but often are *ad hoc*. Censuses are typically restricted to factual questions to which there is a single truthful reply. In surveys on demographic issues an effort has often been made to go beyond fact and seek out interpretations and opinions: what do you think the ideal family size is; why did you move to this area last year; have you been actively seeking work during the past week? By now, official surveys with demographic data have become almost as common as the better known sources (cf. United Nations 1967; Shryock and Siegel 1971: 17–19).

VITAL STATISTICS

The term *vital statistics* was coined by William Farr, who worked at Britain's General Register Office from shortly after its founding in 1837 until his retirement in 1880. He first defined the term to include "the statistics of health, sickness, diseases, and death," but shortly broadened the designation to encompass also marriages and births. In short, **vital statistics** pertain to each person's birth, changes in his civil status throughout his lifetime, and his death. In almost every culture there is associated with each such event a religious ritual to mark it: birth and baptism, marriage and wedding, death and burial service, and so on. The use of church records for demographic analysis, however, is hampered by the fact that there has seldom really been a one-to-one ratio between event and ceremony. Secularization, therefore, has brought an important progress in recording vital events. Apart from the ancient Inca empire in Peru, 17th-century Massachusetts was the first state to record the occurrence and date of the actual events rather than of the subsequent ecclesiastical ceremonies, and the first to shift the responsibility for this registration from the clergy to civil authorities (Gutman 1959).

In spite of this early beginning, the development of vital statistics in the United States has been slow. In contrast to most West European countries, in the United States vital statistics are still collected by local authorities, so that their completeness and reliability have varied greatly from one region to another. In several 19th-century censuses, attempts were made to find a substitute for national vital statistics by asking how many births or deaths had taken place during a designated period before the enumeration date (see Table 2-2). The responses were quite inadequate, however; the census reports themselves estimated that perhaps as many as half the deaths were omitted.

Following such fiascos, the federal government undertook to guide the procedures of local authorities. Model registration laws were written, and the states were urged to enact them. States in which it was judged on the basis of sample counts that the registration was at least 90 percent complete were gradually included in a Death Registration Area (established in 1880) and a Birth Registration Area (established in 1915). In 1933, with the admission of Texas to the Death Registration Area, they both became coextensive with the continental United States, and American birth and death statistics first came into

being on a national scale. Even today the accuracy and completeness of registration still varies from one state to another, though now ordinarily above the
minimum set as the national norm (see pp. 51–52). A new American agency
established in 1960, the National Center for Health Statistics, took over the
responsibility for collating vital statistics. Its functions, as the name implies,
have also included periodic surveys of medical institutions and their patients, of
health manpower, and the like.

The fairly common contrast between relatively advanced and backward areas
of a country is typically reflected in the quality of the vital statistics collected. In
India, as another example, the part known before 1947 as the British Provinces
is now denoted the "registration area," for which a more elaborate statistical
coverage is attempted than for the rest of the country. However difficult it may
be for an underdeveloped nation to set up a national census, to institute the
collection and compilation of vital statistics imposes even greater problems.
The best of a country's technical and administrative skills are ordinarily congregated at the capital and can be mustered for the periodic census. But the regular
registration of vital events must depend on local talents. In Kenya, as one
example, births and deaths are in principle registered by the attendant physician
(usually there is none); or as a second alternative by the headmen, parents, or
other relatives (most are illiterate); or, in fact in most cases, by school registrars
or district clerks (Huxtable 1967).

A count of births and deaths constitutes, of course, only the beginning of the
data needed to analyze fertility and mortality. If persons differ in one or the other
according to their occupation, ethnic group, urban or rural residence, or whatever, we can draw conclusions from such patterns only if the accuracy of registration can be assumed to be the same in all the categories being compared. The
reasonable assumption from the regional differences we have noted, however,
is the contrary—that with improvements, e.g., in controlling early death, there
go improvements in registering those deaths that do occur. Epidemiological
research is based fundamentally on an analysis of deaths classified by cause and
contributing factors, but the cause of death can generally be established only by
a physician, whose very availability means that sickness is under control. Thus,
some 60 percent of the deaths registered in British India up to 1945 (which had
better demographic statistics than most other underdeveloped countries) were
ascribed simply to "fever" and over 25 percent to a catch-all category of "other
causes." In all countries infant mortality is generally less accurately registered
than the deaths of adults, and records of fetal mortality are usually so poor that
one can hardly base any conclusions on them at all.

Data on changes in civil status are inherently more difficult to collect than
those on births and deaths. Since the family, that universal but highly variable
institution, cannot really be analyzed by truly international standards, we shall
never have truly comparable data. For example, consensual unions or common-
law marriages are almost the standard lower-class norm in much of Latin
America, yet some of the countries do not recognize them in their statistics. In

the United States registration areas have been established as one attempt to improve the record. In 1972, the Marriage Registration Area included forty-one states, the Divorce Registration Area only twenty-nine states. It is recognized that these data are quite inadequate,[6] and the personnel of the National Center for Health Statistics are endeavoring to stimulate a demand for more rapid improvement (cf. U.S. Public Health Service 1970; Hetzel 1971).

MIGRATION STATISTICS

If we define **migration** as "the permanent movement of persons or groups over a significant distance," some of the key terms of this definition (*permanent*, *significant*) are ambiguous and in practice have to be delimited by an arbitrary criterion. We know whether someone has been born or has died, but who shall say whether a person has migrated? A farmer who goes to the nearest town on a Saturday to buy a suit, we feel, is not a migrant. A person who leaves his home and goes to another country and settles there for the rest of his life, on the other hand, is a migrant. But between these two extremes lies a bewildering array of intermediate instances; and such criteria as distance, duration of stay, and importance of purpose do not clarify the concept entirely. "No objective, natural criterion exists on the basis of which migrants distinguish themselves from travelers, . . . [and] one should not expect to arrive at a unique criterion or definition of migration" (Lacroix 1949).

The basic distinction in migration statistics is that between **international migration,** in which the migrant crosses the boundary between one country and another, and **internal migration,** in which he does not. A difference is made also in the terms designating the two types of persons: international migrants are called **emigrants** when they leave and **immigrants** when they arrive, while internal migrants are called **out-migrants** when they leave and **in-migrants** when they arrive.

The distinction between internal and international migration is not always clear-cut, for as we have noted territories often have some but not all of the characteristics of independent states. Thus, according to the purpose for which the statistics are gathered, one might designate as either internal or international the movement among the occupied zones of postwar Germany; or between Puerto Rico and the United States; or between Britain and the British dominions, colonies, or mandated territories; and so on through scores of examples of ambiguous sovereignty. Each such case is decided on the basis of particular

---

[6] One important impediment is that states that have made a business of marriage and divorce are reluctant to cooperate in the compilation of complete and accurate statistics on their activities. Since all divorces handed down in Nevada, for example, are to persons legally defined as residents of that state, migratory divorce is not a fact that the Nevada administrators will officially acknowledge. Cf. William Petersen and Lionel L. Lewis, *Nevada's Changing Population* (Carson City, Nevada: State Printing Office, 1963), pp. 34–39.

circumstances, and there are many strange anomalies. To cite one: in the migration statistics of the United Kingdom, citizens of the Republic of Ireland are treated throughout as British subjects! Another instance: a difference in how two federal agencies defined *the United States* resulted in an apparent underenumeration of foreign-born Japanese in 1920. More than half of the population anticipated from the 1910 count plus the probable natural increase during the interim was missing. The "loss" was due, however, to the fact that the Commissioner General of Immigration included the Territory of Hawaii in migration statistics but that the Census Bureau excluded it from the general count of the national population—in both cases usually with no special warning to those using the tables (cf. Petersen 1971: 18).

Another limitation to the internal–international dichotomy is that it tends to obscure processes that cut across it. We usually think of labor mobility or of urban growth, for example, as intranational phenomena, forgetting that much of the movement of workers to cities has been across national boundaries. We speak of the assimilation of immigrants, but usually not of in-migrants. The implication that the difference between national cultures is *always* greater than that between rural and urban is certainly not in accord with the facts: a native of Toronto who moves to Detroit would ordinarily be, in any but a legal sense, less of an alien than an in-migrant from rural Alabama; and this contrast might also hold, for example, in the cases of a Viennese and a French peasant who go to live in Paris. These comments are not meant to imply, of course, that whether or not a migrant crosses an international border is unimportant to any demographic study. The point is rather that, even when an analyst deems this distinction to be irrelevant to the problem with which he is concerned, he must use the two sets of statistics as they have been separately collected; to combine data on international and internal migration is seldom feasible.

International Migration

The statistics of international migration, as collected by the various national governments, are not ordinarily accurate, complete, or comparable. There are three main reasons for this:

1. The statistics collected are an adjunct to a border patrol that many try to evade. The neutral character of modern Western censuses and vital statistics—the fact that they are data collected for their own sake rather than as a step preparatory to unpopular state controls—is thus lacking in the statistics of international migration. Distinctions made for legal or political reasons, moreover, are seldom relevant to a demographic study; for example, the difference in the United States between quota and nonquota immigrants relates only to American law and has no counterpart in the statistics of other countries. Each such specific regulation reduces the international comparability of the statistics based on it.

2. Even apart from variations in migration law, migrants are not classified by a uniform system in different countries. Among the totals entering and leaving a country, designated as **arrivals** and **departures**, the first subclassification is usually between **nationals** and **aliens,** who are both further subdivided between **visitors** and **permanent migrants.** All of these terms are ambiguous to some degree. Between *national* and *alien* there are persons of dual nationality, permanent stateless residents, and others who exemplify the complexities of international law. The distinction between *visitor* and *migrant*, similarly, is hard to draw precisely. The criterion recommended by the United Nations, to define removal for a year or more as "permanent," does not satisfactorily classify persons who remain abroad for more than a year but who intend to return. In the United States, for example, travelers in transit, tourists, businessmen, students, and others may get a visa for a year's stay and still remain "nonimmigrant aliens." It might be better to distinguish between **permanent migrants,** who intend to settle in a new country for the rest of their lives, and **quasi-permanent migrants,** who intend to remain a year or more but to return at some time after that. In any case, the "permanence" is based on the migrants' stated intentions at the time of their arrival, and some may not tell the truth and others may change their minds.

Several classes of international migrants do not fit into this scheme. Refugees, deportees, displaced persons, transferred populations, and the like are often, but not always, admitted under special conditions and outside the legal and statistical framework of "normal" movements. Also, persons who live on one side of an international border and work or shop or perform similar routine activities on the other side ordinarily carry frontier cards, with which they can short-circuit the usual control of passports and visas, and their movement back and forth is usually also segregated in the statistics.

3. The relevance of the data available varies with the problem being studied. An analysis of a country's labor force would obviously have to include seasonal workers and daily commuters, though the latter would not have to be included in a study, e.g., of housing. For an analysis of future population growth, including the children to be born to immigrants, age would be more relevant than citizenship. And for some purposes the total *de facto* population, including even one-day tourists, would be the most useful figure. But migration statistics are not ordinarily compiled so that one can take out just those data that are pertinent.

Internal Migration

Statistics on internal migration are quite limited in most countries. If there are no direct data, it is possible to calculate internal migration as a residue. The difference between births and deaths gives one the natural increase, which, when compared with the total intercensal increase, yields the presumed net movement into or out of the area. Symbolically this can be represented for the simplest case by the following equation:

$$M = P_1 - P_0 - B + D$$

With this method, however, it can happen that the errors in all the other data are added up as part of the assumed migration (Hamilton 1966).

Beginning with the 1850 census, native-born Americans have been asked to name their state of birth. This information, when compared with their state of residence at the time of the census, is a gauge of internal migration, but only a rough one, for the migration could have taken place at any time during the respondent's whole life, and intermediate stopovers, if any, are not given. Even so, the data are sufficient to indicate both the tremendous magnitude of the movement (according to each of the censuses, only about three persons out of four lived in their native state) and the general direction of the streams (that is, East to West, South to North), with sometimes strong presumptive evidence of the country-to-town movement. Place of birth has been recorded also in almost every European census and the indicated movement is usually to the national center—in England to London, in Sweden to Stockholm, in Denmark to Copenhagen, in France to Paris—or in such large countries as Germany, to the regional center (Kirk 1946: chap. 7).

Beginning with the 1940 census, Americans have been asked where they were living 5 years, or 1 year, earlier; and from 1945 on, questions of this kind were introduced into the *Current Population Survey.* The **mobile population,** defined as those who were living in different houses within the United States on the two dates, is divided first of all into **intracounty movers** and **intercounty migrants.** The latter category is further divided according to whether the migration was within the same state, to a contiguous state, or to a noncontiguous state. Migrants to the United States from another country are separately classified. This differentiation between *migrant* and *mover* is intended to distinguish changes in residence that are and are not accompanied by concomitant changes in job, school, type of neighborhood, and so on, but it is not possible to mark this social–economic boundary clearly by a geographical index. Persons who leave a farm and move to a town, who are classified as migrants by rural sociologists, may or may not fall into the category so defined in census statistics. A move from a city center to a suburb often crosses a county line; social theory is not clear on whether this should rate as "migration" or not (Shryock 1964: chaps. 2–3).

According to the data from the census and sample surveys, one American out of five moves each year to another house. In recent years the annual growth of the country's population from both natural increase and net international migration has amounted to between 2 and 3 million persons. Annual migration across county lines is more than three times this figure and that between states more than one and a half times. In many parts of the country, therefore, particularly in the

West, internal migration has been the most important determinant of population size and composition, but it is still the demographic factor we know least about.

ERRORS IN DEMOGRAPHIC DATA

Modern demographic data are no closer to perfection than any other creation of fallible humans, though in the context of social disciplines they constitute a unique reservoir of reliable statistical information. Indeed, it is a measure of the discipline's maturity that today few in it attempt to realize the unattainable. As any count approaches the theoretical total (termed the **universe**, as distinguished from the empirical total, the **population**), each additional reduction in error is bought at a higher cost in effort and money. With respect to sample surveys, the textbook admonition is to obtain only the maximum precision obtainable at the permitted expenditure (e.g., Kish 1965: 25). "The objective of 'optimum design' in sampling is coming to be the objective [also] in census taking. Instead of striving for perfection, we view the task as that of balancing the costs of producing statistics against the losses from errors in the statistics" (Hansen *et al.* 1953). Of course, a count of the whole population and a sample survey are not wholly comparable. The **precision** of a sample survey can be calculated from probability theory alone; given the size and nature of the sample, we know what the sampling error is likely to be. The **accuracy** of a survey, whether sample or complete, is the inverse of the total error, including biases. And there is no simple, efficient mode of measuring accuracy, for the unknown biases present in the original count may be retained in any subsequent check (Kish 1965: 12–13). Even so, inasmuch as accuracy, especially extreme accuracy, is expensive, administrators may decide to aim at no more than "reasonable" completeness and correctness and to use the funds so saved to obtain additional data.

Types of Error and Their Effects

Demographic data, as has been noted with respect to censuses, ought to be universal; that is, every instance of the phenomenon being measured ought to be counted once and only once. **Errors in coverage** can mean, thus, either that a person (or a population characterisic) is omitted or that he (or it) is counted twice. Duplicate registration of vital events is negligible. Duplicate counts in a census, although they exist, ordinarily cause far less error than passing over some of those who should have been counted. In migration statistics too high a count is sometimes made as a result of careless classification, as when a native returning from abroad is treated in the statistics as an immigrant. With respect to all types of population data, however, an undercount is generally more frequent and larger than an overcount.

If we take the American census as an example, the most immediate effect of an underenumeration is directly related to the purpose of the census that is stipulated in the Constitution: to lay a population basis for a new apportionment of congressional districts. If enough persons are passed over, that number lose their representation in national, state, and usually local governments. Moreover, not only political power but many other values are distributed according to the number of inhabitants. It was estimated, for instance, that each uncounted resident of New York City cost the municipal government $35 in lost state aid (*New York Times*, August 25, 1970). Many federal laws—revenue-sharing bills, for instance—include an allocation formula based in part on census data. It is in the manifest interest of each local government, one would suppose, to cooperate fully with the Census Bureau in minimizing the underenumeration in its jurisdiction, but it is only after the count has been completed that most governors and mayors recognize—with howls of anguish—its great importance to themselves. More generally, virtually every set of social or economic statistics is associated with the number of inhabitants in each locality through the routine calculation of rates per unit of the population. To the degree that the denominators of these fractions are off, the country's whole social bookkeeping incurs an additional error, apart from any in measuring the trend being analyzed (cf. Parsons 1972: chap. 1).

Errors of classification should be suspected whenever a reply can give the respondent a lower or a higher social standing. Questions on such matters as income, occupation, and education might be regarded as almost an invitation to boost one's self-esteem by stretching the truth a bit. Paradoxically, the same factor plays some part in misreporting of age (see pp. 64–65). The distortion can be particularly significant when a difference in group norms effects a different mode of response. For instance, the growing influence of sadhus, or holy men, on India's politics and society is in contrast to their number, which has fallen off from 5 million in pre-independence India to less than half a million today. (But the vaguely defined category of sadhus was expanded in the censuses of British India—"the British were eager to swell the figure in order to prove the Indians' reluctance to work"—and contracted in the counts since independence —in an effort "to destroy the image of India as a *yogi*-land."[7])

The misclassification of the "insane" in the 1840 census of the United States is an example of official prejudice so gross that it is difficult to believe. At the time the American Statistical Association and a number of other organizations and individuals criticized the returns for their patent deficiencies. According to one of the memorials submitted to Congress, "In many towns all the colored population are stated to be insane; in very many others, two-thirds, one-third, one-quarter, or one-tenth of this ill starred race are reported to be thus afflicted." The congressional committee to which these criticisms were referred admitted that this and a number of similarly grave errors had been made, but took no steps to correct them or to remove the official sanction from the published census volumes (Wright 1900: 38).

Errors of all kinds can be illustrated from the records of immigration to the United States. Surreptitious crossings take place along the borders of every

[7] Khushwant Singh, "Holy Men of India: In Search of the Seekers of Truth," *New York Times Magazine*, January 8, 1967.

country, of course, and the number entering the United States without benefit of an official welcome has in some periods been quite large. The past movement from Canada, both of Canadians and of transmigrant aliens, is largely unrecorded; according to the author of one study of the subject, his reconstruction of it "has a status intermediate between pure fact and pure speculation" (Keyfitz 1950). About four-fifths of the illegal aliens apprehended are Mexican nationals. The number of these deported increased from 320,241 in 1970 to 387,713 in 1971 to 467,185 in 1972. It cannot be determined, however, how much of this sharp rise was due to increased vigilance by the Immigration and Naturalization Service. In any case, the almost half a million per year who are arrested constitute only a half or even a quarter of the total number of aliens illegally in the country (Fragomen 1973).

To say merely that there were errors in classifying the nationalities of European immigrants is hardly to characterize the record compiled by unbelievably harried officials. According to the Commissioner of Immigration in New York during the 1890s:

The few registry clerks in the office were supposed . . . to take a statement from the immigrants about their nationality, destination and ages, [but] as a matter of fact whole pages did not contain any reply to any of these points. They were nothing more than an index of names of people arriving at the port. It was, as a matter of fact, physically impossible for . . . the port officers to do more. There were but a few of them who had to register sometimes 4,000 or 5,000 in a day. Now, under no circumstances could it be expected from them that they could examine the immigrants as to all these specific points, and put them down, and then expect that when through with the day's work they would make up the statistics.[8]

Apparently immigrants were often listed as natives of the country from which they had sailed, though many more than English left from Liverpool, or Germans from Hamburg. This confusion was particularly likely when the language spoken by the immigrants was not the one associated with their native country; thus, Flemish-speaking Belgians arriving on Dutch boats were often counted as Dutch. And what the immigration officers did with the complex ethnic structures of the empires of Austria-Hungary and Russia, no one really knows. Certainly there is no consistency in the records: Ukrainian immigrants, for instance, were sometimes so listed, and sometimes as Russians, Austrians, Galicians, or Ruthenians; eventually each of these several categories was solemnly totaled.[9]

[8] *Reports of the Industrial Commission*, **15** (Washington, D.C., 1901), p. 179; quoted in Brinley Thomas, *Migration and Economic Growth: A Study of Great Britain and the Atlantic Economy* (Cambridge, England: Cambridge University Press, 1954), p. 45.

[9] This ignorance is not limited to Eastern Europe or to the past. In 1958 the Passport Office of the U.S. Department of State issued some statistics on the number of American tourists that had visited various European countries during the first three quarters of that year. "Holland," with 17,621 visitors, was eighth on the list, and "Netherlands" was eighteenth with 5,110. A few weeks later, the somewhat embarrassed passport authorities issued a revised list, pointing out that these two countries were, of course, the same (*Nieuwe Rotterdamse Courant*, November 1, 1958).

Enumerators in countries otherwise as different as Malaya and the United States have made the same **error in recording**. When a woman who was asked how many children had been born to her answered "None," enumerators noted this reply in a manner that coders later repeatedly interpreted to mean "No answer." The number of childless couples, a most important datum for any analysis of fertility, was thus misstated (El-Badry 1961).

Misclassification need not be the reason that errors are differentially distributed, but rather the fact that either over- or undercounts are typically concentrated in particular portions of a population, particular areas, or particular time periods. For example, in the 1870 census (the first after the Civil War) the enumeration in the South was so inadequate that any interregional comparison based on uncorrected figures would be quite misleading. There is no reason to suppose, similarly, that immigrants from various European countries were randomly distributed between the steerage, where they were counted, and the first and second classes, where for most of the period of heavy immigration to the United States they were not.

Generally speaking, the greatest improvements in demographic data have come with the reduction of **errors in processing.** The importance of improved administration can be illustrated negatively with respect to the agency responsible for collecting immigration data in the United States. This has been shifted a number of times—from the Department of State (1820–74) to the Bureau of Statistics of the Treasury Department (1867–95), to the Bureau of Immigration (1892–1932), to the Immigration and Naturalization Service, first in the Department of Labor (1933–40) and then in the Department of Justice (1940 to date). For some periods, it will be noted, duplicate sets of statistics were taken, but until the 1920s none was satisfactory. A law passed in 1819 required masters of arriving ships to declare the number of their passengers, as well as their age, sex, occupation, and the country "of which it is their intention to become inhabitants." Had these manifests been filled in accurately, they would have furnished a good source of immigration statistics, but actually the records are neither complete nor consistent. In particular, immigrants were not distinguished from visitors in the annual totals, and naturalized citizens returning from abroad were not differentiated from aliens (Hutchinson 1958). When the current series of statistics began in 1892 with the establishment of the Bureau of Immigration, the quality of the data did not improve markedly. In the first decade of the 20th century registration at points of entry along the land borders was introduced and several other improvements were made, so that by 1914 essentially the same system of controls as presently exists was instituted. That is to say, reasonably accurate and complete statistics were begun about the same time that restrictive legislation cut down immigration to a fraction of the pre-1914 flow.

Some of the complexity of immigration statistics is the result of the frequent change in the responsible agency, and of the patent fact that the purposes these records were supposed to serve were neither clear nor constant. Similarly, the first nine United States censuses were supervised by federal marshals as a relatively unimportant portion of their regular duties. Full-time supervisors were appointed for the first time in 1880, and a permanent Bureau of the Census was established only in 1902. The permanent institution had a salutary effect on professional standards, both in the census itself and in the collection of vital statistics. It is now mostly in the stage of the process that cannot be mechanized, the original collection of the data, where most errors occur.

Best statistical results are to be expected, to repeat, when data are gathered for their own sake, rather than as an appendage to some other administrative procedure. One might say *a priori* that in a totalitarian state there would be more reasons than in the democratic West for evading a population count of any type and less opportunity to do so, but there is little evidence to substantiate such a judgment. In the comparative works of international bodies like the United Nations, which include member nations of every political type, the contrast itself is of course never made. In the United States census information is completely private, carefully guarded against even other government bureaus, and never published in a form that would make the identification of individuals possible. The protection of a person against the use of census data to his detriment, according to a 1929 decision in one of the few cases challenging the Census Bureau's defense of this position, "is akin to the protection afforded by the prohibitions against the evidential use of communication between attorney and client, priest and penitent, and physician and patient."[10] Insofar as certainty is possible, Americans know that others will not be permitted to use any information they submit to the Census Bureau.

The enumerator (or, more generally, the person who solicits and records any type of data) should exude an air of sympathetic objectivity, neither resisting nor overstressing the import of any question (e.g., Hanson and Marks 1958; Powell and Pritzker 1965). One can reasonably assume that **rapport** with the respondent, though it can be improved by training, is more fundamentally a function of whether the communication is across the ethnic, regional, class, and other structural lines of a society. One of the important advantages of the mail-out/mail-back procedure that the Census Bureau used in 1960 and 1970 may well be that the information gathering was anonymous in form as well as substance.

Correction of Errors

The best correction of the most common fault, an undercount, is to find and include those who were missed. Shortly after the date of the 1970 census, advertisements appeared in newspapers throughout the United States asking

---

[10] *Brauner* vs. *Mutual Life Insurance Co. of N. Y.*, 4 D & C 2d 106 (1929); see Petersen 1970: 226–267, for further details. During a period of not quite a year there was a partial break in this confidentiality. On December 11, 1961, the Supreme Court ruled in the case of *St. Regis Paper Co.* vs. *United States* that government agencies could subpoena not the reports a company made to the Census Bureau, but the copies of such reports it retained for its own files. Public Law 87–813, signed on October 15, 1962, extended the confidentiality of reports to copies (Corcoran 1963; Rubin 1962; Taeuber 1967).

WERE YOU COUNTED ?

The 1970 Census is now almost finished. It is very important that the census be complete and correct. If you believe that you (or anyone else in your household, including visitors) were NOT counted, please fill out the form below and mail it IMMEDIATELY to: **U.S. Census Office**

(Insert address)

CENSUS '70

PLEASE PRINT OR WRITE CLEARLY

- I have checked with the members of my household, and I believe that one (or more) of us was NOT counted in the 1970 Census.

- On April 1, 1970, I lived at _____

  (House number)   *(Street or road)*   *(Apartment number or location)*

  _____

  (City)   *(County)*   *(State)*   *(ZIP code)*

- This address is located between _____ and _____

  (Name of street or road)   *(Name of street or road)*

- I am listing below the name and required information for myself and each member of my household.

PLEASE INCLUDE	DO NOT INCLUDE
All family members and other relatives living here, including babies.	Any college student who stays somewhere else while attending college.
All lodgers, boarders, servants, hired hands, and other nonrelatives living here.	Any person away from here in the Armed Forces or in an institution such as a home for the aged or mental hospital.
All persons who usually live here but are temporarily away.	
All persons with a home elsewhere but who stay here most of the week while working or attending college.	Any person who usually stays somewhere else most of the week while working there.
Anyone staying or visiting here who had no other home.	Any person visiting here who has a usual home elsewhere.

NAMES OF PERSONS LIVING IN THIS HOUSEHOLD ON APRIL 1, 1970, AND THOSE STAYING OR VISITING HERE WHO HAD NO OTHER HOME.			Print relationship of each person to the head of the household.		Is this person—	When was this person born?		Is this person—
Print names in this order — { Head of the household / Wife of head / Unmarried children, oldest first / Married children and their families / Other relatives of the head / Persons not related to the head }			*For example:* Wife, Son, Daughter, Grandson, Mother-in-law, Lodger, Lodger's wife	Male or Female M or F	White, Negro (Black), American Indian, Japanese, Chinese, Filipino, Hawaiian, Korean, Other (print specific race)			Now married, Widowed, Divorced, Separated, Single (never married)
(If you list more than 6 persons, use an additional sheet)						Month	Year	
Last name	First name	Middle initial						
			HEAD					

- Name of person who filled this form: _____

NOTICE – Your answers are CONFIDENTIAL. The law (Title 13, United States Code) requires that you answer the questions to the best of your knowledge. Your answers will be used only for statistical purposes and cannot, by law, be disclosed to any person outside the Census Bureau for any reason whatsoever.

U.S. Dept. of Commerce
Bureau of the Census
Form D-26

Budget Bureau No. 41-S68107
Approval Expires: 12-31-70

Cut along dotted line

In an effort to correct underenumeration in the 1970 count, the Census Bureau placed this form in various newspapers (*U.S. Bureau of the Census*).

readers in English, Spanish, Italian, Chinese, Yiddish, Polish, Croatian, Serbian, or Hungarian, "Were you counted?" No doubt some of the underenumeration was removed, but this kind of check is probably least likely to reach precisely the type of people who had been overlooked originally. As long ago as in a volume supplementing the 1900 census, Walter Willcox had defined the class most likely to be passed over, and the reason.

Census returns are obtained by enumerators who inquire from dwelling house to dwelling house, [but] a small minority of the population have no dwelling house even in the loose sense in which that term is defined by the Census Office, namely, the place where a person regularly sleeps. Such persons without habitation are somewhat likely not to be counted, and also are likely to be predominantly males. . . . [They also] constitute perhaps a larger proportion of the population in cities and towns than they do in any but the most sparsely settled country districts [U.S. Bureau of the Census 1906: 88].

During pretests of the 1970 census, experimental "casual-setting" interviews were conducted in New Haven and Trenton. Men were accosted on street corners or in saloons to see whether their names were on the lists being developed for the coming count. The responses validated Willcox's insight more than half a century earlier. "It may well be that, for practical purposes, such persons should be considered 'to live' on street corners and in bars, poolrooms, and other 'casual settings' in which censuses are not customarily taken" (Parsons 1972: 31). That the Bureau had gone to such lengths to locate these derelicts indicates how ill informed and unjust many of its critics are.

Once any set of data has been made as complete as possible, it can be checked for its **internal consistency.** In earlier counts this had been done by field supervisors, but in the processing of the 1970 census the computer itself was programed to do preliminary editing. A woman listed as both a wife and single, for instance, the computer changed into "now married." Or, in another example cited from a Bureau release, "assume that a person reported as a 20-year-old son of the household head failed to indicate his marital status. Upon detecting this omission, the computer assigned him the same marital status as that of the last son that was processed in the same age group." This procedure, called "allocation of data," generally results in a greater validity than would distributing persons with missing characteristics uniformly over the whole of the population.

There must also be a **temporal consistency** in any statistical series. Some characteristics, once acquired, are permanent—for example, literacy or legal majority; and a decline in the proportion able to read or to vote, if not due to emigration or a change in age structure or whatever, would make one suspect the accuracy of the data. Age does not remain constant but changes at a regular rate, and an unexplained variation from this pattern would also make one check the figures again.

It is often possible to **compare data collected in different ways** on the same facts, such as country-of-birth returns in the census with immigration records. Or the latter can be contrasted with the statistics maintained by some emigration countries.[11] As a particular kind of such comparisons, it is always possible to

---

[11] In general, the records of the receiving countries are better. For the entire period from the first colonization to the present, overseas emigration totaled over 60 million by the statistics of the receiving countries but about 10 percent less by those of the sending countries (Kirk 1946: 72–73). For specific countries or periods, however, the discrepancy is much

check a census against birth or death registrations. In the 1940 census of the United States an especially careful cross-check of this kind was made. Enumerators filled in a separate card for each infant under four months old on April 1, the official date of the census, and these cards were compared with the registrations of births and infant deaths in each area. The results were appalling. For the entire country only 92.5 percent of births had been registered. In sixteen states the complete figure was below 90 percent, the standard that had been used to admit them to the Birth Registration Area; in six states it was under 85 percent; in South Carolina and Arkansas hardly more than three births in every four had been registered. Partly as a consequence of renewed efforts to improve registration procedures, and partly because of the larger proportion of hospital confinements, a similar check a decade later showed that there had been a considerable increase in the proportion of births registered. In 1950 this was almost 98 percent over the whole nation, and for the South it was 96 percent. Only two states still remained below the standard of 90 percent (Shapiro 1954). Similarly, in 1958 the Census Bureau and the National Office of Vital Statistics conducted a joint study in Memphis, matching the data on death certificates with those listed in the 1950 census and a special questionnaire. Among the 83 percent of the cases that could be matched, only 85.6 percent were identical on the birthplace of the decedent, and only 78.4 percent were within 5 years of the same age (Guralnick and Nam 1959). When one imperfect instrument is used to gauge the accuracy of another, the overall improvement can be great, even though it is not possible by such a comparison to detect parallel errors.

It is also possible to correct errors by an especially careful recount of a small sample of the population (e.g., Lahiri 1958). For example, after the 1950 United States census a **post-enumeration survey** was made using scrupulously selected and specially trained interviewers. About 3,500 small areas were recanvassed in order to gauge the number of households omitted in the original census, and 22,000 households were revisited in order to see how many persons had been miscounted. On this basis, it was estimated that there had been an underenumeration of 3.4 million persons and an overenumeration of 1.3 million in the census, or a net undercount equal to 1.4 percent of the total enumerated population. Errors were relatively more frequent in the South, in rural areas, and among nonwhites. Following the 1960 census, a check through a general sample of the population was supplemented with samples of three particular groups—social-security pensioners, selective-service registrants, and college students. According to two members of the Bureau's staff, however, the post-enumeration survey was effective mainly in locating households that had been missed, but not those

---

greater. For example, "for the years 1916 to 1920, Italian passport statistics indicate 633,000 emigrants to the United States; but the statistics of that country registered only 171,000 Italian immigrants" (Lacroix 1949). Similarly, Dutch statistics show a total of 130,222 departures to *all* countries during 1882–1924, while for this period American statistics alone record 179,258 arrivals from the Netherlands (Willcox and Ferenczi 1931, vol. 2: 125, 737–746).

persons omitted from households included in the original count. They estimated that the resurvey had uncovered only about 40 percent of the net underenumeration (Heer 1968: 61–63).

The post-enumeration survey has been used, moreover, not only to correct a prior count but to set better standards for future ones. It is one type of the continuing research that the Census Bureau conducts in its persistent effort to reduce nonsampling error to a minimum. Self-enumeration was introduced in 1960, for example, partly because of a study of how and why enumerators differed among themselves in 1950, and the extension of the technique in 1970 was based on further research on response variance in 1960. Over the years the Bureau has tried to improve the census and the *Current Population Survey* through experimentation with enumeration procedures, the design of questionnaires, the sample design, and, most generally, methods of identifying and controlling errors in response and measurement (Hansen and Waksberg 1970).

With various controls for the quality of enumeration, one can calculate the "true" size of population sectors and thus the proportion of each that was missed. Coverage improved markedly between 1950 and 1960, both overall and separately for age, sex, and color categories with one important exception: young male blacks, of whom a higher proportion apparently was missed in the latter year (Table 2-4). According to the Bureau's final estimate, in 1970 the net underenumeration of 5.4 million (2.5 percent) comprised 3.5 million whites (1.9 percent) and 1.9 million blacks (7.7 percent). New techniques enabled the Bureau to reach an estimated 2.4 million persons who probably would have been passed over with the methods used in previous enumerations.

A final method of correcting errors in data and particularly of filling in gaps is by the construction of a **mathematical model**. Fertility, mortality, and the age structure are related to each other in such a way that if any two of these are known the range of the third can be determined. The curve of each of the major demographic variables can be smoothed by techniques that yield not precise data but probably more accurate figures for many countries than those obtained by any alternative estimation. The method also has the distinct advantage of being very much less costly than any other.

SUMMARY

Population data are of four main types: the census, vital statistics, international migration records, and those on internal migration. Although partial precursors can be found in previous historical eras, in a strict sense all four types are a product of modern Western culture. It was almost inevitable, therefore, that population theory tended to be ethnocentric, for even after World War II "the good population data on which demographic generalizations are based almost entirely relate to populations of European race" (Kirk 1949). The most important example of this bias was noted in the previous chapter, the supposi-

Table 2-4. Estimated Percentage of Net Underenumeration by Age, Sex, and Color, United States, 1950 and 1960

Age Category	April 1, 1950				April 1, 1960			
	MALE		FEMALE		MALE		FEMALE	
	WHITE	NONWHITE	WHITE	NONWHITE	WHITE	NONWHITE	WHITE	NONWHITE
0–4	4.3	9.9	3.7	9.1	2.0	7.7	1.2	6.4
5–9	3.0	10.7	2.4	9.1	2.4	5.7	1.6	4.8
10–14	1.0	6.6	1.1	6.5	2.5	5.2	1.5	4.2
15–19	4.0	15.2	1.8	10.8	3.8	12.5	2.4	10.1
20–24	5.6	15.9	1.6	7.5	4.3	17.5	2.4	9.6
25–29	4.9	16.6	0.3	7.4	4.2	19.7	1.4	8.7
30–34	4.3	16.6	0.1	8.3	3.1	18.0	0.6	5.9
35–39	2.1	10.8	-1.4	2.9	2.5	14.5	-0.2	6.2
40–44	3.3	16.6	2.0	15.3	1.9	12.8	-0.2	6.4
45–49	2.2	11.6	1.5	10.8	1.6	11.5	0.7	8.4
50–54	2.2	9.9	2.6	13.7	3.6	17.8	4.2	18.2
55–59	5.0	14.4	7.1	23.0	0.4	5.9	1.6	10.0
60–64	3.5	19.5	6.8	26.5	3.0	9.7	4.2	14.1
65+	-2.0	10.8	2.2	4.7	3.8	1.8	2.1	12.2
Total	3.1	12.8	2.1	9.8	2.8	10.9	1.6	8.1

SOURCE: Jacob S. Siegel, "Completeness of Coverage of the Nonwhite Population in the 1960 Census and Current Estimates, and Some Implications," in David M. Heer, editor, Social Statistics and the City (Cambridge, Mass.: Harvard University Press, 1968), pp. 42–43.

tion—almost universally accepted in the 1930s—that the demographic transition in Europe would be followed with no essential change in all underdeveloped areas.

The censuses of the Western world, held every decade or so with few or no interruptions since some date in the 19th century, have gradually become more accurate and broader in the range of questions covered. Today they are an indispensable tool for, among others, statesmen, social scientists, and businessmen. Vital statistics, because of the historical accident that usually they are gathered by local authorities rather than by national governments, have developed more slowly. International migration records, inadequate in a number of ways during the 19th century, were brought up to a reasonable standard of accuracy and completeness only by about 1914 in the United States, the prime country of destination in the prior period. The statistics of many demographic phenomena—for example, marriage and divorce, morbidity, and internal migration—are still quite poor in many economically advanced countries and practically nonexistent in underdeveloped areas.

During the past century, originally as an extension of the national bookkeeping of Western Europe, several international congresses and organizations have tried in various ways to establish worldwide statistical standards. These efforts are wholly laudable, and it is particularly useful that the underdeveloped countries presently beginning their statistical records will be able, at least in some respects, to start from the highest level of the procedures so painfully worked out in Western countries. It must be emphasized, however, that variation in statistical methods is in part accidental—and with sufficient effort and good will this can be reduced—and in part a reflection of differences in national culture. International migration statistics, for example, so long as they are collected as an adjunct to the political control of national borders, will be noncomparable mainly because of the great differences in various countries' migration laws. Or, as another example, what are termed common-law marriages in the United States are very frequent in Latin America, where, however, they are often not recognized either in law or in the statistics, so that thousands of mothers or even grandmothers are classified as single. In short, some standardization of population data is both possible and desirable, but so long as national cultures are not homogenized into a worldwide uniformity, the international comparability of statistics will not be fully achieved.

To avoid errors in demographic statistics, the following conditions must be met:

1. All categories to be measured must be precisely defined.

2. Each instance of the phenomenon being measured must be counted once, and only once.

3. Respondents must be induced to answer truthfully the questions put to them.

4. Answers must be classified in the appropriate categories and subcategories.

5. Errors must not be introduced in the compiling, processing, and publication of the data.

As even this list suggests, perfect accuracy is not attainable. Indeed, it is not sought. The aim in modern demographic statistics is to reduce the error to a small proportion of known range rather than to try to eliminate it altogether. The errors that are made can be detected and in part corrected by checking: (1) any form for collecting information, such as a census schedule or a birth certificate, for internal consistency; (2) data of the same series, such as successive censuses, for serial consistency; (3) data of different types, such as vital statistics and the census, or the census and immigration records, for external consistency; (4) the grosser count with an especially carefully drawn sample; and (5) the components of the population for consistency with a mathematical model.

CITED REFERENCES AND SUGGESTIONS FOR FURTHER READING

The best introductory works are probably the three manuals issued by the United Nations (1949, 1954, 1955); all three contrast recommended procedures with actual practices. Of considerably greater interest and no less importance is Milbank Memorial Fund's symposium (1949), a series of essays on how various demographic concepts are interpreted in various countries. Techniques of population analysis are expounded in Barclay (1958), McArthur (1961), Shryock and Siegel (1971), and, at a more advanced level, Spiegelman (1968).

The U.S. Bureau of the Census's short pamphlet (1970a) describes the Bureau's operations in popular terms. It can be suplemented best by various papers written by Bureau personnel—e.g., Hanson and Marks (1958), Powell and Pritzker (1965), Taeuber (1967), Hansen and Waksberg (1970), several of the papers in Heer (1968), and especially the book by its one-time director (Eckler 1972). The history of the early censuses, given in full and sometimes fascinating detail in Wright (1900), is summarized, as it were, in U.S. Bureau of the Census (1960). The best short statement on new procedures introduced in the most recent American census is in Kaplan (1970); for a fuller discussion, see U.S. Bureau of the Census (1970b). Garland (1972) offers a useful guide to the products of the 1970 census. Benjamin (1970) is an excellent booklet, especially useful to American readers because most of its examples are drawn from the British experience. The Population Research Center (1965) and Blake and Donovan (1971) have surveyed the censuses of other countries, the first broadly and the latter more intensively. Ferris and Lee (1971) offer a number of essays on how the 1970 American census can be used in sociological research.

Gutman (1959) has written the definitive study of America's earliest registration system. Gaete-Darbó (1964) has made a critical appraisal of vital statistics in Latin America, which applies in part to similar difficulties and gaps throughout the underdeveloped world. Various articles on registration in the United States, e.g., Shapiro (1954), indicate both the problems that persist and methods of coping with them. Of the several series the National Center for Health Statistics publishes, the most important are the annual *Vital Statistics of the United States*, the *Monthly Vital*

Statistics Report, and *Vital and Health Statistics.* Two numbers of the last publication (Series 4, no. 12–13, 1970) offer a critical review of the Center's work and the additional data needed for various types of analysis.

In spite of its date, Willcox and Ferenczi (1929–31) is still the best work on historical migration statistics. See, for example, the essay by Marian Rubins Davis, "Critique of Official United States Immigration Statistics" (vol. 2, 645–658), which is brought up to date by Hutchinson (1958). Comparable analyses of American data on internal migration are given by Lee and Lee (1960) and Shryock (1964).

*BARCLAY, GEORGE W. 1958. *Techniques of Population Analysis.* New York: Wiley.

BENJAMIN, BERNARD. 1970. *The Population Census.* London: Heinemann.

BLAKE, JUDITH, and JERRY J. DONOVAN. 1971. *Western European Censuses, 1960: An English Language Guide.* Berkeley: Institute of International Studies, University of California.

BOURGEOIS-PICHAT, JEAN. 1972. "Le troisième congrès mondial de la population (1974) et l'Année mondiale de la population (1974)," *Population,* **27,** 1053–1074.

CICOUREL, AARON V. 1964. *Method and Measurement in Sociology.* New York: Free Press.

CORCORAN, THOMAS F. 1963. "On the Confidential Status of Census Reports," *American Statistician,* **17,** 33–40.

DALZELL, DONALD R. 1970. "Photocomposition of Statistical Tables." Washington, D.C.: U.S. Bureau of the Census. Mimeographed.

*DUNN, EDGAR S., JR. 1967. "The Idea of a National Data Center and the Issue of Personal Privacy," *American Statistician,* **21,** 21–27.

*ECKLER, A. ROSS. 1972. *The Bureau of the Census.* New York: Praeger.

EL-BADRY, M. A. 1961. "Failure of Enumerators to Make Entries of Zero: Errors in Recording Childless Cases in Population Censuses," *Journal of the American Statistical Association,* **56,** 909–924.

FERRIS, ABBOTT L., and EVERETT S. LEE, editors. 1971. *Research and the 1970 Census.* Oak Ridge, Tenn.: Southern Regional Demographic Group.

FISCHER, J. L. 1958. "The Classification of Residence in Censuses," *American Anthropologist,* **60,** 508–517.

FRAGOMEN, AUSTIN T., JR. 1973. *The Illegal Alien: Criminal or Economic Refugee?* New York: Center for Migration Studies.

GAETE-DARBÓ, ADOLFO. 1964. "Appraisal of Vital Statistics in Latin America," *Milbank Memorial Fund Quarterly,* **42,** 86–103.

GARLAND, MICHAEL G. 1972. "A Guide to the Products of the 1970 Census of Population and Housing," *Population Index,* **38,** 409–424.

GLASER, E., D. ROSENBLATT, and M. K. WOOD. 1967. "The Design of a Federal Statistical Data Center," *American Statistician,* **21,** 12–20.

GURALNICK, LILLIAN, and CHARLES B. NAM. 1959. "Census-NOVS Study of Death Certificates Matched to Census Records," *Milbank Memorial Fund Quarterly,* **37,** 144–151.

GUTMAN, ROBERT. 1959. *Birth and Death Registration in Massachusetts, 1639–1900.* New York: Milbank Memorial Fund.

HAMILTON, C. HORACE. 1966. "Effect of Census Errors on the Measurement of Net Migration," *Demography,* **3,** 393–415.

HANSEN, MORRIS G., WILLIAM N. HURWITZ, and LEON PRITZKER. 1953. "The Accuracy of Census Results," *American Sociological Review*, **18**, 416–423.

*_____, and JOSEPH WAKSBERG. 1970. "Research on Non-sampling Errors in Censuses and Surveys," *Review of the International Statistical Institute*, **38**, 317–332.

HANSON, ROBERT H., and ELI S. MARKS. 1958. "Influence of the Interviewer on the Accuracy of Survey Results," *Journal of the American Statistical Association*, **53**, 635–655.

HEER, DAVID M., editor. 1968. *Social Statistics and the City*. Cambridge, Mass.: Harvard University Press.

HETZEL, ALICE M. 1971. "Marriage and Divorce Statistics and the Health Department," *HSMHA Health Reports*, **86**, 616–626.

HOLLINGSWORTH, THOMAS H. 1971. "Population Data Needs and the Use of Such Data in Demographic and Social Analysis," Second European Population Conference, *Report*, Subject V, vol. 4. Strasbourg.

HUTCHINSON, E. P. 1958. "Notes on Immigration Statistics of the United States," *Journal of the American Statistical Association*, **53**, 963–1025.

HUXTABLE, DEANE L. 1967. "Vital Statistics Aid in Developing Nations," *American Journal of Public Health*, **57**, 504–508.

JOHNSTON, DENIS FOSTER. 1966. *An Analysis of Sources of Information on the Population of the Navaho*. Bureau of American Ethnology, Bulletin 197. Washington, D.C.

KAPLAN, DAVID L. 1970. "Plans for the 1970 Census of Population and Housing," *Demography*, **7**, 1–18.

KEYFITZ, NATHAN. 1950. "The Growth of Canadian Population," *Population Studies*, **4**, 47–63.

KIRK, DUDLEY. 1946. *Europe's Population in the Interwar Years*. League of Nations. Princeton, N.J.: Princeton University Press.

_____. 1949. "Problems of Collection and Comparability of International Population Statistics," in Milbank Memorial Fund 1949.

KISH, LESLIE. 1965. *Survey Sampling*, New York: Wiley.

LACROIX, MAX. 1949. "Problems of Collection and Comparison of Migration Statistics," in Milbank Memorial Fund 1949.

LAHIRI, D. B. 1958. "Recent Developments in the Use of Techniques for Assessment of Errors in Nation-wide Surveys of India," *Bulletin de l'Institut International de Statistique*, **36**, 71–93.

LAZARSFELD, PAUL F. 1961. "Notes on the History of Quantification in Sociology—Trends, Sources and Problems," in Harry Woolf, editor, *Quantification: A History of the Meaning of Measurement in the Natural and Social Sciences*. Indianapolis: Bobbs-Merrill.

LEE, EVERETT S., and ANNE S. LEE. 1960. "Internal Migration Statistics for the United States," *Journal of the American Statistical Association*, **55**, 664–697.

LINDER, FORREST E. 1955. "Adherence of National Censuses to International Recommendations," in World Population Conference, 1954, *Proceedings*. New York: United Nations.

MCARTHUR, NORMA. 1961. *Introducing Population Statistics*. Melbourne: Oxford University Press.

*MILBANK MEMORIAL FUND. 1949. *Problems in the Collection and Comparability of International Statistics*. New York.

PARSONS, CAROLE W., editor. 1972. *America's Uncounted People.* Report of the Advisory Committee on Problems of Census Enumeration, National Research Council. Washington, D.C.: National Academy of Sciences.

PETERSEN, WILLIAM. 1970. *The Politics of Population.* Gloucester, Mass.: Peter Smith.

_____. 1971. *Japanese Americans: Oppression and Success.* New York: Random House.

POPULATION RESEARCH CENTER, UNIVERSITY OF TEXAS. 1965. *International Population Census Bibliography.* No. 1: *Latin America and the Caribbean*; No. 2: *Africa*; No. 3: *Oceania*; No. 4: *North America*; No. 5: *Asia*; No. 6: *Europe.* Austin: Bureau of Business Research, University of Texas.

*POWELL, BARBARA A., and LEON PRITZKER. 1965. "Effects of Variation in Field Personnel on Census Results," *Demography*, 2, 8–32.

RUBIN, ERNEST. 1962. "Government Statistics and Confidentiality of Response," *American Statistician*, 16, 27–30.

SHAPIRO, SAM. 1954. "Recent Testing of Birth Registration Completeness in the United States," *Population Studies*, 8, 3–21.

SHRYOCK, HENRY S., JR. 1964. *Population Mobility Within the United States.* Chicago: Community and Family Study Center, University of Chicago.

*_____, and JACOB S. SIEGEL. 1971. *The Methods and Materials of Demography*, 2 vol. Washington, D.C.: U.S. Bureau of the Census.

SPIEGELMAN, MORTIMER. 1968. *Introduction to Demography.* Cambridge, Mass.: Harvard University Press.

SYMONDS, RICHARD, and MICHAEL CARDER. 1973. *The United Nations and the Population Question.* New York: McGraw-Hill.

TAEUBER, CONRAD. 1967. "Invasion of Privacy," *Eugenics Quarterly*, 14, 243–246.

THOMAS, DOROTHY SWAINE. 1938. "The Continuous Register System of Population Accounting," in National Resources Committee, Committee on Population Problems, *The Problems of a Changing Population.* Washington, D.C.: U.S. Government Printing Office.

*UNITED NATIONS. 1949. *Problems of Migration Statistics.* Population Studies, no. 5. New York.

*_____. 1954. *Handbook of Population Census Methods.* Studies in Methods, Series F, no. 5. New York.

*_____. 1955. *Handbook of Vital Statistics Methods.* Studies in Methods, Series F, no. 7. New York.

_____. 1967. *Sample Surveys of Current Interest.* Statistical Papers, Series C, no. 12. New York.

U.S. BUREAU OF THE CENSUS. 1906. "Special Reports. Supplementary Analyses and Derivative Tables." *Twelfth Census of the United States, 1900.* Washington, D.C.

*_____. 1960. *Historical Statistics of the United States, Colonial Times to 1957.* Washington, D.C.

*_____. 1963. "The Current Population Survey: A Report on Methodology." Technical Paper no. 7. Washington, D.C.

_____. 1970a. *We, the Americans—Who We Are.* Washington, D.C.

_____. 1970b. *1970 Census Users' Guide*, 2 parts. Washington, D.C.

U.S. DEPARTMENT OF STATE. 1969. *Status of the World's Nations.* Bureau of Intelligence and Research, Geographic Bulletin no. 2. Washington, D.C.

U.S. PUBLIC HEALTH SERVICE. 1970. *Report of the Twentieth Anniversary Conference of the United States National Committee on Vital and Health Statistics.* Rockville, Md.

*WILLCOX, WALTER F. 1930. "Census," *Encyclopedia of the Social Sciences,* vol. 3, 295–300. New York: Macmillan.

——. 1949. "Development of International Statistics," in Milbank Memorial Fund 1949.

*——, and IMRE FERENCZI, editors. 1929, 1931. *International Migrations:* vol. 1, *Statistics*; vol. 2, *Interpretations.* National Bureau of Economic Research, Publications 14 and 18. New York.

*WRIGHT, CARROLL D. 1900. *The History and Growth of the United States Censuses, Prepared for the Senate Committee on the Censuses.* Washington, D.C.: Government Printing Office.

AGE AND SEX STRUCTURE

3

It is convenient to distinguish **population structure**, or the distribution by sex and age, from **population composition**, or the distribution by other attributes; for the former is in several respects more basic to demography.

1. Sex and age are **universal**. Indeed, some types of occupational pattern and class structure, of religion, of ethnic differentiation, are also to be found in virtually every society, but the effect of such factors on the population varies greatly. If the gods of the ancient Aztecs demanded enormous human sacrifices and Roman Catholicism has inhibited the spread of contraception, one cannot therefore speak of *the* influence of religion on mortality and fertility.

2. Sex and age are **always relevant** and always in roughly the same way. Some religions, to continue with the same example, have no effect on population phenomena, but in every culture throughout the world children are borne only by females in the fecund ages, and the probability of dying within a year is greater among infants and the aged than among young adults. One of the principal modes of refining demographic rates, therefore, is to relate the incidence of such demographic events as births or deaths to a population delimited by its age and sex characteristics.

3. The population structure is the **basis of a population model**, which is the principal subject matter of formal demography (see pp. 2–3). The processes of fertility, migration, and mortality together determine not only the current size of the population of any area but also its structure; and, conversely, to the degree that other factors remain unchanged, the population structure sets the future rates of fertility, migration, and mortality. What is termed a **young population**— that is, one in which young persons are relatively more numerous—is more fecund, less susceptible to many causes of death, and usually more migratory than an **old population**.

QUALITY OF THE DATA

Statistics on sex are generally the best in any demographic record. There is no ambiguity about the meaning of *male* and *female*[1] and seldom any motivation

---

[1] There are no words, it is true, to denote the two sexes only of the human species irrespective of age. In some languages the equivalents of *male* and *female* refer mainly to animals and

for misrepresentation. In the United States the historical record has only two significant gaps: the sex of Negroes before 1820 and the sex of immigrants before about 1850. The data on sex listed for the whole population, however, may be a good deal more accurate than figures for various subcategories. Among foreign-born, for instance, females are less likely to list themselves as natives than males, whose occupation outside the home affords both a stronger motive and a more rapid acculturation. Most casual and migrant laborers, who as we have noted are most likely to be passed over in any population count, are male adults, and although their omission affects overall totals only slightly, this might not be the case for smaller subpopulations.

Data on age, available in almost all types of population records, are also relatively accurate and complete, though far less so than the uninitiated would suppose. Although all peoples have roles specific to infants, children, youth, adults, and the aged, many are alien to a more precise designation of age. In the first population counts undertaken by the European administrators of the various Pacific islands, for example, the only age differentiation attempted was to distinguish children from adults. Then the populations were divided by social-status categories roughly associated with particular age ranges. "Even now, relatively few are conscious of age as the number of years which have elapsed since their birth; if asked their age, many will reply with a number, but often the answer is quite meaningless" (McArthur 1961: 24).

The distribution of ages in populations lacking such data is typically estimated by either of two methods. One is termed, rather loosely, "historical reconstruc-tion." In the 1966 census of Papua and New Guinea, thus, enumerators had been instructed to estimate ages in the following manner: "From a list of notable events the informant was asked to identify an event which he remembered during his childhood. He was then asked to point out a child the same size as he remem-bered himself to be at the time of this event. The child's [estimated] age was then subtracted from the date of this event to give an estimate of the date of birth of the informant" (quoted in Wolfers 1972). The second method, no more satisfac-tory, is to convert the intervals between such physiological markers as puberty and menopause into age categories. But in Negro Africa, for instance, interviewers have systematically raised the ages of married women and mothers toward the middle range of fecundity, starting from a supposed age at marriage higher than the actual and an interval between births assumed to be standard. In the Upper Volta, thus, the number of females of 10–14 years has been underestimated by perhaps 15 to 25 percent, and those of 15–19 years by a smaller but still signifi-cant proportion, with a consequent overestimation of those aged 20 to 40. The error in estimating males' ages, because of the usual difference in the age at

---

thus suggest vulgarity when applied to humans. In Spanish, for instance, columns of age distributions beginning with the first year would be headed *Hombres* and *Mujeres*. In English, similarly, the "perverse" use of *woman* as an adjective (as H. W. Fowler termed it in *Modern English Usage*) has become common in phrases like *woman lawyer* and even *women lawyers*.

marriage, has generally been smaller; this means that the proportions of the two sexes in each age bracket, an important datum for demographic analysis, have also been falsified (Van de Walle 1968).

Present-day recapitulations of the population growth of Western countries are often broken down by age, but in many of the earliest censuses these data were in fact not collected. Thus, in England no question was asked about age in 1801; in 1821 the question was included in the schedule, but persons were required to answer it only "if not inconvenient"; in 1831 the only return concerning age was an estimate of the number of males over 20. Respondents had to state their age only from 1841 on. The age statistics collected in the United States, as another instance, varied even more during the first decades of the national census (Wright 1900: 91):

Free Whites
    1790: Males divided into two categories only—under 16 years, and 16 years and over; females not classified by age.
    1800–20: Males and females each classified as follows: under 10, 10–15, 16–25, 26–44, 45 and over.
    1830–40: Males and females each classified as follows: under 5, 5–9, 10–14, 15–19, 20–29, 30–39, 40–49, 50–59, 60–69, 70–79, 80–89, 90–99, 100 and over.
Colored (except Indians not taxed)
    1790–1810: Divided into slave and free; not classified by sex or age.
    1820: Divided into slave and free and by sex, and each subpopulation classified by age as follows: under 14, 14–25, 26–44, 45 and over.
    1830–40: Divided into slave and free and by sex, and each subpopulation classified by age as follows: under 10, 10–23, 24–35, 36–54, 55–99, 100 and over.

Beginning in 1850, enumerators were instructed to ask for the exact age. Since that date, this has been defined as the age on the last birthday except in 1890, when the question called for age at the nearest birthday. In 1900 and again in 1960, each respondent was also asked for the month and year of his birth, but in processing the latter census the data were grouped into three-month periods. In 1970, as we have noted, information was collected directly on the quarter-year of birth.

Age, in short, can be defined in grosser units than single years. If in years, it can be measured to the last birthday or to the nearest one. Or, most precisely, the date of birth can be asked for. Practice varies considerably from one country to another, and in any country from one type of demographic data to another. The standard certificate for a live birth, for instance, in the form recommended by the U.S. National Center for Health Statistics (1968: 6; cf. Lunde and Grove 1966) calls only for the "age (at time of this birth)" of the mother and the father. This is a less precise designation, particularly of the mother's age, than would be useful in analyzing fertility.

Once persons in a Western society have been asked for their age, it might be supposed that most respondents both could furnish this datum and would be willing to do so. However, even in a country like the United States some report that they do not know their age. Others give it only approximately, either because they do not know it precisely or because they do not recognize the importance of accuracy. They "heap" their stated age at an even number, a number ending in five, or particularly one ending in zero (Myers 1940; Bachi 1954; Zelnik 1961, 1964). How old a person is might be regarded as a relatively neutral characteristic, but the prestige associated with a particular age is likely to be reflected in the record. Thus, Americans often used to overstate the correct figure to heap ages at the 21 years marking majority; presumably this will change to 18 years as this new definition of legal maturity evolves. The ages of infants and young children are frequently overstated, and that is one reason for their usual underenumeration. At least by popular legend, middle-aged women frequently understate their age or refuse to reveal it. The very old, on the contrary, often exaggerate their longevity. The proportion of centenarians enumerated in the censuses has been going down steadily, and breakdowns by urban–rural residence and color suggest that the simpler life of long ago must have been more healthful. The real reason is given in an analysis supplementary to the 1900 census: when the states were ranked by the proportions reportedly 100 years or over and illiterate, there was a correlation of .714 between the two series (calculated from Young 1906).

The problems in interpreting the age data of non-Western population records are similar, though with some interesting differences. In Japan, inasmuch as respondents are asked for their date of birth, there is no tendency to heap replies on ages ending in an even number, five, or zero (this is thus an important additional advantage to phrasing the question in the most precise form). Even so, when data were compared from the same persons in a census and in a sample survey, discrepancies were found in 17 percent of the returns, partly because of errors, partly because of the exaggeration of advanced ages (Morita 1958). In Ghana, similarly, when the dates of registered birth of a sample of children aged up to 8 years were compared with their ages as given in the 1960 census, 35 percent were different (Caldwell 1966).

Among Chinese populations a person is traditionally reckoned to be 1 year old at birth, and then a year older on each following Chinese New Year's day (marking the beginning of the lunar year, which is slightly shorter than the solar year conventionally used in the West). As compared with the Western system, a person so measured is always 1 to 3 years older. Correcting for the difference can be complicated, for in partly westernized populations no one knows what proportion of the Chinese uses each system. When enumerators in Singapore were instructed to ask for the age "according to the English reckoning"— thus in effect requesting the more traditional respondents to calculate their age before replying—it was impossible to know how many in fact complied. The solution is to ask for the totemic animal under which the person was born.

Alfred Murphy, a former slave, attended a literacy class that the WPA ran in Columbus, Ohio. At 105, he thought he was "never too old to learn" (*Ohio Historical Society Library*).

These animals—ox, rat, pig, and so on—recur in a 12-year cycle. Thus, for persons born in the Chinese years falling mainly in 1920, 1932, 1944, 1956, 1968, etc., the totem is the monkey; and if a person so identified gave his age in 1957 as 14, we know that by the Western system it was probably 13. However, there are always two totemic animals in a Western year, since the Chinese New Year falls in either January or February. They can be differentiated by asking whether the birth date was between the New Year's Day and the date of the census (You 1959; Saw 1967).

Errors in reported ages can generally be adjusted by either of two principles, which are termed the *cohort method* and the *smoothing method* (cf. Shryock and Siegel 1971: chap. 8).

A **cohort** constitutes all persons born during the same year (or some other unit of time), who are analyzed as a unit throughout their lifetime.[2] Apart from such factors as, for instance, a migration into or out of the area under study,

[2] More precisely, this is a birth cohort. One can also designate marriage cohorts (all persons married during a given year), cohorts of college graduates, and so on.

each cohort changes from one year to the next only by the proportion of persons who die off at that age—a figure that one can derive from the life table for the population (see pp. 230–233). Whether there is a heaping at age 25, for example, could be shown by a sample survey the following year, when the age of the cohort would be 26.

For any one census, similarly one can assume that under normal conditions there will have been a gradual reduction in the size of cohorts of successive ages. Thus, the number aged 26 should be only slightly less than that aged 25; and if it is not, the age curve can be smoothed by the calculation of **age ratios**, or the number of persons at each age divided by the averages of the number at the adjacent five older and five younger ages (Zelnik 1961). In many cases, however, it is impossible to be sure whether deviations from a smooth curve are the consequence of spurious reporting or of actual differences in the size of certain cohorts. For instance, the age structure of Indonesia in 1961 showed a very large proportion aged 5 to 9, an extraordinarily small proportion aged 10 to 24, and again a larger proportion aged 25 to 44. If one accepts the figures as reported, the plausible reason is that during the Japanese occupation and the subsequent revolution the birth rate was lower and the infant death rate higher (Keyfitz 1965). However, it may be that in Indonesia, as in a number of African countries, young persons on the verge of adult roles tend to understate their ages, and then to overstate them once social adulthood has been achieved (Van de Walle 1966, with a reply by Keyfitz).

THE SEX STRUCTURE

The relation in a population between the number of males and the number of females can be measured with any of three simple measures. If we denote the number of males by P_m, the number of females by P_f, and the total population by P_t, the three equations are as follows:

$$\text{Percent male excess} = \frac{P_m - P_f}{P_t} \times 100$$

$$\text{Proportion male} = \frac{P_m}{P_t} \times 100$$

$$\text{Sex ratio} = \frac{P_m}{P_f} \times 100$$

Which of the three to use is a matter mainly of custom.[3] A generation or so ago, a usual form was the proportion male, but this has been largely displaced by the sex ratio. A population perfectly balanced between the sexes would show

[3] The first two measures could be calculated, of course, to show the percent female excess and the proportion female, but those are implicit in the equations as shown. Some authorities define the sex ratio as the number of males per *1,000* females, thus moving the decimal point in the form as given here. And in some countries of Continental Europe the conventional form is (or used to be) the number of females per 100 (or 1,000) males.

a male excess of zero, a proportion male of 50 percent, and a sex ratio of 100. The three indices calculated for a number of populations are shown in Table 3-1.

The evidence available indicates that many more males than females are conceived and that the proportion male is also higher among fetal deaths. At birth there still are usually more males than females; according to a compilation of data from countries with moderately good reporting, the sex ratio at birth has a worldwide average of between 104 and 107 (Visaria 1967; cf. Rubin 1967). The greater vulnerability of male fetuses and infants means that the better the conditions of gestation and birth, the more likely it will be that the baby is a boy. A study of all registered live births in the United States over more than 20 years showed that the sex ratio at birth differed significantly by color, age of mother, and birth order of the child. Genetic factors may also be important, but the higher proportion of male births among whites suggests an effect of the social–economic–cultural environment on the incidence of fetal deaths. The younger the mother and the fewer prior confinements, the more likely the infant is to be male (Tarver and Lee 1968). There is also the persistent allegation, supported by some seemingly solid evidence, that through a special intervention of providence military losses in a war are often made up by a larger proportion of male births during and immediately after the hostilities. Of the several hypotheses offered to explain this phenomenon, the most reasonable are that the age of marriage, and thus the mean age at childbearing, often fall during wartime, and that the prolonged absence of males from their wives increases the average interval between births. Both shifts would result in a smaller proportion of conceptions ending in fetal deaths (cf. Panunzio 1943; Markle 1974).

Among peoples who practice infanticide, this means mostly the disposal of female infants, with a consequent very high sex ratio of those permitted to enter the society. There are, of course, few exact data on such practices. One of the best records pertains to the Jhareja, who live in Kathiawar (Gujarat) in western India. They were notorious for the proportion of their female infants that they killed off, and the British government undertook to end the custom. To check on the success of their efforts, officials collected a mass of statistics, which have recently been analyzed in an interesting paper (Pakrasi and Sasmal 1970). In 1817, at the time of the first comprehensive inquiry, the sex ratio of this people was 235.8, and over the following decades it gradually fell off, though not to parity. Female infanticide, however, is only one indication—the most extreme— of disparity between the sexes in their life chances. If according to the society's norms young girls and women get less to eat and have to work harder, their less healthful way of life is likely to show up in a difference in age-specific death rates, and thus in the sex ratio (El-Badry 1969; Kennedy 1972).

More generally, the sex ratio of any population is affected by its past fertility, mortality, and migration (Figure 3-1). The higher mortality of males as fetuses and infants continues throughout most of life, for not only are they generally more susceptible to disease but—apart from chilbearing under primitive conditions—their vocations are typically more dangerous. The American sex ratio

Table 3-1. Measures of the Sex Structure, Selected Countries, Between 1965 and 1970

| Country and Date | Population (thousands) | | | Percent Male Excess (or Deficit) $\frac{(1)-(2)}{(3)} \times 100$ | Proportion Male $\frac{(1)}{(3)} \times 100$ | Sex Ratio $\frac{(1)}{(2)} \times 100$ |
| | MALE | FEMALE | TOTAL | | | |
	(1)	(2)	(3)	(4)	(5)	(6)
Kuwait (1965)	286	181	467	+22.5	61.2	158.0
Taiwan (1966)	6,875	6,286	13,161	+4.5	52.2	109.4
Singapore (1970)	1,062	1,012	2,074	+2.4	51.2	104.9
Turkey (1965)	15,997	15,394	31,391	+1.9	51.0	103.9
Australia (1966)	5,816	5,734	11,550	+0.7	50.4	101.4
Eire (1966)	1,449	1,435	2,884	+0.5	50.2	101.0
Sweden (1965)	3,880	3,886	7,766	−0.1	50.0	99.8
Mexico (1970)	24,140	24,237	48,377	−0.2	49.9	99.6
Denmark (1965)	2,362	2,405	4,767	−0.9	49.5	98.2
Luxemburg (1966)	165	170	335	−1.5	49.3	97.1
Rumania (1966)	9,351	9,752	19,103	−2.1	49.0	95.9
United States (1970)	98,912	104,300	203,212	−2.7	48.7	94.8

SOURCES: United Nations, *Demographic Yearbook, 1970* (New York, 1971); U. S. Bureau of the Census, *Census of Population, 1970* (Washington, D.C.: U. S. Government Printing Office).

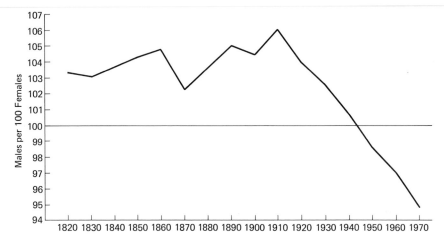

Figure 3-1.   Males per 100 Females, United States, 1820–1970.

SOURCES: U.S. Bureau of the Census, *Historical Statistics of the United States, Colonial Times to 1957; Census of the Population, 1960; 1970* (Washington, D.C.: U.S. Government Printing Office).

of 102.2 in 1870, the lowest up to that point, was partly the consequence of the heavy male losses in the Civil War, probably aggravated by a greater under-enumeration of males. As males and females are seldom balanced in migration, whether internal or international, this also can have an important effect on the sex ratios of both the sending and the receiving areas. In the United States, thus, the highest sex ratio was 106.0, recorded in 1910 after a quarter century of very large male-dominated immigration. In the most recent period, almost all factors have helped lower the sex ratio: immigration was sharply curtailed and shifted in large part to the family movement of refugees; there were sizable male losses in World War II and smaller ones in Korea and Vietnam; and some of the most significant medical advances—particularly in the control of cancers—have been more successful in reducing the deaths of females than those of males.

One reason for studying the sex ratio is its relevance to family formation. The number of marriages possible in monogamous countries and thus also the number of legitimate births depend in part on whether there are as many men as women. A marked and growing disparity has often been viewed as a threat to family stability. Following World War II, when Australia was endeavoring to increase its population through subsidized immigration, the strong male predominance among the immigrants was reinforced by the emigration of Australian females who had married Allied servicemen temporarily stationed in Australia. With such a pattern of net immigration, a country committed to doubling its population was forgoing many of the immigrants' potential progeny by its policy of fostering the influx of single males (Borrie 1949: 93–95).

The sex ratio of the entire population, however, hardly indicates the number of potential new families. The pertinent figure is rather the sex ratio of that

Table 3-2. Sex Ratio of Persons 14 Years and Over, by Marital Status and Region, United States, 1960–70

Region	Single		Married		Separated		Widowed		Divorced	
	1960	1970	1960	1970	1960	1970	1960	1970	1960	1970
Northeast	109.9	106.1	98.7	98.9	63.8	58.6	29.3	23.1	64.1	58.2
North Central	122.7	114.6	99.6	99.4	82.3	68.0	29.5	22.8	74.6	65.3
South	124.5	122.2	90.9	99.1	70.7	68.1	25.5	20.0	67.5	63.7
West	149.1	130.1	100.5	100.0	80.9	69.6	26.6	21.4	79.0	67.6
United States	123.4	117.2	96.8	99.3	71.7	64.2	27.9	21.5	70.9	63.5

SOURCES: U.S. Bureau of the Census, *Census of Population, 1960; 1970* (Washington, D.C.: U.S. Government Printing Office).

portion able to wed. This class is delimited, first, by age (it is conventional in the United States to include that sector of the population aged 14 and over) and, second, by marital status (in a monogamous society, those with one spouse may not take another). If marriageable persons are defined as those denoted as "single" in the American census classification—that is, those aged 14 years and over and never married[4]—their sex ratio was 123.4 in 1960 and still 117.2 in 1970 (Table 3-2). Thus, in spite of the considerable female surplus in the population as a whole, among single adults the balance was reversed. As a consequence of this skewed sex ratio, American men married at an increasing rate during the 1960s but females at a decreasing rate (Akers 1967).

This marriageable class, moreover, is not homogeneous (Rubin 1962). One of the prerequisites to romantic love is that most prosaic characteristic, spatial propinquity, and the availability of partners varies widely from one section of the country to another, as the figures in Table 3-2 roughly indicate. Intermarriage is atypical also across lines set by race, religion, and social class, so that the sex ratio of each of the essentially endogamous subpopulations formed by the composite effect of all such factors is what generally determines the probability of family formation. Particularly among the smaller nonwhite races in the United States, the large surplus of males combined with the small chance of intermarriage made a normal family something of a rarity during the decades of heavy immigration.

THE THREE MAIN AGE CATEGORIES

The most useful single figure summarizing a population's age structure is its **median age**, which divides the population into two equal parts, half older and half younger. In the United States, with the gradual decline in fertility and the rise in life expectancy, the median age rose steadily from the first censuses, when half the white population was under 16 years, to 1950, when the median was almost double that (Table 3-3). During the next two decades it fell slightly, reflecting the postwar revival in the birth rate. This historical record of one Western country is similar to the worldwide range around 1960, when the median ages of various countries ranged between 17.7 (Taiwan) and 36.2 (Sweden). Only 26 percent of the Swedish population was under the Taiwanese median, and only 23 percent of Taiwan's population was older than the Swedish median.

A more detailed representation of a society's age structure can be based on a division of its population into three main age categories: dependent children, aged 14 years and under; the active population, 15 to 64 years; and dependent aged, 65 years and over. This distribution is shown in Table 3-4 for the United

---

[4] Whether to include widowed and divorced persons is a moot point. Legally they are marriageable, but actually in the United States a considerable proportion of the persons so designated in any census will not remarry; and of those that do, many will be too old to bear children.

Table 3-3. Median Age of the Population, by Sex, United States, 1790–1970

	Male	Female	Total
1790[a]	15.9	—	—
1800[a]	15.7	16.3	16.0
1810[a]	15.9	16.1	16.0
1820	16.6	16.7	16.7
1830	17.1	17.3	17.2
1840	17.8	17.7	17.8
1850	19.2	18.6	18.9
1860	19.8	19.1	19.4
1870	20.2	20.1	20.2
1880	21.2	20.7	20.9
1890	22.3	21.6	22.0
1900	23.3	22.4	22.9
1910	24.6	23.5	24.1
1920	25.8	24.7	25.3
1930	26.7	26.2	26.5
1940	29.1	29.0	29.0
1950	29.9	30.5	30.2
1960	28.7	30.3	29.5
1970	26.8	29.3	28.1

[a] White population only.
SOURCES: U.S. Bureau of the Census, *Historical Statistics of the United States, Colonial Times to 1957*; *Census of Population, 1960*; *1970* (Washington, D.C.: U.S. Government Printing Office).

States since 1880, the date at which America's transformation from an agrarian to an industrial society passed its preliminary stage.

Dependent Children

From the first three censuses of the United States until 1940, the proportion of children steadily fell, at first slowly and then more rapidly. In 1850 two-fifths of the population was under 15 years, in 1910 almost one-third, and after the depression of the 1930s one-fourth. The most obvious reason for these changes in the percentage under 15, of course, was the long-term fall in fertility, its revival after World War II, and its subsequent decline. The secular fall in the death rate, since it was concentrated in infant and child mortality, was equivalent to a rise in the birth rate. The effect of immigration was complex; most immigrants were young adults, and the immediate consequence of their entry was to decrease the

Table 3-4.   Percentage Distribution Among the Three Main Age Categories, United States, 1880–1970

Year	Dependent Children (14 YEARS AND UNDER)	Active Population (15–64 YEARS)	Dependent Aged (65 YEARS AND OVER)	Index of Aging $\frac{(3)}{(1)} \times 100$	Dependency Ratio $\frac{(1) + (3)}{(2)} \times 100$
	(1)	(2)	(3)	(4)	(5)
1880	38.1	58.5	3.4	8.9	70.9
1890	35.5	60.4	3.9	11.0	65.2
1900	34.4	61.3	4.1	11.9	62.8
1910	32.1	63.4	4.3	13.4	57.4
1920	31.7	63.4	4.7	14.8	57.4
1930	29.3	65.1	5.4	18.4	53.3
1940	25.0	68.1	6.8	27.2	46.6
1950	26.8	65.3	8.2	30.6	53.5
1960	31.0	59.8	9.2	29.7	67.2
1970	28.5	61.6	9.9	34.7	62.3

SOURCES: Conrad Taeuber and Irene B. Taeuber, *The Changing Population of the United States* (New York: Wiley, 1958), p. 31; U.S. Bureau of the Census, *Census of Population, 1960; 1970* (Washington, D.C.: U.S. Government Printing Office).

proportion of children in the population, but in the somewhat longer run this was countered by their higher than average fertility.

As with the change in median age so also with that in the proportion of children, the progression over time in the United States can be matched with today's range among countries of the world. The poorest countries, like the poorest families, generally have the most children, and in both cases that is an important reason why they are poor (Davis 1965). The future of any country lies with its children, and if their excess numbers make it impossible to afford them adequate care, the prognosis for social progress is likely to be bleak.

For some purposes it is too gross a simplification to classify all children as undifferentiated burdens, for obviously the cost to the parents varies considerably according to a number of factors: among others, the level of living of the country, social class, region, rural–urban location; the number and age of the dependent children; the portion of childrearing costs that are paid by the state; the income that is forgone by a mother (the so-called opportunity cost) who otherwise would work outside the home. If one sums differentially the total child dependency of various subpopulations, one obtains the relative pressures on parents to limit further procreation (Schnaiberg 1973). In an interesting application of this rationale to an African hunter-gatherer tribe presently in transition to a sedentary life, it was shown that the burden of childrearing is becoming markedly less.

For when the band is on the move, the mother has to carry her young child or children. From estimates of the weight of a child of each age and the total distance covered each year, one can calculate the load for each mother, and thus the incentive to space births. In this tribe the first pregnancy comes 3 to 5 years after puberty, and extended lactation keeps the interval between subsequent births to about 3 to 5 years. Thus, "sedentarization alone may trigger population growth, since women may have children more frequently without any increase in work on their part and without reducing their ability to provide for each one" (Lee 1972).

Dependent Aged

The percent of the United States population aged 65 and over rose from 3.4 in 1880 to 9.9 in 1970. Over the same period, while the whole population increased 4.1 times, the number of aged increased 11.6 times. What caused this rise in the proportion of the aged in the United States, as in all Western countries? The common-sense reply to this question might be that it was the combined effect of falling mortality and falling fertility, but such an answer would be misleading. The increase in the *number* of old people was indeed the consequence of improvements in death control. However, because declines in mortality have been greatest among infants and children, the larger proportion who remained alive *retarded* the aging of the population. "In most Western countries the fraction over 65 would be *larger* than it is if mortality rates had remained at their 1900 level. The average age of the population would be *greater* if [control over] mortality had *not* improved" (Coale 1956; cf. Valaoras 1950; Sauvy 1954).

The two influences can be combined into a single figure, as follows:

$$\text{Index of aging} = \frac{\text{Persons 65 years and over}}{\text{Children 14 years and under}} \times 100$$

The long-term rise in this index, shown in Column 4 of Table 3-4, not only slowed down but was actually reversed from 1950 to 1960. This retardation of the aging of the American population, mainly the consequence of the post-1945 rise in fertility, ended when the secular decline in family size was renewed. If the demographic processes continue as now anticipated, by the end of this century 28.8 percent of the population will be aged 65 or over, 12.6 percent 75 or over. And by the year 2020 these percentages will be, respectively, over 40 and almost 14 (Figure 3-2). It is too often forgotten that, even so, "the problem of aging" is "only the pessimistic way of looking at a great triumph of civilization" (Notestein 1954). All cultures aspire to long life; it has been achieved on a mass scale through the science fostered in the modern West.

The life span beyond 65 years comprises two phases, as suggested in Figure 3-2. The first begins when a sizable proportion retire from full participation in the labor force, the second when many of these need constant aid merely to carry on as retired pensioners. This second phase, what may be designated as

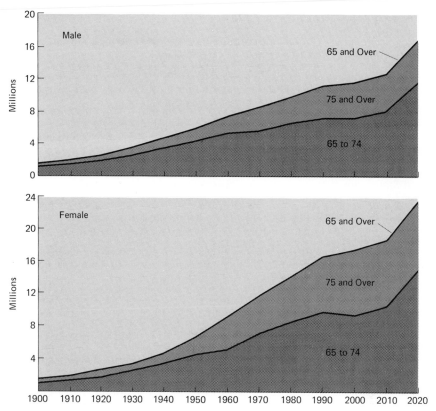

Figure 3-2.   Growth of the Population Aged 65 and Over, by Sex, United States, 1900–2020

SOURCE: Jacob S. Siegel and William O'Leary. "Some Demographic Aspects of Aging in the United States," U.S. Bureau of the Census, *Current Population Reports*, Series P-23, no. 43 (Washington, D.C.: U.S. Government Printing Office, 1973).

true old age, starts in Western countries in the mid-70s (LeGros Clark 1966: 16). Physically, most retired persons are completely self-dependent; in the United States many have moved to states with a pleasant climate, particularly Florida, Arizona, and California, and there begun a new life.

With the aged, there live on the ideas, limitations, and surviving hopes of the past. For example, when today's very old were children, about a quarter of the population of the United States were given no more than 4 years of schooling, an education now considered so inadequate that it is used to define the upper limit of the "functionally illiterate." Similarly, since immigration was sharply curtailed after 1914, the proportion of aged among the foreign-born is much higher than in the native population. The out-migration of young adults from farms, as a third instance, has left disproportionate numbers of the elderly in the rural sector.

The Active Population

The definition of adulthood, although it has a biological base, varies greatly from one culture to another. Children on a farm are assigned their chores; in today's cities child labor is prohibited. Any delimitation of active adulthood in terms of chronological ages rather than functions, therefore, must be approximate and to some degree arbitrary. The definition used here, those aged 15 to 64, conforms with some statistical and legal conventions, but in several respects it overstates the actual size of the active population in a typical Western country. Few outside this age group perform adult roles, and many in it do not, especially those in school beyond age 14 and those who have retired before age 65. In the United States, not only are rather high percentages at either end of the so-called active age range typically not in the labor force, but significant percentages have never worked at all outside the home. If we define the active population by non-economic roles, the same deviations can be noted. The median age at marriage, though it went down after World War II, is still nearer 20 than 15; and women's childbearing period must end between 45 and 50. The age at which young men used to be conscripted was usually around 18, and meaningful military service ends long before 65. Suffrage is now legally available in the United States at age 18, and most states are in the process of setting this age also as the beginning of legal maturity; but actually the very young and the very old vote in smaller proportions than those in the middle age range.

To define the category aged 15 to 64 as the society's producers means, therefore, that for Western countries we are in effect estimating the **labor potential**, the figure to which the labor force might expand in a period of national emergency. The dependency ratio as calculated in the last column of Table 3-4 thus understates the number of persons that the average worker must support (cf. Kleiman 1967). Even with the more conservative index, the ratio rose by more than 20 percentage points between 1940 and 1960, then fell somewhat in 1970.

Table 3-5. Percentage Change in the Labor Force by Age Category, United States, 1960–70 and 1970–80

Age Category	1960 to 1970	1970 to 1980
16–24	**53**	19
25–34	16	**49**
35–44	−1	13
45–54	15	−4
55–64	21	14
65+	−8	6
16–65+	18	18

SOURCE: U.S. Department of Labor, *U.S. Manpower in the 1970s: Opportunity and Challenge* (Washington, D.C.: U.S. Government Printing Office, 1970).

Table 3-6. Dependency Ratios by Demographic and Economic Categories, Major World Areas, 1950, 1960, 1975

World Region	$\dfrac{\text{Population Aged 0-14, 65+}}{\text{Population Aged 15-64}} \times 100$			$\dfrac{\text{Economically Inactive Population}}{\text{Economically Active Population}} \times 100$			Percentage Increase 1960–75	
	1950	1960	1975 (PROJECTED)	1950	1960	1975 (PROJECTED)	TOTAL POPULATION	ECONOMICALLY ACTIVE POPULATION
Africa	75	79	84	125	130	135	30	27
Northern America	55	67	63	137	146	140	27	30
Latin America	74	80	86	171	181	190	51	47
Asia	74	76	79	160	161	166	37	35
Europe	50	54	59	120	126	133	14	11
Oceania	62	66	66	160	167	162	31	33
USSR	59	58	64	123	122	129	28	24
World	67.5	70	75	146	150	156	33	30

SOURCE: Françoise Leridon, "Prévisions de population active: Trois publications internationales," *Population*, **17** (1962), 97–120.

Over the longer run, as one can see from an inspection of its component elements, the ratio varied mainly with changes in the proportion of dependent children.

During the 1960s, when the extraordinarily large numbers born immediately after World War II were entering the labor force, these youngest components were by far its most rapidly growing category. Ten years later, these enormous cohorts will be in the prime working ages, 25 to 34 years (Table 3-5). Other things being equal, the effect on labor productivity, and thus on the economy generally, should be beneficial.

Leridon (1962) combined recent estimates and projections of the economically active population from three international agencies. Whether we measure the dependency ratio by age bracket or by economically active and inactive categories, it is clear that the rise in the dependency burden will generally be greatest in the poorest areas of the world (Table 3-6).

Youth

Especially in an analysis focused on social rather than economic roles, it is useful to separate out the youngest sector of the adult group, the youth of any population (U.S. Bureau of the Census 1973). To define this in terms of its age limits is notoriously difficult. And if we designate it by its "youthful" behavior, we find many roles tailored to fit adults who have never fully matured (Berger 1963). Perhaps the least arbitrary definition of youth is those in the age range 15 to 24, thus including adolescents as well as the first years of legal maturity. Together with children aged 5–14, youth constitute almost the entire enrollment of educational institutions. Most who enter the labor force for the first time are in this age range, and in the United States by far the highest proportion of unemployment is usually among teenagers.

In the 1960s a fascinating manifestation of youth was the so-called generational revolt. A symposium entitled "Youth in Flux" included German feuilletons on young Chinese Communists and on "beats" wandering over Europe; a query from an English playwright on whether this phenomenon is not "simple hooliganism"; articles on delinquency in Israel and "dropouts on the run in the Soviet Union"; and, as an intimation of the apparent new fad, the rising "Concrete Generation" in France.[5] In all these places, except perhaps China, the percentage of youth in revolt was very small; in the United States, for instance, the adolescents in the Boy Scouts and the 4-H Clubs always far outnumbered those participating in demonstrations. Some have on this account called the youth revolt a "myth," but one should remember that revolts and even revolutions are typically generated by a small minority.

---

[5] "Youth in Flux," *Atlas*, March, 1966, pp. 146–162. An especially interesting account of the "nihilists" and "anarchists" in the Soviet Union is given in Darrell P. Hammer, "Among Students in Moscow: An Outsider's Report," *Problems of Communism*, **13** (1964), 11–18. The whole of the Fall, 1968, issue of *Public Interest* is devoted to generally excellent analyses of student movements.

A demographer can more reasonably make two other points that usefully supplement cultural–political analyses of youth rebellions:

1. The proportion of youth grew enormously, as a consequence in Western countries of the baby boom and in underdeveloped countries of the precipitous decline in infant mortality after the end of World War II. In the United States for instance, the birth rate rose immediately after the war and remained about 24 from 1946 to 1960. The persons born in those years will be aged 15–24 over the years 1961 through 1984, and the cohort born in the peak birth year of 1947 reached these ages in 1962 through 1971. The postwar baby boom was shorter in some countries and in others the decline in infant mortality has continued, but in most of the world's nations during the 1960s and early 1970s youth was attaining a new numerical importance. From infancy on, these cohorts burst the bounds of institutions built to accommodate more modest numbers, and as adolescents they saw ahead of them adult societies with too few jobs, swollen and yet inadequate universities, and in general a world seemingly ill prepared to absorb its progeny. In Indonesia, as a non-Western example, entry into the labor force increased from 1.5 million per year in the mid-1960s to more than double that in the early 1970s. "Each entrant will literally bring his brother along, and the brother will want a job as well" (Keyfitz 1965). Indeed, such a stupendous rise constitutes the stimulus to change that some have termed it, but it is less apparent whether a country like Indonesia can respond to the stimulus by developing its economy sufficiently fast.

2. An analysis in terms of cohorts combines the general determinants of behavior based on age with the specific determinants set by each cohort's past history. To take a purely demographic illustration, women aged 40–44, who are close to the end of their fecund period, generally have few children; but the American cohorts born in 1911–15, many of whom postponed getting married— or, if married, having children—during the depression of the 1930s, showed a high fertility late in their reproductive life (see pp. 339, 350). Similarly, one can come to a limited understanding of youthful revolts merely by noting that those tied to their parents as children break away during adolescence in order to achieve adult independence.[6] But however much credence one gives this maxim, it hardly helps in explaining the differential incidence of youth revolt. For example, during the 1920s and again during the 1950s young Americans generally accepted the society that their parents had built, and in the 1930s and 1960s many rebelled against it. This cyclical pattern suggests that what is seen as revolt may in many cases be the contrary, a docile acceptance of one's parents' and

---

[6] The literature on this theme is enormous even if the sizable Freudian or general psychological components are passed over. Among the best known sociological analyses are Kingsley Davis, "The Sociology of Parent-Youth Conflict," *American Sociological Review*, **5** (1940), 523–535; Talcott Parsons, "Age and Sex in the Social Structure of the United States," in *Essays in Sociological Theory, Pure and Applied* (New York: Free Press, 1949), pp. 218–232; Lewis S. Feuer, *The Conflict of Generations: The Character and Significance of Student Movements* (New York: Basic Books, 1969).

professors' ideas: the children of the "Babbitts" became the "quiet generation," and the children of CCNY radicals invented the academic sit-in. Columbia University's radical students were "strikingly similar to the pattern across the nation . . . at a dozen other campuses."

The activists are typically very bright and predominantly Jewish, usually reared in affluent or financially comfortable families in the big cities and suburbs of the Eastern Seaboard. They are students of the humanities rather than the sciences. Their fathers came of age during the Great Depression of the 1930s and were often insecure about money and jobs, if not downright needy. Many of them are now successful in the professions or creative fields. They are permissive parents, politically oriented toward liberalism and the left.

The overwhelming majority of the radical students at Columbia said their parents had been sympathetic to their protests, more loving than judging. The proud "my son, the revolutionary" response of Mrs. Jacob Rudd, mother of Mark [leader on campus of the extremist Students for a Democratic Society, at the time of writing sought by the police on criminal charges], was absolutely typical [*New York Times*, June 10, 1968].

Such an example suggests that the concept of cohort, or what some analysts term a "political generation," can be useful not only in demography but in almost any social, political, or economic analysis of age differentiation.

THE POPULATION PYRAMID

The distribution of a population by age and sex together is usually represented by a special type of bar graph, called a population pyramid. The various bars represent successive ages from the lowest at the bottom to the highest at the top, each divided between the males at the left and the females at the right. The length of all the bars together represents, according to the scale along the horizontal axis, the total population either in absolute figures or as a percentage. Each bar thus designates what proportion that age is of the total. Very often the population represented in a pyramid is broken down into 5-year or larger age brackets, into which the typical misreporting of age is largely absorbed.

The reason for the basic shape of the pyramid is that among those born, e.g., in 1900, some have died in each year since then, gradually reducing the length of the bars representing successively higher ages. The shape is not ordinarily a perfect pyramid, however, because mortality varies from year to year, and because fertility and migration also affect the population structure. Whether recent fertility has been high or low is shown by the relative length of the bottom bar. The depletion caused by a past famine, epidemic, or war, or by a period of particularly low fertility or large emigration, is represented by an indentation from a smooth pyramid; and, on the contrary, a past period of high fertility or of large immigration is represented by a corresponding protuberance. These irregularities remain on population pyramids of successive dates, gradually moving up to the top of the graph and disappearing only when the cohorts

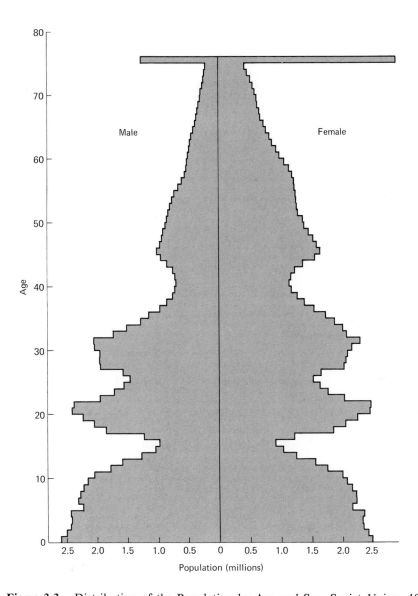

Figure 3-3.   Distribution of the Population by Age and Sex, Soviet Union, 1959

SOURCE: U.S. Bureau of the Census, "Estimates and Projections of the Population of the U.S.S.R., by Age and Sex: 1950 to 2000," *International Population Reports*, Series P-91, no. 23 (Washington, D.C.: U.S. Government Printing Office, 1973).

finally die off. This process can be illustrated best, of course, with the pyramid of a population that has been subjected to the most drastic changes, such as that of the Soviet Union in 1959 (Figure 3-3). From 1914 on, Russia was drained of population by World War I; the revolution and civil war, accompanied by a mass famine and epidemic; the forced collectivization of agricultural land, resulting in another famine; the political purge of the population and the spread of forced labor as an institution; and then, as a climactic bloodletting, World War II. Some of these catastrophes, such as wars, affected males more than females; others, such as famines and epidemics, depleted both sexes impartially. In the worst periods fertility fell off as mortality rose. No accurate count can be taken of such tolls at the time, but their effect can be reliably estimated from the imprint left on the age and sex structure. (The very long bars at the top of the figure represent those aged 75 and over; because of the unreliability of age reporting by the elderly, these are classified here into a single category.)

One pyramid is often superimposed on another, in order to illustrate the contrast between two populations or between the structures of a single population at different times. Figure 3-4, thus, represents the population of the United States at two dates. In 1900 there was a regular progression of age categories in an almost completely regular pyramid, but in 1970 the extremely low birth rates of the 1930s were reflected in a pinched waist, which was reinforced by the larger proportions at higher ages.

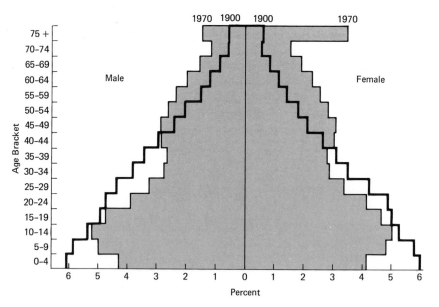

Figure 3-4. Population by Age Interval and Sex, United States, 1900 and 1970

SOURCES: U.S. Bureau of the Census, *Census of Population, 1900; 1970* (Washington, D.C.: U.S. Government Printing Office).

RATIOS AND RATES

The calculations made in analyzing population data depend, of course, mainly on the information available and the analyst's purpose, but very often the tools thus fashioned are closely related to the age and sex structure. Indeed, a gross figure is sometimes more appropriate than any alternative. The datum that the Chinese are increasing by 20 million a year, or that over a particular holiday weekend there were 325 deaths in automobile accidents, could hardly be put more forcibly than as these simple statements. Usually, however, a ratio or a proportion or a rate tells us more.

A **ratio** is of the form $(a/b)k$, where a and b denote sectors of a population and k any convenient constant. One example has already been cited in the text— the sex ratio (males per 100 females). The child–woman ratio (sometimes called the fertility ratio) is the number of children under 5 per 1,000 women in the fecund ages. In one of these cases the value assigned to k is 100 and in the other 1,000. More generally, in both ratios and other types of calculations, k is conventionally fixed according to the relative frequency of the phenomenon, in order to avoid cumbersome decimals. Thus, occupational rates are ordinarily expressed as percentages (Latin for "per 100"), whereas suicide rates are usually given per 100,000. Note that the two components of the sex ratio together make up the whole of any population (males plus females) but that this is not a necessary condition for a ratio (young children and fecund women do not include men, older children, and other sectors).

A **proportion** is of the form

$$\left(\frac{a}{a + b}\right)k$$

that is, a relation between a total and one of its parts. For example, as we have noted, one can express a sex ratio of 100 as the statement that 50 percent of the population is male.

Crude Rates and Standardization

A **crude rate** is of the form $(m/P)k$, where P is the total midyear population and m the number of births, or deaths, or marriages, or other demographic events during that year. Note that m and P are not from the same set of statistical records; in the birth rate, for example, the numerator comes from vital statistics, and the denominator from the census. The two universes, thus, do not refer to quite the same population: that enumerated in the census, or estimated from the successive censuses, is fixed at one particular time; that included in the vital registration fluctuates throughout the year.

A more serious question is whether the total population is the most apposite base. Ideally, a rate should express the relation between the actual and the potential. Suppose we want to compare the military forces of two countries. A direct comparison—Country A has 2 million men under arms as against 4 million in Country B—might for some purposes be the most relevant one. But if we want to judge the relative drain on the population, and thus the relative possibility of expanding the size of the armed forces, the 2 or 4 million can be compared with the respective total population or, better, with the number of men of military age (or men and women, if the latter are to be drafted; or healthy men only, for a further refinement; and so on). In this example, if the proportion of young men of military age is the same in both populations, then it is unimportant whether a rate is calculated with this reservoir or the whole population as the denominator. Or, more generally, if the age and sex structure of two populations being compared are identical, then the crude rates need no refinement. Often this relation more or less holds, and the easily calculated, readily understood crude rate may be more appropriate than a complex substitute, particularly if the requisite data are not thoroughly accurate (see p. 90).

If the structures of the populations differ greatly, however, then crude or insufficiently refined rates can be grossly misleading, as in the following historic examples:

1. In a special Massachusetts state census in 1905 it was pointed out that the average number of children ever born to mothers then living was only 2.77. This figure was compared with that in the previous generation by asking the respondents how many children *their* mothers had borne—namely, 6.47 on the average. The contrast was interpreted as evidence of a very sharp decline in average family size. Actually, of course, the number of children to the respondent mothers—some of whom were still in their teens, others in their 20s, and so on—was compared with the *completed* fertility of a group virtually all of whom had reached the end of their fecund years (Chaddock 1936; see also p. 379).

2. During the Spanish–American War there was great public concern over the large number of soldiers dying in the Philippines. In his annual report for 1899 the Secretary of War replied to the criticism by pointing out that the death rate among the troops was almost identical with that of the civilian population of Washington or Boston. In making a polemical point, he overlooked the fact that soldiers are all young adults while the general population includes infants and old persons, who generally have a higher death rate (Chaddock 1936).

3. The national-quota system underlying American immigration policy for some four decades was based to an important degree on the analysis of Dr. Harry H. Laughlin, associated with the Eugenics Record Office of the Carnegie Institution of Washington. As "expert eugenics agent" to the House Committee on Immigration and Naturalization, he submitted a report entitled "Expert Analysis of the Metal and the Dross in America's Modern Melting Pot."[7] In

[7] U.S. House of Representatives, *Hearings Before the Committee on Immigration and Naturalization, November 21, 1922,* 67th Congress, 3rd Session, Serial 7-G (Washington, D.C., 1923). According to one authority, this report "is often considered the principal basis of the Act of 1924"—Roy L. Garis, *Immigration Restriction: A Study of Opposition to and Regulation of Immigration into the United States* (New York: Macmillan, 1927), pp. 239–240. Cf. Petersen 1970: 195–215.

order to show that social ills are not randomly distributed among the various nationalities in the United States, Laughlin compared for each ethnic group its proportion in the total population with that in prisons, asylums, and similar institutions. For example, in 1910 persons of Italian birth made up 1.46 percent of the total population, and if proportionally represented in the 93 insane asylums that Laughlin surveyed, they would have constituted 1.46 percent of the total number of inmates, or 1,228. Since there were actually 1,938 Italian-born persons in these institutions, the incidence of insanity among Italians was concluded to be more than one and a half times higher than that of the general population.

Among many other flaws in Laughlin's influential analysis, the fundamental ones in this context are that he made no allowance for the regional variation in communal care (institutions were scarce in the immigrant-free South and much more numerous in northern cities, where most of the immigrants lived) and that he ignored the difference in structure of the populations he compared (immigrants were concentrated in the middle male age intervals, which typically show the highest incidence of many social ills).

When the total population is used as the base in calculating a crude birth rate, the "potential" parents include some who can never become actual. The crude death rate is not illogical in the same sense: all persons are mortal. But the probability of dying within a year varies greatly according to age (and to some degree also according to sex), and in practice the two crude rates have the same virtues and limitations. They are simple to calculate from data often available, and if the effect of the age structures on fertility and mortality does not differ greatly in the populations being studied, they give a good basis for comparison. However, when a recent period is contrasted with a relatively distant past, or a Western country with a non-Western one, then the difference in age structure is likely to be so large that a measure that takes it into account is preferable.

If the age-specific birth and death rates of a population with no migration were to remain constant for a century or more, the population structure would also become fixed. Such a **stable population**, in which the proportion of each age interval remains constant, is not necessarily one of constant size, but one whose growth is at a constant rate (which can be negative or zero as well as positive). It is thus to be distinguished from a **stationary population**, or one of which both the age structure and the size are permanently fixed.

As an example of how one can use these two models, consider Figure 3-5, in which there have been plotted the contributions that age structure makes to the actual population growth of various countries. The figures along the horizontal axis are the **crude rates of natural increase** (that is, the crude birth rates minus the crude death rates). If the age structures had been those of a stationary population with the current age-specific vital rates, the rates of natural increase would be less by the figures shown along the vertical axis.

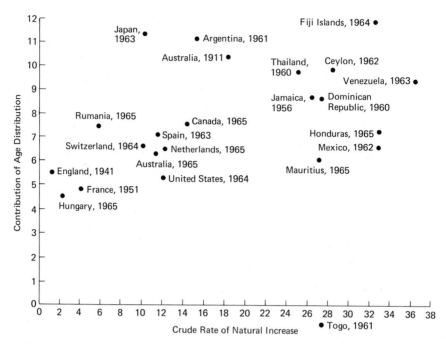

Figure 3-5. The Contribution of Age Distribution to the Crude Rates of Natural Increase, Selected Countries at Recent Dates

SOURCE: Samuel H. Preston, "Empirical Analysis of the Contribution of Age Composition to Population Growth," *Demography*, **7** (1970), 417–432.

For example, in 1960 the Dominican Republic increased by 27.1 per 1,000 population, of which 8.8 units were due to its age distribution. In general, the underdeveloped countries grouped in the upper right corner were growing by about 3 percent per year, and between a quarter and a third of this growth was due to the age structure. In Togo, however, the population was so young that it grew more slowly than it would have under the stipulated conditions. The countries with developed economies, all on the left in the figure, show the characteristically lower rates of natural increase but also have a typically high contribution from the age structure. That is because the "boom babies" born in the years following World War II grew up to become large proportions in the age range most likely to have children themselves.

One of the commonest devices for refining crude measures is **standardization**, or "holding constant" the age structure while comparing the differential effect of other factors. Suppose, for example, that in order to compare the relative efficiency of social welfare in the various states of the United States, we use as one index their crude death rates. Some of the differences among these rates, however, will be due to the extraneous fact that there are proportionately more elderly people, or more infants, in some states than in others. The usual way to remove this effect is to calculate the specific death rates of convenient age categories for each of the states, multiply these by the number of persons of the same ages in the United States (the so-called standard population), thus deriving the number of deaths in each age interval that would have obtained if the structure had been uniform throughout the country. For each state the total of such deaths per 1,000 population is its **standardized death rate.**[8]

The one problem more complex than simple arithmetic relates to the choice of the standard population. For years, the population of England and Wales in 1901 was used as a worldwide standard, but its structure was so different from that of non-Western populations that this was eventually deemed to be a poor choice. A standard population can be any, either actual or constructed, that is similar in structure to the populations whose rates are being standardized. When two populations are being compared, either can be designated as the standard, or, alternatively, a composite containing both, as in the example we have used. No absolute rule applies, but since the standardized rates can differ widely depending on the selection of the standard, this cannot be chosen randomly.

The value of standardization is merely suggested by this discussion. It can be used to "hold constant" any variable while comparing the effect of any other, so long as these are expressed in figures and the data are available. Suppose, as another example, that we wanted to study the effect of occupations on marital status. It would be appropriate to standardize not only for age but also for sex ratio, ethnic and religious homogeneity, and any other possibly relevant demographic characteristic (Kitagawa 1964).

Measures of Fertility

One important method of refinement that such examples suggest is the one we have indicated: to substitute a sector of the population for the whole as the denominator. This principle can be exemplified by several measures of fertility used to supplement, or to replace, the crude birth rate. The simplest of these is the **general fertility rate,** or the number of births per 1,000 women in the fecund ages. Here we have, it would seem, a direct relation of actual procreation to potential procreators, but in fact the difficulty of defining the "potential" has not been overcome entirely. Female fecundity develops gradually during adolescence, slowly declines after age 30 to 35, and disappears between the ages, approximately, of 45 and 50 (see pp. 192–194). Demographers are not agreed on the conventional definition of "the childbearing ages." In Western countries

---

[8] This is the so-called direct method of standardization. If the data needed for it are not available, it is possible to achieve a similar result by multiplying the age-specific rates of the standard population by the number of persons of each age interval in the various states (the so-called indirect method). A more detailed discussion of standardization is included in almost any elementary work on statistics. See, for example, Barclay 1958: 161–166, 175–177; Linder and Grove 1963: chap. 4; Shryock and Siegel 1971: 289–291.

some births are to women aged 15–19 and 45–49, but far fewer relatively than these age intervals comprise of all women able to give birth. Whether or not these ages are included, a decision hard to make on principle (cf. Kuczynski 1928: 102–103), thus effects a considerable difference in the rate.

The basic pattern of relating births to women in the fecund period can be varied as widely as the data permit and the analyst's purpose demands. For example, *legitimate* births per 1,000 *married* women aged 15 to 44 define the **marital fertility rate**. The average number of children ever born to women aged 45 and over defines the **completed family size**. If no vital statistics are available for the country or period being analyzed, data wholly from the census can be substituted to calculate the **child–woman ratio**, already defined as the number of children under 5 years per 1,000 women in the fecund period.

Inasmuch as even within the fecund period the ability to have children varies according to age, a more precise measure is to calculate an **age-specific fertility rate**, defined as the number of births to a specified age bracket per 1,000 women of those ages. Usually the division is made by 5-year periods, as in the illustrative data reproduced in Table 3-7. The figures in Column 3 of this table, for greater convenience of presentation, can be added up to one figure, which is multiplied by 5 in order to relate it to the age of mothers by single years. The resultant figure, called the **total fertility rate** (in this case 495.5 × 5, or 2,477.5), tells us how many children on the average each 1,000 women have while passing through their fecund years. In order to include also the effect of mortality, each age-specific fertility rate can be reduced by the proportion that would not survive, according to age-specific death rates in that year, from birth to the midpoint of each age interval (Columns 4 and 5 of the table). Sometimes the measure is calculated to show rather the number of daughters—that is, future mothers—the females being analyzed would have who would survive. With a sex ratio at birth of 105 (which is the usual figure in the United States), one must reduce the total fertility rate by slightly more than half (multiplying it by 0.488); and it is conventional to give the resultant figure, called the **gross reproduction rate**, per woman rather than per 1,000 women. To get the **net reproduction rate** (Kuczynski 1932), the sum of Column 5 is multiplied by the same series of figures, for the same reasons; thus:

$$\text{Gross reproduction rate} = 495.5 \times 5 \times 0.488 \times 0.001$$
$$= 1.19$$
$$\text{Net reproduction rate} = 478.7 \times 5 \times 0.488 \times 0.001$$
$$= 1.15$$

Of course, the net rate is always smaller than the gross, though when female mortality is as low as presently in the United States the difference is not very significant.

The vital rates of a stable population, called its "true" or **intrinsic birth** and **death rates**, also reflect the fertility and mortality apart from the effect of the

Table 3-7. Age-Specific Fertility and Survival Rates, United States, 1968

Age Category	Estimated Number of Females (–000) (1)	Births to Women of Specified Age Category (2)	Age-Specific Fertility Rates[b] (2) ÷ (1) (3)	Proportion Surviving from Birth to Mid-point of Age Category (4)	Age-Specific Survival–Fertility Rates (3) × (4) (5)
15–19	8,949	600,816[a]	67.1	0.97334	65.3
20–24	7,809	1,306,872	167.4	0.97008	162.3
25–29	6,443	903,890	140.3	0.96620	135.5
30–34	5,607	419,696	74.9	0.96116	71.9
35–39	5,786	206,062	35.6	0.95371	34.0
40–44	6,274	60,438	9.6	0.94246	9.1
45–49	6,205	3,790[a]	0.6	0.92577	0.6
			495.5		478.7

[a] Births to mothers aged under 15 and over 49 are included, respectively, in the first and last rows.
[b] If the figures in Column 1 had been given complete, rather than estimated to the nearest thousand, these ratios would have to be multiplied by 1,000.
SOURCE: U.S. National Office of Vital Statistics, *Vital Statistics of the United States, 1968* (Washington, D.C.: U.S. Government Printing Office).

89

population structure. The difference between them, the "true" or **intrinsic rate of natural increase**, thus, is similar to the net reproduction rate except that it is calculated on an annual rather than a generational basis (Dublin *et al.* 1949: chap. 12; Coale 1968).

How useful are these more elaborate measures of fertility? They are a significant improvement over the crude rate, to repeat, only when the proportion of fecund women in the total population varies greatly; and in any particular society during a period of uniform demographic change, this proportion is likely to be more or less fixed. Even Kuczynski (1928: 17–19), who did more than any other individual to popularize the reproduction rates, pointed out that in the countries of Northwest Europe the percentage of women in the fecund period remained virtually constant between 1860 and 1910. It rose by several points after World War I, when fertility and therefore the relative number of minors declined faster. The issue that this datum suggests was developed by Stolnitz in an interesting paper. He compiled all the reproduction rates available for the period up to the late 1940s, and in each case matched the gross reproduction rate with the birth rate (the obvious analogue among crude vital measures) and the net reproduction rate with the crude rate of natural increase. For example, for France the gross reproduction rate fell from 1.31 in 1904–07 to 1.23 in 1908–13, or by about 6.1 percent, while over the same period the birth rate fell from 20.4 to 19.3, or by 5.4 percent. As in this example, the trend of the reproduction rate was in general not markedly different from that of the crude birth rate.

Among the eleven countries with twenty or more values on record, the coefficient of linear correlation between the two measures was .93 in one instance, .98 to .99 in four cases, and .99 or over in the remaining six. The implications of these results for purposes of estimation are obvious. Perhaps equally interesting is their bearing on traditional methodology. Judging from the past at least, our substantive knowledge of movements in the gross reproduction rate would have been very nearly the same, had it been necessary to rely on the birth rate alone [Stolnitz 1955].

The correlation, though not quite so high, was also sizable between net reproduction rates and crude rates of natural increase. Some of the divergence, moreover, was due to the lesser precision of the reproduction rates, when these had been computed on the basis of life tables some years out of date.

These comparisons do not condemn the reproduction rates altogether, of course, but they do challenge the widespread notion that the more work that goes into a computation, the more precisely its end product reflects reality. The limitations of a crude rate must be pointed out, but in some discussions perhaps they have been stressed too much.

Ansley Coale (1970) devised a new measure of fertility, based on comparing the total fertility rate of any population with the highest one ever recorded. If a woman married at age 15 and, throughout her fecund period, had the same number of children that Hutterites do in each age interval, she would bear an average of 12.6 children during her lifetime. If we take this to be the maximum physiological potential for a population (individual families have of course been larger), the reproduction of less prodigious peoples can be related to this norm by the following equation:

$$\text{Index of Overall Fertility} = \frac{B}{\Sigma\, W_i F_i}$$

where

B = the number of births to the subject population in a given year,
W_i = the number of women in each 5-year age interval from age 15 to age 50, and
F_i = the marital fertility of Hutterite women in each age interval.

The capital sigma indicates, of course, that one should sum the items following it, as in Columns 3 or 5 of Table 3-7. By breaking down the data, one can calculate in the same way the separate rates of legitimate and illegitimate fertility. This is perhaps the most elegant way of controlling for age structure and, in the same measure, indicating also the relation of a particular level of fertility to the most appropriate standard.

SUMMARY

The structure of a population, or its distribution by age and sex, can be analyzed with a number of tools—among others, the sex ratio, median age, and the population pyramid. For some purposes, it is useful to compare the three main age categories of dependent children, the active population, and the dependent aged, and to construct from them indices of aging and of dependency.

The increment to the population of any area can be measured simply by noting the natural increase (births less deaths) and the net immigration (immigration less emigration). In such a preliminary analysis, however, the interdependence of fertility, migration, and mortality has yet to be included. Population structure is relevant to every demographic study because birth, death, and migration rates affect the proportions of the various ages and the two sexes, and in turn are affected by them.

For one who has accustomed himself to think in terms of population structure, many of the generalizations made about all kinds of social behavior are incomplete, if not actually false. All social statistics, no matter what their specific subject matter, must be interpreted with the possible relevance of population structure in mind.

The principal limitation of the simple ratios and crude rates conventional in demographic analysis, similarly, is that the population structure is ignored in them. They are useful, therefore, only when the distribution by sex and age in the populations being compared either is the same or is not pertinent to the question being analyzed. In other cases, some degree of refinement is called for, and this generally means specifying the elements of the population structure sufficiently to compare demographic events independent of its influence.

The two sexes and the several broad age categories are distinguished most fundamentally by physiology and thus, usually in a derivative sense, by their typical social roles. One should beware, however, of the trend to overstate the coherence of these structural elements. Feminist spokespersons and youth partisans claim to represent genuine if still inchoate constituencies, but one can hardly imagine a social or political issue that in fact would excite a consensus among all young people, or among all persons of one or the other sex. For a professional social analyst to designate those of 30 to 34 years, say, as an age "group" (as in previous editions of this work) is inexcusable sloppiness. There are many alternative terms—*category*, or *bracket*, or *interval*—that properly suggest a more or less arbitrary analytical division rather than a self-consciously distinctive entity.

It is useful to distinguish three fixed patterns of interaction between population structure and fertility plus mortality. These three stable populations are (1) **expansive**, with a broad base to the population pyramid, indicating a high proportion of children and a rapid rate of population growth; (2) **stationary**, with

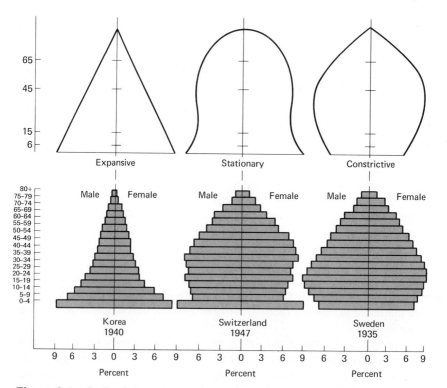

Figure 3-6. Stylized Population Pyramids and Three Comparable Population Structures

a narrower base to the population pyramid, indicating a moderate proportion of children and a slow or zero rate of growth; and (3) **constrictive**, with a base narrower than the middle of the pyramid, indicating a proportion of children insufficient to maintain the population. In Figure 3-6 three stylized pyramids are compared with three actual population structures that approximate their shape. The expansive type could have been exemplified as well by the structure of almost any other Asian or Latin American population. By 1947 Switzerland had already experienced an increase in fertility, so that the bottom bar is longer than it ought to be to represent exactly the stationary type. Any one of several West European countries in the mid-1930s—France, Germany, or England, for example, as well as Sweden—approximated the constrictive type fairly closely. The postwar revival of fertility in all of these countries and the subsequent decline changed the shape of their population pyramids radically.

The three types of population structure also approximate three stages in the demographic transition of Western countries, corresponding to periods of actual or potential rapid growth, little or no growth, and actual or potential decline in numbers. One reason that demographers in the 1930s generally spoke of an "incipient decline" even in Western countries whose populations were still growing was that they knew this increase was more the consequence of the population structure than of the average family size. Once the large proportion of young adults—the temporary heritage of the high birth rates several decades earlier—was reduced, then the true vital rates would become actual. The analysis represented a considerable improvement in method; it failed only because the assumption that fertility would remain constant, or continue to decline, proved to be unrealistic.

CITED REFERENCES AND SUGGESTIONS FOR FURTHER READING

Every general work on population includes an analysis of structure, and many specific topics (e.g., labor force, fertility measures) relate to it very directly. A full bibliography on population structure, therefore, could be almost as long as one on the topic of the whole book, and the following list is highly restricted.

AKERS, DONALD S. 1967. "On Measuring the Marriage Squeeze," *Demography*, **4**, 907–924.

BACHI, ROBERTO. 1954. "Measurement of the Tendency to Round Off Age Returns," *Bulletin de l'Institut International de Statistique*, **34**, 129–138.

BARCLAY, GEORGE W. 1958. *Techniques of Population Analysis.* New York: Wiley.

BERGER, BENNETT M. 1963. "On the Youthfulness of Youth Cultures," *Social Research*, **30**, 319–342.

BORRIE, W. D. 1949. *Immigration, Australia's Problems and Prospects.* Sydney: Angus and Robertson.

CALDWELL, JOHN C. 1966. "Study of Age Misstatement among Young Children in Ghana," *Demography*, **3**, 477–490.

*CHADDOCK, ROBERT E. 1936. "Age and Sex in Population Analysis," *Annals of the American Academy of Political and Social Science*, **188**, 185–193; reprinted in Joseph J. Spengler and Otis Dudley Duncan, editors, *Demographic Analysis*. New York: Free Press, 1956.

*COALE, ANSLEY J. 1956. "The Effect of Declines in Mortality on Age Distribution," in Milbank Memorial Fund, *Trends and Differentials in Mortality*. New York.

———. 1968. "Convergence of a Human Population to a Stable Form," *Journal of the American Statistical Association*, **63**, 395–433.

———. 1970. "The Decline of Fertility in Europe from the French Revolution to World War II," in S. J. Behrman *et al.*, editors, *Fertility and Family Planning: A World View*. Ann Arbor: University of Michigan Press.

DAVIS, KINGSLEY. 1965. "The Population Impact of Children in the World's Agrarian Countries," *Population Review*, **9**, 17–31.

DUBLIN, LOUIS I., ALFRED J. LOTKA, and MORTIMER SPIEGELMAN. 1949. *Length of Life: A Study of the Life Table*, revised ed. New York: Ronald Press.

EL-BADRY, M. A. 1969. "Higher Female than Male Mortality in Some Countries of South Asia: A Digest," *Journal of the American Statistical Association*, **64**, 1234–1244.

KENNEDY, ROBERT E., JR. 1972. "The Social Status of the Sexes and Their Relative Mortality in Ireland," in William Petersen, editor, *Readings in Population*. New York: Macmillan.

KEYFITZ, NATHAN. 1965. "Age Distribution as a Challenge to Development," *American Journal of Sociology*, **70**, 659–668.

———. 1966. "Reply" to Van de Walle, *American Journal of Sociology*, **71**, 556–557.

*KITAGAWA, EVELYN M. 1964. "Standardized Comparisons in Population Research," *Demography*, **1**, 296–315.

KLEIMAN, E. 1967. "A Standardized Dependency Ratio," *Demography*, **4**, 876–893.

KUCZYNSKI, ROBERT R. 1928. *The Balance of Births and Deaths*. Brookings Institution. New York: Macmillan.

———. 1932. *Fertility and Reproduction: Methods of Measuring the Balance of Births and Deaths*. New York: Falcon.

*LEE, RICHARD B. 1972. "The Intensification of Social Life among the !Kung Bushmen," in Brian Spooner, editor, *Population Growth: Anthropological Implications*. Cambridge, Mass.: M.I.T. Press.

LEGROS CLARK, F. 1966. *Work, Age and Leisure: Causes and Consequences of the Shortened Working Life*. London: Michael Joseph.

*LERIDON, FRANÇOISE. 1962. "Prévisions de population active: Trois publications internationales," *Population*, **17**, 97–120.

*LINDER, FORREST E., and ROBERT D. GROVE. 1963. *Techniques of Vital Statistics*. Washington, D.C.: National Office of Vital Statistics.

LUNDE, ANDERS S., and ROBERT D. GROVE. 1966. "Demographic Implications of the New United States Certificates," *Demography*, **3**, 566–573.

MARKLE, GERALD E. 1974. "Sex Ratio at Birth: Values, Variance, and Some Determinants," *Demography*, **11**, 131–142.

MCARTHUR, NORMA. 1961. *Introducing Population Statistics*. Melbourne: Oxford University Press.

MORITA, YUZO. 1958. "The Accuracy of Age-Reporting in the Population Census," *Bulletin de l'Institut International de Statistique*, **36**, 183–189.

MYERS, ROBERT J. 1940. "Errors and Bias in the Reporting of Ages in Census Data," *Transactions of the Actuarial Society of America*, **41**, Part 2, 395–415.

NOTESTEIN, FRANK W. 1954. "Some Demographic Aspects of Aging," *Proceedings of the American Philosophical Society*, **98**, 38–45; reprinted in Joseph J. Spengler and Otis Dudley Duncan, editors, *Demographic Analysis*. New York: Free Press, 1956.

*PAKRASI, KANTI, and BIBHAS SASMAL. 1970. "Effect of Infanticide on the Sex Ratio in an Indian Population," *Zeitschrift für Morphologie und Anthropologie*, **62**, 214–230.

PANUNZIO, CONSTANTINE. 1943. "Are More Males Born in Wartime?" *Milbank Memorial Fund Quarterly*, **21**, 281–291.

PETERSEN, WILLIAM. 1970. *The Politics of Population*. Gloucester, Mass.: Peter Smith.

*RUBIN, ERNEST. 1962. "Aspects of Statistical Aggregate Measures, I: The Sex Ratio," *American Statistician*, **16**, 37–39.

————. 1967. "The Sex Ratio at Birth," *American Statistician*, **21**, 45–48.

SAUVY, ALFRED. 1954. "Le vieillissement des populations et l'allongement de la vie," *Population*, **9**, 675–682.

SAW SEE-HOCK. 1967. "Errors in Chinese Age Statistics," *Demography*, **4**, 859–875.

*SCHNAIBERG, ALLAN. 1973. "The Concept and Measurement of Child Dependency: An Approach to Family Formation Analysis," *Population Studies*, **27**, 69–84.

*SHRYOCK, HENRY S., and JACOB S. SIEGEL. 1971. *The Methods and Materials of Demography*, 2 vol. Washington, D.C.: U.S. Bureau of the Census.

*STOLNITZ, GEORGE J. 1955. "Uses of Crude Vital Rates in the Analysis of Reproductivity," *Journal of the American Statistical Association*, **50**, 1215–1234.

TARVER, JAMES D., and CHE-FU LEE. 1968. "Sex Ratio of Registered Live Births in the United States, 1942–63," *Demography*, **5**, 374–381.

U.S. BUREAU OF THE CENSUS. 1973. "Characteristics of American Youth, 1972," *Current Population Reports*, Series P-23, no. 44. Washington, D.C.: U.S. Government Printing Office.

U.S. NATIONAL CENTER FOR HEALTH STATISTICS. 1968. "The 1968 Revision of the Standard Certificates," *Vital and Health Statistics*, Series 4, no. 8. Washington, D.C.: U.S. Government Printing Office.

*VALAORAS, VASILIOS G. 1950. "Patterns of Aging of Human Populations," in Eastern States Health Education Conference, *The Social and Biological Challenge of Our Aging Population*. New York: Columbia University Press.

VAN DE WALLE, ETIENNE. 1966. "Some Characteristic Features of Census Age Distributions in Illiterate Populations," *American Journal of Sociology*, **71**, 549–555.

————. 1968. "Characteristics of African Demographic Data," in Office of Population Research, Princeton University, *The Demography of Tropical Africa*. Princeton, N.J.

VISARIA, PRAVIN M. 1967. "Sex Ratio at Birth in Territories with a Relatively Complete Registration," *Eugenics Quarterly*, **14**, 132–142.

WOLFERS, EDWARD P. 1972. "On Coming to One's Census," in William Petersen, editor, *Readings in Population*. New York: Macmillan.

WRIGHT, CARROLL D. 1900. *The History and Growth of the United States Censuses, Prepared for the Senate Committee on the Censuses*. Washington, D.C.: Government Printing Office.

*YOU POH-SENG. 1959. "Errors in Age Reporting in Statistically Underdeveloped Countries," *Population Studies*, **13**, 164–182.

YOUNG, ALLYN A. 1906. "Age," in *Supplementary Analysis and Derivative Tables: Special Report on the Twelfth Census.* Washington, D.C.: U.S. Bureau of the Census.

ZELNIK, MELVIN. 1961. "Age Heaping in the United States Census: 1880–1950," *Milbank Memorial Fund Quarterly*, **39**, 540–573.

————. 1964. "Errors in the 1960 Census Enumeration of Native Whites," *Journal of the American Statistical Association*, **59**, 437–459.

4

SUBNATIONS

What characteristics of a population ought to be included in the demographic records we compile? The number of possible classifications is all but infinite. One might, for example, divide a population into blonds, brunets, and redheads in order to relate hair color to other variables, but the results would not be illuminating, except possibly to a physical anthropologist. On the other hand, it is standard to classify the population by skin color—which biologically is hardly more significant than hair color—because the fertility and mortality of a society's various races are usually different, as well as their distribution by region, occupation, education, and so on. That is to say, a population datum is relevant if either demographic or social rates differ by that variable.

Populations are typically classified by a number of principles. For demography the most fundamental is the one described in the previous chapter, the universal structure by age and sex. At the other extreme, the classification of persons by such jurisdictional units as states, counties, and townships (or their equivalents in other countries than the United States), though routine in the presentation of almost all population statistics, is of little use in most social analyses; for the boundaries of such areas almost never set off one distinctive subpopulation from another. Between these two polar types, the kinds of characteristics used to denote a population's composition are parallel to the achieved and the ascribed statuses of an individual. To measure the movement of a person up the social ladder or, analogously, of a nation toward full economic development and cultural modernity, analysts generally use changes in occupation, education, income, and rural–urban–metropolitan residence as indices of social class. This will be discussed in later chapters. In contrast, some classifications are defined by criteria that are (or are perceived to be) more or less immutable: race, origin, national stock, language, citizenship, religion, and region (in the sense of a cultural rather than a political subdivision). These define the social counterpart of what Harold Isaacs (1968) called a person's "basic group identity."

On a world scale, the institution associated with each basic group identity is, of course, the nation—a people linked by common descent from a putative ancestor, a common territory, history, language, religion, and way of life. Obviously not all nations conform to every element of this definition, and some of those fashioned in the last generation lack all except a common territory, which frequently was arbitrarily demarcated by alien powers. Within most nations are smaller units that also depend on the individuals' ascribed statuses. Except for their smaller size, these **subnations** have the main features that we associate with nationality: a common territory, an easier communication inside than outside the group, an actual or putative biological descent from common forebears, a sentimental identification with insiders and thus often a relative hostility toward outsiders. As with nations, not all subnations need show every distinguishing characteristic.

The principal reason that statistics on subnations are generally poor is that the concept itself is muddled. This statement can be illustrated in a number of ways.

1. There is a considerable variety, first of all, in the meanings given to key terms. Some analysts use *ethnic group*, for instance, more or less as I use *subnation* (e.g., Gordon 1964: 27; Barth 1970: 10–11), while others distinguish an "ethnic" from a "racial" group or a "race" (e.g., Berry 1965: 46–47). The common term *minority group*, as another example, does not ordinarily refer to a self-conscious and coherent statistical minority (thus, *not* an elite) but only to a sector, not necessarily comprising less than 50 percent, that is subordinate in the social structure (e.g., Wirth 1945; Blalock 1967). Physical anthropologists use *race* to denote a category distinguished by biological characteristics, but others define it as "a group that is *socially* defined but on the basis of *physical* criteria" (Van den Berghe 1967: 9). Still others hope to eliminate racism through word magic and abjure the term *race* altogether (e.g., Montagu 1964: Appendix B). Though I share the distaste for still more sociological jargon, in this case there is a place for a neologism that is free of the accumulated disorder in the meanings of near synonyms.

2. Even when these other terms are defined precisely, moreover, it is often impossible to associate them clearly with particular peoples. Whether Jews, for example, are a religious group, an ethnic stock, members of a nation partly in exile, carriers of a particular culture, or some combination of these has been the subject of a long and often heated dispute—in which a compiler of statistics has no place. In the statistical record, as we shall see, some "races" are defined by cultural characteristics, some "ethnic groups" by racial characteristics, and so on. The genus *subnation* can be defined conceptually without concern about how species in it are differentiated; and empirical studies of subnations in the United States (race), Belgium (language), Northern Ireland (religion), and other countries strongly suggest that the defining criterion need not be an important determinant of group behavior.

3. That there are individuals marginal to almost any subnation means that its boundaries are generally imprecise and shifting. The dilemma posed by this fact has been resolved by two false doctrines, which can be illustrated with respect to race. The first is to ignore the boundaries and define race as an ideal type, the "pure" stock. The other is to ignore the core of similarity and hold that, because of their indefinite limits, "there are no races." Even biologically both conceptions are fallacious, since from the slightest knowledge of taxonomy we know that not merely subspecies (that is, races) but all classificatory divisions up to and including phyla have both characteristic features *and* vague boundaries, and that this duality follows from the process of evolution itself. To demand precise limits across the board would eliminate virtually all of the distinctions made in social analysis—between rural and urban, between working- and middle-class, between employed and unemployed, even between male and female if we are interested in social roles rather than physiology.

According to the first of two international surveys by the United Nations (the second survey was not essentially different), thirty-nine countries classified their populations by nationality or a corresponding geographical unit, ten by race, eight by culture, twenty-two by a combination of race and culture, eleven by a combination of culture and geography, one or two by the original stock as indicated by the language of the respondent's father, and several by the mode of life.

Even where the concept employed in several countries or census operations is apparently the same, . . . the meaning or definition of the concept may have changed and the amount of detail shown in the final tabulations may differ considerably. . . . The adequacy of the response may be seriously affected by the clarity of the question used, [and] . . . there is always a considerable chance of deliberate falsification in connection with questions having to do with matters affecting social prestige [United Nations 1957: 32–33].

The phenomena to be measured are more or less immutable, some in principle entirely so (place of birth, race, etc.) and others subject to slow and cumbrous change (citizenship, usual language, etc.). But "ethnic group . . . relate[s] to a series of categories which are not uniform in concept or terminology. . . . It is impossible to define these concepts precisely" (United Nations 1964: 38). The difficulties in defining subnations are discussed more fully with respect to three typical indices—one biological (race), one cultural (language), and one geographical (region)—chosen out of the dozen or more characteristics that are used to denote the ethnic structure of various countries.

RACE

As biologists and physical anthropologists define the term, a race is "a population which differs significantly from other human populations in regard to the frequency of one or more of the genes it possesses. It is an arbitrary matter which gene loci, and how many, we choose to consider as a significant 'constellation'" (Boyd 1950: 207). The principal factor inhibiting interbreeding has always been geographical separation. Thus, the "major" races—Caucasoid, Mongoloid, Negroid, American Indian, and Australoid—are each associated with one continent. However, groups in physical proximity often retain a degree of racial separation through rules prescribing endogamy or various other boundary-maintaining features of their cultures.

For physical anthropologists the concept of race, while still a matter of dispute, is thus fairly clear in its broad outline. There are, in the common phrase, no pure races; but in the process of genetic differentiation, characteristics tend to cluster in groups that, as groups, can be distinguished from one another by the relative frequency of specific characteristics. In demography, however (as also in law), the differentiation must be specified in a way that can apply not only to populations but to each individual; therefore, the problem of how to classify intermediate types cannot be evaded. There are five alternative principles by which the race of an individual is established in population counts: genealogy, physical characteristics, reputation, self-identification, and cultural attributes. None of these yields wholly satisfactory results, and in many cases the officials responsible for collecting data have vacillated among several criteria.

To denote a person to be in a particular race by his **genealogy**, if no less than one-half, or one-quarter, or some other fraction of his forebears were in that race, is in itself a procedure in some accord with the notion of race as a breeding group. But there are several problems. Genealogies are typically not available over a sufficient period and, if they are, may not be accurate concerning the forebears' races. When the designated fraction is very small, the definition based on genealogy contradicts the evidence of one's senses. For example, the Five Civilized Tribes in Oklahoma include on the tribal rolls persons who are 1/256 Indian (Beale 1958). In any case, the definition of the races is a function of how officials designate the distinguishing fraction, which typically varies from one jurisdiction or time period to another. Consider, as one example, the official definitions of *mulatto* in the United States. In the 1890 census, after a precise differentiation among blacks, mulattoes, quadroons, and octoroons, the census volume commented: "These figures are of little value. Indeed, as an indication of the extent to which the races have mingled, they are misleading" (quoted in Wright 1900: 187). That "mulattoes" increased from 11.2 percent of all Negroes in 1850 to 20.9 percent in 1910 was due in part to such variations in the definition of the term (Cummings 1918: 208).

The **physical characteristics** used to distinguish races can be any that are known to be hereditary. Those used in traditional 19th-century anthropology were height; cephalic index, or the ratio of the breadth to the length of the head; color of skin, eyes, and hair; texture of hair and degree of the body's hairiness; and special features like the epicanthic fold or steatopygia. Such somatic characteristics generally depend on the interaction of a large number of genes, so that each person falls somewhere along a continuum from short to tall, for example, or from light to dark. More recently anthropologists have preferred to classify races also according to traits that are known to be determined by the action of a single gene, of which the best known are the four blood groups (A, B, AB, and O), the three blood types (M, N, and MN), and the eight Rhesus blood types. With such serological criteria, each individual can be placed into all-or-none categories, but in classifying populations one incurs the same kind of difficulties as with the traditional somatic traits.

The principal objection to all these indices is that they are not, as hypothesized, wholly determined by heredity but also, in some cases at least, markedly affected by environment. Americans of European origin, for example, were generally about 2 inches taller than their parents; and as Boas (1911) demonstrated in a classic study, a new environment can effect within a single generation great changes even in the shape of the skull, which used to be a major criterion of racial differentiation. For a while it was believed that serological traits are neutral with respect to human survival, but this is certainly not the case for at least some of them, which in this respect are little better than somatic traits as classificatory criteria of presumed biological groupings. In a population with considerable miscegenation, moreover, the lines of division differ according to which characteristic is used, for the various indices are not highly correlated.

The **reputation** of a person in the local community has often been used to resolve such dilemmas. For instance, instructions to enumerators of the United States census in 1900, contrary to earlier censuses, did not define race, and according to a subsequent census monograph, the enumerators' "answers reflect[ed] local opinion, and that opinion probably [was] based more on social position and manner of life than upon relative amounts of blood" (U.S. Bureau of the Census 1906: 177). Such a dependence on popular definition may not be haphazard, as in this case, but called for in the census instructions. For example, in 1951 the Union of South Africa redefined a "white" as follows:

A white person is now defined as a person who in appearance obviously is, or who is generally accepted as, a white person, but does not include a person who, although in appearance obviously a white person, is generally accepted as a colored person. This means that the appearance and associations of a person are the main considerations in determining whether he is white or not, rather than the parentage, as in the past [quoted in United Nations 1956: 5].

Self-identification depends on self-perception, which changes with new ideological fashions. There has been a certain change in the attitude toward color in the United States and in Brazil, two countries that now use self-identification to designate race. In the United States, at the time the National Association for the Advancement of Colored People was founded in 1909, *negro* was regarded as a term of abuse. Today, while *Negro* with a capital letter is standard in scholarly discourse (except when it is displaced by such euphemisms as *underprivileged*), black nationalists prefer *Afro-American*, *African*, or *black* (Isaacs 1963: 62–71). In 1960 and 1970, when respondents themselves identified their race, some Negroes might have used the occasion to pass into the white category, while others might have reflected their new pride of race, with blackness defined as a desirable trait. According to the Census Bureau, there was no net difference: "The distribution by color in 1960 was close to that shown by postcensal estimates for 1960 based on the 1950 Census counts by color and estimated population changes during the decade. The increase in the Negro population in particular was consistent with the statistics on its natural increase during this period" (U.S. Bureau of the Census 1963: xi).

Brazil adopted self-identification to classify its population in 1950, and this definition gave "greater precision to the census results" according to the introduction to the census volume. Bertram Hutchinson (1959) speculated, on the contrary, that in 1950 the definition of race was based more on social–economic factors than in earlier censuses. In Brazil the dominant influence in revising self-perception has been Gilberto Freyre, whose apologetic view of Brazilian slavery in *Masters and Slaves* became more indulgent with each succeeding volume of his opus. During the years that he was developing the thesis that for Brazil miscegenation represented not only no defect but her great asset, large numbers of Brazilians of mixed stock were rising to higher status; and their welcome made Freyre "the most influential figure in the last thirty years of Brazilian intellectual history" (Skidmore 1964). His views, once highly regarded also in the United States, have recently been subjected to more criticism. Patterson (1966) holds that Freyre's opinions have been responsible for "romantic nonsense," and according to Stein (1961), "the perfervid regionalist who exhumed the colonial past seems now enamored of a corpse."

Cultural attributes sometimes define the supposedly biological category of race not incidentally, as when local reputations or self-identification are the criteria, but unambiguously and entirely. This is especially so of American Indians. In the censuses of some South American countries, they are defined by their native language; in popular usage, also by their dress. For Mexico, Moore (1951:216) suggested a range of "Indianness," from 100 percent for those who wear Indian clothes and speak only an Indian language, to nil for those who wear European clothes and speak only Spanish. Thus, the charge that the Indian is inferior in industrial tasks is not only true but a truism, for when this inferiority disappears he acquires cultural attributes that redefine him as a non-Indian.

The Indian minority has also been the race most ambiguously defined in the United States. The government volume on federal law pertaining to Indians has a long section aptly titled "Definitions of 'Indian,'" which opens with a warning against any simple interpretations: "Legally speaking, an Indian is what the law legislatively defines, or juridically determines, him to be. General definitions do not suffice" (U.S. Department of the Interior 1958: 4). Each legal definition—for example, enrollment in a tribe, tribal membership, adoption (e.g., of a wholly white person)—has its own background of legislation and court decisions. Each "tribe" (sometimes the status is not clear) may have its own treaty-guaranteed relations with the government. Each individual has the option of maintaining full, partial, or no status in the tribe. Some of the legal disabilities of Indians have been onerous, but sometimes the benefits of government wardship or of membership in a wealthy tribe have been substantial. It is often not only convenient but also possible for a single individual both to be and

"Do you go barefoot, wear sandals, or wear shoes?" asked an enumerator for the 1960 census in a Mexico City slum (*Wide World Photos*).

not to be an Indian, depending on the context. A volume on the Navaho, the largest tribe, distinguishes three possible counts: the *de jure* population, comprising all who are legally classifiable as Navaho; the administrative population, comprising those who as Navahos use the tribe's services or participate in Navaho affairs; and the core population, comprising those with a primary involvement with traditional Navaho culture (Johnston 1966: 12).

Untaxed Indians—that is, those living in Indian Territories or on reservations—were the only group excluded from the census when it was prescribed in the Constitution. They were not counted until 1890, and as the policy varied in subsequent censuses on how to define an "Indian," the number enumerated went up and down, as though until the recent rapid growth the population were suffering from recurrent catastrophes (Figure 4-1). These fluctuating figures must be corrected not only for the effect of the changing directions given enumerators but also for those Indians omitted in all the censuses. In 1950, for instance, the approximately 343,000 Indians enumerated in the census included neither an estimated 75,000 persons who would normally report themselves as Indians on public documents (of whom about 30,000 hybrids were enumerated

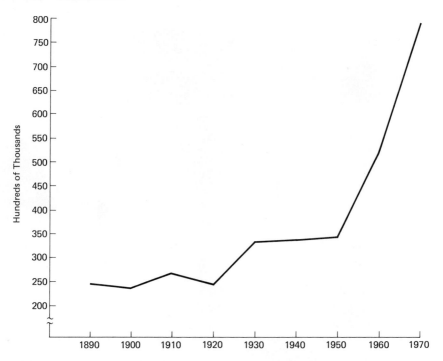

Figure 4-1. Number of Indians Enumerated in United States Censuses, 1890–1970

SOURCES: U.S. Bureau of the Census, *Historical Statistics of the United States, Colonial Times to 1957*; *Census of Population, 1960*; *1970* (Washington, D.C.: U.S. Government Printing Office).

as whites) nor an additional 25,000 persons entitled to legal recognition as tribe members who would not usually report themselves as Indians (Hadley 1957). The indicated increase during the subsequent two decades was certainly genuine, but there is no reason to suppose that the self-identification instituted in 1960 accurately counted Indians as they are designated in the census volumes— including persons of mixed blood "if they are enrolled on an Indian tribal or agency roll or if they are regarded as Indians in their community."

LANGUAGE

Language statistics of the various countries of the world as compiled by the United Nations refer to three different units: (1) "mother tongue," usually defined as the language spoken in the respondent's home during his early childhood; (2) "usual language," defined as the language(s) currently spoken in his home; and (3) all the languages, or all those in a specified list, that the respondent can speak. Of the thirty-seven countries with data, twelve were based on (1), eleven on (2), eleven on (3), and three on some combination of these. Manifestly such compilations are not comparable, even apart from differences in the designated age range, the manner of recording deaf-mutes, the distinction made between "language" and "dialect," and other details (United Nations 1964: 39; cf. Lieberson 1966b).

The difficulties in classifying languages are analogous to those in classifying races, for in both cases the basic problem is how to distinguish clusters in a continuum from one another.

> All languages that are known to be genetically related, i.e., to be divergent forms of a single prototype, may be considered as constituting a "linguistic stock." . . . When we set it up, we merely say, in effect, that thus far we can go and no farther. At any point in the progress of our researches an unexpected ray of light may reveal the "stock" as but a "dialect" of a larger group. The terms dialect, language, branch, stock—it goes without saying—are purely relative terms. They are convertible as our perspective widens or contracts [Sapir 1921: 163–164].[1]

This is equivalent to the sentence quoted earlier from Boyd—that "it is an arbitrary matter which gene loci, and how many, we choose to consider as a significant 'constellation.'" Often linguistic characteristics matter less in determining the designation than the cultural or political status of the group that uses it. For example, Flemish was once the "dialect" of Dutch spoken in Belgium, but now, after the successful effort of Flemish nationalists to establish it as such, "Dutch" or "Southern Dutch" is one of the country's two official "languages."

The place of local speech forms in the national culture has been a political issue also in such other European nations as Ireland, Scotland, Wales, Norway, Finland, the Netherlands, France, Spain, and Yugoslavia, as well, of course, as in virtually all the countries of European immigration, particularly Canada and South Africa. In India, advocates of English, Hindi, and the regional languages have struggled so vigorously that, in the view of one Indian expert, the country "stands the risk of being split up into a number of totalitarian small nationalities" (quoted in Harrison 1960: 3). In the new states of sub-Saharan Africa at least 800 distinct languages are spoken, none by more than 8 percent of the total population (Ornstein 1964). The governments of multilingual countries face demands that are in part irreconcilable: each minority typically wants education, official proceedings, and culture in its own speech, while the continuity of the nation as a whole depends on developing a means of easy communication across the existent, and sometimes growing, language boundaries.

REGION

Odum and Moore began their book on regionalism (1938: 2) by quoting twenty-eight different definitions of *region*, to which they added a twenty-ninth of their own. The basic element of most of these definitions (or sometimes, particularly

---

[1] Copyright, 1921, by Harcourt, Brace and Company, Inc.; renewed 1949, by Jean V. Sapir. This quotation reprinted by permission of the publishers.

among plant and animal ecologists and some geographers, the only element) is the **natural area**, or a physiographic unit delineated by its topography, soil type, climate, and similar features.[2] The natural environment formed by a mountain range, or a river valley, or a seacoast can have a considerable influence on the lives of its inhabitants. For example, an invisible boundary running from eastern North Dakota to western Texas divides an area to the east with an annual rainfall of more than 20 inches from one to the west with less than this amount, and to this day the semi-arid Rocky Mountain region between this isogram and the coastal area is the most sparsely populated in the United States. In Dr. C. A. Bentley's 1916 report of the Indian Medical Service, now a classic of epidemiology, he presented a map of Bengal showing the relative incidence of malaria, which depended on the distribution of mosquito-breeding areas. When this map is compared with one showing the relative increase in population from 1901 to 1911 (the two maps are reproduced in Stamp 1964: 22–23), it is clear that the differential pattern of mortality, supplemented perhaps by migration to more healthful areas, largely set the regional growth pattern.

A second meaning of *region*, the **culture area**, was developed by such anthropologists as Clark Wissler and, following his lead, Kroeber (1939), who divided the pre-Columbian population of North America into groups of contiguous tribes with similar patterns of life. From the substantial overlap between physical and cultural elements, it could be assumed that the history of each culture area had been essentially self-contained and more or less determined by the natural environment. There was not, however, a perfect correlation between natural and culture areas: eastern tribes living in the same type of habitat were sometimes not at all alike, and the Navaho and Hopi, although occupying the same natural area in the Southwest, had markedly different native cultures.

Geography, in other words, determines the limits of a group's development, but within these limits a considerable variation in culture is possible. In the often quoted words of Vidal de la Blache, "Nature is never more than an advisor." Some degree of identity between natural and culture areas is thus usual, particularly among primitive peoples, but the greater the control over its natural environment a society has, the smaller this correlation will generally be and the less can one regard it as an inescapable cause–effect relation. A reasonable stance can be based neither on geographic determinism nor on the denial that geographic factors are sometimes decisive, particularly in the past (and on occasion the quite recent past), in underdeveloped countries, and in those regions of advanced economies subject to extremes of climate or topography. That the correlation between natural and cultural region depends on technical skill means that time is also relevant. Historical areas retain their local character

---

[2] Unfortunately, human ecologists have also used the term *natural area* to designate a homogeneous neighborhood of a city, even though most of its characteristics, of course, are culturally determined. In this usage, *natural* means developing outside of policy decisions rather than from the forces of nature. This confusing double meaning of a key term is probably too well established to be eliminated, but it will not be followed in this book.

until the unifying effect of the national culture permeates every corner of a country. Thus, the regional boundaries drawn today may be obsolete tomorrow, when the topography has been conquered and the frontier between contiguous cultures has disappeared.

In the United States few concepts of social history have generated more interest, and less agreement, than "the frontier." "The West" began to evolve as a self-conscious section when it was still to the east of the Appalachians. By the first quarter of the 19th century, the frontier was at the Mississippi; by 1850 at the Missouri and in California; and by 1900 in the Rocky Mountains. This east-to-west social evolution, according to Frederick Jackson Turner, perhaps the most influential American historian of his day, "worked a political transformation." The frontier "promoted the formation of a composite nationality," in part by decreasing America's dependence on England. He saw this fusion as the dominant theme of 19th-century American history, compared with which "the slavery question is an incident." The Middle West was "the typically American region," "democratic and non-sectional," where frontier individualism has most successfully developed into American democracy (Turner 1949).

Beginning in the 1930s Turner and his thesis began to be challenged and rejected, and defended anew. Of the principal criticisms the most interesting to a demographer was the attack on Turner's "safety-valve"—the proposition that the availability of free land on the frontier cut down economic discontent in eastern cities by drawing off the surplus urban population to the farm. This was no more effective, however, than "a whistle on a peanut roaster," for class conflict was actually extremely sharp just during the decades that free land was available. The dominant migration, in fact, was in the wrong direction: for each industrial laborer who moved to the land, at least twenty farmers moved to the city. The free land did not even absorb the rural natural increase: for each farmer's son who became the owner of a new farm other than his father's, ten moved to the city (Shannon 1949).

Each step taken so far in the formulation of *region* has increased the complexity of defining this ambivalent concept. A natural region is not typically sharply bounded; its overlap with a cultural region is usually only partial; and the frontier, the border between a developed and an undeveloped region, remains a subject of scholarly dispute. The demographer's concept of a region combines these three compromises with yet one more, which can be illustrated with the "regions" of the United States. Whether *New England, the South, the Great Plains*, and so on denote regional subcultures is a question that can be answered empirically, but the answer will vary greatly according to where the boundaries between them are drawn. Regions, however defined, merge into one another, but for a statistical analysis the lines between them must be sharp. And if the regional division is to have the greatest practical use, the boundaries must correspond to those of the administrative units by which census data are segregated—that is, states or counties.

The presentation of United States census data by region developed gradually

(Mood 1965). The ordering of data in the 1790 census—a list of states from north to south, followed by the western territories—was maintained with appropriate additions and slight changes until 1840. In a work based on that census, *Progress in the United States in Population and Wealth* (1843), George Tucker held that the states and territories "naturally arranged themselves" into five divisions, based both on their "geographical position" and "modes of industry and commercial interest," or into only four when the east–west contrast was crossed with one between states with and without slaves. The 1870 census, prepared under Francis A. Walker as superintendent, introduced two innovations. State data were presented alphabetically, thus seemingly abandoning the prior concept of regionalism; but for the first time the census statistics were illustrated with maps, which clearly showed the regional distribution of many variables. Walker assigned one of his staff, Henry Gannett, to work out a new basis for a regional system, and his schema has been maintained, with minor variations, to the present day. Gannett divided the country into three topographical units—the Atlantic region, the Mississippi valley, and the West—and subdivided the first two along the Mason–Dixon line (with an approximate westward extension) into two units differing mainly in history and social structure.

The four regions presently used by the Bureau of the Census are shown in Figure 4-2. On the whole, this breakdown represents accurately the major geographic areas in American history: the Northeast (equivalent to *the North* of the 19th century), the South, the North Central region (equivalent to *the Middle West*), and the West. Each region is broken down further into **divisions**: the Northeast between the two historic areas of New England and the Middle Atlantic states, the North Central region between an eastern division of five industrial–agricultural states and a western one of seven grain-producing states, and the West between the five Pacific states and the semi-arid Mountain states.[3] So long as this official pattern lasts, it determines the presentation of regional data and thus our perception of this country's regions. One should not assume, however, that the Census Bureau's present schema is necessarily fixed. For example, the prestigious Committee for Economic Development published a work that both departs from the Census Bureau denotation of regions in a number of significant respects (Perloff 1963: 15) and better represents the present distribution of at least some important variables. In France, as another example, the *départements* that Napoleon had fashioned in order to break up the old

---

[3] The breakdown of the South, however, is less satisfactory. The subcultural areas defined by most indices would seem to be the intermediate region between the South and the South-west, which is adequately represented by the West South Central division; the Deep South, from the Carolinas west to Mississippi or farther; and the border states, from Delaware west to Missouri. Odum and Moore, following some earlier precedents, even assigned Delaware, Maryland, West Virginia, and the District of Columbia to the North. The line between the South Atlantic and the East South Central divisions, on the contrary, groups these states with the Carolinas and Georgia, and Kentucky with Mississippi and Alabama.

Figure 4-2.   Regions and Geographic Divisions of the United States, 1970, as Defined by the U.S. Bureau of the Census

provinces were recently recombined into twenty-one regions, plus Paris. It is generally recognized that French society is too highly centralized, and one reason has been that other regions had no effective administrative units (*New York Times*, January 26, 1974).

To sum up: Out of the dozen or so ethnic indicators used by various countries, three—race, language, and region—have been examined in some detail in order to see how the objective reality, as seen by specialized scholars, is translated into demographic data. In all three cases (and this is generally true of ethnic indicators), the demographer is faced with the same paradox: the incidence of the variable tends to cluster, marking the significant differences that exist; but since the clusters are not sharply bounded, the assignment of intermediate units must be more or less arbitrary.

The subnations of any society, then, are classified only partly according to their objective characteristics, partly also according to such other criteria as the view that the politically dominant group has of the whole society. The dominant subnation, whether in numbers or in power, is typically given the most statistical attention; but even after this relative power declines, it may retain its earlier place in the official classification. A subnation with a designation that it deems to be derogatory may demand not merely a new term but a reclassification. More generally, the designations are often changed from one synonymous term to another because of shifts in their emotional or political connotation. A decision not to classify a population by subnations, although it is often justified by a statement that ethnic differentiation is unimportant, is usually based, on the contrary, on a reluctance to publicize significant ethnic–class or ethnic–political correlations (Petersen 1969; cf. Farley 1968; Levy 1960, 1962).

ETHNIC VARIABLES AND SOCIAL STRUCTURE

A subnation defined by one criterion very often comes to be differentiated also by others. French Canadians, for example, differ from English Canadians not only in language but also in dominant religion, region, traditional occupations, degree of urban concentration, and general way of life. American Negroes are distinguished from whites not only by genetic characteristics but also by most social–economic indices. The effect of such a pattern on a nation's social structure can be illustrated conveniently by examining an extreme case, the caste system of Hindu India.[4] The English word *caste* is used to translate two Hindi words, *varna* and *jati*, which must be differentiated. The literal meaning of *varna* is "color," and although there is no absolute color line along any dimension, color marks a significant differentiation. The population of the North is usually fairer than that of the South, and the highest castes are generally lighter than the Untouchables. "A light skin color is valued almost universally. . . . In many Indian languages the words *fair* and *beautiful* are often used synonymously. . . . Virginity and a light skin color are among the most desirable qualities in a bride" (Béteille 1967). There are four varnas: in hierarchical order, *Brahmin*, the priest or scholar; *Kshatriya*, the warrior-ruler; *Vaishya*, the merchant; and *Sudra*, the peasant or craftsman. This four-level hierarchy makes the caste system of one region of India intelligible in another, though usually with some oversimplification or distortion. In fact, the more significant broad classification divides Hindu India into only three parts: the "twice-born," who undergo a *rite de passage* that makes them full members of society (the first three varnas);

---

[4] *Caste*, it is true, is sometimes used as a generic concept to denote any subnation separated by a considerable number of ethnic indicators, but most Indologists agree that "the only genuine parallels to Hindu caste are to be found in communities which, though professing other faiths, live with or near Hindu communities" (Srinivas 1959: 149). According to some interpretations the system originated in an attempt to distinguish the prehistoric fair invaders from the darker peoples they conquered. This theory was propounded by Sir Herbert Risley, the director of the 1901 census, who made the first systematic attempt to classify the Indian population by race. Today his conclusions are more or less accepted by some (e.g., Ghurye 1961) and rejected by others (e.g., B. S. Guha, cited in Béteille 1967).

the "once-born" *Sudras*; and the Untouchables (or Avarnas, "noncaste persons"), who are below the varna system altogether.

However, "it is necessary for the sociologist to free himself from the hold of the varna-model if he wishes to understand the caste system" (Srinivas 1962: 66). Hinduism divides Indian society not into three to five broad orders but into perhaps 3,000 castes and subcastes—some subunits of varnas, some associated with particular territories or traditional occupations, some the consequence of the spread of Hinduism to tribal peoples, and so on (Hutton 1963: 2). These smaller units are the *jatis*, the breeding units of the Indian population. The word derives from *jan*, "to give birth to," and jati "comes closer to the meaning of 'race' than perhaps any other word in popular usage" (Béteille 1967). As caste defines the units of endogamy, one should not be surprised that both of the words to denote it reflect a concern with genetic purity.

Ghurye (1961: chap. 1) has defined six main features of Hindu society before it was markedly affected by Western ideas, as follows:

1. Each subcaste typically restricts marriage to within its own group, and so famous an anthropologist as Westermarck termed this **endogamy** "the essence of the caste system." The one important traditional exception is that in some areas a man may take a wife of lower caste; but, apart from this hypergamy, intercaste marriage is condemned more strongly than almost any other transgression of Hindu tradition. All castes of good position, moreover, are bound by its *sapinda* rule, which prohibits the union of any two persons with a common ancestor not more than six degrees removed on the male side, or four degrees on the female side. Thus, some 2,121 kinds of relatives are excluded, as compared with thirty by the relatively rigid rules (for the West) of the Anglican Church. In part as a consequence of these restrictions, the lack of suitable mates compels even rigid high castes to take lower-caste women as wives. "But in such cases both the husband and his caste connive at their own deception and, if they are willing to ignore custom, are very unwilling that the fact should be generally known" (Blunt 1931: 48, 60).

2. Caste segments society into distinct units, each **governed by a caste council** (or *panchayat*), which has the power to impose strong sanctions on those members who break its rules. (Yet, more generally, the values that define the hierarchy are not imposed from the top but permeate all levels, even in modern times. When Nehru tried to bring up an Untouchable girl together with his daughter, the parents were delighted until they heard that she ate with Brahmins; they then withdrew her in horror.) To the extent that their lives are so governed, caste members are not members of a general society. There is no overall moral norm in Hinduism, no revealed divine laws, no equivalent to sin, hardly even a universal deity. All the rules and the ritual depend on the individual's subcaste, which is analogous to an extended family. Beyond this the individual in practice recognizes no society or community; "the Hindu has become an abstraction, a sociological fiction" (Panikkar 1933: 17).

3. Not only the varnas but also the subcastes are **ranked in a hierarchy** down through a varying, often disputed, ordering to the lowest of several categories of Untouchables at the bottom. The widely divergent rules cover every facet of life—the length of twig with which one brushes one's teeth, the size of wheel a potter must use, the color of the flower one may wear, the type of house that may be built, the clothing that may be worn, the punishment to be meted out for identical misdeeds, and so on and on through a catalog that includes both life's fundamentals and its minutiae. The rigidity with which such rules were enforced in British India "would put to shame even the Great Inquisition" (ibid.: 9).

4. The ranking of castes is denoted by **restrictions on social intercourse**. Members of higher castes are polluted by the touch of a lower-caste person (a modern Brahmin physician attending a Sudra wraps his patient's wrist in a piece of silk before taking his pulse), by his shadow, or even by his presence closer than at a certain number of paces. The most important indicator of rank is the transfer of water: one takes water from one's equals or superiors, not from one's inferiors. Food therefore is divided into two types: *kachcha*, cooked with water and therefore subject to the strictest rules, and *pakka*, cooked with ghee (or clarified buffalo butter) and thus subject to less stringent restrictions. The most familiar sanction that panchayats use to force members to adhere to the infinity of commandments, to forbid a fellow member from giving them water or receiving it from them, in effect excommunicates the delinquents from the caste system.

5. Since defilement can be by any member of specified groups, efforts to avoid it go beyond setting up institutions that regulate the relations among individuals. Untouchables typically live in segregated areas at the outskirt of the village and sometimes, particularly in the South, various other castes also have their own **segregated quarters or streets**, to which in extreme cases they are restricted. Brahmins, the traditional priests of Hinduism, administer two types of ritual—the very holy Vedic for themselves and other "twice-born," and the Puranic, of lesser sanctity, for such as Sudras—whereas to Untouchables no Brahmin would minister at all.

6. Castes are sometimes associated with **a traditional occupation**, in which case many in the caste, perhaps between half and three-quarters, make their living in it (Davis 1951: 168; cf. Driver 1962). Beyond this, the choice of occupation is restricted at both ends, with the priesthood excluded to all but Brahmins and all caste members forbidden to do work defined as degrading or polluting.

In principle, the caste system is fixed: every person is born into the status that he will retain throughout his life, and the social structure summing up this complete lack of social mobility is also stable. In fact, the structure has never been immutable, in part because it is both one system and many systems. The key concept is "pollution," but who or what pollutes and under which circumstances varies widely and inconsistently. As with modern totalitarianism, which has undergone certain revisions in its original and supposedly unchanging struc-

A village of ex-Untouchables, Tondiarpet, India (*Camera Press—PIX*).

ture, one must try to distinguish within-system changes from changes in the system.

Apart from the kind of excommunication already mentioned, most social mobility in caste society is of groups rather than of individuals. It is convenient to classify changes in the social structure and resistance to them into several types:

1. Over a generation or two, lower castes (thus, not Untouchables) have always been able to rise by what Srinivas (1962: 42–62) terms sanskritization, that is, the conscious adoption of certain of the customs, rites, and beliefs of the Brahmins. Moreover, "a caste which owned land exercised an effective dominance regardless of its ritual status" (Srinivas 1959: 140). This means that at any particular time the precise order of local subcastes may be in dispute; in one village of highland Orissa, the third rank, immediately under Brahmins and Warriors, was held jointly by four occupations (Bailey 1957: 8). A jati that succeeds in rising typically acquires "all the intolerance of the parvenu"

(Blunt 1931: 103), so that whatever social mobility takes place by this route tends to strengthen adherence to the system rather than to disrupt it.

2. Individuals, or occasionally whole subcastes, have attempted to rise in Indian society by joining one of the non-Hindu religions. The principal result of this process, however, has been to recreate the caste system among Moslems, Christians, Buddhists, and Jews. Four centuries after their conversion, Goan Catholics have still sought mates for their children from the appropriate caste (Zinkin 1962: 2). Through an analogous process the primitive tribal peoples of central India assimilate to Hinduism by becoming another jati, usually at the bottom of the caste ordering but above the line of pollution (cf. Srivastava 1966).

3. "The village communities," Sir Charles Metcalfe wrote in 1832, "are little republics, almost independent of any foreign relations." The intrusion of British influence on this Hindu world was of several kinds. The principle of equality before the law undercut "the whole basis of Hindu justice," by which "punishment or penalties did not merely depend upon the nature of the crime committed but also on the caste of the criminal and that of the victim" (Sinha 1965). Political democratization, started in British India and greatly accelerated since independence, has in many respects undercut the caste hierarchy, but at least one analyst holds that "the power and activity of caste have increased in proportion as political power passed increasingly to the people from the rulers" (Srinivas 1962: 23). For what seem to be disputes between political parties or language or regional groups are often, a half-inch below the surface, manifestations of persistent caste hostilities.

4. Industrialization and urbanization also attacked the village-based social structure. New occupations did not fit into the traditional ranking; greater migration afforded more opportunities to escape from local hierarchies; in the crowded city the rules concerning touchability are unenforceable among an anonymous population; the main criterion of pollution, accepting water from an inferior, is all but impossible to apply to a municipal supply that comes from a tap.

5. The greatest change relates to the 65 to 95 million ex-Untouchables, as Isaacs terms Indians below the line of pollution.[5] The "Scheduled Castes" are now favored by special provisions in the Indian Constitution, the Untouchability (Offenses) Act of 1955, and quotas in colleges and in civil-service jobs. Important advances have been made in some respects, but hardly in all. One response to the ambiguity is "semi-passing"—"passing in public while not passing in private" (Isaacs 1965: 147)—which permits a person to take advantage of new opportunities, but does not cut him off completely from his caste com-

---

[5] As with so many of the world's depressed classes, the name used to refer to them is not neutral. *Untouchables* is wholly accurate only for the past; *Exterior* or *Scheduled* castes are officialese at its most pompous; *Harijans*, the term bestowed by Gandhi, means "children of God"—that is, persons conceived illegitimately (Isaacs 1965; chap. 2). According to the 1961 census, there were 64.4 million in Scheduled Castes plus 30.1 million in Scheduled Tribes. Together they made up 21.5 percent of India's population.

munity, through which such crucial affairs as marriage typically must still be arranged.

"Shall we have democracy or shall we have caste?... That we cannot have both of them at the same time is certain" (Panikkar 1933: 37). On balance, there has been a decline in the importance of caste except in the barrier against intermarriage, which remains almost unbreached. Yet the caste system—ancient, ingrained, not disturbed by flagrant inconsistencies—has also retained a degree of invulnerability. Some caste organizations have responded to the challenge of modernization not with passivity or retreat but with educational institutions, fraternal orders, social agencies, and other means of helping good caste members solve, within the framework of the caste, the problems that urban–industrial society poses. In the view of perhaps the foremost scholar of the subject, "Caste is so tacitly and so completely accepted by all, including those who are most vocal in condemning it, that it is everywhere the unit of social action" (Srinivas 1962: 41).

ASSIMILATION AND THE QUEST FOR COMMUNITY

The Hindu social structure, particularly in its classical, pre-British form, had the maximum overlap of the social–economic statuses with ethnic indices. A person's position in society and also that of his subcaste are in theory fixed; the assimilation of minorities into the broader society is in principle impossible. In contrast, this section discusses the various types of assimilation as these take place in an open society like the United States. In both cases, of course, the model has been less fully realized: just as the caste system was never as rigid as it was supposed to be, so the equal opportunity guaranteed in the American creed has in some instances been unequally available.

The interaction of ethnic minorities and the larger society has been known by a number of terms—among others, *assimilation, acculturation, integration, adjustment,* in addition to such nationally specific ones as *Americanization, Australization,* and so on. Sometimes these have a loose association with academic disciplines (sociologists—assimilation, anthropologists—acculturation), sometimes with a more or less invidious tone. But generally they are used without clear distinctions (cf. Gordon 1964: chap. 3). It is convenient to retain **assimilation** as the generic term denoting the entire process by which nations and the subnations comprising them penetrate each other and become more similar.

During the last decades of the 19th century, when the "hordes" entering the United States made an important political issue of assimilation, this was seen as an all-or-none process. Natives urged those born in other countries to be "hundred-percent" Americans, not Swedish-Americans or Italian-Americans or other "hyphenated" Americans. In 1908 Israel Zangwill's *The Melting Pot* was produced in New York, proclaiming the message that in this new land all European strains would disappear and blend into a nobler American compound.

The hero, like the playwright a Russian Jewish immigrant, marries the immigrant daughter of the tsarist official responsible for the pogrom in which his own parents were killed. As literature, *The Melting Pot* was on a level with a later counterpart, *Abie's Irish Rose*; and within a few years Zangwill abandoned his assimilationist thesis and became a Zionist. But the ideology of his work endured, given a more respectable exposition in the works of Robert E. Park, perhaps the most important sociologist of the 1920s, and his many students and imitators. "Changes in race . . . inevitably follow, at some distance, changes in culture. . . . When migration leads to conquest, either economic or political, assimilation is inevitable" (Park 1950: 345–356). Or, more succinctly still, in a later work: "Assimilation . . . goes on wherever contact and communication exist between groups. . . . It is as inevitable as it is desirable. The process may be hastened or delayed; it cannot be stopped" (Davie 1949: 498–499).

Today, when intergroup conflict seems to be increasing all over the world, few would accept so one-sided a generalization. Indeed, the immigrant generation proffered the concept of melting pot mainly in order to defend themselves against native Americans' hostility: however different we may be now, they were in effect saying, in a few decades we will all be like you. The debate whether to limit immigration was one of the main political issues from the 1890s to the 1920s, and liberals—including in particular liberal scholars—who were opposed to restrictions typically argued their case with the immigrants' self-defensive metaphor. But an answer to xenophobia that consists principally in covering over genuine group differences implicitly affirms the premise that such differences are reprehensible. The Zangwills were at first too insecure to face the issue squarely, and their evasion set a precedent that still dominates discussions.[6] The concentration on such negative features, the definition of the field as "the study of hostile policies directed towards groups ascriptively distinguished by either physical or cultural characteristics" (Rex 1970: 134), is typical of that considerable number of sociologists who endeavor not to understand society but to improve it. *Ethnocentrism*, coined by William Graham Sumner as a neutral term, has also acquired a negative connotation. *Cultural pluralism*, perhaps the best obverse to *melting pot*, is too closely tied to Horace Kallen's specific views to be useful as a general denotation. That one must search for a word meaning the social expression of individuals' search for their basic group identity is indicative of how lopsided the study of subnations has become.

For such a term, I have adapted to a new use the title of Robert Nisbet's historical study, *The Quest for Community* (1953). In the large populations of

---

[6] As one index, take the *International Encyclopedia of the Social Sciences* (1968), generally an excellent survey of contemporary social thought. The two main articles on "Assimilation" and "Acculturation" are reinforced by papers that denote the failure to assimilate as social problems: "Prejudice," "Segregation," "Race Relations," and so on. The contrary process of differentiation, analyzed under "Nativism and Revivalism," is mainly about this phenomenon among primitive peoples, but the author notes in passing that in developed societies the term can refer to a "rejection of alien persons or culture."

modern societies, an individual's relations with those outside his family are likely to be partial, based on particular roles rather than an association between whole persons. There is a consequent rise of what Durkheim called anomie, what Marx called alienation. Efforts to counter this trend can be of various types, but they all constitute essentially a reinforcement of social identity. The two processes, assimilation and the quest for community, thus continually interact; the pressures to disappear into an undifferentiated One World excite counter-pressures to reassert group distinctions. Any new definition of an *in-group* means a redesignation of the *out-group*. As a counterpart to *segregation*, the expression of outsiders' hostility, there is what might be termed *congregation*, or the preference of persons of any subnation to live among their conationals. That residence patterns are typically analyzed as expressions solely of the first and without reference to the second is the consequence not of genuine difficulty in distinguishing between them empirically so much as of a general and almost routine bias.

In the United States, it is true, European additions to the Anglo-Saxon base have melted down into a relatively homogeneous people. Neither the dichotomy between Old and New Immigrants (that is, those from Northwestern Europe and those from Southern and Eastern Europe) nor that between natives and aliens retains nearly so much salience as they had a half-century ago. It is possible with census data to differentiate the foreign-born and their native-born offspring (who together are termed the **foreign stock**), but native-born of native-born parents merge into the general population. For the third and higher generations, since few reliable data on European background are available, theories about whether European identities are retained necessarily are impressionistic.[7]

The proportion of foreign-born whites has fallen off rapidly since the restrictionist laws of the 1920s. Native-born increased from 85 percent of the population in 1920 to 95 percent in 1970, and those with native-born parents from

[7] Nevertheless the immigration quotas set in the 1920s were based on the "national origins" of the American population. It was necessary to calculate "the number of inhabitants in continental United States in 1920 whose origin by birth or ancestry is attributable to [each] geographical area" designated in the immigration statistics as a separate country, and this task was undertaken by the Bureau of the Census, assisted by two experts paid by the American Council of Learned Societies. The frequent and untraceable marriages across ethnic lines, however, made it impossible to divide the 1920 population itself into distinct ethnic groups, and the committee undertook instead to measure the proportionate contribution of various national stocks to the total white American gene pool. It began by dividing the country's original white population by national origin, principally from the family names as enumerated in the 1790 census. As the committee itself pointed out, however, there was a "considerable element of uncertainty" in such a classification, and even small discrepancies in 1790, when increased geometrically from that date until 1920, made a substantial difference in the size of the quota each country was allowed. To this base were added immigration figures, such as they were, and—for lack of a breakdown by ethnic groups—an overall rate of natural increase (U.S. Senate 1928). In short, the paucity and the poor quality of the available statistics made it impossible to carry out the committee's assignment, yet until 1965 American immigration law was based on the results of this calculation. See Petersen 1970: 195–215 for a fuller discussion.

slightly over 60 to about 82 percent. The foreign stock, a small proportion already, is getting smaller still, both because it includes relatively few new arrivals and because its age structure results in a higher mortality. At the height of the immigration, the newcomers were mostly young adults: they were born into American society, so to speak, at the age of 20 and ranged upward from that figure. This age structure (as well as old-country family norms) resulted in a very high fertility; and in 1890 the country's youngest ethnic class was the native-born of foreign-born or mixed parentage. But today the typical foreign-born American is near the age of retirement, and his older sons are middle-aged.

If this statistical summary suggests that the assimilation of European immigrants is all but completed, it is only because the statistics pass over the subtleties. The interaction between the natives and the foreign stock was far more complex than a count of the two categories can convey. By definition, acculturation involves contact with cultures of which all concerned are more or less ignorant; it is, thus, an interrelation between groups in terms of two stereotypes. As Walter Lippmann wrote in *Public Opinion* (the work that introduced *stereotype* in this sense), "For the most part we do not first see, and then define; we define first and then see. . . . Americanization, for example, is superficially the substitution of American for European stereotypes." The picture that the typical immigrant had of America was a composite of the fables circulating in his home country with generalizations drawn from an extremely limited experience after he arrived. And, on the other side, even American immigration officials were puzzled by the complex multiplicity of European peoples, as we have seen from the records that they collected.

In the 19th century, the Germans and Irish came from self-conscious groups that had not yet achieved legal unity; they were nations but not yet states. The Norwegians and Swedes, on the contrary, came from states that were not yet nations; only the upper classes were self-conscious bearers of the national culture (cf. Glazer 1953). This variation was to be found also among the later immigrants. An East European, for example, as he saw himself when he first arrived in the United States, had four identities. He was a subject of a particular state, for example, Russia; he spoke a particular language, for example, Lithuanian; he was an adherent of one or another religion; and he regarded a certain village or province as "home." Typically the peasant emigrants had no special feeling of identification with Russia or "Lithuania." This was often true even of emigrants from a nation that had achieved political unity: an "Italian," for instance, was much more likely to look on himself as a Sicilian or Calabrian.

In many cases it was only after they had left it that migrants learned to identify themselves with "their" country. They were taught this first of all by the native Americans, who demanded a simple, understandable answer to the question, "What are you?" Having learned that they belonged to a nation, some of the immigrants became nationalists. They submerged their provincialisms into a broader patriotism, their local dialects into languages. The first Lithuanian newspaper was published in the United States; the Erse revival began in Boston; the Czechoslovak nation was launched at a meeting in Pittsburgh; the very name of Pakistan was coined by students in London. Yet the nativism of such groups was often one facet of their acculturation, paradoxical as this may seem.

The paradox is even more striking in the phenomenon known as the nativism of the third generation, based on the psychological certainty that in all essential respects one's integration into American society has been completed. While immigrants to the United States were linked to their native countries by childhood memories and nostalgia, as well as by immigrant-aid societies, national churches, and other ethnic organizations, their acculturation was not ordinarily impeded by a conscious reluctance to give up these old-country remnants. On the contrary, most immigrants tried to be more American than a Mayflower descendant, and this aspiration was taken over a little more realistically by the second generation, which typically attempted to learn nothing of the language and other culture traits of its European forebears. It has been suggested (e.g., Handlin 1951) that some of the characteristics specific to the American family derived from the fact that the immigrant father had an ambivalent authority over his native-born son, who spoke English without a foreign accent and also in other respects was likely to be more successful in American society. The third generation, however, has often tried to organize a revival of old-country culture. Thus, the procession of ethnic groups that came to the United States in some instances at least was followed two generations later by a succession of amateur historical societies, folklore associations, and other organized efforts to keep alive specific elements of the various overseas cultures. In short, it is an "almost universal phenomenon that what the son wishes to forget the grandson wishes to remember" (Hansen 1938; but see also Appel 1960, 1961).

In sum, most white minorities went through a more or less difficult period of initial adjustment, then achieved (sometimes in the first but often only in the second or third generation) a far more comfortable niche in American society, while stopping short of full assimilation in all respects. In the first edition of *Beyond the Melting Pot*, Glazer and Moynihan (1963) argued that colored minorities were following the same succession in about the same way. That this cogently analyzed and seemingly perceptive view had to be revised in a second edition indicates how fast ethnic relations have been changing in the United States. "Race has exploded to swallow up all other distinctions, or so it would appear at the moment. . . . Adjustments to the reality of race and ethnic difference have now taken the center of the stage" (Glazer and Moynihan 1970: viii, xxviii). In analyzing more fully the balance between assimilation and quest for community, it is useful to divide the discussion according to some of society's major institutions—economic, social and religious, reproductive, and political. These are discussed in turn.

Economic Structure

No other type of human intercourse, perhaps, is so likely to remain partial as one based on economic relations. The interdependence of different peoples through trade, an example of the type of adaptation human ecologists term *symbiosis*, can remain absolutely stable in this truncated form, particularly if the effort to keep the groups separate in other respects acquires ideological legitimacy and institutional form. An obvious example is the Jewish minority in Gentile societies. Ever since the diaspora, Jews have generally been in continuous commercial relations with the peoples among whom they lived; the degree of integration varied considerably from one country or era to another, but Jews were seldom completely assimilated. Their merging with the broader society was generally prevented by the anti-Semitism of Gentiles and the pro-Semitism of Jews, as well as the ghettos and similar institutions that both reflected these attitudes and helped perpetuate them.

In the modern West, and particularly in the United States, economic integration has been more closely linked with other types of assimilation. To Europeans of every nationality, the democratic system of the overseas republic was an attraction of enormous strength, and particularly the fact that the democracy extended also to social and economic relations. It was necessary to work hard in the new country, but during the decades when immigration was at its height what a man produced was his own to enjoy.

The per-capita expense of government was only one fourth that of the Netherlands and less than a tenth that of England. No percentage was deducted as tithes for the clergy or as rates for the poor. Though the United States had about the same population as Prussia, the standing army of the latter was fifty times as large. It was amazing that a farm that kept eight horses paid a tax in America of only twelve dollars [Hansen 1951: 158].

Immigrants themselves strongly reinforced this established trend toward egalitarian social relations. Of humble birth in overwhelming majority, ignorant of one another's background, they were impatient with class distinctions that rested on family pedigree or even on what Tocqueville called "the natural aristocracy of knowledge and virtue." There was a country to be built, and when it was built it would be theirs. This sense of participation in a joint venture, founded in American law and tradition but more subtle than either, is the key to the successful assimilation of millions of Europeans of such diverse backgrounds.

The part that each immigrant group played in building the American economy, however, was largely specific to it, so far as inadequate sources permit us to judge. Apart from agriculture few skills developed in Europe were transferred to the United States (Jewish tailors and furriers were an exception). In general the young immigrants, including most Jews, found work in occupations that were new to them. Employment opportunities in the United States varied considerably from one period or region to another, and each nationality was typically shunted into a particular type of occupation. There was a good deal of overlap in occupation among nationalities arriving during the same decades, but sometimes also marked differences. The Irish, for instance, who immigrated in great numbers from the 1840s on, did not become farm laborers or farmers but stayed in the towns in spite of their peasant background. Such a trend, once started, tended to continue. Each immigrant found work alongside men who could speak his language, drawn there both by that fact and by directives from immigrant-aid groups, clergymen, or employment agents of his nationality. Thus, for example, a National Society for German Emigration was in operation by the early 1850s; and "after his arrival the [German] immigrant could proceed from city to city, receiving advice at each stage" from compatriots who had already established themselves (Hansen 1951: 302). A similar network, either formally organized or not, existed for each of the immigrant nationalities.

The resultant differences are suggested in Table 4-1, in which only Scots and Irish are compared for only two censuses and a few occupations. The index numbers for each nationality express the proportion engaged in the given occupation as a percentage of the proportion of all native whites in that occupation. Thus, in 1890 there were relatively 7.39 times as many miners among those born in Scotland as among native white males, but only 2.32 times as many among the Irish-born. Among those born in Scotland, work in the mines or cotton mills was relatively most frequent, but the highest proportion among the Irish-born was servants. From 1890 to 1900 the relative proportion of Scots working as miners fell by almost half, and those working in cotton mills by two-thirds. The miners were replaced by Central Europeans and the textile workers by Jews or Italians, while the Scots were becoming clerks or even physicians. In 1900 there were proportionately more doctors among sons of Scots immigrants than in the native white population generally. The Irish moved up too, by a different route: here the next higher rung for most of the second generation was a job as a clerk.

If such a table could be expanded to include all the major nationalities and occupations and the whole of the past century and a half, then we would have a good picture of the interrelation between country of birth and occupation in the United States. Lack of data precludes so complete a study, but Hutchinson has squeezed all that could be gotten out of the record. He sums up his work on this subject as follows:

In 1919 the foreign-born white male workers were most heavily concentrated in some branches of the clothing industry, . . . among bakers, and in several semiskilled or unskilled employments. . . . Relatively few were found in clerical work and the learned professions; but they were well represented in the artistic professions and among welfare and religious workers. In 1950 they are much less identified with unskilled labor, and more concentrated than formerly in the clothing industry . . . and have become relatively numerous in a wider variety of occupations than before. . . . Although still underrepresented in the learned professions and clerical work as a whole they have made considerable progress in these fields of employment [E. P. Hutchinson 1956: 216].

More generally put, all white immigrants were congregated at the bottom of the social scale on their arrival, but in different occupations. And all of them, or their children, moved up from these several starting points, but along different

Table 4-1. Index Numbers of Relative Participation of Scots and Irish Males in Certain Occupations, United States, 1890–1900

Occupation	Total Native White	Scots			Irish		
		1890, FIRST GENERATION	1900 FIRST GENERATION	1900 SECOND GENERATION	1890, FIRST GENERATION	1900 FIRST GENERATION	1900 SECOND GENERATION
Miners	100	739	441	329	232	188	153
Cotton-mill workers	100	417	140	80	263	140	100
Servants	100	212	200	120	358	340	180
Clerks	100	92	105	155	44	55	160
Teachers	100	27	33	83	17	17	50
Physicians	100	53	86	114	19	29	57

SOURCE: Brinley Thomas, *Migration and Economic Growth: A Study of Great Britain and the Atlantic Economy* (Cambridge, England: Cambridge University Press, 1954), p. 145; data from U.S. censuses.

routes and by varying degrees. This hypothesis—which the data available merely suggest—marks one important limitation to the melting-pot thesis. Total assimilation by ethnic background is possible only if nationalities are randomly distributed among all occupations; for to the degree that the contrary is the case, variation by ethnic background tends to persist in the form of class differences.

The relative position of various European nationalities in 1950, the date at which Hutchinson's analysis ends, is given in Table 4-2. The median occupational rank according to the Alba Edwards scale was computed for ten nationalities, each divided by generation and standardized for age and residence. The highest possible rank, for a nationality of which all were professionals or high-level technicians, would be 6.00; the median for native-born workers of native parents, not differentiated by color, was 3.72. Among the foreign-born, three nationalities ranked higher, and among the second generation six out of ten. The data do not permit a cross-classification by religion, but one can assume that many of the Russians and some of the Germans and Austrians were Jewish. In 1969, according to a publication of the Census Bureau (1971a), the median family income was highest among Russian Americans and second highest

Table 4-2. Median Occupational Rank of Selected European Nationalities, by Generation, United States, 1950

	Foreign-born		Second Generation	
			Russians	4.87
	Russians	4.47		
			Swedes	3.97
	English and Welsh	3.92	English and Welsh	3.92
			Norwegians ⎱ Irish ⎰	3.91
			Germans	3.78
	Germans	3.75		
3.72[a]			Austrians	3.70
	Austrians	3.55		
	Swedes	3.50		
	Norwegians	3.43		
			Czechs	3.41
			Italians	3.39
			Poles	3.24
	Czechs	3.08		
	Italians	3.04		
	Irish	2.99		
	Poles	2.97		

[a] Median for native-born workers of native parents.
SOURCE: Charles B. Nam, "Nationality Groups and Social Stratification in America," *Social Forces*, **34** (1959), 328–333.

among Polish Americans, but again it was presumably the Jewish components of these nationalities that lifted them to these places.

In Table 4-3 information is shown for a total of 9,593 respondents questioned in seven NORC surveys between 1963 and 1972. In spite of their lacks, these data have the advantage of permitting a cross-classification of nationality and religion. As other studies have suggested, Jews ranked highest in education, occupational level, and income. Immediately under them came Irish Catholics, whose substantial advance is masked when they are grouped either with other Catholics or with Protestant Irish, most of whom live in the rural South and share its generally low social–cultural level. Similarly, British Protestants (commonly known by the somewhat opprobrious term *Wasps*) include sub-sectors as divergent as Boston Brahmins and Appalachian miners, but their overall level is lower than one might have supposed. "Other Protestant," "Other Catholic," and "Others" are not distinct subnations, of course, but residual categories that include especially those respondents unable to specify one dominant ancestral line. The table shows that those groups of which the largest proportion took advantage of the public education that was available to all generally moved into higher occupations and received greater incomes, but there were also alternative routes to a well-to-do status (cf. Greeley 1973).

Whether the occupational status of nonwhites in 1970 was favorable or not depends on how the question is put (cf. Farley and Hermalin 1972). Compared with the 11 percent nonwhite of the whole labor force, somewhat smaller proportions were employed in the higher occupations and considerably larger proportions in the lower ones (Table 4-4). The shift from 1960 to 1970, however, was almost revolutionary: the number of Negroes employed as household workers or farm laborers fell off drastically, while those in the top and middle ranks increased even faster. In 1969 the median family income of nonwhites was $6,191, or 63 percent of the comparable figure for whites. This contrasts with 51 percent in 1947 and still only 52 percent in 1959 (U.S. Bureau of the Census 1971b). In short, by a variety of indices the improvement in the status of blacks was faster than that of whites during the 1960s, and faster probably than at any prior time. This does not mean that the social–economic differences between the races disappeared, but it does mean that the trend was in that direction.

The improvement in the whole black race, moreover, averages two quite diverse subgroups: those Negroes who took full advantage of the improved opportunities during the 1960s and those who, because of age, region, or family structure, found it difficult or impossible to do so. If we control for these three factors, the difference in income between the races disappears: "There was no apparent difference in 1970 between the income of white and Negro husband–wife families outside the South where the head was under 35 years" (ibid.).

Now this is surely an event: young couples from an oppressed minority starting their lives as full equals, in income terms at least, of their contemporaries in the

Table 4-3. Indices of Social Class by Nationality–Religion, United States, 1963–72

Years of Schooling		Percent White-Collar		Occupational Prestige		Family Income	
East European Jewish}	13.3	East European Jewish	79	German Jewish	5.36	Sephardic Jewish	$11,218
Sephardic Jewish	13.3	Sephardic Jewish	73	East European Jewish	4.77	East European Jewish	11,114
German Jewish	12.9	German Jewish	57	Sephardic Jewish	4.38	German Jewish	9,326
Irish Catholic	12.2	British Protestant	53	Irish Catholic	4.27	Irish Catholic	9,255
No religion	12.0	Irish Catholic	49	British Protestant	3.98	No religion	9,046
British Protestant	11.9	No religion}	45	German Catholic	3.88	German Catholic	8,903
Oriental	11.6	German Catholic	45	Others	3.72	British Protestant	8,309
Scandinavian Protestant}	11.3	Others	44	No religion	3.49	Other Catholic	8,105
German Catholic	11.3	Scandinavian Protestant	42	Italian Catholic}	3.48	Italian Catholic	7,979
Others	11.2	Other Protestant	41	Slavic Catholic[a]	3.48	Polish Catholic	7,940
German Protestant}	11.0	German Protestant	40	German Protestant}	3.46	Oriental	7,918
Other Catholic	11.0	Italian Catholic	39	Other Catholic	3.46	Scandinavian Protestant	7,869
						German Protestant	7,858
						Slavic Catholic[a]	7,693
						Others	7,654
NATIONAL MEAN 10.9		NATIONAL MEAN 39		NATIONAL MEAN 3.42		NATIONAL MEAN 7,588	
Italian Catholic	10.7	Irish Protestant}	38	Scandinavian Protestant	3.38	French Catholic	7,478
Irish Protestant	10.6	Other Catholic	38	Other Protestant	3.33	Other Protestant	7,275
Other Protestant	10.5	Oriental	35	French Catholic	3.30	Irish Protestant	7,022
Slavic Catholic[a]	10.4	Polish Catholic	34	Irish Protestant	3.17	"Spanish" Catholic[b]	6,145
French Catholic}	10.0	Slavic Catholic[a]	31	"Spanish" Catholic[b]	3.10	Negro	5,425
Polish Catholic	10.0	French Catholic	25	Polish Catholic	2.69		
Negro	9.7	"Spanish" Catholic[b]	24	Oriental	2.60		
"Spanish" Catholic[b]	9.3	Negro	18	Negro	2.47		

[a] Does not include Poles, who are listed separately; includes such non-Slavic East Europeans as Hungarians and Lithuanians.
[b] Includes in addition to immigrants from Spain and their descendants also Puerto Ricans, Mexican Americans, and other "Spanish-speaking" groups.

SOURCE: Seven surveys by the National Opinion Research Center, University of Chicago, as reported in Andrew M. Greeley, "The Demography of Ethnic Identification," unpublished, 1972.

125

Table 4-4. Employment Status by Occupational Group, Color, and Sex, United States, 1970

Occupational Group	Employed in 1970 (−000)		Percentage Change, 1960–70		Percentage Nonwhite 1970	Unemployment Rate, 1970			
						Male		Female	
	WHITE	NONWHITE	WHITE	NONWHITE		WHITE	NONWHITE	WHITE	NONWHITE
Professional and technical	10,374	766	45	131	7	1.8	2.0	2.3	2.2
Managers, officials, and proprietors	7,991	298	16	67	4	1.2	2.0	2.1	1.2
Clerical	12,601	1,113	36	121	8	3.2	5.2	3.9	8.1
Sales	4,675	179	13	77	4	2.7	4.0	4.9	13.3
Craftsmen and foremen	9,467	691	16	67	7	3.7	5.2	4.1	2.5
Operatives	11,904	2,004	13	42	14	5.7	7.5	9.1	11.6
Service workers, except private household	6,608	1,547	37	27	19	4.7	6.8	5.1	8.1
Private household workers	906	653	−9	−34	42	1.3	[d]	3.5	5.4
Nonfarm laborers	2,859	866	10	−9	23	9.1	10.5	11.8	11.6
Farmers and farm laborers	2,797	328	−35	−61	11	2.1[a]	4.5[a]	2.8[a]	11.0[a]
TOTAL	70,182	8,445	19	22	11	{ 4.0[b] / 3.6[c]	7.3[b] / 6.6[c]	5.4[b] / 4.6[c]	9.3[b] / 7.7[c]

[a] Farm laborers.
[b] Total, civilian labor force.
[c] Total, experienced labor force.
[d] Base too small to compute a meaningful rate.

SOURCE: U.S. Bureau of the Census, "The Social and Economic Status of Negroes in the United States, 1970," *Current Population Reports*, Series P-23, no. 38, July 1971.

"majority" group. Not only they, but their children. This is not the end of it. In young families outside the South, where both husband and wife worked, black incomes are *higher* than white. For those with heads under 35, black earnings were 104 percent of white. For those with heads under 25, black earnings were 113 percent of white! It would thus be reasonable to state that these young black couples, starting their lives together, beginning to send their children to school, beginning to look for a house perhaps, have the highest median family incomes [for persons of their age] ever recorded in the history of the world ($9,777 as against $8,678 for whites). Surely this says something about the recent past, and hopefully also about the future [Moynihan 1972].

Religion

Whether religious affiliation should be included in census schedules and other demographic forms is a matter of dispute. In its recommendations for the 1950 and 1960 censuses, the United Nations did not mention religion, but for the 1970 censuses it was among the "other useful topics" that governments might include at their option. A number of the more important countries of immigration, such as New Zealand and Canada, have collected detailed statistics on the religions of their variegated populations. In the United States there is a law permitting the Census Bureau merely to compile the existent statistics of the various denominations, and during the 19th century this authority was sometimes interpreted rather broadly. In this century there were four such "censuses" of religious bodies—in 1906, 1916, 1926, and 1936. In 1946 Congress refused to allocate the funds needed to continue the series, and a decade later no one in Congress was enough interested in these data even to propose its renewal. The compilation is now made by the National Council of Churches and is published in its *Yearbook* and, more accessibly, in the *World Almanac*.

This compilation of membership figures, however, is deficient in a number of respects. The data depend on the voluntary cooperation of the denominations, which is lacking in some cases (Christian Scientists prohibit the publication of their membership figures) and meaningless in others (store-front churches are not equipped to maintain an accurate register). In any case, *membership* is defined differently: for Catholics and some Protestants, it means all who have been baptized, and for most Protestants all who have been confirmed. An unknown but significant number of Americans are not members of any church; about these the ecclesiastical records of course say nothing.

The U.S. Census Bureau made a nationwide survey on religious affiliation in 1957 (*Current Population Reports*, Series P-20, no. 79, February 2, 1958), and it was planned to include such a question in the 1960 census questionnaire. Because of loud opposition from a small number of organizations, the idea was abandoned (cf. Petersen 1970: 248–270). The only data on religion in the United States, as we have suggested, are the figures collected by private polling organizations from small samples and usually incidentally to other issues (cf. Bogue 1959: 697 ff.). The church membership claimed by ecclesiastical officials is not the same as these religious preferences reported by individuals. The figures needed for social analysis—the proportion of each denomination living in cities and in the countryside; with large, medium, and small incomes; and so on—are even less precise than the totals. Yet it is only with such data that one could give an empirical reply to the basic question of the sociology of religion: what are the social effects of religious faith?

One official doctrine in the United States is that a faith has no social consequences of any importance, so that immigrants urged to acculturate in every other sense were guaranteed the right to religious freedom by the Constitution itself. On the other hand, it would not be accurate to describe the separation of church and state in the United States as absolute. Americans now pledge allegiance to one nation "under God," and it is taken for granted that churches are partly supported out of public funds: the institutions themselves pay no taxes even on their nonecclesiastical property, and individuals may deduct donations from their taxable income.

Undoubtedly the ambiguity surrounding the social effects of religious faith, and thus the definition of religious freedom, has encouraged some zealots to go beyond the legitimate limits of politics under the guise of religion. During the 19th century Protestant ministers often confused orthodoxy with persistence of the old-country language, and among Lutherans the dispute between proponents of English and German "provoked riots and bloodshed" (Hansen 1951: 75). About the time of World War I, the Calvinist ministers of the Michigan Dutch community attempted to establish what they termed a "Christian society," with a Calvinist political party, a Calvinist newspaper, Calvinist trade unions, a Calvinist school system of which Calvin College still exists. The Irish Catholic Benevolent Society had even broader plans: separate banks, steamship companies, hotels, labor unions—"in fact almost a complete Irish Catholic economic system," but these fanciful aspirations were never realized (Kane 1951). Much of whatever interreligious hostility exists has been the consequence of the Catholic Church's effort to have the entire population—rather than only its own constituents—governed in accordance with its specific norms ruling birth control, abortion, divorce, and censorship; of Fundamentalist Protestants' attempts to make Prohibition the law of the land or forbid public schools to teach evolution; of Zionists' endeavors to influence American foreign policy in the Middle East. In short, what is termed religious bias is often (indeed, not always) due rather to the overlap of religion with other dimensions of American subnations.

An analysis of the social correlates of religion cannot be satisfactory if it is made in terms of denominations, some of which comprise up to twenty-five subdenominations. The divisions are based first of all on differences in doctrine important enough to have caused schisms. Partly because of the persistence of old-country languages, differences in national origin affect social attitudes even within the same church (e.g., Abramson and Noll 1966). For most denominations, there is also a heavy concentration in particular regions, as can be most clearly seen from maps representing their distribution (Zelinsky 1961). Members of the religions established in this country for a longer period are more likely to be in the upper middle class, though as we have seen with important exceptions.

Not surprisingly, social analysts have not agreed on whether in the United States religion indeed has a significant effect on behavior patterns. To determine this, one would have to isolate this often vague adherence to ill defined faiths from the social variables correlated with it, and then establish how the secular behavior of those of various religions (and of none) differs independently. Perhaps the most notable effort to isolate this "religious factor" is Lenski's work (1961), but even he failed to convince some that in the United States today religion in itself is an important determinant of social behavior (e.g., Babbie 1965; Winter 1967).

Amalgamation

The ultimate assimilation, according to many analysts, is achieved when the diverse physical types merge into a new one through successive generations of intermarriage. This was the original meaning of *melting pot* in Zangwill's play: "Celt and Latin, Slav and Teuton, Greek and Syrian—black and yellow, . . . East and West, and North and South, . . . how the great Alchemist melts and fuses them with his purging flame!" In this physiological sense the melting pot has been quite inefficient. Marriage is still atypical across lines set by racial, religious, nationality, or class differences. Indeed, one might say that inter-marriage is atypical by definition, for if an initial hostility no longer persists toward a marriage between blonds and brunets, for instance, then one no longer characterizes such a union as intermarriage.

Much has been written on intermarriage, but so little of quality that the basic theory is still to be worked out. Is it true even that intermarriage breaks down structural lines (e.g., C. A. Price 1966: A22 ff.)? Sometimes the person who converts to Catholicism in order to marry a Catholic becomes the most doctrinaire member of the Church. Even a person with "a trace of Negro blood" has typically been classified as a Negro in the United States, and sometimes the light-skinned Negro is more antiwhite than darker ones (cf. Richardson 1962). What is the effect of intermarriage on the social structure when there is a sort of exchange of values along two structural dimensions—when, for example, a Negro professional marries a lower-class white woman (e.g., Bertram Hutchinson 1957; Merton 1941)? The empirical data with which to answer such questions are often lacking, and when data are available the rates to measure inter-marriage are sometimes inappropriate. The most obvious confusion in measure-ment is between rates based on the number of persons who intermarry and those based on the number of marriages (Rodman 1965; Besanceney 1965). It is also not clear how such factors as the subnations' age structure and sex ratio should be reflected in the rates (C. A. Price and Zubrzycki 1962a, 1962b; Lieberson 1966a).

Most American marriages are class-endogamous, and in the interclass marriages that do occur, the man usually marries down and the woman up. Interclass marriage is so little analyzed, probably because statistics are even poorer than for other kinds of intermarriage, that such broad generalizations sum up most of our knowledge. In particular it is all but impossible to judge to what degree the opposition to interracial, interreligious, or internationality marriage is specific, and to what degree rather it is an index of an all but unexpressed opposition to interclass marriage.

Marriages across nationality lines used also to be atypical. According to an early study, three out of four marriages were within the same group, and the fourth between two of closely related cultures (Bossard 1939). But in one city in-group marriages among Italians fell from 71 percent in 1930 to 27 percent in 1960, and among Poles from 79 percent to 33 percent over the same period (Bugelski 1961). According to another study, intermarriage across nationality lines is becoming relatively common, so long as both partners are Protestant or Catholic or Jewish (Kennedy 1944, 1952; cf. Herberg 1955), but this much cited finding may be out of date.

Marriage across religious lines is generally opposed by clergymen of all denominations, and this attitude is often reflected also in the advice given by secular marriage counselors. Yet some local studies have indicated that interfaith marriages are far more numerous than is generally recognized (e.g., Thomas 1951; Chancellor and Monahan 1955; Chancellor and Burchinal 1962); and in Canada—a somewhat similar culture with better data—the trend in interfaith marriages has been upward (Heer 1962). The serious concern that has been expressed about the out-marriage of Jews (e.g., Cahnman 1963) is not based on reliable evidence. The only national datum available is the Census Bureau's 1957 survey, according to which only 3.6 percent of those who identified themselves as Jews had non-Jewish spouses. The rate seems to be higher in some cities, for example Washington, but not in others, for example Providence (Goldstein and Goldscheider 1966).

Interracial marriages are apparently at the lowest rate of all types of intermarriage. Until recently they were forbidden by law in the South, the border states, and most of the West. In 1967, when this prohibition remained in force in sixteen states, it was abolished by a sweeping, unanimous decision of the U.S. Supreme Court. Even where legal, marriages across racial lines offer the greatest affront to conventional norms, which generally are strong enough to be effective without a legal reinforcement. According to a special survey associated with the 1960 census, only 0.12 percent of all marriages were between a white and a black. A similar survey in 1970, not yet published at the time of writing, is expected to show a moderate increase in interracial marriages from this extremely low level, but not a significant one. If the present trend is projected into the future, it would take—depending on various assumptions—between

351 and 27,000 years for amalgamation to be completed (Heer 1966). It has been surmised that, on the contrary, Negroes are becoming physiologically more sharply distinguished from the white population. Extramarital relations between white males and black females, probably less common than they once were, at any rate result less often in conception. Persons who range in physical type between Negro and white may be more likely than some decades earlier to move into one or the other race, rather than building a bridge between them (cf. Rose 1948: 47–48).

Interracial marriage of Asians, also uncommon on the mainland, is remarkably frequent in Hawaii. The most striking evidence of the degree of racial admixture is in a study by three geneticists at the University of Hawaii. The racial identification of parents listed on the birth certificates of 179,327 babies born from 1948 to 1958 was adjudged substantially accurate when checked against evidence based on samples from the Hawaii blood clinic. Each father and each mother were placed in one of the following races: Caucasian, Hawaiian, Chinese, Filipino, Japanese, Puerto Rican, and Korean, plus combinations of each of these primary categories with each of the other six. With thirty possible racial identifications for each parent, there were 900 possible crossings, of which 524 were included in the record. According to the serological evidence, "Hawaiians" have an 8.5 percent Caucasian mixture and a 13.7 percent Chinese mixture, and the other presumably pure racial groups include a smaller but usually also notable element from other components of the Islands' population (Morton *et al.* 1967). Hawaii, in short, represents the amalgamation that may occur in a mixed population when the typical link between race and social–economic status begins to disappear.

On the other hand, one can easily overstate the degree of amalgamation present even in this world-famous melting pot. It is true that the offspring from some of these marriages lose their ethnic identity (or acquire the developing one of "Cosmopolitan"), but culturally—rather than racially—most remain in the subnation of only one of their parents. The two dominant races in the Islands, whites and Japanese, remain entirely distinct, with their edges barely blurred. In the post-1945 years the Japanese succeeded in eliminating the earlier discrimination against them in public life, while at the same time maintaining a good measure of their private life in recreational and civic associations based on ethnic identification. A subnation that in less than a generation went from wartime obloquy to political and economic power, not surprisingly, is thoroughly conscious of its race (cf. Petersen 1971: chaps. 9–10).

Political Integration

Every nation-state, virtually by definition, expects all its ethnic groups to be loyal to it. But these subnations often have some ties to other nations, and the issue of divided loyalty arises frequently. Not only in colonial days but also in the 19th century, some immigrants to America believed that they were carrying the superior culture of the Old World to a benighted backwoods area (and, indeed, there was sometimes substance to this sentiment). The Germans who settled in Missouri or Wisconsin, the Scandinavians who settled in Minnesota, did not come with the idea of giving up their native language and way of life. From its side, the American government did little more to foster the assimilation of early immigrants than to prohibit their formal segregation by nationalities. In 1818, when Irish immigrant-aid societies petitioned Congress for a land grant on which to settle some of the charitable cases they were attempting to help, this request was denied on the ground that it would be undesirable to concentrate alien peoples geographically. "Probably no decision in the history of American immigration policy possesses more profound significance" (Hansen 1948: 132). By the natural cohesion from their common background, the immigrants from each country tended in any case to congregate in the same region of the Middle West, or later in the same quarters of eastern cities; but the fact that there was no formal boundary greatly facilitated contacts with the native culture.

Integration did not proceed, however, in an altogether laissez-faire framework. Policy decisions on other matters often resulted in the dissemination of the native culture. The public school system, gradually set up during the first half of the 19th century, was based on the general principle that democracy, to be viable, must rest on a literate electorate. But the influence of public schools was also decisive in establishing English as the native language of all immigrant groups, at the latest among the second generation. Foreign-language publications, which numbered 1,350 in thirty-six languages about the time of World War I, declined sharply from this high point. The principal function of these newspapers and magazines has not been to retain foreign languages—they all but disappear anyway among the native-born—but to facilitate acculturation. In their political ideas, their advertising of American goods, and their use of cartoons and similar features, these newspapers and magazines often imitated their larger English-language counterparts. Now that the issue is dead and we know that the nativist fear of a polyglot America had no substance, we can wonder whether the victory of English was not too great. The national interest of the United States is not served by the fact that so few Americans can speak even one other language. Even so, the United States has become a bilingual country, since it is now possible for immigrants who know no English to become naturalized by taking the oath of allegiance in Spanish.

Logically, giving newcomers the official right to participate in the running of a nation would seem to be the ultimate stage of assimilation; and so it is in many countries. Immigrants to full-fledged democracies like France or Switzerland may be entirely ineligible for citizenship, and it is not automatically granted even to their native-born offspring. Compared with the regulations even of other major countries of immigration, American criteria for naturalization—apart from the law barring citizenship to foreign-born Asians, now no longer in force—have been markedly lax. When a West European expresses puzzlement at the concept of "un-American activities," the reason is that being Swedish, for example, is seen to be more a consequence of biology, less a matter of political faith, than being American. Many countries of Northwest Europe now depend to a varying degree on alien laborers, but in most cases they are not permitted—or, at best, not encouraged—to become citizens. In Switzerland, to take one example, in the late 1960s there were about 660,000 aliens with work permits (daily commuters, seasonal workers, or workers with permits good for one year) and only 180,000 aliens with the right to reside permanently in the country. The latter may apply for Swiss citizenship after 12 years' residence, but whether it is granted is entirely at the discretion of the state (cf. Gruner and Junker 1968: 57).

The rate of naturalization, though frequently used in the United States as an index of acculturation, is in fact ambiguous, for the seeming relation between nationality and the proportion applying for citizenship is often spurious. Some nationalities became farmers and settled in the Middle West, in relative isolation until rather recently from national or state politics; and these Old Immigrants were slow in seeking naturalization. About the nationalities that settled mainly in cities, on the other hand, the complaint voiced by James Bryce in his classic *American Commonwealth* (1889, vol. 2: 95) was typical of many.

The immigrants vote . . . after three or four years' residence at most, and often less. (Federal law prescribes a residence of five years as the prerequisite for naturalization, but the term which enables a vote to be acquired is often shorter under state laws.) But they are not fit for the suffrage. . . . Incompetent to give an intelligent vote, but soon finding that their vote has a value, they fall into the hands of the party organizations. . . . Such a sacrifice of common sense to abstract principles has seldom been made in any country.

In any case, acquiring citizenship may mean that the shift in allegiance has been completed, or that the allegiance is itself a critical public issue—as it was for those of German birth, for instance, around the time of either of the world wars.

It has become a commonplace of political journalism that subnations generally vote as blocs, but this fact—if it is a fact—has only recently come to the surface. It used to be a prime shibboleth of liberal politics that a person's ethnic or religious affiliation can have no possible effect on the way he votes, that only a reactionary ignoramus could refer to "the Jewish vote," "the Polish vote," and so on. Typical of the present view and better than many alternative presentations is a book called *The Future of American Politics* (Lubell 1956), which offers not only an analysis of public-opinion polls and elections but also a reinterpretation of much of American history. As the successive waves of immigrants arrived in the United States, fitting in at the bottom of the economic scale, they were opposed in social-class terms to their Anglo-American employers. Whenever social conflict was expressed in political terms, thus, it tended also to result in a confrontation of ethnic groups. For example, in the middle of the 19th century most of the eastern cities were governed by Republican machines led by men of English stock. The Irish immigrants joined the Democratic opposition, and by their success built a link between Catholic and Democratic that to a large degree persists to the present day. In national politics, by Lubell's analysis, the vestigial link of the various ethnic groups to Europe has had an important influence on American foreign policy. The isolationism before World War II, for instance, he interprets as not a withdrawal from European politics but the contrary. The descendants of German and Scandinavian immigrants tended to be pro-German, and the Irish to be anti-English; but as it was patently impossible to involve the United States on the side of Germany, this sympathy was expressed by the demand that America remain at home minding its own business. Even the Yankee descendants of the original settlers, on the other hand, voted to assist England when her need was great enough.

It is almost impossible to determine how much truth there is in the now routine analysis that Lubell's book typifies. As we have noted, adequate statistics exist in the United States on neither nationality (except for the first two generations) nor religious affiliation; and even if the data existed, linking them with secret votes involves all the well known faults of ecological correlations. Even if the correlations were well founded, moreover, they would not be sufficient to establish a cause–effect relation. Take as an example the 1960 election of John F. Kennedy as president. According to the estimates of all the polling organizations, between 75 and 80 percent of the Catholic voters, but only about 35 percent of the Protestant, supported Kennedy. The general conclusion was that the American electorate was strongly prejudiced; according to so responsible a person as Reinhold Niebuhr, the anti-Catholic bias in the United States, "unmatched in any other nation," had reached "the level of paranoia" (*New Leader*, December 12, 1960). But we know even from our poor statistics that Catholics were concentrated in social categories with high proportions of Democrats—northern cities, trade unions, such ethnic minorities as Puerto Ricans and Mexicans—and that the businessmen, midwestern farmers, and others who voted Republican in large proportion were predominantly Protestant. Whether religion actually influenced the vote or was merely an accidental characteristic could have been determined only by analyzing several factors at once. Among trade-union members, for instance, or among farmers, was the vote for and against Kennedy split along religious lines? This the polling firms did not tell the public, nor could they; for their samples are usually too small to permit the simultaneous analysis of several variables. Concerning the 1940 election, the one that Lubell stressed most, one of America's foremost political scientists concluded from a detailed analysis that "foreign policy seemed to have far less bearing on the vote than did questions of domestic policy.... The data indicate a comparatively mild relation between attitudes on foreign policy and vote shifting" (Key 1966: 50). Whether or not those who analyze elections in terms of subnational blocs are empirically correct, virtually everyone now assumes them to be so.

Under the Constitution subnations have no legal existence. The famous decision of Justice Harlan in *Plessy* v. *Ferguson* (1896), though given as a dissenting opinion, expressed the dominant ethos of American law both before and since that date: "There is no caste here. Our Constitution is color-blind, and neither knows nor tolerates classes among citizens. In respect of civil rights, all citizens are equal before the law. The humblest is the peer of the most powerful." To the extent that subnations acted as interest groups, then, they used to be required to rationalize their demands in terms of the national interest of the United States. English, Polish, or Jewish interventionists, German or Irish isolationists, debated America's attitude toward what was to become World War II in the name of multinational parties or other similar broad institutions. The Irish associated anonymously, as it were, in the Roman Catholic Church, in the Democratic Party, in trade unions and professional societies, but specifically as Irish only in an organization like the Ancient Order of Hibernians; and the same was true of every other nationality.

During the 1960s there developed a fundamental contradiction in the legal identity of subnations. The long struggle to realize the American creed of equality before the law reached a climax in the Civil Rights Act of 1964, which again, and in stronger language, guaranteed every individual equal treatment. Yet over the same years the federal government itself pressured business firms, trade unions, and particularly universities to take "affirmative action"—that is, to pay particular attention precisely to the color, ethnic identity, and sex of aspirant employees, faculty, and students. The new trend went even farther in the new rules (repealed after the election) governing the 1972 convention of the Democratic Party, which in effect redefined democracy to mean that one can be represented only by a person of the same age–sex–subnation category.

The notion that a person should be judged, or represented, according to his sex or skin color or nationality is poor policy, first of all, because persons have many identities and only they can best choose which is most important for them in a particular context. The boundaries of subnations, to repeat, are notoriously imprecise. It was pointed out in the last chapter that the term *age group* is typically a misnomer. Similarly, "ethnic groups" may indeed be bounded by regular institutionalized roles and characteristic informal behavior, but they also may be closer to social aggregates.

For any study of group relations this distinction is essential. . . . The sections of an ethnically and culturally divided population may, according to circumstances, be institutionalized groups related to one another in a system of stratification, or they may be groups living side by side and related in other ways. Ethnic divisions may simply be categories of the population [Morris 1968].

Professional Indians, professional Italians, the professional ideologues of every subnation invariably testify to the cohesion of those they claim to speak for, but their testimony is hardly disinterested. No pressure or interest "group" typically represents all of its supposed members (cf. Olson 1968). Those who have "made it" on their own, or hope to do so, generally find it disadvantageous, if not obnoxious, to associate with the subnation's noisier, more activist organizers.

In the view of the German Jews, the more numerous East European Jews who came to the United States a generation or so later were less fellows than a threat; "lace-curtain" Irish tried mightily to avoid identification with "shanty" Irish. To outsiders, all in a subnation are the same (and this is particularly so of racists' view of racial groups), but the same kind of internal division, whether sharp or blurred, probably exists in every subnation. One black professor distinguished between "competent blacks" and "'authentic' ghetto types" (Sowell 1970), another between "the nationalist" and "the integrationist" (Hamilton 1972). However one designates the two types, much that is written about Negroes pertains to only one of them (cf. Lieberson 1973). Those in Type A are by and large peaceable; those in Type B sometimes advocate and often practice violence, with Type A blacks as their chief victims. Those in Type A seek to move into the general society and, if possible, to achieve middle-class status; the most extremist of Type B would destroy society as it now exists, and for them "middle-class" is a summation of evil. Type A are for desegregation, Type B usually for resegregation. Whether we speak of principles, immediate program, or the means of achieving it, the differences are fundamental.

SUMMARY

The "composition" of a population (as contrasted with its "structure") pertains to its *subnations*, or the groups defined by such characteristics as race, national origin, language, religion, and region. The distribution by any of these indices typically shows a decided clustering, indicating that subnations are significantly different from the general population, but also a tendency for these clusters to be linked by intermediate instances. In a literary analysis one can concentrate on the clusters and ignore the others. But when a population count is made, each individual person must be categorized according to each of the classifications being used, so that demographers are forced to define subnations, however arbitrarily, with precise boundaries. No resolution of this dilemma can be wholly satisfactory, and time series of ethnic data often reflect changes in the units' definitions.

The social structure associated with a population composition depends in part on whether the various types of ethnic differentiation overlap or, on the contrary, cut across one another. The greatest inequality is realized in a caste system, which can conveniently be analyzed in terms of the Hindu tradition. The assimilation of subnations into the broader society can be along several routes, ranging from the adoption of culture traits to intermarriage. Assimilation, thus, is not an all-or-none process, but rather a continuum from total assimilation to total nonassimilation, with various degrees and types of adaptation in between.

Assimilation can be facilitated by a number of factors, of which the most important seem to be the following:

1. A relatively small difference between the interacting cultures, either actual or as defined by the participants: in particular, if differences are defined as immutable, then assimilation is ruled out as impossible.

2. Agreement between the interacting groups that one of the cultures, the same one, is superior: a minority finds it rankling to be dominated by a group whose culture it sees as inferior to its own.

3. The relative size of the minority: for maximum acculturation, it should be large enough to furnish psychological security to its members, but small enough to be integrated without difficulty.

4. A long period of interaction between the groups: however, the generalization that the longer the contact, the more acculturation, is not invariably true, for some patterns of partial interrelation have remained constant over centuries.

If these generalizations about assimilation are tested against trends in the United States, they prove to be tentative with respect to whites and often completely invalid when applied to nonwhites. Negroes have been in America longer even than most of the Old Immigrants; whereas among whites Daughters of the American Revolution are a rare phenomenon, a probable majority of Negroes are descended from the Africans brought here during the 18th century. More significantly still, American Negroes have no vestigial tie to their "homeland"; in spite of ideological sympathies with new African states, their real world is defined almost wholly in American terms. Asians and the other smaller minorities are so tiny that one might have expected them to sink into the white sea. Obviously neither the size of a minority, nor its period of residence, nor the strength of its ties to other cultures, determines its relative integration in American society—if the minority is not white.

That such minorities have not been assimilated in American culture is sometimes explained by their greater "visibility." One suspects, however, that the visibility of an ethnic group is less a cause than a symptom of its nonassimilation. It is easy to distinguish a Jew, for example, by his "hooked nose, oily skin, thick lips"; the only difficulty is that these features typify not real Jews but the abstraction attacked by anti-Semites. And to recognize as Negro such a man, for example, as Walter White, a blue-eyed blond who for many years was a leader of the National Association for the Advancement of Colored People, was something of a feat. On the other hand, an American is quite likely not to recall, say, the color of the eyes of a person he met casually a week or so ago. Skin color is more "visible" than eye color because one is, and the other is not, a symbol of social differentiation.

Racial minorities remain separate groups in American society mainly because of the laws, behavior patterns, and attitudes that have forced them to be so. Any analysis of these minority races must consist in large part of an examination of the special means by which their differences from the white population are maintained and accentuated. The purpose of such laws and institutions was usually to discriminate against the minority, but sometimes (for example,

Indian reservations or Negro colleges) it was the opposite. In either case, the distinctive behavior due to these special institutions is often confused with biological variation.

With respect to any subnation, the will to assimilate can be strongly countered by a quest for its own identity, by the attempt to establish, or re-establish, a community built from its own foundations. Mere separation, thus, cannot be taken as an index of segregation, imposed from the outside by a more powerful sector, for some or all of it may derive from congregation, the desire of members of a subnation to live and associate with others of their kind. Particularly in the United States, as a heritage from the period of heavy immigration, the concentration on assimilative processes has induced some analysts to pass over the re-grouping of subnations. Yet the dominant trend the world over would seem to be the rise of national and subnational sentiment, whether defined by racial, linguistic, religious, or other criteria.

CITED REFERENCES AND SUGGESTIONS FOR FURTHER READING

The analysis of population composition overlaps with a number of other disciplines, and each of several of the topics briefly discussed in this chapter—caste or inter-marriage, for instance—has an enormous literature. In a demographic context, some of the best data in the United States are the *Current Population Reports* on either ethnic structure as a whole (e.g., U.S. Bureau of the Census 1971a, 1973a) or particular subnations (e.g., U.S. Bureau of the Census 1973b). Of the generally excellent 1960 census monographs, one (D. O. Price 1969) is on the Negro population. But official data in the United States do not include such fundamental dimensions of ethnic variation as religion, not to say attitudes based on nationality or region; and for such topics one must seek guidance from a broader range of works. An especially good series of booklets on particular subnations throughout the world is published by the Minority Rights Group in London.

The starred items are recommended either as a better than average presentation of the subject in general or, especially, as a work particularly relevant to a demographic analysis.

ABRAMSON, HAROLD J., and C. EDWARD NOLL. 1966. "Religion, Ethnicity, and Social Change," *Review of Religious Research*, **8**, 11–26.

APPEL, J. J. 1960. "New England Origins of the American Irish Historical Society," *New England Quarterly*, **33**, 462–475.

———. 1961. "Hansen's Third Generation 'Law' and the Origins of the American Jewish Historical Society," *Jewish Social Studies*, **23**, 3–20.

BABBIE, EARL R. 1965. "The Religious Factor—Looking Forward," *Review of Religious Research*, **7**, 42–53.

BAILEY, F. G. 1957. *Caste and the Economic Frontier: A Village in Highland Orissa.* Manchester, England: Manchester University Press.

BARTH, FREDRIK. 1970. *Ethnic Groups and Boundaries: The Social Organization of Culture Difference.* London: Allen & Unwin.

BEALE, CALVIN L. 1958. "Census Problems of Racial Enumeration," in Thompson and Hughes 1958.

BERRY, BREWTON. 1965. *Race and Ethnic Relations*. Boston: Houghton Mifflin.

BESANCENEY, PAUL H. 1965. "On Reporting Rates of Intermarriage," *American Journal of Sociology*, **70**, 717–721.

*BÉTEILLE, ANDRÉ. 1967. "Race and Descent as Social Categories in India," *Daedalus*, **96**, 444–463.

BLALOCK, HUBERT M., JR. 1967. *Toward a Theory of Minority-Group Relations*. New York: Wiley.

BLUNT, E. A. H. 1931. *The Caste System of Northern India, with Special Reference to the United Provinces of Agra and Oudh*. London: Oxford University Press.

BOAS, FRANZ. 1911. "Changes in Bodily Form of Descendants of Immigrants," in U.S. Senate Immigration Commission, *Report*, vol. 38. Washington, D.C.

BOGUE, DONALD J. 1959. *The Population of the United States*. New York: Free Press.

BOSSARD, JAMES H. S. 1939. "Nationality and Nativity as Factors in Marriage," *American Sociological Review*, **4**, 792–798.

*BOYD, WILLIAM C. 1950. *Genetics and the Races of Man: An Introduction to Modern Physical Anthropology*. Boston: Heath.

BRYCE, JAMES. 1889. *The American Commonwealth*, 2 vol. London: Macmillan.

BUGELSKI, B. R. 1961. "Assimilation Through Intermarriage," *Social Forces*, **40**, 148–154.

CAHNMAN, WERNER J., editor. 1963. *Intermarriage and Jewish Life: A Symposium*. New York: Herzl Press.

CHANCELLOR, LOREN E., and LEE G. BURCHINAL. 1962. "Relations Among Interreligious Marriages, Migratory Marriages and Civil Weddings in Iowa," *Eugenics Quarterly*, **9**, 75–83.

————, and THOMAS R. MONAHAN. 1955. "Religious Preference and Interreligious Mixtures in Marriages and Divorces in Iowa," *American Journal of Sociology*, **61**, 233–239.

CUMMINGS, JOHN. 1918. *Negro Population, 1790–1915*. Washington, D.C.: U.S. Bureau of the Census.

DAVIE, MAURICE R. 1949. *World Immigration, with Special Reference to the United States*. New York: Macmillan.

DAVIS, KINGSLEY. 1951. *The Population of India and Pakistan*. Princeton, N.J.: Princeton University Press.

DRIVER, EDWIN D. 1962. "Caste and Occupational Structure in Central India," *Social Forces*, **41**, 26–31.

*FARLEY, REYNOLDS. 1968. "The Quality of Demographic Data for Nonwhites," *Demography*, **5**, 1–10.

————, and ALBERT HERMALIN. 1972. "The 1960s: A Decade of Progress for Blacks?" *Demography*, **9**, 353–370.

GHURYE, G. S. 1961. *Caste, Class and Occupation*. Bombay: Popular Book Depot.

GLAZER, NATHAN. 1953. "America's Ethnic Pattern," *Commentary*, April, pp. 401–408.

*————, and DANIEL P. MOYNIHAN. 1963–70. *Beyond the Melting Pot*, 2nd ed. Cambridge, Mass.: M.I.T. Press.

*GOLDSTEIN, SIDNEY, and CALVIN GOLDSCHEIDER. 1966. "Social and Demographic Aspects of Jewish Intermarriage," *Social Problems*, **13**, 386–399.

GORDON, MILTON M. 1964. *Assimilation in American Life: The Role of Race, Religion, and National Origins.* New York: Oxford University Press.

*GREELEY, ANDREW M. 1973. "Making It in America: Ethnic Groups and Social Status," *Social Policy*, 1, 21–29.

GRUNER, ERICH, and BEAT JUNKER. 1968. *Bürger, Staat und Politik in der Schweiz.* Basel: Lehrmittelverlag.

*HADLEY, J. NIXON. 1957. "The Demography of the American Indians," *Annals of the American Academy of Political and Social Science*, 311, 23–30.

HAMILTON, CHARLES V. 1972. "The Nationalist vs. the Integrationist," *New York Times Magazine*, October 1.

HANDLIN, OSCAR. 1951. *The Uprooted: The Epic Story of the Great Migration that Made the American People.* New York: Grosset & Dunlap.

*HANSEN, MARCUS LEE. 1938. *The Problem of the Third Generation Immigrant.* Rock Island, Ill.: Augustana Historical Society; reprinted in *Commentary*, November 1952, pp. 492–500.

———. 1948. *The Immigrant in American History.* Cambridge, Mass.: Harvard University Press.

———. 1951. *The Atlantic Migration, 1607–1860: A History of the Continuing Settlement of the United States.* Cambridge, Mass.: Harvard University Press.

HARRISON, SELIG S. 1960. *India: The Most Dangerous Decades.* Princeton, N.J.: Princeton University Press.

HEER, DAVID M. 1962. "The Trend of Interfaith Marriages in Canada, 1922–1957," *American Sociological Review*, 27, 245–250.

*———. 1966. "Negro-White Marriage in the United States," *Journal of Marriage and the Family*, 28, 262–276.

HERBERG, WILL. 1955. *Protestant, Catholic, Jew: An Essay in American Religious Sociology.* Garden City, N.Y.: Doubleday.

HUTCHINSON, BERTRAM. 1957. "Some Evidence Related to Matrimonial Selection and Immigrant Assimilation in Brazil," *Population Studies*, 11, 149–156.

———. 1959. "Race Differences in Fertility: A Note on Their Estimation in Brazil," *Population Studies*, 13, 151–156.

*HUTCHINSON, E. P. 1956. *Immigrants and Their Children: 1850–1950.* New York: Wiley.

HUTTON, J. H. 1963. *Caste in India: Its Nature, Function, and Origin*, 4th ed. Bombay: Oxford University Press.

ISAACS, HAROLD R. 1963. *The New World of Negro Americans.* New York: Viking-Compass.

*———. 1965. *India's Ex-Untouchables.* Bombay: Asia Publishing House.

*———. 1968. "Group Identity and Political Change: Nationalism Revisited," *Survey*, no. 69, pp. 76–98.

JOHNSTON, DENIS FOSTER. 1966. *An Analysis of Sources of Information on the Population of the Navaho.* Bureau of American Ethnology, Smithsonian Institution, Bulletin 197. Washington, D.C.

KANE, JOHN J. 1951. "Protestant-Catholic Tensions," *American Sociological Review*, 16, 663–672.

KENNEDY, RUBY JO REEVES. 1944. "Single or Triple Melting Pot? Intermarriage Trends in New Haven, 1870–1940," *American Journal of Sociology*, 49, 331–339.

———. 1952. "Single or Triple Melting Pot? Intermarriage Trends in New Haven, 1870–1950," *American Journal of Sociology*, 58, 56–59.

KEY, V. O., JR. 1966. *The Responsible Electorate: Rationality in Presidential Voting, 1936–1960.* Cambridge, Mass.: Belknap Press.

KROEBER, A. L. 1939. *Cultural and Natural Areas of Native North America.* Berkeley: University of California Press.

LENSKI, GERHARD. 1961. *The Religious Factor.* Garden City, N.Y.: Doubleday.

LEVY, PAUL M. G. 1960. *La querelle du recensement.* Brussels: Institut Belge de Science Politique.

———. 1962. "La mort du recensement linguistique," *Revue Nouvelle*, **18**, 145–154.

*LIEBERSON, STANLEY. 1966a. "The Price-Zubrzycki Measure of Ethnic Intermarriage," *Eugenics Quarterly*, **13**, 92–100.

———. 1966b. "Language Questions in Censuses," *Sociological Inquiry*, **36**, 262–279.

*———. 1973. "Generational Differences Among Blacks in the North," *American Journal of Sociology*, **79**, 550–565.

LUBELL, SAMUEL. 1956. *The Future of American Politics*, 2nd revised ed. Garden City, N.Y.: Doubleday-Anchor.

MERTON, ROBERT K. 1941. "Intermarriage and the Social Structure: Fact and Theory," *Psychiatry*, **4**, 361–374.

MONTAGU, ASHLEY. 1964. *Man's Most Dangerous Myth: The Fallacy of Race.* New York: World.

*MOOD, FULMER. 1965. "The Origin, Evolution, and Application of the Sectional Concept, 1750–1900," in Merrill Jensen, editor, *Regionalism in America.* Madison: University of Wisconsin Press.

MOORE, WILBERT E. 1951. *Industrialization and Labor: Social Aspects of Economic Development.* Ithaca, N.Y.: Cornell University Press.

MORRIS, H. S. 1968. "Ethnic Groups," *International Encyclopedia of the Social Sciences.* New York: Macmillan and Free Press.

MORTON, NEWTON E., CHIN S. CHUNG, and MING-PI MI. 1967. *Genetics of Interracial Crosses in Hawaii.* New York: S. Karger.

*MOYNIHAN, DANIEL P. 1972. "The Schism in Black America," *Public Interest*, no. 27, pp. 3–24.

NAM, CHARLES B. 1959. "Nationality Groups and Social Stratification in America," *Social Forces*, **34**, 328–333.

NISBET, ROBERT A. 1953. *The Quest for Community: A Study in the Ethics of Order and Freedom.* New York: Oxford University Press.

ODUM, HOWARD W., and HARRY ESTILL MOORE. 1938. *American Regionalism: A Cultural-Historical Approach to National Integration.* New York: Holt.

OLSON, MANCUR, JR. 1968. *The Logic of Collective Action: Public Goods and the Theory of Groups.* New York: Schocken.

ORNSTEIN, JACOB. 1964. "Patterns of Language Planning in the New States," *World Politics*, **17**, 40–49.

*PANIKKAR, K. M. 1933. *Caste and Democracy.* London: Hogarth Press.

PARK, ROBERT EZRA. 1950. *Race and Culture.* New York: Free Press.

PATTERSON, H. O. L. 1966. "Slavery, Acculturation, and Social Change: The Jamaican Case," *British Journal of Sociology*, **17**, 151–164.

PERLOFF, HARVEY S. 1963. *How a Region Grows: Area Development in the U.S. Economy.* New York: Committee for Economic Development.

*PETERSEN, WILLIAM. 1969. "The Classification of Subnations in Hawaii: An Essay in the Sociology of Knowledge," *American Sociological Review*, **34**, 863–877.

PETERSEN, WILLIAM. 1970. *The Politics of Population.* Gloucester, Mass.: Peter Smith.
*———. 1971. *Japanese Americans: Oppression and Success.* New York: Random House.

*PRICE, CHARLES A. 1966. *Australian Immigration: A Bibliography and Digest.* Canberra: Australian National University.

———, and JERZY ZUBRZYCKI. 1962a. "The Use of Intermarriage Statistics as an Index of Assimilation," *Population Studies,* **16,** 58–69.

———, and ———. 1962b. "Immigrant Marriage Patterns in Australia," *Population Studies,* **16,** 123–133.

PRICE, DANIEL O. 1969. *Changing Characteristics of the Negro Population.* Washington, D.C.: U.S. Government Printing Office.

REX, JOHN. 1970. *Race Relations in Sociological Theory.* New York: Schocken.

RICHARDSON, ALAN. 1962. "A Note on Mixed Marriage as a Factor in Assimilation," Research Group for European Migration Problems, *Bulletin,* **10,** 115–119.

RODMAN, HYMAN. 1965. "Technical Note on Two Rates of Mixed Marriage," *American Sociological Review,* **30,** 776–778.

ROSE, ARNOLD. 1948. *The Negro in America.* Boston: Beacon.

SAPIR, EDWARD. 1921. *Language: An Introduction to the Study of Speech.* New York: Harcourt, Brace.

SHANNON, FRED A. 1949. "A Post Mortem on the Labor Safety-Valve Theory," in Taylor 1949.

SINHA, V. K. 1965. "Secularism and Indian Democracy," in S. P. Aiyar and R. Srinivasan, editors, *Studies in Indian Democracy.* Bombay: Allied Publishers.

*SKIDMORE, THOMAS. 1964. "Gilberto Freyre and the Early Brazilian Republic: Some Notes on Methodology," *Comparative Studies in Society and History,* **6,** 490–505.

SOWELL, THOMAS. 1970. "Colleges Are Skipping Over Competent Blacks to Admit 'Authentic' Ghetto Types," *New York Times Magazine,* December 13.

*SRINIVAS, M. N. 1959. "Caste: A Trend Report and Bibliography," *Current Sociology,* **8,** 135–183.

———. 1962. *Caste in Modern India and Other Essays.* Bombay: Asia Publishing House.

SRIVASTAVA, RAM P. 1966. "Tribe–Caste Mobility in India and the Case of Kumaon Bhotias," in Christoph von Fuerer-Haimendorf, editor, *Caste and Kin in Nepal, India, and Ceylon.* Bombay: Asia Publishing House.

STAMP, L. DUDLEY. 1964. *The Geography of Life and Death.* London: Fontana.

STEIN, STANLEY J. 1961. "Freyre's Brazil Revisited: A Review of *New World in the Tropics: The Culture of Modern Brazil,*" *Hispanic American Historical Review,* **41,** 111–113.

*TAYLOR, GEORGE ROGERS, editor. 1949. *The Turner Thesis Concerning the Role of the Frontier in American History.* Boston: Heath.

THOMAS, JOHN L. 1951. "The Factor of Religion in the Selection of Marriage Mates," *American Sociological Review,* **16,** 487–491.

THOMPSON, EDGAR T., and EVERETT C. HUGHES, editors. 1958. *Race: Individual and Collective Behavior.* New York: Free Press.

TURNER, FREDERICK JACKSON. 1949. "The Significance of the Frontier in American History," in Taylor 1949.

UNITED NATIONS. STATISTICAL OFFICE. 1956. "1960 World Population Census Pro-

gramme: 1945–1954 Experience—Ethnic Characteristics and Native Customs."
Mimeographed.

———. 1957. *Demographic Yearbook, 1956*. New York.

———. 1964. *Demographic Yearbook, 1963*. New York.

U.S. BUREAU OF THE CENSUS. 1906. "Special Reports. Supplementary Analysis and Derivative Data," *Twelfth Census of the United States, 1900*. Washington, D.C.

———. 1963. *U.S. Census of Population, 1960*. Subject Reports: *Nonwhite Population by Race: Social and Economic Statistics for Negroes, Indians, Japanese, Chinese, and Filipinos*, Final Report PC(2)-1C. Washington, D.C.

———. 1971a. "Characteristics of the Population by Ethnic Origin," *Current Population Reports*, Series P-20, no. 221.

*———. 1971b. "Differences between Income of White and Negro Families by Work Experience of Wife and Region, 1970, 1969, and 1959," *Current Population Reports*, Series P-23, no. 39.

———. 1973a. "Characteristics of the Population by Ethnic Origin, March 1972 and 1971," *Current Population Reports*, Series P-20, no. 249.

———. 1973b. "Persons of Spanish Origin in the United States, March 1972 and 1971," *Current Population Reports*, Series P-20, no. 250.

U.S. DEPARTMENT OF THE INTERIOR. 1958. *Federal Indian Law*. Washington, D.C.

U.S. SENATE. 1928. "Immigration Quotas on the Basis of National Origin," *Miscellaneous Documents 8870*, vol. 1, no. 65. 70th Congress, 1st Session. Washington, D.C.

VAN DEN BERGHE, PIERRE L. 1967. *Race and Racism: A Comparative Analysis*. New York: Wiley.

WINTER, GIBSON. 1967. "Methodological Reflections on 'The Religious Factor,'" in Richard D. Knudten, editor, *The Sociology of Religion: An Anthology*. New York: Appleton-Century-Crofts.

WIRTH, LOUIS. 1945. "The Problem of Minority Groups," in Ralph Linton, editor, *The Science of Man in the World Crisis*. New York: Columbia University Press.

WRIGHT, CARROLL D. 1900. *The History and Growth of the United States Censuses, Prepared for the Senate Committee on the Censuses*. Washington, D.C.

ZELINSKY, WILBUR. 1961. "An Approach to the Religious Geography of the United States: Patterns of Church Membership in 1952," *Annals of the Association of American Geographers*, **51**, 139–193.

*ZINKIN, TAYA. 1962. *Caste Today*. Institute of Race Relations. London: Oxford University Press.

MALTHUSIAN THEORY AND ITS DEVELOPMENT

5

"The" population problem as most persons define it has little to do with the topics discussed so far. It pertains rather to the world's explosive growth, the dearth of food, the means by which the disparity between numbers and resources can be reduced and, one hopes, eventually eliminated. Although the struggle to survive has always been the fundament of human existence, the serious analysis of this effort did not begin until modern times. It started in England of the early 19th century, the birthplace of the industrial revolution, and from the name of the principal theorist the designation of the problem became "the Malthusian dilemma."

Malthus has the faults of a pioneer, but his *Essay on the Principle of Population* is more directly relevant today than the works of any predecessor, and even of many successors. He saw the potential for the rapid growth that has indeed taken place since he wrote, and for the deterioration in human welfare that this increase in numbers can effect. He saw also how control over such multiplication could be established—by the gradual inculcation in each person of a higher aspiration, which would induce him to forgo a numerous progeny in exchange for other values. Malthus's work is important also for a significant line of development from it, the theory of population optimum. The question, what size of population is best suited to a given environment, is hardly more than a modern paraphrase of the issue that Malthus analyzed. Malthus's relevance to the world today will be apparent in subsequent chapters on specific countries or elements of demographic analysis. Here we shall look at the theory as he developed it and its more general ramifications.

Thomas Robert Malthus (from childhood on he was known as "Robert") was born in 1766, one of eight children of a country gentleman. He was educated privately and at Jesus College, Cambridge, where he read English and French literature and ancient history, won prizes in Latin and English declamation, and was graduated with honors in mathematics. At the age of 22 he took orders so as to realize, he wrote, "the utmost of my wishes, a retired living in the country." For a short period he was curate at Okewood, Surrey, a village "truly remarkable throughout the 18th century for its enormous number of baptisms and its small number of burials" (James 1966: 7). From 1793 until he forfeited it by his marriage in 1804, he held a fellowship at Jesus College. In the latter year he

144

became Professor of History and Political Economy in the newly founded East India College, soon to be domiciled at Haileybury. This was the first professorship in political economy established in Britain, and he filled the post with distinction until his death in 1834.

Malthus was one of the founders of 19th-century economics, a direct successor of Adam Smith,[1] a good personal friend of David Ricardo, and a telling influence on neoclassicists. Ricardo incorporated Malthus's principle of population virtually intact into economic theory and, indeed, carried it even farther than the author himself. In one respect, however, Malthus stood outside the main line of development of classical theory: in the 1930s, when Keynes started a new trend in economics by emphasizing "effective demand," this concept was revived from an insight of Malthus's that had been neglected for more than a century.

Malthus's most important work in the context of this book, and also the one for which he is most honored and maligned, is his *Essay on the Principle of Population*. It was first published anonymously in 1798, when the author was 32 years old. This short work was written with an aggressive confidence, a dashing style that passed over exceptions, anomalies, and minor points, and swept on to the main conclusion with youthful confidence. It brought the author immediate fame and notoriety, but if he had been content to let it rest with this version, his name would not be known to every educated person today. Malthus spent a good portion of the rest of his life collecting data on the relation between population and environment in various cultures, bringing his theory in accord with these facts, and adjusting it to criticism. (There were seven editions of the *Essay* in all, the last published posthumously in 1872.) Since most countries of the Western world were just beginning to compile reliable demographic statistics, this empirical orientation required an extraordinary effort.[2] The second edition of the *Essay*, issued after five years of travel and study, was four times as long as the first. The style is much more sober: "If I had confined myself to general views, I could have entrenched myself in an impregnable fortress," Malthus wrote in the preface. "I was willing to sacrifice all pretensions to merit of composition to the chance of making an impression on a larger class of readers."

BACKGROUND TO MALTHUS'S THEORY

As his critics have often pointed out, Malthus's ideas were not wholly original with him. According to the author of the *Essay* himself, before he wrote the first edition he had read the works of only four writers on population—David Hume,

[1] Before Malthus traveled to Scandinavia, he jotted down the topics he was interested in under the heading "Smith's Questions": "Interest of money. Corn laws. Inland merchants & at the Ports. Recompence of Laborer. Relative prices of provisions & manufactures at different times. Bills & Bankers. Religious establishments & sects" (James 1966: 24).

[2] James (1966: Appendix 1) has printed on facing pages the chapter "On the Checks to Population in Norway" and the travel notes on which this was based. It is a fascinating exposition of Malthus's method of work.

Adam Smith, Robert Wallace, and Richard Price—and of these only Wallace is really relevant to Malthus's specific theory. For Hume and Smith population was a relatively subordinate subject, and Price was convinced that England's depopulation was proceeding apace. Although in his later study Malthus found a much longer list of men who had anticipated him, the *Essay* was original in an important sense. By putting these ideas that other men had expressed into a larger framework and examining in detail the relation of population growth to economic and political development, Malthus did more than any of his predecessors or all of them together. He wrote a book that, whether as guide or as butt, has become for all the beginning of modern population theory. And although in certain respects the *Essay* was derivative, in more important ways it opposed two strong schools of thought, mercantilism and revolutionary utopianism.

Mercantilism is a modern term, first used by German writers in the 1860s to denote what Adam Smith had called the "mercantile system" of roughly the 15th to the 18th centuries. Smith and, following him, those who built classical economics used mercantilism as an overall target, so that there is a point-by-point differentiation between it and the liberal doctrine that they developed. The highly centralized nation–state deemed to be necessary in mercantilist theory is to be contrasted with laissez-faire, the belief that the economy works best with the minimum regulation; the assumption that each nation could benefit only at the cost of others, with the promotion of free trade, which it was held permitted each nation to exchange its surpluses for the goods it lacked; the advice to each state to hoard gold, with the thesis that the true "wealth of nations" lies in their ability to produce usable goods.

Just as it hoarded bullion, so the mercantilist state hoarded people, and for the same reason, to increase its economic, political, and military prowess. The trade in slaves was seen to be indispensable (Dorn 1963: 261–262). Armies were amalgams of native and foreign riffraff; many of the mercenaries "had been kidnapped, forcibly dragged from taverns, swept up from the streets or released from the prisons. It was the pinch of poverty, however, that drove the great mass of mercenary soldiers into enlistment" (ibid.: 83). The function of the mass of the population was to produce for the greater power of the state, and to this end no child was too young to begin working.

Whereas from the beginning of the 19th century onwards, after tentative beginnings, stronger and stronger measures were taken to limit child labor by law, under mercantilism the power of the state was exerted in precisely the opposite direction. ... In a decree of 1668 affecting the lace-making industry in Auxerre, ... [Colbert] commanded ... that all the inhabitants of the town should send their children into this industry at the age of six, on pain of a penalty of 30 *sous* per child [Heckscher 1935, vol. 2: 155].

Wages should be at subsistence but never higher. A worker, in William Petty's words, should be able only to "live, labor, and generate," and "if you double wages, then he works but half so much as he could, or otherwise would."

The population theories and policies of the mercantilist period, though they varied from one nation or time to another, were remarkably consistent. "An almost fanatical desire to increase population prevailed in all countries" (ibid.: 158). France under Colbert in particular attempted to stimulate fertility and to proscribe emigration. The most important of the pronatalist measures (1666) exempted those who married early from certain taxes and granted pensions to the fathers of ten or more living legitimate children. These stimulants had little or no effect and were revoked in 1683, but the idea behind them survived in a considerable "repopulationist" literature during the 18th century (Spengler 1942: chap. 3).

In spite of the axiom that a large population is good and a larger one better, mercantilist writers continually noted the "overcrowding" evidenced by a high incidence of vagrancy and crime. Anxious about both the insufficiency of people and their unemployment, they never reconciled these two positions. "French writers failed to recognize, explicitly and completely, the dependence of the population upon the food supply" (ibid.: 19). The way to solve overcrowding in the mercantilist framework was to ship the surplus to colonies, where they could aggrandize the state's power in another quarter of the globe. And here the same cycle was started again, with renewed efforts to increase the overseas population as rapidly as possible. Whole boatloads of women, usually corralled from houses of correction but sometimes also young country girls, were sent to the French colonies, where soldiers who refused to marry them were punished. In the innumerable letters back and forth, these females were quite clearly seen simply as breeders. "In the same breath mention is made of shiploads of women, mares, and sheep, the methods of propagating human beings and cattle being regarded as roughly on the same plane" (Heckscher 1935, vol. 2: 300).

Modern demography began with the efforts of mercantilist states to keep track of their populations. William Petty (1623–87), a man of a wide range of talents and immense energy, was the first exponent of what he called "political arithmetic." John Graunt (1620–74) constructed the first crude life table and combined various sets of approximate data to estimate the population of London (cf. Zito 1972). Gregory King (1648–1712), the son of a mathematician and himself a practicing accountant and skilled genealogist, constructed population estimates based on actual local enumerations, which he corrected for technical errors.

It was Petty who proposed a central government statistical office and a system of census taking. He anticipated William Farr in estimating the economic loss due to mortality. Many of his calculations, however, do not stand up to the tests of consistency that Graunt would have applied. It seems to be generally agreed that Graunt made an immeasurably greater contribution to demography [Benjamin 1968].

Both Petty and Graunt influenced a later Continental demographer, Johann Peter Süssmilch (1707–67), who used Protestant parish records throughout Prussia to estimate trends in fertility and mortality. Trained in mathematics, he worked out a crude theory of probability that long antedated later, independent developments. Richard Cantillon (1680?–1734) was born in Ireland, lived for most of his life in France and the Low Countries, and died (of murder) in London. Far less of a moralist than Süssmilch and less of a nationalist than the typical mercantilist writer, he analyzed population trends in an almost modern manner. Internal migration, deaths, and especially marriages and therefore births varied, he held, according to the prevailing standards of living and the structure of demand for labor. As the "first of the moderns" (Spengler 1954), Cantillon probably influenced the subsequent development of economic–demographic thought more than any of his predecessors and contemporaries except perhaps François Quesnay (1694–1774), who founded what eventually came to be called physiocratic thought. Though Quesnay was little interested in population as such, the economic system as he analyzed it implicitly set the bounds of its growth. In one sense at least, the Physiocrats were typical of the Enlightenment: they took the "natural order" of medieval thought, secularized it, and made of it the machine that ran the circular flow of economic life.

Revolutionary Utopianism, a new conception of humanity, gradually evolved during the 18th century, particularly in the writings of the French political philosophers. With respect to demographic theory and policy, however, there was neither a clear line of development nor a clean break with mercantilism (Spengler 1942: chap. 6). One recurrent theme was the strong probability, or even inevitability, of human betterment, and those who believed this also generally held that growth in numbers was a social good, a clear index of the nation's health. Convinced on the contrary that the population of France, and indeed of the whole world, had diminished because of "interior vice and bad government," Montesquieu also recommended that Colbert's laws, which rewarded only the prodigiously fertile, be broadened into a more general pronatalist policy. According to Voltaire, a nation was fortunate if its population increased by so much as 5 percent a century. Saint-Just, later one of the instigators of the Jacobin terror, proclaimed that misery could never follow from overpopulation, but only from social institutions. One can usually depend on nature "never to have more children than teats," but to keep the balance in the other direction nature needs the state's assistance. His notion of a just family law, inspired by Rousseau, was that marriage should be encouraged by state loans, and a couple still childless after seven years ought to be forcibly separated (Fage 1953).

In the context of a discussion of Malthus, two revolutionary ideologues are especially relevant, Condorcet and Godwin. The first edition of Malthus's *Essay*, as its very title indicated, was intended to reply to "the speculations of Mr. Godwin, M. Condorcet, and other writers."

Marie-Jean-Antoine-Nicolas Caritat, Marquis de Condorcet (1743–94), was an ardent revolutionary, a prominent member of the Girondin faction. In 1793, after the more radical Jacobins had gained full control, Condorcet was tried *in absentia* and sentenced to death. He remained in Paris, hiding in a students' boarding house, and over the next six months, while the tumbrils were rolling by almost under his window, he wrote his famous *Esquisse d'un tableau historique des progrès de l'esprit humain*, a history of human progress from its earliest beginnings to its imminent culmination in human perfection. According to Condorcet, all inequalities of wealth, of education, of opportunity, of sex, would soon disappear. Animosities between nations and races would be no more. All persons would speak the same language. The earth would be bountiful without stint. All diseases would be conquered, and if man did not become immortal, the span of his life would have no assignable upper limit. The question of whether production would always suffice to satisfy the people's wants could not be answered, for the problem would not have to be faced for ages to come, by which time man would have acquired new types of now still unimagined knowledge. In this rational age to come, men would recognize their obligation to those not yet born and to the general well-being both of their society and of all humanity, and "not to the puerile idea of filling the earth with useless and unhappy beings." At that time a limit could be set to population other than by the premature death of a portion of those born. "Thus we find in Condorcet the entire genesis [though indeed no more than this hint] of the Malthusian population law, but in France these ideas remained unnoticed" (Fage 1953; cf. McCleary 1953: 86–88).

France's Revolutionary Assembly, like the earlier philosophers, was in the main pronatalist. The principal instrument used by the republican government to stimulate population growth was the same as Colbert's, differential taxation; single persons 30 years old and over paid a surtax of 25 percent. As defined in the new constitution itself, "No one can be a good citizen who is not a good son, a good father, a good brother, a good husband" (Reinhard 1946). Membership in the *Conseil des Anciens* was constitutionally restricted to married men. A national celebration to honor Husbands and Wives provoked a deluge of sentimental panegyrics. A campaign against celibates was reflected both in legislation and in crackpot ideas of fanatics—for example, that all celibates be required to wear clothing of a specific color, so that they might not escape the just ridicule of the people; or the petition to the Convention that celibacy be made a capital offense (Fage 1953; Glass 1940: 146).

Population policy under Napoleon represented a compromise. Pronatalist decrees continued; in 1813, though the need for soldiers was great, married men were exempted from military service. Under the Civil Code, marriage remained a civil contract and divorce was possible, though difficult. The authority of the father was strengthened, both over his children and over his wife. As under the Republic, primogeniture was supplanted by a law requiring each owner of property to divide the bulk of it equally among all his children; and at one time some analysts believed that this clause had effected a decline in French fertility, particularly among the peasants, for whom a numerous progeny would mean a rapid subdivision of the farm into uneconomic plots. Actually, however, even before the revolution equal division of property had been the usual practice

William Godwin, 1756–1836 (*N. Y. Public Library, Victorian Collection*).

except among the nobility, so that the decline in family size cannot be ascribed to the law, and certainly not to its purpose (Blacker 1957).

The same year in which Condorcet went into hiding, a book expressing the same ideas that he espoused was published across the Channel, *An Enquiry Concerning Political Justice*. Its author, William Godwin (1756–1836), had a more direct influence on Malthus's development than any other representative of utopian thought, and it is instructive to review once again their famous confrontation (cf. Petersen 1971).

Population was a recurrent theme of Godwin's writings, but he offered little that was positive. Since in his view "myriads of centuries of still increasing population may pass away, and the earth be yet found sufficient for the support of its inhabitants," he thought it idle to be discouraged by so remote a contingency (*Political Justice*, vol. 2: 518). In the far future, when a zero rate of population growth would become necessary, this would be realized in a world without births or deaths. Since "one tendency of a cultivated and virtuous mind is to diminish our eagerness for the gratification of the senses, . . . the men whom we are supposing to exist when the earth shall refuse itself to a more extended population will probably cease to propagate. The whole will be a people of men, and not of children. Generation will not succeed generation, nor truth have, in a certain degree, to recommence her career every thirty years" (ibid.: 528). This dissipation of the sexual urge would be matched by a total conquest of death, brought about by "the immediate and unavoidable operation of an improved intellect"—not, as in others' speculations on this topic, by improvements in the medical art. For if "mind will one day become omnipotent over matter," then "why not over the matter of our own bodies?" Disease then would be completely conquered by cheerfulness, which "gives new elasticity to our limbs and circulation to our juices," and reason, which abolishes confusion, "in all instances the concomitant" of disease. But "the surest source of cheerfulness is benevolence." In short, "the term of human life may be prolonged [indefinitely, simply] by the immediate operation of the intellect beyond any limits which we are able to assign" (ibid.: 519–529).

This vision of men transformed into sexless angels with a life span "beyond any limits we are able to assign"—in Godwin's half-secularized sermon a "matter of probable conjecture"—constituted his own principal contribution to demography. The vast bulk of his writings on population was negative, a detailed criticism of Malthus, who responded initially by a considerable revision of his first statement.

Just as Godwin started with an overemphasis (according to his own later view) on the power of reason to control human behavior and thus to transform society, Malthus began, on the contrary, by analyzing merely the imbalance between two biological drives, hunger and sexuality, with no role at all given to rationality. The first edition of the *Essay*, which Godwin praised for its major idea, he also criticized for this overemphasis on physiology.

[Malthus] appears to me to have made as unquestionable an addition to the theory of political economy as any writer for a century past. The grand propositions and outline of his work will, I believe, be found not less conclusive and certain than they are new. For myself I cannot refuse to take some pride insofar as by my writings I gave the occasion, and furnished an incentive, to the producing of so valuable a treatise. . . .

[But] is it necessary that we should always preserve the precise portion of vice and misery which are now to be found in the world, under pain of being subjected to the most terrible calamities? . . . Another check upon increasing population which operates very powerfully and extensively in the country we inhabit is that sentiment, whether virtue, prudence, or pride, which continually restrains the universality and frequent repetition of the marriage contract. . . . Everyone, possessed in the most ordinary degree of the gift of foresight, deliberates long before he engages in so momentous a transaction. He asks himself again and again how he shall be able to [support] the offspring of his union. . . . Is it not in the human character to reason after this manner in such a situation? The more men are raised above poverty and a life of expedients, the more decency will prevail in their conduct, and sobriety in their sentiments. . . . Where a man possesses every reasonable means of pleasure and happiness, he will not be in a hurry to destroy his own tranquility or that of others by thoughtless excess [*Parr's Spital Sermon*: 55–74].

Responding directly to Godwin's amicable critique, Malthus accepted the proposition that sexuality can be controlled by reason and, in the second and subsequent editions of the *Essay*, therefore added "moral restraint" to his "positive checks." In the view of the mature Malthus, man was no longer at the mercy of forces outside human control; population would grow faster than the means of subsistence only if this control was not exercised. Over his lifetime, even if with certain lags, Malthus moved from a biological to a sociological analysis, from principled pessimism to cautious optimism, and from a direct contradiction of Godwin to an accommodation to his main criticisms.

Godwin's responses to Malthus's revisions of his theory are something of a puzzle. To the simplistic views of the first edition, which Malthus had offered as a direct challenge to Godwin's utopianism, Godwin had responded with over-generous praise. But after Malthus had moved a good distance toward Godwin, not only accepting the criticisms of his principle of population but working for changes in society that would help obviate the preventive checks, Godwin replied with a long silence and then—a decade and a half after the *Essay*'s second edition, which had incorporated the main points that Godwin contributed to Malthus's thought—with *Of Population*. No other work except *Political Justice* itself so thoroughly commanded Godwin's attention. Not a day passed without a record in his diary of pages written and rewritten. But Godwin at age 62 lacked his old vigor. While at work on the book, he suffered a slight stroke, and during the ensuing period his journal recorded a "prevailing sensation of somewhat failing bodily powers" (Paul 1876, vol. 2: 258–259).

Of Population, 626 pages long, is prolix and difficult to summarize. Essentially it made four points: that Malthus had changed his position from the first edition (indeed!); that the world is not full (which confuses the distinction between potential and actual); that the ratios misrepresent the possible increase of man-kind and of its subsistence (Godwin also had changed his view); and that popu-lation statistics particularly for North America, which he took as Malthus's crucial example, did not support the argument of the *Essay*. More important today than his lack of factual or methodological precision, however, is Godwin's repeated falsification of the theory he was attacking. Throughout most of the work he took the *Essay*'s first edition as his principal target, ignoring except in an occasional passage the fact that Malthus had accepted his earlier criticisms and incorporated them into a completely reworked principle of population.

THE PRINCIPLE OF POPULATION

"In an inquiry concerning the improvement of society," Malthus begins the final edition of the *Essay*, the natural procedure is to investigate past impediments to "the progress of mankind towards happiness" and the probability that these would be totally or partially removed in the future. He does not pretend to be able to discuss so large a subject in its entirety, but "one great cause" is "the constant tendency in all animated life to increase beyond the nourishment prepared for it."

Population, "when unchecked," doubles once every generation. Among plants and "irrational animals," the potential increase is actual, and its "superabundant effects are repressed afterwards by want of room or nourishment." The matter is

Thomas Robert Malthus, 1766–1834.

"more complicated" in the human species, for man, a rational being, can consider the effects of his potential fertility and curb his natural instinct. With man there are two types of controls of population growth, which Malthus terms the **preventive** and the **positive checks**. "In no state that we have yet known, has the power of population been left to exert itself with perfect freedom."

The principal preventive check is "moral restraint," or the postponement of marriage with no extramarital sexual gratification. Other types of preventive checks he terms "vice," namely, "promiscuous intercourse, unnatural passions, violations of the marriage bed, and improper arts to conceal the consequences of irregular connections"—or, in modern terminology, promiscuity, homosexuality, adultery, and birth control (or abortion).

Positive checks include "wars, excesses, and many others which it would be in our power to avoid"; but in a country already fairly densely populated (Malthus used Great Britain as an example, and specifically excluded the America of his day), lack of food is the decisive factor. If the average produce from the land were doubled over one generation, or about 25 years, this would be "a greater increase than could with reason be expected." A second doubling in the following 25 years "would be contrary to all our knowledge of the properties of land."

That is to say, the "tendency" or "power" of every species, including the human one, is to increase at a geometric rate, while under the most favorable circumstances usually to be found, its subsistence increases at an arithmetic rate. Thus, "the human species would increase as the numbers, 1, 2, 4, 8, 16, 32, 64, 128, 256; and the subsistence as 1, 2, 3, 4, 5, 6, 7, 8, 9. In two centuries the population would be to the means of subsistence as 256 to 9; in three centuries as 4,096 to 13, and in two thousand years the difference would be almost incalculable." Lack of food, then, is the principal ultimate check to population growth but "never the immediate check, except in cases of actual famine."

Apart from migration, the population growth of any area depends on the preventive and positive checks taken together, or, in modern terminology, on practices affecting fertility and those affecting mortality.

The preventive and the positive checks [, moreover,] must vary inversely as each other; that is, in countries either naturally unhealthy, or subject to a great mortality, from whatever cause it may arise, the preventive check will prevail very little. In those countries, on the contrary, which are naturally healthy, and where the preventive check is found to prevail with considerable force, the positive check will prevail very little, or the mortality be very small.

Or, as we would say today, fertility and mortality, apart from transitional periods, are generally either both high or both low.

Population tends to oscillate around its means of subsistence. If a country with a population of 11 million, say, has food adequate for this number, then in most cases the population would increase sooner than the subsistence, which eventually would have to be divided among perhaps 11.5 million. Because of the consequent distress among the poor, more would put off getting married (the high negative correlation between the price of wheat and the marriage rate that Malthus noted has been repeatedly confirmed in subsequent studies). With a fall in the wage rate, farmers would be encouraged to hire more hands to "turn up fresh soil and to manure and improve more completely what is already in tillage," until the food supply was again on a par with the population, and the cycle began again. In primitive societies, where there is no market system, the same kind of oscillation takes place more directly. "When population has increased nearly to the utmost limits of the food, all the preventive and the positive checks will naturally operate with increased force . . . till the population is sunk below the level of the food; and then the return to comparative plenty will again produce an increase, and, after a certain period, its further progress will again be checked by the same causes" (cf. pp. 369–370).

The tension between population and subsistence, which Malthus saw as the major cause of misery and vice, could also have a beneficial effect. A man who postpones marriage until he is able to support his family is driven by his sexual urge to work hard. Malthus was therefore opposed to contraceptives, for their use permits sexual gratification free, as it were, and does not generate the same drive to work as would either a chaste postponement of marriage or children to care for. If a misunderstanding of Malthus's meaning was possible in the first edition, this should have been removed by a very specific denunciation of birth control that he made originally in the appendix to the 1817 edition, answering one James Grahame:

> I should always particularly reprobate any artificial and unnatural modes of checking population, both on account of their immorality and their tendency to remove a necessary stimulus to industry. If it were possible for each married couple to limit by a wish the number of their children, there is certainly reason to fear that the indolence of the human race would be very greatly increased, and that neither the population of individual countries nor of the whole earth would ever reach its natural and proper extent. But the restraints which I have recommended are quite of a different character. They are not only pointed out by reason and sanctioned by religion, but tend in the most marked manner to stimulate industry [*Essay*: 512].

Not only did Malthus accept the norm of moral restraint but he advocated more fully, also in part under Godwin's influence, the social democracy in which this deterrent would best flourish. In Malthus's writings, the negative correlation between station in life and number of children was increasingly stressed as the clue to the population problem. In order to bring the lower classes up to the self-control and social responsibility exercised by those with more money and education, Malthus asserted that the poor should also be given more money and education.

Wages are determined by the amount of money available to pay workers and the level of demand that they set, and generally, Malthus held, these two factors change together. For "when the funds for the maintenance of labor are rapidly increasing and the laborer commands a large portion of necessaries, it is to be expected that, if he has the opportunity of exchanging his superfluous food for conveniences and comforts, he will acquire a taste for these conveniences, and his habits will be formed accordingly" (*Principles*: 224–225). That is to say, workers who move into the middle-class income range will come to aspire to a middle-class style of life, including the smaller number of children typical among that class. This rise in economic status can be greatly facilitated by an appropriate political setting:

> Of all the causes which tend to generate prudential habits among the lower classes of society, the most essential is unquestionably civil liberty. No people can be much accustomed to form plans for the future who do not feel assured that their industrious exertions ... will be allowed free scope.... [Moreover,] civil liberty cannot be permanently secured without political liberty, ... [which] teach[es] the lower classes of society to respect themselves by obliging the higher classes to respect them [ibid.: 226–227].

In line with these ideas, Malthus advocated a system of universal free education. He considered it a "great national disgrace" that the education of the lower classes was left to a few Sunday schools, which could include in their instruction "any kind of bias which they please." The main argument against mass education, that the common people would be able to read "such works as those of Paine," thus increasing the tendency toward "a spirit of tumult and discontent," he regarded as plainly false. For "an instructed and well informed people would be much less likely to be led away by inflammatory writings," since they could better judge the "false declamation of ambitious demagogues." In sum,

In most countries, among the lower classes of people, there appears to be something like a standard of wretchedness, a point below which they will not continue to marry and propagate their species. . . . The principal circumstances which contribute to raise [this standard] are liberty, security of property, the diffusion of knowledge, and a taste for the comforts of life. Those which contribute principally to lower it are despotism and ignorance [*Essay*: 436–441].

CRITICISM AND ANALYSIS

It is standard that important books are more often cited than read, but in the whole development of the social sciences, there has probably never been anyone attacked and defended with so little regard for what he had written as Malthus. The errors and misrepresentations have been so general and so persistent that an account of his theory cannot be considered complete until some attention has been paid them. Accounts in responsible works are sometimes mistaken even on matters of simple, easily ascertainable facts—when Malthus was born, where and in what he was educated, what his profession was, whether he was married, how many children he had, how many editions there were of the *Essay*, and so on. Those most interested in Malthus, whether to praise or to damn him, have often started out with a misconception so fundamental that it enveloped the whole man. The "Malthusian" (later "Neo-Malthusian") Leagues sometimes took several generations to discover that the person whose name they used had been opposed in principle to the birth control they advocated.

And the opponents of Malthus have often propagated the myth that he was a reactionary, that "the *Essay on Population* chimed with a growing tendency to repress—discussion, association, political organization were becoming less free, as the wars became more exacting and more intense" (Beales 1953). A widely used text (Roll 1956) denounces Malthus as "an apologist for feudalism on a capitalist and utilitarian basis"—feudalism in England of 1800! Malthus's actual political effect has been aptly analyzed by Halévy (1955: 244) as follows:

The influence of the [*Essay*] will be better understood if a comparison be made between two speeches about the Poor Law made by one member of Parliament, Samuel Whitbread, in 1796 and 1807. In 1796, he demanded [only] that the justices of the peace should be authorized to fix the wages of labor at every three months' session. . . . Eleven years later, Whitbread, applauded by Malthus, proposed a bill whose principal features were a regularization and democratization of the right of suffrage in parochial assemblies, and a system of universal popular instruction.

Between 1796 and 1807, the influence of Malthus had been felt by the Liberal party. It was a democratic influence. As concerns the education of the poor in particular, the radical theory of popular instruction is Malthusian in origin.

This appraisal of Malthus's influence, even from so authoritative an analyst as Halévy, must certainly strike most of today's students of the subject as novel, even forced. The repeated vilifications by Godwin, Marx, and their followers have all but carried the day.

That "willful misinterpretation," as an anonymous reviewer of Godwin's attack on Malthus termed it, has become established doctrine is best indicated by the meaning of *Malthusian* as a supposedly neutral term. Is this word ever used to designate, say, the first significant economist to recognize the importance of effective demand and thus the only 19th-century figure in the main line of classical economic thought to suggest the serious lacks in laissez-faire policies; or, in social thought, a pioneer advocate of universal education, the initiator of political science as a university discipline; or, specifically with respect to population, the theorist who analyzed both the relation between humans and resources and the effect of social man's rising aspirations on his fertility? Very little of the full and well rounded thought of Professor Thomas Robert Malthus is ordinarily recalled in the commentary even of professional demographers.

To reject the frequent errors and misrepresentations in discussions of Malthus's work does not mean that we must accept it as gospel. He is still worth studying today because he forcefully posed a few very important questions, but his answers to them are inadequate by the best of modern standards. These deficiences derive in large part from three contradictions in his work that were never wholly resolved.

Moralist Versus Scientist.   To this day, social theorists find it difficult to separate an analysis of what is from what, in their opinion, ought to be. Malthus wrote at a time when such subjects as population were ordinarily discussed in the context of "moral philosophy"; he himself was a trained mathematician who helped found the Royal Statistical Society and, as already mentioned, was England's first professor of political economy. The pages of his books, reflecting this transition from a moralist to a scientific frame of reference, are sprinkled with allusions to "the Creator" and what He would prefer. The modern reader, even a pious one, finds such stylistic mannerisms inappropriate to a work in social science.

Sometimes the competition between the two analytical systems comes to the surface. Consider the proposition that "vice" leads to "misery." This might be the topic of a sermon, and Malthus the moralist would be pleased with the formulation. Malthus the scientist could hardly be. The main impetus to rapid population growth, and thus, in his system, to misery, came from early marriage. Although he strongly advocated "moral restraint," he never quite designated the failure to exercise it—getting married—as "vice." And, on the other hand, as pointed out in an interesting footnote, some vice—for example, extramarital intercourse—may "have added to the happiness of both parties and have injured no one."

These individual actions, therefore, cannot come under the head of misery. But they are still evidently vicious, because an action is so denominated which violates an express precept, founded upon its general tendency to produce misery, whatever may be its individual effect; and no person can doubt the general tendency of an illicit intercourse between the sexes to injure the happiness of society [*Essay*: 9].

Or, as a present-day sociologist would put it, no society can be viable if it lacks so fundamental an institution as the family, which, to persist, must be protected by a principle of legitimacy and moral injunctions against extramarital relations. In the *Essay* a hint of such a functional analysis is sometimes perceptible, intertwined with "moral philosophy."

As another example, compare his opposition to birth control with that in traditional Catholic dogma. When contraceptives are denounced as "unnatural," there is no way of translating this moral judgment into scientific language. Malthus disapproved of them "both on account of their immorality and their tendency to remove a necessary stimulus to industry," and of the two reasons he stressed the second. Birth control was what modern sociologists would term "dysfunctional." Malthus was partly wrong on this point, of course: man's ambition can be excited by other stimulants than his sexuality. But the interesting point is that Malthus was not satisfied with labeling birth control as "immoral"; he tried to state his opposition also in an empirical context, in which he *could* be proved wrong.

Although Marx and others habitually referred to him as "Parson Malthus," many clergymen found his interpretation of Providence not to their liking, and one went so far as to charge the author of the *Essay* with atheism (Bonar 1924: 365). The population theory appropriate to a "parson," they felt, was something along the lines of Martin Luther's adage, "*Gott macht Kinder, der wird sie auch ernähren*"—God makes children, and He will also nourish them. The principle of population, on the contrary, brought man fully into nature, one species among others. As Darwin himself remarked, his casual reading of the *Essay*, "for amusement," furnished the first clue out of which the theory of evolution developed. Thus, in the dispute between evolutionists and traditional theologians, a momentous struggle that set the tone of intellectual life during the whole second half of the 19th century, the role of Malthus was not that of a theologian but rather a forerunner of scientific biology.

Deductive Versus Inductive System. The principle of population, as enunciated in the first edition of the *Essay*, was wholly deductive. It started with axioms and proceeded to conclusions drawn from them. Subsequent editions, as we have seen, were based also on a mass of empirical data, gathered to check and support the original thesis. In its final statement, Malthus's theory is not clearly either deductive or inductive, but a sometimes confusing mixture of the two (Davis 1955). But this is very often true of scientific discourse, particularly in the social disciplines. One reason that Malthus continued to express his thoughts in deductive terms was his training as a mathematician, and many passages in the *Essay* are verbalizations of general mathematical formulas (Rubin 1960).

Nevertheless, the shuttling back and forth between empirical data and axiomatic theses muddled the theory, so that the meaning of a number of key terms is ambiguous. In the phrase, "the ultimate check to population appears to be a want of food," what is the meaning of "ultimate"? Sometimes it seems to mean "in the long run" (if the potential population increase is realized, then ultimately the lack of food will become the most important check), but Malthus emphasized that the potential had never been fully realized and, if moral restraint became general, the population need never press on the means of subsistence. Sometimes "ultimate" seems to mean "fundamental, underlying all other checks" (for both vices and moral restraint were often the consequence of hunger, or of the fear of it), yet Malthus also emphasized that the standard of living could rise above the subsistence level, so that hunger would be completely irrelevant to actual population trends, as indeed it has become in the countries of the West since his day.

A more important symptom of the confusion between Malthus's deductive and inductive systems is the ambiguity of the concept *tendency* (see the interesting exchange between Malthus and Nassau Senior, reprinted in McCleary 1953: 114–128). In the sentence, apart from "extreme cases, . . . population always increases where the means of subsistence increase," the tendency seems to be a summary of empirical data. In other contexts, however, the "tendency" of population to increase up to the means of subsistence signifies its "power . . . when unchecked."

Biological Determinist Versus Sociologist. Malthus's emphasis on the fact that man is an animal, with sexual passions and the need for food, has often been taken as the sum of his theory. Godwin was not the only critic to ignore Malthus's lifelong effort to improve the initial statement of his theory. In any case, the remaining emphasis on man's biological nature, which to some may sound like an insistence on the obvious, was not entirely pointless. Many in Malthus's day believed that the fecundity of the human species was being reduced by its urban setting or by the food it was then eating. Sadler (1829: xxviii), for instance, was not the first to contend that "the fecundity of human beings under similar circumstances varies inversely as their numbers on a given space"; or Doubleday (1842: 7), that abundant food destroys the physiological ability to reproduce, so that "in a nation highly and generally affluent and luxurious, population will [necessarily] decrease and decay." And according to Godwin, if sexual intercourse were stripped of "all its attendant circumstances, . . . it would be generally despised." Against such adversaries, it was relevant to stress man's physiological drives and needs.

That still today the biological element is often taken to be the whole of Malthus's theory is particularly strange, since he dissented on just this point from the others, particularly David Ricardo. For him, as for most who helped develop classical economics, the problem to be analyzed was production, and consumption was viewed rather mechanically in terms of a reified Economic Man. For Malthus, on the contrary, the standard of living was not simply a biological factor but also a cultural norm. The automatic circuit posited by Ricardian theory, the notion that the very production of commodities creates the ability to buy them, was countered by the suggestion that some purchasing power might be siphoned off into unused "hoards." It is worth recalling again the debt Keynes acknowledged to Malthus on this point:

The idea that we can safely neglect the aggregate demand function is fundamental to Ricardian economics, which underlie what we have been taught for more than a century. Malthus, indeed, vehemently opposed Ricardo's doctrine that it was impossible for effective demand to be deficient; but . . . Ricardo conquered England as completely as the Holy Inquisition conquered Spain. . . . [Malthus was one of] the brave army of heretics, . . . who, following their intuitions, have preferred to see the truth obscurely and imperfectly rather than to maintain error, reached indeed with clearness and consistency and by easy logic, but on hypotheses inappropriate to the facts [Keynes 1935: 32, 371].

If it is true that the principle of population and the principle of effective demand were competitive in Malthus's mind and works, it is also true that the trend over his life was from the former to the latter. The final chapter of the *Essay*'s last edition, titled "Of Our Rational Expectations Respecting the Future Improvement of Society," draws up a balance that is far from the gloom of the first edition.

The prudential check to marriage has increased in Europe; and it cannot be unreasonable to conclude that it will still make further advances. . . . Norway, Switzerland, England, and Scotland are above all the rest in the prevalence of the preventive check; and . . . from the little that I know of the continent, I should have been inclined to select them . . . as rather above than below their neighbors in the chastity of their women, and consequently in the virtuous habits of their men. Experience therefore seems to teach us that it is possible for moral and physical causes to counteract the effects that might at first be expected from an increase of the check to marriage. . . .

From a review of the state of society in former periods compared with the present, I should certainly say that the evils resulting from the principle of population have rather diminished than increased, even under the disadvantage of an almost total ignorance of the real cause [*Essay*: 477, 480].

Whether Malthus was correct about the pressure of population on resources can still be a polemical issue, since resources as well as numbers of people have grown. But his vision that the lower classes might acquire a taste for middle-class life, and thus the self-restraint to work for it, is incontrovertible.

POPULATION OPTIMA

If the term *neo-Malthusian* had not been appropriated by the advocates of birth control, it would be an apt designation for the economists who developed the concept of population optimum. In this sense, as in the usual one, the new Malthusianism would mean not merely a continuation of his ideas but their projection to a new level. The mathematical formulation of Malthus's principle could be called no more than a first approximation: population tends to increase by a geometrical ratio and food by an arithmetical ratio; therefore, population tends to press against the means of subsistence. These two progressions can be reformulated in terms of the **law of diminishing returns**, as follows: To produce food, two factors are required—land and labor. If to a fixed amount of land more and more labor is added, the result will generally be a declining per-capita return. For while the two factors are interchangeable to some degree (as can be seen in the difference between extensive and intensive agriculture), eventually increasing the workers per acre by x percent will result in a rise of production by less than x percent. The first statement of population optimum was essentially a development from such a simple model.

In his discussion of a newly settled area like America, Malthus sometimes half-intimated that population increase there was not only no problem but an actual benefit. If he meant to say this, he certainly did not say it clearly, and the first improvement on his theory is to posit **underpopulation** as well as **overpopulation** as a possible relation between people and land. Or, to continue with the same simple model, if to a fixed number of acres, more and more laborers are added, the first result may be a greater than proportionate increase in per-capita production, then a proportionate increase, and only finally a decreasing return. This model was developed principally by two economists, in Sweden by Knut Wicksell (1851–1926) and, somewhat later and apparently independently, in Britain by Edwin Cannan (1861–1935). As the latter put it, "If we want to preserve the phrase 'diminishing returns,' we must take the point of maximum return as the starting point and say that returns diminish in either direction, all commodities or industries being always and everywhere subject to this 'Law of diminishing returns'" (Cannan 1928: 59). The second emendation of Malthus's theory was no less important: the correction of his almost exclusive concern with food. Even the simplest list of economic factors includes land, labor, and also capital, and of the three the last is crucial in many circumstances. And if we analyze not only agriculture but also industry, then land is only one of the relevant natural resources that can be exhausted by growing numbers.

For all the similarity in the abstract formulations that Wicksell and Cannan offered, their views were diametrically opposed, partly because of the different climates of opinion when the two men wrote but partly also because of their contrasting personalities. All his life Wicksell espoused radical causes, from free speech to atheism, from women's rights to anarchism; on one occasion his politics landed him in prison, and toward the end of his career he proposed that the Soviet Union annex Sweden. Neo-Malthusianism, in the long array of such reforms, was for him the first, the most durable, and the most basic. His first publications were two pamphlets arguing that drunkenness is caused fundamentally by overpopulation, and he began to study economics seriously in an

Overpopulation—an engraving by George Cruikshank, 1792–1878 (*The Bettmann Archive, Inc.*).

effort to lay a sounder base to such theses (Gårdlund 1958: 73). In an essay contest sponsored by the French academy of sciences, he shared the third prize with two others for a paper prophesying that industrial production would decline in the coming decades, so that, if the level of life was to be maintained, a decrease in the population would be needed (ibid.: 150–151). In a pamphlet written in prison, he exemplified this idea with respect to Sweden:

As in every other European country [the population optimum] has been greatly *exceeded*; thus the way to prosperity lies not in an increase in the population but, on the contrary, in a sharp, continuous *decrease*. . . . The only expedient course would be to bring about a radical decrease in the population, to about *3 million*, for example (instead of the present 5.5 million), which would guarantee an adequate though modest livelihood for everyone forever [ibid.: 257–258; cf. Wicksell 1924].

In his last years, when the advocacy of contraception was no longer very radical, Wicksell campaigned for the legalization of abortion, though he admitted that he would not like to be a member of an investigating committee that "might have to pass sentence of death, as it were, on an innocent budding life" (Gård-lund 1958: 317–318).

If in Wicksell's view Malthus had understated the dangers of overpopulation, Cannan held consistently that these were exaggerated. Even when he seemed to be agreeing with Malthus, he let the reader know that this was not the case. For example, that the substantial decline in infant mortality had been the main cause of the modern increase of European peoples he took to be a contravention of Malthus's principle. For this cut in mortality was not uniform, and a "greater will and capacity for tending their offspring would be likely to be accompanied by greater energy and capacity in other directions." If superior peoples are more likely to increase in numbers, it is difficult to separate the effects of population growth from the effects of this superiority. "We cannot usefully speculate on what would be the condition of the world if its population were greater or smaller than it actually is, *other things being equal*, since it is perfectly certain that they would not be equal" (Cannan 1929: chap. 4). In a collection of his essays entitled *Economic Scares*, one of the bogeys that he deprecated was "Overpopulation," for in the early 1930s it had become obvious that, at least for the time being, Europe's surge of rapid growth was over. Cannon did not, however, join the gloomy prophets of imminent doom (see pp. 546–547).

I agree with J. S. Mill that it is well that population should become stationary long before necessity compels it. After all, the increase must stop some time, and watching the effect of stoppage will be a very interesting experience which I should like to have been born late enough to enjoy [Cannan 1933: 107].

However distinct in their details, the criticisms of Malthus by Wicksell and Cannan resulted in a wide acceptance of "the optimum" as the number of inhabitants of any country that produces the highest per-capita economic return. In the writings of various analysts, this "return" has been specified as total production per head, or real income per head, or the point at which the marginal and the average product per laborer are equal. Which criterion is used is less important than the idea that it should be an exact measure of specifically economic welfare. Such a definition of a population optimum, however, has been challenged on a number of grounds.

Actual or Optimum Institutional Framework?

The issue between Godwin and Malthus, or between Malthusians and Marxists (cf. pp. 670–674), is relevant also to the definition of optimum population. The famous dispute in the 1920s between Keynes and Beveridge about whether England was overpopulated, as another example, was largely terminological. As Warren Thompson (1935: 436) later summarized it:

If we are thinking of overpopulation as a condition which cannot arise so long as there are conceivable ways in which more people can be employed so as to produce larger real incomes, then apparently Sir William [Beveridge] was right, and there is no overpopulation in England or in Europe. . . . On the other hand, if we think of overpopulation as a condition in which there are too many people to be employed at good real wages under the conditions which actually exist and which appear likely to exist for some time to come, it would seem that Professor Keynes was fully justified in saying that England and Europe are overpopulated.

In more recent years, the issue has often arisen with respect to the new nations of Asia and Africa, whose present population pressure is ascribed to the imperial powers' maladministration during the earlier colonial period. By such an analysis, none of the newly established nations can be described as overpopulated. As we shall see, Soviet spokesmen generalized this kind of argumentation in preposterously utopian terms.

In order to discuss the concept of optimum at all, one must first agree, then: that population *is* a factor in economic welfare, no matter what the social organization, and that it is the present institutions, with whatever changes may be reasonably expected, that are relevant—not those of the past ("imperialism") or of the supposed future ("socialism").

Economic or General Welfare?

As the separate discipline of demography developed, population theorists began to wonder whether the economists had not delimited the optimum too narrowly. Attempts were made to restate it in terms of general welfare rather than income or production per head. Sometimes the new measure chosen was a demographic one, such as expectation of life, but once a reasonably precise economic standard was abandoned as too narrow, the tendency was toward broader, vaguer criteria. By one definition, for example, the optimum population is "the number socially desirable" (Penrose 1934: 90). The income and welfare concepts of optimum population are identical, in this view, "on the assumption that this income is spent in the consumption of the kinds and amounts of goods and services that make the maximum contribution to welfare." For example, all the money for food should be spent in accord with a consensus among biochemists on the kind and amount needed for optimum physiological welfare, and similarly for other products (ibid.: 74–83). There is, of course, no such consensus, even within any one culture. The concept of a general-welfare optimum, more broadly, "does not give sufficient weight to the influence of culture patterns upon *how* given needs are satisfied, [and] it ignores the influence of the culture pattern upon the *number* of needs that must be satisfied" (Spengler 1938: 274–275).

One of the cultural elements that are relevant is the level of aspiration. Quite often, as the real income of a country (or of one social class) goes up, the people see their situation as deteriorating, for their expectations rise still faster. Thus, in the words of a League of Nations study committee, "Overpopulation may be said to exist, not so much in actual figures as in the consciousness of the country concerned" (quoted in F. C. Wright 1939: 80). With such a definition, *the* optimum is indeterminate. As Adolphe Landry put it, "A country is overpopulated in relation to another country when its standard of living is lower than in the latter. Thus country *A*, though underpopulated with reference to an absolute optimum, may consider itself overpopulated in relation to its neighbor *B*" (International Studies Conference 1938: 122).

An economic measure and a more general one are both indices of the same variable, the first more reliable and the second more valid. But is the people's welfare the only objective that a nation seeks with its population policy? In particular, is the number of people that produces the maximum income per capita necessarily the same as the one best able to defend the country at war? Obviously not, yet these are only two out of several possible goals of policy. Sauvy listed a number of such different national objectives, each of which would have a different optimum population associated with it. Rather than maximum wealth, a country may seek a maximum rate of increase in wealth, or the conservation of its natural resources for future generations, or power, whether military or other, or full employment, or the maximum distribution of knowledge and culture among its people, or general well-being, as measured by health or longevity or otherwise. He concluded:

> The optimum population is that which insures the realization of a given objective in the most satisfactory manner. . . . The concept is nothing more than a convenience at the present time. The demographer may use it as an intermediary tool in the same way that the mathematician uses imaginary numbers [Sauvy 1952: 50–53].

Over two or three decades, thus, the concept of optimum population became so rarefied as to lose all real meaning; and the various attempts to coalesce these diverse goals into a single definition of optimum cannot be regarded as very successful (Ferenczi 1938). Perhaps the very word *optimum* was too moralistic to serve aptly as a scientific term. Originally it meant the number of people that would make best use of a given economy, but it gradually came to mean simply "the best population," with each analyst furnishing his own yardstick of what is "good." An optimist might hold that there is an inherent tendency in every population to move toward the optimum, which therefore could differ only slightly from the actual number (Carr-Saunders 1922: chap. 9). A nature enthusiast might call for more and larger national parks, with the optimum over large areas set at zero. A nationalist might be affronted at the very notion that there could be too many natives of his country. A utopian derides the proposition that population size has any economic or other effect at all in an optimum social environment. It cannot be the function of one definition to decide such questions, or even to take sides on them.

The Economic Optimum

The **optimum population** of any area is the number of people that, in the given natural, cultural, and social environment, produces the maximum economic return. The definition does not imply that this environment ought, or ought not, to be changed. Nor does it state that the maximum economic return is the only legitimate goal of a nation's population policy. These are different questions, and specifying the economic effects of population size is in itself a difficult enough problem.

The *size* of a population, first of all, is a very gross measure of its economic relevance. Among purely demographic characteristics, the rate of growth is of almost equal significance, not to mention health, literacy, skill, and especially age structure. Western Europe is too populous, let us suppose with Wicksell, in the sense that a smaller number of people would enjoy a higher average real income, and it is agreed that an attempt should therefore be made to reduce the rate of growth. This can be done in only three ways: by increasing mortality (which is, of course, ruled out as a policy in nontotalitarian countries), decreasing fertility, and increasing net emigration. But either a decline in births or a rise in emigration cuts down the proportion of young people, and thus aggravates Europe's other demographic problem—the large proportion of dependent aged. "These conditions pose a dilemma—to grow or to age—a conflict between population structure and population size" (Sauvy 1953: 119).

Moreover, the relation between population and resources in "Malthusian" terms, and that between population and economic growth in Keynesian terms, are quite different. Ultimately, the former model is still relevant even in wealthy countries; in the long run, maximum numbers are indeed set by the total resources available and the skill in exploiting them. However, in the long run, as Keynes once remarked, we are all dead. Within any one industrial country with a capitalist or mixed economy, over a period of, say, one generation, rapid growth not only uses up some of the resources but—and this is often the more important point—keeps the economy going.

In classical economic theory, just as every feasible demand elicits a supply, so supply creates its own demand; for in a free economy the production of goods in itself gives the eventual consumers the power to purchase them. True, the commodities produced may not wholly coincide in kind with those in demand; that is, local, specific crises are possible, but these are checked by the automatic adjustment between supply and demand. But a *general* economic crisis—a general fall of prices to below cost, general overproduction, general unemployment— is impossible by the very nature of the economic system. This doctrine, usually termed Say's Law (after Jean-Baptiste Say, who gave it its best known formulation), had been challenged by Malthus and, in different terms, by Marx, but among orthodox economists it held its own until Keynes upset it by reviving the Malthusian concept of effective demand.

According to Keynes, the automatic circuit posited by classical theory is completed only in the special case when planned savings and planned investment are equal; in all other cases, a part of the potential purchasing power is siphoned off into idle savings, or "hoards." It is particularly in wealthy countries (that is, also those whose populations were presumed to be in "incipient decline") that investment tends to be inadequate, for two reasons: because a smaller share of the national income is consumed and thus a larger share is left to be invested, and because the larger existent capital stock means that new investment opportunities are more difficult to find. Thus, as the stock of capital grows in any one country, the possibilities for new investment are less; or, in Keynesian terms, other things being equal, the marginal efficiency of capital is the lower, the greater the existing amount of capital. Why should this long-term decline in the marginal efficiency of capital not have been operative during the 19th century? Because, as Keynes put it, "the growth of population and of invention, the opening up of new lands, the state of confidence and the frequency of war over the average of (say) each decade seem to have been sufficient" (Keynes 1935: 307). Keynes's primary concern was with another problem; but his few *obiter dicta* on population encouraged other economists to formulate a tentative theory of demographic economic development. "With increasing population, investment can go roaring ahead, even if invention is rather stupid; increasing population is therefore actually favorable to employment. It is actually easier to employ an expanding population than a contracting one, whatever arithmetic would suggest" (Hicks 1936).

Thus, on the one hand, an increasing population requires a larger investment in capital equipment; but, on the other hand, in a capitalist country with a developed economy, this very demand keeps investment roaring ahead and the economy healthy. That is to say, if the number of a country's inhabitants is at its optimum point by one economic criterion, by another it may be too small, or, better, its rate of growth may be too low. There are at least two economic optima, a population–resources one and a Keynesian one. The first is the population that, in terms of present or prospective technology and institutions, affords the highest per-capita level of living; the second is the population growing at the rate that, in terms of . . . etc. Though it is obvious that these are not the same concept, they are often treated as though they were. Thus, as one example out of many, the argument of the 1930s against immigration to Australia (that its empty land was largely uninhabitable desert) was answered by post-1945 proponents of immigration in part within the same framework (by pointing out the potentialities of irrigation), but principally in Keynesian terms (a rapidly growing population is beneficial to the economy). A Keynesian analysis, however, is appropriate only when "Malthusian" pressure is not acute. On a true Sahara, more people bring no benefits.

An interesting extension of the Keynesian model appeared in a work by a Swedish economist, Ester Boserup (1965). For Malthus, the growth of population depends on other factors; but in Boserup's view, "the main line of causation is in the opposite direction: population growth is here regarded as the independent variable which in its turn is a major factor determining agricultural developments" (p. 11). Necessity is the mother of invention, in short. Most of her examples, however, merely deduce from a rough correlation a causal effect in the hypothesized direction. One illustration of her thesis is Tokugawa Japan

(p. 61), though in this instance the system of agriculture changed in spite of the virtually static population (see below, pp. 455–456). One can certainly find instances of "the vicious circle of sparse population and primitive techniques" (the title of her Chapter 8), and it is useful to point to these; but they do not obviate the more familiar vicious cycle of a dense, rapidly growing population and techniques inadequate to feed it properly. Boserup's model may explain some specific cases, but it is less general in its applicability than the contrary one associated with Malthus.

The ambiguity between population-resources and Keynesian economics has been aggravated by the tendency of economic thought to follow not the specifics of a case so much as the fashion of the day. Malthus's principle of population, once established as part of economic theory, went virtually unchallenged among professional economists for half a century, then after 1900 was subjected to greater and more sweeping criticism. In the 1920s Keynes was among those who led an international Malthusian revival, which was dissipated a decade later in the widespread fear of Western depopulation. In the most recent period, apart from an occasional echo of Communist or Catholic points of view or such an anomaly as Boserup, Western social scientists generally have come again to perceive overpopulation as a serious threat. The revival of the more pessimistic element of Malthusian thought is based, moreover, not merely on population projections but also on actualities. Malthus is relevant whether we observe underdeveloped countries, with their sometimes critical and growing shortage of food, or industrial nations, whose superior economies use up irreplaceable resources at prodigious rates and substitute for them a vast pollution. With the swing of the pendulum, a noisy clamor has built up. Population numbers are assigned the responsibility for virtually all problems in society: actual or pro-jected or imagined shortages in food, natural resources, and energy; pollution of the environment; deficiencies in education, health, urban life, and well-being; "life styles and human values" (Singer 1971). Essentially such ideological effu-sions have abandoned the notion of optimum, replacing it with a faith in two axioms, neither of which stand up to serious analysis: the growth of population brings mainly, or only, negative consequences to the economy, society, and culture; and population is a principal determinant of virtually all institutions and trends. In order to avoid the superficiality of this global view, it is useful to divide the population–resources balance into a number of genuinely relevant portions.

FOOD

As in Malthus's day, the most obvious limitation to population growth is the supply of food, and—also as in Malthus's day—there is wide disagreement between optimists and pessimists. In fact, the statistical base is too poor to resolve the issue. For sizable portions of the world—including its most populous nation, Communist China—no records are available on food production. A

[ABOVE] A thoroughly eroded terrain, c. 1930, since reclaimed by the Tennessee Valley Authority (*U.S. Information Agency—National Archives*). [BELOW] When land is plowed along the contour lines, as is this field in Clayton County, Iowa, each furrow catches the runoff (*Soil Conservation Service—U.S. Department of Agriculture*).

portion of those data that do exist must be taken only as rough estimates. Much of the food grown in most underdeveloped countries comes from very small family plots, whose produce is seldom included in overall statistics. In many places, moreover, peasants dispose of some of their crop secretly on a black market or hide part of it in order to avoid requisitions or taxes. On the other hand, any official encouragement of increased agricultural production is likely to result in a no less official exaggeration of the consequent successes. The several weaknesses of the statistical base are typically aggravated, finally, by the general practice of extrapolating a supposed trend to, for example, *Famine—1975!*, the title of an egregious work by the Paddock brothers. Though written in a more hyperbolic style, this book reflected much sober opinion during the 1960s, when it was generally held that on a world scale population was increasing faster than subsistence.

According to the U.S. President's Science Advisory Committee (1967, vol. 1: 12), for example, if the world's numbers continued to increase at the 1965 rate, the caloric requirements would grow by more than half in 1985. If one optimistically assumed an overall decline by 30 percent in fertility, caloric requirements would still increase by 43 percent by that date. According to the estimates of the Food and Agriculture Organization (FAO), as another instance, the total food production of the world remained static during the 1965–66 harvest year, while population increased by some 70 million. Such global averages give only a first indication of how serious the shortages were seen to be, for the differences are enormous between rich and poor nations and, within each of them, between regions and between social classes. In the most underdeveloped countries, in particular, improvements in agriculture apparently failed to keep pace with the growth in numbers. Over the period 1939 to 1965, according to FAO estimates, per-capita food production declined by 2.8 percent in the Far East (excluding Communist China), by 4 percent in Africa, and by 5.7 percent in Latin America. Presumably the widespread hunger in the major agricultural countries would have deteriorated into gigantic famines except for massive shipments of foodstuffs from such urban societies as the United States, Canada, and Australia. The barometer of the FAO annual reports, which on occasion had reflected an almost sanguine expectation of progress, turned gloomier than ever. According to the 1966 report,

The outlook is alarming. In some of the most heavily populated areas the outbreak of serious famines within the next five to ten years [that is, by 1970 to 1975] cannot be excluded. . . . The world food situation is now more precarious than at any time since the period of acute shortage immediately after the Second World War.

Yet the very next year the FAO report asserted that "the world food and agricultural situation is now in a state of transition and hope," for by its calculation world food production per capita had increased by 0.5 percent during 1967. And by 1970 the mood was cautiously optimistic. World food supplies were described as adequate; and even extrapolations to 1985, though based on an assumption that population growth would continue at the current rate, did not lead to the massive food shortages that had been predicted a few years earlier. According to what was termed an "indicative world plan for agricultural development," the earlier search for new land was to be largely supplanted by a more efficient use of land already under crops.

Even in those countries where a choice was permitted by unutilized land resources, intensification was chosen as the main component of increases in agricultural production, . . . [for] in general the returns . . . are higher than those accruing to development of new land and water resources. The diminishing cost of modern technology (as embodied in high-yielding varieties, fertilizers, plant-protection measures, and mechanization) relative to labor is the crucial factor influencing the shift towards the relatively higher economic attractiveness of intensification [FAO 1970: 51].

Thus, the recommendation was to increase the land permanently under crops in all underdeveloped countries from 210 million hectares in 1962 to only 223 million in 1985! In India, as one important example, the proposed increase from 161 to 164 million hectares over this period would cut the average size of cultivated area per unit of the agricultural population from 0.50 to 0.34 hectares (ibid.: 23).

This new stance represents a fundamental shift—from an attempt to spread the relatively primitive food-raising practices of peasant countries over a greater area to an effort, rather, to improve those practices. The enormous gap in agricultural productivity between developed and underdeveloped areas is not due merely to differences in soil or climate. Demonstration farms in various peasant countries, when cultivated under the guidance of technicians sent by such international agencies as FAO, have frequently produced as much food per acre as in technically advanced countries. That is, if the best farming practices were adopted throughout the world, its present population could probably be fed at an adequate level of subsistence. But using traditional techniques, some countries with three-quarters of their populations engaged in agriculture cannot feed themselves and, to one degree or another, have depended on imports from industrial nations. At the other extreme, the United States, where well under a tenth of the labor force produces all the country's food, built up a curious "farm problem" —a government subsidy to limit agricultural stockpiles.[3] The paradox that industrial nations have helped feed agricultural ones suggests why it is so difficult really to overcome the world's food shortage more than temporarily and thus somewhat precariously. Raising the level of agricultural production is not, as it

[3] These surpluses, which for several decades provided a cushion against crop failures anywhere in the world, were seriously depleted in the mid-1960s and early 1970s by especially large grants and sales to agricultural countries, followed in 1973 by the worst weather in a century. Some publicists, therefore, called for a change in American farm policy: "With surpluses dwindling and a hungry world to be fed, there's no longer any justification for a policy that restricts production and burdens taxpayers. It's time to turn the farmers loose" (Meyers 1966). In the early 1970s, when a beginning turnabout in American farm policy was attempted, it went painfully slowly, for subsidies to pay for nonproduction had become institutionalized.

Hens laying eggs on production line, Georgia. They eat and drink from troughs that refill automatically, while another conveyor belt takes away the droppings. One man can care for 7,000 chickens with a daily production of 4,000 eggs (*Burk Uzzle, Leviton-Atlanta*).

is often pictured, simpler and easier than industrialization and overall modernization. Indeed, the two are in large part the very same process.

To analyze potential sources of a future food supply, one can divide possible developments into several types:

Conventional approaches begin with **irrigation**, which was the basis of large population concentrations in the preindustrial era. To provide water for today's much larger numbers, however, is a task for an industrial society, for projects on the scale required involve much more than control of agricultural water. The World Health Organization, in commenting on the deleterious effects of African irrigation projects, referred to bilharziasis as a "man-made sickness." *A fortiori*, the large-scale desalination of sea water, a recourse of nations with an ample supply of cheap power, probably must wait for the development of commercial atomic energy.

Fertilizers were once provided through the "night-soil" (or human feces) collector, whose function it was to return nutrients to the farm. And in the agriculture of early-modern Europe, crops were carefully balanced with livestock, whose main product was manure. But on today's scale, fertilizers in sufficient quantity must be synthesized—which implies, once again, an industrial economy. One expert held that

the general distribution of fertilizers would be the quickest way to increase food production in the hungry parts of the world. . . . Except in acute emergencies, therefore, it would seem preferable to send fertilizers rather than food to areas of need, for they not only give a better return on the costs of transport but also start a useful cycle of technical development and objective thinking about the processes of agriculture [Pirie 1963].

In any underdeveloped country sizable portions of the recorded harvest, say between 5 and 10 percent, are routinely lost to rodents, other pests and diseases, theft, and spoilage (Farmer 1969). For each dollar spent on the **pesticides and medicines** that an industrial economy can furnish and trained agronomists can administer, the return in increased production is four or five times as much. However, as we shall see, one possible cost of some pesticides is pollution. The effective life of pesticides, moreover, is typically limited by the tendency of attacked species to develop resistant strains. This is markedly true of insects, for with their short life cycles genetic change can occur very quickly on a human scale. But it is the case also, for instance, of rats. These destructive rodents are finicky eaters, suspicious of new foods and particularly those that have a strange odor or taste. Most poisons, therefore, though often dangerous to other animals, are relatively ineffective against rats. In the early 1940s a professor of biochemistry at the University of Wisconsin discovered warfarin, an odorless and tasteless chemical that kills them slowly—by internal bleeding—and they are not warned away from foods containing it. This was so effective that all government- and university-sponsored research on rodenticides stopped, and in mid-1972 there was not a single project under way. But after about a decade of its first use rats began to develop an inherited immunity, and experts predicted that by the late 1980s every rodent in the United States will be resistant to warfarin.

Transportation is one of the main controls of famines, which can often be kept to local dimensions if food is shipped in promptly from more productive areas or central storehouses. The traditional famines of India, thus, were successfully combated with the railroads that the English built, and without today's imports of staples, India's ever recurrent shortages would indeed have developed into mass starvation. To build and maintain transportation facilities adequate to the task of distributing food throughout the world is, again, a problem only an industrial society can cope with. And this is even truer concerning such subsidiary processes as canning, refrigerating, dehydrating, freezing, and so on.

Ocean farming, the **synthesis of foodstuffs**, and various other unexploited or underexploited modes of producing nutrients are sufficient in combination, it has sometimes been argued, to feed not only the present world population but its projected increase for an extended period. Apart from the technical problems involved, however, one must consider the conservatism with which peoples, particularly in agrarian societies, adhere to their traditional diets. The United States, with its affluent and cosmopolitan population, is probably less tied to dietary tradition than any other culture. Yet a generation ago, when a number of enthusiasts for the soybean tried to popularize this excellent and inexpensive source of vegetable protein, they had little effect. One can imagine the response to a suggestion that Americans, who depend on beef, pork, and fish as their main sources of essential amino acids, might supplement these expensive products with such other good sources of high-quality protein, consumed enthusiastically by

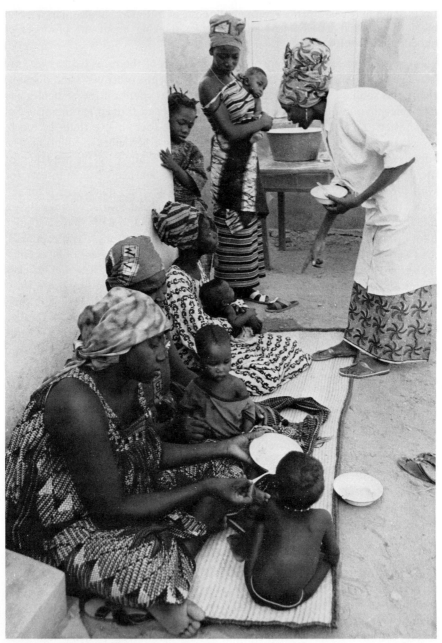

A nurse in Niger is explaining to several mothers how to make a millet gruel that contains all the elements needed by an infant that is being weaned (*World Health Organization*).

some peoples, as horsemeat, dogs, rats, locusts, and snakes. To achieve an adequate subsistence, it would be necessary in many countries not only to furnish more food but to develop an acceptance of better food.

The Africans in general are very conservative in their habits, . . . [and they] have never achieved a satisfactory diet. Almost all those examined are short of fats, vitamins, and mineral substances, and all except those of pastoral tribes, of protein also. . . . Ignorance and social custom often operate badly; eggs and mutton are taboo for women, especially pregnant women, among some tribes in Uganda; milk is not taken by the men. . . .

This vicious circle, malnutrition and ignorance preventing improvement, and lack of improvement increasing poverty, could never be broken without help from outside [Russell 1954: 234–236].

The main reason, of course, for the shift from deep pessimism in the late 1960s to relative optimism in the early 1970s was the so-called green revolution—the development of new varieties of food grains (Saitō 1971). Where these were successful, they overwhelmed all earlier predictions. In West Pakistan, to take a prime instance, a dwarf, short-stemmed race of wheat, with seeds imported from Mexico, was introduced on an experimental 10-acre plot in the winter growing season of 1964–65. The yield per unit of land doubled, and by 1970 the strain was growing on 6.5 million acres. The production of rice rose almost as spectacularly with the introduction of the dwarf IR-8 "miracle" variety.

These superplants had been produced by a long and tedious process, transferring the male pollen from one species to the female receptable of another. Nature does not accommodate readily to such induced interbreeding: the main criterion by which species are ordinarily defined is that reproduction is possible only within each. Those seeds that nevertheless did develop were then planted, in order to see whether, as hypothesized, the offspring were indeed superior to the parents. When it turned out that two excellent qualities were combined into a new strain, this was typically sterile (like a mule, a counterpart among vertebrates), so that each year the seeds to be sown have had to be artificially produced anew. It may be that these shortcomings will shortly be circumvented. Three research biologists at the Atomic Energy Commission's Brookhaven National Laboratory successfully produced a hybrid of two tobacco species by a method that bypassed the plants' sexual apparatus. They extracted cells from sterilized leaves of the two species and, in a suitable medium, induced them to combine and to develop into a hybrid plant. Since it has all the genes of naturally reproduced organisms, a plant created by what the authors call parasexual hybridization will in all probability be completely fertile, producing its own seeds generation after generation. "The potential offered by somatic hybridization may be expected to [transgress] the limitations imposed by sexual processes, and extend the possibilities of combining widely divergent genotypes of plants" (Carlson *et al.* 1972).

The superplants now in use have not adapted well to all environments. For example, in East Pakistan, much of which is subject to periodic flooding, the dwarf rice was not successful and agriculture stagnated. Over all, there was more food than before in Pakistan, but the economic disparity between the two halves of the country increased so much that it contributed substantially to the eventual break between them. In the spring of 1972 U.N. officials were predicting that within a few weeks the food shortages in Bangladesh would escalate to a mass famine, for chronic lacks had been aggravated by the partial destruction of the transportation system, a spiraling inflation, and the continuing effects of the war of independence. Officials in neighboring India, meanwhile, were looking for export markets for the novel surplus of 8 million tons of wheat and rice anticipated at the year's end. Their euphoria was short-lived. The monsoon in 1973 was termed disastrous, yet in the spring of that year India was planning to import only about 2 million tons of grain, or about as much as it had granted in aid to Bangladesh. Even in the countries where it worked best, the green revolution brought no permanent solution to growing populations but rather a respite of a decade or two during which, one hopes, effective means might be found to reduce fertility.

Unfavorable weather was not limited to India, and by 1973 the world's cereal stocks had fallen to the lowest level in two decades. Shortages were typically aggravated by rising prices. Following a prolonged drought, several countries of sub-Saharan Africa were suffering from acute shortages, which in some areas became a mass famine. In the new reports of the FAO director general, little remained of the optimism of the late 1960s.

It was becoming clear, moreover, that in those countries that had had a stupendous rise in agricultural production, this had not been achieved without a considerable potential cost. The more primitive races of plants from which the new strains were bred varied much more in all of their characteristics, including susceptibility to diseases, than the superplants. With their extremely narrow genetic base, the latter are more vulnerable to mass destruction. If the Mexican wheat should become susceptible to a new disease—say, a mutation of an existent organism—this might be a catastrophe of unprecedented proportions, for the rapidly growing populations have come to depend on the higher yields of the superplants. The most familiar of these in the United States, the new strain of corn, suggested what might happen to the crops of wheat and rice. In 1970 a leaf blight, a new mutant strain, attacked only this single type of corn—which was grown, however, by almost every farmer in the country. It devastated 15 percent of the crop, and that the blight was brought under control the following year was due mainly to the happy accident of favorable weather. In part as a response to this near disaster, the National Academy of Sciences undertook a study of the genetic susceptibility of food crops, which concluded that "most major crops are impressively uniform and impressively vulnerable."

The improvement of peasant agriculture is impeded not only by traditional cultures but also, and perhaps even more, by the traditional institutional structure. The low productivity and high population density of a subsistence economy are closely interrelated. Significant proportions of the agrarian populations of

Views of the Uttar Pradesh Agricultural University, Pantnagar, India (*Frances M. Foland—Institute of Current World Affairs*).

many underdeveloped countries are economically surplus—in the specific sense that if these workers left the land, the amount of food produced would not be less. This "hidden unemployment," as it is sometimes called, is not corrected in a family enterprise. A peasant does not "fire" a kinsman who is not needed to work the family plot: because the relation is not merely contractual, it continues even when it is no longer economically efficient.

On the other hand, the successful breakthrough in agricultural productivity that the new varieties represented helped shatter the earlier relatively static social structure. The high-yield plants demand large amounts of fertilizers and water, and productivity is greatest on farms big enough to warrant mechanization. Thus, those peasants who had been relatively well off were best able to adopt the new techniques, and it was they who personally profited from them (for a comparable effect in 18th-century England, see pp. 439–442). Francine Frankel (1971: chap. 7) analyzed this dual effect in five widely separated districts of India, a country that has tried valiantly both to raise agricultural production and to establish greater equality in the rural population. The programs that the government set up to help all agriculturists share in the benefits from the superplants exclude those at the bottom (the landless, both laborers and sharecroppers, as well as peasants with submarginal plots); and many of the smallholders who are eligible under the law are afraid to apply for production loans, for if a crop should fail they would lose their land. The Fourth Five-Year Plan (1969–74), which started with a backlog of some 9 or 10 million unemployed, itself estimated that the number would increase to about 13 or 14 million by the end of the period. And many of those not classified as unemployed are losing the relative security that traditional poverty had afforded them, for the well-to-do peasants are becoming market-oriented businessmen. There is, as a consequence, increasing social antagonism between landlords and both tenants and laborers. Just in those provinces that have succeeded most in raising agricultural production, three revolutionary parties are busy organizing. It may be that *green revolution* is not only a catchword to suggest that a fundamental problem is being partly solved, but also an all too apt designation of the social–political changes that the new agriculture is helping to effect.

In sum, the state of the world's food is too complex to support the simplistic extrapolations of either the sanguine optimists or the more typical doom-sayers. The risks incurred in so sharply narrowing the genetic base of major food plants are horribly great. But contrary to almost all recent predictions, the world's food supply has increased per capita, and, even more significantly, biologists are seemingly on the brink of new methods of genetic manipulation that will circumvent a clumsy imitation of the birds and the bees.

NATURAL RESOURCES AND POLLUTION

The fear that the increasing numbers of humans would outgrow their food supply, though a constant theme of neo-Malthusian propaganda, was recurrently undercut by the actual trends. By the end of the 19th century many—perhaps even most—economists rejected Malthus's principle of population, partly because in Western countries fertility had declined appreciably but partly also because far more food was available than he had anticipated. However, both the industrialization underlying this improvement in agricultural productivity and the better means of transportation from new overseas sources expended other resources than the land on which Malthus had focused his attention. As early as 1865 a work appeared entitled *The Coal Question: An Inquiry Concerning the Progress of the Nation and the Probable Exhaustion of Our Coal-mines,* by W. S. Jevons, one of the greatest and most original of English economists. And in the Malthusian revival of the 1920s, this theme was given far greater emphasis: Harold Wright (1923), for instance, both quoted at length from Jevons and extended his argument to iron, cotton, wool, and by implication all the ingredients of an industrial society. In the current wave of Malthusian thought, thus, it is no novelty to forecast the coming shortages not only of arable land, and thus of food, but also of all other natural resources.

These predictions of the imminent depletion of this or that have seldom been accurate. Gifford Pinchot, generally regarded as the founder of the conservation movement in the United States, wrote in 1910: "We have timber for less than 30 years, ... anthracite coal for but 50 years. ... Supplies of iron ore, mineral oil, and natural gas are being rapidly depleted" (quoted in Barnett 1967). In the very year that the Paley report (U.S. President's Materials Policy Commission 1952), as another instance, predicted that the prices of raw materials would rise steadily compared with those of finished goods, the terms of trade turned against many raw materials, for which new substitutes had been found or invented. It would serve no purpose here to review all the more recent efforts to prophesy how fast various resources are being used up. Perhaps the most pretentious attempt to trace the exponential increases of population, food production, industrialization, and pollution has been in a work titled *The Limits of Growth.* Sponsored by a group of private citizens that calls itself The Club of Rome, the analysis was guided through the computer by a Massachusetts Institute of Technology team headed by Donella H. Meadows (1972). The resulting book was designed for mass consumption, with translations announced into half a dozen languages; in the view of such a popular pundit as Anthony Lewis of the *New York Times,* it was "likely to be one of the most important documents of our age." According to its prognosis, the highest possible level of living that the entire world can enjoy was said to be about half that of the United States today. The authors recommended, therefore, that both population growth and capital investment should cease, so that the modest benefits of a reduced world industry could be distributed equally among all the world's peoples.

In a discussion of the possible depletion of "natural resources," it is useful to begin by dividing this somewhat heterogeneous category into major classes. One of the most important, timber, not only is renewable but is being renewed. At the present time virtually all the trees cut for commercial uses are wild plants, comparable to the scrawny corn harvested by pre-Columbian American Indians. But a genetic improvement of some species began in the United States in the mid-1950s, and the forest management instituted by such pace-setting firms as Weyerhaeuser Company in the Pacific Northwest makes the best use of the superior crop. It is expected that the new strains of Douglas fir will grow to maturity almost twice as fast as their wild predecessors, with a doubling of the yield per acre. The green revolution that has transformed the production of food plants, with all of its advantages but also some of its limitations, is in prospect for timber-producing trees.

According to the classical "law" of diminishing returns (which was developed, the reader will recall, as a refinement of Malthus's principle), the total quantity of one or more factors in production is permanently fixed, so that entrepreneurs, starting with the best source of each material, must gradually make do with less and less suitable stocks. The long-run trend (as the examples of superplants and supertrees suggest) has sometimes been, on the contrary, from less good to better. As another instance, the main sources of energy, in order, have been first dung and wood; then peat, charcoal, or coal; then water power, either as itself or transformed into electricity; currently for many uses oil and gas; and soon nuclear power. The order of metals has been similar: copper and tin first, then iron, the light metals last. "The assumption that man will utilize best resources first and then lesser ones, thereby descending a quality gradient as population grows, is erroneous in a dynamic world" (Barnett 1971).

It is true of course that the most easily available sources of metals, the richest deposits in the ground, are used first and that as these are depleted it becomes profitable to move on to ores of a lower grade. According to the late Samuel G. Lasky, an American geologist and a sort of Malthus-in-reverse, each such arithmetic reduction in the grade of porphyry copper ore mined would open up vast marginal reserves, so that the amount of available metal would increase geometrically (Faltermayer 1972). The timing of this process, since it depends on both how great the ready supply is and how extensive the demand, differs for each of the commercial metals. To extrapolate the availability of any one of them into the future requires the combined technical knowledge of research geologists and industrial managers (plus some inspired guesswork), and summing these imprecise projections into an overall forecast is doubly precarious. One should note, in any case, that the quantities of the various elements are fixed, the same a million years ago as today or a million years hence. As the supplies of a particular metal from mining operations become less relative to the demand for it, it is more and more profitable to recycle scrap containing it. Moreover, if it is deemed to be useful, this market operation could be hurried along by either of two policy intrusions: to charge mining companies for what economists call the "externalities" of their operations—that is, the pollution and erosion that typically accompany unregulated mining; and, second, to tax metal commodities enough to make recycling profitable sooner. Both these corrections of the market would raise the cost of the goods to the consumer.

The surprising fact is that raw materials are not at the moment very costly, and moreover their cost relative to the cost of finished goods has not been increasing. The gross national product in the United States is more than $4,500 per capita and the raw-materials component per capita is less than $100, [relatively] no higher now than at the beginning of the century [Coale 1970].

From a concentration on natural resources, one constituent among others, one ought to move to considering how resources are interrelated with the many other factors in social change. The analysis then becomes inordinately complex, and most discussions evade it. But the frenzied attack on one target, temporarily defined by zealots as *the* criticial issue of the month, has typically aggravated the overall problem. During the early 1970s, to take a good example, American environmentalists tried, usually with some success, to postpone or block the building of a pipeline to transport oil from Alaska, in order to preserve the natural habitat of the wildlife there; to block construction of oil refineries on the East Coast and of nuclear power plants anywhere, because of possible pollution; to limit offshore drilling and to oppose oil imports, because of the danger of spills; to halt strip mining, because of the damage to the countryside; and to discourage the construction of port facilities for importing liquefied natural gas, because of a general hostility to industrial society. Predictably, the "environmental crisis" was followed by an "energy crisis," which, also predictably, was denounced by some of the same persons and groups that had contributed to it.

How much the energy crisis of the early 1970s was caused by genuine shortages, and how much by politics, both international and domestic, the incompetence of administrative agencies, and the maneuvers of oil companies, it would take a separate study to work out. Shortages were genuine and serious in such industrial countries as Japan and most of Western Europe, which lack their own energy supplies. But if we continue to restrict the discussion to the United States, the situation was both more complex and less drastic. There are large supplies of natural gas, which is readily available, convenient for many uses, relatively cheap, and nonpolluting. Deposits of coal are tremendous, but this fuel is used to supply only 17 percent of the country's energy requirements. The Bureau of Mines has developed techniques by which most of the sulfur can be removed (Osborn 1974), and there is every reason to anticipate that this process can be made cheaper and more effective. In the long run, indeed, the fossil fuels will be exhausted, but one should recall that for all the dire warnings over the past century or more, the known supplies have generally been going up. And when this source of energy will have been depleted, another will have taken its place—unless the technological development over the past two centuries is mysteriously interrupted.

There has been a rising demand, of course, to abolish the pollution of the natural environment. That overzealous social reformers can overshoot their mark and hurt their own cause can be illustrated by a number of instances in this effort. The Water Quality Control Act of 1972, for example, has as its stated objective to achieve 100-percent clean water by 1985. According to expert testimony before a congressional committee, testimony that was not seriously disputed, the cost of realizing this would be approximately $2.3 trillion, or more than the entire world's gross national product for a year. But if members of Congress voted against "clean water," they feared they would be labeled advocates of "dirty water"; and indeed in the 1972 election environmentalists concentrated an attack on twelve members up for re-election, whom they denounced as the "Dirty Dozen." Thus, this preposterous bill passed unanimously in the Senate and in the House against only fourteen nay votes.

Perhaps the best estimate to date of the cost of reducing air and water pollution to "acceptable levels" (with no attention given to such comparatively less obtrusive problems as noise pollution) is a volume prepared jointly for the U.S. Council on Environmental Quality and the Environmental Protection Agency (1972). According to this estimate, the minimum program it considered will cost, in constant 1958 dollars, 872.2 billion over 1972–76 and 956.9 billion over 1972–80. If we ignore the increase in costs from inflation and take the annual average of the 5-year period, about $175 billion, this amounts to 22 percent of the national income in 1970. The ancillary costs, moreover, are not equally distributed over the fifteen industry groups surveyed, and those hardest hit will suffer greatly. To install adequate pollution-control equipment on automobiles, for instance, would add only about $350 to the manufacturing cost, and even if the increased price were to cut the sales somewhat and shift some purchases to cheaper models, the maximum reduction in jobs in the industry would be by only 1.8 percent over 5 years. In the canning industry, in contrast, it is anticipated that the added cost of reducing pollution will squeeze small and even medium-sized plants out of the market.

The potential impact of dislocations may be borne disproportionately by areas which already lag the nation in economic health. Approximately 90 percent of the employees of processing plants are relatively unskilled and only part-time employed. This large segment of the total labor force required is not generally mobile and would have difficulty relocating [ibid.: 122].

Of the 1,200 canning plants included in the survey, it was expected that one-third would have to close down, resulting in a loss of jobs by approximately 28,000 workers. Moreover, if the farmers in these areas were unable to find alternative markets for their products, they also might be pushed into bankruptcy.

As a consequence of the frenetic environmentalist propaganda, the general public has become aware of the "pollution crisis," but the support for reforms would seem to be well short of what they would cost. According to one apparently typical local survey, 74 percent of the respondents believed that environmental pollution is a "serious problem" in the nation as a whole, but only 13 percent in their local community, which by objective data was worse than the national average (Murch 1971). When several cities, including Chicago as the largest, banned the sale of detergents containing phosphates, many of the housewives affected sought their favorite brands in suburban stores. Thus, in just one

Oak Lawn supermarket across the street from Chicago's city limits, the sales of Tide, the largest-selling phosphate detergent, jumped from less than twenty cases a week to about a hundred cases a day. Some months later a federal judge ruled that the ban is unconstitutional and then went on to assert that not only are phosphates safe but they do a good job in getting clothes clean (*Wall Street Journal*, August 10, 1972; March 7, 1973). Manifestly, the economic and political problems associated with the protection of the environment are still poorly understood; and once they are spelled out, it is not likely that a majority of the electorate will soon support a sizable cut in their consumption level in order to bring about an environment reasonably free of pollution.

In sum, the actual or potential shortages of food or other natural resources, the actual or potential destruction of the natural environment, are serious problems—far too serious to be dealt with by those who substitute an apocalyptic stance for the expertise they lack.

Whatever general validity there may be in the prophecies of doom, in a work on population one should emphasize that the contribution of population size and growth to the supposed catastrophe has generally been overstated. If the automobile uses up oil and iron and emits unpleasant and potentially dangerous fumes, the broader background to this phenomenon includes, apart from engineering factors, the affluence of the United States, which has made it possible for almost every family to acquire a personal means of locomotion; the degeneration of the rail system and the failure to construct alternative means of mass transport comparable in efficiency to the railroads of Western Europe, for instance, or the underground of London or Toronto; the sheer size of the country, which meant that the commitment to automobiles and highways, once it was made, constituted an expenditure of billions in capital investment, not easily discarded for any alternative transportation system. Population in itself is hardly significant, even as an aggravating factor.

In a country like the United States, moreover, it is not typically the number of people that contributes to ecological imbalances but their dense concentration in relatively tiny portions of the land's total area. Such a concomitant of metropolitan living as congestion is obviously not based on the very low national density. And even in the large cities, where congestion is much discussed, it is not seen as a serious enough problem to have stimulated corrective action. The staggering of work hours, which would cost almost nothing in money and rather little in relative inconvenience, has often been suggested—it is obvious enough—but applied almost nowhere. One must conclude that urban life, even including what are called the typical urban problems, holds more appeal for many people than rural or small-town alternatives.

SUMMARY

Malthus's *Essay on the Principle of Population*, in spite of its faults and limitations, marks the beginning of scientific demographic theory. His main ideas in present-day terms are the following: Man's physiological ability to reproduce is great enough to permit any population to double each generation (true). Actual fertility was never so high as this fecundity (probably true). In most cases, however, the checks on population growth imposed by reduced fertility were less important than those effected by heavy mortality (generally true of Malthus's day and of prior periods, though the postponement of marriage had also been a significant factor). The most important reason for late marriage, and for high death rates, was usually an actual or threatened shortage of food (the postponement of marriage had been enforced by institutionalized regulations; at least in Europe, disease was more significant than hunger as the cause of early death).

Malthus's population theory is neither wholly acceptable nor wholly defective. It suffers from inconsistencies and ambiguities. Yet Malthus's work helped establish two valid theses: (1) Contrary to beliefs widely held in his day, the population was growing rapidly. Wise social policy consisted in the opposite of pronatalist decrees, an effort to substitute the control of fertility for high death rates. (2) Contrary to utopian dogmas, man is not only a social being but also a biological one. The population of even a perfect society depends on births and deaths, and thus on the sexual drive and food.

The difficulty that Malthus had in separating scientific from ethical canons has persisted in various formulations of the optimum, a development from the population–resources dilemma that he analyzed. It is certainly correct that any conceivable index of the population optimum could not be "of very great precision." "We could hardly hope to determine the optimum, for any given area at any given time, more closely than within a range of, say, 5 percent on either side" (Dalton 1928). Even the restrained optimism of this "hope" is not warranted in many cases. For example, Spengler (1938: 273) wrote that France's population of 42 million (in 1938) ought to be cut down by a quarter to maximize the per-capita income, while Sauvy (1952: 186) set the optimum in the postwar period at somewhere between 50 and 75 million. When two men so eminently qualified to discuss the population of France differ to this degree, others may wonder whether the concept has any utility. Myrdal (1940: 26–27), for instance, termed the theory of optimum population "one of the most sterile ideas" ever developed in economics. "Its elaboration has not increased its scientific significance or practical applicability. The theory stands mainly as an excuse for, and also as an actual inhibition of, the proper posing of the problem of the economic effects of population changes."

Even if we stipulate the meaning of *optimum* as the population that is best according to a quite specific economic criterion, we cannot advance very far beyond that conceptual clarification. There are two economic optima, here called the market and the ecological, and neither one can be applied very precisely to real populations. Several empirical and theoretical studies challenging Keynes's concepts have brought into fundamental question at least the present relevance of the market optimum, but this challenge is not accepted by all economists. And if we do hold that under some circumstances a growing population stimulates an economy that otherwise might falter, no formula exists for reconciling this proposition with the one that a growing population is undesirable because it eats up resources more quickly. It is possible to designate an optimum size or rate of growth, in fact, only in the sense that extremes of any kind are associated with special problems. The argument in favor of instituting a population policy in a country like the United States, thus, is typically made on the basis of an extrapolation to some future time, when its present rather low population density and relatively comfortable relation to natural resources will presumably have disappeared.

Yet the idea underlying the concept of optimum, that national income can sometimes be increased by adjusting the population to the economy, is the rationale behind many specific policies, including, for example, the pronatalist program that Myrdal helped work out in Sweden. If the theory of population optimum is to be at all useful, however, it is necessary first of all to set aside both the heavy ideological luggage and the legitimate scientific questions to which we can as yet give no definite answers. Second, we must recognize that any measure of the optimum must be crude: to say that India is overpopulated is meaningful and correct, but with respect to a country like France it is perhaps pointless to ask whether it is under- or overpopulated.

In the recent revival of Malthusian ideas, the forecasts have been not only of mass famines but, concomitantly, of the depletion of natural resources and the increasing pollution of the environment. A typical example of this genre, though perhaps more influential than most, is *The Limits of Growth* (Meadows 1972). The profoundly pessimistic projections in this work were based on a rather simple fallacy: the estimated past trends of several important variables were extrapolated into the future, but with the constant assumption that there would be no appreciable change in the most dynamic factor of all—technology. In spite of the facade of elaborate expertise, it is a model as simple as that in the first edition of Malthus's *Essay*. An increasing population will require, for example, an ever increasing amount of "food" (with no suggestion of what this is likely to encompass over the period of the projection), which must be produced on a limited area of "arable" land (the significance of this adjective changed radically almost while the computer was grinding out its message of disaster). As was pointed out in *The Economist's* review of the book (March 11, 1972), "In 1872 any scientist could have proved that a city the size of London was impossible, because where were Londoners going to stable all the horses and how could they avoid being asphyxiated by the manure?"

CITED REFERENCES AND SUGGESTIONS FOR FURTHER READING

In order to know what Malthus said, it is necessary to read him. The first edition of the *Essay* is readily available in an Ann Arbor Paperback and, together with an abridged version of the seventh edition, in a volume of the Modern Library. The seventh edition, which in this chapter has been cited from the original 1872 printing, is also available in a recent Everyman reprint. An appreciation of Malthus's method of work can be had from his superbly edited travel diaries (James 1966); and for a full understanding, one must know also his *Principles of Political Economy* (see also Spengler 1945). A delightful biographical sketch of Malthus is given by Keynes (1933); more detailed accounts, together with sympathetic analyses of his theory, are given by Bonar (1924) and McCleary (1953). The short biography in James (1966) corrects several widespread errors.

The literature on the Malthusian debate is enormous. Spengler (1942) gives a conscientious summary of French 18th-century thought; for a comparable analysis of Malthus's English predecessors, see Hutchinson (1967). A bibliography "intended to cover the genesis and course of the Malthusian controversy in Britain" from Godwin to only 1880 takes more than thirty pages (Glass 1953: 79–112); for analyses of the controversy see Coontz (1957), Eversley (1959), and Hutchinson (1967). I have written earlier on Marx versus Malthus and on Keynes's theories of population (Petersen 1970: 46–89). Apart from the essay on which a portion of this chapter is partly based (Petersen 1971), there is very little discussion of Godwin's works on population. Raymond A. Preston, the sympathetic editor of one modern edition of Godwin's *Political Justice* (New York: Knopf, 1926), omitted Chapter 7, "Of the Objection to This System from the Principle of Population," as "more than ordinarily conjectural and . . . altogether superseded by the more careful considerations of the same subject made later by Malthus, his followers, and his refuters, including Godwin himself" (p. 280).

Wolfe (1926), Robbins (1927), Sauvy (1960), Day and Day (1965), and Hutchinson (1967) are among the better discussions of population optimum. Of the vast flood of writings on natural resources and pollution, very little can be recommended—except as horrendous examples of the pollution of academic publications. Two of the best collections of papers are by Brown and Hutchings (1972) and the National Academy of Sciences (1971).

BARNETT, HAROLD J. 1967. "The Myth of Our Vanishing Resources," *Trans-action*, **4** (7): 6–10.

*_____. 1971. "Population Problems—Myths and Realities," *Economic Development and Cultural Change*, **19**, 545–559.

BEALES, H. L. 1953. "The Historical Context of the *Essay on Population*," in Glass 1953.

BENJAMIN, BERNARD. 1968. "John Graunt," *International Encyclopedia of the Social Sciences*, **6**, 253–255. New York: Macmillan and Free Press.

BLACKER, J. G. C. 1957. "Social Ambitions of the Bourgeoisie in 18th-Century France, and Their Relation to Family Limitation," *Population Studies*, **11**, 46–63.

*BONAR, JAMES. 1924. *Malthus and His Work*. New York: Macmillan.

BOSERUP, ESTER. 1965. *The Conditions of Agricultural Growth: The Economics of Agrarian Change Under Population Pressure*. Chicago: Aldine.

BROWN, HARRISON, and EDWARD HUTCHINGS, JR., editors. 1972. *Are Our Descendants Doomed? Technological Change and Population Growth*. New York: Viking.

CANNAN, EDWIN. 1928. *Wealth: A Brief Explanation of the Causes of Economic Welfare*, 3rd edition. London: King.

CANNAN, EDWIN. 1929. *A Review of Economic Theory*. London: King.

———. 1933. *Economic Scares*. London: King.

CARLSON, PETER S., HAROLD H. SMITH, and ROSEMARIE D. DEARING. 1972. "Parasexual Interspecific Plant Hybridization," *Proceedings of the National Academy of Sciences*, **69**, 2292–2294.

CARR-SAUNDERS, A. M. 1922. *The Population Problem: A Study in Human Evolution*. Oxford: Clarendon.

*COALE, ANSLEY J. 1970. "Man and His Environment," *Science*, **170**, 132–136.

COONTZ, SYDNEY H. 1957. *Population Theories and the Economic Interpretation*. London: Routledge & Kegan Paul.

DALTON, HUGH. 1928. "The Theory of Population," *Economica*, **8**, 28–50.

DAVIS, KINGSLEY. 1955. "Malthus and the Theory of Population," in Paul F. Lazarsfeld and Morris Rosenberg, editors, *The Language of Social Research: A Reader in the Methodology of Social Research*. New York: Free Press.

DAY, LINCOLN H., and ALICE TAYLOR DAY. 1965. *Too Many Americans*. New York: Delta.

DORN, WALTER L. 1963. *Competition for Empire, 1740–1763*. New York: Harper.

DOUBLEDAY, THOMAS. 1842. *The True Law of Population Shewn to Be Connected with the Food of the People*. London: Simpkin, Marshall.

EVERSLEY, D. E. C. 1959. *Social Theories of Fertility and the Malthusian Debate*. Oxford: Clarendon.

*FAGE, ANITA. 1953. "La révolution française et la population," *Population*, **8**, 311–338.

FALTERMAYER, EDMUND. 1972. "Metals: The Warning Signals Are Up," *Fortune*, October, pp. 109 ff.

*FARMER, B. H. 1969. "Available Food Supplies," in Joseph Hutchinson, editor, *Population and Food Supplies*. Cambridge, England: Cambridge University Press.

FERENCZI, IMRE. 1938. *The Synthetic Optimum of Population: An Outline of an International Demographic Policy*. League of Nations. Paris: International Institute of Intellectual Co-operation.

FOOD AND AGRICULTURE ORGANIZATION. 1970. *Provisional Indicative World Plan for Agricultural Development*, vol. 1. Rome.

*FRANKEL, FRANCINE R. 1971. *India's Green Revolution: Economic Gains and Political Costs*. Princeton, N.J.: Princeton University Press.

GÅRDLUND, TORSTEN. 1958. *The Life of Knut Wicksell*. Stockholm: Almqvist & Wiksell.

GLASS, D. V. 1940. *Population Policies and Movements in Europe*. Oxford: Clarendon.

———, editor. 1953. *Introduction to Malthus*. New York: Wiley.

GODWIN, WILLIAM. 1946. *Enquiry Concerning Political Justice and Its Influence on Morals and Happiness*, 3 vol. Toronto: University of Toronto Press.

———. 1964. *Of Population: An Enquiry Concerning the Power of Increase in the Numbers of Mankind, Being an Answer to Mr. Malthus's Essay on that Subject*. New York: Kelley.

———. 1968. *Thoughts Occasioned by the Perusal of Dr. Parr's Spital Sermon*, reproduced in facsimile in Jack W. Marken and Burton R. Pollin, editors, *Uncollected Writings . . . by William Godwin*. Gainesville, Fla.: Scholars' Facsimiles & Reprints.

*HALÉVY, ELIE. 1955. *The Growth of Philosophic Radicalism*. Boston: Beacon Press.

HECKSCHER, ELI F. 1935. *Mercantilism*, 2 vol. London: Allen & Unwin.

HICKS, J. R. 1936. "Mr. Keynes' Theory of Employment," *Economic Journal*, **46**, 238–253.

HUTCHINSON, E. P. 1967. *The Population Debate: The Development of Conflicting Theories up to 1900*. Boston: Houghton Mifflin.

INTERNATIONAL STUDIES CONFERENCE. 1938. *Peaceful Change: Procedures, Population, Raw Materials, Colonies*. League of Nations. Paris: International Institute of Intellectual Co-operation.

*JAMES, PATRICIA, editor. 1966. *The Travel Diaries of Thomas Robert Malthus*. New York: Cambridge University Press.

KEYNES, JOHN MAYNARD. 1933. *Essays in Biography*. New York: Harcourt, Brace.

———. 1935. *The General Theory of Employment, Interest, and Money*. New York: Harcourt, Brace.

*MALTHUS, T. R. 1872. *An Essay on the Principle of Population*, 7th ed. London: Reeves and Turner.

———. 1936. *The Principles of Political Economy*, 2nd ed. Tokyo: International Economic Circle.

*McCLEARY, G. F. 1953. *The Malthusian Population Theory*. London: Faber & Faber.

MEADOWS, DONELLA H., et al. 1972. *The Limits of Growth: A Report for the Club of Rome's Project on the Predicament of Mankind*. New York: Universe Books.

MEYERS, HAROLD B. 1966. "It's Time to Turn the Farmers Loose," *Fortune*, December, pp. 141 ff.

MURCH, ARVIN W. 1971. "Public Concern for Environmental Pollution," *Public Opinion Quarterly*, **35**, 100–106.

MYRDAL, GUNNAR. 1940. *Population: A Problem for Democracy*. Cambridge, Mass.: Harvard University Press.

NATIONAL ACADEMY OF SCIENCES. 1971. *Rapid Population Growth: Consequences and Policy Implications*. Baltimore: Johns Hopkins Press.

OSBORN, ELBURT F. 1974. "Coal and the Present Energy Crisis," *Science*, **183**, 477–481.

PADDOCK, WILLIAM, and PAUL PADDOCK. 1967. *Famine—1975! America's Decision: Who Will Survive?* Boston: Little, Brown.

PAUL, C. KEGAN. 1876. *William Godwin: His Friends and Contemporaries*, 2 vol. London: King.

PENROSE, E. F. 1934. *Population Theories and Their Applications with Special Reference to Japan*. Stanford, Calif.: Food Research Institute.

PETERSEN, WILLIAM. 1970. *The Politics of Population*. Gloucester, Mass.: Peter Smith.

———. 1971. "The Malthus–Godwin Debate, Then and Now," *Demography*, **8**, 13–26.

PIRIE, N. W. 1963. "Future Sources of Food Supply: Scientific Problems," in Royal Statistical Society, *Food Supplies and Population Growth*. Edinburgh: Oliver & Boyd.

REINHARD, MARCEL. 1946. "La révolution française et le problème de la population," *Population*, **1**, 419–427.

*ROBBINS, LIONEL. 1927. "The Optimum Theory of Population," in T. E. Gregory and Hugh Dalton, editors, *London Essays in Economics in Honour of Edwin Cannan*. London: Routledge.

ROLL, ERIC. 1956. *A History of Economic Thought*, 3rd ed. Englewood Cliffs, N.J.: Prentice-Hall.

RUBIN, ERNEST. 1960. "The Quantitative Data and Methods of the Rev. T. R. Malthus," *American Statistician*, **14**, 28–31.

RUSSELL, E. JOHN. 1954. *World Population and World Food Supplies*. London: Allen & Unwin.

SADLER, MICHAEL THOMAS. 1829. *Ireland, Its Evils and Their Remedies*. London: Murray.

*SAITŌ, KAZUO. 1971. "On the Green Revolution," *Developing Economies*, **9**, 16–30.

SAUVY, ALFRED. 1952–54. *Théorie générale de la population*. Vol. 1: *Economie et population*. Vol. 2: *Biologie sociale*. Paris: Presses Universitaires de France.

––––––. 1953. *L'Europe et sa population*. Paris: Editions Internationales.

––––––. 1960. "Evolution récente des idées sur le surpeuplement," *Population*, **15**, 467–484.

SINGER, S. FRED, editor. 1971. *Is There an Optimum Level of Population?* New York: McGraw-Hill.

SPENGLER, JOSEPH J. 1938. *France Faces Depopulation*. Durham, N.C.: Duke University Press.

––––––. 1942. *French Predecessors of Malthus: A Study in Eighteenth-Century Wage and Population Theory*. Durham, N.C.: Duke University Press.

*––––––. 1945. "Malthus's Total Population Theory: A Restatement and Reappraisal," *Canadian Journal of Economics and Political Science*, **11**, 83–110, 234–264.

––––––. 1954. "Richard Cantillon: First of the Moderns," *Journal of Political Economy*, **62**, 281–295, 406–424.

THOMPSON, WARREN S. 1935. *Population Problems*, 2nd ed. New York: McGraw-Hill.

*UNITED STATES. COUNCIL ON ENVIRONMENTAL QUALITY and ENVIRONMENTAL PROTECTION AGENCY. 1972. *The Economic Impact of Pollution Control: A Summary of Recent Studies*. Washington, D.C.: U.S. Government Printing Office.

––––––. PRESIDENT'S MATERIALS POLICY COMMISSION. 1952. *Resources for Freedom*, 5 vol. Washington, D.C.: U.S. Government Printing Office.

––––––. PRESIDENT'S SCIENCE ADVISORY COMMITTEE. 1967. *The World Food Problem*, 3 vol. Washington, D.C.: The White House.

WICKSELL, KNUT. 1924. "The Crux of Malthusianism," *Birth Control Review*, **8**, 171–172.

WOLFE, A. B. 1926. "The Optimum Size of Population," in Louis I. Dublin, editor, *Population Problems in the United States and Canada*. Boston: Houghton Mifflin.

WRIGHT, FERGUS CHALMERS. 1939. *Population and Peace: A Survey of International Opinion on Claims for Relief from Population Pressure*. League of Nations. Paris: International Institute of Intellectual Co-operation.

WRIGHT, HAROLD. 1923. *Population*. New York: Harcourt, Brace.

ZITO, GEORGE V. 1972. "A Note on the Population of 17th-Century London," *Demography*, **9**, 511–514.

THE GENERAL DETERMINANTS
OF FERTILITY

6

"General" determinants of fertility are those not specific to any particular culture. The ones most clearly general in this sense are the biological character- istics of the human species relevant to conception and childbearing, and these are discussed in the first section of this chapter.

It is atypical in almost any society, however, to realize the physiologically maximum family size. The actual number of children is reduced both by birth control and by value systems and institutional patterns that influence fertility even though this is not their purpose. As these social usages are manifestly part of what we mean by a culture, one might discuss them as part of the analyses of particular societies, rather than in a chapter on the general determinants of fertility. However, some of these culture traits are universal. For instance, most anthropologists agree (even if with some haggling) that the nuclear family exists in all societies and that all of its varieties are similar in a number of basic respects. And it is convenient in this preliminary look at fertility to consider also the range of such variables as the age at marriage, which exemplifies a social pattern with a wide variation from one society to another.

BIOLOGICAL DETERMINANTS
OF FECUNDITY

The analysis of fertility trends, especially though not exclusively by 19th-century theorists, has been an egregious example of the common confusion between biological and cultural determinants of human behavior. Did the smaller families in cities, for instance, result from an impairment of the physiological ability to have children or from the desire for fewer children that the urban setting stimulated? The facts available to the earliest investigators, mainly that the urban middle classes were leading the trend toward lower fertility, could be used to support either theory, and indeed the two were often not sharply distinguished.

The terms *fecundity* and *fertility*, originally used synonymously, were differentiated from one another only gradually. In 1934 the Population Associa- tion of America officially endorsed the distinction between **fecundity**, the physiological ability to reproduce; and **fertility**, the realization of this potential, the actual birth performance as measured by the number of offspring.[1] Now that the distinction is made conceptually, it is still difficult to apply it in practice. For at the present level of medical knowledge, the only absolute evidence that a person is fecund is the production of an offspring, in which case fecundity and fertility are operationally identical. The successful fertilization of a human egg, in one sense the beginning of a new life, is also the climax of a process complex enough to make the number of elements in an analysis of fecundity extremely large. Moreover, with rapid advances in obstetrics, the dominion of the "natural" has constantly given way to medical controls. Some of those working in the new discipline of molecular biology, moreover, predict a revolution in it with incalculable effects on some of the topics examined in this chapter. As recently as 1953, it was discovered that one substance, the DNA (for deoxyribonucleic acid) molecule, controls the germ plasm of all living things, and in 1961 its structure was determined. If it becomes possible to adjust genetic factors to human desires, then the meaning of *hereditary* will be altered immeasurably. (For one account of this fascinating research that is intelligible to a nonbiologist, see Lessing 1966.)

The available data indicate that the fecundity of each of the partners can be affected by several physical factors, of which the most important are discussed briefly in the following paragraphs.

Heredity

Although the evidence is not clear, it seems that one influence on the innate ability to reproduce is the relative fecundity of one's forebears. Such a physiological determinant is often very difficult to estimate, of course, for whenever children remain in the same social–economic situation as their parents—which is the typical case—a similar size in the two generations may be due merely to the continuing pressure of this unchanged environment. It is only at the two extremes of the fecundity range that hereditary influence is definitely perceptible. On the one hand, fecundity can be impaired by any one of a number of defects in the sexual organs; and a predisposition toward such constitutional impediments can be inherited. Certain of such hereditary defects inhibit reproduction altogether, and with others offspring die before they in turn can procreate. The inheritance of a high level of fecundity, on the other hand, is suggested by the

---

[1] This distinction is not always made in nonprofessional writings, but it is now fairly consistently maintained in demographic works written in English. The etymological equivalents of *fertility* and *fecundity* in Romance languages are used, however, in the opposite sense; thus, the French *fécondité* or the Spanish *fecondidad* is translated by "fertility," and *fertilité* or *fertilidad* by "fecundity." It should also be noted that physicians often use the two terms more loosely. The definitions given in Norman L. Hoerr and Arthur Osol, editors, *Blakiston's New Gould Medical Dictionary*, 2nd ed. (New York: McGraw-Hill, 1956), pp. 440, 443, agree with demographers' usage; but in *Stedman's Medical Dictionary*, 17th rev. ed. (Baltimore: Williams & Wilkins, 1957), pp. 514, 517, the meanings are not distinguished.

fact that the proportion of multiple births, which seems to be correlated with general fertility, differs significantly both from one family line to another and from one race to another. In one notable case, when one of a set of quadruplets married one of a pair of twins, they had thirty-two children in eleven pregnancies (Pearl 1939: 34–36, 58–65). The rate of twinning is several times higher among American Negroes than among American whites. How little still is known of this factor is suggested by a recent authoritative summary:

The variability of the dizygotic twinning rate in different races and the constancy of the monozygotic twinning rate suggest that dizygotic, but not monozygotic, twinning is under hereditary control. It is generally believed today that this is so and that the mode of inheritance is confined to the mother. It was suggested by several earlier investigators that the father might also play a role in the inheritance of twinning, but it now seems likely that these results were due to bias in the collection of the data [Bulmer 1970: 113].

Health

Like any other animal, a human being with a certain innate reproductive capacity has the highest possible fecundity when he or she is in a state of vigorous health. Certain infections, such as syphilis, gonorrhea, or tuberculosis of the genital tract, impede or prevent procreation directly (Retel-Laurentin 1973; Wilde 1973). And if a person's health is impaired by other causes—such as, among others, a nonvenereal disease (e.g., Ballew and Masters 1954) or nutritional deficiency (Hulme 1951; Williams 1962: chaps. 5–6)—this also affects his or her reproductive capacity adversely.

The seemingly obvious statement that good health is correlated with fecundity does not follow, however, simply and directly from the empirical evidence. On the contrary, human misery and high fertility are very frequently associated, and some analysts have interpreted this correlation to mean that the relatively healthful and comfortable life of the middle class in Western countries has reduced the average fecundity. Thus, Charles (1936: 182–183) suggested that the decline in the size of the Western family was due to factors like "the widespread habit of excessive washing"; Castro (1952) that it was due to the high-protein diet of well-to-do classes and nations. Contrary to such interpretations, most demographers today would agree that cleanliness and good food, together with all other conditions conducive to good health, increase reproductive capacity to the degree that they affect it at all, but that these physical factors have often been negated in industrial societies by the higher social valuation put on small families.

Age

Procreation is a function primarily of young adults. The capacity to reproduce, entirely lacking in childhood, begins to appear at puberty, develops gradually during adolescence, and reaches a high point at maturity. There follows a decline in middle age, relatively rapid and complete in females, slow and apparently sometimes only partial in males (cf. Vincent 1958). Individual cases vary widely: children have been born to a mother of 6.5 years, at one extreme, and to one of 59 or possibly even 63 years, at the other (Pearl 1939: 57–58; Kuczynski 1935: 106–110). That the range between the averages of social groups is narrower suggests that some of the seemingly physiological variation may be related to differences in their cultural environment.

In the female the **menarche**, or first menstruation, is usually taken to define puberty. The many studies analyzing the age at menarche (Pearl 1939; Kumar 1967) clearly indicate several patterns. The better the food, the lower the age; e.g., among a sample of urban Yugoslav girls, it was 14.10 years $\pm$ 0.111 among those subsisting mostly on carbohydrates and 12.65 $\pm$ 0.133 among those fed ample proteins. Certain diseases apparently delay the onset of menstruation. Because of these two factors, there is a difference in the average age according to the country's social development: in the United States and Europe it is below 14 years, in African countries above 14 years, and in Asian countries between the two. In advanced countries, similarly, the gradual improvement in the level of living has resulted in a decline in the average age at menarche: in Norway, the country with the longest record, it fell from above 17 years in 1844 to about 13.2 in the early 1950s. On a world scale (omitting a Bantu sample because of their especially poor diet), during the past three decades the average age fell by 1.5 years to about 13.66 years. This suggests that the earlier interest in sex so much discussed in Western countries probably has a physiological basis. Indeed, from the thin data available Cutright (1972) concluded that earlier maturation was the only genuine change that the "teenage sexual revolution" represented.

The menarche is only one step, the most clearly marked one, in a long process, and the regular development of healthy ova usually begins later. The earliest evidence of this fact came from a number of ethnographers who found, among various widely separated peoples, a puzzling conjunction of premarital sexual intercourse without contraceptives and an almost total absence of illegitimate births (Montagu 1957: 8–22). It is now recognized that for several years, during a period of **adolescent subfecundity**, the young person is able to produce a child but the probability that he or she will do so with a given degree of exposure is less than at maturity. According to tests using the basal body temperature as an index, more than half of the female's cycles during the first years of adolescence are anovular (that is, produce no eggs) or subfecund. The maximum proportion of normal cycles is reached only at ages 26 to 30 (Döring 1969). Children born to mothers under the age of full sexual maturity, roughly 18.25 years, are more likely to have physical, psychological, and social defects (cf. Oppel and Royston 1971).

Corresponding to the gradual rise of fecundity during adolescence, there is from middle adulthood on a gradual decline, which in females is termed the climacteric. **Menopause**, or the cessation of menstruation, is relatively the sharpest manifestation of this process and is therefore typically used to mark, though only approximately, the end of a woman's fecund period. According to several studies, the age at natural menopause varies only slightly among a number of populations (MacMahon and Worcester 1966). One of the two ages conventionally used by demographers, 45 years, is on the low side; and the other, 50 years, is higher than most studies would suggest. In any case, there is a gradual decline in fecundity, parallel to its gradual development, from early middle age to its cessation at menopause. The sexual prowess of males also falls off with age, but there seems to be nothing comparable to the climacteric.

Ovulation Cycle

The human female, like all other female mammals, produces ova periodically rather than continuously. In most subprimate species, the same hormone that controls this ovulation cycle also regulates the female's sexual desire. When the egg is ready to be fertilized, the female animal is "in heat" (**estrus**) and accepts, or seeks, the male's advances; and at all other times (during **anestrus**) she rejects them. Sexual union in such species is, in two senses, narrowly physiological: its timing is determined by the animal's glandular flow, and the union has the single function of physical reproduction.

In most primate species the female exhibits this estrus-anestrus cycle in a vestigial form. The vaginal skin of the female chimpanzee, for example, tightens and reddens at the time of ovulation, and the greater prominence of the sexual organ stimulates the male to more frequent copulation. In most respects, however, the sexual behavior of monkeys and apes resembles that of humans rather than that of mammals lower on the evolutionary scale. As with humans, there is a menstrual cycle, overlapping with the ovulation cycle. And, as with humans, the female is accessible to the male at any time, not only when she is estrous. Among primates, that is to say, the sex drive serves two functions: to reproduce the species, and to induce a mating couple to form a permanent union (cf. Washburn and DeVore 1961).

In the normal cycle of the human female during the years of sexual maturity, one or more ova are released from each ovary once every 28 days. Each month, while they are developing, the wall of the uterus swells, preparatory to receiving a fertilized ovum. If copulation takes place during the short portion of the cycle when fertilization is possible, a new life may ensue. The length of this period, as judged from studies of the survival of sperm and ova within the female, is certainly less than 72 hours and probably less than 48 hours. No agreement exists, however, whether the average is closest to 12, 24, or 36 hours (Potter 1961). If an ovum is not fertilized, the female is sterile until the following cycle. In that case the ova and the wall of the uterus disintegrate, discharging blood through the vagina. There is thus also a menstrual cycle of 28 days, with each menstruation spaced about halfway between two ovulations. Human females, however, have no remnant of the estrus–anestrus cycle. On the contrary, if women experience a cyclical variation in sex drive, they are likely to feel the strongest desire just before and just after menstruation, when fertile copulation is normally impossible, and the weakest desire just at the time of ovulation (Katharine Davis 1929: chaps. 8–9; Pearl 1939: 32–34).

Lactation and the Interval Between Pregnancies

After a woman has given birth, if she does not breast-feed the child, the menstrual cycle normally begins again after about two months and the ovulation cycle two months later still. The recurrence of regular ovulation, and thus the probability of another pregnancy, are usually impeded as long as the mammary glands remain active. This relation was long in dispute, but several studies during the past decade or so have furnished better evidence. One of these was made in several Punjab villages in India.

When an infant survived one month or more, lactation usually lasted well over a year, and the median length of postpartum amenorrhea was eleven months. If the child was stillborn or died in the first month of life, the mother did not lactate and the median length of postpartum amenorrhea was in the vicinity of two months [Potter et al. 1965; cf. Cantrelle and Leridon 1971; Perez et al. 1971; Kippley and Kippley 1972].

In some societies, however, the physiological relation is obscured by the prohibition of intercourse with a woman who is still breast-feeding an infant, as in the polygynous families of East Africa (Saxton and Serwadda 1969).

Sex Drive

The social dominance of the male in most cultures means that his sexuality is more likely than the female's to determine coital incidence. According to nine American and European studies, the average frequency of marital coitus is very slightly more than ten times per month (Pearl 1939: 69). Kinsey gives a much lower overall figure, 1.06 times per week (Kinsey et al. 1948: 568). If what anthropologists are told on this matter can be accepted, the frequency is considerably higher among nonindustrial peoples. "In most of the [primitive] societies on which information is available, every adult normally engages in heterosexual intercourse once daily or nightly during the periods when coitus is permitted" (Ford and Beach 1951: 78; cf. Nag 1972). In all cultures the range of individual differentiation is wide. And whether any of these data are trustworthy may be questioned, for they are distorted both by the inclination everywhere to preserve the privacy of the sexual act and the tendency, probably no less universal, of at least the male to exaggerate his virility. The comment of a physician in Central Africa may well be relevant generally: "We have interrogated a small proportion of our patients about the frequency of intercourse in young married couples, but do not wish to publish the results of the poll taken, because the answers, usually given rapidly, tend to cluster around two standards which are maybe in the mind of the people as much as in their practice; these two standards are three intercourses per week and three intercourses per day, the latter being much rarer" (Barlovatz 1955).

The negative data on the cases that physicians treat for subfecundity are generally more reliable. Of a long series of such patients over a 5-year period, 5.5 percent of the infertile males had semen of normal quality and wives whom gynecologists had judged to be potentially fertile. The impotency was psychological and could be treated mainly be psychiatric methods (Dubin and Amelar 1971; 1972). According to an interesting study by three Yugoslav physicians, men who had migrated from the countryside to a city and there obtained work in a noisy factory were particularly susceptible to infertility during an adjustment period of about 3 years (Milojković et al. 1972). This is one of the very few analyses of human data that seemingly validate the studies made with lower animals, whose fertility is often cut by the stress associated with excessive crowding (see p. 380). In this as in other respects, the human species is governed more by cultural standards than by physiological checks.

Analysts of Latin American fertility have often referred to the effect on family size of the males' grossly exaggerated virility, but this *machismo* has seldom been put in historical context. According to one account, it is an expression of lower-class braggadocio, an attempt to reverse the relative positions of social classes or of two nations. For example, a Mexican folk song popular when General Pershing was trying to capture Pancho Villa went as follows:

> Qué pensarán los bolillos tan patones
> Que con cañones nos iban a asustar;
> Si ellos tienen aviones de a montones
> Aquí tenemos lo mero principal.

(What did those gringo bigfeet think, that they can scare us with cannon? If they have lots of airplanes, we have what really counts.) The deliberately vulgar sexual humor of the American frontier around the time of Andrew Jackson, similarly, may have expressed the feeling of inferiority to European culture. And in present-day United States, according to the thesis, the counterpart to Mexican machismo is found principally among lower-class blacks (Paredes 1971).

Given the approximate length and timing of the fecund period, one can calculate the relation between the frequency of intercourse and the probability of conception. One such model, based on alternative assumptions that the probability of intercourse on a given day does or does not depend on the time since the last coitus, comes to the not surprising conclusion that the probability of conception is greatly influenced by the pattern of intercourse (Glasser and Lachenbruch 1968).

Pregnancy Wastage

Out of every 100 pregnancies in the West, about 2 result in stillbirths, between 10 and 20 in spontaneous abortions, and between 78 and 88 in live births. The lower of the two figures reflects the number of miscarriages typically recorded, but many are not reported and some occur even before the woman is aware that she is pregnant (Potter 1963). Manifestly these proportions depend greatly on the particular society's level of culture, so that the difference in pregnancy wastage is considerable between developed and underdeveloped countries or between the present and the past.

Fecundability

To indicate the sum of all these factors as they affect the probability that a woman will become pregnant, one uses the term **fecundability**, which seems to have been coined by the Italian demographer Gini (1924). He defined it as the probability of conception during any one month in the absence of contraception and outside the periods of gestation and of sterility following a childbirth.

Of course, the concentration on the female—so common in various types of demographic research—is wholly appropriate only in the rare case of a virgin birth. In fact, though not as the term is commonly understood, fecundability is a characteristic of the couple; and with the development of diagnostic skill, it should become possible to devise a reasonably accurate criterion of fecundity by combining measures of the various relevant physical characteristics of the two partners. Indeed, an attempt to construct such an index was made in one study of a sample of subfecund couples. They had all tried unsuccessfully to conceive for a year or more, and none had had any children. Males were divided into two fecundity classes, "good" and "poor," on the basis of a sperm count and several other measurable characteristics of the spermatozoa. Females were divided into two age brackets and, within each, into the same two classes according to such characteristics as the regularity of the menses and ovulation and the state of the Fallopian tubes. As can be seen from Table 6-1, on the basis of this diagnostic differentiation in fecundity, the authors were able to predict to some degree the actual birth performance of various couples. That the age of the wife is a most important factor is evident from these data. When the wife was under 30, the rate of pregnancy was markedly low only when the fecundity of *both* partners was rated as "poor." But if a wife of 30 years or over had "poor" fecundity, the "good" fecundity of her husband did not much increase the probability of pregnancy. It should be stressed that the highest figure in the table, 40 percent, pertains to only a year of exposure of a sample of subfecund couples. According to another study, similarly, the cumulative conception rates over a longer period showed that about 60 percent of the younger and only relatively more fecund patients conceived within 3 years (Lamb 1972). In a study of New Orleans whites, "sterile" or subfecund women had as many children

Table 6-1. Percentage of Pregnancies Within a Year of Exposure, by Diagnosed Fecundity of the Marriage Partners and Age of the Wife

Husband's Fecundity	Fecundity of Wife			
	UNDER 30 YEARS		30 YEARS AND OVER	
	"GOOD"	"POOR"	"GOOD"	"POOR"
"Good"	40	23	18	8
"Poor"	25	3	16	4

SOURCE: John MacLeod *et al.*, "Correlation of the Male and Female Factors in Human Infertility," *Fertility and Sterility*, **6** (1955), 112–143. Copyright American Society for the Study of Sterility.

as the fully fecund; among Negroes the difference was only between 2.38 and 3.32 children, respectively (Harter 1970). A very small proportion of these unexpected offspring, it is true, had been adopted or were stepchildren. But with the downward trend in family size among the general population and, on the other hand, the considerable improvement in treating subfecundity, there has been a convergence of family sizes of the two categories. In other words, in a modern population subfecundity has little or no effect on the overall reproduction.

The Fecundity of Populations

A reproductive potential can be assigned to individuals, somewhat more realistically to couples, or, at least in theory, to populations. Since it is possible to designate each couple's approximate fecundity, one could add up these figures for any population and get a measure of its biological potential; but this has never been done. Two approximations are commonly used, the incidence of sterility (and, sometimes, of subfecundity) and the recorded fertility of populations that are presumed not to practice contraception (e.g., Smith 1960).

The rather common assumption that deliberate contraception is more or less limited to modern Western societies, so that among either primitives or preindustrial civilizations fecundity is equivalent to the recorded fertility, can be challenged on a number of grounds (see pp. 379–380, 415–416). A good example is an analysis of a 19th-century isolated Swedish population "without family limitation." Among married women aged 15–39 years, the 12 percent that had no children (or their husbands) were deemed to be sterile; the proportion varied from 2 percent of the women who had married at ages 15–19 to 20 percent of those who had married at ages 30–39 (Hyrenius 1958). As Carlsson (1966) has shown, however, the variation among preindustrial communities itself suggests that some were systematically controlling births. Of the almost 300 judiciary

A Dutch couple and their children (*Copyright Anfoto, Amsterdam*).

districts (or *harad*) in Sweden, 73 were overwhelmingly agrarian and nonurban still in 1930. As far back as 1860, the considerable range in marital fertility was based *not* on different degrees of urban influence but on quite stable parochial patterns of family formation. "This preindustrial variation strongly suggests that fertility was in fact controlled long before 1880, [and] not only among urban middle-class families." Completed family size in a number of underdeveloped countries has ranged from 5.1 to 6.2 children per woman, 5.9 to 6.6 per wife, and 6.5 to 7.3 per mother (Freedman *et al.* 1959: 412). The maximum family size attainable under optimum conditions, when fecundity is enhanced by modern health measures, is suggested by the fertility of the Hutterites, a fundamentalist sect whose members practice no birth control. They average 10.4 births per couple (Eaton and Mayer 1954: 20. Cf. pp. 90–91).

The rather frightening number of children actually born to some populations, moreover, cannot be taken as the maximum achievable. Guttmacher (1952) deduced from a number of American and English studies that on the average a woman in these countries who nurses all her children can give birth each twenty-four months, and one who does not each nineteen months. According to this timetable, if a girl marries at age 16, if the couple remains married and fecund for 30 years, if there are no fetal deaths, and if all babies are breast-fed, the average completed family size resulting from uncontrolled normal inter-course would be fifteen children (but cf. Henry 1961; Vincent 1961; James 1963).

SOCIAL DETERMINANTS
OF FERTILITY

Fertility is often perceived as the resultant of fecundity and birth control: biology sets a maximum number of possible births, and man contrives by one means or another to reduce it. But such purposive action on the part of the parents—or, in an attempt to work through parents, of churches or governments—is only one subclass of a broader category, **fertility determinants**, which include any of a society's policies, laws, institutions, styles of life, and so on that influence the average family size, whether or not this is their sole or even conscious purpose or generally known effect. A number of analysts have suggested, for instance, that one reason for the lower fertility in cities is that the competitive diversions of urban life result in a lower incidence of marital coitus. In an instance like this, the persons involved may be completely unaware of the cause–effect relation. Another example would be the factors, whatever they may be, that determine the "proper" age at which to marry. In this case, while the effect on fertility is patent, this is not necessarily the purpose of the behavior pattern.

Deviant Sexual Practices

The "total sexual outlet," to use Kinsey's term, includes intercourse with objects unlikely or unable to conceive—a prostitute, a person of the same sex, an animal, an imagined partner. Such relations absorb in the aggregate a large portion of the total sexual energy expended in virtually any society, but because some or all are everywhere defined as vice and the moral pressure of the community induces most persons to conform most of the time, these deviant practices are concentrated among a minority of "perverts," experimenting adolescents (masturbation, homosexuality in the United States),[2] and adults lacking a marital outlet (nocturnal emissions, intercourse with prostitutes) or seeking a supplement to such an outlet (intercourse with prostitutes, homosexuality in the Levant). In short, the usual pattern is that these practices represent an addition to marital intercourse rather than a substitute for it, and thus probably do not affect fertility significantly.

Religiously inspired celibacy is a deviancy of a different kind, but also with little effect on population growth. In the United States, of the total of almost 48 million Roman Catholics in 1970, only about 0.5 percent were celibates. According to various surveys, moreover, the shortage of new priests was due

---

[2] Kinsey *et al.* 1948: chap. 21. Of Kinsey's male sample, 37 percent had had some homosexual experience to the point of orgasm, usually during their adolescence, but only 4 percent were exclusively homosexual throughout their lives. Probably no section of Kinsey's work excited more adverse comment than the one on homosexuality; for a balance criticism, see William G. Cochran *et al.*, *Statistical Problems of the Kinsey Report on Sexual Behavior in the Human Male* (Washington, D.C.: American Statistical Association, 1954), pp. 142 ff. and *passim*.

School for young Tibetan lamas in Dalhousie, India. They will remain celibate all their lives (*T. S. Satyan, Camera Press*).

in large part to the potential recruits' opposition to a celibate life. The 1971 Synod of Bishops, assembling in Rome from all over the world, reaffirmed the traditional requirement, but on some of the specific points the vote was close. In Tibet, where the tradition used to be that one male child in three was assigned to the clerical order, celibacy probably did reduce the country's fertility considerably, though even in this extreme case the supposition cannot be proved.[3]

Family Formation

The sex drive is sufficient to induce copulation and thus reproduction, but this biological link between man and woman is almost everywhere reinforced by ethical norms. A society's demographic and cultural persistence depends on the

[3] The gross effect of celibacy on Tibet's population growth would have to be distinguished from that of the widespread polyandry, the high incidence of venereal diseases, and the possibility that fecundity is impaired by the country's extreme altitude. Population estimates before 1950 were most approximate, usually ranging between 1.0 and 1.5 million, and figures released since the Chinese conquest of 1953, though expressed more precisely, are not necessarily more accurate. *Cf.* Leo A. Orleans, "A Note on Tibet's Population," *China Quarterly*, **27** (1966), 120–122.

fact that the physical care, socialization, and social placement of its young are not left to the sometimes haphazard dictates of sexuality alone. The family, in short, is not merely a biological group but one held together also by complementary economic needs, moral codes, and the integrative force of the whole social structure. In particular, the bond between father and offspring, which physiologically is the weakest in the nuclear family, is culturally reinforced by what Malinowski termed "the principle of legitimacy," which designates one man (usually though not necessarily the biological father) as responsible for each infant born into the society. In some societies or subcultures where illegitimacy is relatively common (e.g., portions of Latin America, lower-class blacks in the United States), this lack of a two-adult team working in the interest of their offspring makes socialization markedly less efficient.

While the nuclear family is designated as the basic social unit in all cultures, the wider structures built from this center differ greatly. Incest taboos, all but universal within the nuclear family, are extended to include cousins and other relatives of second and higher degrees according to a number of different patterns; and these various limitations on the choice of a marriage partner reinforce the kind of society from which they derive. Family types and the kind of social structure with which they are generally associated, moreover, may together encourage different levels of fertility (Kingsley Davis and Blake 1956). *A priori* one can assume, for instance, that the relative importance of the family in any society strongly influences its fertility. Although the marital state is the norm everywhere, the pressure to follow it differs according to the social structure. Since in a traditional agrarian setting many wants can be satisfied only through the family, persons are induced to form one early; on the contrary, since the many other industrial–urban institutions make the family relatively less important, there is less pressure on any individual to marry, or to marry early. In the abstract, then, the average age at marriage, to the degree that it is rationally determined, would seem to depend primarily on two factors: how much preparation the two partners need in order to take over adult roles, and how much assistance they can expect.

It is not easy, however, to spell out these plausible generalizations with empirical data from various societies. The few works on the joint family, for instance, do not altogether support the thesis, derived deductively from reasonable postulates, that this type of institution encourages a large progeny (see pp. 414–415). Similarly, the notion that the precarious condition of life among primitive peoples necessitates a compensating high fertility, and thus an early age at marriage, is not wholly validated by ethnographic data (Nag 1962). The shift from tradition that accompanies industrialization is not consistent: India and Ireland, two countries noted for their very low and very high ages at marriage and, related to these, their low and high proportions who never marry, are both in their different ways traditionalist (see pp. 414, 543). And the effect on fertility of such a family type as polygamy is also difficult to measure empirically, in part because one cannot judge whether such marriages include a high proportion of exceptionally virile men and of barren women. According to the best study, the main *raison d'être* of polygyny, to afford the *man* a greater number of offspring, is realized, but *each wife* has fewer children on the average than one in a monogamous union (Muhsam 1956).

More generally, a cross-cultural analysis must be based on data that are neither complete nor wholly comparable. Only eighty-one geographic units (including some nonsovereign districts) provide data on marriages by the ages of bride and groom. These sparse data, moreover, are based on the various definitions of "marriage" in different cultures and, it would seem, on systematically misstated ages in at least some instances. For example, "in some countries there appears to be an abnormal concentration of marriages at the minimum marriageable age and at the age at which valid marriage may be contracted without parental consent, indicating perhaps an overstatement in some cases to comply with the law. Factors which may influence age reporting, particularly at older ages, include an inclination to understate the bride's age in order that it may be equal to or less than that of the groom" (United Nations 1972: 5–14, 49).

Behavior Patterns Within Marriage

The ethical norms by which the family is maintained—for example, the prescription of absolute filial obedience in traditional China or India—may strongly influence attitudes toward family size. The discussion here is restricted to a more direct determinant of fertility, sexual continence other than that intended as a means of birth control.

Virtually all societies impose periods of sexual abstinence within marriage. Many of these are set by female physiology: intercourse is often banned during menstruation, during the gestation period or at least the last portion of it, and for some time after the birth of a child. These taboos generally have little effect on fertility, except perhaps indirectly through promoting the health of the woman or increasing coital incidence when conception is possible. Other prescriptions of periodic abstinence may represent a denial of pleasurable experience, analogous to fasting, during a time when solemnity or mourning is appropriate. Or they may be determined by occasions when the man's virility is deemed to be particularly important (thus, among many primitives during a war and, in our own culture, during the training period of a professional athlete). As many of these miscellaneous bans are enforced by a religious sanction, they may be more important in agrarian than in industrial societies.

It is convenient to exemplify such impositions of sexual abstinence with the traditional practices of China, for in most Western texts the Chinese family is cited as an institution adapted to virtually unlimited procreation. In fact, marital coitus is inauspicious or even dangerous on the first, seventh, fifteenth, twenty-first, twenty-eighth, and twenty-ninth days of each lunar month; on the sixteenth day of the fifth month; during solar or lunar eclipses, the days of equinoxes and solstices; when there is an earthquake, rain, thunder and lightning, great heat, or great cold; after washing the hair, a long trip, heavy drinking or eating; when the man is tired, very excited, too old; during the woman's menstruation, for one month following the birth of a child, and after the woman has reached 40; during twenty-seven months following the death of a parent; permanently after the birth of a grandchild. In various texts only some of these rules are stressed, but books and astrological calendars denoting the auspicious and inauspicious days still circulate today in Taiwan (and, one presumes, possibly still in Mainland China). If all the basic rules are observed, only about a hundred days per year are auspicious for intercourse. In addition, the traditional Chinese family typically uses *coitus interruptus* and an inaccurately based "safe period" deliberately to control conception. Even the enormous stress in Confucian teaching on the overriding importance of male progeny should not lead one to pass over these other determinants of family size (Eberhard and Eberhard 1967).

In traditional China and also, among other civilizations, Hindu India, there has been a widespread belief that semen is a great source of strength and good health, so that men are much concerned about losing too much of it through coitus. Nag (1972) quotes an ethnographic monograph by a physician who had practiced in rural India concerning the many fantasies surrounding the belief. "Celibacy was the first requirement of true fitness, because every sexual orgasm meant the loss of semen, laboriously formed." Not only physical but also moral strength can be accumulated by conserving one's semen. Like Confucianism, therefore, Hinduism also sets many days when marital coitus is forbidden on pain of going to hell, "where dung and urine must be his food"—for example, the eighth and fourteenth days of the half-month, the days of the new moon and the full moon, the day when the sun comes into a new house of the zodiac, as well as during menstrual and postpartum periods.

METHODS OF BIRTH CONTROL

One of the most important social determinants of fertility is **birth control**, or the conscious use of any practice that permits heterosexual intercourse while reducing the likelihood of conception. The term thus includes not only the use of mechanical or chemical contraceptives but also such practices as "withdrawal" and the "safe period," for the important factor is not the means used but the intention to control conception. Indeed, some of the most interesting of recent analyses have been those rather few studies showing that persons who feel "powerless," unable to control anything else, also do less to try to control conception (e.g., Groat and Neal 1967, 1970; Bauman and Udry 1972).

Why are [lower-class Negro women] not more strongly motivated to limit their families? In good part, . . . they are not motivated because they do not believe they have much chance of success; lack of hope reduces the likelihood of making a serious effort, particularly in the context of a marital relationship in which they cannot expect close cooperation with their husbands. The end result of such a situation, having children without specifically wanting them, merely confirms the self-conceptions they have developed of being moral, hard-pressed, hapless creatures [Rainwater 1965: 233].

What may be the commonest method of birth control throughout the world is the simplest, **coitus interruptus**, or male withdrawal just before ejaculation. This was said to be "the most popular, widely diffused method of contraception, ... probably nearly as old as the group life of man" (Himes 1936: 183–184). It requires no preparations or appliances, costs nothing, is available at all times. It has, however, the disadvantage that it requires the male to be strongly motivated enough to frustrate his desire at the moment of highest excitation. We should expect to find, therefore, that *coitus interruptus* is less frequently practiced in societies or societal sectors where the economic and social responsibility for the child is borne by the mother or the broader kin group, rather than mainly or entirely by the father.

The postnatal mode of "birth control," **infanticide,** however barbarous by modern Western standards, also goes back immemorially. Moral compunctions aside, infanticide has the disadvantage of exposing the mother to pain and risk to no purpose, but it is also the only method of controlling family size that permits a selection among offspring. Wherever infanticide is practiced, female infanticide is the rule (cf. p. 67), supplemented by the elimination of defective and unhealthy offspring and those undesirable by reason of some magical (e.g., multiple births) or social (e.g., illegitimacy) factor. Infanticide is thus associated with the higher valuation of males, as in a hunting society (Eskimos), among certain polyandrous peoples (the Toda, a primitive tribe of southern India), and in many of the great agrarian civilizations (traditional China and India and even Japan well into the 20th century, as well as medieval and early-modern Europe). In contemporary Western societies infanticide is a rarity (but see pp. 259–260) not only because of moral and legal sanctions, but also because contraception reduces the number of unwanted children born and when, in spite of contraceptives and abortions, these do arrive, they can sometimes be disposed of by offering them for adoption.

Abortion has also been termed perhaps "the most widely used single method in the world today" to control fertility (Freedman 1965). In many countries the operation is (or was until recently) against the law, and whatever statistics exist are not accurate or complete. Even the connotation of the basic terms is indefinite and in flux. The dictionary definition of *abort* is "to give birth prematurely" or "to cause to be delivered prematurely," but *abortionist* is defined as "one who practices the producing of criminal abortions." The word *abortion* takes on both colorations: as used by physicians it relates to the physiological process, but as used by lawyers it typically refers to a law prohibiting persons from inducing premature birth. The World Health Organization has recommended that the word be avoided altogether and that "fetal death" be substituted for it in all contexts. Principled opponents of abortion, finally, commonly call it "feticide" (the killing of a fetus), which associates the act with homicide, patricide, and so on.

Preindustrial societies, lacking any effective contraception, have often sanctioned some crude form of abortion as a means of controlling births. In industrial societies, with some exceptions (the Soviet Union and its European satellites, Japan after 1945), the typical law used to permit induced abortions only when the mother's life was endangered or under other special circumstances. This does not mean, of course, that no other operations have been performed. According to a summary of several studies in the 1960s, "about one out of every five pregnancies in the United States terminate[d] in illegal abortion" (Bates and Zawadzki 1964: 3). But other analysts found such estimates greatly exaggerated (e.g., on Britain, Goodhart 1973).

Throughout the West the trend in the incidence of abortions has been subject to very rapid change in their legal and medical settings. Britain adopted the Abortion Act of 1967, permitting the operation under a variety of specified social or medical conditions (cf. James 1971), and some seventeen American states passed similar laws. It was estimated that over 200,000 legal abortions were performed in the United States during 1970, and a number of hospitals and clinics combined to set up a Joint Program for the Study of Abortion. According to a report of more than 40,000 records submitted by sixty-four of the participating institutions, the modal patient was a young single white woman, pregnant for the first time. Approximately 21 percent of the abortions were done after thirteen weeks or more of gestation, including 3 percent after the twentieth week. (In a very few cases in New York State, the operation was performed so late in the pregnancy that the fetus survived, and those opposed to the new trend made much of these examples.) More than 10 percent of the women experienced some complications, including many relatively minor ones. The rate of complications varied with the method (with suction, presently the prevalent method, having a relatively low rate), the period of gestation, the status of the patient (whether private or not—a combined measure of social class and type of service), and the patient's age (Tietze and Lewit 1971; cf. Tietze et al. 1973; Tietze and Dawson 1973).

At the beginning of 1973, the U.S. Supreme Court held that the right of a woman to decide herself whether and, within broad limits, even when to terminate her pregnancy was guaranteed by the Constitution. Until a fetus is viable, by the Court's reckoning for the first six or "usually" seven months of gestation, no restriction whatever may be placed on this personal liberty. After viability has been reached, the fetus is not a person "in the whole sense," though the "potential life" may be subject to constitutional protection, depending on how the several states legislate on the issue. In short, during the first six or seven months of pregnancy, abortion must be granted on demand; thereafter, it may be granted if it is required to preserve the health of the mother, appraised by a medical judgment "exercised in the light of all factors—physical, emotional, psychological, familial, and the woman's age—relevant to the well-being of the patient." However one judges the moral issue, the decision was one of the clearest instances of legislation by a judicial body. "Never before in British or American law has a baby in the last stages of pregnancy been so exposed to destruction at the desire of the parent" (Noonan 1973).

Sponges and tampons placed in the vagina go back to before the Christian era. They are still used throughout the world, mainly as improvised contraceptives among the poor. **Douches** are also a frequent household contraceptive.

The **condom**, made of intestines of sheep or other animals, first appeared in 18th-century England. Today's product is of rubber. Since 1938, when the Food and Drug Administration began to control their quality, an estimated 997 out of every 1,000 sheaths sold in the United States have been free from defects. In the early 1960s American production totaled between 720 million and 864 million units per year, of which perhaps a fifth were exported (Tietze 1963).

An important new factor in Western fertility during the second half of the 19th century was the development of improved contraceptive devices. In the 1880s, the **diaphragm** (also called pessary or cervical cap) was invented by Dr. W. P. J. Mensinga, later a professor of anatomy at Breslau. In the following decades a considerable improvement in **chemical spermicides** took place. A diaphragm used with spermicidal jelly or cream was the means that most American physicians and clinics recommended until a decade or two ago. Mechanical and chemical contraceptives were novel in several senses. With their use, the control is put at the beginning of the procreative process, so that the woman's health and life are not endangered by repeated unwanted pregnancies, and Western ethical injunctions against abortion and infanticide can be obeyed. On the other hand, in contrast to continence and *coitus interruptus*, contraceptives permit full expression to one of man's strongest natural drives. The link between the sexual instinct and reproduction, absolute in lower animals and mitigated in primates, is made subject to man's will. These contraceptives, however, have been more or less restricted to industrial societies, for agrarian countries are generally unable or unwilling to either manufacture or import them in sufficient quantities.

The most popular middle-class contraceptive in the United States today is "the pill," a steroid tablet that when taken orally prevents ovulation. **Oral contraceptives** have the prime advantage of convenience and efficiency, as well as some disadvantages. "Probably no drugs have ever aroused such public controversy or been the subject of such sensational journalism. Legislative hearings have added their confusion to the issue. The controversy has become so heated that it is difficult to tell fact from fiction" (Preston 1971). According to two authoritative reviews of research in Britain and the United States, by Preston (ibid.) and Andrews (1971), the number of well based conclusions about possible deleterious side-effects is small. The one more or less solid fact is that the use of oral contraceptives, particularly those containing higher doses of estrogens, raises slightly the incidence of blood clotting. According to one study, thus, deaths from pulmonary embolism or cerebral thrombosis attributable to the use of oral contraceptives by healthy women amounted to 1.3 per 100,000 users aged 20–34, and 3.4 per 100,000 users aged 35–44. Even these very low figures, typical of those from other studies, cannot be accepted without question, since they are generally based on retrospective analyses of relatively small samples. The widespread fear that the use of oral contraceptives might result in cancer was founded on laboratory experiments showing that the same steroid substances, when given to subprimate animals in very large doses over a long period of time, can produce tumors, some of them malignant. The authors of both of the summary articles conclude that there is no valid evidence at present linking oral contraceptives with cancers in humans. Conversely, however, no evidence exists to exonerate them. Perhaps the most reasonable stance was that taken in Britain by the Committee on Safety of Medicines, which in 1972 concluded a 6-year study of the relation between oral contraceptives and cancer. Because of its mainly negative findings, ten new oral contraceptives were approved for sale in Britain. However, the report also recommended that women taking any of the pills should be carefully watched for signs of breast cancer (*New York Times*, October 29, 1972). Other side-effects, such as the nausea that some women report, are less serious or, at least in some instances, apparently not the consequence of the contraceptives (Goldzieher *et al.* 1971). In sum, oral contraceptives are not absolutely safe but, according to the composite findings from the modest amount of research to date, are safer than the pregnancies that would ensue without them or a suitable alternative.

Intra-uterine devices (or IUDs) were first developed in the 1920s by a Berlin physician named Ernst Gräfenberg. They consist of a small ring, loop, Y-shape, or other compressible device, made of metal, silkworm gut, or plastic, which when inserted into the uterus expands to its original shape and holds in place. How it prevents conception is not known precisely, possibly by impeding the implantation of the ovum on the uterus wall. A small proportion of users, differing according to the device used, have reported bleeding or other side-effects, and others have ejected the device, sometimes without knowing it. As an extremely cheap and relatively effective contraceptive, it was used mainly in underdeveloped countries, then also in Japan and Israel, more recently also in the United States and Western Europe. In mid-1973 hearings were held before a congressional committee to investigate whether IUDs should be brought under the control of the Food and Drug Administration (cf. Thomsen 1973). As with oral contraceptives, there is some risk of serious complications (perforation of the uterus, pelvic infection) and even death (estimated at less than 2 per 100,000), but the risks from pregnancy are far greater. Also as with oral contraceptives, the research is inconclusive and the reports are often biased for or against (*Newsweek*, June 25, 1973; Tietze 1965).

Sterilization in females is ordinarily accomplished by salpingectomy, or the cutting or tying of the Fallopian tubes through which ova pass from an ovary. Ordinarily, this is a major operation, but at the time of childbirth it can be performed with minimal added discomfort and danger. Male sterilization, or

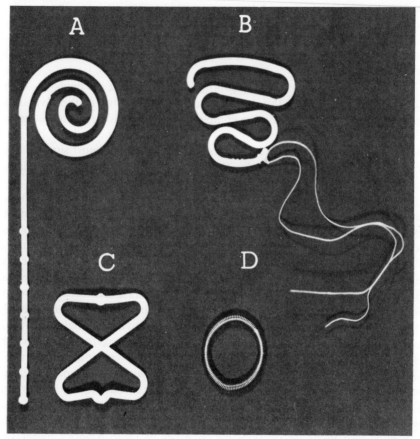

Four of the intra-uterine devices used in various countries (actual size) are: A—Margulies, B—Lippes loop, C—Birnberg, and D—Ball ring (*Planned Parenthood/World Population*).

vasectomy, can be performed expeditiously with only local anesthesia; risk to life is practically nil. In a very small proportion of cases contraception is not achieved, but more generally either type of sterilization is wholly effective. In many societies the operation is hedged in by magical fears and legal restrictions, but in Puerto Rico it is one of the most popular methods of birth control, and it is becoming more prevalent in such other countries as India and, seemingly, the mainland of the United States. According to a very thorough worldwide survey (Presser 1970), the number of sterilizations is considerable in many other countries as well. The major medical and psychological limitation to this mode of contraception is that, with present methods, the patient cannot be assured that the operation can be reversed (ibid.; Johnson 1972; Bumpass and Presser 1972). By those who have all the children they want, however, this permanence—

combined with simplicity and low cost—may be seen as advantageous. For individuals with low or moderate incomes, or for underdeveloped countries looking for a means of drastically reducing high-parity births, sterilization is an especially appropriate method of birth control (Wood 1967; Konotey-Ahulu 1973).

The **rhythm** method, or periodic continence, is based on the ovulation cycle. If coitus is avoided during the short period each month that mature ova are in place, in theory conception can be completely avoided. However, to determine this period precisely is not easy. As used for centuries, the method was based on fallacious physiology; the present system derives from the almost simultaneous work of two physicians, Kyusaku Ogino in Japan and Hermann Knaus in Austria, who correctly placed the fecund period as roughly "fourteen days *before* the onset of menstruation" (Knaus 1964: chap. 6). For women with any but absolutely regular menstrual periods, this is not a precise specification. As rhythm is now used, the woman must be completely continent for a number of months while a trained worker determines how regular the menstruation and ovulation cycles are, and thereafter periodic abstention must be practiced not only during the assumed ovulation phase but also for several days before and after it. Under such circumstances, the method "offers a satisfactory degree of protection against unwanted pregnancy to rigorously selected and carefully instructed wives who, with their husbands, are intelligent and strongly motivated. For others and for those to whom pregnancy would be dangerous, the effectiveness of the method in preventing conception is not considered adequate" (Tietze *et al.* 1951). Many American Catholics begin with rhythm and then, after the birth of several unwanted children, shift to more efficient means. According to a 1965 survey, more than half of the Catholic couples in the United States used methods condemned by the Church (*New York Times*, December 3, 1966; cf. Westoff and Bumpass 1973). Some countries of Latin America honor Dr. Ogino by calling the children inadvertently born to parents using rhythm "oginitos."

For more than a decade research has been under way to use changes in body temperature, in the count of blood enzymes, or in other indicators as a more accurate index of the ovulation cycle (Pincus 1965: 206 ff.). The Human Life Foundation, set up in 1968 with a grant from the American Catholic bishops, is an independent, self-governing, nonsectarian research institute focused on improving methods of family planning with periodic abstinence. During a three-day conference in 1972 that the foundation sponsored jointly with the National Institute of Child Health and Human Development, there was a thorough review of the current status and prospects of what was termed natural family planning. The conclusion was similar to that in the paper published in 1951: "natural family planning is a feasible method of contraception for couples with sufficient motivation and a willingness to accept a measurable risk of pregnancy." More reliable timetables were often not used because of a lack of trained personnel. "All participants agreed that natural family planning must be improved if a significant number of new couples, both Catholic and non-Catholic, are to use it" (Gilder *et al.* 1972).

The effectiveness of contraceptives, as this is ordinarily measured, means not their theoretical efficacy under ideal conditions but how they work when used by a sample of fallible humans. The usual index until recently, sometimes called "Pearl's formula," was the failure rate per 100 years of use:

$$R = \frac{\text{Number of accidental pregnancies} \times 1200}{\text{Total months of use}}$$

The rate of accidental pregnancies, so calculated, varies greatly for different contraceptive methods (Table 6-2). With this formula, however, one gets merely an approximation of the actual proportion of failures. Among any group of women that start to control births, those that discontinue over the following period are not representative of the whole. Those who find the particular method objectionable shift to another. Those that have an accidental pregnancy are presumably less conscientious or less skillful users, possibly more fecund. Month by month, the original mixed population is reduced to a more and more homogeneous residue of satisfied, highly motivated users, including all of the sterile and most of the subfecund. Thus, the rates of accidental pregnancies calculated at intervals of several months start higher than R and gradually

Table 6-2.   Accidental Pregnancy Rates per 100 Years of Exposure, by Method of Contraception

Type of Contraception	Various Studies	Metropolitan American Families	Composite from Six Studies
Oral progestin–estrogen	0.1–1.1	—	—
Intra-uterine devices	0.9–8.5	—	—
Condom		13.8	14
Diaphragm and spermicide		14.4	12
Withdrawal		16.8	18
Spermicide alone		—	20
Rhythm		38.5	24
Douche		40.5	31
Others		30.3	—
No contraception, with lactation	50		
No contraception, no lactation	63		

SOURCES: Gregory Pincus, *The Control of Fertility* (New York: Academic Press, 1965), pp. 297–299; Alan F. Guttmacher, "Fertility of Man," *Fertility and Sterility*, **3** (1952), 281–289.

Table 6-3. A Comparison of Observed and Adjusted Pregnancy Rates

Months of Exposure	Pregnancies per 100 Years of Exposure	
	OBSERVED	ADJUSTED
1–3	29.1	28.8
4–6	11.5	11.6
7–9	5.7	5.7
10–12	3.5	3.5
13–20	1.3	1.5
1–20	10.4	8.3

SOURCE: Robert G. Potter, Jr., "Additional Measures of Use-Effectiveness of Contraception," *Milbank Memorial Fund Quarterly*, **41** (1963), 400–418.

decline to a figure lower than R (Table 6-3, observed rates). To correct this, one can adapt the life-table model to the risk of pregnancy, obtaining the adjusted rates in Table 6-3 (Potter 1967).

Moreover, the efficiency of a contraceptive cannot be equated with the reduction in fertility of the population that uses it. One with an 80 percent efficacy, for instance, reduces fertility by about half. A single failure may result in conception, but a contraceptive success must be repeated at each new ovulation. "A little contraception is a nugatory thing" (Ryder 1965).

SUMMARY

Fecundity, the physiological ability to procreate, varies with a number of physical characteristics, of which the most important are heredity, health, age, the ovulation cycle, lactation, and sex drive. The distribution of these characteristics, particularly age, determines the relative ability of populations to reproduce themselves.

Determinants of fertility include both the deliberate control of births and social usages or institutions that influence birth rates, even with no such purpose and sometimes without a general awareness of the connection. In a traditional society many social wants can be satisfied only through the family, and persons are thereby induced to form one early, while in the institutional complex of an industrial society, on the contrary, the family is relatively less important, and there may be less pressure on any individual to marry, or to marry early. Thus, although the marital state is the norm everywhere, the age at marriage and the proportion married may depend on how important the family is in the social structure.

In Table 6-4 fertility determinants have been divided into four broad types according to the point in the physiology of reproduction they affect: continence,

Table 6-4. Types of Fertility Determinants

Fertility Determinant	Conscious Means of Birth Control	Significant Effect on Fertility
CONTINENCE		
Permanent celibacy	No	Generally not, except possibly Tibet
Premarital	Generally not; yes in Ireland	Yes in Western societies
Intermarital	Generally not	Often
Intermittent	No, except "rhythm"	Yes, particularly "rhythm" and magical rules
VICES	No	Generally not
CONTRACEPTION		
Coitus interruptus	Yes	Yes
Chemical, mechanical	Yes	Yes in industrial societies
Sterilization	Generally yes	Not usually; yes in Puerto Rico, portions of India, etc.
Oral	Yes	Yes, especially in wealthy societies
Intra-uterine devices	Yes	Yes, especially in a few underdeveloped countries
FETAL MORTALITY		
Spontaneous miscarriage	No	Yes
Induced abortion	Yes	Yes, especially in non-industrial countries, the USSR and its satellites, France, Japan, and now also Britain and USA
INFANT MORTALITY		
Unintended	No	Yes in nonindustrial societies, though less than before 1945
Infanticide	Yes	Yes in nonindustrial societies

213

contraception, fetal mortality, and infant mortality (Kingsley Davis and Blake, 1956). For each type the relative importance of deliberate and nondeliberate regulation is indicated. The overriding differentiation that this table suggests— though less now than several decades ago—is that between industrial and nonindustrial societies. An industrial society, first of all, is one with more knowledge of the natural world and better techniques to control it. Infant mortality and, to a smaller degree, fetal mortality are reduced, and effective contraceptives obviate the need for clumsier, more dangerous methods of birth control later in the physiological process. This improved control of both fertility and mortality means that institutional patterns have a less significant influence on the birth rate. Industrialization loosens the social structure of an agrarian society: the sharp increase in both geographical and social mobility means that more and more persons are removed from the influence and control of the extended kin group to the relatively anonymous life of the large city. This very anonymity, however, probably increases the importance of the emotional tie between husband and wife. The normative system of the agrarian society, in particular its religious values, may also be weakened by this loss of its institutional base, which is challenged as well by the higher valuation of rationality in an industrial setting. Fertility, in brief, tends to be associated with social structure, technological standards, and specific prescriptions or taboos; and all three of these determinants have been markedly changed by industrialization.

However, the theory that associates industrial societies and low fertility, while valid up to a point, has important flaws. As we shall note in subsequent chapters, such exceptions as the low fertility of Tokugawa Japan and the unanticipated rise of Western birth rates after World War II have never really been fitted into the general analysis. More pertinently, the assertion that industrialization results in a small-family system, even if absolutely valid, is of little practical value. For in much of the underdeveloped world, the large-family system is efficiently blocking efforts to create an industrial economy.

CITED REFERENCES AND
SUGGESTIONS FOR FURTHER READING

Excellent guidance through the enormous literature on fertility, including elements not covered in this chapter, is provided by Freedman (1961–62), Liu (1968), and Driver (1971).   Many of the works cited here have more specialized bibliographies.

No attempt is made to cover analyses of fecundity by physiologists or physicians, except for the two evaluations of contraceptives by the AMA.   The book by Raymond Pearl (1939), though marginal to the social sciences and in some respects out of date, is still a fascinating pioneer's effort. Good analyses of fecundity by those in the social disciplines include the works by Eaton and Mayer (1954), Kumar (1967), and Harter (1970).

The advances in contraception have been so rapid, and sometimes so technical or controversial, that books and even research papers soon go out of date. The best summary up to the date of its publication was probably the one by Pincus (1965). Some of the journal articles to be recommended are those of Potter, Tietze, Presser (1970), Preston (1971), Andrews (1971), and Goldzieher *et al.* (1971).

There are remarkably few works on the general sociology of fertility. Kingsley Davis and Blake (1956), Meier (1959), and Goode (1963) are interesting. Among the best of the more recent efforts to break new ground are Stycos (1962), Blake (1965), Carlsson (1966), and Easterlin (1970). Hawthorn (1970) gives an excellent review of the field.

AMERICAN MEDICAL ASSOCIATION. COMMITTEE ON HUMAN REPRODUCTION. 1967. "Evaluation of Intrauterine Contraceptive Devices," *Journal of the American Medical Association*, **199**, 141–143.

———. COUNCIL ON DRUGS. 1967. "Evaluation of Oral Contraceptives," *Journal of the American Medical Association*, **199**, 144–147.

*ANDREWS, WILLIAM C. 1971. "Oral Contraception: A Review of Reported Physiological and Pathological Effects," *Obstetrical and Gynecological Survey*, **26**, 477–499.

BALLEW, JOHN W., and WILLIAM H. MASTERS. 1954. "Mumps: A Cause of Infertility," *Fertility and Sterility*, **5**, 536–543.

BARLOVATZ, A. 1955. "Sterility in Central Africa," *Fertility and Sterility*, **6**, 363–364.

BATES, JEROME E., and EDWARD S. ZAWADZKI. 1964. *Criminal Abortion: A Study in Medical Sociology*. Springfield, Ill.: Thomas.

BAUMAN, KARL E., and J. RICHARD UDRY. 1972. "Powerlessness and Regularity of Contraception in an Urban Negro Male Sample: A Research Note," *Journal of Marriage and the Family*, **34**, 112–114.

*BLAKE, JUDITH. 1965. "Demographic Science and the Redirection of Population Policy," in Sheps and Ridley 1965.

BULMER, M. G. 1970. *The Biology of Twinning in Man*. Oxford: Clarendon Press.

BUMPASS, LARRY L., and HARRIET B. PRESSER. 1972. "Contraceptive Sterilization in the U.S.: 1965 and 1970," *Demography*, **9**, 531–548.

CANTRELLE, P., and H. LERIDON. 1971. "Breast Feeding, Mortality in Childhood and Fertility in a Rural Zone of Senegal," *Population Studies*, **25**, 505–533.

*CARLSSON, GÖSTA. 1966. "The Decline of Fertility: Innovation or Adjustment Process," *Population Studies*, **20**, 149–174.

CASTRO, JOSUÉ DE. 1952. *Geography of Hunger*. London: Gollancz.

CHARLES, ENID. 1936. *The Menace of Under-population*. London: Watts.

CUTRIGHT, PHILLIPS. 1972. "The Teenage Sexual Revolution and the Myth of an Abstinent Past," *Family Planning Perspectives*, **4**, 24–38.

DAVIS, KATHARINE BEMENT. 1929. *Factors in the Sex Life of Twenty-two Hundred Women*. New York: Harper.

*DAVIS, KINGSLEY, and JUDITH BLAKE. 1956. "Social Structure and Fertility: An Analytical Framework," *Economic Development and Cultural Change*, **4**, 211–235.

DÖRING, GERHARD K. 1969. "The Incidence of Anovular Cycles in Women," *Journal of Reproduction and Fertility*, Supplement 6, pp. 77–81.

*DRIVER, EDWIN D. 1971. *World Population Policy: An Annotated Bibliography*. Lexington, Mass.: Lexington Books.

DUBIN, LAWRENCE, and RICHARD D. AMELAR. 1971. "Etiologic Factors in 1294 Consecutive Cases of Male Infertility," *Fertility and Sterility*, **22**, 469–474.

DUBIN, LAWRENCE, and RICHARD D. AMELAR. 1972. "Sexual Causes of Male Infertility," *Fertility and Sterility*, 23, 579–582.

*EASTERLIN, RICHARD A. 1970. "Towards a Socio-economic Theory of Fertility: A Survey of Recent Research on Economic Factors in American Fertility," in S. J. Behrman, Leslie Corsa, Jr., and Ronald Freedman, editors, *Fertility and Family Planning: A World View*. Ann Arbor: University of Michigan Press.

EATON, JOSEPH W., and ALBERT J. MAYER. 1954. *Man's Capacity to Reproduce: The Demography of a Unique Population*. New York: Free Press.

EBERHARD, WOLFRAM, and ALIDE EBERHARD. 1967. "Family Planning in a Taiwanese Town," in Wolfram Eberhard, *Settlement and Social Change in Asia*. Hong Kong: Hong Kong University Press.

FORD, CLELLAN S., and FRANK A. BEACH. 1951. *Patterns of Sexual Behavior*. New York: Harper.

*FREEDMAN, RONALD. 1961–62. "The Sociology of Human Fertility: A Trend Report and Bibliography," *Current Sociology*, 10–11, no. 2.

———. 1965. "Family Planning Programs Today: Major Themes of the Geneva Conference," *Studies in Family Planning*, no. 8, supplement.

———, PASCAL K. WHELPTON, and ARTHUR A. CAMPBELL. 1959. *Family Planning, Sterility, and Population Growth*. New York: McGraw-Hill.

GILDER, STANLEY, WILLIAM URICCHIO, and PHILIP CORFMAN. 1972. "Status and Prospects of Natural Family Planning," *Studies in Family Planning*, 3, no. 8.

GINI, CORRADO. 1924. "Premières recherches sur la fécondité de la femme," *Proceedings of the International Mathematics Congress*. Toronto.

GLASSER, JAY H., and PETER A. LACHENBRUCH. 1968. "Observations on the Relationship between Frequency and Timing of Intercourse and the Probability of Conception," *Population Studies*, 22, 399–407.

GOLDZIEHER, JOSEPH W., *et al.* 1971. "A Placebo-Controlled Double-Blind Crossover Investigation of the Side Effects Attributed to Oral Contraceptives," *Fertility and Sterility*, 22, 609–623.

GOODE, WILLIAM J. 1963. *World Revolution and Family Patterns*. New York: Free Press.

GOODHART, C. B. 1973. "On the Incidence of Illegal Abortion," *Population Studies*, 27, 207–233.

*GROAT, H. THEODORE, and ARTHUR G. NEAL. 1967. "Social Psychological Correlates of Urban Fertility," *American Sociological Review*, 32, 945–959.

———, and ———. 1970. "Alienation Correlates of Catholic Fertility," *American Journal of Sociology*, 76, 460–473.

GUTTMACHER, ALAN F. 1952. "Fertility of Man," *Fertility and Sterility*, 3, 281–289.

*HARTER, CARL L. 1970. "The Fertility of Sterile and Subfecund Women in New Orleans," *Social Biology*, 17, 195–206.

*HAWTHORN, GEOFFREY. 1970. *The Sociology of Fertility*. London: Collier-Macmillan.

HENRY, LOUIS. 1961. "Some Data on Natural Fertility," *Eugenics Quarterly*, 8, 81–91.

HIMES, NORMAN E. 1936. *Medical History of Contraception*. Baltimore: Williams & Wilkins.

HULME, HAROLD B. 1951. "Effect of Semistarvation on Human Semen," *Fertility and Sterility*, 2, 319–331.

HYRENIUS, HANNES. 1958. "Fertility and Reproduction in a Swedish Population Group Without Family Limitation," *Population Studies*, **12**, 121–130.

JAMES, WILLIAM H. 1963. "Estimates of Fecundability," *Population Studies*, **17**, 57–65.

———. 1971. "The Incidence of Illegal Abortion," *Population Studies*, **25**, 327–339.

JOHNSON, DIANA S. 1972. "Reversible Male Sterilization: Current Status and Future Directions," *Contraception*, **5**, 327–337.

KINSEY, ALFRED C., WARDELL B. POMEROY, and CLYDE E. MARTIN. 1948. *Sexual Behavior in the Human Male*. Philadelphia: Saunders.

KIPPLEY, SHEILA K., and JOHN F. KIPPLEY. 1972. "The Relation between Breast-feeding and Amenorrhea: Report of a Survey," *Journal of Obstetrics, Gynecology and Neonatal Nursing*, **1**, 15–21.

KNAUS, HERMANN H. 1964. *Human Procreation and Its Natural Regulation*. New York: Obolensky.

KONOTEY-AHULU, F. I. D. 1973. "Medical Considerations for Legalizing Voluntary Sterilization: Sickle-Cell Disease as a Case in Point," Second International Conference on Voluntary Sterilization, Geneva.

KUCZYNSKI, ROBERT R. 1935. *The Measurement of Population Growth: Methods and Results*. London: Sidgwick & Jackson.

KUMAR, JOGINDER. 1967. "Age at Menarche: A Comparative Study," paper presented at the 1967 Annual Meeting of the Population Association of America.

LAMB, EMMET J. 1972. "Prognosis for the Infertile Couple," *Fertility and Sterility*, **23**, 320–325.

LESSING, LAWRENCE. 1966. "Into the Core of Life Itself," *Fortune*, March.

LIU, WILLIAM T. 1968. "Selected Works on Fertility and Family-Planning Studies in the United States, 1960–1967," *Journal of Marriage and the Family*, **30**, 346–366.

MACMAHON, BRIAN, and JANE WORCESTER. 1966. *Age at Menopause, United States, 1960–1962*. National Center for Health Statistics, Series 11, no. 19. Washington, D.C.: U.S. Government Printing Office.

MEIER, RICHARD L. 1959. *Modern Science and the Human Fertility Problem*. New York: Wiley.

MILOJKOVIĆ, ALEKSANDAR D., SERĆO F. ŠIMIĆ, and MEHMED S. DŽUMHUR. 1972. "Migration and Place of Work as a Cause of Male Sterility," in William Petersen, editor, *Readings in Population*. New York: Macmillan.

MONTAGU, ASHLEY. 1957. *The Reproductive Development of the Female, with Especial Reference to the Period of Adolescent Sterility: A Study in the Comparative Physiology of the Infecundity of the Adolescent Organism*. New York: Julian.

MUHSAM, H. V. 1956. "Fertility of Polygamous Marriages," *Population Studies*, **10**, 3–16.

NAG, MONI. 1962. *Factors Affecting Human Fertility in Nonindustrial Societies: A Cross-Cultural Study*. New Haven, Conn.: Department of Anthropology, Yale University.

———. 1972. "Sex, Culture, and Human Fertility: India and the United States," *Current Anthropology*, **13**, 231–237.

NOONAN, JOHN T., JR. 1973. "Raw Judicial Power," *National Review*, March 2.

OPPEL, WALLACE C., and ANITA B. ROYSTON. 1971. "Teen-age Births: Some Social, Psychological, and Physical Sequelae," *American Journal of Public Health*, **61**, 751–756.

PAREDES, AMÉRICO. 1971. "The United States, Mexico, and *Machismo*," *Journal of the Folklore Institute*, **8**, 17–37.

PEARL, RAYMOND. 1939. *The Natural History of Population*. New York: Oxford University Press.

PEREZ, A., P. VELA, R. POTTER, and G. S. MASNICK. 1971. "Timing and Sequence of Resuming Ovulation and Menstruation after Childbirth," *Population Studies*, **25**, 491–503.

PINCUS, GREGORY. 1965. *The Control of Fertility*. New York: Academic Press.

POTTER, ROBERT G., JR. 1961. "Length of the Fertile Period," *Milbank Memorial Fund Quarterly*, **39**, 132–162.

———. 1963. "Birth Intervals: Structure and Change," *Population Studies*, **17**, 155–166.

*———. 1967. "The Multiple Decrement Life Table as an Approach to the Measurement of Use Effectiveness and Demographic Effectiveness of Contraception," in International Union for the Scientific Study of Population, *Proceedings*. Sydney.

———, MARY L. NEW, JOHN B. WYON, and JOHN E. GORDON. 1965. "Applications of Field Studies to Research on the Physiology of Human Reproduction," *Journal of Chronic Diseases*, **18**, 1125–1140.

*PRESSER, HARRIET B. 1970. "Voluntary Sterilization: A World View," *Reports on Population/Family Planning*, no. 5.

*PRESTON, S. N. 1971. "The Oral Contraceptive Controversy," *American Journal of Obstetrics and Gynecology*, **3**, 994–1107.

*RAINWATER, LEE. 1965. *Family Design: Marital Sexuality, Family Size, and Contraception*. Chicago: Aldine.

RETEL-LAURENTIN, ANNE. 1973. "Fécondité et syphilis dans la région de la Volta Noire," *Population*, **28**, 793–815.

RYDER, NORMAN B. 1965. "The Measurement of Fertility Patterns," in Sheps and Ridley 1965.

SAXTON, G. A., JR., and D. M. SERWADDA. 1969. "Human Birth Interval in East Africa," *Journal of Reproduction and Fertility*, Supplement 6, pp. 83–88.

*SHEPS, MINDEL C., and JEANNE CLARE RIDLEY, editors. 1965. *Public Health and Population Change: Current Research Issues*. Pittsburgh: University of Pittsburgh Press.

SMITH, T. E. 1960. "The Cocos-Keeling Islands: A Demographic Laboratory," *Population Studies*, **14**, 94–130.

STYCOS, J. MAYONE. 1962. "A Critique of the Traditional Planned Parenthood Approach in Underdeveloped Areas," in Clyde V. Kiser, editor, *Research in Family Planning*. Princeton, N.J.: Princeton University Press.

THOMSEN, RUSSEL J. 1973. "Statement on Regulation of Medical Devices (Intrauterine Contraceptive Devices)," *Hearings before a Subcommittee of the Committee on Government Operations*, House of Representatives, 93d Congress, 1st Session. Washington, D.C.: U.S. Government Printing Office.

TIETZE, CHRISTOPHER. 1960. "Probability of Pregnancy Resulting from a Single Unprotected Coitus," *Fertility and Sterility*, **11**, 485–488.

———. 1963. "The Condom as a Contraceptive," in Society for the Scientific Study of Sex, *Advances in Sex Research*. New York: Harper & Row–Hoeber.

———. 1965. "History and Statistical Evaluation of Intrauterine Contraceptive Devices," in Sheps and Ridley 1965.

TIETZE, CHRISTOPHER, *et al.* 1951. "Clinical Effectiveness of the Rhythm Method of Contraception," *Fertility and Sterility*, **2**, 444–450.

———, *et al.* 1973. "Mortality with Legal Abortion in New York City, 1970–1972: A Preliminary Report," *Journal of the American Medical Association*, **225**, 507–509.

———, and DEBORAH A. DAWSON. 1973. "Induced Abortion: A Factbook," *Reports on Population/Family Planning*, no. 14, pp. 1–56.

———, and SARAH LEWIT. 1971. "Legal Abortions: Early Medical Complications," *Family Planning Perspectives*, **3**, no. 4.

UNITED NATIONS. 1972. *Demographic Yearbook, 1971*. New York.

*VINCENT, PAUL E. 1958. "Variations de la fertilité selon l'âge: Méthode de recherche: Aperçu de quelques résultats d'enquête," *Bulletin de l'Institut International de Statistique*, **36**, 218–226.

———. 1961. "Recherches sur la fécondité biologique: Étude d'un groupe de familles nombreuses," *Population*, **16**, 105–112.

WASHBURN, S. L., and IRVEN DEVORE. 1961. "The Social Life of Baboons," *Scientific American*, Reprint 614.

WESTOFF, CHARLES F., and LARRY BUMPASS. 1973. "The Revolution in Birth Contro Practices of U.S. Roman Catholics," *Science*, **179**, 41–44.

WILDE, MAX. 1973. "The Barren Wives of Barama," *People*, October, pp. 26–27.

WILLIAMS, ROGER J. 1962. *Nutrition in a Nutshell*. Garden City, N.Y.: Doubleday.

WOOD, H. CURTIS, JR. 1967. *Sex Without Babies: A Comprehensive Review of Voluntary Sterilization as a Method of Birth Control*. Philadelphia: Whitmore.

THE GENERAL DETERMINANTS
OF MORTALITY
AND MORBIDITY

7

Though there are no terms analogous to *fecundity* and *fertility*, the determinants of mortality are also biological and social. As with birth so also with death, the ultimate factor is physiology; no matter how much life is prolonged, man remains mortal. And the social determinants of mortality, as of fertility, can also be classified into two types. "Accidents," "acts of God," and similar concepts are in part cultural constructs, for each society defines for itself the area that is beyond human control. When a consensus reigns that man can do nothing to mitigate it, such a condition or mishap is part of "nature." When this consensus breaks down, the evil is redefined as a "social problem"; antagonistic interest groups polemicize first over whether there can, or may, be a solution, and only then over what it is. Once a new consensus develops that one type of mortality is *not* part of nature, it becomes subject to a process analogous to birth control, comprising all the efforts to reduce, say, a kind of disease. This death control is thus one variable species of the larger genus, the social determinants of mortality, which include also all the social customs and structural elements that affect the death rate, even though this is not their purpose or, in some instances, their known effect.

Like all other forms of life, human beings must have a regular supply of food, and they have a better chance of surviving when living in an environment relatively free of their natural enemies, especially the microscopic organisms that cause various diseases. Each of these truisms, on closer examination, turns out to be less simple than this first statement would indicate. Man's ability to resist infection, or to remain healthy with less than the optimum amount of food, differs greatly from one individual to another; and this variation depends on both biological and social factors. And concerning the less direct influences on the death rate, it is often still more problematic where physiology ends and culture begins.

INDIVIDUAL FACTORS IN MORTALITY

The organism that dies is the individual. A social analysis of mortality, thus, is an attempt to relate general determinants to the distribution in a particular population of the several personal characteristics that, to one degree or another,

220

set each individual's relative chance of dying within a certain period. The most important are reviewed here.

Inherited Longevity

Long life seems to depend to some degree on an inherited capacity, but whenever children remain in essentially the same social and economic situation as their parents, a similar average length of life in the two generations may be due either to a genetic proclivity or to the continued influence of the unchanged environment, or to both. What is inherited, moreover, is not a trait but a predisposition to react in certain ways to various environments, so that if these change, the significance of the inheritance may change with them. Notwithstanding these methodological difficulties—the same that were met in analyzing the heredity of fecundity—the genetic factor in mortality can sometimes be suggested.

Several investigators have studied the average length of life in successive generations of various families in order to see whether a trend is discernible. According to the combined results of a number of such studies, a quarter century ago in the United States a favorable ancestry would have added 2 to 4 years to one's expectation of life from age 25 (Dublin et al. 1949: 117). And in 1915 having long-lived parents supposedly had added 7 more years to one's expectation of life than the utmost that medical science could then achieve (Pearl 1922: 165). A later monograph by Pearl and his wife (1934) is still worth reviewing. Nonagenarians were shown to have a significantly higher percentage of longevous parents than the general population. However, the study hardly attempted to differentiate between biological and cultural influences: in the four-page questionnaire on which the study was based, only two questions related to social variables. More generally, Pearl and other early investigators have been criticized for their methodological flaws; according to a study at Johns Hopkins University, the hereditary element in longevity and mortality seems to be more questionable than Pearl asserted (Cohen 1965). In any case, with each advance in medicine the significance of the hereditary element generally becomes less, and this has been true especially of some of the more notable conquests of genetic deficiencies.

It is known that the incidence of some diseases varies markedly from one race to another (Damon 1969). Although this datum suggests that susceptibility to them may be inherited, here again the evidence is muddied by the difficulty of distinguishing biological from environmental factors. The first meeting of two peoples previously isolated from one another frequently marks in a dramatic way the effect of such race differences. For example, when the whites took measles with them to the South Seas, it was transformed from a relatively minor illness to a raging epidemic; and when Columbus's men brought syphilis to Europe from the West Indies, its virulence was also much greater among this fresh population. Such events may indicate a genetic factor: if the constitutional immunity to any disease originally varies in a population, an epidemic kills off the more susceptible, and the survivors pass on to their progeny their greater

Fugen, a Japanese Buddhist god, patron of those who practice "ecstatic contemplation" in order to live longer. Guimet Museum, Paris (*The Bettmann Archive, Inc.*).

inherent resistance. It may be, however, that sometimes the relative immunity to an endemic disease is acquired not genetically but by a mild, perhaps unrecognized, case of it in infancy or childhood.

In the United States the link between genetic diseases and particular subnations has recently altered the financing of medical research. When Senator Edward Kennedy asserted, for example, that he was convinced that "this country has the ability and the concern to provide the necessary research resources to mount an effective attack against this crippling killer," he was not referring to heart disease or cancer, but to thalassemia major, sometimes called Cooley's anemia. This disease affects no more than perhaps 10,000 to 15,000 persons, but it strikes with devastating selectivity at Italian Americans, Greek Americans, and others originally from the Mediterranean basin, nationalities that are well represented among the Massachusetts electorate. With surprising speed both houses of Congress approved a control program costing $11.1 million. Not to be outdone, Rep. Louise Day Hicks of Boston introduced a bill to set up an institute that would combat dysautonomia, a genetic disease characterized by defective secretion of tears, skin blotching, and poor motor coordination; it is especially prevalent among Jews.

The most prominent of such programs pertains to sickle-cell anemia, which affects only Negroes. About 2 million American blacks carry the gene for this disease, in most cases without being aware of it. When two such carriers have children, one out of every four—or an estimated total of between 25,000 and 50,000 persons—will have sickle-cell anemia. With a deficiency of healthy red corpuscles, the patients are susceptible to infections, failure of the heart or kidneys, and shock. Many die as children, but if they survive to adulthood, the severity and frequency of attacks are often diminished. Before this became a faddish issue, the federal government was spending about $1 million on research. At the beginning of 1971 President Nixon proposed that the figure be upped to $6 million, but Congress, without a dissenting vote in either house, authorized a total of $115 million over 3 fiscal years. The screening program that was set up was opposed by black spokesmen, and others demanded that research funds be given mainly to blacks, irrespective of their capabilities. Even if some of the programs to control these genetic diseases do succeed, medical researchers are generally distressed that one important criterion for allocating federal funding has become the pressure of ethnic blocs.

Sex Differences

Except during their childbearing years, females generally have lower age-specific death rates than males; and in modern Western societies the rule holds without this exception (but see p. 67). The older the age bracket, therefore, the higher the usual proportion of females: in 1970 the sex ratio in the United States ranged from 103.8 for those aged under 5 years to 72.2 for those 65 and over. The contrast between the two sexes' death rates, moreover, has been increasing over the past half century (Table 7-1).

Table 7-1. Ratio of Male to Female Age-Adjusted[a] Death Rates, United States, 1900–70

Year	White	Nonwhite
1900[b]	110	106
1910[b]	116	107
1920[b]	108	97
1930[b]	121	109
1940	132	117
1950	148	125
1960	164	136
1970[c]	175	163

[a] Standardized on the basis of the age distribution of the United States population in 1940.
[b] States in the Death Registration Area.
[c] Provisional.
SOURCE: Metropolitan Life Insurance Co., *Statistical Bulletin*, December 1971.

Some of the sex difference in mortality is almost certainly innate. The much larger proportion of males who die in infancy (and probably also in the uterus, though here the evidence is not firm) cannot be explained by any systematic variation in the environment. Although for most adults it is difficult to distinguish biological from environmental influences, such a differentiation was made by comparing the mortality of Catholic monks and nuns engaged principally in teaching. The life patterns of these two groups were very similar, especially in the absence of sex-linked activities most relevant to mortality—namely, childbearing for females and dangerous occupations and strains for males. In these culturally standardized groups the divergence in expectation of life by sex was greater than in the population as a whole, and it had also been increasing over the past decades, suggesting that biological factors are more important than social–cultural ones in effecting the differentiation in death rates by sex. The author proposed as a hypothesis:

> *Under conditions of equal stress* women may be no more resistant to the *infectious* and *contagious* diseases than men—perhaps even less so—and . . . the gains which women have been making over men in this century may be chiefly bound up with a greater constitutional resistance to the *degenerative* diseases. . . . The growing advantage of American women over men is a function of the transition from conditions when infectious and contagious diseases were the main causes of death to conditions wherein the degenerative diseases play this role [Madigan 1957].

Most analysts agree, thus, that many more males than females die of heart disease, though the pattern is confused by the changing and sometimes ambiguous criteria of diagnosis (Klebba 1966: 16; Tracy 1966). In the white population, the age-specific death rate from cancers, as another example, was 65 percent higher for females in 1900, about equal between the two sexes in 1947, and 21 percent higher for males in 1963. Between 1960–61 and 1966–67 deaths from cancers increased by 5 percent for males, but fell off by 1 percent for females (Metropolitan Life Insurance Co. 1972). The principal reason would seem to be that the diagnosis and cure of cancers most frequent among females, breast and uterus, improved faster than of those most frequent among males, digestive system and lungs.

Senescence

The most important characteristic related to innate susceptibility to death is age. The power of self-renewal and the ability to reproduce the species, the principal features that distinguish living beings from inert matter, both decline with advancing age. One index of this process is the rate at which body lesions heal. If persons of various ages sustain a wound of 20 square centimeters, under otherwise identical conditions this will heal in twenty days on the body of a child of 10 years, in thirty-one days with a person of 20, in forty-one days with one aged 30, in seventy-eight days with one aged 50, and in a hundred days with one aged 60 (DuNoüy 1936: 154–155). A child of 10 thus typically cicatrizes a wound at five times the rate of a man of 60. Among the other physiological functions that have been intensively studied—for instance, the amount of physical work one can do, the speed of nerve conduction, the amount of acid secreted by the mucous membranes of the stomach, the maximum rate at which one can breathe, the cardiac output, and the maximum filtration rate of the kidney—in each case there is an annual loss of only about 1 percent of the initial capability by around age 30.

Yet by the time we have lost about 40 percent of [such] a function, ... the probability of death will have increased almost a thousandfold. ... It is not yet possible to explain fully the decline in physiological function with age, the real key to the aging process. It is clear that, if function did not change with time, the probability of dying would be a constant [Strehler 1967].

In fact, the probability of death of human beings doubles about every 8 or 9 years in the age range from 35 to 90.

However, the rate at which one ages, whether by these or any other indices, varies widely according to life conditions. A person of any particular age combines the effects of physiological senescence, which we may take as the same for the whole of the species, with those of his own particular experience. It would be useful to separate these two elements into what has been termed *chronologic age*, or the number of years lived, and *biologic age*, or the person's relative functioning capacity as determined by the sum of genetic and environmental factors, including his chronologic age (Benjamin 1947). Although this distinction cannot yet be finely drawn, an approximation is sometimes attempted. Whether or not a life insurance company grants a policy to any applicant, for instance, depends not only on the probability that someone of his chronologic age will die but also on such rough indications of his biologic age as his parents' longevity, his personal and medical history, his present state of health, and his occupation.

It is now possible to retard senescence to some degree, and this control may improve during the coming decades. In that case, as the proportion of aged in the population increases, the physiological and psychological characteristics typical of elderly persons might also change. We still know rather little about how much the biological process of senescence can be altered by a favorable medical, social, and psychological environment.

A priori, it is often assumed that aging is accompanied by measurable and meaning-ful mental deterioration, and this negative assumption is the starting point for much of the research in gerontology. An examination of the literature reveals that most information has been obtained from senile inmates of mental institutions and homes for the aged and that the findings from such studies have been generalized to the aged at large. ... [There has been a general] failure to control pertinent variables which may have far more influence on the experimental findings than age *per se* [Arnhoff 1955].

This appraisal, completely valid when it was written some two decades ago, has remained pertinent.

Class in human anatomy at the Ohio Medical University, Columbus, c. 1900 (*Ohio Historical Society Library*).

How far can the conquest of nature go? When will the remarkable advances in medical science reach the impassable barrier? The utopian vision of Condorcet—an era free from disease, in which old age and death could be postponed indefinitely—has recently attained a certain respectability from well known personages who extrapolated from the growing number of actual achievements to a dream of continuing and unlimited progress. Opposed to this rosy perspective is one that emphasizes the rise of new ailments associated, actually or supposedly, with modern industrialism: cancers from smoking and x-rays, ailments from polluted air and water, allergies from detergents and synthetics, and so on. Some responsible physicians, moreover, have begun to express concern about the indefinite "medicated survival" of those too senile or too deficient physiologically ever to be able to function.

DIFFERENTIALS IN MORTALITY BY AGE

In any society, then, a person's age and sex are important factors in the probability that he or she will die within that year; and with the convergence of some other differentials, these physiological determinants have become relatively more significant in recent years. The **crude death rate**, or the number of deaths in a year per 1,000 persons in the midyear population, thus has the same virtues and limitations as the crude birth rate (see pp. 83–84): it is easy to calculate from data often available, but it blurs the effects of age and sex distribution on the level of overall mortality. For a more refined analysis, age- and sex-specific rates can be calculated, and in a number of particular instances this is usual.

The shape of the curves in Figure 7-1, showing the age-specific death rates for

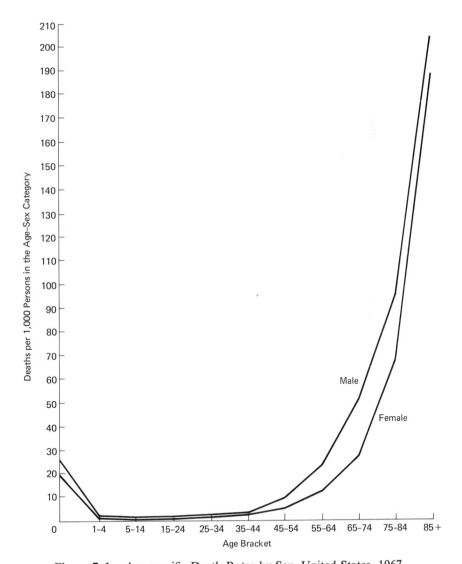

Figure 7–1.   Age-specific Death Rates by Sex, United States, 1967

SOURCE: U.S. National Office of Vital Statistics, *Vital Statistics of the United States, 1967,* vol. II, Part A (Washington, D.C.: U.S. Government Printing Office).

males and females, is characteristic. Wherever modern death control has not been fully established, infancy and early childhood are dangerous periods; but for those who survive them the death rate is relatively low until senescence becomes a significant factor, at the age of 40 or 50. As the greatest advance has been in the control of infectious diseases, the sharpest drop was in the mortality of infants and young children. Even so, the probability of dying during infancy is still greater than during childhood or early adulthood. That is to say, some sort of U-shape or J-shape describes the age-specific death rates of all cultures, no matter how primitive or advanced. If one imagines superimposed on such a curve another one representing age-specific fecundity—that is, inverted to ∩—one can see why age structure can have so great an effect on population growth: the young adults who are most likely to have children are also the persons least likely to die within a given year.

Infant and Fetal Mortality

In any analysis of general mortality, it obviously makes good statistical sense to segregate so important a class of deaths as those of the very young and consider it separately. This is done in the **infant mortality rate**, or the number of deaths between birth and age 1 year per 1,000 live births.[1] For the United States in 1968, for example, it was:

$$\text{Infant mortality rate} = \frac{\text{Deaths at age 1 year or under}}{\text{Live births}} \times 1,000$$

$$= \frac{76,263}{3,501,564} \times 1,000 = 21.8$$

Infant mortality is high relative to that at other ages for two reasons—because a baby, if barely born alive, may not be able to remain so very long, and because any baby, even if born healthy, is especially susceptible to disease. These two causes of infant mortality have been termed **endogenous**, referring to what might be considered a postponed fetal death, and **exogenous**, referring to a death that differs from general mortality only in the age of the person affected (Bourgeois-Pichat, 1946–51). The differentiation is important in that it separates causes of death difficult or impossible to control at the present level of medical knowledge (inherent weakness of the mother or fetus, extraordinary difficulty in delivery, etc.) from those that can be prevented by modern medicine and public-health

---

[1] Since both the numerator and the denominator designate these categories during any one calendar year, the ratio does not really indicate the risk of dying before one's first birthday, for some of the children born in any calendar year die the following year but still before they are a year old. That is to say, the infant mortality rate assumes a constant fertility, and a large and rapid change in the number born will introduce a significant error (see Moriyama and Greville 1944). In most cases, however, the rate as conventionally calculated is satisfactory without adjustment. An age-specific death rate for those aged 1 year and under would be still less accurate, because the census count of young babies is generally less complete than the registration of births.

measures. The same distinction can be made in statistical terms, though only approximately, by separating deaths during the first 28 days from those during the rest of the first year. The first class, **neonatal mortality**, represents that part of infants' deaths that until a few years ago was regarded as the irreducible minimum. More recently, marked improvements in obstetrics have cut down the critical period to the week after birth, or less.

According to the definition recommended by the World Health Organization (WHO), **fetal mortality** is "death prior to the complete expulsion or extraction from its mother of a product of conception, irrespective of the duration of pregnancy; the death is indicated by the fact that after such separation the fetus does not breathe or show any other evidence of life." The WHO also suggested that fetal mortality be classified into four groups according to the duration of the gestation period, as follows: early fetal deaths, twenty weeks or less; intermediate fetal deaths, twenty to twenty-eight weeks; late fetal deaths, twenty-eight weeks or over; and gestation period not classifiable. The term *stillbirth*, according to this recommendation, would be abandoned, and stillbirths would be classified either as late fetal deaths or neonatal deaths, according to whether any sign of life was evident after the complete expulsion of the fetus.

As is implied in the distinction between endogenous and exogenous infant mortality, deaths shortly before and shortly after birth may not be different in principle. The two types are grouped together as **perinatal mortality**, meaning deaths between the time when the fetus becomes viable to the time after birth when prenatal causes of death are no longer operative. Although usage differs, it may be that the most useful definition of perinatal mortality includes that between the twentieth week of gestation and the first week after birth.[2]

As the reader may have found this multiplicity of definitions confusing, it will be well to review the principles underlying them, for on these there is more agreement. An effort is being made to refine the natural notion, which has been the basis of most demographic rates, that human life begins with birth. In one sense, life begins with conception, and from that point on one can designate several stages of development: (1) a viable fetus, (2) birth, and (3) a time after birth when endogenous causes of death are no longer significant. The precise designation of these three stages must be somewhat arbitrary, and conventions have not yet been universally accepted. Even *birth*, which is less vague than the other two, must be very precisely defined to avoid confusion; the variation at one time in the meaning of *stillbirth* used to make international comparisons of infant or especially of neonatal mortality somewhat dubious.

Another reason for the differences noted in definitions is that all these rates represent something of a compromise between an abstract ideal and the measure

[2] Unfortunately, there are two ways of calculating the perinatal mortality *rate* (cf. Dorn 1956). The usual method is to relate the appropriate sum of prenatal and postnatal deaths to the number of live births, as in calculating the infant mortality rate. It makes better sense, however, to calculate perinatal mortality as a proportion of the total number of viable fetuses conceived, whether or not they survive till after the birth.

most useful with the data actually available. If five out of six fetal deaths still remain unreported, it can be questioned whether it is worth while using a refined rate incorporating such incomplete data, but some analysts nevertheless prefer to do so.

The Life Table

A **life table** (or, as it is sometimes called, a mortality table) shows what the probability is of surviving from any age to any subsequent age, according to the age-specific death rates prevailing at a particular time and place. This information is the basis of life-insurance rates, and the life table also has a much wider range of uses. It is assumed, as a convention, that 100,000 babies are all born on the same day, and the experience of this cohort is followed until its last surviving member finally dies. The life table does not show what will happen, but what *would* happen if the age-specific death rates remained constant. When the control of death is rapidly improving, as generally in the modern period, life tables have to be revised frequently. Sometimes they are calculated for a period of several years in order to eliminate the effect of short-term fluctuations.

A full life table, by single years of age, gives more detail than is needed for most purposes. It is often abridged as in Table 7-2, which will be used in a brief explanation of each of the columns.

The figures in column 1, the year of age, are precise; that is, 0 is the date of birth, 1 is the date of the first birthday, and so on. The first of the two figures (which sometimes is the only one given) is denoted in subsequent column headings by x.

The figures given in column 2 ($_nq_x$) are *not* the usual age-specific death rates but the probability of not surviving from one birthday to the next one given in column 1. (The highest probability, absolute certainty, is conventionally denoted by unity; but in order to avoid a long series of decimals, the figures in column 2 are sometimes, though not in this example, multiplied by 1,000.) Thus, of those born 2.02 percent do not survive to age 1; of those alive on their first birthday, 0.34 percent die before they reach precise age 5; and so on.

Column 3 (l_x) is the number surviving at precise age x given in column 1. The convention, as we have noted, is to begin with a cohort, called a **radix**, of 100,000. From this figure, each successive one is obtained by subtracting the number who died in the previous interval, obtained from column 4 ($_nd_x$). Thus

$$100,000 - 2,016 = 97,984$$
$$97,984 - 331 = 97,653$$
$$97,653 - 205 = 97,448$$

and so on.

Column 4, the number dying, is calculated for each row by multiplying the number that survived (column 3, l_x) by the proportion that die during the interval (column 2, $_nq_x$). Thus

$$0.0202 \times 100,000 = 2,016$$
$$0.0034 \times 97,984 = 331$$
$$0.0021 \times 97,653 = 205$$

and so on. Note, However, that because of the rapid decline in the rates during the first 5 years of life, the first two figures in column 4 are not precisely the products called for by the formula.

Columns 5 and 6 both refer to what is called a **stationary** (or life-table) **population**, i.e., one that does not change in either its age composition or its size. While the assumptions underlying a life table are unrealistic (no immigration or emigration, the birth each year of a new cohort of 100,000, and no change in the age-specific death rates), the concept of a stationary population is often useful as a model. Much can be learned by comparing this hypothetical population with a real one that shares some of its characteristics.[3]

Column 5 ($_nL_x$) gives the number of persons in the stationary population in the age interval indicated in column 1. A census taken of a population based on the assumptions of the life table—100,000 births annually and age-specific deaths in accordance with column 2—would on any date show, say, 481,825 persons aged 20–25. Column 6 (T_x) gives the total number of years lived by the survivors in the year x and all subsequent years. It is derived from column 5 by calculating a cumulative total, beginning with the highest age. For age 85 and over, thus, the two columns have the same figure, and successive figures are calculated as follows:

$$122,292 + 140,305 = 262,597$$
$$262,597 + 213,104 = 475,701$$
$$475,701 + 297,788 = 755,489$$

and so on.

Column 7 (^0e_x) gives the average number of years of life remaining at the beginning of the age interval or, in the usual phrase, the average life expectancy from age x. Column 6 (T_x) gives the *total* number of years to be lived by all the survivors in the cohort, and column 3 (l_x) gives the number of survivors in the cohort at each age; the average is calculated by dividing the total years by the number of persons. Thus,

$$7,085,472 \div 100,000 = 70.9$$
$$6,987,283 \div 97,984 = 71.3$$
$$6,596,139 \div 97,653 = 67.5$$

and so on. This, for our purposes the most important column in the life table, measures mortality conditions independent of the effect of age structure. The first figure in the column, the expectation of life at birth (70.9 years in this case),

---

[3] Compare the definition of stable population, pp. 92–93. Note also the discussion of the net reproduction rate, pp. 88–90.

Table 7-2. Abridged Life Table for the Total Population, United States, 1970

Age Interval	Proportion Dying	Of 100,000 Born Alive	Number Dying During Age Interval	Stationary Population		Average Remaining Lifetime
PERIOD OF LIFE BETWEEN TWO EXACT AGES STATED IN YEARS (1)	PROPORTION OF PERSONS ALIVE AT BEGINNING OF AGE INTERVAL DYING DURING INTERVAL (2)	NUMBER LIVING AT BEGINNING OF AGE INTERVAL (3)	NUMBER DYING DURING AGE INTERVAL (4)	IN THE AGE INTERVAL (5)	IN THIS AND ALL SUBSEQUENT AGE INTERVALS (6)	AVERAGE NUMBER OF YEARS OF LIFE REMAINING AT BEGINNING OF AGE INTERVALS (7)
x to $x + n$	$_nq_x$	l_x	$_nd_x$	$_nL_x$	T_x	$°e_x$
0–1	0.0202	100,000	2,016	98,189	7,085,472	70.9
1–5	.0034	97,984	331	391,144	6,987,283	71.3
5–10	.0021	97,653	205	487,712	6,596,139	67.5
10–15	.0020	97,448	198	486,793	6,108,427	62.7
15–20	.0055	97,250	535	485,022	5,621,634	57.8
20–25	.0074	96,715	713	481,825	5,136,612	53.1
25–30	.0072	96,002	690	478,310	4,654,787	48.5
30–35	.0086	95,312	821	474,602	4,176,476	43.8
35–40	.0123	94,491	1,161	469,745	3,701,876	39.2
40–45	.0187	93,330	1,745	462,599	3,232,130	34.6
45–50	.0288	91,585	2,640	451,806	2,769,531	30.2
50–55	.0436	88,945	3,876	435,607	2,317,725	26.1
55–60	.0660	85,069	5,611	412,091	1,882,118	22.1
60–65	.0956	79,458	7,600	379,204	1,470,027	18.5
65–70	.1386	71,858	9,960	335,334	1,090,823	15.2
70–75	.1976	61,898	12,234	279,788	755,489	12.2
75–80	.2885	49,664	14,330	213,104	475,701	9.6
80–85	.4035	35,334	14,257	140,305	262,597	7.4
85 and over	1.0000	21,077	21,077	122,292	122,292	5.8

SOURCE: U.S. Public Health Service, *Vital Statistics of the United States, 1970*, Vol. 2, Section 5: *Life Tables* (Washington, D.C., 1973), Table 5-1.

is usually the best index of mortality whenever a crude death rate is not sufficiently accurate.

Since the average life expectancy at birth is based in part on the considerable number who die during the first year, it indicates an expected life shorter than at any subsequent age. Indeed, some of the figures given in column 7 are smaller, but they indicate the expectation of life from year x, which increases for each row. Obviously, the total years lived is the sum of each figure in column 7 and the appropriate value for x. Thus—

$$70.9 + 0 = 70.9 \text{ total years lived}$$
$$71.3 + 1 = 72.3$$
$$67.5 + 5 = 72.5$$

and so on. The **median expectation of life** (or what is sometimes called the "probable lifetime") is always greater than the average. It is the age to which a person has a 50–50 chance of living or, from birth, the age at which the original cohort of 100,000 will be reduced to 50,000. In this example, then, at age 71 (the *average* life expectation) about 60 or 61 percent of the original cohort is still alive (column 3); the median expectation is close to 75 years.

The life table given in Table 7-2 is for the total population of the United States in 1970. Since there are appreciable differences in mortality by sex, race, occupation, and other structural dimensions, it is usual to calculate separate life tables for the appropriate segments of the population when this additional information is needed. For example, in 1970 the life expectations from birth for the designated sectors of the population were as follows:

Male, total	67.1
White	68.0
Nonwhite	61.3
Female, total	74.8
White	75.6
Nonwhite	69.4

Adult Male Mortality

The most puzzling trend of the recent past is that in most advanced countries the mortality of middle-aged and elderly men has *risen*. In Norway, for example, the expectation of life from age 40, which had been 35.5 years in 1951–55, fell to 34.6 years in 1961–65. The same decline is to be seen in most of the other countries of Northwest Europe (cf. Hansluwka and Smith 1971) and in the United States (Klebba 1971). The typical greater longevity of females that was noted earlier could hardly explain why male rates should go up.

No explanation would appear to be fully satisfactory. If it were an excess mortality of veterans, one would not find the same situation in countries whose experience of war had been very different. If automobile accidents were the cause, France ought to be included among the countries with a rising mortality; moreover, these accidents affect least men of advanced age [Henry 1972].

Preston (1970) considered three hypotheses to explain the reversal of past progress, rejected two of them, and argued persuasively for the third: (1) While it is likely that with the earlier sharp decline of infant and child mortality some persons with inherently weak constitutions were kept alive, the evidence suggests the contrary: cohort death rates at younger and older ages are *positively* correlated. In any case, why should the less robust survivals be only males? The explanation, then, is not the genetic deterioration of the stock. (2) And while it has often been alleged that stress associated with modern civilization, especially for adult males who have moved up the social ladder, results in more deaths from heart diseases, the evidence is shaky in every particular. The economic growth and urbanization concomitant with *early* development are probably far more "stressful" than the relatively comfortable life in fully advanced economies. Such broad changes as modernization or its various components, presumed to effect so vague a condition as stress, do not constitute a satisfactory explanation. (3) The diseases that most distinguish male from female deaths among adults include lung cancer, arteriosclerotic heart disease, bronchitis, and emphysema (a disease of the lungs characterized by the distention and rupture of their air sacs). All of these have been connected through exhaustive epidemiological studies to cigarette smoking. Indeed, the causal inference from this association has been challenged (e.g., Brownlee 1965; Greenberg 1969), but seemingly with less and less assurance. According to one effort to pinpoint the relation, in 1962 smoking accounted for almost half of the sex difference in life expectancy between the ages of 37 and 87, and for three-quarters of the increase in this difference between 1910 and 1962 (Retherford 1972).

Cigarette smoking clearly represents the most plausible explanation of excessive adult male mortality considered here. The mortality risk from smoking is un-equivocal; smoking has increased several-fold since 1930; older male mortality is much more responsive to the habit than that of other groups; the three diseases most closely associated with smoking affect the mortality deviations in nearly the same ratio and at the same level as is predicted by prospective studies of cigarette smokers. . . . Rather than representing victimization by nature or by hostile social forces, the current abnormal rates of dying among older males appear to be largely self-imposed and avoidable [Preston 1970].

With the alarming rise in the incidence of diseases plausibly assigned to cigarette smoking, public officials have sought means of guarding the community's health without either infringing on individuals' civil rights or damaging unnecessarily the countries' economies. In Britain, the Royal College of Physicians recommended that cigarette advertising be curbed, and some time later it was abolished altogether from that country's commercial television. The Danish National Society for the Combating of Cancer recommended that advertising be cut down or abolished and that smoking in public be restricted and forbidden to minors. The U.S. Surgeon General issued reports officially affirming the scientific indictment of cigarettes, and the industry was first required to place a label on each package warning against its contents and then was forbidden to advertise on television. In Sweden a leading tobacco company found a way to promote health and sales simultaneously. According to its full-page advertisements, "The further in on the cigarette you smoke, the less filter effect you get. Therefore extinguish more than 1 centimeter before the filter, ... or 2–3 centimeters without filter" (Corwin 1972). Particularly but not exclusively in the United States, those who would like more stringent regulations are probably deterred by the manifest failure of Prohibition and, more recently, of the criminal sanctions against marijuana.

After a setback during the 1960s, the American tobacco industry is again booming, selling more than ever before in its history. In 1971 the total was 538 billion cigarettes; in 1972, according to preliminary estimates, it was 554 billion. The principal reason, it would seem, is the very rapid growth of the cohorts aged 25 to 44, who constitute the main market for cigarettes.

There has been an increase in heavy smoking among women, and it may be that the sex difference in adult mortality will be eliminated not by a decline in male rates but by a rise in female ones. Studies suggest that increased cigarette smoking has increased the incidence of coronary heart disease among females (Spain *et al.* 1973), as well as that of perinatal mortality when the women are pregnant (Rush and Kass 1972).

HEALTH AND MORBIDITY

The death rate and the average life expectancy, certainly meaningful indices of a population's level of health, were almost the only ones ever used until the 1930s. It is true, of course, that there can be a wide discrepancy between either of these and morbidity. Some diseases with virtually no effect on mortality may bring about a considerable decline in efficiency, a high degree of discomfort, or other impairments of well-being. The common cold, for instance, is not a direct cause of death, but it is a leading reason for absenteeism among school children and industrial workers. Trachoma, an infection of the eye prevalent in the Near East, is another example; those afflicted with it and not treated eventually become blind, but they do not die appreciably earlier than their uninfected neighbors. Blindness is one example of what is called a "permanent total disability"; the very term emphasizes that life can continue for a period with well-being markedly below the optimum level. It would be useful, then, to devise other measures of health in order to supplement mortality statistics. Any alternative would be difficult to apply with the grossly inadequate morbidity data presently available, but presumably this deficiency could be remedied in the future. A more significant obstacle is to define "health" in terms that make it possible to collect meaningful statistics. Death is a precise event, occurring only once for each person and at a time that can be specified fairly exactly. It is hard, on the other hand, even for the person affected or for a physician always to distinguish a morbid condition precisely from acceptable good health.

Because of the differences between illness and mortality or fertility, the measures of disease frequency are not merely counterparts of the standard demographic rates. One index is the **prevalence rate,** or the number of persons diagnosed as having the disease on a given day (or other time period) per unit of the total population. Such an instantaneous count of patients, however, passes over the fact that disease is not an event but a process, so that those designated as ill at a particular time typically range from beginning cases to convalescents. For many purposes, therefore, it is preferable to calculate an **incidence rate**, or the number of new cases during a specified period per unit of the midpoint population. The prevalence varies as the product of the incidence and the average duration from the disease's onset to its termination; or, if one can reasonably assume that the incidence and duration remain constant over the relevant period, then

$$P = I \times D$$

In other words, a change in the prevalence may reflect a change in the incidence, the duration, or both.

Two other differences from the usual demographic rates should be noted. Since births and deaths are relatively far more common than most diseases, the constant used to remove a long series of decimals from disease rates is not 1,000 but rather 100,000 or even 1,000,000. More significantly, crude rates are more usual in epidemiology than in demography; though susceptibility to different ailments generally varies considerably by age and sex, most of the standard compilations include only rates per unit of the total population.

Cross-cultural comparisons of health are precarious. Illness or disability is typically penalized by the loss of one's function, income, prestige, and so on, but the severity of the penalty varies greatly from one society to another. More-over, each individual's state of health depends in part on his personality: he may imagine diseases and produce real symptoms, or he may ignore actual impairments and function efficiently in spite of them. Such difficulties have been aggravated by the tendency to conceptualize "health" not merely negatively, as the physical condition that inhibits mortality, but positively. The World Health Organization has made the distinction with a utopian fervor that hardly fits in with its important tasks in the real world: "Health is a state of complete physical, mental, and social well-being, and not merely the absence of disease or infirmity."

Self-healing

One of the principal characteristics of life, as we have noted, is the power of self-regeneration. A malfunctioning of the body from whatever cause triggers a curative process, which may or may not dispel the malady irrespective of any therapy. A most convincing test of this assertion is the behavior of wild animals— as recounted, for example, in a classic paper by Schultz (1939). Of 118 skeletons of wild adult gibbons that he collected, 42 (or 36 percent) had fractures that had healed in varying degrees of restoration to the normal state.

It seems that not many fractures can end fatally and that they do not, as a rule, incapacitate the apes sufficiently to lead to death by starvation or through capture by their many enemies. . . . In spite of [their] manifold afflictions they manage to survive. All this in populations of apes in their natural environment . . . casts serious doubt on the often assumed prevalence of health and normality in nature and on the efficiency of natural selection.

The power of self-therapy, though general to all living beings, varies in any species from one individual or population to another, a fact that can be best illustrated by considering the differential resistance to infectious diseases. If a germ is not prevented from entering the body by public-health measures, and if it is not destroyed in the body by medicaments, will the germ cause an infection, and if so how virulent will it be?

Every infectious disease is the result of a struggle between two variables—the pathogenic powers of the bacteria on the one hand, and the resistance of the subject on the other—each of these again modified by variations in the conditions under which the struggle takes place. . . . The concepts "resistance," "immunity," and "susceptibility" are relative terms which can never be properly discussed without consideration of all modifying conditions [Zinsser et al. 1940: 106].

These modifying conditions may include an inherited resistance to the particular disease, whether on the part of the race or of the particular individual. They may include an acquired immunity, the consequence of either an inoculation or an earlier case of the same disease. The will to live may be relevant. Variations in the environment, as in the temperature, may reduce the body's resistance. The virulence of the germ itself may be markedly increased or weakened by, for example, passage through the body of an animal of a different species.

These changes in the relation between germs and their human hosts have resulted occasionally in the disappearance of diseases, and in the appearance of new ones. Bubonic plague, which devastated Europe in the 14th century and struck again in the 17th, has not occurred in epidemic proportions anywhere in the Western world for more than a century. Leprosy, similarly, was all but unknown in Europe by the 17th century. On the other hand, the first reliable evidence of infantile paralysis in epidemic form dates from 1840, and there are other examples of new maladies. Sometimes a terrifying plague appears briefly and then completely and inexplicably vanishes. The most remarkable instance is the so-called English sweating disease, of which there is no mention either before 1485 or after 1552, but which during that short time disorganized English society (Zinsser 1935: chap. 5; cf. Shrewsbury 1964).

During the past decade or two, there have been some extraordinary developments in immunology (Sigel and Good 1972). A young child, the son of an Air Force officer, was admitted to the Walter Reed Hospital some nineteen times over 4 years suffering from one serious infection after another. His blood should have been producing great amounts of gamma globulins, or antibodies; but when it was tested none at all could be detected. In fact, the boy was prone to recurrent severe infection just because his body was incapable of manufacturing this particular protein, and the trouble stopped when it was regularly injected. In 1952, when Dr. Ogden C. Bruton published a paper on this case, it was the first reported instance of disease due to a defect in the body's immune system. Since then, medical researchers have diagnosed more than 3,000 cases of various defects in patients' ability to produce antibodies, which usually could also be supplied artificially.

More recently, the concept of immunity has developed beyond the prior understanding of the power of a person to resist an *infection*. The body's immune system, it is now believed, rejects not only invading micro-organisms but anything that it recognizes as alien: transplanted skin or organs, for example, or any of the substances that cause allergies, or the malignant cells that the body itself generates in nonviral cancers. According to this theory, susceptibility to both infectious and noninfectious malignancies varies according to the individual's relative efficiency in producing immunity. This ability declines with age, which is why most who contract almost any type of cancer are well along in years. If the present research in a half-dozen academic disciplines converges into a fundamental advance in our knowledge of immunity, in other words, it may mean a cure for some of today's more important diseases.

Psychotherapy

However the body goes about building up resistance to disease or debility of any kind, this process can be stimulated by psychological means. A placebo, or an inert substance prescribed merely to please the patient, is often therapeutic. Indeed, all treatments possess placebo components, for one variable in the effectiveness of any treatment is the authority with which it is prescribed and thus the faith that the patients have in it. For example, of two groups of persons treated with a placebo for bleeding ulcers, a *physician* told the first that they would undoubtedly get relief from this new medicine, and a *nurse* told the second that they were being given an experimental medicine of unknown efficacy. Some 70 percent of the first group, but only 25 percent of the second, responded favorably to the treatment. The trust that a patient places in a doctor, moreover, is likely to depend in part on characteristics irrelevant to his skill—his ethnic or religious affiliation, for instance. The placebo effect depends also on the patient's suggestibility, which seems to vary with his religiosity but to be independent of his intelligence (Liberman 1961).

The placebo phenomenon explains the sometimes amazing results of pseudo-therapies based on superstitions or false notions of physiology. Among most primitive peoples, the cause of illness or death, as of any other misfortune, is typically sorcery, and the cure is therefore magic. Similar beliefs are common in Latin America and also among Mexican Americans, who are likely to see an illness as the work of a witch and particularly chronic ailments as punishment for sin (e.g., Saunders 1954). Nor are belief systems that compete with modern medicine necessarily dissipated in the middle classes of an advanced country (Frank 1963; Torrey 1972). Most Christian Scientists, who hold that all disease is "error," are moderately well educated, as well, it would seem, as many of the patients of chiropractors and naturopaths. Certainly those who spend months or years in psychoanalysis have good incomes, and they are not dissuaded by the fact that the practitioners of the several schools have patients who produce dreams, fantasies, and childhood recollections that substantiate contradictory theories. Since not even the most efficient medicine eliminates all pain and death, such competing faiths will never lack clients. Yet it is probable that superstitions of this type are more common among primitives and, in advanced societies, among the lower classes; thus, a *portion* of the social–economic differences in mortality probably derives from the greater readiness of the better educated to accept soundly based medical advice. "Medicine is part of the value system of the higher social classes" (Watts 1966).

Cross-cultural comparisons of health and illness are also hampered by the differential delimitation of "nature." Among all peoples there is a tendency to confuse a statistical norm with a medical–ethical one. States of the body that a Western physician defines as morbid, in part because scientific controls have reduced their incidence, others perceive as part of everyday life, requiring neither explanation nor remedial action.

[Among] the Bantu of South Africa . . . coughs and colds, fever and rheumatism need no explanation. They come and go, are treated by the patient himself or by the family members with what we should call domestic remedies, and little is thought of them. . . . Even such a disease as yaws in its primary and secondary stages does not call for interpreting. It is so common that the Mano merely says, "Oh, that is not a sickness, everybody has that" [Sigerist 1967: 125–126].

Food and Health

The supply of nutrients obviously relates to health, but the specification of this relation, however one makes it, is not simple. The most obvious question in a demographic context, whether there is (and will be) enough food to feed the world's people, presumably would depend on only three sets of data: the growth of the population, the total production of all types of food and its probable development, and the minimum requirements per person. As we note in other contexts, the first two terms are extremely difficult to establish within a satisfactory range of error, and the third—which one might take to be the easiest—can also not be set with any assurance.

Food nourishes man in two ways, by supplying fuel for energy and warmth, and by providing the material with which the body is built, maintained, and regulated. Food requirements, thus, include both a certain amount and a certain balance among various types of nutrients. Either a deficiency in quantity or an imbalance has as its successive consequences a less than optimum well-being, sickness, and ultimately death.

An individual's calorie requirements depend on a large number of variables: among others, his age, sex, basal metabolism rate, body type, occupation and avocation, the climate he lives in, and the type of clothing he wears. In a sizable population, of course, most of these factors balance out. The Committee on Calorie Requirements of the FAO used an arbitrarily defined "Reference Man," 25 years old, healthy and moderately active, weighing 65 kilograms (or about 144 pounds), and living in a moderate climate. This man was said to require 3,200 calories per day. The Committee that came to this conclusion had no disagreements among its fourteen members. "The report is, in fact, orthodox. It is unlikely that substantial changes in its recommendations will be necessary—at least in this century" (Passmore 1963). There are, unfortunately, other orthodoxies. A moderately active, mature person, living in a temperate climate, requires, according to the Food and Nutrition Board of the U.S. National Research Council, 3,000 calories per day for a 154-pound man (thus, 200 calories less for a man weighing 10 pounds more) and 2,400 per day for a 123-pound woman (MacLeod and Sherman 1951). One cannot extend these "recommended allowances" (*not* "standards") to other countries without considering temperature and other factors, and whether they should be accepted even for the United States is disputed. A different authority recommends 18 calories per pound of ideal body weight for the average woman (or 2,214 calories per day for the 123-pound woman, rather than 2,400) and 21 calories per pound for the man (or 3,234 per day for the 154-pound man rather than 3,000) (Goodhart 1964). According to still another authority, "the orienting philosophy behind [the National Research Council's recommendations] has been to emphasize the frequency and danger of undernutrition and to promote an abundance of food supplies" (Keys 1951b). Actually, in Keys's view, caloric inadequacy is a far less significant cause of ill health in Western countries, even in times of economic depression, than overeating and obesity, and various surveys indicate that eating less than the recommended allowance is not only not detrimental but, within limits, beneficial to health.

Energy requirements are ordinarily provided mainly out of carbohydrate staples, which in wealthy countries are strongly reinforced by fats and proteins. These latter are also essential nutrients, though in what amount is not known. "It is not yet possible to state definitely a reasonable allowance for fat in the diet" (Goodhart 1964). "The minimum daily protein requirement . . . can be approximated only crudely" (Albanese and Orto 1964).

The optimum ingestion of other nutrients is no more determinate. The etiology of the major food-deficiency maladies (scurvy, pellagra, goiter, beriberi,

Albert Szent-Györgyi von Nagyrapolt (1893–), Hungarian chemist, who in 1937 won the Nobel Prize for his discovery of vitamin C (*World Health Organization*).

and others) was established before the end of the 19th century, but only in the sense that certain rough dietary rules were stipulated. Scurvy, for example, was clearly described in the Ebers papyrus, which dates from about 1500 B.C. Its cause was established by Dr. James Lind of the British navy in a classic experiment: out of a dozen equally scorbutic members of one ship's crew, he subjected two to each of the six cures then in vogue, and the pair who were given oranges and lemons made a dramatic recovery. The active ingredient of citrus fruits was identified as vitamin C, or ascorbic acid, only in the 1920s, and about 5 years later it was synthesized. Scurvy is now a rare disease in developed countries, but it is probable that much subclinical ascorbic-acid deficiency exists.

The term *vitamin* was coined by Casimir Funck, a Polish chemist, in 1912. As they were isolated one after the other, vitamins were labeled with successive letters; but with the rapid expansion of knowledge only a few of these original names have remained an adequate denotation. "Vitamin B," for example, turned out to be a complex of a dozen substances. The vitamins and a number of minerals are essential elements of human diet in small amounts. With some of them—for example, calcium and vitamins A and C—the consumption of larger amounts than the minimum required seems to confer corresponding increases in well-being, while with others this apparently is not the case. Moreover, the interaction among food elements means that the correct amount of any one varies also according to the amounts of others consumed (Harte and Chow 1964).

Whether malnutrition short of starvation contributes substantially to mortality is not entirely clear. One view, to which the FAO holds in most of its publications, is that the inadequacy of food in poor countries has always contributed directly to a high death rate. But apart from infancy and childhood, when the continued growth of the body depends on good nutrition, and from certain ailments, the most important of which is tuberculosis, whether the susceptibility to disease is *directly* affected by malnutrition remains an open question. "Definitive statements on the relationship of specific dietary components to resistance to infection are difficult to make" (Axelrod 1964). On a mass scale, the effects of famine can seldom be distinguished from those of social disorder. In Nazi-occupied Holland and Greece, where the mass starvation was not accompanied by a general breakdown of society, the typical association of famine and epidemic was lacking, whereas the 1946 diphtheria epidemic in Germany, on the other hand, seemed to affect the well nourished American occupation troops as severely as the underfed German population (Keys 1951a).

The Measurement of Health

It is possible to compile morbidity data from existent medical records, as collected by physicians, clinics and hospitals, or health-insurance plans of one type or another. However, the incidence of disease as measured in medical records depends on the existence of physicians to generate the data; and in this sense the more medical facilities that are available, the higher is the incidence and thus the lower the apparent level of health. A second, less obvious fault of such records is that the unit is typically the case rather than the person; thus, those who go to more than one physician during a year or who are hospitalized more than once can be interpreted as several patients. Efforts have been made in several countries to establish a system of record linkage, which would not only eliminate such duplications but also clarify the physiological or social connections between various illnesses. No country has a full system, but Britain has gone some distance toward it (cf. Acheson 1968).

If the state of health is to be measured independently of the differential access to medical care, the index cannot be a by-product of existent records. It was not until recently, however, that special health surveys were made. In 1949, in an effort to improve the morbidity statistics then available in the United States, a National Committee on Vital and Health Statistics was established, and a number of important local studies of health conditions followed. In 1956 Congress passed an act under which the U.S. Surgeon General is authorized to gather data regularly on the health of the whole country's population. In this continuing Health Household-Interview Survey, the concept of morbidity is defined as "a departure from a state of physical or mental well-being, resulting from disease or injury, of which the affected individual is aware." Similarly, *illness* is defined as a period when a person considers himself to be "sick" or "injured."[4] However inaccurate these subjective reports may be in one sense, they undoubtedly reflect fairly precisely the behavior of the respondents. A man must be quite sick or disabled before he is deprived completely of choice of action; short of that state, the way he himself defines his health is an important determinant of what he does. In 1972, thus, when the incidence rate of acute illnesses or injuries was estimated to be 219.7 per 100 persons, this resulted in an average of 9.5 days of restricted activity and 4.1 days in bed (U.S. National Center for Health Statistics 1973).

These subjective reports are supplemented, moreover, by a periodic Health Examination Survey made by physicians of a sample of the population. Its purpose is not to prescribe therapy but only to provide comparable national estimates of the incidence of important diseases for which accurate and simple diagnostic criteria exist. Because of its high cost, it must be limited to a relatively small sample, which is further restricted by the fairly large number of persons who refuse to be examined.

During the few years that the National Health Survey has been in existence, it has only begun to grapple with the difficult conceptual and methodological problems inherent in its work. As the third element of its function, the service conducts its own methodological studies (e.g., Cartwright 1959, 1963). To measure precisely and for the whole country the economic cost of illness and disability, for instance, requires a new combination of several types of non-comparable data—gross national product, attitude surveys, physicians' diagnoses, census classifications, and concepts specific to the survey itself (cf. Nagi 1969).

Another measurement of health, both mental and physical, is made by the U.S. Army when it checks whether those drafted are suited for combat duty—thus, for a function considerably more demanding than many civilian occupations. The population so tested, moreover, is not wholly representative of young American males, because it excludes those who volunteered and were accepted (who are qualified by definition) and those deferred on grounds other than health (who may be qualified in higher proportion), but the results were disturbing nonetheless (Table 7-3).

Since data on health are by their very nature inferior to those on mortality or fertility, some demographers have been reluctant to extend the domain of their discipline to include this new territory. Others have argued persuasively that the study of such qualitative characteristics of populations is just as important as the analysis of quantatitive data (Feldman 1958; Linder 1967). Most of the analysis of diseases still remains, however, in the related discipline of epidemiology, which is typically more closely allied to medicine than to the social sciences.

[4] U.S. Public Health Service, *Origin and Program of the U.S. National Health Survey* and *Concepts and Definitions in the Health Household-Interview Survey*, Series A-1 and A-3, Health Statistics from the U.S. National Health Survey, Publications 584-A1 and 584-A3 (Washington, D.C.: U.S. Government Printing Office, 1958).

Table 7-3. Percentage Distribution of Combined Results of Pre-induction and Induction Examinations of Draftees, by Army Area, United States, 1965

Army Area	Quali-fied	Disqualified				
		TOTAL	FOR ADMIN-ISTRATIVE REASONS	MENTALLY[a]	MEDI-CALLY	MENTALLY AND MEDI-CALLY
First[b]	48.9	51.1	1.7	16.4	30.5	2.5
Second[c]	51.8	48.2	1.4	16.5	26.8	3.5
Third[d]	40.4	59.6	0.9	33.9	21.5	3.3
Fourth[e]	47.3	52.7	1.2	23.5	25.4	2.6
Fifth[f]	58.0	42.0	1.7	12.0	27.4	0.9
Sixth[g]	51.4	48.6	3.3	12.1	31.8	1.4
Outside Zone of Interior[h]	34.1	65.9	1.8	46.8	12.8	4.5

[a] Includes both those who failed a mental test known as the Armed Forces Qualification Test (or its Spanish equivalent), and those classified in an aptitude test as "Trainability Limited."
[b] Connecticut, Maine, Massachusetts, New Hampshire, New Jersey, New York, Rhode Island, Vermont.
[c] Delaware, District of Columbia, Kentucky, Maryland, Ohio, Pennsylvania, Virginia, West Virginia.
[d] Alabama, Florida, Georgia, Mississippi, North Carolina, South Carolina, Tennessee.
[e] Arkansas, Louisiana, New Mexico, Oklahoma, Texas.
[f] Colorado, Illinois, Indiana, Iowa, Kansas, Michigan, Minnesota, Missouri, Nebraska, North Dakota, South Dakota, Wisconsin, Wyoming.
[g] Arizona, California, Idaho, Montana, Nevada, Oregon, Utah, Washington.
[h] Alaska, Hawaii, Guam, Mariana Islands, Puerto Rico, Panama Canal Zone, and Virgin Islands.
SOURCE: U.S. Army, Office of the Surgeon General, *Supplement to Health of the Army*, "Results of the Examination of Youths for Military Service, 1965," **21** (July 1966), 25.

THE ETIOLOGY OF MORTALITY

The concept of *cause* is slippery, and death is typically the effect of a number of factors, both intrinsic and extrinsic. Before we look at the way that mortality statistics are actually compiled, it may be useful to consider again some of the inherent complexities.

Let us suppose that a number of persons were in an accident and sustained identical injuries. Two-thirds recovered after being treated. In most types of analysis this fact alone would make us hesitate in describing the accident as the "cause" of death for the others. Of those that died, let us suppose, one was an elderly man, whose lesions healed too slowly; one had a chronically weak heart; one had had an appendectomy, the scar of which released a thrombus; one, a Negro, was denied admission to the nearest hospital. For all these persons the accident would be listed as the immediate cause of death; and of the other circumstances and those like them, some might be included as contributory factors, but many would not be mentioned or even known to the person compiling the statistics.

A child had died of diphtheria. At the clinical pathological conference, the pathologist demonstrated the organs, showed the culture of diphtheria bacilli isolated from the lesions and expressed regret at the relatively uninstructive program of the morning. The case was so straightforward, the cause of death so evident. An elderly physician in the audience then rose to say that he did not believe the real cause of death had been brought out at all; that he had other information. The birth of the child had never been reported to the responsible authority. As a consequence the family was not visited at the child's first birthday, as was the practice of the Health Department, to present to the father and mother the advantages of immunization against diphtheria and the means to obtain that service. The child was not immunized. The cause of death was social, and [not only] biological.[5]

In 1958 a British doctor issued a death certificate listing as the cause "carcinoma [cancer] of bronchus due to excessive smoking." The registrar refused to accept so unorthodox a juncture of "natural" and social causes, and there had to be an inquest. The coroner, an unrepentant smoker, declared that the physician had been attempting "to judge the habits of [his] fellow men. That must be the province of the coroner." His verdict was death from natural causes. Two years later an American sued Liggett & Myers Tobacco Company for $1,250,000, charging that from smoking the company's Chesterfield cigarettes he had developed cancer in one lung. As experts did not then agree on the relation between smoking and cancer, the judge directed the jury to return a verdict in favor of the company; but a new suit was filed on essentially similar grounds.

When an inhabitant of Los Angeles with a weak heart died during one of the city's recurrent bouts of smog, the physician called the smog "a significant condition contributing to death." The coroner refused to accept the certificate. "Los Angeles smog is not a disease," he declared, and added: "We would be opening the gates to litigation against the Board of Supervisors if we accepted such a certificate."

These examples could be multiplied, but these should suffice to indicate the range of difficulties that would ensue if a serious attempt were made to list the main cause, the ancillary causes, and the significant contributing factors leading to each death. The analytic problem can perhaps be clarified by recalling the several types of causation that Aristotle and the medieval schoolmen used. The proximate factor, the **efficient cause** of death, is what physicians have generally concentrated on. Their job is to keep their patient alive, not to understand the whole social context of dying.

Lawyers, on the other hand, are concerned with the **formal cause** of death. From their point of view, all deaths are divided into "violent" and "natural,"

[5] John E. Gordon, "Discussion," in Milbank Memorial Fund, *Trends and Differentials in Mortality*, New York, 1956, pp. 43–47.

depending on whether they do or do not involve the law. For some types of death this differentiation is of such practical importance that it is given by physicians on death certificates.

The **material cause** is the particular susceptibility of the organic system affected. In the same sense that one can say a house burned down because it was built of combustible material, so one can say that a person died of enteritis only because his intestinal tract was too weak to withstand an attack of the germs (cf. Pearl 1922: chap. 2). If the building had been made of concrete, or if the man's intestines could be made more resistant to this disease, then neither the arsonist nor the germ could have caused any damage. With the transplantation of organs, a branch of surgery likely to develop in the next decades, this classificatory principle may acquire a new relevance.

The **first cause** of death, on the other hand, is that ultimate beginning of a chain of occurrences that eventually led to the one being analyzed. In such a view, any death takes place only because unicellular animals, which in a favorable environment live until they split into two,[6] began to evolve into more complex beings.

The **final cause** of anything is its plan or design. A building has two stories, for example, because it was so drawn in the architect's blueprint. Although it is difficult outside a religious context to discuss such a teleological principle with respect to natural phenomena, one can say that death does have a function in nature. It makes possible the evolution of the species by removing one generation and replacing it with its slightly different successor. Natural selection can operate only because living beings are not immortal.

In the recent period our concept of the cause of death has in some cases been broadened to include much more than the proximate factor. This is particularly manifest when legal responsibility for automobile accidents, e.g., is now shared by the manufacturers of defective vehicles. If Los Angeles indeed were held responsible for deaths resulting from its smog—the legal principle that the city's coroner found abhorrent and ridiculous—this would provide the most efficacious goad imaginable to corrective action by public agencies.

Even physicians are re-examining their conception of *death*. A prestigious committee of the Harvard Medical School recently suggested that "responsible medical opinion is ready to adopt a new criterion for death to have occurred in an individual sustaining irreversible coma as a result of permanent brain damage." For with the new techniques available, it is possible in some cases to restore "life," as defined by the present criteria of persistent respiration and continua-

---

[6] Contrary to what one might suppose, thus, death is not the inevitable concomitant of life, but only of specialized forms of life. In a favorable environment unicellular bodies have been observed to live for millions of generations with no diminution of vitality; and to the degree that the word has any empirical meaning, they can be called "immortal." In the laboratory a portion of a chicken's heart has been kept alive much longer than the natural span of the species. The question arises, then, whether the present link between specialization and death is inevitable, or whether a suitable change in environment might alter it.

tion of the heart beat, even when there is not the remotest possibility that the individual will ever recover consciousness. As the committee sees it, the problem is a purely medical one, for the legal definition of death, whenever a question arises, depends on the testimony of a physician. The medical question is how to determine whether a brain is *permanently* nonfunctioning even when other organs continue to function; the main symptom is a flat electro-encephalogram (Beecher *et al.* 1968).

The Certification of Death

In all advanced countries the fact and circumstances of each death are certified by a physician or other responsible person; and the statements made on these death certificates, as compiled in central statistical bureaus, become the raw material of demographers' analyses of mortality. In the United States there have been nine editions of the standard death certificate, the first in 1900 and the latest in 1968; over the period the number of items increased from forty-two to sixty, with additional information on the cause of death an important component of the expansion. Under the law the certificate must ordinarily be signed by the physician who last attended the deceased. But when a person dies without prior medical attention, or his identity or the cause of his death is unknown, or violence was involved or suspected, in most states the form must be signed by a medical examiner or coroner. It is estimated that about one-fifth to one-quarter of all certificates fall under this stipulation. The two forms differ only slightly, with the basic information the same on both.

The accompanying photograph shows the usual death certificate, in this case for a death in Ohio. Note that the cause of death is divided into three categories: "immediate cause," "conditions which gave rise to immediate cause," and "other significant conditions." *A priori*, one might suppose that many diagnoses entered on a death certificate would be mistaken: the very fact of death means that, for one reason or another, the doctor has not been able to carry out his function of keeping the patient alive and facilitating his recovery. And when diagnoses are checked by a postmortem autopsy, this supposition is often verified. According to various studies, half of the cases of terminal pulmonary embolism (a blood clot in the lungs) were wrongly diagnosed *ante mortem*, a third of the cases of gastro-intestinal hemorrhage, fifty-three out of eighty-five cases of abscess of the liver, eighty-three out of a hundred cases of syphilitic aortitis (inflammation of the main artery resulting from syphilis), forty out of forty-three cases of sacroidosis (a chronic infectious disease of unknown cause), and so on. In short, an "antemortem diagnosis is frequently refuted, clarified, modified, or elaborated by postmortem examination" (Prutting 1967). As one might expect, a long series of medical discoveries derived from knowledge gained from autopsies (Prutting *et al.* 1968). Even so, except for deaths that come under a medico-legal authority, few autopsies are performed. Opposition to them

OHIO DEPARTMENT OF HEALTH
Reg. Dist. No. _____
Primary Reg. Dist. No. _____
DIVISION OF VITAL STATISTICS
CERTIFICATE OF DEATH
State File No. _____
Registrar's No. _____

DECEASED

DECEASED—NAME *First*	*Middle*	*Last*	SEX	DATE OF DEATH *(Month, Day, Year)*
1.		2.	3.	

RACE *White, negro, american indian, etc. (Specify)*	AGE—*Last birthday (years)*	UNDER 1 YEAR *Mos.* *Days*	UNDER 1 DAY *Hours* *Min.*	DATE OF BIRTH *(Month, Day, Year)*	COUNTY OF DEATH
4.	5a.	5b.	5c.	6.	7a.

CITY, VILLAGE, OR LOCATION OF DEATH — 7b.   INSIDE CITY LIMITS *(Specify yes or no)* 7c.   HOSPITAL OR OTHER INSTITUTION—NAME *(If not in either, give street and number)* 7d.

STATE OF BIRTH *(If not in U.S.A., name country)* 8.   CITIZEN OF WHAT COUNTRY 9.   MARRIED, NEVER MARRIED, WIDOWED, DIVORCED *(Specify)* 10.   SURVIVING SPOUSE *(If wife, give maiden name)* 11.

SOCIAL SECURITY NUMBER 12a.   WAS DECEASED EVER IN U. S. ARMED FORCES? *(Yes, no, or unknown)* 12b.   *(If yes, give war or dates of service)*

USUAL RESIDENCE WHERE DECEASED LIVED. IF DEATH OCCURRED IN INSTITUTION, GIVE RESIDENCE BEFORE ADMISSION.

USUAL OCCUPATION *(Give kind of work done during most of working life, even if retired)* 13a.   KIND OF BUSINESS OR INDUSTRY 13b.

RESIDENCE—STATE 14a.   COUNTY 14b.   CITY, VILLAGE OR LOCATION 14c.   INSIDE CITY LIMITS *(Specify yes or no)* 14d.   STREET AND NUMBER 14e.

PARENTS

FATHER—NAME *First* *Middle* *Last* 15.   MOTHER—MAIDEN NAME *First* *Middle* *Last* 16.

INFORMANT—NAME 17a.   MAILING ADDRESS *(Street or R.F.D. no., city or village, state, zip)* 17b.

CAUSE

PART I.   DEATH WAS CAUSED BY: *(ENTER ONLY ONE CAUSE PER LINE FOR (a), (b), AND (c))* 18.   APPROXIMATE INTERVAL BETWEEN ONSET AND DEATH

IMMEDIATE CAUSE (a)
DUE TO, OR AS A CONSEQUENCE OF:
Conditions, if any, which gave rise to immediate cause (a), stating the underlying cause last (b)
DUE TO, OR AS A CONSEQUENCE OF:
(c)

PART II. OTHER SIGNIFICANT CONDITIONS: *Conditions contributing to death but not related to cause given in part I (a)*   AUTOPSY *(Yes or no)* 19a.   IF YES were findings considered in determining cause of death 19b.

ACCIDENT, SUICIDE, HOMICIDE, OR UNDETERMINED *(Specify)* 20a.   DATE OF INJURY *(Month, Day, Year)* 20b.   HOUR 20c. M   HOW INJURY OCCURRED *(Enter nature of injury in part I or part II, item 18)* 20d.

INJURY AT WORK *(Specify yes or no)* 20e.   PLACE OF INJURY *At home, farm, street, factory, office bldg., etc. (Specify)* 20f.   LOCATION 20g.   *(Street or R.F.D. no., city or village, state, zip)*

PHYSICIAN CERTIFIER

CERTIFICATION—PHYSICIAN: I ATTENDED THE *Month Day Year* 21a. DECEASED FROM   TO *Month Day Year* 21b.   AND LAST SAW HIM/HER ALIVE ON *Month Day Year* 21c.   I DID/DID NOT VIEW THE BODY AFTER DEATH. 21d.   DEATH OCCURRED (HOUR) 21e. M.   At the place, on the date, and, to the best of my knowledge, due to the cause(s) stated.

CORONER CERTIFIER

CERTIFICATION—CORONER: *On the basis of the examination of the body and/or the investigation, in my opinion, death occurred on the date and due to the cause(s) stated.* 22a. M.   Hour of death 22b.   The decedent was pronounced dead *Month Day Year Hour* M.

CERTIFIER—NAME *(Type or print)* 23a.   SIGNATURE 23b.   Degree or title   DATE SIGNED 23c.

MAILING ADDRESS—CERTIFIER 23d.   STREET OR R.F.D. NO.   CITY OR VILLAGE   STATE   ZIP

BURIAL

BURIAL, CREMATION *(Specify)* 24a.   DATE 24b.   NAME OF CEMETERY OR CREMATORY 24c.   LOCATION 24d.   *(City, village, or county) (State)*

NAME OF EMBALMER 25.   (LIC. NO.)   FUNERAL DIRECTOR'S SIGNATURE 26.   (LIC. NO.)

FUNERAL FIRM AND ADDRESS 27.   (STREET NO.)   (CITY)   (STATE)   (ZIP)

DATE REC'D BY LOCAL REG. 28.   REGISTRAR'S SIGNATURE 29.   DATE PERMIT ISSUED 30.   SIGNATURE OF PERSON ISSUING PERMIT 31.   DIST. NO.

TYPE OR PRINT IN PERMANENT INK

V.S. 11 5152.06 Rev. 1/68

The standard death certificate, adapted for use in Ohio.

is sometimes strong, based on either superstition or religious guidance (e.g., Jakobovits 1958), and there is a decided shortage of competent pathologists.

As specified by a physician and later included in a nation's vital statistics, each cause of death is ideally in accordance with the International Statistical Classification of Diseases, Injuries, and Causes of Death. This schedule has evolved gradually over the past century—from 1853, when the First Statistical Congress commissioned two of its leading members to work up an improvement in the alphabetical list of causes of death then in general use, to January 1, 1968, when the Eighth Revision went into effect.

The Classification, arranged in seventeen main sections, deals first with diseases caused by well defined infective agents; these are followed by categories for neoplasms, and endocrine, metabolic, and nutritional diseases. Most of the remaining diseases are arranged according to their principal anatomical site. . . . The last section provides a dual classification of injuries, according to the "external cause" giving rise to the injury and according to the "nature of injury," such as puncture, open wound, or burn. . . .

The Detailed List consists of a list of 671 categories of disease and morbid conditions, plus 182 categories for classification of the external cause of injury and 187 categories for classification of injuries according to the nature of the lesion. . . . The detailed categories of the classification are designated by three-digit numbers. . . . The fourth-digit subcategories provide further specificity or more information regarding etiology or manifestations of the disease [U.S. Public Health Service 1967: xxiii–xxiv].

For example, venereal diseases are designated by the first two digits 09; among these, 090 indicates congenital syphilis, and 090.2 indicates "early congenital syphilis, unspecified." Or, as another example, neoplasms (tumors or cancers) run from 140 to 239; the first two digits 15 indicate a malignant neoplasm of the digestive organs, 151 specifies the stomach, and 151.1 the pylorus (or the opening of the stomach into the intestines).

While the International Classification is an enormously valuable instrument, to which some of the best epidemiologists and demographers over the past century have devoted much thought, in analytical terms it remains inelegant. As a practical statistical tool, it reflects compromises made with the current state of medical knowledge, international differences in usage, and the greater or lesser relevance, with respect to any category, of medicine, anatomy, or law. International comparisons must be based on the statistics compiled by the various countries, which may differ somewhat in how accurate, consistent, and up to date their reporting on the cause of death is. Over all, the proportion of deaths assigned to unknown or ill defined causes has declined, but not at the same rate or in the same way in every country.

There is no satisfactory procedure for reducing the spurious trends introduced by the increasing specificity of diagnosis. . . . Exact diagnosis, in the sense of choosing the initiating condition in a sequence of morbid events, is very difficult for an increasing number of deaths in industrialized countries. . . . While diagnostic accuracy has undoubtedly improved, a randomly chosen diagnosis made in 1965 is likely to be no more reliable than one made in 1900, in the sense of denoting *the* underlying cause of death, because of the changing cause and age structure of death [Preston *et al.* 1972: 30–34].

The most obvious characteristic of such a trend is the sharp reduction in deaths due to infectious diseases, in some cases to nil, with the consequent greater significance of such noncommunicable causes of death as heart diseases, cancers, stroke, and some types of accidents. This transformation is illustrated in Table 7-4, which lists the top ten causes of death in the United States in 1900 and in 1969. Today important frontiers of medical science lie somewhere beyond infections, in the difficult terrain of "morbid conditions," psychosomatic ailments, allergies, and "positive health." That in advanced countries morbid

Table 7-4.   Death Rates by Selected Causes, United States, 1900 and 1969

Disease or Other Cause of Death	Rank of Cause		Deaths per 100,000 Population	
	1900[a]	1969	1900[a]	1969
Influenza and pneumonia, except pneumonia of newborn	1	5	202.2	33.9
Tuberculosis, all forms	2	< 10	194.4	2.8
Gastro-enteritis	3	< 10[b]	142.7	1.3[b]
Diseases of the heart	4	1	137.4	366.1
Vascular lesions affecting the central nervous system ("stroke")	5	3[c]	106.9	102.6[c]
Chronic nephritis	6	< 10[d]	81.0	4.0[d]
All accidents	7	4	72.3	57.6
Malignant neoplasms ("cancers")	8	2	64.0	160.0
Certain diseases of early infancy	9	6	62.6	21.4
Diphtheria	10	—	40.3	0.0
General arteriosclerosis	< 10	9	—	16.4
Diabetes mellitus	[e]	7	[e]	19.1
Other diseases of the circulatory system	< 10	8[f]	12.0	16.6[f]
Other bronchopulmonic diseases	< 10	10[g]	12.5	16.0[g]
All causes			1,719.1	951.9

[a] Death-Registration Area.
[b] Enteritis and other diarrheal diseases.
[c] Cerebrovascular diseases.
[d] Chronic and unqualified nephritis and renal sclerosis; because of the change in classification, the rates are not comparable for the two years.
[e] Not comparable because of a change in classification.
[f] Hypertension, plus other diseases of arteries, arterioles, and capillaries.
[g] Acute bronchitis and bronchiolitis, plus bronchitis, emphysema, and asthma.
SOURCES: U.S. Public Health Service, *The Facts of Life and Death*, 1965, Table 14; "Advance Report—Final Mortality Statistics, 1969," *Monthly Vital Statistics Report*, **21**, no. 4, Supplement 2, 1972.

conditions now cause more deaths than infectious diseases can be interpreted in two ways. In one sense, the statement is simply a tautology, meaning no more than that with medical science we can control what we understand. At one time, for instance, the condition of the body called "fever" was regarded as the cause of much mortality; today it is interpreted as a symptom associated with the action of many different germs. What we term "heart disease" is a current example of such a composite term, and, similarly, cancer is not a single clear-cut disease entity but a group of diseases, involving a multitude of possible causative factors. That is to say, some morbid conditions are simply those diseases about

Table 7-5. Average Percentage of Newborns Who Would Ultimately Die of Specified Causes, by Life Expectancy and Sex, 1960s

Sex and Expectation of Life at Birth	RESPIRATORY TUBERCULOSIS	OTHER INFECTIOUS AND PARASITIC DISEASES	NEOPLASMS	CARDIOVASCULAR DISEASES	INFLUENZA, PNEUMONIA, BRONCHITIS	DIARRHEAL DISEASES	CERTAIN DEGENERATIVE DISEASES	MATERNAL DISEASES	CERTAIN DISEASES OF INFANCY	VIOLENCE	ALL OTHER, AND UNKNOWN	Number of Populations
Males												
<35	7.67	12.48	1.27	7.99	25.98	5.11	1.74	—	6.67	4.71	26.37	3
35–39	8.00	11.89	2.72	14.05	17.99	7.80	1.75	—	5.93	4.49	25.38	5
40–44	11.19	9.47	2.98	15.25	19.06	7.28	2.95	—	3.89	4.53	23.39	9
45–49	6.68	7.38	4.88	19.73	13.30	8.17	4.32	—	4.33	5.55	25.63	15
50–54	5.50	5.32	7.15	19.80	13.79	4.71	3.54	—	3.86	7.49	28.84	6
55–59	5.45	4.48	9.39	26.36	10.73	2.61	6.29	—	3.23	7.33	24.11	21
60–64	4.03	2.60	12.46	32.63	8.18	1.62	5.39	—	2.36	6.43	24.30	36
65–69	2.35	.97	16.56	45.35	6.65	.58	4.18	—	1.81	6.52	15.03	55
70–74	.87	.71	18.61	48.53	5.21	.43	3.01	—	1.33	5.96	15.34	15
Females												
<40	7.43	12.31	2.74	11.92	21.13	7.42	1.38	1.62	5.54	1.45	27.06	6
40–44	10.08	8.98	4.20	16.95	17.22	7.88	2.56	1.73	3.80	1.78	24.80	7
45–49	7.17	8.69	5.43	19.30	15.68	7.55	2.75	1.25	3.27	1.86	27.07	9
50–54	5.08	6.20	6.80	24.86	12.63	7.88	4.25	.98	3.59	1.79	25.95	10
55–59	5.58	4.65	9.42	24.09	13.67	3.94	4.28	1.09	2.90	2.13	28.25	11
60–64	4.37	3.54	12.27	30.58	9.76	2.16	5.28	.96	2.37	2.82	25.89	20
65–69	2.59	2.04	13.24	37.71	8.70	1.54	5.61	.61	1.82	2.88	23.88	31
70–74	.96	.68	15.83	52.13	6.21	.67	3.70	.17	1.31	3.70	14.63	58
75+	.31	.45	18.31	51.49	6.05	.45	3.44	.12	.83	4.33	14.21	8

SOURCE: Samuel H. Preston, Nathan Keyfitz, and Robert Schoen, *Causes of Death: Life Tables for National Populations* (New York: Seminar Press, 1972), Tables I-1a and I-1b.

which we know too little either to effect cures or to classify except in such a composite grouping.

Or, to make the same point in a different way, the category of diseases known as "chronic" is usually defined operationally simply in terms of their duration, either as a morbid condition lasting for three months or more (U.S. National Health Survey) or as one that is permanent, nonreversible, or requiring a long period of care (Commission on Chronic Illness). Once it is known what causes a morbid condition, however, in many cases it is no longer chronic in this sense, and this can be so whether the cause is genetic (hyperthyroidism) or environmental (pellagra). In the recent past a considerable number of both types of chronic diseases have become subject to therapy, either wholly or in part.

The greater importance of morbid conditions as causes of death may be due, however, not merely to ignorance but to inherent, irremovable weaknesses in the human body. As more and more of the controllable causes of death are brought under control, the residual group acquires a greater and greater relative importance. Cures for infectious diseases effected a sharp reduction in infant and child mortality, and an increase in life expectancy to ages when organic senescence is significant.

When national populations are ranked by the expectation of life at birth, as in Table 7-5, it is possible to estimate from cause-specific life tables the percentage that would die from each of the major categories of causes. Very roughly, in other words, the temporal change that was indicated in Table 7-4 is reproduced spatially by the contrast between underdeveloped and modernized countries. The same decline in infectious, pulmonary, and infant diseases is to be seen, and the same rise in cancers and heart diseases.

SOCIAL DISORDERS

The shift from infectious diseases to morbid conditions, however, marks only one of the important trends. In recent decades the causes of substantial proportions of both mortality and morbidity cannot be adequately classified as a purely medical category of any kind, for the behavioral component is both too important and too obvious. Involved in these causes are some malfunctioning of social institutions, some type of deviance from the norm for optimum health, and often an infraction of some law. Of course, *any* preventable death can be seen as a failure of the social order, and throughout the ages philosophers have dreamed of a conflictless world. The causes congregated here as symptoms of "social disorder" have not been defined by a criterion of perfection, but rather by a reasonable expectation of how a modern society might function. Data on these phenomena, like crime statistics generally, are often poor and difficult to interpret; for instance, a rise in the incidence may be genuine or may reflect only increased vigilance. Though some of the diseases discussed under this heading are infectious (e.g., venereal diseases) or chronic in the usual sense (e.g., addictions), even in these instances a narrowly medical or demographic analysis can be no more than suggestive. On the other hand, some of the topics discussed elsewhere in this chapter (in particular, the effects of cigarette smoking) might also have been included here. The ordering of the types of social disorder that are discussed here is more or less arbitrary, running from addictions through family and sex to various patterns of violence.

Drinking and Alcoholism

Alcoholism is notoriously difficult to define, and neither medical texts nor legal statutes are ordinarily precise and consistent. Nor can one, from the point of view of legitimate social control, easily distinguish an addiction to alcohol from "public intoxication," stipulated as an offense in many legal codes; or from "driving under the influence of alcohol"—that is, below the level of intoxication; or even from "social drinking" on the scale of a typical Frenchman, who might consume 2 or 3 liters of wine a day and, without ever becoming drunk, eventually die of the effects of alcohol on his system.

Various methods have been used to gauge the numbers of persons deleteriously affected by alcohol. From the sales records of beverages one can get a rough comparison of national populations. Among the top ten developed countries in the late 1960s, the rank order in per-capita consumption, ranging from 6.53 to 2.20 gallons of absolute alcohol per year, was: France, Italy, Switzerland, West Germany, Australia, Belgium, United States, New Zealand, Czechoslovakia, and Canada. Some populations noted for heavy drinking ranked remarkably low by this index; Sweden was thirteenth, Ireland only sixteenth (U.S. Dept. of HEW 1971: 17). For obvious reasons, arrest records or their converse, the membership rolls of organizations like Alcoholics Anonymous, do not necessarily correlate highly with average consumption figures. In the United States several sample surveys have given a basis for distinguishing types of users by their social characteristics (ibid.: chap. 2):

Abstainers (and usually also Infrequent Drinkers), likely to be female or, among males, older, of lower social class, living in the South or rural areas, of native-born parents, with a high degree of religiosity in conservative or fundamentalist Protestant denominations, relatively alienated from society and unhappy with their lot in life.

Light or Moderate Drinkers, the dominant pattern, including almost half of the adult males and more than a third of the females.

Heavy Drinkers, likely to be young adults, male (21 percent of the total) rather than female (5 percent), of Irish or British parentage, of urban residence (particularly rural in-migrants) and the lower classes, with persistent family difficulties (e.g., from a broken home, themselves single or divorced), irreligious or associated with Catholic or liberal Protestant churches, and (like Abstainers) relatively alienated from society and unhappy with their lot in life.

Perhaps the best index of alcoholism, particularly in a demographic context, is the number of deaths from associated ailments. Alcohol is not digested like other foods but is absorbed directly from the walls of the small intestine into the blood stream. If the liver is required to process excessive amounts of it, a progressive destruction of the liver cells, known as cirrhosis, takes place. Not all alcoholics, however, develop cirrhosis, and not all cirrhosis results from excessive drinking. According to a formula devised by Elvin M. Jellinek (1947), the number of alcoholics (A) can be estimated from the following equation:

$$A = (PD/K)R$$

where

> $P =$ the proportion, separately for the two sexes, of deaths from cirrhosis assignable to alcoholism,
> $D =$ the deaths in any year from cirrhosis of the liver,
> $K =$ the percentage of "alcoholics with complications" (previously termed "chronic alcoholics") who die of cirrhosis, and
> $R =$ the ratio of all alcoholics to "alcoholics with complications."

Several of the terms, as Jellinek pointed out, are specific to a particular time and place and change with, for example, a variation in the diet. As estimated from this formula, the number of alcoholics in the United States in 1948 was nearly 4 million. Most subsequent estimates showed a substantial rise, but apparently often for spurious reasons. According to a first-rate review of the most significant papers (Keller 1962), there was no rise in the basic rate of alcoholism from the mid-1940s, when Jellinek's first estimate appeared, to 1960, when the number of alcoholics was almost 4.5 million, of whom 840,000 were "alcoholics with complications." The increase reflects the change in population number and structure rather than in prevalence.

Conceivably it might be possible to improve the estimate by extending Jellinek's formula from cirrhosis to other pathological conditions primarily or partly caused by alcohol abuse. These include a number of other ailments of the digestive system, various brain disorders, myopathy (or diseased muscle) especially of the heart, atrophy of some endocrine glands, and of course deaths from automobile accidents or other injuries.

Drug Addiction

Whatever has happened to the incidence of drug abuse, certainly there has been a colossal increase in public awareness and analysis, leading to a frustrating multiplication of contradictory "solutions." The discussion here is limited to a small but crucial element, the problems of measurement in the United States.[7] Some of the increase is due to the proliferation of marijuana, which is omitted

---

[7] The variation in national statistical systems makes a meaningful cross-cultural comparison in drug abuse impossible; see U.N. Commission on Narcotic Drugs, *Summary of Annual Reports of Governments Relating to Opium and Other Narcotic Drugs, 1964*, New York, 1966.

from this account as in a different class from hard drugs like heroin. And some other portion may well be due to the increased activity of law-enforcement officials at various levels.

According to the compilation of federal, state, and local records that the U.S. Bureau of Narcotics keeps, the number of active addicts roughly doubled from 1956 to 1969 (Table 7-6). In this growing total, the proportion of blacks fell from 60 percent to a bit under half; in other words, however much attention is given to the drug addiction of middle-class whites, it is still mainly a problem of lower-class blacks. And the supposed spread of the habit to teen-agers is not validated by these data: the percentage remained well below that in the base year, and the absolute number rose slightly above that in 1956 only as late as 1969. Indeed, the major shift in age category has been the contrary, the doubling of the percentage of addicts in their 30s, representing an absolute increase by three and a half times.

As with alcohol, one alternative means of getting information on drug use is to administer a questionnaire, hoping that the inclination to lie will be mitigated by assurances of anonymity. Perhaps the best survey of this type was given to a sample of 2,547 military personnel in Vietnam, of whom 2,372 filled in usable schedules. The very small number of company-grade officers included few who used drugs, and the adequate sample of NCOs an even smaller proportion; the problem was heavily concentrated among privates. Very much of the information collected pertained to marijuana, which was used by almost a third of the incoming soldiers and half of those leaving Vietnam. The largest relative increase was in the use of opium, from 5.5 to 17.4 percent. The percentages using heroin/morphine or hallucinogens, on the other hand, dropped by about half during the time spent in Vietnam. There was a slight positive relation between exposure to enemy fire and frequency in the use of marijuana. At least according to this one report, public concern was somewhat exaggerated: "marijuana and some other illicit drugs may actually *help* certain types of individuals to function on the job by assisting them in maintaining an adequate psychological adjustment." Somewhat in the same vein is the very mild summary statement that "certainly all these illicit substances can have dangerous effects, especially when used to excess" (Stanton 1972; cf. Greden and Morgan 1972). According to a House committee, on the other hand, some 10 to 15 percent (or 30,000 to 40,000) of U.S. servicemen in Vietnam were "addicted" just to heroin; but this very much larger estimate was used as a basis for the proposal, obviously supported also on other grounds, that the withdrawal of draftees should be accelerated (*Congressional Quarterly Weekly Report*, June 4, 1971).

Again as with alcohol, perhaps the best index of narcotics addiction is the number of deaths assigned to it as the cause. About half the addicts in the United States, it is estimated, live in New York City, and the record there is suggestive. According to statistics reported by the city's Chief Medical Officer, the rise that began in the mid-1950s skyrocketed during the 1960s (Figure 7-2). It is possible, of course, that because of the growing public concern about drugs

Table 7-6. Active Narcotic Addicts, United States, 1956 and 1965–69

End of Calendar Year	Total Recorded	Sex		Age Bracket				Race		
		MALE	FEMALE	>21	21–30	31–40	41+	WHITE[a]	NEGRO	OTHER
				Percentage Distribution						
1956	35,835	77.7	22.3	12.3	59.7	17.0	11.0	37.8	60.0	2.2
1965	57,199	82.3	17.7	3.5	46.4	37.7	12.4	47.8	51.5	0.7
1966	59,720	82.5	17.5	3.5	45.9	37.5	13.1	49.0	50.4	0.6
1967	62,045	82.8	17.2	3.6	45.8	37.0	13.6	49.8	49.7	0.5
1968	64,011	83.4	16.6	4.2	46.6	35.3	13.9	50.5	49.0	0.5
1969	68,088	84.4	15.6	7.1	48.9	31.2	12.8	50.8	48.8	0.4
				Index of Absolute Numbers (1956 = 100)						
1956	100	100	100	100	100	100	100	100	100	100
1965	159.6	169.1	126.6	44.8	124.1	354.1	180.5	201.8	137.2	49.3
1966	166.7	177.0	130.7	48.1	128.1	367.6	198.3	216.4	139.9	44.0
1967	173.1	184.5	133.6	50.4	132.7	377.7	213.8	228.1	143.4	43.5
1968	178.6	191.9	132.5	61.0	139.2	371.9	225.6	238.8	146.0	37.1
1969	190.0	206.5	132.8	109.7	155.6	348.6	221.7	255.3	154.7	33.6

[a] Includes Puerto Ricans and Mexican Americans.
SOURCES: U.S. Bureau of Narcotics, *Traffic in Opium and Other Dangerous Drugs* (Washington, D.C., various dates).

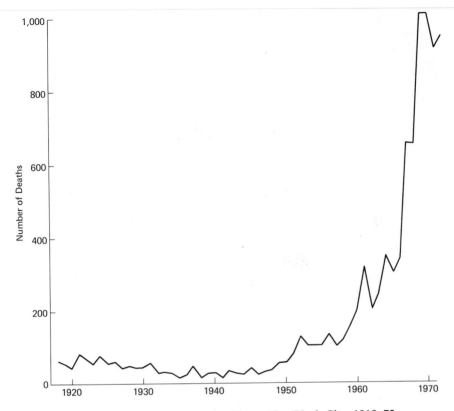

Figure 7–2.   Deaths from Narcotics Abuse, New York City, 1918–72

SOURCE: Milton Helpern, "Fatalities from Narcotic Addiction in New York City," *Human Pathology*, **3** (1972), 13–21. Reproduced with permission of the author.

an increasingly higher proportion of deaths from narcotics was correctly diagnosed; but even if that is the case, it means only that part of the acceleration is spurious, not the very high numbers in recent years. There is good reason to suppose, on the contrary, that the number of addicts who die from drug abuse is often understated. In an especially careful study (Lerner and Nurco 1970), the authors compared the deaths reported to the Chief Medical Examiner of Maryland during the period 1951–66 with the names listed on that state's drug-abuse register. They concluded that 386 of the fatalities (excluding those from anesthesia) were in fact due to drug abuse; almost 60 percent had been classified as suicides, and almost 20 percent each as accidents and as undetermined or unknown. The circumstances were not typical of the deaths assigned to narcotics: about 70 percent of the deaths were from barbiturates, a slight majority of the deceased were female, about 60 percent were 40 years and over, a vast majority were white. One recurrent reason for the misclassification, presumably, is the stereotype of a young male, often black, dying from heroin.

Sir Alexander Fleming (1881–1955), British bacteriologist, who was awarded the Nobel Prize in 1945 for his discovery of penicillin (*World Health Organization*).

Health and the Family

As one might suppose, both alcoholism and drug addiction are less common among those embedded in the protective environment of a stable family. The cause–effect relation probably works in both directions: his family withdraws from an addict, and a person isolated from strong personal bonds is more likely to become addicted. The same pattern has been discerned also with a number of other causes of death.

The relative risks of attempted suicide, of accidental injury, and of having tuberculosis are respectively seven, five, and four times as great for those who have been orphaned as for those reared in an intact family. . . . There are several categories of disease in which those who are unmarried or no longer married have very much higher mortality rates than those who are married. These are influenza and pneumonia, syphilis and cirrhosis of the liver, "violence," and tuberculosis [Chen and Cobb 1960].

Three factors seem to be operating: the absence of mutual care (influenza and pneumonia), sexual promiscuity and self-indulgence (venereal diseases and addictions), and social isolation (suicide and accidents). The sudden imposition of such social isolation by the death of a spouse can lead to what has been termed the "mortality of bereavement" (Rees and Lutkins 1967). In this study, the risk of mortality within one year of the death of a close relative was shown to be seven times that of a control group matched by age, sex, and marital status. "People who die following a bereavement are on the average slightly

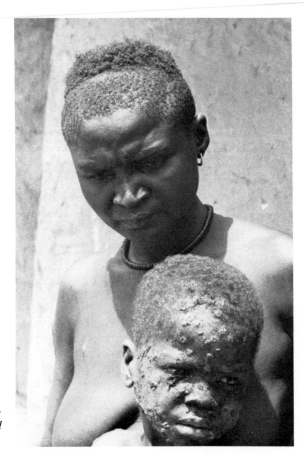

A single injection of penicillin can cure yaws (*World
Health Organization*).

younger than the relatives who predeceased them, and they die at an earlier age
than is usual for the community in which they live." This would seem to be a
better test than the mere correlation between the married state and greater
longevity, which is subject to misinterpretation (cf. Sheps 1961; Berkson 1962).
More generally, a slight decline in the death rate occurs at the time of such
ceremonial occasions as the person's birthday, important elections, and, among
Jews, the Day of Atonement (Phillips and Feldman 1973). The presumed effect
of the heightened will to live can be interpreted as the correlative of the mortality of bereavement.

The family is not always a haven; it can be a dangerous environment. During
the past decades the American public has become aware of what is termed the
"battered-child syndrome" (Kempe *et al.* 1962), the clinical condition of infants
or young children subjected to serious physical abuse, usually by their parents.
When radiologists first noticed that child patients being examined for other
reasons sometimes showed fractures of the skull or limbs, they assumed that

these must have been due to accidents, for which the parents were culpable only in the sense that they had been careless. In fact, many of the infants and young children were beaten or badly burnt or otherwise intentionally hurt; the responsibility was direct and in any other context it would have involved criminal sanctions. But under both common and statutory law the parents' right to control the upbringing of their children could not be easily abridged, particularly since both physicians and social workers were ordinarily reluctant to interfere. In rapid order all fifty states passed new laws making parents more accountable for the physical abuse of their children, and once this new definition of the situation took effect, hundreds of cases of child abuse were recorded in one jurisdiction after another. This is a prime instance of a statistical series created not from given levels of incidence (which for all we know may have been constant) but out of a sharply increased awareness (Gil 1970).

Whether sexual promiscuity has increased or has only become more prominent is also not known, but the deleterious effects of random mating—illegitimacy and venereal disease—have gone up.

The venereal diseases, syphilis and gonorrhea, have reached epidemic proportions throughout the United States. Reported cases of gonorrhea have been increasing yearly at an alarming rate of 10–15 percent and in fiscal year 1970 increased by 79,000 cases to reach an all-time high of 573,000. After four years of decline, reported infectious syphilis increased by 1,500 cases in fiscal year 1970 [U.S. National Commission on Venereal Disease 1972: v].

This is a worldwide phenomenon, and the United States is not the worst country. In the list of incidence rates for gonorrhea in 1970, for instance, the American rate of 285 per 100,000 compared with one of 400 for Sweden.

The new epidemic, paradoxically, is the consequence of a number of developments that were all seen as manifestations of progress. Because of penicillin,

"A message from the Minnesota VD Awareness Committee" (*Minneapolis Tribune*). The control of venereal disease is only secondarily medical; the primary task is to induce patients to volunteer for treatment and then to help trace the paths of infection.

the scourge of syphilis was apparently headed for extinction, so that federal programs to control it and its sister diseases were cut back drastically. Few physicians, whether specialists or general practitioners, any longer acquired an adequate training in this field of medicine, and research by both biological and social scientists was slighted. The earlier contraceptives, as another point, were largely replaced by the more convenient, more effective pill, but the condom (and to some degree even the pessary) had also acted as a prophylactic. The earlier puritanical stance that impeded efforts to control syphilis and gonorrhea—in the 1930s newspapers would not print the very words (Locke 1939)—was dissipated, but the seemingly greater sexual activity was not accompanied by a genuine objectivity: many venereal patients are still unwilling to seek medical help from established authorities and especially to help them trace the path of infection.

Accidents

One might suppose that accidents, virtually by definition, are less amenable to control than other causes of death, but this is not entirely so. The toll fluctuates considerably: in the United States the deaths from this cause fell in 1970 by about 2,000 to an estimated 113,000, but in each of the two following years it rose again by 2,000 to a total of 117,000 in 1972. The principal site of accidents used to be the place of work, and these were halved during some three decades, partly because of the sizable shift of workers to less dangerous office work but also because public controls forced factory owners to maintain much more effective safety standards. According to poor data, deaths and injuries from accidents in the home seem to have increased. Regulations exist for the construction of new residences, the maintenance of tenant-occupied homes, the manufacture of electrical and some other household equipment, and so on. But the enforcement of such regulations frequently conflicts with a strong competing norm, the privacy of the home and the right of each adult to determine for himself the environment in which he and his children live.

Accidents involving motor vehicles constitute the fourth leading cause of death in the United States. The causes that generally rank higher—cardiovascular diseases, cancers, and strokes—are concentrated in the upper ages, while motor-vehicle accidents rank first for persons aged 1–24 years, and they are responsible for 40 percent of all deaths of those in the 15–24 age bracket (National Safety Council 1970: 8). This concentration, typical also of European statistics (Table 7-7), represents a great social cost, for persons are removed after much of the expenditure in rearing and education has been made but before society receives much of a return on this investment in a productive life.

Traffic fatalities have not increased over the years proportionate to the growth of population (Klein and Waller 1970: 4). The rise in rank is due to the relative decline of deaths from communicable diseases. One can even argue that the safety improvements in vehicles and highways and from motorists' registration

Table 7-7. Motor-Vehicle Deaths as a Percentage of All Deaths, by Age Category, Selected European Countries, 1967

Country	All Ages	15–25 Years
West Germany	3.6	50.2
Netherlands	3.8	47.3
Denmark	3.2	45.6
Belgium	2.9	44.2
France	3.6	43.8
Austria	3.7	43.3
England and Wales	1.8	41.9
Northern Ireland	2.2	41.0
Sweden	2.0	35.3
Switzerland	3.8	34.2
Scotland	1.8	33.2
Finland	3.3	32.5
Greece	2.3	28.8
Czechoslovakia	2.5	28.1
Ireland	1.7	28.0
Norway	1.8	27.2
Iceland	3.1	24.1
Portugal	2.5	21.6
Bulgaria	2.3	20.3
Poland	1.8	14.9
Hungary	1.3	14.4

SOURCE: Alfred Sauvy, "Les conséquences démographiques des accidents de la route," *Population*, **27** (1972), 1138–1140.

have been increasingly effective, for in the United States the death rate per 100 million vehicle-miles fell almost steadily from about 55 in the mid-1920s to less than 5 in 1971. Over this same period, however, the number of vehicles (as well as the average distance traveled) grew so fast that the effect of safety controls was more than canceled. According to a Census Bureau survey (*Current Population Reports*, Series P-65, no. 44, February 1973), in 1972 some 81 percent of all households in the United States owned one or more motor vehicles, almost 40 percent owned two or more, and 8.4 percent owned three or more.

Most of the records on automobile accidents are collected as adjuncts to police regulations or insurance coverage, and neither set of statistics is entirely appropriate for an analysis of etiology. Before an effective policy can be formulated, this paucity of relevant data will have to be repaired.

It is hardly a complicated matter to conceive what basic national data ought to be collected: rates for deaths, injuries, and accidents; geographical and temporal distribution of such; types of vehicles involved; types of drivers involved; types of roadway and environmental failures. That would be a beginning. Most of the data could be gathered by standard sampling techniques (Moynihan 1966).

According to the data now available, there is a consistent variation in accident rates by important characteristics of the persons involved: age, sex, race, marital status, and social class. Since society deprecates accidents, there is a prima-facie plausibility in denoting them a type of "social deviance" (Suchman 1970), but the concept, whether or not it is analytically fitting, has not been useful in getting anyone to accommodate to the general norm. Others have argued, on the contrary, that such values as aggressive competition, risk taking, and violence when "necessary" are likely to encourage behavior conducive to accidents (Klein and Waller 1970: 185–194). But the personality factors associated with so simple a decision as whether or not to use a safety belt would not seem to confirm either of these more grandiose hypotheses (Robertson *et al.* 1972). In short, there is not only the standard need for research, but for research based on cooperation among social scientists, engineers, and lawyers (e.g., Miller 1972).

Murder and Suicide

Crime statistics are notoriously inadequate, and this is especially so when an analysis is attempted across cultural lines. In a society lacking efficient law enforcement, the record of crimes committed, not to say data on arrests and imprisonment, will give no clue to the state of civil order. The American West at its most rambunctious can be exemplified by Nevada, an area with few natural attractions to in-migrants apart from the gold and silver booms. The men who came to raw mining towns were not by and large what one would term responsible citizens; the state's newspapers carried almost daily accounts of murder on the streets. Yet, according to the census of 1870, during the year ending on June 1 of that year only 132 persons had been convicted of any crime, and on that date only 99 were in prison—figures that, compared with a population of more than 40,000, might suggest a thoroughly law-abiding state. The truth was, of course, that law-enforcement agents were too few, often too weak, and sometimes too dishonest to protect citizens even against murder.

Homicide is a subject, moreover, that social scientists have found remarkably unsusceptible to analysis. A generally law-abiding person who commits murder under emotional stress, a psychopath, a professional killer for organized crime—these are not individuals who can easily be fitted into the social categories with which a sociologist works. Each year in the mid-1960s there were some 8,500 reported murders in the United States, or only slightly fewer than the deaths from all forms of tuberculosis. The number has been rising, as well as the disparity between the United States and other industrial countries (Table 7-8). In the mid-1950s homicide rates for white Americans had been at about the same level as in France and Japan, but they declined sharply in those two countries and rose in the United States. The stupendous rates for nonwhites, both male and female, set this category apart from almost any comparable groups in the world. The patterns of violence poignantly described in such a work as Kenneth Clark's *Dark Ghetto* are part of the basic substance of lower-class Negro life;

Table 7-8. Average Annual Death Rates from Homicide per 100,000 Population by Sex, Age Category, and Color, Selected Developed Countries, Recent Dates

Country	1956–57			1966–67			1968		
	15–24	25–44	45–64	15–24	25–44	45–64	15–24	25–44	45–64
						MALE			
United States	9.0	13.0	7.9	13.2	19.7	11.1	16.7	23.1	13.2
White	3.9	5.3	4.4	5.7	8.8	6.2	7.8	10.5	7.4
Nonwhite	45.0	81.6	43.9	65.4	108.7	58.4	77.3	126.4	69.7
Canada	1.4	1.7	2.0	1.6	2.6	2.1	1.8	3.7	2.2
Scandinavia and the Netherlands	0.3[a]	0.5	0.7	0.4[a]	0.8	0.8	0.4[a]	0.7	0.8
United Kingdom	0.6	0.5	1.5	1.1	1.1	0.7	0.9	0.9	0.7
France	3.1	4.8	2.0	0.7	1.6	1.0	0.6	1.3	1.1
West Germany	1.1	1.2	1.1	1.1	1.8	1.9	b	b	b
Japan	3.4	3.9	2.2	1.8	2.5	1.4	1.6	2.4	1.4
						FEMALE			
United States	2.9	4.0	2.2	3.7	5.5	3.0	4.0	5.6	2.9
White	1.4	1.9	1.6	2.1	2.9	2.0	2.2	2.9	2.0
Nonwhite	12.4	20.5	9.0	14.3	24.3	11.9	16.1	24.9	11.3
Canada	0.7[a]	1.2	1.1	1.2	1.7	1.1	1.5	1.9	1.4
Scandinavia and the Netherlands	0.5[a]	0.5	0.4	0.4[a]	0.6	0.5	0.4[a]	0.4[a]	0.6[a]
United Kingdom	0.3[a]	0.5	0.4	0.9[a]	0.6	0.4	0.7	0.7	0.5
France	0.4	0.6	0.6	0.5	0.8	0.6	0.6	0.8	0.4
West Germany	0.6	0.5	0.4	1.4	1.1	0.7	b	b	b
Japan	1.1	1.1	1.2	0.7	1.0	0.8	0.7	0.8	0.7

[a] Rate based on 10–20 deaths. b Data not available.

SOURCE: Metropolitan Life Insurance Co., *Statistical Bulletin*, December 1972.

and during the 1960s, when there was a substantial improvement in the civil rights, income, and general well-being of many blacks, the threat increased from murder—in the main by other blacks. Most people would see these data as an index of a crisis calling for desperate measures to reverse the trend. Many black leaders, on the contrary, have evinced a blanket hostility to all police and courts, and on a broader scale the U.S. Supreme Court made it more and more difficult to bring palpable criminals to justice. The *Statistical Bulletin* from which the table was copied speaks of "the increasing concentration of nonwhites and of the poor in central cities" (it has *not* been increasing, but the contrary) and of the "decline in traditional values in many segments of the population" (too vague a diagnosis to suggest an appropriate therapy). Those most concerned about the welfare of blacks might well consider whether more and better police should not be one of their primary demands.

Even in countries with a good registration system, the accuracy and significance of suicide data vary widely (Barraclough 1972). Religious and other cultural inhibitions induce an indeterminate, but probably sometimes large, amount of underreporting. In one of the classics of sociology, Durkheim (1951: 152–170) noted that the rate was consistently lower for Catholics than for Protestants, Jews, or atheists; and he explained the difference by the stronger cohesion of the Catholic Church and thus the greater insulation of each individual Catholic from "suicide-generating currents." Another likely—more likely?—interpretation is that because suicide is a greater sin for Catholics, they take greater care than others to disguise it as a normal death, enlisting the support of sympathetic family doctors and even coroners in what all are prone to see as a white lie. "For some time, some reasonable men have rejected the use of 'public,' or even any form of statistical, data for the study of suicide" (Wilkins 1967). Those who use the figures that are recorded typically offer no defense of them except that nothing better exists. Possibly the best mode of analysis is to combine epidemiology with case studies (Sainsbury 1972).

Probably the analysis of suicide should be based on the postulate that it is a symptom of quite diverse causative factors, which are confused when the phenomenon is congregated into overall rates. Those who interpret suicide as a reflection of an inadequate social system, for instance, are puzzled by the fact that the rates are generally highest in the most organized states of the West—Sweden and Denmark especially—and have been rising there particulary among males aged 15–24. In Japan, on the contrary, rates were very high as a reflection of the distinctive national culture, but in this age–sex category they fell by 70 percent in one decade. In the United States and Canada, male rates have risen sharply at ages under 45 but declined at higher ages. In those countries, where the traditional values strongly affirm the maintenance of life, the decline of such norms may be taken as the ultimate reason for whatever rise in suicide there has been. Such suppositions do little to help one interpret the quite diverse changes in industrial countries (Table 7-9), which cannot all be explained as due only to differences in the accuracy of the records.

Table 7-9. Reported Suicides per 100,000 Population, Industrial Countries, Recent Dates

Country	Average 1956–57	Average 1966–67	Percent Change
Austria	23.6	22.8	−3
Sweden	20.1	20.9	+4
West Germany	18.7	20.9	+12
Switzerland	21.6	20.0	−7
Denmark	22.3	17.7	−21
France	17.0	15.5	−9
Belgium	14.8	14.7	−1
Japan	24.5	14.7	−40
United States	9.9	10.9	+10
England and Wales	11.9	10.1	−15
Portugal	9.2	9.5	+3
Canada	7.5	8.8	+17
Norway	7.3	7.1	−3
Netherlands	6.7	6.7	0
Italy	6.6	5.3	−20

SOURCE: J.-C. Chesnais, "L'évolution de la mortalité par suicide dans divers pays industrialisés," *Population*, **28** (1973), 419–422.

War

Over the centuries the deadliness of weapons has increased considerably, and to the extent that this is the decisive factor, the number of casualties should have gone up proportionately. According to one reckoning, thus, the proportion of the armed forces of four major European powers that were killed or wounded increased from less than 5 percent in the 13th and 14th centuries to more than 16 percent in the 19th (Sorokin 1937: 337). By another estimate, on the contrary, military casualties decreased from about 30–50 percent of the armed forces in the Middle Ages to about 6 percent in World War I (Wright 1942, vol. 1: 242). One reason for such divergencies, obviously, is that statistics are not only sparse but systematically falsified. An account deserving no credence at all was, in Napoleon's phrase, "false as a bulletin," and his own reports fit the pattern (Dumas and Vedel-Petersen 1923: 22).

Although the data are too poor to make precise comparisons over several centuries, one can reasonably assert that there has been a downward trend in the human cost of war if we include in this class also deaths from war-related disease. Before the development of modern surgery, a serious wound was more or less equivalent to death, and in the past the epidemics that wars stimulated were deadlier than battles. Zinsser (1935) has a chapter entitled, "On the influence of epidemic diseases on political and military history, and on the relative unimportance of generals." Disease was the decisive factor in many of the

One of the main squares of Rotterdam, before (ABOVE) and after (BELOW) the Germans bombed it in 1940. This was not a military action but rather a punishment of the Dutch for having resisted the Nazis' invasion of their country (*Royal Dutch Airlines—KLM*).

wars of the preindustrial world—in the Crusades, in the struggle between Catholics and Protestants during the Reformation, in the wars of the Napoleonic period (particularly the disastrous retreat from Moscow), in colonial wars (independent Haiti was established mainly because 22,000 of the 25,000 invading French troops died of yellow fever).

Sorokin's main thesis that war is especially characteristic of modern, rationalized, so-called sensate societies is questionable. Industrialism spread from England during the 19th century, and its rise coincided with a phenomenon unheard of in the annals of Western civilization—a century of peace in Europe. From 1815, the end of the Napoleonic wars, to 1914, the beginning of World War I, "apart from the Crimean war—a more or less colonial event—England, France, Prussia, Austria, Italy, and Russia were engaged in war among each other for altogether only eighteen months. A computation of comparable figures for the two preceding centuries gives an average of sixty to seventy years of major wars in each" (Polanyi 1944: 5). To equate industrialism with belligerence is obviously inadequate.

One can distinguish three types of military conflict—absolute war, in which the annihilation of the enemy is sought without rules; instrumental war, in which the cost of gaining access to values that the enemy controls is calculated against possible benefits; and agonistic fighting, which is very closely regulated by strict observance of rules (Speier 1952: 223–229). Such a social definition of the purpose of war—annihilation of the enemy, relative advantage (economic or other), or glory—has had a greater effect on mortality than the efficacy of the weapons used.

Absolute war is waged at all levels of society—among certain primitive peoples, for whom this is a way of life (Wright 1942, vol. 1: Appendixes 9, 10, 13); by advanced civilizations, particularly against those enemies defined as "savages" or "infidels"; and by the present-day totalitarian powers. By the 12th century, when Sorokin's figures begin, the social controls of feudal society had been established in Europe; wars were fought for limited aims and, when Christians opposed other Christians, according to the code of chivalry. With the breakdown of feudalism, this chivalric norm disappeared, and the religious and civil conflict of the following centuries took a much greater toll. In the 19th century, with bourgeois industrial society well established in Europe, a new code—the balance-of-power system—effectively limited warfare and mortality from it.

The military conflicts since 1914 have been more devastating principally because the international structure of the 19th century has broken down. In the two world wars, regulations of various kinds have successively been abrogated—concerning places (e.g., open cities), concerning weapons (tanks, poison gas, atomic bombs), concerning forms (declaration of war, treatment of prisoners), and concerning values (e.g., setting limits to the spoliation of property or of persons).

Comparing the total (military and civilian) casualties in the two world wars, we find that the estimated number of dead increased from 9.7 to 54.8 million and of wounded from 21.1 to 35.0 million.[8] This greater mortality was concentrated among the nationals of only a few countries, particularly Germany, Poland, and the Soviet Union, whereas for the other European belligerents World War II proved to be considerably less deadly than World War I. In the case of France, for example, military casualties amounted to about 200,000, or about one-seventh of those in 1914–18 (Vincent 1946); France's total loss of life due to World War II, including both direct and indirect mortality, amounted to about 1,130,000, which was made up in a few years by the unusually high postwar fertility. This decline in casualties was due in part to the improvement in military technology, with which the Nazi armies were really able to conduct a "lightning war."

In Germany, from one world war to the next, the number of military dead increased by about half (from 2,037,000 to 3,050,000), but the number of civilian dead by more than four times (from 500,000 to 2,050,000). Of the approximately 25 million adults killed in the Soviet Union during the war of 1941–45, more were civilians (some 15 million) than soldiers (see pp. 701–703). These figures illustrate what is perhaps the most important change that total war has effected with respect to mortality—the all but complete disappearance of the prior distinction between military and civilians as legitimate targets. Indeed, with the most devastating of modern weapons, the hydrogen bomb, such a distinction is hardly possible.

What would be the effects on the American population of a nuclear attack? No one knows, of course, but it is possible to speculate against a background of relevant knowledge. Two of the patterns of bombing analyzed by defense experts, depending on whether the raids were primarily at military targets or at both military and industrial targets, might result in an overall fatality ranging from 18 to 30 percent of the population. Since either kind of attack would be directed mainly at urban centers, the sectors of the population concentrated there—Catholics, Negroes, highly educated, and so on—would presumably suffer even greater losses than these figures. American institutions would be transformed by the postattack manpower shortages. Greater public controls would have to be substituted, at least for a period, for the free market in goods and services; larger welfare payments would demand heavier taxes to pay for them; with the state responsible both for the care of orphans and for urgent stimulation of greater fertility, the family system would be changed appreciably (Heer 1965).

The costs in human life of the Vietnam war have been surprisingly slight, despite repeated allegations to the contrary. Whether it was in the national interest of the United States to get involved in that war is a question on which a difference of opinion is reasonable, but this difference has often affected the

[8] German Federal Government, Press and Information Office, *Germany Reports* (Wiesbaden, 1953), pp. 101–103. For World War I, cf. also Dumas and Vedel-Petersen 1923.

ABOVE. Assembling place for wounded in the American Civil War, Savage Station, Virginia (*The Bettmann Archive, Inc.*).

BELOW. A MUST (Medical Unit Self-contained Transportable) Unit, comprising three compact elements, was used in the field in the Vietnam war. The shipping container, when unfolded, served as a modern facility for surgery; the inflatable shelter, with all the basic equipment of a hospital ward, could accommodate twenty combat casualties; and the self-contained utility system provided electric power, air conditioning, heating, hot and cold running water, and waste-water disposal (*U.S. Army*).

reporting of presumed facts. From 1961 through 1971, battle deaths among American forces totaled 45,629—including not only those killed in action but those who later died of wounds and those known to be dead among the men originally reported as captured or wounded. Over the 11 years, this total averages less than twelve men per day. Similarly, the *New York Times* and other news media repeatedly reported heavy civilian casualties from the "carpet bombing" of United States forces over North Vietnam, in spite of the fact that Hanoi Radio itself reported very few deaths. After reporters were able to get into Hanoi, the denials of the Air Force were validated. "United States air strikes against legitimate military targets in Hanoi seem to have been carried out with almost surgical precision. . . . Hanoi's people, contrary to some reports, seem to have had an easier war than some. . . . The city is hardly touched" (*Washington Star-News*, April 1, 1973).

In sum, there are three main determinants of military deaths, and the trend has not been consistent with respect to all three. The most important is the ability of the quartermaster corps to maintain supplies, both for military and supporting civilian forces, and of the medical corps to impede infections of wounds; here the improvement has been phenomenal. The second most important is the political–institutional type of the belligerent countries—whether or not they observe certain conventions even in fighting an all-out war. With the rise of totalitarianism during the 20th century, the trend has been toward the obliteration of all limits to killing, but the civilizing inhibitions are still usually intact among most Western nations. The third variable, the development of weapons of devastating power, is potentially the most important, but whether hydrogen bombs will ever be used depends on politics rather than technology.

SUMMARY

It would be useful to divide mortality into two types analogous to fecundity and fertility, but in practical terms such a classification is hampered by the fact that in most deaths biological and environmental influences are too closely interlinked. The physiological causes of death pertain to the individual organism, whereas most measures of death control operate through social institutions. One can pair the findings of nutritionists on the individual's food requirements with economists' data on the world's food production, or the characteristics that influence the individual's susceptibility to disease with the social organization of medical facilities, but at our present level of knowledge these are not equations that yield precise answers. In areas where food production and disease control are efficient, accidents, homicide, and other reflections of social disorder have been relatively more important causes of death. And if the world should engage in another all-out war, fought with weapons of unique destructive power, the devastation could be greater than at any time in all history. This must be noted as a possibility in spite of the fact that through the war of 1939–45 and beyond improved military (including medical) technology generally was associated with a proportionate decline in casualties.

The progress in medical science that has taken place during the lifetime of today's adults is probably greater than during the previous five millennia. If *all* mortality up to the age of 40 had been eliminated and age-specific rates for ages 41 and over had remained the same as they were in 1948, it was pointed out shortly after that year, the average expectation of life at birth would be 70.7 for white males and 75.0 years for white females (Dorn 1952)—or about the figures that have actually been achieved in the countries with the best control over mortality. Any appreciable decline in death rates from their present level will be attained, if at all, less by a simple extension of past improvements than by the introduction of radically new factors, especially some control over senescence. In some respects, there has been a retrogression—the rise of age-specific death rates of adult males, the sharp increase in the incidence of some diseases, and particularly the maladies associated with a partial breakdown of the social order.

How much has life expectation increased over the whole of human existence? The average length of life about doubled from prehistoric times to the Middle Ages, and then remained more or less static until the 19th century. During the last 150 years it has doubled again. The increase from roughly 18 to roughly 35 years, which took place before the development of industrial society, was due in the main to social innovations—in particular, the consolidation of large areas over which a powerful state maintained effective social control. The second doubling, from about 35 to about 70 years, can be ascribed in large part to technical improvements in agriculture, medicine, and public health, whose efficacy is so great that they tend to obscure other relevant factors. The successful application in underdeveloped countries of the most recent innovations in death control is almost completely independent, as we shall see in Chapter 15, of whether or not these nations are able to effect concomitant rises in social welfare. It is hardly an exaggeration to say that the social determinants of mortality have been reduced more and more to the single decisive one, whether the fruits of modern Western science are available.

CITED REFERENCES AND
SUGGESTIONS FOR FURTHER READING

The subject matter of this chapter overlaps with several related disciplines, from actuarial demography to epidemiology, from public health to the sociology of medicine. The works listed here comprise only a small portion of those that might be listed.

The methods of constructing a life table, a subject beyond the scope of this book, are fully discussed in a number of works focusing on formal demography: Barclay 1958: chap. 5 and Appendix; Spiegelman 1968: chap. 5; Shryock and Siegel 1971: chap. 15; the manual by the U.S. National Center for Health Statistics (1964). In spite of its date, the book by Louis Dublin and his associates (1949) is still one of the best primers on the uses of the life table.

A good introduction to the rapidly growing field of nutrition is by Williams (1962), written for the lay public by an authority in the discipline. Wohl and Good-hart (1964) is a professional text; the *Handbook of Nutrition* by the AMA Council on Food and Nutrition is medically authoritative and readable. Berg (1973) relates what is known of nutritional requirements to programs in underdeveloped countries.

Perhaps the most stimulating work on the general biology of death is by that pioneer, Raymond Pearl (1922). Such experts on epidemiology as Zinsser (1935) and Winslow (1952), and such a historian as Shrewsbury (1964), have written for the general reader, and those who enjoy following this type of detection might well supplement these works with the more popular book by Roueché (1955). Among the better items on the sociology of medicine, one might mention those by Mechanic (1968) and Scott and Volkart (1966). Stimulating discussions of the political–economic issues in health care include the works by Lerner and Anderson (1963), Kosa *et al.* (1969), and Ginzberg (1969).

ACHESON, E. D., editor. 1968. *Record Linkage in Medicine.* London: E. & S. Livingstone.

ALBANESE, ANTHONY A., and LOUISE A. ORTO. 1964. "The Proteins and Amino Acids," in Wohl and Goodhart 1964.

AMERICAN MEDICAL ASSOCIATION. COUNCIL ON FOODS AND NUTRITION. 1951. *Handbook on Nutrition,* 2nd ed. New York.

ARNHOFF, FRANKLYN N. 1955. "Research Problems in Gerontology," *Journal of Gerontology,* 10, 452–456.

AXELROD, A. E. 1964. "Nutrition in Relation to Acquired Immunity," in Wohl and Goodhart 1964.

BARCLAY, GEORGE W. 1958. *Techniques of Population Analysis.* New York: Wiley.

*BARRACLOUGH, B. M. 1972. "Are the Scottish and English Suicide Rates Really Different?" *British Journal of Psychiatry,* 120, 267–273.

BEECHER, HENRY K., *et al.* 1968. "A Definition of Irreversible Coma: Report of the Ad Hoc Committee of the Harvard Medical School to Examine the Definition of Brain Death," *Journal of the American Medical Association,* 205, 337–340.

BENJAMIN, HARRY. 1947. "Biologic versus Chronologic Age," *Journal of Gerontology,* 2, 217–227.

BERG, ALAN. 1973. *The Nutrition Factor: Its Role in National Development.* Washington, D.C.: Brookings Institution.

BERKSON, JOSEPH. 1962. "Mortality and Marital Status: Reflections on the Derivation of Etiology from Statistics," *American Journal of Public Health,* 52, 1318–1329.

BOURGEOIS-PICHAT, JEAN. 1946–51. "De la mesure de la mortalité infantile," *Population,* 1, 53–68; 6, 233–248, 459–480.

BROWNLEE, K. A. 1965. "A Review of 'Smoking and Health,'" *Journal of the American Statistical Association,* 60, 722–739.

*CARTWRIGHT, ANN. 1959. "Some Problems in the Collection and Analysis of Morbidity Data Obtained from Sample Surveys," *Milbank Memorial Fund Quarterly,* 37, 33–48.

————. 1963. "Memory Errors in a Morbidity Survey," *Milbank Memorial Fund Quarterly,* 41, 5–24.

*CHEN, EDITH, and SIDNEY COBB. 1960. "Family Structure in Relation to Health and Disease: A Review of the Literature," *Journal of Chronic Diseases*, 12, 544–567.

COHEN, BERNICE H. 1965. "Family Patterns of Longevity and Mortality," in James V. Neel, Margery W. Shaw, and William J. Schull, editors, *Genetics and the Epidemiology of Chronic Diseases*. Washington, D.C.: U.S. Public Health Service.

CORWIN, EMIL. 1972. "Roses, Music, Misocapnists, and Smoking," *Health Service Reports*, 87, 491–495.

*DAMON, ALBERT. 1969. "Race, Ethnic Group, and Disease," *Social Biology*, 16, 69–80.

DORN, HAROLD F. 1952. "Prospects of Further Decline in Mortality Rates," *Human Biology*, 24, 235–261.

————. 1956. "Some Problems for Research in Mortality and Morbidity," *Public Health Reports*, 71, 1–5.

*DUBLIN, LOUIS I., ALFRED J. LOTKA, and MORTIMER SPIEGELMAN. 1949. *Length of Life: A Study of the Life Table*, rev. ed. New York: Ronald.

DUMAS, SAMUEL, and K. O. VEDEL-PETERSEN. 1923. *Losses of Life Caused by War*. Carnegie Endowment for International Peace. Oxford: Clarendon.

DuNOÜY, PIERRE. 1936. *Biological Time*. London: Methuen.

DURKHEIM, EMILE. 1951. *Suicide*. New York: Free Press.

FELDMAN, JACOB J. 1958. "Barriers to the Use of Health Survey Data in Demographic Analysis," *Milbank Memorial Fund Quarterly*, 36, 203–220.

*FRANK, JEROME D. 1963. *Persuasion and Healing: A Comparative Study of Psychotherapy*. New York: Schocken.

*GIL, DAVID G. 1970. *Violence against Children: Physical Child Abuse in the United States*. Cambridge, Mass.: Harvard University Press.

*GINZBERG, ELI. 1969. *Men, Money, and Medicine*. New York: Columbia University Press.

GOODHART, ROBERT S. 1964. "Criteria of an Adequate Diet," in Wohl and Goodhart 1964.

GREDEN, JOHN F., and DONALD W. MORGAN. 1972. "Patterns of Drug Use and Attitudes toward Treatment in a Military Population," *Archives of General Psychiatry*, 26, 113–117.

GREENBERG, B. G. 1969. "Problems of Statistical Inference in Health with Special Reference to the Cigarette Smoking and Lung Cancer Controversy," *Journal of the American Statistical Association*, 64, 739–758.

HANSLUWKA, HAROLD, and ALWYN SMITH. 1971. "The Demographic Aspects of Differential Mortality and Morbidity According to Age and Sex in Europe: Their Social and Economic Consequences, Especially in the Field of Excess Male Mortality," Second European Population Conference, *Report*. Strasbourg: Council of Europe.

HARTE, ROBERT A., and BACON CHOW. 1964. "Dietary Interrelationships," in Wohl and Goodhart 1964.

HEER, DAVID M. 1965. *After Nuclear Attack: A Demographic Inquiry*. New York: Praeger.

HENRY, LOUIS. 1972. "The Population of Norway During the Past Two Centuries," in William Petersen, editor, *Readings in Population*. New York: Macmillan.

JAKOBOVITS, IMMANUEL. 1958. "The Dissection of the Dead in Jewish Law: A Comparative and Historical Study," *Tradition*, 1, 77–103.

JELLINEK, ELVIN M. 1947. "Recent Trends in Alcoholism and in Alcohol Consumption," *Quarterly Journal of Studies on Alcohol*, **8**, 1–42.

*KELLER, MARK. 1962. "The Definition of Alcoholism and the Estimation of Its Prevalence," in David J. Pittman and Charles R. Snyder, editors, *Society, Culture, and Drinking Patterns*. New York: Wiley.

KEMPE, C. HENRY, *et al.* 1962. "The Battered-Child Syndrome," *Journal of the American Medical Association*, **181**, 105–112.

*KEYS, ANCEL. 1951a. "Caloric Undernutrition and Starvation, with Notes on Protein Deficiency," in AMA 1951.

————. 1951b. "Energy Requirements of Adults," in AMA 1951.

KLEBBA, A. JOAN. 1966. *Mortality Trends in the United States, 1954–1963*. National Center for Health Statistics, Series 20, no. 2. Washington, D.C.: U.S. Government Printing Office.

————. 1971. *Leading Components of Upturn in Mortality for Men, United States, 1952–67*. National Center for Health Statistics, Series 20, no. 11. Washington, D.C.: U.S. Government Printing Office.

KLEIN, D., and J. A. WALLER. 1970. *Causation, Culpability and Deterrence in Highway Crashes*. Washington, D.C.: U.S. Government Printing Office.

KOSA, JOHN, AARON ANTONOVSKY, and IRVING KENNETH ZOLA, editors. 1969. *Poverty and Health: A Sociological Analysis*. Cambridge, Mass.: Harvard University Press.

LERNER, MONROE, and ODIN W. ANDERSON. 1963. *Health Progress in the United States, 1900–1963*. Chicago: University of Chicago Press.

*————, and DAVID N. NURCO. 1970. "Drug Abuse Deaths in Baltimore, 1951–1966," *International Journal of the Addictions*, **5**, 693–715.

*LIBERMAN, ROBERT. 1961. "An Analysis of the Placebo Phenomenon," *Journal of Chronic Diseases*, **15**, 761–783.

LINDER, FORREST E. 1967. "The Health of the American People," *Statistical Reporter*, **67**, 113–118.

LOCKE, HARVEY J. 1939. "Changing Attitudes Toward Venereal Diseases," *American Sociological Review*, **4**, 836–843.

MACLEOD, GRACE, and HENRY C. SHERMAN. 1951. "Recommended Dietary Allowances," in AMA 1951.

*MADIGAN, FRANCIS C. 1957. "Are Sex Mortality Differentials Biologically Caused?" *Milbank Memorial Fund Quarterly*, **35**, 202–223.

MECHANIC, DAVID. 1968. *Medical Sociology: A Selective View*. New York: Free Press.

METROPOLITAN LIFE INSURANCE CO. 1972. "Cancer Mortality in the 1960s," *Statistical Bulletin*, March.

MILLER, RICHARD S. 1972. "The Needs and Potential for Cooperation between Human Factors Specialists and Lawyers in Research and Development of Automobile Accident Law," *Human Factors*, **14**, 25–33.

MORIYAMA, IWAO M., and THOMAS E. N. GREVILLE. 1944. "Effect of Changing Birth Rates upon Infant Mortality Rates," *Vital Statistics—Special Reports*, **19**, no. 21.

MOYNIHAN, DANIEL P. 1966. "The War Against the Automobile," *Public Interest*, no. 3, pp. 10–26.

*NAGI, SAAD Z. 1969. *Disability and Rehabilitation: Legal, Clinical, and Self-Concepts and Measurement.* Columbus: Ohio State University Press.

NATIONAL SAFETY COUNCIL. 1970. *Accident Facts: 1970 Edition.* Chicago.

PASSMORE, R. 1963. "Estimation of Food Requirements," in Royal Statistical Society 1963.

PEARL, RAYMOND. 1922. *The Biology of Death.* Philadelphia: Lippincott.

———, and RUTH DeWITT PEARL. 1934. *The Ancestry of the Long-Lived.* Baltimore: Johns Hopkins Press.

PHILLIPS, DAVID P., and KENNETH A. FELDMAN. 1973. "A Dip in Deaths before Ceremonial Occasions: Some New Relationships between Social Integration and Mortality," *American Sociological Review*, **38**, 678–696.

POLANYI, KARL. 1944. *The Great Transformation.* New York: Rinehart.

*PRESTON, SAMUEL H. 1970. "An International Comparison of Excessive Adult Mortality," *Population Studies*, **24**, 5–20.

———, NATHAN KEYFITZ, and ROBERT SCHOEN. 1972. *Causes of Death: Life Tables for National Populations.* New York: Seminar Press.

*PRUTTING, JOHN. 1967. "Lack of Correlation between Antemortem and Postmortem Diagnoses," *N.Y. State Journal of Medicine*, **67**, 2081–2084.

———, et al. 1968. "Medical Progress and the Postmortem: A Symposium," *Bulletin of the N.Y. Academy of Medicine*, **44**, 792–861.

REES, W. DEWI, and SYLVIA G. LUTKINS. 1967. "Mortality of Bereavement," *British Medical Journal*, **4**, 13–16.

RETHERFORD, ROBERT D. 1972. "Tobacco Smoking and the Sex Mortality Differential," *Demography*, **9**, 203–216.

ROBERTSON, LEON S., et al. 1972. "Factors Associated with Observed Safety Belt Use," *Journal of Health and Social Behavior*, **13**, 18–24.

ROUECHÉ, BERTON. 1955. *Eleven Blue Men and Other Narratives of Medical Detection.* New York: Berkley.

ROYAL STATISTICAL SOCIETY. 1963. *Food Supplies and Population Growth.* Edinburgh: Oliver & Boyd.

RUSH, DAVID, and EDWARD H. KASS. 1972. "Maternal Smoking: A Reassessment of the Association with Perinatal Mortality," *American Journal of Epidemiology*, **96**, 183–196.

SAINSBURY, PETER. 1972. "The Social Relations of Suicide: The Value of a Combined Epidemiological and Case Study Approach," *Social Science and Medicine*, **6**, 189–198.

SAUNDERS, LYLE. 1954. *Cultural Difference and Medical Care: The Case of the Spanish-speaking People of the Southwest.* New York: Russell Sage Foundation.

*SCHULTZ, ADOLPH H. 1939. "Notes on Diseases and Healed Fractures of Wild Apes," *Bulletin of the History of Medicine*, 7, 571–581.

SCOTT, W. RICHARD, and EDMUND H. VOLKART, editors. 1966. *Medical Care: Readings in the Sociology of Medical Institutions.* New York: Wiley.

SHEPS, MINDEL C. 1961. "Marriage and Mortality," *American Journal of Public Health*, **51**, 547–555.

SHREWSBURY, J. F. D. 1964. *The Plague of the Philistines and Other Medical-Historical Essays.* London: Gollancz.

SHRYOCK, HENRY S., and JACOB S. SIEGEL. 1971. *The Methods and Materials of Demography.* Washington, D.C.: U.S. Government Printing Office.

SIGEL, M. MICHAEL, and ROBERT A. GOOD, editors. 1972. *Tolerance, Autoimmunity and Aging*. Springfield, Ill.: Thomas.

SIGERIST, HENRY E. 1967. *Primitive and Archaic Medicine*. New York: Oxford-Galaxy.

SOROKIN, PITIRIM A. 1937. *Social and Cultural Dynamics*, vol. 3: *Fluctuations of Social Relationships, War, and Revolution*. New York: American Book Company.

SPAIN, DAVID M., HENRY SIEGEL, and VICTORIA A. BRADESS. 1973. "Women Smokers and Sudden Death," *Journal of the American Medical Association*, **224**, 1005–1007.

SPEIER, HANS. 1952. *Social Order and the Risks of War*. New York: Stewart.

SPIEGELMAN, MORTIMER. 1968. *Introduction to Demography*, rev. ed. Cambridge, Mass.: Harvard University Press.

STANTON, MORRIS D. 1972. "Drug Use in Vietnam," *Archives of General Psychiatry*, **26**, 279–286.

STREHLER, BERNARD L. 1967. "The Origins of Senescence," *Society of Actuaries Transactions*, **19**, Part II, pp. D429–440.

SUCHMAN, E. A. 1970. "Accidents and Social Deviance," *Journal of Health and Social Behavior*, **11**, 4–15.

TORREY, E. FULLER. 1972. *The Mind Game: Witchdoctors and Psychiatrists*. New York: Emerson Hall.

TRACY, RICHARD E. 1966. "Sex Difference in Coronary Disease: Two Opposing Views," *Journal of Chronic Diseases*, **19**, 1245–1251.

*U.S. DEPARTMENT OF HEALTH, EDUCATION, AND WELFARE. 1971. *First Special Report to the U.S. Congress on Alcohol and Health*. Washington, D.C.: U.S. Government Printing Office.

U.S. NATIONAL CENTER FOR HEALTH STATISTICS. 1964. *Comparison of Two Methods of Constructing Abridged Life Tables by Reference to a "Standard" Table*. Vital and Health Statistics, Series 2, no. 4. Washington, D.C.: U.S. Government Printing Office.

———. 1973. *Current Estimates from the Health Interview Survey, United States, 1972*, Series 10, no. 85. Washington, D.C.: U.S. Government Printing Office.

U.S. NATIONAL COMMISSION ON VENEREAL DISEASE. 1972. *Report*. Washington, D.C.: U.S. Department of Health, Education, and Welfare.

U.S. PUBLIC HEALTH SERVICE. 1967–68. *Eighth Revision, International Classification of Diseases, Adapted for Use in the United States*, 2 vol. Washington, D.C.: U.S. Government Printing Office.

VINCENT, PAUL. 1946. "Conséquences de six années de guerre sur la population française," *Population*, **1**, 429–440.

WATTS, DOROTHY D. 1966. "Factors Related to the Acceptance of Modern Medicine," *American Journal of Public Health*, **56**, 1205–1212.

WILKINS, JAMES. 1967. "Suicidal Behavior," *American Sociological Review*, **32**, 286–298.

WILLIAMS, ROGER J. 1962. *Nutrition in a Nutshell*. Garden City, N.Y.: Doubleday.

WINSLOW, C.-E. A. 1952. *Man and Epidemics*. Princeton, N.J.: Princeton University Press.

*WOHL, MICHAEL G., and ROBERT S. GOODHART, editors. 1964. *Modern Nutrition in Health and Disease: Dietotherapy*, 3rd ed. Philadelphia: Lea & Febiger.

WRIGHT, QUINCY. 1942. *A Study of War*. Chicago: University of Chicago Press.

*ZINSSER, HANS. 1935. *Rats, Lice and History: . . . The History of Typhus Fever*. Boston: Little, Brown. (Reissued as a Bantam paperback, 1960.)

————, JOHN F. ENDERS, and LEROY D. FOTHERGILL. 1940. *Immunity: Principles and Application in Medicine and Public Health*, 5th ed. New York: Macmillan.

THE GENERAL DETERMINANTS OF MIGRATION

8

The modern era has seen sizable movements of peoples in various parts of the world—for instance, the migration of Chinese into Southeast Asia, of Indians to Eastern and Southern Africa, or of Africans to the Americas. The most significant in terms of both numbers and the diffusion of culture patterns was the emigration of Europeans. In the great awakening of Western civilization that we term the Renaissance, European man began to explore not only the Greek and Roman foundations of his civilization and the physical and biological laws of nature, but also the world beyond the Mediterranean basin and the eastern Atlantic. The ships of Spain and Portugal, of England and Holland, worked their way down the coast of Africa and, around the middle of the 15th century, found a sea route to Asia. At the end of the century, 3,000 miles to the west, they discovered a veritable New World, vast, rich in every natural resource, and virtually unpeopled. During the two centuries following, tiny bands of explorers sought gold, glory, or salvation, establishing dominion over a million square miles by the planting of a flag.

The age of discovery and colonization merged into the Great Migration. The mass movement from Europe in the 19th century was on a scale new in human history. Of the 67 million persons who crossed an ocean from 1800 to 1950, some 60 million were Europeans, and of these two out of every three went to the United States. That analysts of migration, and particularly the Americans among them, should derive their precepts entirely from this prototype is perhaps understandable, for the strong tendency in all of us toward ethnocentrism is here reinforced by the universal significance of this element of American civilization. We shall attempt to avoid that trap. Migration does not always follow whatever laws can be derived from the transatlantic movement during the 19th century; for all its importance, it should be seen as one type among others.

When we speak of the general determinants of migration, we cannot begin with an analogy to fecundity and the biology of mortality. Migration is not universal: we are all born and we all die, but only some of us migrate. Even the strongest motivation results in migration only when it has been translated into action by human will. And the migration that does take place, on the other hand, often completely lacks any biological incentive. As was noted in the earlier discussion

279

A group of immigrants, segregated by sex, waiting for further processing at Ellis Island, ca. 1910 (*The Bettmann Archive, Inc.*).

of migration statistics (see pp. 41–45, 46–47), the concept is riddled with ambiguity. When one speaks of migratory birds, or migrant laborers, or nomads, the connotation is not of a permanent move from one area to another, but rather of a permanently migratory way of life, which often means a cyclical movement within a more or less restricted area. On the other hand, the sense associated with the word's derivation from the Latin *migrare*, "to change one's residence," is rather to change one's community. A person who moves from one home to another in the same neighborhood and who therefore retains the same social framework is ordinarily not deemed to be a migrant. "Change of community" as an index of migration affords a very rough gauge of the meaning to be assigned to such indeterminate words as *permanent* and *significant* in the usual definition of **migration**—the relatively permanent movement of persons over a significant distance.

MIGRATION AND POPULATION GROWTH

That individual migrants become permanent residents of the new country does not mean that one can merely add them up to derive the demographic effect of the migration. Common sense tells us that if 1,000 persons migrate from Country *A* to Country *B*, the population of Country *A* is decreased by 1,000 and that of Country *B* is increased by the same number. However, in all probability the shift will bring about changes in the population structure, economy, and social conditions of both countries, and these changes in turn will influence the population growth of each. If we take these indirect effects into account, the relation between migration and population is a good deal more complex than it would seem at first sight (cf. Tabah and Cataldi 1963).

1. Under some circumstances, particularly in large international movements, the effect of migration on the sending country may be nil. As we have seen, one of Malthus's principal theses was that, other things being equal, the population of any area generally tends to increase up to the maximum that the economy can support. Wherever this is indeed the case, the effect of migration on the size of the population of either of the areas involved cannot be very great: emigrants will eventually be replaced through a higher natural increase, and immigrants will merely take the place of natives who would otherwise have been born (or, if born, would have stayed alive). People leaving a country like India or China, thus, have practically no effect on the eventual number remaining.

Under such conditions migration effects a real shift in population only when those who move have special skills, so that there is a concomitant shift in what Benjamin Franklin termed "the state of the arts." In general, emigration was for Malthus "a slight palliative," "a partial and temporary expedient" with "no permanent effect on population" (*Essay*, 7th ed., Book 3, chap. 4). It must be noted, however, that with respect to policy Malthus's usual emphasis was not on this presumed absence of long-term effects but on the more immediate, temporary consequences. He considered emigration "well worthy the attention of the government, both as a matter of humanity and policy" (ibid.). The evidence that he gave before the Second Select Committee on Emigration in 1827 was based on these considerations rather than on the hypothesis that emigration would have no permanent effect on the size of the Irish population. Similarly, Warren Thompson (1948: 154–155) concluded from a study of the movement from Shantung and Hopei to Manchuria that "emigration can do little or nothing to mitigate the actual physical poverty of the densely settled lands of Asia." This judgment, again, did not determine the policy he recommended: "Permitting these peoples to migrate even though relatively few could actually move would help greatly in creating a better atmosphere in which to discuss the problems of population pressure and the better distribution of the world's resources."

In one of the first efforts to add up Europe's population, Willcox (1906) estimated that it had increased from 130 million in 1750 to 500 million in 1900, and "the persons of European stock living outside of Europe in 1900 were three-fourths as many as the entire number of inhabitants of that continent in 1750." "Instead of draining off Europe's population, the steady stream of emigrants promoted its unprecedented growth, [for] the removal of the excess population prevented catastrophes such as those which had formerly destroyed peoples and economies" (Kulischer 1948: 28). Or, with respect to a specific country, "it is arguable that the population of Italy is not less than it would have been if emigration had not taken place, and perhaps is greater" (Foerster 1924: 469).

2. However, movement out of an area, particularly one with a small population to begin with, can remove the base from which subsequent recuperation would have taken place. Migrants are characteristically young adults, and their departure typically means a rise in the country's average age and thus an increase in its death rate. And as they take with them, as it were, their future progeny, the birth rate typically falls. Most countries in which either urban growth or emigration from the countryside has been sizable have complained recurrently of rural depopulation, even in nations that as a whole suffer from agrarian overpopulation. The effects of emigration on certain districts in southern Italy, for example, "have been officially compared with those of a pestilence. . . . Here are villages all but abandoned, the houses uninhabited and in decay, grass growing in the streets, and in the gardens weeds choking whatever vegetables come up. Far and wide, it is the aged, the women, and the children who constitute the labor force" (ibid.: 449). In the United States, similarly, the out-migration from New England left behind some half-abandoned villages; Lyme, N.H., having reached a maximum size around 1830, thereafter lost people to the new land in the West and later to the manufacturing towns (Goldthwait 1927). Very often the abandoned land is marginal in one sense or another, either because of its low fertility (as in the Southeast of France), or because of particularly oppressive relations with landowners (as sometimes in Italy), or because of the decline of rural industries (as in parts of England; cf. Saville 1957: 20–30).

Rural depopulation can affect whole districts or even whole countries. The classic examples are Ireland and Scotland, in particular the island of Skye. More recently, an interesting case study was made of the Greek island of Ithaca. In the 19th-century tradition, the island's population was supported in large part by seamen, who after long separations came home to settle down with their families. Around 1910 this somewhat precarious balance was disturbed by the new opportunities opening up in the United States and other immigration countries, so that many of the young men who sailed away never returned. With the radically altered sex ratio, marriages were fewer and at a later age, and the strong patrifocal extended family started to fall apart. With the shortage of labor, between 1896 and 1951 the cultivated land declined by more than a quarter and the value of agricultural production by almost half. Over these same years the island's population fell off by almost half, or from 11,409 to 5,877 (Lowenthal and Comitas 1962).

3. The effect of migration to cities on urban populations has been enormous. In the early modern period, when infections spread uninhibited through the dirty congested quarters of the growing towns, these usually had higher death rates than the surrounding countryside. After some control was established over urban mortality, the low birth rate of cities still kept the natural increase relatively low. The stupendous rise of urban centers over the past two centuries, thus, has been in large part the consequence of in-migration.

4. The possible effect of immigration on the population of the receiving

Table 8-1. Recorded Immigration to the United States, by Decades, 1819–1970

Period	Number (− 000)	Rate[a]
1819–30	152	1.2
1831–40	599	3.9
1841–50	1,713	8.4
1851–60	2,598	9.3
1861–70	2,315	6.4
1871–80	2,812	6.2
1881–90	5,247	9.2
1891–1900	3,688	5.3
1901–10	8,795	10.4
1911–20	5,736	5.7
1921–30	4,107	3.5
1931–40	528	0.4
1941–50	1,035	0.7
1951–60	2,515	1.5
1961–70	3,321	1.7
1819–1970	45,162	3.7

[a] The immigration during the period, divided by the sum of the annual estimates of the population totals during that period, times 1,000.
SOURCE: U.S. Bureau of the Census, *Statistical Abstract of the United States, 1971* (Washington, D.C.: U.S. Government Printing Office, 1971), Table 130.

country can be illustrated with the United States. Immigration to that country from the beginning of the statistical record in 1819 is summarized in Table 8-1. The number arriving rose after 1880 both absolutely and as a proportion of the resident population, fell off during the depression of the 1890s, and after the turn of the century again set new records. In the fiscal year ending June 30, 1907, the high point of 1,285,349 was reached, and in each of five other years up to 1914 more than a million immigrants were recorded. Even at the peak of this wave, however, the proportion of newcomers to the resident population—perhaps a more meaningful index than the absolute number—did not rise much above that in the 1840s and 1850s. But the immigration of more than a million in one year was a fact that stayed in one's mind. And it was not only, not even principally, a question of numbers. Until the 1880s the "Old" Immigrants had come from Northwest Europe, and from that date on the increasing proportion of "New" Immigrants came from Southern and Eastern Europe. Arguments for restriction of numbers were based in many instances on hostility to Italians, Poles, and Russian Jews.

The fluidity of analytical postulates on this matter can be illustrated by the several articles of Francis A. Walker, superintendent of several censuses and among post-Civil War Malthusians "probably the most influential writer on population," who molded a dozen or more important economists and demographers (Spengler 1933). At the beginning of the 19th century one Elkanah Watson noticed that without immigration, which had been interrupted by the wars in Europe, the population of the United States had increased by about one-third during each of the two decades following the 1790 census. His population projection at the same high rate of growth up to 1900 was widely accepted (see p. 336). In 1873 Walker wrote an article gently deriding Watson's thesis. When a geometrical progression is found in human affairs, "the most improbable supposition which could be formed respecting it is that it will continue." In fact, the natural increase had not been maintained at the projected rate; American fertility began to fall with the shift of the people from agriculture to manufacturing, from country to town. That nevertheless the population increase was maintained for several decades was due to "a flood of immigration unprecedented in history" (Walker 1873).

Twenty years later the same man wrote three more articles on the relation between immigration and population growth (Walker 1891, 1892, 1896). He used Watson's projection again, but this time as a criterion for judging the actual population growth. Immigration, he now found, "instead of constituting a net reinforcement to the population, simply resulted in a replacement of native by foreign elements," for the American "was unwilling himself to engage in the lowest kind of day labor with these new elements ... [and] even more unwilling to bring sons and daughters into the world to enter that competition." For Walker, the essential question was how to protect "the quality of American citizenship from degradation through the tumultuous access of vast throngs of ignorant and brutalized peasantry" from the countries of Eastern and Southern Europe.

That Walker was hostile to New Immigrants is not the point, but rather that a social scientist of his high standing reversed himself on a key demographic question in an attempt to validate that political stance. In the 1870s he found that America's fertility was falling because of the transformation into an urban–industrial society, and the only effect of immigration was to "cover from the common sight" the decline in the natural increase. In the 1890s he asserted that fertility would have remained at its projected high level but for the economic competition of immigrants. In the 1870s the geometrical progression was dismissed out of hand; in the 1890s Walker was one of the most prominent "Malthusians." The contrasts underline not only one man's inconsistencies, but also the complexity of the apparently simple question: what *is* the effect of migration on population growth?

The crucial test of Walker's thesis was to specify the date when the decline in fertility began. Using census data and the child–woman ratio, Willcox (1911) showed that, except for the single decade 1850–60, fertility had declined steadily from 1810 on. It was the rise in fertility during those 10 years, probably the consequence of the heavy immigration of young adults, that had led previous investigators to conclude that the birth rate had been increasing or stationary up to the Civil War. In short, Walker's "theory had its value as a challenge of the current belief that immigration regularly increased the population by an amount equal to its number. But it is almost equally incorrect to maintain that it did not increase the population at all" (Willcox and Ferenczi 1929–31, vol. 1: 103).

In summary, the relation between migration and population growth[1] can be analyzed with three components: (1) the direct movement of the migrants themselves; (2) the effect of the movement on the population structure of the two areas, which ordinarily increases the size of the transfer; and (3) the effect on social–economic conditions in the two areas, which may reduce or cancel the results of the transfer. In the abstract, one can say that all three of these factors are always relevant. In the concrete, their total impact is discernible only in such extreme cases as, for example, emigration from a very densely settled country like India or immigration to a relatively empty country like the British colonies in America; the latter was Malthus's prime example of a population increase due to migration.

Total Versus Net Migration

In the discussion thus far of how migration affects the population growth of the two areas concerned, it has been assumed that all the movement is in one direction. The official immigration figures cited in Table 8-1, for instance, are deceptive, for they list merely the numbers who came into the United States and ignore those who left. Yet during the height of the mass immigration of 1890–1910, an estimated 40 percent of the foreign-born emigrated (Kuznets and Rubin 1954: Table 7). Conclusions drawn from gross migration data are likely to be grossly inaccurate with respect to not only the size of the movement but also all its other characteristics.

Movement In Versus Out. Most attempts to analyze migration, as we shall see, are based on the premise that in various ways one area is more attractive than the other, so that these countermovements are not explained. It is more reasonable to posit a differentiation by type of migrant: young people move out of Florida seeking better employment, whereas the old move in to one of the state's retirement settlements. One of the few attempts to develop such a broader theory was made by William Burton Hurd, a Canadian professor of political

[1] Other attempts to sum up these diverse possibilities and the schools of thought concerning them (e.g., Gonnard 1927: 285–286, 323–324) suggest the range of possible views. According to Gini (1946), when the population of a country is in a state of equilibrium, neither immigration nor emigration affects the total numbers in the long run. On the other hand, if migration takes place from an overpopulated country, or to an underpopulated one, this movement does change the total population. It would be difficult to put the case less well.

science who imported Walker's theory to that country, also in an effort to bolster his opposition to non-British immigrants. Hurd's thesis that *immigration causes emigration* follows the essence of Walker's argument: because immigrants created an economic and social environment unpalatable to native-born Canadians, these moved out to the United States. Immigration thus effected not an addition to Canada's population, but only a substitution of less desirable for more desirable sectors. The hypothesis was not valid in the Canadian case, and Hurd made no effort to exemplify it with other data (cf. Petersen 1955: 202–210).

More generally, it can be hypothesized with respect to both internal and international movements that "for every major migration stream, a counterstream develops" (Lee 1966). The reasons given are three: improved communication between two areas facilitates movement in both directions; the original attractions at the first destination may lessen or disappear, in part even as a consequence of the increased numbers; and some of those who moved in may always have intended to leave.

Remigrants—those who leave their country (or area) for a period and then return to it—typically make up a large portion of any countermovement. They ordinarily differ from the emigrants who remain abroad, but not necessarily according to any consistent pattern. Particularly during an economic depression, some immigrants leave the new country when they lose their jobs (Berthoff 1953: 73). Sometimes, on the contrary, it is the relatively successful that return, either to find a wife (Borrie 1954) or to retire. The rise of nationalism in the old country often attracts back some of the incompletely assimilated emigrants (Saloutos 1956). Even a small percentage of the subsidized migrants to Australia and Canada return to Britain (Appleyard 1962; Richmond 1968; Richardson 1968).

The differences between Old and New Immigrants to the United States are far less when measured by net migration than by gross. For the period 1908 to 1923—that is, from the beginning of the record on the immigration of aliens to just before the establishment of the national-quota system—the average remigration amounted to 35.2 percent of the immigration. But for the different nationalities this percentage varied as follows (Willcox and Ferenczi 1929–31, vol. 2: 206–207):

Chinese	130	Lithuanian	25
Bulgarian, Serbian,		Syrian	24
and Montenegrin	89	Scandinavian	22
Turkish	86	African	22
Korean	73	French	21
Rumanian	66	English	21
Hungarian	66	Mexican	19
Southern Italian	60	Dutch and Flemish	18
Cuban	58	Armenian	15
Slovak	57	Scottish and Welsh	13
Russian	52	Irish	11
Finnish	29	Jewish	5

From this list it is evident that a much larger percentage of New Immigrants returned home than of Old Immigrants. (Of course, special factors influenced the remigration rate of certain of the nationalities, particularly the two extremes —the Chinese, of whom more departed than arrived, and the Jews, most of whom were undoubtedly classified elsewhere.) There is no reason to suppose that this was not true also of the period before 1908, for which direct data are not available. Indeed, one of the arguments that the advocates of restriction offered was that immigrants at the end of the century were less likely to settle permanently than those a generation or two earlier. Almost by definition, the remigrants were less able to acculturate to their new environment than the immigrants who remained, but few valid generalizations can be added to that truism.

Transmigrants, those who move into an area for a period and then out of it, can sometimes be identified as such in the statistics of international migration, but not necessarily. For example, a person intending to immigrate to the United States but not able to get a visa may live in a neighboring country while waiting for it, and one of Hurd's complaints against immigrants to Canada was that many used that country only as a passageway. He could not substantiate this charge, for, as is usually the case, transmigrants merge into general statistics in and out, and thus by their double count artificially raise both numbers.

Similarly in internal migration, it is known from sample surveys that each year approximately one American in five moves to a new residence. However, according to a detailed analysis of one particular community (Goldstein 1954), a sizable proportion of this large percentage is made up of persons who move more than once during a year and who are atypical also in other ways. A study of repeated migration in Denmark suggests that the phenomenon is not restricted to the United States (Goldstein 1964).

MIGRATORY SELECTION

Even the demographic effect of a migration, not to say the economic or cultural effect, depends on how many move and on their characteristics. In a study of migrants to Aberdeen, that is, of movement within Scotland over only a few years, it was found useful to classify respondents into a number of types. These included, among others, professionals advancing their careers, young persons seeking an education, workers taking specific jobs, casual laborers looking for employment, wives and children joining the heads of families, and remigrants (Illsley *et al.* 1963). The conclusions to be drawn differed to some degree for each of these categories. If it is useful to specify to this degree the types moving within a relatively homogeneous area, then manifestly it is so with respect to migration encompassing the whole world and all of history. A general analysis of migration, in other words, must begin with the various motives that determine why in any situation some leave and others stay, and since these motives are not usually established directly, they must be inferred from the differential migration rates.

Given a sedentary population and an inducement to leave, migrants become differentiated from nonmigrants by the fact that neither category is a random sample of the whole population. This process of migrants' self-selection according to various social characteristics is called **migratory selection** (or "selective migration"). Whether the decision is made by the migrants themselves is not a crucial distinction in a demographic context. Two centuries ago a slave-trader raiding the African coast would have chosen only young, healthy Negroes; or, more recently, various governments have established quotas by which the immigration of some classes is fostered and that of others is impeded or prohibited. Such regulations by an outside force, while quite dissimilar in some respects from a process of self-selection, are also examples of what we term migratory selection.

Age

With respect to age differentiation, all migration is one: in both internal and international movements, adolescents and young adults usually predominate. This is one of the most firmly established generalizations in demography. Between two-thirds and four-fifths of the immigrants to the United States in the 19th century were aged between 15 and 40 years (Willcox and Ferenczi 1929–31, vol. 2: 212–213). The proportion in internal migration is typically just as large: for example, the median ages of persons who had moved within the United States during the year 1949–50 ranged, according to their color and the size of their 1949 place of residence, from 19.8 to 30.5 years (Duncan and Reiss 1956: 83–87). Even those inclined to doubt whether rural–urban migration is selective by other characteristics hold that it is so with respect to age and, to a lesser degree, sex (e.g., Sorokin and Zimmerman 1929: 582). That young adults predominate does not mean, of course, that other persons never migrate. Families that move, particularly within a single country, may include young children (Shryock 1964: 352) or, less frequently, elderly parents; and in recent years some of the migration within the United States has been the movement of retired persons.

One reason for the high proportion of young adults would seem to be that any migration involves a certain amount of adjustment at the destination, and youth connotes a better ability to adapt to new circumstances. A second reason, relevant when geographical mobility is a concomitant of job changes, is that these are more frequent among persons who have only recently started to work.

The age bracket of young adults is also distinguished from the rest of a population by many other characteristics, both physiological and social, and a comparison between migrants and nonmigrants is therefore misleading unless age is held constant.

Age is such an important discriminant for mobility status that we need to be sure that a difference in, for example, the migration rates of two social–economic groups is not simply attributable to differences in age composition of these groups. In many of the available statistics, however, there is no cross-classification by age, and recourse must be made to an analysis by indirect methods [ibid.: 30–31].

Migrants generally enter the labor force in proportionately larger numbers than a sedentary population. In the years before World War I, it was often pointed out that immigrants to the United States had a much higher birth rate than the native population, and until recently some of the new suburbs used to look like mass nurseries. In both cases the real difference in fertility was exaggerated by the atypical age structure.

Sex

Selection by sex is also usual, but whether males or females predominate depends on the circumstances. One of Ravenstein's famous "laws" was that "females are more migratory than males," but even he noted that this was more true for short distances than for longer ones (Ravenstein 1885–89; cf. Lee 1966). The 19th-century movement into European towns from the surrounding countryside, the local movement that Ravenstein alluded to, was made up in large part of young farm girls who found work as domestic servants in the homes of the urban middle class. An international migration that does not involve great distances or the crossing of an important cultural boundary may also show a predominance of females, and for the same reason. Thus, for example, most of those who left Germany for the Netherlands in the interwar years were also domestic servants, so that in this international migration the sex ratio was typically very low (Kirk 1946: 117n.). Another example is the settlement of Irish servants in England or even the United States. A 19th-century farm boy, on the other hand, acquired no skills useful to him in getting established in the city; if he left the farm, he would be more likely to go to a place where his youthful energy and physical strength were at a premium.

The characteristics of any frontier town, like those of the white populations of the American West a century ago or of New Guinea today, derive in part from its very high sex ratio and the consequent almost total lack of family life. In Colorado in 1860, for example, only 3.2 percent of the total population consisted of women in the reproductive ages. Similarly, males are likely to predominate during the first stages of emigration from any country, no matter what the destination. Thus, among pre-1914 migrants to the United States, the sex ratio of those from Southern and Eastern Europe was very much higher than of those from Northwest Europe, even though at that time most newcomers of whatever nationality settled in cities. These were certainly not a frontier in the usual sense, but until a sizable Polish or Italian community, for example, was built up in America, there were more males among the immigrants from those countries.

Characteristically, then, internal migrants are predominantly female and international ones predominantly male, but this generalization cannot aptly

Table 8-2. Percentage Distribution of Population Aged 5 and Over, by Place of Birth, Residence in 1965 and in 1970, Sex, and Age Bracket, United States, 1970

| Sex and Age Bracket | Native-born, Living in: | | | | | | | | Foreign-born |
| | State of Birth in 1970 | | | Not State of Birth in 1970 | | | | | |
	STATE OF BIRTH, 1965	DIFFERENT STATE, 1965	ABROAD[a] IN 1965	SAME STATE, 1965 AND 1970	STATE OF BIRTH, 1965	DIFFERENT STATES, 1965 AND 1970	ABROAD[a] IN 1965	OTHER	
Male									
5–9	73.5	1.7	3.3	5.7	5.9	2.2	1.1	5.6	1.2
10–14	73.2	1.5	2.0	9.8	3.4	2.5	0.8	5.4	1.4
15–19	69.2	1.3	1.7	12.0	4.9	2.5	1.0	5.7	1.8
20–24	54.1	2.7	2.9	11.4	12.2	5.0	2.0	6.8	2.9
25–29	49.9	5.3	3.9	15.0	6.6	6.9	2.7	5.8	4.0
30–34	52.5	3.0	1.8	19.9	4.3	5.9	1.8	5.7	5.1
35–44	54.4	1.9	1.2	24.1	2.6	4.3	1.4	5.3	4.9
45–54	55.2	1.0	0.9	28.4	1.4	2.5	0.8	5.0	4.8
55–64	54.5	0.7	0.7	28.0	1.1	1.5	0.5	5.2	7.8
65–74	48.8	0.7	0.7	26.2	1.3	1.6	0.5	5.8	14.4
75+	44.2	0.5	1.0	24.5	1.0	1.1	0.5	7.0	20.3
5–75+	59.3	1.8	1.8	18.1	4.1	3.2	1.2	5.6	4.9

Female

Age									
5–9	73.5	1.7	3.4	5.7	5.9	2.2	1.1	5.5	1.1
10–14	73.2	1.6	2.0	9.8	3.4	2.5	0.8	5.4	1.4
15–19	70.2	1.4	1.8	12.2	4.1	2.3	0.8	5.3	1.8
20–24	58.9	2.3	2.4	12.7	9.3	4.1	1.1	5.9	3.4
25–29	52.9	3.5	2.1	17.3	6.5	5.8	1.3	5.6	4.9
30–34	53.0	2.6	1.6	21.3	3.7	4.9	1.2	5.6	6.1
35–44	55.1	1.6	1.2	24.7	2.2	3.3	0.9	5.2	5.8
45–54	56.0	0.9	0.9	27.8	1.3	2.0	0.7	5.0	5.3
55–64	55.0	0.8	0.9	27.1	1.2	1.5	0.6	5.2	7.7
65–74	50.5	0.8	0.9	25.7	1.3	1.4	0.6	5.5	13.4
75+	47.2	0.7	1.3	24.7	1.1	1.2	0.7	7.0	16.1
5–75+	59.8	1.6	1.7	18.8	3.6	2.7	0.9	5.5	5.4

[a] Includes those whose residence was not reported.

SOURCE: U.S. Bureau of the Census, *Census of Population, 1970*. Subject Reports: "Lifetime and Recent Migration," Final Report PC(2)-2D (Washington, D.C.: U.S. Government Printing Office, 1973), Table 1.

be designated a "law" that applies to non-Western societies. In both cases the reason for the sex ratio is that the social conditions at the destinations favor one or the other sex. Most who left India were contract laborers, and thus male, and only somewhat later did the more successful of overseas Indians have females brought over as brides. Those who have moved within India from village to town, however, have also been predominantly male. In the only four large cities with adequate statistics, the average sex ratio of in-migrants in 1931 was 154 (Davis 1951: 135). Single girls have generally been too closely bound to traditional village roles to be able to leave independently, and when husbands have gone to the city, they very often have left their families at home and returned to them as soon as they could. The sex ratio of a city in underdeveloped areas, that is to say, is usually high, and it thus has some of the social characteristics of a frontier town (cf. pp. 497–498).

How significant an effect international migration may have on sex ratios can be suggested by comparing the proportions of the two sexes in immigration and emigration countries. In Western Europe, where emigration was at a peak around the middle of the 19th century, the sex ratio was well under 100 by 1900; but in Eastern Europe and Japan, where the high point came later, it declined from about 100 in 1900 to about 90–95 in 1950. The one important exception to this pattern is Ireland, the emigration country par excellence, where the ratio actually increased; the reason presumably is the already noted sizable number of *female* domestic servants who had left. In receiving countries, on the contrary, with the influx of males to frontier areas, the sex ratio tended to be high in 1900 and to approach parity over the next half-century, as the size of the immigration decreased in many cases and the frontier was pushed back.

If the sex ratio of international migrants is high, that of remigrants, judging by the period for which American data are available, is still higher, and what is true of gross immigration must again be corrected to apply to the more meaningful category of those who came to stay. Because of the several legal provisions favoring female immigrants, they have been the predominant sex since the 1930s (Rubin 1966), but even in this period the sex ratio of remigrants remained well above 100.

Many of these generalizations still hold in present-day United States. Some of them, however, seem to be less valid now than in the past, as we can see from the results of the 1970 census. From questions posed to respondents, it was possible to locate them at three points in their lifetime: their date of birth, in 1965, and in 1970 (cf. Taeuber *et al.* 1968). Of course, these three residences constitute only a rough index of migration: those included in the first column of Table 8-2 (who resided in their state of birth in both 1965 and 1970) might have moved either within the state or out of it and back. But if we take this column to designate the nonmigrants, the difference between the sexes (59.3 versus 59.8 percent) is insignificant. Note also that among young adults, those aged 25 to 29 years, the two sexes again differed only between 49.9 and 52.9 percent. Similarly, those living in the same state in both years but not the state of their birth (who perhaps can be presumed to have moved only once, at some time before 1965) comprised 18.1 of the males and 18.8 percent of the females. From this table it would seem, in short, that selectivity by either age or sex is remarkably less than it used to be in other cultural contexts, because of many of the changes in American society. With the greater participation of females in the labor force, they are more likely to move about in the same proportion as males. And with the lesser proclivity of middle-aged and elderly persons to stay put, what once was the migration of single persons has often become that of whole families.

Family Status

The older generalization that migrants are typically *single* young adults was true of two of the characteristic types of the past, male pioneers and female domestic servants. Why, in greater detail, should this contrast between unmarried transients and relatively fixed families now hold less than it used to?

Urban growth was at one time predominantly a movement of single persons, but as cities grew larger and older a tendency developed to move out of the crowded centers to the suburbs. The continuing in-migration of unmarried persons was then matched by an out-migration of families. In the United States today not only do married couples move about as well as single persons, but they are often motivated to do so precisely because of their family life—in order to have a larger house for an increasing number of children, in order to live in a "nicer" neighborhood or close to a better school, and so on (Rossi 1955).

It is possible that there has been a shift in the marital status also of international migrants. In the 19th century the typical European who went overseas was a young unmarried adult trying to establish himself economically. The exodus of Jews from Eastern Europe during the decades before World War I, however, did not fit into this pattern. Having been induced to leave not merely for economic reasons but because of the threat of persecution or actual pogroms, Jewish migrants included a much larger proportion of females and children than other nationalities (Hersch 1931). With the rise of totalitarian states and the consequent shift from economic to political motivations, both the stimulus to family migration and the difficulties in realizing it have increased.

Occupation

The effect of international migration on the labor force of the two countries is complex. In the Liberal economic theory of the 19th century, free movement was justified on the ground that those in an overcrowded occupation tended to go wherever their skill was in short supply, so that this natural functioning of the international labor market benefited everyone concerned, both the migrants and the two nations. The principle has a certain validity, but it must certainly be qualified:

1. The principle does not hold for migration that is not wholly economically motivated; and the persecution of minorities, the fear of another war, and other political considerations play a large if usually indeterminate role. According to a study of post-1945 refugees in the United States (Davie 1947: 132–135), their occupation in the new country was shaped by two contradictory factors. Many had to accommodate to less comfortable circumstances. Thus, of the females who had been housewives in Europe (more than half), about 40 percent took work, presumably menial in most cases, outside the home. And those whose livelihood had depended on facility in their native language (writers, teachers, and so on) obviously faced the most difficult adjustment, particularly if their profession was culture-bound also in other respects (jurists). Thus, of the refugee lawyers in the sample, only 5.8 percent were practicing law. On the other hand, many who left for political reasons could transfer their well paid professional and craft skills, so that in fact there was less of a shift in occupations among refugees than among the mass of economically motivated migrants.

2. More generally, the assumption in the Liberal principle that skills are fixed is not warranted. In many cases, selection by occupation is less significant than the *change* of occupation that takes place as a concomitant of migration. Only a very small proportion of the villagers who flocked to the United States in the decades before 1914 became farmers, and the work that they and their sons did generally had nothing to do with what they had learned in Europe. Four-fifths of the immigrants had had no previous experience in manufacturing or mining, the sectors of American industry in which most of them found jobs as unskilled laborers (Davie 1949: 238). That America was a "land of opportunity" meant precisely that it was a country whose economy was expanding rapidly enough to enable a man to earn his living with aptitudes never used before and then possibly to rise from that beginning status.

3. Apart from other factors, economic competition for labor is weighted in favor of the area with the higher standard of living. For example, immediately after World War II, when Europe needed all its building workers for reconstruction, many of them left nevertheless; for they were wanted also for the development programs of the overseas countries, which could offer more attractive prospects. Occupational self-selection operating in the form of the so-called brain drain (BD) has become something of an international issue (see p. 591). The term is very often loosely used; the emigration of highly qualified technicians and scientists from Britain has been widely publicized, whereas that from France (cf. Monroe 1966), which proportionately is almost equivalent, is barely noted. An adequate measure of brain drain ought to control for both the size of the general emigration and the proportion in the population of persons with the skill being drained out (Grubel, in Gollin 1966: 16; cf. Grubel and Scott 1967; Mills 1966). If the issue concerns physicists, thus:

$$BD = \frac{\text{Physicists migrating from Country } A \text{ to Country } B}{\text{Total migrants from Country } A \text{ to Country } B}$$

$$\div \frac{\text{Physicists in Country } A}{\text{Total population of Country } A}$$

If there is simply a large migration, including a large but proportionate number of the highly skilled, by this index BD is equal to unity; if there is a small general migration and a larger, though still not highly visible, migration of professionals, BD is greater than unity. It is true, on the other hand, that if a migration is stimulated by other factors, those with qualifications guaranteeing successful integration may well depart in larger numbers. Thus, the roughly 300,000 Cuban refugees in the United States in the mid-1960s included nearly 2,000 physicians, plus a sizable number of medical students and nurses. This is hardly a brain drain in proportion to the total migration, but it certainly could be considered one in terms of the island's needs, a factor not included in Grubel's formula. More generally, data on the migration of high-level manpower are often too poor to substantiate reasoned argument, not to mention changes in legislation (Bayer 1968).

The simplest case of brain drain is an unimpeded migration with no change of occupation. For example, of all those trained as nurses in Chile, about half used to leave the country and, of that half, most went to the United States and practiced nursing (John Useem, in Gollin 1966: 30; cf. Beijer 1966). In many cases, however, the motivation of the migrant is at least partly to evade one or another regulation governing, for instance, the status of students. If an Israeli graduate student in science returns home immediately after receiving his American doctorate, he can begin in the civil service in grade C and be eligible for promotion to grade B after about four years, while if he remains in the United States for a year or two he will start in grade B (Paul Ritterband, in Gollin 1966: 26).

Often brain drain is partly balanced by what has been termed "brain gain," a movement in the opposite direction. In one recent year there was a net immigration to Sweden of only five persons with university degrees, but they were the difference between 135 who entered the country and 130 who left it (Table 8-3). Emigration seemed to be to places with a higher standard of living (United States), a better climate (Spain), or specific openings (Africa); much of the immigration was from the rest of Scandinavia, including Finland and Iceland.

4. The brain drain has attracted so much scholarly attention partly because it contradicts the plausible generalization that most migrants come from the lower social levels of the sending country. Usually their assimilation has therefore had to be a dual process, both to an alien culture and to the somewhat higher social class into which many were rising. The widespread hostility to free immigration that developed in the United States between the 1880s and the 1920s was probably less xenophobic in general than specifically focused on how the "tumultuous hordes" of illiterates would damage the democratic system. One way of resolving the dilemma is to import laborers but to deny them, by one device or another, the means of attaining civil status. Mexican nationals working in the Southwest of the United States, for instance, are usually temporary and sometimes illegal migrants, who participate in America's economy but ostensibly not in its society or culture. It would seem that everyone benefits from the arrangement—the workers, who earn more than they could at home; the employers, who get labor cheaper than they otherwise could; the sending country, which has its unemployed reduced and its monetary balance improved; and the receiving country, which acquires a supplementary work force anxious to take jobs that natives will not accept. But the pattern generates difficulties, and usually it is eventually opposed on several grounds.

An anomaly in American immigration history, *Gastarbeiter* (or "guest workers," as they are called in German and often also in English texts) have become a significant sector in Western Europe. In 1973, the percentages of alien workers (or quasi-alien, like the colored Commonwealth migrants in Britain) in the labor force of some European countries were as follows:

Switzerland	27
West Germany	11
France	9
Austria	9
Great Britain	7
Sweden	6
Belgium	6

Most of the temporary workers have come from the countries of the Mediterranean basin—Turkey, Greece, Yugoslavia, Italy, and Spain, supplemented in particular cases by Algerians (to France), Africans (to England), and Finns (to Sweden). With their families the *Gastarbeiter* in Western Europe numbered about 15 million in 1973—the tenth member of the Common Market, as they are sometimes called, as populous as the Netherlands and growing much faster. So long as they were fewer, they seemed to be a boon; they collected the garbage, washed the hotel dishes, performed all the unpleasant and ill paid tasks that Northwest Europeans are generally unwilling to do for themselves. They lived cheaply, for example in the notorious *bidonvilles* (or shantytowns) surrounding Paris. But as their numbers grew, problems grew with them. Young men living alone sought female company and sometimes excited the jealousy of native males; but if families moved in with the migrants, a considerably larger investment in housing, schools, and other infrastructure was required. Sentiment developed to limit their further influx, particularly in Switzerland, with over a quarter of its labor force made up of aliens, but also in France, West Germany, and Britain. There is no easy solution, for Northwest Europe's rapidly expanding economy has come to depend on these alien workers, but to grant all of them the possibility of naturalization would radically change the European concept of nationality (cf. Mayer 1972; Ball 1973).

5. The economic factor shaping the international movements of migrants has typically been broader than occupational selection, even when this was operative. According to several careful studies, if conditions in the home country were such as to build up a general desire to leave, the volume, direction, and timing of the movement were set largely by business conditions in the receiving

Table 8-3.   Migration of University-Educated Manpower, Sweden, c. 1960

Country	Net Migration		Dominant Disciplines
	FROM SWEDEN	TO SWEDEN	
United States	24–25		Social sciences, law, technical
Switzerland	18–19		Economics, other social sciences, law
Great Britain	10		Technical, humanities
France	6–7		Economics, other social sciences, technical
Spain	6–7		Technical, humanities
Italy	5–6		Humanities
Africa	4–5		Technical, economics
Asia	3		Technical
South America	2		Technical, economics
Australia	1–2		Technical
Canada		1–2	Technical
Iceland		5	Medical
Germany		9	Dentistry, technical, humanities
Norway		12–13	Technical
Austria		18	Medical, technical
Finland		20	Various
Hungary		20–21	Technical, medical
Denmark		42	Medical, technical
TOTAL	130	135	

SOURCE: Göran Friborg and J. Annerstedt, *Brain Drain and Brain Gain of Sweden* (Stockholm: Swedish Natural Science Research Council, 1972), Table 1.

country. The correlation between the business cycle in the sending country and emigration was not negative, as might be expected, but "positive and fairly high"; for it was the pull of opportunities overseas that determined the migration rate, and in their broad trends business cycles tend to be international (D. S. Thomas 1925: 148; cf. D. S. Thomas 1941).

Selection by occupation among internal migrants takes place to some degree, but it is difficult with the data ordinarily available to pin down motives for what has become, at least in the United States, so casual an act as moving to another home or job. Except to the degree that the motivation of migrants is implicit in the timing and direction of their movements, we know very little about it (cf. Shryock 1964: chap. 12).

Several times the U.S. Census Bureau has asked a sample of the population their motives for moving. The reasons were classified into the following categories: to take a job, to look for work, housing problems, change in marital status, to join the head of the family, to move with the head of the family, health,

A few of the several thousand Italian workers at the Volkswagen factory, Wolfsburg, West Germany, who live in a nearby village that the firm built specially for them. Not only Germany but most of the countries of Northwest Europe depend for crucial proportions of their labor forces on alien workers, who are typically not permitted to immigrate permanently or to become naturalized citizens. Like the men in this photograph, these *Gastarbeiter* often seem to be lonely, somewhat lost in their temporary environment (*Wide World Photos*).

and "other" (of which the most frequent instances were to attend school or to live in a different climate). These reasons are obviously not all of the same order. Many studies of migratory selection are based on the assumption, usually left implicit, that all migrants choose whether or not to move and that they make their choice in response to social–economic forces. Let us designate those of whom this assumption is valid **resultant migrants**, who make up only the first three classes in this list of motives. Those with no choice whether to move (for example, children taken by their parents) and those who decide to move for reasons not associated with social–economic forces (but rather, for example, because of their health or the climate) are termed **epiphenomenal migrants** (Hobbs 1942: 43–44). How important this differentiation can be is suggested in Table 8-4. The postulate that migration is a function primarily of economic circumstances is obviously not true in a direct sense: in 1945–46 more than 70

Table 8-4.   Percentage Distribution of Internal Migrants, by Motive, United States, 1945–46 and 1962–63

Motive	1945–46			1962–63, Male
	TOTAL	MALE	FEMALE	
Resultant Migrants				
Job-related	22.6	41.1	6.2	58.1
Housing	6.4	9.8	3.3	11.3
Epiphenomenal Migrants				
Family migration	61.7	38.1	82.7	16.3
Health	1.2	1.8	0.8	2.8
Other reasons	8.9	10.3	7.6	11.5

SOURCES: U.S. Bureau of the Census, *Current Population Reports*, Series P-20, no. 4, October 7, 1947; Series P-20, no. 154, August 22, 1966.

percent of the migrants were epiphenomenal. This very high proportion probably reflected postwar adjustments, with more families moving about than in a normal period. A full comparison is not possible with the later survey, when only males were interviewed but when over 30 percent of the male migrants moved for reasons not related to either a job or housing. Since the sex ratios of the two types of migrants differ considerably, one can presume that the percentage would be higher if women were included. The age structure varies even more sharply: virtually all migrants under 14 and over 65 are epiphenomenal. The many generalizations concerning migratory selection based on the (sometimes tacit) assumption that all migrants are resultant, thus, can be valid only when family migration is insignificant.

Another limitation to the postulate that migrants mainly move to new jobs is the paradox that the flow of blacks to the large cities of the North and West was seemingly not impeded by the lack of occupational opportunities there. Since unemployment rates of certain age–sex–race categories (in particular, Negro males aged 15 to 24) sometimes ranged as high as a third or a half, continued in-migration was manifestly not economically motivated in the usual sense. It seems probable that some of the movement was based on a different kind of economic differential: the higher or lower welfare payments available in various jurisdictions supposedly stimulated a flow from the South, where by and large recipients received least, to those cities where with the minimum bureaucratic control they got the most. According to data from the 1970 census, however, this relation did not hold in the six cities with at least a half million blacks (New York, Philadelphia, Chicago, Detroit, Los Angeles, and Washington). The analysis does not completely invalidate the hypothesis (gaps in the enumeration were concentrated among lower-class blacks in the specified age interval, and other faults in the data are apparent), but it is suggestive.

Moving day in a Los Angeles housing development (*J. R. Eyerman—Life. © Time, Inc.*).

For the six cities with the largest black populations, . . . blacks who are most likely to be poor and on welfare are those born and raised in the city and living there at the time of the 1970 census. Only recent (since 1965) arrivals from the South were found to have rates of poverty and welfare dependence as high as blacks who were born and raised in their city of 1970 residence [Long 1973; cf. Blevins 1971].

The finding suggests that poverty and welfare dependence may be due to two seemingly contradictory factors. Recent in-migrants often are unemployed during their adjustment to a new environment, but this effect is dissipated within a few years. On the other hand, the level of aspiration of blacks raised in the North or West has sometimes risen faster than their capabilities, so that they are less willing to accept low-level jobs. Long supports this latter supposition from earlier studies on the slight relation between migration and such other social problems as delinquency and rioting.

Psychological Factors

The study of factors like the level of aspiration differs from that of the usual demographic variables in several respects. (1) In the definition of the characteristic: When a person tells us that he is 27 years old and married, this is information on a different level from, for instance, the results of intelligence tests. (2) In the amount of data available: Questions on age, sex, and marital status are included in all censuses and in virtually all special studies of migratory selection. Census data are lacking on factors like intelligence; and of the smaller number of specific studies that include such variables, many are based on inadequate research methods. (3) In the time of its first appearance: A statement that a person was single when he left and that he married after settling in his destination is unambiguous. But if a migrant turns out to be a criminal or psychopathic, it is usually impossible to choose among three possible causes: (a) It may be that the home country or area has a higher incidence than the destination. This is perhaps the most common popular explanation of observed differences: thus, Italians are "prone to be criminals"; villagers are "dim-witted." (b) It may be that migratory selection takes place—that is, that persons with a predisposition to "criminality" or mental illness or whatever tend to leave in larger proportion. Or (c) it may be that the newcomers fail to adapt successfully to the strange conditions and therefore exhibit one or another form of social pathology.

A priori one can argue that either the less or the more intelligent tend to leave any particular area: (1) In the competition to achieve satisfactory living conditions, by and large the more intelligent will succeed more often, and the less so will thus be forced to seek their fortunes elsewhere. Or (2) in any population it will be the more adaptable, that is to say, the more intelligent, who will respond first to an impetus to emigrate, and the duller who will remain behind.

Whether selection by intelligence takes place in international migrations is still an open question. Indeed, many I.Q. tests have been made of the foreign stock, particularly in the United States, but it is difficult to say what these prove. Immigrants generally score lower, but one reason is certainly their less adequate knowledge of English and of the American culture generally. If this deficiency could be removed, probably the group differences would disappear with it; but the various attempts to devise a culture-free intelligence test probably have not been wholly successful. In any case, the testing of newcomers to the United States, whatever importance it may have for other reasons, is irrelevant to a study of migratory selection, for it is made at the wrong end of the journey. The question is not how German immigrants, for example, compare with native Americans, but rather how those Germans who leave compare with those who remain in Germany.

Selectivity by intelligence in internal migration has often been discussed. Some analysts have attempted to prove, sometimes with inadequate methods, that urban growth selected the more intelligent in the rural population, but others have challenged this conclusion. It is difficult, in view of the small number of good studies and their contradictory results, to come to overall conclusions. Dorothy Thomas (1938: 125) does not believe that any generalization at all can be made: "Migration may, under given circumstances, select the intelligent; under other circumstances, the less intelligent; and under still other circumstances, be quite unselective with regard to intelligence." The tentative conclusion offered by Sorokin and Zimmerman (1929: 571) is that "cities attract the extreme while the farms attract the mean strata in society." An essay by the Dutch sociologist Hofstee (1952) dispels some of the confusion around this question. Most of the previous discussion had centered on so-called *push* factors, that is, conditions at home that induce some persons to leave. Hofstee shifted the argument to *pull* factors, that is, conditions that attract migrants. Everything that we know about selectivity by more easily defined characteristics, such as sex, indicates the greater importance of pull factors: the dominance of males or of females is generally determined less by the conditions at home than by the opportunities for one or the other at the destination. In the same way, selection by intelligence depends mainly on the level of opportunities available. Since many urban occupations both require a greater mental capacity and offer more income and status, there is a tendency for the more intelligent in a rural population, particularly if they are well educated, to migrate to the towns.

Several studies on the relation between urbanization and the incidence of mental disease indicate both the possibilities of improving on the research methods of earlier analyses and the difficulties, even so, in reaching a firm conclusion. According to a monograph based on an analysis of first admissions to New York State mental institutions, in-migrants were represented in much higher proportion than those born in the state, even when migrants and non-migrants of the same age were compared. Among whites the in-migrants' age-standardized rate was twice, among nonwhites about three times that of the native born. The admission rate of in-migrants who had lived in the state for more than five years was higher, but only slightly higher, than that of native New Yorkers (Malzberg and Lee 1956).

These data suggest that all three of the causes noted above are relevant: (a) Since the standards of institutional care are relatively good in New York State, the incidence of mentally ill *outside hospitals* is higher in the population of many other states, particularly in the South and among Negroes. (b) In many cases admission to a mental hospital took place so soon after arrival in the state that the disease must have been well advanced prior to the migration. This implies (though only an investigation at the point of origin could prove this) that the mentally ill tend to migrate in greater proportion; but in that case some of those originally resident in New York presumably would have left. (c) The sharp contrast between recent migrants and those in the state more than

five years is a clear indication that the strains of adjustment to a new environment are also etiologically significant (see also Lee 1958, 1963).

Two other studies on the relation between mental illness and migration
supplement these findings. A comparison of first admissions in three states,
New York, Ohio, and California, confirmed the datum that in-migration *per
se* was "a major determinant" of admission to hospitals. "However, nonwhite
natives have very much higher relative rates . . . than do corresponding classes
of whites. . . . It seems, therefore, to be *not* nativity but color that determines
the pattern" (Lazarus *et al.* 1963).[2] According to a study in Jerusalem, "emotional disorder" was related to "status inconsistency" as measured by a discrepancy in either direction between an immigrant's educational level and that
of his occupation (Abramson 1966).

Even more evasive than intelligence or mental illness is the typical migrant's
personality and character. In several essays, Hansen (1948: 66–67) has examined
the popular picture of the immigrant as pioneer, radical, innovator—and
found it faulty. During the 19th century, he wrote, the American immigrants
stayed in the settled areas, following the advice of those few who had left them
and generally returned: "Let the Americans start the clearing; they alone
possess the specialized technique." Thus, "the first white man to pioneer in any
township was not a Schultz or a Meyer, a Johnson or an Olson. He was a
Robinson, a McLeod or a Boone. He was a descendant of that old Americanized
stock which had learned frontiering in the difficult school that was in session
from 1600 to 1800." The immigrant was a pioneer only in the sense that he left
his native country and braved the hardships of the journey, often considerable
in the days of sailing ships.

Most of the immigrants were politically and culturally conservative, both
in the old country and in the United States. The contrary notion grew out of
the prominence of the small minority of political refugees—Carl Schurz and a
few thousand like him as against the more than a million Germans who migrated
to America during the 1850s. In Germany, "the areas of political disturbance did
not coincide with the areas of emigration. From the cities that had witnessed
bloody street fighting the emigrants were few; from the peaceful country districts the departing throngs threatened to depopulate the land" (ibid.: 80).
In the American Federation of Labor, the continual re-election of Samuel
Gompers, whom his opponents termed a renegade to his class, "was due largely
to the support of trade organizations in which immigrant membership was

[2] As in other studies based on census data, "a major difficulty arose because of ambiguity
in the census 'color' classification of the population. In New York and Ohio . . . 'nonwhites' were overwhelmingly Negro, . . . but in the California population this category was
only 69 percent Negro, the other 31 percent being predominantly Japanese, Chinese, and
other so-called 'minor races.' Inasmuch as the nonwhite category could not be reallocated
in the denominators of rates, this ambiguous classification had to be retained in the numerators." The Census Bureau no longer uses the term *nonwhite*, but many of the tables based
on the 1970 census are still divided into the same two racial categories, whites and all others.

strong" (ibid.: 90). The populist movement was almost wholly native. Immigrants voted against suffrage for women; "the reminiscences and reports of the suffrage missionaries agree that their opposition was perhaps the most formidable obstacle to overcome" (ibid.: 92). This strong conservatism derived principally from three sources—the immigrant's liking for the free-enterprise system and the opportunities it offered him; the influence of the immigrant churches, which were not only religious institutions but guardians of the old ways; and the new-comer's typical aspiration to be *plus royaliste que le roi.*

In Hansen's opinion, the desire for greater liberty did exist as one motive for migration, but it achieved its prominence in the public mind because other motives were depreciated. For an immigrant to speak of his material incentives would emphasize his economic competition with the natives, and to say that his sons had been growing up lazy and shiftless in a country where they could find no work would give point to the argument that foreigners were depraved and worthless.

> Hence . . . the newcomer said, "I came to the United States to enjoy the blessings of your marvelous government and laws," [and] the native warmed to him and was likely to inquire whether there was not something he could do to assist him. Immigrants soon learned the magic charm of this confession of faith. They seized every opportunity to contrast the liberty of the New World with the despotism of the Old. . . . So the tradition was established, and the desire for political freedom was accounted one of the principal causes for the immigration [ibid.: 78–79].

According to a recent survey of British migrants to Australia, they also rationalized motives like feelings of insecurity or inadequacy into the most acceptable one, which in this instance was not love of, liberty but an aspiration to economic advancement (Appleyard 1964).

The process of migratory selection is obviously of great practical importance; to a large degree, it defines the meaning of any movement for the two areas concerned. Unfortunately, as this discussion has indicated, it is a subject about which we still know rather little. We have seen that migrants are in most respects not a random sample of the populations they leave and enter. In most cases adolescents and young adults predominate. With respect to other character-istics—sex and occupation, possibly intelligence and mental health—selection usually seems to depend more on conditions at the destination than on those at the origin.

POLITICAL FACTORS

Political influences on the number of migrants and their characteristics are of two broad types—inhibitions or encouragements to movement and migrations under duress or by force. Examples of both can be cited from movements within the boundaries of totalitarian states (see pp. 695–698), but most of the data relate to international migration.

Immigration Restrictions

A number of standard works on American immigration policy, using absolute freedom of migration as a standard, find that "free immigration" ended about 1830 (e.g., Garis 1927), when some of the states along the eastern seaboard established controls, mostly ineffective. But this was before the massive flow from Europe even got under way. Just as a society can be meaningfully free though it has prisons, so to deny admission to obviously antisocial elements, as the eastern states attempted to do, is not inconsistent with the principle of free migration. The exclusion of criminals, prostitutes, and others with specific objectionable personal characteristics we will denote as the **regulation** of migration, which is to be distinguished from both **numerical restriction**, by which a certain maximum immigration is set for each year, and **qualitative restriction**, by which entry is denied to specified broad social or ethnic classes.

In the United States, restriction was enacted after World War I, following several decades of intense national debate. The exclusion of Southern and Eastern Europeans was first sought indirectly, by proposing that admission should be denied to all adults not able to read and write some language. Of the two dozen such literacy bills introduced in Congress, four were passed, to be vetoed successively by Presidents Cleveland, Taft, and Wilson. The law stipulating a literacy test, finally passed in 1917 over Wilson's second veto, kept out some Southern and Eastern Europeans, but not nearly so many as had been anticipated. Also in that year all immigration from the "barred zone" of Asia was banned; with earlier laws excluding Chinese and sharply limiting the immigration of Japanese, the new act all but eliminated movement from that continent to the United States. The law of 1921, enacted as a stopgap measure until the problems could be studied, limited European immigration to 3 percent of the number of foreign-born of each nationality residing in the United States at the time of the last available census figures, those of 1910. A second law, passed in 1924, set up another temporary system, more restrictive in two respects than its predecessor: the 3 percent quota was reduced to 2 percent, and the base population was changed from the 1910 to the 1890 census, when the proportion from Southern and Eastern Europe was smaller. In 1929 this base population was changed again to those in the total population of each "national origin" (see p. 117, n. 7). The Immigration and Nationality Act of 1952 (usually known as the McCarran–Walter Act) continued to use national origins as the main criterion of eligibility, but in the ensuing period this principle was gradually eroded by a series of *ad hoc* laws that permitted refugees and others to immigrate outside the quota limitations. The national-quota system was finally abandoned in the Immigration Act of 1965, which went into effect in mid-1968.

The success of the immigration legislation in achieving the restrictionists' purpose is indicated in Table 8-5. The total immigration from Europe, 8.1 million in 1901–10 and 4.4 million in 1911–20 (the latter would have been larger if migration had not been suspended during the war), was cut down to a decen-

Table 8-5.   Immigration Quotas Under Successive Laws, United States, 1921–64

Area of Origin	1921	1924	1929	1952[a]
Northwest Europe[b]	197,630	140,999	127,266	125,631
Southern and Eastern Europe	159,322	20,423	23,225	23,966
Asia	492	1,424	1,423	3,690
All other countries	359	1,821	1,800	4,874
TOTAL	357,803	164,667	153,714	158,161
		PERCENT		
Nothwest Europe[b]	55.2	85.6	82.8	79.4
Southern and Eastern Europe	44.5	12.4	15.1	15.2
Asia	0.1	0.9	0.9	2.3
All other countries	0.1	1.1	1.2	3.1
TOTAL	99.0	100.0	100.0	100.0

[a] As amended; 1964 quotas.
[b] British Isles, Scandinavia, Germany, Low Countries, France, Switzerland.
SOURCES: President's Commission on Immigration and Naturalization, *Whom We Shall Welcome* (Washington, D.C., 1953), pp. 76–77; U.S. Bureau of the Census, *Statistical Abstract of the United States, 1965* (Washington, D.C., 1965), Table 114.

nial quota of about 1.5 million. And the Old Immigration, which made up only about a quarter of the *gross* movement during the last 25 years of unrestricted influx, was assigned approximately 85 percent of the European quotas, or roughly the same proportion as in the immigration around 1880. The two purposes of numerical and qualitative restriction had thus been achieved; under the 1965 law a restriction on numbers was retained but with no specification of quality as defined by national origin.

The immigration policy of the United States before it was changed in 1965 has its counterpart in most of the countries to which sizable immigration might be expected. Although the formal law of Canada is different, the policy developed from it is precisely parallel (cf. Petersen 1955: chap. 7; Timlin 1965). The "White Australia" policy and its New Zealand version have a long history (Price 1966; Ross 1967; Rivett 1967). Britain imposed restrictions on the free immigration of British subjects from other members of the Commonwealth. Latin America has in general followed a similar policy. Even some of the countries of Asia have erected bars against the immigration of coolies from their Asian neighbors.

Subsidized Migration

The bar to members of certain nationalities or races has in some cases been countered by special inducements to those of other nationalities to migrate.

In Britain, after several years of preparation, the Empire Settlement Act (1922) authorized the government to pay up to half the costs of settling suitable persons in the overseas dominions. From the receiving side, the dominions have granted assistance to immigrants of British and, since 1945, various other European nationalities. In a number of emigration countries in addition to Britain, prospective migrants have been subsidized in various ways (cf. Petersen 1955: chap. 3). Whether financial assistance greatly increases the size of migration is questionable in most instances, but it gives a country somewhat greater control over the classes of migrants to be admitted or sent out.

Refugees

A far greater impetus to migration in the modern world has come from the various social catastrophes generating refugee streams. In the present age of total wars and totalitarian regimes, political motivations have set not only "Europe on the move" (Kulischer 1948) but also, sometimes as reverberations from European disturbances, much of the rest of the world. To take a notable example, the partition of British India into the nations of India and Pakistan was accompanied by one of the largest migrations in human history, in part induced by terrorists on both sides, in part arranged under state auspices (Schechtman 1963: chap. 7). In 1972, when East Pakistan became the new nation of Bangladesh, this marked the culmination of another tumultuous period with again a movement of tens of thousands of refugees in both directions.

In earlier ages whole nations were dispersed in a diaspora—the Jews or the Armenians. Sectors of populations were expelled—the Jews from medieval Germany and later from Spain, the Gypsies from England, the Protestants from France. But before the 20th century it was mostly the exiled notable individuals who captured a place in history books—the French royalists living as émigrés after 1789, or revolutionaries like Marx or Mazzini whose native countries were inhospitable.

The status of refugee, one of a mass of émigrés, developed in fact after World War I. Fridtjof Nansen, whom the League of Nations appointed High Commissioner in 1921, devoted his main effort to the succor of Armenians fleeing the Turks and of Russians fleeing the revolution; those unable to return home were eligible for the so-called Nansen passport. Such efforts were much enhanced after the founding of the United Nations, whose activities on behalf of certain categories set administrative definitions of the major terms. "Refugees," thus, did not include those who had fled Communist regimes.[3] Those who had been

[3] Immediately after its founding the United Nations defined *refugee* as "a person who has left, or who is outside of, his country of nationality or of former habitual residence, and who, whether or not he has retained his nationality, belongs to one of the following categories: victims of Nazi or fascist regimes or of regimes which took part on their side in the Second World War, ... persons who were considered refugees before the outbreak of the Second World War for reasons of race, religion, nationality, or political opinion, ...

"displaced" from such countries were to be sent back "as soon as possible."[4] Among the 2 million refugees delivered to Soviet authorities by Western military officials and, later, UNRRA and IRO, there were many thousands repatriated against their will, as indicated by the high incidence of suicide among them. This policy continued until mid-1948, when the wartime alliance between the Soviet Union and Western democracies, already past its prime, was ended by the coup in Czechoslovakia and the blockade of Berlin (Kulischer 1949). "Stateless persons" were also eligible for certain kinds of assistance, unless their actions violated the "purposes and principles" of the United Nations (including its treatment of refugees from Communist totalitarianism?).[5] Although the blatant political bias of this period has dissipated to some degree, assistance to refugees through official agencies continues to depend, obviously, on the administrative definitions of the term.

In customary (unwritten) international law there is no such thing as a generally accepted definition of "refugee." It follows that it has no meaning to speak of "refugees in the juridical sense" or [the concept of refugees] except in the context of a particular legal instrument. . . . To delimit the category . . . can be neither right nor wrong, but it can undoubtedly be more or less fitting [Grahl-Madsen 1966, vol. 1: 73–74].

The principal international agency, governed by the U.N. High Commissioner for Refugees, has a narrowly restricted prime mandate: to assist persons who do not want to return to their country because of actual or feared racial, religious, or political persecution; and it may also extend its "good offices" to certain other limited categories. This definition does not include several numerically important classes of uprooted peoples: (1) Those who had fled from local political disturbances but remained within the boundaries of the same state; for example, those who fled from various outrages in Negro Africa were or were not "refugees" depending on whether they ended up on one side or the other of newly established and often artificial boundaries. (2) Those who are forcibly moved about within the boundaries of a single state; for example, the nationals

---

[who are] unable or unwilling to avail [themselves] of the protection of the Government of [their] country of nationality or former nationality" (*Yearbook of the United Nations, 1946–47*, New York, 1947, p. 816).

[4] A *displaced person* was defined as one who "has been deported from or has been obliged to leave his country of nationality or of former habitual residence, such as persons who were compelled to undertake forced labor or who were deported for racial, religious, or political reasons. . . . If the reasons for such displacement have ceased to exist, they should be repatriated as soon as possible" (ibid.).

[5] A *stateless person* was defined as one "who is not considered as a national by any state under the operation of its laws," excluding, however, criminals, those who received protection or assistance from the United Nations High Commissioner for Refugees, and those "guilty of acts contrary to the purposes and principles of the United Nations" (United Nations, Economic and Social Council, *Conference on the Status of Stateless Persons*, E/Conf. 17/5, 54-26300, 1954).

Chinese refugees in Macao, who in the early 1970s numbered about 65,000, compared with about 200,000 in the nonrefugee population (*United Nations*).

of the Baltic states incorporated into the Soviet Union, who were then deported to forced-labor camps in Soviet Asia. (3) Those who had been forced to "return" to what is now defined as "their" country, after having lived "abroad" sometimes for generations; for example, the persons of French origin expelled to France from Algeria.

As official U.N. definitions of *refugee* and similar categories are tied to restricted activities, the statistics issued by U.N. agencies understate the number of refugees more broadly defined. Data from the other main sources, the various private agencies, are not consistently compiled or equally accurate, and since the agencies generally receive funds on the basis of the number of persons aided, one can reasonably expect their figures to be on the high side. Unfortunately no demographer or other scholar has defined the term so as to lay a basis for data independent of such biases.

Schechtman (1963) is in one sense an exception to this assertion. He views "refugees" in a Zionist perspective and thus excludes any "ingathering" into a counterpart of Israel. For example, almost a quarter of the West German population in 1960 was made up of some 9.3 million expellees from East Germany, 3.3 million ethnic Germans from various countries of East Europe, and 230,000 non-German refugees. The successful integration of this vast throng was something of a miracle (cf. Paikert 1962), which is not obliterated by a definition of "refugee" that excludes all but the last, and smallest, of the

Table 8-6. Estimated Refugee Population of the World, by Country of Origin and Asylum, 1969–70

Refugees		Estimated Number	
FROM	TO	1969	1970
China	Hong Kong	2,035,000	2,000,000
China	Macao	73,000	65,000
China	USSR	70,000	[a]
USSR	China	1,000	1,000
China	Thailand	7,300	7,300
China	West Borneo	60,000	40,000
West Borneo	Nationals[b]	40,000	40,000
West Irian	Papua and New Guinea	6,000*	[c]
South Vietnam	Nationals[b]	1,197,000	3,500,000
South Vietnam	Cambodia[d]	20,000	200,000
Cambodia	South Vietnam[c]	—	200,000
Cambodia	Nationals[b]	—	500,000
Laos	Nationals[b]	260,000	300,000
North Vietnam	Thailand	40,000	40,000
Burma	Thailand	30,000	30,000
Tibet	Bhutan	6,000	6,000
Tibet	Nepal	8,000	8,000
Tibet	Sikkim	5,000	5,000
Tibet	India	55,000	56,000
Tibet	Switzerland	600	700
Tibet	United States	70	70
East Pakistan	India	2,000,000	4,450,000
West Pakistan	India	1,000,000	—
India	Pakistan	260,000	260,000
Palestine	Egypt	45,000	3,000
Palestine	Gaza Strip	307,700	311,800
Palestine	Jordan[e]	761,500	778,700
Palestine	Lebanon	171,500	176,000
Palestine	Syria	154,300	158,700
Various countries	Israel	54,000	—
Various countries	Lebanon	—	5,200*
Circassians (USSR)	Syria	8,000	8,000
Middle East, various countries	Middle East, various countries	350,000	350,000
Various countries	Egypt	1,000*	5,300*
Various countries	Morocco	3,000	3,300
Sudan	Ethiopia	20,000	20,000
Somali Republic	Ethiopia	70,000	70,000

310

Table 8-6 (continued)

Refugees		Estimated Number	
FROM	TO	1969	1970
Ethiopia	Somali Republic	189,000	189,000
French Somaliland	Somali Republic	12,000	12,000
Kenya	Somali Republic	218,000	218,000
Congo	Sudan	7,500	6,500
Ethiopia	Sudan	38,000	48,000
Zanzibar	Dubai	200*	250*
North Africa	Italy	2,500	2,500
Congo, Zambia	Angola	6,500	7,500
Congo, Rwanda	Burundi	92,000	46,000
Burundi	Rwanda	12,600	12,500
Chad, Congo, Sudan	Central African Republic	24,500*	27,500*
Various countries	Democratic Republic of Congo	581,500	669,000
Uganda	Kenya	—	5,000
Various countries	Kenya	700	700
Mozambique	Malawi	15,000	15,000
Various countries	Tanzania	56,700	59,600
Congo, Rwanda, Sudan	Uganda	176,000*	177,000*
Various countries	Zambia	12,200	14,800
Nigeria	Nationals[b]	3,500,000	[c]
Nigeria	Various countries	42,200	[c]
Various countries	Dahomey	12,000	12,000
Portuguese Guinea	Senegal	63,000	68,000
South Africa	Africa, various countries	2,500	2,500
Angola	Botswana	4,000*	4,000*
Africa, various countries	Africa, various countries	500	51,700*
Europe	Asia, various countries	2,000	2,000
Eastern Europe	Austria	35,800*	33,000*
Eastern Europe	Germany	114,700*	114,100*
Eastern Europe	Switzerland	30,500	32,300
Eastern Europe	Italy	14,800*	14,500*
Eastern Europe	Netherlands	8,000*	8,000*
Eastern Europe	Norway	—	6,200
Eastern Europe	Sweden	17,000*	17,000*
Eastern Europe	Greece	8,000*	8,000*
Eastern Europe	Australia	45,000	47,200
Eastern Europe	New Zealand	3,000*	3,000*
Eastern Europe	Hong Kong	—	1,000
Eastern Europe	Turkey	10,000	10,000

311

Table 8-6 (continued)

Refugees		Estimated Number	
FROM	TO	1969	1970
Czechoslovakia	South Africa	600	600
Czechoslovakia	United States	1,800	2,000
Eastern Europe	Canada	10,000	15,200
Eastern Europe	Latin America	110,000*	110,000*
Albania	Yugoslavia	26,000*	26,000*
Various countries	United Kingdom	161,000	161,000
Various countries	France	310,000	183,100
Cuba	United States	493,300	457,500
Cuba	Puerto Rico	14,900	7,500
Cuba	Latin America	48,500	3,000
Cuba	Spain	23,700	15,000
Haiti	Bahamas	15,000	15,000
Haiti	Dominican Republic	5,000	300,000
Haiti	Puerto Rico	5,000	5,000
Haiti	United States	6,000	50,000
Honduras	El Salvador	—	40,300
Chile, Bolivia, Paraguay	Argentina	1,000,000	17,000
Various countries	United States	550,000	550,000

*Some or all are entitled to protection and/or assistance from the U.N. High Commissioner for Refugees. Palestinian refugees are given aid by another international agency, the U.N. Relief and Works Agency.
[a] No information available.
[b] Refugees who have remained in their home country; not generally recognized under international law.
[c] Refugees listed in previous year presumably were repatriated.
[d] Detainees.
[e] Including the West Bank of the Jordan River, occupied by Israel.
SOURCE: U.S. Committee for Refugees, *World Refugee Report* (New York, 1971).

three components. In a different sense the late Eugene Kulischer was also an exception. If he had lived to continue his studies, the demography of war and revolution might have attained a general acceptance. But as defined by the U.N. population and statistical commissions, migration "excludes population transfers, . . . deportations, refugee movements, and the movement of 'displaced persons,'" all of which fall outside "the migratory movements of normal times." That an international body which includes some of the states most responsible for forced migrations should exclude them from its demographic analyses is understandable, but it is unfortunate that most independent students of migration accept this arbitrary and misleading delimitation of their subject.

A count of refugees, then, can be no more than a rough approximation. The figures listed in Table 8-6, assembled from a wide variety of sources, are knowl-

A Palestinian refugee settlement at Ein-Sultan, near Jericho, Jordan, 1966—one of more than fifty camps administered by the U.N. Relief and Works Agency (*United Nations*).

edgeable estimates. The categories marked with an asterisk are the only ones in the compilation included among "refugees" as defined by the principal international agency, the U.N. High Commissioner for Refugees. Part of the discrepancy comes from the exclusion of certain types, in particular those who are ousted from their homes but do not cross a national border. When a person who has been a refugee ceases to be one is also ambiguous, for the process of integration is not clearly or consistently designated. In Table 8-6, for example, none of the millions of North Vietnamese who fled to South Vietnam are included, though it was estimated that in 1970 some 3.5 million South Vietnamese remained refugees in their own country. As another instance, the migration of refugees from Cuba to the United States totaled almost half a million by 1970, but at that date only 175,000 were still so designated by the U.S. Office of Refugee and Migration Services. Whether refugees become integrated in their new society depends on several factors, many beyond their control. Thousands of "hard-core" cases, left over from the Spanish Civil War of the mid-1930s, lived in camps in France until they died, prohibited from residing elsewhere or getting regular jobs. The Palestinian refugees scattered throughout the Middle East, as another example, have been maintained in their precarious status in part as political pressure against Israel.

However one calculates the flow into and out of the status of refugee, it is clear that the total is growing rapidly. The world over, the estimated number increased from 9.8 million in 1965 to 17.6 million in 1970, then fell off to 15.7 million in 1972 (U.S. Committee for Refugees 1973). Even if these are taken to be inflated figures, the phenomenon they reflect is staggering in its magnitude. The implication of the data can be better grasped when we recall that the usual estimate of the total migration from all of Europe between 1800 to 1950 is 60 million, or only about eight times the *increase* in the number of refugees over 5 years.

MODELS OF MIGRATION

The various mathematical formulas that summarize migration trends omit political factors altogether. The simplest takes into account nothing but distance: within any area homogeneous with respect to all the other factors that affect the propensity to migrate, the number of migrants will be inversely related to the miles covered. One can express this relation in an equation, as follows:

$$M = \frac{aX}{D^b}$$

where M stands for the number of migrants, D for the distance over the shortest transportation route, and X for any other factor that is thought to be relevant; a and b are constants, ordinarily set at unity. In one version of this equation, the so-called $P_1 P_2 / D$ hypothesis, the populations of the end points of the movement are taken as the X factors (Zipf 1949). Another variation is the proposition that "the number of persons going a given distance is directly proportional to the number of [employment] opportunities at that distance and inversely proportional to the number of intervening opportunities" (Stouffer 1940). When "opportunities" were defined operationally as the number of in-migrants, the hypothesis could be validated in a number of instances (Catton 1965; Galle and Taeuber 1966). According to a detailed comparison of the two, Stouffer's formulation is better than Zipf's, since in effect measuring "opportunities" corrects the total figures for the amount of unemployment in the two areas (Anderson 1955).

In both Stouffer's original study and several of the replications, the hypothesis leaves out not only all noneconomic factors but also some of the influences on job-hunting migrants. In a subsequent analysis, Stouffer (1960) introduced the factor of competing migrants: "Everything else being equal, the attractiveness of city Y for migrants from city X will depend, at least to some extent, on how many potential migrants are closer to Y than are the potential migrants in X." In a study of migration among Dutch provinces, the analyst extended the range of variables farther: when he included per-capita income, percentage un-employed, degree of urbanization, quality of dwellings, and recreational resources, he found that the correlation between these and net migration was about 0.9 (W. H. Somermeijer, cited in ter Heide 1963).

Social Models

The framework of hypotheses like Zipf's or Stouffer's is essentially psycho-logical: each potential migrant, operating as an individual even if within the context of social–economic forces, decides on the basis of relative personal gains whether or not to leave. In fact, however, this decision is usually made not merely by the calculation of "pleasure" versus "pain" but in part through social contagion. By what is called the axiom of cumulative inertia, "the longer a person remains in a given location, the lower [is] the probability that he will leave it" (Myers *et al.* 1967). Once migration is well begun, correlatively, its continuation is semi-automatic; in a study of interstate labor mobility in the United States during 1955–60, Greenwood (1969) found that prior internal migration accounted for 72 percent of the variance.

The Petersen-Greenwood hypothesis [as it is termed in one study] is based upon the sound, logical procedure that current or future human behavior (as it pertains specifically to interstate movement) must be based upon the regularities, uniformities, and patterns of previously observed behavior. . . . People's past actions serve as a guide to future behavior. . . . A strong case can be made that Zipf's hypothesis is much more mechanistic than the Petersen-Greenwood hypothesis [Tarver and McLeod 1973].

In fact, the understanding of migration as a group process rather than the sum of individual events is well established. Movement from and to Southern Appalachia was analyzed with the help of the concept **migration system**, which is "composed of two or more areas of origin and destination which 'interact' in terms of significant migratory interchange to form migratory patterns" (Hillery *et al.* 1965). The movement of Italians to the United States, as another example, took place through **chain migration**, defined as "movement in which prospective migrants learn of opportunities, are provided with transportation, and have initial accommodation and employment arranged by means of primary social relationships with previous migrants" (MacDonald and MacDonald 1964). Perhaps the most general term is **migration stream**, or the totality of a movement from one area to another, conceived in social rather than psychological terms. Occasionally, however, analysts have ignored the continuity of the pro-cess, as in the several papers using a Markovian analysis (Goodman 1961, 1962; Li 1970). A so-called Markov chain (named after the Russian mathematician A. A. Markov) is a chance process with the specific characteristic that from a knowledge of its present state one can predict its future just as well as from a knowledge of its entire past. The cumulation of causal influences, in other words, is implicit rather than explicitly studied in a long-term analysis.

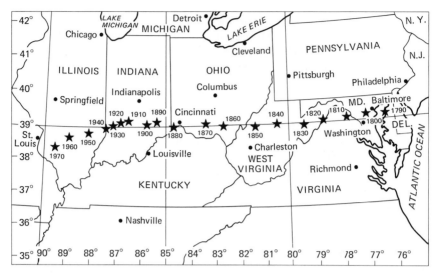

Figure 8-1. Center of Population of Conterminous United States, 1790 to 1970
SOURCE: U.S. Bureau of the Census.

One of the most important factors in American history, the continuous migration to the West, can be used to explicate migration as a stream. The point marking the center of the United States population has moved steadily westward along the 39th parallel at the rate of 4 or 5 miles per year, from northeastern Maryland in 1790 to southeastern Illinois in 1970 (Figure 8-1). If the two new states of Alaska and Hawaii were included, the shift would of course be farther westward. Though markedly affected by land grants, gold rushes, and transportation facilities, as well as by the several major geographical barriers on the way to the Pacific and beyond, the westward migration was more or less continuous. After a lull during the depression of the 1930s, it was greatly stimulated by the government's policy of establishing industrial plants on the Pacific Coast, as an aid to the war against Japan. Until World War II, the West had imported a substantial portion of the goods it consumed; and the cost of the long haul from the centers of manufacturing, often aggravated by discriminatory freight rates, created the equivalent of a protective tariff wall behind which even marginal manufacturing plants could be set up. With the growth of the population, the consumer market was no longer too small to attract industries; once new enterprises were established, the employees who came into the area to work in one factory or office comprised a market for other new businesses.

Four of the major migration streams in American history converged on California: in addition to the westward movement, the exodus from relatively impoverished areas, the movement from the countryside to cities, and the migration from other countries to the United States (Morrison 1971; Hernández 1971). Some time between the 1960 and 1970 censuses, California passed New

York and became the most populous state; its growth during the decade was from 15.7 to 20.0 million, including a net in-migration of some 2.1 million. In 1970, 18.5 million persons, or not quite 93 percent of the state's population, lived in its metropolitan areas. The prodigious growth generated enormous disequilibria in the state's institutions and, under the conditions prevailing, also a prodigious growth in environmental pollution (Cook 1966).

A GENERAL TYPOLOGY OF MIGRATION

If we try to expand these observations on the conditions and effects of migration, we shall not be able to formulate valid "laws," for the empirical regularities do not always hold. The ultimate generalization in this case is a typology, associating the various settings of migration with its probable effects (Heberle 1956). Perhaps the widest-ranging effort to construct such a typology is a paper by Howard Becker (1930–31), "an implicit and explicit criticism of all theorizing about . . . population movement which is not based on culture case study." As he illustrates with a fascinating collection of examples, migration can involve numbers from a single person to whole peoples, a distribution by age and sex no less wide in its range, a variety in the spread of the movement, its warlike or pacific intent, the geographic and political characteristics of the sending and receiving areas, and so on. Rich in details as the discussion is, it ends with only a catalogue of the factors, with no attempt to weave them into an interrelated whole.

We have noted the crude first step frequently made in this direction, the contrast between "push" and "pull" factors—that is, between circumstances at home that repel and those abroad that attract. This conceptualization is inadequate, first of all, because it implies that man is everywhere sedentary, remaining fixed until he is induced to move by some force. Like most psychological universals, this can be matched by its opposite: man migrates because of wanderlust. And, like all such universals, these cannot explain differential behavior: if all men are sedentary (or migratory) "by nature," why do some migrate and some not? If a simplistic metaphor is used, it should be at least as complex as its mechanical analogue, which includes not only the concept of forces but also that of inertia.

Thus, one might better say that a social group at rest, or a social group in motion (e.g., nomads), tends to remain so unless impelled to change; for with any viable pattern of life a social structure and a value system are developed to support that pattern. To analyze the migration of Gypsies, for example, in terms of push and pull is no better than to explain modern Western migration, as Herbert Spencer (1892, vol. 1: 566) did, in terms of "the restlessness inherited from ancestral nomads." If the principle of inertia is accepted as valid, then the difference between gathering and nomadic peoples, on the one hand, and agricultural and industrial peoples, on the other hand, is fundamental with respect to migration. For once a people has a permanent place of residence, the relevance of push and pull factors is presumably much greater.

If wanderlust and what might be termed *sitzlust* are not useful as psychological universals, they do suggest a criterion for a significant distinction. If persons leave as a means of achieving the new, let us term such migration **innovating**. If, on the contrary, they respond to a change in conditions by trying to retain what they have had, moving geographically in order to remain where they are in all other respects, let us term such migration **conservative**. When the migrants themselves play a passive role, as in the case of African slaves being transported to the New World, the movement is termed innovating or conservative depending on how it is defined by the activating agent, in this case the slave-traders.

The fact that the familiar push–pull polarity implies a universal sedentary quality, however, is only one of its faults. The push factors alleged to "cause" emigration ordinarily comprise a heterogeneous array, ranging from agricultural crises to the spirit of adventure, from the development of shipping to over-population. No attempt is generally made to distinguish among underlying causes, facilitative environment, precipitants, and motives. In particular, if we fail to distinguish between personal motives and social causes—that is, if we do not take the emigrants' level of aspiration into account—our analysis must lack logical clarity.

No principled difference is usually made between what is sometimes termed "absolute overpopulation," which results in hunger and starvation, and milder degrees of "overpopulation," which reflect not physiological but cultural standards (cf. pp. 160–164). In the first case the aspiration of emigrants can be ignored, for it is a bare physiological minimum that can be taken as universal, but in the second case it is the level of aspiration itself that defines the "over-population" and sets the impetus to emigrate. Similarly, economic hardships can appropriately be termed a "cause" of emigration only if there is a positive correlation between hardship, however defined, and the propensity to leave. The mass exodus from Europe in modern times, it must be recalled, developed together with a marked *rise* in European levels of living; and this inverse relation is not exceptional. In short, it is probably true that most transatlantic migrants were economically motivated, but not that the propensity to leave was directly associated with economic conditions in the home country. As has been noted, the correlation was rather with the business cycle in the receiving country, and even this explains fluctuations in the migration rate more than its absolute level.

Nor can the class differential in the rate of emigration be ascribed simply to economic differences. Although the European bourgeoisie lived in more comfortable circumstances than the workers, for many a move to America would also have meant a definite material improvement. During the period of mass exodus, however, this was stereotyped as lower-class behavior, a bit unpatriotic for the well-to-do. For a son of a businessman to emigrate meant a break with the established group pattern, and from this class, thus, only marginal types like idealists or black sheep left the country, and these for relevant *personal* reasons. Once a migration has reached the stage of a social movement, however, such individual motivations are generally of little interest to the analyst.

This kind of confusion is not limited to economic factors. Religious oppression or the infringement of political liberty was often a *motive* for leaving Europe, but before the rise of modern totalitarianism emigrants were predominantly from those countries least marked by such stigmata. An increasing propensity to emigrate spread east and south from Northwest Europe, together with democratic institutions and religious tolerance. Again, we are faced with the anomaly that those who departed "because" of the persecution came from countries where there was less of it than elsewhere.

When the push–pull polarity has been refined in these two senses, by distinguishing innovating from conservative migration and by including in the analysis the migrants' level of aspiration, it can form the basis of a typology of migration. Five broad classes are defined, which are designated as primitive, forced, impelled, free, and mass. It should be noted that while these words are terms in common usage rather than neologisms, since they are here more precisely defined than in most contexts, they denote a narrower range of meaning. Free migration, thus, is *not* all migration that is not forced, for it is one of five rather than two classes.

Primitive Migration

The first class is that consequent from an ecological push, which is termed **primitive migration**. In this context, then, this does not define the wandering of primitive peoples as such, but rather a movement related to man's inability to cope with natural forces. However, since the reaction to a deterioration in the physical environment can be either remedial action or emigration, depending on the technology available to the people concerned, primitive migrations in this narrower sense are often by primitive peoples.

Many of the treks of preindustrial folk, it would seem, have been conservative as we have defined this term here. "There is often a strong tendency for [such] a migrating group to hold conservatively to the same type of environment; pastoral peoples, for example, attempt to remain on grasslands, where their accustomed life may be continued" (Dixon 1933). The impetus to leave, the route, and the destination are set not by push and pull, but by the interplay of push and *control*. If they are indifferent about precisely where they are going, men migrate as liquids flow, along the lines of least resistance. Their way is shaped by barriers, both natural and manmade—both mountains, rivers, or rainfall or the lack of it, and the Great Wall of China or other, less monumental evidences of hostility toward aliens. Conservative migrants seek only a place where they can resume the old way of life, and when this is possible, they are content. Sometimes it is not possible, and any migration, therefore, may be associated with a fundamental change in culture.

The usual designation for treks of prehistoric primitives used to be "wandering of peoples," a translation from the German that, however inelegant, is nevertheless appropriate, for it denotes two of the characteristics that define it. It is usually a people as a whole that moves about and not merely certain families or groups, and they leave without a definite destination, as *wander* implies in English. Let us, then, term such migrations as those induced by ecological pressure **wandering of peoples**. Unintended movements over the ocean—an analogous type of primitive migrations, which can be termed **marine wanderings** —have occurred more frequently than was once supposed (Numelin 1937).

Contemporary primitives also often move about in a way directly related to the low level of their material culture. A food-gathering or hunting people cannot ordinarily subsist from what is available in one vicinity; it must range over a wider area, moving either haphazardly or back and forth over its traditional territory. Such movements are called **gathering**. The analogous migrations of cattle-owning peoples are called **nomadism**, from the Greek word for *graze*. Gatherers and nomads together are termed **rangers**.

The way of life of rangers is to be on the move, and their culture is adapted to this state. Their home is temporary or portable; some Australian peoples have no word for *home* in their language. Their value system adjudges the specific hardships of their life to be good. Although they are ordinarily restricted to a particular area, bounded by either physical barriers or peoples able to defend their territories, rangers are presumably more likely to migrate over longer distances (apart from differences in the means of transportation) simply because they are already in motion. Whether any particular nomad people settles down and becomes agricultural does not depend merely on geography. Geography determines only whether such a shift in their way of life is possible— it is barely feasible on the steppe, for example. But even when physical circumstances permit a change, the social pattern of ranging may be too strong to be broken down. Thus, the Soviet program of settling the Kirghiz and other nomad peoples on collective farms succeeded only because it was implemented by sufficient terror to overcome their opposition. That is to say, ranging, like wandering, is typically conservative.

A primitive migration of an agrarian population takes place when there is a disparity between the produce of the land and the number of people subsisting from it. This can come about either suddenly, as by drought or an attack of locusts, or by the steady pressure of growing numbers on land of limited area and fertility. Persons induced to migrate by such population pressure can seek another agricultural site elsewhere, but in the modern era the more usual destination has been a town. That is to say, the migration has ordinarily been innovating rather than conservative. The Irish immigrants to the United States in the decades after the Great Famine, for example, resolutely ignored the Homestead Act and other inducements to settle on the land; in overwhelming proportion, they moved to the cities and stayed there. Let us term such an innovating movement **flight from the land** (again an inelegant but useful translation from the German).

Table 8-7.   Types of Primitive Migration

Primitive	Wandering	Wandering of peoples
		Marine wandering
	Ranging	Gathering
		Nomadism
	Flight from the land	

To recapitulate, primitive migration has been divided as shown in Table 8-7. These are the types set by a physical push and geographical or social controls.

Impelled and Forced Migrations

The activating agent in migration is often not ecological pressure, but rather the state or some equivalent social institution. It is useful to distinguish **impelled migration**, when the persons involved retain some power to decide whether or not to leave, from **forced migration**, when they do not have this power. Often the boundary between the two, the point at which the choice becomes nominal, may be difficult to set. Analytically, however, the distinction is clear-cut, and historically it is often so. The difference is real, for example, between the Nazis' policy (roughly 1933–38) of encouraging Jewish emigration by various anti-Semitic acts and laws, and the later policy (roughly 1938–45) of herding Jews into cattle trains and transporting them to extermination camps.

A second criterion by which we can delineate types of forced or impelled migration is its function, as defined by the activating agent. If persons are induced to move simply to be gotten rid of, since this does not necessarily bring about a change in the migrants' way of life, it is analogous to conservative migration and can be subsumed under it. Others are moved in order that their labor power can be used elsewhere, and such a migration, which constitutes a shift in behavior patterns as well as in locale, is designated as innovating. Four types are thus defined, as shown in Table 8-8. Each of these will be discussed briefly.

Table 8-8.   Types of Impelled and Forced Migrations

Function	Impelled	Forced
To be rid of migrants (conservative)	Flight	Displacement
To use migrants' labor (innovating)	Coolie trade	Slave trade

In all of human history, **flight** has been an important form of migration. Whenever a stronger people move into a new territory, it may drive before it the weaker former occupants. The invasion of Europe during the early centuries of the Christian era, thus, was induced not only by the power vacuum consequent from the disintegration of the Roman Empire, but also by a series of successive pushes, originating from either the desiccation of the Central Asian steppes (Huntington 1924) or the expansion of the Chinese empire still farther east (Teggart 1939).

Many more recent migrations have also been primarily a flight before invading armies (Kulischer 1948). In modern times, however, those induced to flee have often been only certain groups among the population, rather than everyone occupying a particular territory. Indeed, political dissidents had always been ousted when they became a danger to state security, but with the growth of nationalism, ethnic as well as political homogeneity has been sought. The right of national self-determination proclaimed by the Treaty of Versailles, thus, included no provision for the minorities scattered through Central Europe; and in the interwar period the League of Nations negotiated a series of population transfers designed to eliminate national minorities from adjacent countries or, more usually, to legitimate expulsions already completed (Ladas 1932).

A forced movement intended merely to remove a dissident population is here called **displacement**. One purpose of the forced migrations under both Nazi and Soviet auspices has typically been to remove a hostile or potentially hostile group from its home. For example, after Poland was divided between Nazi Germany and Communist Russia in 1939, the more than a million Poles deported to Asiatic Russia were chosen not merely on the basis of actual or alleged opposition to their country's invasion, but more often as members of a large variety of occupational groups defined as potentially oppositionist.

Regarded as "anti-Soviet elements," and so treated, were administrative officials, police, judges, lawyers, members of Parliament, prominent members of political parties, noncommunist nonpolitical societies, clubs, and the Red Cross; civil servants not included above, retired military officers, officers in the reserve, priests, tradesmen, landowners, hotel and restaurant owners, clerks of the local Chambers of Commerce, and any class of persons engaged in trade or correspondence with foreign countries—the latter definition extending even to stamp collectors and Esperantists. . . . Many artisans, peasants, and laborers (both agricultural and industrial) were banished too, so that, in effect, no Polish element was spared [Rozek 1958: 39].

A second purpose of forced migrations has often been to furnish an unskilled labor force. During World War II, for example, Germany imported workers from all occupied countries to keep its economy going. This modern variant of the **slave trade** differs in some respects from the overseas shipment of Africans during the mercantile age, but the two criteria that define the type are the same—the use of force and the supply of manpower.

The analogous form of impelled migration is termed **coolie trade**. This includes not only the movement of Asians to plantations, the most typical form, but also, for example, that of white indentured servants to the British colonies in the 18th century. Such migrants, while formally bound only for the period of a definite contract, often are forced to go into debt and therefore to extend their service almost indefinitely (e.g., Purcell 1951: 348). Many coolies eventually return to their homeland.

Free Migration

In the types discussed so far, the will of the migrants has been a relatively unimportant factor. A primitive migration results from the lack of means to satisfy basic physiological needs, and in the forced (or impelled) type the persons involved are wholly (or partially) passive. We now consider the type in which the will of the migrants is the decisive element, or what is termed **free migration**. One of the principles established by the American and French revolutions was that, as the French constitution of 1791 put it, "the liberty of all to move about, to remain, or to leave" is a "natural and civil right." Among the founders of the United States, this tenet was axiomatic.[6]

Overseas movements from Europe during the 19th century can be discussed most conveniently in terms of one illustrative example, and because of the excellence of its formal analysis, Lindberg's monograph on emigration from Sweden to the United States has been chosen for this purpose (cf. Quigley 1972). Lindberg (1930) begins by distinguishing three periods, each with a characteristic type of emigrants. During the first stage, beginning around 1840, they came principally from the two university towns of Upsala and Lund, "men with a

---

[6] In the Declaration of Independence itself, one of the complaints voiced against George III was that, in his endeavor "to prevent the population of these States," he had obstructed the naturalization of foreigners and refused "to encourage their migration hither." Jefferson enunciated "the natural right which all men have of relinquishing the country in which birth or other accident may have thrown them, and seeking subsistence and happiness wheresoever they may be able, or may hope to find them." Or, in the words of Washington, "The bosom of America is open to receive not only the Opulent and Respectable Stranger, but the oppressed and persecuted of all Nations and Religions, whom we shall wellcome to a participation of all our rights and privileges, if by decency and propriety of conduct they appear to merit the enjoyment." This country was ordained as a haven for "the wretched refuse of [Europe's] teeming shores"—to quote Emma Lazarus's words as inscribed on the base of the Statue of Liberty.

There was, of course, also a dissident minority that challenged this basic value system, but the strength of xenophobia in American life has very often been exaggerated. If the Alien and Sedition Acts were enacted under Adams, it is no less significant that they were repealed under Jefferson, and in the aftermath were an important reason for the eclipse of the Federalist Party that had made them law. The nativist movement of the 1830s, the Know-Nothing Party of the 1850s, the American Protective Association of the early 1890s, the Ku Klux Klan reborn in 1915—all these movements indicate both the persistence of antiforeigner sentiment in America and also the fact that it has usually been limited to noisy groups of merely local importance.

good cultural and social background, mostly young and of a romantic disposition" (ibid.: 3). As the risks overseas were great and impossible to calculate in a rational manner, those who left tended to be adventurers or intellectuals motivated by their ideals, especially by their alienation from European society during a period of political reaction. The significance of this **pioneer migration** was not in its size, which was never large, but in the example it set: "It was this emigration that helped to break the ice and clear the way for the later emigration, which included quite different classes" (ibid.: 7). These pioneers wrote letters home; their adventures in the New World were recounted in Swedish newspapers. Once settled, they helped finance the passage of their families or friends.

Imperceptibly, this first stage developed into the second, the period of **group migration**—the departure, for example of pietist communities under the leadership of their pastor or another person of recognized authority. Even when not associated through their adherence to a dissident sect, emigrants banded together for mutual protection during the hazardous journey and against the wilderness and the often hostile Indians at its end. The significance of this group movement also lay not in its size but in the further impulse it gave. Those leaving during the decade beginning in 1841 averaged only 400 persons annually, and during the following decade still only 1,500.

Mass Migration

Free migration is always rather small, for individuals strongly motivated to seek novelty or improvement are not commonplace. The most significant attribute of pioneers, as in other areas of life, is that they blaze trails that others follow, and sometimes the number who do so grows into a broad stream. Migration becomes a style, an established pattern, an example of collective behavior. Once it is well begun, such a movement is semi-automatic in its growth: the principal cause of emigration is prior emigration. Other circumstances operate as deterrents or incentives, but within the attitudinal framework as already defined; all factors except population growth are important principally in terms of the established behavior.

As we have already noted, when emigration has been set as a *social* pattern, it is no longer relevant to inquire concerning *individual* motivations. For the individual is, in Lindberg's phrase, in an "unstable state of equilibrium," in which only a small impulse in either direction decides his course; thus, the motives he ascribes to his emigration are either trivial or, perhaps more likely, the generalities that he thinks are expected (cf. p. 304).

Migration as collective behavior can be aptly illustrated, again, by the Swedish case. The decade 1861–70, when the average number of emigrants jumped to 9,300 per year, began the transition to the third stage of **mass migration.** Transportation facilities improved. Railroads connected the interior with the port cities, and the sailing ship began to be replaced by the much faster and safer steamer. Not only was the geographical distance cut down, but also what Lindberg terms the social distance: as communities in the new country grew in size and importance, the shift from Sweden to America required less and less of a personal adjustment. Before someone left to go to a Swedish-American settlement, he started his acculturation in an American-Swedish milieu, made up of New World letters, photographs, mementoes, knick-knacks. There developed what the peasants called "America fever." In some districts there was not a farm without relatives in America, and from many all the young people had gone overseas. According to a government report that Lindberg quotes, children were "educated to emigrate," and he continues: "When they finally arrived at a decision, they merely followed a tradition which made emigration the natural thing in a certain situation. In fact, after the imagination and fantasy had, so to speak, become 'charged with America,' a positive decision *not* to emigrate may have been necessary if difficulties arose" (ibid.: 56–57).

The Swedes who migrated to Minnesota became farmers or small-town craftsmen or merchants. In a more general analysis, it is useful to distinguish two types of mass movement according to the nature of the destination—**settlement**, such as Lindberg described, and **urban growth**, or mass migration to a larger town or city. No distinction is made here between internal and international migration; for the fundamentals of the rural–urban shift so characteristic of the modern era are usually the same whether or not the new city dwellers cross a national border.

The typology developed here is summarized in Table 8-9. These are so-called ideal types, analytical constructs derived from historical examples but stripped of accidental, specific features in order to make them of more general significance. The most useful distinction in the typology, perhaps, is that between mass

Table 8-9. General Typology of Migration

Type of Interaction	Migratory Force	Class of Migration	Type of Migration	
			CONSERVATIVE	INNOVATING
Nature and man	Ecological push	Primitive	Wandering	Flight from the land
			Ranging	
State (or equivalent) and man	Migration policy	Impelled	Flight	Coolie trade
		Forced	Displacement	Slave trade
Man and his norms	Higher aspirations	Free	Group	Pioneer
Collective behavior	Social momentum	Mass	Settlement	Urban growth

migration and all other kinds, for this emphasizes the fact that the movement of Europeans to the New World during the 19th century, the instance with which we are most familiar, does not constitute the whole of the phenomenon. After World War I, largely because of new political limitations imposed by both sending and receiving countries, there was a change to a different type, and this was very often interpreted as the end of significant human migration altogether. A world in which hardly anyone dies in the place where he was born, however, cannot be termed sedentary.

SUMMARY

Migration changes the size of population and the rate of growth of the two areas involved but usually not in the simple fashion that common sense suggests. Most migrants are young adults, and their movement changes the age structure and thus the birth and the death rates of both areas. And if the migration affects the social–economic determinants of fertility and mortality, the movement can be negated or, on the contrary, reinforced. Since remigration and transmigration are common, the net figures rather than the gross should be used to gauge the effect on population.

Given a sedentary population and a stimulus to migrate, typically some leave and some do not. There is a self-selection by age, sex, family status, and occupation, as well as possibly by intelligence, mental health, and independence of character. Such generalizations are based on migration that is predominantly economically motivated but not on the presently larger flow of refugees.

Migration is not unitary; it differs from fertility and mortality in that it cannot be analyzed, even preliminarily, in terms of supracultural, physiological factors but must be differentiated even at the most abstract level with respect to the social conditions obtaining. This means that the most general statement that one can make concerning migration must be in the form of a typology, rather than a law. Although few today would follow Ravenstein's example and designate their statements "laws," most discussions of migratory selection still imply an almost equal degree of universality. Actually, selection ranges along a continuum, from total migration to total nonmigration, and the intermediate cases vary not only in the proportion that leave but also in the typical characteristics of those that do. The predominance of females in rural–urban migration that Ravenstein noted for England must be contrasted with male predominance in, for example, India's urban growth. In Table 8-10 a principle of selection is suggested for each type of migration. How accurate this is in each instance is an empirical question, and further research may make a revision necessary. But we know enough now to assert that migratory selection does vary considerably, and that a search for universal generalizations would be fruitless.

Table 8-10. Migratory Selection by Type of Migration

	Types	Destination of Migrants	Migratory Selection	Comments; Examples
Wandering	Wandering of peoples	None	Survival of the fittest?	Prehistoric migrations
	Marine wandering			
Ranging	Gathering	Greener pastures; commutation	None	Migratory way of life
	Nomadism			
	Flight from the land	More fertile land (or towns)	?	"Malthusian" pressure
	Flight	Place of safety	None; or minority groups	Emigrés and refugees
	Coolie trade	Site of work, usually plantations	Young males	Large remigration
	Displacement	Any	None; or minority groups	Population exchanges
	Slave trade	Site of work	Young adults	Mercantile or industrial
	Pioneers	Frontier lands	Young males	Individually motivated
	Group migration	New lands	Dissident groups	
	Settlement	Rural areas	Young males predominate	Social momentum
	Urban growth	Towns	Young females predominate (in Europe)	

327

CITED REFERENCES AND
SUGGESTIONS FOR FURTHER READING

Of the enormous literature on particular migrations, a few works contribute to a broader understanding of the whole subject. The collection edited by Shimm (1956), an excellent compilation on American immigration policy, is brought up to date in the Summer 1970 issue of *International Migration Review*. Historical perspective on the migration to the United States is given by Higham (1956), Hansen (1948), and several of the chapters in Hutchinson (1966). Perhaps the best view of the movement from the perspective of the European sending countries is in the several chapters by Kirk (1946); it is brought up to date by, among others, Danieli (1971) and Mayer (1972), both of whom correctly stress the movement within Europe rather than from it. The books by Kulischer (1948) and Petersen (1955) supplement works that analyze only economic determinants. Several of the works on Australia—e.g., by Borrie (1954), Zubrzycki (1960), and especially Price (1966)—try to use the insights from the larger and earlier American experience to analyze the phenomenon in this different setting. The collection by Jansen (1970) includes some of the best studies from various countries.

Of the monographs on internal migration, the most ambitious is by the Population Studies Center (1957–64), which is summarized by Kuznets and Thomas (1958). The collection of studies in Goldstein (1961), more modest in scope, is also stimulating. Perhaps the best single analysis of internal migration is by Illsley and his colleagues (1963). Much of the methodological work uses internal migration as its substantive element; two of the more interesting items out of a large literature are by Wilber (1963) and Tabah and Cosio (1970).

Isaac's standard work (1947) on the economics of migration should be supplemented by the more interesting analysis of Brinley Thomas, which recently appeared in a revised edition (1972). The best studies of migratory selection up to that date were compiled by Dorothy Thomas (1938), and the most significant addition since then is the short work by Hofstee (1952). Very few analysts have attempted to construct typologies similar to the one in this chapter, but see those by Fairchild (1925: chap. 1), Becker (1930–31), Heberle (1956), Das Gupta (1959), and Price (1966), as well as the lesser works that they cite. The view of migration by Hoffman-Nowotny (1970) should be specially enlightening to non-Europeans.

The two most extensive bibliographies are by Brinley Thomas (1961) and Price (1966, 1971); the first is heavily economic in its emphasis, the second more sociological.

ABRAMSON, J. H. 1966. "Emotional Disorder, Status Inconsistency and Migration," *Milbank Memorial Fund Quarterley*, **44**, 23–48.

ANDERSON, THEODORE R. 1955. "Intermetropolitan Migration: A Comparison of the Hypotheses of Zipf and Stouffer," *American Sociological Review*, **20**, 287–292.

APPLEYARD, R. T. 1962. "The Return Movement of United Kingdom Migrants from Australia," *Population Studies*, **15**, 214–225.

———. 1964. *British Emigration to Australia*. Toronto and Canberra: University of Toronto Press and Australian National University.

BALL, ROBERT. 1973. "How Europe Created Its 'Minority Problem,'" *Fortune*, December.

BAYER, ALAN E. 1968. "The Effect of International Interchange of High-Level Manpower on the United States," *Social Forces,* **46,** 465–477.

BECKER, HOWARD. 1930–31. "Forms of Population Movement: Prolegomena to a Study of Mental Mobility," *Social Forces,* **9,** 147–160, 351–361.

BEIJER, GÜNTHER. 1966. "Selective Migration and 'Brain Drain' from Latin America," *International Migration,* **4,** 28–36.

BERTHOFF, ROWLAND TAPPAN. 1953. *British Immigrants in Industrial America, 1790–1950.* Cambridge, Mass.: Harvard University Press.

BLEVINS, AUDIE L., JR. 1971. "Socioeconomic Differences Between Migrants and Nonmigrants," *Rural Sociology,* **36,** 509–520.

*BORRIE, W. D. 1954. *Italians and Germans in Australia.* Melbourne: Cheshire.

CATTON, WILLIAM R., JR. 1965. "Intervening Opportunities: Barriers or Stepping Stones?" *Pacific Sociological Review,* **8,** 75–81.

COOK, ROBERT C. 1966. "California: After 19 Million, What?" *Population Bulletin,* **22,** 29–57.

DANIELI, L. 1971. "The Demographic and Social Pattern of Migrants in Europe, Especially with Regard to International Migrations," in Second European Population Conference, *Report.* Strasbourg: Council of Europe.

DAS GUPTA, AJIT. 1959. "Types and Measures of Internal Migration," in International Union for the Scientific Study of Population, *International Population Conference.* Vienna.

DAVIE, MAURICE R. 1947. *Refugees in America: Report of the Committee for the Study of Recent Immigration from Europe.* New York: Harper.

———. 1949. *World Immigration, with Special Reference to the United States.* New York: Macmillan.

DAVIS, KINGSLEY. 1951. *The Population of India and Pakistan.* Princeton, N.J.: Princeton University Press.

DIXON, ROLAND B. 1933. "Migration, Primitive," in *Encyclopedia of the Social Sciences,* **10,** 420–425. New York: Macmillan.

DUNCAN, OTIS DUDLEY, and ALBERT J. REISS, JR. 1956. *Social Characteristics of Urban and Rural Communities, 1950.* New York: Wiley.

*ELDRIDGE, HOPE T. 1964. "A Cohort Approach to the Analysis of Migration Differentials," *Demography,* **1,** 212–219.

FAIRCHILD, HENRY PRATT. 1925. *Immigration: A World Movement and Its American Significance,* rev. ed. New York: Macmillan.

FOERSTER, ROBERT F. 1924. *The Italian Emigration of Our Times.* Cambridge, Mass.: Harvard University Press.

GALLE, OMER R., and KARL E. TAEUBER. 1966. "Metropolitan Migration and Intervening Opportunities," *American Sociological Review,* **31,** 5–13.

GARIS, ROY L. 1927. *Immigration Restriction: A Study of the Opposition to and Regulation of Immigration into the United States.* New York: Macmillan.

GINI, CORRADO. 1946. "Los efectos demográficos de las migraciones internacionales," *Revista Internacional de Sociología,* **4,** 351–388.

GOLDSTEIN, SIDNEY. 1954. "Repeated Migration as a Factor in High Mobility Rates," *American Sociological Review,* **10,** 536–541.

———. 1964. "The Extent of Repeated Migration: An Analysis Based on the Danish Population Register," *Journal of the American Statistical Association,* **59,** 1121–1132.

*GOLDSTEIN, SIDNEY, editor. 1961. *The Norristown Study*. Philadelphia: University of Pennsylvania Press.

GOLDTHWAIT, JAMES WALTER. 1927. "A Town That Has Gone Downhill," *Geographical Review*, **17**, 527–552.

GOLLIN, ALBERT E., editor. 1966. *The International Migration of Talent and Skills*. Washington, D.C.: Bureau of Social Science Research.

GONNARD, RENÉ. 1927. *Essai sur l'histoire de l'émigration*. Paris: Valois.

GOODMAN, LEO A. 1961. "Statistical Methods for the Mover–Stayer Model," *Journal of the American Statistical Association*, **56**, 841–868.

———. 1962. "Statistical Methods for Analyzing Processes of Change," *American Journal of Sociology*, **68**, 57–78.

GRAHL-MADSEN, ATLE. 1966–72. *The Status of Refugees in International Law*, 2 vol. Leiden: A. W. Sijthoff.

GREENWOOD, MICHAEL J. 1969. "An Analysis of the Determinants of Geographic Labor Mobility in the United States," *Review of Economics and Statistics*, **51**, 189–194.

GRUBEL, H. G., and A. D. SCOTT. 1967. "Determinants of Migration: The Highly Skilled," *International Migration*, **5**, 127–138.

*HANSEN, MARCUS LEE. 1948. *The Immigrant in American History*. Cambridge, Mass.: Harvard University Press.

*HEBERLE, RUDOLF. 1956. "Types of Migration," Research Group for European Migration Problems, *Bulletin*, **4**, 1–5.

HERNÁNDEZ, JOSÉ. 1971. "Foreign Migration into California," in Kingsley Davis and Frederick G. Styles, editors, *California's Twenty Million: Research Contributions to Population Policy*. Berkeley: Institute of International Studies, University of California.

HERSCH, LIEBMANN. 1931. "International Migration of the Jews," in Willcox and Ferenczi 1929–31, vol. 1.

HIGHAM, JOHN. 1956. "American Immigration Policy in Historical Perspective," in Shimm 1956.

HILLERY, GEORGE A., JR., JAMES S. BROWN, and GORDON F. DeJONG. 1965. "Migration Systems of the Southern Appalachians: Some Demographic Observations," *Rural Sociology*, **30**, 33–48.

HOBBS, ALBERT HOYT. 1942. *Differentials in Internal Migration*. Philadelphia: University of Pennsylvania Press.

*HOFFMANN-NOWOTNY, HANS-JOACHIM. 1970. *Migration: Ein Beitrag zu einer soziologischen Erklärung*. Stuttgart: Ferdinand Enke.

HOFSTEE, E. W. 1952. *Some Remarks on Selective Migration*. Research Group for European Migration Problems. The Hague: Nijhoff.

HUNTINGTON, ELLSWORTH. 1924. *Civilization and Climate*, 3rd. rev. ed. New Haven, Conn.: Yale University Press.

HUTCHINSON, EDWARD P., editor. 1966. "The New Immigration," *Annals of the American Academy of Political and Social Science*, vol. **367**.

*ILLSLEY, RAYMOND, ANGELA FINLAYSON, and BARBARA THOMPSON. 1963. "The Motivation and Characteristics of Internal Migrants," *Milbank Memorial Fund Quarterly*, **41**, 115–143, 217–248.

ISAAC, JULIUS. 1947. *Economics of Migration*. London: Kegan Paul, Trench, Trubner.

*JANSEN, CLIFFORD J., editor. 1970. *Readings in the Sociology of Migration*. London: Pergamon Press.

KIRK, DUDLEY. 1946. *Europe's Population in the Interwar Years.* League of Nations. Princeton, N.J.: Princeton University Press.

*KULISCHER, EUGENE M. 1948. *Europe on the Move: War and Population Changes, 1917–47.* New York: Columbia University Press.

———. 1949. "Displaced Persons in the Modern World," *Annals of the American Academy of Political and Social Science,* **262,** 166–177.

*KUZNETS, SIMON, and ERNEST RUBIN. 1954. *Immigration and the Foreign Born.* New York: National Bureau of Economic Research.

*———, and DOROTHY SWAINE THOMAS. 1958. "Internal Migration and Economic Growth," in Milbank Memorial Fund 1958.

LADAS, STEPHEN P. 1932. *The Exchange of Minorities: Bulgaria, Greece and Turkey.* New York: Macmillan.

LAZARUS, JUDITH, BEN Z. LOCKE, and DOROTHY SWAINE THOMAS. 1963. "Migration Differentials in Mental Disease," *Milbank Memorial Fund Quarterly,* **41,** 25–42.

LEE, EVERETT S. 1958. "Migration and Mental Disease: New York State, 1949–51," in Milbank Memorial Fund 1958.

———. 1963. "Socio-Economic and Migration Differentials in Mental Disease, New York State, 1949–51," *Milbank Memorial Fund Quarterly,* **41,** 249–268.

———. 1966. "A Theory of Migration," *Demography,* **1,** 47–57.

LI, WEN L. 1970 "Matrix Analysis of Migration Streams," *International Migration,* **8,** 174–181.

LINDBERG, JOHN S. 1930. *The Background of Swedish Emigration to the United States: An Economic and Sociological Study of the Dynamics of Migration.* Minneapolis: University of Minnesota Press.

LONG, LARRY H. 1973. "Poverty Status and Receipt of Welfare Among Migrants and Nonmigrants in Large Cities," paper presented at the annual meeting of the Population Association of America, New Orleans.

LOWENTHAL, DAVID, and LAMBROS COMITAS. 1962. "Emigration and Depopulation: Some Neglected Aspects of Population Geography," *Population Review,* **6,** 83–94.

MACDONALD, JOHN S., and LEATRICE D. MACDONALD. 1964. "Chain Migration, Ethnic Neighborhood Formation, and Social Networks," *Milbank Memorial Fund Quarterly,* **42,** 82–96.

MALZBERG, BENJAMIN, and EVERETT S. LEE. 1956. *Migration and Mental Disease: A Study of First Admissions to Hospitals for Mental Disease, New York, 1939–1941.* New York: Social Science Research Council.

MAYER, KURT B. 1972. "International Migrations of European Workers," *New Community,* **1,** 1–10.

*MILBANK MEMORIAL FUND. 1958. *Selected Studies of Migration Since World War II.* New York.

MILLS, THOMAS J. 1966. "Scientific Personnel and the Professions," in Hutchinson 1966.

MONROE, J. J. 1966. "Regional Variation in French Emigration Rates," *International Migration,* **4,** 186–198.

MORRISON, PETER A. 1971. "The Role of Migration in California's Growth," in Kingsley Davis and Frederick G. Styles, editors, *California's Twenty Million: Research Contributions to Population Policy.* Berkeley: Institute of International Studies, University of California.

MYERS, GEORGE C., ROBERT MCGINNIS, and GEORGE MASNICK. 1967. "The Duration of Residence Approach to a Dynamic Stochastic Model of Internal Migration: A Test of the Axiom of Cumulative Inertia," *Eugenics Quarterly*, **14**, 121–126.

*NUMELIN, RAGNAR. 1937. *The Wandering Spirit: A Study of Human Migration.* Macmillan: London.

PAIKERT, G. C. 1962. *The German Exodus: A Selective Study on the Post-World War II Expulsion of German Populations and Its Effects.* Research Group for European Migration Problems. The Hague: Nijhoff.

*PETERSEN, WILLIAM. 1955. *Planned Migration: The Social Determinants of the Dutch-Canadian Movement.* Berkeley: University of California Press.

POPULATION STUDIES CENTER. UNIVERSITY OF PENNSYLVANIA. 1957–64. *Population Redistribution and Economic Growth, United States, 1870–1950.* American Philosophical Society, *Memoirs*, vols. **45**, **51**, **61**.

*PRICE, CHARLES A., editor. 1966–71. *Australian Immigration: A Bibliography and Digest*, 1st and 2nd eds. Canberra: Australian National University.

PURCELL, VICTOR. 1951. *The Chinese in Southeast Asia.* London: Oxford University Press.

QUIGLEY, JOHN MICHAEL. 1972. "An Economic Model of Swedish Emigration," *Quarterly Journal of Economics*, **86**, 111–126.

RAVENSTEIN, E. G. 1885–89. "The Laws of Migration," *Journal of the Royal Statistical Society*, **48**, 167–235; **52**, 241–305.

RICHARDSON, ALAN. 1968 "A Shipboard Study of Some British-born Immigrants Returning to the United Kingdom from Australia," *International Migration*, **6**, 221–238.

RICHMOND, ANTHONY H. 1968. "Return Migration from Canada to Britain," *Population Studies*, **32**, 263–271.

RIVETT, KENNETH. 1967. "A Proposal for Change in Australia's Immigration Policy," in S. Chandrasekhar, editor, *Asia's Population Problems.* London: Allen & Unwin.

ROSS, ANTHONY CLUNIES. 1967. "Asian Migration—An Australian Failure?" in S. Chandrasekhar, editor, *Asia's Population Problems.* London: Allen & Unwin.

ROSSI, PETER H. 1955. *Why Families Move: A Study in the Social Psychology of Urban Residential Mobility.* New York: Free Press.

ROZEK, EDWARD J. 1958. *Allied Wartime Diplomacy: A Pattern in Poland.* New York: Wiley.

RUBIN, ERNEST. 1966. "The Demography of Immigration to the United States," in Hutchinson 1966.

SALOUTOS, THEODORE. 1956. *They Remember America: The Story of the Repatriated Greek-Americans.* Berkeley: University of California Press.

SAVILLE, JOHN. 1957. *Rural Depopulation in England and Wales, 1851–1951.* London: Routledge & Kegan Paul.

SCHECHTMAN, JOSEPH B. 1963. *The Refugee in the World: Displacement and Integration.* New York: Barnes.

*SHIMM, MELVIN G., editor. 1956. "Immigration," *Law and Contemporary Problems*, **21**, no. 2.

SHRYOCK, HENRY S., JR. 1964. *Population Mobility within the United States.* Chicago: Community and Family Study Center, University of Chicago.

SOROKIN, PITIRIM A., and CARLE C. ZIMMERMAN. 1929. *Principles of Rural-Urban Sociology.* New York: Holt.

SPENCER, HERBERT. 1892. *The Principles of Sociology*, 3rd rev. ed. New York: Appleton-Century-Crofts.

SPENGLER, JOSEPH H. 1933. "Population Doctrines in the United States, 2: Malthusianism," *Journal of Political Economy*, 41, 639–672.

STOUFFER, SAMUEL A. 1940. "Intervening Opportunities: A Theory Relating Mobility and Distance," *American Sociological Review*, 5, 845–867.

———. 1960. "Intervening Opportunities and Competing Migrants," *Journal of Regional Science*, 2, 1–26.

TABAH, LÉON, and ALBERTO CATALDI. 1963. "Effets d'une immigration dans quelques populations modèles," *Population*, 18, 683–696.

———, and MARIE-EUGÉNIE COSIO. 1970. "Mesure de la migration interne au moyen des recensements: Application au Mexique," *Population*, 25, 303–346.

TAEUBER, KARL E., LEONARD CHIAZZE, JR., and WILLIAM HAENSZEL. 1968. *Migration in the United States: An Analysis of Residence Histories*. Public Health Monograph no. 77. Washington, D.C.: U.S. Government Printing Office.

TARVER, JAMES D., and R. DOUGLAS McLEOD. 1973. "A Test and Modification of Zipf's Hypothesis for Predicting Interstate Migration," *Demography*, 10, 259–275.

TEGGART, FREDERICK J. 1939. *Rome and China: A Study of Correlations in Historical Events*. Berkeley: University of California Press.

TER HEIDE, H. 1963. "Migration Models and Their Significance for Population Forecasts," *Milbank Memorial Fund Quaterly*, 41, 56–76.

THOMAS, BRINLEY. 1961. *International Migration and Economic Development: A Trend Report and Bibliography*. Paris: Unesco.

———. 1972. *Migration and Economic Growth: A Study of Great Britain and the Atlantic Economy*, 2nd. ed. National Institute of Economic and Social Research. Cambridge, England: Cambridge University Press.

THOMAS, DOROTHY SWAINE. 1925. *Social Aspects of the Business Cycle*. New York: Dutton.

———. 1941. *Social and Economic Aspects of Swedish Population Movements, 1750–1933*. New York: Macmillan.

*———, editor. 1938. *Research Memorandum on Migration Differentials*. New York: Social Science Research Council.

THOMPSON, WARREN S. 1948. *Plenty of People: The World's Population Pressures, Problems, and Policies, and How They Concern Us*. New York: Ronald.

TIMLIN, M. F. 1965. "Canadian Immigration Policy: An Analysis," *International Migration*, 3, 52–70.

U.S. COMMITTEE FOR REFUGEES. 1973. *World Refugee Report, 1973*. New York.

WALKER, FRANCIS A. 1873. "Our Population in 1900," *Atlantic Monthly*, 32, 487–495.

———. 1891. "Immigration and Degradation," *Forum*, 11, 634–644.

———. 1892. "Immigration," *Yale Review*, 1, 124–145.

———. 1896. "Restriction of Immigration," *Atlantic Monthly*, 77, 822–829.

WILBER, GEORGE L. 1963. "Migration Expectancy in the United States," *Journal of the American Statistical Association*, 58, 444–453.

WILLCOX, WALTER F. 1906. "The Expansion of Europe in Its Influence upon Population," in James Hayden Tufts *et al.*, editors, *Studies in Philosophy and Psychology by Former Students of Charles Edward Garman*. Boston: Houghton Mifflin.

WILLCOX, WALTER F. 1911. "The Change in the Proportion of Children in the United States and in the Birth Rate in France During the Nineteenth Century," American Statistical Association, *Publications*, no. 93.

*———, and IMRE FERENCZI. 1929–31. *International Migrations*, 2 vol. New York: National Bureau of Economic Research.

ZIPF, GEORGE K. 1949. *Human Behavior and the Principle of Least Effort*. Reading, Mass.: Addison-Wesley.

ZUBRZYCKI, JERZY. 1960. *Immigrants in Australia*, 2 vol. Melbourne: Melbourne University Press.

9

PROJECTIONS AND FORECASTS

Demographers are called on not only to furnish data about the present size and composition of the population and their past development, but also to estimate their future trend. Such a prognosis, however it is made, is likely to be incorrect, but this does not mean that it is useless. It may be compared in many respects to a weather prediction by a meteorologist. In both cases, the estimate by a competent expert will generally be more accurate than a layman's guess. Moreover, much of what we know about the weather or about the determinants of population growth has been learned by comparing false predictions with the actual events and trying to understand why the error was made. In one respect, however, there is an important difference between a meteorologist's and a demographer's forecasts. If the weather bureau predicts that it will rain on a certain day, this statement has no effect on the weather; but a population forecast, if it is made a basis for government policy, itself becomes one of the determinants of population change. One analyst speaks of a "law of forecast feedback": "If a system of forecasting achieves a significant reputation for infallibility, its forecasts tend to become part of the chain of events, affecting the outcome in an unpredictable manner" (Smith 1964). The very predictions of incipient population decline in the 1930s, for example, may have helped reverse the trend and thus make the forecasts false. Or, on the smaller scale of urban planning, it is well known that a new road or a new school or any other new facility, constructed in accord with carefully estimated rates of in-migration and natural increase, often attracts many more families to the area than had been anticipated.

TYPES OF POPULATION PROJECTIONS

A chronological account of population projections is largely a history of developing methodology. The linear extrapolations of the 19th century gave way to a search for a natural law of population growth and, most recently, to attempts to analyze separately changes in fertility, mortality, and migration as these relate to population structure. It is convenient to trace this development with examples pertaining mainly to the population of the United States.

335

Projections of Total Population Growth

The simplest type of projection is an extrapolation of the past growth of the total population. The most famous, perhaps, of the several calculations of this type made early in American history was that by Elkanah Watson, a minor figure of the revolutionary period. He noticed that the population of the United States had increased by about a third during each of the first two decades following the 1790 census, and in a two-page article he calculated the growth if this decennial rate were to continue (Watson 1856: 257–258). Until 1860 this forecast proved to be extraordinarily close to the actual population growth. For 1840 the projected figure was 17,116,526 and the census count 17,069,453, representing an error of about 0.3 percent. For 1850 the projected figure was 23,185,368 and the census count 23,191,876, representing an error of about 0.03 percent almost 40 years after the calculation was made!

An only slightly more elaborate extrapolation by Francis Bonynge (1852) also predicted actual growth over a considerable span. He divided the population into the three classes of whites, slaves, and free Negroes, and applied a rate of decennial increase to each. Watson's forecast was reasonably accurate for 50 years, Bonynge's for 70 years.

In the 1840s a more thorough analysis of population growth was made by George Tucker, a professor of political economy and moral philosophy at the University of Virginia. He calculated fertility ratios from 1800 on and deduced that the family size had been decreasing since that date. This decline in fertility had begun, according to Tucker, because of "moral causes," but the decisive factor would eventually become the "difficulty of subsistence." The rate of growth would fall, therefore, unless immigration steadily increased. He predicted a population of 74 to 80 million in 1900 (the census count was 76 million) and one of 200 million in 1940 (compared with the actual 132 million) (Spengler 1936).

J. D. B. DeBow, superintendent of the 1850 census, believed that the most likely figure in 1900 was 100 million, but that thereafter the rate of growth would fall off sharply. He predicted the 1950 population of 150 million precisely. Toward the end of the century, several efforts were made to fit the past growth to a more elaborate curve. H. S. Pritchett, who used a third-degree parabola, forecast the population of 1900 within 2 percent and that of 1910 within less than 3 percent; but by the year 2900, according to his series, the United States would have 40 billion inhabitants.

How is it that these men, some of them wholly untrained (Bonynge was a retired China merchant), all of them using crude methods, were able to forecast the growth of the population over many decades? The astounding accuracy was a fluke; until 1860 the population counted in successive censuses increased by a regular proportion, and the formulas used by these early forecasters were usually not much more complex than this record. Most of the predictions were off by considerable amounts for the later dates, but even so they are enough of a curiosity to excite any student's wonder. None of the technically more pretentious efforts to project population growth has been nearly so successful over so long a period as the best of these early forecasts.

A well known effort to find a general growth pattern is the Pearl–Reed logistic curve, as enunciated in several books and articles and applied to the populations of various countries and times. Raymond Pearl was a zoologist, and he developed his theory from analyzing the actual multiplication of fruit flies with a given amount of food in a closed bottle. As the adult drosophilae able to propagate increased from the original pair, their number went up at an ever accelerating rate until the limiting factor of the fixed food supply became relevant. Then the S-shaped growth curve gradually flattened out, approaching but never quite reaching a maximum level fixed by the subsistence available.

The populations of a number of countries were fitted to logistic curves of various formulas, with at first a good deal of success.[1] For example, a forecast that Pearl and Reed made in 1920 predicted the 1950 population of the United States with an error of only about 1 percent (Pearl and Reed 1920). In the meantime, however, since Logistic I had predicted a population in 1940 some 3.5 percent higher than the census count in that year, Pearl and his associates calculated Logistic II, which missed the 1950 population by 7 million rather than by 2 million.

A decisive test of his theory was to be found, according to Pearl, in the one instance of a self-contained population on which adequate statistics had been maintained over a considerable period.

The native Algerian population ... affords a crucial case. It is a human population which has virtually completed a cycle of growth according to the logistic curve within the period of recorded census history. One can now feel more certain that this curve is a first and tolerably close approximation to a real *law* of growth for human populations than was possible when the completion of a cycle for a human population demanded extrapolation of the curve for many years beyond the period of the observation [Pearl 1925: 125–126].

When his first projected figure, 5.2 million in 1931, was short of the actual population by some 300,000, Pearl fell back on the explanation that a law in 1919 had extended political rights to certain of the native Algerians and had thus changed the influences on growth. As social changes of this importance are frequent occurrences in every country, it meant that the theory, even if valid on other grounds, was far less precise than he had suggested in his first statement

---

[1] It was used, for instance, by Janisch in Germany, Yule in England, and Maclean in Canada. See F. Janisch, *Das Exponentialgesetz als Grundlage einer vergleichenden Biologie*, Berlin, 1927; G. Udny Yule, "The Growth of Population and the Factors which Control It," *Journal of the Royal Statistical Society*, **88** (1925), 1–58; M. C. Maclean, "The Growth of Population in Canada," in Canada, Dominion Bureau of Statistics, *Seventh Census of Canada, 1931*, **1**: *Summary*, Ottawa, 1936, 99–132. For a critical comment on the last, see William Petersen, *Planned Migration: The Social Determinants of the Dutch-Canadian Movement* (Berkeley: University of California Press, 1955), pp. 204ff.

of it. Sometimes he combined two logistic curves of different equations into a single growth curve. In the case of Germany, for example, the shift from one equation to another was supposedly necessitated by the change from a predominantly agricultural to an industrial society; but an exactly comparable change in, for example, American society did not require a compound curve (ibid.: 14, 21).

In retrospect, the success of the logistic curve, like that of the earlier predictions, must be regarded as coincidental. What most condemns it is the biological rationale on which it is based. The relative abundance of food, which in Pearl's basic model was the only determinant of population growth, in a country like the United States is hardly even a relevant factor—except possibly in the very long run. In Pearl's extension of this model the limit was not merely food but the total physical resources as developed by the technology of the period. While this seems reasonable enough, it is actually not a very useful theory on which to base forecasts. This is so for two seemingly contradictory reasons: (1) In the modern period the control over the environment becomes more effective year by year. To set a maximum population (the asymptote that the logistic curve will never quite reach) in terms of present technology would be unrealistic, but to set it in terms of an extrapolation of improving technology involves a guess no less hazardous than the projection of the number of people. On the other hand, (2) the population pressure that will later develop may be felt immediately, for human decisions are made not merely in response to physical difficulties but often in anticipation of them. The ultimate limit to growth, that is to say, is not a useful guide to the future rate of increase, because that limit will change and, in any case, its effect may be significant much before the ultimate point.

The growth rate of human populations did not decline because of hunger, as with the fruit flies, but mainly because, for various reasons possibly including hunger, parents decided to have fewer children. For a period mortality fell faster than fertility, and the population increased rapidly; then fertility fell faster and the curve began to flatten out. That is to say, the S-shaped curve, to the degree that it has actually described the growth of human populations, has done so because of the demographic transition, not because of the biological determinants that Pearl posited.

Reproduction Rates

Both the gross and the net reproduction rates, it will be recalled (see pp. 88–90), are population projections, though half-disguised as measures of, respectively, fertility and natural increase. A projection based on wholly unrealistic assumptions—such as that the demographic rates of any one year are a permanent fixture—is often a useful device; although we know this will not happen, let us see what the consequences would be if it did. But the synthetic cohort of the model is not the same as an actual cohort. If one forgets that these assumptions were made, the tool is less helpful than misleading (Stolnitz and Ryder

1949). The average net reproduction rate of the United States during the 1930s was 0.98, or 2 percent below the replacement level of 1.0. The annual age-specific birth rates during that one decade, however, were not a good indication of what the completed family size of any cohort would be. Older women, who had borne children in the 1920s, refrained in greater numbers from having more; and younger women put off having children until the 1940s. Thus, what was widely interpreted as the first step toward the impending decrease in population was in fact a temporary phenomenon.

In 1931 Dublin presented two forecasts based on the principles underlying the net reproduction rate. According to the first, which in his opinion was "altogether too optimistic," the population of the United States with no migration would reach a maximum of 154 million between 1980 and 1990 and then decline to 140 million by 2100. By the second, "more reasonable" estimate, the maximum of 148 million would be reached by 1970, followed by a decline to 140 million by 2000 and to 76 million by 2100! "These predictions are remarkable not so much for their specific numerical values as for the fact that a prominent American demographer had stated publicly that the population of the United States almost certainly would decline in the very near future. The most pessimistic of previous forecasters had assumed merely that the rate of increase would approach zero at some distant time" (Dorn 1950).

The main reason that reproduction rates are inappropriate as predictive instruments, to sum up, are that they are ordinarily (though not necessarily) based (1) on the fertility and mortality of a single year and (2) on the assumption that these will remain constant for a century or so after that. The rates "are analogous to the speedometer on a car in that they measure the approximate speed or force of reproduction at a given time but not necessarily the actual distance being covered or the actual time required to reach the destination. The 'speed' fluctuates too much [to be a] reliable measure of distance" (Grabill et al. 1958: 73; cf. ibid.: 313–314, 360).

Component Projections

In virtually all projections made today the total population is not extrapolated as such but is rather divided up first into its component parts and, as it were, reassembled at successive future dates. The growth in an area during any particular period is the consequence of its natural increase and the net migration. If one analyzes separately the trend in the three components—fertility, mortality, and migration—the most important determinant is almost always the age and sex structure. Since childbearing is physiologically possible only to women between the ages, roughly, of 15 and 45, the proportion of the total population in this particular age category of females is a relevant factor in judging its future fertility. Similarly, since the probability of dying within the next year is higher for infants and the old than it is for children or young adults, mortality will also vary according to the age structure. Migration, finally, is a behavior typical of young adults or, to a lesser degree, of the young children or elderly persons that they may take with them. A component projection, then, is made by applying simultaneously age-specific rates of fertility, mortality, and migration to a given population in the process of gradual change in both size and structure.

The method can be illustrated by the forecasts that Warren S. Thompson and P. K. Whelpton made in the 1930s for the Committee on Population Problems of the National Resources Committee (1938). This example is worth discussing both because it had a great impact on public opinion of the time and because it illustrates very well the reasons why demographers in the 1930s (and also very often for a considerable period thereafter) believed that population would soon stop growing or even begin to decline.

Thompson and Whelpton tried to judge the future growth by assessing recent trends in mortality, fertility, and immigration, both in the United States and in other Western countries. Their appraisal is summarized in the following paragraphs.

Death Rates. The major advances in the past, the authors pointed out, had been made through the decline in death rates of infants and young children, especially by the greater control over infectious diseases. They believed that one important cause of death among adults, pneumonia, would decline rapidly, but others—in particular, heart disease, cancer, nephritis, and cerebral hemorrhage—were "likely to prove much more difficult to control than such former scourges as smallpox, tuberculosis, typhoid fever, and diarrhea and enteritis." They estimated, therefore, that the lowest possible mortality in 1980 could effect only a moderate decline, with expectations of life at birth at that date of 72 years for males and 74 for females. With the highest probable mortality, these figures would be 65.6 and 68.4 years, respectively, levels close to what had already been attained by New Zealand and some other countries with a Western culture. The most likely figures, in their opinion, were based on a medium assumption—68.8 years for males and 71.2 for females; and these were the ones used in most of the projections.

Birth Rates. "It seems far easier to judge what can be done in lowering death rates in the future than to judge what people may want to do regarding the size of their families; hence the relative difference between high and low birth rate assumptions . . . is roughly four times as great as that between the high and low death rate assumptions." "In view of the past trend in the United States, and the lower rates that prevail in certain other nations," the highest future fertility trend that seemed reasonable was that the age-specific birth rates of 1930–34 would continue unchanged until 1980. During that period the completed family size was less than 2.2 children per woman, or about 2.4 children per wife, or about 2.9 per mother. According to the probable lower limit, the decline in birth rates would continue until 1980, though at rapidly diminishing rates. In 1980, by this assumption, there would be 1.5 children per woman, or about 2 children per mother. "This is approximately the present situation in California and Washington, D.C., as well as in all of England." In the opinion of the authors, the most likely trend was a medium one, by which fertility would fall by 13 percent over the next 50 years, ending with completed family sizes in 1980 of 1.9 children per woman, or slightly more than 2.5 per mother.

The Committee on Population Problems rejected the high estimate as too improbable to consider. In some regions of the country, it believed, fertility would continue to fall off, and "it seems extremely unlikely that this decline will be offset by increases of such magnitude, in areas where birth rates are low, as to cause fertility rates for the nation as a whole to remain constant. Accordingly, emphasis is here placed on the estimates based on 'medium' and 'low' assumptions as regards fertility, combined with the 'medium' assumption as regards mortality."

Immigration.   Under the quota laws in effect in the 1930s, 153,714 immigrants were permitted to enter each year from quota countries and an unlimited number from other countries. In an Executive Order of 1930 consular officers had been instructed to be especially careful in screening out aspirant immigrants likely to become public charges. Actually, in every year from 1931 to 1935 there had been a net emigration. Thompson and Whelpton chose to calculate projections with two alternative assumptions concerning migration—no immigration and the net arrival of 100,000 immigrants. The Committee seemed to lean toward the first as the more probable. New permanent restrictions were likely, it believed, in particular the extension of the quota principle to the Western Hemisphere.

With three assumptions concerning mortality, three concerning fertility, and two concerning immigration, the total number of possible projections is their product, or eighteen. Of these, however, only seven were worked out at all, and three were considered by the Committee to be most probable: (1) medium fertility and mortality with 100,000 immigrants per year; (2) medium fertility and mortality with no immigration; and (3) low fertility, medium mortality, and no immigration. The projected populations in 1950 and 1980 based on these three sets of assumptions were, respectively: (1) 142 and 158 million, (2) 141 and 153 million, and (3) 137 and 134 million.

Looking back at these estimates from today's perspective, one can very easily judge them too harshly. It must be emphasized that the appraisals of future trends were made in the light of what seemed to be reasonable expectations on the basis of everything that was known in the 1930s. Unlike Pearl, Thompson and Whelpton did not attempt to develop a "natural law" of population growth. And, unlike those who became so enamored of the net reproduction rate that they assumed *a priori* that the age-specific birth and death rates were fixed, Thompson and Whelpton attempted to judge this question empirically from the social and economic conditions then prevailing. So long as the depression continued the forecasts made by this method were accurate, even amazingly so. The figure for 1940 that Thompson and Whelpton had calculated in 1933 was more precise than the census count itself before this was corrected for underenumeration!

Table 9-1. Some Early Component Projections, Population of the United States (millions)

	1930	1940	1950	1960	1970	1980	1990	2000
Census population	122.8	131.7	150.7	179.3	203.2			
Scripps Foundation:								
1928	123.6	138.3	151.6	162.7	171.5	—	—	186.0
1931		132.5	139.8	143.9	144.6	142.9^a		
1933:								
High		134.5	148.5	—	—	190.0		
Low		132.5	140.5	—	146.0	145.0^a		
1935:								
High		132.6	146.1	159.5	172.8	185.8		
Medium		132.0	141.6	149.4	155.0	158.3^a		
Low		131.2	136.2	137.1	134.0	127.6^a		
1943:								
High			145.0	156.5	167 9	179.4	189.4	198.7
Medium			144.4	153.4	160.5	165.4	167.1	166.6^a
Low			143.0	147.7	148.7	145.8	138.9	129.1^a
1947:								
High			148.0	162.0	177.1^b			
Medium			146.0	155.1	162.0^c			
Low			144.9	149.8	151.6^a			
Census Bureau								
1949			149.9	160.0				

^{a} Declines thereafter.
^{b} Increases thereafter.
^{c} Increases until about 2000, then declines.
SOURCES: Various, as compiled in Harold F. Dorn, "Pitfalls in Population Forecasts and Projections," *Journal of the American Statistical Association*, **45** (1950), 311–344.

For the period after the depression, however, the forecasts made in its social–economic context were off by a wide margin. Several of the most important calculated before the 1950 census are shown in Table 9-1 (the ones dated 1935 are essentially the same as those prepared for the National Resources Committee, discussed in detail above). The succession of figures suggests what happened. The projection made in 1928, just before the onset of the depression, overstated the population of 1940 by 6.6 million and that of 1950 by almost a million, but understated that of 1960 by 16.6 million. The following projections, beginning with the one made in 1931, were adjusted to the expected population of 1940 with much greater accuracy, but they were much farther off in 1950 and thereafter. Note that not a single estimate for 1960, high, low, or medium, comes close to the actual population of 179.3 million, and only one series (the high estimate made in 1947) approaches this figure even by 1970.

The main reason these projections were so far off was the baby boom of the 1940s and the continuing high fertility of the 1950s. In the 1930s most demographers would have gone along with the Committee on Population Problems in rejecting the assumption that birth rates would remain static at the 1930–34 level, Thompson and Whelpton's highest estimate of fertility. The misjudgment concerning fertility was compounded, moreover, by errors in the same direction with respect to mortality and immigration. Death rates went down, and immigration went up, faster than was anticipated.

Once the fact of the baby boom was absorbed into demographers' calculations, there was a tendency to extrapolate from this higher fertility. Quite unexpectedly, however, birth rates in the early 1970s fell to levels close to what Thompson and Whelpton had anticipated—though one can hardly say that they were therefore correct, for their conclusion had been based on reasoning that proved to be false. Mortality also moved closer to their pessimistic prediction: as we have noted, age-specific rates of some portions of the population not only stopped declining but rose during recent decades. The failure to predict correctly the fertility of the 1970s underlines the fact that there has been no improvement in probable accuracy since the 1930s.

PROJECTIONS VERSUS FORECASTS

In the gradual development of new techniques for extrapolating population growth, it has become usual to distinguish two types of estimates. When all of the independent variables are given in demographic terms—for example, certain age-specific birth and death rates and net migration at a given annual rate— the extrapolation of the past trend is termed a population **projection**. When at least some of the independent variables are given in social or economic terms, or the greater or lesser probability of demographic variables is posited in a social–economic framework, the same extrapolation is termed a population **forecast**. Many extrapolations are not clearly in either one class or the other. Let us consider first those that are.

Demographers often project the future population that will result from the current rate of increase not in order to make a valid forecast but, on the contrary, to demonstrate that the present growth *cannot* continue. An extreme example can be cited from the Australian demographer George Knibbs (1928: 49n.): If a population grew from a single couple at the annual rate of 1 percent, at the end of 10,000 years it would require 248,293,000,000,000,000,000 earths to furnish the material for the bodies of the people. The actual rate of growth of the world population from 1950 to 1965 was at 1.8 percent. In 1971 the world's population was increasing by an estimated 2.0 percent per year, that of various countries of South America or Africa by 3.4 percent per year. These latter figures mean that the populations would double in, respectively, 35 and 21 years. With such a calculation as Knibbs made, one is struck by the fact that the current rate of increase of the human species is a temporary phenomenon, which could not have begun very long ago and cannot endure for very much longer.

In a short but elegant paper, two archeologists used the same logic to show that the growth of population in the Near East during the Neolithic must have been very slow. At the beginning of the era, 8000 B.C., they took the initial population to be 100,000—an arbitrary but not unreasonable figure. With the lowest rate of annual increase they considered, 0.5 percent (or only a quarter of the rate at which the world's population was growing in the early 1970s) the 100,000 in 8000 B.C. would have become 46.2 trillion in 4000 B.C.

The choice of a rate of even 0.13 percent results in a total population for the Near East in 4000 B.C. of over 18 million, which still appears excessive. . . . The increase in population that occurred during the Neolithic period was *not* "exceedingly rapid" [as many have assumed]. It was, in fact, only on the order of one-tenth of one percent per year. For a village of 100 this rate of increase is equivalent to a net gain of only one person over a 10-year period [Carneiro and Hilse 1966].

Of course, there were fluctuations over these several millennia. In especially favored areas or periods, the increase was undoubtedly considerably faster, but that means that in other places and times it was even less than 0.1 percent. Over all, the growth was so slow as to be imperceptible during anyone's lifetime, and during the whole of the era the fertility and mortality were more of less in balance. This is not a fact that could be concluded so plausibly from any alternative line of reasoning.

On the more modest scale of extrapolations of one country's population growth over a few decades, such projections are much less useful. To point out that the likely trends in immigration, mortality, and fertility will together favor an increase in the population of the United States, and that if such a process were to continue for several centuries there would be "standing room only," does not help us determine what the population will probably be a decade hence. It is only in countries where the population pressure is both already great and increasing rapidly, as in India or Egypt, that an extrapolation over even a relatively short period helps demonstrate that present growth rates cannot continue, and may encourage policy-makers to consider whether they would prefer a decreased fertility or an increased mortality.

At the other extreme from a projection that specifically does not forecast there is a forecast that is placed fully in the economic and social context of population change. There is no reason why a population analyst should be expected to know, for example, whether and when an economic depression will occur, or a war, or a cure for cancer, or any of the other hundred significant changes in the economy, technology, society, cultural patterns, that are relevant to population growth.[2] Even a specialist in these various fields is not only generally unable to predict their future development but also often unable to summarize their past trend accurately. For instance, the crucial error of the demographers, their failure to predict postwar fertility correctly, was based in part on the sociologists' analysis of urbanism. Since it was believed that in a Gesellschaft all social relations are atomized, it was reasonable to conclude that increasing urbanization would also transform the family from an "institution" to "companionship" (see p. 548). This too was a false prognosis.

It is within the province of the demographer to consider, however, "the determinants and consequences of population trends" (as it was put in the title of the well known United Nations publication), and these, too, cannot ordinarily be assessed with precision. The question is not whether there will be a war, or a depression, or whatever, but if there is such a break in normal development, what the demographic consequences will be. Most of the forecasts of the 1930s, for instance, were hedged with the condition that there would be no major war over the period of the projection; for the excess mortality resulting from it, together with the loss in fertility from the subsequent unbalanced population structure, would mean a faster decline in population growth. The war came, but for most of the belligerent countries the consequence was the opposite of what had been anticipated. Similarly, the effect of an economic depression on the birth rate is not really well understood. Indeed, family size fell off during

---

[2] A list compiled in the mid-1960s of 100 technical innovations "likely" before the end of the 20th century (Kahn and Wiener 1967; cf. Petersen 1967) included the following *directly* relevant to population trends:

Mortality and health

Wider application of lasers to surgery.

Major reduction in hereditary and congenital defects.

Extensive use of mechanical aids or substitutes for human organs, senses, limbs; more frequent transplantation of organs.

Effective control of appetite and weight.

New improvements in food plants and animals.

Human "hibernation" for short periods for medical purposes.

Ocean "farming."

Cheap, widely available, and extremely destructive weapons.

Postponement of aging; limited rejuvenation.

Fertility

Cheap, convenient, and reliable birth control.

Ability to designate the sex of unborn children; improved ability to change sex.

Other genetic controls.

Population distribution

Some control over weather.

Practical large-scale desalination.

Labor force

Automated or more mechanized housekeeping.

Use of nuclear reactors for power, excavation, mining, etc.

General use of automation in management and production.

the 1930s, but in part because the economic crisis came as a culmination of many other depressants on fertility. The fact that the well-to-do had the smallest families and the men on work–relief the largest should warn us against a simplistic economic interpretation of fertility trends. If there were another depression of a given severity—measured, let us say, by the precise proportion of the labor force that is unemployed—no demographer would be able to estimate how much the birth rate would fall as a result.

Moreover, the effect of population growth on the society and thus back on itself has seldom or never been included except in such broad and abstract forecasts as the theory of the demographic transition: an improved efficiency in death-control measures increased the rate of population growth, which stimulated the need or desire for birth control. We do not know enough to discuss this kind of interaction in the framework of a specific short-term projection.

Both projections and forecasts, if these words are narrowly defined, are thus useful primarily for a rather loose analysis over a relatively long period. Most population extrapolations are a little of both, in form purely mathematical calculations of what would happen under certain demographic conditions, but in actuality with premises chosen because they seem reasonable in the given social and economic context. The difference, some critics have intimated, lies only in the temerity of the analyst. In the 1930s, when the accuracy of the extrapolations was sometimes uncanny, they were termed "forecasts," while the less successful efforts of the postwar period, though based on precisely the same type of calculations, are called "projections." And if the demographer tries to hold to the differentiation, he is put under pressure to abandon it.

Maintaining the distinction between population projections and population forecasts is not easily done. Once assumptions have been spelled out and the consequent arithmetic has been done, it seems difficult to remove the aura of predictions from the resulting numbers. Hard-pressed planners in government and business and in all other endeavors which need indications of future developments ask simply for a number. What they seem to want is a forecast, and sometimes they express impatience with the explanation that a forecast is exactly what is not available. And when confronted with several numbers and the statement that, though they differ widely, each of these is a reasonable number, there is sometimes a tendency to pick one of the numbers and treat it as though it were a forecast [Taeuber 1957].

One way out of the dilemma might be to bring the implicit gradient of probabilities to the surface and estimate both the future population trend and the degree of uncertainty of alternative projections (Muhsam 1956; Iklé 1967), even though no techniques yet exist by which the relative probability of various assumptions can be reliably judged. Meteorologists now dare to put their weather predictions in the form that there is a 20, or an 80, percent chance of rain. This puts the responsibility of choosing on the expert rather than on the laymen who must use his products.

FORECASTS OF THE AMERICAN POPULATION

If one follows the example of Thompson and Whelpton in their report to the National Resources Committee and attempts to appraise the relative influence of the factors that will determine the population growth of the United States over the immediate future, one must admit that this cannot be done any more reliably today than in the 1930s. The one thing demographers have learned in the interim, perhaps, is how little they really know. The one thing that they can anticipate with definite assurance is that events will surprise them.

The Lessons of the 1950s

It is convenient to take as a starting point the assumptions underlying two series of Census Bureau projections made in 1955 and 1958.[3] The premises on which the 1955 projection was based were critically discussed by Whelpton (1956) and Taeuber (1957), and some of these criticisms were taken into account in the revised projection. This contrast of several points of view offers a good basis for the discussion of current practice.

Immigration. In the first of the two Census Bureau projections, it was assumed that the net arrival of 1.4 million immigrants during 1950–55 would be duplicated during 1955–60, and that subsequently the figure would fall off to 1.2 million per 5-year period. Over the 20 years from 1955 to 1975, this would make a total of 5 million net arrivals or, assuming the same age structure and consequently the same fertility and mortality as for those who entered during 1950–55, a total of 6.5 million persons added by immigration and the natural increase of the immigrants.

In the second projection the postulated net immigration for the entire period was 1.5 million per quinquennium, or roughly the number of net arrivals during the years 1951–56. Assuming again that the age structure, fertility, and mortality remain the same as in this base period, by 1980 a total of 10.2 million persons (rather than 6.5 million by 1975) would be added by immigration and the natural increase of the immigrants.

Presumably this revision in the assumed number of future immigrants was based primarily on the experience between the dates of the two projections. In 1956 and again in 1957 about 325,000 immigrants were admitted, or more by a considerable margin than in any previous postwar year. It is true, nevertheless, that immigration made up only a small part of the average population growth during the 1960s of almost 2.4 million per year. As Taeuber pointed out, a dramatic event like the defeat of the Hungarian revolution added only some 38,000 refugees to the inflow.

Mortality. In the first of the two projections the Census Bureau assumed that age-specific death rates for each sex would continue to decline at the same

[3] U.S. Bureau of the Census, *Current Population Reports*, Series P-25, no. 123, October 20, 1955; no. 187, November 10, 1958.

rate as during the 1940s until 1955–60, but after that date there would be no change up to 1970–75. This slow decline was postulated on the general premise that there would be "no disastrous war, major economic depression, epidemic, or other catastrophe" during the period of the projection. Actually, the extension of life that was anticipated over two decades was completed in one year!

According to the assumptions on which the 1958 projection was based, the crude death rate would decline from 9.5 to 8 per thousand or slightly more, depending on whether fertility was high or low. In an important innovation, the 1958 projection was based on an attempt to forecast deaths by their cause. "Hypothetical low and high age-specific death rates, by sex, for the year 2000 were arrived at by applying assumed high and low percentages of reduction between 1953 and 2000 of death rates by age, sex, and ten broad groups of causes of death, to the corresponding rates for 1953, and converting the results to age-sex-specific rates for all causes combined." Although this method may not result immediately in greater accuracy, it is certainly a step in the right direction. The future decline in mortality, if any, depends not on the past rate of decline (except possibly indirectly) but on future advances in the control of death. That it is admittedly difficult to predict such advances accurately is irrelevant to the point.

In their report to the National Resources Committee in the 1930s, it will be recalled, Thompson and Whelpton pointed out that control over the major infectious diseases had become so efficient that it would be more difficult to effect further reductions in mortality. Yet a notable improvement was actually attained during the next quarter-century; the average expectation of life at birth increased considerably for all sectors of the population. Existent cures had been made available more widely, and there had also been dramatic, unexpected innovations in every relevant field—diagnosis, medicine, surgery, and public health.

It is much truer today than it was in the 1930s that the major communicable diseases have been brought under control and that further advances depend on significant medical discoveries or innovations. A layman hardly dares suggest whether, or how soon, these will be made. Will there be a conquest of fetal mortality comparable to that of infant mortality during the past half century? Will the considerable amount of research on cardiovascular ailments and cancers produce substantial results over the next decade or two? Will the health insurance now enjoyed through private plans or through Medicare and local counterparts spread through the rest of the population? In short, will the improvement in death control consist only in the extension of known methods to more people and to peripheral areas of infectious diseases, or will there again be new types of control?

Prognosis is still more difficult with respect to that wide range of "social disorders" now responsible for a sizable proportion of morbidity and mortality. When by various measures the incidence of fatalities from automobile accidents, alcoholism, drug addiction, homicide, and so on seems to have risen, one does not simply project the downward curve of mortality into the future. To reduce deaths from causes of this type involves skills far beyond the range conventionally defined as medical, and we can hardly guess what the trend is likely to be.

The Crucial Question of Fertility.   As against our uncertainty about the future trends in immigration and mortality, we are almost totally ignorant concerning future fertility. Compared with one hypothesis for immigration and one for mortality in each of the two projections, thus, the Census Bureau used four alternative assumptions about the trend of fertility. But only 3 years after the 1955 projection, the actual population was 360,000 greater than the projection with the highest fertility, and almost 2 miilion greater than that with the lowest. In the 1958 projection, therefore, the assumed fertility was increased considerably.

The range in the projected populations, as well as in the three Scripps–Michigan series (Freedman *et al.* 1959: Table 11-1), can be suggested by citing the figures even for a single year. The various estimates of the 1975 population (in millions) are as follows:

Census Bureau, 1955	Census Bureau, 1958	Scripps–Michigan, 1958	
AA: 228.5	I: 243.9	High:	239.3
A: 221.5	II: 235.2	Medium:	222.5
B: 214.6	III: 225.6	Low:	205.4
C: 206.9	IV: 215.8		

Note the increase in the range from high to low estimates; it is 21.6 million in the 1955 projection, 28.1 million in the 1958 Census Bureau projection, and 33.9 million in the Scripps–Michigan projection. All series of all three, however, indicate a substantial increase from the 1955 population of 165 million.

The three Scripps–Michigan projections were calculated with a method superior to previous efforts in two important respects. First, the calculation was based on the fertility of cohorts, which in principle is better than that based on age-specific births (see pp. 551–557). One reason for the baby boom, for instance, was the lower mean age at which females married. A decline in the age at marriage affects fertility in two ways—actual, but temporary, and permanent, but only potential. The sharp increase in the number of newlyweds, and thus in the number of first and second births, raised the crude birth rate for a certain period. But earlier marriage also extended the number of years from the birth of the last *wanted* child to the woman's menopause, and thus increased the risk of *unwanted* pregnancies. The two types of influence can best be separated with a cohort analysis. As a second example, another reason for the baby boom was that many women who had postponed having children during the depression of the 1930s had them in the 1940s, relatively late in their fecund period. Once this special circumstance was no longer relevant, one could expect that the birth rates of women over 40, or perhaps even of those over 30, would fall off. That is, age-specific birth rates depend both on the general determinants of fertility and on the specific past experiences of each cohort.

The estimate of future fertility, moreover, was not simply one or another extrapolation of past trends but an interpretation of a nationwide sample survey on the expected completed family size. It is true, of course, that what married women say about the number of children they expect to have is an insecure base for fertility forecasts, yet presumably even such inaccurate and incomplete data are better than no direct contact with the presumed parents-to-be.

Postulates Underlying Forecasts of the 1960s and the 1970s

During the mid-1960s the U.S. Bureau of the Census issued a series of *Current Population Reports* which revised the method of analysis, the premises underlying the figures selected, and thus the projected populations. Only one postulate was offered concerning the trend in mortality and one concerning immigration. The analysis of fertility was based on the completed family size of successive cohorts, understood as a limit of the recorded trend for those females still in the childbearing ages. Even though completed family size had risen and was expected to continue to rise ("at least" for the cohorts born in 1910–35 and ending their childbearing years in 1958–83), all of the four alternative fertility levels implied a decline from the number of children in the mid-1960s. This followed from survey data of the Michigan–Scripps project, which suggested that later cohorts "expected" smaller families on the average. However, the evidence from the same study that "many women have more children than they want" was not projected into the future (Siegel and Akers 1964).

The range in the completed family sizes was as follows:

Series A	3.35 children
Series B	3.10
Series C	2.78
Series D	2.48

The presumed decline in offspring per family could not be translated into a decline in annual birth rates, for the large cohorts born in the mid-1940s would move into the principal childbearing years from the mid-1960s on. Thus, from 1964 the number of women aged 20–29 would increase by 26 percent in 1970 and by 70 percent in 1985, so that only a drastic decline in age-specific rates could forestall another baby boom (ibid.).

The rationale developed by the Census Bureau at the end of the 1960s can be indicated from its own summary of population projections.

The population of the United States is bound to grow substantially in the coming years, but how much is uncertain. . . . The projected population falls between 240 and 275 million in 1985 and between 280 and 360 million by the year 2000. This is to say that in the next 33 years or so, the country might grow by anywhere from 80 to 160 million. . . .

The increase of population of 80 million in 33 years, according to the lowest fertility assumption, is more than the total population of the country in 1900. It would be the equivalent of adding the present population of England and France to the United States. The higher figure of a 160 million increase would be equivalent to the annexation of West Germany, too. . . .

Births are the great unknown. They have fluctuated widely over the last 50 years and could well do so again. . . . The rate was low during the depression years of the 1930s, was high just after World War II, and is now falling again. . . . By 1966, it had fallen to 18.6 per 1,000, a drop of 22 percent since 1960. It is not likely to drop below 17.0 and might return to 25.0. Even the lower rate is nearly twice the death rate and will assure a rapid rate of growth [U.S. Bureau of the Census 1968].

In 1968, when this passage was published, the American birth rate was 17.6, and 2 years later it had risen to 18.2. But in 1972 the crude birth rate was down to 15.6, in spite of the large proportion of the population in the prime reproductive ages. The general fertility rate (the number of births per 1,000 women aged 15–44) was 73.4 in 1972, or several units under the lowest point of the 1930s (75.8 in 1936). This dramatic decline can be best represented perhaps in absolute numbers, as in Figure 9-1. The rising slope of the mortality curve reflects mainly the growth of the population: in spite of the very great improvement in the

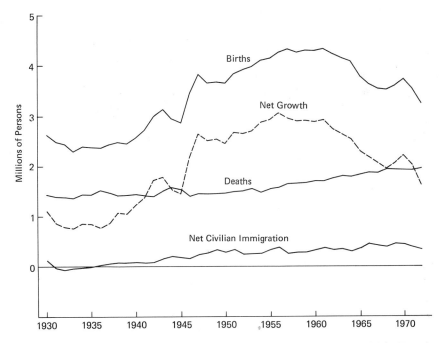

Figure 9-1. Estimated Births, Deaths, Net Civilian Immigration, and Net Population Growth, United States, 1930–72

SOURCE: U.S. Bureau of the Census, "Estimates of the Population of the United States and Components of Change, 1972," *Current Population Reports*, Series P-25, no. 499, May 1973.

control of early death over this period, more persons died because there were so many more living. For the same reason one would expect the number of births to go up: since the base population was larger and since in particular the base population of potential parents was larger, only a very drastic decline in the number of families formed and the number of children per family could result in a fall in the number of births. One should note, however, that the frequent comment in the early 1970s that "zero population growth" had been reached was based on a fundamental misunderstanding. If each two parents have an average of 2.1 children (thus, with the decrement to allow for infant and child mortality, exactly replacing themselves), this does *not* mean necessarily that the whole population is just replacing itself. This can be seen more easily if we divide a population into three age categories and make a few simplifying assumptions concerning them: those aged 50 and over, those in the reproductive ages, and recently born infants and children. Balance in the whole population is between the number in the older category who die off and the number of new births, but the sum of balanced families represents a relation, rather, between young adults and their offspring. If a generation of parents has so few children as to achieve zero population growth, these children—in order to maintain the population growth at zero—will have to have far larger families on the average, since there will be so few of them. Only if the age-specific birth and death rates were to remain constant for several generations and the age-sex structure became fixed would one be able to add up the fertility of individual families to get a rate for the whole nation (cf. U.S. Bureau of the Census 1970). The often announced goal of "zero population growth" by the year 2000, thus, requires not merely a reduction of average family size but an adjustment of fertility to the changing age structure, as well as presumably to the continuing changes in mortality.

With the sharp and totally unanticipated decline in fertility, the four postulates (see p. 350) on which earlier projections had been based were extended to include two new ones:

Series C	2.8 births per woman
Series D	2.5
Series E	2.1
Series F	1.8

Based on these alternative assumptions, the projected population in the year 2000 would range between 251 and 300 million, and in the year 2020 between 265 and 392 million (Figure 9-2).

Since the widest fluctuation in population projections stems from our inability to guess what future fertility will be, it follows that short-range forecasts of the adult population, all of whom have been born at the date of the projection, can be far more accurate. The Census Bureau regularly publishes estimates of the future trend in, for example, the school population, the labor force, and the electorate. These are typically quite accurate representations of the numbers of

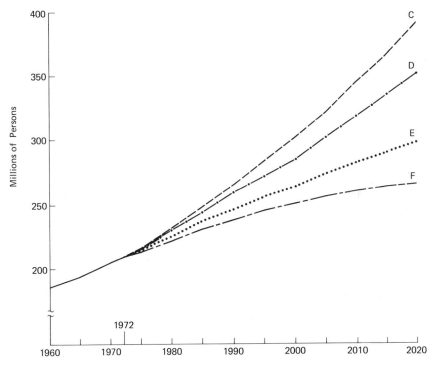

Figure 9-2. Projections of the Total Population, United States, 1972 to 2020

SOURCE: U.S. Bureau of the Census, "Projections of the Population of the United States, by Age and Sex, 1972 to 2020," *Current Population Reports*, Series P-25, no. 493, December 1972.

persons who, by their age and sex, might play the designated roles; but they have little to do with the actual trends. In the presidential election of 1972, thus, only about 55 percent of the electorate voted. And in 1973, in spite of the continuing rise in the number of persons of college age, enrollments in colleges throughout the nation fell off. The difference between the potential and the actual labor force is often large (thus shifting also the unemployment rate) because many adolescents and married women enter or leave on slight provocations. That is to say, even when a projection is completely accurate in its demographic terms, its usefulness depends on how precisely one can forecast the social–economic behavior of particular population segments.

For a country as large as the United States, even an accurate projection of the total population is almost useless for many purposes. Both government bureaus and business firms require estimates of local trends, which are far more difficult to extrapolate. Net migration into the United States is small relative to the natural increase, and both the number and the age–sex distribution of the migrants are measured with reasonable accuracy. Internal migration, on the contrary, has been the dominant element of the population change of some areas, and estimates of the number and characteristics of migrants are notoriously poor. Some of the unanticipated fluctuation in mortality or fertility may cancel out over so large a population as a whole nation, but these aberrations from an assumed trend can affect the smaller local populations much more decisively. Efforts have been made to project the growth of cities, metropolitan areas, states, and regions, but in general the results have been disappointing.

During the 1960s an alternative rationale was developed for local projections: rather than extrapolating the trends in fertility, mortality, and migration, as the Census Bureau does, one takes the population growth as a dependent variable and attempts to forecast the change in the local economy and thus in the number of job opportunities. This alternative method was developed especially by the National Planning Association (1967; see also Kupinsky 1967), the Stanford Research Institute (cf. Siegel and Akers 1964), and such state administrations as the California Department of Finance (Hollman 1967). "That demographic projections cannot be made *in vacuo* is beginning to be appreciated by demographers; the National Planning Association reports represent a first major attempt to blend economic and demographic projections into a coherent and internally consistent whole" (Rosenberg 1967). The new method, however, is not likely to produce more accurate estimates. Projecting the growth of a local economy can hardly be done precisely, and the postulate that there is a necessary and determinate relation between the economic base, the labor force, and the total population can be challenged on a number of grounds. In 1973, after 13 years of surveying consumers' expectations, the Census Bureau abandoned this activity because the results were too poor to be worth the cost. But if consumers themselves do not know how many homes, automobiles, appliances, and so on they are likely to purchase over the next several months, the business activity that depends on these decisions is hardly more predictable.

THE FUTURE POPULATION OF THE WORLD

For a country with good population data and stable institutions, as we have seen using the United States as an example, it is barely possible to construct projections that are accurate enough to be useful. One cannot pretend to even that level of precision for the whole world, and the purpose of a projection can only be to suggest the approximate dimensions of growth. However, as the aggregate is both very large and growing very fast, great accuracy is not required to show that enormous numbers of people will be added over the next generations. The world's population in any year is derived from national totals whose probable accuracy ranges from high to low. For instance, when the surprising results of China's census-registration in 1953 were announced (see pp. 720–721), the world total for 1950 was raised from 2.4 to 2.5 billion, or by more than 4 percent. There is hardly any of the world's population that is not increasing, but the rates vary greatly from one nation or region to another (Table 9-2).

Table 9-2. Estimated and Projected Demographic Statistics of the World's Major Countries and Regions, mid-1973

Region or Country[a]	Population (millions)	Rate of Population Growth (percent)	No. of Years to Double Population	Crude Birth Rate	Crude Death Rate
World	3,860	2.0	35	33	13
North America					
Canada	22.5	1.2	58	15.7	7.3
United States	210.3	0.8	87	15.6	9.4
Middle America	75	3.2	22	43	11
Mexico	56.2	3.3	21	43	10
Guatemala	5.6	2.6	27	43	17
El Salvador	3.8	3.2	22	42	10
Honduras	3.0	3.2	22	49	17
Nicaragua	2.2	2.9	24	46	17
Costa Rica	2.0	2.7	26	34	7
Panama	1.6	2.8	25	37	9
Caribbean Area	27	2.2	32	33	11
Cuba	8.9	1.9	37	27	8
Haiti	5.6	2.4	29	44	20
Dominican Republic	4.8	3.4	21	49	15
Jamaica	2.1	1.5	47	35	7
Trinidad and Tobago	1.1	1.1	63	24	7
South America	165	1.4–3.4	21–50	23–45	7–19
Venezuela	11.9	3.4	21	41	8
Colombia	23.7	3.4	21	45	11
Ecuador	6.7	3.4	21	45	11
Peru	14.9	3.1	23	42	11
Brazil	101.3	2.8	25	38	10
Bolivia	5.0	2.4	29	44	19
Paraguay	2.7	3.4	21	45	11
Uruguay	3.0	1.4	50	23	9
Argentina	25.3	1.5	47	22	9
Chile	10.4	1.7	41	26	9
Europe	472	0.7	99	16	10
Ireland	3.0	0.5	139	22.4	11.2
United Kingdom	57.0	0.3	231	14.9	11.9
Norway	4.0	0.7	99	16.6	10.0
Sweden	8.2	0.3	231	13.8	10.4
Denmark	5.1	0.5	139	15.8	10.2
West Germany	59.4	0.0	—	11.5	11.7
Netherlands	13.4	0.8	87	16.1	8.5

355

Table 9-2. Continued

Region or Country[a]	Population (millions)	Rate of Population Growth (percent)	No. of Years to Double Population	Crude Birth Rate	Crude Death Rate
Belgium	9.8	0.2	347	13.8	12.0
France	52.3	0.6	117	16.9	10.6
Spain	34.2	1.1	63	19.4	8.2
Portugal	9.8	1.0	70	21.3	11.1
Switzerland	6.5	1.0	70	14.4	8.7
Austria	7.5	0.1	700	13.8	12.6
Italy	54.9	0.7	99	16.8	9.6
Finland	4.8	0.3	231	12.7	9.6
East Germany	16.3	−0.2	—	11.7	13.7
Poland	34.0	0.9	77	17.4	8.0
Czechoslovakia	15.0	0.5	139	16.5	11.5
Hungary	10.4	0.3	231	14.7	11.4
Rumania	21.0	1.0	70	19.6	9.5
Yugoslavia	21.2	0.9	77	18.2	9.1
Bulgaria	8.7	0.6	117	15.3	9.8
Albania	2.3	2.8	25	35.3	7.5
Greece	9.1	0.8	87	15.9	8.3
USSR	250	1.0	70	17.8	8.2
Asia	2,204	2.3	30	37	14
Communist China	799.3	1.7	41	30	13
Hong Kong	4.5	2.4	29	20	5
North Korea	15.1	2.8	25	39	11
South Korea	34.5	2.0	35	31	11
Japan	107.3	1.2	58	19	7
Taiwan	15.0	2.2	32	27	5
Philippines	42.2	3.3	21	45	12
North Vietnam	22.5	—	—	—	—
South Vietnam	19.1	—	—	—	—
Laos	3.2	2.5	28	42	17
Cambodia	7.8	3.0	23	45	16
Thailand	39.9	3.3	21	43	10
Malaysia	11.8	2.7	26	38	11
Singapore	2.3	2.2	32	23	5
Indonesia	132.5	2.9	24	47	19
Burma	29.8	2.3	30	40	17
Bangladesh	83.4	—	—	—	—
Nepal	12.0	2.2	32	45	23
India	600.4	2.5	28	42	17
Ceylon	13.5	2.2	32	30	8

Table 9-2. Continued

Region or Country[a]	Population (millions)	Rate of Population Growth (percent)	No. of Years to Double Population	Crude Birth Rate	Crude Death Rate
Pakistan	68.3	3.3	21	51	18
Afghanistan	18.3	2.4	29	51	27
Iran	31.1	2.8	25	45	17
Iraq	10.8	3.4	21	49	15
Turkey	38.6	2.5	28	40	15
Lebanon	3.1	—	—	—	—
Syria	6.8	3.3	21	48	15
Jordan	2.6	3.3	21	48	16
Israel	3.1	2.4	29	28	7
Saudi Arabia	8.4	2.8	25	50	23
Yemen[b]	7.6	2.9	25	50	23
Africa	374	2.5	28	46	21
Egypt	36.9	2.1	33	37	16
Sudan	17.4	3.1	23	49	18
Libya	2.1	3.1	23	46	16
Tunisia	5.6	2.2	32	38	16
Algeria	15.5	3.3	21	50	17
Morocco	17.4	3.4	21	50	16
Mauritania	1.3	2.1	33	44	23
Mali	5.5	2.3	30	50	27
Niger	4.2	2.9	24	52	23
Chad	4.0	2.3	30	48	25
Nigeria	59.6	2.6	27	50	25
Dahomey	2.9	2.6	27	51	26
Upper Volta	5.7	2.0	35	49	29
Togo	2.0	2.5	28	51	26
Ghana	9.9	2.9	24	47	18
Ivory Coast	4.6	2.4	29	46	23
Liberia	1.2	2.7	26	50	23
Sierra Leone	2.8	2.3	30	45	22
Guinea	4.2	2.3	30	47	25
Senegal	4.2	2.4	29	46	22
Cameroon	6.2	2.0	35	43	23
Central African Republic	1.6	2.1	33	46	25
Congo (Republic of)	1.0	2.1	33	44	23
Zaïre	18.7	2.1	33	44	23
Angola	6.1	2.1	33	50	30
Zambia	4.7	2.9	24	50	21

Table 9-2. Continued

Region or Country[a]	Population (millions)	Rate of Population Growth (percent)	No. of Years to Double Population	Crude Birth Rate	Crude Death Rate
Ethiopia	26.8	2.1	33	46	25
Somalia	3.0	2.2	32	46	24
Kenya	12.0	3.0	23	48	18
Uganda	9.3	2.6	27	43	18
Rwanda	3.9	2.9	24	52	23
Burundi	3.9	2.3	30	48	25
Tanzania	14.3	2.6	27	47	22
Malawi	4.8	2.5	28	49	25
Malagasy Republic	7.5	2.1	33	46	25
Mozambique	8.2	2.1	33	43	23
Rhodesia	5.6	3.4	21	48	14
South Africa	21.7	2.4	29	41	17
Lesotho	1.1	1.8	39	39	21
Oceania	21	2.0	35	25	10
Australia	13.3	1.9	37	20.5	8.5
New Zealand	3.0	1.7	41	22.1	8.5
Papua-New Guinea	2.6	2.4	29	42	18

[a] Including all countries with an estimated population of a million or more.
[b] Yemen consists of two countries, officially the Yemen Arab Republic and the People's Republic of Yemen, but in the early 1970s moves were taken to reconcile their differences and possibly reunite them.
SOURCE: Population Reference Bureau, *1973 World Population Data Sheet*, Washington, D.C., reporting latest available data or estimates from the United Nations and other sources.

The difference in growth rates of the various nations has a number of important implications. If countries are listed from the slowest to the fastest growing, most of the underdeveloped areas fall at the latter end. In the future increase of the world's population, that is to say, the proportion of persons living in industrial countries (most of whom are of European stock) will decline (cf. Durand 1967). The difference in age structure is striking: between 1960 and 2000, those aged up to 14 years will increase by a third in the developed countries but will double in the underdeveloped ones, and in the latter case this broad population pyramid will stimulate a continued high rate of growth. The relative shifts in the size of the labor force, and thus in the dependency ratio, will also be in sharp contrast (Vávra 1967).

According to a statement by the United Nations in 1958, "Barring either a catastrophe, or a deterioration of social conditions for progress in health of global proportions, a world population of between 6,000 and 7,000 million by the end of the century should now be expected almost as a matter of certainty." Some years later, based on the hope that growth would decelerate in both developed and underdeveloped regions, the projected population in the year 2000 was estimated at between 5.4 and 7.0 billion (Durand 1968), or in the year 2100 between 5.7 and 15.1 billion (Frejka 1973). The increased range reflects the lesser assurance of later and more cautious forecasters.

SUMMARY

The need for estimates of future population growth is too great to be denied. Government agencies, both national and local; business firms and their customers; colleges, churches, and other cultural institutions—the list of those using population forecasts includes all who deal on a sizable scale with people and attempt to plan their operations some way into the future. The demand has if anything increased, in spite of the conspicuous failure of some recent projections to predict accurately. As John Hajnal once remarked, the true function of a population projection is to give an administrator the basis for action. If the forecast proves to be correct, he will continue on course; if incorrect, he will make the necessary adjustment. But in either case he will have been given the necessary stimulus to act.

So long as a population is growing at a uniform rate or is changing according to a regular pattern, one can predict its future with very simple techniques, as was done by a number of men in the 19th century. However, it is a useful rule of thumb in social analysis that any trend, once it goes beyond a certain point, tends to build up a resistance that eventually leads to a reversal. Merely extrapolating the decline in the rate of population growth, for example, was satisfactory for a period, but only for a period. In order to understand a change in population, one must divide it into its three components of fertility, mortality, and net migration; try to judge how these will be affected by the probable social and economic developments; and apply variable age-specific rates to a population changing in both size and structure.

The principal difficulty in making an accurate forecast is in judging the probable trend of fertility. In the 1930s demographers generally believed both that the incentives that had induced the middle class of Western nations to reduce its average fertility would eventually establish a one-child (or even childless) family as the norm in that class, and that this example would spread through the social structure to other classes and to other countries undergoing modernization. In the mid-1940s, however, the gradual decline in the average size of the family over the past century or more was reversed. The postwar trend in most industrial countries has been toward a relatively constant norm of a small to middle-sized family, not always large enough to divert analysts from renewed speculation about "depopulation." And in many underdeveloped areas *the* crucial social–economic problem is how to reduce fertility.

The probable growth of the world's population, to between 6 and 7 billion by the year 2000, will show the largest proportional gain in the underdeveloped areas. The total for Europe, the Soviet Union, the United States, Canada, Oceania, and Japan, which comprised about 30 percent of the world's population in 1965, will be perhaps 22 percent at the end of the century.

CITED REFERENCES AND SUGGESTIONS FOR FURTHER READING

Spengler (1936) and Pearl (1925) are interesting on early projections. Dorn (1950) and Whelpton (1956) offer two of the more penetrating criticisms of the projections of the 1950s, the crucial period when the lessons of the baby boom were being incorporated into demographers' thinking. Siegel and Akers (1964), two Census Bureau analysts, give a more complete exposition of the rationale behind the Bureau's projections than is generally available. The papers by Durand (1967) and Vávra (1967) both stress the contrasting growth rates of developed and underdeveloped regions. Of the various projections of other countries' populations that could be cited, a recent paper on Algeria (Bourcier de Carbon 1973) is listed because that country was used by Pearl as his prime example. A view from the Pacific is given by the Australian demographer Borrie (1971). An elementary manual by the United Nations (1956) explains the techniques of population projection, with examples drawn from various countries. Keyfitz (1972) gives a good exposition of the principles behind some of these techniques.

BONYNGE, FRANCIS. 1852. *The Future Wealth of America*. New York: Author.

BORRIE, W. D. 1971. "'Predicting' Populations," *Australian Outlook*, 25, 275–284.

BOURCIER DE CARBON, PHILIPPE. 1973. "Projections de la population algérienne jusqu'en 2001," *Population*, 28, 291–334.

CARNEIRO, ROBERT L., and DAISY F. HILSE. 1966. "On Determining the Probable Rate of Population Growth during the Neolithic," *American Anthropologist*, 68, 177–180.

*DORN, HAROLD F. 1950. "Pitfalls in Population Forecasts and Projections," *Journal of the American Statistical Association*, 45, 311–334.

DURAND, JOHN D. 1967. "A Long-Range View of World Population Growth," *Annals of the American Academy of Political and Social Science*, 369, 1–15.

FREEDMAN, RONALD, PASCAL K. WHELPTON, and ARTHUR A. CAMPBELL. 1959. *Family Planning, Sterility, and Population Growth*. New York: McGraw-Hill.

FREJKA, TOMAS. 1973. "The Prospects for a Stationary World Population," *Scientific American*, 228, no. 3, 15–23.

GRABILL, WILSON H., CLYDE V. KISER, and PASCAL K. WHELPTON. 1958. *The Fertility of American Women*. New York: Wiley.

HOLLMAN, WALTER P. 1967. "Population Projections for Counties and Metropolitan Statistical Areas in California," in American Statistical Association, *Proceedings*, Social Statistics Section, pp. 8–15.

IKLÉ, FRED CHARLES. 1967. "Can Social Predictions Be Evaluated?" *Daedalus*, 96, 733–758.

KAHN, HERMAN, and ANTHONY J. WIENER. 1967. "The Next Thirty-three Years: A Framework for Speculation," *Daedalus*, **96**, 705–732.

KEYFITZ, NATHAN. 1972. "On Future Population," *Journal of the American Statistical Association*, **67**, 347–363.

KNIBBS, GEORGE HANDLEY. 1928. *The Shadow of the World's Future: Or the Earth's Population Possibilities & the Consequences of the Present Rate of Increase of the Earth's Inhabitants*. London: Benn.

KUPINSKY, MANNIE. 1967. "Metropolitan Area Population Projections: Use of Regional and National Economic Frameworks," in American Statistical Association, *Proceedings*, Social Statistics Section, pp. 2–7.

MUHSAM, H. V. 1956. "The Utilization of Alternative Population Forecasts in Planning," *Bulletin of the Research Council of Israel*, **5c**, 133–146.

NATIONAL PLANNING ASSOCIATION. 1967. *Economic and Demographic Projections for 224 Metropolitan Areas*. Washington, D.C.

*NATIONAL RESOURCES COMMITTEE. COMMITTEE ON POPULATION PROBLEMS. 1938. *The Problems of a Changing Population*. Washington, D.C.: U.S. Government Printing Office.

PEARL, RAYMOND. 1925. *The Biology of Population Growth*. New York: Knopf.

———, and LOWELL J. REED. 1920. "On the Rate of Growth of the Population of the United States Since 1790 and Its Mathematical Representation," *Proceedings of the National Academy of Sciences*, **6**, 275–288.

PETERSEN, NORMAN V. 1967. "A National Plan for Century III," *Journal of the American Institute of Planners*, **33**, 222–233.

ROSENBERG, HARRY M. 1967. "Discussion," in American Statistical Association, *Proceedings*, Social Statistics Section, pp. 21–25.

*SIEGEL, JACOB S., and DONALD S. AKERS. 1964. "Outlook for Population at Mid-Decade," in American Statistical Association, *Proceedings*, Business and Economic Statistics Section, pp. 358–366.

SMITH, GEORGE CLINE. 1964. "The Law of Forecast Feedback," *American Statistician*, **18**, 11–14.

SPENGLER, JOSEPH J. 1936. "Population Projections in Nineteenth-Century America," *American Sociological Review*, **1**, 905–921.

STOLNITZ, GEORGE J., and NORMAN B. RYDER. 1949. "Recent Discussion of the Net Reproduction Rate," *Population Index*, **15**, 114–128.

TAEUBER, CONRAD. 1957. "The Census Bureau Projections of the Size and the Age and Sex Composition of the Population of the United States in 1975," in Donald J. Bogue, editor, *Applications of Demography: The Population Situation in the U.S. in 1975*. Oxford, Ohio: Scripps Foundation for Research in Population Problems.

UNITED NATIONS. 1956. *Methods for Population Projections by Sex and Age*. Population Studies, no. 25. New York.

U.S. BUREAU OF THE CENSUS. 1967. "Projections of the Population of the United States by Age, Sex, and Color to 1990, with Extensions of Population by Age and Sex to 2015," *Current Population Reports*, Series P-25, no. 381.

———. 1968. "Summary of Demographic Projections," *Current Population Reports*, Series P-25, no. 388.

———. 1970. "Projections of the Population of the United States, by Age and Sex, 1970 to 2020," *Current Population Reports*, Series P-25, no. 448.

VÁVRA, ZDENĚK. 1967. "Future Trends in World Population Growth," *Demography*, **4**, 497–514.

WATSON, WINSLOW C., editor. 1856. *Men and Times of the Revolution; or Memoirs of Elkanah Watson.* New York: Dana.

WHELPTON, PASCAL K. 1956. "Census Projections: Some Areas of Doubt," *Conference Board Business Record*, **13**, 2–6.

PART II

The Population of Various Societal Types

THE POPULATION OF PRIMITIVE SOCIETIES

10

Population data concerning either prehistoric or contemporary primitive societies are of a completely different order from those based on even inadequate statistics. It is not merely that population size, structure, movements, and so forth must be inferred from indirect evidence, but also that this evidence is incomplete and very often biased. Information concerning present-day primitive peoples comes mainly not from themselves but from representatives of advanced societies, who usually began to record fairly reliable observations only after a considerable period of contact. Reconstructing the true primitive culture, entirely free of influence from civilized peoples, is thus almost as difficult with contemporary as with prehistoric examples.

As the population of a primitive society depends very directly on its economy, it is reasonable to combine data on the prehistoric period with those on contemporaries in the same "stage" of development. Peoples do not live in economic stages, of course; they operate economies, which are often combinations of such ideal types as collecting, hunting, fishing, cultivation, and stock raising. However, so long as we keep in mind that these are abstractions, they can be useful in analyzing the various ways that real societies at different cultural levels acquire their food. Between the physical environment and the number of people that subsist on it, there is always an intervening variable, the culture pattern; but the less efficient the technology, the closer the relation is between habitat and population.

Any study of primitive economics deals largely with the production and consumption of food. This is so partly because of the directness of the nutritional aim and the absence of intermediaries such as an entrepreneur and a money payment; partly because of the relatively small range of objects of economic interest; and partly because of the extensive use of food for other than purely nutritive purposes [Firth 1950: 37–38].

TYPES OF PRIMITIVE ECONOMY

The geologic period that runs from about 2 million to some 10,000 or 15,000 years ago is called the Pleistocene, or "most recent." Four times during this era enormous ice sheets expanded to cover substantial portions of Eurasia and North America. Forms of life suited to milder climates perished unless they adapted to the cold or migrated southward. At the beginning of the Pleistocene, or perhaps even earlier, in the Pliocene epoch, hominids began to evolve, and from these there gradually developed the new species of *Homo sapiens*. Prehistorians now recognize four phases in the probable continuum of human evolution—Australo-pithecine, Pithecanthropine, Neanderthal, and Modern—but these are merely the points for which there happens presently to be the most fossil evidence (Brace and Montagu 1965: chap. 7).

Our understanding of the prehistoric past depends in great part on how precisely we can date the materials that are dug up. At one time the best that could usually be accomplished was "sequence dating," or arranging artifacts or fossils in an order from the oldest to the most recent, and "cross-dating," or linking two such ordinal series. The intent is now more often to date absolutely, to place settlements on a calendar. The most accurate measure, counting the rings of very old trees, is of course limited to such areas as the American South-west, where such trees grow. The technique most widely used depends on the fact that each radioactive element is transformed into a stable counterpart at a more or less fixed rate, so that by measuring the ratio of the radioactive com-ponent to its inert end product, one can estimate the time elapsed since a fossil or artifact was deposited. The conversion of carbon 14 into ordinary carbon, thus, became the usual basis for establishing dates during the past 50,000 years, but in fact, for reasons that are not well understood, the decay rate varies con-siderably. Carbon 14 is being supplemented with radioactive potassium and argon, and other techniques depend on the thermoluminescence of ancient pottery or the hydration rate of obsidian. According to a recent review (Michels 1972), the prognosis for precise chronometric techniques is "very good," but most of the dating incorporated into already published works was grossly in-accurate (cf. Brace and Montagu 1965: 228).

We do know that the evolution from primates through hominids to man, wherever and whenever it occurred, produced a species qualitatively different from all that had preceded it. However "wild" the first man in the fossil record may seem to us, he was much closer to present-day humans than to his animal forebears. He used tools to hunt; he kept himself warm with fire; he almost certainly spoke a language; he even had an occasional ability to represent his world on the walls of caves.

Modern archeological research, including the way that inferences are drawn from scanty data, can be exemplified by the excavation of a mesolithic site at Star Carr, near Scarborough, Yorkshire (Clark *et al.* 1954). Everything recovered from the digging was plotted on a yard-square grid, and a density of 36 or more fragments of flint per square yard was taken to define the area of occupation. It was assumed that, as among contemporary Eskimos, women were mainly responsible for preparing skins, so that the presence of skin-working tools "argues for the presence of women" (ibid.: 11). "No trace was found of culti-vated plants or domesticated animals and it is evident that subsistence was based entirely on such activities as plant-gathering [and] hunting" (ibid.: 13). The nonhuman bones identified at the site were mostly of small animals—various birds, hare, wolves, hedgehogs, wild pigs, but also two species of deer, elk, and oxen (ibid.: chap. 3). Tools were found fabricated out of flint, stag antlers, and bone. Some of the antlers were cut seemingly to fit the head, and one can suppose —again following leads from contemporary primitive cultures—that they were used for stalking or for magic (ibid.: 170).

Some of the deductions, in short, are based on what is called ethnographic analogy: since it is likely that the life of prehistoric man was not too different from that of the most primitive of peoples alive today, these can be used to fill in the details in our account of ancient man. The link is not a necessary one and must be used with discretion. The succession of culture stages that 19th-century theorists expostulated, with living peoples interpreted as "fossils" of types that had elsewhere disappeared, has few defenders today. "Modern savages have a history precisely as long as that of the most civilized peoples, even if it does not happen to have been written down. . . . Existing peoples can only be used as sources for reconstructing the lives of prehistoric peoples with extreme caution and within well defined limits" (Clark 1965: 171–172). In a demographic analysis, stretching the plausibilities of ethnographic analogy does not carry one very far, for the record of contemporary primitives is extraordinarily free of solid statistics and analyses about population. The painstaking compilations by Krzywicki (1934) and Kirsten (1956) are collections of data mostly too poor to be useful, and in the several decades since they appeared, in spite of the excellence of particular studies, the overall picture has improved but little. We know more about kin structure than family size, more about beliefs in the afterworld than causes of death, more about the structure of roles than of age categories.

The contemporary primitives used to round out our knowledge of our earliest forebears should preferably be a food-gathering tribe, which has not domesticated either plants or animals and which has been little influenced by more advanced cultures. The Xetá of the Brazilian interior, or the Semang, a Negrito people of the Malay peninsula, typify a class that we have termed Rangers— "peoples who (1) live very largely by gathering fruits and nuts, digging roots, collecting shellfish, and devouring reptiles, insects, and vermin; (2) have no permanent dwelling, but erect windbreaks, live in caves, or put up very slight and temporary huts of boughs or palm leaves; (3) have no spinning and weaving except in the form of plaiting, no pottery, no metal, and very poor canoes; (4) no domestic animals except the dog and possibly a few pets" (Hobhouse *et al.* 1930: 17). Because of the restricted resources of any one locality, both the Xetá and the Semang live in bands of no more than twenty or thirty persons, including children. Each one of such bands has a traditional territory of some 20 square miles over which it slowly wanders, gathering food on the way. Temporary shelters are made of branches and leaves, and abandoned each time a move is made. From one end of his life to the other, a Semang remains with his

Members of a primitive food-gathering people, the Xetá, who numbered about 100. They were discovered in 1958 in an isolated area of Paraná State in southern Brazil. Note the stone ax (*José Loureiro Fernandes—University of Paraná*).

small group, occasionally seeing other bands of similar size but total strangers only rarely. The Xetá, even more isolated, were discovered by whites just a few years ago. "This limited range of contact and stimulus is of fundamental importance in understanding the stability and slowness of change among the simpler societies of man" (Forde 1952: chap. 2; Loureiro Fernandes 1959).

The surviving Lower Hunters may be unrepresentative precisely because they have remained at this level, pushed off into an unhospitable corner by their more robust neighbors, fearful of contact with anyone outside their tiny group. The prehistoric men who shared their habitat with as many large animals of various species as were to be found, say, on the African veld a generation ago were undoubtedly more enterprising; and if Carleton Coon (1955: chap. 3) is correct in his interesting reconstruction, the people of that era subsisted mainly from the chase. The hunting techniques of paleolithic man, the use of fire especially, made him a formidable opponent even of much more powerful and ferocious beasts. A band of five to ten men, armed with spears or bows and arrows and accompanied by dogs, could bring back a ton of meat from a successful hunt.

The economy of such primitive hunters is suggested by that of the Plains Indians before their whole culture was transformed by the acquisition of the horse. Until about 1750 the Blackfoot, for instance, were pedestrian hunters, carrying their scanty possessions on dog sledges or the backs of females. A buffalo hunt was conducted in the following fashion. Women gathered downwind from the herd and placed their sledges upright in the earth so as to form a semi-circular fence. Several swift-running men upwind from the herd drove the buffalo into this enclosure. Shouting women and barking dogs confused the animals, and in the turmoil hunters were able to rush in and with lance or bow and arrow kill a number of the herd. With such a method of garnering food, the camp had to consist of ten to thirty tents, for the hunt depended on the cooperation among that many persons but did not furnish enough food for more. With only primitive means of transportation, the aged, sick, and infirm were left behind to die whenever the camp moved (Ewers 1955).

Among food gatherers, fishing peoples are most likely to enjoy a more regular subsistence, and they are not compelled to be on the move constantly following their food supply. Their level of culture and also their population density are typically higher than those of hunters. This observation can be exemplified by the several Indian tribes living along the Pacific coast of the United States and Canada, "whose common culture is one of the most specialized in North America and perhaps the most advanced found among any nonagricultural people." Indeed, before the white man arrived they were on the verge of developing independently the domestication of fish and plants. If the run of salmon in a particular stream began to fall off, the Nootka "restocked it, obtaining spawn from another river at the breeding season and carrying it back in moss-lined boxes to start a new generation in the depleted stream." And two of the tribes, the Tlingit and the Haida, cultivated a tobaccolike plant that was chewed for its narcotic effect. Some of the tribes carried on a primitive trade, exchanging fish for vegetable products gathered inland by neighboring groups. The houses were substantial, built in permanent settlements of thirty or more, with each village thus having a population of several hundred (Forde 1952: chap. 6).

For perhaps 98 percent of his time on earth, man has lived from gathering food. Some 8,000 years ago, probably somewhere in the area between Afghanistan and Abyssinia, he learned to domesticate both plants and animals. This momentous innovation, it is believed, arose not from hunger but from leisure. These very first steps toward civilization depended on an economic surplus that was not absorbed into a population increase. Usually the conundrum of how this could take place is solved by assuming the development of a hierarchical structure, of which the top layers were well fed from the excess produced by the lower ones (e.g., Herskovits 1952: 412–413). The solution helps little with respect to the small bands of hunter–gatherers, who are assumed—by ethnographic analogy and common sense—to have had a relatively unstructured society. Over the longer run, in Thomas Hobbes's well known summation, the life of man in a state of nature may well have been "solitary, poor, nasty, brutish, and short"; but this normal state was presumably interrupted by favored periods of perhaps several generations, a mere instant in archeological time. It was during these prosperous intervals, according to one hypothesis, that the first progress was achieved.

A contrary, narrowly materialist interpretation of prehistoric societies is encouraged, of course, by the fact that material artifacts typically constitute the sole basis for every reconstruction of their institutions. And this bias was strongly reinforced by the considerable influence of Gordon Childe, whose talent as an archeologist was magnified by his adeptness in finding memorable phrases ("the neolithic revolution," "the urban revolution") in his highly readable popularizations. In Childe's work the effect of economic factors on any society was dictated by a certain simple-minded Marxism; rather few Western scholars cited Stalin to validate a professional point (Childe 1951: 35). Braidwood and Howe (1960: chap. 1), as they phrased it, were "strongly influenced" by Childe and set out to validate his thesis in the field. But as they tried to test his notions, they established a more and more independent conceptual base, rejecting altogether such terms as *mesolithic* and *neolithic*, which group together chronology, technical innovation, and cultural interpretation. Rather than combining all of these *a priori* and thus imprecisely, Braidwood and Howe analyzed them separately to the degree that this was possible. In an even more forthright denial of the axioms on which Childe's theorizing had been based, Binford (1968) challenged the postulate that early man was continuously trying to increase his food supply and, thus, that he had time to elaborate his culture only when he was freed from this preoccupation.

> While hunting–gathering populations may vary in density between different habitats in direct proportion to the relative size of the standing food crop, nevertheless within any given habitat the population is homeostatically regulated *below* the level of depletion of the local food supply. . . . Not only [do] hunter–gatherers have adequate supplies of food but they enjoy quantities of leisure time, much more in fact than do modern industrial or farm workers, or even professors of archeology.

This view was presented also in a symposium on the relation between population and resources in an ethnological context (Spooner 1972). According to the diverse opinions of the participants, the limit of the food supply is the main restriction to population growth, or, on the contrary, that limit acts as a stimulus to technical and institutional innovation. Perhaps both views are correct, and neither generalization is valid for the whole transition from gathering bands to established settlements.

In the still dominant view, the boundary between the paleolithic and the neolithic ages is marked by a shift from food gathering to food producing. The earliest domesticated breeds of both plants and animals were, of course, indistinguishable from the wild ones. Even in areas that concentrated on them, the new modes of livelihood did not displace hunting and gathering. Early husbandry was not efficient, and the yield from hunting was not only food but also bone, antlers, hides, and even, one might suppose, sport (Clark 1952: 48). Where agriculture resulted in higher density of population, thus, there was also an increased pressure on wild foods (ibid.: 58). The earliest cultivators established a life only slightly less mobile than hunting, *Brandwirtschaft*, or slash-and-burn culture. A patch of woodland was cleared and burnt, the seeds planted in the ash-strewn soil with a primitive digging stick or hoe; and then, when the soil was exhausted, the process was repeated elsewhere. Among Europeans this mode of agriculture survived longest among Finno-Ugrians, who until the 1870s obtained very large yields of grain but only for one or two seasons, and thus at an appalling cost in timber (ibid.: 92–93, 98). If one compares the present productivity of hoe and plow cultures in an area where both are used, it is found that the former takes three times as many man-hours as the latter to raise one hectare of corn (Lewis 1949). The neolithic production with a digging stick required still more work, and the plot had to be constantly watched to protect it against predatory animals.

Specialized agriculture or stock raising as the sole basis of food seems to have been a later development from the earlier domestication of plants *and* animals. Many of the pastoral peoples of Asia are "denuded agriculturists," induced to abandon half of their prior economy by "unsettled political conditions" (Forde 1952: 404–405). Flight to the steppe, which is difficult or impossible to cultivate, made such a specialization necessary. Nomads depend on their animals for their food, clothing, and shelter, and their culture must thus accommodate itself to the seasonal search for pasture. Such a society could subsist only in small mobile units: a Mongol camp consists ordinarily of six to ten tents of five to six persons each, or a group only about twice as large as a food-gathering band.

All the elements of the neolithic economy—hunting, hoe culture, and nomadism—implied a migratory way of life, and by 2000 B.C. the essential pattern had spread throughout Eurasia, from Ireland to China. Each local culture was specific, distinguished by its particular balance between cultivation and stock breeding, by the plants or animals raised, by adaptations to the climate or other natural features, by accidental variations. But overlying this diversity were not only the production of food, the basic invention of neolithic man, but also tools of polished rather than chipped stone, pottery, and houses.

THE POPULATION OF NONLITERATE SOCIETIES

In most discussions of modern populations, the analyst passes over the most basic question: what entity is being measured? The persons residing in a particular juridically bounded area, typically a national state or one of its subdivisions, ordinarily constitute a "population," though as we have seen this fact does not specify the concept unambiguously. As archeologists use the word, a population often has the same meaning as in zoology: a breeding group. But archeological data on mating and fertility are of course poorer than those concerning other demographic processes. The time span represented in a single dig can go over centuries, during which much—or nothing—may have happened to the population(s) that once lived there. The puzzle is typically solved by classifying whatever data the archeologist (or paleontologist or anthropologist) has accumulated and then associating a population with each of the classes. But there is no necessary or fixed association between the style of pottery or residential structures or whatever and a particular population; the first can change over time or space with no change in the other, and that the first remains the same over time or space does not mean a necessary constancy in the second (cf. Brothwell 1970). As we have seen, the most elaborate classificatory systems, which divide the human species into races or language groups, permit neither a sharp nor a consistent delimitation of distinct populations.

In both historic and prehistoric demography, it would seem that one of the simplest operations is to relate the inhabited area to the number of persons that once lived on it. Such estimates, however, involve several recurrent difficulties, none of which can be overcome completely. An archeological excavation typically includes only a portion of the site, and to generalize from the known segment to the whole must ordinarily result in some slippage. Is the population density deduced from the completely excavated dwellings specific to them? Were all of the houses inhabited at the same time, or do they represent a number of successive generations living in different houses on adjacent plots? Thompson (1971), for example, pointed out that among the Maya it was the custom to bury a dead person in his hut and then abandon it and, on another scale, to move from one site to another as good soil became exhausted (but cf. Haviland 1972). In Central Mexico, similarly, "sites may represent those segments of a living community which have been abandoned during normal community operations. All contemporary communities studied in detail in the Teotihuacán Valley have some structures unoccupied at any given time" (Charlton 1972). The dwellings inhabited seriatim would presumably have been constructed over a few decades at the most, or too short a period to be distinguished by almost any dating technique.

Trying to generalize on a world scale involves more problems, for population density is likely to vary with the climate, the usual mode of construction, the number and type of nonresidential buildings, and the like. From eighteen ethnographic studies, Naroll (1962) estimated very roughly that each person in a primitive society requires 10 square meters of roofed living space (cf. LeBlanc 1971). From California Indian tribes, Cook and Heizer (1968) derived 12 square meters per person. Given the wide range of errors implicit in the calculations, however, the two ratios, 10 and 12, can be interpreted as essentially identical, especially since the total populations derivative from either one are usually very small.

Though the population–area ratio of a settlement would seem to imply an average household size, calculating the latter involves additional dubious assumptions.[1] The size of a nuclear family is one of a number of interrelated demographic variables, but there is no way of estimating how the nuclear family relates to the size of a household. As Allen and Richardson (1971) pointed out, the reconstruction of kinship from archeological data—which is difficult enough in itself—is made more so by the confusion among ethnologists concerning contemporary residence patterns. The apparently clear distinctions drawn a generation ago among types of residence rules have proved to be inadequate, and in any case the actual practice in many societies differs significantly from the presumed norm. Among thirteen American Indian tribes, the floor area of the house assumed to contain a single nuclear family ranged between 119.5 and 322 square feet (Cook 1972: Table 1), and if worldwide data were compiled the variation would presumably be even greater. In a stratified society, moreover, the average number of persons in a household or the average amount of space they occupy would probably differ considerably from the mode. However, by calculating a total population from the area of an entire settlement, one can reasonably expect that some of these several types of variation will average out.

Natural Increase

One way of deducing prehistoric man's rate of natural increase is to show that it could not have been very great over the period since *Homo sapiens* evolved (cf. pp. 9–10). Starting from a single pair, man would have had to double his numbers only thirty-one times in order to reach 4.2 billion, or well over the present population of the world. Under conditions most conducive to growth each doubling takes 25 years, and with such a "Malthusian" projection the increase from two persons to the present world's population would have taken slightly under eight centuries. As we know that man began to evolve many hundreds of thousands of years ago, we know also that the rate of growth in the modern world is anomalous, and that during the whole of the paleolithic period man's numbers must have been close to stationary.

This conclusion is substantiated by another line of reasoning. The balance of

---

[1] Rough guesses have been made about the size of households from the capacity of cooking jars (Turner and Lofgren 1966), or about the size of populations from the skeletal remains (e.g., Howells 1960) or even the animal bones in garbage heaps (e.g., Phillips 1972). One wonders whether even the most ingenious argumentation can develop a plausible estimate from such data.

births and deaths of hunting peoples depends a good deal on the natural environment, but under all circumstances the population densities of food gatherers are very low. They were estimated for contemporary primitive cultures by Friedrich Ratzel, one of the great 19th-century pioneers of human geography, and his summary of an array of data is reproduced in Table 10-1. Neither the peoples living in such especially unfavorable habitats as the Arctic or semi-arid regions nor those subsisting on fish or domesticated animals are pertinent to a general discussion. The population density of typical food gatherers, given relatively advantageous conditions, is likely to be that of the Xetá and the Semang, or on the order of one per square mile. The total land surface of the earth is about 57 million square miles, including Antarctica, the Arctic region, mountains, and deserts. The habitable portion, counting both optimum and marginal areas, is only slightly more than half this figure. If we assume one person per square mile as the average population density in the paleolithic era, then the *maximum* world population in that period was on the order of 30 million. If we restrict the area to that archeologists know to have been inhabited at that time, it could hardly have been more than 5 million.

The domestication of plants and animals, even at the neolithic level of efficiency, increased the *potential* population of the earth enormously. For example, the prehistoric population of the present area of France, as estimated from a detailed survey of archeological findings, was never more than about 20,000 so long as food gathering furnished its subsistence. During the fourth millennium B.C., when the first agricultural settlements appeared, the population grew to 500,000, and over the next thousand years to 5 million (Nougier 1954), which is also the theoretical carrying power of an area of this size with primitive agriculture. It is a reasonable inference that the spread of domestication to the rest of Europe and the world also effected an increase, though not by so large a jump as in this case (cf. p. 344).

The growth in numbers brought about by neolithic inventions was a cause as well as a result of social efficiency. Some tasks cannot even be attempted by a

Table 10-1. The Density of Hunting Populations According to Ratzel's Estimates

Type of Population	Square Miles per Capita	Persons per Square Mile
Hunting and fishing peoples in the Arctic	75–200	
Hunting peoples in semi-arid regions (Bushmen, Patagonians, Australians)	45–200	
Hunting peoples with some agriculture or trade with agricultural tribes	0.5–2	
Shepherd nomads		1.8–4.7
Fishing peoples (North America, Polynesia)		4.5

SOURCE: Friedrich Ratzel, cited in A. B. Wolfe, "The Fecundity and Fertility of Early Man," *Human Biology*, 5 (1933), 35–60.

small group. When Robinson Crusoe was joined by Friday, the work the two could do together was much more than double what Crusoe had been able to accomplish alone, and this greater than proportionate increase in economic production with each new addition to the population continues up to a certain number. Food-gathering bands have an optimum size of about twenty-five to thirty persons, and one that grows much beyond this splits into two. Similarly, peasant agriculture can be carried on most efficiently by a village of about 500 to 1,000 persons; up to this number, the gain from new hands more than offsets the loss to new mouths. A village does not grow into a town, but rather founds daughter villages in the near distance. With conditions that favor continuous increase, the ultimate pattern is like that in sections of India or Java, with thousands and thousands of small villages making up a dense but generally nonurban population.

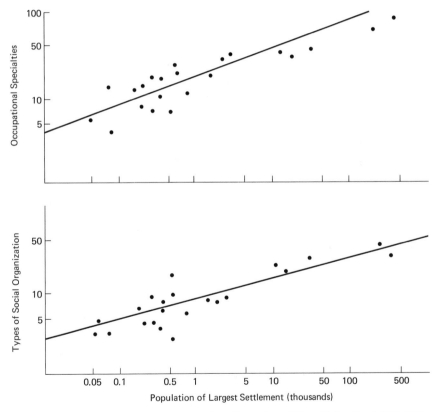

Figure 10-1.   Relation Between Population Growth and Two Other Social Variables in Twenty-two Societies

SOURCE: Raoul Naroll, "A Preliminary Index of Social Development," *American Anthropologist*, **58** (1956), 687–715.

The precise relation between population size and the other features of a primitive society in part dependent on it has been formulated in an interesting study by Naroll. As can be seen in Figure 10-1, if the population of the largest settlement (P) of each of twenty-two peoples is plotted on a logarithmic grid, together with the number of occupational specialties (S) or the number of types of social organization (r) in each culture, the points tend to fall along two straight lines. The two regression lines shown have the equations:

$$P = \left(\frac{S}{2}\right)^3 \quad \text{and} \quad P = \left(\frac{2r}{3}\right)^4$$

This means that if the largest settlement grew from a hamlet of 500 to a town of 10,000, say, the average number of occupational specialties in the culture would increase from sixteen to forty-two, and the number of types of social organization from seven to fifteen.

Mortality

Some information on the diseases of prehistoric man is obtainable from the archeological record. The number of skeletons that have been recovered is small, of course, and we do not know to what degree they represent a typical sample. But there is no question that even before *Homo sapiens* evolved, his forebears were suffering from disease: the femur of one specimen of Java Man has marked exostoses, or knoblike protuberances, indicating a pathological condition of great severity.

Of course, the conclusion from a surviving skeleton (or worse, only part of one) can only be tentative. A diagnosis based only on the bones of a person recently deceased is difficult, and during the centuries that ancient man's skeletons endured they usually underwent many changes that make a diagnosis considerably more difficult. "When we remember the many ways in which a pseudo-pathological appearance can be produced—or a genuine lesion obscured—it no longer seems extraordinary that paleopathologists occasionally make a wrong diagnosis. The wonder is that we ever make a right one" (Wells 1967).

Nor, once again, is it possible to round out the evidence very much from ethnographic analogy. Contact with higher cultures has ordinarily influenced the mortality of primitives so much, both negatively and positively, that one can hardly reconstruct the life chances of isolated hunter–gatherer bands. According to a summary of sixteen ethnographic studies in various parts of the world, the proportion dying under 1 year of age ranged from 10 to 35 percent, that under 5 years from 30 to 70 percent, and that under 18 from 26 to 35 percent (Polunin 1967). Some of the variation is undoubtedly due to the different methods used in the surveys, as is evident from the fact that the last figures are inconsistent with the first. But there is also no reason to anticipate an overall uniformity among primitive peoples independent of their habitat, standards of sanitation, nutritional norms, patterns of violence, and therapeutic skills. In some areas, for example, food shortages have contributed greatly to mortality and morbidity, but among the native Hawaiian population famines were relatively infrequent and mostly local, causing more out-migration than deaths. The one exception was the famine caused by the civil wars of 1780–96, not an instance that fits in with the Darwinian model (Schmitt 1970). As this example suggests, the deaths from organized violence are far from limited to those killed directly, and any estimate of the mortality "caused" by war must be very loose indeed. Yet we know that there is a worldwide range from the Zulus, whose whole livelihood derived from preying on other tribes, to the entirely pacific Indian tribes of California.

Perhaps disease caused the death of primordial man less often than the drownings, burns, wounds, and fractures associated with his dangerous life. Judging from the number of skeletons that show marks of heavy blows or arrow and spear points, combat was also an important cause of death. Some skeletal remains show evidence of a continued life after a serious injury and of its final healing, and these indicate at least the possibility of some skill in surgery (but see p. 237). Among eighteen instances of fractures in prehistoric skeletons, one paleontologist found only three that had healed badly, and he came to the conclusion that early man was amazingly skillful at setting broken bones (Moodie 1923: 89). One of the more spectacular operations was trepanation, or the boring or scraping of a hole into the skull. When this is performed in modern surgery, it is usually to relieve the pressure from a brain tumor; early man, like those contemporary primitives that follow this practice, probably opened the skull also in order to release an evil spirit from the body. In a few prehistoric groups trepanation was practiced quite frequently. "In one burial mound in France yielding the bones of 120 individuals more than 40 showed the effects of trepanation. . . . A few ancient skulls reveal five cruel openings, which had all healed. The patient had survived them all" (ibid.: 100).

Any but the most elementary estimate of mortality depends on an appraisal of the population's structure, which is not easy for an archeologist to make. The sex of skeletal remains is often problematic. In the extreme case of the scrappy bits of Australopithecus recovered from several sites in East Africa, what earlier investigators had taken to be the male and female of a single species, Pilbeam (1972) interpreted as two manlike species, one "robust" and one "gracile," coexisting in the same general area. In the best case determining the sex of a skeleton demands so much skill that a layman must depend on experts' testimony, which unfortunately is not entirely consistent. Certainly no measurable characteristic of any one bone can serve by itself to distinguish the sex of an individual. Working on Egyptian mummies, Wood Jones found pelvises that he would have characterized definitely as male except that there were fetuses in the wombs. With the whole skeleton and his own method of determination, Genovés (1970a) believed that he could classify 99 percent of all remains correctly; but with partial skeletons or less accurate techniques, the probability of an accurate classification has in his opinion fallen as low as 20 percent. In any case, a completely correct dichotomy of a population into males and females is not much use for demographic analysis unless it is accompanied by a reasonably accurate classification into age categories.

One criterion for estimating the age of skeletal remains is the degree of wear on teeth, but as Vallois (1960) pointed out no common standard exists on how rapidly the teeth of either fossil men or existing populations have worn down. Vallois would use the condition of the teeth to judge age only up to about 12 or 13 years, with the closing of cranial sutures as the principal index thereafter. According to Genovés (1970b), however, the obliteration of sutures in the skull "does not follow a well defined pattern." The most discouraging report (McKern and Stewart 1957) is an analysis of the skeletons of American soldiers killed in Korea, all of known age. According to their data, there is almost no point where one can draw a line and say a person having reached this stage must have been so many years old; the variation is very great, and any correlation with age is at best an approximation.

In an important early paper, Vallois (1937) noted the decline in the proportion that had died at age 20 or under, from 55 percent of 20 Neanderthal remains to 34–37 percent of 167 Upper Paleolithic or Mesolithic (Table 10-2). If, as seems likely, the very high proportion of infant deaths was underrepresented among the surviving skeletons, the usual age at death would be lower than these figures suggest. Subsequent compilations by Vallois or others indicate the same general range. Very roughly, then, there have been—to repeat—two doublings of the expectation of life from birth, from under 20 years in the earliest prehistoric period to 35–40 years in preindustrial civilizations and then to 70–75 years in today's advanced societies. With the mortality obtaining in prehistoric times, anyone who managed to survive to age 40 would by that fact become the Old Man of the band. Fewer than half of those born would live long enough to become parents themselves.

Table 10-2. Estimated Age at Death of 187 Human Fossil Remains

Age	Neanderthal		Upper Paleolithic		Mesolithic	
	NO.	PERCENT	NO.	PERCENT	NO.	PERCENT
0–11	8	40	25	24.5	20	30.8
12–20	3	15	10	9.8	4	6.2
21–30	5	25	28	27.4	32	49.3
31–40	3	15	27	26.5	6	9.2
41–50	1	5	11	10.8	1	1.5
51+	—	—	1	1.0	2	3.0
TOTAL	20	100	102	100.0	65	100.0

SOURCE: Henri V. Vallois, "La durée de la vie chez l'homme fossile," *Anthropologie*, **47** (1937), 499–532.

Fertility

The measurement of fertility is a far less obvious operation than it might seem. The significance of a "family" is ambiguous even in our own culture (does it include grown children who have moved away, or not?), and with the variety of kin structures to be found the world over simple queries can often be misunderstood. Many peoples, out of a sense of privacy or a taboo, are reluctant to discuss any family matters with a stranger. In a fertility survey in East Africa, for instance, "a man who refused to give any information to the first two investigators finally gave the names of two children to the third. . . . [He] later admitted to ten children but still concealed a second wife in another village" (Richards and Reining 1954: 362). And if questions are fully and accurately answered, the data are not always interpreted properly even by professional social scientists. For example, a survey of three "generations" on Eddystone, one of the Solomon Islands, seemingly showed a calamitous decline in the number of children per marriage, from 2.16 to 1.28 to 0.65 (Rivers 1922: 98). In fact, since there was no control for the age of the mother, the contrast was mainly between the completed fertility of the older women and the partial families of the younger. In general, the critical datum for any long-term analysis is not an annual rate, which can fluctuate widely, but the total number of children that the average couple bring into the world.

No direct data exist, of course, on the fertility of early man. From the suppositions that his mortality was, by our standards, extraordinarily high and that his population was not depleted, one concludes that the fertility must have been close to the physiological maximum. Indeed, most demographers of a generation ago assumed that this condition more or less obtained until the modern era, when the development of effective contraceptives and the dissolution of traditional norms presumably led to the first substantial decline in family size. This reconstruction has been proved wrong for most present-day primitives and presumably for most of preindustrial history.

In Tikopia, for example, deliberate control of population growth was effected by a number of traditional means: nonmarriage, more or less enjoined on young men without land; *coitus interruptus*, commonly used in both extramarital and marital sex; abortion, generally restricted to extramarital pregnancies; and infanticide, sanctioned at the discretion of the father irrespective of the child's sex. Exposure to the risk of pregnancy was typically not over the whole of a woman's fecund years: marriage was later than at puberty, and the remarriage of widows was rare. These conscious mechanisms were supplemented by the effects of such other traditional practices as interisland voyages and wars, by which many young males were lost (Firth 1957: 163, 373–374). From an early survey of primitive cultures, Carr-Saunders (1922) concluded that *all* of them include customs whose primary function is to restrict the increase of population: abstention from marriage, delayed marriage, periodic abstention from intercourse, *coitus interruptus*, prolonged lactation, other types of contraception, abortion, and/or infanticide. Whatever fault one may find with this generalization, it is certainly far more valid than its contrary—that primitives ordinarily follow the Darwinian model.

If we speculate about the beginnings of primitive population control, ethnographic analogy can take us only to a choice of models. When the population density of lower animals becomes too high, in many species the check to further growth through mortality is supplemented by a physiological or instinctive behavioral adjustment of the fertility. Popularizers like Konrad Lorenz have extended this process to humans, but with little evidence to support their notion. In the human species the control of fertility is mainly cultural, only incidentally physiological. If only through infanticide, ancient man always had the capability of limiting the number of his offspring, and the question is when and under what conditions he would be motivated to exercise this control. There is no reason to suppose that the transition took place in a single "stage"; rather, if mortality varied from one prehistoric culture to another as much as we have suggested, one should expect a parallel variation in the development of fertility control from the occasional practice of individuals to the institutionalized norms of societies. Moreover, there is no reason *a priori* to date this process late in the prehistoric era, but rather the contrary. As we noted earlier (see pp. 73–74), the transition of a gathering band to a sedentary life reduces the incentive to control fertility and may bring about a larger number of children per woman. "It is the demand for oysters and champagne, not for the basic bread and butter, that triggers off social conventions which hold human populations down" (Douglas 1966).

THE DEPOPULATION OF PRIMITIVE PEOPLES

An important limitation to the analogy that we have drawn between paleolithic populations and those of contemporary primitives results from the effect that advanced cultures have had, or may have had, on the latter. The usual contention is that food-gathering peoples, even the most isolated, have suffered a loss in numbers as compared with an earlier "natural" state; but this depopulation among primitives, though much debated, is still a subject on which there is little agreement. Almost half a century ago the English anthropologist Pitt-Rivers (1927: 19) commented on this process in the Pacific islands, and what he wrote is to a large degree true today:

> During the past fifty or sixty years the dying out of the native Pacific populations has frequently been the subject of official and unofficial inquiries, and it is remarkable that there is as little agreement on the subject now as when it was first investigated. Not only does the failure in diagnosis remain as evident as before, but little or no progress has been made in methods of investigation. No satisfactory system or method has been established, and, largely in consequence of this, during the whole period few exact vital statistics are obtainable which might throw light upon the matter and establish the correctness or otherwise of diagnostic attempts.

Pitt-Rivers went on to compile an amusing table, listing the "causes" of depopulation among South Sea islanders in two columns. In the first was, for example,
the allegation that the abolition of head-hunting, by depriving the natives of their
chief interest in life, had brought about a despondency that eventually led to a
decline in their fertility; and in the second, on the other hand, the fact that head-
hunting still continued and contributed to a high mortality. In the first, again,
were listed various types of European foods or clothing that had been condemned
as unsuitable, and in the second various types of native food, clothing, housing,
etc., that had been condemned as unsanitary (ibid.: 48). Analysts have found it
all too easy to ascribe as the cause of depopulation any prior condition, either
the continuation of elements of the native culture, or the change in these by
acculturation, or whatever. *Post hoc, ergo propter hoc* has seldom been applied
so freely to any problem.

Where it has taken place, depopulation can be ascribed to the following factors:

1. In any struggle with higher cultures, primitives have invariably lost out.
The establishment of control over an area has very often been through a war in
which their opponents' more effective weapons proved to be a decisive advantage.
Wherever it has been introduced, slavery has probably decreased the population
of the enslaved peoples. The attacks in which slaves are taken result not only in
many deaths but very often in the disorganization of the native society (cf.
Curtin 1968). The low population density of Negro Africa, for example, is at
least in part the result of over a millennium of slave-raiding, first among the
African tribes themselves, then by Arabs and Europeans. In the Pacific islands,
slave-raiders generally carried off young males, and the females left behind were
often unable to marry and have children.

2. Depopulation was less the consequence of violence and servitude, however,
than of disease. This is always more virulent in a fresh population, for its effect
is later reduced by the natural selection of those best able to resist it, as well as
often by an acquired immunity from mild childhood cases in areas where it has
become endemic (see pp. 221, 237). The transfer of diseases, moreover, has
usually been from advanced to primitive peoples, since the latter are relatively
isolated, almost by definition, and are thus more likely to meet any infection for
the first time. Europeans have transported to other parts of the world syphilis,
malaria, tuberculosis, measles, whooping cough, chicken pox, dysentery,
smallpox, and even the common cold; and all of these were more often fatal
among the new hosts than in Europe. Venereal diseases in particular spread
rapidly between a dominant and a subordinate population. "Brazil would appear
to have been syphilized before it was civilized. The first Europeans . . . did not
bring civilization, but there is evidence to show that they did bring the venereal
plague. . . . [A] 'barbarous superstition' held that those suffering from gonorrhea
would be cured if they contrived to have intercourse with a [slave] girl at the
age of puberty" (Freyre 1946: 91, 325). According to one of the most careful
surveys of depopulation in the Pacific islands, "the cause of native decay is

largely disease" (Lambert 1934: 41). "Gonorrhea alone has created enough havoc to merit a major role in the dispeoplement of the Carolines" (Lessa 1955). In the New Hebrides, "diseases of the respiratory organs . . . are undoubtedly claiming the most victims, chiefly in the form of tuberculosis, influenza, bronchitis, and pneumonia" (Felix Speiser, in Rivers 1922: 26). Just smallpox was responsible for cutting the populous Mexican Indians by about a third, and the smaller Indian populations north of Mexico by substantial proportions (Stearn and Stearn 1945; cf. Borah and Cook 1960).

Epidemics are of course more visible, but endemic disease may disrupt a society as much. A people infected by malaria, for example, lacks energy, and anthropologists are likely to describe it as suffering from melancholia. Endemic syphilis may kill few, but it prevents the birth of many. The full effect of disease on a society is therefore not at all easy to measure, particularly in retrospect from incomplete and inaccurate records.

3. The introduction among primitives of the elements of a more efficient culture *sometimes* has the consequence, even with no purposeful action on the part of either group, of reducing their population. It is hardly necessary to point out that steel knives and repeating rifles have made their wars more deadly. Elements of a European diet, even when wholesome if consumed together, were considerably less so after a partial transfer to other peoples. This is especially so of alcohol, which has had a deleterious effect on many primitives. According to a missionary in Melanesia,

> Of all the evil customs introduced by civilization the wearing of clothes is probably the greatest. . . . As a skirt becomes ragged another is superimposed, while the rags beneath gradually rot off. Clothes are worn till they cease to exist as recognizable garments. . . . The custom is disastrous, [particularly since] the rainfall is abnormally heavy, the average being half an inch a day all the year round. . . . Such goods as trousers, shirts, and coats should be forbidden, or so heavily taxed as to make the price prohibitive to ordinary natives [W. J. Durrad, in Rivers 1922: 7–8, 22].

It was usually missionaries, however, who forced Pacific islanders to wear clothing unsuitable to the climate—which they might have done in any case, since European garments were the clearest mark of higher status.

4. The disruption effected by the infiltration of such alien elements can be cumulative. The social structure of a primitive people, though sometimes resilient in the face of reverses associated with traditional culture, often proves to be fragile in an encounter with a higher one. When the chief whose authority rests on his military prowess is decisively beaten, when the magic of the shaman is ridiculed and his direst spells have no effect, the whole social fabric can begin to erode. The social constraint of a nonliterate society typically rests, in Durkheim's terms, on mechanical rather than organic solidarity. "Restriction of excesses was a matter of external order and not, as Christian teaching endeavors to make it, a thing of inward righteous feeling. For a time at least, Christianity tends to loosen the bonds of restraint, for it removes the terror of punishment that would have been meted out by the chiefs of former days" (ibid.). According to one interpretation, such a decay of the culture is transformed on the individual level into a cause of death. "The new diseases and poisons, the innovations in clothing, housing, and feeding, are only the immediate causes of mortality. It is the loss of interest in life underlying these more obvious causes which . . . allows them to work such ravages upon life and health" (Rivers 1922: 96).

5. In a world that is falling apart, normal day-to-day activities like raising children may no longer seem to be worthwhile. Among the Pelly Bay Eskimos, Rasmussen noted thirty-eight cases of female infanticide out of ninety-six births in eighteen families. Among the Rendille, a tribe of some 6,000 in Kenya who depend almost solely on their camel herd, population is held down by, among other measures, killing off boys born on Wednesdays. Since the means of restricting population growth exist in the culture, they can be applied; and when the family declines as an institution, the consequent reduction in the birth rate may on occasion have been substantial. One wonders, however, whether the elasticity of such regulation has been in only one direction. If for certain magical reasons fertility is impeded, these taboos conceivably could be relaxed. "A rumor was current among the Yapese in 1948 that a secret meeting on the depopulation [had been] held by the chiefs and religious leaders in 1946. These men supposedly decided that most of the former taboos on coitus should be discontinued" (Hunt *et al.* 1954). More generally, if indigenous authority breaks down through European dominance, the lapse in controls might result, one would think, in the abandonment of taboos of this type.

Apart from such questions, this list of causes of depopulation is so impressive that it proves too much. How was it that primitives anywhere have survived at all? Yet although some nonliterate peoples, particularly Polynesians and American Indians, undoubtedly underwent a loss in numbers during a period, this was not the case universally. Where it took place, moreover, depopulation varied greatly in its severity. For example, among three 17th-century peoples in the Caribbean area, the Indians of Hispaniola (Haiti) were nearly extinct within a single generation, the Omagua were reduced by half within 40 years, and the neighboring Cocama have retained about their original numbers to the present day (Steward 1949). In the New Hebrides, the population of some islands increased—for instance, "Tanna, Malo, Paama, Merelava, and probably Tongoa" (Felix Speiser, in Rivers 1922: 51). The Angmagssalik Eskimos on the east coast of Greenland, who numbered 413 when Holm discovered them in 1884, increased apparently without interruption to 2,249 in 1971. Dispersal of the population into smaller settlements "became necessary because of the rise in population over the last 50 years induced by improvements in living standards and health facilities." With the addition of market products to their traditional subsistence economies, there has been a general increase in Eskimo populations and, except for the coastal villages along the Bering and Beaufort Seas, seemingly without a prior decrease (Hughes 1965).

The range in population changes among various primitive peoples, from complete extinction to an increase, results from a complex interplay of a no less full range of factors, some of which are related to the native culture. Disease, generally the most important cause, ordinarily did not effect a permanent loss of population except in conjunction with other factors. If conditions favor growth, losses from even a calamitous epidemic can be made up in a few generations.

There is good reason to believe, moreover, that the depletion of primitive peoples has probably been exaggerated in many cases (McArthur 1968). There are several reasons why this may be so, as follows:

1. Primitives, of course, keep no record of their own population, and the later estimates by anthropologists or other Westerners are seldom securely based. Table 10-3 shows, as one example, five estimates of the number living in the Americas at the time of Columbus's first voyage. The range in the total from 8.5 to 112.6 million is by more than thirteen times.

Table 10-3. Estimates of Native American Population (–000), c. 1492

	Sapper (1924)	Kroeber (1939)	Rosenblat (1945)	Steward (1949)	Dobyns (1966)
North of Mexico	2,000– 3,500	1,001	1,000	1,001	9,800–12,250
Mexico	12,000–15,000	3,000	4,500	4,500	30,000–37,500
West Indies and Central America	8,000–10,000	200[a]	1,100	961	11,243–14,054
South America	15,000–20,000	4,300[a]	6,785	9,129	39,000–48,750
Total	37,000–48,500	8,501	13,385	15,591	90,043–112,554

[a] Central America included with South America.

SOURCES: Julian H. Steward, "The Native Population of South America," in Julian H. Steward, editor, *Handbook of South American Indians*, Smithsonian Institution, Bulletin 143 (Washington, D.C.: U.S. Bureau of American Ethnology, 1949), vol. 5, Part 3, p. 656. Henry F. Dobyns, "Estimating Aboriginal American Population: An Appraisal of Techniques with a New Hemisphere Estimate," *Current Anthropology*, 7 (1966), 395–415.

The population estimates of the aboriginal population of Pacific islands, in any case of no great precision, have subsequently been mistranslated, misquoted, and otherwise garbled in later works. One principal source is Captain Cook, and we can take his estimate of the population of Tahiti as an example. On May 14, 1774, Cook projected the population of Tahiti from an enormous fleet of war canoes that he saw. A similar fleet representing all of the districts of Tahiti, he wrote, would "require Sixty eight Thousand able bodied men and as these cannot amount to One third part the number of both Sex the whole Island cannot contain less than two hundred and four thousand inhabitants."

Unfortunately, Cook's figure was immediately mistranslated in its first French edition, which rendered the crucial sentence as "... toute l'isle contient au moins deux cent quarante mille habitants." . . . The erroneous figure of 240,000 has been unsuspectedly quoted by [eleven authorities]. . . . Others even misquoted the mistranslation. Cook's figure was given as 140,000 by Nordmann, 130,000 by Sasportas, 100,000 by Seurat, and 30,000 by Lesson. . . .

Although Cook's 1774 estimate for Tahiti is but one of many made for the island during the 1760s and 1770s, it is virtually the only one to be either quoted or misquoted. At least seven others were reported by early visitors, and many more were offered by later authorities [Schmitt 1972].

Cook's estimate of the number of Maori in New Zealand was 100,000, and other guesses ranged as high as five times that. From 1858, when the first census was taken, to 1896, when the downward trend was reversed, the Maori population fell from about 56,000 to about 42,000 (Borrie 1959). Mortality was high during these 38 years, probably no higher in the earlier period. If as a rough gauge we extrapolate the loss of 368 persons per year back to the time of the first substantial interaction with whites, Cook's estimate seems to be on the high side.

The first figures for any area are likely to be set by missionaries or administrators, who may exaggerate them for bureaucratic reasons; thus, those cited from Kroeber in Table 10-3 had all been reduced from the Spanish sources. A supposition that a large and prosperous people flourished before the Europeans came is often given support by nativist accounts of the more or less legendary past. Anthropologists sometimes generalize from the most horrible examples—which are also the most striking—of population decline. Dobyns (1966), thus, estimated the "nadir," or lowest level of population, from modern censuses, then multiplied it by a measure of depopulation based on various guesses. For the whole of the Central Andes, for instance, Dobyns based his depopulation ratio on areas that had suffered an estimated loss of 15/16 or even 24/25, whereas according to a detailed analysis of just this region (Smith 1970), the depletion may have been from something over 400,000 to something under 100,000— certainly dramatic enough for most tastes.

2. When no figures are available at all, one common method of estimating the past numbers is to calculate the maximum population of the territory a primitive people inhabited. The figures cited from Sapper in Table 10-3, for example, were based on the assumed carrying power of various types of soil, given the level of technology and the type of land use of the various Indian peoples. He assumed that the population in each case was the greatest possible with food gathering or primitive agriculture, and by this exclusive attention to economic factors he altogether neglected the effect of intertribal warfare or human sacrifices, to cite only the most obvious of other relevant factors. In a painstaking and entirely plausible argument, as one instance, Cook (1946) showed that from the late 14th to the early 16th centuries human sacrifice and war may have accounted for as much as one-fifth of the mortality in Central Mexico. He was unwilling, however, to accept the religious significance of propitiation of the gods, or of the waging of war in part to replenish a waning supply of victims. His straightforward account of these ideational motives is muddled by the supposition that because "the margin of subsistence was becoming some-what precarious," there was a "social urge" to check population growth. It is a remarkably restrictive view of history to hold that the mass slaughter ostensibly in support of an ideology in fact must mask an unfavorable balance between population and resources. The population density of what is now the eastern portion of the United States, as another example, was certainly well below what one could deduce from its carrying power. That is to say, peoples at the same technical level, even if as widely separated in time as prehistoric savages and contemporary primitives, have a population *potential* of the same general order. Whether this is realized, however, depends on more than ecological or technical or economic factors. An implicit assumption that the social–cultural milieu of primitives is optimum with respect to their numbers will generally result in an overestimate.

3. If approximations of aboriginal populations before contact with another culture tend to run too high, those of the current numbers are often too low. To the degree that racial mixture and acculturation take place, non-Europeans "disappear" not in a physical but in a statistical sense. "When is a Maori a 'Maori'?" (Pool 1961) is a question that, appropriately specified, must be posed as the prelude to virtually every analysis of the population growth of primitives. Moreover, even those peoples that indubitably underwent a decline in the past have in many instances experienced a more recent population growth, sometimes at a prodigious rate (e.g., Pool 1967; Jones 1967; Schmitt 1968; cf. pp. 102–104).

4. The most typical response of primitives to disaster perhaps was not to wait for its culmination but rather to move away. With the poor statistics available to present-day compilers, such migrations are likely to be interpreted as depopulation, for those escaping from oppression in one area were hardly likely to advertise their presence in another.

PREHISTORIC MIGRATIONS

If, as prehistorians and anthropologists now generally agree, *Homo sapiens* evolved from some lower primate form only once, then the existence of humans over the whole of the world indicates that a series of prehistoric migrations took place from mankind's birthplace, wherever that was. How can we imagine that ancient man was able to anticipate by many eons the extraordinary feats of the Age of Discovery, when Europeans first pushed beyond the outer frontiers of the Mediterranean basin and sailed around Africa to the South Seas and across the Atlantic to the "New" World? These primeval migrations are explicable by several of their characteristics. The passage from what is now one continent to another was made possible by the fact that the succession of Pleistocene glaciations absorbed a large portion of the oceans' water into ice sheets, so that land bridges may have been in existence across the Mediterranean, for example, and (more certainly) down through the East Indies, facilitating the movement away from the climate of the northern hemisphere. It must be recalled that the glaciations, which foreshortened in retrospect may seem cataclysmic, took place so slowly as to cause no perceptible fall in average temperature during the whole of a lifetime. The push to migrate, though real, was exerted so gradually as to effect a movement by stages.

Food gatherers and hunters, because of the limitations of their economy, must be on the move; they are rangers. Herdsmen and primitive agriculturists, as we have seen, are hardly more sedentary. While today such people move over a limited area that is theirs by tradition, in a world relatively unpopulated by humans each band would follow wherever the available subsistence led it. Most prehistoric migrations, as we can imagine them, constituted movements of groups of twenty or thirty persons, walking a few miles a day, as do the Semang, in order to collect their food supply. Similarly, one can explain the wide distribution of the neolithic Danubian cultivators by their nomadic agriculture: "Assuming quite short shifts of territory every twelve years or so, it would take only a few centuries for a modest initial population to spread from say the Drave to the Harz" (Childe 1950: 93). In geologic time, at the rate and with the prodigious waste of a natural process, food-gathering or agricultural bands separated by thousands of miles and became nuclei of discrete populations (cf. Edmonson 1961).

It is possible, then, to state that prehistoric migrations took place, to time some of them within wide limits by carbon-dating or an alternative technique, and to offer plausible hypotheses about routes and the rate of movement. To fill in these generalizations with details on specific migrations, however, is extraordinarily difficult. A prehistoric migration, by definition, is one of which we have no written record, and of which we must therefore reconstruct all the details from circumstantial evidence.

The reconstitution of prehistoric migrations from any type of current data ordinarily consists of three steps: (1) classifying the data into a spatial pattern, (2) discounting the factors other than migration that might have changed the pattern, and (3) inferring migrations from the remaining systematic differences in the pattern. Embedded in the schema at point (2) is that hoary dispute concerning repeated invention versus diffusion from a single source, and in its current phase the argument is sometimes still as dogmatic as in the 19th century. Thus, Coon's (1962) argument, offered with an expertise that seemingly would have demanded respectful attention, that the human species evolved through a convergence of discrete hominid stocks most scholarly reviewers rejected out of hand. In the major (if not only) work on folklore methodology, as a completely different instance, it is axiomatic that "the variants being compared all go back to one parent form. . . . Even one single independent reoccurrence of a complicated form—for example, the Cinderella tale—as the result of the general similarity of human fantasy or pure chance is highly unlikely." Variations, moreover, generally "increase progressively in the direction of migration." The analysis of folklore as so conceived consists in the search for the *Urform*, its geographical placement, and the tracing of routes of diffusion from that nucleus (Krohn 1971: 58, 126–127).

Perhaps the simplest example of a reconstructed past migration is that given in Kenneth Jackson's masterful work on the relation between Brittonic (the language that the Celts had brought to Britain) and early English. He uses geographic place names, especially of rivers, to mark the westward movement of the Angles and the gradual retreat of the Celts (Figure 10-2). East of a line running north from the Isle of Wight, Brittonic names are rare and are confined almost entirely to large and medium-sized rivers. At the other extreme, Monmouthshire remained Brittonic until at least the Norman conquest, most of Cornwall until the 18th century, and much of Wales to the present day; and in this area the names of rivers are overwhelmingly Celtic. "From the evidence of place names it is clear that in point of fact the British population was nowhere completely exterminated, though it certainly survived more fully in some areas than in others" (Jackson 1953: 234). This seems a very large conclusion from so slight a base. If we were to ask what relation the existence of Indian place names in the American Middle West has to an Indian population, or Spanish names in California to Spanish, or Polynesian names in Hawaii to native Hawaiian, we would impose a stricter test than Jackson puts to his own thesis.

Nor does an attempt to reconstruct prehistoric migrations from the present distribution of human races (e.g., Taylor 1928) lead to an unambiguous conclusion. And even when the probability of diffusion is accepted, one cannot reasonably infer a migration from it, or no migration from a lack of it.

Migrations . . . form the crass instances of the process, easily conceived by a simple mind. That a custom travels as a people travels carrying it along is something that a child can understand. The danger is in stopping there and invoking a national migration for every important culture diffusion, whereas it is plain that most culture changes from without have occurred through subtler and more gradual or piecemeal operations [Kroeber 1948: 473].

If a prior movement *is* deduced from a similarity among the surviving artifacts, one still cannot know in every case which way the prehistoric bands went. For instance, after citing four archeologists who have reconstructed a neolithic migration from the Danube basin to what is now Macedonia, Childe suggested— "reluctantly"—that the movement had been in the opposite direction (Childe 1950: 50). An analogous state of knowledge with respect to modern migration would leave us in doubt as to whether Englishmen had populated the United States, or Americans England.

SUMMARY

The direct evidence on paleolithic populations is so slight that it was necessary to consider ways by which it might be extended. Following the recent trend in anthropology, certain features of the life of contemporary food-gathering

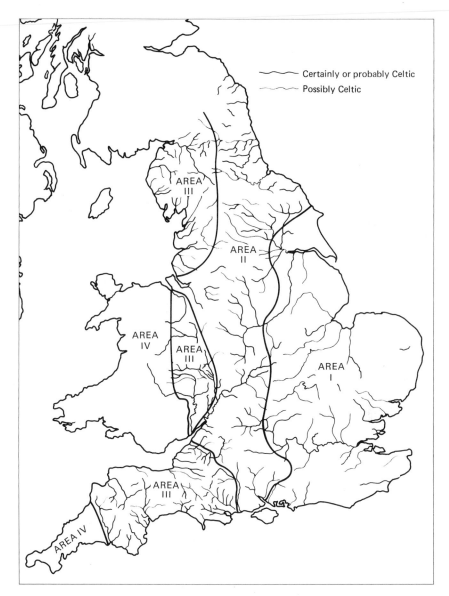

Figure 10-2.   Zones of Relative Penetration of the English into Celtic England, as Estimated from the Etymology of River Names

SOURCE: Kenneth Jackson, *Language and History in Early Britain: A Chronological Survey of the Brittonic Languages, First to Twelfth Centuries, A.D.* (Cambridge, Mass.: Harvard University Press, 1953), p. 220. Reproduced with permission from the Edinburgh University Press.

primitives have been accepted as a probable close counterpart to that of pre-agricultural peoples. Combining archeological with anthropological data, we can conclude that the average density of paleolithic man was of the order of one person per square mile, and that therefore no more than about 30 million or, more probably, around 5 million lived in the entire world. Population was all but static, growing slowly in relatively favorable periods and being reduced sharply in time of distress. Expectation of life at birth was probably less than 20 years, and the maximum span not much more than double that figure. Fertility must have been high in order to offset the high mortality. But there is no reason to assume that ancient man lacked either the desire to control the number of his offspring or the means of realizing it.

Contact with advanced cultures has often resulted in a decline of population among primitives. The factor generally most responsible was the new diseases brought by Europeans. There is good reason to believe, however, that this depopulation has often been exaggerated.

It can be assumed that the present geographical pattern of both physical and cultural traits is related in a distant way to a series of prehistoric migrations, but so many other factors have influenced it that it is not possible to trace this relation except in the most tentative fashion. The methodological problem to be solved—namely, to infer prior motion from static data—can be indicated by a rather farfetched analogy. Suppose that there are several species of beetles, each of which leaves a track of a different color when it walks. We have only a broken and scratched pane of glass over which various beetles, long since dead, have passed, and the task is to reconstruct their movements from the color pattern. The first step, obviously, is to classify the colors themselves: orange must be distinguished from red, green from blue, and each intermediate case must be put into one or the other category. Then all irrelevant influences must be considered and their effect taken into account: other insects may have marked the glass, portions of it may have faded in the sun, and so on. Only then, finally, can an attempt be made to reconstruct the beetles' movement over the glass.

CITED REFERENCES AND SUGGESTIONS FOR FURTHER READING

Demographers have generally shown little interest in analyzing the populations of either prehistoric or primitive peoples, and until very recently prehistorians, archeologists, and anthropologists were no more involved in building a bridge from the other side. Demography has been treated inferentially in works on physical anthropology, prehistory, and especially economic anthropology: Firth (1950), Herskovits (1952), Forde (1952), Coon (1955), and so on. One of the best of such works, in spite of its date, is the classic volume by Hobhouse and his colleagues (1930). Of the various works on the population of specific primitive peoples, some of the best are by Steward (1949), Nougier (1954), Borrie et al. (1957), Johnston (1966), Schmitt (1968, the early chapters), McArthur (1968), and Romaniuk and Piché (1972). Of the various volumes that reflect a new and growing interest in the topic of this chapter, the more stimulating include those edited by Brothwell and Sandison (1967), Spooner (1972), and Siegel *et al.* (1972).

*ALLEN, WILLIAM L., and JAMES B. RICHARDSON III. 1971. "The Reconstruction of Kinship from Archeological Data: The Concepts, the Methods, and the Feasibility," *American Antiquity*, **36**, 41–53.

BINFORD, LEWIS R. 1968. "Post-Pleistocene Adaptations," in Sally R. Binford and Lewis R. Binford, editors, *New Perspectives in Archeology*. Chicago: Aldine.

BORAH, WOODROW, and S. F. COOK. 1960. *The Indian Population of Central Mexico, 1531–1610*. Berkeley: University of California Press.

BORRIE, W. D. 1959. "The Maori Population: A Microcosm of a New World," in J. D. Freeman and W. R. Geddes, editors, *Anthropology in the South Seas*. New Plymouth, N.Z.: Avery.

————, RAYMOND FIRTH, and JAMES SPILLIUS. 1957. "The Population of Tikopia, 1929 and 1952," *Population Studies*, **10**, 229–252.

BRACE, C. L., and M. F. ASHLEY MONTAGU. 1965. *Man's Evolution: An Introduction to Physical Anthropology*. New York: Macmillan.

*BRAIDWOOD, ROBERT J., and BRUCE HOWE. 1960. *Prehistoric Investigations in Iraqi Kurdistan*. Chicago: University of Chicago Press.

BROTHWELL, DON. 1970. "Stones, Pots and People: A Plea for Statistical Caution," in Don Brothwell and Eric Higgs, editors, *Science in Archeology: A Survey of Progress and Research*. New York: Praeger.

————, and A. T. SANDISON, editors. 1967. *Diseases in Antiquity: A Survey of the Diseases, Injuries and Surgery of Early Populations*. Springfield, Ill.: Thomas.

CARR-SAUNDERS, A. M. 1922. *The Population Problem: A Study in Human Evolution*. Oxford: Clarendon.

CHARLTON, THOMAS H. 1972. "Population Trends in the Teotihuacán Valley, A.D. 1400–1969," *World Archeology*, **4**, 106–123.

CHILDE, V. GORDON. 1950. *Prehistoric Migrations in Europe*. Instituttet for Sammenlignende Kulturforskning. Oslo: Aschehoug.

————. 1951. *Social Evolution*. New York: Henry Schuman.

CLARK, J. GRAHAME D. 1952. *Prehistoric Europe: The Economic Basis*. London: Methuen.

*————. 1965. *Archeology and Society: Reconstructing the Prehistoric Past*. New York: Barnes and Noble.

————, et al. 1954. *Excavations at Star Carr: An Early Mesolithic Site at Seamer near Scarborough, Yorkshire*. Cambridge, England: Cambridge University Press.

COOK, SHERBURNE F. 1946. "Human Sacrifice and Warfare as Factors in the Demography of Pre-Colonial Mexico," *Human Biology*, **18**, 81–100.

————. 1972. "Prehistoric Demography," Module 16. Reading, Mass.: Addison-Wesley.

————, and ROBERT F. HEIZER. 1968. "Relationships among Houses, Settlement Areas, and Population in Aboriginal California," in K. C. Chang, editor, *Settlement Archeology*. Palo Alto, Calif.: National Press Books.

COON, CARLETON S. 1955. *The Story of Man: From the First Human to Primitive Culture and Beyond*. New York: Knopf.

————. 1962. *The Origin of Races*. New York: Knopf.

CURTIN, PHILIP D. 1968. "Epidemiology and the Slave Trade," *Political Science Quarterly*, **83**, 190–216.

DOBYNS, HENRY F. 1966. "Estimating Aboriginal American Population: An Appraisal of Techniques with a New Hemisphere Estimate," *Current Anthropology*, **7**, 395–415.

*DOUGLAS, MARY. 1966. "Population Control in Primitive Groups," *British Journal of Sociology*, **17**, 263–273.

EDMONSON, MUNRO S. 1961. "Neolithic Diffusion Rates," *Current Anthropology*, **2**, 71–102.

EWERS, JOHN C. 1955. *The Horse in Blackfoot Indian Culture, with Comparative Material from Other Western Tribes*. Smithsonian Institution, Bulletin 159. Washington, D.C.: U.S. Bureau of American Ethnology.

FIRTH, RAYMOND. 1950. *Primitive Polynesian Economy*. New York: Humanities Press.

———. 1957. *We, the Tikopia: A Sociological Study of Kinship in Primitive Polynesia*, 2nd ed. Boston: Beacon Press.

FORDE, C. DARYLL. 1952. *Habitat, Economy, and Society: A Geographical Introduction to Ethnology*. New York: Dutton (reprinted as a Dutton paperback, 1963).

FREYRE, GILBERTO. 1946. *The Masters and the Slaves: A Study in the Development of Brazilian Civilization*, 4th ed. New York: Knopf.

GENOVÉS, SANTIAGO. 1970a. "Sex Determination in Earlier Man," in Don Brothwell and Eric Higgs, editors, *Science in Archeology: A Survey of Progress and Research*. New York: Praeger.

———. 1970b. "Estimation of Age and Mortality," in ibid.

HAVILAND, WILLIAM A. 1972. "Estimates of Maya Population: Comments on Thompson's Comments," *American Antiquity*, **37**, 261–262.

HEIZER, ROBERT F., and SHERBURNE F. COOK, editors. 1960. *The Application of Quantitative Methods in Archeology*. Chicago: Quadrangle Books.

HERSKOVITS, MELVILLE J. 1952. *Economic Anthropology: A Study in Comparative Economics*. New York: Knopf.

*HOBHOUSE, L. T., G. C. WHEELER, and M. GINSBERG. 1930. *The Material Culture and Social Institutions of Simpler Peoples: An Essay in Correlation*. London: Chapman & Hall.

HOWELLS, W. W. 1960. "Estimating Population Numbers through Archeological and Skeletal Remains," in Heizer and Cook 1960.

*HUGHES, CHARLES CAMPBELL. 1965. "Under Four Flags: Recent Culture Change among the Eskimos," *Current Anthropology*, **6**, 3–69.

HUNT, EDWARD E., JR., *et al.* 1954. "The Depopulation of Yap," *Human Biology*, **26**, 21–51.

JACKSON, KENNETH. 1953. *Language and History in Early Britain: A Chronological Survey of the Brittonic Languages, First to Twelfth Centuries, A.D.* Cambridge, Mass.: Harvard University Press.

JOHNSTON, DENIS FOSTER. 1966. *An Analysis of Sources of Information on the Population of the Navaho*. Smithsonian Institution, Bulletin 197. Washington, D.C.: U.S. Bureau of American Ethnology.

JONES, L. W. 1967. "The Decline and Recovery of the Murut Tribe of Sabah," *Population Studies*, **21**, 133–157.

KIRSTEN, ERNST. 1956. *Raum und Bevölkerung in der Weltgeschichte*, vol. 1: *Von der Vorzeit bis zum Mittelalter*. Würzburg: Ploetz.

KROEBER, A. L. 1948. *Anthropology*, rev. ed. New York: Harcourt, Brace.

KROHN, KAARLE. 1971. *Folklore Methodology*. Austin: University of Texas Press.

KRZYWICKI, LUDWIK. 1934. *Primitive Society and Its Vital Statistics*. London: Macmillan.

LAMBERT, S. M. 1934. *The Depopulation of Pacific Races*. Special Publication 23. Honolulu: Bishop Museum.

LEBLANC, STEVEN. 1971. "An Addition to Naroll's Suggested Floor Area and Settlement Population Relationship," *American Antiquity*, **36**, 210–211.

LESSA, WILLIAM A. 1955. "Depopulation of Ulithi," *Human Biology*, **27**, 161–183.

LEWIS, OSCAR. 1949. "Plow Culture and Hoe Culture—A Study in Contrasts," *Rural Sociology*, **14**, 116–127.

LOUREIRO FERNANDES, JOSÉ. 1959. "The Xetá—A Dying People in Brazil," *Bulletin of the International Committee on Urgent Anthropological and Ethnological Research*, no. 2, pp. 22–26.

MCARTHUR, NORMA. 1959. "Fijians and Indians in Fiji," *Population Studies*, **12**, 202–213.

*———. 1968. *Island Populations of the Pacific*. Honolulu: University of Hawaii Press.

MCKERN, THOMAS W., and T. D. STEWART. 1957. *Skeletal Age Changes in Young American Males Analysed from the Standpoint of Age Identification*. Environmental Protection Research Division, Technical Report EP-45. Natick, Mass.: Quartermaster Research & Development Center, U.S. Army.

MICHELS, JOSEPH W. 1972. "Dating Methods," in Siegel *et al.* 1972.

MOODIE, ROY L. 1923. *The Antiquity of Disease*. Chicago: University of Chicago Press.

NAROLL, RAOUL. 1956. "A Preliminary Index of Social Development," *American Anthropologist*, **58**, 687–715.

*———. 1962. "Floor Area and Settlement Population," *American Antiquity*, **27**, 587–589.

NOUGIER, L. R. 1954. "Essai sur le peuplement préhistorique de la France," *Population*, **9**, 241–271.

PHILLIPS, PATRICIA. 1972. "Population, Economy and Society in the Chassey-Cortaillod-Lagozza Cultures," *World Archeology*, **4**, 41–56.

PILBEAM, DAVID. 1972. "Adaptive Response of Hominids to Their Environment as Ascertained by Fossil Evidence," *Social Biology*, **19**, 115–127.

PITT-RIVERS, G. H. L. F. 1927. *The Clash of Culture and the Contact of Races*. London. Routledge.

POLUNIN, IVAN V. 1967. "Health and Disease in Contemporary Primitive Societies," in Brothwell and Sandison 1967.

POOL, E. I. 1961. "When Is a Maori a 'Maori'?" *Journal of the Polynesian Society*, **73**, 206–210.

———. 1967. "Post-war Trends in Maori Population Growth," *Population Studies*, **21**, 87–98.

RICHARDS, AUDREY I., and PRISCILLA REINING. 1954. "Report on Fertility Surveys in Buganda and Buhaya, 1952," in Frank Lorimer, editor, *Culture and Human Fertility*. Paris: Unesco.

RIVERS, W. H. R., editor. 1922. *Essays on the Depopulation of Melanesia*. Cambridge, England: Cambridge University Press.

ROMANIUK, ANATOL, and VICTOR L. PICHÉ. 1972. "Natality Estimates for the Canadian Indians by Stable Population Models, 1900–1969," *Canadian Review of Sociology and Anthropology*, **9**, 1–20.

SCHMITT, ROBERT C. 1968. *Demographic Statistics of Hawaii: 1778–1965*. Honolulu: University of Hawaii Press.

———. 1970. "Famine Mortality in Hawaii," *Journal of Pacific History*, **5**, 109–115.

*———. 1972. "Garbled Population Estimates of Central Polynesia," in William Petersen, editor, *Readings in Population*. New York: Macmillan.

SIEGEL, BERNARD J., ALAN R. BEALS, and STEPHEN A. TYLER. 1972. *Annual Review of Anthropology*, vol. 1. Palo Alto, Calif.: Annual Reviews.

SMITH, C. T. 1970. "Depopulation of the Central Andes in the 16th Century," *Current Anthropology*, **11**, 453–464.

*SPOONER, BRIAN, editor. 1972. *Population Growth: Anthropological Implications*. Cambridge, Mass.: M.I.T. Press.

STEARN, E. WAGNER, and ALLEN E. STEARN. 1945. *The Effect of Smallpox on the Destiny of the Amerindian*. Boston: Bruce Humphries.

STEWARD, JULIAN H. 1949. "The Native Population of South America," in Julian H. Steward, editor, *Handbook of South American Indians*. Smithsonian Institution, Bulletin 143. Washington, D.C.: U.S. Bureau of American Ethnology.

TAYLOR, GRIFFITH. 1928. *European Migrations: Past, Present and Future*. Sydney: Dey.

THOMPSON, J. ERIC S. 1971. "Estimates of Maya Population: Deranging Factors," *American Antiquity*, **36**, 214–216.

TURNER, CHRISTY G., and LAUREL LOFGREN. 1966. "Household Size of Prehistoric Western Pueblo Indians," *Southwestern Journal of Anthropology*, **22**, 117–132.

VALLOIS, HENRI V. 1937. "La durée de la vie chez l'homme fossile," *Anthropologie*, **47**, 499–532.

———. 1960. "Vital Statistics in Prehistoric Population as Determined from Archeological Data," in Heizer and Cook 1960.

WELLS, CALVIN. 1967. "Pseudopathology," in Brothwell and Sandison 1967.

THE POPULATION OF PREINDUSTRIAL CIVILIZATIONS

11

The neolithic inventions of agriculture and stockherding not only gave primitive food-gathering tribes a valuable supplement to their prior means of subsistence, but also became the technical base for the urban civilizations that flourished in the Near East at the dawn of written history. By 3000 B.C., in Egypt and Mesopotamia the domesticated ox was put in front of a wooden plow, furnishing man the first source of energy apart from his own muscles. At about the same time metallurgy was developed, and coppersmiths became the first full-time craftsmen. The wheel was already in existence, and the same harness used to pull a plow could be attached to a cart. With this technical base, true agriculture (the word is from the Latin *ager*, "field") could supplant the tillage of small plots.

With respect to population growth, there was no social change of comparable significance until several millennia later, when the industrial revolution transformed Western Europe in the 18th and 19th centuries. Preindustrial civilizations developed populations that, though still rather small by present standards, were tremendous compared with the food-gathering cultures of prehistory. (The term *preindustrial*, one should note, is more precise than *nonindustrial*, for today's underdeveloped areas are altogether different: the population growth, economic development, and cultural transformation of such countries as modern India or China are markedly influenced by the industrial civilizations of the West and Russia.) Man's first urban settlements were concurrent with his first massive technical advances. During peaceful, prosperous times the number of people in the new civilizations grew to new dimensions, but periodically it was cut back by pestilence, famine, or the breakdown of social order. Even so, the average expectation of life may have increased from less than 20 years at the beginning of the neolithic era to something over 30 years.

Great contrasts can be noted, of course, between ancient Rome and Manchu China, or Tokugawa Japan and medieval Europe. But the demographic characteristics of these and similar societies differed no more, perhaps, than those of cultures dependent on gathering and on fishing. It is not distortive to classify all pre-urban peoples or, as in this chapter, all preindustrial civilizations as one analytical unit.

One trait these civilizations had in common is that they maintained records, sometimes even had so-called censuses. Until rather recently these partial and ambiguous data were analyzed by only a few historians and virtually no demographers. As one of this rare tribe wrote a generation ago, "There is no subject of the first importance in ancient scholarship in which our thoughts are vaguer, in which we almost refuse to think (because the evidence is unsatisfactory), than that of population" (Gomme 1933: 1). A historian's analysis of population data, moreover, does not differ essentially from any of his other efforts. Scholarship is based fundamentally on what the great German historian Leopold von Ranke called *Quellenkritik*: using both his technical skill and his detailed knowledge of the whole social context, the historian judges the comparative worth of documents to decide which is most likely to be true. There are some questions, however, that this method is ill equipped to answer.

The historian accustomed to working with literary sources would attack the question whether family limitation was being practiced before the Industrial Revolution by searching for references in contemporary writing to abortion or to contraceptive devices and practices. Such evidence is peculiarly difficult to find, for there was a considerable taboo against even the mention of such things, and they are usually referred to by euphemisms—sometimes impenetrable ones. . . . Furthermore, such references as we do have do not indicate how widespread the practice was, or in what social groups at what times it could be found [Vann 1969].

But population differs from other topics of historical analysis in that it is to some degree a self-contained process, invariant irrespective of the cultural context. To take the simplest example: since any person aged 25, if he survives one year, will be 26 years old, any series of reported ages can always be checked for internal consistency (see pp. 65–66). Since the population of any area is equal to that population at an earlier date plus the intervening natural growth and net in-migration, if some of these elements are known the others can be derived or estimated. More fundamentally, since in any society infants and the elderly are more likely to die within a year than adolescents and young adults, and since childbearing is physiologically limited to females in the same favored age range, there is a necessary relation among mortality, fertility, and the age structure. As A. J. Lotka pointed out as early as 1907, these three elements of any population are associated by the following equation (cf. Coale and Demeny 1966: 9–10):

$$c(a) = be^{-ra}p(a)$$

where

    $c(a)$ = the proportion of the population at age a,
      b = the birth rate,
      e = the base of natural logarithms,
      r = the annual rate of increase, and
    $p(a)$ = the proportion surviving from birth to age a.

In other words, if two of the three factors (fertility, mortality, and the age–sex structure) are known with a given degree of certainty, the range of the third can be stipulated (cf. Brass 1953).

Mathematics of even this modest difficulty is beyond the ken of most traditional historians, and the field was transformed when men adept in such techniques applied them to historical data. One pioneer was Louis Henry, who had been trained as an engineer and became a demographer in his adult years. His analyses of some sets of 18th-century data started a boom in French historical demography, which was encouraged by a manual on the techniques specific to the subdiscipline (Henry 1970), the founding of a Société de Démographie Historique, the publication of its *Annales*, and even a computer program to facilitate this type of analysis (Beauchamp *et al.* 1973). The French school has been only somewhat more productive than its counterparts in Britain (e.g., Hollingsworth 1969; Wrigley 1966b, 1969), Italy, the Netherlands, and Hungary. In each of these countries, the works of historians writing about population in the framework of a *Quellenkritik* are being supplemented by analyses based on the physiological patterns of demographic factors. No one supposes that the historical expertise is dispensable, but few any longer doubt the superiority of the joint product.

SOURCES OF INFORMATION

Henry (1970: ix) calls the historical era after the establishment of systematic mass records but before demographic data were collected for their own sake "protostatistic." The kinds of data compiled in the several preindustrial civilizations differ considerably, and also the portion of the record that has survived from each area or period. Underlying this variation, however, there are several common features, which can be exemplified by specific instances.

The most detailed information available usually comes from the accounts of economic transactions. In this class, for instance, are the lists of grain shipments from the whole empire to the city of Rome; but to translate these into population figures requires a rather hazardous guess as to what the per-capita consumption was. Economic and demographic data for particular localities are sometimes known in meticulous detail. In 9th-century France, for instance, abbeys maintained an estate book listing all their landed property and its production; and "we know today the name of almost every man, woman, and child who was living on these little *fiscs* [or estates] in the time of Charlemagne, and a great deal about their daily lives" (Power 1954: 17). But one never can be certain how representative such figures are for larger areas. The most famous survey of this type, and the only one covering a considerable territory, is the Domesday Book, the inventory of his lands that William the Conqueror had made in 1086. According to the man historians know as the "Saxon chronicler," "there was not one single hide nor rood of land, nor—it is shameful to tell but he thought it no shame to do—was there an ox, cow, or swine that was not set down in the writ."

Most population data were collected as part of the administration of taxes, military conscription, and similar governmental functions. Whenever it was possible, of course, people evaded such counts; and they ordinarily pertained, moreover, only to certain sectors, so that it is necessary in each case to estimate the number of inhabitants from an unknown fraction. Sometimes the enumerated portion was rather large; the Roman head-tax introduced under Diocletian, for example, apparently was imposed on the entire labor force and thus excluded only children and women, the aged, and the feeble-minded. The Roman census was narrower; originally it was a count of certain adult males primarily for military conscription. Similarly, studies based on the genealogies of nobility or the life histories of monks, two medieval classes about whom good data sometimes exist, are obviously not of universal relevance.

Even when statistics were not specific to particular portions of the population, such a limitation was often effected by their nature. One of the better sources on mortality in Rome is the life table drawn up by Ulpian, a famous jurist of the 2nd and 3rd centuries A.D.; since, however, this was used by courts to settle property disputes, it was presumably based on the death rates of the well-to-do. The inferences to be drawn from old epitaphs concerning the range in the age at death, and thus the general mortality conditions, are similarly selective. In ancient Rome, "tombstones with ages were an essentially middle-class and lower middle-class institution. The governing classes, . . . having many more interesting things to say about themselves and their relatives, generally did not give ages; and the really poor could not afford tombstones" (Burn 1953). And these were seldom erected for infants, who constitute a very important sector in any study of mortality. Several times Henry questioned the validity of even approximate conclusions about age–sex structure derived from tombstone inscriptions (e.g., Henry 1957), but his most persuasive argument was to show how deceptive such data are even in a modern Western country. Of 1,253 tombstones in a Lyon cemetery counted and classified in the year 1834, most for persons who had died over the previous two decades, 54 percent were for males and 46 percent for females—an unlikely distribution. In France during the years 1831–1835, the percentage of males that died under age 15 was 43.7 (compared with 10.6 of the cemetery sample), and of females it was 39.4 (compared with 8.2). The difference was not a demographic aberration of this particular city; it was based rather on customs governing who should be buried with a tombstone and who not (Henry 1959).

Within the social class or classes to which any set of data pertains, moreover, the unit often was not the individual but the family. A good portion of the information we have about late-medieval Europe, for example, is based on the so-called hearth taxes. In order to obtain the total population in any area, one must multiply the given figure by a number equivalent to the size of the family, including parents, children, and others living with them. What this index should be for various countries and periods is not known precisely (Mols 1954, vol. 2: 100–109; Laslett 1969, 1970; Nixon 1970; Herlihy 1972). A parallel problem is how to judge the population of a community, given certain other data about it. It is often possible from archeological research (in recent years sometimes

Two well preserved Roman tombstones of the type from which demographic data are extracted. Note that the translations require a thorough knowledge not only of the language but also of the conventional abbreviations and usages (*Dr. Hilding Thylander, Stockholm*).

ABOVE: "Diis Manibus [to the ancestral spirit gods]. Albia Urbica erected [this tomb] to her very sweet stepson, Marcus Octavius Aerius, who lived 10 years, 7 months, and 19 days." Marble plaque, 41 × 35 cm., attached to the wall of a tomb in Isola Sacra, Italy; date uncertain.

BELOW: "Diis Manibus [to the ancestral spirit gods]. Ampliatus, slave of the emperors, has erected [this tomb] for Claudia Soteris, his wife, who well deserved it. She lived 19 years." Marble plaque, 24 × 35 cm., Isola Sacra, Italy; second half of the 2nd century, A.D.

supplemented by aerial surveys) to calculate rather exactly the area inside the walls of ancient or medieval cities, so that with a guess as to what their average density was one can estimate the number of their inhabitants.

Even within the same political unit there was seemingly little uniformity in any of the conditions surrounding the collection of statistics. Over such areas as the Roman empire or ancient China, tax or conscription laws, or the stringency with which they were enforced, or the care with which records were kept, certainly varied greatly from one time or locality to another. The number enumerated in the Roman census, for instance, increased abruptly from about 900,000 in 69 B.C. to over 4 million in 28 B.C. A jump by four and a half times in 40 years obviously did not reflect only a growth in population, but scholars are not agreed on whether it represented a rapid extension of citizenship, or the inclusion of females in the count, or what (Russell 1958: 48). Or, as an even more striking example, the supposed population of China increased by 78 million from 1911 to 1912 (Ho 1959: 79). The obvious reason for so great a discrepancy, one can assume, is the very large underenumeration reflected in the first figure, though this was generally accepted as substantially accurate until the new one was published.

In summary, the extant statistical data on the population of various preindustrial civilizations are almost all indirect, and require a good deal of interpretation. It is ordinarily necessary to estimate the total from the number of persons, or even of families, in one particular sector. Figures on such classes as minors and females, slaves and aliens, are usually especially poor. And when the data do relate to the total population (as on grain deliveries or the areas of cities), it is nevertheless difficult to use these statistics for demographic analyses.

The estimates by different scholars, made by manipulating these unsatisfactory sources in various ways, often have a wide range. For instance, of fourteen figures cited by Maier (1954) for the population of Rome at the time of Augustus (who reigned from 27 B.C. to A.D. 14), the low is 250,000 (Lot) and the high 1.6 million (Lugli). The population of the empire of the same period was estimated by Beloch at 50 to 60 million, by Lot at 60 to 65 million, by Stein at 70 million. The range for the 3rd century is even wider: Delbrück suggested 90 to 100 million; Bury, 70 million; and Stein, only 50 million (Boak 1955: 5–6). Nor is it possible to assume that, because of improvements in method or in the sources available, later estimates are necessarily better.

A much greater degree of consensus, however, is to be found on other questions. Although classical scholars differ concerning the population of the Roman empire at any one date, they all agree that it fell off by a considerable proportion from roughly the 3rd century on, that the density in Italy was higher than in most of the provinces, that slavery and plagues had an important influence on population trends, and so on. That is to say, one can examine the determinants, general trends, and possible effects of population growth in preindustrial civilizations even though certain data are approximate or lacking.

One should not, moreover, draw too sharp a distinction between protostatistical and statistical eras; the improvements came gradually, and even after they had been instituted at the center, the periphery of a country sometimes lagged several generations behind. The shift from ecclesiastical to civil authority in the maintenance of vital statistics, for instance, ultimately improved the coverage fundamentally; but the early data gathered by civil authorities were grossly defective (in the United States, as we have seen, until well into this century) and the earlier parish records, on the other hand, can be used with great profit. One of Henry's fundamental contributions was to extend such analyses to the general population, developing a technique for reconstituting all of a community's family genealogies from its parish records. It is laborious to extract the maximum information out of the usually incomplete and not wholly accurate lists, and the technique consists essentially in filling in gaps on the basis of the highest probabilities. In the community of Crulai, for instance, twelve persons appeared in the record (four through death, five through marriage, and three otherwise) without ever having had their births registered. Though these twelve constituted only 2.2 percent of the total population, they were neither ignored nor merely distributed proportionately among the whole. The twelve nonregistered births had taken place in ten families, and of the sixty-six registered births in those families, thirteen infants had died before their first birthday, nineteen others had died before getting married, fourteen had married, and the remaining twenty had incomplete records. "This distribution can be considered to represent that of the families in which the dates of some births are lacking" (Henry 1970: 14–15). Wrigley (1966b: chap. 4) adapted the methods of family reconstitution to the types of data found in England, and in an important paper Henry (1968) summarized how one verifies data in historical demography.

In sum, Hollingsworth (1969: 43–44) gives the following list of sources for historical demography, more or less in order of decreasing precision and usefulness: censuses, vital statistics, bills of mortality, such ecclesiastical records as parish registers, fiscal documents, military records, inventories of property, genealogies, wills, marriage settlements, eye-witness estimates, long-term price series, number and extent of towns, archeological remains, methods of agricultural economy, ecclesiastical and administrative geography, new buildings, colonization of new land, and skeletons and tombstone data. Most of the items near the top of the list are not available for the earlier period, of course, or are available only for limited areas. The data on which the discussion in the previous chapter was based, on the other hand, are typically near the bottom of the list. The step from prehistoric to historical demography, from archeological and paleontological remains to any kind of written records, was of fundamental importance.

THE GENESIS OF PREINDUSTRIAL CITIES

Whatever their other characteristics, the distinguishing mark of ancient civilizations—as the etymology of the word suggests—was the development of human settlements larger and more complex than in earlier epochs. Until agriculture and stock raising became efficient enough to provide a sizable surplus, every person had to devote himself to caring for his basic needs. In a food-gathering band, everyone is a food gatherer. And in the late neolithic period, when hunting had been supplemented by primitive agriculture, only metal working and magic were likely to be full-time specialties. The development of the first cities meant that the division of labor was extended beyond these few examples to become a basic principle of social structure. The distinction between a village and a town or city is not primarily one of size but one of function; a village is a focal point of agriculture, a city is complementary to rural life. The very existence of a city suggests that its inhabitants—though often only a small portion of them—live off the agricultural surplus and perform nonagricultural functions. Occupational differentiation is characteristic also within the urban sphere; there is no generalized urban "husbandry." Each urban dweller is a specialist and by this fact may also be more efficient. The urban populations in the Near East were the centers of a new level of culture and the site of a number of important inventions associated with bureaucracy (writing, accounting, censuses), religion (a solar calendar and, through astronomy, the beginnings of science), and to some degree technology (bronze and iron). These developments, and parallel ones in India and China, marked the threshold between primitive cultures and higher civilizations, and between prehistory and history.

The occupational specialization characteristic of town life was often incomplete, related to a continuing osmosis between the rural and urban worlds. In Mesopotamia, "many of the townspeople worked their own fields, and the life of all was regulated by . . . the succession of the seasons" (Frankfort 1956: 62). In West Africa during precolonial times nearly all the Yoruba engaged in some agriculture, and it has been estimated that many of the inhabitants of the Aztec capital did the same (Trigger 1972). In 14th-century England, as still another instance, many town dwellers cultivated their own plots just outside the walls and grazed cattle or sheep on the common pasture.

In 1388 it was laid down by Parliamentary Statute that in harvest time journeymen and apprentices should be called on to lay aside their crafts and should be compelled "to cut, gather, and bring in the corn." . . . Even London was no exception to the rule of a half-rustic life. . . . No Englishman then was ignorant of all country things, as the great majority of Englishmen are today [Trevelyan 1942: 28].

Yet in an age when literacy, wealth, and political power were largely concentrated in cities, the distance along these dimensions between their upper classes and the rural mass was greater than in any developed nation today.

Archeologists generally agree that cities were first established during the fourth milennium B.C. in Mesopotamia and then Egypt, and that subsequently they appeared—whether by diffusion or independent invention is not always clear —during the third millennium in the Indus valley, the second in China, and the first in the Andes. In every case initial urban growth was a slow process, seemingly the synthesis of juxtaposed subenvironments that could be exploited symbioti-cally (Braidwood and Willey 1962; Kraeling and Adams 1960). The city's most elementary function was to furnish a haven, a place of protection. The English word *town*, like the Russian equivalent *gorod* (cf. Leningrad, for example), originally meant "enclosure"; the German *Burg* (related to the French *bourgeois* and the English *burgher* and *borough* and hundreds of place names—Hamburg, Pittsburgh, etc.) means "fortress." In medieval Europe one important criterion of a city, a feature that distinguished it from a village, was that it had a wall surrounding it. It was, in the common phrase, a "walled city."

A second important reason for establishing an urban center was to provide a nucleus to the religious communicants. "The temple community, . . . this urban form of political organization, . . . is a man-made institution overriding the natural and primordial division of society into families and clans. It asserts that habitat, not kinship, determines one's affinities" (Frankfort 1956: 76–77). Fustel (1956) developed essentially the same theme with respect to the cities of ancient Greece and Rome, and Wheatley (1967), in a provocative and stimulating essay, generalized it to the origins of urban settlements in both the Old World and the New. These were essentially ceremonial centers, "instruments for the creation of political, social, economic, and, above all, sacred space at the same time as they were symbols of cosmic, social, and moral order." With this limited function, the town needed to accommodate only a corps of priests and resident craftsmen, and during most of the year, in the interim between seasonal festivals, it would be nearly empty.

For an era when religion was but weakly separated from nascent forms of the state, however, the distinction between a ceremonial and an administrative center is often artificial. For example, in Uruk, an ancient city on the Mesopotamian plain, the head of the temple community seems also to have been the secular lord, taking a central role in both cult and military activities. The priestly office was a politico-religious one, designed to direct economic management in part through propitiation of the gods. The word *sanga* on the Uruk tables is some-times translated as "priest," sometimes as "accountant." This union of what we see as two institutions was completed when the king made a successful claim to personal divinity (Adams 1966: chap. 4). Once such states attained the power associated with a developed institutional structure, they typically conquered neighboring peoples, establishing new administrative centers from which their control could be exercised. The rise and decline of urbanization in the Uruk-Warka region over seven millennia are summarized in Figure 11-1. The con-comitant changes in the polity and economy, fairly well substantiated for this well researched area, are plausible also for many other early urban sites.

This interpretation of the first cities as spiritual–managerial centers, which seems to be the dominant one today, contrasts with an emphasis on material factors. What Childe (1951: 116) termed "the urban revolution," for instance, was a shift "from self-sufficing food production to an economy based on special-ized manufacture and external trade." Indeed, all elements of communal life

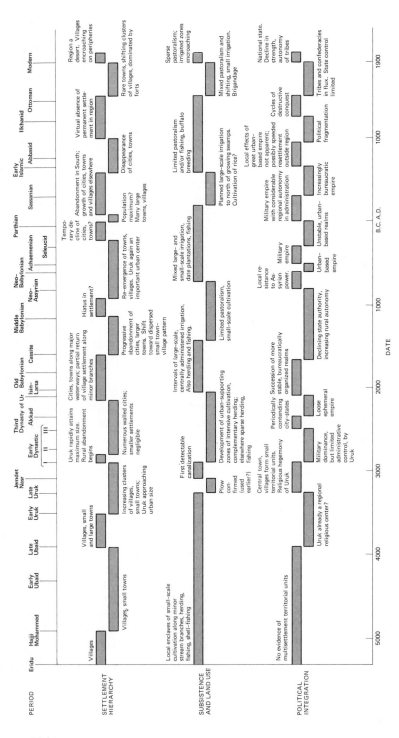

Figure 11-1. Seven Millennia of Social-Political Change in the Uruk Countryside, Modern Mesopotamia.

Note: The periods listed at the top begin at the line directly under their names and continue to the next line.

SOURCE: Robert McC. Adams and Hans J. Nissen, *The Uruk Countryside: The Natural Setting of Urban Societies* (Chicago: University of Chicago Press, 1972), End paper. © 1972 by The University of Chicago Press. Used by permission.

underwent a basic transformation, and the question is which came first and thus could indeed be the causal factor. "During the phase of active generation of temple cities," according to Wheatley (1967), "technology appears, on present evidence, to have almost invariably remained more or less static." Childe's neo-Marxist position is reminiscent of Marx's own dogma that religion, a part of the "superstructure," is wholly derivative from the material base, as contrasted with Max Weber's thesis that "the Protestant ethic" both was prior in time and helped bring about the industrial revolution.

According to Wittfogel (1957), the characteristics of ancient urban society and particularly of its administration derived mainly not from the material base as a whole but from a single technical innovation. He divides agriculture into two types, that based on rain and that on large-scale irrigation. Rain agriculture, the usual form in all of the Western world, led to a minimum of social cohesion among a dispersed peasantry. In the great civilizations of the ancient Near East, India, China, and portions of pre-Columbian America, all based on vast irrigation and flood-control works, a leading stratum had to keep a record of available manpower, recruit it when necessary, assign it to designated jobs—both the direct construction or maintenance of dams and channels and such subsidiary tasks as assembling building materials or food for the workers. In such a **hydraulic civilization**, as Wittfogel terms it, those whose function it was to administer the complex task of maintaining the works were uniquely prepared to wield supreme political power. Once the institutional framework of bureaucratic control over the whole of the society was established for one purpose, it spread from this to military operations; a people based on rain agriculture could flee before a stronger foe, but one that had spent generations in building irrigation works had to try to defend them. Hydraulic civilizations built Great Walls and other massive defenses, as well as highways and postal systems that provided, given the technical level, excellent communications across enormous empires. Corvée labor was also used to construct grandiose monuments—palaces, temples, tombs—to the glorification of the despotic ruler.

In Wittfogel's analysis, the keynote of West European feudalism is decentralization, the diffusion of power in many competing hands. The king, the titular head of the state, had a contractual relation with his vassals, who owed him so much allegiance but no more and were jealous of their own prerogatives. In certain periods the church was more powerful than the emperor, and in late feudalism the free cities were in some respects more powerful than either. The keynote of hydraulic civilizations, on the other hand, is centralization. All power derives from the bureaucratic apparatus, and in most cases from the person of the despot. His "vassals" owe him total and immediate obedience, and symbolize their utter degradation by such rituals as prostrating themselves before him. Religion is not an antagonistic or even an independent force, but is assimilated as the state's main ideology; in the most developed form the head of the state is also the god to be worshipped. In short, the state is stronger than the society of Oriental despotism. "The hydraulic state is a genuinely managerial state, . . . [which] prevents the nongovernmental forces of society from crystallizing into independent bodies strong enough to counterbalance and control the political machine" (ibid.: 49).

In order to appraise Wittfogel's thesis, it is useful to divide it into two parts. His assertion that irrigation systems were the major cause of "Oriental despotism" has been fairly generally rejected (for a trenchant summary of criticisms, see Wheatley 1971: 289–297); one might better say that, in certain places and periods, the development of an agriculture based on large-scale control of the water supply aggravated the already existent tendency toward the centralization of all governmental functions. But the differentiation between two types of civilization that Wittfogel made has much more validity. The distinction was sharper in the analysis offered by Max Weber, for whom "an urban 'community,' in the full meaning of the word, appears as a general phenomenon only in the Occident":

> To constitute a full urban community a settlement must display a relative predominance of trade-commercial relations, with the settlement as a whole displaying the following features: (1) fortification; (2) a market; (3) a court of its own and at least partially autonomous law; (4) a related form of association; and (5) at least partial autonomy and [an administration by authorities that the burghers help to elect] [Weber 1958: 80–81; cf. Weber 1950: chap. 23].

In Murvar's slight modification of the typology (1966), Weber's differentiation between the Occidental and the Oriental city is summarized as follows: Unlike its Western counterpart, the Oriental city was juridically indistinguishable from the village (except that it might be the residence of the ruler or the site of a local administrator) in that it had no fiscal or political autonomy. Unlike even absolute monarchs of the West, the Oriental ruler had power approximating totality, often with a monopoly of military, economic, religious, and political control in the hands of one god-king; and since the sole function of the merchants and artisans who lived in an Oriental city was to serve the officialdom, they were in any case closely tied to its interests. The principle of residence, the key to urban autonomy in the West, never superseded that of kinship in determining the social organization of the Oriental city. Only Western cities established their own military forces, "a brotherhood in arms for mutual aid and protection," so that eventually no Western ruler was able to overcome all of the many interdependent urban powers. The crucial difference is that "the Oriental city was unable to create or foster [the] conditions necessary for the growth of the bourgeoisie."

One can develop the differentiation further by following Pirenne's analysis of the cities of medieval and early-modern Europe, which he divided into two types. The function of the first, the center of a duchy or a diocese, was purely administrative; it was the residence of a political or religious official, together with a small class of servants and craftsmen. If the town had a market, this was only to distribute local produce, a task that required no special urban class to carry it out. As the new urban function of long-distance trade began to develop, however, a distinction arose between "burghers" (who lived in the "new burg," or mercantile quarter) and the "castellani" or "castrenses" (who lived in the "old burg," or administrative center). Merely by plying their trade, the merchants gradually evolved the elements of bourgeois society. "From a simple social group given over to the carrying on of commerce and industry, [the middle class] was transformed into a legal group, recognized as such by the princely power. . . . Courts whose members [were] recruited from among the burghers were able to render them a justice adequate to their desires and conforming to their aspirations" (Pirenne 1956: 82–83). Inside the walls of the cities, whatever their differences in wealth, all men eventually were of equal civil status. A serf who fled to a city and lived there for a year and a day could not be ejected without a court trial; in the words of the German proverb, *Die Stadtluft macht frei*—the air of the city makes one free. The middle class were not consciously missionaries, but by their independent existence they challenged, and gradually eroded, the hierarchical social structure of feudalism. It was in this sense that "the" city was restricted to the Occident.

It is instructive to compare the parallel development in several civilizations other than the Western Europe that Pirenne analyzed. Islam, as another example, "was destined from the beginning to a predominantly urban history" (Benet 1963). For Mohammed, the clearest sign that the desert tribes had accepted the new religion was their settlement in towns. (*Hegira*, literally "flight," denotes of course the Prophet's journey to Medina, but today Arab sociologists use it also to mean in-migration to cities, with overtones of spiritual improvement.) The Bedouin nomad was not regarded as trustworthy; according to the Koran (9:98), he is strong "in unbelief and in hypocrisy and more apt not to know the limits of what Allah hath [proclaimed through] His messenger." As Islamic tradition developed, to return to the tribe from the city came to be considered a kind of apostasy. Wherever the conquering Arabs went, thus, they built new cities (Benet lists several dozen). For "only in a city, that is, a settlement harboring a central mosque fit for the Friday service and a market (and preferably a public bath), can all the requirements of the faith be properly fulfilled" (Grunebaum 1954: 173). But those Islamic centers that did not acculturate to Western civilization often disappeared in a generation or two; "the feeble cities needed the sap of the strong tribes." During their sometimes brief life, moreover, cities had no "community" institutions in Weber's meaning. On the contrary, "the war of village against village and of quarter against quarter is eternal in the history of the oasis" (Benet 1963). The influence of such cities on Islamic society was to civilize in the sense of spreading the faith, but certainly not to secularize. In the light of Western norms, the result often seems to be self-contradictory. In some respects, for instance, Mohammed raised the status of women from the general Levantine level (they were given free disposal of their property and could inherit with fewer encumbrances), but it was also the Islamic city that enforced the veil, which in Mohammed's day had apparently been limited to Meccan ladies of status (Grunebaum 1954: 174).

The contrast with classical China is especially pertinent in specifying the distinctive characteristics of medieval Europe. One fundamental difference, as we have noted, is that the Oriental despot was given absolute and unlimited obeisance, while the feudal lord was due only as much homage as was stipulated in the relation between him and his vassal. "A strongly contractual basis is, in my opinion, essential to the feudal condition" (Wheatley 1971: 201, in this particular echoing one of Wittfogel's principal arguments). Around 500 B.C. the unified state of China began to break up, and during the following several centuries of general strife there developed what one might term, by an analogy with late-medieval European history, nascent national states. In the course of the wars, much land was abandoned by its noble owners and often taken over by former serfs. Cities grew both in number and in total population, and as in Europe at a later date they were of two types: "the rectangular, planned city of the Chou conquerors, a seat of administration; and the irregularly shaped city which grew out of a marketplace and became only later an administrative center." The considerable independence of the latter is suggested by the fact that some of them issued their own currency. Up to the 18th century, China's long-distance trade was as great as Europe's or greater. "An observer to whom the later Chinese history was not known," Eberhard (1960: 51–56) remarks, "could have predicted the eventual development of a capitalistic society out of the apparent tendencies." The evolution of the merchant class, however, was crucially different. Merchants took over the task of collecting state taxes and thus became provincial officials, tied to the provincial (or, later, central) administrative class, and they invested their surplus money in land. In short, instead of becoming a bourgeoisie in the Western sense, the Chinese merchants contributed to the evolution of the gentry. The Chinese city, thus, remained "the seat of the administration, . . . the home of officials," parallel with the "old burg." There were no city charter, no municipal law, no "concept of the city as an independent unit" (Eberhard 1956).

THE POPULATION OF PREINDUSTRIAL CITIES

In sum, there were important political and cultural differences between the free cities of Europe and the administrative centers of the Orient, but in other respects the cities in all these societies were similar. The urban population was everywhere small, in two senses: the proportion living in towns never was more than a few percent of the total, and the size of even the large towns was modest by today's standards. The famous Ur had only about 25,000 inhabitants, Uruk (or Erech) about the same. Much later, around 1600 B.C., Thebes at the height of its splendor as Egypt's capital may have had as many as 225,000 by a liberal estimate (Davis 1955). Rome was certainly the largest city of antiquity. The exact number of its inhabitants, as we have seen, is not known. After a careful consideration of the evidence, Russell (1958: 63–68) has suggested 350,000 as the probable maximum in the 1st century A.D., equivalent to a density of about 250 persons per hectare, which would seem rather high for a city with many open squares and public buildings. From this figure, Rome declined to about half by the middle of the 4th century. Of the Holy Roman Empire's approximately 3,000 "cities" (in the sense of walled enclosures with charters) at the end of the Middle Ages, 2,800 had populations ranging between 100 and 1,000 (Dickinson 1951: 290). And the others also were not large. Table 11-1 summarizes the more detailed data that Russell has compiled from a variety of sources. All the cities with an estimated population of 30,000 or more are included, together with a few others that might be of interest—London, with 18,000 in the 11th century; or Nuremberg, whose medieval aspect has survived in part today, with only 23,000 in the 15th century. Even if we grant that these are rough approximations and in an extravagant gesture double the number of inhabitants, these medieval towns would still be classified today as small.

The city of preindustrial civilizations was different from its modern counterpart also in its occupational structure. The various handicrafts were typically grouped together in, for example, a "street of the goldsmiths," and the in-group solidarity of such neighborhoods was strengthened by the guild, which closely regulated the conditions of work. Generally membership in a guild was a prerequisite to the practice of almost any urban occupation, and apprentices were ordinarily chosen on the basis of kinship rather than universalist standards. Not

Table 11-1.   Population Estimates of Some Large Medieval European Cities

City	Date of Estimate	Population	Persons per Hectare
London	{1086	18,000	108
	{1377	35,000	121
Milan	13th century	52,000	166
Naples	1278	27,000	133
Paris	1292	59,000	157
Padua	1320	41,000	117
Bruges	1340	25,000	58
Ghent	1356	60,000	93
Venice	1363	78,000	240
Bologna	1371	32,000	76
Florence	{1381	55,000	107
	{1424	37,000	73
Nuremberg	1449	23,000	165
Bourges	1487	32,000	289
Genoa	early 16th century	38,000	129
Barcelona	1514	31,000	118
Rome	1526	55,000	40

SOURCE: J. C. Russell, "Late Ancient and Medieval Population," *Transactions of the American Philosophical Society*, **48**, Part 3 (1958), Tables 63, 64, 65.

only the family but also religion (each guild had its patron saint) and even magic were interwoven with economic activities. In short, very few of what the modern Western world sees as "the" urban characteristics, as specified, for instance, in Louis Wirth's well known article (see p. 475), apply to preindustrial cities.

The town also was a structural element of its region, and its "hinterland" was also transformed through urban growth. "It required the city to bring [the peasant] into existence. There were no peasants before the first cities. And those surviving primitive people who do not live in terms of the city are not peasants" (Redfield 1953: 31). In the simpler economy of preindustrial societies, setting the boundaries of regions may be easier than in today's more complicated world, but few general principles held everywhere. Islands usually constituted more or less independent entities, but the coast of medieval Sicily was more closely bound to southern Italy than to the island's interior. River basins were natural areas, as well as such other geographical features as plains or plateaus. But any such ecological factors could be canceled by historical accident.

Understanding the structure of the region from a demographic standpoint requires a study of the *size* of cities, of the *spacing* of cities in respect of each other and within the population of the region, and of the *functioning* of demographic factors such as migration and differing economic groups within the cities and the region [Russell 1972: 18].

Cities grew in large part by in-migration from the countryside since the very beginning of urban growth. The differentiation between the two sectors of any population was reinforced by this pattern, for it was probably the pre-urban types, then as later, who moved to the town, leaving behind a more purely rural remnant.

FAMILY AND FERTILITY

Preindustrial civilizations were urban in the sense that a new type and level of culture flourished in their cities, but the large majority of the people were still rural. The depopulation of the Roman empire, for instance, cannot reasonably be ascribed to merely the decline of fertility in the city of Rome, although the implicit assumption has sometimes been made that the urban norms, about which we know much more, were general throughout the society. It is perhaps more accurate, though also arbitrary, to posit an ideal type, the "familistic" society, or one in which the family has a range of functions far wider than those associated with the domestic unit Americans are familiar with. In societies that lack other facilities, each person depends on his kin for services rendered in the modern West by employment agencies, banks, schools, trade unions, and so on. And since the family is important in so many contexts, one can hypothesize that the pressure is great to produce a numerous progeny. Yet the fertility was markedly different in various preindustrial societies, all of which can be classified as familistic to one degree or another.

Ancient Greece and Rome

The principal evidence on the age at marriage and, with estimates of the expectation of life from various ages, on the average duration of marriages comes from inscriptions on tombstones set up by spouses. One study of Roman epitaphs suggests that the average ages at marriage were 18 for females and 26 for males (Harkness 1896). If these figures could be taken as representative, and if the life expectation from birth was 25 years, this would indicate a mean duration of first marriages of 18 years (Hopkins 1965). According to a later paper by the same author, however, the median age at marriage of girls "of the respectable classes" was 15 years or less, and the median and average ages at death of Roman women were 26 and 29.6 ($N = 82$). Thus, the median and average lengths of married life were roughly between 10 and 14.6 years. "It seems clear that the length of marriage was recorded if it was something to be proud of"—so that the entire set of data is systematically unrepresentative (Hopkins 1966).

Although under Roman law the purpose of marriage was procreation, which public officials praised as a civic duty, fertility was certainly far below what these figures would imply in a population with no controls. That some means of controlling fertility were used does not tell us which ones. In many of the ancient Greek city-states, infanticide had not only been permitted but under some conditions prescribed; in Rome it was limited by various legal restrictions and finally, in the 4th century A.D., made a capital offense. The increasing stringency of the prohibition itself suggests that the practice was not exceptional, and the high incidence probably continued during the following centuries. Out of a list of twenty-two ancient medical writers (all whose works are extant and not on irrelevant topics), eleven discussed contraceptive methods, and fifteen methods of inducing abortion, apart from the fact that in some texts the two were confused (Hopkins 1965). It is reasonable to suppose that all physicians could obtain the current knowledge on birth control, only a portion of which was efficacious. Aëtios, whose passage on contraception is relatively rational and complete, also recommended magic charms: "Wear the liver of a cat in a tube on the left foot, . . . or else wear part of the womb of a lioness in a tube of ivory. This is very effective." Even Soranus, whose work has been depicted as "the most brilliant and original account of contraceptive techniques written prior to the 19th century" (Himes 1936: 88–92), passed on the standard combination of superstition and effective practice. On the one hand, he recommended that the woman hold her breath during the sexual act or sneeze and drink something cold immediately after it; on the other hand, he prescribed spermicides that physicians were still advocating in the 1930s (Hopkins 1965). Several analysts assert that the most common method was *coitus interruptus*, though one cannot base this supposition on classical references.

It has been surmised that slavery constituted one important factor in reducing Rome's fertility (Landry 1936; cf. Noonan 1965: 20–21). The slaves themselves had few offspring, first of all because their masters wanted it that way. So long as it was possible, their owners found it more advantageous to purchase adults than to pay for the raising of children. After the price went up (in Rome about the time of Augustus), apparently the birth rate still remained low, partly because the masters did not perceive their interest immediately, partly because the slaves themselves often wanted even less to reproduce. The slave population, thus, could be maintained only by continuous recruitment; when this lagged, it moved toward extinction. The number of slaves is unknown, but estimates for both Greece and Rome run as high as one-third of the free population—a large enough proportion to have a considerable effect on reproductive trends. The fertility of freed men was also very low. In Rome manumission was generally based on the condition that the slaves promised never to marry, for if they died without legitimate issue, their property reverted to their former owner. Slavery may also have been a significant depressant on the birth rate of the free population. Among the upper classes a man who owned a female was not induced to marry by either his sexual drive or his need for someone to care for his household.[1] Casual unions with slaves were generally infertile, as were, of course, the frequent homosexual ones in Greece.

One indication that the family size of Rome was effectively cut is the pronatalist sentiment expressed by various writers and officials, particularly by Augustus, emperor at the beginning of the Christian era. Three famous laws— *Lex Julia de adulteriis coercendis, Lex Julia de maritandis ordinibus,* and *Lex Papia et Poppaea*—were intended to raise the family's prestige and thus to encourage marriage and reproduction. The unmarried and childless were penalized by various legal disabilities; fathers were given preferential treatment in the allocation of public offices; "matrons" (probably the mothers of three or more children) were given the right to wear distinctive clothes. These laws were repeatedly modified, but in one form or another they remained in effect for a considerable period, finally to be rescinded by Justinian in the middle of the 6th century. Landry (1934: 95) believed that they had a beneficial effect on family life and helped to raise the birth rate. Their influence, however, cannot have been great, for beginning in the 3rd century at the latest, the population of the empire declined. This was especially true of the center, from which there was a considerable migration to the periphery. "As every Roman citizen had much better opportunities of earning a living in the provinces, Italy was constantly drained of her best men, and the gaps were filled by slaves. When an abundant supply of slaves ceased to be available, Italy began to decay in her turn, for the process of emigration never stopped, as one land after another was opened up for settlement" (Rostovtzeff 1956, vol. 1: 375).

---

[1] According to the Greek historian Polybius (circa 140 B.C.), "the whole of Greece has been subject to a low birth rate and general decrease of the population," for men have fallen into "such a state of pretentiousness, avarice, and indolence that they did not wish to marry, or if they married to rear the children born to them, or at most as a rule but one or two of them" (Polybius, *The Histories,* vol. 4. London: Loeb Classical Library, 1927, Book 36, Para. 17.6–13).

The interrelation between population decline and the rise of Christianity has been analyzed in various ways. One hypothesis is that the depopulation during the late-ancient and early-medieval periods brought about an economic, social, and intellectual depression, the "Dark Ages," and thus a stronger interest in religion (Russell 1941). There may have been an influence also in the other direction. Although the Christian doctrine of the inestimable worth of every human soul, no matter how humble its vehicle, led the early Church to favor population growth, its opposition to sexuality *per se* blocked the development of an effective pronatalist policy. Church doctrine was too confused and too vacillating to become the sole ethical force even among all its own adherents (cf. Noonan 1965, *passim*). Even the injunctions against infanticide, which were certainly less ambivalent than rules on other sexual and family matters, became effective only when they were reinforced by foundling hospitals. The first of these were established in the early Middle Ages, but their number grew very slowly; "the strong sense always evinced in the Church of the enormity of unchastity probably rendered the ecclesiastics more cautious in this than in other forms of charity" (Lecky 1955, vol. 2: 33). As late as the 17th century, when St. Vincent de Paul established the order associated with his name, one impetus to his act was the continuing high incidence of infanticide.

The Joint Family

The societies of classical India and China were both based on the **joint family**, "a group of people who generally live under one roof, who eat food cooked at one hearth, who hold property in common, and who participate in common family worship and are related to each other as some particular type of kindred" (Irawati Karve, quoted in Madan 1963; cf. Lee 1953). The strength and resilience of this institution are so great that one can discuss it in an almost timeless perspective, exemplifying its characteristics indifferently with historical or contemporary data, except of course for the family in Communist China.

The adult sons of a joint family do not leave the ancestral home when they marry but bring their wives into it, so that three or more generations live under one roof as a social, religious, and economic unit. The property and the income from it, along with the earnings of all the family members, constitute a common fund out of which the needs of all are met. Everything is formally administered by the oldest male, the patriarch, to whom all others owe absolute obedience. The larger the joint family, the greater the patriarch's realm and honor: according to legend, the head of a family of nine generations who lived during the T'ang dynasty was visited and decorated by the emperor in person. The decision when and whom to marry does not rest with the two participants but with their elders; the Confucian classics define *marriage* as "a union between two persons of different families, the dual object of which is to serve the ancestors in the temple and to propagate the coming generation." The strength of the Chinese institution, thus, was based not only on its current structure but on its intergenerational continuity, with ancestor worship reaching into the past and emphasis on a numerous progeny into the future. Although this ideal of the Chinese family was realized only among the gentry, the more numerous peasantry seemingly also accepted it as their standard and strove to imitate the upper class to the degree that their poverty permitted (Lang 1946; Kulp 1925).

A joint household facilitates early marriage: adolescents can undertake such roles as parenthood while they are still socially immature, for they will not bear the main responsibility for caring for their children. In classical China marriage was typically entered at an early age; in India, by an aberration from the joint-family pattern, it was, and is, still earlier, often before puberty. The betrothal at the groom's house (the *shadi*) often takes place in early childhood or even infancy, and at puberty the bride returns to the groom's home and after a second ceremony (the *gauna*) the marriage is consummated. Marriage is virtually a universal state; in India in 1961 only one female in 200 was still single at the end of the fecund period.

It is true that India's earlier tradition was changed slightly by restrictive legislation. In 1860, sexual intercourse with a wife under 10 was prohibited; in 1904, the minimum age for females was raised to 12 years (though still, on the guardian's petition, it was 9 years); in the Sarda Act of 1929, the minimum ages at marriage were raised to 18 for boys and 14 for girls (the law resulted in a temporary *decline* in the mean age at marriage, for parents rushed their children to wed before the law went into effect); and in 1955, the minimum age for girls was again raised to 15 (Goode 1963: 234). According to the best study of the question, the average female age at marriage gradually rose from 12.77 years in 1891–1901 to 15.38 in 1941–51, or by an average of half a year per decade. The male age declined over the same period from 20.01 to 19.93 years. "On the whole the Sarda Act, which was enacted to restrict child marriages, seems to have some effect, at least among females. . . . Surprisingly enough, there seems to be a slight tendency towards increased child marriages among males" (Agarwala 1962: 229).

The effect of the increase in age at marriage on Indian fertility is not so simple as one would suppose. According to a sample survey of rural households near Banaras, total fertility was 730 per 1,000 females married at 14 years or less, and 680 for those married at 17 to 19 years. This is what one would expect: with a shorter period of exposure there are fewer births. However, one must consider also the factor of adolescent subfecundity: with the rise in the age at marriage, the interval to the first birth decreased appreciably. The decline in fertility from the loss of the early reproductive period, thus, was far less than one would suppose from a calculation of the years of nonexposure (Rele 1962; cf. Collver 1963).

Western sociologists often explain the rise in the marriage age, such as it was, by industrialization and urbanization, which supposedly bring about a gradual deterioration of the joint family and thus an increased age at marriage (e.g., Goode 1963; Ross 1961). However, with size of household as an index, the incidence of joint families did not decline, and may even have risen, from 1911 to 1951 (Orenstein 1961; cf. Desai 1964). At least among one small sample, even the attitude toward living in joint families has become more favorable (K. M. Kapadia, cited in Orenstein 1961). Indeed, it is no longer certain that in contemporary India the family type influences fertility. According to two studies, the family was smaller, though not significantly so, in joint than in simple families (Pakrasi and Malakar 1967). Whether the pattern one would expect from family theory has been reversed is not yet settled, if only because of the loose definition of the two types, and in any case perhaps one can assume that the theory holds for historic India, before modernizing disturbances had become significant.

Western Europe

The marriage pattern of most of [Western] Europe as it existed for at least two centuries up to 1940 was, so far as we can tell, unique or almost unique in the world. ... The distinctive marks of the "European pattern" are (1) a high age at marriage and (2) a high proportion of people who never marry at all [Hajnal 1965].

When precisely this pattern began to develop is not known. The evidence from the medieval period is fragmentary, largely imprecise (in a literary reference to "late" marriages, what is the meaning of the key word?), and in any case contradictory. On the one hand, only about 4 percent of a sample of medieval London merchants remained bachelors; and one can surmise that the typical ages at marriage among this class were 20–24 for males and 13–14 for females (Thrupp 1962: chap. 5). On the other hand, we are told that the Middle Ages was "as familiar as our own day with the independent spinster" (Eileen Power, cited in Hajnal 1965). Perhaps the best evidence that the European pattern developed at an early date is etymological. The word *husband* derives from two words meaning "house" and "dwell," and its original meaning (still preserved in *husbandman* and *husbandry*) was a householder, a man who had a home. The Middle English word for an unmarried man was *anilepiman*. These two terms, one referring to the management of property and the other to marital status, gradually became associated as opposites, *anilepiman* coming to mean a man who had no living and therefore could not marry, and *husband*, a man who was able to care for a family and therefore could get (or, eventually, was) married (Homans 1941: 136-137).

Another line of argumentation relates to the family organization that developed to prevent the partition and repartition of family plots. In the **stem family** (sometimes given its French name of *famille souche*, from the usage of Frédéric LePlay, the first to analyze it at length), the entire property goes to a single heir, and his siblings either move away or do not marry. The typical household, thus, consists of a peasant, his wife and minor children, his unmarried brothers and sisters, and perhaps his aged father and mother. When this system was operative, farmhands were in some respects almost members of a farmer's family, sleeping and eating in and under no social pressure to marry early, or at all. An English report (1824) on the poor laws discussed the "old system" in the countryside by which men "did not marry until they were perhaps near 30 years of age, and until they had got a little money and a few goods about them" (Griffith 1926: 109). This type of three-generation household once prevailed in much of Europe and still exists in a number of rural areas. In the towns many occupations were governed by guilds, which generally inhibited marriage until after an apprentice had finished his training period and moved up to the next level.

According to the sparse data available, then, the age at marriage in Western Europe started to rise either in the Middle Ages (if we accept merely indicative evidence) or in any case well before the 18th century. In Venice, to take one striking example, the ages at marriage in 1701–84 fluctuated between 29.9 and 31.7 for males and between 28.0 and 29.8 for females (Daniele Beltrami, cited in Hajnal 1965). The one country where this extraordinary postponement of marriage survived is Ireland, and the more accurate and extensive data of this country can be used to analyze the demographic effect of "the European pattern" (see pp. 542–544).

MORTALITY

Age-specific death rates *per 1,000 deaths* in three regions of Roman Italy, as calculated by Beloch from tombstone inscriptions, are shown in Table 11-2.

Table 11-2. Age-Specific Deaths per 1,000 Deaths, Roman Italy, as Calculated from Epitaphs

Age Bracket	Male	Female	Total
0–15	315	252	289
16–30	331	428	370
31–45	171	169	170
46–60	81	71	76
Over 60	102	80	95

SOURCE: Julius Beloch, *Die Bevölkerung der griechisch-römischen Welt* (Leipzig: Duncker & Humblot, 1886), p. 48.

The small proportion for those aged 15 and under certainly reflects only the fact that tombstones were seldom erected for infants or young children. Note that for the relatively small number of minors represented, the sex ratio is 125, while for the major reproductive period it is 84. Childbirth apparently was dangerous to mothers, and by inference also to their children (cf. Russell 1958: Tables 3 and 4; Burn 1953). It is worth remarking also that in Beloch's more detailed table giving rates by single years of age, a very definite tendency is discernible to heap at ages ending in 5 and 0, exactly as in the returns from modern censuses. Even in so personal a datum as the inscription on one's tombstone, age was rounded off.

Median expectations of life as calculated by Beloch are given in Table 11-3. These figures have the same limitations, of course, as the "death rates" on which

Symbol of death with his scythe, depicted in mosaic on the floor of a Pompeiian villa. The motto reads KNOW THYSELF (*The Bettmann Archive, Inc.*).

they are based. In particular, it is impossible to calculate the expectation of life from birth, for data are too poor on the mortality of infants and young children. However, if the probability was that children of 10 would live only to their 20s, then the expectation of life from birth, which would take into account the certainly larger infant mortality, could not have been more than a bit over 20 years. In Figure 11-2, the two heavier lines indicate the percentages of males alive at the beginning of successive 5-year age intervals that survived the 5 years, according to two model life tables based on expectations of life from birth to 20 and 30 years, respectively. The sharp downward slopes at the left reflect the very high infant and child mortality, typical of all cultures that lack modern medicine and sanitation. The upward slope of the curves for four regions of the Roman empire, thus, is not the consequence of an aberrant pattern of mortality but of the inadequate statistics on early deaths.

Table 11-3. Median Expectations of Life, Roman Italy, as Calculated from Epitaphs

From Age	Males	Females
10	17–18	15–16
20	16–17	10–11
30	15–16	11–12
40	15–16	15–16
50	10–11	10–11
60	10–11	8

SOURCE: Julius Beloch, *Die Bevölkerung der griechisch-römischen Welt* (Leipzig: Duncker & Humblot, 1886), p. 51.

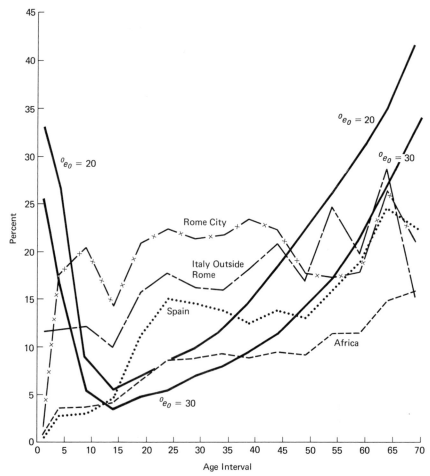

Figure 11-2. Percentage of Males Alive at the Beginning of Successive 5-Year Intervals That Survived the 5 Years, According to Data from Four Regions of the Roman Empire and Two Model Life Tables

SOURCE: Keith Hopkins, "On the Probable Age Structure of the Roman Population," *Population Studies*, **20** (1966), Figure 2.

This lack of data for the younger ages is an all but irremediable fault of mortality statistics of all preindustrial civilizations. That these data are also unrepresentative of the class structure is less of a fault, however, for it is reasonable to suppose that the mortality of especially favored groups was probably at the lowest level the particular culture could achieve. Among the members of all Europe's ruling houses, for example, mortality began to fall, especially among infants, long before the development of modern medicine. Infant deaths after the first week, which numbered 104 per 1,000 live births in 1500–99, rose to 171 in the following century. But during 1700–99 this index dropped to 106 and then more sharply to 45 in 1800–99 and 3 in 1900–35. Between 1500 and 1849 the average life expectancy increased by some 13.5 years for males and 12 years for females (Peller 1965). Data on the English royal house can be carried back farther than 1500. For its members born before 1348, the year that the Black Death struck England, the expectation of life at birth was generally slightly above 30 years. It fell during the plague period to 17, and then rose very slowly over the next 75 years again to something over 30. Life tables for a small sample of monks, another favored group, give about the same figures (Russell 1948: 178–193). Perhaps the most detailed of such studies is Hollingsworth's analysis (1957) of 1,908 legitimate offspring of British kings, queens, dukes, or duchesses, all who were born between 1330 and the end of 1954. The expectations of life at birth rose without a break from 24 years (male) and 33 years (female) in the 14th century to 55 years (male) and 70 years (female) in the early 20th century. A part of the consistently favored position of females can be explained by the males' deaths from violence.

More generally, the causes of high mortality cannot, of course, be specified in terms of the modern classification. We know very little about why people died in a "normal" year; but over a longer period a large proportion died as the consequence of famines, epidemics, or the breakdown of the social order (including war). Some overall data on these three types of catastrophe are available for the whole of the historic era.

Famine

Medieval Europe suffered from severe famines, such as that in 1315–17 (Lucas 1930), and these recurred well into the modern era. In the 1690s a succession of poor harvests created a subsistence crisis throughout most of Europe; in 1698 the death rates in two regions of Sweden rose to 90 and 160 per 1,000 population. The winter of 1708–09, long remembered in France as "*le grand hiver,*" brought to that country among several others intense misery and heightened mortality (Helleiner 1965). In the last great famine of the Western world, in Ireland in the 1840s, several hundred thousand persons died of starvation and the already large emigration was given a mighty stimulus; on the Continent a less disastrous failure of the potato crop intensified the destitution of the poor. Yet only occasionally did these recurrent food shortages develop into a true famine, and then typically only in certain regions or countries. However disastrous they might seem to a citizen of a 20th-century Western country, on the scale of world history Europe's food shortages have always been relatively puny.

The normal death rate of the great civilizations of Asia, on the contrary, "may be said to contain a constant famine factor." Between 108 B.C. and A.D. 1911, China withstood 1,828 famines, or nearly one per year in some of the provinces during these two millennia (Mallory 1926: 1). Most of them were over only a portion of the country; the worst were nationwide. But everywhere throughout China, every district experienced a famine at least several times during each normal lifetime. And even this record understates the probable catastrophic effects of crop failures, droughts, floods, and locusts and other pests, for the information in general official works "often fails to indicate the scope and severity of a famine." A good example is provided by the province of Hupei, for which Ho (1959: 228–229, 292–300) calculated year by year the number of counties affected by natural calamities (including also epidemics) from 1644 to 1911. Out of this period of 267 years, there were only 27 entirely free of disaster (including those for which the record is known to be incomplete). Droughts occurred in 92 of the years, floods in 190. In the average year slightly more than one-tenth of the province was hit.

One of the worst famines of modern China struck four northern provinces in 1877–78. Communications were so poor that almost a year passed before news of it reached the capital. Cannibalism was common, and local magistrates were ordered "to connive at the evasion of the laws prohibiting the sale of children, so as to enable parents to buy a few days' food." The dead were buried in what are still today called "ten-thousand-men holes." From 9 to 13 million, according to the estimate of the Foreign Relief Committee, perished from hunger, disease, or violence during these two years (ibid.: 231–232).

Of course, it is not possible to measure the mortality from Asiatic famines directly. The registration of deaths, never very accurate at best, breaks down completely during such a period. But one can estimate the mortality in India due to the famines during the 1890s, for example, by comparing the country's natural increase in this decade with that in the ones before and after it:

In the previous decade [the population of India] grew 9.4 percent, and in the following decade 6.1 percent. If the 1891–1901 decade had experienced the average rate of growth shown by these two decades, it would have grown by 7.8 percent instead of 1 percent. The difference is a matter of some 19 million persons, which may be taken as a rough estimate of loss due to famines. It should be borne in mind, however, that relief measures were functioning at this time and that this saved the lives of millions of persons who otherwise would have died [Davis 1951: 39].

This contrast between the famine-ridden civilizations of China and India and those of medieval and early-modern Europe, relatively free of this cause of death, cannot be explained by a difference in technical skill. If anything, the Chinese peasant was a better agriculturist than his Western counterpart. One reason for the difference is geographical: the uncertainty of rainfall in India is probably the biggest single factor influencing life there, and the same might be said of monsoon Asia in general. In both India and China, agriculture was based to a large extent on irrigation and flood-control works, which, as we have noted, probably contributed to the rise of Oriental despotism. The rapacious bureaucracy endemic in this type of society, as well as the routine banditry and civil war, made it difficult to store food against times of need. (For a first-hand account of the "political causes of famine" in China, see Mallory 1926: chap. 3.)

To this day the transportation system of either China or India is poor. Most famines are local, at least in origin. If food cannot be shipped in from other areas, however, the starving people leave their homes and steal food where they can, spreading the famine and often pestilence as they go. A final reason for the difference was probably the higher fertility in Asia. Although family size was controlled by means of *coitus interruptus*, abortion, and particularly infanticide, China and India certainly had a higher fertility than other preindustrial civilizations. Their populations therefore may have pressed more closely on the subsistence available to them.

Pestilence

With respect to diseases, however, the preindustrial civilizations were more or less on a par. We can illustrate their common characteristics with examples from ancient Egypt. In contrast to primitive medicine, in which the magical, the religious, and the empirico-rational are inextricably combined, in Egypt there was at least a partial segregation. In place of the single role of medicine man or shaman, three types of healer were distinguished—the physician, the priest of Sekhmet, and the sorcerer (Sigerist 1967: 267). The latter two combated the evil spirits that caused disease with incantations, amulets, manipulations, and various mixtures of strange ingredients. Often the sorcerer probably had better results than the physician, for "magician and priest were able to put the sick in a frame of mind in which the healing power of the organism could do its work under the best conditions" (ibid.: 280). The rational medicine of Egypt is expounded especially in Papyrus Ebers and Papyrus Edwin Smith, both of which date from the first half of the 16th century B.C. and summarize a much earlier lore. Papyrus Edwin Smith is a fragment on surgery; partly because of this subject matter, its recommended practices are almost entirely free of magic. The Ebers Papyrus is a complete medical compendium, which combines a magical element, a largely obsolete materia medica, and a wealth of information on related topics in a more or less rational perspective. Incantations, for instance, are recommended in only twelve types of cases, most of which were defined as hopeless.

Judged by our physiology and medicine, the doctors of Egypt as of other preindustrial civilizations did not know the cause of most ailments and usually had little success in curing them. As one would expect, the best information we have concerns the most devastating—the plague, malaria, cholera, and the other major epidemic diseases (Russell 1958: 35–45; Davis 1951: 42–61).

The plague appears in three forms—pneumonic, septicemic, and bubonic. A person infected with the first type, the least important of the three, is directly contagious. The other two are spread by a complex interaction among the bacillus, its host (the flea), and the flea's hosts (the rat and man). The bubonic plague was the most terrible of the epidemics of the ancient and medieval worlds. It struck in the first half of the 6th century and then again some 800 years later.

The path of the 14th-century epidemic, the famous Black Death, is shown in

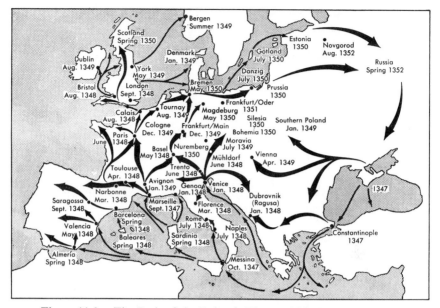

Figure 11-3. The Path of the Bubonic Plague, 14th-Century Europe

SOURCE: Ernst Kirsten, *Raum und Bevölkerung in der Weltgeschichte* (Würzburg: Ploetz, 1956). © 1956 by A. G. Ploetz-Verlag, Würzburg.

Figure 11-3. The first cases were in Constantinople in 1347; and the presumption is that the infection came from China, where it may have been endemic. By the fall of 1347 it was reported in Sicily. During the spring of 1348 it spread throughout the Mediterranean basin to Italy, France, and Spain, reaching Paris in June, London in September. From London it went west to Dublin (1349), north to York (1349) and Scotland (1350). From Italy and France it traveled to various German cities, reaching East Prussia in 1350 and Russia in the spring of 1352. In each place it struck in epidemic form several times—in England, for example, in 1348–50, 1360–61, 1369, and 1375—and continued endemic for some 80 years. The mortality throughout Europe was appalling. Contemporary figures reflect the variation from one place to another and are often exaggerated, but even the more conservative estimates of present-day scholars indicate an unparalleled loss of life. One analysis is by Russell (1948: 214–232; 1958: 40–45), who believes that most European nations sustained a depletion of 20 to 25 percent in the first attack of 1348–50, and of 40 percent by the end of the century.[2]

---

[2] Ohlin (1966) gives a detailed but excessively harsh criticism of Russell's calculations (cf. Russell and Thrupp 1966). According to the more judicious appraisal by Hollingsworth (1969: 58), Russell has been "as indefatigable as Mols in collecting material, . . . a pioneer more than anyone previously mentioned [in a long list of historical demographers] except Graunt." As a pioneer, he "must be expected to make mistakes. . . . Russell's chief virtue, in fact, is that he gives others something to refute. All his figures may be altered eventually, but the debt to him will remain."

Site of the English village of Tusmore, which was totally depopulated by the Black
Death. It lay to the northeast of Oxfordshire, some five miles north of Bicester. In
1279 it comprised twenty-three households, in 1355 none. The village's earthworks
appear on the photograph as ridges in a grass field; a low-lying area to the left,
which was dammed in modern times, is now a pool.

SOURCE: M. W. Beresford and J. K. S. St. Joseph, *Medieval England: An Aerial Survey*
(Cambridge, England: Cambridge University Press, 1958), Figure 43.

Urban death rates were probably higher than the average, because of the greater
contagion in congested areas, and the depopulation of cities was aggravated by
a mass exodus of their terror-stricken inhabitants. Since pregnant women seem
to have been particularly susceptible, the stupendous loss could not be quickly
repaired. "Only one disease, the plague, seems to have been lethal enough to
destroy population faster than humanity could restore it in the late ancient and
medieval period" (Davis 1951: 45).

The total mortality from other major diseases, however, was also great. It is
not possible in most cases even to suggest their rates of incidence, except to state
that they were high. There is a marked difference in the relative susceptibility of
various age groups. The plague strikes heaviest at the aged, which is presumably

A 17th-century woodcut of a physician during a London plague. The nosepiece filled with strong herbs supposedly protected him against the miasmas; the leather coat, leggings, and gloves were to prevent contagion (*The Bettmann Archive, Inc.*).

one reason why the best known personages of 14th-century Europe died in such an overwhelming proportion during the first attack of the Black Death. Tuberculosis, on the contrary, typically infects young children and kills at the beginning of their adult life, thus placing the burden of support on society with no economic or demographic return. The age differential for malaria is parallel to that for general mortality, very high in infancy, low in the teens, and gradually rising with adult ages.

The Breakdown of Social Order

That famine and pestilence ordinarily appear together suggests a direct relation between them, but apparently the usual reason is that both the supply of food and public health depend on—and can affect—the maintenance of social order (see p. 242). People who have witnessed hundreds of their neighbors die of hunger or disease do not themselves continue to carry out their usual pursuits in accordance with established norms. Often they flee from their homes, carrying the blight with them.

The interaction of these three major factors in mortality can be illustrated by some pages from the history of the late Roman empire. The process began as early as the reign of Trajan (A.D. 98–117), whose military successes, according to Rostovtzeff (1956, vol. 1: 358–359) brought "the empire to the verge of ruin."

The dread symptom of this decay was the depopulation of the peninsula and the concurrent decline of Italian agriculture. . . . Nerva endeavored to repopulate the country by reviving the plan of distributing land to poorer citizens. . . . Trajan forbade emigration from Italy and settled Roman veterans in the immediate vicinity of Rome; he forced senators to acquire land in the mother country; and he helped Italian landowners in general, both large and small, to improve their situation by supplying them with cheap credit.

Over the following several hundred years these remedies would be applied again and again, with less and less effect (Boak 1955: chap. 2). The capital's disorganization was reflected in a virtual civil war in the countryside. During a 50-year period in the 3rd century, there were twenty-seven official emperors in Rome and twice that many aspirants. Armies broke up into antagonistic units, which successively requisitioned (or stole—the distinction was not sharp) standing crops, food stores, and livestock, leaving impoverishment and starvation in their wake. At the end of the century, barbarians invaded Italy and also ravaged the countryside. The cultivators were mostly either slaves, who took the opportunity to escape, or *coloni* (tenant farmers), who also often fled from their holdings. The brigand bands that they formed in some cases constituted veritable armies, in Gaul large enough to menace cities. In the middle of the 3rd century Italy was infested by the plague, which was rapidly spread by the movement of troops and irregulars.

Efforts to repair the damage often increased it. Much land had gone out of cultivation, and Rome was deprived both of its produce and of taxes. In the 4th century a system evolved by which these abandoned plots were assigned to adjoining estates, so that their owners would both cultivate them and pay the land tax again. Rather than accept what was often an intolerable burden, many gave up their own properties. With land out of use and drainage systems neglected, breeding places for mosquitoes multiplied, and malaria became a greater threat to the population, killing many and sapping the strength of others. Early in the 4th century the *coloni*, who had been using their contractual right to leave their farms, were bound to the soil. They became serfs. Their status was gradually imposed also on the free agricultural workers, so that by the 5th century the prior distinction between them and *coloni* had all but disappeared.

The decisive break with the civilization of antiquity did not come from the German infiltration or the attendant circumstances that made it possible. The barbarians did not so much cause the downfall of Rome as fit into a process of gradual disintegration well under way before they became a significant factor. Constantine (306–337) had forced a treaty on the Visigoths, who agreed to supply soldiers to the Roman army in return for yearly payments, and over the following period the Roman army was gradually germanized. Assigned to frontier duty, German soldiers acquired land there and in many places became the dominant element of the population. After Ulfilas (or Wulfila, 311–381), a bishop of Arian convictions, translated the Bible into Gothic, a large number of Germans were converted to Christianity and thus even more subject to Roman influence than before. In the following period the distinction between "Roman" and "barbarian" became vaguer. The relation between the two cultures was not so often a confrontation on the field of battle as a divided loyalty of marginal men—for example, Alaric, the leader of the Visigoths who sacked Rome, a romanized German, a former officer in the Roman army, a Christian; or Stilicho, the *de facto* emperor at that time, a German by descent who had reached this high post through a successful army career.

The aim of the invaders was not to destroy the Roman empire but to occupy and enjoy it. By and large, what they preserved far exceeded what they destroyed or what they brought that was new. . . . [The civilization of the empire] outlived its authority. By the Church, by language, by the superiority of its institutions and law, it prevailed over the conquerors. . . . They barbarized it, but they did not consciously germanize it [Pirenne 1956: 5; cf. Bury 1928].

The decisive rupture came much later, in the 8th and 9th centuries, when Europe was unable to repel invasion. Moslems conquered Spain and threatened Constantinople; Norsemen plundered the coasts of the North Sea and of every river that emptied into it; the Hungarians swept in from Asia. "The devastation was so complete that, in many cases indeed, the population itself disappeared." Too weak to defend its periphery, Europe turned inward. "The Empire of Charlemagne . . . was essentially an inland one, . . . a State without foreign markets, living in a condition of almost complete isolation" (Pirenne 1956: 19, 21).

During most of the first millennium of the Christian era, then, the civilization of antiquity was in decline. It is not easy, and in this context not relevant, to distinguish such a general social disintegration, inevitably aggravated by combat, from formal warfare. Present-day Americans are likely to conceptualize war in terms of their own experience—a process in which young men are trained, sent overseas to fight, and welcomed home on their usually victorious return. War in the country where the battles are fought, particularly when a defeated army breaks up into small marauding bands, is much less clearly distinguished from civilian life.

Another striking example is the Taiping Rebellion of 1851–64, which Ho (1959: 236–246, 275) terms "the greatest civil war in world history." Indeed, as he writes, "in sheer brutality and destruction it has few peers." In the usual tactics against the rebels, not only were all prisoners summarily slaughtered but a scorched-earth policy was used to starve the armies into submission. In one area of some 6,000 square miles no trace of human habitation was left. The usual estimate of the number who died, 20 or 30 million, is too low in Ho's opinion. The devastation is merely suggested by the fact that in 1953 the population of three of the provinces most affected—Chekiang, Anhwei, and Kiangsi (see the map on p. 731)—was still 19.2 million, or 14 percent, under the estimated number in 1850.

POPULATION CYCLES

The main emphasis in demographic analysis is usually on population growth, and this is appropriate in either of two contexts. With respect to the term of

Homo sapiens on earth, the dominant trend has been an increase in numbers. And in the modern world, from roughly 1650 on, this increase has been at a rapid and usually accelerating rate. But a closer view of preindustrial civilizations reveals a striking exception to the rule: their populations typically grew and declined in a cyclical pattern.

The gradual development of classical antiquity as a unit, for example, was certainly accompanied by a substantial rise in population. The depopulation of the Roman empire as a whole probably began in the 3rd century A.D. and continued for several hundred years. The nadir was reached around 600, and Europe's population remained more or less static at this low level for almost 400 years. The epidemic of the bubonic plague with which this period was opened, possibly the most devastating in history, was followed by the Moslem, Norse, and Hungarian invasions (Russell 1958: chap. 8).

By 950 Europe had developed enough power to protect its borders, and the ensuing four centuries constitute the "medieval increase," as Russell (ibid.: chap. 9) terms it. From the middle of the 11th century to just before the Black Death, the population of England, for example, increased from 1.1 to 3.7 million, that of France (territory of 1328) from 4.0 to 13.5 million. Similarly, Bloch speaks authoritatively of "the two ages of feudalism," and one index of his differentiation is demographic rates (1961: 60–61, 69). Throughout Europe the decline that started with the outbreak of the plague in 1348 continued for about 80 years. From 1430 to the present day, the population of Europe has grown steadily, though at different rates at various times.

The evidence concerning Asia also suggests a cyclical pattern.

During the two thousand years that intervened between the ancient and the modern period India's population ... must have remained virtually stationary. ... In "normal" times, ... the customs governing fertility would provide a birth rate slightly higher than the usual death rate. This would build up a population surplus as a sort of demographic insurance against catastrophe. Inevitably, however, the catastrophe would come in the form of warfare, famine, or epidemic, and the increase of population would suddenly be wiped out [Davis 1951: 24].

In Ho's reconstruction of China's population history, there has been an irregular increase—from 65 million in 1400, to 150 million in 1600 and still in 1700, to 313 million in 1794, 430 million in 1850, and 583 million in 1953. Other scholars (e.g., Usher 1930; Taylor 1950), while agreeing that growth occurred over this period, have stressed more its irregularity.

What is the meaning of these long cycles? In what way are they associated with trends in economic and social life? Depopulation in the late Roman empire coincided with the disintegration of classical society, and the low point was during the Dark Ages; from 950 to 1350 marked a new rise in population and the evolution of medieval culture to its high point; the subsequent increase from 1430 on coincided with the Renaissance and beginning of modern Europe. There certainly is a correlation here. But in which direction is the causal relation? Is population size an effect of the economic level or, on the contrary, a cause of a more general development or decline? Or is the cause–effect relation both more variable and more complex than either of these alternatives? Let us consider these questions with respect to depopulation, which is atypical in human history and therefore the most interesting feature of preindustrial civilizations.

The decline of Europe's population in the second half of the 14th century was indubitably caused by the Black Death. The unreliable rainfall of monsoon Asia is indeed the greatest influence on the life of its inhabitants. That is to say, sometimes a single factor is so dominant that analysts have no hesitation in designating it as the cause of demographic processes. But even in such cases, it must be emphasized, these factors operate within a certain cultural–social–economic context. India's dependence on rainfall, for example, was mitigated by irrigation systems and increased by family-building norms that pushed the population always close to the subsistence available. And more often there is no such single factor on which all scholars agree but a multiplicity of causes, each emphasized by a different writer. In explaining the depopulation of the ancient world, for instance, Landry (1936) singled out the fall in fertility. Others have stressed the high mortality, sometimes even that from a single disease (e.g., Jones 1907). Still others have paid greatest attention to the gradual disintegration of the state's political control, and its eventual effect on everything from family life to agricultural production. Such separate factors can be identified in order to examine them more thoroughly, but the most reasonable hypothesis usually is that the decline in numbers was brought about not by any single one but by the interaction of all.

Nor is it any easier to analyze the effects of depopulation on the rest of society. The first to be noted is that on military prowess. While there is not a simple one-to-one relation, it is true that states of grossly different sizes can wield power more or less proportionate to their populations; and this was even more the case in the past, when there were not such great differences in military technology. As its title indicates, this is one principal theme of Boak's book, *Manpower Shortage and the Fall of the Roman Empire in the West* (1955: 115–116). In order to maintain the boundary of the empire safe against incursions, Rome—as we have seen—had to recruit an increasing number of Germans into its army. A vigorous and expanding Roman population could have absorbed this barbarian element, but, as it was, the Germans not only came to dominate the ranks and officer corps but were well represented among commanding generals. Even so, the manpower shortage continued, and in the next stage treaties were signed by which nominally dependent—though actually autonomous—German tribes were paid to defend the frontiers. And the proximate cause of the fall of the city of Rome was a struggle between the Latin and German parties in the empire. A loss of military power, moreover, can be cumulative. One reason that Europe was unable to defend its borders against Saracens, Norsemen, or Hungarians was its lack of manpower; and, vice versa, one reason that this low population level remained characteristic of the Dark Ages is the effects, both direct and indirect, of the continued raids that Europe had to withstand. Yet, it should be noted, Boak concludes this discussion as follows: "I should be the last person to claim that the fall of the West Roman Empire can be explained solely in terms of a problem of shortage of recruits for the army."

It is a reasonable hypothesis that the transition to the rapid growth of the modern era began with a change in this cyclical pattern. "It was the peaks rather than the plateau of mortality that were lowered. . . . The disappearance of plague above all, but also a very sensible mitigation of subsistence crises seem to have been chiefly responsible for the increase in life expectancy" (Helleiner 1965).

SUMMARY

The term *preindustrial civilizations* has been used to designate a class of societies based on agriculture and trade but with no industry, with an urban population and a high culture but few of the characteristics associated with urbanism in the modern West. These societies, particularly ancient Rome, medieval Europe, and classical China and India, have certain important elements in common.

It is important to distinguish, however, between the free cities of Europe and the administrative centers either there or elsewhere. The former gave rise to the new bourgeois class, which later helped develop Europe's technological advance and democratic society. The cities of other preindustrial civilizations, though associated in their earliest stage with stupendous innovations, did not become nuclei from which the same type of society could develop.

The population of preindustrial civilizations generally grew to a maximum and then declined sharply but temporarily as the consequence of famines, epidemics, and the breakdown of social order. This cyclical pattern was characteristic of all of them, but differences can be noted between Asia and ancient or medieval Europe. In the former, females generally married at or soon after puberty, and virtually all adults of both sexes were married, while in Europe postponement of marriage and nonmarriage of some adults cut the fertility to well below the physiological maximum. Because of this partial control of procreation, the European population did not press so closely on its means of subsistence, with the probable consequence that it was less often devastated by famine. In Asia, on the contrary, starvation seems to have been more important even than disease as a cause of high mortality.

During the downswing of a cycle the population, economy, and culture have often declined together, and this correlation has given rise to a variety of theories. In the most general terms, the cause of the periodic depopulation was that much larger numbers survived to maturity during favorable periods than could be maintained permanently. On the other hand, though the loss of population was often an important factor in the decline in political power, economy, and culture, it cannot generally be designated as "the" cause.

CITED REFERENCES AND
SUGGESTIONS FOR FURTHER READING

For several decades theories concerning the genesis of cities stressed sometimes the material preconditions to large settlements—e.g., Childe (1951), Davis (1955), Wittfogel (1957)—and sometimes rather the spiritual motivations for establishing them—e.g., Frankfort (1956), Fustel (1956). In their interpretation of new archeological and historical evidence, such recent authorities as Adams (1966) and Wheatley (1967) generally confirm the latter view.

The interpretation of the demographic data of preindustrial civilizations has moved beyond what traditional historians or such pioneers as Beloch (1886) accomplished. The most important innovators were Henry (1968, 1970), as well as Wrigley (1966b, 1969) and Hollingsworth (1969). Some good papers in the new spirit are included in the collections edited by Glass and Eversley (1965) and Revelle (1968).

The most difficult topic to analyze with the data available is probably fertility. Nag's monograph (1962) is a good summary of data and theories on nonindustrial societies (thus including primitive and underdeveloped, as well as preindustrial). Two of the better papers are by Hajnal (1965) and Wrigley (1966a). The best analyses of mortality pertain, as one would expect, to the most devastating losses of life in various cultures—e.g., Russell (1948), Davis (1951), and Ho (1959).

Chiao *et al.* (1938) offer a useful warning against those who accept population data too uncritically. Thrupp (1961) and Russell (1965) are good bibliographic essays.

ADAMS, ROBERT McC. 1966. *The Evolution of Urban Society: Early Mesopotamia and Prehispanic Mexico.* Chicago: Aldine.

———, and HANS J. NISSEN. 1972. *The Uruk Countryside: The Natural Setting of Urban Societies.* Chicago: University of Chicago Press.

*AGARWALA, S. N. 1962. *Age at Marriage in India.* Allahabad: Kitab Mahal.

BEAUCHAMP, PIERRE, HUBERT CHARBONNEAU, and YOLANDE LAVOIE. 1973. "Reconstitution automatique des familles par le programme 'Hochelaga,'" *Population*, **28**, 39–58.

BELOCH, JULIUS. 1886. *Die Bevölkerung der griechisch-römischen Welt.* Leipzig: Duncker & Humblot.

BENET, F. 1963. "The Ideology of Islamic Urbanization," *International Journal of Comparative Sociology*, **4**, 211–226.

BLOCH, MARC. 1961. *Feudal Society.* London: Routledge & Kegan Paul.

BOAK, ARTHUR E. R. 1955. *Manpower Shortage and the Fall of the Roman Empire in the West.* Ann Arbor: University of Michigan Press.

BRAIDWOOD, ROBERT J., and GORDON R. WILLEY, editors. 1962. *Courses Toward Urban Life: Archeological Considerations of Some Cultural Alternates.* Viking Fund Publications in Anthropology, no. 32. New York.

BRASS, W. 1953. "The Derivation of Fertility and Reproduction Rates from Restricted Data on Reproductive Histories," *Population Studies*, **7**, 137–166.

BURN, A. R. 1953. "Hic Breve Vivitur: A Study of the Expectation of Life in the Roman Empire," *Past and Present*, no. 4, pp. 2–31.

BURY, J. B. 1928. *The Invasion of Europe by the Barbarians.* London: Macmillan.

CHIAO, C. M., WARREN S. THOMPSON, and D. T. CHEN. 1938. *An Experiment in the*

Registration of Vital Statistics in China. Oxford, Ohio: Scripps Foundation for Research in Population Problems.

CHILDE, V. GORDON. 1951. *Man Makes Himself*. New York: New American Library, Mentor Books.

COALE, ANSLEY J., and PAUL DEMENY. 1966. *Regional Model Life Tables and Stable Populations*. Princeton, N.J.: Princeton University Press.

COLLVER, ANDREW. 1963. "The Family Cycle in India and the United States," *American Sociological Review*, **28**, 86–96.

*DAVIS, KINGSLEY. 1951. *The Population of India and Pakistan*. Princeton, N.J.: Princeton University Press.

―――. 1955. "The Origin and Growth of Urbanization in the World," *American Journal of Sociology*, **60**, 429–437.

DESAI, I. P. 1964. *Some Aspects of Family in Mahuva*. Bombay: Asia Publishing House.

DICKINSON, ROBERT E. 1951. *The West European City: A Geographical Interpretation*. London: Routledge & Kegan Paul.

*EBERHARD, WOLFRAM. 1956. "Data on the Structure of the Chinese City in the Preindustrial Period," *Economic Development and Cultural Change*, **4**, 253–268.

―――. 1960. *A History of China*. Berkeley: University of California Press.

FRANKFORT, HENRI. 1956. *The Birth of Civilization in the Near East*. Garden City, N.Y.: Doubleday-Anchor.

FUSTEL DE COULANGES, N. D. 1956. *The Ancient City: A Study of the Religion, Laws and Institutions of Greece and Rome*. Garden City, N.Y.: Doubleday-Anchor.

GLASS, D. V., and D. E. C. EVERSLEY, editors. 1965. *Population in History*. Chicago: Aldine.

GOMME, A. W. 1933. *The Population of Athens in the Fifth and Fourth Centuries B.C.* Oxford: Blackwell.

GOODE, WILLIAM J. 1963. *World Revolution and Family Patterns*. New York: Free Press.

GRIFFITH, G. TALBOT. 1927. *Population Problems of the Age of Malthus*. Cambridge, England: Cambridge University Press.

GRUNEBAUM, GUSTAVE E. VON. 1954. *Medieval Islam: A Study in Cultural Orientation*, 2nd ed. Chicago: University of Chicago Press.

*HAJNAL, J. 1965. "European Marriage Patterns in Perspective," in Glass and Eversley 1965.

HARKNESS, ALBERT GRANGER. 1896. "Age at Marriage and at Death in the Roman Empire," *Transactions of the American Philological Association*, **27**, 35–72.

*HELLEINER, K. F. 1965. "The Vital Revolution Reconsidered," in Glass and Eversley 1965.

HENRY, LOUIS. 1957. "La mortalité d'après les inscriptions funéraires," *Population*, **12**, 149–152.

―――. 1959. L'âge au décès d'après les inscriptions funéraires," *Population*, **14**, 327–329.

*―――. 1968. "The Verification of Data in Historical Demography," *Population Studies*, **22**, 61–81.

*―――. 1970. *Manuel de démographie historique*, 2nd ed. Paris: Librairie Droz.

HERLIHY, DAVID. 1972. "Mapping Households in Medieval Italy," *Catholic Historical Review*, **58**, 1–24.

HIMES, NORMAN E. 1936. *Medical History of Contraception.* Baltimore: Williams & Wilkins.

*HO PING-TI. 1959. *Studies on the Population of China, 1368–1953.* Cambridge, Mass.: Harvard University Press.

HOLLINGSWORTH, T. H. 1957. "A Demographic Study of the British Ducal Families," *Population Studies,* **11,** 4–26.

*———. 1969. *Historical Demography.* London: Hodder and Stoughton.

HOMANS, GEORGE CASPAR. 1941. *English Villagers of the Thirteenth Century.* Cambridge, Mass.: Harvard University Press.

HOPKINS, KEITH. 1965. "Contraception in the Roman Empire," *Comparative Studies in Society and History,* **8,** 124–151.

*———. 1966. "On the Probable Age Structure of the Roman Population," *Population Studies,* **20,** 245–264.

JONES, W. H. S. 1907. *Malaria: A Neglected Factor in the History of Greece and Rome.* Cambridge, England: Macmillan & Bowes.

KRAELING, CARL H., and ROBERT MCC. ADAMS, editors. 1960. *City Invincible: A Symposium on Urbanization and Cultural Development in the Ancient Near East.* Chicago: University of Chicago Press.

KULP, DANIEL HARRISON. 1925. *Country Life in South China: The Sociology of Familism.* New York: Teachers College, Columbia University.

LANDRY, ADOLPHE. 1934. *La révolution démographique: Etudes et essais sur les problèmes de la population.* Paris: Sirey.

———. 1936. "Quelques aperçus concernant la dépopulation dans l'antiquité gréco-romaine," *Revue Historique,* **61,** 1–33.

LANG, OLGA. 1946. *Chinese Family and Society.* New Haven, Conn.: Yale University Press.

LASLETT, PETER. 1969. "Size and Structure of the Household in England over Three Centuries," *Population Studies,* **23,** 199–223.

———. 1970. "The Decline of the Size of the Domestic Group in England," *Population Studies,* **24,** 449–454.

LECKY, W. E. H. 1955. *History of European Morals from Augustus to Charlemagne,* 2 vol. New York: Braziller.

LEE SHU-CHING. 1953. "China's Traditional Family, Its Characteristics and Disintegration," *American Sociological Review,* **18,** 272–280.

LUCAS, HENRY S. 1930. "The Great European Famine of 1315, 1316, and 1317," *Speculum,* **5,** 343–377.

MADAN, T. N. 1963. "The Joint Family: A Terminological Clarification," in John Magey, editor, *Family and Marriage.* Leiden: Brill.

MAIER, F. G. 1954. "Römische Bevölkerungsgeschichte und Inschriftenstatistik," *Historia,* **2,** 318–351.

MALLORY, WALTER H. 1926. *China: Land of Famine.* New York: American Geographical Society.

MOLS, ROGER. 1954–55. *Introduction à la démographie historique des villes d'Europe du XIVe au XVIIIe siècle,* 3 vol. Gembloux, Belgium: Duculot.

*MURVAR, VATRO. 1966. "Some Tentative Modifications of Weber's Typology: Occidental versus Oriental City," *Social Forces,* **14,** 381–389.

NAG, MONI. 1962. *Factors Affecting Human Fertility in Nonindustrial Societies: A Cross-Cultural Study.* New Haven, Conn.: Department of Anthropology, Yale University.

NIXON, J. W. 1970. "Size and Structure of the Household in England over Three Centuries: A Comment," *Population Studies*, **24**, 445–447.

NOONAN, JOHN T., JR. 1965. *Contraception: A History of Its Treatment by the Catholic Theologians and Canonists.* Cambridge, Mass.: Belknap–Harvard University Press.

OHLIN, GORAN. 1966. "No Safety in Numbers: Some Pitfalls of Historical Statistics," in Henry Rosovsky, editor, *Industrialization in Two Systems: Essays in Honor of Alexander Gerschenkron.* New York: Wiley.

ORENSTEIN, HENRY. 1961. "The Recent History of the Extended Family in India," *Social Problems*, **8**, 341–350.

PAKRASI, KANTI, and CHITTARANJAN MALAKAR. 1967. "The Relationship Between Family Type and Fertility," *Milbank Memorial Fund Quarterly*, **45**, 451–460.

PELLER, SIGISMUND. 1965. "Births and Deaths Among Europe's Ruling Families Since 1500," in Glass and Eversley 1965.

*PIRENNE, HENRI. 1956. *Medieval Cities: Their Origins and the Revival of Trade.* Garden City, N.Y.: Doubleday-Anchor.

POWER, EILEEN. 1954. *Medieval People.* Garden City, N.Y.: Doubleday-Anchor.

REDFIELD, ROBERT. 1953. *The Primitive World and Its Transformation.* Ithaca, N.Y.: Cornell University Press.

*RELE, J. R. 1962. "Some Aspects of Family and Fertility in India," *Population Studies*, **15**, 267–278.

REVELLE, ROGER, editor. 1968. "Historical Population Studies," *Daedalus*, **97**, no. 2, Special Issue.

ROSS, AILEEN D. 1961. *The Hindu Family in Its Urban Setting.* Toronto: University of Toronto Press.

ROSTOVTZEFF, M. 1956. *The Social and Economic History of the Roman Empire*, 2nd rev. ed. Oxford: Clarendon.

RUSSELL, J. C. 1941. "The Ecclesiastical Age: A Demographic Interpretation of the Period 200–900 A.D.," *Review of Religion*, **5**, 137–147.

*_____. 1948. *British Medieval Population.* Albuquerque: University of New Mexico Press.

*_____. 1958. "Late Ancient and Medieval Population," *Transactions of the American Philosophical Society*, **48**, Part 3.

_____. 1965. "Recent Advances in Medieval Demography," *Speculum*, **40**, 84–101.

_____. 1972. *Medieval Regions and Their Cities.* Bloomington: Indiana University Press.

_____, and SYLVIA THRUPP. 1966. "Effects of Pestilence and Plague, 1315–1385," *Comparative Studies in Society and History*, **8**, 464–483 (article by Russell, comments by Thrupp).

SIGERIST, HENRY E. 1967. *A History of Medicine*, vol. 1: *Primitive and Archaic Medicine.* New York: Galaxy–Oxford University Press.

SJOBERG, GIDEON. 1960. *The Preindustrial City: Past and Present.* New York: Free Press.

TAYLOR, K. W. 1950. "Some Aspects of Population History," *Canadian Journal of Economics and Political Science*, **16**, 301–313.

THRUPP, SYLVIA L. 1961. "The Creativity of Cities: A Review Article," *Comparative Studies in Society and History*, **4**, 53–64.

_____. 1962. *The Merchant Class of Medieval London (1300–1500).* Ann Arbor: University of Michigan Press.

TREVELYAN, G. M. 1942. *English Social History: A Survey of Six Centuries, Chaucer to Queen Victoria.* London: Longmans, Green.

*TRIGGER, BRUCE. 1972. "Determinants of Urban Growth in Pre-industrial Societies," Reprint 11. Andover, Mass.: Warner Modular Publications.

USHER, ABBOTT PAYSON. 1930. "The History of Population and Settlement in Eurasia," *Geographical Review,* **20,** 110–132.

*VANN, RICHARD T. 1969. "History and Demography," *History and Theory,* Special no. 9, pp. 64–78.

WEBER, MAX. 1950. *General Economic History.* New York: Free Press.

————. 1958. *The City.* New York: Free Press.

*WHEATLEY, PAUL. 1963. "What the Greatness of a City Is Said to Be: Reflections on Sjoberg's 'Preindustrial City,'" *Pacific Viewpoint,* **4,** 163–188.

*————. 1967. "Proleptic Observations on the Origins of Urbanism," in Robert W. Steel and Richard Lawton, editors, *Liverpool Essays in Geography: A Jubilee Collection.* London: Longmans.

————. 1971. *The Pivot of the Four Corners: A Preliminary Enquiry into Origins and Character of the Ancient Chinese City.* Chicago: Aldine.

WITTFOGEL, KARL A. 1957. *Oriental Despotism: A Comparative Study of Total Power.* New Haven, Conn.: Yale University Press.

*WRIGLEY, E. A. 1966a. "Family Limitation in Pre-Industrial England," *Economic History Review,* **19,** 82–109.

*————. 1969. *Population and History.* New York: McGraw-Hill.

————, editor. 1966b. *An Introduction to English Historical Demography.* New York: Basic Books.

POPULATION DURING
THE INDUSTRIAL REVOLUTION

12

The development of industrial societies must be a recurrent theme in any work on population. It has been discussed in the most general terms as the major factor in the demographic transition, and in this chapter we shall take a closer look at two places where the immediate effect of industrialization can conveniently be studied—England from roughly 1760 to 1840 and Japan from 1868 to World War I. The major emphasis will be on the former, where an industrial society first developed. But Japan, the only wholly non-Western country to become a major industrial power, affords an opportunity to check the conclusions derived from the sparse, often dubious, sometimes contradictory data concerning the interrelation of economic and demographic trends in Britain.

THE ENGLISH MODEL

The phrase *industrial revolution* does not define a precise period on which all agree; and its various elements, though overlapping and interacting, are also in some senses discrete. It is important, in any case, not to interpret the term too narrowly. Many present-day readers, misled by the label, would miss the point of the story about the schoolboy who began his theme on The Industrial Revolution with the sentence, "About 1760 a wave of gadgets swept over England." One must remember that while the metamorphosis was greater in manufacturing, it was also momentous in mining, transportation, and agriculture; and that while the significance of all the new machines and the technological processes together was tremendous, their impact was also "revolutionary" because they were accompanied by no less dramatic changes in the social structure. More important even than the building of factories was the creation of a factory *system*, with the gradual amalgamation of industrial entrepreneurs and urban workers into two new social classes.

Did industrialism improve urban living conditions? The controversy over this question between scholars who have come to be known as "optimists" and "pessimists" began during the industrial revolution itself and has continued intermittently ever since. In the 1830s Andrew Ure so admired the new order that he could compare factory children to "lively elves" at play, while Thomas Carlyle saw the world of the millhand as "a dingy prison-house" (Taylor 1960). In the

435

later decades of the century, as "the voice of the social reformer mingle[d] with that of the historian," the gloomier view came to be generally accepted, not only by liberals like Arnold Toynbee (*Lectures on the Industrial Revolution in England*, 1884), but especially by the considerable number of socialists who wrote about the period—in particular Sidney and Beatrice Webb, G. D. H. Cole, and J. L. and Barbara Hammond. Their prime inspiration was a book written in 1849 by Marx's friend and collaborator, Frederick Engels (1958); and, while they did not use the whole elaborate schema developed by Marx, they, like him, explained the social history of this period principally as an opposition between "exploiting" and "exploited" classes. In the 1920s there appeared a number of works which struck a less dismal note. Several of these—by Griffith, Buer, and George—were in large part about population movements, and the most important, J. H. Clapham's *Economic History of Modern Britain* (1926), attempted to show that real wages had risen during industrialization. Even apart from the point of view expressed, this recourse to new types of statistical data opened up the dispute again.

Analysts today interpret early English industrialization in terms of an ideology somewhere along the scale from Stalin to Hayek, but typically with a more careful attention to sources than some of their 19th-century predecessors. Unfortunately, many of the primary data are also biased; their ambiguity reflects, at least in part, an ambivalence among the lower classes themselves toward the great changes in their life. It would be impossible here to reconcile these several points of view; a whole volume would be needed merely to spell out in full the variety of interpretations deriving from different approaches or methods of analysis. Some of the polemical areas, however, are too important to pass over altogether. The following discussion will emphasize factors in the population growth, using the rather thin statistical base to the degree that this is possible, and relating the demographic changes inferentially to those taking place in England's institutional structure.

No characteristic of the population remained unchanged in this transformation of the economy and society. The movement of laborers, even though retarded by legal impediments, became greater than ever before. Growth in numbers, which had been relatively slow from the beginning of the modern period, accelerated. Authorities agree in designating this a natural increase: the overseas emigration was about balanced in this period by immigration from Ireland. However, whether it was the consequence of a rise in births or a fall in deaths—or, if both, in what proportion—has also been the subject of a learned discussion.

Sources of Information

In the second half of the 18th century, no one knew whether the population was increasing or decreasing. The debate on the social and demographic effects of industrialization was in full swing, with sometimes more vehemence than logic.

From the fact that fewer were dying, Richard Price, for instance, argued that there were fewer to die—that the population was decreasing (George 1925: 23). Even after the first censuses were taken, the dispute continued. For William Cobbett, thus, the returns of the 1821 census were "the biggest lie ever put in print, even in romance." The huge population increase they showed was fanciful: "the size of the churches alone was sufficient to convince any man of sound judgment that there had been a prodigious decrease!" (Fay 1947: 83).

At least in contrast to this confusion one can speak of an advance in knowledge. Late-medieval and early-modern England, excepting the period of the Black Death, had a population well under 4 million. At the end of the 17th century, according to the estimate that Gregory King made from hearth-tax returns, England and Wales had some 5 million inhabitants, and a century later there were more than 9 million. Virtually all of this increase, moreover, was in the second half of the 18th century, during the first decades of quickening industrialization. This growth is summarized in Table 12-1.

Table 12-1.   Estimated Population of England and Wales, 1086–1841

Date	Population (Millions)	Source of Information
1086	1.1	Domesday Book
1348	3.7	Poll tax times estimated family size
1377	2.2	Same, after Black Death
1545	3.2	Chantry lists
1695	4.8–5.5[a]	Gregory King's estimate
1801	9.2	First census (corrected)
1811	10.2	
1821	12.0	Census returns
1831	13.9	
1841	15.9	

[a] The larger figure is King's; Glass has suggested the range given, with the most probable figure above its midpoint.
SOURCES: J. C. Russell, *British Medieval Population* (Albuquerque: University of New Mexico Press, 1948); D. V. Glass, "Two Papers on Gregory King," in D. V. Glass and D. E. C. Eversley, editors, *Population in History* (Chicago: Aldine, 1965).

The details to fill in this picture, however, are another matter. The first English census was taken only in 1801, and both it and its immediate successors were less accurate and less complete than those taken later in the century. "There were fears that the census of 1801 was to be the basis for new taxes (the triple assessment and the income tax were fresh in people's minds) or for the levy of men for the unpopular and, at the same time, unsuccessful war" (Krause 1958). National vital statistics date from 1837. For much of the key period, from 1760 to 1840, we must depend mainly on parish records (cf. Krause 1965).

John Rickman, the director of the first four censuses, compiled the basic data from which both he and several later analysts attempted to describe the population growth during the previous century. He had a questionnaire sent to every "Rector, Vicar, Curate, or Officiating Minister," asking them to extract from their parish records the numbers of baptisms and burials, distinguishing between male and female, for each decade from 1700 to 1780 and for each following single year up to 1800. How well this formidable task was performed is a question to which no definite reply can be given, though it is reasonable to suppose that there must have been great lacunae in data so collected (B. Hammond 1928). In any case, these Anglican parish registers did not include Dissenters, some paupers, and others. To reconstruct birth and death rates, therefore, one must increase the given figures on baptisms and burials by a more or less arbitrary proportion, representing the best guess on the total size of the several deficiencies. Then, working back from the census count of 1801 (corrected for its substantial underenumeration), one can calculate the population totals and crude rates. The method depends, thus, on three assumptions: (1) that the corrected 1801 count was accurate, (2) that the underregistration in the parish records was at the estimated rates, and (3) that there was no net migration.

1. We can accept the corrected 1801 census figure as substantially accurate. At the very least, it is the best datum up to that time.

2. The disparity in the ratio of births to baptisms, and in that of deaths to registered burials, was a symptom of the transformation the country was undergoing. So long as the relatively stable agrarian society persisted, one could assume that underregistration was at a constant proportion (although even then there may have been some oscillation with the business cycle, for one factor in reducing the later registration was that many Anglicans were unwilling to pay the relatively high fees for their rites). However, as the center of population moved from the South to the new industrial regions in the North, churches and clergy were left behind. The migration from villages to towns was marked by the same lag. "The London parish of Marylebone, with 40,000 inhabitants, had church accommodations for only 200" (Krause 1958). The war also had its effect on the record, for while soldiers died in higher proportion than equivalent civilian cohorts, they escaped ecclesiastical registration. It is more or less certain, then, that the birth/baptism and death/burial ratios varied considerably from one year or one locality to another; but this means that any average for the nation as a whole or for a decade or longer period can be only the roughest guess.[1] For any particular parish with reasonably complete records still extant, it would be possible to improve on the national estimates; see, for example,

---

[1] Griffith (1926: 18) raised the recorded baptisms by 15 percent and the burials by 10 percent; he has been criticized—correctly, I would judge—for assuming that the two ratios remained constant. "There is . . . much reason to believe that the registration of deaths deteriorated sharply between 1781 and 1821 and improved thereafter. Farr's estimated death-burial ratios, 1.23 in 1801–10, 1.33 in 1811–20, 1.16 in 1821–30, and 1.12 in 1831–40, are plausible in so far as the trend is concerned" (Krause 1958).

Chambers's discussion of Nottingham (1965c). The country was far less an integrated unit than it was to become, and many of the determinants of population trends were narrowly circumscribed. These local surveys, thus, are decidedly pertinent but also often quite unrepresentative.

3. The postulate that net migration was zero is even less well based statistically. Adequate migration data were compiled only after this transitional period was long past, and what records exist up to 1840 hardly form the basis for an informed guess. Emigrants from the United Kingdom were officially counted only from 1815 on, and the statistics were a by-product of a law, frequently evaded, introduced to compel ship masters to assign a specific minimum space to each passenger. Accuracy at a usable level begins in 1840, when the first Cunard steamships went into service and the Colonial Land and Emigration Commission was established (Thomas 1954: 36). Whether the unknown number of emigrants from England and Wales was matched, as is generally assumed, by an equal number of Irish and Scottish immigrants also cannot be established. The English census of 1841, the first to include such data, recorded 419,000 residents of Irish birth; and this figure, even if it were wholly accurate, would represent only a portion of the Irish who had taken up residence in England during the previous 80 years (Redford 1926: chaps. 8–9). If we accept the hypothesis that the total numbers of persons entering and leaving England were the same, the age structure of the immigrants and emigrants, and consequently their fertility and mortality, presumably differed considerably.

In short, the national data concerning population growth up to 1840 have to be supplemented by analyses of parish records, and important work is being done in this respect (e.g., Wrigley 1966 and, for a useful summary, Wrigley 1969: chap. 5).

Establishing a more accurate numerical base, to the degree that it is possible, is still only preliminary to analyzing *why* the changes in mortality and fertility occurred. What we propose to do here is to examine the theory of the demographic transition in the context of English social history, reinforced with statistical data only when these are reasonably precise. According to this theory, it will be recalled, the population growth of an area undergoing modernization is divided into three stages: (1) a more or less static population at high levels of fertility and mortality, (2) a period of constant fertility and falling mortality, with a consequent rapid increase in population, and (3) a more or less static population at more efficient levels of birth as well as death control.

The Transformation of English Agriculture

The first step toward understanding the population developments during the industrial revolution is to survey the momentous changes that took place in the English countryside. In the first half of the 18th century, the agrarian system of the Middle Ages still persisted in full force over a great portion of England. All cultivation of land, whether by proprietors or by tenants, was in accord with decisions of the village council, following practices made impregnable by tradition. Arable land was divided into three strips, of which one was left fallow each year and two were planted in coarse grains. Pasture was ordinarily inadequate, and the animals fed from stubble and heath. Since there was little or no hay to store, most of the herd was killed in the autumn and eaten through the winter as salt meat. Available pasture was usually held in common, as well as woods (for both hunting and firewood) and water (which included fishing rights). Attached to most villages were a number of squatters, who were permitted to eke out a miserable living though they had no legal right to the use of the joint property.

Landlords and tenants were equally ignorant and sunken in routine, while mutual suspicion divided them; for the landlord feared that the farmer would exhaust the land by forcing a few richer crops out of his fields during the last years of his tenancy, and therefore refused to grant leases for a fixed period, preferring the unstable state of things known as tenure at will. As a result, any spirit of enterprise, any undertaking that involved a considerable period for its completion, were out of the question for the farmer, since he lived under the constant threat of instant dismissal and of the loss of a whole year's labors. Thus the effect of backwardness was to make for more backwardness [Mantoux 1952: 162].

This whole mode of agriculture was transformed in the second half of the 18th century. In a series of individual acts of Parliament, the common land of villages was transferred to the private ownership of families with some ancient right to it. Deprived of the use of the commons, the squatters and cottagers often suffered a decline from even their modest living conditions. The more substantial cultivators, who were recompensed in land or money (the amount was set by the parliamentary commissioners, and no appeal could be made from their decision), were sometimes unable or unwilling to maintain themselves in the new circumstances, and some of them also sank into tenancy or pauperism. But if the social cost was high, it paid for an astounding advance in English agriculture (for a good summary, see McKeown et al. 1972). The first act of the new owner was always to enclose the open field with a hedge, in order to protect it against grazing cattle. "The age of enclosure was also the age of new methods of draining, drilling, sowing, manuring, breeding and feeding cattle, making of roads, rebuilding of farm premises and a hundred other changes, all of them requiring capital" (Trevelyan 1942: 376). Potatoes and other root crops became staples. New breeds of farm animals were developed. Feed was grown that could be stored during the winter, the prior custom of converting the major portion of a herd into salt meat was abandoned. The improved methods were applied also to waste land, of which about 2 million acres were brought under cultivation during the 18th century.

There is hardly a question, then, that the food supply improved enormously in both quantity and variety.[2] The issue, rather, is what happened to the country

[2] Some analysts, it is true, have argued the contrary. From the increasing use of the potato, "the cheapest and one of the most efficient single foods man has as yet cultivated in the temperate zones," Salaman (1949: chaps. 25–26) concluded that the living conditions deteriorated.

people. "Enclosure was fatal to three classes: the small farmer, the cottager, and the squatter. To all of these classes their common rights were worth more than anything they received in return" (Hammond and Hammond 1932b: 73). For many years it was held that these classes, ousted from the village, were the raw material out of which the industrial labor force was formed. Indeed, this "Marxist doctrine," as Chambers terms it, may have been the model that the Soviet planners followed in the 1930s (see pp. 675–678). In 18th-century England, however, the main factor in supplying the developing urban industry with workers was not the displacement of villagers but rather the growth of the total population. While there was a good deal of migration to the towns, this did not result in the "rural depopulation" that Cobbett and others feared at the time. "The period 1780–1840 saw only a sporadic exodus . . . from the rural areas, . . . and side by side with it an actual filling up of empty spaces and a steady rise in the great majority of established centers of rural population" (Chambers 1965b; cf. Redford 1926: 58–69; Saville 1957; Lawton 1967). If numbers were increasing in both town and country, as was certainly the case at least for the period covered by the census records, then the supposed sharp decline in rural levels of life may well have been exaggerated.

The population grew and also the subsistence; what of the balance between them? Was the food per capita more or less plentiful, better or worse on the average? Did real wages rise or fall? It is not possible to answer such questions altogether satisfactorily, mainly because this was a period of rapid and all-encompassing change. At almost any time during these decades the situation of some in the lower classes was improving, and that of others deteriorating. For example, we can reasonably deduce from the data available that the real wages of cotton operatives went up steadily, and this may even have been so of factory workers generally. But the most important determinant of many workers' incomes was not their wage rate but how regularly they were employed. In the words of Hobsbawm (1957), "No discussion which overlooks the massive waves of destitution which swamped large sections of the laboring poor in every depression can claim to be realistic." His view of "realism" is, on the contrary, to minimize the rise in wages of the employed workers.

And if the amount of money received by workers varied widely, what they could buy with their wages varied even more. The cost of all foodstuffs differed greatly from one part of the country to another, and in any one locality "the price of a loaf of bread or a pound of beef might double or halve within the course of a few months or even weeks" (Ashton 1954a). Since this condition resulted from the primitive consumer market rather than specifically from food production, one can conclude that there was a similar variation in the prices of all essential commodities. For Hobsbawm (1957), "the discussion of food consumption . . . throws considerable doubt on the optimistic view." And Habakkuk (1965) also concludes: "The scantiness of the evidence makes any judgment dangerous, but the surviving examples of laborers' diets hardly suggest that any improvement in their diet can have been substantial." Another conclusion is that, "all in all, conditions of labor were becoming better, at least after 1820, and that the spread of the factory played a not inconsiderable part in the improvement" (Ashton 1954a).

Perhaps the best evidence that diets improved during this period is the lower incidence of food-deficiency diseases, and especially their virtual disappearance as causes of death. Drummond and Wilbraham (1957: 392), who lean toward the pessimistic view, note that by 1830 scurvy had become so rare that a well known physician was unable to diagnose its symptoms. They conclude, even if somewhat reluctantly, that the incidence of rickets also declined, possibly in part because of the beginning use of cod liver oil as a specific. This would have an important influence on fertility as well as mortality, for rickets frequently causes pelvic deformations and thus fetal and maternal deaths.

The Revolution of Rising Expectations

If objective criteria like the trend in real wages are difficult to establish in themselves, this is doubly so because the subjective meaning of such measures was also undergoing a rapid change. The "standard" of living includes the norms by which conditions are judged to be better or worse. Industrialism was frequently compared with an idyllic preindustrial society. To idealize the past was characteristic of Romanticism, which flourished during these same decades; revolutionary socialists wrote prose poems celebrating the Good Old Days (Engels 1958: 10–11); and representatives of the landed gentry opposed the developing factory system in part because they saw it as a challenge to their social and political power. The last point of view especially is well represented in the parliamentary hearings. The "too liberal use of weak tea, as extremely debilitating to the stomach," was only the most frequent proof of moral degradation deduced from changes that to us would suggest economic and social advance.

Thackrah lamented the fact that children were no longer contented with "plain food" but must have "dainties." The Reverend G. S. Bull deplored the tendency of girls to buy pretty clothes "ready-made" from shops instead of making them themselves, as this practice unfitted them to become "the mothers of children." Gaskell saw decadence in tobacco. "Hundreds of men may be daily seen inhaling the fumes of this extraordinary plant." He also saw moral decline in the growth of workmen's combinations [that is, trade unions]. The men were no longer "respectful and attentive" to their "superiors" [Hutt 1954].

If here tea-drinking and smoking were taken as signs of lower-class degeneration, for Hobsbawm (1957) the *slow* adoption of these new customs is proof, on the contrary, that consumption standards were lagging. The example indicates how difficult it is to distinguish what consumers wanted and could not buy from what they did not want. How many of the imprecisely recorded shifts reflected a change merely in taste?

The factory system, it would seem, was generating a new type of lower-class person, who fitted ill into the traditional class structure. "The ideological break with traditionalism," as Bendix (1956: 74) terms it, was based on Joseph

Townsend's proposition that "the slave must be compelled to work, but the free man should be left to his own judgment and discretion." In expostulating his principal theme of "the role of ideas in the management of economic enterprises," Bendix traces in detail the process by which the prior master–servant relation was gradually supplanted by one between the two new urban classes, the entrepreneurs and the factory workers, whose legitimacy evolved together with their growth in numbers. During the transition, it is true, a kind of medieval paternalism was often carried over into factory management: the responsibility of the upper classes was interpreted as including the duty, and the right, to control every move the workers made. In one factory the doors were locked during working hours. It was prohibited to drink water in spite of the heat. Fines were imposed for washing oneself or for being dirty, for putting out the light too soon or not soon enough, and so on (Hammond and Hammond 1932a: 19–20). Those regarded as the best of the new employers were often the most painstaking in preserving the preindustrial master–servant relation. Robert Owen, for example, who is usually cited as a prototype of the modern manager, gave his employees marks for their moral conduct—bad, denoted by black; indifferent, by blue; good, by yellow; and excellent, by white—"during every day of the week, Sundays excepted, for every year they remained in my employment." Workers in his model factory at New Lanark had to attend dancing lessons for the sake of their health, and some quit their jobs on that account (Plumb 1950: 145).

The reader is likely to sympathize with the worker who rebelled against constraints of this kind. The situation is more complex, however, when it was the workers who tried to preserve traditional patterns, and particularly such abhorrent ones—to the 20th-century Westerner—as child labor. Although the prefactory system of spinning and weaving varied greatly, one common element was that the family constituted an economic unit. The place of manufacture (literally, "making by hand") was the countryman's cottage, and the manufacturers were the cottager, his wife, and his children. The kinship base of this domestic system, as it is termed, survived for a while the shift to the factory.

Witnesses before the parliamentary committees from 1816 through 1819 testified consistently that masters allowed the operative spinners to hire their own assistants (piecers, scavengers, etc.) and that the spinners chose their wives, children, near relatives, or relatives of the proprietors. Many children, especially the youngest, entered the mill at the express request of their parents. . . . Most of the early trade unions' rules explicitly prohibited members from recruiting assistants outside the narrowly defined classes of children, brothers, orphan nephews, etc. [Smelser 1959: 188–189].

Parents retained, thus, their traditional authority over their children, who learned their trade while contributing to the family income. "Little wonder, then, that the conditions of child labor did not offend spinners interviewed by Factory Commissioners in 1833" (ibid.: 190). But both improved technology

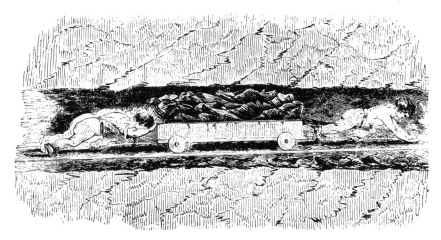

An illustration from Children's Employment Commission, *First Report of the Commissioners: Mines* (London: H.M. Stationery Office, 1842), one of the many white papers reporting the government's investigations of labor conditions in 19th-century England. The accompanying text (pp. 81–82) follows:

"By far the greater number of Children and persons employed in coal-mines are engaged in propelling and drawing tubs laden with coal, from the face to the pit-eye, or the main-levels in those pits where they have horses. This is done by placing the hands on the back of the waggon, and propelling it forward with as great velocity as the inclination of the mine, the state of the road, and the strength of the waggoner admit of. The mines in this district [Lancashire and Cheshire] are for the most part laid with rails, and the waggon runs on wheels. . . . There are, however, mines . . . where the old mode of drawing the baskets or wooden sledges (called in Lancashire 'sleds') is still retained. The drawer is in this case harnessed by means of a chain attached to the 'sled'; the other end of the chain passes between his legs, and fastens in front to a belt round the waist. When thus harnessed, and moving along on his hands and feet, the drawer drags after him the loaded basket; if he is not sufficiently strong he has a helper rather younger than himself." . . . [The figure] represents three young Children hurrying or drawing a loaded waggon of coals. The Child in front "is harnessed by his belt or chain to the waggon; the two boys behind are assisting in pushing it forward. Their heads, it will be observed, are brought down to a level with the waggon, and the body almost in a horizontal position. This is done partly to avoid striking the roof, and partly to gain the advantage of the muscular action, which is greatest in that position. It will be observed the boy in front goes on his hands and feet: in that manner the whole weight of his body is in fact supported by the chain attached to the waggon and his feet, and consequently his power of drawing is greater than it would be if he crawled on his knees. These boys, by constantly pushing against the waggons, occasionally rub off the hair from the crowns of their heads so much as to make them almost bald."

and structural changes in the factory system led to a greater differentiation of roles, and thus both broke down the economic authority of the father–spinner over his children–assistants and in many cases reduced the composite wage that he received. *Some* of the misery of the period, as seen by those who suffered it, was due to the decline of this semi-apprenticeship system based on kinship; and the "array of threats to the family's traditional organization underlay much of the turmoil among operatives and others between 1825 and 1850" (ibid.: 199).

In short, the way that the participants in England's early industrialization defined their situation helped determine their behavior. What the members of parliamentary committees, or their witnesses, or factory operatives saw as problems became the main content of the data collected. This "bias" is especially difficult to cope with, since most of the people living through that turbulent period must have been confused concerning what it was they really wanted. And we aggravate this confusion if we assume that the common people must have demanded "progress" as a present-day liberal defines it, and that their protest *for* child labor or for a *longer* workday, because they seem to be anomalies, can best be ignored.

We have argued, then, that it is all but impossible to find conclusive evidence on the trend in living conditions during this period, and that this difficulty has typically been compounded by the fact that most data were gathered and interpreted as part of a political dispute. Many of the causal links implied in this long debate, moreover, are not necessary ones.

What happened to the standard of life of the British working classes in the late decades of the 18th and the early decades of the 19th centuries? Was the introduction of the factory system beneficial or harmful in its effect on the workers? These, though related, are distinct questions. For it is possible that employment in factories conduced to an increase of real wages but that the tendency was more than offset by other influences, such as the rapid increase of population, the immigration of Irishmen, the destruction of wealth by long years of warfare, ill devised tariffs, and misconceived measures for the relief of distress [Ashton 1954a].

From roughly 1790 to 1815, England was at war with France; and this was "the central economic characteristic of these years." Some 3 to 5 percent of the population, and, of course, a far higher proportion of the labor force, were in military service. The rise in the real cost of many commodities, especially of imports and therefore some foodstuffs, was more the consequence of the war than of any other factor (Rostow 1948: 13–14). As another instance, the fact that homes in the rapidly growing cities were ramshackle, and if not worse than the hovels of the rural areas then also not much better, still does not settle the question of why this was so. The state deflected requisite materials and labor to the prior demand of military necessity, and this was an important reason for the inadequacy of the rapidly constructed homes of the new industrial towns. A new word was added to English—*jerry-built*, from the nautical word *jury* (as in "jury mast"), meaning "temporary," "emergency" (Ashton 1954b). The shortage of houses persisted, however, and these "temporary" residences were occupied for decades.

To sum up, evidence concerning the trend in living conditions is typically ambiguous enough to permit judgments to vary considerably; and this tendency has often been compounded because of the political implications to be drawn from the conclusion that real wages were rising, or falling. Actually, the political argument is not only scientifically unfortunate but also often unwarranted, for whatever happened to the average Englishman's living conditions was not the consequence merely of "capitalism," or the factory system, or any other single factor.

MORTALITY IN BRITAIN

There is no question that the population increased substantially from, say, 1760 to 1840. Was this growth the consequence, either wholly or mainly, of a decline in mortality, as is assumed in the model of the demographic transition? Perhaps the best answer to this question is that by two medical historians, McKeown and Brown (1965; cf. McKeown *et al.* 1972). They divided the possible causes of a reduction in mortality into three broad classes, which we consider in turn.

1. A change in the balance between the virulence of the infective organism and the resistance of the host. In certain instances—for example, the transformation of scarlet fever from a frequently fatal disease to a relatively trivial complaint—this was probably the decisive factor. The general effect of such changes on the long-term trend in the death rate, however, was slight.[3]

[3] A seeming exception is the bubonic plague, which was still endemic in Eastern Europe during the 18th century. In 1720 an infected ship brought the disease to Marseilles, and in the furious outbreak about 40,000 of the city's 90,000 inhabitants died. It spread through Provence and a few adjoining districts with smaller losses. Inexplicably the plague stopped short, and in a bit over a year it was all over (Helleiner 1965).

Louis Pasteur (1822–1895), French chemist, helped prove the germ theory of disease. Until the last quarter of the 19th century, practitioners had not taken the first step toward the control of infectious diseases—the recognition that they are the consequence of an invasion by microorganisms (*World Health Organization*).

2. Specific preventive or curative therapy. Most treatments of the various important causes of death can be discounted for the period earlier than the middle of the 19th century. It is a moot question whether fever hospitals, for example, helped restrict contagion by the semiquarantine they imposed or, on the contrary, raised the death rate by the fact that virtually all persons who entered them would be infected. So long as bleeding was the first treatment for illness, the contribution that physicians made to their patients' health was minimal; so long as something like half of surgical patients died of infection, it can be questioned whether surgeons saved more patients than they killed. "It might safely be said," McKeown and Brown conclude, "that specific medical treatment had no useful effects at all, were it not for some doubt about the results of the use of mercury in syphilis, iron in anemia, cinchona in malaria, and inoculation against smallpox."

Of the four diseases, the last was by far the most important in England of the 18th century, when it is estimated that one out of every five persons died from smallpox, typically in childhood. The terror it caused can be imagined. "Men would not marry until or unless the lady had had smallpox, servants were advertised for who had had it" (Griffith 1926: 248). Inoculation with a small, nonfatal amount of infected liquid, it was discovered, could establish immunity. This practice was introduced in the 1720s and used intermittently through the rest of the century, but medical historians disagree on its effect. It was dangerous to the patient if not skillfully administered, and unless he was segregated he could spread the disease to others. In 1798 Edward Jenner discovered that vaccination with cowpox germs, which causes only a minor skin irritation, also effects im-

Edward Jenner (1749–1823), an English country doctor, discovered that vaccination with cowpox germs provides immunity against smallpox (*World Health Organization*).

"The Cow Pock," a print by James Gillray, 1802, shows the alleged effects of vaccinations with cowpox serum (*The Bettmann Archive, Inc.*).

munity against smallpox. In part because of the ambivalent results from inoculation, there was some opposition at first also to vaccination, and we do not know how rapidly its practice spread.[4] In sum,

> Virtually nothing was known about the etiology and natural history of disease before the late 19th century. Effective measures were few and their use was largely misunderstood. Surgery was limited without anesthesia and dangerous without knowledge of antisepsis.... Inevitable risks [were] associated with hospital care [McKeown *et al.* 1972].

3. Improvement in living conditions, by which McKeown and Brown mean "any change which would have reduced the risk of infection, or increased the

---

[4] Griffith (1926) argues that there was a sharp fall in the death rate from 1800 to 1810, largely the consequence of a reduced incidence of smallpox, and that the subsequent rise was partly due to the increased mortality from this disease until it was discovered that immunity must be periodically renewed. But the evidence is not clear on any of his allegations: We do not know whether the death rate fell in the century's first decade; many authorities believe it rose. We do not know whether Jenner's discovery was much used only two years after it was made; a widespread system of free vaccination was established only in the 1840s and there were serious outbreaks of smallpox still after that date. We do not know, finally, whether the effective control of one important disease, supposing that it took place, would have reduced substantially the death rate of a society with so few guards against epidemic diseases in general.

survival rate among those infected: under the first are such measures as improvements in housing, water supply, or refuse disposal; under the second influences affecting the general standard of health, of which by far the most important was probably nutrition." It is not likely that there could have been a very great improvement in living conditions in the first sense; on the contrary, the risk of infection almost certainly increased, assuming that the villagers' style of life remained essentially the same after they migrated to the towns, or even that it improved somewhat. Lower-class urban quarters were probably no more squalid than their rural counterpart, but the higher population density made of cities the graveyard of countrymen, to cite that graphic aphorism. Both in England and elsewhere in the Western world urban death rates were higher than rural until the last quarter of the 19th century, by which time public sanitation was sufficiently established to cancel the biological effect of crowded living quarters (cf. Rosenberg 1966).

There was little direct incentive to control urban filth, for the theory relating it to disease was by no means universally accepted. The understandable desire to mitigate the stink of even middle-class homes was probably more relevant. In any case, public sanitation was not much improved before 1840 (cf. Hennock 1957), as can be illustrated by the fact that so important a step as the separation of sewage from drinking water was taken only very gradually. During the first half of the 18th century excrement was dumped out of town windows on to the street, and from about 1750 on scavengers gathered the "night-soil" in the better-class neighborhoods. The water closet, invented toward the end of the century, emptied into either large vaults under the houses or, later, into sewers that flowed into a river. Until 1850 one of London's drinking-water companies still had its intake within a few feet of the mouth of the Westbourne, which had become the Ranelagh common sewer! (Buer 1926: 108). The cholera epidemic of 1831–32, which came just when urban sanitation was at its worst, is considered by some to have been almost a blessing, for it helped the physicians in their effort to establish minimum norms of public health.

To sum up, while it is impossible to document it with the precision that we would prefer, there was probably a more or less continuous decline in mortality roughly from 1760 to 1840. Medical advances had little to do with this, except possibly in the single case of smallpox (which in any case was largely replaced by measles as one of the most important killers). The debate over what caused the decline continues from one learned paper to the next. There has been a paradoxical tendency on the part of analysts to discount the effect of the factor they studied most intensively. "Surprisingly, these medical historians [McKeown and Brown] argued that . . . medical advances, with the exception of vaccination, were demographically irrelevant, and that environmental changes, mainly economic, were at work. Their view, thus, contradicts that of T. H. Marshall, the economic historian, who held that economic factors were unimportant, and that medical factors were responsible" (Krause 1958).

As other possible factors are partly eliminated, the improvement in the food supply would seem to be a major cause of any important decline in mortality before about 1850, and McKeown and Brown believe it to be the principal reason for the population growth of the late 18th and early 19th centuries. The only other plausible factor is a kind of *deus ex machina*, a fortuitous change in the environment that, perhaps with no one being aware of it, happened to reduce the virulence of particular diseases. It has been suggested, for example, that the species of host rats changed, and thus made the spread of the plague to man less likely. Or, as another instance, perhaps the decisive factor in the sharply reduced incidence of typhus was the shift from woolen to cotton clothing and the improved cleanliness that this facilitated. Characteristically, Engels (1958: 78–79) cited this change to cotton as one further proof that the living conditions of the English working class had deteriorated.

The evidence for either of these changes, whether improvement in the average nutrition or an exogenous shift in the environment, is at best probable, sometimes hardly that; and the pessimistic view that there was a decline in consumption and health can also be supported with plausible data, particularly for the war years. In any case, was the decline in mortality sufficient to account for the population increase—taking only the period measured by censuses—from roughly 9.2 million in 1801 to 15.9 million in 1841? Or is there not a *prima facie* case here for the probability that fertility rose while mortality declined?

FERTILITY IN BRITAIN

The population of early industrial England has been studied principally by economic historians, who, as one would expect, have tended to stress economic factors. While this emphasis can lead to a reasonably good understanding of mortality trends, the state of the economy is not the most important determinant of fertility. One economic historian, thus, finds the "sociological weakness" of his colleagues' studies to be "striking."

Allowing for exceptions such as Marshall and Glass, British researchers have tended to slight the analysis of the social determinants of birth rates, nuptiality, and the other components of population change. They have placed most of their emphasis on material considerations—Malthusian checks and their shifting incidence—and to such proximate relations as the immediate influence of the birth and death rate on population. And they have perhaps been too quick to assume away the significance of nonmaterial factors: witness Habakkuk's statement that "within any given social group marriage habits might be expected to be stable"; or the neglect of socially determined changes in fertility as a possible factor in population growth [Landes 1958].

As was noted earlier, the growth of population in medieval Europe was held to well below the physiological maximum by ethical and institutional norms. The principle that a man ought to be able to support a family before he married and had children was embodied in the regulations of the major medieval institutions. In the old system, as it functioned in both town and countryside, a male assistant or apprentice, or a female domestic, generally lived in as a subordinate member of the master's family. As a consequence, the morals of adolescents were supervised; sexual dalliance meant the possible loss of one's position in a secure world. Young people were not under economic pressure to marry early, since they were meaningful members of a functioning household. At the same time, parents may have restricted the number of their children because extended kin were also included in the family economy.

Virtually all urban occupations were governed by guilds, which particularly in England prohibited their members from marrying until they had completed their apprenticeship. Guild regulations apparently were still enforced in England during the first half of the 18th century, but pamphleteers were finding them unnecessary and onerous. By 1775 the system was in an advanced state of decay (Griffith 1926: 114, 116), but—as we have seen—it persisted for a while even in some of the new factories, where operatives retained the prerogatives of master craftsmen. As England was still predominantly rural, national population trends were set principally by what was happening in the countryside. Whatever effect the enclosure movement had on living conditions generally, it certainly tended to release the average countryman from traditional bonds, whether he stayed in the village or migrated to the towns, whether he retained his prior status or sank into pauperdom.

Indeed, the distinction between a worker and a pauper became tenuous during this period. In 1795 the magistrates of Berkshire County met at Speenhamland, a suburb of Newbury, in order to fix and enforce a minimum wage. Instead, they drew up a scale of doles to be paid on the basis of three factors—the wages earned, the price of bread, and the size of the worker's family. This so-called Speenhamland scale, which was imitated over a large portion of England, was popular with almost everyone concerned. The poor were safe from extreme want under all market conditions. Employers could find workers at almost any wage, no matter how low, for it was supplemented up to the subsistence level out of taxes. And the general public found the system good, both because it gave charity to those in need of it and because it inhibited, it was believed, the spread of revolutionary ideas from France.

In spite of its popularity, the Speenhamland system was what Malthus (*Essay*, Book 3, chaps. 5–7; Book 4, chap. 8) termed it, "a pernicious evil." It is true that the alms mitigated the distress suffered by individuals, but it is no less true that in overall terms the Berkshire scale aggravated and prolonged the misery occasioned by the rapid social change.[5] With the massive shift taking place from agrarian to industrial occupations, when a prime economic need consequently was a mobile labor force, the new poor law restricted free movement. A man who

---

[5] "The right solution would have been the enforcement of a legal minimum wage in agriculture. This the laborers demanded in the 1790s, appealing to the Elizabethan Statute of Artificers (1563). But the appeal was useless, for the Wages sections were by this time inoperative, and they had never been used as a lever for raising wages beyond the prevailing competitive level" (Fay 1947: 92).

left one parish and remained for a full year in another lost his right to relief in the first and established it in the second.

For this reason parish authorities were reluctant to receive outsiders, and employers who were large ratepayers would sometimes offer work only for a period short of a full year. If before a laborer had gained a settlement in a new parish he fell on evil days, he could be moved back summarily to the parish from which he had come, and this made him think twice before leaving his native village to seek work far away [Ashton 1948: 110].

By a wide margin, the cost of poor relief was the major item in local taxation. From 1782 to 1793, its average annual cost was £2 million, as compared with £0.2 million for all other local expenditures; in 1813 the figures were £7 million and £1.5 million (Trevelyan 1942: 353, 470). The main burden of poor relief fell on the small farmer, who paid taxes but, unlike the new gentry, got no cheap labor in return. The decline of the yeoman class was certainly quickened by the administration of the poor law, and undoubtedly at least some of those pushed down themselves became paupers.

In the long run the result was ghastly. Although it took some time till the self-respect of the common man sank to the low point where he preferred poor relief to wages, . . . little by little the people of the countryside were pauperized. . . . But for the protracted effects of the allowance system, it would be impossible to explain the human and social degradation of early capitalism [Polanyi 1944: 80].

It is usual to conceptualize the dynamics of Western fertility patterns in terms of the changes that took place in the second half of the 19th century—the erosion of the preindustrial norms and the gradual evolution of the small-family system. We tend to think, following the logic of the demographic transition, that a breakdown of traditionalism always results in a lower fertility; but this is nonsense. The control of family size, no matter what means is used, demands *self*-control; and self-control is likely to prevail only in a society in which individuals have strong motives for imposing it. The smaller family of the urban middle class developed, that is to say, principally because in a mobile society a man with fewer children could advance farther. But in the period we are discussing, and particularly for the mass of the people, there was no question of achieving self-improvement through self-control. Here the breakdown of the ethical and institutional norms, with the limitation to procreation they had set, meant a probable rise in fertility.

The dissolution of village society could result in a rise in fertility because of (1) less frequent or less effective control of conception within marriage, (2) a higher incidence of illegitimacy, (3) a lower age at marriage, together with a higher proportion marrying, and (4) a change in the age structure. Let us examine each of these factors briefly, beginning with the most hypothetical.

Less Effective Birth Control. The main point to be made here is that this change was *possible*. Once again, we tend to view this period in terms of irrelevant comparisons. It is true that the mechanical and chemical contraceptives developed in the last century are more efficient than prior methods, but it must not be supposed that the latter cannot reduce fertility substantially. The average family size in the United States began to fall at the beginning of the 19th century, and in France probably even earlier, in both cases presumably because of the more frequent practice of *coitus interruptus*. If England's marital fertility was held in check by this method in the 18th century, a matter on which we have no information, and if self-control was reduced during the transitional period as we have hypothesized, then—. Not a firm conclusion, but the contrary one is no firmer, and is generally believed.

Illegitimacy.   Data on illegitimacy are poor (cf. Laslett and Oosterveen 1973). In 1830, by one estimate, 5 percent of all births were outside marriage (Griffith 1926: 125–126), but this figure may be "far too low"; "the rate for 1851–60 was 6.5 percent, and it had been falling" (Marshall 1965). If we accept this view and assume that, say, 7 to 8 percent of the births in all regions and all social classes were illegitimate, then for the particular declassed villagers evolving into the new proletariat the rate must have been higher.

Under the law in effect from 1808 to 1834, an unmarried mother could force support from the man she claimed to be the father. Whether she married thus made little difference to her financially. It was held that under the Speenhamland system the mother of enough illegitimate children could support herself by breeding: "There was one thing better than to marry and have a family, and that was to marry a mother of bastards. . . . As one young woman of 24 with four bastard children put it: If she had one more, she should be very comfortable" (*Report on Labourers' Wages*, 1824, quoted in Redford 1926: 71). The conditions of work, particularly in the mines, afforded temptations and opportunities for extramarital intercourse, which is frequently mentioned in the reports of the period. If the breakdown of village institutions meant a concomitant decline in the moral standards associated with them, as we should expect in theory, then a considerable proportion of the population must have become indifferent to the distinction between marital and illegitimate conception.

Decline in the Age at Marriage.   The reports of the period are full of complaints that young people were marrying irresponsibly as a consequence of the Speenhamland system. According to a Factory Report of 1833, thus, operatives often married before they were 18 and the usual age was probably not even so high in rural areas affected by enclosures. "Much of the evil [of improvident marriages] would be remedied," the *Poor Law Report* of 1831 tells us, "if the farmers would return to . . . keeping their unmarried [farmhands] as servants in the house, boarding them and lodging them and giving them pecuniary wages" (Griffith 1926: 105, 109). Malthus (*Essay*: 474) shared the prevalent opinion that poor relief fostered early marriages and large families, and for this reason he advocated that public relief be abolished. The one exception he would have made was families with six or more children, whose misery could be alleviated without encouraging still more procreation. As Habakkuk (1965) points out, "Malthus's views on this subject are apt to be misinterpreted. He did not argue that people had more children in order to profit from the earnings of the children in factories, or to enjoy larger poor-law benefits. His point was that the prospect of parish relief and the earning capacity of children at an early age reduced the force of the incentive to postpone marriage."

Though the alleged relation between the dole and the size of the family cannot be proved statistically, there is good circumstantial evidence to support it. As the amount of the relief payment was based in part on the size of the pauper–worker's family, employers were able to pay lower wages to those with more children. "As the farmers have under the scale system a direct inducement to employ married men rather than single, in many villages . . . they will not employ the single men at all. In others they pay them a much lower rate of wages for the same work in the hope of driving them to seek work out of the parish" (*Reports on the Poor Laws*, 1834, quoted in Griffith 1926: 263). Or, as seen from the point of view of the workingmen,

Men who receive but a small pittance know that they have only to marry, and that pittance will be augmented in proportion to the number of their children. . . . An intelligent witness, who is much in the habit of employing laborers, states that when complaining of their allowance they frequently say to him: "We will marry, and you must maintain us" [*Report on Labourers' Wages*, 1824, quoted in Redford 1926: 71].

In the four counties in which industry was most important, in 1821 there were 677 children under 5 per 1,000 women aged 15–49, as contrasted with only 580 in the rest of England. Since there is good reason to believe that infant and child mortality was greater in the first category, the higher child–woman ratio there is doubly impressive (Krause 1958).

The implied causal relation is not proved, of course; it is just as likely that the breakdown of the traditional society increased both the average relief and fertility. In fact, it is rather unfortunate that the factual question of whether the birth rate rose has so long been associated with the policy question of whether Speenhamland was a just and efficient poor law. It is always difficult to analyze the effect of such subsidies or quasi-subsidies on the size of the family.[6] Even those instituted in the 20th century, for which accurate fertility data are available, are not easy to separate from a dozen other factors that may have influenced family size.

Change in the Age Structure. A rise in the birth rate for any other reason may become cumulative by increasing in the next generation the proportion of persons physiologically capable of parenthood. As at this time a large proportion died in the first years of life, most of whatever decline in the death rate took place

---

[6] Blackmore and Mellonie (1927–28), with what Marshall (1965) termed "a touching faith in the sanctity of even the shadiest figures," proved to their own temporary satisfaction that the Speenhamland system had effected a *decline* in the birth rate. Some months later, however, they offered "a second analysis" showing that there was no relation between the subsidy and fertility.

was equivalent to an additional rise in the birth rate. Even a relatively small change in each of the several factors affecting fertility or mortality, thus, could have brought about a substantial population increase over several generations.

During this transitional period, we can hypothesize in summary, there were three European family types in existence concurrently.[7] In the **traditional** family typical of the preindustrial period, the postponement of marriage, plus the nonmarriage of a considerable portion of the secular population, constituted an onerous but efficient means of reducing fertility. With the **proletarian** family, typical of the mass of either rural or urban workers who had been released from these institutional and normative restrictions, social control was barely strong enough to force a marriage even if a child had been conceived. Once the sexual urge developed, there was certainly no effective bar to marriage. In the **rational** family type, which arose first among the middle class and during the 19th century spread to the rest of the society, a sense of parental responsibility and, with it, a limitation of family size reappeared. The average age at marriage rose again, and the same end was also achieved with less privation by the use of more efficient contraceptives. In order to trace the change in fertility in detail, thus, we would need the statistics on completed family size by social class going back at least as far as 1750. While such data will never become available, we can be reasonably certain that the shifts in the overall crude birth rate were largely the consequence of the gradual substitution of one of these family types for another.

THE JAPANESE MODEL

England affords one framework for analyzing population trends in a country undergoing modernization, but it is also atypical in that it was the first country to develop an industrial society. All subsequent modernization, and especially that currently under way in underdeveloped areas, has been far more rapid in some respects and thus more disruptive. And all countries that have imitated England's example have done so, to one degree or another, under the direction of the state. Among other industrial powers, Japan is most often cited as both a guide to underdeveloped Asia and a model for analysis.

Japan is a happy hunting ground for the demographer, for . . . it provides an opportunity, if not to answer, at least to add substantially to the evidence concerning one important question: how truly universal is the association of the "demographic revolution" with industrialization? Does the same configuration of trends as was observed in Western societies recur also in societies with entirely different cultural traditions? [Dore 1959].

The Japanese case has the neatness of a laboratory experiment. The Tokugawa regime (1603–1868) cut off the country almost completely from alien

[7] This tripartite typology derives from E. W. Hofstee, [Regional Differentiation in Dutch Fertility during the Second Half of the 19th Century], in Dutch, in Koninklijke Nederlandse Akademie van Wetenschappen, *Akademie-Dagen*, **7** (1954), 59–106. Amsterdam: Noord-Hollandsche Uitgevers.

influences and thus from most Western contacts; along many dimensions, there-fore, the ensuing burst of modernization started from virtually zero. For much of this epoch, moreover, the population was as stable as it is supposed to be during Stage I of the demographic transition; between 1726 and 1852 the total fluctuated slightly around 25 million, with the low and the high during this century and a quarter differing by less than 10 percent (Taeuber 1958: 21). The reason for this stability was *not*, however, that unrestrained procreation was cut back by a commensurate mortality. Indeed, the death rate was high, but fertility was set (as in early-modern Europe) at well below the physiological maximum. Conscious family limitation was achieved in part through the post-ponement of marriage, contraception, and abortion, but in greater part appar-ently through infanticide, euphemistically termed *mabiki* (literally, "thinning," as of rice seedlings when some are pulled up to encourage the growth of the remainder). As in the familistic culture of classical China, so also in its adaptation to the straitened economy of the Japanese islands, the dominant goal was that the family be continued through the male line. In China this was realized in principle through a numerous progeny, but in Japan by sacrificing numbers to quality (ibid.: 31).

Few analysts would have forecast from the Meiji "restoration" in 1868 any-thing like the subsequent remarkable rise in productivity. The country was in chaos for a decade or more, and social order was restored by the samurai, once a class of warrior knights who had become obsolescent in this traditional func-tion. They combined old and new with a marvelous adeptness, refurbishing the imperial office and the established religion and even increasing their prior authority and, on the other hand, taking over wholesale Western technology and education, Western legal codes, details of Western political administration down to the postal system. The meteoric rise to full industrial power, in such dramatic contrast with the static misery of most underdeveloped countries, has of course stimulated much analysis: what were the crucial reasons for Japan's success?

One frequent explanation is based on the ideology of nationalism.

> Nationalism is a *sine qua non* of industrialization, because it provides people with an overriding, easily acquired, secular motivation for making painful changes. National strength or prestige becomes the supreme goal, industrialization the chief means. ... To the degree that the obstacles to industrialization are strong, nationalism must be intense to overcome them. Nationalism was a potent element in the industri-alization of Japan, Germany, and Russia [Davis 1955].

Although Japan is invariably cited as prime evidence for this argument, it is not clear that this nation's ideology was merely one instance of a universal category. The etymological meaning of *nation* (the word derives from the Latin for "to be born") suggests a people linked by common descent from a putative ancestor; and other accepted characteristics are a common territory, history, language, religion, and way of life. The list, compiled from various political theorists as an introduction to an analysis of newly established African states, underlines how different they are from Japan. Since "nearly all the new African nations lacked *all* these elements except a common territory, and even that has been lately and arbitrarily demarcated by alien power," whether in these instances nation-building has fostered modernization is far from clear (Perham 1962: 26). In such cases, on the contrary, one can reasonably argue that nationalism generally blocks the modernization of new nations. As in so many other characteristics, so also in this one, Japan is close to unique: there nationalism could rest securely on all of the listed foundations. Before the advent of the Meiji regime, the country was homogeneous in ethnicity, language, and religion, and this multiple unity was reinforced not only by its geographical separation from the mainland but also by the lack of any basis for transnational loyalties similar to Pan-Africanism or Pan-Arabism. A small but crucial minority were literate, and the new regime almost immediately used the universal compulsory education it established (and, for adults, classes in the conscripted army) to breed patriotism. By 1940, the "almost total uniformity of educational experience in the first six school years of the life of every Japanese child" produced "a homogeneity of popular intellectual culture which has probably never been equaled in any society of 70 million people" (Dore 1964). In short, Japan's nationalism could be generated largely from the natural unity of her population, and the mythical element, always a necessary supplement, was inculcated with an inimitable efficiency.

The characteristics of Japan's preindustrial civilization that made her rapid modernization feasible, however we specify them, were associated with the country's urban population. In the Tokugawa period there were three large cities—Edo, with a population variously estimated between half a million and a million, and Kyoto and Osaka, each with perhaps a third of a million—plus hundreds of castle towns, temple towns, market centers, ports, and post towns. "Japan in 1800, though an outwardly feudal land, was almost as urbanized as were the leading industrial countries at that time" (Reischauer 1957: 82). The urban aggregates most important for Japan's future development, surprisingly, were the castle towns, which were gradually transformed from the seats of "feudal" power into the nuclei of modern authority. Just as Edo, the capital of the Tokugawa shogun, became the capital of new Japan under the new name of Tokyo, so the shift of local authority followed. Of the forty-six prefectural capitals today, thirty-four were castle towns in Tokugawa times, and in most cases the modern prefecture is named after its capital rather than the pre-Meiji province. "The city, its life and its institutions, was in reality basically antagonistic to the type of land-centered military regime envisaged by the Tokugawa authorities. The urban environment, from its inception, was destined to have a contradictory effect upon the feudal class" (Hall 1955; Carpenter 1960; but cf. Bellah 1957: 43). If this interpretation is correct, Pirenne's thesis concerning the cities of early-modern Europe (see pp. 406–407) is partly true also of Japan.

From 1875–79, shortly after the Meiji regime was installed, to 1915–19, when

Table 12-2. Population and Vital Rates, Japan, 1875–1939

Five-year Period[a]	Mid-period Population (–000)	Average Annual Rate per 1,000 Mid-period Population		
		BIRTH	DEATH	NATURAL INCREASE
1875–79	35,111	25.2	18.0	7.2
1880–84	37,079	26.3	19.5	6.8
1885–89	39,081	28.3	21.5	6.8
1890–94	41,093	28.4	21.1	7.3
1895–99	43,248	30.6	20.7	9.9
1900–04	45,984	32.0	20.4	11.6
1905–09	48,759	32.0	20.9	11.1
1910–14	52,140	33.6	20.2	13.4
1915–19	55,527	32.4	22.5	9.9
1920–24	57,285	35.9	22.3	13.6
1925–29	61,526	34.8	19.6	15.2
1930–34	66,267	32.7	18.0	14.7
1935–39	70,031	29.8	17.5	12.3

[a] From 1875 to 1919, based on registration of the population with legal domiciles in Japan; from 1920 to 1939, based on census data.
SOURCE: Various compilations of official data, as reported in Irene Taeuber, "Japan's Demographic Transition Re-examined," *Population Studies*, **14** (1960), Table 1.

the initial phase of rapid industrialization was over, the population—according to official statistics, such as they are—increased from 35.1 million to 55.5 million (Table 12-2). During and immediately after this period the birth rate rose from about 25 to well over 30, the death rate remained more or less constant at around 20, and the natural increase began its stupendous rise—for which, in later years with better records, it became world-famous. To the degree that these figures can be accepted as accurate, then, the initial rise in population was *not* the consequence of a substantial decline in mortality, as one would anticipate from the transition theory, but of a rise in fertility—ignoring the slight effect of migration.

As always during a period of rapid social change, however, there is a good possibility that the figures are spurious, for undoubtedly over the time span included in the table one can assume an improvement in the completeness and accuracy of the records on which the vital rates are based. If the actual birth rate remained constant but with a higher proportion of births recorded, this would show up as a rising rate; and if the actual death rate fell but with a higher proportion of deaths recorded, this would show up as a more or less constant rate (cf. Morita 1963). As in England at an earlier date, thus, determining the true trend depends on one's manipulation and interpretation of dubious figures. Irene Taeuber, certainly the principal authority in the English language on the population of Japan, was not able to resolve the issue. Her conclusion that "in Japan the initial impact of economic modernization tended toward an increase in fertility" (1958: 55) was not substantiated in the later paper (1960). On the other hand, the fertility rate in the early 1920s rose sharply, contrary to the "anticipation of declining fertility with increasing industrialization," and for this period there is no question of dismissing the apparent rise as spurious. It was a genuine increase in fertility, the consequence, according to Taeuber's interpretation (1958: 232–233), of changes in mortality, age structure, and marriage rate.

As we have noted, there is considerable research under way in England, France, and other countries of Europe to reconstruct early population trends from local data. Some similar work is being done in Japan, and it may be that one day a compilation of village studies will provide a better basis for estimates of national trends. A study of one village during the Tokugawa period indicates a decline of the average birth rates from a high of 33.1 in 1830–34 to 18.3 in 1859–63, thus suggesting the possibility of a sharp increase with any improvement in conditions.

A population pyramid drawn for [the village of] Fujito would have a very different shape from the usually pictured fan-shape of the typical underdeveloped country of today. . . . The sides would be almost perpendicular up to the 30-to-35 age group. The relatively narrow base and high peak were obviously caused by a relatively low birth rate and a relatively long life span for much of the population [Hanley 1972].

The low birth rate was realized partly through a high age at marriage, which for females averaged between 23.4 and 25.7 years over the last seven decades or so of the Tokugawa era. Abortion and infanticide were undoubtedly known to the villagers and presumably practiced. The sex ratio did not deviate enough from parity to suggest a frequent exposure of female infants, and Taeuber (1960) concluded from a similar finding based on national statistics that "there is no way by which the high infant mortality that was normal in 19th-century Japan can be separated into its natural and its deliberate components."

However, . . . one could hypothesize that women would keep the first several children, whatever the sex, and exercise selection only when they had all or most of the children they desired. Therefore sex ratios were calculated for the last-born children of mothers in various marriage and/or birth cohorts. . . . The sex ratio of the children last born to women married between 1841 and 1863 but whose marriages or childbearing years terminated prior to 1863 is 1.7, which is over 5.4 standard deviations away from the universe mean [Hanley 1972].

By a decree of 1871 the customary family registers were made mandatory, and for the Meiji era (1868–1912) these can be used to supplement other local data. It is sometimes difficult, however, to distinguish the natural family from the household—a crucial distinction in a demographic analysis. Adoption, moreover, had (and has) a far wider function in Japan than in Western countries (cf. Petersen 1971: 195), and without careful control those adopted can be mistaken for natural children. According to one village compilation, thus, out of a total population that grew from 806 in 1876 to 939 in 1887, 112 persons had been adopted. Of these sixty-four were male, forty-eight female; their ages were concentrated in the 10–19 bracket but ranged from shortly after birth up to 40 years (Aymans 1969). As so often with family or parish records, those in Japan help answer some questions but also raise others.

Apart from whatever conclusion one reaches from such efforts to extend and interpret the sparse and inadequate statistics, there are three reasons for postulating a probable rise in fertility: the disparity between the population growth and the probable decline in mortality, the disappearance of the once prevalent practice of infanticide, and the subsidiary case of Taiwan. Let us look at each of these briefly.

None of the early demographic data are accurate, of course, but the growth of the population by a very substantial proportion is indisputable. According to estimates in Table 12-2, the population about doubled from the beginning of the Meiji era to just before World War II. Did living conditions improve sufficiently, particularly during the first decades after the Meiji restoration, to reduce mortality enough to bring about so fast a growth in numbers? The hyperrapid and supremely successful industrialization during the Meiji era was not achieved without heavy cost, and this was borne almost entirely by the peasantry. The new land tax of 1873 provided 94 percent of the government's tax revenue at the time of the decree, and over half until almost 1900. However startling the rise of the country as a whole, for several generations most of the peasants remained mired in the poverty that had been their lot during the prior century or more. Economic difficulties were aggravated by political unrest, which culminated in the Satsuma rebellion of 1877.

Japanese geographers have reconstructed a number of local economies, and their findings seldom suggest that the mortality could have declined substantially. An extreme case, perhaps, was the small island of Oshima in Yamaguchi Prefecture, the subject of two detailed studies (Doi 1957; Ishikawa 1967). Since its population was too densely settled to subsist from farming and fishing alone, men traditionally took on such secondary occupations as carpentry or stone-cutting, and their wives wove cotton at home. After the routinely dismal life was worsened by a typhoon and landslide, the daily meal as recorded at the time consisted mostly of buckwheat and bean-curd refuse, flavored with aromatic leaves. The central government distributed food to the worst stricken, who only thus were saved from death by starvation. Subsequent improvement in the local economy was due less to any relaxation of population pressure than to assistance from emigrants established abroad; in a single year, according to an actual count, 27,326 overseas parcels were received in Oshima. In short, if the figures on population growth are accepted as substantially accurate (and no one has disputed the upward trend), there is even less basis than McKeown and his associates found in England for postulating the requisite decline in Japan's mortality. Once again, there is an implicit case for a rise in fertility.

On the other hand, to the extent that industrialization improved certain classes' well-being, in many cases the result was to lessen the tight control over fertility. Restriction of family size had been achieved by a postponement of marriage to well beyond puberty, crude contraceptives and abortion (one method was a *moxa*, or cautery, burnt in the navel), and especially infanticide. Every account of late Tokugawa and early Meiji Japan notes the widespread prevalence of *mabiki*, and yet by the end of the 19th century it had disappeared except possibly from some isolated rural areas, without then being replaced by modern contraceptives. Those who doubt the rise of fertility during the transition must ask themselves, what happened to all the children who by the earlier norms would have been exposed. "The necessary conclusion from the Japanese experience is that the role of family limitation in premodern societies may have been underestimated and the motivating factors oversimplified" (Taeuber 1958: 33).

Taiwan, which Japan acquired as its first colony in 1895, became an amalgam of Japanese and Chinese cultures, administered as "one of the most successful colonial programs in the world" (Barclay 1954: 7) and with a time series of population data that are uniquely complete and accurate for a country in the first stage of development (Figure 12-1). Fertility definitely rose, not merely the crude birth rate shown in the graph. Up to around 1920, the birth rate fluctuated around 40, then during the 1920s it climbed to a new plateau at around 45, which was maintained for about a decade. The postwar rise to a new high of 50 in the

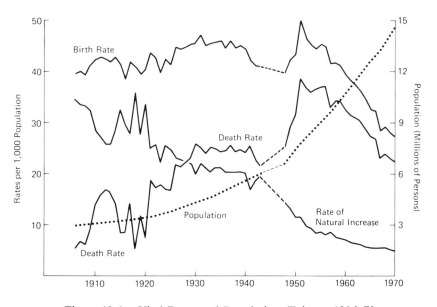

Figure 12-1. Vital Rates and Population, Taiwan, 1906–70

SOURCES: 1906–43: *Tung Chi Yao Lin* [Statistical Summary of the Past 51 Years] (Taipei: Taiwan Provincial Government, Bureau of Statistics, 1946), Table 96. 1948–51: United Nations, *Demographic Yearbook, 1952* (New York, 1953). 1952–70: Republic of China, Council for International Economic Cooperation and Development, *Taiwan Statistical Data Book, 1971* (Taipei, 1971).

year 1951 is also suggestive, but in this context the portion of the record following 1920 is more pertinent: the beginning of the characteristic decline in mortality was accompanied by a rise in fertility. Whether we regard Taiwan as a reflection of Japanese norms or as an independent example, it constitutes another challenge to the dogma that modernization and economic development inevitably bring about an immediate decline in the birth rate.

SUMMARY

During the 80 years or so following 1760, England's economy and social structure underwent a complete transformation, commonly known as the industrial revolution. In agriculture, the medieval three-field system was supplanted by enclosed fields, resulting in both a greatly increased productivity and new social relations in the rural areas. Manufacturing, which had been scattered through the countryside, was concentrated into factories, around which new urban centers rapidly developed. The prior rural isolation ended with the construction of roads and canals, by which both men and goods could move about more easily. These economic changes constituted the first fundamental advance since the establishment of preindustrial cities several millennia before.

All the authorities who have analyzed it agree that England's population grew at an unprecedented rate during these 80 years, and that this was primarily a natural increase, since the emigration of Englishmen was more or less balanced by the immigration of Irish and Scots. Differences arise over whether the greater numbers resulted mainly from a decline in the death rate (Griffith, McKeown and Brown, et al.) or from a rise in the birth rate (Malthus, Habakkuk, Krause, et al.). It is worth stressing that there is nothing in logic against accepting each set of arguments as partly correct, assuming the actual process was more complex than either side has pictured it. During this transitional period, in all likelihood, birth and death rates were simultaneously rising and falling in different sectors of the population. Institutional bars to early marriage still kept the birth rate low; their erosion permitted it to rise; and the small-family system, based on both the postponement of marriage and birth control, began to be established among the middle class. Death rates, similarly, certainly differed from one area or social class to another, varying with diets, styles of life, and other conditions affecting mortality. It is just this variety, compounded by the teasingly thin statistical data, that has made possible the continuous dispute over what really happened.

For England the theory of the demographic transition more or less accurately sums up the period from 1850 (or even 1875) to 1945—that is, from the time when medicine and public sanitation really effected a rapid decline in mortality, particularly of infants and children, to the postwar baby boom. For earlier decades, most death-control measures were too inefficient to have been so clearly the principal factor in the demonstrable population growth. During the first three-quarters of the 19th century, it must be emphasized, the trend in England's birth rate was upward. The secular decline in fertility that began in the year of the Bradlaugh–Besant trial (cf. pp. 516–517), that is to say, did not start from the high plateau that is assumed in the theory.

The differences between the English and the Japanese cases are manifest, but there is also a surprising similarity, some of which seems to challenge the theory of the demographic transition.

1. In both societies fertility in the preindustrial period was at well below the physiological maximum, in England mainly because of postponement of marriage and permanent secular celibacy of many adults, in Japan because of widespread infanticide. Defined by the means to achieve a relatively low fertility, the European family pattern was almost unique, as Hajnal termed it (cf. p. 415). But defined by a small family size irrespective of how this was achieved, the norm of Tokugawa Japan was more European than Asian. This is a crucial difference from the postulated Stage I of the conventional theory of the demographic transition.

2. According to that theory, modernization can affect fertility only to reduce it, and that notion seems to be the impetus behind some attempts to defend it (cf. Kammeyer 1970). However, in a society in which controls of family size are built into traditional institutions that are related to the traditional economy, a break with tradition would result, *a priori*, in a certain impulse toward a higher fertility. In both England and Japan the poor statistical record is at least consistent with this conclusion, and the same is true of such other countries as, for example, the Netherlands (Petersen 1960).

3. In both cases whether there was an early decline in mortality is debatable, and, if there was, the reasons are not clear. That the period of rapid growth depends entirely on the fall of the death rate seems to be valid only after 1870, say, in England or 1920 in Japan—that is, not until some decades after the increase in population began.

CITED REFERENCES AND SUGGESTIONS FOR FURTHER READING

Of the considerable literature on the industrial revolution in England, two of the older works are still among the best, by Ashton (1948) and Mantoux (1952). The view that the mass of the people suffered as a direct result of the country's industrialization is dramatically presented by, for example, the Hammonds (1932a, 1932b) and convincingly countered in the exciting volume edited by Hayek (1954). No book-length discussions of England's population during the social and economic transformation are wholly satisfactory. Though out of date in many respects, those by Griffith (1926) and Redford (1926) are still important. The recent heightened interest in historical demography is represented best in the volume edited by Glass and Eversley (1965); that edited by Wrigley (1966) is partly a manual on methods of historical demography, partly a summary of conclusions about the growth of England's population.

On the population of Japan, the massive book by Taeuber (1958) comes close to being definitive, and she has supplemented it with a paper (1960) especially pertinent to the discussion in this chapter. Dore's review-essay on Taeuber's book (1959) is interesting, and his paper on Japan as a model of economic development (1964) gives a distinguished scholar's summary view on this question.

ASHTON, T. S. 1948. *The Industrial Revolution, 1760–1830.* London: Oxford University Press.

*————. 1954a. "The Standard of Life of the Workers in England, 1790–1830," in Hayek 1954.

————. 1954b. "The Treatment of Capitalism by Historians," in Hayek 1954.

AYMANS, GERHARD. 1969. "Die Meiji-zeitlichen Familienregister als Quelle bevölkerungsgeographischer Studien," in Wilhelm Lauer, editor, *Beiträge zur geographischen Japanforschung: Vorträge aus Anlass des 50. Todestages von Johannes Justus Rein (1835–1918).* Bonn: Dümmlers.

BARCLAY, GEORGE W. 1954. *Colonial Development and Population in Taiwan.* Princeton, N.J.: Princeton University Press.

BELLAH, ROBERT N. 1957. *Tokugawa Religion.* New York: Free Press.

BENDIX, REINHARD. 1956. *Work and Authority in Industry: Ideologies of Management in the Course of Industrialization.* New York: Wiley.

BLACKMORE, J. S., and F. C. MELLONIE. 1927–28. "Family Endowment and the Birth-Rate in the Early Nineteenth Century," I and II. *Economic History* (Supplement to the *Economic Journal*), **1**, 205–213 and 412–418.

BUER, M. C. 1926. *Health, Wealth, and Population in the Early Days of the Industrial Revolution.* London: Routledge.

CARPENTER, DAVID B. 1960. "Urbanization and Social Change in Japan," *Sociological Quarterly*, **1**, 155–166.

CHAMBERS, J. D. 1965a. "The Course of Population Change," in Glass and Eversley 1965.

*————. 1965b. "Enclosure and Labour Supply in the Industrial Revolution," in Glass and Eversley 1965.

————. 1965c. "Population Change in a Provincial Town, Nottingham 1700–1800," in Glass and Eversley 1965.

DAVIS, KINGSLEY. 1955. "Social and Demographic Aspects of Economic Development in India," in Simon Kuznets *et al.*, editors, *Economic Growth: Brazil, India, Japan.* Durham, N.C.: Duke University Press.

DOI YATARŌ. 1957. [A History of Emigration to Hawaii from Oshima District, Yamaguchi Prefecture], in Japanese, *Yamaguchi Daigaku Nōgakubu gakujutsu hōkoku*, **8**, 775–848.

DORE, R. P. 1959. "Japan: Country of Accelerated Transition," *Population Studies*, **13**, 103–111.

*————. 1964. "Japan as a Model of Economic Development," *European Journal of Sociology*, **5**, 138–154.

DRUMMOND, J. C., and ANNE WILBRAHAM. 1957. *The Englishman's Food: A History of Five Centuries of English Diet*, rev. ed. London: Cape.

ENGELS, FREDERICK. 1958. *The Condition of the Working Class in England in 1848*, translated and edited by W. O. Henderson and W. H. Chaloner. New York: Macmillan.

FAY, C. R. 1947. *Life and Labour in the Nineteenth Century.* Cambridge, England: Cambridge University Press.

GEORGE, M. DOROTHY. 1925. *London Life in the XVIIIth Century.* New York: Knopf.

*GLASS, D. V., and D. E. C. EVERSLEY. 1965. *Population in History.* Chicago: Aldine.

GRIFFITH, G. TALBOT. 1926. *Population Problems of the Age of Malthus.* Cambridge, England: Cambridge University Press.

*HABAKKUK, H. J. 1965. "English Population in the Eighteenth Century," in Glass and Eversley 1965.

*HALL, JOHN W. 1955. "The Castle Town and Japan's Modern Urbanization," *Far Eastern Quarterly*, **15**, 37–56.

HAMMOND, BARBARA. 1928. "Urban Death-Rates in the Early Nineteenth Century," *Economic History* (Supplement to the *Economic Journal*), **1**, 419–428.

HAMMOND, J. L., and BARBARA HAMMOND. 1932a. *The Town Labourer, 1760–1832: The New Civilisation,* 2nd ed. London: Longmans, Green.

———, and ———. 1932b. *The Village Labourer, 1760–1832: A Study in the Government of England Before the Reform Bill.* London: Longmans, Green.

*HANLEY, SUSAN B. 1972. "Toward an Analysis of Demographic and Economic Change in Tokugawa Japan: A Village Study," *Journal of Asian Studies*, **31**, 513–537.

HAYEK, F. A., editor. 1954. *Capitalism and the Historians.* Chicago: University of Chicago Press.

HELLEINER, K. F. 1965. "The Vital Revolution Reconsidered," in Glass and Eversley 1965.

HENNOCK, E. P. 1957. "Urban Sanitary Reform a Generation before Chadwick?" *Economic History Review*, **10**, 113–119.

HOBSBAWM, E. J. 1957. "The British Standard of Living, 1790–1850," *Economic History Review*, **10**, 46–61.

HUTT, W. H. 1954. "The Factory System of the Early Nineteenth Century," in Hayek 1954.

ISHIKAWA TOMONORI. 1967. [A Social-Geographical Study of Japanese Indentured Emigrants to Hawaii from Kuga Village, Oshima District, Yamaguchi Prefecture], in Japanese, *Chiri Kagaku*, **7**, 25–38.

KAMMEYER, KENNETH C. W. 1970. "A Re-examination of Some Recent Criticisms of Transition Theory," *Sociological Quarterly*, **11**, 500–510.

*KRAUSE, J. T. 1958. "Changes in English Fertility and Mortality, 1781–1850," *Economic History Review*, **11**, 52–70.

———. 1959. "Some Implications of Recent Work in Historical Demography," *Comparative Studies in Society and History*, **1**, 164–188.

———. 1965. "The Changing Adequacy of English Registration, 1690–1837," in Glass and Eversley 1965.

LANDES, DAVID S. 1958. "Discussion," *Journal of Economic History*, **18**, 531–536.

LASLETT, PETER, and KARLA OOSTERVEEN. 1973. "Long-term Trends in Bastardy in England," *Population Studies*, **27**, 255–286.

LAWTON, RICHARD. 1967. "Rural Depopulation in Nineteenth-Century England," in Robert W. Steel and Richard Lawton, editors, *Liverpool Essays in Geography: A Jubilee Collection.* London: Longmans, Green.

MALTHUS, T. R. 1872. *An Essay on the Principle of Population,* 7th ed. London: Reeves and Turner.

MANTOUX, PAUL. 1952. *The Industrial Revolution in the Eighteenth Century: An Outline of the Beginnings of the Modern Factory System in England*, rev. ed. London: Cape.

MARSHALL, T. H. 1965. "The Population Problem During the Industrial Revolution," in Glass and Eversley 1965.

*McKEOWN, THOMAS, and R. G. BROWN. 1965. "Medical Evidence Related to English Population Changes in the Eighteenth Century," in Glass and Eversley 1965.

―――, ―――, and R. G. RECORD. 1972. "An Interpretation of the Modern Rise of Population in Europe," *Population Studies*, **26**, 345–382.

MORITA, YUZO. 1963. "Estimated Birth and Death Rates in the Early Meiji Period of Japan," *Population Studies*, **17**, 33–56.

PERHAM, MARGERY. 1962. *The Colonial Reckoning: The End of Imperial Rule in Africa in the Light of the British Experience*. New York: Knopf.

*PETERSEN, WILLIAM. 1960. "The Demographic Transition in the Netherlands," *American Sociological Review*, **25**, 334–347.

―――. 1971. *Japanese Americans: Oppression and Success*. New York: Random House.

PLUMB, J. H. 1950. *England in the Eighteenth Century*. Harmondsworth, England: Penguin.

POLANYI, KARL. 1944. *The Great Transformation*. New York: Rinehart.

REDFORD, ARTHUR. 1926. *Labour Migration in England, 1800–50*. Manchester: University of Manchester Press.

REISCHAUER, EDWIN O. 1957. *The United States and Japan*, 2nd ed. Cambridge, Mass.: Harvard University Press.

ROSENBERG, CHARLES E. 1966. "Cholera in Nineteenth-Century Europe: A Tool for Social and Economic Analysis," *Comparative Studies in Society and History*, **8**, 452–463.

ROSTOW, W. W. 1948. *British Economy of the Nineteenth Century*. Oxford: Clarendon.

SALAMAN, REDCLIFFE N. 1949. *The History and Social Influence of the Potato*. Cambridge, England: Cambridge University Press.

SAVILLE, JOHN. 1957. *Rural Depopulation in England and Wales, 1851–1951*. London: Routledge & Kegan Paul.

SMELSER, NEIL J. 1959. *Social Change in the Industrial Revolution: An Application of Theory to the British Cotton Industry*. Chicago: University of Chicago Press.

*TAEUBER, IRENE. 1958. *The Population of Japan*. Princeton, N.J.: Princeton University Press.

―――. 1960. "Japan's Demographic Transition Re-examined," *Population Studies*, **14**, 28–39.

*TAYLOR, A. J. 1960. "Progress and Poverty in Britain, 1780–1850: A Reappraisal," *History*, **45**, 16–31.

THOMAS, BRINLEY. 1954. *Migration and Economic Growth: A Study of Great Britain and the Atlantic Economy*. Cambridge, England: Cambridge University Press.

TREVELYAN, G. M. 1942. *English Social History: A Survey of Six Centuries, Chaucer to Queen Victoria*. London: Longmans, Green.

WRIGLEY, E. A. 1969. *Population and History*. New York: McGraw-Hill.

*―――, editor. 1966. *An Introduction to English Historical Demography, from the Sixteenth to the Nineteenth Century*. New York: Basic Books.

CITIES OF THE MODERN WORLD 13

In Chapter 11, on the rise of urban civilizations, most of the problems associated with the analysis of cities were ignored, partly because the archeological and historical data embodied enough difficulties of their own, partly because in that simpler epoch the urban–rural contrast had a reality that has since been largely dissipated. The conviction remains, however, that the mere distinction between town and country is still fundamental, and the most unpretentious papers on social differentiation are likely to include this factor. More serious efforts to cope with the complexities of spatial distribution, on the other hand, have evolved into a number of subdisciplines—human ecology, population geography, urban economics, regional science, and city planning—of which the partly distinctive jargons and personnel are likely to insulate parallel studies from one another. As the basic data became less and less manageable, a propensity developed to retreat into more and more abstruse mathematical models. A volume transgressing these disciplinary boundaries (Hauser and Schnore 1965), however valuable as a review of the several perspectives, in fact reflected all too accurately the chaos in the field.

The impediments to a systematic examination of the rural–urban continuum start with defining key terms. A walled city of medieval or early-modern Europe had a fixed boundary and thus a specific population, which was unambiguously distinct from the rural mass, moreover, in culture (literacy was an attribute mainly of city dwellers), in economic function (rural was equivalent to agricultural, urban to administrative or mercantile), and even in politics (these were often "free cities," independent of outside control). Setting off a modern city from its hinterland or, *a fortiori,* the urban sector from its rural counterpart cannot be so artless, for along any one of these dimensions the opposition between the two is far from a sharp dichotomy. Where shall we set the limits of an "urban place" if its administrative border does not coincide with a densely populated "settlement"? Having defined urban places ranging from a few thousand inhabitants to several million, how shall we divide this congeries into meaningful subclasses? Having done so according to the statistics of particular years, may we arrange this series in a temporal order to indicate "urban growth"? If we succeed in establishing a satisfactory historical record for one country, and then for a number of countries with different definitions, different patterns of

467

urban concentration, different city functions, how far can we legitimately carry a comparative analysis? And, finally, how much substance is there in the contrast: in the West "urban" qualities have spread throughout the population, and in underdeveloped areas peasants have swarmed into cities in such overwhelming numbers that in some respects even the largest have become "rural." No firm answers exist to such questions, and this one chapter can no more than suggest how some of the inescapable ambivalences have been mitigated in demographic analysis.

Like most verbal nouns, *urbanization* can connote either a state or a process. *Population* used to be similarly ambiguous (see the quotation from the Declaration of Independence, p. 323, n. 6), but in modern texts the word is typically used only to denote a static count of an area's inhabitants and is thus set off from *population growth*. Analogously, **urbanization** means the percentage of a population living in urban places, and **urban growth** means a change in that percentage over time. These definitions depend on the more fundamental one of "urban place," which we consider first in the narrower context of the American society and then more broadly.

"RURAL," "URBAN," AND "METROPOLITAN"

As is typical with all but the most basic items in the census schedule, those designed to measure America's urban growth were added only after this process was well under way. For the first century of the nation's life, the only meaning of *urban* was to designate a place granted a charter by a state government. According to criteria set by the various states, the minimum population ranged from 100 to over 1,000. In New England town governments often had authority over adjacent villages, whose populations were counted as part of the "town." As late as 1850, the superintendent of the census apologized for not having separated the urban from the rural sectors; enumerators ought to have had explicit instructions to set apart the returns from "all places having an aggregation of over fifty or a hundred persons, with a store, tavern, blacksmith shop, or schoolhouse and post office" (DeBow 1854: 192). Nothing was done about the matter in the two following censuses. In 1874, finally, the following superintendent published a *Statistical Atlas* giving the population density of each of the nation's counties, and in the analysis of the data towns of 8,000 inhabitants or more were defined as urban and the rest of the population as rural. Over the next several decades attempts were made both to refine this definition and to construct a residential classification from the first census onward.

Aggregation of data had at first to be based on existent territorial units: the counties, subdivisions of the county, and the incorporated places. The last of these categories, as we have seen, varied greatly in population and in any case were often too small to be classified as part of the urban sector of a nation developing great cities. Counties ranged in size from about 20 to about 20,000 square miles, and they were far less stable than one might suppose. Depending on the topography, the survey techniques, the policy of the public-land office, the date of statehood, and the size and population of the state, a county's size may have been altered several times, in some cases disappearing altogether. In each decade between 1790 and 1900, at least one county was partitioned in every state except three of the smallest (Connecticut, Rhode Island, and Delaware). The county's population was also influenced by its function, which was minimal in New England, strongly governmental in the South, and coordinated with minor civil units in the North and West (Golicz 1972).

The very names given to townships suggest how much they differed in size and function. They were called "towns" or "boroughs" (Connecticut), "hundreds" (Delaware), "militia districts" (Georgia), "beats" (Alabama), "jury wards" (Louisiana), "commissioner's," "justice's," or "election precincts" (Texas), "election precincts" (Colorado), and "judicial townships" (California). In 1900 the average size of this civil unit in the several census divisions ranged from 26.5 to 364.9 square miles.

"In summary, all three forms of local government differed among the states in at least one of two ways crucial to comparative studies of population distribution, either in territory or in minimal population criteria for incorporation" (ibid.). Better progress was made after a permanent Census Bureau was established and aggregate data did not depend entirely on the vagaries of local definitions, but the complexity of the distribution between town and country also increased.

The gradual development of the U.S. Census Bureau's definitions of *rural, urban,* and *metropolitan,* summarized in Table 13-1, illustrates the problem of assigning statistical indices to rapidly changing social entities. The division that had been established almost incidentally in the *Statistical Atlas* of 1874 was projected back to 1790, and eventually this series was continued until 1920. In the same census of 1880, however, a new definition was established: urban = an aggregate of 4,000 or more, rural = the balance. Even with this simple dichotomy, the division between rural and urban was complicated by the existence, particularly in New England, of large townships with low population density, and in almost all censuses some special provision has had to be made to adjust these to the national definition. In 1900 a three-way division was made between "urban" (population of 4,000 or more), "semi-urban" (incorporated places of less than 4,000), and "rural" (unincorporated places). This census, thus, introduced two novelties—a departure from the rural–urban dichotomy and the simultaneous use of two indexes.

In a supplementary analysis of the 1900 census (1906), a population of 2,500 or more was taken as the basic definition of *urban,* and this has remained standard to this day. *Cities* were defined as aggregates of 25,000 or more, and this was the first step toward the later separation of metropolitan units. In a special 1920 monograph both the urban and the rural sectors were divided into farm and nonfarm, and this differentiation has been maintained for the rural population in subsequent censuses.

Table 13-1. The Definition of *Urban* and *Rural* in Successive Censuses, United States, 1874–1970

Date of Definition	Period for Which Used	Urban		Rural	
1874	1790–1920	8,000+		Residue	
1880	1880–1900	4,000+		Residue	
1890	[a]				<1,000
1900	1900	4,000+		*Semi-urban:* incorporated and <4,000	Unincorporated and <4,000
1906	1900–10	*Cities* 25,000+	*Urban* 2,500+	*County districts* residue	
1910	1880–1970		2,500+ and incorporated	<2,500 or unincorporated	
1920	1920–70			Rural nonfarm	Rural farm
1930	1930–50	Population of 10,000, plus density of 1,000/sq. mi.			
1940	1940	*Metropolitan district:* city of 50,000+ with contiguous areas			
1950	1950–70	Urbanized Area[b] SMA[c]	New definition of urban[b]	1,000–2,500	<1,000
1960	1960–70	Standard Consolidated Area[b] SMSA[b]			

[a] In 1890 the rural population was subdivided into *compact bodies* of 1,000 or more and the remainder, but this division was not included in the census, apparently inadvertently.
[b] For definition, see text.
[c] Standard Metropolitan Area, the original designation of what is now termed SMSA.
PRINCIPAL SOURCE: Leon E. Truesdell, "The Development of the Urban-Rural Classification in the United States, 1874 to 1949," in U.S. Bureau of the Census, *Current Population Reports*, Series P-23, no. 1, August 5, 1949.

470

A number of new concepts and procedures were introduced in the 1950 census. The size-of-place classification was extended to segregate two classes of villages, those of 1,000 to 2,500 inhabitants (whether incorporated or not), and those of fewer than 1,000. A new definition of *urban* was adopted, by which this population comprises all persons living in (1) incorporated places of 2,500 or more (except in New England and other states where *towns* are subdivisions of counties); (2) the urban fringe (cf. Duncan and Reiss 1956: 117–118), whether incorporated or not, around cities of 50,000 or more; and (3) unincorporated places of 2,500 or more outside an urban fringe. The remaining population was classified as *rural*.

Two new metropolitan units were also established in 1950. An **Urbanized Area** is made up of at least one city (or a pair of contiguous twin cities) of 50,000 or more, plus the surrounding densely settled, closely spaced, urban fringe. A **Standard Metropolitan Statistical Area** (or SMSA), as it is now termed, is defined as one or more contiguous nonagricultural counties containing at least one city of 50,000 or more (or, again, a pair of contiguous twin cities of at least this joint size), and having a generally metropolitan character based on the counties' social and economic integration with the central city (U.S. Bureau of the Budget 1967). Whether Urbanized Area or SMSA is the preferable unit depends on the use to which it is put. The first measures primarily the residence pattern in a city and its immediately adjoining area, the second the broader economic and social integration of whole counties. By the definition of both metropolitan units, a city's effective population is no longer the number of persons who happen to live within its corporate limits. What is commonly termed the "greater" city is a much more realistic measure of the actual social aggregate, and these new census definitions approximate it in different ways. In both, formal administrative borders are ignored also in other respects: Urbanized Areas include either incorporated or unincorporated places; both they and SMSAs extend over state lines (cf. Berry 1967).

Only minor revisions were made in the classification in 1960 and 1970. The name and the precise definition of the SMSA were changed slightly. A new megalopolitan unit was set, the **Standard Consolidated Area**, and two such areas were delimited: the New York–Northeastern New Jersey SCA comprises four SMSAs plus two New Jersey counties, and the Chicago–Northwestern Indiana SCA comprises two adjacent SMSAs.

The development of the rural–urban differentiation, to repeat, is almost as complex as the social reality it partly reflects. The details of the changing classification are of little importance to a nonspecialist, but for any analyst of American society it is essential to recognize how intricate residential differentiation has become. At the beginning of the 19th century, residents of the *countryside* were *farmers* living in *unincorporated* places; and any one of these three elements could be taken as a sufficiently accurate measure of the composite status. In its continuing attempts to measure the subsequent transformation, the Census Bureau has experimented with a number of indices, of which the most important were political status (e.g., incorporated or unincorporated), occupation (e.g., rural–farm), population density (e.g., the classification added in 1930), population size (with 2,500 becoming the dividing point between urban and rural), and social and economic integration (e.g., the number of telephone calls between the central city and the suburban ring, one of the criteria by which counties are included in an SMSA). These guidelines, in any case a composite of several types of criteria, have not been followed consistently, especially when an area once included in an SMSA resists a reclassification out of it (Rosenwaike 1970).

International Comparisons

A generation ago, the U.N. Population Division conducted a detailed survey on how the rural–urban continuum is classified throughout the world, and the results, as one might expect, were even less helpful to analysis than the historical record of the United States. Of the fifty-three countries with one or more censuses that were examined, only two (Costa Rica in 1927 and Thailand in 1947) did not divide the population according to urban or rural residence, though three others (Netherlands, Belgium, and Japan) were also partial exceptions. Some countries classified places as urban if they had a political status (e.g., "incorporated"); some, if they constituted divisions similar to townships with a certain minimum size of population, which ranged from 2,000 for Austria to 20,000 for the Netherlands; some, if they performed an administrative function (similar to that of a county seat), for example, Brazil, Colombia, Peru, Egypt, and Turkey. Among countries that defined *urban* by an aggregation of population, the minimum size ranged from 250 in Denmark to 25,000 in Mexico (United Nations 1950). The population most commonly used to define an urban place, 2,000 persons or over, was implicitly proposed as an international standard. To adopt it as a measure would have changed the percentage urban in Iceland (1940) from 71.7 to 46.7, in the Netherlands (1947) from 54.6 to 72.5. In spite of the range in definitions, there was a correlation of 0.84 between the percentage "urban" as each country designated this sector and the percentage living in cities of 100,000 or more (United Nations 1953: chap. 1).

According to the latest detailed review (United Nations 1968: chap. 1), the comparability of the data has not improved in the interim. Moreover, even when the ostensible criteria were identical, one cannot assume that the figures have the same denotation. Words in the definitions carried different meanings, or the same meanings were applied to different units. In the last available yearbook (United Nations 1972: Table 5), Costa Rica is listed as having a rural–urban breakdown, but Thailand still is not. A number of other changes were made in the definitions of *urban* in countries we have cited as examples, but with little evidence of any trend toward approximate uniformity. Among those countries that use size of population as one criterion of urban status, this ranged from 200 (Greenland, Faeroe Islands) through 5,000 (Madagascar, Republic of Korea)

Table 13-2. Distribution of the World's Population by Rural and Urban Residence, 1950–70

Date	Percent		Total (–000,000)
	RURAL	URBAN	
1950	71.8	28.2	2,502
1960	67.0	33.0	3,013
1970[a]	62.0	38.0	3,605
1970[b]	61.4	38.6	3,628

[a] Based on a sum of the projections of the populations of individual countries.
[b] Based on projections of the world's total population and of its urban sector, assuming that the rate of growth during 1950–60 would be continued during 1960–70.
SOURCE: Kingsley Davis, *World Urbanization 1950–1970*, vol. 2: *Analysis of Trends, Relationships, and Development* (Berkeley: Institute of International Studies, University of California, 1972), Table 1.

to 10,000 (Malaysia, Switzerland). To adopt a definition of 2,000 or more as urban would still radically change the urban sector of many countries.

The designation of areas as urban or rural is so closely bound up with historical, political, cultural, and administrative considerations that the process of developing uniform definitions and procedures moves very slowly. Not only do the definitions differ one from the other, but in actual fact they may no longer reflect the original intention of distinguishing urban from rural. The criteria . . . become fixed and resistant to change [United Nations 1968: chap. 1].

In sum, "about thirty definitions of urban population are in current use, but none of them is really satisfactory . . . in making international comparisons" (Macura 1961). For whatever this means, the percentage of the world's population living in urban places increased from about 28 in 1950 to about 38 in 1970 (Table 13-2).

If the statistics as given are virtually useless for cross-cultural analyses, serious work in that direction must begin with constructing an alternative data base. This has been done by Davis (1970–72), at the cost of a decade of concentrated effort. He limited his perspective to urban or metropolitan agglomerations with a minimum population of 100,000, which he termed "Cities."[1] This legitimate

[1] It would be convenient if this terminology were generally adopted. Among the various terms that the U.S. Census Bureau used to demarcate the larger units of the urban sector, one was *City*, which is in accord with the distinction in American English between *city* and *town* on the basis of size. In England *city* is commonly used in the same sense, but more precisely it is an honorary title granted by royal charter, or by the Church of England to an episcopal see. In the latter sense, *cities* range from substantial metropolitan settlements like Birmingham down to Wells, with a 1961 population under 7,000, or the famous City of London, with about 5,000. Thus, what is called *city planning* in the United States becomes *town planning* in Britain, and the same difference holds for similar locutions.

restriction passes over, of course, the considerable proportion of the world's population that is considered urban by more inclusive criteria. Moreover, as Arriaga (1970) pointed out, if most of a country's urban dwellers live in a single City and the rest of the area is thinly settled, the percentage urban will be too high to suit our preconceptions; thus, at about the same dates Hawaii was as "urban" by this index as England and Wales, or Kuwait as Israel.

The most important difference, however, between Davis and many of the national statistical bureaus is that he used a strictly demographic criterion to measure urbanization. Defining an "urban place" by the number of its inhabitants does not, of course, eliminate all difficulties. One must set a cut-off figure, and one must decide between a town and a population settlement irrespective of administrative boundaries. In the United States, Europe, and Oceania "underbounded" cities are common—that is, administrative urban units that comprise only part of a continuous bloc of nonagricultural population. In such other parts of the world as the Philippines, one finds "overbounded" cities—single administrative units made up of both an urban nucleus and a rural periphery (Gibbs 1961: 17). Such impediments to measuring urbanization, great as they are, are less serious than when this is confused with **urbanism**, by which we mean the culture of cities, the way of life of town dwellers. The essential analytical question of all the disciplines concerned with cities is whether, and if so how, urban characteristics are causally related; specifically, whether large and densely settled populations generate a contrast in social features. Measurements that confuse urbanization with urbanism, supposed cause with supposed effect, make any such calculation virtually useless. Yet we have noted how typically definitions of urban places confound several kinds of criteria, at least three in addition to population size and density:

1. The most common distinguishing feature, to repeat, is to denote an urban place by its administrative function. The equivalent of a county seat in an area with a thin population acquires a special significance even though, as DeBow wrote, it has no more than fifty or a hundred inhabitants.

2. Economic criteria are used especially to distinguish the agriculture of the countryside from the service functions of a market town. Thus, some analysts have designated the sum of the two interacting parts a *community*:

Structurally speaking, the community is a unit of local organization having a center and an outer zone, with the two connected by radial routes of travel. If the center possesses a market and various specialists whose activities serve the entire unit, it is at least an incipient urban center. . . . [However,] the progress of urbanization renders the concept of community less and less useful, . . . [for] as the scale of organization increases the boundaries of locality become blurred and indistinct [Hawley 1971: 10–11].

For example, we certainly cannot mark the boundaries of a community area today by so simple an index as the source of consumer goods. The food eaten in any American city can include not only milk from the immediate locality but also (if we restrict the list to domestic products) California vegetables, Florida fruit, Wisconsin cheese, Idaho potatoes, Kansas corn and pork, and so on through all the specialized commodities of America's rationalized agriculture. On the other hand, the urban influences impinging on rural regions, while they may be transmitted through the nearest town (in the form, say, of the local newspaper or television station), are as likely as not to have originated in New York or Washington or Hollywood. Even the market town of a preindustrial society that related only to the surrounding countryside was less likely, as we have noted, to develop full urban characteristics than either an administrative center or, especially, a depot of long-distance trade.

3. Cultural criteria supposedly distinguish the essential characteristics of urban life. When so defined, the city is "a state of mind, a body of customs and traditions, and of the organized attitudes and sentiments that inhere in these customs and are transmitted with this tradition" (Park 1925).

The larger, the more densely populated, and the more heterogeneous a community, the more accentuated the characteristics associated with urbanism will be. . . . The bonds of kinship, of neighborliness, and the sentiments arising out of living together for generations under a common folk tradition are likely to be absent or, at best, relatively weak. . . . Competition and formal control mechanisms furnish the substitutes for the bonds of solidarity that are relied upon to hold a folk society together. . . . The city is characterized by secondary rather than primary contacts. The contacts of the city may indeed be face to face, but they are nevertheless impersonal, superficial, transitory, and segmental. . . . Whereas, therefore, the individual gains, on the one hand, a certain degree of emancipation or freedom from the personal and emotional controls of intimate groups, he loses, on the other hand, the spontaneous self-expression, the morale, and the sense of participation that comes with living in an integrated society [Wirth 1938].

Sometimes the contrast with a nonurban way of life is expressed as a contrast between two polar types. In the usual formulation, rural–urban is more or less identified with Gemeinschaft–Gesellschaft or nonindustrial–industrial. Redfield (1947), for example, designated *urban society* as the contrary of *folk society*, which he defined as follows:

Such a society is small, isolated, nonliterate, and homogeneous, with a strong sense of group solidarity. The ways of living are conventionalized into that coherent system which we call "a culture." Behavior is traditional, spontaneous, uncritical, and personal; there is no legislation or habit of experiment and reflection for intellectual ends. Kinship, its relationships and institutions, are the type categories of experience and the familial group is the unit of action. The sacred prevails over the secular; the economy is one of status rather than of the market.

These three classes of urban characteristics—administrative, economic, and cultural—supposedly interact with the demographic characteristics that, as in a well designed experimental model, we designate the independent variable. This is only secondarily population size; the several hundred thousand farmers, herders, and miners scattered over the Mountain West manifestly do not comprise a city. The crucial feature of an urban population is its concentration within a small compass, the high density relative to the nonurban sector.

POPULATION DENSITY

The measurement of density is deceptively simple: one merely divides the number of persons in an area by the size of that area (cf. Day and Day 1973). The resultant figure, however, depends largely on the choice of denominator. In 1970, the three American states with the densest populations were, in order, New Jersey (953 persons per square mile), Rhode Island (902), and Massachusetts (727). What distinguishes these three states is their small size, not that they contain mamoth cities like New York, Chicago, or Los Angeles (New York State had a density of 381, Illinois one of 199, and California one of 128). The point, one would think, is fairly obvious, but if the population densities of the states (or of nations, as another example) are close to meaningless, why should they be computed and given in almost every sourcebook?

The implied assumption in the simple calculation of a density figure is that the population is distributed more or less uniformly over the whole area. In most cases this is patently false. Minor adjustments can be made—thus, calculating the number of rural persons per unit of *agricultural* land, or the number of urban persons per unit of *residential* land—but typically the improvement in the ratio is not great. Usually density figures are meaningful only if they refer to rather small areas, particularly if these are drawn (as are census tracts) in order to demarcate relatively homogeneous units.

The overall density of a large city or a metropolitan area is also an almost useless datum, and the attention of analysts has focused rather on density gradients. The first serious attempt in the United States to generalize concerning the patterning of business districts and residential neighborhoods was made by a number of sociologists at the University of Chicago, particularly Ernest W. Burgess. He first offered his theory of urban zones in a paper read before the American Sociological Society in 1923 and developed it into a mature statement by 1929. According to his formulation, all modern American cities (in the first statement he had spoken of "any town or city") are spatially divided into five concentric zones: (1) a central business district, (2) a "transitional" zone of deteriorating real property used as boarding houses, and three residential areas: (3) working-class, (4) middle-class, and (5) upper middle-class. The highest density, thus, was at the center, where business firms competed for the most valuable space, and it fell off with increasing distances from the center according to the following equation:

$$d_x = d_0 e^{-bx}$$

where

d_0 = the population density at the center,
d_x = the density at distance x from the center,
e = the base of natural logarithms, and
b = the density gradient, showing the rate at which density diminishes with distance from the city center.

According to a paper published as late as 1963 (Berry *et al.*), "almost a hundred cases are now available, with examples drawn from most parts of the world for the past 150 years, and no evidence has yet been advanced to counter . . . the universal applicability of [this] equation."

For a full generation or more, the density gradient dominated both theory and research in urban sociology, particularly at Chicago. Monographs were written on the spatial distribution of crime and delinquency, family patterns, mental disorders, and other social characteristics; and all seemed to validate the theory. Then a decade or two after its initial formulation, the hypothesis of concentric circular zones was subjected to a good deal of criticism, both theoretically and empirically based. Although the studies of some cities in addition to Chicago seemed to confirm the hypothesis (St. Louis, Rochester), others apparently had more complex and altogether different spatial patterns (New Haven, Boston, Pittsburgh, New York, Flint). According to even a sympathetic critic, "The hypothesis of concentric zones as formulated by Burgess needs to be seriously modified if, indeed, it can be defended at all" (Quinn 1950: 135). Similarly, Amos Hawley, though he has sometimes been characterized as the culmination of the traditional school (e.g., Guest 1973), presented a judiciously balanced view of Burgess's theory, assigning it to a chapter titled the urban center "in the 19th century" (1971: chap. 5) and giving full attention to all criticisms except the most basic, on which Alihan (1938) had concentrated her attention. A summary of these failings is still a convenient way of considering the complexities of any attempt to generalize about how urban density is patterned.

1. Human ecology—the name of the subdiscipline, its key processes ("competition," "succession," and so on), and the Social Darwinist rationale behind them—derived from plant and animal ecology; and like other biological metaphors in social analysis, in the long run this one was less helpful than confusing. There is indeed a "struggle for existence," as Robert Park was fond of pointing out, and business firms do compete for desirable space, as Burgess was likely to rephrase the dictum, but these processes rarely take place outside a limiting normative framework that has no counterpart in lower forms of life. However one measures the effect of implicit planning (such as the spread of the grid pattern), the occasional plans of whole cities (with Washington as the prime but not sole example), the City Beautiful movement (especially prominent in Chicago, the usual site of early ecological studies), and the development of zoning laws (which at least fixed the location of such nuisance enterprises as slaughterhouses and later often set the social class of each residential area), to analyze urban structures while ignoring the influence of such controls is a caricature of social analysis.

2. Decentralization could be realized on a mass scale only with the rise of good transportation systems, first trolley cars and then automobiles and good roads, electric railroads, and a telephone network (McKelvey 1963: chap. 5; Winsborough 1963). As McKenzie (1933: 69) stated in a summary phrase of his pioneering study, the metropolitan community is "the direct result of motor transportation and its revolutionary effect upon local spatial relations." The increasing concentration into American cities up to about 1920 was countered after that date by an out-migration to the suburbs, and in the most recent period many city centers (or central cities of metropolitan areas) have on balance lost population.

3. Remarkably, Burgess had no place in his schema for industry, even though this is one of the principal determinants of residential patterning. From 1900 or before, factories were being built around the periphery of industrializing cities, either in so-called industrial parks or in the suburbs (e.g., McKelvey 1963: chap. 2). The well-to-do who used their affluence to avoid the dirt and noise of an industrial district never enjoyed a monopoly of the outer ring; from before its inception, the schema of concentric rings was too simple a model.

4. The popular notion, therefore, that "the" suburb is a middle-class or upper middle-class dormitory is not entirely correct. On the one hand, some suburbs are thoroughly working-class in all their characteristics (Berger 1960; Clark 1963). And on the other hand, neighborhoods of older cities that have enjoyed a long period of gentility sometimes retain—or even recover if they lost them—the upper-class residents associated with that way of life (Firey 1947). The importance of sentimental attachment to a family home and neighborhood is negatively related, one can hypothesize, with social mobility. For the *nouveaux riches* typical of the United States, the place where one was born has counted for far less than a brand new home in a "nice neighborhood," well away from one's childhood associations. In Budapest, as a contrasting case, land uses were arranged not around a central business district but around the nobility's residential quarter (Beynon 1943).

"Sentiment and symbolism as ecological variables" (Firey 1945) can be exemplified with the central plaza of Latin America. Following a carefully developed urban policy embodied in the 16th-century Laws of the Indies (Nuttall 1921–22), cities as far apart as Bogatá in Colombia and Concepción in Chile, as well as practically every one in between, were built according to the same overall plan. "A uniformity of city layout has been rubber-stamped all over the face of the continent no matter what the site, hill or dale, valley or pampa" (Violich 1944: 28). The dominant feature of this all but universal city plan is the main plaza, which though based on a European model is socially far more important in Spanish America than in Spain (Ricard 1950, 1952). Still today, the preference of the upper middle class for the environs of the plaza

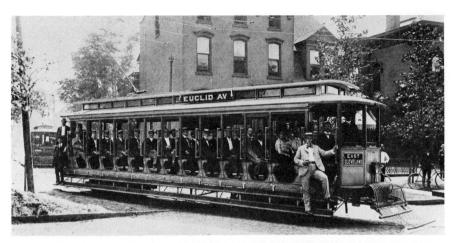

Decentralization of urban populations into suburbs developed together with transportation facilities. Around 1915, the Euclid Avenue streetcar was the means of commuting in Cleveland (*Cleveland Public Library*). Today, with heavy automobile traffic, Los Angeles has built a four-layer crossover (*J. R. Eyerman, courtesy of Life.* © *1953 Time, Inc.*).

affects the whole city. It is generally difficult to move schools or other public buildings from their traditional central location to a presently more convenient site, and business firms also seek the prestige associated with the plaza. "Over-centralization is probably the most serious problem in the Latin American city" (Gakenheimer 1959).

A study of Mérida, the capital of Yucatan State in Mexico, is especially inter-esting in that it suggests how important the relation is between social structure and the spatial pattern (Hansen 1934). The residential differentiation that the Spaniards set was "as stable as the social and cultural situation of which it was a part": the whites lived around the central plaza, the Indians in the barrios (literally, *quarters*) some distance off; and as the city grew the barrios were moved farther out. The correlation was so high that one could designate social class by referring to spatial position—"the people of the center" versus "the people of the barrios" or *barrianos*. Each barrio was both a lower-class quarter of the city and in some respects a semi-autonomous village, with a community life, organized around its own square, under the rule of an Indian cacique. In the 1880s a man who had been to the United States tried to subdivide his land outside the city into a middle-class suburb, but both this venture and a subse-quent one several years later failed completely. The traditional pattern was partially broken in the 1890s when a sharp rise in the price of sisal, the area's main commodity, set off a real-estate boom. Though the plantation owners and substantial professionals retained their attachment to the plaza, the new rich moved to a new suburb on the far side of the barrios, reached by a new boule-vard. Thus sandwiched between two parts of the growing city, the barrios were gradually transformed from more or less discrete communities into precincts.

5. If persons are not tied to a home as a symbol of intergenerational family continuity, then the age of the house is likely to determine the social class of those living in it. And since houses in a neighborhood are generally built at more or less the same time, one can relate the date of their construction to their state of deterioration and thus to the average income of those living in them. This theme is elegantly illustrated in a study of housing cohorts in Cleveland (Guest 1973). In Figure 13-1, the curves represent the changes in population density in par-ticular sectors of the city, dated according to when they reached two dwelling units per acre. The data from successive censuses are supplemented by those from an inventory of real property in 1934, which provided the ages of struc-tures before 1920. Note that in the earlier period, when transportation was less available, density built up rapidly, but after it was easier to commute over longer distances, the rise in density was at a slower rate to a much lower maximum. The earliest tracts, those that had been built up by 1905, were losing population from 1920 on. There is no evidence from this study of—by American standards— a middle-aged city to support the generalization that density increases as metro-politan areas become larger. The one important exception to this finding, one would suppose, may be public housing, where low-income families are given dwellings of an age they could not afford in the free market. Such housing develop-

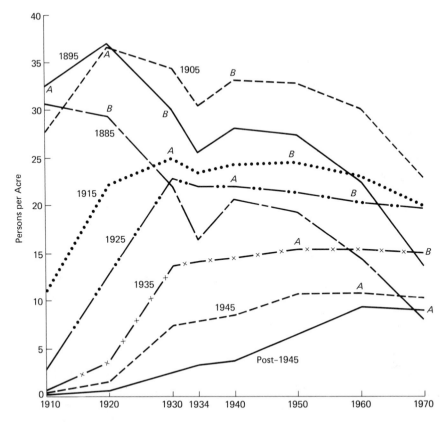

Figure 13-1. The Relation Between Age of Housing and Population Density, Cleveland, Ohio, 1910–70

Note: The dates on the curves indicate when the sector of the city reached a density of two dwellings per acre. *A* and *B* mark the approximate dates 15 and 35 years thereafter, respectively.

SOURCE: Avery M. Guest, "Urban Growth and Population Densities," *Demography*, **10** (1973), 53–69.

ments are often high-rise apartments with a dense population, but in some instances their rate of deterioration has been far faster than the norm. Apart from this exception, the generalization apparently holds that the density of particular portions of a city or metropolitan area depends mainly on the transportation available and the age of the dwellings.

Antipathy to urban life has been traditional in Western thought from the ancient Greeks to the Chicago sociologists and beyond. That the censures summarized in Louis Wirth's famous paper (p. 475) should be echoing in current books and articles is not surprising, for cities indeed have become dirtier, more disorderly, more dangerous. How desperate mayors have become is suggested by an experiment that Philadelphia initiated in 1973—a sort of urban Homestead Act. The city sold several hundred empty houses in a racially mixed neighborhood for $1 each plus a pledge that the buyer would rehabilitate the house and occupy it for 5 years, after which he would acquire unconditional title to the property. In Wilmington, Delaware, where some 1,500 houses had been abandoned, a similar plan was under way. Even without such measures, a model that explains the development of slums in part by the aging of residences implies an eventual reversal, for when structures are too old to be serviceable at all they are razed and replaced by new ones. In many cities throughout the United States such a transformation of particular neighborhoods has taken place. Moreover, the phenomenon of "urban malaise" is misnamed, for the antipathy is not to cities but rather to the very largest cities, particularly those that in one sense or another are inefficiently administered (Fischer 1973; cf. Franke 1974).

Effects of Density and Crowding

In his presidential address to the Population Association of America, Hawley (1972) reminded his audience that, parallel with the list of supposed or actual deleterious effects, population density brings a corresponding array of typical

Demolition of the Pruit-Igoe Housing Project, St. Louis, after it had deteriorated into crime-infested squalor. Children had used the stairways for toilets. Hoodlums had smashed windows and wrecked vacant apartments. Narcotics peddlers, drug addicts, and muggers had made a jungle of this high-rise slum within a few years of its construction. No ameliorative measures were effective, and eventually twenty-three buildings were closed down and three of them razed (*Michael J. Baldridge of the St. Louis Post-Dispatch*).

benefits: institutional support in attaining one's goals, extraordinary opportunities to gratify one's desires, selective association with persons compatible in values and behavior, mutual assistance in achieving access to scarce facilities, automatic exposure to education and innovative ideas. "The psychological as well as the economic analysis of physical density," he concluded, "should be submitted to a cost-benefit treatment."

The difficulties in such a procedure are suggested by the durability of stereotypes concerning the alleged effects of population density on health and mortality. The widely held folk belief, which was cited earlier, that towns are "the graveyard of countrymen" has had the implicit support of much sociological theory; according to a "census of opinion" from ancient times to several decades ago, 95 percent of those who expressed a view believed that rural life is more healthful than urban (Sorokin *et al.* 1930, vol. 1: 143). A century or two ago, perhaps one town dweller in twenty died during an epidemic year, but what urban death rates were in other periods we do not know. Contemporary opinion held not only that urban mortality was higher than rural but that it was increasing. Indeed, so long as sanitation and public health were relatively primitive, the greater concentration of population increased the dangers of infection. A part of the recorded difference, however, is often spurious: one reason for the higher death rate of the towns of the past is that a better count was made there than in the countryside. In the 20th century public-health measures and new medicines have cut the importance of infectious diseases as causes of death, eliminating in the West the epidemics that used to decimate town populations. Air pollution, traffic, overcrowding, and the stress of urban life still represent special hazards, but the medical care available to city dwellers of all classes has become better than that in rural areas, which in the United States, for instance, have generally been supplied with proportionately smaller numbers of physicians, dentists, nurses, technicians, and every other class of medical personnel except untrained midwives and possibly chiropractors. The interaction of these two factors—the greater hazards of life in the city and the better medical care available there—has resulted in a complicated pattern, with a convergence of rates in recent decades. According to a careful review of the evidence (Cassel 1971), the current relation between population density and health is ambiguous and negligible.

For a better control of causal relations, one should distinguish between **density** (measured in persons per square mile or another large areal unit) and **crowding**, sometimes termed congestion (measured in persons per room). There is no necessary relation between the two, as Table 13-3 shows. In modern cities density and crowding are more or less independent of each other, with typical correlations below 0.3 (Carey 1972), and the presumed effects of frequent close association on health, whether through infection or stress, are more likely to be felt within the close confines of a crowded apartment than in a densely populated city. In one study, controlling for social class and ethnicity reduced the apparent relation between density and pathologies to levels not significantly different from

The building of the Long Island Expressway near Central Islip, 1965. Even before the road was completed, real estate developers had established a new suburban community, whose residents helped crowd the highway as soon as they were permitted on it (*Drennan Photos*).

zero; crowding, on the other hand, "may be an important factor" in the rates of fertility, mortality, public assistance, and juvenile delinquency, but not mental health (Galle *et al.* 1972). This finding has been supported in other papers, but one study of Honolulu showed on the contrary that density explained more of the variance in pathology rates than did crowding (Schmitt 1966). Of forty

Table 13-3.   Typical Relations Between Population Density and Residential Crowding, United States

Persons per Areal Unit	Persons per Room	
	BELOW AVERAGE	ABOVE AVERAGE
Below average	Stereotype of suburbia	Slums in Western cities (e.g., Oakland, Watts)
Above average	High-rise luxury apartments; high-rise public housing	Stereotype of an urban tenement district

SOURCE: Adapted from George W. Carey, "Density, Crowding, Stress, and the Ghetto," *American Behavioral Scientist*, **15** (1972), 495–509.

analyses of the relation between housing and health, twenty-six showed a positive relation (good housing, including a lack of overcrowding, resulting in good physical and mental health; bad housing in poor health), eleven showed either no relation or an ambiguous one, and three showed a negative relation (one pertained to tuberculosis, one to death rates, and one to admissions to mental hospitals). Taking off from this review, Wilner and Walkley (1963) measured the health and "adjustment" of the members of 300 lower-class black families that moved from a slum to public housing, comparing them over a 3-year period with a matched control group of the same size that remained in the slum. During an interim period of about five months, illness and disability rates were *higher* for persons under 20 in the families that had moved to better quarters. Over the longer span the move seemingly reduced the morbidity of persons under 35, especially children, but there was no significant difference between the test and control groups for persons aged 35 and over. "Adjustment," measured by mild pathological manifestations, changed little if at all.

To summarize: Population density—that is, the seemingly relevant demographic characteristic of urban life—has little or no independent effect on morbidity and other pathologies, and the frequent assumption that it causes the typical characteristics of cities is even less well founded. That crowding should be the cause of high rates of illness would seem to be plausible, but studies of the relation are far from unanimous in confirming this supposition. One should recall that overcrowding is a symptom of the complex known as poverty, and probably no analyst has succeeded completely in separating the interrelated strands of that condition.

SYSTEMS OF CITIES

Definitions of *urban* vary so much from country to country because the meaning of a human conglomeration differs according to the broader setting. Iceland, with an area of just under 40,000 square miles (about the same as Kentucky's) and an estimated 1970 population of 200,000 (Kentucky's was 3.2 million), is not populous enough to have sizable cities. Reykjavik, its capital and largest settlement, had a 1970 population of only some 81,600, and regional administrative centers were much smaller; yet in the context of this nation these were economic–cultural centers of far greater import than their size would suggest.

Or, as another example, the influence of SMSAs in the United States cannot be measured merely by their size independent of their surroundings. The 247 SMSAs identified in the 1970 census, whose total population comprised over two-thirds of the nation, ranged from New York City, with its 11.5 million, down to Meriden, Conn., population 55,959. Generalizations covering so wide a compass are likely to be rather thin. In densely settled areas of the country, smaller metropolises are both centers of their immediate region and adjuncts to their larger neighbors. Denver had a 1970 population of something over 1.2 million, considerably less than the almost 1.9 million living in Newark. Yet Denver retained much of its earlier status as the transportation, financial, and even cultural center of the Mountain West, while Newark was in most respects a satellite of New York. In short, the significance of a single urban unit can be understood fully only in relation to the whole of the urban sector.

Social Characteristics by Type of Urban Place

Attempts to classify the rural–urban continuum into meaningful clusters can be based on any measurable characteristic of interest to a particular analyst. The chapters in a *City Classification Handbook* (Berry 1972b), thus, arrange cities according to their economic function, the characteristics of their nonwhite or their suburban populations, their political history, the residential pattern of their social classes, and so on. And in a critique of the book's other chapters (Alford 1972), it was proposed that "a far broader range of data should be included in the materials on which city classifications are built." How feasible it is to handle such masses of statistics can be suggested by Berry's attempt (1972a) to devise a new functional classification of American cities. For each of 1,762 urban places with a population of 10,000 or more in both 1950 and 1960, he collected 97 variables. He went through a factor analysis of the $1,762 \times 97$ data matrix, ending up with fourteen "latent dimensions." Earlier efforts had done no more, as he pointed out, than differentiate "between mining towns, manufacturing cities, service centers, college towns, and the like"; and these four types, plus military centers, made up five of his own categories. The other factors were no more novel: "functional size of cities," recent population growth and expansion of employment opportunities, participation of females and of elderly males in the labor force, proportions of nonwhites and of foreign-born, and so on. As a technique of manipulating data, factor analysis is likely to bring to the surface either trivialities or the generalizations implicit in the researcher's assumptions. A prior step should be a full conceptual clarification, such as Schnore's distinction (1957) between a suburb (the dormitory of commuters) and a satellite (a smaller city of a metropolitan area with its own economic structure).

A classification by size, though routine in presenting data, is also beset with difficulties, as the dichotomy between "urban" and "metropolitan" suggests. Within the category of SMSAs, the 1972 *Statistical Abstract of the United States*, as one example, gives detailed information only on those with 200,000 or more inhabitants, merely listing the names of the smaller ones. In most breakdowns (e.g., U.S. Bureau of the Census 1971), it is usual to divide the metropolitan population between the sectors living inside and outside the central cities. No analysis of more recent data is as full, and therefore as illuminating, as the census monograph on the population of the United States in 1950 (Duncan and Reiss 1956), and in spite of its date this is worth a review. In it, the urban–rural continuum was divided into the eleven size classes shown in Table 13–4. So detailed a breakdown proves its utility in their analysis, in part by differentiating those characteristics that increase (or decrease) regularly through the continuum from those whose relation to size of place is more complex. The correlation between size of place and personal income is the most striking. The median income of males (columns 7 and 8) ranged from $3,078 to $1,379 among whites and from $2,226 to $569 among nonwhites. The considerably lower incomes of females, whether considered as a unit or divided by race, were also directly correlated with size of place. For either sex the progression was in part a reflection of regional differences (the South, in particular, had the lowest median income as well as the least urbanization), but within each region income still varied together with size of place, even when educational level and type of occupation were held constant. As the money a person earns is an important determinant of a wide variety of social characteristics, one would expect to find, were the data available, a gradient in style of life by size of place.

When the effect of the age structure was eliminated, the proportion of the whites married was correlated with the size of place, especially among females (columns 3 and 4). The data suggest that the age at first marriage was higher in larger places, and that the proportion of marriages dissolved was greater. Partly as a consequence of these differences in family formation, there was also the expected correlation between size of place and fertility, as measured by the number of children under 5 years per 1,000 women aged 20 to 44 (column 5). The median age (column 2), which in part reflects the fertility, varied as one would anticipate except that villages, especially small ones, deviated from the gradient.

The sex ratio (column 1), on the other hand, had a different pattern altogether: the whole population was more or less the same except "other rural," which was ten to fifteen points higher. That is to say, except in the West, the excess of females obtained in all sizes of urban places.

The relation between internal migration and size of place was different again. The percentage of the population living in the same house in 1949 and 1950 (column 6) formed a $\bigcup$-shaped curve. While there was a considerable variation among the four regions (the percentages nonmobile were: Northeast, 87; North

Table 13-4. Selected Social Characteristics by Size of Place, United States, 1950

Size of Place	Sex Ratio	Median Age	Married[a] WHITE MALE	Married[a] WHITE FEMALE	Child–Woman Ratio[b]	Percent Non-Mobile[c]	Median Income[d] WHITE	Median Income[d] NONWHITE
	(1)	(2)	(3)	(4)	(5)	(6)	(7)	(8)
Urbanized Areas								
3,000,000 or more	94.0	33.7	−2.5	−4.2	433	85.1	$3,078	$2,213
1,000,000 to 3,000,000	94.3	32.0	−2.4	−4.1	478	83.4	3,026	2,226
250,000 to 1,000,000	94.0	31.5	0.5	−2.6	503	78.9	2,779	1,695
Under 250,000	93.5	30.9	1.0	−1.8	510	79.9	2,692	1,543
Places outside Urbanized Areas								
25,000 or more	93.7	30.4	0.7	−1.8	522	77.5	2,554	1,407
10,000 to 25,000	93.0	30.3	1.9	−0.7	525	77.8	2,484	1,275
2,500 to 10,000	93.1	29.9	2.6	1.3	570	79.0	2,354	1,134
1,000 to 2,500	94.3	30.2	3.1	3.2	609	81.0	2,268	1,092
Under 1,000 (incorporated)	93.8	32.3	2.7	4.9	629	82.1	1,935	807
Other rural								
Nonfarm	105.7	26.5	0.5	6.2	717	76.5	2,029	974
Farm	109.5	26.1	−0.2	8.4	766	85.2	1,379	569
TOTAL United States	97.6	30.2	0	0	587	81.1	2,572	1,341

[a] Deviation from percent expected on the basis of age structure.
[b] Children under 5 years per 1,000 women aged 20 to 44.
[c] Percent of population 1 year and over living in same house in 1949 and 1950.
[d] Median income of males 14 years and over with an income, 1949.

SOURCE: Otis Dudley Duncan and Albert J. Reiss, Jr., *Social Characteristics of Urban and Rural Communities, 1950* (New York: Wiley, 1956), Tables 3, 4, 6, 15, 21, and 38. Copyright © 1956 by the Social Science Research Council.

Central, 83; South, 77; and West, 73), within each region the same relation with size of place held.

Several general conclusions, not essentially different from those derived from later statistics, can be drawn from the data reported in this table: (1) The conventional division between rural and urban, a population of 2,500 and over, does not mark an important break in any of the series. Nor is any alternative dividing point any better. The social world is too complicated to be analyzed any longer by a simple dichotomy, as the Census Bureau itself has in effect recognized in the growing complexity of its statistical indexes. *Rural* and *urban*, at least with respect to contemporary United States, designate contrasting poles of a continuum rather than categories. (2) The "rural nonfarm" population does not fit into the size-of-place continuum. The reason, as one might suspect from its very name, is undoubtedly that it is too composite a grouping. (3) Some social characteristics vary with size of place (for example, income, marriage patterns, fertility), but this is not true of all (for example, sex ratio, mobility).

The Analysis of Primacy

Primacy is the ratio of the largest urban aggregate of a city system (for example, all the cities of one nation) to a designated portion of the remainder of the urban population. If one ranks cities by size, then according to Pareto's rule,

$$P_n = P_1 n^b$$

where P_1 is the population of the largest city and P_n that of the city of rank n. In the special case when $b = -1$, an equation analyzed by Zipf (1949), for any country the nth-ranking city has a population equal to $1/n$th of the largest city. Using a variation of Pareto's formula, Mitra calculated the expected size distribution of Indian cities and compared it with the actual distribution; from the difference he devised an "index of differential composition," Δ, shown in the last column of Table 13-5. This is the sum of either the positive or the negative percentage differences; thus, in this example, only 3.21 percent of the total would have to be shifted between the expected and observed distributions to obtain a perfect correspondence between them.

If one is interested less in the entire rank-size distribution than in its upper segment, which for most purposes is more important, it is convenient to indicate the primacy of a city system by a simpler index, conventionally,

$$\frac{P_1}{P_2} \quad \text{or} \quad \frac{P_1}{P_2 + P_3 + P_4}$$

where these symbols represent the populations of a country's cities ranked by size (Browning and Gibbs 1961). Which of these indices one uses is a matter of indifference; for eighty-two countries throughout the world, the coefficient of correlation between the two was 0.94 (Davis 1962). According to this study, high primacy was loosely associated with low economic development, small size

Table 13-5.   Comparison of Observed and Expected Distribution of Urban Places by Size Class, India, 1961

Size Class (−000)	Percentage of Urban Population		Difference Between Observed and Expected
	OBSERVED	EXPECTED	
	(1)	(2)	(1) − (2)
5–10	8.09	8.96	−0.87
10–20	14.44	13.90	0.54
20–50	20.08	18.50	1.58
50–100	12.35	11.80	0.55
100–200	10.92	11.89	−0.97
200–500	10.68	12.05	−1.37
500+	23.44	22.90	0.54
TOTAL	100.00	100.00	$\Delta = 3.21$

SOURCE: S. Mitra, "The Changing Pattern of Population Concentration in Indian Cities," *Eugenics Quarterly*, **12** (1965), 154–161.

of country and total population, and a traditional centralization of culture and political power. In Latin America, the region with the highest primacy, the only three countries with an index below unity—Brazil, Colombia, and Ecuador—have a topography (as well as, in the case of Brazil, an enormous size) that impeded the development of national unity, with a consequent rise of important regional capitals. More generally, the relatively small countries of Latin America have concentrated their administrative, political, religious, and cultural life very heavily in one major city, the national capital in every case but Ecuador. Nor have economic forces generally fostered the growth of competing centers. A transshipment point for the raw materials that Latin America produces (ores and metals, petroleum, various agricultural products) is not likely to develop from this function, and the Latin American equivalent of a market town has typically been too much dominated by the neighboring hacienda to grow into an important regional center. A person who wants to escape from this domination, whether a peon who migrates to a big city or a young man beginning a professional career, is induced to go to the only place, if that, where the hacendado's power does not reach. This dominance by the hacienda is not, of course, a recent development (cf. Morse 1962), and the high primacy of Latin American city systems also goes back to the 16th century.

Apart from such political and cultural factors, are primacy and economic development generally related? According to one study, the association of uniformly defined "Metropolitan Areas" with modernization "becomes closer as the extent of urbanization increases" (Wilkinson 1960). Another analyst found that "different city-size distributions are in no way related to the relative economic development of countries" (Berry 1961). Yet another concluded that the primacy of city systems "does not appear to be a function of the level of economic development, industrialization, or urbanization," but rather that high primacy is associated with "small areal and population size" (Mehta 1964). At most, one can conclude that whatever association there may be between the two factors is loose and easily negated by other characteristics of the city system.

OCCUPATIONAL AND SOCIAL CATEGORIES

It is manifest that the division between town and countryside is related to the way any population breaks down by occupation and thus by social class, but the association is seldom simple. Not only is the urban–rural division set, as we have seen, by partly arbitrary criteria, but this is true also of the classification of occupations and of the distinction between those who are and are not economically active. The ambiguities in the definition of the labor force are discussed in terms of four successively smaller subdivisions:

1. In any population only a certain portion, designated as its **labor pool**, is capable of gainful work. The very young and the very old are dependent on the intermediate age group, but at what ages does a person move from one category to the next? In the United States, as we have noted earlier, the minimum age of those in the labor pool was twice raised, from 10 to 14 years between the 1930 and the 1940 censuses, and from 14 to 16 in 1967. This reflects the virtual elimination of child labor in this country, but the present dividing line is hardly relevant to the situation in many other cultures. Among the potentially active population demarcated by age, moreover, some are mentally or physically disabled, or for other reasons not capable of performing useful work. Here again, the norms of each society partly define the limits of this category, though in any case the number of incapacitated is small relative to that of dependent young and aged.

2. A greater proportion of any society's labor potential can be realized during such a national emergency as a major war, for in a normal period several categories are omitted from the **labor force**: those who maintain childhood roles beyond the age defining economic maturity (i.e., students) or who retire before the supposed end of their working life, and also those who work in their own household without remuneration (i.e., most adult females). Thus, around 1960 between 59 percent (industrial countries) and 52 percent (underdeveloped countries) of all males were listed as economically active, but only about a quarter of all females (Sadie 1967). In fact, it is prudent in such international comparisons to omit females altogether, since the way their economic activity is recorded varies too much from country to country. However, this kind of ambiguity also characterizes male peasants' activities, which also constitute both an extension of their domestic establishment and a participation in the national economy. In particular, it would be hazardous to take as an implicit model for cross-cultural analysis the situation in the United States, with its highly rationalized agriculture and the generally sharp separation between economic and other social roles.

3. The distinction between armed forces and the **civilian labor force** is usually clear-cut (an area in which guerrillas are operating is not generally one where statistics of any kind can be collected).

4. Note that **occupied** and **employed** are not synonymous: a person not at work on a specific day may nevertheless be employed; one unemployed but seeking a job is occupied. As of January 1967, the slightly revised definition of an unemployed person in the United States was as follows: one who during a periodic survey is not gainfully employed, is currently available for work, and actively sought a job during the past four weeks. Those absent from a job during the survey week because of such factors as illness, a strike, or bad weather are classified as employed even if they are seeking another job. In peasant countries it is more difficult to delimit employed from unemployed, for between them there is a loosely defined category of "hidden unemployment"—comprising all those economically surplus on a job who are retained because of family ties or other economically irrelevant considerations.

In the United States, which can be used as an example of how industrial countries analyze their labor force, persons are identified by occupations (listed in a massive *Dictionary of Occupational Titles*), which are classified into "occupational categories" (of which there were 441 in 1970, as compared with only 297 in 1960). These are then combined into the "major occupational groups" that sociologists typically use as one index of social class. In the 1970 census schedule, the standard query on the "kind of work" the respondent did was supplemented by two others, asking for his job title and his major activities. Changes over the decade reflected both the development of the country's technology (the number of occupations in the computer field went from none to five, for instance) and a greater effort to improve the presentation of the data. Categories were made more specific, more homogeneous, in some cases smaller (Greene *et al.* 1969). As in all such revisions, any improvement over earlier classification systems makes temporal comparisons more difficult.

The choice of an occupational classification partly determines the patterns of social stratification and social mobility that the historian will find. . . . They determine which shifts between specific jobs can be considered instances of vertical mobility and which differences of occupation between people can be said to indicate differences of status or class. . . . I would contend [that] the schemes used in most contemporary sociological research and by the United States Bureau of the Census have confused two objectives: the study of occupational structure and the study of occupational mobility [Katz 1972].

Cutting across the classification by occupation is a no less complicated one by industry. A mechanic or a physician may be self-employed, or he may work for a government agency or for a private corporation, and if the latter it may be engaged in manufacturing, construction, or whatever. As with occupations, a major effort was made to improve the 1970 classification of industries, which comprised 226 industry groups as compared with 150 a decade earlier. These revisions again reflected both an attempt to organize the data better and important changes in the society, with new categories added in such services as education and health and such technical fields as computer programing (Greene 1969).

If it were possible to rank occupations, or even occupational categories, by the social status associated with each, changes in the proportion of the labor force engaged in each would be a good index of social mobility. Differences over time in the still more heterogeneous major occupational groups give a rough indication of a significant overall advance (Table 13-6). The greatest proportionate increase during this century was in white-collar jobs, both clerical and professional. The greatest decline over the long run was in agriculture: the percentage employed in this sector fell from an estimated 83 in 1820 to 53 in 1870 to a little

Table 13-6. Percentage Distribution of Experienced Labor Force by Major Occupational Group, United States, 1900–70

Major Occupational Group	1900	1930	1960	1970[a]	Percent Change 1900–70	Percent Change 1960–70
Professional, technical, and kindred workers	4.3	6.8	11.2	13.5	+214	+21
Farmers and farm managers	19.9	12.4	3.9	2.4	−88	−38
Managers, officials, and proprietors, except farm	5.8	7.4	8.4	10.5	+81	+25
Clerical and kindred workers	3.0	8.9	14.4	17.4	+480	+21
Sales workers	4.5	6.3	7.2	6.1	+36	−15
Craftsmen, foremen, and kindred workers	10.5	12.8	13.5	12.9	+23	−4
Operatives and kindred workers	12.8	15.8	18.4	17.6	+38	−4
Private household workers	5.4	4.1	2.7	1.9	−65	−30
Service workers, except private household	3.6	5.7	8.4	10.1	+181	+20
Farm laborers and foremen	17.7	8.8	2.2	2.4	−86	+9
Laborers, except farm and mine	12.5	11.0	4.8	5.0	−60	+4
Occupation not reported	—	—	4.9	—	—	—
TOTAL	100.0	100.0	100.0	100.0		

[a] Employed persons as of June, based on a Bureau of Labor Statistics survey.
SOURCES: U.S. Bureau of the Census, *Historical Statistics of the United States*, 1960; *Census of the Population, 1960*, 1964. U.S. Department of Labor, *Employment and Earnings*, vol. 18, 1971.

over 30 in 1910, and from that date the decline continued not only relatively but in absolute numbers. In the most recent period those employed in agriculture fell from 7.4 million in 1950 to 5.4 in 1960 and 3.7 in 1971 (U.S. Bureau of the Census 1972). Apart from agriculture, the largest proportionate losses were in the bottom categories, unskilled and household labor. This record, although its dimensions are related to the size, wealth, and social democracy of the United States, reflects also the shift linked anywhere with the advance of industrialism—out of low-level menial jobs and to service industries and professions.

CITIES IN ECONOMIC DEVELOPMENT

We all know, of course, that industrialization and urbanization have been related in the past. Before 1850 no society of the world was predominantly urban, and by 1900 only Great Britain had become so; today all industrial nations are highly urban. Recently, however, the city growth historically associated with the rise of industry has been even faster in some underdeveloped areas and not unambiguously as an accompaniment or precursor of development.

Spelling out this commonplace numerically is impeded, once again, by the considerable ambiguity in quantitative measures. The usual index of "economic development" is the per-capita Gross National Product (GNP), or the total monetary value of all the goods and services produced during a given year. This datum can be approximated with moderate accuracy for industrial countries, but for those going through the developmental process estimates are subject to large and systematic errors of unknown size. Among the 122 nations included in a handbook of economic indicators (Russett *et al.* 1964: 149), thus, only eleven had a probable margin of error of only ± 5 percent, while for the twenty-nine countries at the other end of the continuum the margin "should be under ± 50 percent, but it is impossible to say how much under." The incomparability derives not only from a varying accuracy in the data collected but, more fundamentally, from a continual shift in the size of the universe. Much of peasant countries' produce is not marketed but consumed directly; like the work of housewives in advanced economies, the food grown in small private plots is either excluded from the GNP by definition or is brought in through the wildest of guesses. Since the extension of the market economy means precisely that a larger and larger proportion of this household production is shifted to cash crops or paid work, a recorded increase in GNP can reflect either that transformation of the distribution system or a higher overall production, or both in an unknowable ratio. Morgenstern (1963: 300) held that rates of growth in GNP are "worthless in view of the exacting uses to which they are being put"; that is, they provide a loose suggestion of broad distinctions but not an acceptable basis for exact differentiation.

And if the numerators of rates of GNP per capita can be adequately estimated, the denominators still involve assumptions that are often unwarranted. That the populations are not known precisely is a minor matter—except in those countries (such as Communist China) that lack even a pad from which guestimates can be launched. But dividing the approximated GNP by the approximated population, if the resultant average is to have a general significance, implies a more or less even distribution of goods and services throughout the society. Russett *et al.* (1964: 155) placed Kuwait first in an ordered list of nations because it had a 1957 GNP per capita of $2,900 as against $2,577 in the United States, which was ranked second. In less extreme contrasts, such a pair of averages is ordinarily taken to be a genuine reflection of the two countries' welfare. Much of what is included in "development," moreover, has little to do with the material well-being of any social class; such typical projects as national airlines or mammoth steel plants may be not so much useful elements of the economy as status symbols. How much of the capital fund is diverted into these counterparts of the ancient pyramids depends in part on how each analyst appraises genuine utility, but it is often too great a proportion to be safely ignored.

Not surprisingly, then, the data compiled to compare the various nations' GNP per capita are inherently implausible. Of the 122 countries listed in Russett *et al.*, half showed $105 or less, ranging down to $45 for Nepal. Two systematic errors are built into these preposterous figures, the already mentioned underestimates of production outside the market and, probably more important, the noncomparability for such purposes of the world's currencies. As the authors put it (ibid.: 149), "A man would surely starve on an annual income of $100 in the United States, but given the price of staple foods in Burma [for instance] the same amount, converted into Burmese *kyat*, keeps him alive at least at the subsistence level." But if converting *kyat* into dollars at the rate used in international trade tells us nothing of the purchasing power of the typical Burmese, one wonders what the purpose of the exercise can be.

In his analysis of what he termed a **dual economy**, Boeke (1953: 68–78) distinguished between "village money," circulating mainly within the community, and "dualistic money," which comes from the outside, passes through the village, and ends up again beyond its limits. In the Netherlands East Indies, Boeke's principal example, the two items that had to be imported into the local economy were kerosene and salt; in most other respects, it was self-subsistent. Villagers spent the market days buying and selling their wares for amounts as low as half a guilder-cent (or about $0.0012). The name of the currency was the same, but in fact there were two media of exchange, separated by the level at which ordinary purchases could be made. No peasant could ever accumulate enough village money to convert it into a meaningful number of guilders of dualistic money; and, vice versa, when some enterprising fishermen tried to make their fortune by selling to urban traders, they were "excommunicated"—that is, denied access to agricultural produce and village services. Some leakage was possible in both directions but by far not enough to warrant an assumption that both types of money were parts of the same system, convertible into dollars at a single rate.

A dual economy differs from a monistic one in much more than this gross disparity in prices. According to Boeke's thesis, the European sector operated in accordance with the interrelated postulates of Western economic theory—that consumers' wants are unlimited, that the economy is based on a money exchange, that each consumer acts as an individual in the market (or often in both a local and an international market). But these premises did not apply, or applied only in part, to the native sector of the dual economy. In the pre-independence Indonesian village, the economic unit was not the individual but the family. Work was done to satisfy needs set by physiology and hereditary status; apart from the number of dependents they were therefore relatively fixed. As a family grew larger, the person responsible for its care had to work harder; but if it was small, he worked only enough to maintain his charges at their appropriate level. The consequences for the operation of elementary economic "laws" were bizarre.

When the price of rice or coconuts is high, the chances are that less of the commodities will be offered for sale; when wages are raised, the manager of the estate risks that less work will be done; if three acres are enough to supply the needs of the household a cultivator will not till six; when rubber prices fall the owner of a grove may decide to tap more intensively, whereas high prices may mean that he leaves a larger or smaller portion of his tappable trees untapped [ibid.: 40].

Implicitly we have defined *development* narrowly, relating it only to change in the economy, and the broader transformation of the society that is commonly termed *modernization* is of course still more difficult to measure. Ness (1970: 8–9) noted some sixty-eight variables that have been used as indices of development and/or modernization, ranging from the number of items of domestic mail per capita through population density to the percent of the total vote for various types of political parties. Even apart from the paucity and inaccuracy of most of the data, the correlation among them is usually not impressive. The typical underlying assumption—that development and modernization are inevitably linked in a rather simple fashion—hardly fits the two nations outside the Western sphere that have been industrialized, Japan and the Soviet Union. From those precedents, should we not anticipate that whatever kinds of society evolve in India, Latin America, and black Africa will combine in each instance elements of the local tradition with the universals of modernization into an amalgam specific to itself?

A priori, if one accepts Boeke's thesis as a plausible statement of the confrontation of two economic systems,[2] the metropolises of underdeveloped areas

[2] Of the several economists who have criticized Boeke, Bauer (1965: 15, 17, 23) can be taken as a typical defender of academic orthodoxy. On the one hand, he admits the possibility that Western economic theorems may not apply universally: "Of course the institutional framework of the community limits and directs the operations of its economic activities; and this framework in underdeveloped countries is often very different.... The readiness of response varies with all sorts of factors and influences, and in stable and stratified societies with strong traditions wants may be less expansive than in other more fluid societies." On the other hand, he asserts that "those who dispute the relevance of the propositions of economics to underdeveloped countries usually base their arguments on the differences in

functioned as loci from which Western (that is, modernizing) influences disseminated. Many of these cities were the outright creation of Europeans; others grew from small towns or villages mainly as a consequence of Western influences.

In 1800, Rangoon, Saigon, and Singapore did not yet exist in city form; Bangkok, the new capital of Thailand, was less than twenty years old; Manila and Batavia (Jakarta), though then about 200 years old, were merely small coastal towns. They began to grow rapidly after the middle of the 19th century [and] . . . the consolidation of Western control, direct or indirect, over most of Southeast Asia in the 1890s [Ginsburg 1955].

So cosmopolitan are such Asian centers still that typically each can be paired with a subcenter of the native culture; thus, Shanghai–Nanking, Rangoon–Mandalay, Jakarta–Jogjakarta, Manila–Cebu, and so on. Similarly, "the modern African town did not grow out of the needs of, and in service to, its own hinterland; its primary relationship is to Europe" (McCall 1955). The alienation of the peasant mass from such cities was based first of all on their foreignness. In the period after 1945, when many of the world's colonies achieved independence (or, as in the case of Thailand, greatly expanded their range of prior nominal independence), there was some sentiment in the Southeast Asian nations to select as their capitals cities that had a native tradition and were located near the countries' geographical centers. In fact, almost without exception they chose cities created by Western trade and imperial rule, typically the largest urban aggregate and in some cases the only real one—Karachi, Colombo, Rangoon, Bangkok, Kuala Lumpur, Jakarta, Manila, and of course Singapore. As the capitals took on the many tasks of administering these new nations, including a sizable portion of their economies, the populations of these metropolises increased even more rapidly than at Southeast Asia's generally high rate of natural increase and urban growth. In short, even if occasionally with a fresh name to recall the precolonial grandeur, the centers of new nationalism are indisputable products of the colonial rule (Murphey 1957; cf. Fryer 1953).

TYPES OF RURAL–URBAN MIGRATION

That modernization forces are so heavily concentrated in the large cities of underdeveloped areas means that, at least to some degree, what might be termed the classical model of rural–urban migration (cf. pp. 325–326) applies. In the development of Western nations, the urban sector has grown by its own natural

---

attitudes and institutions, . . . [but] these views reflect incomplete observations or imperfect understanding of economics." There follow several anecdotes to show that in some instances non-Westerners behave as they are supposed to in Western economic theory, but in sum these add up to much less than the contrary instances cited by Boeke, not to mention works in a similar vein about India or Africa. In any case, one would expect a society in transition to exhibit psychological norms derivative both from traditional institutions and from modern ones; and which attitudes are modal in any area is an empirical question, not a doctrinal one.

increase, by the annexation of new territory, and, as the most important factor, by the massive migration of countrymen out of agriculture into city occupations. Those who have made this move are rewarded with better jobs and incomes, more varied and comfortable living. Under these conditions, the migration to the cities of a relatively homogeneous society results in its greater diversification, which starts with the very process of the migrants' self-selection according to characteristics relevant to success in urban pursuits.

One variation of this model common in underdeveloped areas results in a markedly different urban society. In both Africa and Asia it used to be that commercial interests, in an attempt to acquire an urban labor force without paying for a city, fostered the migration of young males to industrial sites while inhibiting the development there of any normal social life. The workers' settlements once attached to African mines, for instance, were often large enough to be designated "cities," but in their truncated function, and thus in their age and sex structure, they more closely resembled enormous army camps (Mitchell 1961; Elkan 1960). In the past decade or two, it is true, such African firms as the Copperbelt mining companies have come to recognize that a stabilized labor force brings a substantial commercial benefit (Steel 1961). Similarly, the European or Japanese directors of government bureaus and commercial enterprises once fostered a separation of their employees' lives between economic functions in a city and social ones in a nearby village; and many reasons have remained why in Asia or Africa a countryman who wants to supplement his peasant's income migrates to a mine or city alone and temporarily, eventually to return to his village, his wife and children, his extended-family associations, his share of the tribal land. Urban housing and transportation are poor; there are no adequate substitutes, in the form of social welfare or high wages, for the communal services of the village. As Schapera (1947) pointed out in his classic study of Bechuanaland, a period of employment in the city where a young man can sow his wild oats came to be seen almost as a necessary prelude to full tribal manhood; once such a pattern developed, it reinforced the traditional reluctance to submit the females of one's family to the damaging entanglements, if not actual physical dangers, of urban slums. For all these reasons, in contrast to the low sex ratio of the movement into Western cities, in-migration to the cities of underdeveloped areas, and thus the urban populations themselves, have been predominantly male. Thus, even when rural–urban migration has been a response to economic opportunities in the city, it has not necessarily resulted in the separation of an advanced sector of the population from its rural base and the full development of a town-based subculture.

Although the rapid urban growth of underdeveloped areas thus derives in part from the fact that better paying industrial jobs are located in the cities, the prevalent rural stagnation is much more important. In the language of the conventional schema, the predominance of pull factors has given way to push factors. Nonindustrial countries have enjoyed a remarkable decline in rural mortality; medicines, technicians, and other death-control measures, disseminated from industrial nations through international agencies (cf. chap. 15), have shattered the prior balance between the traditional economy and the rural population. And corrective efforts to raise productivity, when they have succeeded, also increased the proportion of the peasants economically surplus to the agricultural sector. The effects of the growing disparity between the countryside's resources and the numbers dependent on them have been aggravated, moreover, by a rise in expectations so rapid as to surpass any conceivable improvement in the actual situation. When even the most isolated hamlet catches glimpses of metropolitan glamor, the simple life that satisfied parents and grandparents is likely to be seen as too confining; as against the village's rigid social structure, the city appeals even more for its greater anonymity, its wider range of personal freedom.

A very large portion of this new type of in-migrants lack the most elementary urban facilities—water supply, sewerage, even a right to their hovels. Almost all large cities of underdeveloped countries are ringed by squatter settlements, shantytowns of self-constructed huts, which in Latin America, for instance, constitute a third (Caracas) or even half (Maracaibo) of the city's population. As the squatters have no legal right to the land, they invade it quickly and *en masse*, suddenly confronting authorities with the established fact of their presence. For example, on a single night of December 1954, some 5,000 persons established a

One of the families living in a shantytown on the periphery of Brazilia, the new capital of Brazil (*Paul Conklin—PIX*).

new *barriada* in Lima, Peru. Previously the quasilegal promoters had organized the invasion, assigning a plot to each applicant. During the night each family rushed to throw up some kind of dwelling in order to establish squatters' rights to the land (Matos 1961). Though few details are known with any certainty of how a typical slum dweller lives, assumptions have helped protract the dispute over the social function of large cities.

Half of the inhabitants of Latin America, to take that area as a prime example, live in cities, more than a quarter in the ten metropolises with over a million each. Most of the anticipated very rapid growth of the population (Table 13-7), moreover, will end up in the cities. Over the 15 years from 1965 the rural sector is expected to grow by something over 30 million persons, but the urban by almost 100 million. Not even the most sanguine optimist could hope that urban facilities will expand rapidly enough to accommodate this flood. In the late 1960s the Inter-American Development Bank estimated the housing shortage in

Table 13-7. Percent Urban, Estimated and Projected Population, Principal Countries of Latin America, 1960–80

Country	Percent Urban, Latest Census Year		Population (millions)		
			1965	1970	1980
Uruguay	81	(1963)	2.7	2.9	3.3
Argentina	74	(1960)	22.5	24.4	28.2
Chile	68	(1960)	8.7	9.8	12.2
Venezuela	67	(1961)	9.1	10.8	15.0
Colombia	53	(1964)	18.7	22.2	31.4
Mexico	51	(1960)	42.7	50.7	71.4
Peru	47	(1961)	11.6	13.6	18.5
Brazil	46	(1960)	81.0	93.2	124.0
Panama	44	(1960)	1.2	1.4	1.9
Nicaragua	41	(1963)	1.7	2.0	2.8
El Salvador	39	(1961)	2.9	3.4	4.9
Ecuador	36	(1962)	5.1	6.0	8.4
Paraguay	36	(1962)	2.0	2.4	3.5
Costa Rica	35	(1963)	1.5	1.7	2.3
Bolivia	35	(1950)	4.1	4.7	6.0
Guatemala	34	(1964)	4.6	5.3	7.0
Dominican Republic	30	(1960)	3.7	4.3	6.2
Honduras	23	(1961)	2.2	2.6	3.7
Haiti	12	(1950)	4.6	5.2	6.8
TOTAL			230.6	266.6	357.5

SOURCES: U.N. Economic Commission for Latin America, *Statistical Bulletin*, March 1971; October 1971.

A slum district of Guay-
aquil, Ecuador (*Paul
Conklin—PIX*).

Latin America at between 12 and 14 million units, which would cost a total of
$30 billion or, with modest community facilities, as much as $50 billion (Casasco
1969). One need only ponder where such an amount could come from to recognize that the slum is an inescapable fact; official efforts to ameliorate the situation, if not based on this premise, have usually been unsuccessful. Some have
aggravated the problem. If police clear out the area of settlement, the squatters
spread to other parts of the city and start again at a still lower level of hope and
subsistence. If adequate housing is constructed, the result commonly is to attract
still more in-migrants to the city and even to that housing project. In 1958 the
Venezuelan housing agency constructed ninety-seven apartment blocks in
Caracas at a total cost of some $200 million, designed to house about 180,000
persons. An additional 4,000 families invaded the apartments and lived there
illegally; other thousands built a shantytown on the project site. After a year
unpaid rents totaled $5 million, augmented by half a million per month in
maintenance losses. "The accompanying social, economic, and administrative
difficulties" mounted into "civil anarchy." According to an international study

team called in to analyze the project's problems, it was the massive program itself that had attracted many rural migrants to the area, and the experts recommended that the government postpone the building of such residential units until it had established a "housing policy related to the economic and social development of the country and within a process of national planning and construction" (Carlson 1959).

Sometimes it is difficult, on the contrary, to induce squatters to leave their dwellings and settle in new housing. For example, when a slum near the center of Lagos, the capital of Nigeria, was torn down and its residents were transferred to a new project on the outskirts, some were delighted by the change. For others the move was "disastrous."

They were isolated from their work, their markets, and their relatives, at the end of a long and expensive bus journey. Unable to meet the expenses of suburban life, some of the husbands sent their wives home to their families, and distributed their children among relatives. Wives, finding no opportunities for trade, left to live with their own relatives nearer the center of town; others simply deserted when their husbands could no longer support them. Old people who had lived before in a family house, where they paid no rent, and were cared for, now found themselves neglected. Craftsmen and traders who had lost their customers sold up and at last determined to go abroad out of reach of wives and children and all family responsibilities, in the hope of recovering their fortunes. For these, the kind of domestic life for which the estate was planned was a luxury they could not afford [Marris 1960; cf. Marris 1961; Gans 1962].

Marris's conclusion was that "many Lagos families have neither the desire nor the means to accept the social reforms which are being imposed upon them."

These reservations about slum clearance have been generalized in a vivid passage:

In a housing famine there is nothing that slum clearance can accomplish that cannot be done more efficiently by an earthquake. The worst aspects of slum life are overcrowding and excessive shelter cost. Demolition without replacement intensifies overcrowding and increases shelter cost. . . . Actually, the provision of public housing is an independent undertaking that need not be part of the clearance operations. . . . Worse than slums is a slum shortage that provides no shelter, good or bad [Abrams 1964: 126–128].

In countries as different as the United States, Nigeria, and Peru, that is to say, the efforts of public authorities to combat what they view as virulent social diseases have been based on a number of dubious preconceptions. Antipathy to squatter settlements is at least in part an expression of the very common aversion to cities, and particularly to large cities. In a few instances—Gandhi or the landed upper class of Latin America—the antipathy is, more fundamentally, to industrialism; but more usually policymakers want to acquire the benefits of modernization while preventing the growth of the "megalopolis," its typical site, and substituting a multiplicity of smaller towns. In the early 1950s, there was a reported "widespread agreement concerning the desirability of decentralization, the governments of Burma, Ceylon, Hong Kong, India, Indonesia, Pakistan, the Philippines, Singapore, and Vietnam having generally accepted this principle as one of the bases for housing and town and country planning" (ILO 1953: 85). As some of the countries on this list suggest, one of the problems that concerned the officials was not metropolization *per se* but the refugees who fled from Pakistan to India, from India to Pakistan, from China to Hong Kong, from North to South Korea, and so on. It is misleading to illustrate the disadvantages of large cities from conditions in such a commonly chosen example as Calcutta (e.g., Wurster 1962; Bose 1965), for the true comparison here is less with small towns or the countryside than with refugee camps.

Very often the separation of metropolitan centers from the rural mass is designated as one reason for such a hostile policy; small urban centers constitute "a more effective bridge between city and country" (Wurster 1955: 8). But this very fact that a small city is likely to be thoroughly embedded in its hinterland and thus markedly influenced by traditional norms suggests that the metropolis is a more effective instrument for the creation of a society that deviates from those norms. Sometimes the policy is to concentrate on agriculture and in effect to ignore the city. But the improvement of peasants' social and legal status, however desirable it may be on other grounds, need not stem the rural–urban flow. In Mexico, after half a century of vigorous land reform (supplemented in demographic terms by the absorption of some of the surplus agricultural labor into temporary jobs in the United States), cities have grown at rates high even for Latin America.

The more or less specific objections to the metropolis are strongly reinforced by general theory. In the conventional wisdom of American sociology (which has markedly influenced that in other countries), the social changes associated with the type of urbanization prevalent in underdeveloped nations (or even with urbanization altogether) are denoted as "social disorganization," or the breakdown of viable patterns of community life. "Personal disorganization, which is the subjective aspect of social disorganization, is manifest in such conditions as juvenile delinquency, crime, and vice" (Hauser 1957). One flaw in this concept is the premise that in the countryside a viable community exists, virtually by definition, and that it is the movement to an urban setting that *dis*organizes it. The very sparse data available suggest that typically the residents of shanty-towns are not disoriented by urban life nearly so much as by the rural one they finally escaped. According to the 1956 census of fifty-six *barriadas* in Lima, most of the migrants came seeking employment and only one in a hundred failed to find some remunerative job (Matos 1961). Studies of in-migrants to a number of Asian cities found that the attraction of "city lights" was of no significance: "economic hardship in varying degrees was the real reason for practically all migration" (Unesco 1956: Introduction).

Like *disorganization*, the concept of *overurbanization* has become a commonplace in writings on underdeveloped areas. The term, which derives originally

Homeless sleeping in a Calcutta street. As in other instances of extreme overcrowd-ing, congestion from the normal in-migration to Calcutta was aggravated by an influx of refugees (*James Burke, courtesy of Life. © Time, Inc.*).

from an article by Davis and Golden (1954), offers a framework for analyzing the two types of rural–urban migration we have noted. As they use the concept, those countries with a greater urban population than is typical at their level of industrialization are "overurbanized." Thus, with the percentage of the country's population in cities of over 100,000 and the percentage of economically active males in agriculture as the two indices, Egypt, for example, was notably overurbanized. "The densely settled and impoverished countryside of Egypt is pushing people into the cities because they have no other alternative"; this kind of urban growth is generated by intolerable conditions at its source rather than mainly by the pull of opportunities in urban industry. The implicit confusion of statistical and ethical norms is not by design; as the authors use it, overurbanization "has only a statistical meaning, with no overtone of evaluation intended." But the word was poorly chosen to convey such a neutral meaning, and most who have adopted the concept made a policy recommendation with it. Two years after Davis and Golden's article appeared, thus, the summary report of a United Nations conference on the growth of cities in Asia noted that "urbanization has generally tended to move ahead of economic development" and that, since this differential development had various deleterious effects, "it is probably true to say that Asia is overurbanized in relation to its degree of economic development" and thus "consideration was given to ways in which the 'overurbanization' in many Asian countries could be combated" (Hauser 1957). Or, as another representative example: "It may well turn out that urbanization in Asia is proceeding at too rapid a rate, and that urban populations tend to be too heavily concentrated in a few primate cities. . . . At present the countries of South Asia may be regarded, on the whole, as 'overurbanized'" (Hoselitz 1957).

Such a blanket appraisal is beside the point, as would also be a blanket rejection of it. The crucial problem, both for analysis and for policy, is to distinguish between two types of shantytowns. They cannot be differentiated necessarily by the physical condition of the hovels; it took policymakers decades to learn that the characteristic feature of a slum is not poor housing but the lack of a viable community life. There are "slums of hope" and "slums of despair" (Casasco 1969). Perhaps the best analysis of this distinction is by William Mangin (1967a, 1967b), who spent a decade in more or less continuous study of the squatter settlements in Peru and who, more recently, has edited a book on rural in-migrants throughout the world (1970).

In the Peruvian *barriadas*, by avoiding government control and the requirements of lending institutions, the people have built houses to their own desires and on the basis of first things first. Because they needed shelter immediately, they built walls and a roof and left bathrooms and electricity to be added later. They want flat roofs and strong foundations so that they can add a second story. They want a yard for raising chickens and guinea pigs, and a front room that can serve as a store or a barroom. They have dispensed with the restrictive residential zoning and construction details that middle-class planners and architects consider essential for proper housing [Mangin 1967b].

The community is organized, as we have pointed out, even before the new residents move in and put up their homes. It is run by membership organizations, which Mangin describes as more democratic than the government of Peru. They are strong enough to levy taxes (in the form of "dues"), screen new applicants, resolve land disputes, and organize cooperative projects. At best, such a shanty-town can be reasonably viewed as the site of a transition from a rural origin in a place no longer able to support its growing population to full-fledged urban life. In terms of this analysis, good policy consists of activities based on two premises: the rural–urban flow is unavoidable, and efforts to block it are likely to be futile or counterproductive; and, second, efforts to facilitate the acculturation of rural in-migrants should not confuse the physical setting with spiritual vitality. Furnishing a sewerage system can be a boost to community morale, but this depends more on the availability of jobs than perhaps any other factor. But according to another survey, dissatisfaction was greatest concerning the lack of municipal services (street paving, water, garbage collection, police, and so on) and the location of medical services; general satisfaction was expressed concerning schooling and public transportation (Andrews and Phillips 1970).

The two types of rural–urban migrants, then, are based on the generalization that much current movement is based far less on opportunities in the city than on stagnation in the countryside, and there is no reason to doubt the widespread validity of that premise. It may be, however, that migratory selection is similar in the two types. It would be useful, as also in international migration, to distinguish between gross and net movement and to base one's conclusions on the latter. In Thailand, for instance, the gross in-migration to Greater Bangkok over the period 1955–60 totaled just over 7 percent of the city's 1960 population, but the net migration was under half that and, for some age categories, less still (Goldstein 1972: 16). Generally we must depend on gross figures, which presumably include more of those who fail to acculturate and thus probably understate the degree of initial selectivity. According to Mangin (1967b), the educational level in Lima's *barriadas* is higher than the country's average. In Mexico, migrants to the city of Monterrey were positively selected by education and occupation (Browning and Feindt 1969), and a study directly comparing migrants and nonmigrants in a rural area showed the same pattern (Rengert and Rengert 1973). Abu-Lughod (1961) found that those leaving rural areas for Cairo comprised both the standard bright pre-urban young males and what she termed "non-selective" migrants; the thesis was given inconclusive support in a partial replication (Petersen 1971). In sum, any generalization must be tentative and may not apply to all countries or to all stages of a continuing movement, but it would seem likely that many of the in-migrants to cities of the underdeveloped countries, however low their education and level of skill, are better than the average of the villagers they left behind.

SUMMARY

What is loosely called urban growth is really a combination of two phenomena: the development of large concentrated aggregates of human beings, and the rise of new culture patterns, the new ways of thinking and behaving, characteristic of these cities. In order to discuss the relation between the two, one must keep the concepts separate: *urbanization*, the state of population concentration, and *urbanism*, the way of life of city dwellers. The effect of density on culture patterns is important, but not absolute; that is, the correlation between urbanization and urbanism is high, but not perfect.

In order to test this relation empirically, it is necessary to have clear and consistent definitions of the independent variable. In fact, the statistical criteria of *urban* and *rural* differ greatly from country to country and, in any one series, from one decade to the next. The simple dichotomy hardly suffices any longer; either a more complex classification (e.g., metropolis, city, village, farm) or a continuum by size of place is more useful.

In the development of mankind from its savage state, the two major advances were closely associated with urbanization, both the beginnings of civilization in the ancient Near East and the rise and spread of industrialism. In the broadest sense, then, human progress and the city have been linked for several millennia. This correlation, it is true, has not been a one-to-one relation. As we noted in Chapter 10, several of the most distinguished analysts of preindustrial cities divided them into subcategories, the free mercantile cities of Europe and the administrative centers of either Europe or other civilizations, on the ground that the first generated fundamental social change while the second, on the contrary, usually coalesced the traditions of those societies into more durable forms. In the analysis of underdeveloped countries today, somewhat similar attempts have been made to classify cities into types, according to whether they do or do not foster the development of an industrial society. It is hypothesized here that in-migrants to cities, even those motivated by nothing more than a desire to escape the destitution of the village, are potentially more suitable human resources in modernization than those who remain more fully enmeshed in traditional norms and probably less willing to risk a new way to the future. Not only has the criticism of the large city as parasitic often been based on "loose thinking and remarkably little actual research," but some of this criticism might better be diverted to the rural social structure, especially though not exclusively of Latin America (Browning 1958).

Yet most governments attempt to impede the growth of cities, particularly of large cities; they would like to acquire the benefits of a modern industrial economy without paying the price, as they see it, of a cosmopolitan urban society. The typical attitude in underdeveloped countries toward town and country is succinctly put in two chapter headings of a United Nations work (1959: chaps. 11, 13): "Programmes of Rural Development" and "Programmes and Measures for Meeting Problems of Rapid Urbanization." The transformation of the villager ordinarily entails some costs, but one should always remember that high urban rates of various social pathologies are at least partly spurious, since urbanization is associated with better statistics, higher standards of efficiency, and greater visibility of social ills. Apart from the "disorganization" it supposedly generates, the city is too seldom seen as a process. The ties of American urban sociology with human ecology, of French or Dutch studies with urban geography, of American and especially British city planning with architecture, all tend to emphasize the locus of urban events rather than the social change that an urban environment fosters.

No urban place is spatially homogeneous, and its growth can be studied by analyzing the changing relationship of its several parts. Since about 1920, the rings of metropolitan areas in the United States have been increasing much faster than the central cities; and in the most recent period there has also been a decentralization of business and light industry. To some degree, lower classes and especially Negroes have concentrated in the central cities and successively higher classes at greater and greater distances from it. This Burgess model is often not true, however, of the urban or metropolitan structure in other countries, where the attraction to the center is frequently greater.

The very rapid urban growth of many underdeveloped countries is largely based on a new type of migrant, less attracted to the city by the opportunities that accompany industrialization than expelled from the countryside by the imbalance between the rural economy and its population. These newcomers lack the elements of lower-class life: a regular job, a home, a neighborhood. They have had to create all of these for themselves, and in at least some instances they have succeeded remarkably well. The squatter towns surrounding many large cities can be festering sores, but sometimes they are transitional zones in which some of the surplus peasantry learn to adapt to a new way of life.

CITED REFERENCES AND
SUGGESTIONS FOR FURTHER READING

A possible reading list peripheral to the subject matter of this chapter could be almost as long as one wanted to make it. The work edited by Hauser and Schnore (1965) includes chapters on the subdisciplines of history, geography, political science, sociology, and economics that pertain to urbanization. It has also been a developing interest in anthropology; see, for example, the excellent papers by Little (1971) and Epstein (1972). The book edited by Gibbs (1961) is a good collection on methods of urban analysis. The new edition of Hawley's text (1971) is a first-rate statement by one of the country's leading ecologists. Davis's several works represent the most thoroughgoing attempt to transcend the limitations of existent data in international comparisons. Among the books devoted specifically to the cities of underdeveloped countries, the short work by Breese (1966) is a brief but adequate statement; for a fuller analysis see the book of readings edited by Breese (1969) and especially the one by McGee (1971). Americans' frequent lack of interest in demographic history does not extend to the rise of cities. McKelvey's masterful history (1963) is excellent sociology as well; Lampard's long paper (1955) summarizes well the economic function of cities; and some of the best recent studies are included in the work edited by Thernstrom and Sennett (1969). Two books concentrate more narrowly on urban policy: that by Beijer (1963) is a bibliographic study of European countries, and Rodwin (1970) calls his work "a comparison of strategies for urban growth."

ABRAMS, CHARLES. 1964. *Man's Struggle for Shelter in an Urbanizing World.* Cambridge, Mass.: M.I.T. Press.

ABU-LUGHOD, JANET. 1961. "Migrant Adjustment to City Life: The Egyptian Case," *American Journal of Sociology*, **67**, 22–32.

ALFORD, ROBERT R. 1972. "Critical Evaluation of the Principles of City Classification," in Berry 1972b.

ALIHAN, MILLA A. 1938. *Social Ecology: A Critical Analysis.* New York: Columbia University Press.

ANDREWS, FRANK M., and GEORGE W. PHILLIPS. 1970. "The Squatters of Lima: Who They Are and What They Want," *Journal of Developing Areas*, **4**, 211–224.

ARRIAGA, EDUARDO E. 1970. "A New Approach to the Measurements of Urbanization," *Economic Development and Cultural Change*, **18**, 206–218.

BAUER, P. T. 1965. *Economic Analysis and Policy in Underdeveloped Countries.* London: Routledge & Kegan Paul.

BEIJER, G. 1963. *Rural Migrants in Urban Setting: An Analysis of the Literature on the Problem Consequent on the Internal Migration from Rural to Urban Areas in 12 European Countries (1945–1961).* The Hague: Nijhoff.

BERGER, BENNETT M. 1960. *Working-Class Suburb.* Berkeley: University of California Press.

BERRY, BRIAN J. L. 1961. "City Size Distributions and Economic Development," *Economic Development and Cultural Change*, **19**, 573–588.

————. 1967. "Generalization of the Metropolitan Area Concept," in American Statistical Association, *Proceedings, Social Statistics Section.* Washington, D.C.

————. 1972a. "Latent Structure of the American Urban System, with International Comparisons," in Berry 1972b.

————, editor. 1972b. *City Classification Handbook: Methods and Applications.* New York: Wiley.

————, JAMES W. SIMMONS, and ROBERT J. TENNANT. 1963. "Urban Population Densities: Structure and Change," *Geographical Review*, **53**, 389–405. Reprinted in George J. Demko *et al.*, editors, *Population Geography: A Reader.* New York: McGraw-Hill, 1970.

BEYNON, ERDMAN D. 1943. "Budapest: An Ecological Study," *Geographical Review*, **33**, 256–275.

BOEKE, J. H. 1953. *Economics and Economic Policy of Dual Societies, as Exemplified by Indonesia.* New York: Institute of Pacific Relations.

BOSE, NIRMAL KUMAR. 1965. "Calcutta: A Premature Metropolis," *Scientific American*, **213**, 91–102.

BREESE, GERALD. 1966. *Urbanization in Newly Developing Countries.* Englewood Cliffs, N.J.: Prentice-Hall.

*————, editor. 1969. *The City in Newly Developing Countries: Readings on Urbanism and Urbanization.* Englewood Cliffs, N.J.: Prentice-Hall.

BROWNING, HARLEY L. 1958. "Recent Trends in Latin American Urbanization," *Annals of the American Academy of Political and Social Science*, **316**, 111–120.

————, and JACK P. GIBBS. 1961. "Some Measures of Demographic and Spatial Relationships among Cities," in Gibbs 1961.

————, and WALTRAUT FEINDT. 1969. "Selectivity of Migrants to a Metropolis in a Developing Country: A Mexican Case Study," *Demography*, **6**, 347–358.

BURGESS, ERNEST W. 1929. "Urban Areas," in T. V. Smith and Leonard D. White, editors, *Chicago: An Experiment in Social Science Research*. Chicago: University of Chicago Press.

*CAREY, GEORGE W. 1972. "Density, Crowding, Stress, and the Ghetto," *American Behavioral Scientist*, **15**, 495–509.

CARLSON, ERIC. 1959. "High-Rise Management: Design Problems as Found in Caracas Studied by International Team," *Journal of Housing*, **16**, 311–314.

CASASCO, JUAN A. 1969. "Slums of Hope and Despair," *Américas*, **21**, 13–20.

CASSEL, JOHN. 1971. "Health Consequences of Population Density and Crowding," in National Academy of Sciences, *Rapid Population Growth: Consequences and Policy Implications*. Baltimore: Johns Hopkins Press.

CLARK, S. D. 1963. "The Society of Suburbia," in William Petersen and David Matza, editors, *Social Controversy*. Belmont, Calif.: Wadsworth.

DAVIS, KINGSLEY. 1962. "Las causas y efectos del fenómeno de primacía urbana, con referencia especial a América Latina," in Mexican Sociological Society, *Proceedings of the 14th Annual Congress*. Sonora: Hermosillo.

*————. 1970–72. *World Urbanization, 1950–1970*, vol. 1: *Basic Data for Cities, Countries, and Regions*, rev. ed.; vol. 2: *Analysis of Trends, Relationships, and Development*. Berkeley: Institute of International Studies, University of California.

————, and HILDA HERTZ GOLDEN. 1954. "Urbanization and the Development of Preindustrial Areas," *Economic Development and Cultural Change*, **3**, 6–24.

DAY, ALICE TAYLOR, and LINCOLN H. DAY. 1973. "Cross-National Comparison of Population Density," *Science*, **181**, 1016–1023.

DEBOW, J. D. B. 1854. *Statistical View of the United States*. Washington, D.C.: Superintendent of the U.S. Census.

*DUNCAN, OTIS DUDLEY, and ALBERT J. REISS, JR. 1956. *Social Characteristics of Urban and Rural Communities, 1950*. New York: Wiley.

ELKAN, WALTER. 1960. *Migrants and Proletarians: Urban Labour in the Economic Development of Uganda*. London: Oxford University Press.

*EPSTEIN, A. L. 1972. "Urbanization and Social Change in Africa," in William Petersen, editor, *Readings in Population*. New York: Macmillan.

FIREY, WALTER. 1945. "Sentiment and Symbolism as Ecological Variables," *American Sociological Review*, **10**, 140–148.

————. 1947. *Land Use in Central Boston*. Cambridge, Mass.: Harvard University Press.

FISCHER, CLAUDE S. 1973. "Urban Malaise," *Social Forces*, **52**, 221–235.

FRANKE, DAVID. 1974. *America's 50 Safest Cities*. New Rochelle, N.Y.: Arlington House.

FRYER, D. W. 1953. "The 'Million City' in Southeast Asia," *Geographical Review*, **43**, 474–494.

GAKENHEIMER, RALPH A. 1959. "The Spanish King and His Continent: A Study of the Importance of the 'Laws of the Indies' for Urban Development in Spanish America." Unpublished master's thesis in regional planning, Cornell University.

*GALLE, OMER R., WALTER R. GOVE, and J. MILLER MCPHERSON. 1972. "Population Density and Pathology: What Are the Relations for Man?" *Science*, **176**, 23–30.

GANS, HERBERT J. 1962. *The Urban Villagers: Group and Class in the Life of Italian-Americans*. New York: Free Press.

*GIBBS, JACK P., editor. 1961. *Urban Research Methods*. New York: Van Nostrand.

GINSBURG, NORTON S. 1955. "The Great City in Southeast Asia," *American Journal of Sociology*, **60**, 455–462.

GOLDSTEIN, SIDNEY. 1972. *Urbanization in Thailand, 1947–1967*, rev. ed. Bangkok: Institute of Population Studies, Chulalongkorn University.

GOLICZ, LAWRENCE J. 1972. "The U.S. Census and the Study of Urban Population Distribution in the 19th Century." Paper presented at the meeting of the Population Association of America, Toronto, Canada.

GREENE, STANLEY. 1969. "The 1970 Census of Population Industry Classification System," *Statistical Reporter*, no. 69–10, pp. 155–161.

————, JOHN PRIEBE, and RICHARD MORRISON. 1969. "The 1970 Census of Population Occupation Classification System," *Statistical Reporter*, no. 70–6, pp. 77–84.

GUEST, AVERY M. 1973. "Urban Growth and Population Densities," *Demography*, **10**, 53–69.

HANSEN, ASAEL T. 1934. "The Ecology of a Latin American City," in E. B. Reuter, editor, *Race and Culture Contacts*. New York: McGraw-Hill.

HAUSER, PHILIP M. 1957. "Summary Report," in Joint U.N.-Unesco Seminar on Urbanization in the ECAFE Region, *Urbanization in Asia and the Far East*. Calcutta: Unesco.

————, editor. 1961. *Urbanization in Latin America*. New York: Columbia University Press.

————, and LEO F. SCHNORE, editors. 1965. *The Study of Urbanization*. New York: Wiley.

*HAWLEY, AMOS H. 1971. *Urban Society: An Ecological Approach*. New York: Ronald Press.

*————. 1972. "Population Density and the City," *Demography*, **9**, 521–529.

HOSELITZ, BERT F. 1957. "Urbanization and Economic Growth in Asia," *Economic Development and Cultural Change*, **6**, 42–54.

INTERNATIONAL LABOUR ORGANISATION. 1953. *Workers' Housing Problems in Asian Countries*. Geneva.

KATZ, MICHAEL B. 1972. "Occupational Classification in History," *Journal of Interdisciplinary History*, **3**, 63–88.

*LAMPARD, ERIC E. 1955. "The History of Cities in the Economically Advanced Areas," *Economic Development and Cultural Change*, **3**, 81–136.

LITTLE, KENNETH. 1971. "Some Aspects of African Urbanization South of the Sahara," McCaleb Module in Anthropology.

MACURA, MILOŠ. 1961. "The Influence of the Definition of the Urban Place on the Size of the Urban Population," in Gibbs 1961.

*MANGIN, WILLIAM. 1967a. "Latin American Squatter Settlements: A Problem and a Solution," *Latin American Research Review*, **2**, 65–98.

————. 1967b. "Squatter Settlements," *Scientific American*, **217**, 21–29.

————, editor. 1970. *Peasants in Cities: Readings in the Anthropology of Urbanization*. Boston: Houghton Mifflin.

MARRIS, PETER. 1960. "Social Change and Social Class," *International Journal of Comparative Sociology*, **1**, 119–124.

————. 1961. *Family and Social Change in an African City: A Study of Rehousing in Lagos*. London: Routledge & Kegan Paul.

MATOS MAR, JOSÉ. 1961. "Migration and Urbanization: The 'Barriadas' of Lima, an Example of Integration into Urban Life," in Hauser 1961.

McCALL, DANIEL F. 1955. "Dynamics of Urbanization in Africa," *Annals of the American Academy of Political and Social Science*, **298**, 151–160.

*McGEE, T. G. 1971. *The Urbanization Process in the Third World: Explorations in Search of a Theory*. London: Bell.

McKELVEY, BLAKE. 1963. *The Urbanization of America (1860–1915)*. New Brunswick, N.J.: Rutgers University Press.

McKENZIE, R. F. 1933. *The Metropolitan Community*. New York: McGraw-Hill.

MEHTA, SURINDER K. 1964. "Some Demographic and Economic Correlates of Primate Cities: A Case for Revaluation," *Demography*, **1**, 136–147.

MITCHELL, J. CLYDE. 1961. "Wage Labour and African Population Movements in Central Africa," in K. M. Barbour and R. M. Prothero, editors, *Essays on African Population*. London: Routledge & Kegan Paul.

MITRA, S. 1965. "The Changing Pattern of Population Concentration in Indian Cities," *Eugenics Quarterly*, **12**, 154–161.

MORGENSTERN, OSKAR. 1963. *On the Accuracy of Economic Measurement*, 2nd ed. Princeton, N.J.: Princeton University Press.

MORSE, RICHARD M. 1962. "Latin American Cities: Aspects of Function and Structure," *Comparative Studies in Society and History*, **4**, 473–493.

MURPHEY, RHOADS. 1957. "New Capitals of Asia," *Economic Development and Cultural Change*, **5**, 216–243.

NESS, GAYL D., editor. 1970. *The Sociology of Economic Development: A Reader*. New York: Harper & Row.

NUTTALL, ZELIA. 1921–22. "Royal Ordinances Concerning the Laying Out of New Towns," *Hispanic American Historical Review*, **4**, 743–753; **5**, 249–254. (The first of the two articles gives the Spanish text of the ordinances, a short commentary, and a garbled translation; a correct translation is given in the second.)

PARK, ROBERT E. 1925. "The City: Suggestions for the Investigation of Human Behavior in the Urban Environment," in Robert E. Park and Ernest W. Burgess, editors, *The City*. Chicago: University of Chicago Press.

*PETERSEN, KAREN KAY. 1971. "Villagers in Cairo: Hypotheses versus Data," *American Journal of Sociology*, **77**, 560–573.

QUINN, JAMES A. 1950. *Human Ecology*. Englewood Cliffs, N.J.: Prentice-Hall.

REDFIELD, ROBERT. 1947. "The Folk Society," *American Journal of Sociology*, **52**, 293–308.

RENGERT, ARLENE C., and GEORGE F. RENGERT. 1973. "Who Moves to Cities: A Multivariate Examination of Migrants from Rural Mexico." Paper presented at the annual meeting of the Population Association of America, New Orleans.

RICARD, ROBERT. 1950. "La plaza mayor en España y en América Española," *Estudios Geográficos*, **11**, 321–327.

———. 1952. "Apuntes complementarios sobre la plaza mayor española y el 'rossio' portugues," *Estudios Geográficos*, **13**, 229–237.

RODWIN, LLOYD. 1970. *Nations and Cities: A Comparison of Strategies for Urban Growth*. Boston: Houghton Mifflin.

ROSENWAIKE, IRA. 1970. "A Critical Examination of the Designation of Standard Metropolitan Statistical Areas," *Social Forces*, **48**, 322–333.

RUSSETT, BRUCE M., *et al.* 1964. *World Handbook of Political and Social Indicators*. New Haven, Conn.: Yale University Press.

SADIE, JAN L. 1967. "Labor Supply and Employment in Less Developed Countries," *Annals of the American Academy of Political and Social Science*, **369**, 121–130.

SCHAPERA, ISAAC. 1947. *Migrant Labour and Tribal Life: A Study of Conditions in the Bechuanaland Protectorate*. London: Oxford University Press.

SCHMITT, ROBERT. 1966. "Density, Health and Social Organization," *Journal of the American Institute of Planners*, **32**, 38–42.

*SCHNORE, LEO F. 1957. "Satellites and Suburbs," *Social Forces*, **36**, 121–127.

SOROKIN, PITIRIM A., CARLE C. ZIMMERMAN, and CHARLES J. GALPIN. 1930. *A Systematic Source Book in Rural Sociology*, 2 vol. Minneapolis: University of Minnesota Press.

STEEL, R. W. 1961. "The Towns of Tropical Africa," in K. M. Barbour and R. M. Prothero, editors, *Essays on African Population*. London: Routledge & Kegan Paul.

THERNSTROM, STEPHAN, and RICHARD SENNETT, editors. 1969. *Nineteenth-Century Cities: Essays in the New Urban History*. New Haven, Conn.: Yale University Press.

TRUESDELL, LEON E. 1949. "The Development of the Urban–Rural Classification in the United States, 1874 to 1949," U.S. Bureau of the Census, *Current Population Reports*, Series P-23, no. 1. Washington, D.C.: U.S. Government Printing Office.

TURNER, ROY, editor. 1962. *India's Urban Future*. Berkeley: University of California Press.

UNITED NATIONS. 1950. "Data on Urban and Rural Populations in Recent Censuses." St/SOA/Series A, Population Studies, no. 8. Reprinted in part in Gibbs 1961.

———. 1953. *Demographic Yearbook, 1952*. New York.

———. 1959. *International Survey of Programmes of Social Development*. New York.

———. 1968. *Demographic Yearbook, 1967*. New York.

———. 1972. *Demographic Yearbook, 1971*. New York.

UNESCO. 1956. *The Social Implications of Industrialization and Urbanization: Five Studies in Asia*. Calcutta.

UNITED STATES. BUREAU OF THE BUDGET. 1967. *Standard Metropolitan Statistical Areas: 1967*. Washington, D.C.: U.S. Government Printing Office.

*———. BUREAU OF THE CENSUS. 1971. "Social and Economic Characteristics of the Population in Metropolitan and Nonmetropolitan Areas: 1970 and 1960," *Current Population Reports*, Series P-23, no. 37. Washington, D.C.: U.S. Government Printing Office.

———. ———. 1972. "Farm Population of the United States: 1971," *Current Population Reports*, Series P-27, no. 43. Washington, D.C.: U.S. Government Printing Office.

VIOLICH, FRANCIS. 1944. *Cities of Latin America: Housing and Planning to the South*. New York: Reinhold.

WILKINSON, THOMAS O. 1960. "Urban Structure and Industrialization," *American Sociological Review*, **25**, 356–363.

*WILNER, DANIEL M., and ROSABELLE PRICE WALKLEY. 1963. "Effects of Housing on Health and Performance," in Leonard J. Duhl, editor, *The Urban Condition: People and Policy in the Metropolis*. New York: Basic Books.

WINSBOROUGH, HAL H. 1963. "An Ecological Approach to the Theory of Suburbanization," *American Journal of Sociology*, **68**, 565–570.

WIRTH, LOUIS. 1938. "Urbanism as a Way of Life," *American Journal of Sociology,* **44**, 1–24.

WURSTER, CATHERINE BAUER. 1955. "The Optimum Pattern of Urbanization: Does Asia Need a New Type of Regional Planning?" in United Nations, *Seminar on Regional Planning.* Tokyo.

———. 1962. "Urban Living Conditions, Overhead Costs, and the Development Pattern," in Turner 1962.

ZIPF, GEORGE K. 1949. *Human Behavior and the Principle of Least Effort: An Introduction to Human Ecology.* Cambridge, Mass.: Addison-Wesley.

Mortality and fertility change for three kinds of reasons: technical advances in medicine and contraception, differences in social groups' access to the more advanced techniques, and changes in their attitudes toward using them. The third factor is occasionally significant with respect to mortality (as in the opposition to vaccination or the persistence of folk medicine), but the high value placed on good health and long life generally transcends social boundaries. With respect to fertility, however, attitudes are decidedly more relevant. Because the number of children desired differs among social groups, a couple with knowledge of contraceptives, physical access to them, and no moral inhibitions about their use still may or may not exercise birth control. The analysis of fertility is therefore more complex than that of mortality.

It is convenient to divide the discussion of fertility by societal types—industrial countries in this chapter and underdeveloped ones in Chapter 16. The present analysis, thus, picks up themes that were discussed earlier. The section on Malthus leads, even if by a route that he did not mark, into the rise of the neo-Malthusian movement; the discussion of the physiology of reproduction as this relates to contraception is a necessary introduction to the analysis here of differential attitudes toward birth control. Such links are obvious, but the reader should also note that the rise of urban–industrial society, the overall background to Part II of this book, is the main dimension along which birth rates can be meaningfully differentiated.

THE BIRTH-CONTROL MOVEMENT
AND ITS OPPONENTS

The battle for what Himes termed the democratization of birth control constitutes one of the most interesting episodes in the history of ideas. Neo-Malthusianism was no less an invention of the 19th century than, say, the vulcanization of rubber, which made possible the development of more efficacious contraceptive devices. From one country or period to another, one can distinguish differences in dogma; and occasionally the same country had several competing birth-control leagues, which opposed each other with all the vehemence of political or religious sects. Underlying the variation, however, a fundamental agreement on several key doctrines evolved from the works of the English and American pioneers (Himes 1936: chaps. 9–10):

1. Control of family size is both physically possible and morally desirable.

2. The ultimate decision whether and when to have children should be made by parents, rather than by fate, or tradition, or church, or state.

3. A relatively small number of children is a social good, both because of favorable effects within the family and because a too rapid population growth is a serious danger to social welfare.

The first book to recommend contraceptive measures as a substitute for Malthus's moral restraint appeared in England in 1822—*Illustrations and Proofs of the Principle of Population*, by Francis Place; a modern edition was edited by Himes (Boston: Houghton Mifflin, 1930). Though derivative from a number of predecessors (among them Benjamin Franklin), Place was original in that he gave the birth-control movement its first systematic social theory and ethical rationale. The postponement of marriage that Malthus advocated, he argued, is too onerous a means of limiting population growth ever to be widely adopted. Marriages between young people, in his view, are generally happier ones, for older persons cannot adjust to each other so readily. If one accepts Malthus's thesis that too rapid a population growth leads inevitably to social and economic distress—and Place repeated it in a simplified version—then "to avoid these miseries, the answer is short and plain": the use of contraceptives.

On the other side of the Atlantic, the first book on birth control, *Moral Physiology* (1830), was written by Robert Dale Owen (the oldest son of Robert Owen), shortly to be followed by Charles Knowlton's *Fruits of Philosophy* (1832). Unlike Place and Owen, Knowlton was a physician, and in medical terms his pamphlet was an improvement over its predecessors. "Perhaps it is no exaggeration to say that Knowlton's treatment of contraceptive technique is the first really important account after those of Soranos and Aëtios two millennia earlier" (Himes 1936: 227). Place and his associates had recommended a sponge, and Owen *coitus interruptus*; Knowlton's chief method was a douche with an astringent solution.

In England, neo-Malthusianism was beginning to attract some of the best minds of the period, in particular, Jeremy Bentham and John Stuart Mill. The most important figure in the middle of the century was George Drysdale, author of *The Elements of Social Science* (1854), a book of some 600 finely printed pages. In medical terms, the author was less accurate than Knowlton or even Place, but by his extensive and sympathetic exposition of classical economic theory, he established a firmer link between it and neo-Malthusian doctrine than had existed previously. During half a century *The Elements* appeared in thirty-five English editions and was translated into at least ten languages.

After five decades of obscurity, in 1876–77 the birth-control movement was suddenly given wide publicity by the prosecution of two of its advocates, Charles Bradlaugh and Annie Besant. They had organized a firm for the express purpose of publishing and distributing Knowlton's *Fruits of Philosophy*, and thus testing a court decision banning it. Arrested and tried, for four days the defendants argued their case in social as well as legal terms. It was desirable, they held, that the poor should be informed on contraceptive means. The trial was reported in both the national and the local press, often with long verbatim passages from their testimony and even quotations from Knowlton's book itself. The sale of *Fruits of Philosophy*, which had been only 700 copies a year, jumped to some 125,000 in three months, not including a flood of imitations and pirated editions. The defendants were convicted and sentenced to six months' imprisonment and a fine of £200; they appealed and a year later were acquitted on a technicality. As a direct consequence of the publicity furnished by the Bradlaugh–Besant trial and a number of other prosecutions of birth-control proponents, a new Malthusian League was founded, with Charles R. Drysdale (brother of George) as president and Mrs. Besant as secretary. The League grew rapidly, receiving a sympathetic reception from a portion of the population not only in large cities but in remote villages (Himes 1936: chap. 10; Banks and Banks 1954; Glass 1940: 38).

The United States went through a similar cycle a generation later. In 1913 Mrs. Margaret Sanger, then a visiting nurse in New York's East Side slum, went to England, Holland, and France in search of information on reliable contraceptive methods. On her return she opened a clinic and served thirty days in prison for maintaining a "public nuisance." She started the *Birth Control Review*, a propaganda organization, another clinic, and a research bureau, the National Committee on Maternal Health. As early as 1922, she helped set up birth-control movements in Hawaii, Japan, and China (Sanger 1931, 1938). That contraceptives were made legal in most of the United States was due in considerable degree to the courage and perseverance of this one woman.

The transatlantic interaction between English and American pioneers marked the start of the movement the world over (see also Field 1967; Micklewright 1961). It was their stimulus, as publicized especially by the Bradlaugh–Besant trials, that induced similar social reformers to start parallel efforts in France (Bergues 1960) and Scandinavia (Sutter 1960; Mangin 1962), among other countries. Through such scholars as Wicksell (see pp. 161–163), the advocacy of contraception was also associated with the development of population theory.

Traditional Opposition

In all countries the birth-control movement has been shaped to a considerable degree by the opposition to it, which was generally based on one of three competing groups of ideologues: nationalists, who emphasized the importance of a large population in realizing their country's legitimate aspirations (pp. 618–619); socialists, for whom the population–resources balance merely deflected attention from the only important issue, the reorganization of the economy and society (pp. 670–674); and traditionalists, who defended the integrity of the family

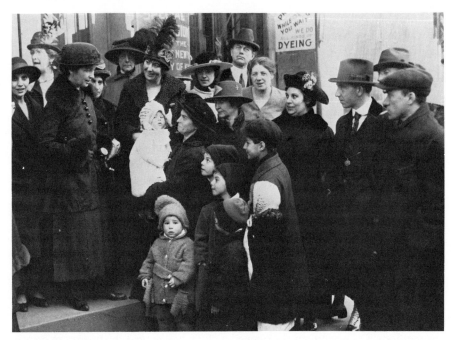

Admirers welcome Margaret Sanger after she is released from jail (*Planned Parent-hood/World Population*).

against what they saw as an invitation to license. In the traditional view children come as gifts of God, and should be accepted gratefully, unquestioningly. To subject the process of reproduction to man's will is "unnatural." One difficulty with this view is that it makes no allowance for the no less unnatural death control that has been achieved in the modern world. An inefficient check to fertility, combined with modern medicine, public sanitation, insecticides, and so on, results in a population growth so great that, indeed, the balance with nature is endangered.

The notion that parents should be permitted to determine the size of their family began everywhere as the point of view of an embattled minority, the sort of people who held and expressed unpopular opinions of all kinds. Bradlaugh, for instance, was a militant atheist; Mrs. Besant was an ardent feminist, later a theosophist. More generally, the advocacy of birth control tended to overlap with support of other sectarian views—pacifism, temperance, vegetarianism, and secularism but not feminism (see Banks and Banks 1964); and when the link did not exist in substance, it was often created in form by the libertarians who defended anyone whose freedom of speech had been infringed. Like any other social reform, then, neo-Malthusianism was opposed first of all because of its novelty, its affront to conventionality. And in this case the automatic rejection was strengthened by the specific proposal, particularly in so prurient a nation as

Victorian England. One of the worst offenses of Bradlaugh and Besant was their plain speaking, their threat to what *The Times* termed "certain reserves and proprieties surrounding the first law of Nature and the domestic hearth" (Banks and Banks 1954).

The principal institution that preserves the cultural tradition concerning family norms is the church, and religious thought throughout the world is generally favorable to family life and thus to procreation. Yet the opposition to birth control that some see as implicit in this normative stance is often lacking either from sacred works or from recent exegeses. Even a brief review of the major religions suggests that the range is wide—from strong and explicit condemnation, through a frequent ambivalence that depends on interpretation to give it concrete meaning, to a positive endorsement of contraception. Of the three important sources of religious thought in the West—Judaism, Protestantism, and Roman Catholicism—the first two have gradually moved away from an earlier traditionalist opposition to birth control, so that the Catholic doctrine is now anomalous and, if only for that reason, of especial interest.

Judaism.   Relevant passages in the Old Testament, as also in Christian thought, have been subjected to various interpretations. According to modern exegesis, the sin of Onan (Genesis 38:9) was not *coitus interruptus*, but rather the refusal to beget offspring by his deceased brother's wife, as required under the law of the levirate. A more pertinent imperative is "Be fruitful and multiply" (Genesis 1:28), which the orthodox interpret as a prohibition of both contraception and celibacy and, above all, as an abhorrence of childlessness (Patai 1959: chap. 5). But according to certain commentators, the Talmud permitted contraception and even made it mandatory if the health of the mother or the welfare of previous children so indicated. "The Jewish attitude never considered the function of intercourse to be for procreation only" (Glasner 1961). In 1959, the parent body of American Reform Judaism passed a resolution against all legal barriers to contraception and in favor of its wider public dissemination through both public and private agencies (General Assembly, Union of American Hebrew Congregations, November, 1959). This more or less represents the present stance, apart from the most orthodox, of Jews throughout the world.

While **Protestantism** hardly constitutes a single entity on this question, it has followed a path parallel to that of Judaism. Opposition to birth control was general at the time of the Reformation. For Calvin *coitus interruptus* was "doubly monstrous," for "it is to extinguish the hope of the race and to kill before he is born the son who was hoped for." Luther, while less specific on contraception, condemned it by implication (Noonan 1965: 353). Such views were all but universal in world Protestantism up to the 19th century. The change since then can be illustrated by the successive statements of Anglican bishops at the Lambeth conferences.

In 1908 they spoke out unambiguously against the use of contraceptives. In 1920 they were still opposed, but Bishop Kirk, the leading Anglican authority on moral theology, sensed the beginnings of permissiveness on the subject. The Lambeth Conference gave clear permission for the conscientious use of contraceptives in 1930, and was even more forthright in 1948 in presenting the case for birth control. This development is significant, partly because Anglican bishops ... look for guidance to a considerable extent to the Catholic tradition of moral theology and are often cautious about taking any action that widens the separation between their Church and the Roman Church [Bennett 1959].

In the United States, the Federal Council of the Churches of Christ in America published a report in 1931 approving contraception in principle; and more recently a number of Protestant denominations have taken the stand that "responsible family planning is today a clear moral duty" (this is the wording of one such statement, by the Council for Christian Social Action, United Church of Christ, January 30, 1960).

The Catholic Positions on Birth Control

Roman Catholicism is the one important world religion that still upholds its opposition to contraception, though here too the doctrine is in disarray. The present position "may appear as metaphysical hair-splitting," as one priest put it (Gibbons 1956); and strong pressure to resolve the contradictions has been exerted not only by non-Catholics (who resent the Church's influence on the general society's law and public policy) and Catholic laity, but by a considerable section of the hierarchy itself. No account of this ongoing debate in a book not devoted exclusively to that subject can be complete or, probably by the time this is read, up to date.

Of the flood of printed matter on Catholics and birth control, the best by a wide margin is *Contraception*, by John T. Noonan, Jr., at the time a professor in the Notre Dame Law School and director of its Natural Law Institute. Neither the punishment of Onan nor any other passage, in his opinion, establishes biblical authority for the prohibition of birth control. Given the quite specific Jewish laws against homosexuality, against bestiality, against temple prostitution, against marital intercourse during menstruation, "it is surely strange that ... the illegality of contraception should be left to inference, if the compilers of the Pentateuch believed contraception to be unlawful" (Noonan 1965: 35). As the early Church lacked a clear guide from either Testament, it gradually worked out a position in opposition to competing movements. On the "left" were the Gnostics, who regarded themselves as "royal sons" of the Lord and thus bound by no law; they scorned marriage and lived as libertines. On the "right" were the Manichees and various other neo-Platonist groups, who believed that sexuality is evil and only absolute continence is wholly good.[1]

---

[1] Compare: "In a fully populated world a substantial proportion of men and women should lead celibate lives, ... [which] would hardly be possible at all except in a Catholic community. ... The only real answer [to population pressure] is that the whole world should become Christian in the course of the next century or so" (Russell 1958).

The most important figure in the early development of Catholic doctrine, Augustine, was of course a Manichee for some decades before his conversion, and these imprints were "never effaced from his mind; his concern with evil, his concern with sexuality, were Manichean" (ibid.: 119). Augustine purged himself of his background by denouncing Manichean morals, including in particular contraception by the method the Manichees had taken over from Greek medicine, the fallacious use of the sterile period. It is indeed "piquant that the first pronouncement on contraception by the most influential theologian teaching on such matters should be a vigorous attack on the one method of avoiding procreation accepted by 20th-century Catholic theologians as morally lawful" (ibid.: 120). The Augustinian doctrine was given a more definite form in early medieval penitentials, which classified the criteria by which confessors were to judge the relative gravity of sins. These were concerned to an overwhelming degree with sexuality;[2] during the same period there evolved also the rule on priestly celibacy and the cult of virginity (cf. May 1931). Contraception was condemned as a form of homicide, a ruling preserved in Catholic law until 1917 (Noonan 1965: 168–169, 232–237). A numerous progeny was recommended for its own sake, for "the more offspring, the bigger the population of heaven" (ibid.: 275–276).

How important this last theme became can be illustrated by the writings on birth control in the Jesuit journal *America* from its first issue in 1909 to the 1960s (Reiterman 1965). By far the major emphasis up to 1930, when *Casti connubii* was promulgated, was on the simple value of procreation, the moral worth of large families irrespective of any contrary considerations. "Suppose a child is born deaf, dumb, blind, idiotic, in utter poverty, and that its parents know beforehand that such would be its condition." Suppose, in another example, that there is a "tubercular father with no prospects of supporting his family." Suppose, in a third example, that a wife is told by "a very modern physician" that "she could not give birth to her child without imperiling her own life." In all these cases, *America*'s answer was the biblical injunction to "increase and multiply." "To be born, even with a strong probability of future infirmity, is better than not to be born." Similarly: "We must make every effort to accommodate the increased numbers which God, in His wisdom, sees fit to place upon the earth through men" (Kelly 1960: 75). "The family which courageously and even heroically rears a large number of children in an overpopulated area merits special praise for its virtue" (Zimmerman 1957: 103).

"The most independent critique of the Christian sexual ethic undertaken by an orthodox critic" was made by Martin LeMaistre (1432–81), who was the first (!) to "establish the general lawfulness of the marital act" (Noonan 1965:

---

[2] It is interesting to compare the schedule in traditional China, where transgressors are assigned to one of the eight hells according to the gravity of their sins. Apart from homosexuality, sodomy, incest, and adultery only "if the adulterer talks about it," all other sexual acts are sinful only if they are related to religion. Thus, "the worst sin is a sexual act with a Buddhist saint" (Eberhard 1967: 61–63).

306–312). "Between 1450 and 1750 there was a substantial rejection of the Augustinian view that intercourse may be initiated only for procreation" (ibid.: 339). Contraception was still banned mainly because, following Aquinas, it was seen as "unnatural," but various statements in the 1820s and 1830s "encouraged a belief that the Church was about to modify its position on contraception" (ibid.: 403). The change came only in 1930, with the papal encyclical *Casti connubii* ("On Christian Marriage"), a small section of which was interpreted, against much ecclesiastical opposition, to sanction the rhythm method if there is a "serious motive" for avoiding childbearing (ibid.: 438–447; Sulloway 1959: chap. 7).

How shall this "serious motive" be defined? In present-day Catholic doctrine. as expressed in the Code of Canon Law, "The primary end of marriage is the procreation and education of offspring; the secondary end, mutual aid and the remedying of concupiscence" (quoted in Gibbons 1956). Under some circumstances, Catholic doctrine defines it as licit to serve the secondary ends (mitigating the sex drive and mutual aid, which is interpreted to include increasing the bond of marital affection) even when conception is impossible; for example, persons known to be sterile may enjoy marital relations without sin. It might seem that intercourse during a wife's sterile period is free from sin in the same way, and indeed the Catholic Church's stand has seemingly moved toward this interpretation. According to Pius XII (1951), it is legitimate for a Catholic couple to restrict intercourse to the sterile period "always and deliberately" under a wide array of loosely specified conditions:

There are serious motives, such as those often mentioned in the so-called medical, eugenic, economic, and social "indications," that can exempt for a long time, perhaps even the whole duration of the marriage, from the positive and obligatory carrying out of the act [of procreation]. From this it follows that observing the nonfertile periods alone can be lawful only under a moral aspect. Under the conditions mentioned it really is so [quoted in Schmiedeler 1952: 3–23].

From "every attempt to hinder procreation is immoral" (*Casti connubii*, 1930) to the "so-called medical, eugenic, economic, and social" exceptions to this dictum (1951), a considerable distance was covered.

The argumentation for the exclusive legitimacy of periodic abstinence has been openly attacked by respected members of the hierarchy throughout the world. "Schema for a Document on Responsible Parenthood," the position paper submitted in 1966 by a *majority* of the papal birth-control commission (*National Catholic Reporter*, April 19, 1967), marks the high point of this line of criticism. The text condemned abortion and declared that sterilization "is generally to be excluded," but made no other specification of a licit method of contraception. The means should be selected by "the couple" on the basis of the following criteria: (1) "The whole meaning of the mutual giving and of human procreation [shall be] kept in a context of true love," and extramarital contraception is barred. (2) The method used shall have an appropriate "effectiveness." (3) There shall be the "least possible" number of negative side-effects, whether biological, hygienic, or psychological. (4) No absolute rules shall apply, for the best means may depend on the situation of "a certain couple."

The commission submitted its majority and minority reports to Pope Paul VI on June 28, 1966, and for two years the world wondered whether the Catholic Church would accept the majority's recommendation and abandon its opposition to "artificial" birth control. In an encyclical issued in March 1967, *Populorum progressio* ("Development of Peoples"), the Pope pointed to the population problem of underdeveloped areas and the need for family planning—though by what means was left indefinite. But in another encyclical, *Humanae vitae* ("Of Human Life"), issued on July 29, 1968, the traditional doctrine was reaffirmed:

> Marriage and conjugal love are by their nature ordained toward the begetting and education of children. Children are really the supreme gift of marriage and contribute very substantially to the welfare of their parents. . . . In the task of transmitting life, therefore, [the parents] are not free to proceed completely at will, as if they could determine in a wholly autonomous way the honest path to follow; but they must conform their activity to the creative intention of God. . . . Each and every marriage act must remain open to the transmission of life. . . . Abortion, even if for thera-peutic reasons, [is] absolutely excluded, . . . [as is also] sterilization, whether per-petual or temporary, whether of the man or of the woman. Similarly excluded is every action which, either in anticipation of the conjugal act, or in its accomplish-ment, or in the development of the natural consequences, proposes, whether as an end or as a means, to render procreation impossible [*National Catholic Reporter*, August 7, 1968].

The sanctioning of the rhythm method was affirmed, provided its use is "for just motives," not further specified.

"It can be foreseen," one sentence of the encyclical reads, "that this teaching will perhaps not be easily received by all." Indeed, considerable numbers of Catholic laity, priests, and higher prelates openly challenged not only the wisdom of the ban on contraceptives but, more fundamentally, this application of the Church's magisterium, its teaching authority. *America*, which we have used to trace the development of American Catholic thought during the early decades of this century, completed its conversion in the issue of September 30, 1967. The view that would prevail in the Church, it hoped, was that expressed by "a distinguished Catholic physician": "Contraception is essential for a sound Catholic family life" (cf. Blake 1966a). Demographers have concentrated on hostile comment (e.g., Thomlinson 1972), but the dispute generated much support of the Pope's position as well. In the most complete review of world opinion on the encyclical, some 4,000 citations were compiled and translated from fifteen languages (Joannes 1970). In Latin America the orthodoxy was contrasted with what is termed "Pentagonism," that is, the application of Presi-dent Johnson's maxim that $5 spent in family planning brings a better return than $100 spent for development. Some support of the doctrine, on the other hand, may have been seen as an embarrassment; for instance, the African bishops pointed to the similarities between Paul VI's pronouncements and those of native fertility cults.

That it is possible to speak realistically of Roman Catholic *positions* on contraception is the most dramatic fact that can be adduced in any discussion of the doctrine. With the Church's teaching in disorder, one can assume that its effectiveness has been reduced. In the United States opinion polls indicated a growing convergence of Catholic and non-Catholic contraceptive practices.

By 1970, two-thirds of all Catholic women were using methods disapproved by their Church; this figure reached three-quarters for women under 30. Considering the fact that most of the one-quarter of young Catholic women conforming to Church teaching had never used any method, the percentage of those deviating may well reach 90 as these women grow older and the problems of fertility control become more important. . . .

The defection has been most pronounced among the women who receive Communion at least once a month. . . . That many Catholics can continue in their other religious practices and simultaneously deviate on the issue of birth control is an interesting commentary on the process of social change [Westoff and Bumpass 1973].

According to less complete data on Catholics in other countries, the same trend seems to be underway throughout the world (Jones and Nortman 1968).

CLASS DIFFERENCES IN FERTILITY

The social analysis of a nation's population is made by comparing the rates of relatively homogeneous categories. How should they be delimited? Differential rates have been calculated by region or urban–rural residence (suggesting the impact of urbanization on demographic trends), by social class (as measured by education, occupation, income, or some combination of such factors), and by religion or ethnic group (indicating a vestigial element of traditional culture). The comparison of such categories, even if at a single point in time, is often implicitly dynamic. For the demographic rates of any sector suggest that its way of life affects fertility and mortality, and if others seem to be imitating that way of life, then the trend of one segment may indicate the future of the whole population. The lower birth and death rates of the urban middle classes, to take the most obvious example, have often been seen as a kind of forecast of the levels to which rural or working-class rates would fall some time later. By the rationale of the demographic transition, thus, social sectors are roughly of two types, those that introduce and help disseminate modernizing attitudes and behavior patterns and those that, for whatever reasons, lag behind.

Rural–Urban Differences

Irrespective of other variations, urban fertility in the West has almost always been lower than rural. Very often the decline in the birth rate was greatest in the largest cities. From the last decades of the 19th century to the 1930s, completed family size in Norway and the Netherlands, to take two disparate examples, fell steadily; but the earliest and most rapid declines were in Oslo and Amsterdam and the latest and slowest in the rural areas, while the smaller towns stayed between the two extremes (Johnson 1960).

What is the meaning of the rural–urban contrast? It has often been pointed out that urban living conditions favor smaller families in a number of ways. City apartments permit expansion less comfortably than the one-family houses typical of villages and farms. Children are more expensive to rear when everything has to be bought than when at least a portion of the food is home-produced. On a farm minors help earn their keep by doing chores from a very young age on, whereas under urban conditions parents get no financial return, as it were, on their investment in offspring. In towns women are more likely to find alternative roles to being a housewife and thus to postpone procreation or even to put it off altogether. In judging the probable weight of these factors, it is useful to distinguish the physical constraints of rural and urban life from the city's ideas and culture patterns—that is, urbanization from urbanism.

Since the United States lacks adequate registration data for the 19th century, particularly for the early decades, the primary measure available is the child–woman ratio, or the number of children under 5 per 1,000 women in the fecund period, however this is specified. For well over a century the urban child–woman ratio fluctuated at under two-thirds of the rural one. The factors underlying the long-term decline in fertility from 1810, when it began, to 1940, when at least temporarily it ended, have been allocated as follows: 24 percent because of the continuing decline in the size of town families, 20 percent because of rural–urban migration, and 56 percent because of the decreased fertility in the countryside (Grabill et al. 1958: Tables 7–8; cf. Okun 1958: 99–101). This rural–urban contrast, even apart from complicating factors, has several half-hidden implications. Since cities have grown largely by the in-migration from smaller places, and since one might suppose that for several reasons those who make this move will have fewer children on the average than the settled population, the difference by size of place may partly reflect one by migration status. A study designed to test this hypothesis, however, reached the tentative conclusion that migration has no effect on fertility (Ritchey and Stokes 1972). One might hypothesize also that, since those who move to the city take some time to acculturate to urban norms, what are taken to be city rates are in fact a composite of fully urban and vestigial rural family-building practices. When two-generation urbanites were compared with rural migrants to Detroit, the difference in their fertility proved to be larger than that between religious or class categories of the fully urbanized sector. Moreover, since most rural in-migrants take low-level jobs when they go to the city, some of the difference by social class reflects the higher fertility of farm-reared city dwellers (Goldberg 1959). At least for a nation like the United States, where one can hardly speak of peasantry, one should not stress too much the direct influence of habitat on family size. A country population that is literate and in close touch with the city-based culture assimilates, even if partially and more slowly, the behavior patterns that originate there. But if the city is seen less as an ecological unit than as a center from which innovations and new attitudes flow, then rural–urban contrasts are in large part an index of the differences by social class.

Inverse Correlation Between Class and Fertility

In traditional societies the class differentiation is more or less the same with respect to both mortality and fertility. For where long life and a numerous progeny are seen as good, the classes with the greatest control over their destiny ordinarily live longer and also have larger families. The pattern is well illustrated by a study of twenty villages of 20th-century Poland. Among two successive peasant generations, the wealthier the couple was, the more children they had. "Rich peasant girls, being much sought after as marriage partners, marry earlier than poorer girls, begin to bear children sooner, and bear them more frequently and up to a later age." Even among the present generation, where the contrast was less because a few women were practicing contraception, the average number of children born ranged from about three in families with 1 hectare or less of land up to more than nine in those with 15 to 20 hectares (Stys 1957).

In modern Western societies, on the contrary, the typical pattern has been that the better a family is able to afford children, the fewer children it has. The details differ according to the index used, but the general conclusion in the United States, for instance, is the same as far back as our information will take us. Using whatever data were available for the first several decades of the 19th century, Jaffe (1940) divided the inhabitants of New York, Boston, and Providence by the taxes they paid; those of the rural counties of New York State by their per-capita ownership of agricultural property; and those of the counties of several southern states by the number of slaves owned. In each case he found an inverse relation between wealth and family size, largest in the cities but significant also in the rural areas.

In several United States censuses, women were asked how many children they had ever borne. For a female past her fecund years, this figure is known as the **completed family size,** a remarkably simple and direct measure of natality. Table 14-1 shows the completed family size of women aged 45 to 49 according to the major occupational group of their husbands. The contrast between urban and rural is sharp for each group at all three dates, especially when (as in the table) the sponge class of "rural nonfarm" is eliminated. It should be kept in mind that the women had had most of their children when they were in their 20s and early 30s—thus, some two decades before the census dates given. At the end of the 19th century (1910 census) a tendency was discernible within each residence class toward an inverse correlation of occupation and fertility, but after World War I (1940 census) there was some convergence. During the 1930s (1950 census), however, a clear progression in family size by occupational group was re-established,

Table 14-1.   Completed Family Size,[a] White Population, by Major Occupational Group of Husband and Place of Residence, United States, 1910, 1940, and 1950

	1910		1940		1950	
Major Occupational Group	URBAN	RURAL-FARM	URBAN	RURAL-FARM	URBAN	RURAL-FARM
Professional, technical, and kindred workers	2.8	4.3	2.0	2.9	1.7	3.0
Managers, officials, and proprietors, except farm	3.3	4.8	2.1	3.4	1.9	2.7
Clerical, sales, and kindred workers	3.1	4.7	2.0	3.0	1.9	2.8
Craftsmen, foremen, and kindred workers	4.0	5.2	2.6	4.0	2.3	3.5
Operatives and kindred workers	4.1	5.6	2.7	4.4	2.5	4.2
Service workers, including private household	3.9	[b]	2.5	[b]	2.3	3.5
Laborers, except farm and mine	4.8	5.5	3.2	4.4	3.1	4.4
Farmers and farm managers	4.2	5.6	2.7	4.1	3.1	3.6
Farm laborers and foremen	4.4	5.1	[b]	4.4	3.6	4.2

[a] Children ever born to women aged 45–49 years, married once, whose husbands were still living with them at the time of the census. Data are for white women in 1950, for native white women in 1910 and 1940.
[b] Rates are not shown when there were fewer than 1,200 women in 1910 or 3,000 in 1940.
SOURCE: Wilson H. Grabill, Clyde V. Kiser, and Pascal K. Whelpton, *The Fertility of American Women* (New York: Wiley, 1958), Table 54. Copyright © by The Social Science Research Council.

especially among the urban population. More than any other datum, these figures on family building during the 1930s rule out a simple economic interpretation of fertility. During a major depression, when economic burdens weighed heavily on all groups but most on those at the bottom of the social scale, the inverse relation between social class and fertility not only did not disappear but was more firmly established than in prior decades.

Differentials by the education of the wife are parallel to those by the occupation of the husband, except that the contrasts stand out even more clearly. Education has several advantages over occupation as an index of social class. There is no question about ordering: under all circumstances, college can be ranked above high school, but the same cannot be said of a professional, for example, as compared with a managerial position. Also, comparisons by husband's occupation often reflect the fact that young men start in low-level jobs and rise during their lifetime. Since in any one year their wives will usually have more children while they are younger, an annual rate (such as the birth rate, though not a cumulative rate, like the completed family size) will generally exaggerate class differences in fertility. Education, however, is ordinarily completed as a unit and then becomes a fixed attribute of adults for the rest of their lives.

Another advantage of education as an index is that it applies to all women and not, like the occupation of the husband, only to those who are married. There is a significant effect on the fertility of women who do not marry or marry at a relatively advanced age: the gradients for completed family size, thus, are somewhat steeper per woman than per wife. Among white women aged 45 to 49 in 1950, for example, a quarter of the college graduates had never married, as compared with less than 6 percent of those with eight years or less of schooling (Grabill *et al.* 1958: Table 67). According to a later study, however, the higher education of a sample of college-trained women made very little difference in their fertility values and expectations (Westoff and Potvin 1967).

The Dumont–Banks Model

These differences by social class in the United States were parallel with those in England (Innes 1938; Glass and Grebenik 1954), France, the Low Countries, Scandinavia, and Western nations generally. The contrast was usually especially marked in each country when its birth rate began to fall. "As national birth rates turned downward, class fertility differentials increased greatly" (Wrong 1958). The pattern strongly suggests that the decline in fertility was started by the middle classes, whose smaller families were gradually imitated by the rest of Western populations.

In the theory of the demographic transition, it is assumed that mortality fell first and that the subsequent decline in fertility was largely a response to the resultant increase in population. In the West, there is more validity to the converse of this thesis. The norm proscribing reproduction before a suitable place was available for the wife and children, which had been embedded in preindustrial institutions, was shattered with the advent of the industrial society. Thus, among some social classes the incidence of marriage rose and the average age at which it occurred went down, resulting in a rise in fertility and a sharp increase of population. Together with other analysts of the day, Malthus proposed a return to the practice by which marriage was postponed until a living had been established for the future family. In what is sometimes termed "the" Malthusian doctrine, he warned that if prudence did not govern sexual passion, the population would be cut back instead by food shortages and other "positive" factors. In a second thesis more applicable to Western countries, Malthus held that those with an opportunity to advance themselves would reduce the family obligations they incurred in order to improve their chances of success. Not malnutrition but the best possibility of moving to a higher social rung induced the middle classes to adopt the norm of small families.

Any man tends to rise from inferior positions in society to higher ones. This tendency can be blocked by the material or other obstacles that immobilize him, but the tendency itself is beyond question. . . . —to climb unceasingly, as oil rises in a lamp wick, toward a marvelous ideal which attracts and seduces [him]. . . . For one who starts at the bottom to arrive at the top, it is necessary to run fast and not to be encumbered with baggage. Thus, while an ambitious man can be served by a good marriage, either because of the wealth or the contacts it brings him, his own children, particularly if they are numerous, almost inevitably slow him down [Dumont 1890: 106, 110].

The best study of this process of "social capillarity" is a work titled *Prosperity and Parenthood: A Study of Family Planning among the Victorian Middle Classes* (Banks 1954). During the 19th century, Britain became the world's wealthiest nation and the urban middle classes her wealthiest social stratum. To move into that favored position was possible for many, but aspirants had to set and maintain an appropriate pattern of expenditures. One full-time servant, the minimum index of social respectability, constituted only the opening wedge. "With three servants—cook, parlormaid, and housemaid, or cook, housemaid, and nursemaid—a household was considered complete in all its functions. Further extensions were merely variations on this theme" (ibid.: 76). The paraphernalia of gentility at the next step up included a carriage, of which the endless varieties provided a ladder of social status, from a humble pony and gig to a luxurious coach with three powdered footmen in elegant livery. An annual holiday away from home, which had been reserved for the wealthiest, came to be seen as a necessary part of middle-class life. The cost of children, particularly of the upbringing that would fit them for a suitable career, increased steadily. While at the beginning of the century seven boarding schools had sufficed to educate the sons of the aristocracy and upper gentry, some forty new public schools were established between 1840 and 1870 for the far more numerous progeny of the advancing middle class. During this period a university degree became useful, if not indispensable, in more career lines. In short, during "the twenty years leading up to the Great Depression [that began in 1873], . . . there took place a striking expansion in the numbers of the English middle classes, in their wealth, and in their level and standard of living" (ibid.: 113). The depression, far from reversing the trend among the nouveaux bourgeois, intensified the competition for the fewer opportunities for social advancement. There was thus a greater incentive to cut down on some expenditures, "especially those not directly relevant to their appearing affluent to the eyes of the world" (ibid.: 133).

The limitation in family burdens was effected first of all by a postponement of marriage. Among the clergymen, doctors, lawyers, members of the aristocracy, merchants, bankers, manufacturers, and others of the gentleman class who married between 1840 and 1870, the average age was a shade under 30 years (ibid.: 48). So long as the industrial expansion continued unabated, late marriage was for most in the middle classes a sufficient check on reproduction, though undoubtedly some practiced birth control as well. By 1876–77, the dates of the Bradlaugh–Besant trials, many were finding it "increasingly difficult to preserve the kind of differential standard to which they had become accustomed," and the trials acted as a catalyst to the earlier partial and surreptitious spread of contraceptives. "Anthony Trollope's advice to a young lady: 'Fall in love, marry the man, have two children, and live happily ever afterwards,' seems neatly to sum up the outlook of this later period" (ibid.: 166–168).

What general prerequisites to a decline in fertility can be deduced from Banks's study? (1) Reproduction must be perceived not in a "natural" but in a "rational" perspective—that is, as legitimately subject to human control. For this reason, one author terms it the "Weber–Banks hypothesis" (Beshers 1967: chap. 4). As we have seen, however, to some degree rationality is a typical element of family formation in all cultures; the change in 19th-century Western countries was in degree rather than in kind. To behave responsibly and postpone marriage to the "proper" age was a norm in part taken from the European tradition, and limiting family size by contraception was undoubtedly adopted in practice long before it was publicly accepted in respectable circles. (2) The social structure must be open, with social advance possible for those who curtail their family responsibilities. "The widespread desire for self-advancement economically, which is such an outstanding characteristic of capitalistic civilization, is fundamental" (Himes, cited in Banks 1954: 8). As we have noted, the upper classes of static societies typically reflect their favored position in high fertility, the correlative of their low mortality. Similarly, the lower classes respond to their poorer chances for social advancement with a lesser control over their reproductive capacity. (3) The crucial element is the social class's aspirations: as its income level goes up, its hope for greater wealth goes up faster. When a middle-class woman says she cannot "afford" another child while women with much lower incomes can and do, the difference obviously does not lie in the cost of subsistence or even of comforts. (4) The propaganda for family limitation and even the increased efficacy of contraceptives are relevant mainly as catalysts, reinforcing motivations that derive from the social structure.

During the first decade of this century, more or less, the pioneering upper middle classes passed on the leadership to groups lower on the social scale. The route by which the small-family norm was disseminated varied, of course, from one country to another, but typically it was the lower middle and the upper working classes that next adopted it. In England just before World War I, the birth rate of members of a sickness-benefit society (mostly small shopkeepers and skilled workers) fell more than twice as fast as that of the general population. "The birth rate was falling most conspicuously, if not exclusively, not among the wealthy or the middle class as such, but among those sections of every class in which there is much prudence, foresight, and self-control" (Webb 1913). As another instance, among French civil servants above a certain income, this was positively correlated with family size as early as 1906. In short, "before 1910 the upper classes led the decline in fertility, but after 1910 the intermediate groups assumed the lead" (Wrong 1958). In a number of instances, thus, the relation between social class and fertility formed a J-shaped curve: among families of successively lower incomes, the number of children decreased slightly and then, from the upper-middle bracket down, increased steadily.

VARIATIONS ON THE DUMONT–BANKS MODEL

Banks's analysis manifestly describes not only the behavior of middle classes in Victorian England but that of the sectors of various Western populations at some phase in the historic decline of family size. But whether the model fits France and the United States, the two countries where fertility fell first, depends on how specifically one defines the various factors. Dumont held that the breakdown of social barriers in the French Revolution accelerated interclass mobility, but according to a subsequent analysis his thesis applied better to 18th-century France: "Social promotion was not so difficult that all ambition was stifled; it was not so easy that unlimited fertility did not constitute a serious handicap in the struggle to rise in the social scale" (Blacker 1957). The contraction of family size in France was associated, however, not with a dynamic social class attempting to establish an industrial society, but with the contrary.

> There was in the economy of the old regime a distinct configuration of wealth, noncapitalist in function, that may be called "proprietary." It embodied investments in land, urban property, venal office, and annuities. The returns it yielded were modest, ranging between one and five percent, but they were fairly constant and varied little from year to year. They were realized not by entrepreneurial effort, which was degrading, but by mere ownership and the passage of calendar intervals. Risk was negligible. . . .
>
> Both before and after the Revolution, the social values of the old elite dominated the status-conscious men and women of the wealthy Third Estate. Avid for standing, they had little choice but to pursue it as the aristocracy defined it, and the result was a massive prejudice that diverted . . . wealth into comparatively sterile proprietary investments [Taylor 1967].

Those who sacrificed to acquire these various types of noncapitalist wealth preferred rent to profit, security to risk, tradition to innovation, gentility to skill. France displayed nearly all the traits of a traditional society as Rostow (1960: chap. 2) defined it, yet this unlikely population constituted another source from which the small-family system spread. The most striking overlap with the Dumont–Banks model is that the French *propriétaire* limited the size of his family in order to acquire status as defined by another class. The relative insignificance of contraceptives is also apparent. The reason French fertility declined farther than in the rest of the Western world, one might hypothesize, is that the two contexts of a small-family system, the proprietary and the industrial-bourgeois, eventually reinforced each other.

The Decline of American Fertility

The very high fertility of the American colonies in the 18th century was noted by a number of contemporaries—Malthus, Benjamin Franklin, and Jefferson, among others; and it is also the conclusion of modern analysts using several techniques to manipulate various kinds of inadequate data. According to the consensus of these estimates, both contemporary and modern, around the end of the 18th century each married woman bore an average of almost 8 children (e.g., Lotka 1927). The decline in white fertility began in 1810 and continued steadily until 1940. During this period the child–woman ratio of the white population fell from 1,358 to 419—about one-third by 1850, about three-quarters by 1900, and the remainder in the 20th century. The fertility of Negroes began at a higher point in 1850 (prior data are not available) but decreased more rapidly, reaching parity with the whites in 1920 (Grabill *et al.* 1958: Table 6).

When women who have passed their childbearing period are divided into successively older categories, the number of children they report gives an approximate indication of the decline in family size over a considerable time, as shown in Table 14-2. The main sources of error with this measure derive from the facts that underreporting probably increases with age, particularly for the higher ages, and that there is some relation (though not a simple one) between longevity and completed family size (ibid.: 400–404). In the table the rows for women aged 45–49 and 55–59 at successive censuses indicate that the discrepancy is not serious. On the other hand, the jump over only 5 years between two successive rows, women aged 45–49 in 1910 and those aged 70–74 in 1940, is probably based in part on the fact that the women in the latter—that is, very much older—age bracket are less representative of their complete cohort.

In any analysis of fertility, it is important to include marriage trends. We know virtually nothing about the age at marriage in the 19th century even for the whole of the American population, not to speak of its various sectors. The proportion of the females who never married, as shown in column 7 of Table 14-2, forms a ⋂-curve, with low points among cohorts having their children in the third quarter of the 19th century and the second quarter of the 20th century, and an intermediate high point among those having their children just before World War I. As at least nine out of ten married during all periods in the past century, the loss to fertility by nonmarriage was probably never greater than one-tenth.

Childless couples, equivalent so far as fertility trends are concerned to persons who remain single, are a class particularly difficult to analyze, for they are made up of two quite different categories—sterile marriages and those in which the forces toward smaller families have reached the ultimate point. Some authorities hold that on the average one marriage in ten is naturally sterile (see p. 198). The figures at the top of column 8 suggest both that this estimate is too high and that deliberate childlessness was all but nonexistent in the middle of the 19th century. A large part of the decline in fertility can be accounted for by the rise in the number of childless couples, which constituted one out of every five in the period just preceding World War II.

Note that up to the 1940s there was also a steady but gradual decline in the completed size of families with at least one child (column 11). The average number of children per mother, estimated at more than eight in 1800, was less than six in the third quarter of the century, just four in the first quarter of the 20th

Table 14-2. Completed Family Size, United States, 1910–70

Age of Women at Given Date					Main Child-Bearing Period[b]	Percent Never Married	Of Ever Married, percent Childless	Children Ever Born[c]		
1910	1940[a]	1950[a]	1960[a]	1970[a]				PER WOMAN	PER WIFE	PER MOTHER
(1)	(2)	(3)	(4)	(5)	(6)	(7)	(8)	(9)	(10)	(11)
70–74					1858–1882	6.5	7.7	5.0	5.4	5.8
65–69					1863–1887	6.5	7.9	5.0	5.4	5.8
60–64					1868–1892	7.3	8.2	4.8	5.3	5.7
55–59					1873–1897	7.2	8.3	4.8	5.2	5.7
50–54					1878–1902	8.4	8.9	4.5	5.0	5.5
45–49					1883–1907	9.0	9.5	4.3	4.7	5.2
	70–74				1888–1912	10.0	12.5	3.4	3.8	4.4
	65–69				1893–1917	10.0	14.0	3.2	3.6	4.2
	60–64				1898–1922	9.5	15.0	3.0	3.4	4.0
	55–59				1903–1927	9.0	16.5	3.0	3.3	3.9
	50–54				1908–1932	9.1	16.3	2.8	3.1	3.7
	45–49	55–59			1913–1937	8.9–8.0	16.1–16.9	2.7–2.7	3.0–2.9	3.5–3.5
		50–54			1918–1942	8.0	18.0	2.5	2.7	3.3
		45–49	55–59		1923–1947	8.4–8.4	19.5–20.0	2.3–2.2	2.5–2.5	3.1–3.1
			50–54		1928–1952	7.8	20.0	2.1	2.3	2.9
			45–49	55–59	1933–1957	6.6–6.4	17.1–16.8	2.2–2.2	2.4–2.4	2.8–2.8
				50–54	1938–1962	5.6	12.9	2.4	2.6	2.9
				45–49	1943–1967	5.2	9.9	2.6	2.8	3.1

[a] Whites only.

[b] Dates over which the middle cohort (aged 72 in 1910, for example) was 20 to 44 years old.

[c] Converted from columns headed children ever born "per 1,000 women," "per 1,000 women ever married," and "per 1,000 women who bore at least one child."

SOURCES: Wilson H. Grabill, Clyde V. Kiser, and Pascal K. Whelpton, *The Fertility of American Women* (New York: Wiley, 1958), Tables 9 and 16. Copyright © by The Social Science Research Council. U.S. Bureau of the Census, *U.S. Census of Population, 1960*, vol. 1: *Characteristics of the Population, U.S. Summary*, Table 190. *U.S. Census of Population, 1970*, vol. PC(1)-D1: *Detailed Characteristics, U.S. Summary*, Table 212 (Washington, D.C.: U.S. Government Printing Office).

century, and less than three in the second quarter. Even ignoring the women who remained single and the increasing proportion of married women who were child-less, the completed family size decreased by almost one child per generation.

It is worth emphasizing the date when this transformation started. The decline began when the United States was a relatively empty country with a wide-open frontier, when it was still overwhelmingly rural and agricultural (although the rural sector was becoming increasingly involved in the town-oriented market economy), when the very term *birth control* had not yet been coined and contra-ceptive means were more or less limited to *coitus interruptus*—when almost all of the factors cited in the later studies as causes of the decline were still in the future. Does the United States fit the Dumont–Banks model? Certainly the new industrialists that transformed the country after the Civil War were the provin-cial cousins of their English counterparts. But whether the opportunity of social mobility alone brought about the decline in family size two generations earlier could be answered only by a study in depth—in fact, a replication of Banks's volume using American data.

Working Wives

In its original formulation the Dumont–Banks thesis applied exclusively to males. It was the men with an opportunity to rise who decided to have fewer children; their wives, who bore the children, fitted passively into the background. This was an accurate enough representation of at least the outward forms of family life in Victorian England, but most students of stratification have contin-ued to define the status of couples exclusively by the husband's occupation, ignoring the increasing proportion of married women who work outside the home and the effect of this trend on family life (Day 1961). The possibility of rapid social mobility is far greater, of course, if a young husband and wife both work, post-poning reproduction until the man is established at a higher level. We should expect the inverse correlation with fertility to be higher than with the social mobility of the male alone, for it is especially burdensome for the female to combine childrearing with employment outside the home. The cause–effect relation, moreover, can work in both directions: a woman with no children is more likely to seek a job, and a woman who is earning a wage is more likely to prevent conceptions.

Work for females outside the home, which is relatively rare in underdeveloped economies, has increased appreciably in almost all Western countries. The main reason is that the trend of advanced economies is toward a greater concentration of the labor force in occupations in which females had been traditionally dom-inant—such middle-level, service-oriented professions as nursing, social work, teaching, librarianship, as well as office or factory jobs of a relatively low skill that can easily be shifted from one part of a bureaucratic structure to another, such as stenographers and typists, textile workers (Oppenheimer 1970). Within this general context, motivations vary greatly. Most studies cite economic deprivation as an important reason that married women work, and this applies in an absolute sense to a minority, especially those with husbands absent or dead. The fact, however, that the employment of married women has increased greatly during a period of economic prosperity indicates that the "deprivation" is often measured against rising expectations.

The question has an answer that borders on the cliché: "Why do you work?" "For money." . . . Somewhere between 55 and 90 percent of the answers will be in terms of money, depending on the particular sample of women being questioned, the phrasing of the question, etc. . . . A young professional woman said to her secretary, "It's all right for you to have a baby; it only costs you $4,000 to quit your job. But it would cost me $9,500, so I can't afford it" [Nye and Hoffman 1963: 22–25].

In the United States, the proportion of females in the labor force remained static at about one-quarter of those aged 14 and over from 1910 to 1940. Then, with the labor shortage during World War II, it rose to 29 percent in 1950 and, surprisingly, continued to rise to 34.5 in 1960. In 1970, 42.6 percent of females aged 16 and over were in the labor force, and according to conservative extrapolations there is good reason to anticipate the proportion will continue to rise (Oppenheimer 1973). Under the Civil Rights Act of 1964 it became unlawful to discriminate on the basis of sex in hiring, job retention, and promotion. One may prohibit the hiring of married women, for instance, only if the ruling applies to married men as well.

Of the growing number of females in the labor force, the percentage married and with husband present—only 14.7 in 1940—rose to 23.8 in 1950, 30.5 in 1960, and 40.8 in 1970. And of the 31.7 million women in the labor force in March 1971, almost two-fifths had children under 18, divided as follows:

With children under 3 years	2.3 million mothers
With children 3–5 years (none under 3)	2.0
With children 6–17 years (none under 6)	7.9
TOTAL: 25.7 million children	12.2 million mothers

Five-sixths of the 12.2 million mothers were married with husband present. This number was the highest ever, comparing with 8 million working mothers of children under 18 in 1960, only 1.5 million in 1940. According to the 1971 survey, the occupations of working mothers were distributed in more or less the same proportions as all females in the labor force; there seems to have been little or no special discrimination against mothers in either hiring or placement.

So long as there were strong legal and cultural norms against combining marital and nonfamilial roles, females were generally obliged to choose one or the other; if they married, and particularly if they had minor children, they were more or less barred from many types of employment. It was widely held, therefore, that the elimination of discriminatory rules, and the encouragement of a greater female participation in the labor force, would be one means of reducing fertility. But as the numbers involved continued to rise, there developed various adjustments between occupational and familial duties, facilitating the relatively easy union of work outside the home with a moderate number of children.

In judging the large number of analyses of labor-force participation and the size of the family, therefore, one must carefully note the date and country of the statistics and thus the legal and normative framework that they reflect. Studies of the relation between the two variables differ markedly also according to the discipline of the analysts. Family sociologists have built up a large corpus validating the conventional view that the proper place of mothers is in the home; much of this was summarized and partly answered by Nye and Hoffman (1963). For demographers, the object of analysis is fertility, and work outside the home is seen as one of the independent variables that affect it (e.g., Collver 1968). For economists, on the contrary, the problem is how the marriage and childbearing of women influences their participation in the labor force (e.g., Cain 1966). To some degree the points of view of prior studies by sociologists and economists were combined by Rosenberg (1972, 1973), who analyzed the intervening variables that help determine both the timing and the number of children of women in the labor force.

The Fertility of American Subnations

In most countries of the Western World, Jews and the irreligious have by far the smallest families, Protestants of various denominations are in the intermediate range, and Catholics have the largest. According to public-opinion polls in the United States, the three groups generally fall in the same order with respect to the number of children desired and expected, and the approval and use of contraception (Freedman *et al.* 1961). The significance of these findings depends to some degree on the interpretation of the researcher. In an analysis of Western fertility concentrated on overall long-term trends, differences in religion and similar culturally defined characteristics can be regarded as minor, residual to the differentiation by social class. In the process of modernization that the growth of cities and of urban-based social classes effects, one typical consequence is secularization, the tendency of religious–cultural differences to become smaller. Thus, the effect of religion *per se* on the reproductive behavior of most persons in the West is now probably close to nil. What may seem to be a religious influence often reflects the fact that the members of any denomination are typically concentrated in a very few places in the social structure as defined by occupation, education, income, or any other of the usual indices.

In the analysis of fertility differences among the nationalities and races of the American population, similarly, it was ordinarily held until recently that these were mainly indicative of the various family-forming patterns associated with social-economic categories. The higher birth rate of Negroes, thus, derived from their residence in the rural South—the region and the economic sector with the greatest fertility irrespective of race. And the low birth rate of American Jews also reflected their locus in society—their high proportions in professional and managerial occupations and their virtual absence from such sectors as the rural South. There is some validity in such interpretations, but a supplementary hypothesis has now been developed.

The new theory was developed first in several papers summarizing Calvin Goldscheider's dissertation on the Jewish population of Providence, R.I. Like Jews elsewhere in the Western world, the study population had small families, which could be differentiated by denomination (Orthodox, Conservative, and Reformed), by social class (upper, middle, and lower), and by generation (foreign-born, second, and third). These three classifications were not distinct, of course, and it was necessary to separate the strands whenever possible. When differences in family size by religious division were controlled for social class, they almost disappeared; that is, the Orthodox hostility to contraception was not an important factor in the fertility of that group (Goldscheider 1965). The low fertility of second-generation Jews, thus, was not due to their rejection of Orthodoxy, nor was it a reflection simply of their class position.

Second-generation Jews were economically mobile, [and] most had the benefits of a secular education and desired acculturation. Nevertheless, their rejection of the ghetto life of the first-generation Jews and their non-acceptance in the general community created a sense of insecurity. Thus, the minority status of Jews, coupled with the economic depression of the 1930s, led to drastic reductions in the size of second-generation Jewish families, and many delayed their marriages. . . .

The economic depression of the 1930s [however] was not the key factor in the decline of Jewish fertility as it was for the general population. Jewish family size (2.0 children) was lower at that time than that of the non-Jewish population. . . . [Similarly] although the third generation had found more security than previous generations, the general insecurity of their minority status, their fear of discrimination, and their values of high achievement retained for them lower fertility than their non-Jewish neighbors [Goldscheider 1966; cf. Goldscheider 1967; Goldscheider and Uhlenberg 1969].

In short, Jews have been remarkably successful in realizing their aspiration to higher status, and they have had to climb up the social ladder against frequent impediments of anti-Semitism.

If the thesis is correct, it should apply also to those other subnations that share the Jews' characteristics. The closest parallel is Japanese Americans, who also have suffered from discrimination, have overcome it in a remarkable record of upward mobility, and have a lower fertility than the American norm (Goldscheider 1971: 291–292). Whether it fits American Negroes depends on whether one analyzes them as a single group (cf. Sly 1970).

In Chapter 13 (pp. 497–506), it was suggested that the current urban growth of underdeveloped nations is of a different type from that in the historic West, and the move to cities by blacks is a partial parallel. In both cases the migration has been less of self-selected persons qualified to succeed in urban pursuits than the push from the countryside of poverty-stricken, declassed peasants (Farley 1970: chap. 3). That under such conditions urban growth is not accompanied by an immediate decline in fertility may be regarded as a negative confirmation of the Dumont–Banks hypothesis. Birth control by any method is based fundamentally on self-control, which socially mobile persons exercise because their restraint is rewarded with an improvement in social–economic status. But those ill prepared for urban–industrial jobs (or blocked from them by race prejudice—the demographic effect is the same) lack such an incentive. Indeed, those with little hope of economic stability may not have the personal prerequisites of family stability. During the early period of English industrialization, it will be recalled, the urban paupers and new industrial workers, raw from the deteriorating village culture, probably had more children, legitimate and illegitimate, than their immediate forebears (pp. 450–455).

The traditional Negro family in the United States, a residue of slavery, was highly matricentric, with barely enough cohesion to retain the husband–father in the household. With the shift of lower-class Negroes to a new metropolitan environment, this weak institution disintegrated further. One important index is the absent father who "haunts the Negro family" (Lincoln 1965). In spite of a decline in widowhood, the proportion of Negro women who state that they have ever been married and are now living alone is between a fifth and a quarter at the youngest ages, rising to almost a third in middle age. Obviously such data are less accurate than those on morally neutral questions. In reply to the census questions, women may state that they were married even if they were not, that their absent husbands died even if this was not the case, or that their husbands were presently living with them even if they were alone. As such evasions are possible, the figures may understate actual proportions, though it is impossible to guess by how much (cf. Farley and Hermalin 1971).

The Negro women who in so many cases must carry unaided the full financial burden and moral responsibility for their children would have, one would think, the maximum incentive to exercise birth control. But it is the Negroes with higher education, stable families, and middle-class aspirations who have small families. "The excess of nonwhite over white fertility is concentrated among couples with ... children in addition to the number desired" (Whelpton *et al.* 1966: 349). Lower-class Negro women sometimes have moral objections to contraception, and many are ignorant of the most effective means, but the crucial factor is apathy. "They seem to regard the burden of numerous children with the same fatalism (and, perhaps, despair) with which they 'accept' their extreme poverty" (ibid.: 356). One consequence is an extraordinarily high proportion of illegitimate births (cf. Cutright and Galle 1973), well over one-quarter in the 1960s and rising (Table 14-3).[3]

---

[3] One of the values that money can buy is privacy, and many illegitimate births to middle-class women are not recorded as such. According to one important study, unwed mothers in the middle class do not differ greatly from a random sample of other white middle-class females (Vincent 1961). However, even if the white rate in Table 14-3 is raised substantially

Table 14-3.   Illegitimate Births, by Color, United States, 1940–68

	Number (–000)		Percent Illegitimate of All Live Births	
	WHITE	NONWHITE	WHITE	NONWHITE
1940	40	49	2.0	16.8
1945	56	61	2.4	17.9
1950	54	88	1.8	18.0
1955	64	119	1.9	20.2
1960	83	142	2.3	21.6
1965	124	168	4.0	26.3
1966	133	170	4.4	27.7
1967	142	176	4.9	29.4
1968	155	184	5.3	31.2

SOURCES: U.S. Bureau of Labor Statistics, *Recent Trends in Social and Economic Conditions of Negroes in the United States*, BLS Report no. 347 (Washington, D.C., 1968), p. 23; U.S. Bureau of the Census, *Current Population Reports*, Series P-23, no. 36, April, 1971.

The rapid cultural change that the nonwhite population is undergoing has left its mark on fertility differences between whites and nonwhites. We find that nonwhite couples have had and expect more births than white couples, and that this difference is brought about partly by the unusually high fertility of a minority of nonwhite couples who live in the rural South, and partly by the moderately high fertility of the many nonwhite couples who have Southern farm origins. Nonwhite couples with no Southern farm background have and expect about the same number of births as similar white couples. These differentials suggest that as the influence of Southern rural patterns of mating and childbearing diminishes, the fertility differences between whites and nonwhites will decline (Whelpton *et al.* 1966: 369).

As we noted in another context (p. 196), it is misleading to classify all Negroes together, since in many respects their behavior patterns form a bimodal curve. Above age 30 the frequency of childlessness and of one-child families is higher among Negroes than among whites; less than half of Negro women, as compared with two-thirds of white women, have two to four children; but these differences are masked by the higher proportion of black women with five or more children (Table 14-4). Some blacks, for whatever reason, make little or no effort to rise in social scale; and associated with this apathy, as both cause and effect, there is a typically large progeny. Negroes who do move up in educational and

---

in order to include an approximation of such hidden births out of wedlock, the rate for nonwhites will still be several times larger. One should note, also, that the rate for "nonwhites" (or "Negro and other races," the current locution) is lower than that for blacks, since it includes such components as Orientals, who typically do not breed outside of wedlock.

Table 14-4. Children Ever Born, by Race, Age Category, and Marital Status of Women, United States, 1969

Race and Age Category	Children Ever Born (–000)	Percent of Women Ever Married by Children Ever Born					Children Ever Born	
		TOTAL	0 OR 1	2 TO 4	5 OR MORE		PER WOMAN	PER EVER MARRIED WOMAN
Negro								
15–19	157	100	73	27	—		0.1	1.1
20–24	581	100	48	47	5		1.0	1.8
25–29	600	100	29	51	20		2.3	2.8
30–34	584	100	26	43	32		3.1	3.5
35–39	584	100	22	38	40		3.7	4.0
40–44	609	100	31	37	32		3.5	3.6
15–44	3,115	100	33	42	25		2.0	3.1
White								
15–19	925	100	91	9	—		0.1	0.6
20–24	4,411	100	71	28	—		0.7	1.0
25–29	4,802	100	34	62	4		1.8	2.0
30–34	4,611	100	18	69	13		2.7	2.9
35–39	4,931	100	17	64	19		3.0	3.1
40–44	5,340	100	18	64	18		2.9	3.0
15–44	25,021	100	33	56	11		1.7	2.4

SOURCE: U.S. Bureau of the Census, "The Social and Economic Status of Negroes in the United States, 1970," *Current Population Reports*, Series P-23, no. 38, 1971, Table 96.

occupational level generally have to overcome a high barrier of prejudice, and their small families exemplify the Dumont–Banks thesis as clearly as any sector in the American population.

Fertility can be influenced not only by the hostility of others but also, at least in some instances, by the efforts of the subnation's leaders to enhance its power by increasing its size. The nationalist opposition to birth control (pp. 618–619), in other words, is voiced—sometimes even more vehemently—by those striving for relative advantage within the population of a single nation. Many Jewish spokesmen have expressed concern about the supposed numerical decline of American Jewry, whether by secularization, intermarriage, or low fertility. Black nationalists in the United States have denounced birth-control clinics as genocide. In Canada, French spokesmen have advocated *la revanche des berceaux*—getting even with the English by filling the cradles.

However often ideologues sought a larger power base through pronatalist measures, in most instances the effect of their advocacy has been too small to distinguish it from all the other determinants of group fertility. The one important exception would seem to be the Catholic sector of a mixed population. Even before the erosion of the Church's doctrine, the prohibition of effective contraceptives was never enough to explain Catholic fertility. France, at least nominally a Catholic country, was the first in the West to establish the small-family system (Goldscheider 1971: 156–161). The fertility of Italy's northern, more industrial provinces has generally been as low as anywhere in the world, and even that of the southern, typically agrarian provinces has been intermediate on the world scale (Seppilli 1960).

American Catholics reflect a number of influences. As peasant immigrants they carried old-country norms with them, and they typically fitted in the American occupational structure at a low level, with a correspondingly high fertility. In the 1930s the birth rate of Catholics was higher than that of non-Catholics but declining faster, and the general prognosis was that the difference would eventually disappear. "It is quite clear that the main reason why Catholic fertility is falling more rapidly arises from the fact that it has farther to fall; because there has been, in fact, a cultural lag" (Himes 1936: 413). In the postwar period several analysts have challenged this prognosis (e.g., Kirk 1955), and others have confirmed it (e.g., Brooks and Henry 1958). According to one Princeton study, Catholics desire larger families than other Americans, but in part because "the more fundamentalist Protestant sects found in the southern and rural parts of the country" were omitted from the sample (Westoff *et al.* 1961: 179). Even so, the range in the mean number of children desired, unchanged in a later study, was very small—from 3.6 by two Catholic parents to 2.7 by two Jewish parents (ibid: 180; Westoff *et al.* 1963: 89). When a Catholic had been married to a non-Catholic by a priest, the wife wanted 3.3 children on the average; when not by a priest, she wanted 3.0 children. The stated preference among the eight Protestant denominations surveyed ranged between 2.8 and 3.1 children. Among Catholics the mean number of children desired was highest in the professional class (4.0) and lowest in the unskilled (3.4). From those data the authors concluded that "religion exerts a strong influence on fertility" and that "the comparative influence of class appears negligible" (Westoff *et al.* 1961 : 191). But when differentials along all dimensions contract to so narrow a range, it is a more or less arbitrary decision whether to stress one or another among the remaining differences. That middle-class Catholics have had a higher fertility than others in the middle class may be because "their minority status has developed a sect type of mentality in its most committed membership" (Hunt 1967).

The most detailed analysis was Van Heek's study (1954, 1956) of Dutch Catholics, whose fertility has been extremely high by Western standards. Oppressed by Protestants in the 17th and 18th centuries, the substantial bloc of Catholics in the Netherlands acquired a fighting spirit that persisted long after their full emancipation. This religious élan was expressed in their stricter discipline and their more rigid adherence to dogma (cf. Petersen 1966). The control was maintained, moreover, through a variety of Church-related agencies, which in the predominantly Catholic South intruded into the life of every family (Van 't Veer 1972). The thesis has been applied to Catholic minorities in other countries (Burch 1966; Day 1968; Kennedy 1973b). In every case, the analysis is difficult, for Catholic minorities may act according to both the Goldscheider and the Van Heek theses, striving both to reduce their family responsibilities in order to rise in the social scale and, on the contrary, to enhance the power of their religious bloc through a rapid growth in numbers. The ambivalence exists not only in the differential behavior of members of the denomination but often in the confused and half-contradictory norms of individual Catholics. No analysis, however perceptive, need remain valid for very long. Thus, the Dutch Catholicism that Van Heek and Van 't Veer studied represented the ultramontane wing of the world Church, but by the mid-1960s this had become the most obstreperously independent of the national churches.

The Irish Pattern of Late Marriage

In common with the rest of Western Europe, Ireland in the 18th century lived by the tradition that a young man ought not to marry until he had a patch of land to cultivate, so that in general he had to wait for his inheritance. By 1780 several factors together increased the amount of free land available: under the impetus of mercantilist encouragements to the cultivation of grain, pastureland was converted to agriculture; much swampland was drained; the potato, introduced from America, increased greatly the food value per unit of tilled land. An adolescent boy with a small holding could now build a hut and grow enough potatoes to raise a family. Girls were typically mothers by their early teens, and in a country with no birth control this decrease in the age at marriage had a decisive effect. In six decades the population of Ireland more than doubled, increasing from 4.0 million in 1781 to 8.2 million in 1841 (Connell 1950). This growth stimulated a large emigration, which became a mass exodus after the failure of the potato crop and the great famine of the 1840s. At mid-1956 the estimated population of Eire and Northern Ireland together was 4.3 million, or only slightly more than it was in 1781, at the start of the tremendous increase. This massive depopulation, unique among modern Western countries, was effected only in part by emigration. The age at marriage in Ireland has generally been the highest in the world, and the proportion that never marry the greatest, so that in spite of a high rate of marital fertility, the natural increase was only moderate (cf. Walsh 1972).

An analysis of the long-term trend in age at marriage cannot be made from vital statistics. Until about a decade ago the exact age was not recorded, and the data from which it can be estimated are not available for every census. The proportions reported single in each census, which are an alternative index of family formation, are indicative. In recent decades between half and three-quarters of the males, and between a third and a half of the females, were still single at about 30 years, and more than a quarter did not marry while they still could have children. Since many single persons emigrated, the extraordinary proportions of the population in Ireland counted as single at the time of each census in fact understate the reluctance of the Irish to accept family responsibilities (Kennedy 1973a: chap. 7).

In their aspiration for a better life, the Irish did not differ from other peoples of Western Europe, and that they sought to reduce the size of their families by an extended postponement of marriage was also in accord with general European norms. The Irish pattern differs in degree. The discrepancy between actual conditions and those aspired to was probably especially great in Ireland, whose poor inhabitants received regular reports from relatives and friends on the comparative affluence in America and England. While other populations gradually shifted to contraception, the clergy, the law, and the pressure of public opinion made this adaptation difficult in this strictly Roman Catholic country.

Until very recently, it was illegal to advocate, advertise, or sell contraceptives, on pain of a fine up to £50 and/or imprisonment up to six months. The ban on importing contraceptives for personal use, in effect for nearly four decades, was declared unconstitutional only in 1973. The following year the small Irish Family Planning Association won a suit challenging its right to distribute contraceptives; it does not sell them but accepts voluntary contributions.

The marital fertility particularly but not exclusively of the non-Catholics has fallen in recent years, indicating that some Irish control conception. The commonest means used, Kennedy believes, may be prolonged continence. The negative attitude towards sexuality in the Augustinian tradition, which has remained especially strong in Irish Catholicism, may also have induced some young people to postpone marriage out of a fear or disgust even of licit sex between husband and wife.[4] With the rise in life expectancy during the second

[4] "Most of us," one Irishwoman recalls, "remember with a shiver those three-day retreats at school, [after which] . . . the confessor put questions to us concerning sex habits of which in our genuine innocence we had never dreamed in the worst nightmare and which so shocked and sickened us that we remained sex-frightened for years" (Maura Laverty, in O'Brien 1953).

half of the 19th century, sons had to wait longer to inherit their fathers' holdings, and some that put off marriage eventually decided not to marry at all. With many unmarried males, institutions developed that catered to their special wants; celibacy was not so lonely a state with so many to share it. As bachelors, most men can count on their mothers to keep house for them—or those unmarried sisters who remain in this man's land rather than emigrating. In the opinion of some Irish women, "the men are cagey, spiritless, selfish, and spoiled by their mothers." One of them called Ireland "a paradise for the male. It is not that the young man in modern Ireland cannot afford to get married. It is that he cannot get married and still afford his car, his club, his betting, his poker, his golf, and his holidays" (Seán O'Faolain, in O'Brien 1953).

The late marriage of many Irish and the nonmarriage of many others are linked to the rest of the country's social–demographic processes. The tie to emigration is well known: the high proportion of females leaving the country reflects a search for both husbands and a style of married life less oppressive than the norm. Not so obviously, the same pattern holds for much of the internal migration. Irish women move to cities, leaving behind a surplus of males and building up a surplus of urban females (Table 14-5). Though it is usually assumed that permanent celibacy is characteristic of the countryside, in fact there are proportionately more spinsters in the towns.

Table 14-5. Percentage Single among Persons Aged 25–29 and 45–54, by Sex and Rural–Urban Residence, Ireland, 1926–66

Sex and Year	Aged 25–29 Years				Aged 45–54 Years			
	TOTAL	RURAL	URBAN[a]	RURAL EXCESS	TOTAL	RURAL	URBAN[a]	RURAL EXCESS
Male								
1926	80	86	68	+18	31	34	25	+9
1936	82	89	71	+18	34	37	25	+12
1946	80	86	68	+18	32	37	23	+14
1961	67	80	54	+26	30	36	20	+16
1966	58	73	46	+27	29	36	19	+17
Female								
1926	62	65	58	+7	24	22	27	−5
1936	64	57	61	+6	25	23	28	−5
1946	58	58	57	+1	26	24	29	−5
1961	45	47	44	+3	23	20	26	−6
1966	38	40	37	+3	21	18	24	−6

[a] Places with 1,500 or more inhabitants.
SOURCE: Robert E. Kennedy, Jr., *The Irish: Emigration, Marriage, and Fertility* (Berkeley: University of California Press, 1973), Table 57.

The Control of Fertility in Postwar Japan

Japan's rapid population increase—the consequence of a rise in fertility, a decline in mortality, and the remigration from the lost empire of administrators and settlers—had become intolerable by the end of World War II. The response was equally dramatic. Japan's birth rate fell from 34.3 in 1947 to 17.2 in 1957, or by almost exactly half in a decade, and this remarkable record has been widely cited as a goal for such countries as India.

It can hardly be said that the Japanese government guided the people into adopting a program of planned parenthood. The measure under which the subsequent population policy developed did not have this overt intention: the stated purpose of the Eugenic Protection Law of 1948 was "to prevent the increase of the inferior descendants from the standpoint of eugenic protection and to protect the life and health of the mother as well." The law was not, in Taeuber's opinion (1958: 269, 372), merely "a devious route by which the government could sponsor abortions as a means of 'solving' the population problem," even though it was true that "its major advocates were those who favored the diffusion of contraception." Under the law, the state provided voluntary and in some cases compulsory sterilization, abortion facilities, and "practical guidance in adjustment of conception" when there were eugenic or medical reasons for preventing births. In an amendment the following year, economic factors were added, and the program quickly developed into a mass state-subsidized effort to reduce natality, as its liberal sponsors had originally intended. The official fee for an abortion was from 1,000 to 2,000 yen, but the actual amount paid under insurance plans and health services was usually about 300 yen (or less than $1), and in at least one place the cost to the woman was only 15 yen. By 1953 there were 692 public clinics, as well as 55 private ones. The number of abortions performed under the law rose from 320,000 in 1950 to 1,128,000 in 1958 (or from 137 to 682 per 1,000 live births). After 1958 efforts were made to encourage contraception, and the number of abortions declined slightly from this high point. According to one estimate for the year 1955, the number of births would have been 1.4 to 2.1 million larger (depending on varying estimates of fecundity) if there had been no legal abortions (Muramatsu 1960).

Indeed, the control of Japanese fertility was so successful that eventually the government called for a reversal of the trend. The chairman of the semi-official Population Problems Inquiry Council submitted a report recommending that the net reproduction rate be raised to unity in order to avoid an imminent labor shortage (Kurushima 1970). His proposal was shortly repeated in a statement by the prime minister, who thus marked it as official policy. This reversal was made in spite of the facts that at the current rate Japan's population would continue to increase until well into the next century, and that even today this is the world's most crowded nation (Boffey 1970; Nizard 1970).

Japan's record is the best one to test the common notion that abortions are intrinsically injurious to the woman's health—that is, apart from the conditions prevailing in countries where they are illegal. In Japan trained physicians perform aseptic operations and prescribe penicillin for every patient. On the other hand, while the program was being set up, there were some unskilled practitioners, and operations were permitted up to the seventh month of pregnancy rather than only before the end of the third month, as medical opinion generally considers mandatory. The inconclusive evidence to date suggests that one or two abortions under optimum medical conditions are not typically harmful, but repeated abortions may be (as are also repeated deliveries in many cases). For this reason, the sentiment developed in Japan to shift the major emphasis in the state clinics from abortion to contraception or sterilization, or both. A typical view was expressed in a 1967 book by Tenrei Ota, a socialist gynecologist and the inventor of the intra-uterine contraceptive device that bears his name.[5] His basic aim, to protect the health of mothers especially in the poorer classes, would in his opinion be best served if the physician could at his own discretion prescribe the most effective contraceptive or induced abortion or sterilization, depending on the circumstances. In a 3-year program to introduce contraception among a large sample of railroad workers, the birth rate was cut from 40.8 to 19.4, with a small and decreasing proportion of unwanted pregnancies ended by abortion (Koya 1962). In other words, since postwar Japan is not hampered by tradition, religion, or any other ideology from responding rationally to population pressure, any efficacious means of reducing fertility could work fast.

"DEPOPULATION," THE BABY BOOM, AND THE BABY BUST

Changes in the class differentials in fertility, which have been analyzed to exemplify a historic era, were typically seen during that process as both an expression and a cause of the degeneration of Western societies. The inverse correlation between education and fertility, and thus implicitly between innate intelligence and family size, was widely interpreted as the means by which the genetic quality of Western populations was being reduced. This theory is especially associated with right-wing politics, but it was shared, for instance, by Sidney Webb, one of Britain's best known socialist intellectuals.

It is the differential character of the decline in the birth rate, rather than the actual extent of the decline, which is of the gravest import. . . . In Great Britain at this moment [1913], when half, or perhaps two-thirds, of all the married people are regulating their families, children are being freely born to the Irish Roman Catholics and the Polish, Russian, and German Jews, on the one hand, and to the thriftless and irresponsible, . . . on the other. . . . This can hardly result in anything but national

---

[5] [*The Prohibition of Induced Abortion and the Eugenic Protection Law*], in Japanese; see the book review by John Y. Takeshita in *Milbank Memorial Fund Quarterly*, **45** (1967), 467–471.

deterioration; or, as an alternative, in this country gradually falling to the Irish and the Jews [Webb 1913].

As the norm of small families spread down through the social structure and the fertility of whole societies declined, concern shifted from the comparative quality of new cohorts to their small size. The advantages that accrued to married couples from reducing the number of their offspring, whether in less expense or in more convenience, were the greater the smaller the number of children; and once persons saw family formation in this perspective and had the means of limiting births, the trend seemed to be toward one-child or no-child families (cf. Rossi 1968). Even liberals came to see the fact that potential parents were able to control conception as what Carr-Saunders (1964: 244) termed "the small-family problem": "If for any reason, however remote, trivial, selfish, or unsubstantial, parents do not want a child, the child does not come. Consequently there is no assurance whatever that children will come in sufficient numbers to prevent a decline of population and ultimate extinction." Indeed, in all Western countries demographers spelled out the gloomy implications of this analysis. For instance, Enid Charles (1935, 1938) projected the population of England and Wales on the basis of three postulates with respect to fertility and mortality: (1) that fertility and mortality would continue at the 1933 rate; (2) that fertility and mortality would continue to fall as they had in recent years; and (3) that fertility would rise to the 1931 level, or to about 10 percent higher than in 1933, while mortality would continue to fall. In a book published three years later, the substance of the memorandum was republished but the estimate based on the third assumption, the one closest to what turned out to be the actual trend, was omitted altogether. A summary of this "classic study" was incorporated in Reddaway's exposition of Keynesian theory, called *The Economics of a Declining Population* (1939). The "more reasonable forecast" was taken to be that the population of England and Wales would start to decline in 1939 and would be reduced by nine-tenths over the following century. Yet Reddaway's book was published in 1939, four years after the low point of British fertility, when the actual population was larger than the upper limit in Charles's projection. According to a forecast that Louis I. Dublin presented in 1931, with no migration the population of the United States would reach a maximum of 154 million between 1980 and 1990 and then decline to 140 million by 2100. Since in his opinion this prognosis was "altogether too optimistic," he offered a second, "more reasonable" estimate, by which the maximum of 148 million would be reached by 1970, followed by a decline to 140 million by 2000 and to 76 million by 2100 (cited in Dorn 1950; cf. above, pp. 339–343).

Curiously, one reason that professional demographers went so far astray is that, unlike the general public, they knew that a portion of even the low fertility of the 1930s was the consequence of a relatively favorable age structure. In most Western countries large numbers had been born in the pre-1914 decade, and the proportion of potential parents in the 1930s, therefore, was far greater than it would be when the later, much smaller cohorts grew to maturity. This important qualification to any understanding of the current birth rate was incorporated in the reproduction rates, which became very popular during the 1930s.[6] Properly understood, these rates have their uses. Unfortunately demographers sometimes forgot that reproduction rates are in fact population projections, half-disguised as measures of fertility or natural increase. Charles (1936: 104) categorically asserted the contrary: "In parts of Europe and America the population has already ceased to be capable of maintaining its numbers. It cannot be too clearly emphasized that this statement is not a prediction of future events ... but a description of what is actually happening at the moment." The comment of Carr-Saunders (1964: 258) that England's "reproduction rate is about 25 percent below replacement rate" was also subject to misunderstanding. Net reproduction rates, it must be stressed, do *not* show that populations are increasing or decreasing. A rate of more than unity does *not* mean that a population is increasing or that it will necessarily increase in the future. A net reproduction rate of 0.75 means not that the growth of population *is* 25 percent under replacement, but that it *would* decline if the current age-specific fertility and mortality continued without change for several generations.

That demographers' population forecasts were wrong is indisputable, but one must recall also that their view of future trends fitted in with what was being predicted in other social sciences as well. The notion that the family was being transformed from an institution to "companionship," to quote the title of a very widely used college text (Burgess and Locke 1945), prevailed; and even after the rise in fertility was well under way it took years before commentators revised their analyses. In 1946, Talcott Parsons (1949: 251–274), whom many regarded as the country's foremost sociological theorist, explained the decline in fertility in the most general terms. The growing girl, he wrote, discovers that "she must compete for masculine favor and cannot stand on her own feet," and this discovery cannot but be a source of insecurity and hence aggression. The aggression, in turn, "underlies the widespread ambivalence among women toward the role of motherhood, which is a primary factor in the declining birth rate." A full 5 years after the upturn in the birth rate, David Riesman (1950) based his whole analysis of the American "character structure" on a presumed "incipient decline" in the country's population. It would be possible to add to these prominent examples a full array of economists, sociologists, journalists, and others, virtually all of whom held that Oswald Spengler's "decline of the West" was being enacted in literal fact.

[6] It will be recalled (see pp. 88–90) that a gross reproduction rate is the ratio of female births in two successive generations, assuming no change in the age-specific birth rates and no deaths before the end of the childbearing period, and a net reproduction rate is the ratio of female births in two successive generations, assuming no change in the age-specific birth and death rates. That is, the gross rate measures fertility only, the net rate the natural increase. Both rates are related to the stable population—that is, the population of fixed age and sex distribution that would develop if the present age-specific fertility and mortality were to continue without change for about a century.

Pronatalist Measures

According to one view of the decline in fertility, it was a "birth strike," a refusal of potential parents to reproduce until their onerous economic burdens were reduced—that is, borne in part by nonparents. The countries that initiated such programs ranged politically from Nazi Germany or the Soviet Union to Britain or Sweden, and the philosophies underlying pronatalist policies were similarly diverse:

1. Catholic doctrine: The natural unit of society is not the individual but the family, and wages should therefore be paid at least in part according to family needs, rather than individual economic worth.

2. Egalitarianism: Since in general there is a negative correlation between income and family size, family subsidies help effect a more equitable distribution of income.

3. Social welfare: The children of large families are often those who most need assistance.

4. Nationalism: To the extent that the secular decline in the birth rate has been caused by economic factors, it can be checked by family subsidies, thus increasing the manpower and military prowess of the nation.

These four principles are ranked in order of decreasing importance, from a fundamental norm to a contingent expedient of unproved value. In general, thus, the earliest and strongest advocates of family subsidies were Catholics, especially in countries (such as France) with very low natality. Fascist countries (and, since the middle 1930s, the Soviet Union) also uniformly adopted some mode of family endowment, particularly because of the assumed value to the nation of a rapidly growing population (see pp. 618–619). Socialists and liberals, on the other hand, were less consistent. In Anglo-Saxon countries, they were sometimes among the most vigorous proponents of a family wage (for example, Eleanor Rathbone in Britain, Paul Douglas in the United States); but the historic role of Continental socialist parties and their affiliated trade unions was forthright opposition, petering down to acquiescence. In line with the trade-union slogan, "Equal pay for equal work," members of the French trade-union federation went so far in the 1920s as to refuse to accept family benefits after the system had been established; members of the metalworkers union in Berlin threatened to leave the organization unless the system was effectively opposed. However, it became increasingly difficult, particularly during the depression of the 1930s, to align this stand with fundamental socialist principles; for one could hardly find a more direct translation into social action of "To each according to his needs" than a law regulating workers' pay according to the number of minor children they had to support. Fundamental opposition to family subsidies, therefore, tended to give way to differences over administration and other details.

Some pronatalist means were repressive, such as taxes on bachelors in Italy or more stringent prohibition of contraception and abortion in Germany. Other measures constituted positive attempts to induce young persons to marry or couples to have more children, in return for cash grants (or their converse, re-duced taxes) or for preference in acquiring housing, government posts, or other values in short supply. In general, to the degree that one can separate the govern-ments' efforts from other determinants of fertility, the pronatalist policies were a failure. "In one case only—Germany since 1933—does there appear to have been any marked success, and even in that case the reasons for success are not clear" (Glass 1940: 370). One determinant there may have been the "psychic rebirth" afforded by Nazi Germany's bloodless victories over Western Europe in the 1930s. Glass held, however, that "material measures [were] more impor-tant than 'psychic' changes and that, in particular, the suppression of illegal abortion [was] a major factor" (ibid: 312).

The reasons for the usual failure of pronatalist measures vary from case to case. In some instances the policy was administered blindly, with little regard for the underlying causes of the decline in fertility, but the time and intelligence that Sweden devoted to a full and painstaking analysis proved to be of no avail. Repressive measures failed because, except in Germany, they were not well en-forced. Monetary inducements and, *a fortiori*, allowances in kind were "not large enough to cover the additional costs of family life. . . . However urgently governments may have declared their desire to increase the supply of births, they have nevertheless persistently tried to buy babies at bargain prices" (ibid.: 371).

Postwar Rise in Fertility

In most countries of the Western world, after various kinds of pronatalist policies had failed, the birth rate increased during and immediately after World War II, when Europe suffered from shortages of housing and even of food and all of these countries lacked some of the material comforts that their affluent classes had come to expect. Europe's fertility rose enough to make nonsense of the dire forecasts of depopulation, as well as of the theory underlying most family-subsidy programs, yet on a global scale the increase was to only a modest figure. For the five years 1956–60 Europe's average annual rate was 19 births per 1,000 population (contrasted with 36 for the whole world), and the crude rates of natural increase for that quinquennium were, respectively, 8 and 18 per 1,000. In the United States the birth rate also rose dramatically, reaching 26.6 in 1947 (compared with 18.4 in 1933 and 1936, the low points during the inter-war depression).

The crude birth rate, of course, gives only a first impression of the trend. Because the base population eventually included all the boom babies, the very increase in fertility was, paradoxically, one reason why the rising rate decelerated and then fell off. Like the reproduction rate, crude rates generally relate to the data of a single year and thus exaggerate minor fluctuations. For a long-term analysis, the only adequate index is completed family size—the average number of children that women bear during the whole of their lifetime—but it has the obvious disadvantage that it cannot be used to measure current trends. A partial answer to this question can come from a cohort analysis (Grabill *et al.* 1958: chap. 9). A birth cohort, it will be recalled, constitutes all those born at the same time, who are analyzed as a unit through their lifetime. For example, those born during the twelve months centering on January 1, 1900, constitute the cohort of 1900. Table 14-6 illustrates how useful this method is in breaking down the several factors in any fertility rate. The first row concerns girls who were born during 1936–40 and were aged 15 to 19 years at the beginning of 1955; that is, on January 1, 1955, the average age of the girls in the cohort of 1940 was exactly 15 years, for those in the cohort of 1939 it was exactly 16 years, and so on. The next column gives the cumulative birth rate; this means that the five cohorts had had a total of 77 births per 1,000, of which 65 were first births, and so on.

It is evident that a large part of the baby boom was due to the higher fertility of young women, reflecting the decline in the age at marriage (Table 14-7). For females the median age fluctuated between 1890 and 1940 and then in the following two decades fell off by 1.2 years. For males, similarly, there was a decline by 3.3 years from 1890 to 1960. In part as a reflection of this lower age, the proportion married of those aged 14 and over increased from somewhat more than half in 1890 to over two-thirds in 1960. The decline in age at marriage was greatest among those with most education, so that the class differential along this dimension fell off appreciably (Tietze and Lauriat 1955; Lauriat 1959). The interval between marriage and the birth of the first child is usually short, and "more young wives than formerly are having their second child relatively soon after their first, and their third relatively soon after their second" (Grabill *et al.* 1958: 330). The trend toward earlier marriage, in other words, was generally linked to the increase in fertility, even though effective contraceptives might have broken this relation.

Marriage at young ages is surprising, for over the same period the amount of preparatory training needed to begin remunerative work certainly increased on the average, and in particular the proportion of adolescents attending college went up sharply. But the pattern of social maturation changed. Sons of the middle class, who once made up the larger part of the college population, had a regular progression prescribed for them: earn a degree, find a job, and get established in it, marry, then, and not before, have children. This postponement of family formation until his late 20s or early 30s was the price a young man paid to start in a good position. Whether the pattern would have survived the spread of college education to greater numbers and different social classes can perhaps be questioned. In any case, it was shattered by World War II. Veterans going to college were years older than the standard student body, and in other respects still more mature. They could live, single or married, on their income under the so-called G.I. Bill and its supplements. In 1947, thus, an estimated 200,000 college students were married; and once the pattern was set, it continued without the impetus of veterans' benefits. By the fall of 1956, one out of every four college students was married.

Table 14-6. Cumulative Birth Rates, by Order of Birth, for Cohorts of Native White Women, United States, 1910–55

Cohorts of—	January 1 of—	All Births	Order of Birth							
			1ST	2ND	3RD	4TH	5TH	6TH	7TH	8TH+
EXACT AGES 15 TO 19[a]										
1936–1940	1955	77	65	11	1	b	...	...	...	...
1931–1935	1950	67	57	9	1	b	...	...	...	...
1926–1930	1945	44	39	5	1	b	...	...	...	...
1921–1925	1940	44	39	5	b	b	...	...	...	...
1916–1920	1935	41	36	4	b	b	...	...	...	...
1911–1915	1930	49	43	5	b	b	...	...	...	...
1906–1910	1925	51	45	5	b	b	...	...	...	...
1901–1905	1920	43	38	5	b	b	...	...	...	...
1896–1900[c]	1915	49	43	5	b	b	...	...	...	...
1891–1895[c]	1910	50	44	6	b	b	...	...	...	...
EXACT AGES 20 TO 24[a]										
1931–1935	1955	789	479	222	67	17	4	1	b	b
1926–1930	1950	636	427	159	39	9	2	b	b	b
1921–1925	1945	520	348	125	36	9	2	b	b	b
1916–1920	1940	453	308	108	29	7	1	b	b	b
1911–1915	1935	454	300	112	32	8	2	b	b	b
1906–1910	1930	526	340	133	40	10	2	1	b	b
1901–1905	1925	560	358	144	44	11	2	1	b	b
1896–1900[c]	1920	533	339	138	44	10	2	b	b	b
1891–1895[c]	1915	557	349	146	48	12	2	b	b	b
1886–1890[c]	1910	568	349	151	50	14	3	b	b	b

1926–1930	1955	1,642	757	519	233	87	30	10	3	2
1921–1925	1950	1,389	715	415	163	60	22	8	3	1
1916–1920	1945	1,188	621	337	140	57	22	8	3	1
1911–1915	1940	1,064	555	293	127	55	22	8	3	1
1906–1910	1935	1,149	567	320	151	69	28	10	3	2
1901–1905	1930	1,275	604	357	178	83	34	13	4	2
1896–1900c	1925	1,331	618	373	191	91	37	14	5	2
1891–1895c	1920	1,335	619	372	194	91	37	15	5	2
1886–1890c	1915	1,417	629	389	220	109	46	17	5	2
1881–1885c	1910	1,453	632	394	228	119	52	19	6	3

1921–1925	1955	2,126	845	648	346	158	69	32	15	12
1916–1920	1950	1,857	789	554	274	126	60	29	14	11
1911–1915	1945	1,638	715	462	230	115	59	30	15	12
1906–1910	1940	1,639	689	445	238	129	69	37	18	14
1901–1905	1935	1,795	704	478	277	159	88	48	23	17
1896–1900c	1930	1,938	724	510	310	183	105	57	29	20
1891–1895c	1925	2,016	742	521	326	198	113	62	31	23
1886–1890c	1920	2,076	747	533	340	209	118	68	35	26
1881–1885c	1915	2,175	757	544	362	230	136	76	40	30
1876–1880c	1910	2,282	759	545	380	256	163	95	48	36

(Continued)

Table 14-6—*Continued*

Cohorts of—	January 1 of—	All Births	1ST	2ND	3RD	4TH	5TH	6TH	7TH	8TH +
						Order of Birth				
				EXACT AGES 35 TO 39[a]						
1916–1920	1955	2,278	839	653	376	195	99	53	29	35
1911–1915	1950	2,046	782	567	316	168	91	53	30	38
1906–1910	1945	1,987	748	524	299	172	100	61	36	46
1901–1905	1940	2,112	745	533	327	201	123	78	47	58
1896–1900[c]	1935	2,300	760	563	366	234	149	97	60	71
1891–1895[c]	1930	2,448	780	581	393	260	168	111	69	86
1886–1890[c]	1925	2,567	791	597	414	280	184	125	79	98
1881–1885[c]	1920	2,707	802	615	438	305	204	140	90	112
1876–1880[c]	1915	2,873	809	630	464	335	235	162	103	135
1871–1875[c]	1910	3,051	812	632	486	367	270	192	125	167
				EXACT AGES 40 TO 44[a]						
1911–1915	1955	2,224	799	597	350	196	111	66	40	64
1906–1910	1950	2,174	770	557	331	196	118	75	47	79
1901–1905	1945	2,274	761	554	348	219	140	93	60	100
1896–1900[c]	1940	2,473	770	579	384	254	168	115	76	125
1891–1895[c]	1935	2,656	791	597	414	283	191	133	91	156
1886–1890[c]	1930	2,828	803	616	440	309	213	154	106	186
1881–1885[c]	1925	3,010	816	636	467	337	238	174	123	218
1876–1880[c]	1920	3,206	824	654	494	367	265	199	144	260
1871–1875[c]	1915	3,424	828	662	521	399	300	231	171	312

EXACT AGES 45 TO 49[a]

1906–1910	1955	2,209	773	561	335	200	122	78	50	89
1901–1905	1950	2,313	764	557	352	223	143	96	63	114
1896–1900c	1945	2,510	772	581	387	257	172	119	81	143
1891–1895c	1940	2,703	792	599	417	286	195	138	96	180
1886–1890c	1935	2,887	805	618	443	313	218	159	113	217
1881–1885c	1930	3,084	817	639	471	342	244	182	131	258
1876–1880c	1925	3,292	826	657	498	372	273	207	153	307
1871–1875c	1920	3,515	830	666	526	405	308	239	181	360

EXACT AGES 50 TO 54[a]

1901–1905	1955	2,315	764	557	352	224	144	96	63	115
1896–1900c	1950	2,512	772	581	387	257	172	119	81	144
1891–1895c	1945	2,705	792	599	417	286	195	138	96	182
1886–1890c	1940	2,891	805	618	443	313	218	160	113	221
1881–1885c	1935	3,088	817	639	471	342	244	182	132	261
1876–1880c	1930	3,299	826	657	498	372	273	207	153	312
1871–1875c	1925	3,521	830	666	526	405	308	240	181	365

[a] The year in which these ages were reached is given in the second column from the left. For example, the cohorts of 1936–40 reached ages 15 to 19 at the beginning of 1955; i.e., on January 1, 1955, the average age of the women in the cohort of 1940 was exactly 15 years; for those in the cohort of 1939 it was exactly 16 years; etc.

[b] 0.5 or less.

[c] The rates for the cohorts of 1896–1900 and earlier are preliminary estimates, subject to minor changes.

SOURCE: Scripps Foundation for Research in Population Problems, cited in Wilson H. Grabill, Clyde V. Kiser, and Pascal K. Whelpton, *The Fertility of American Women* (New York: Wiley, 1958), Table 114. Copyright © by The Social Science Research Council.

Table 14-7. Age at Marriage and Proportion Married, United States, 1890–1970

Years	Median Age at First Marriage		Of Persons Aged 14 and Over, Percent Now Married	
	MALES	FEMALES	MALES	FEMALES
1890	26.1	22.0	52.1	54.8
1900	25.9	21.9	52.8	55.2
1910	25.1	21.6	54.2	57.1
1920	24.6	21.2	57.6	58.9
1930	24.3	21.3	58.4	59.5
1940	24.3	21.5	59.7	59.5
1950	22.8	20.3	68.0	66.1
1960	22.8	20.3	69.5	66.0
1970	23.2	20.8	65.7	61.2

SOURCES: U.S. Bureau of the Census, *U.S. Census of Population: 1950*, Vol. 2, *Characteristics of the Population*, Part 1, *U.S. Summary* (Washington, D.C., 1953), p. 1–97; *Current Population Reports*, Series P-20, no. 105, November 2, 1960; *U.S. Census of Population: 1970, Detailed Characteristics, U.S. Summary* (Washington, D.C., 1973); *Current Population Reports*, Series P-20, no. 242, November, 1972.

The consequences for fertility of the lower age at marriage can be seen in Table 14-6. The cumulative birth rate of cohorts aged 15–19 years increased from 50 in 1910 to 77 in 1955, that of those aged 20–24 from 568 to 789, that of those aged 25–29 from 1,453 to 1,642. Note that the percentage increase declines for higher ages. The 1955 cumulative birth rates for cohorts aged 30–34 years, while higher than for the immediately preceding period, were lower than for 1910; and those for cohorts aged 45 and over were lower in 1955 than at any preceding date.

What of the order of births? Of course, most of the teen-age girls giving birth were having their first baby; but in 1955, 11 per 1,000 births to mothers aged 15–19 were second births, and one per 1,000 was a third one. Compare the women aged 20–24 in 1955 with those of the same age in 1940, the last group before the baby boom started. That there should have been more first and second births one expects, but the rate went up from 29 to 67 for third births (an increase of 130 percent in 15 years), from 7 to 17 for fourth births (140 percent), from 1 to 4 for fifth births (300 percent), from less than 0.5 to 1 for sixth births (at least 100 percent). It is true that these increases are calculated from the period of lowest fertility, but note that for the women aged 20–24 the cumulative birth rates in 1955 are also higher than those in 1910 for every order of births up to the sixth!

Another reason for the baby boom was that women who postponed having children during the depression of the 1930s often had them after 1945, relatively late in their fecund period. This can also be illustrated from Table 14-6. Note the cohorts born in 1911–15 in the third deck: their cumulative birth rate at ages 25–29 was 1,064 per thousand, or the lowest of any group of cohorts of this age. In 1955, when the 1911–15 cohorts were aged 40–44, their cumulative birth rate was 2,224. Of the increase, 244 (799 − 555) units represented first births to women aged 30–44 years.

The annual average number of births to native white women increased from 1.90 million in 1930–39 to 3.01 million in 1945–54, or by 58.7 percent. These are the dimensions of the baby boom. What caused this unprecedented and wholly unanticipated rise in natality? Four factors are relevant (Grabill *et al.* 1958: 365–371):

1. The population increased, so that there were more people to have children.
2. The age at marriage went down, and a larger proportion married.
3. Of those who married, a larger proportion had children.
4. The average number of children per family increased.

In an especially interesting paper, Frank Notestein (1950) made a *post factum* analysis of why demographers in the 1930s, he himself included, had been mistaken in their expectations with respect to fertility. His thesis is that they had been wrong in their timing but not fundamentally.

In the first place, the downward trend got under way in a differential fashion, spreading from the upper urban classes of the population down through the social–economic structure and outward from the city to the rural region. By the end of the interwar period the highest rates were the ones that were declining most rapidly, the lowest were declining least rapidly, and no evidence of a real upturn was in sight. In the second place, the differences in fertility were closely correlated with differences in the prevalence and effectiveness of contraceptive practice, and there was every indication that contraceptive materials were becoming more abundant, and that the knowledge of their use was spreading. In the third place, the middle-class standards, which had been such a strong factor in the motivation for small families, appeared to be spreading throughout the mass of the population. Thus the nature of the trends, the means by which they were brought about, and the nature of the pressures and incentives motivating restrictionist practices all suggested a pattern of decline that had not run its course.

Decline in American Fertility

It was generally anticipated that, as the cohorts born in the years immediately following World War II attained the age to start childbearing, there would be an echo of the baby boom. Even if the size of families remained the same or declined slightly, the very large number of potential parents would result in a higher birth rate. The cohort born in 1947, the high point of the baby boom, reached age 21 in 1968. From 1960 to 1968 there was a steady decline in the birth rate, from 23.7 to 17.5. Thereafter, after a slight rise during two years, the rate fell still lower (Figure 14-1). The failure of demographers to forecast this downward trend was no less notable than their inability to predict the baby boom.

Figure 14-1. Estimated Crude Birth Rate, United States, 1855–1970

SOURCES: U.S. Bureau of the Census and National Bureau of Vital Statistics, various publications.

Breaking down the data by birth parity or by age of mother (Table 14-8) does not help explain it, for the decline was across the board. From 1955–59 to 1968, age-specific birth rates to the oldest mothers (aged 35–44) fell off by 40 percent, and for ages under 35 the decline was well over 30 percent. Nor is it generally helpful to divide the population into social or areal categories. Except for illegitimate births, which rose sharply during the 1960s, fertility typically fell among all sectors—whites and Negroes, rural and urban, all regions of the country. There was, however, a continuing negative relation between educational attainment and family size, especially sharp among black women (U.S. Bureau of the Census 1971).

Of the several factors that have been cited to explain the decline in fertility, the most obvious is the improvement in the efficacy of contraceptives, the change in attitudes toward them and abortion, and the readier access to both. According to two Gallup polls, the percentage holding that the decision whether to have an abortion should be made exclusively by the patient and her physician rose from 15 in 1968 to 64 in 1972; it would be hard to think of another turnabout on such an important issue in so short a time. Not only did the U.S. Supreme Court validate this trend in popular opinion (see p. 206) but, under various decisions by lower courts and provisions by federal and state agencies, family planning and abortions were provided gratis to indigent women.

That the means to control reproduction was at hand, however, can explain only a portion of the decline in fertility. Puzzled social scientists ranging from Philip Hauser to Margaret Mead fell back on a "small-family fad" to explain the small families. Undoubtedly there is some truth in such an assertion: the

Table 14-8.   Age-Specific Birth Rates, United States, 1940–44 to 1971

Time Period	15–19	20–24	25–29	30–34	35–39	40–44
Age of Mother						
5-year average						
1940–44	57.6	152.4	135.7	91.6	49.5	15.4
1945–49	71.0	186.2	159.6	105.4	56.5	16.1
1950–54	86.8	217.3	179.2	110.9	55.5	15.6
1955–59	92.6	254.9	196.7	116.8	58.9	16.0
1960	89.1	258.1	197.4	112.7	56.2	15.5
1961	88.0	253.7	197.9	113.3	55.6	15.6
1962	81.2	243.7	191.7	108.9	52.7	14.8
1963	76.4	231.2	185.8	106.2	51.3	14.2
1964	72.8	219.9	179.4	102.9	50.5	13.8
1965	70.4	196.8	162.5	95.0	46.4	12.8
1966	70.6	185.9	149.4	85.9	42.2	11.7
1967	67.9	174.0	142.6	79.3	38.5	10.6
1968	66.1	167.4	140.3	74.9	35.6	9.6
1969	66.1	165.7	143.1	73.5	33.3	8.8
1970	69.6	166.2	144.7	73.1	32.3	8.2
1971	66.8	150.1	134.5	68.0	29.1	7.3

SOURCE: U.S. Bureau of the Census, "Fertility Indicators: 1970," *Current Population Reports*, Series P-23, no. 36, 1971.

norms governing desired family size do spread somewhat in the manner of other styles. But at least according to what was reported to Gallup interviewers, there was no significant change in the ideal family size during the years from 1953 to 1966 (Blake 1967). If the reasoning from trend to "fad" is not to be merely circular, it must be checked against such an outside datum as the results of opinion polls—which in this case suggest that, while the fertility declined, the ideal family size remained more or less constant.

The most plausible explanation of both the baby boom and the lack of an echo has been offered by Richard Easterlin (1961; cf. Sweezy 1971). During the 1930s, when the cohorts who produced the baby boom were growing up, the straitened economy developed modest expectations in most of them. But when these young people entered the job market in the late 1940s and early 1950s, their competitive position was excellent—for a number of reasons:

1. Because of the low birth rates 20 years earlier, there was a shortage of young workers.

2. Earnings were therefore high, and they rose faster in lower-income occupations than in the rest of the labor force.

3. These earnings were supplemented by very much expanded transfer payments in the form of veterans' benefits and unemployment insurance.

4. The many who used the veterans' benefits to extend their education both improved the competitive position of the remaining younger workers and, after they graduated, were themselves able to compete against older men, who lacked their up-to-date training.

5. The promotion of young men into higher levels of many occupations was therefore much more rapid than in earlier decades.

In sum, the income and prospects of young people were exceptionally favorable in the late 1940s and early 1950s, especially when measured against the near penury of their usual childhood. The percentage of nonfarm dwelling units owned by persons aged 15–34 rose from 33 in 1940 to 56 in 1949; young people were able to afford even such a major purchase as a home of their own. In fact, they could afford all the material possessions they wanted and also marry young and have a middle-sized family.

By the 1960s each of these conditions was repeated in reverse. The boom babies, growing up in homes where rising prosperity was seen as the rule, extrapolated this upward trend in their own anticipations. A much larger proportion went to college than in earlier generations. Because of their extraordinarily large numbers, they were a glut on the job market, very often for occupations demanding graduate degrees as well as for those lower on the social scale. Expecting more from life than their fathers and able to get less, they took steps to reduce their family responsibilities. The periods of both high and low fertility, thus, were the consequence not merely of economic conditions—a simplistic argument—but of these combined with the relative size and social aspirations of the cohorts entering the labor force.

Fertility in Western Europe

The recent trend in other Western countries, though with important differences among them, was generally similar to that traced for the United States (Table 14-9). In Italy, Spain, and Portugal, the decline continued from the relatively high rates of the 1930s, but in every other country of Western Europe the general fertility rate rose from before to after World War II. True, there was no evidence of a return to very large families. The proportions of married women with four or more children continued to fall, but so did those of childless or one-child families. Somewhat as in the United States, the family size seemed to be leveling off at two to three children, with a convergence along the structural lines of European societies.

In fact, however, this seeming stability was as evanescent as in the United States. The high point of fertility, in most West European nations around the year 1964, was largely the consequence of early marriages and rapid childbearing, a phenomenon that soon came to an end. Even so, because of the large cohorts

Table 14-9. Live Births per 1,000 Women Aged 15–49 Years, Western Europe, Selected Years

Country	Approximate Periods				
	1935–39	1950–54	1955–59	1960–64	1965–69
Eire	84[a]	94[a]	96	103	102
England and Wales	54	62	67	77	76
Norway	55	76	78	76	79
Sweden	54	64	61	62	64
Finland	74	88	80	74	64
Denmark	66	73	71	72	71
West Germany	68[b]	60[a]	64[a]	75[a]	71
Netherlands	77	90	90	89	81
Belgium	60	68	72	76	67
France[c]	60	80	82	82	74
Switzerland	55	68	70	76	72
Austria	—	58	67	80	75
Italy	90	70	—	73	72
Spain[d]	90	72	—	84	81
Portugal	105	90	91	94	87

[a] Single-year rates for the second year of each period.
[b] Prewar territory of Germany, 1937.
[c] It is not clear whether live-born children who died before registration are included.
[d] Single-year rates for 1940, 1950, 1960, and 1969.
SOURCES: 1935–64: Various, as compiled in D. V. Glass, "Fertility Trends in Europe Since the Second World War," *Population Studies*, **22** (1968), 103–146, Table 4. 1965–69: Calculated from United Nations, *Demographic Yearbook* (New York, various years).

of potential parents, the more recent decline was also generally unanticipated. In a paper published in 1972, two French demographers foresaw the same convergence, though toward a lower level, that others had foreseen earlier.

Except in Finland, the Netherlands, Portugal, and perhaps Germany, the downward trend of the annual fertility rates seems to have decelerated, if not actually stopped. If a stable period were to ensue, it would be characterized by the diffusion of the French pattern: a continuing decline of large families but, more remarkably, also of childless couples [Marchal and Rabut 1972; cf. Tabah 1971].

We ought to have learned one thing from the postwar baby boom: that parents can rationally choose to have children, as against alternative ways of life. In the 1930s it was believed that the most probable choice for a couple, once contraception was made available in both physical and moral terms, was to help establish a norm of childless marriages. For all the reasons that potential parents had for preventing the conception of a fifth or sixth child seemed to apply *a fortiori* to the first child, which cost them the most in money, time, effort, and loss of freedom. The conceptual framework in which population extrapolations were made was a simple equation: middle-class rationality added to access to contraceptives ultimately will effect an average family too small to maintain the population. But potential parents' decisions on whether to have children are determined not only by their "selfish" desire for "comfort" but also by selfish "pride in progeny." Now that birth control is all but universal in Western countries, it is the relation between these conflicting goals of parents that principally determines the size of the family—and the accuracy of population projections. The forces that impelled the decline in American fertility from the beginning of the 19th century on did not suddenly disappear in 1940; some of the values and styles of living still push toward a decline in the birth rate. On the other hand, the counterforces that resulted in the baby boom throughout the Western world are also a reality, not merely an aberration from the downward trend.

ATTITUDES AND FAMILY SIZE

The analysis of familial events by such broad categories as social classes is based on the premise, validated by the small range of differentiation within any one of them, that by and large persons in the same place in the social structure, subject to the same pressures, will usually make more or less the same decisions. But children are born to a single pair of parents, and it is really their decisions, if they make any, that help determine the size of their family and the spacing of their children. In some ways, then, it makes sense to shift the focus of research from social groups to individuals, from sociological to social–psychological concepts, from demographic to public-opinion data. The new trend developed in part because the convergence of class fertility rates induced analysts to look for finer distinctions, but attitude research had become so important a preoccupation in sociology generally that in any case one could have expected its use in demographic analysis.

Against the important gains that this new type of research brings to the discipline, one must mark certain limitations. Standard demographic data are perhaps the best in any social science, collected at government expense by highly qualified experts; attitude polls, typically made from small samples by either commercial firms or research teams, are ordinarily of a lower quality. Stated preferences concerning family size undoubtedly relate to actual fertility, but not necessarily closely. In perhaps the best study ever made of the matter, the correlation between the stated preference and the actual number of children 20 years later was only 0.30, or separately 0.45 for those who did and 0.19 for those who did not plan every pregnancy (Westoff et al. 1957; cf. Westoff et al. 1963; Freedman et al. 1965). Even when the preferred and the actual number of children coincide, it is difficult to say which is the independent variable; for instance, Catholic mothers who refuse to use efficient contraceptives and therefore expect to have large families may also say that this is what they desire.

According to thirteen public-opinion polls in the United States between 1936 and 1966, the mean family size considered ideal ranged from 2.9 to 3.5 children (men) and from 2.7 to 3.6 (women). During the depression of the 1930s, World War II, and the years of postwar prosperity, reported shifts were within a range of less than one child (Blake 1966b, 1967). That the changes in actual fertility were greater may mean that responses to poll questionnaires merely approximate the actual decisions concerning family size or that a significant proportion of fertility was not subject to rational control, or both (cf. Blake 1974).

The Indianapolis Study

Of the various analyses in the United States that concentrated on psychological factors, the first sizable one was the Indianapolis study, "Social and Psychological Factors Affecting Fertility." This was published in thirty-three articles in the *Milbank Memorial Fund Quarterly*, and later bound in five volumes.[7] It was truly a pioneer effort, with the virtues and also the faults one might expect from any attempt to break new ground, particularly concerning psychological motivation. A miscellaneous list of twenty-three hypotheses on factors possibly affecting either planned or actual family size were tested. Of these, three pertained to the effect of economic security, five to the family background and health of the potential parents, five to their expressed interest in children and their home, eight to their personality characteristics (feelings of inadequacy, fear of pregnancy, general tendency to plan, conformity to group patterns, etc.), and two to the relations between husband and wife. One of the hypotheses, for instance, was the following paraphrase of the Dumont–Banks thesis: "The greater the difference between the actual level of living and the standard of living desired, the higher the proportion of couples practicing contraception effectively and the smaller the planned families." To test this, respondents were asked what they would like in order to live in a satisfactory manner, and their reply was compared with their actual mode of living. Very often a person with a second-hand car, for instance, expressed the desire for a new one, whereas someone who owned a new Cadillac, say, indicated his satisfaction with it. Economic tension decreased with greater incomes, rather than the contrary, as it should have to validate the hypothesis. Yet probably no demographer doubts the at least partial validity of the thesis as stated; indeed, when it was negated, the analysts rejected their own

[7] See in particular the final article, by Kiser and Whelpton (1958), which includes references to previous articles in the series and to various discussions of the study. After a preliminary household survey of most of Indianapolis (from which it was possible to compare the fertility of religious denominations), couples were divided into "relatively fecund" and "relatively sterile" classes, depending on whether there had been any considerable periods during which intercourse without birth control had not resulted in conception. A more detailed analysis was restricted to a sample of 1,444 relatively fecund native white Protestant couples, who had been married during 1927–29 and had lived in a large city most of the time since then. Of this group, 98 percent reported some experience with contraception; 14 percent had planned the number, and an additional 28 percent both the number and spacing of all pregnancies.

findings. We cannot measure levels of aspiration nearly so accurately as the behavior patterns associated with them, so that if respondents say one thing but do another, we accept the latter as the more meaningful.

Another of the hypotheses tested in the Indianapolis study was the following: "The stronger the interest in and liking for children, the lower the proportion of couples practicing contraception effectively and the larger the planned families." If one grants that it is possible to measure "liking" for children with reasonable accuracy from what people say, and if this proves to be positively correlated with the size of the family, then it would seem to be just as likely (as the analysts themselves point out) that couples who have children have learned to like them as *vice versa*. A more probable cause–effect relation, both in this instance and generally, is that the independent variables in the twenty-three hypotheses and the supposed effects of planned and actual family size were both consequences of the relatively undifferentiated culture pattern of this white Protestant sample of a midwestern city. As the authors put it, "Our measures of psychological characteristics probably were too crude to afford precise differentiations, [and] it may be little wonder that the Study failed to indicate strong and consistent relations of fertility behavior to psychological characteristics" among so homogeneous a sample (Kiser and Whelpton 1958: 323). "The chief lesson" to be learned from the Indianapolis study, according to the men who directed it, is that fertility is generally more closely related to "broad social factors (including the economic)" than to psychological. Both family planning and actual fertility were clearly correlated with social–economic status; but when this variable was held constant, "the observed relation of fertility behavior to most of the psychological characteristics considered was generally much less pronounced or less regular" (ibid.: 318–319).

The Indianapolis study set the pattern for two series of monographs, one called the "Growth of American Families" (or GAF) studies, under the direction of P. K. Whelpton and, after his death, Ronald Freedman (see Kiser 1967), and the Princeton fertility surveys, conducted by Charles Westoff and his associates. These were based on national samples rather than a sample of one supposedly representative city, and the techniques of analysis became considerably more elaborate. The amount of detail in all these volumes makes them difficult to summarize. For all their virtues, they share the basic lacks of all analyses based on stated preferences rather than actual birth performances. In spite of the avidity with which the subject was pursued, no one was able to predict the remarkable decline in American fertility in the early 1970s.

The Micro-economics of Family Formation

In Victorian England, the reference group of the rising middle class—the benchmark against which it measured its own welfare—was still higher in the social scale. But for many in the United States today the reference group constitutes persons of equivalent age and occupation. Thus, "an income above the average for one's status is associated with more children, but being in a higher absolute income class means fewer children if the higher income is only what is usual for the husband's age and occupation" (D. S. Freedman 1963; cf. Kunz 1965). In other words, the inverse correlation between class and fertility, which was instituted by the social ambitions of the upwardly mobile, tends to disappear among those who measure their well-being by that of their own kind. That is, the well-to-do of an affluent society could opt for *both* a middle-sized family *and* greater material welfare. The first realization of this possibility may well have been in Sweden during the 1930s. Among a considerable sample of Stockholm families, the correlation between social class and fertility was positive throughout the income range, and this association was strengthened when class was defined jointly by income and education (Edin and Hutchinson 1935). In the sizable number of tests of the Dumont–Banks hypothesis since 1945, the results have generally depended on how wealthy the country was and how open its social structure. Most of the studies in the United States and one in Australia (Tien 1961) showed no relation between mobility and family size, while research in France, Belgium, Denmark, and Brazil supported the hypothesis.

The American findings may indicate what happens in a society when mobility becomes so predictable and routine as to minimize its social and monetary costs and when the goal of mobility is a life style which includes a moderate number of children. . . . In a society with high mobility even the nonmobile may limit family size simply to maintain their place in the social order. They must run in order to stand still [R. Freedman 1961–62: 60].

That mobility into the small and highly restricted upper class of the United States, rather than into the well-to-do middle class, *is* negatively correlated with family size (Baltzell 1953) would seem to validate Freedman's explanation.

According to the best estimates the costs of childrearing have risen greatly during the past generation or so, both to the parents and to the community as a whole. In North Carolina around 1965, as one example, the sum of federal, state, and local expenditures over the first 25 years of life for relevant health, education, and welfare budgets amounted to $3,187 per person (Leasure 1967). That economic factors can play an important part in potential parents' decisions on whether to have a child, or another child, has led some economists to use the theory of demand for consumer durables as a framework for analyzing the "demand" for children. The first formal statement of this thesis was by Gary Becker (1960):

A family must determine not only how many children it has but also the amount spent on them—whether it should provide separate bedrooms, send them to nursery school and private colleges, give them dance or music lessons, and so forth. I will call more expensive children "higher-quality" children, just as Cadillacs are called higher-quality cars than Chevrolets. . . . If more is voluntarily spent on one child than on another, it is because the parents obtain additional utility from the additional expenditure, and it is this additional utility which we call higher "quality." . . . A change in the cost of children is a change in the cost of children of given quality, . . . [but] a secular increase in expenditures on children [is] often interpreted as a rise in the cost of children. . . .

Economic theory . . . suggests that a rise in income would increase both the quality and quantity of children desired.

The appraisal of Becker's paper has seemingly depended on the discipline of the critic. Economists have used words like *seminal*, and indeed the 1960s saw an important revival of economic analyses of fertility. Sociologists, on the other hand, have derided the notion that parents view their offspring as durable commodities (e.g., Blake 1968). If we try to steer a path between these polar positions, a number of points can be made.

1. In its essence Becker's thesis is not an advance over prior theory. When he called it "a generalization and development" of Malthus, he was referring only to that portion of Malthus's theory contained in the first edition of the *Essay*—in Becker's words, "that an increase in income would lead to a relatively large increase in family size." In fact, as we have noted in some detail (pp. 154–156), Malthus later developed a first statement of what we have termed the Dumont–Banks thesis, which Becker paraphrased in another jargon.

2. Like many other economic theories, Becker's is related to the rest of the social world by an unanalyzed factor, in this case "tastes": "The relative preference for children—or, in other words, 'tastes'— . . . may, in turn, be determined by a family's religion, race, age, and the like. This framework permits, although it does not predict, fertility differences that are unrelated to 'economic' factors." In analyzing fertility trends, sociologists have typically considered both economic factors and cultural ones, with the latter usually related to the concept of *reference group* rather than *taste*. As we have seen, Easterlin's analysis of the baby boom included the suggestion that the cohorts of young parents had acquired rather modest tastes during their childhood; that is, for Easterlin *taste* was not an unanalyzed residual but a generic term for the living standard bred into particular sectors of the population. In several papers (e.g., 1966, 1970, 1973), Easterlin has tried to extrapolate from his earlier monograph to a general synthesis of the economics and sociology of fertility.

3. The postulates on which economics is based—that everyone acts rationally in his own best interest, that all choices are possible to all men, and so on—fit behavior in the market with less distortion than the process of family formation. The social constraints are far greater in the second situation. If a man decided to purchase two Chevrolets rather than one Cadillac, no one would gainsay him; but it is hardly conceivable that a middle-class American would choose to have four children who could go only to high school rather than two that he could send to college. Within the parameters set by cultural standards, moreover, decisions are generally made according to rather vague impulses (which social psychologists term *attitudes*), and to designate both the desire to save money on family expenditures and the desire to continue the family as "utility" does not

convert them into the same mensurable units, with which one could be compared meaningfully with the other. As James Duesenberry remarked in a comment on Becker's paper, "Economics is all about how people make choices. Sociology is all about why they don't have any choices to make."

4. More pointedly, it is questionable whether *any* decision-making model is appropriate to the understanding of how some conceptions take place. All planning, including family planning, is based on an implicit belief in the future— which many in the lower classes, those typically with the largest number of children, seemingly lack. If one attempts to measure such feeling states as "meaninglessness," "powerlessness," "normlessness," and "social isolation," one sometimes finds a significant correlation between them and fertility (Groat and Neal 1967, 1970; Bauman and Udry 1972). By construing the process of conception as a completely rational one, Becker omitted altogether the portion that constitutes the most serious social problem and the most interesting analytical one.

> Some respondents speak of family planning in a matter-of-fact, cut-and-dried way; family limitation for them is a well established habit. Others seem less sure of what they are doing, more bothered by the possibility of accidents, less confident in the method, or they look forward with uncertainty to a time when they will begin using contraception. Finally some respondents are quite passive and fatalistic about family planning; they do nothing because they do not think anything will help, or they go through the motions of using a method in which they have little confidence (and therefore do not use it very consistently) [Rainwater 1965: 201].

Among Rainwater's sample, some 14 percent of middle-class Catholics responded in the passive, fatalistic manner, and 24 percent of unskilled workers. But among the so-called lower-lower class, casual workers and unemployed, the percentage among a sample of both whites and Negroes was 63; that is, almost two out of every three families did not believe enough in the future to plan anything, including their families.

5. Even if one accepts the postulates of Becker's thesis, finally, it is hardly subject to empirical testing. The cost of a child, unlike that of a Cadillac, is so complex an entity that it is virtually impossible to come up with a reasonable estimate *post factum*; and if parents do make rational choices based on comparative costs, they do so on the basis of very inadequate information. An important component, first of all, is the so-called opportunity cost, or the income that the mother forgoes during the period she is not working. But whether she would work outside the home, and if so how much she would earn, can be only guessed at, using data on women who, since they made the contrary decision, are more or less beside the point. In circles where females are expected to contribute fully to a joint household, those who find office or factory work boring might become pregnant in order to escape it. The expenditures for children, second, are made over the whole of their minority (say, up to age 18), with the typical expectation that prices will rise and the hope that the family will improve

Table 14-10. Estimated Average Annual Cost, Per Child and Total, for the Children in the Three-Child Family at Three Levels of Income, United States, 1960–61

Income Level	Average Annual Cost to Age 18				Total Cost as a Percent of Income Earned[a]			
	FIRST CHILD	SECOND CHILD	THIRD CHILD	COMBINED COST	FIRST CHILD	SECOND CHILD	THIRD CHILD	COMBINED COST
Lower[b]	$2,049	$ 956	$ 967	$3,250	37.8	17.2	17.1	59.1
Middle[c]	2,231	1,079	1,085	3,596	29.8	14.1	13.9	47.4
Upper[d]	2,538	1,293	1,299	4,198	23.9	11.8	11.7	38.8

[a] The income is estimated for the appropriate period, 18 years for each child and, with the standard spacing of the children, 22 years for the combined cost.

[b] An annual income of $4,564 when the household head is aged 26.8, rising to $5,879 at age 43.8, and declining thereafter.

[c] An annual income of $6,326 when the household head is aged 27.9, rising to a maximum of $8,120 at age 45.9.

[d] An annual income of $9,007 when the household head is aged 30.1, rising to a maximum of $11,698 at age 50.1.

SOURCE: Thomas J. Espenshade, "Estimating the Cost of Children and Some Results from Urban United States," University of California, Preliminary Paper No. 4, Berkeley: International Population and Urban Research, February, 1973.

its standard. The common simplifying assumption that costs are the same irrespective of birth order or the child's age are quite unrealistic. Using a selected portion of a Consumer Expenditure Survey conducted by the U.S. Bureau of Labor Statistics in 1960–61, Espenshade calculated the expenditures on children as related to three levels of income for a three-child family (Table 14-10). Costs both per child and for all the children increase with income, but not proportionately; relative to family income, children are *less* expensive at upper than at lower levels. As the author is well aware, the assumptions on which the calculation was based are no better than several possible alternatives.

SUMMARY

The birth-control movement that arose in Europe and the United States during the 19th century gradually legitimized the small-family norm. The route by which this norm was disseminated to the various sectors of Western populations was class differentiation in fertility. The secular decline began in the urban middle classes, and from them spread to the urban working class and then to the rural sector. It seems that the small family became established more by the diffusion of urban ideas to rural areas than by the migration of rural persons to urban places. It is necessary to look for causes, thus, not so much in the living conditions in cities as in the ideas and aspirations of city people. More precisely, the modern small-family system originated among persons rising in the social scale. Not only can one move farther and faster with fewer dependents, but in an upwardly mobile family aspirations are typically higher than any income can satisfy, so that, however paradoxical it may be in simple economic terms, persons of middle incomes are often under heavier financial pressure than those who earn less. Implicit in this Dumont–Banks hypothesis is the corollary that among the upper class, as distinguished from those moving up into it, the rule might be large families, which often constitute one exception to the negative correlation. As the small-family norm spread down the social structure, the first consequence was an overall reduction in fertility, with smaller class differences in family size than before. In rich societies those who reached the top were in many cases able to set their own family norm, which often included a moderate number of offspring. With such a decline of differentials by social class, those by residual factors like religion and ethnicity became more prominent.

In the 1930s almost every demographer thought in terms of a stylized picture of Rational Man and believed that the downward trend in fertility would continue. Once it became general to adjust family size according to the loss in money and convenience incurred from having children, it was thought that many couples, perhaps eventually most, would have none at all. In the postwar decade, however, there was a wholly unexpected revival of births. In general, this was most marked among the social classes that previously had shown the greatest decline, so that the trend seemed to be toward a greater convergence in fertility, with both social–

economic extremes moving toward a central norm of a middle-sized family (or, according to the trend in the 1970s, one on the smaller side), with possibly a *positive* correlation between social class and family size over a very small range. Students of the recent period, therefore, have generally concentrated on religious–cultural differences in fertility and turned to a new source of data, public-opinion polls on attitudes that relate the desired to the actual family size.

Analysts of the fertility of subnations, using different ones to exemplify their theses, have argued plausibly for two contradictory patterns. Members of minorities subject to discrimination who have the will and ability to rise in the social scale are likely to have very small families, reflecting the Dumont–Banks thesis in an extreme form. Ideologues of the same minorities, however, may want their numbers to increase as a means to greater power. Probably the ambivalence often exists not only in groups' behavior but in personal attitudes.

During the 1960s a sizable number of economists applied their technical skills to the analysis of fertility—a welcome addition to those studying an important and puzzling phenomenon. Men respond to economic stimuli in terms of the standards they have assimilated, and an analysis of how early socialization affects family size was a crucial part of the best explanation of the baby boom. It was widely anticipated that the high fertility would produce an echo, for when these large cohorts reached the age of marriage and childbearing the birth rate was almost certain to go up. Instead, it declined sharply in the early 1970s, presumably again because the potential parents were not easily able to acquire the economic base of the life they had been taught to expect. Paradoxically, as the American birth rate fell to its lowest point in history, the first official commission on "population and the American future" was assembling a massive antinatalist report (U.S. Commission 1972). Western countries are plagued by many problems, but too rapid population growth is hardly one of the most urgent.

CITED REFERENCES AND
SUGGESTIONS FOR FURTHER READING

The bibliography on the fertility of Western nations, already tremendous, grows rapidly year by year. Some of the references appended to Chapters 6, 9, 12, and 16 might be repeated here, but an effort was made to restrict the list to the narrow subject of the modern (rather than long-term historical) trend of fertility in Western societies. Freedman's bibliographic guide (1961–62) is useful, and Hawthorn's short work (1970) is probably the best brief introduction to the sociology of fertility. Easterlin's efforts to combine a sociological with an economic analysis (1970, 1973) build on his earlier empirical analysis (1961).

The definitive history of the birth-control movement is still to be written. The work by Himes (1936), originally intended as the first of two volumes, remains the best book-length study. It can be usefully supplemented by many articles, such as those by Micklewright (1961) and Banks and Banks (1954). The history of the American movement is given in fascinating detail by Field (1967) in a book all but forgotten but now available again in a reprint.

The monograph by Banks (1954) is indispensable in understanding the social background of the secular decline in fertility, and Wrong (1958) gives an excellent summary of the relation of demographic trends to changes in the social structure. The several large-scale studies of trends in the United States, which deserve a fuller analysis from a student particularly interested in fertility, have been discussed in this chapter only partially, in connection with particular topics. For overall reviews, see the critiques by Goldberg (1960), Kiser (1967), and Westoff *et al.* (1963: chap. 2). Of all the works that combine demographic analysis with attitude studies, the best is still that by Freedman, Whelpton, and Campbell (1959). Two publications of the U.S. Bureau of the Census (1971, 1973) give an excellent basis for attempting to interpret the anomalous trend in the early 1970s.

BALTZELL, E. DIGBY. 1953. "Social Mobility and Fertility within an Elite Group," *Milbank Memorial Fund Quarterly*, **31**, 411–420.

*BANKS, J. A. 1954. *Prosperity and Parenthood: A Study of Family Planning among the Victorian Middle Classes*. London: Routledge & Kegan Paul.

————, and OLIVE BANKS. 1954. "The Bradlaugh–Besant Trial and the English Newspapers," *Population Studies*, **8**, 22–34.

————, and ————. 1964. *Feminism and Family Planning in Victorian England*. Liverpool: Liverpool University Press.

BAUMAN, KARL A., and J. RICHARD UDRY. 1972. "Powerlessness and Regularity of Contraception in an Urban Negro Male Sample: A Research Note," *Journal of Marriage and the Family*, **34**, 112–114.

BECKER, GARY S. 1960. "An Economic Analysis of Fertility," in National Bureau of Economic Research 1960.

BENNETT, JOHN C. 1959. "Protestant Ethics and Population Control," *Daedalus*, **88**, 454–459.

BERGUES, HÉLÈNE, *et al.* 1960. *La prévention des naissances dans la famille: Ses origines dans les temps modernes*. Paris: Presses Universitaires de France.

BESHERS, JAMES M. 1967. *Population Processes in Social Systems*. New York: Free Press.

BLACKER, J. G. C. 1957. "Social Ambitions of the Bourgeoisie in 18th-Century France, and Their Relation to Family Limitation," *Population Studies*, **11**, 46–63.

BLAKE, JUDITH. 1966a. "The Americanization of Catholic Reproductive Ideals," *Population Studies*, **20**, 27–43.

*————. 1966b. "Ideal Family Size Among White Americans: A Quarter Century's Evidence," *Demography*, **1**, 154–173.

————. 1967. "Family Size in the 1960s—A Baffling Fad?" *Eugenics Quarterly*, **14**, 60–74.

————. 1968. "Are Babies Consumer Durables? A Critique of the Economic Theory of Reproductive Motivation," *Population Studies*, **22**, 5–25.

————. 1974. "Can We Believe Recent Data on Birth Expectations in the United States?" *Demography*, **11**, 25–44.

BOFFEY, PHILIP M. 1970. "Japan: A Crowded Nation Wants to Boost Its Birth Rate," *Science*, **167**, 960–962.

BROOKS, HUGH E., and FRANKLIN J. HENRY. 1958. "An Empirical Study of the

Relationships of Catholic Practice and Occupational Mobility to Fertility," *Milbank Memorial Fund Quarterly*, **36**, 222–281.

BURCH, THOMAS K. 1966. "The Fertility of North American Catholics: A Comparative Overview," *Demography*, **3**, 174–187.

BURGESS, ERNEST W., and HARVEY J. LOCKE. 1945. *The Family: From Institution to Companionship*. New York: American Book Co.

CAIN, GLEN G. 1966. *Married Women in the Labor Force: An Economic Analysis*. Chicago: University of Chicago Press.

CARR-SAUNDERS, A. M. 1964 (reprint of the 1936 edition). *World Population: Past Growth and Present Trends*. London: Cass.

CHARLES, ENID. 1935. *The Effect of Present Trends in Fertility and Mortality upon the Future Population of England and Wales and upon Its Age Composition*. London: Royal Economics Society, Memorandum no. 55.

———. 1936. *The Menace of Under-Population: A Biological Study of the Decline of Population Growth*. London: Watts.

———. 1938. "The Effect of Present Trends in Fertility and Mortality upon the Future Population of Great Britain and upon Its Age Composition," in Lancelot Hogben, editor, *Political Arithmetic: A Symposium of Population Studies*. New York: Macmillan.

COALE, ANSLEY J., and MELVIN ZELNIK. 1963. *New Estimates of Fertility and Population in the United States*. Princeton, N.J.: Princeton University Press.

COLLVER, O. ANDREW. 1968. "Women's Work Participation and Fertility in Metropolitan Areas," *Demography*, **5**, 55–60.

CONNELL, K. H. 1950. *The Population of Ireland, 1750–1845*. Oxford: Clarendon.

CUTRIGHT, PHILLIPS, and OMER GALLE. 1973. "The Effect of Illegitimacy on U.S. General Fertility Rates and Population Growth," *Population Studies*, **27**, 515–526.

DAY, LINCOLN. 1961. "Status Implications of the Employment of Married Women in the United States," *American Journal of Economics and Sociology*, **20**, 390–398.

———. 1968. "Natality and Ethnocentrism: Some Relationships Suggested by an Analysis of Catholic–Protestant Differentials," *Population Studies*, **22**, 27–50.

DORN, HAROLD F. 1950. "Pitfalls in Population Forecasts and Projections," *Journal of the American Statistical Association*, **42**, 311–334.

DUMONT, ARSÈNE. 1890. *Dépopulation et civilisation: Etudes démographiques*. Paris: Lecrosnier et Babé.

*EASTERLIN, RICHARD A. 1961. "The American Baby Boom in Historical Perspective," *American Economic Review*, **51**, 869–911.

*———. 1966. "On the Relation of Economic Factors to Recent and Projected Fertility Changes," *Demography*, **3**, 131–153.

———. 1970. "Towards a Socio-economic Theory of Fertility: A Survey of Recent Research on Economic Factors in American Fertility," in S. J. Behrman, Leslie Corsa, Jr., and Ronald Freedman, editors, *Fertility and Family Planning: A World View*. Ann Arbor: University of Michigan Press.

———. 1973. "The Economics and Sociology of Fertility: A Synthesis," 2nd draft. Unpublished paper.

EBERHARD, WOLFRAM. 1967. *Guilt and Sin in Traditional China*. Berkeley: University of California Press.

EDIN, KARL A., and EDWARD P. HUTCHINSON. 1935. *Studies of Differential Fertility in Sweden*. London: King.

FARLEY, REYNOLDS. 1966. "Recent Changes in Negro Fertility," *Demography*, **3**, 188–203.

———. 1970. *Growth of the Black Population: A Study of Demographic Trends.* Chicago: Markham Publishing Co.

———, and ALBERT I. HERMALIN. 1971. "Family Stability: A Comparison of Trends Between Blacks and Whites," *American Sociological Review*, **36**, 1–17.

FIELD, JAMES ALFRED. 1967 (reprint of the 1931 edition). *Essays on Population and Other Papers.* Port Washington, N.Y.: Kennikat Press.

FREEDMAN, DEBORAH S. 1963. "The Relation of Economic Status to Fertility," *American Economic Review*, **53**, 414–426.

*FREEDMAN, RONALD. 1961–62. "The Sociology of Human Fertility: A Trend Report and Bibliography," *Current Sociology*, **10–11**, no. 2.

———, LOLAGENE C. COOMBS, and LARRY BUMPASS. 1965. "Stability and Change in Expectations about Family Size," *Demography*, **2**, 250–275.

*———, PASCAL K. WHELPTON, and ARTHUR A. CAMPBELL. 1959. *Family Planning, Sterility, and Population Growth.* New York: McGraw-Hill.

———, ———, and JOHN W. SMIT. 1961. "Socio-economic Factors in Religious Differentials in Fertility," *American Sociological Review*, **26**, 608–614.

GIBBONS, WILLIAM J., S.J. 1956. "Fertility Control in the Light of Some Recent Catholic Statements," *Eugenics Quarterly*, **3**, 9–15 and 82–87.

GLASNER, SAMUEL. 1961. "Judaism and Sex," in Albert Ellis and Albert Abarnel, editors, *Encyclopedia of Sexual Behavior.* New York: Hawthorn.

GLASS, D. V. 1940. *Population Policies and Movements in Europe.* Oxford, Clarendon.

*———. 1968. "Fertility Trends in Europe since the Second World War," *Population Studies*, **22**, 103–146.

———, and E. GREBENIK. 1954. *The Trend and Pattern of Fertility in Great Britain: A Report on the Family Census.* London: H. M. Stationery Office.

*GOLDBERG, DAVID. 1959. "The Fertility of Two-Generation Urbanites," *Population Studies*, **12**, 214–222.

———. 1960. "Some Recent Developments in American Fertility Research," in National Bureau of Economic Research 1960.

GOLDSCHEIDER, CALVIN. 1965. "Ideological Factors in Jewish Fertility Differentials," *Jewish Journal of Sociology*, **7**, 92–105.

———. 1966. "Trends in Jewish Fertility," *Sociology and Social Research*, **50**, 173–186.

———. 1967. "Fertility of the Jews," *Demography*, **4**, 196–209.

———. 1971. *Population, Modernization, and Social Structure.* Boston: Little, Brown.

*———, and PETER R. UHLENBERG. 1969. "Minority Group Status and Fertility," *American Journal of Sociology*, **74**, 361–372.

*GRABILL, WILSON H., CLYDE V. KISER, and PASCAL K. WHELPTON. 1958. *The Fertility of American Women.* New York: Wiley.

*GROAT, H. THEODORE, and ARTHUR G. NEAL. 1967. "Social Psychological Correlates of Urban Fertility," *American Sociological Review*, **32**, 945–959.

———, and ———. 1970. "Social Class and Alienation as Predictors of Catholic Fertility," *American Journal of Sociology*, **76**, 460–473.

*HAWTHORN, GEOFFREY. 1970. *The Sociology of Fertility.* London: Collier-Macmillan.

HIMES, NORMAN E. 1936. *Medical History of Contraception*. Baltimore: Williams & Wilkins.

HUNT, CHESTER L. 1967. "Catholicism and the Birthrate," *Review of Religious Research*, **8**, 67–80.

INNES, J. W. 1938. *Class Fertility Trends in England and Wales, 1876–1934*. Princeton, N.J.: Princeton University Press.

JAFFE, A. J. 1940. "Differential Fertility in the White Population in Early America," *Journal of Heredity*, **31**, 407–411.

*JOANNES, F. V., editor. 1970. *The Bitter Pill: Worldwide Reaction to the Encyclical Humanae Vitae*. Philadelphia: Pilgrim Press.

JOHNSON, GWENDOLYN Z. 1960. "Differential Fertility in European Countries," in National Bureau of Economic Research 1960.

JONES, GAVIN, and DOROTHY NORTMAN. 1968. "Roman Catholic Fertility and Family Planning: A Comparative Review of the Research Literature," *Studies in Family Planning*, no. 34, pp. 1–27.

KELLY, GEORGE A. 1960. *Overpopulation: A Catholic View*. New York: Paulist Press.

*KENNEDY, ROBERT E., JR. 1973a. *The Irish: Emigration, Marriage, and Fertility*. Berkeley: University of California Press.

————. 1973b. "Minority Group Status and Fertility: The Irish," *American Sociological Review*, **38**, 85–96.

KIRK, DUDLEY. 1955. "Recent Trends in Catholic Fertility in the United States," in Milbank Memorial Fund, *Current Research in Human Fertility*. New York.

KISER, CLYDE V. 1967. "The Growth of American Families Studies: An Assessment of Significance," *Demography*, **4**, 388–396.

————, and P. K. WHELPTON. 1958. "Summary of Chief Findings and Implications for Future Studies," *Milbank Memorial Fund Quarterly*, **36**, 282–329.

KOYA, YOSHIO. 1962. "A Family Planning Program in a Large Population Group," *Milbank Memorial Fund Quarterly*, **40**, 319–327.

KUNZ, PHILLIP R. 1965. "The Relation of Income and Fertility," *Journal of Marriage and the Family*, **27**, 509–513.

KURUSHIMA, HIDESABURO. 1970. "An Opinion on the Reproductivity Trend in Our Country," *Studies in Family Planning*, no. 56.

LAURIAT, PATIENCE. 1959. "Marriage and Fertility Patterns of College Graduates," *Eugenics Quarterly*, **6**, 171–179.

LEASURE, J. WILLIAM. 1967. "Some Economic Benefits of Birth Prevention," *Milbank Memorial Fund Quarterly*, **45**, 417–425.

LINCOLN, C. ERIC. 1965. "The Absent Father Haunts the Negro Family," *New York Times Magazine*, November 28.

LOTKA, ALFRED J. 1927. "The Size of American Families in the Eighteenth Century," *Journal of the American Statistical Association*, **22**, 154–170.

LUNDE, ANDERS S. 1965. "White–Nonwhite Fertility Differentials in the United States," *Health, Education, and Welfare Indicators*, September.

MANGIN, MARIE-REINE. 1962. "La politique néo-Malthusienne au Danemark," *Population*, **17**, 75–96.

MARCHAL, FRANCE, and ODILE RABUT. 1972. "Evolution récente de la fécondité en Europe occidentale," *Population*, **27**, 838–874.

MAY, GEOFFREY. 1931. *Social Control of Sex Expression.* New York: Morrow.

*MICKLEWRIGHT, F. H. AMPHLETT. 1961. "The Rise and Decline of English Neo-Malthusianism," *Population Studies,* **15**, 32–51.

MURAMATSU, MINORU. 1960. "Effect of Induced Abortion on the Reduction of Births in Japan," *Milbank Memorial Fund Quarterly,* **38**, 153–166.

*NATIONAL BUREAU OF ECONOMIC RESEARCH. 1960. *Demographic and Economic Change in Developed Countries.* Princeton, N.J.: Princeton University Press.

NIZARD, ALFRED. 1970. "Le Japon vingt ans après la loi eugénique," *Population,* **25**, 1236–1262.

*NOONAN, JOHN T., JR. 1965. *Contraception: A History of Its Treatment by the Catholic Theologians and Canonists.* Cambridge, Mass.: Belknap–Harvard University Press.

NOTESTEIN, FRANK W. 1950. "The Population of the World in the Year 2000," *Journal of the American Statistical Association,* **45**, 335–349.

NYE, F. IVAN, and LOIS WLADIS HOFFMAN. 1963. *The Employed Mother in America.* Chicago: Rand McNally.

O'BRIEN, JOHN A., editor. 1953. *The Vanishing Irish: The Enigma of the Modern World.* New York: McGraw-Hill.

OKUN, BERNARD. 1958. *Trends in Birth Rates in the United States Since 1870.* Baltimore: Johns Hopkins Press.

*OPPENHEIMER, VALERIE K. 1970. *The Female Labor Force in the United States: Demographic and Economic Factors Governing Its Growth and Changing Composition.* Berkeley: Institute of International Studies, University of California.

———. 1973. "Demographic Influence on Female Employment and the Status of Women," *American Journal of Sociology,* **78**, 946–961.

PARSONS, TALCOTT. 1949. "Certain Primary Sources and Patterns of Aggression in the Social Structure of the Western World," *Essays in Sociological Theory, Pure and Applied.* New York: Free Press.

PATAI, RAPHAEL. 1959. *Sex and Family in the Bible and the Middle East.* Garden City, N.Y.: Doubleday.

PETERSEN, WILLIAM. 1966. "Fertility Trends and Population Policy: Some Comments on the Van Heek–Hofstee Debate," *Sociologia Neerlandica,* **3**, 2–13.

RAINWATER, LEE. 1965. *Family Design: Marital Sexuality, Family Size, and Contraception.* Chicago: Aldine.

REDDAWAY, W. B. 1939. *The Economics of a Declining Population.* London: Allen & Unwin.

*REITERMAN, CARL. 1965. "Birth Control and Catholics," *Journal for the Scientific Study of Religion,* **4**, 213–233.

RIESMAN, DAVID, et al. 1950. *The Lonely Crowd: A Study in the Changing American Character.* New Haven, Conn.: Yale University Press.

RITCHEY, P. NEAL, and C. SHANNON STOKES. 1972. "Residence Background, Migration, and Fertility," *Demography,* **9**, 217–230.

ROSENBERG, HARRY M. 1972. *The Influence of Fertility Strategies on the Labor Force Status of American Wives.* Springfield, Va.: National Technical Information Service, Report PB 213–743.

———. 1973. "Fertility Strategies as Intervening Determinants of Wives' Labor Force Status." Paper presented at the meeting of the Population Association of America, New Orleans.

ROSSI, ALICE S. 1968. "Transition to Parenthood," *Journal of Marriage and the Family*, **30**, 26–39.

ROSTOW, W. W. 1960. *The Stages of Economic Growth: A Non-Communist Manifesto.* Cambridge, England: Cambridge University Press.

RUSSELL, JOHN L. 1958. "Christian Theology and the Population Problem," *The Month* (London), **19**, 197–208.

SANGER, MARGARET. 1931. *My Fight for Birth Control.* New York: Farrar & Rinehart.

———. 1938. *Margaret Sanger—An Autobiography.* New York: Norton.

SCHMIEDELER, EDGAR, editor. 1952. *Moral Questions Affecting Married Life.* Washington, D.C.: National Catholic Welfare Conference.

SEPPILLI, TULLIO. 1960. "Social Conditions of Fertility in a Rural Community in Transition in Central Italy," *Annals of the New York Academy of Sciences*, **84**, Article 17.

SLY, DAVID F. 1970. "Minority-Group Status and Fertility: An Extension of Goldscheider and Uhlenberg," *American Journal of Sociology*, **76**, 443–459.

STYS, W. 1957. "The Influence of Economic Conditions on the Fertility of Peasant Women," *Population Studies*, **11**, 136–148.

SULLOWAY, ALVAH W. 1959. *Birth Control and Catholic Doctrine.* Boston: Beacon.

SUTTER, JEAN. 1960. "Bilan de la politique néo-malthusienne en Suède (1939–1957)," *Population*, **15**, 677–702.

SWEEZY, ALAN. 1971. "The Economic Explanation of Fertility Changes in the United States," *Population Studies*, **25**, 255–267.

TABAH, LÉON. 1971. *Rapport sur les relations entre la fécondité et la condition sociale et économique de la famille en Europe; leurs répercussions sur la politique sociale.* Council of Europe, Second European Population Conference. Strasbourg.

TAEUBER, IRENE B. 1958. *The Population of Japan.* Princeton, N.J.: Princeton University Press.

*TAYLOR, GEORGE V. 1967. "Noncapitalist Wealth and the Origins of the French Revolution," *American Historical Review*, **72**, 469–496.

THOMLINSON, RALPH. 1972. "Prevented Births, Naturalness, and Roman Catholic Doctrine," *Journal of Sex Research*, **8**, 73–100.

TIEN, H. YUAN. 1961. "The Social Mobility/Fertility Hypothesis Reconsidered: An Empirical Study," *American Sociological Review*, **26**, 247–257.

TIETZE, CHRISTOPHER, and PATIENCE LAURIAT. 1955. "Age at Marriage and Educational Attainment in the United States," *Population Studies*, **9**, 159–166.

*U.S. BUREAU OF THE CENSUS. 1971. "Fertility Indicators: 1970," *Current Population Reports*, Series P-23, no. 36. Washington, D.C.: U.S. Government Printing Office.

———. 1973. "Birth Expectations and Fertility: June 1972," *Current Population Reports*, Series P-20, no. 248. Washington, D.C.: U.S. Government Printing Office.

U.S. COMMISSION ON POPULATION GROWTH AND THE AMERICAN FUTURE. 1972. *Report: Population and the American Future.* Washington, D.C.: U.S. Government Printing Office.

VAN HEEK, F. 1954. *Het geboorte-niveau der Nederlandse Rooms-Katholieken.* Leiden: Stenfert Kroese.

*VAN HEEK, F. 1956. "Roman-Catholicism and Fertility in the Netherlands: Demographic Aspects of Minority Status," *Population Studies*, **10**, 125–138.

VAN 'T VEER, ANTHON J. 1972. "Roman Catholic Fertility in Tudderen: An Analysis of One Factor," in William Petersen, editor, *Readings in Population*. New York: Macmillan.

VINCENT, CLARK E. 1961. *Unmarried Mothers*. New York: Free Press.

WALSH, BRENDAN M. 1972. "Trends in Age at Marriage in Postwar Ireland," *Demography*, **9**, 187–202.

WEBB, SIDNEY. 1913. *The Decline in the Birth-Rate*. London: Fabian Society.

*WESTOFF, CHARLES F., and LARRY BUMPASS. 1973. "The Revolution in Birth Control Practices of U.S. Roman Catholics," *Science*, **179**, 41–44.

*————, ELLIOT G. MISHLER, and E. LOWELL KELLY. 1957. "Preferences in Size of Family and Eventual Fertility Twenty Years After," *American Journal of Sociology*, **62**, 491–497.

————, ROBERT G. POTTER, JR., PHILIP C. SAGI, and ELLIOT G. MISHLER. 1961. *Family Growth in Metropolitan America*. Princeton, N.J.: Princeton University Press.

————, ————, and ————. 1963. *The Third Child: A Study in the Prediction of Fertility*. Princeton, N.J.: Princeton University Press.

————, and RAYMOND H. POTVIN. 1967. *College Women and Fertility Values*. Princeton, N.J.: Princeton University Press.

WHELPTON, PASCAL K., ARTHUR A. CAMPBELL, and JOHN E. PATTERSON. 1966. *Fertility and Family Planning in the United States*. Princeton, N.J.: Princeton University Press.

WRONG, DENNIS H. 1958. "Trends in Class Fertility in Western Nations," *Canadian Journal of Economics and Political Science*, **24**, 216–229.

ZIMMERMAN, ANTHONY F. 1957. *Overpopulation*. Washington, D.C.: Catholic University of America Press.

MORTALITY IN THE MODERN WORLD

Differences in the level of fertility have grown smaller among Western nations and the social classes within them, and the overall contrast between the fertility of advanced and that of underdeveloped countries has become more pronounced. With respect to mortality, on the contrary, the worldwide range has narrowed. The reason, obviously, is that the control over the number of children that is exercised inside each family varies greatly from one culture to another, whereas the control of early death has become in great part independent of the will of the persons affected. Thus, it is convenient to discuss in this one chapter the mortality of all the world, while the analysis of fertility has been divided into two parts. The arrangement is designed to emphasize the chronology: (1) the fall of birth rates in the West, which began before the substantial decline in Western death rates; (2) the decline in mortality throughout the world (this chapter); and (3) the attempts to bring the fertility of underdeveloped countries under control, following the sizable decline in mortality. This is not to suggest, however, that the effect of life-saving techniques has been the same in the rest of the world as in the historic West. Over the decades, as new medicines, surgical practices, and medical institutions were invented in Europe or its overseas extensions, these improvements were used to bring about a gradual reduction in mortality; but in many underdeveloped areas the control of early death went from witchcraft to antibiotics in one fantastic leap.

DECLINE OF MORTALITY IN THE WEST

The most remarkable fact about modern death control is how recently it began. As we noted in Chapter 11, the probable decline in English mortality around 1800 is difficult to explain. Only toward the middle of the 19th century was a serious attempt made to separate sewage from drinking water, and most of the specifics against various infections did not become available until several decades later.

From the middle of the 19th century on, it is possible to trace international mortality trends with life tables, of which about 250 were available by the mid-1950s (Stolnitz 1955–56). The gains in life chances of West Europeans from the 1840s to the 1940s—or, more precisely, mainly in the second half of that

Table 15-1.   Proportion Surviving[a] in Five West European Countries, by Sex, 1840s and 1940s

Country	1840s				1940s			
	1_1		1_{15}		1_1		1_{60}	
	MALE	FEMALE	MALE	FEMALE	MALE	FEMALE	MALE	FEMALE
Netherlands	776	814	615	644	967	973	805	839
Sweden	835	859	710	741	966	974	759	802
England and Wales	836	865	673	697	952	963	722	799
France	822	847	659	676	943	957	684	776
Belgium	836	864	655	670	936	951	673	772

[a] The symbol 1_x denotes the number of an original 1,000 live births that survive to age x (see pp. 230–233). Early values for France cover the period 1840–59, for England and Wales 1838–54. Later values for all countries except Sweden are for postwar years.
SOURCE: George J. Stolnitz, "A Century of International Mortality Trends: I," *Population Studies*, **9** (1955), 24–55.

century—were probably greater than those over the previous two millennia (Table 15-1). Just before World War I, the pattern of Europe's mortality followed that of its economic development. In Northwest Europe—that is, the British Isles, the Low Countries, Germany, Switzerland, and Scandinavia—only 15 persons died in each year per thousand of the population; in France, Italy, and the western portion of Austria–Hungary this death rate was about 20; and in Spain and the Balkans it was about 25 (Kirk 1946: chap. 4). Since that time death rates have fallen steadily—apart from the two world wars—throughout Europe, and this regional variation all but disappeared. The very acquisition of an urban–industrial culture, once the major travail of the transition was past, invariably generated a substantial decline in mortality.

Direct information on mortality in the United States before 1900 is limited to surmises from local figures (Taeuber and Taeuber 1958: 269–272). These indicate that expectation of life at birth at the beginning of the 19th century was probably not much higher than 35 years, or about half what it is today. In Massachusetts, the first state to collect vital statistics systematically, the expectation of life at birth went up from 38.3 years in 1850 to only 46.1 years in 1900–1902 for males, and from 40.5 to 49.4 for females (Dublin *et al.* 1949: 48). Data on deaths throughout the country go back only to 1933, when the last state was admitted to the Death-Registration Area (see pp. 39, 52), and national rates for earlier dates are generally based on the assumption that the death-registration states were typical. As there is every reason to believe, on the contrary, that greater control over death developed together with better statistics concerning it, such a series probably understates the decline in mortality that has taken place over the long term, substantial as the record showed it to be.

According to the most ambitious extrapolation from local life tables to national trends, expectation of life improved slowly from 1850 to 1900, much more rapidly from 1900 to 1950, and again more slowly since 1950; and these stages have affected the differential pattern of mortality by race and sex (Rao 1973).

The most remarkable improvements were in the control of deaths at the earliest ages. The fall in infant mortality can be illustrated by the example of Sweden, which has both the longest historical series of accurate statistics and, at the present time, one of the world's best records for effective control. From 1750 to about 1810 infant mortality in Sweden fluctuated around 200 per 1,000 live births; that is, at that time one child out of every five born died before its first birthday. During the rest of the 19th century the rate fell slowly but consistently, reaching 100 by 1900 and, after a much faster decline, 21 by 1950 and slightly more than 15 in 1962. The reduction in infant mortality over 150 years, thus, was by about 90 percent. For the most recent decades, death rates are available by shorter periods than the whole of the first year, and these are suggestive. From 1915 to 1945 the proportion of deaths under the age of one week remained essentially constant at about 16 per 1,000 live births, while deaths from age one week to one year fell off by about 70 percent (United Nations 1954: 29–35). By 1970 Sweden had the lowest infant mortality rate in the world, having cut it enough to pass the Netherlands and Norway, which 20 years earlier had ranked first and second.

In the United States the infant mortality rate fell from 95.7 in 1915–19 to 19.8 in 1970 (Table 15-2). Up to 1933, when the figures excluded some of the states with the highest mortality, the decline was probably slower than that indicated, and much of the improved control was stimulated by the work of vital statisticians. The American Association for the Prevention of Infant Mortality, organized in 1909, devoted its main effort during its first years to campaigning for the extension and improvement of birth and death registrations. As more accurate statistics on infant mortality became available, these denoted both the seriousness of the problem and the causes of death that most urgently required medical attention. The rate continued to fall in the more recent period but more slowly, particularly as compared with the continued improvement in Northwest Europe (note the position of the United States in Table 15-3). The reason for this lag, it was usually supposed, was the superior medical care available through state-run facilities in Europe, as contrasted with the mixture of private and socialized medicine in the United States. Among the "many social, economic, and program issues" to explain the difference in rates, thus, "high on the list would be a lag in community facilities, . . . difficulties experienced by the in-migrant [blacks] in taking advantage of their new medical-care environment, overcrowding, and low income" (Shapiro et al. 1968: 137).

However, when the independent variable is merely designated by the name of a country, as in Table 15-3, it is difficult to specify it more precisely. The different systems of medical care would seem indeed to be a plausible factor, as well as possibly variations in geography, the characteristics of the populations, or the

Table 15-2. Infant and Neonatal Mortality Rates per 1,000 Live Births, by Color, Birth-Registration Area of the United States, 1915-70

Time Period	Infant Mortality Rate			Neonatal Mortality Rate		
	TOTAL	WHITE	NONWHITE	TOTAL	WHITE	NONWHITE
1915–19	95.7	92.8	149.7	43.4	42.3	58.1
1920–24	76.7	73.3	115.3	39.7	38.7	51.1
1925–29	69.0	65.0	105.4	37.2	36.0	47.9
1930–34 [a]	60.4	55.7	92.9	34.4	32.8	45.5
1935–39	53.2	49.2	81.3	31.0	29.5	41.4
1940–44	42.4	39.0	66.9	26.2	24.9	35.6
1945–49	33.3	31.0	49.4	22.9	21.8	30.3
1950–54	28.1	25.4	44.7	19.8	18.6	27.5
1955–59	26.4	23.4	43.7	19.1	17.6	27.7
1960–64 [b]	25.3	22.3	41.6	18.3	16.8	26.3
1965	24.7	21.5	40.3	17.7	16.1	25.4
1966	23.7	20.6	38.8	17.2	15.6	24.8
1967	22.4	19.7	35.9	16.5	15.0	23.8
1968	21.8	19.2	34.5	16.1	14.7	23.0
1969 [c]	20.7	18.4	31.6	15.4	14.1	21.6
1970 [c]	19.8	17.4	31.4	14.9	13.5	21.6
1971 [c]	19.2	16.8	30.2	14.3	12.9	20.8

[a] In 1932–34, Mexicans were included with "Nonwhites."
[b] In 1962–63, figures by color exclude data for residents of New Jersey.
[c] Preliminary.
SOURCES: 1915–39 and 1951–64: U.S. Public Health Service, *Vital Statistics of the United States*, various dates. 1940–50: U.S. Public Health Service, *Vital Statistics—Special Reports*, vol. 45, no. 1, 1957, Tables 2 and 4. 1965–70: U.S. Bureau of the Census, *Statistical Abstract of the United States, 1973* (Washington, D.C.: U.S. Government Printing Office, 1973), Table 82.

type and adequacy of reporting (cf. Chase 1969). In the best comparative analysis (Chase 1967), all of these were examined but with no clarification. This came, however, from a detailed study of one cause of infant mortality: prematurity, or birth before the full term of about forty weeks. This is generally (though not entirely accurately) measured by the weight at birth. During the first three months of 1950, as a typical range, neonatal death rates in the United States ranked unilinearly from 871.7 per 1,000 live births of babies weighing 1,000 grams or less at birth down to 5.6 of those weighing 3,501–4,000 grams, the optimum range for the American population. The critical weight is usually stipulated as 2,500 grams or less. By the criterion of birth weight a relatively higher proportion of the births in the United States were premature—increasing, moreover, from 7.7 percent in 1959 to 8.2 percent in 1964. In Great Britain over the same period, the proportion remained constant at 6.6 to 6.7 percent; and in

Table 15-3. Infant Mortality Rates, Selected Western Countries, 1935, 1950, 1970

Country	Infant Mortality Rate and Rank Among Countries			Percent Decline	
	1935	1950	1970	1935–70	1950–70
Sweden	45.9 (3)	21.0 (1)	11.7[a] (1)	75[a]	44[a]
Netherlands	40.0 (1)	26.7 (2)	12.7 (2.5)	68	52
Norway	44.2 (2)	28.2 (3)	12.7 (2.5)	71	55
Denmark	71.0 (6)	30.7 (6)	14.2 (4)	80	54
England and Wales	56.9 (5)	29.9 (5)	18.1 (5)	68	39
Scotland	76.8 (7)	38.6 (7)	19.6 (6)	74	49
United States	55.7 (4)	29.2 (4)	19.8 (7)	64	32

[a] Data for 1969 rather than 1970.
SOURCES: Helen C. Chase, *International Comparison of Perinatal and Infant Mortality: The United States and Six West European Countries*, U.S. National Center for Health Statistics, Series 3, no. 6 (Washington, D.C., 1967); United Nations, *Demographic Yearbook, 1971* (New York, 1972); Norway, Central Bureau of Statistics, *Statistical Yearbook of Norway, 1972* (Oslo, 1972).

the other countries, which did not keep records on weight at birth, unofficial estimates suggested that the percentages were as low as 5.5 percent (Netherlands) or even 5.04 percent (Sweden). In the United States, in other words, a significantly higher (and growing) proportion of premature babies were delivered, with the relative risk of neonatal mortality in those cases rising by more than a hundred times. Compared with Sweden or the Netherlands (the two countries with the best recorded control of infant mortality), the attempts of American obstetricians to save a higher proportion of infants with a dangerously low birth weight accounted for 85–90 percent of the difference in neonatal mortality (ibid.: 63).

DIFFERENCES BY SOCIAL CLASS

That an inverse correlation exists between almost any index of social class and mortality would seem to be so obvious that one hardly demands any proof. Those at the upper levels have less dangerous occupations, live under more healthful conditions, and can more easily afford medical attention when it is necessary. But with the mass control of infectious disease, the influence of living conditions on mortality is not so great and direct as it once was; and the development of free clinics, group health insurance, and similar institutions has made adequate medical care much more widely available than formerly. The evidence from various studies suggests that class differentials are becoming smaller or even disappearing, and it is very important, thus, to keep this chronology in mind and note the date of any statistics being analyzed.

In interpreting any comparison of death rates by occupation, four general factors can be important. (1) The number of deaths comes from death certificates, and the number of persons in the occupational category from the census. A "physician" is almost certain to be so listed on both, but miscellaneous categories (as, for instance, "mechanics, not otherwise specified") are probably so designated much more often on the certificate than in the census, thus inflating the rate by an unknown proportion (cf. Stockwell 1961; Hart 1972). (2) There is a self-selection by physique and state of health into appropriate occupations. If tailors have a higher rate than miners, say, one might infer that this is the reason. (3) Most obviously, occupations vary in the danger to life associated with them. Among professionals, physicians typically have higher rates than clergymen or lawyers; among miners, those in tin or copper mines have higher rates than those in iron mines. (4) Occupations are associated, finally, with particular social classes, which may differ in income, knowledge, way of life, and other attributes relevant to health.

Some of the earliest studies of differences in mortality by occupation were made by the most distinguished statisticians of several countries—Alphonse Bertillon in France, William Farr in England, Louis Dublin in the United States. Daric (1951) brought together these studies and offered a commentary on them that was so judicious that the U.S. National Office of Vital Statistics published it in translation. One table that he reproduced is given here (Table 15-4), for it contains a number of interesting features. Each figure is a **standardized mortality ratio**, or the death rate of each social class expressed as a percentage of that of the whole age–sex category. Note that the spread over the five classes fell

Table 15-4. Standardized Mortality Ratios, All Causes of Death by Social Class, Persons Aged 20–64 Years, England and Wales, 1921–23 and 1930–32

Social Class	1921–23 MALES (EXCLUDING NONCIVILIANS)	1930–32 MALES (INCLUDING NONCIVILIANS)	1930–32 MARRIED WOMEN BY CLASS OF HUSBAND	1930–32 OCCUPIED SINGLE WOMEN
I (high)	82	90	81	—
II	93	94	89	—
III	94	97	99	95
IV	99	102	103	102
V (low)	121	111	113	112
TOTAL	100	100	100	100

SOURCE: Great Britain, *Registrar General's Decennial Supplement, England and Wales, 1931,* Part IIa, "Occupational Mortality," p. 20, Table E. Reproduced in Jean Daric, "Mortality, Occupation, and Socio-economic Status," U.S. National Office of Vital Statistics, *Vital Statistics—Special Reports,* **33,** no. 10, September 1951, (Washington, D.C.: U.S. Government Printing Office).

from 48 percent in 1921–23 to 24 percent in 1930–32 for males, with the sharpest differentiation in both periods between skilled and unskilled workers. Women classified by the occupations of their husbands were ranked in the same order but with a sharper rise, suggesting that a good environment favored women even more than men (cf. Logan 1954).

One of the early comparable studies in the United States was an analysis of death rates by occupation in 1930 (Whitney 1934). The range was restricted to the ten states with data sufficiently accurate to warrant analysis (Massachusetts, Connecticut, New York, New Jersey, Ohio, Illinois, Wisconsin, Minnesota, Kansas, and Alabama) and to those occupations with at least 500 deaths during the year from all causes. Within these limitations, there was a rough inverse correlation by occupation, though with a good deal of variation in the detailed tables giving rates by cause. But when the occupations were grouped into social classes according to the Alba Edwards scale, this irregularity all but disappeared. For all gainfully occupied males, the rates per 1,000, standardized according to the age distribution of all gainfully occupied males in the ten selected states, were as follows:

Agricultural workers	6.21
Professionals	7.00
Proprietors, managers, and officials	7.38
Clerks and kindred workers	7.40
Skilled workers and foremen	8.12
All gainfully occupied males	**8.70**
Semiskilled workers	9.86
Unskilled workers	13.10

The very low rate for agricultural workers, found also in other studies (e.g., Moriyama and Guralnick 1956), is almost certainly spurious, based at least in part on the less complete registration of deaths in rural areas. In an interesting paper Higgs (1973) estimated the rural death rate with the following equation:

$$M = b \cdot M_r + (1 - b)M_u$$

where M is the aggregate crude death rate, M_r and M_u are the crude rates of the rural and urban populations, and b is the proportion of the population living in rural areas (defined as having fewer than 10,000 persons). While urban death rates fell from 23–29 in 1870–80 to 15–17 in 1910–20, according to this formula the rural rates fell over the same period from 21–23 to 14–15. The cause of this decline was neither an improvement in medical facilities and personnel nor better control of public health, but the effect of a marked rise in the real income of the farm population.

Stockwell (1961) noted in a review of the literature that as early as the 1950s some analysts were challenging the continued validity of the inverse relation between social class and mortality. The argument seemed to depend on whether

The D & C Warehouse in Cleveland, where some thirty squatters made their home during the depression of the 1930s (*Cleveland Public Library*).

A home in Appalachia, southeastern Ohio (*Ohio Historical Society Library*).

the topic was total mortality or only that from particular causes, whether the same measures were used to denote class, and which countries or regions were included in the sample. Roberts *et al.* (1970) grouped disease into six categories, hypothesizing that the social class of a census tract is not related to death rates from degenerative diseases, senility, and other ill defined causes, but that it is related to those from infections, diseases associated with maternity and infancy, those with "social causes," and thus those from all causes together. In an ecological study of Houston, the hypotheses were validated for the years 1959–61. Indeed, when analyses included cause of death, in some cases the highest social class showed *higher* age-standardized death rates than those immediately below it (e.g., Ellis 1957). It has been especially widely held that the upper classes, presumably because of the greater stress their members undergo, die more often from the major cardiovascular diseases, but Antonovsky (1968) challenged this opinion in an impressive review of thirty-five studies of mortality and twenty-one of morbidity:

> No fewer studies report inverse class gradients than direct gradients, and both are outnumbered by the number of studies showing no clear gradient. . . . There would often seem to be a curvilinear relation between class and disease. This would suggest that social class is a highly important variable in the study of cardiovascular diseases, even if the relation is not simplistic. . . . At least in the United States, class differences in the factors which might be related to heart disease, e.g., diet, have tended to disappear. This might account for the cumulating evidence that there is no longer—if there ever was—much of a class differential.

Elements in the Relation Between Social Class and Health

Given the ambiguity of the results of prior studies, it would not seem to be useful to go on analyzing the simple relation between social class, however defined, and mortality or morbidity. In an interesting paper, Lerner (1968) suggested some of the main strands that have to be separated; his schema, somewhat changed, is reproduced in Table 15-5. Whether his tentative conclusions are correct is less important than the framework of his analysis.

1. Occupation. In the prior literature the main factors considered were the frequency of accidents (e.g., miners, truck drivers) and the physical dangers inherent in the type of work (e.g., sand blasters, deep-sea divers). More pertinent today is whether the occupation is sedentary or involves physical activity. While the work week of the working class has been reduced to 40 hours or less, many executives spend perhaps 45 to 48 hours in their offices, plus a considerable addendum nights and weekends at home. The heavy responsibility generates severe strains and tensions, which are believed to be a factor in several stress-related diseases. Though the evidence is lacking, Lerner believes that the poverty population probably resembles the working class in this respect.

2. Level of living, including such specifics as food, housing, transportation, and the like. Relative to the rest of the American people, the poverty population

Table 15-5. Elements of the Life Styles of Three Social Classes That Help Determine Their Level of Health, United States, c. 1970

Element of Life Style	Poverty Population	Working Class	Middle Class
1. Occupation	+ ?	+	−
2. Level of living	−	+	+ +(− ?)
3. Social milieu	−	−	+
4. Knowledge of health care	−	+	+ +
5. Access to private medical care	−	+	+ +

SOURCE: Adapted from Monroe Lerner, "The Level of Physical Health of the Poverty Population: A Conceptual Reappraisal of Structural Factors," *Medical Care*, 6 (1968), 355–367.

is manifestly deprived and the working class much better off. According to Lerner's supposition, the middle class may score *too* highly, eating too much and too richly. A simple continuum is often manifest in traditional agrarian societies: a peasant is thin, and a member of the upper class demonstrates in his physique his access to more food. Though data are sparse, this seems not to be the case in the United States. According to one study based on a sample of white elderly couples in Providence, the relation between social class and obesity is the opposite of what it would be in a peasant society, particularly among females. In order to control for the effect of subcultural cuisines, the sample was divided into Italian, Irish, other Catholic, Protestant, and Jewish. Among all these subnations, a higher proportion of lower-class women were overweight or, among the three Catholic groups, obese (Burnight and Marden 1967). One can speculate that income is a factor (starchy foods cost less than proteins or vegetables), but perhaps the constraint imposed by the middle-class style of slimness influences eating habits more. Differences in foods given to infants and small children affect both their immediate health and their life expectation (Fomon and Anderson 1972).

3. Social milieu, including such specifics as the degree of economic security and the type of neighborhood. Concerning the degree of protection against economic hazards, Lerner puts the first two classes on a par and both lower than the middle class. But the situation varies greatly within the working class: those in large firms, with group health insurance and a factory clinic available, are treated for minor ailments more readily than many in the middle class. The condition of neighborhoods is a crucial contribution to deaths related to social disorganization (cf. pp. 252–265), as well as to the relative efficiency of any health-related institutions.

4. Knowledge of health care can be a significant variable, which Lerner omits from his schedule. According to the responses to thirty-six questions in fourteen national surveys between 1941 and 1962, knowledge about health is positively

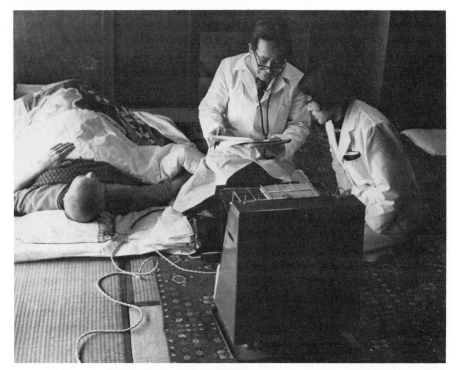

As in all advanced countries, in Japan heart disease is an important cause of death. Here a patient is getting emergency treatment in his home; he will be transferred to a special ward for acute cardiovascular ailments (*World Health Organization*).

related to education, income, and occupational status; is negatively related to age; is greater among females than males; is likely to derive from notable news events rather than the specific utility of the information (Wade 1970). According to a study with better controls, health knowledge does not differ significantly by social class, age, or sex, but mainly by the level of education (Samora *et al.* 1962). In the most recent period, the health of the poverty population has seemed to be less the consequence of low income than of poor education (Lefcowitz 1973). Even when differences are controlled for years of schooling, however, for several generations a person's ethnic background can affect his perception of illness and the expression of its symptoms (Croog 1961).

How much of what a physician tells his patients, using lay language and carefully avoiding medical jargon, is the typical person able to understand, and how much does this understanding vary by social characteristics? In one study, a roster of fifty words was compiled from the tapes of actual interviews between physicians and their patients, screened to eliminate unusual or difficult terms. The words were put into simple sentences, and a very loose test of adequate comprehension was applied to a sample of lower-class patients, divided into native English-speaking whites, Negroes, and Spanish Americans. Only four words out of the fifty were understood by nine out of ten of the patients: *vomit*, *relieve*, *appointment*, and *constipated*. Fewer than half could make anything of seventeen of the terms, including *digestion*, *tissue*, *therapy*, *nerve*, and so on (Samora *et al.* 1961).

If the patient is unable to come to the physician, one might suppose that the physician should move closer to the patient.

> By knowing well the cultural background of the patient, the physician can view the universe through the eyes of the patient. . . . If we wish really to understand a patient's mode of thinking we must delve deeply into his history, culture, and tradition. . . . This is true of all peoples and all nationalities [Savitz 1952].

Dr. Savitz is a Jew, and he illustrates this dictum with several anecdotes about Jewish patients whom he helped in part because he knows Hebrew, the Talmud, and Jewish history. But the notion of pairing off doctor and patient in a multi-ethnic society like the United States strikes one not only as impracticable but rather frightening in its implications.

5. Access to medical care, which Lerner restricted to the private medical-care system, varies as he noted: inadequate among the poverty population, adequate for the working class, and superior for the middle class. But it is arbitrary to omit public health care, which was instituted to redress this imbalance.

> Need and publicly financed care act in conjunction to produce the inverse relationship found in the [most recent] tabulations of physician utilization and income. Low-income persons not only have a higher need and therefore a higher use, but also the availability of publicly financed care seems to stimulate use even when need, as measured by restricted activity days, is not present [Monteiro 1973].

In one respect, the very ability of middle-class patients to pay for care means that their physicians may choose to continue treatment rather than referring them to someone better qualified. In a study of patients suffering from head or neck cancer, for which prompt therapy by a specialist is essential, lower-class patients were referred sooner and in a larger proportion than the well-to-do (Miller 1973).

From an array of data such as those presented here, Lerner reached a conclusion in sharp contradiction to the conventional wisdom:

> The working class is likely to have the best overall mortality record of the three strata. This good record occurs because its mortality rates from the communicable diseases, and during infancy and at younger ages, are likely to be as low, or nearly as low, as the rates of the middle class, and much lower than those for the poverty population. On the other hand, its mortality rates during the older ages and from the diseases associated with the aging process are likely to be as low, or nearly as low, as the rates of the poverty population, and much lower than the rates for the middle-class population.

Differences by Type of Medical Service

In his work on the population of Europe, Kirk (1946: 180–182) found a way of dramatizing the superior death control practiced in Holland, whose recent record is comparable to Sweden's. He contrasted the number of deaths in each country with the number there would have been if Holland's age-specific rates in 1939 had obtained, and then he calculated the difference as a percentage of the total and labeled this "excess deaths." On this basis, in that year excess mortality for Europe as a whole amounted to 35 percent, and for Northwest and Central Europe alone it was 23 percent (cf. Guralnick and Jackson 1967; Burgess *et al.* 1966). Since this variation in mortality was not based on a difference in medical techniques, which were more or less identical all over Western Europe, the reasons for it must be sought in the country's social history.

The rise of Dutch industry and the development of social-welfare legislation in Holland were almost simultaneous. There were only three decades of un-controlled urban growth—from about 1870, when industrialization really got under way, to 1900, when the first housing act was passed. The evils associated with the factory system of England, to take a classic example, existed in the Netherlands, but on a proportionately much smaller scale and for a much shorter period. The impetus to develop this social-welfare program, moreover, came in large part from such traditionalist institutions as the churches, which thus established for themselves a significant function in relation to the new society. As one consequence, the best of modern medical science was made available to the people through institutions connected with religious or other groups to which they were bound by strong sentiments. The Dutch equivalent of the Red Cross, for example, is three "Cross Societies," associated respectively with the Catholic, the Protestant, and the secularist sectors of the population. Similarly, the Dutch medical profession itself established a health-insurance plan, which

A horse-drawn ambu-lance, c. 1911, of the Black and Wright Am-bulance Service, Cleve-land (*Cleveland Public Library*).

has remained private in the sense that the physicians and the member–patients control it, but health insurance is now compulsory for all wage and salary earners, with half of the premiums paid by the employers (cf. U.S. Social Security Administration 1964: 140–141). The age-adjusted death rates of six occupational groups in Amsterdam in 1947–52 showed a marked lack of variation by social class: the ratio of worst to best (117:100) was barely above the level of statistical significance. In contrast with a number of studies made in other countries, the rates for unskilled and skilled workers were the same. Only the clerical group had relatively high death rates, presumably because of their poor physiques (Antonovsky 1967).

Britain's National Health Service, established in 1948 as the culmination of a long trend toward separating medical care from the ability to pay for it, has generated a considerable body of polemical writings. The best account of the background and early years is Eckstein's book (1958), which judiciously balanced achievements against shortcomings and concluded with an overall positive appraisal. The costs were not as great as had been feared; the erosion of the physician–patient relation, in his view, was an obsolete and almost meaningless issue; the main reason for the shortcomings was "the sheer dilapidation and disorganization of the medical system inherited by the Health Service authorities" (ibid.: 253). In retrospect, it can be seen that Eckstein seriously underestimated several faults, particularly the effects of the hostility of the medical profession. He noted that "young men were not discouraged from entering a medical career by the Health Service; in the first three years of the Service [the number of students in medical schools] grew from 1,734 to 2,115" (ibid.: 225). But each year during the 1960s between a fifth and a third of the graduates of the medical schools emigrated, stimulating the Health Minister to complain that "Britain simply cannot afford to train doctors for the purpose of swelling the membership of the American Medical Association." The system continued to function only because of the brain drain *to* Britain of Indians and Pakistanis, who constituted almost half of the country's junior medical staff, and the partly successful effort to induce some of the emigrants to return (*New York Times*, September 16, 1966; January 7, 1968).

The system continued to deteriorate during the late 1960s and early 1970s, reflecting structural weaknesses that were built into the service from its inception. The lack of a fee encouraged the public to consult doctors for trivial complaints, with the consequence that facilities became too overloaded to give adequate care to the genuinely sick. As one practitioner put it:

Ask any doctor in general practice today how much of his time is spent doing the job for which he has been so methodically trained. About half of his working week is spent in listening to tales of family woe, marital stress situations, and with other problems still further removed from medicine: filling in forms, administering his practice, making claims and writing letters to the Executive Council and, of course, in dealing with those frivolous and trivial complaints when the patient only consults the doctor because the service is free and it is the doctor's duty to be available. . . . It is a ridiculous waste of national resources to train a man . . . and then force him to spend most of his working day in dealing with problems that require no skill at all, . . . meanwhile importing less well trained doctors from overseas on the pretext that there are not enough doctors in this country [Linklater 1973].

One should not imagine that this was the aberrant complaint of an embittered individual. According to a survey of a random sample of English general practitioners, the frustrations generated by the system are pervasive. Relative to the population, the number of GPs declined. Since their remuneration was based on the number of doctors rather than the amount of work, with an increasing workload doctors earned less per unit of work. Two-thirds of the respondents had more than 2,500 patients to care for, almost a sixth had more than 3,500. They complained that their professional quality suffered from the need to work fast, to make spot diagnoses. In 1965, and again in 1970, a vast majority of the GPs working in the National Health Service submitted undated resignations from the system, to be used to strengthen their position in negotiations with the government for higher remuneration and improvements in the general structure (Mechanic 1968; Mechanic and Faich 1970; Battistella and Chester 1973).

Sweden's health service, which has been widely praised in the United States, is also in serious trouble. The cost of medical services is very high, though because of the difference in the manner of payment exact comparisons are not possible. Most of the money comes from taxation, and Swedes are the most heavily taxed people in the world. A family of four with an income of about $12,500 pays a total of about 55 percent in taxes (excluding those on property but including all others), compared with about 20 percent in the United States. In 1970 there was a general reorganization of the Swedish system, which in some respects suggested a potential decline in quality. And in 1973 the out-of-pocket fee to patients was almost doubled.

In order to see a doctor, a Swede must ordinarily wait weeks or months or, for some types of treatment, as much as a year. Like its British counterpart, the system is beset by a proliferating bureaucracy. Persons are assigned to whatever doctor happens to be available at each visit, so that it is only by chance that a doctor sees the same patient twice. The main supposed benefit—that all patients are treated equally irrespective of their income—holds only within any one institution; there is a serious maldistribution of personnel and facilities, with the best services and the most physicians concentrated in the larger towns. Even so, according to a number of indices Sweden's medical services seem to be more efficacious. The sharpest contrast, however, is in the infant mortality rate, which as we have seen (p. 581) is a spurious indicator. That the life expectancy is greater in Sweden than in the United States is due in part to the lower infant mortality and in part to such other factors as the homogeneity of its population (which reduces sharply the complexity of genetic components in disease) and its generally good housing. The physicians themselves seem no longer to be certain that the difference can be ascribed to Sweden's socialized medicine (Altman 1973).

In the United States, the fundament of the medical system is still private practice, under which the physician and the patient come together as individuals, based on the latter's desire for care, choice of his doctor, and ability to pay for the service. In the view of its proponents, the advantages of private practice are that the consumer's free choice of medical care, like free enterprise generally, effects the maximum quality of the product or service; that patient–doctor relations are at their best; and that physicians are more efficient because their income is commensurate with their long training and high level of skill. The overwhelming disadvantage is that adequate care would depend on private income rather than medical need, so that for decades a complementary system of services was built up, organized through churches, insurance companies, municipalities, the states, or the federal government.

In the United States, **health insurance** began in the 1930s, initiated for the employees of various large corporations or the members of trade unions, and then through such organizations as Blue Cross and Blue Shield. In the middle 1960s, it was estimated by the health-insurance association that almost 80 percent of the civilian population was covered by some form of hospital or health insurance (Reed 1965). Such insurance spreads the costs of medical care over periods of health and sickness and between well and sick, thus rendering the burden easier to carry for middle-income groups. Under many schemes, such advantages of private practice as the free choice of a physician are retained. However, the sector of a population least able to pay for medical care (the bottom fifth) is typically also not included in insurance plans.

In 1965 two amendments to the Social Security Act brought Medicare into existence: all those aged 65 years and over and entitled to old-age, survivors', or disability insurance (OASDI), totaling initially some 19 million persons, were enrolled free in a hospital-insurance plan and permitted to participate in a low-cost supplementary medical-insurance plan (cf. Myers 1966). The program is supported out of separate taxes, paid at the same rate by employers, employees, and the self-employed (West 1967). Only one year after it went into effect, it was obvious that Medicare would have a number of probably unanticipated side-effects. Since the aged now constituted a source of considerable income, nonaccredited hospitals and medical laboratories had a strong incentive to improve their services sufficiently to meet the conditions for participation in the program. One such condition, specified in Title VI of the Civil Rights Act of 1964, was that hospital care must be offered without discrimination, and Medicare became a basis for enforcing this guarantee more effectively (Stewart 1967).

The most important side-effect, however, was to help accelerate the rise in medical costs, which in any case had been going up faster than other consumer prices (cf. Ginzberg 1969). From 1946 to 1960, when prices of the entire "market basket" of goods and services increased by an average of 3 percent per year, the increase of every item in medical care was greater. With the advent of Medicare and reimbursement on the basis of reasonable costs, hospitals throughout the country have raised particularly the notoriously low wages of employees below the professional level. Physicians' incomes rose because they increased their customary charges and because they no longer applied a sliding scale of fees to low-income aged clients (Price and Horowitz 1967). For middle-class patients the inflation in medical costs, particularly for illnesses that required a relatively long stay in a hospital, outdistanced the resources of the typical family. A partial reversal in the upward trend was effected through so-called Health Maintenance Organizations, which charge a fixed fee whether clients are sick or well. The principle gives doctors a powerful incentive to provide care good enough to prevent the development of serious ailments (Rothfeld 1973). The concept overlaps what is now termed **preventive medicine**, which is "not so much *preventive* as *social* medicine—concerned with interacting *social* variables." According to one survey, the physicians in this field are generalists rather than specialists, interested not only in the full range of medical topics but also in biostatistics and the organization of health services. Practitioners try to synthesize their skills with insights from social disciplines in order to achieve control of diseases not patient by patient but on a broad basis (Backett 1964).

Implicit in the criticisms of American medicine is frequently a comparison with the British system, and in a number of stimulating papers this contrast has been made explicit (Mechanic 1971; Glazer 1971; Klein 1972). The comparisons are often difficult to interpret, but some facts are well established. The American system is far more expensive: in the United States expenditures for health absorbed 7.0 percent of the national income in the early 1960s and 8.2 percent in the late 1960s, growing by 10.4 percent per year; and in Britain the comparable figures were 5.0, 6.0, and 9.2. Britain has fewer doctors but more nurses per unit of population, yet one symptom of the "crisis" in the United States is generally the alleged shortage of physicians. One solution, in the words of a planning council that Glazer quotes, would be to redefine "many health service tasks so that lesser trained personnel can take them on"; but it is a remedy seemingly needed as much in Britain as in the United States. A far larger proportion of the costs in Britain is paid out of general taxes, but the lack of the mild deterrent that a "reasonable" fee would mean has resulted, as we have seen, in overloading doctors with unsick clients. Nor is there a necessary and continuing relation between rising income and improved health care: as Lerner noted in his discussion of the complex range of what determines good health, on balance the American working class is better off than those with higher incomes (cf. Klarman 1974).

DECLINE OF MORTALITY IN UNDERDEVELOPED COUNTRIES

The death rate, the number of deaths per 1,000 population, requires both vital statistics and a census count. Even for those underdeveloped areas with a reasonably accurate census, therefore, it is often impossible to calculate it directly, since underregistration is still generally too great. The mortality of such countries can be estimated, however, from the age structure in successive census years. Using this method, Davis (1951: 36) concluded that India's death rate before 1920 fluctuated between 40 and 50 and that after that date it fell off to an average of 36.3 in 1921–31, and 31.2 in 1931–41. The precise reasons for this decline are hard to establish, since any explanation has to embrace medical, economic, political, and social factors. Some of the causes Davis suggested seem to be relevant mainly to an earlier period: the elimination of war and banditry, which was completed long before the decline began; improvement of the food supply, which was undertaken on a large scale from the middle of the 19th century on and was efficient enough by 1900 to prevent nationwide famines. The trend in diseases is difficult to analyze; up to 1945, 60 percent of all registered deaths in British India were acribed simply to "fever" and over 25 percent to a catch-all "other causes." Nevertheless, it is reasonable to suppose that three of the most important epidemic diseases—plague, smallpox, and cholera—became less important as causes of death.

The experience of British India is typical of a fairly large number of under-developed areas. At the beginning of usable records, crude death rates were generally around 45 or 50; and one can assume that still earlier, before the social order permitting the collection of statistics was established, even higher rates sometimes prevailed. During the several decades prior to World War II, mortality in various nonindustrial countries underwent a gradual decline, the consequence of a no less gradual improvement in the level of living (Bourgeois-Pichat and Pan 1956). Subsequent progress was faster than it had been in Western countries, for of course it was not necessary to duplicate the slow process by which each medical or technological innovation had been developed.

Ceylon

The most startling instance of a new pattern was in Ceylon, where the estimated expectation of life at birth increased from 43 years in 1946 to 52 in 1947. The gain achieved in this one year had taken half a century in most Western countries. This amazing decline in mortality seemed to derive essentially from one factor— DDT, an insecticide that had been developed during World War II, which when sprayed from airplanes over low-lying areas all but eliminated malaria, the principal cause of death, by killing the mosquitoes that carry it. "The anti-malaria campaign is estimated to have contributed 60 percent of the rise in the rate of [Ceylon's] population growth since the war, resulting in a population size that by the end of 1960 was a million larger than it otherwise would have been" (Newman 1965: 69). But this interpretation has been challenged by a number of other analysts (Frederiksen 1960, 1961; Meegama 1967), with a response from Newman (1970). The differences among them are interesting,

Paul Herman Müller (1899–1965), Swiss chemist, who won the Nobel prize in 1948 for his discovery of DDT (*World Health Organization*).

for they highlight the difficulties in interpreting what at first appeared to be a simple cause–effect relation.

Malaria was virtually eliminated, all three agree, as a cause of death. However, since before the war and after it almost three-quarters of the population lived in nonmalarial areas, this direct effect was not in itself sufficient to explain the extraordinary decline in mortality. In view of the primitive reporting of diseases in Ceylon, it was hardly possible to specify the changes in mortality by cause of death. Two frequently cited causes of death are *rathe* (literally, "redness"), loosely applied to a variety of symptoms that may or may not be related to the fatal disease, and *mandama* (literally, "wasting"), under which are subsumed food-deficiency states. "'*Grahaniya*,' which . . . was at one time the name of a she-demon who pursued the lives of young children, now appears to be a synonym for '*mandama*' and is coded as such" (Padley 1959). Newman (1965: 78–79) stressed the indirect effects of the spraying—the reduced incidence of other insect-borne diseases and especially the mitigation of the debility that malaria brings to those it does not kill. Frederiksen and Meegama emphasized that the food shortages during the war were suddenly eased at its end; for example, the importation of milk and milk products almost doubled from 1945 to 1946. The number of hospitals on the island increased from an average of 146 in 1941–46 to an average of 247 in 1947–50, the number of maternity homes from 26 to 79, the number of midwives from 492 to 951, the number of health centers from 476 to 634, the number of pregnant women under care in centers from 126,125 to 288,646 (Meegama 1967). The crucial test, it would seem, is to determine what would have been the course of Ceylon's death rate if only malaria had been brought under control without these other measures. According to Newman, the control by spraying was just as effective in reducing mortality in British Guiana, where the high incidence of the disease had been the consequence of agricultural practices rather than natural conditions (see also Mandle 1970). But according to Meegama, in Guatemala the contrary was true: from 1958 to 1959, the number of deaths reported as due to malaria fell sharply from 6,238 to 124, yet the general death rate was cut only from 21.3 to 17.3, and it remained more or less constant at that level for the subsequent decade.

Coupled with the decline in mortality, however one analyzes its causes, there was an appreciable increase in the fertility of Ceylon, due in part to the migration of young persons into previously malarial areas, in part to a change in the age structure. Newman (1965: 39) speculated that there may also have been a more direct relation, because of the decline in the number of malaria-related miscarriages; and one can plausibly argue as well that there may have been a higher incidence of marital coitus in a population no longer weakened by endemic malaria. Certainly the population grew at an alarming pace. "If the sequence of events in Ceylon," Frederiksen (1961) wrote, "had demonstrated that economic development is no longer a prerequisite for a decline in the death rate, it might have seemed plausible to postulate that modern public health measures would tend to reduce per-capita income as well as mortality." And that conclusion, however unwelcome it may be to a conscientious practitioner of public health, seems to follow from the record no matter how one interprets its background. Ceylon's work force, thus, will increase from 3.4 million in 1956 to an estimated 7.1 million in 1981, and unemployment was rising already in the early 1960s. According to an official of Ceylon's Department of National Planning, "the high rate of population growth observed recently in Ceylon imposes serious strains on the economy and restricts its capacity to expand rapidly" (Selvaratnam 1961).

The General Pattern

That the decline in Ceylon's death rate had nothing to do specifically with the country's culture, its social structure, or its economy is shown by the fact that the stupendous success achieved there was repeated elsewhere. In India, as another example, the incidence of malaria fell from more than 100 million cases annually before World War II to less than 50,000 in 1966. In Mauritius the remarkable government campaign to combat malaria resulted in a "spectacular drop in mortality within a year [that] almost precisely duplicated the pattern of postwar mortality control . . . in Ceylon" (Titmuss and Abel-Smith 1961: 49).

In the United States, a National Malaria Eradication Program was set up in 1946, and within a few years mortality from this cause, which had ranged between 200,000 and 400,000 annually, was eliminated completely. In 1955 the World Health Organization undertook to eradicate malaria altogether, and during the following decade almost $1 billion was spent on this momentous task. Of the total world population (excluding Communist China) of some 2.5 billion at the end of 1964, almost 1.6 billion lived in areas that were or had been malarious. According to WHO estimates, in the mid-1960s 28.5 percent of this latter population enjoyed a completely malaria-free environment and 46.3 percent could observe eradication in progress. Only 25.2 percent were in areas where such programs had not yet been started (Hinman 1966: 102).

The effort to eliminate malaria, which before World War II had been the world's most potent single cause of sickness and death, has not been without reverses. Spraying insecticides from airplanes, by far the cheapest means of mass control, was found to be less effective than hand spraying in and around homes. Of the roughly sixty species of Anopheles that transmit most of the world's malaria, some seventeen became highly resistant to both DDT and other insecticides that were substituted for it. Yet one researcher regarded this fact as no more than "annoying," for the development of still more deadly insecticides was under way (ibid.: 90). The spraying program worked best when supplemented with some new medicaments, especially chloroquine. In British Guiana, eight weeks after a law was passed requiring the admixture of some chloroquine into all salt sold in the country, no new cases of the disease appeared. But this miracle was also short-lived; a strain of malaria evolved that proved to be resistant to this new specific, and the American servicemen in Vietnam down with malaria were treated with that old standby, quinine. It was also found that man is susceptible to monkey malaria, so that even if the disease is eradicated in the entire world population of humans, reservoirs of infection would remain among their simian cousins (Gilmore 1966). A more startling block was the campaign, especially in the United States, to prohibit the use of DDT. A large portion of a special issue of the *WHO Chronicle* (May 1971) was devoted to this threat; various experts agreed that biologic and genetic methods of vector control are generally not beyond the research stage. The cost of withdrawing DDT before the development of an equally efficient substitute, in their joint opinion, would be an immense resurgence of malaria.

In spite of such setbacks, the mass attack on human disease with insecticides is as significant an innovation as the development of Western public sanitation a century ago. It is true that the wholesale destruction of insect life inevitably disturbs the ecology of any area, often to the detriment of man, but in this war the odds are that scientific ingenuity will outwit the blind adaptations of nature. Malaria control can be started with a mass assault, but to be completely successful this must be followed up with a continuous, careful check of the infected areas and populations—the kind of program likely to succeed fully only in a country with a stable and effective government. Yet it is also true that, since antimalarial campaigns have been carried out largely through such international agencies as WHO, they are independent of whether any particular country has the personnel, equipment, funds, and drive to exert these efforts itself.

A second postwar development, potentially no less important than insecticides,

An Indian eradication team spraying insecticide in a malarial area (*P. N. Sharma—World Health Organization*).

is the use of sulfa compounds and antibiotics to combat still other diseases on a mass scale. Trachoma, endemic syphilis, yaws (Hinman 1966: chaps. 11–12), as well as infections better known to the West, yield to such treatment readily. Peasants all over the world who know nothing of modern medicine in any other sense have become quite familiar with penicillin. These preparations are rather expensive, but the cost of both supplying and dispensing them is generally borne in large part by advanced countries, acting through the dozen international agencies helping to reduce mortality in underdeveloped areas.

One of the first major diseases that modern nations were able to control completely among their own populations was smallpox. With the present world-wide vaccination campaign, the estimated number of cases had been cut from 500,000 in 1951 to 50,000 in 1965. An extended program adopted by the WHO

Assembly in 1966 had as its objective the acceleration of past efforts and the complete elimination of the disease in one more decade, and in 1973 the United States and several other countries discontinued compulsory vaccination. Indeed, some epidemiologists were dubious about the new policy, for it meant that the disease might spread quickly in a susceptible population. But they represented a minority in the profession.

As recently as 1942, the very idea was strange that it was feasible to eradicate infectious diseases throughout the world.

Many workers in the control of mosquito-borne disease have been reluctant to accept the idea that man has it in his power to eradicate any mosquito anywhere. ... Psychologically, it is apparently much easier to visualize the geometric increase of a species from a single gravid female to the millions of *gambiae* existing at one time in Northeast Brazil than it is to picture the reverse process, as all possible breeding places in a region are treated week after week with [insecticides]. ... The traditional ingrained philosophy that species eradication is impossible, ... and that when species disappear they do so only in response to "cosmic" or "biological" rather than man-made factors, is most persistent [F. L. Soper and D. B. Wilson, cited in Hinman 1966: 40].

Eradication goes beyond control. In practical terms, it means that a regularly tested area can be considered clear of a disease when no new case appears for

Table 15-6. Measures of Mortality, Selected Countries at Recent Dates

Country	Crude Death Rate	Infant Mortality Rate	Life Expectation at Birth		
			MALE		FEMALE
Sweden	10.5 (1969)	11.7 (1969)	71.69	(1969)	76.50
Netherlands	8.4 (1970)	12.7 (1970)	70.7	(1970)	76.5
New Zealand	8.8 (1970)	16.7 (1970)	68.67	(1965–67)	74.84
United States	9.3 (1971)	19.2 (1971)	66.8	(1969)	74.3
Japan	6.8 (1969)	14.2 (1969)	69.05	(1968)	74.30
Mexico	9.9 (1970)	68.5 (1970)	61.03	(1965–70)	63.73
Trinidad and Tobago	6.8 (1970)	39.7 (1970)	62.15	(1959–61)	66.33
Venezuela	6.8 (1969)	49[a] (1970)	61.2	(1960)	65.6
Mauritius	7.8 (1970)	57 (1970)	58.66	(1961–63)	61.86
Egypt	14.4 (1969)	119[a] (1969)	51.6	(1960)	53.8
Taiwan	5.1 (1969)	19 (1968)	65.84	(1965)	70.44
India	16.7 (1967–70)	124[b] (1965)	41.89	(1951–60)	40.55

[a] The U.N. Statistical Office considers these data to be of questionable reliability.
[b] Data corrected for underregistration as reported in S. Chandrasekhar, *Infant Mortality, Population Growth and Family Planning in India* (Chapel Hill: University of North Carolina Press, 1972), pp. 342–343.
SOURCES: National data as collated by the U.N. Statistical Office; *Population Index*, vol. **38** (1972), no. 3–4; United Nations, *Demographic Yearbook* (New York, various dates).

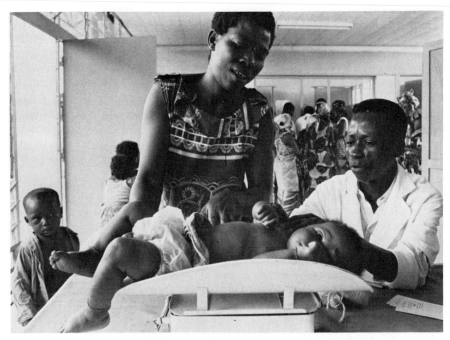

Maternal and infant death rates are high in many parts of Black Africa. In Zaïre (formerly Belgian Congo; *above*) and Uganda (*below*), centers are in operation that the WHO and UNICEF established jointly (*World Health Organization*).

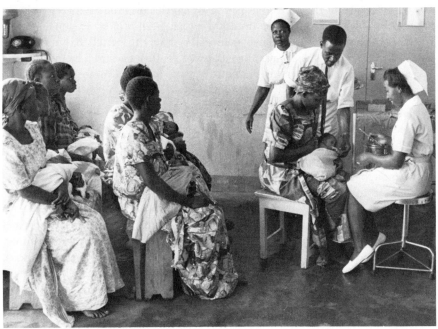

three years. In its literal sense, "pulling out by the roots," eradication implies action on a world scale, and while no disease has been totally defeated in this sense, the notion may no longer be utopian.

The consequences of such campaigns are illustrated in Table 15-6. For comparison the table lists mortality measures of three Western countries with the best controls (Sweden, the Netherlands, and New Zealand), as well as the United States and Japan. The underdeveloped countries are those on three continents with readily available recent data. When Western nations were at a social–economic level comparable to these latter countries, the infant mortality was of the order of 200. Because, without exception, the populations of under-developed areas include a very high percentage of children and young adults, there are proportionately few who die of old age. Thus, once the major causes of early death have been brought under control, the crude death rates are lower in many cases than in advanced industrial countries with excellent social-security systems. The life-expectation figures, which are independent of age structure, are often hardly more than 10 years less than those in advanced industrial countries. The remarkable decline in mortality has been associated in at least some instances with a rise in fertility (e.g., in Algeria, Tabutin 1974), rather than the conventionally anticipated lack of change or very slow decline.

The Social–Economic Context of Mortality Control

Before 1940 the effective operation of most death-control measures depended on a rise in the general welfare, which, when it occurred, took place slowly. The crucial difference in the post-1945 period is that this prior link between a rise in the level of living and a decline in mortality has been broken to some degree. How permanent are these declines in mortality likely to be (cf. Balfour 1956)? One way of getting an approximate answer to this question is by dividing diseases according to the mode of control that is feasible (Table 15-7).

1. Control or eradication of insect vectors depends almost wholly on the availability of funds to use appropriate technical facilities. When an insecticide is sprayed over a whole area from the air, the people affected are not involved at all, and when it is sprayed over the walls of each house, the occupants generally still have no voice in the matter. In the latter case, the skills involved are ordinarily slight enough so that the personnel needed for eradication campaigns can be recruited from the local work force. This is a type of control, in short, that can be exercised without any prior change in the cultural–economic level.

2. Immunization campaigns are also organized on a mass scale, and each person's decision whether or not to participate may be no more than nominal. If the preventive means is wholly effective (e.g., vaccination against smallpox), the eradication campaign can succeed with hardly any more direct involvement of the general population than in an effort to bring a species of insects under control. Some of the diseases listed, which require early diagnosis for effective treatment, come closer to the third category of clinical treatment.

Table 15-7.   Measures for Control or Eradication of Specified Diseases

Control or Eradication of Insect Vectors	Vaccination or Immunization	Clinical Treatment	Control of Human Wastes
Malaria	Smallpox	Yaws	Hookworm
Typhus	Typhus	Malaria	Bilharziasis
Plague	Whooping cough	Leprosy	Roundworm
Encephalitis	Poliomyelitis	Tuberculosis	Cholera
Onchocerciasis	Typhoid fever	Syphilis	Amebiasis
Filariasis	Tuberculosis	Bejel	Dysentery
Yellow fever	Influenza	Pinta	
	Cholera	Trachoma	
	Plague		
	Yellow fever		

SOURCE: U.S. Senate, Committee on Government Operations, *The Status of World Health*, 86th Congress, 1st Session, Senate Report 161, April 10, 1959, p. 58.

3. Some cures are so simple and effective (e.g., quinine for malarial symptoms) that no medical facilities are required. More generally, if diseases are to be controlled through clinical treatment, a sufficient number of highly trained professionals and quite elaborate facilities must be available to a widely dispersed population. Thus, any treatment that depends on a physician's direct diagnosis and care is linked to the shortage of physicians typical of underdeveloped countries. In Mauritius, to take one of the best studied small areas, there was one doctor per 4,500 persons—a relatively favorable ratio. There were more students in medical schools abroad than practicing physicians, but from past experience it was known that a large proportion would not return to the island after their graduation (Titmuss and Abel-Smith 1961: 178–181). In Africa generally, according to the regional director of WHO, the ratio in the mid-1960s was one doctor per 25,000 to 50,000 people. In twenty-six African countries that WHO surveyed, the total number of physicians *fell* from 4,700 in 1962 to 4,400 in 1965. In one country there were no doctors at all; in another the ratio was one to a million persons.

4. The control of human waste is likely to conflict with cultural patterns. Promiscuous defecation, with the subsequent transmission of pathogens to a new host via water, food, insects, or dust, is an important channel by which diseases are spread in most underdeveloped countries. In the West the chain was broken by public action—the construction of sewerage systems, the enactment of pure-food laws, and so on. To duplicate the physical equipment would be vastly more expensive than antimalarial campaigns, for instance, and not necessarily effective. "Mere provision of sanitary latrines is no solution to this problem, as field experience [in India] has shown. For latrines to be used, traditional behavior and attitudes must change as well" (Yankauer 1959).

In Ethiopia, a relatively favored country by African or even worldwide standards, some 300 physicians of about fifteen different nationalities operate one of "the best public health programs in Africa." The ratio of doctors to population is 1:10,000, or precisely the worldwide goal that WHO has set, and training facilities promise an increase in professional medical personnel. Yet the level of health is low, mainly because virtually all water supplies are contaminated.

People who do not know about germs and disease transmission are not concerned with wells and latrines. Even the capital city of almost half a million people has no sewerage system. . . . Probably the most efficient sanitation corps in the country is in the town of Harar, where each night large numbers of hyenas roam the streets and pick them clean. . . . Teachers are probably as important to the development of health in Ethiopia as are doctors [Torrey 1967].

In 1873, when the pioneer Max von Pettenkofer wrote on "the value of health to a city," he compared the crude death rate of his Munich, 33 per 1,000, with the 22 in London. The reasons for the difference, he said, were that the Londoners lived better, with more and better food per capita, better housing, and warm clothing, all organized under a spirit of *noblesse oblige*. Each of Munich's 170,000 inhabitants was sick an average of twenty days per year, and the total annual cost (taking the average earnings at a florin per day) was 3.4 million florins. This first crude attempt at a benefit/cost study of public health set a precedent in the West; how relevant is it to presently underdeveloped countries?

1. "Benefit/cost analysis for health studies . . . [is] ill adapted for areas where underemployment of labor is the critical characteristic. To diminish mortality and morbidity in such instances . . . serves markedly to retard rates of general economic growth" (Perlman 1966). This is the most general criticism: does it serve economic or humanitarian ends if the consequence of health programs is not an improvement of the level of life but merely an increase in the number who survive at subsistence or starve? One reply is that an effective public-health program may lay the basis for continued improvement, first of all by establishing a more vigorous people. Someone determined to retain "optimism and some faith" may even hold that "with encouragement and independence the people will resist a lowering of their standard of living" and therefore limit the size of their families (Balfour 1956). The eradication of malaria from Venezuela more than doubled the portion of that country that is habitable by humans (Arnaldo Gabaldón, quoted in Rubel 1966), and thus in effect may have doubled the potential food supply, space, and other values that a rapid population increase threatens.

To the question often asked, "Is malaria eradication a good thing, bearing in mind its contribution to the population explosion?" I would reply that this question cannot be answered scientifically, since it depends on one's judgment regarding the value of human life. My own feeling is that no one should take it on himself to withhold such effective, and marvelously cheap, methods of improving the general health of a people and, indeed, that the campaigns should be pressed with considerable vigor, since we now know that the indirect effects can be very great. But those embarking on such campaigns should be fully aware, and should make their governments aware, of the enormous demographic effects in several endemic countries, and should be prepared to push even harder for economic development in the decade or so following eradication [Newman 1965: 6].

2. If one accepts the moral stance that to save lives is good even if the consequent population increase creates problems that may be insoluble, the question remains, which lives shall be saved? In other words, given a certain amount of money, a certain number of personnel, to be used in health programs, how shall they be allocated in a country rife with preventable or curable diseases? If most of the effort is expended on the easiest, "marvelously cheap" means, are the quick returns likely to be permanent, or will the masses saved from death by malaria succumb to malnutrition and cholera? As the list of diseases in Table 15-7 suggests, a reduction in mortality that is effected by eradication of only some infectious diseases may mean not a permanent fall but a shift in the usual cause of death. This would be analogous to the shift to cancers and heart diseases that has taken place in advanced countries, but with potentially much more disastrous consequences.

3. Allocations can be made not only among different ways of spending money for public health but also between public health and such other benefits as, particularly, education. Like individual parents in the Dumont–Banks model, governments may choose quality rather than quantity. Under some circumstances an expenditure for education will result in a greater productive capacity than the same expenditure for public health (Enke 1963: 410–413). The direct benefits to mortality control may be greater from education once health projects advance to the point where the government requires the informed, intelligent participation of the general population. As we have seen, even a physician believes that in a country like Ethiopia the improvement of health depends as much on teachers as on doctors.

Taiwan

It is perhaps easier to understand the generalizations concerning the control of mortality if they are put in the context of one country's development. One might choose any underdeveloped area to illustrate various points, but perhaps the most remarkable record of effective death control, documented by excellent data, has taken place in Taiwan (cf. Petersen 1967). To duplicate this achievement is the best that any underdeveloped country could hope to do.

The Taiwan that Japan took over in 1895 was notorious as a malarial death-trap, with more rainfall than any part of Mainland China and in the lowlands a subtropical climate throughout the year. The island was poor in agriculture and almost without other economic activities, truly an inauspicious first colony in Japan's new empire. The crude death rate, not recorded, was certainly well above 40, possibly closer to 50. The conditions in the 19th century can be suggested by the record of the Japanese expeditionary forces. Of an army that landed on Taiwan in the spring of 1895, four out of five were either sick or dead of cholera, malaria, dysentery, typhus, pneumonia, or beri-beri by the end of September.

In 1896, the plague spread to Taiwan from Hong Kong, and over the next 22 years 30,000 persons were stricken and 24,000 died of it. It was wiped out largely by harsh but effective police power, through the isolation of patients, burning of contaminated houses, extermination of rats, and quarantine at ports. Serious outbreaks of cholera occurred in 1902, 1912, 1913, and 1920, but by the last of these years, the public-health system was sufficiently developed to prevent a recurrence. Compulsory vaccination, initiated in 1903, reduced the incidence of smallpox, of which the last serious outbreak was in 1918–20. By 1920, thus, three major epidemic diseases—the plague, cholera, and smallpox—were under effective control. In that year also the growing number of Western-style physicians exceeded for the first time the declining number of Chinese herbalists.

The most troublesome remaining problem was malaria, which had ranked as the first or second cause of death each year from the beginning of the century to 1916, after which date the Japanese measures began to pay off. They eventually set up as many as 200 antimalaria stations equipped to analyze the blood of local populations, and persons found to be infected were given free a compulsory treatment with quinine and mepacrine. When this costly program broke down during World War II, malaria epidemics again swept the island. Beginning in 1951, the new government undertook a continuous antimalaria program using the pesticides developed during the war and concentrating its efforts in areas that according to periodic checks of the school population were most seriously affected. The incidence of malaria has been reduced to a few dozen cases, and it has all but disappeared as a cause of death. As elsewhere in the world, the control of this disease has contributed also to the improvement in general health and the reduction of mortality from other causes.

In the late 1960s and early 1970s, Taiwan's crude death rate was around 5 per 1,000, or the lowest in the world. How accurate is this astounding datum? Apart from the war period, registration has in general been reasonably complete and accurate, but the reporting of infant deaths has been deficient, mainly because of the effect of folk beliefs that persist in rural areas. To speak of a dead child is a bad omen for the living ones. Parents should not grieve for a child that dies before the age of 12, for whom neither a coffin nor a funeral service is appropriate by traditional usage. According to field studies in three townships, in the late 1950s the corrected infant mortality rate was of the order of 50 per 1,000 live births, and up to 30 percent of the infant deaths may not have been registered (Chow and Hsu 1960). If one assumes that later rates were deficient in the same proportion, the corrected crude death rate would be about one-tenth higher than the official one, or still an extremely low figure.

To have transformed a notorious death trap into a nation with the world's lowest death rate in about 70 years is a unique achievement. What generalizations does this experience suggest? (1) The prewar controls laid a broad base for effective utilization of postwar techniques. The precipitous decline in mortality that we have noted in Ceylon and elsewhere was not duplicated in Taiwan; there was rather a continuation of the earlier advances, which the war and Japan's defeat had interrupted. (2) Mortality control was based as much on political and social factors as on purely medical ones. The Japanese administrators established what an American analyst has termed "one of the most successful colonial programs in the world" (Barclay 1954: 7), and one important consequence was the institutionalization of effective public health. (3) The increase of population has become a serious problem, which the government has tried to mitigate by a family-planning program. (4) Even so, the island has enjoyed an enormous economic progress, based in part on monetary and technical assistance from the United States but more fundamentally on the ability of the Taiwanese to put this to good use. In mid-1965, since the economy was adjudged able to continue under its own momentum, American economic aid was discontinued after a "graduation" ceremony. The deterioration of Nationalist China's diplomatic position culminated in 1971–72 with the expulsion from the United Nations and President Nixon's journey to Peking; but this setback did not interrupt the continuing economic advance. Subsequently the Taiwan government signed a contract to have its first integrated steel mill built by Vöest of Austria, and when Philips Gloeilampenfabrieken opened a factory to make television picture tubes, it became the island's largest single foreign investor.

SUMMARY

According to the scattered data available from the beginning of the 19th century, the average expectation of life at birth in Western Europe and its overseas extensions was 35 to 40 years. In the most favored nations the present figure is double that. The major causes of the improvement in the early and middle decades of the century were general rather than specific—public sanitation, better personal hygiene, the overall rise in the level of living, as well as vaccination against smallpox. In the next period there was a great improvement in cures of most infectious diseases, a process that reached its climax with the development of antibiotics. Recent medical advances have also included progress in surgical techniques, particularly in obstetrics; in diagnosis and medicaments; and in institutional forms of care—blood banks, medical teams, group health insurance, and so on. The recent advances in death control, ignoring deaths associated with social disorganization, have almost eliminated all mortality before the age of 40.

Now that infectious diseases are relatively unimportant in mortality, they have been replaced by cancers, diseases of the heart, and fatal crimes and accidents.

This shift in the causes of death has meant that differentials by age, sex, and social group have also changed markedly. The sharpest decline was in the mortality of infants and young children, whereas for the advanced ages improvement in control of death has been at best slow and moderate. The difference in death rates between the sexes is large and can be expected to increase still more. All social differentials—by urban–rural residence, by social class or occupational group, by race—are converging. In the United States, that between whites and Negroes is still significant, in part because Negro mortality is tied in with a lower-class culture.

In the years since 1945 insecticides and antibiotics have made possible enormous advances in the mass control of mortality in underdeveloped countries. A major portion of the cost of these measures is ordinarily borne by Western countries, acting through international agencies. The death rate can fall, though of course not inevitably, to around 10 per 1,000 population irrespective of the culture, the economy, or the government. Until fairly recently a people did not achieve a higher average life expectation until this was earned—as it were— through better food, more healthful living conditions, and an economy able to carry more people. Now the very fact that people are kept alive so easily makes it more difficult to realize these other goals.

CITED REFERENCES AND SUGGESTIONS FOR FURTHER READING

Some of the works listed at the end of Chapter 7 (pp. 272–278) can be recommended again. The compilation by Stolnitz (1955–56) is an especially able comparison of international trends. Concerning the place of the United States with respect to infant mortality, the several papers of Chase (1967, 1969, 1972) are indispensable. On the more specific comparison between the United States and Britain, the articles by Glazer (1971) and Mechanic and Faich (1970) dispel many of the myths once surrounding the National Health Service. Differentials by social class are competently analyzed by Moriyama and Guralnick (1956) and by Antonovsky (1967), but this traditional approach to the analysis of mortality was raised to another level by Lerner (1968).

The recent record of mortality in underdeveloped countries has seldom been analyzed in the round. Some of the difficulties of using the poor data to reach firm conclusions about the causes of the dramatic decline are illustrated by the debate between Newman (1965, 1970) and Frederiksen (1960, 1961) or Meegama (1967). The best book-length studies pertain to particular countries, such as those on India by Davis (1951) and Chandrasekhar (1972), with only some chapters on mortality.

ALTMAN, LAWRENCE K. 1973. "Swedish Medicine Is Troubled," *New York Times*, December 23, 24, 25.

ANTONOVSKY, AARON. 1967. "Social Class, Life Expectancy and Overall Mortality," *Milbank Memorial Fund Quarterly*, **45**, 31–73.

*_____. 1968. "Social Class and the Major Cardiovascular Diseases," *Journal of Chronic Diseases*, **21**, 65–106.

BACKETT, E. MAURICE. 1964. "The Teaching of Preventive Medicine in Europe and in the United States," *Milbank Memorial Fund Quarterly*, **42**, 22–44.

BALFOUR, MARSHALL C. 1956. "Some Considerations Regarding the Permanence of Recent Declines in Mortality in Underdeveloped Areas," in Milbank Memorial Fund 1956.

BARCLAY, GEORGE W. 1954. *A Report on Taiwan's Population*. Princeton, N.J.: Office of Population Research.

BATTISTELLA, ROGER M., and THEODORE E. CHESTER. 1973. "Reorganization of the National Health Service: Background and Issues in England's Quest for a Comprehensive–Integrated Planning and Delivery System," *Milbank Memorial Fund Quarterly*, **51**, 489–530.

BOURGEOIS-PICHAT, JEAN, and CHIA-LIN PAN. 1956. "Trends and Determinants of Mortality in Underdevoloped Areas," in Milbank Memorial Fund 1956.

BURGESS, ALEX M., JR., THEODORE COLTON, and OSLER L. PETERSON. 1966. "Avoidable Mortality: Some Practical Aims for Regional Medical Programs," *Archives of Environmental Health*, **13**, 794–798.

BURNIGHT, ROBERT G., and PARKER G. MARDEN. 1967. "Social Correlates of Weight in an Aging Population," *Milbank Memorial Fund Quarterly*, **45**, 75–92.

CHANDRASEKHAR, S. 1972. *Infant Mortality, Population Growth, and Family Planning in India*. Chapel Hill: University of North Carolina Press.

*CHASE, HELEN C. 1967. *International Comparison of Perinatal and Infant Mortality: The United States and Six West European Countries*. National Center for Health Statistics, Series 3, no. 6. Washington, D.C.: U.S. Government Printing Office.

––––––. 1969. "Registration Completeness and International Comparisons of Infant Mortality," *Demography*, **6**, 425–433.

––––––. 1972. "The Position of the United States in International Comparisons of Health Status," *American Journal of Public Health*, **62**, 581–589.

CHOW LIEN-PIN, and HSU SHIH-CHU. 1960. "Statistical Studies on Mortality in Taiwan During the Last Decade," *Industry of Free China* (Taipei), **14**, 7–34.

CROOG, SYDNEY H. 1961. "Ethnic Origins, Educational Level, and Responses to a Health Questionnaire," *Human Organization*, **20**, 65–69.

DARIC, JEAN. 1951. "Mortality, Occupation, and Socio-economic Status," U.S. National Office of Vital Statistics, *Vital Statistics—Special Reports*, **33**, no. 10. Washington, D.C.: U.S. Government Printing Office.

DAVIS, KINGSLEY. 1951. *The Population of India and Pakistan*. Princeton, N.J.: Princeton University Press.

DUBLIN, LOUIS I., ALFRED J. LOTKA, and MORTIMER SPIEGELMAN. 1949. *Length of Life: A Study of the Life Table*, rev. ed. New York: Ronald.

ECKSTEIN, HARRY. 1958. *The English Health Service: Its Origins, Structure, and Achievements*. Cambridge, Mass.: Harvard University Press.

ELLIS, JOHN M. 1957. "Socio-economic Differentials in Mortality from Chronic Diseases," *Social Problems*, **5**, 30–36.

ENKE, STEPHEN. 1963. *Economics for Development*. Englewood Cliffs, N.J.: Prentice-Hall.

FOMON, SAMUEL J., and THOMAS A. ANDERSON, editors. 1972. *Practices of Low-Income Families in Feeding Infants and Small Children, with Particular Attention to Cultural Subgroups*. Washington, D.C.: U.S. Maternal and Child Health Service.

FREDERIKSEN, HARALD. 1960. "Malaria Control and Population Pressure in Ceylon," *Public Health Reports*, **75**, 865–868.

FREDERIKSEN, HARALD. 1961. "Determinants and Consequences of Mortality Trends in Ceylon," *Public Health Reports*, 76, 659–663.

GILMORE, C. P. 1966. "Malaria Wins Round 2," *New York Times Magazine*, September 25.

*GINZBERG, ELI. 1969. *Men, Money, and Medicine.* New York: Columbia University Press.

*GLAZER, NATHAN. 1971. "Paradoxes of Health Care," *Public Interest*, no. 22, pp. 62–77.

GURALNICK, LILLIAN, and ANN JACKSON. 1967. "An Index of Unnecessary Deaths," *Public Health Reports*, 82, 180–182.

HART, JULIAN TUDOR. 1972. "Data on Occupational Mortality, 1959–63," *The Lancet*, no. 7743, pp. 192–193.

*HIGGS, ROBERT. 1973. "Mortality in Rural America, 1870–1920: Estimates and Conjectures," *Explorations in Economic History*, 10, 177–195.

HINMAN, E. HAROLD. 1966. *World Eradication of Infectious Diseases.* Springfield, Ill.: Thomas.

KIRK, DUDLEY. 1946. *Europe's Population in the Interwar Years.* League of Nations. Princeton, N.J.: Princeton University Press.

*KLARMAN, HERBERT E. 1974. "Major Public Initiatives in Health Care," *Public Interest*, no. 34, pp. 106–123.

KLEIN, RUDOLF. 1972. "The Political Economy of National Health," *Public Interest*, no. 26, pp. 112–125.

LEFCOWITZ, MYRON J. 1973. "Poverty and Health: A Re-examination," *Inquiry*, 10, 3–13.

*LERNER, MONROE. 1968. "The Level of Physical Health of the Poverty Population: A Conceptual Reappraisal of Structural Factors," *Medical Care*, 6, 355–367.

LINKLATER, JOHN. 1973. "The Collapse of the NHS," *The Spectator*, January 6, pp. 26–27.

LOGAN, W. P. D. 1954. "Social Class Variations in Mortality," *Public Health Reports*, 69, 1217–1223.

MANDLE, JAY R. 1970. "The Decline in Mortality in British Guiana, 1911–1960," *Demography*, 7, 301–315.

MECHANIC, DAVID. 1968. "General Medical Practice in England and Wales: Its Organization and Future," *New England Journal of Medicine*, 279, 680–689.

———. 1971. "The English National Health Service: Some Comparisons with the United States," *Journal of Health and Social Behavior*, 12, 18–29.

*———, and RONALD G. FAICH. 1970. "Doctors in Revolt: The Crisis in the English National Health Service," *Medical Care*, 8, 442–455.

MEEGAMA, S. A. 1967. "Malaria Eradication and Its Effect on Mortality Levels," *Population Studies*, 21, 207–237.

*MILBANK MEMORIAL FUND. 1956. *Trends and Differentials in Mortality.* New York.

*MILLER, MICHAEL H. 1973. "Who Receives Optimal Medical Care?" *Journal of Health and Social Behavior*, 14, 176–182.

MONTEIRO, LOIS A. 1973. "Expense Is No Object: Income and Physician Visits Reconsidered," *Journal of Health and Social Behavior*, 14, 99–115.

MORIYAMA, I. M., and L. GURALNICK. 1956. "Occupational and Social Class Differences in Mortality," in Milbank Memorial Fund 1956.

MYERS, ROBERT J. 1966. "The Impact of Medicare on Demography," *Demography*, 3, 545–547.

NEWMAN, PETER. 1965. *Malaria Eradication and Population Growth, with Special Reference to Ceylon and British Guiana*. Bureau of Public Health Economics, Research Series, no. 10. Ann Arbor: University of Michigan School of Public Health.

———. 1970. "Malaria Control and Population Growth," *Journal of Development Studies*, 6, 133–158.

PADLEY, RICHARD. 1959. "Cause-of-Death Statements in Ceylon: A Study in Levels of Diagnostic Reporting," *Bulletin of the World Health Organization*, 20, 677–695.

PERLMAN, MARK. 1966. "On Health and Economic Development: Some Problems, Methods, and Conclusions Reviewed in a Perusal of the Literature," *Comparative Studies in Society and History*, 8, 433–448.

PETERSEN, WILLIAM. 1967. "Taiwan's Population Problem," in S. Chandrasekhar, editor, *Asia's Population Problems*. London: Allen & Unwin.

PRICE, DOROTHY P., and LOUCELE A. HOROWITZ. 1967. "Trends in Medical Care Prices," *Social Security Bulletin*, 30, 13–28.

RAO, S. L. N. 1973. "On Long-term Mortality Trends in the United States, 1850–1968," *Demography*, 10, 405–419.

REED, LOUIS S. 1965. *The Extent of Health Insurance Coverage in the United States*. Social Security Administration, Research Report no. 10. Washington, D.C.: U.S. Government Printing Office.

ROBERTS, ROBERT E., GEORGE W. MCBEE, and ELEANOR J. MACDONALD. 1970. "Social Status, Ethnic Status, and Urban Mortality: An Ecological Analysis," *Texas Reports on Biology and Medicine*, 28, 13–28.

ROTHFELD, MICHAEL B. 1973. "Sensible Surgery for Swelling Medical Costs," *Fortune*, April, pp. 110–119.

RUBEL, ARTHUR J. 1966. "The Role of Social Science Research in Recent Health Programs in Latin America," *Latin American Research Review*, 2, 37–56.

*SAMORA, JULIAN, LYLE SAUNDERS, and RICHARD F. LARSON. 1961. "Medical Vocabulary Knowledge Among Hospital Patients," *Journal of Health and Human Behavior*, 2, 83–92.

———, ———, and ———. 1962. "Knowledge about Specific Diseases in Four Selected Samples," *Journal of Health and Human Behavior*, 3, 176–185.

SAVITZ, HARRY AUSTRYN. 1952. "The Cultural Background of the Patient as Part of the Physician's Armamentarium," *Journal of Abnormal and Social Psychology*, 47, 245–254.

*SELVARATNAM, S. 1961. "Some Implications of Population Growth in Ceylon," *Ceylon Journal of Historical and Social Studies* (Colombo), 4, 33–49.

SHAPIRO, SAM, EDWARD R. SCHLESINGER, and ROBERT E. L. NESBITT, JR. 1968. *Infant, Perinatal, Maternal, and Childhood Mortality in the United States*. Cambridge, Mass.: Harvard University Press.

STEWART, WILLIAM H. 1967. "The Positive Impact of Medicare on the Nation's Health Care Systems," *Social Security Bulletin*, 30, 9–12 and 50–51.

*STOCKWELL, EDWARD G. 1961. "Socio-economic Status and Mortality in the United States," *Public Health Reports*, 76, 1081–1086.

*STOLNITZ, GEORGE J. 1955 and 1956. "A Century of International Mortality Trends," *Population Studies*, 9, 24–55; 10, 17–42.

TABUTIN, DOMINIQUE. 1974. "Mortalité infantile et juvénile en Algérie du Nord," *Population*, **29**, 41–60.

TAEUBER, CONRAD, and IRENE B. TAEUBER. 1958. *The Changing Population of the United States*. New York: Wiley.

TITMUSS, RICHARD M., and BRIAN ABEL-SMITH. 1961. *Social Policies and Population Growth in Mauritius*. London: Methuen.

TORREY, E. FULLER. 1967. "Health Services in Ethiopia," *Milbank Memorial Fund Quarterly*, **45**, 275–285.

UNITED NATIONS. 1954. *Foetal, Infant and Early Childhood Mortality*, 2 vol. Population Studies, no. 13. New York.

U.S. SOCIAL SECURITY ADMINISTRATION. 1964. *Social Security Programs Throughout the World*. Washington, D.C.: U.S. Government Printing Office.

WADE, SERENA E. 1970. "Trends in Public Knowledge About Health and Illness," *American Journal of Public Health*, **60**, 485–491.

WEST, HOWARD. 1967. "Health Insurance for the Aged: The Statistical Program," *Social Security Bulletin*, **30**, 3–16.

WHITNEY, JESSAMINE S. 1934. *Death Rates by Occupation, Based on Data of the U.S. Census, 1930*. New York: National Tuberculosis Association.

*YANKAUER, ALFRED. 1959. "An Approach to the Cultural Base of Infant Mortality in India," *Population Review*, **3**, 39–51.

FERTILITY, POPULATION INCREASE, AND ECONOMIC STAGNATION IN THE UNDERDEVELOPED WORLD

16

What is termed *industrialization* or *economic development* is never merely a change in techniques of production. Although an underdeveloped country that lacks basic scientific knowledge and ability can assimilate much so-called know-how, even minor technical innovations, if they are alien to a society, may eventually disrupt the institutional structure. In the long run, industrialization is possible only as part of a much deeper social change, and in the shorter run, the industrializing country acquires benefits but also the burdens of a painful transition. To appraise the social effects of industrialization, then, we cannot merely compare the birth rates, for example, of advanced and underdeveloped countries. Such a comparison implies that the transitional phase, which is the only one that the present generation will know, is too short and insignificant to be analyzed *per se*, and that once it is passed the social concomitants of the advanced economy will necessarily be the same as can be observed in presently developed countries. Neither assumption is well based.

That the fertility of underdeveloped countries has not fallen nearly so fast as their mortality is what we should expect from both the population history of the West and our knowledge of social behavior. Indeed, it would have been *more* amazing if the decline in Ceylon's death rate by one-third within a single year, to cite that example again, had been matched by a comparable decline in the birth rate. For no matter how underdeveloped areas vary in their cultural values, these generally include a hatred and fear of early death and thus a more or less willing acceptance of any life-saving technique that has proved its efficacy. Moreover, the acquiescence of each person is neither asked for nor required in the mass spraying of insecticides or often even mass inoculations. The control of fertility, on the contrary, must operate by influencing the personal behavior of individuals who are potential parents. It is a crucial question, then, what values underlie decisions concerning family size, and whether and how fast those values are changing.

We can try to come to grips with these matters with three quite different sets of data, on: (1) ideologies, (2) attitudes, and (3) social structure, each interpreted in terms of (4) demographic theory.

1. People's behavior is governed to some degree by religions, nationalist myths, or superstitions; and concerning these broad determinants there is a mass of written evidence available. But which of such norms actually influence behavior, and which are as effective as the Sermon on the Mount is in setting the pattern of life in Christian countries?

2. From survey data we can get attitudes of the actual participants in procreation toward immediately relevant issues like the number of children desired and the relative acceptance of various means of contraception. But are replies to such questionnaires frank and complete enough to give the analyst a reliable indicator of subsequent behavior?

3. Any constraint on individuals' acts generally derives less from an ideology than from their place in a social structure, and the differential analysis of fertility has therefore constituted the mainstay of research in advanced countries. But it is seldom possible merely to use the same categories (e.g., "urban" versus "rural") in an analysis of quite different cultures, and the sociological analysis of the fertility of underdeveloped countries is just beginning.

4. That fertility has seemingly risen in a number of underdeveloped countries contradicts the expectation from conventional theory, which must also be amended. Birth rates are changing in response to impersonal social–economic forces, as before, but in part also to governments' efforts to control family size; and this shift means that some of the postulates underlying earlier demographic theories are no longer valid.

In other words, the four types of data can each contribute to our understanding, but each has specific limitations. The high birth rates typical of nonindustrial societies constitute not only a massive social problem but one to which we have no assured answer. Programs designed to reduce fertility have occasionally been successful, but only in small, homogeneous countries with stable governments and advancing economies.

TRADITIONAL IDEOLOGIES AND MODERNIZING MOVEMENTS

When a Brahmin bride bows to her elders, the traditional blessing is, "Be the mother of eight sons and may your husband live long." In Pakistan, children are referred to as "blessings of God." In Latin America the cult of *machismo* (literally, "maleness") induces men to prove their virility with a large progeny (see p. 196). How relevant are such common ceremonies, symbols, and myths to actual attitudes and behavior? Until recently most Western demographers assumed that, indeed, the world's peasant masses saw reproduction in a traditional perspective. So long as out of every four infants born one died in its first year and a considerable additional proportion before maturity, the society could continue to exist only with a value system and institutional structure that effectively encouraged a generous procreation. Children were said to be economic assets: set to work at an early age, each offspring later helped provide for his parents in their declining years. "The head of a large family gains social importance in the rural setting of India and the prospect of children to look after him in his old age adds to his feeling of security both economically and emotionally" (Mathen 1962). Thus, the weight of traditionalist thought and the logic of functionalist theory together supported the notion that parents wanted the large families characteristic of peasant societies.

Yet both the premises leading to this conclusion are subject to reasonable challenge. According to the same analyst of Indian data, just because of the high incidence of infant and child mortality—"the household survey showed that at least 50 percent lost one or more children"—persons were said to be more favorably disposed to a family-planning program (ibid.). And while the norms taught by the great religions of Asia reinforce, as do their European counterparts, the high valuation of family life and a numerous progeny, there is typically a far greater ambiguity on the key issue of contraception than in Christian fundamentalism of whatever denomination.

Religion

The frank sexuality in **Hinduism** is matched by the call to *dama*, or self-restraint. "We should reduce our wants and be prepared to suffer in the interest of truth. Austerity, chastity, solitude and silence are the way to attain self-control" (Radhakrishnan 1953: 109). Among the most orthodox, marital coitus is a semireligious rite, often associated with the recital of hymns and prayers, the wearing of talismans and charms. "Sexual contact in wedlock is only permissible specifically for procreation of the species, coitus otherwise being considered vulgar, if not sinful" (Shah 1961). Accepting this Hindu heritage, a secularist like Gandhi—once he was too old to be driven by the sexual urge himself—stipulated absolute continence as the only permissible means of limiting births. In a discussion on how to cope with India's population pressure, he once remarked that "perhaps we need some good epidemics." He laughed as he said this, for a professed humanist cannot offer such a proposal seriously; but he *was* serious in holding to his absolute opposition to contraceptives, no matter what the demographic consequences (Fischer 1942: 89; cf. Gandhi 1959).

Yet compare this passage from the Upanishads themselves:

Now the woman whom one desires [with the thought] "may she not conceive," after inserting the member in her, joining mouth to mouth, he should first inhale and then exhale and say, "with power, with semen I reclaim the semen from you." Thus she comes to be without semen. . . .

Now the woman whom one desires [with the thought] "may she conceive," after inserting the member in her, joining mouth to mouth, he should first exhale and then inhale and say "with power, with semen I deposit semen in you." Thus she becomes pregnant [Radhakrishnan 1953: 324].

Manifestly, the desire of the man either to ensure conception or to prevent it is seen as licit, though the efficacy of the method may be questioned.

Buddhism can be represented by the denomination dominant in Ceylon, Burma, Thailand, and Cambodia (Hinayana, or Theravada).

Buddhist texts say nothing directly upon the subject of contraception, nor do they even provide such injunctions as "Be fruitful and multiply." . . . Villagers [in Ceylon] generally look upon any conscious attempt to prevent conception other than through restraint as being "unnatural," "sinful," . . . [but] Buddhist priests [have not] concerned themselves [Ryan 1954].

A questionnaire on this subject was administered to eighty-six monks and priests, who split sharply according to how much schooling they had had. Not one of the best educated found in Buddhism any opposition to contraception, but 41 percent of a middle group and 90 percent of the least educated disagreed, asserting usually that willfully to prevent birth is tantamount to killing (ibid.).

Confucianism was in China the principal ethical underpinning of what is ordinarily termed a familistic culture. Under the traditional Chinese system, it is often stated, "whenever economic circumstances permit, the family membership will continue to grow" (Lee 1953). As we have noted already (pp. 203–204), noneconomic factors cannot be entirely dismissed, and the economic pressure that reduced normative obligations was a constant of Chinese society. It is true that Confucian scholars condemned abortion and infanticide (the modes of population control of, respectively, the urban gentry and the peasantry), but to little effect. The transformation of Chinese familism in traditional Japan (see p. 456) indicates how susceptible the system is to a new environment.

Islam also emphasizes that offspring, especially sons, are essential to a marriage. A barren wife is a hapless creature, who to this day may induce her husband to take a second spouse, either in the superstitious hope that she herself will then become fruitful, or with the simple desire to bring children into her home (Patai 1959: 79). That the family line must be continued does not necessarily imply, however, a ban on contraception. "The stand of the Koran on methods of fertility control is not specific and . . . is subject to various interpretations" (Yaukey 1961: 7). *Azal*, a man's desire that his wife shall not conceive, is permitted in one saying ascribed to the Prophet, forbidden in another; the two rules are said to relate to different situations. One verse of the Koran reads, "And do not slay your children for fear of poverty. We give them sustenance and yourselves, too." Some authorities interpret this ban to include prospective children as well as infants already born (Lorimer 1954: 186–187). Among the Egyptian fellahs that Gabriel Baer interviewed in 1956, it was the almost unanimous opinion that their religion forbids the planning of families (Schieffelin 1967: 37). On the other hand, as early as 1936 the birth-control movement succeeded in obtaining a *futwa* (that is, a formal legal opinion on canon law) from the Mufti of Egypt permitting the use of contraception. A more recent authoritative Islamic stance was given in a reply to a physician's question by His Excellency Ayatollah (a title of the highest ecclesiastical order) Hajji (one who has made a pilgrimage to Mecca) Sheikh Bahaedin Mahallati. The exchange, in 1964, was as follows:[1]

I request that you send me a formal answer to the following question: Would you permit a physician temporarily to prescribe drugs or contraceptive devices [in order to prevent] excessive human reproduction, and is this religiously licit?—Dr. Mohammad Sarram.

In the name of God: From the standpoint of the divine law, the use of drugs or contraceptive devices, especially if it is temporary, to control human fertility does not seem to be illicit if this practice does not damage the female's fecundity and make her barren.—Bahaedin Mahallati.

The great non-Western religions, in short, are ambivalent on the question of whether contraception is permissible, so that typically their moral teachings become explicit only by exegesis. The influence of the West in reinforcing modernist ideas might have resolved the ambiguity, but the most direct transmission of Europe's ethical dicta was through missionaries, typically even less receptive to new ideas than their counterparts at home. In any case, Christian pretensions to a monopoly of religious truth often emerged as partisan support of the imperial power or the white race, and each denomination's proselytizing was undercut by its Christian competitors, so that the long-term religious effects of Asian and African missionaries may be close to nil (Panikkar n.d.: Part VII).

The only Western religion with a significant hold in underdeveloped areas is the Roman Catholicism of Latin America. The faith espoused in the Spanish colonies had been that of the Counterreformation—fervently orthodox, crusading, resourceful. In the revolutions that established the republics, the Church was indifferent or, more often, hostile to nationalist aspirations; Leo XII distributed an encyclical in support of "our dearly beloved son Ferdinand, the Catholic King of the Spains." Until very recently, this history set a pattern in Latin America, with the Church generally the defender of reaction and all who hoped for a better world often pushed to an anticlerical stance (Arciniegas 1967). Following the disarray of Catholic orthodoxy on the question of birth control (see pp. 520–524), the Church in Latin America has begun to reflect all the positions in the continuing dispute. According to surveys in three large cities, a majority of Catholic women, whether or not they were actively involved in their religion, used contraceptive means condemned by the Church (Table 16-1). In three cities of Chile, just under one woman in four interviewed had had at least one induced abortion; 42 percent of the admissions to hospital emergency services were abortion cases. When these data were published in 1962, they prompted parallel studies in a number of other Latin American countries, which uncovered abortion rates ranging from 75 percent of all pregnancies in Uruguay to 15 percent in Guatemala (Stycos 1966). As a Colombian priest noted, the difficulties of "millions of well intentioned couples" in reconciling the licit

---

[1] I am indebted to Dr. Ali A. Paydarfar for a translation from the Arabic original.

Table 16-1. Percentage of Married Catholic Women Who Have Used Contraceptives Forbidden by the Church, Three Latin American Cities, 1960s

Frequency of Church Attendance	Panama City	Rio de Janeiro	San José, Costa Rica
Once a week or more	59	58	65
Once or twice a month	64	47	54
Several times a year	—	51	53
Once a year	58	60	62
Once in several years	—	64	78
Never	50	58	72

SOURCE: Carmen A. Miró and Ferdinand Rath, "Preliminary Findings of Comparative Fertility Surveys in Three Latin American Countries," *Milbank Memorial Fund Quarterly*, **43**, no. 4, Part 2 (1965), 36–62.

ends of marriage "are leading to conflict, perversion of conscience, abandonment of the Church, and a loss of harmony between the spouses" (Pérez 1966).

Nationalism

While the general mass of the population has continued to follow a folk or religious tradition, most of the leaders of the underdeveloped countries have been driven by a secularist faith in nationalist aspirations. In the view of many analysts, nationalism is a *sine qua non* of industrialization, even though it works both ways (cf. pp. 456–457). In the new nations it tends to block modernization because: (1) it reinforces the already existent hostility to the West, the prime source of modernizing institutions; (2) it is often based on an exaggerated reaffirmation of ancient preindustrial models; and (3) the large element of myth in protestations of superiority and reconstructions from a prehistoric past blocks the ready development of rational solutions to the problems of societal transition (e.g., Stycos 1963). And, in particular, (4) the shift of fervor from religion to a new credo does not dispel the ambiguity concerning contraception.

India, for instance, established a courageous and expensive birth-control program, but it took some time for it to get under way. In the first years after independence, most national leaders were either opposed to contraception on moral grounds (especially Gandhi and his followers) or, at best, indifferent to family planning as a social program.

In the first flush of national awakening, Indian leaders became acutely conscious of the poverty of the masses and they believed that it was increasing year after year and that its main cause was economic exploitation by Britain. To this accusation the British reply was that the growing poverty of the people of India was a result of population growth and the people of India were themselves responsible for it. This gave the cue to the nationalist leaders to argue that . . . India was a land of infinite and rich natural resources which could support a much larger population at a considerably higher standard of living than that obtaining in recent times. . . . This [dispute] prevented for a very long time an objective appraisal of the population situation [Sovani 1952].

Reflecting this point of view, Nehru in 1948 termed India "an underpopulated country": "If we increase our production, agricultural and other, if this population is put to work for production, then we are not overpopulated" (quoted in ibid.). Only three years later was a population policy held to be "essential to planning." Apparently some remnant of the earlier position has persisted. China's invasion of India in 1962, thus, made Indians less willing to accept the government's birth-control program. "With 700 million marching on the northern frontier, people began wondering why they should reduce their population" (Dr. K. N. Rao, in Muramatsu and Harper 1965: 62).

Not merely in India but in almost all the new nations, the ruling elite is to some degree motivated by what has been termed a kind of ideological *machismo*—"the feeling on the part of the intellectual classes that to reduce or to slow down the rate of population growth or the fertility of a nation is a kind of cultural castration," which offends all who believe that because the nation is good, therefore it must grow (J. M. Stycos, in ibid.: 180). In a statement summarizing a survey of Mexican males, population growth was equated with power and prestige:

Mexico was once weak, divided and helpless, her people were dominated by alien conquerors, and she was underpopulated, her lands were taken by foreign invaders. But Mexico is growing. There is strength in numbers. True, numbers bring problems, but we are forging these numbers into a great nation [Stycos 1965].

To N. Viera Altamirano, the influential editor of San Salvador's *El Diario de Hoy*, population is an almost mystical force in promoting Latin American grandeur. "To populate America is to civilize America. To oppose population is to oppose civilization" (quoted in ibid.). When nationalism is tinged with socialism, as it so often is in underdeveloped countries, the Marxist hostility to the planning of fertility can reinforce this kind of sentiment.

In Argentina, as a final example, the government announced its concern that the growth of the country's population was far below that of its Latin American neighbors. According to *Las Bases*, a magazine that often reflects the opinion of Juan Perón, "When the year 2000 is at hand, we will have overpopulated neighbors with great food problems, and we, on the contrary, will have three million square kilometers of land, practically unpopulated. We will not have the labor to work this immense and rich territory, and if we do not do it there will be others who will" (*New York Times*, March 17, 1974). In the hope of doubling the country's population over the next generation, the government issued a decree restricting the sale of contraceptive pills.

Planned Parenthood

In the West traditional and religious opposition to the use of contraceptives had been confronted by a countermovement, neo-Malthusianism, which evolved its own rationale for the ethics it advocated. The birth-control associations established in many underdeveloped countries have all had a short life. In Pakistan, for instance, from the founding of the first private family-planning group (in Lahore in 1952) to the institution of a government program (Rs. 30.5 million allocated in the Second Five-Year Plan, 1961–65) was less than a decade. More fundamentally, the birth-control movement is not equipped to cope with the problems of underdeveloped areas.

Even in the West, wherever the use of contraceptives became general enough to dissipate conventional opposition, the transition was accompanied by a change in the character of the movement itself. In Britain the early emphasis on the economic effects of population growth gave way to a narrower concentration on family budgets or the health of the mother; political economists were supplanted by social workers or physicians; and in 1927 the role of the Malthusian League, which disbanded itself at a celebration dinner, was taken over by the Society for Constructive Birth Control, headed by Marie Stopes, a physician. A similar shift of emphasis, even if not accompanied by a change in organization, took place also in other countries, with the new value orientation indicated by the substitution of "planned parenthood" or "child spacing" for "neo-Malthusianism" or "birth control." Reflecting this transition, the international planned-parenthood movement tried to establish itself in underdeveloped countries "as a medical program, directed by medical personnel, dealing with medical problems" (Stycos 1962). This conventional approach helped a tiny westernized elite to control its reproduction, but it was almost irrelevant to the staggering problem of population growth on a scale unimagined by the 19th-century pioneers. In the late 1960s and early 1970s, echoing the views of demographers and ecologists and often extrapolating them to extremist assertions, the birth-control movement again swung back to a social view; the main issue was no longer maternal health but the national economy or the world's resources. But some procedures were fixed, in particular the exclusion of the contraceptive means that had proved largely responsible for declines in fertility elsewhere: *coitus interruptus* and the condom in the West, abortion in Japan, sterilization in Puerto Rico. Merely making contraceptives available, even if gratis, has not ensured a reduction in family size, for unless the population shares Western middle-class values it will not use the means to control its births.

SURVEY DATA ON FERTILITY DETERMINANTS

What are the attitudes of the peasant masses concerning the use of contraceptives, the size of the ideal family, and other matters that help determine the trend in fertility? A reply to such a question based on deductions from ideologies or from actual family size is not sufficient. As we have seen, neither religions nor modernist ethical systems have been consistent in their stance toward fertility determinants; thus, how could an analyst guess which of several leads, if any, the people were following, or whether large families were the consequence of ignorance or apathy, rather than of the acceptance of pronatalist doctrines? Manifestly, direct data on people's attitudes, if they were of reasonable quality, would constitute an important addition to our knowledge.

Polling is fraught with methodological difficulties even in Western countries and even with questionnaires that do not touch on questions as private as coitus and birth control. What kind of response should one anticipate from a peasant population that anywhere in the world is likely to follow the Chinese proverb, "Before a stranger it is better to express only a third of your opinion"?

In a traditional folk society [like Taiwan] it is almost impossible to get a clear individual opinion on many problems. What are problems for the modern are not considered problems by these people, because they are connected with un-questionable mores. Some of our queries were considered just too foolish to answer. Other questions were looked on as impolite or of bad omen [Chen *et al.* 1963].

In Pakistan a question on the number of years of cohabitation elicited only a comment to the interviewer, "You are shameless" (Choldin *et al.* 1967). The reader may recall another example (p. 379), from an analysis of fertility in Uganda:

Complete refusals to answer questions were very rare, although it was sometimes necessary to visit a house three times in order to get cooperation. ... A more common form of refusal was a civil greeting, followed either by reluctance to give any information or by quite obvious misstatements ... or frivolous answers. For instance, a man who had refused to give any information to the first two investigators finally gave the names of two children to the third investigator. ... [He] later admitted to ten children, [while] he still concealed a second wife living in another village [Richards and Reining 1954].

If the study is so designed, it is possible to check survey data for **reliability,** or their consistency with a variation in conditions that should have no effect on the response. Whether the husband or the wife informs the researcher concerning their marital practices, for instance, should make no difference, but in a Calcutta study in which both were separately asked questions about birth control, only 22 percent completely agreed when the husbands were professionals or executives, only 14 percent when they were manual laborers (Poti *et al.* 1962). Or, as another example, the age that adult Ceylonese gave in a first visit was "often" incon-sistent with that declared in a second visit (Kinch 1962; cf. Choldin *et al.* 1967 on Pakistan). In a survey in Tanganyika the age given to a doctor and that computed by a sociologist were the same in only 35 percent of the cases (Richards and Reining 1954).

Even if data are completely reliable, this affords no guarantee concerning their **validity,** or their agreement with objective reality. For example, in the Calcutta study both husbands and wives often stated that an accidental preg-nancy had actually been planned. "Errors of these types are systematic in nature and extremely difficult to eliminate, no matter what efforts the inter-viewers make" (Poti *et al.* 1962). It is often insignificant or peripheral questions that are easiest to validate. "The most important misstatements were with respect to the number of children, as was expected" (Richards and Reining 1954).

The already great difficulties in establishing the truth concerning questions about fertility have been enormously aggravated by what is termed **action-research**: the researcher, in conscious ignorance of the consequences of his acts, undertakes simultaneously to right a social wrong and to understand its causes. But neither goal is well served by combining them. The poor and powerless who are the usual objects of this type of reform are used as laboratory animals. And if the disinterested search for scientific propositions is compromised by merging it with social action, persons will be pressured to respond to questions in the manner that helps realize the program's goals. Thus, rather than concentrating on a questionnaire that will elicit valid responses to queries on the desired size of family, attitudes toward contraceptives, and so on, one attempts to get the "respondents" to accept contraceptives that are made available to them. The "acceptors," then, have both indicated a positive response and acted on it; two steps in the development of the small-family pattern have been collapsed into one. Or have they?

A study, set up by WHO in the early 1950s at the request of the Indian government, was conducted by Dr. Abraham Stone, for years the national director of the Planned Parenthood Association in the United States. He was restricted to investigating the feasibility of using the rhythm method, the only one, in the opinion of the Indian Minister of Health at that time, that would not come into conflict with India's "traditions, culture, or mores."[2] About three-quarters of the couples interviewed wanted information on how to control conception, but of these only 4 percent were still using rhythm at the end of the observation period of almost 2 years. The method was therefore declared to

[2] The difficulties of teaching the rhythm method to an illiterate population posed special problems, which Dr. Stone overcame with great ingenuity. "I constructed a special necklace containing twenty-eight beads, one bead for each day of an average cycle. There are orange beads to indicate the days of the menstrual flow, green beads to indicate the days of the cycle which are safe from conception, and red beads for the fertile days. The beads could be strung for the individual woman on the basis of the duration of her cycles by the physician or health worker, and the woman could then be instructed to move one bead daily from one side of the string to the other, beginning with the first day of her menstrual flow. During the time that the green beads appear, she will be in her safe period; but when the red ones come around, sexual relations should be avoided" (Stone 1953).

"No one anticipated how many snags there were going to be in translating this apparently simple device into effective action. After a week the women came to the clinic with the complaint that they could not distinguish the color of the beads in the middle of the night. An improvement was effected in retaining the color but changing the shape of the beads into round and square ones: round red beads were unsafe, square green beads were safe. . . . Some women simply forgot to push the beads. Some decided not to wear the necklaces because they didn't want the whole village to know that they were practicing family planning. And some mistook the beads for charmed amulets distributed through the courtesy of the Government of India. They thought it was enough to simply push the beads to space or limit their families" (Chandrasekhar 1967a).

be "scarcely favorable" (C. P. Blacker 1955), yet this enormous gap between the proportion that express initial interest and the very much smaller proportion that effectively practice contraception does not depend on the method advocated. "It is somewhat depressing, but not exactly surprising, to find that though 92 percent of the women [surveyed in Madras] were definitely desirous of limiting their families, only 4 percent did anything about it" (Gopalaswami 1962). Of a rural sample in India (Ramanagran), three out of four expressed interest in learning a method of controlling births but only 14 percent of those "interested" actually learned it (Mauldin 1965).

The famous Khanna study (Wyon and Gordon 1971), conducted in seven test Punjabi villages over a period of 6 years and at a total cost of about $1 million, was the first major field study of birth control in India. It was also the only important study anywhere in the world that was subjected to a detailed on-the-spot review by an independent analyst (Mamdani 1972). As in scientific work generally, the possibility of comparing one man's findings with another's critique is a useful path to the truth. As someone told Mamdani (ibid.: 23): "But they were so nice, you know. And they came from distant lands to be with us. . . . All they wanted was that we accept the [foam] tablets. I lost nothing and probably received their prayers. And they, they must have gotten some promotion." Indeed, one interviewer had been fired halfway through the study—according to his later statement, because of his "low performance" (ibid.: 33). Most of the "acceptors" threw the pills away, but one man had a habit of making use of everything. He built a tiny sculpture of the rectangular boxes and bottles; together with calendar prints of gods and godesses, movie stars, and national leaders, it helped to decorate the room. Few wanted to be what the men conducting the study termed "resisters"; it was easier for everyone to become "acceptors." As another villager told Mamdani, "It is sometimes better to lie. It stops you from hurting people, does you no harm, and might even help them" (ibid.: 32). A draft of the original report had declared, "Nearly 90 percent were in favor of contraceptives."

Indeed, the number of women to appear at a newly established clinic and accept its services is generally taken to be a valid index of how successful the program is. "In terms of new acceptors, 1970 was Taiwan's finest year. More loops were inserted; new pill users almost doubled over 1969; and condoms, reintroduced to give couples a wider choice, proved surprisingly popular" (Finnigan and Keeny 1971). Let us suppose that, in this instance, none of the "acceptors" were merely being kindhearted by telling a white lie. But, as even the passage suggests, some of those who chose one way to limit family size merely shifted from another means. One reason may have been to save money, since in underdeveloped countries a portion of the cost of birth control is borne by the government or, in fact, by the American taxpayer. If these substitutions were from one effective contraceptive to another, presumably the women concerned got some personal benefit, though not a reduction in their family size. And if any of the modern means supplanted traditional contraceptives of more limited but nevertheless genuine efficacy, the presumed impact of the program would still be only a fraction of what was implied by counting the "acceptors."

If it were possible to demonstrate which "acceptors" actually use the contraceptives they take, as well as what proportion of these had not been controlling their fertility prior to being recorded, this would not mean that one can equate the remnant—the new "acceptors"—with a decline in family size. The contraceptives most commonly distributed in Taiwan, to continue with that case, are still intra-uterine devices. In the best individual case, a Lippes loop is very effective in preventing a single conception, but many IUDs (the proportion varies from one sample to another) either expel themselves or are deliberately removed because they cause excessive bleeding or too much pain (see p. 208). According to one estimate based on Taiwan data, of the 635,826 IUDs inserted over a 6-year period, only 251,000 to 266,000 were still *in situ* at its end! The prevalence rate ranged, depending on the postulates on which one based the estimate, between 14.3 and 15.2 percent (P. T. Liu and Chow 1971). Those sectors of the female population most likely to remove an IUD were also, as one would expect, least likely to have another inserted (Hermalin and Chow 1971). Moreover, as with any other long-term contraceptive, it is important to distinguish "effective retention" from "effective prevalence." IUDs carried by widows, divorcees, sterile or subfecund women, or wives of sterile or subfecund men prevent few or no conceptions.

In spite of their lacks, what information can be gained from attitude surveys? In addition to the almost routine questioning of the American population, as early as the mid-1960s surveys had been completed or were in process in a remarkably large number of countries, both developed and underdeveloped (Mauldin 1965):

East Asia	Africa and Middle East	Europe	Latin America
Ceylon	Egypt	Czechoslovakia	Argentina
India	Ghana	Greece	Brazil
Indonesia	Israel	Hungary	Chile
Japan	Lebanon	Italy	Colombia
Korea	Tunisia	United Kingdom	Costa Rica
Pakistan	Turkey		Jamaica
Taiwan			Mexico
			Panama
			Peru
			Puerto Rico
			Venezuela

Most of these studies were technically inferior to the few administered with full attention to methodological difficulties, and it is likely that their biases are consistently on the optimistic side, reflecting the patent wishes of the researchers that fertility would soon decline. But even if we accept the data at face value, polls on the ideal size of family give little basis for optimism. According to most of the surveys in India, the mass of the people wanted an average of close to four children. In Santiago de Chile and in Taiwan, in underdeveloped countries generally, more than half of the respondents held four *or more* children to be ideal. Only in Jamaica and Puerto Rico were smaller families becoming the ideal (Blake 1965; Mauldin 1965). The percentages wanting four or more children ranged up to 88 in Ghana, 71 in the Philippines, 65 in Korea, 62 in Thailand (Berelson 1966b: Table 5; cf. Udry *et al.* 1973). After listing these figures, Berelson showed that there was a rough correlation with the proportions illiterate, with the per-capita GNP, even with the percentages of the population living in large cities. This relation with structural features would seem to suggest that, so long as those fundamental characteristics are not changed, it may not be feasible to use mere propaganda to reduce the size of the desired family. The same conclusion was reached by Freedman (1963) in a paper reviewing the family-size norms in underdeveloped areas:

> Social norms support the moderately to very high fertilities found in the so-called underdeveloped societies. . . . High fertility and high fertility norms are not a result of unrestrained maximum fecundity but rather are an adjustment mainly to the [earlier] high mortality and to dependence on kinship-based local institutions. . . . The complex continuum from underdeveloped to developed societies is best represented for our purpose by a continuum from major dependence on relatively small local units to increasing interdependence in larger social units in which kinship plays a decreasing part. In this shift to larger units of interdependence, education and literacy not only have an important part to play but may lead other elements in their effect on fertility.

THE FERTILITY OF UNDERDEVELOPED AREAS

The analysis of quantitative data so far in this chapter has been based on the results of surveys, typically undertaken in order to achieve a better understanding of the reasons for the generally high fertility and thus of means by which it can be controlled. But how high really is the fertility, and what has its trend been over the past several decades? Paradoxically, these are questions on which the data in many cases are so inadequate that some analysts have preferred to shift from the "hard" empirical fact of a birth to the relatively "soft" one of an attitude concerning it. Yet the more important datum, both in itself and as a check on the validity of opinion polls, pertains to family size, its present level and its probable trend in the countries seeking to establish an industrial base for their economies.

Quality of the Data

The statistical data of underdeveloped nations are generally scanty and of poor quality, but also steadily improving. When we try to assess any of the social transformations these countries are undergoing, we must keep in mind that our measuring rods are in all probability changing as rapidly as anything else in the society. Some types of statistics are today fairly satisfactory for some countries, but in almost every case this level of accuracy is too recent to permit equally firm comparisons with those of several decades earlier.

The best past data were collected in a number of European colonies, and we can take British India as an example of an underdeveloped country with an exceptionally good statistical record. The directors of the 19th century censuses included great scholars of Indian civilization—historians, anthropologists, and linguists as well as, later, statisticians. From 1870 on, the censuses they supervised represent "the most fruitful single source of information about the country, ... an accomplishment of which India may be justly proud" (Davis 1951: 5). This judgment should not be interpreted to mean, however, that the censuses were accurate by modern Western standards. For example, when the population count of British India in 1871 was corrected for underenumeration and areas not included, the number was raised from 203.4 to 236 million, and by Davis's estimate the actual population was 255.2 million (ibid.: 26–27). Similar though smaller corrections must be made for each of the subsequent counts at least through that for 1901. These figures of gross population are, of course, only the most basic demographic data, and breakdowns by any classification are typically less rather than more accurate.

A uniform system of vital statistics was established in British India in 1864, but a reasonable level of completeness was never achieved. For the first four decades of the 20th century, the underregistration of births and deaths certainly exceeded 30 percent at all times and was probably nearer to half (ibid.: 34, 67). In independent India, the roughly half-million village headmen are required by law to register vital events, and the record is still very poor (Chandrasekhar 1960, 1972: Appendix 2).

A more general appreciation of the population statistics of underdeveloped areas in the recent past can be had by browsing through the *Demographic Survey of the British Colonial Empire*, to which Kuczynski (1948–53) devoted the last ten years of his life. It is hardly possible to summarize this massive work except to say that no generalization is valid, not even the obvious one that all the statistics analyzed in it are poor. British colonial officers were long required to give basic demographic information in their regular reports, and when they lacked statistics, they furnished the results of their limited observations and general impressions.

Thousands of reports ... submit as facts what are actually reasoned guesses. [The demographer] finds over and over again a consensus of opinion without any real evidence to support this opinion.... A considerable portion of this Survey had, therefore, to be devoted to reinterpretation of the statistical data.... [But] to appraise fertility, morbidity, mortality, or migration is about as difficult in most African Dependencies as to appraise the frequency of adultery in [Great Britain] [ibid.: vol. 1, v–vi].

Kuczynski rigorously judges "censuses," "counts," poll-tax estimates, and vital statistics, and the authority with which he dismisses many of them makes this work much livelier reading than its subject matter would suggest.

At least in quantity, and generally also in quality, the period since 1945 has seen a considerable improvement in the demographic statistics collected in underdeveloped areas. As early as the decade centering on 1950 about four-fifths of the world's population was enumerated in some kind of census, a larger proportion than had ever been counted previously. The United Nations has been pushing for an expansion of this program, as well as for an improvement in the accuracy of the data collected (see pp. 24–26). The statistics available are published annually by the United Nations in its *Demographic Yearbook*, a uniquely valuable compilation. Laymen must learn to use it with care, however, and to pay very close attention to the comments on the estimated adequacy of the data. In general, statistics are printed as they are received from the various national governments and coded as "C," meaning that the coverage was judged to be reasonably complete; "U," meaning that this was not so; or ". . . .," meaning that no judgment was possible. The alternative procedure, to apply different correction factors to various sets of data, would require not only detailed knowledge of each country's statistical procedures, but also the willingness to offer affront in assessing the degree to which official figures are probably incorrect. By their very nature, the anonymous teams working for international agencies do not qualify on either count.

How divergent some of the census data are from presumed reality is suggested by a review of some counts in Latin America. When it was estimated that underenumeration was great, the census officials raised the totals by 4.6 percent (Chile, 1952), 7.5 percent (Peru, 1940), 8.4 percent (Bolivia, 1950), or even 10 percent (Honduras, 1950). Sometimes such augmentations are "due to fraudulent adulterations" (Guatemala, 1940). "In some cases, local census officials with misconceived motives of prestige, introduce fantastic additions; . . . in other cases, census takers, paid proportionally by the number of persons enumerated, add nonexistent individuals or households." The accuracy of data on subpopulations is especially doubtful. In Brazil in 1950, for instance, an estimated half million women aged 30 to 69 declared their ages as 15 to 29 (Mortara 1964).

Because censuses are carried out in one concentrated effort of the central government, their results are generally better than registration data, which depend on a nationwide administrative system that operates continuously. As of the early 1960s birth registrations were reasonably accurate and complete in only twenty-three underdeveloped countries, plus the Colored and Asian populations of the Union of South Africa (see list at top of page 628). Among these twenty-five populations, few had adequate registration as recently as 1945, so that a direct establishment of trends is usually impossible. As can be seen from the list, these populations are hardly representative of underdeveloped countries. Note, too, the large overlap with those in which survey data have been collected (p. 624). With the notable exceptions of India and, more

East and Central Asia	Africa and Middle East	Latin America	
Ceylon	Mauritius	Argentina	Martinique
Malaya	Tunisia	British Guiana	Mexico
Réunion	Union of South Africa	Chile	Panama
Ryukyu Islands	Colored	Costa Rica	Puerto Rico
Singapore	Asian	El Salvador	Surinam
Taiwan		Guadeloupe	Trinidad and Tobago
		Guatemala	Venezuela
		Jamaica	

recently, several countries of South America, most of the demographic polls have been taken in countries with the best conventional population statistics.

It would serve little purpose to bring this account of poor statistics up to date. What is needed is not the data that can be copied from various compilations but reviews by such knowledgeable scholars as Mortara, which do not appear as soon as the figures are published. The reader should not, however, facilely assume that censuses and vital statistics are everywhere getting better and better. In Nigeria, for instance—or for that matter in much of Africa south of the Sahara—the political turmoil has disrupted both the population and administrative functions, and efforts to count those remaining after thousands died or fled have not necessarily improved on the sorry record of the colonial period. "The achievement of adequate birth registration may in fact be viewed as an indicator of a country's modernization" (Ridley 1965; cf. Gaete-Darbó 1964).

Also in the past history of many Western countries, census data were of acceptable quality long before the registration system became adequate. One adjustment to this situation was to substitute the child-woman ratio for other measures of fertility (see pp. 284–285). For lack of anything better, this is still used in analyzing the natality of underdeveloped countries, but it is an especially defective index for temporal or cross-cultural analyses. (1) The age data on which the ratios are based are quite poor, and the errors are greater in the number of children than of women. This constitutes a hindrance to comparative analysis especially when the censuses of some countries, or of some sectors of populations, are improving much faster than others. (2) The undercount of children may vary greatly. (3) Wherever infant mortality used to be high and has since fallen dramatically, the relative level of the child-woman ratio rose very fast. In such instances there has been an increase in what could be termed effective fertility but not necessarily in the number of births.

With a statistical base that is often so insecure, one may well ask, how is it possible to discuss in detail and with assurance the population trends of underdeveloped areas? If any data exist at all, even if quite faulty, a demographer can often derive better estimates with various techniques. At the most elementary level, these are the ones already discussed under the heading, "Correction of

Errors," in Chapter 2. For example, when the results of a 1953–54 sample census in the Indian state of Uttar Pradesh were compared with the registration records, it was found that about 30 percent of births had been omitted and an additional 20 percent had been lost in the transmission of the records to the central office for compilation (Das Gupta 1958). Census data can be used to estimate fertility not only with the child-woman ratio but also by calculating back from the number of survivors at specified ages, given certain assumptions about mortality, to the fertility rates that must have obtained (Table 16-2). In this example not only are the two sets of data calculated from the census somewhat different but even their trends are not the same over the eight decades. A periodic National Sample Survey, which the federal Indian government has made about twice a year since 1950–51, indicated a birth rate of 34 in the mid-1950s, or still about 20 percent under the estimated correct level. Indeed, this was a considerable improvement over figures derived from registration or censuses, but the level of accuracy was hardly satisfactory (cf. Sabagh and Scott 1967; Romaniuk 1967). In the mid-1960s the official rate was "adjusted" from 22.6 in 1963 to 41.0 the following year; the latter is a decidedly more plausible figure, but not necessarily an accurate one.

Incomplete and inaccurate data can be rounded out also by checking the

Table 16-2. Index Numbers (Crude Birth Rate of 40 = 100) of Birth Rates as Estimated from Various Data, India, 1891–1970

Census Year	Official Registration Statistics	Reverse-Survival Calculated from Cohorts Aged	
		0–4	0–9
1891	—	111	122
1901	87	98	115
1911	94	108	120
1921	92	100	123
1931	83	112	116
1941	85	97	113
1951	68	90	98
1961	58	—	—
1966	102[a]	—	—
1970	98	—	—

[a] Adjusted rate.
SOURCES: 1891–1951: Ajit Das Gupta, "Determinants of Fertility Level and Trend in Defective Registration Areas," *Bulletin de l'Institut International de Statistique,* 36 (1958), 127–136. 1961–70: S. Chandrasekhar, *Infant Mortality, Population Growth and Family Planning in India* (Chapel Hill: University of North Carolina Press, 1972), Appendix 4.

Table 16-3. Parameters of a Stable Female Population with Various Expectations of Life at Birth and Gross Reproduction Rates

Expectation of Life at Birth (Years)	Gross Reproduction Rate						
	0.80	1.00	1.50	2.00	2.50	3.00	4.00
PROPORTION AT AGES 0–14							
20	0.099	0.129	0.198	0.257	0.308	0.351	0.420
30	0.117	0.152	0.230	0.294	0.348	0.393	0.464
40	0.129	0.167	0.251	0.319	0.374	0.420	0.491
50	0.138	0.178	0.266	0.336	0.393	0.439	0.510
60	0.144	0.186	0.277	0.349	0.407	0.453	0.524
70	0.148	0.192	0.286	0.359	0.417	0.464	0.534
PROPORTION AT AGES 65 AND OVER							
20	0.168	0.135	0.086	0.059	0.042	0.032	0.020
30	0.180	0.143	0.088	0.058	0.041	0.031	0.018
40	0.189	0.149	0.090	0.059	0.041	0.030	0.018
50	0.198	0.155	0.091	0.059	0.041	0.030	0.017
60	0.206	0.160	0.093	0.060	0.041	0.029	0.017
70	0.215	0.166	0.096	0.061	0.042	0.030	0.017

SOURCE: Ansley J. Coale, "Birth Rates, Death Rates, and Rates of Growth in Human Population," in Mindel C. Sheps and Jeanne Clare Ridley, editors, *Public Health and Population Change* (Pittsburgh: University of Pittsburgh Press, 1965).

consistency among fertility, mortality, population increase (if migration is a significant factor), and a stable population structure—or the one, it will be recalled, that would result from the prolonged continuation of unchanged age-specific birth and death rates (Rele 1967). Recorded gross reproduction rates have ranged between 0.80 (Austria, 1933) and 4.17 (Cocos-Keeling Islands, 1928–32). Mortality as measured by the expectation of life at birth has ranged from about 20 (in areas before accurate records were taken) to above 70 (in various advanced countries). These two schedules, thus, designate the possible combinations of fertility and mortality, and each pair is associated with a particular stable population structure. The relation is illustrated with the proportions of young and aged females in Table 16-3. The approximate nature of a rule of thumb used by some demographers, that in underdeveloped countries the sector aged 0–14 constitutes 40 percent of the total (e.g., Naraghi 1960: 101–107), is suggested in this table.

The postulate in the stable-population model that age-specific birth rates remain unchanged approximates the actual situation in many underdeveloped areas, while that pertaining to fixed age-specific death rates, of course, does not. A quasi-stable model, or the age structure that would result from unchanging age-specific birth rates and age-specific death rates falling in a specified pattern, can also be a useful tool (Rele 1967; Coale 1963; Demeny 1965).

The Trend in Fertility

By making use of this interrelation among fertility, mortality, and population structure, Collver (1965) calculated crude birth rates for twenty **Latin American** countries as far back as the incomplete and inaccurate data permit. At the earliest date (Chile in 1850–54) the estimated crude birth rate was 46.6, and in no country except Uruguay did it fall below 40 until after World War I. For the most recent period it is useful to compare Collver's estimates with those of the United Nations (Table 16-4). Apart from the most advanced countries (Uruguay, Argentina, Chile, and Cuba), all had birth rates of 40 or over. More disturbingly, over this decade Collver's figures generally show a slight *upward* trend, which the more approximate U.N. estimates confirm in a few cases (Costa Rica, Venezuela). In general, El-Badry's figures for the most recent period merely average the range given for a decade earlier, but he suggests that there will be a decline in fertility over the following decade and a half.

In all the four regions some fertility decline is anticipated, but in view of the socio-economic and cultural conditions the decline is expected to be slow and amount to about 10 percent of the gross reproduction rate in each region in 15 years. This trend is slower than that anticipated in Asia. . . . If the assumptions underlying the projections turns out to be true, Middle America would still have a gross reproduction rate of 2.8 and a crude birth rate of 40.2 by 1980–85 [El-Badry 1971].

Apart from Egypt, **Arab countries** have few reliable data on fertility, and births in Egypt are underregistered in those rural areas lacking health bureaus. The crude birth rate corrected for this deficiency, which fluctuated just under 50 in 1934–41, fell to 44.8 in 1959. The uncorrected rate of 42.6 in 1959 compares with an average uncorrected figure of 42.8 in 1960–64 and 41.6 in 1965 (El-Badry 1965). Jordan's "birth registration is officially recognized to be deficient and to vary in extent from one year to the next." Palestinian refugees, who constitute a sizable portion of the population, have maintained a birth rate of 50 in other countries, where more accurate records are kept. According to the 1961 census of Jordan's Maan District, the completed family size of ever-married women was 7.8 children (ibid.). The Syrian birth rates published in the U.N. *Demographic Yearbook*, ranging around 25 in the 1950s, are based on perhaps half the actual number of births. The annual population increase of 3.5 percent estimated for the 1950s may be under the actual rate, for instead of the shortage of land typical of the Middle East, "there exist vast fertile areas in the Northeast which have adequate water supply and which are still inadequately exploited" (ibid.). Between 1951 and 1960, Lebanon's reported birth rate fluctuated erratically between 24 and 41, presumably reflecting temporary improvements in registration (ibid.). According to a sample survey, completed family size in Lebanon

Table 16-4. Crude Birth Rates in Latin America, Estimated 1945–70 and Projected 1970–85

Region and Country	Collver 1945–49	ECLA 1945–50	Collver 1955–59	ECLA 1955–60	El-Badry 1965–70	El-Badry 1970–75	El-Badry 1975–80	El-Badry 1980–85
Middle America
Mexico	44.5	44–48	45.8	44–47	43.2	42.1	40.5	39.3
Guatemala	49.1	48–52	49.0	48–52	43.2	41.6	40.4	39.4
Honduras	44.5	45–50	46.0	45–50	49.0	48.5	47.8	46.1
El Salvador	44.8	44–48	47.9	44–48	46.9	46.5	46.3	45.8
Nicaragua	—	45–52	—	45–52	46.0	46.8	47.4	45.9
Costa Rica	42.7	44–48	45.3	45–50	45.1	44.5	44.1	42.8
Panama	38.3	38–42	40.5	39–42	41.1	40.9	40.9	40.4
Caribbean
Cuba	30.0	32–36	—	30–34	26.6	25.4	24.4	23.4
Haiti	—	42–50	—	42–50	43.9	43.6	43.2	42.4
Dominican Republic	—	48–54	—	48–54	48.5	48.1	47.0	45.5
Tropical South America
Colombia	43.4	44–47	45.1	43–46	44.6	43.9	42.1	39.1
Venezuela	43.6	44–48	44.3	45–50	40.9	40.3	37.9	34.3
Ecuador	45.9	45–50	46.5	45–50	44.9	43.4	42.2	40.9
Peru	44.9	42–48	46.2	42–48	41.8	39.8	38.2	37.1
Brazil	—	43–47	—	43–47	37.8	36.9	36.0	35.0
Bolivia	47.0	41–45	—	41–45	44.0	44.0	43.9	42.9
Temperate South America
Paraguay	—	45–50	—	45–50	44.6	44.6	43.7	41.7
Argentina	25.2	25–26	24.1	23–24	22.5	21.7	21.0	20.2
Chile	37.0	34–37	37.6	35–38	33.2	31.1	29.7	28.5
Uruguay	—	20–23	—	19–22	21.3	20.9	20.8	20.6

SOURCES: O. Andrew Collver, Birth Rates in Latin America: New Estimates of Historical Trends and Fluctuations (Berkeley: Institute of International Studies, University of California, 1965); U.N. Economic Commission for Latin America, Boletín Económico de América Latina, 7 (1962), Table 4; M. A. El-Badry, "Latin American Population Prospects in the Next Fifteen Years," Population Studies, 25 (1971), 183–192.

ranged from 8.09 children among Shiite Moslems down to 6.56 among Maronite and other Catholics; and for those still in their reproductive years the total fertility rate per woman ranged from 7.65 among Shiites to 4.08 among Orthodox Christians (Yaukey 1961: 29).

Following from the results of the 1966 census of Algeria, the country's national statistics bureau calculated alternative projections up to the end of the century. Fertility was estimated assuming that an effective policy of control would be, or would not be, instituted. In the latter case, the gross reproduction rate would remain constant at 3.61, and in the former it would fall to 1.80. How probable it was that the government would set up "a vigorously executed population policy to take effect during the whole of the 15 years" the demographic staff did not state (Bourcier de Carbon 1973).

In **Tropical Africa** crude birth rates as calculated in particular studies have generally ranged upward from about 40 to well above 50 (T. E. Smith 1963). A number of such case studies were assembled in one volume and compared with estimates from a stable-population model.

The assembly of these estimates in a table and a map has the almost inevitable effect of betraying the cautionary warnings given by each author of the case studies. . . . It cannot be emphasized too strongly that the estimates are very uneven in quality. . . . [But] the broad distinction between high and low fertility areas is consistent in the two forms of estimation. . . .

The most striking feature . . . is the very large range, with birth rates varying from about 30 to about 60 per thousand and total fertility—the number of children that would be born during the lifetime of each woman experiencing the given fertility rates—ranging from about 3.5 to over 8. . . . [But] the variations in fertility should not be allowed to convey a false impression that the average fertility of tropical Africa is anything other than very high. The birth rate for all of the populations analyzed combined is about 49 per thousand, and the average total fertility for tropical Africa is probably about 6.5 children [Coale and Lorimer 1968].

While the fertility of westernized sectors of African populations is lower, the relative size of these subpopulations is too small to affect national rates (e.g., Caldwell 1967). Low natality is sometimes due to venereal disease; for example, a survey in the former Belgian Congo in 1956–57 found that the areas with birth rates under 40 had the highest rates of syphilis, and in these localities some 20 to 30 percent of the women of 45 years and over had borne no children (T. E. Smith 1963). According to another study made in the 1950s, however, the relatively low fertility in one area of northeast Tanganyika had resulted from the breakdown of tribal controls over marriage customs, with a consequent high proportion of unmarried adults and particularly women (Roberts and Tanner 1959). The fertility of the settled population of Sudan has been rising from very high levels (Henin 1968).

In terms of sheer numbers, the enormous populations of **Asia** are more significant than the generally much smaller ones noted thus far. Communist China, the most populous nation of the world, is discussed in the following chapter. In mid-1973 the other Asian giants' estimated populations and annual rates of growth were as follows:

Country	Millions	Percent
India	600	2.5
Pakistan	68	3.3
Bangladesh	83	?
Indonesia	133	2.9

At the present rate of growth, during each 5-year period India, for instance, must accommodate an *additional* number about equal to the populations of East and West Germany, or more than those of Australia and New Zealand.

As we have intimated (see Table 16-2), India's birth rate fell from around 50 in the 1890s to around 40 in the 1960s. The official rate, after being adjusted to a more realistic level, declined from 41 in 1964 to 39 in 1970, then went back to 42 in 1973. These slight differences are well within the range of error of the data; one can deduce that there was substantially no change during the period that the government's program to institute family planning might have begun to show nationwide results.

Pakistan's demographic statistics are poor even compared with those of other major underdeveloped countries.

Vital statistics in Pakistan are extremely meager and highly understated. In urban areas they are maintained by the extremely uninterested municipal authority; in rural areas they depend on reports made by illiterate and uninterested *chawkidars* (village watchmen) who, having as a rule to travel on foot considerable distances to make their reports, are inclined to neglect a very troublesome duty even today [Ahmed 1966].

Pakistan's birth rate as estimated from a stable-population model was 60.3 in 1951 (62.2 among Moslems, 50.7 among non-Moslems), or close to the highest ever observed anywhere in the world (cf. Cooke 1969). If a family-planning program did not take effect quickly, it was anticipated that fertility would remain constant or even undergo a short-term increase "because of the peculiar responses of reproduction to changes in various socio-economic factors" (ibid.). Between 1951 and 1961 the population increased by an estimated 2.16 percent per year, during the several years following the latter date by 2.6 to 2.8 percent or more (Querishi 1967).

The estimated birth rate of Indonesia, 43 in the early 1960s and 47 in the early 1970s, was about the same as in the 1930s. In the interim, with World War II and the Japanese occupation, the rate may have been as low as 20 (or if much higher, then negated by an increase in infant mortality). The consequent strange population structure in 1961 will greatly affect the proportion of new parents in the years to come:

Aged	0–9	33.6 percent
	10–19	16.5
	20–34	24.6
	35–44	11.5
	45 and over	13.8

"There are no signs yet as to probable changes in the future course of the overall level of fertility" (Hawkins 1967).

In summary, the birth rate of the major underdeveloped areas of the world, to the degree that imprecise data can tell us, is close 40 or above. Where it is possible to indicate a trend, sometimes there has been a probable decline (India), sometimes a probable rise (much of Latin America).

DIFFERENTIAL ANALYSIS

A decline in family size, should it come about, would of course not take place evenly throughout any society. As earlier in the West, so also in underdeveloped countries today, the inducements to control fertility vary according to one's place in the particular social structure. The best indication of probable future trends, therefore, could be derived from a differential analysis, though of course in areas where even the overall fertility is known only approximately, that of sectors of the population would have to be estimated very cautiously.

Urban–Rural Residence

In the history of the West cities constituted the main driving wedge of the new social order, but the role of cities in underdeveloped areas, as we have seen, is more complex (see pp. 497–506). Thus, some evidence suggests that cities in underdeveloped areas, like their earlier Western counterparts, are leading the population toward a smaller family. According to one analysis, in Latin America as of 1950 "the lower the general rate of reproduction in a country, the greater the rural–urban differentiation" (T. Lynn Smith 1958). With urban growth proceeding apace, this conclusion implies a certain optimism: "as the urban population becomes a more significant proportion of the total population, national birth rates are likely to fall, perhaps sharply" (ibid.). It is now manifest that this conclusion does not apply to all countries undergoing development. In his analysis of pre-independence Indian data, Davis (1951: 81) found a sizable gap between cities and countryside, but he did not feel that this indicated a future decline in fertility. "The rural–urban differentials are certainly present, and are correlated with size of city, but they have not increased in fifty years." This distinction between rural and urban natality, according to a number of more detailed studies of local areas, disappeared (Coale and Hoover 1958: 47–48). In Egypt, as a third example, the estimated levels of fertility in the cities and countryside were substantially the same after the differential underregistration had been taken into account. Urban mortality, on the other hand, is much lower: the installation of a sewerage system in Cairo during World War I resulted in an almost immediate decline in the city's death rate by five units, and between 1945 and 1947 Cairo's death rate fell again from about 33 to about 25. With fertility equal to that in rural areas and a substantially lower mortality (estimated in the mid-1950s to be 16 per thousand as against 22–24), Egypt's cities grew largely by their natural increase, contrary to the conventional doctrine that in-migration is always the main source of urban growth (Abu-Lughod 1964).

In short, the lower urban fertility that has been routine in the West is only one of several patterns in underdeveloped areas. "Instead of uniformity, there is a spectrum" (Robinson 1963). For various dates from 1950 to 1960, the child–woman ratios of urban populations ranged from barely more than half the rural up to two-thirds larger than the rural (Table 16-5).

Table 16-5. Urban Child–Woman Ratios as a Percentage of Rural, Selected Underdeveloped Countries, 1950–60

Nigeria	165.4	Sudan	88.7
British North Borneo	121.9	Libya	85.7
Burma	107.0	Ceylon	81.7
Algeria	105.8	Union of South Africa,	
Malaya	105.5	"Natives"	69.3
Pakistan	97.8	Morocco	64.2
Nepal	96.1	Chile	63.6
India	96.0	Jamaica	58.8
Iran	91.0	Brazil	55.3
Mauritius	90.3	Cuba	51.4

SOURCE: Warren C. Robinson, "Urbanization and Fertility: The Non-Western Experience," *Milbank Memorial Fund Quarterly*, **41** (1963), 291–308.

The first question that these figures pose is whether the relation is spurious. Not only is the child–woman ratio, as we have noted, a deceptive measure for cross-cultural analysis, but any international comparison can be thrown off by the fact that the rural–urban distinction is not based on uniform criteria. In Mexico, for instance, data are collected according to *municipios* (equivalent to townships), and an analysis of differential fertility has to be based on an elaborate manipulation of the census figures (Burnight *et al.* 1956). In some cases, however, the lack of a rural–urban difference in fertility cannot be explained as merely an artifact of the data.

In the main, urban–rural differentials derive not from the direct effect of the urban or rural physical environments but from the fact that social influences on family size are associated with the size of the community, at least in the West. But a society in transition has two overlapping class structures, one more or less equivalent to that in Western societies and the other vestigial from the earlier hierarchy of social classes. In the former structure we should anticipate an inverse correlation between an index of social class and fertility, in the latter case possibly a positive one. Moreover, in plural societies the class structure and the hierarchy of ethnic minorities often overlap, so that it may be difficult to distinguish the social from the cultural differences in fertility determinants (cf. J. G. C. Blacker 1959).

1. The simplest situation to understand, obviously, is the one closest to the pattern that one would anticipate from Western antecedents. Thus, judging from studies in Santiago de Chile, Rio de Janeiro, and Lima, these cities of Latin America show the standard progression of family size inversely correlated with social class (Miró 1964). However, if the small-family sector is a westernized elite, in most underdeveloped countries it will constitute a very small segment of the whole population. In one Indian study, for instance, C. Chandrasekaran found that completed family size ranged from more than six children for women with no more than primary schooling, to five for women with high school, down to two for women with a college education, but the number of women with more than primary schooling was too tiny to have a measurable effect on national rates (cited in Coale and Hoover 1958: 48).

2. For some of the in-migrants to cities, the geographical move is not associated with one toward the social situation that induces smaller families. According to a study in Brazil, migrants to cities who advanced in social class underwent the expected fall in fertility. But nearly a quarter of the in-migrants who had been born into a nonmanual status moved down to lower positions, and among this sample the mean family size increased by 8 percent from one generation to the next (Hutchinson 1961).

3. Some of the variations both over time and between cities, thus, depend on the degree to which "urban" populations consist in fact of recent in-migrants who have not yet been able either to absorb the city's cultural norms or take advantage of its broader opportunities for social advancement. The changes in India between 1921 and 1951 "probably tended to favor modest increases in the urban fertility ratios," for Indian cities are "clusters of villages full of recent migrants from the rural areas, quite unlike the stable cities of a few decades ago" (Robinson 1961). Since rural–urban migration in India has been predominantly of males who leave wives and children in their home villages, elsewhere the effect of migration on the fertility potential could be greater than this cautious conclusion suggests. For example, the urban populations of Africa are said to differ according to whether they are "country-rooted" or "town-rooted" (Mayer 1961). And the sizable migration to the world's shantytowns, so far as data exist, seems not to be strongly selective by sex.

One of the best studies illuminating this relation between in-migration and fertility is a survey of a large sample of adult males in Monterrey, Mexico (Zarate 1967a). The Monterrey metropolitan area, with a population in 1965 of just under one million, is an important center of heavy industry; in 1960, 43 percent of the economically active males were employed in manufacturing. In this urban–industrial center, however, the mean number of live births to the wives of men aged 51 to 60 was 6.03, about one child more than the highest completed family size in other Latin American studies. An inverse correlation was found between fertility and education, occupational level, or income. The most interesting datum is that the mean number of live births was also significantly related to the size of the respondent's birthplace, obtained from the census closest to his date of birth (cf. Zarate 1967b).

4. The most complex pattern is to be found in a country where the correlation between social class and family size is both positive (among the traditionalist sector) and negative (among the modernist one). In either sector higher status is marked by some of the same indices (wealth, education, etc.), and many inhabitants of a society in transition are not so much in *either* sector as partially in *both*; thus, one should not expect clear indications of class differentials. Several studies of fertility in Egypt suggest such a dual pattern (but cf. Khalifa 1973). Urban fertility was negatively correlated with education, one index of social class, but in the countryside women of the lowest class, as designated by either their own education or that of their husbands, had fewer children than the barely literate (Table 16-6). In each of three villages that Rizk analyzed, there was the same positive correlation of fertility and class as indicated by occupational status:

Agriculturists	4.04 children
Unskilled laborers	4.18
Skilled laborers	4.47

El-Badry (1956) suggests that the association may be due to differential under-reporting or to the higher incidence of miscarriages among the lower-class women. It may also be, however, that the higher social levels of the rural sector (and in most underdeveloped countries, of course, this sector constitutes the greater portion of the population) use their greater wealth to realize the goal of a larger family. According to an earlier study of differential reproduction by occupational level, thus, the highest fertility rates in Egypt were among those most imbued with traditional values (religious employees, teachers, and merchants, in that order) and the lowest among Western-type professionals, while those of agricultural and nonagricultural laborers fell in between (see also A. M. Zikry, cited in G. W. Roberts 1967).

Differential Analysis by Other Factors

In the classical studies of Western fertility, the sharpest differentiation was typically by social class, of which rural–urban residence was one index—a convenient one, for it also classified the population by education, income, and even religion. It is very difficult to adapt this model to underdeveloped countries. The significance of education or income, as we have seen, may be ambivalent;

Table 16-6. Average Number of Children per Married Woman, Standardized for Length of Marriage, by Years of Schooling and Urban–Rural Residence, Egypt, 1960

Sex and Schooling	Urban Governorates	Rural Governorates
Wives		
None	4.51	4.13
1–2 years	3.94	4.68
3 years	3.68	4.42
4–5 years	3.86	3.76
6+ years	2.39	—
Husbands		
None	4.45	4.31
Elementary	4.71	4.54
Secondary	3.95	—
University	2.78	—

SOURCE: Hanna Rizk, reported in M. A. El-Badry, "Trends in the Components of Population Growth in the Arab Countries of the Middle East: A Survey of Present Information," *Demography*, **2** (1965), 140–186.

and in any case the numbers that rank high by either criterion are too small to affect general rates very much. Religion is also a variable difficult to use: the doctrines on contraception, as we noted in the survey at the beginning of the chapter, are often ambiguous or even self-contradictory. In fact, the differences to be studied in any society depend on its own structure, which in part is specific to itself. The variables to be compared in a competent analysis, that is to say, can be derived only to some degree from general models based on Western experience; to some degree they must be generated by a full and detailed acquaintance with the society being analyzed. In an important paper Driver (1972: 101–125) showed that "the social ideology held by family-planning experts, including demographers, is [often] invalid with regard to the sociocultural reality present in the nations or societies." The statement holds for much of the world; Driver exemplified it by contrasting the concepts and premises of Americans who have written on their attempts to introduce family planning in India with those of scholars of Indian culture and society. The demonstration of the formers' incompetence, in one sense almost comic, is also important enough to be worth summarizing at length:

In Indian society, the individual and the couple are *not* the basic social units, but rather the extended family, caste, village, and language community. Villages do *not* constitute a homogeneous rural population but vary considerably in their mode of life. Each village is *not* an isolated social unit, but is closely linked with others through extended kin, caste, economic, political, and marital ties, and visiting patterns. Persons with similar interests are likely *not* to join in voluntary associations or formal organizations in order to pursue their common goal, for castes both largely fulfill this function and strongly inhibit alternative groupings. The ultimate values are *not* health and wealth, but nonmaterial or supernatural meanings and norms. Traditionalism is *not* in total and simple conflict with modernism; rather than a dichotomy, there is a variety of configurations that generate neither cultural nor mental conflict. The official language of the region is *not* comprehensible to every inhabitant; an announcement in standard Hindi, for instance, that "there will be a show of healthy babies up to the age of three" was interpreted by some persons as "there will be a wrestling match of three-year-old children." Languages are *not* equivalent to one another, and some ideas, even the "simplest," can therefore *not* be translated; for example, the English *uncle, aunt,* and *cousin* create only confusion when they are converted into an Indian language. Knowledge (as in "knowledge–attitude–practice") is *not* a prime determinant of behavior, as is shown by the persistence of regional attitudes toward irrigation, which has been used in India for millennia. The credibility and effectiveness of an agent of change are *not* functions of his education or experience but of his kin and caste relationships. In sum, "the failure of family-planning programs is due to the false assumptions about society on which they are organized rather than to difficulties of a simple administrative nature."

The contrast that Driver made, it should be noted, is not between Americans and Indians, or between demographers and anthropologists, but rather between family-planning experts intent on "action-research" and scholars. No one who has written about the population of India has been more acutely aware of the problems it poses than Davis, and in his classic work on the subject one of the best chapters is on caste; or, as another example, the speculations about the effect of family structure in the Davis–Blake paper on the determinants of fertility stimulated a series of research papers (see pp. 212–214). When the aim is to change rather than to understand, on the other hand, researchers native to the country can also be diverted from a sympathetic comprehension of how others see their situation.

For example, the Khanna study, already mentioned (p. 623), was conducted by Westerners with a long background in India, assisted by an all-Indian staff. The alienation of the researchers was in class terms rather than nationality; the result was the same. Villagers who "resisted" the program were defined as "ignorant" or "prejudiced." But the distinction between "acceptors" and "resisters" did not lead to a differential analysis. Mamdani (1972: chap. 4), who was hostile to the family-planning technicians, compared sectors of the population in order to explain their behavior. Most of the inhabitants of the subject villages lived off the land but not all in the same way. Those well enough off to own a tractor had no rational need for children; they had large families in response to both public pressure and tradition. But the smallholders who worked their land were responding to a rational demand. It is true that eventually, when the land was divided up among the children, large families would result in greater fragmentation. But the more immediate problem of the smallholders was how to make ends meet.

> Given a very small income, to have to hire even one farmhand can mean disaster. If such a farmer is merely to survive, he must rely on his family for the necessary labor power. . . . Every farmer interviewed in this group expressed the hope that with a large enough family . . . a few children could be spared to live away from the family land, thus accumulating some savings and perhaps buying more land, land which could be worked with the manpower available within the family itself. . . . "Why pay 2500 rupees for an extra hand? Why not have a son?" [ibid.: 76–77].

The situation is similar with respect to landless farm laborers. Partial mechanization—that is, some machinery but not yet tractors—has stimulated the demand for farm labor, though mostly only during certain seasons. The laborers are typically paid a share of the crop, which the entire family—males and females, adults and children—gather together. "The more hands a family can muster, the more land it can contract from the cultivator" (ibid.: 94).

That it is in the rational interest, correctly conceived, of the lower agricultural classes to have large families does not mean that the large population growth that results is beneficial to the society. Even at the level of abstract theory, no one has ever been able really to link micro- with macro-economics, to build a bridge between the behavior of persons acting in their own individual interest and the societal trend resulting from the sum of these acts. In the market, as this developed in Western societies, Adam Smith's hand of providence does ordinarily equate the best interest of each person and of the whole, but not in every instance. The Indian economy is governed only to some degree by the rules of the market. It lacks, most fundamentally, the premise that each man seeks the maximum utility for himself; the very first misunderstanding that Driver listed was the notion that the individual is the basic unit of Indian society.

Has Fertility Increased?

Demographers typically assume that social–economic development results in a sizable decline in natality. The evidence for this is overwhelming if we compare the fertility levels of economically advanced and underdeveloped countries. In the long run, it is certainly true, modernization is associated with a smaller average family, but the crucial question is what happens during the transitional stage, which in the best cases must be measured in decades. The dogma handed down in the transition theory is that fertility declines, and the data to challenge this are typically too poor to make an indisputable case. All of the indices are approximate; the proportion of births measured by any index generally increases with successful modernization, and any upward movement that is accepted as valid may be merely a short-term fluctuation (e.g., Davis 1964). In Taiwan, one of the few areas with reasonably accurate statistics over the whole period of early economic development, the birth rate rose from the low 40s to above 45 before it began to decline, and this was not a spurious trend based on improved registration. Is Taiwan an anomaly in this respect; and, if not, what modernizing forces can result in a higher fertility?

1. Improved health leads to higher fecundity. Most strikingly, the efforts to bring venereal disease under control in Tropical Africa will reduce the widespread sterility that we have noted exists there and, *ceteris paribus*, will result in a sizable rise of the birth rate (A. Romaniuk, cited in Heer 1966). Any improvement in health, as from antimalaria projects or better nutrition (e.g., M. and R. G. Kamat, cited in Mauldin 1965), is likely to stimulate greater reproduction; and this applies to the health of both sexes. Of females in the fecund ages in one rural township of Taiwan, the percentage of widows fell by about half from 1905 to 1935. By the prolongation of *males'* life expectancy, thus, women's effective reproductive period was extended almost 3 years, and their completed family size by about one more child (Tuan 1958).

2. Whatever means the traditional society used deliberately to reduce population growth may not survive modernization. In Japan of the late Tokugawa period, for instance, infanticide was practiced in all regions of the country. While the practice persisted in a few backward communities, the official effort to prohibit it was almost completely successful within several decades after the institution of the new regime in 1867. The fertility of the Meiji period, according to a reconstruction from defective data, rose until the 1880s or 1890s, then remained at a high plateau until after the turn of the century (see pp. 455–462).

3. If in the traditional society the usual age at marriage is well past puberty, the transition to an urban–industrial society may break down the social controls by which this pattern is maintained. The classic case is Western Europe, which almost alone among preindustrial civilizations had established a high average age at marriage as the general norm (see pp. 415–416). Elsewhere in the world other kinds of changes in marital patterns can also effect a rise in reproduction.

4. Village taboos and religious practices unintentionally inhibiting fertility may break down; "the loosening of bonds of tradition . . . can also lead to the abandonment of practices that kept Indian fertility rates from being even higher" (Coale and Hoover 1958: 60). For example, among four social classes of rural India fertility was more or less equal for the first 15 years of marriage, but the completed family size of upper-class Hindus was "substantially lower" because fewer were willing to tolerate the remarriage of widows (Rele 1963).

5. To the degree that traditional norms favoring a large family persist, moreover, an improved economy may push fertility upward. It has been known for many decades that marriage rates (and thus, after a certain lag, birth rates) fluctuate with good or poor harvests, the business cycle, or other indices of relative economic prosperity (see pp. 154, 370, and for other analyses also those cited in Heer 1966). If efforts to improve the economy succeed, then, those who had refrained from marrying or, if married, from having children solely because

of economic pressures may respond to their improved situation with a more numerous progeny.

6. Most remarkably, family-planning programs can themselves result in a rise in fertility. If we assume from polling data that persons in the target population want to have about four children—particularly sons, say—then the ready availability of contraceptives may result in lowering the age at marriage and childbearing. Just because they are more confident that they will be able to avoid unwanted pregnancies later, young women may seek to concentrate their childbearing in their younger years, as is common in the West. In Taiwan, thus, the tendency of younger women to shorten the intervals between low-parity births contributed to a *rise* in their age-specific birth rates (Schultz 1969: 5–6; Freedman *et al.* 1972). And during the whole of the 1960s the fertility rates of wives aged 15–24 rose markedly (Finnigan and Keeny 1971). Given the high proportion of females in their 20s (the cohorts born at the peak of Taiwan's fertility), this negative influence cannot be dismissed as insignificant. Since no contraception works perfectly, some of the women will add another child to their planned family during the many years of their remaining fecundity. And even if this were not the case, the timing itself is an important element of incremental growth.

The direct effect of economic development [in short] is to increase rather than decrease the level of fertility. If this hypothesis is true, the historical fact that fertility over the long run has declined in all present-day industrial societies as their income advanced must then be explained by an inverse association between fertility and other social factors which tend to be positively associated with income [Heer 1966].

Among the most important of such factors are education, which opens up a wider range of possible living styles and thus affords both the incentive to reduce family size and the knowledge of how this can be done; lower infant and child mortality, which by increasing effective fertility reinforces all the pressures to reduce the number of children born; and social mobility, the mechanism by which society both offers potential parents other values in exchange for forgoing some reproduction and, as they move up the social ladder, changes the concept of suitable care so as to increase the cost per child (ibid.).

If Heer's thesis is correct and, indeed, the effect of modernization is partly to increase fertility and in other ways, thus only partly, to decrease it, the prospects are of course much less favorable than they had seemed. So long as one assumed that *traditional* and *modern* described homogeneous trends totally opposed to each other, and that all "traditional" ways of life and modes of thinking were pronatalist and all "modern" ones antinatalist, then any slapdash encouragement to social change would, by definition, reduce the average family size. As we have seen in several contexts, every item in that overoptimistic statement has proved to be fallacious. In order to reduce fertility effectively, one must proceed with a program based on a better appreciation of how complex the matter is.

GOVERNMENT PROGRAMS TO REDUCE FERTILITY

Efforts to induce "respondents" to become "acceptors" have been discussed as a mode of polling, but they are also, of course, an attempt to cut fertility. It has become a commonplace that rapid population growth in at least some underdeveloped countries is a serious block to economic growth and modernization, and most critics of family-planning programs do not challenge this underlying premise. Nor is it merely the issue of whether people or food will increase faster. Coale and Hoover's *Population Growth and Economic Development in Low-Income Countries* (1958), for example, goes well beyond the issue of subsistence. This interesting and important work attempts to give a specific answer to the question, how would India's overall economic development have been affected if its birth rate, instead of remaining constant, had fallen by half during the next generation? The population of the country was projected from 1956 to 1986, assuming that the probable sharp fall in mortality would take place, together with one of three alternative hypothetical courses in fertility: (1) no change or (2) a decline by half between 1966 and 1981 or (3) between 1956 and 1981. The population of 357 million in 1951 would increase, depending on the trend in the birth rate, to 775, 634, or 590 million in 1986, respectively, and the rate of continued growth in that year would be 2.6, 1.0, or 1.0 percent per annum. Growth is cumulative; the failure to control fertility early will present the next generation with the same problem of population pressure in much aggravated form.

In a country like India economic development depends very largely on how much of the national income can be invested. A rapidly increasing population diverts income, instead, to current consumption of food, housing, education, and general "social overhead." Cutting the birth rate, the authors show, would raise total production, which would have to be divided, moreover, among a smaller number. The real income per consumer of the low-fertility population thus would be *at least* 38 percent higher in 1986, and growing much faster than with the alternative projections. If a rise in real income is possible with a rapidly increasing population, that is to say, it would be substantially greater if births were controlled.

Economists can demonstrate that *if* population growth is not curtailed, economic development is hindered or, in the worst cases, blocked. But the influence operates also in the other direction. The principal lesson to be learned from the historical decline of family size in the West, which we have summarized in the Dumont–Banks model, indicates that the economy and thus the social structure must be flexible enough to motivate some, and then others, and finally virtually all to exercise self-control over procreation in exchange for improved chances to climb the social ladder. But if the economy is stagnant (in part because of rapid population growth), then for most this avenue to the small-family system is not available. The countries outside the Western core where the birth rate has fallen well below 40 are generally economically developed (Japan,

Israel) or marginal to the category of "underdeveloped" (Argentina, Chile); those at an early stage of development afford no clear indication of what level of fertility should be expected in the "normal" course of change. Nor is an analysis of such a "natural" trend necessarily a good guide to the probable future.

In the years since World War II, more and more nations and international agencies have come to see population growth, and thus also fertility, in a new light. At one time nontotalitarian governments viewed an increase in numbers as a social good or, if not, as outside the range of legitimate intervention. Still in the mid-1960s, official concern about population in most of Latin America was expressed only by sponsoring conferences or research centers to study the problem, while private groups attempted to institute birth-control programs (Delgado 1966). In the present perspective of some other underdeveloped countries, population is not merely a dependent variable but one element in the complex interrelation of economy, social structure, and culture. A society attempting to plan its transition to a modern industrial level cannot leave this crucial factor to "nature," while policy decisions control every other one.

The Problem of Evaluation

Among American demographers and sociologists, a good deal of attention has been paid to a number of small areas, mainly in Asia, where family planning was introduced under joint government–private auspices.

> The years 1963–64 very probably will go down in demographic history as one of the great landmarks of social-science research progress. In twelve months from June 1963 to June 1964 researchers in fertility control began to get a string of successes that left no doubt that by planned intervention they had induced a down-ward change in the birth rate in high-fertility populations. . . . Six ingredients are the necessary and sufficient conditions for intervention . . . : (1) awareness of the possibility and benefits of family planning; (2) knowledge of how to implement family planning; (3) impersonalization, desexualization, and public discussion of family planning, primarily through private, informal personal interaction; (4) legitimation and social reinforcement of family planning; (5) self-involvement in family planning; (6) supplies through convenient and nonpunitive channels [Bogue 1964].

In a later statement of the same thesis, Bogue (1967) titled his paper "The End of the Population Explosion"! Projecting the same mood of self-congratulation, Frank Notestein asserted that "within two decades the rate of population growth may well be brought to 1 percent or 1.5 percent throughout the major sectors of the newly developing world" (Berelson *et al.* 1966a: 829).

We have intimated that by another opinion programs of "action-research" were not highly successful in eliciting the genuine attitudes toward family size and the use of contraceptives, and we shall shortly question whether they were in fact effective in cutting the family size of the subject population. Such programs can do several useful things. For those willing to listen, they correct misinformation and tell people about efficient contraceptives, how to use them, and where they are available. And they may "change attitudes" in the sense of resolving whatever conflicts of values exist in persons undergoing a process of social change. Thus they may help some persons overcome an aversion to birth control and reduce the number of their children to the family size they desire— which is, to repeat, about four children in most underdeveloped areas (but see also Hyrenius and Åhs 1968). But really to evaluate the effect of a family-planning program on a country's fertility, one must be able to distinguish between it and all the other factors that help determine the average family size. To separate one strand from a complicated interaction is a problem that can perhaps be best explicated with the help of a schematic typology (Table 16-7). Let us consider each of that table's quadrants in turn.

Table 16-7. A Schematic Comparison of Planned and Actual Change

	Actual Change	
Planned Change	NO	YES
No	1. "Natural" stability	2. "Natural" change
Yes	3. "Unsuccessful" planning	4. "Successful" planning

1. "Natural" stability. If there is neither any deliberate policy to reduce fertility nor in fact any decline, one might conclude that everything affecting the birth rate has remained constant; but that conclusion might well be mistaken. The proportion of women in the prime childbearing ages might have risen, for instance, and at the same time the age at marriage might have gone up just enough to cancel the effect of this change in the age structure. More generally, of the myriad influences on either the proportion of young people currently having children or on the completed family size, several factors may have changed in such a way as to result in no net difference in the fertility. Even a competent demographer may be completely unaware, say, that certain days are regarded as inauspicious for marital conception (as in Taiwan) and certainly unaware, therefore, whether the impact of such a superstition is lessening or not.

The relation of this argument to public policy is seldom recognized. When a social phenomenon is the composite effect of many norms and institutions, of which some are unknown and some of the known ones cannot be measured, then no analysis can be more than partial. In particular, a program to effect a deliberate change in such a phenomenon cannot be evaluated with full certainty. Since we are unable to analyze all of the "natural" determinants of fertility and thus are unable to predict its course independent of any family-planning program, we cannot say at all precisely how much that program deflected the trend of the birth rate from its "natural" course.

2. "Natural" change. By "natural" we mean only beyond the realm of policy, and the view of what is possible and legitimate can change at any time. The most important step toward successful rain-making, for instance, may well have been the first, the supposition that we *can* do something about the weather. To the extent that planning connotes an attempt to establish rational control over human affairs, in other words, it results in a contraction of "nature." Such a contraction, once started, is likely to spread: it is a commonplace of social history that persons who grow up in modern industrial societies are less apt to act according to "mere" tradition, more apt to weigh one probable outcome against another and choose the action with the best overall result. We must beware of translating this truism into the notion that rationality is a monopoly of modern man. The propensity to reproduce among Indian agriculturists derived, as we have noted, not merely from the considerable influence of continuing tradition but mainly from the rational choice of the potential parents, who seek their own maximum utility through a numerous progeny.

3. "Unsuccessful" planning. The true test of a policy is its failure, which is parallel to the negation of a scientific theory. It is principally by proved deficiencies in specific plans (or theories) that policy making (or knowledge) as a whole can advance. Yet in the vast number of papers, studies, and monographs reporting on efforts to induce a decline in fertility, extremely few give negative self-evaluations. Indeed, there have been criticisms by other analysts, though on balance not very many. From the annual reports to the several world-wide surveys, the general temper is self-applause—in contrast to the continuing high fertility in most underdeveloped areas.

4. "Successful" planning. At a simplistic level, a successful policy constitutes planned change that is congruent with actual change. The analytic question is: when may one reasonably substitute *the determinant of* for *congruent with*? In any but the simplest social policies, establishing a causal link between purposive acts and their possible consequences involves a full analysis of all actual or possible factors. If there are multiple purposes to the policy, as is often the case, some may be realized and others not; is the policy then successful? The stated aims of a policy may be realized but with unintended deleterious side-effects; is the policy then successful? Sometimes the effect is greater than had been envisaged (as in the effort to cut Japan's fertility and the subsequent reversal of policy). Seriously stipulated, *success* is an enormously intricate concept (cf. Simmons 1971: chap. 5; Wolfers 1969).

The commonest means of adapting this schema to the real world is to compare an experimental population, which is subjected to the stimulus, with a control population, which is not. In the Khanna study, thus, the six villages on which family-planning efforts were focused were contrasted with six others (on the assumption, which Driver challenged, that each village is a world unto itself). There was a temporary decline in the birth rate, but it began before the program got under way, continued at the same rate for a certain period, occurred among both the test and the control populations, and was due to a rise in the age at marriage rather than the increased use of contraceptives. The Khanna study, in short, was a failure in its professed aim of inducing a reduction in fertility, but we know that it was a failure only because—quite atypically—the analysis of its results included a control. In most instances, the sequence program–decline would have been sufficient to apply the common principle: *post hoc, ergo propter hoc*.

Taiwan

Some of the most enthusiastic reports of successful family-planning projects pertain to Taiwan, and it may be useful to consider that case more closely. A significant decline in the birth rate began in 1951 and then, after an interruption, continued from 1955 (see Figure 12–1, p. 461). The reason for this decline, whether broad changes in the society or the program to induce smaller families, is the issue.

In 1962 a fertility survey was conducted in the city of Taichung under the joint auspices of the Taiwan Population Studies Center and the University of Michigan Population Studies Center, with financial aid from the Population Council. This survey indicated that with the spread of modern ideas more women might be willing to plan their families if given the opportunity. On the basis of this hypothesis, an intensive program was initiated in the same city to test the inhabitants' receptivity to family planning and to furnish contraceptives to those willing to use them. Two years later some 250 private physicians agreed to participate in a program to expand family planning from Taichung to eighteen of the island's twenty-two counties and city districts. They inserted Lippes loops and gave after-care when necessary for the equivalent of $1.50, half ordinarily to be paid by the patient and half by the Joint Commission on Rural Reconstruction, the main agency through which American aid has been distributed.

During 1964 almost 50,000 IUDs were inserted, with the number rising rapidly from 516 in January to 6,822 in December. According to a follow-up study a year later, fewer than 1 percent of the loops recorded had not been inserted (presumably the physicians had filled in the forms fraudulently in order to collect the 75 cents), 6.35 percent of the patients had expelled the loop, and 12 percent had had it removed for reasons other than a desire for pregnancy (Gillespie 1965). Taiwan's total fertility rate fell by 3.7 percent in one year, and a number of analysts extrapolated this downward trend with a greater enthusiasm than would seem to be warranted. The two senior American researchers wrote a book with contributions from other members of the team (Freedman and Takeshita 1969), and this can be taken as their considered appraisal of the project. Whether even the tempered optimism of this work is well based, however, can be challenged on a number of points.

The relevance of the Taichung study is said to be broad—namely to the population problem that "exists in many countries," for which "in several ways Taiwan's program has become a model . . . to guide the increasing number of national family-planning programs" (ibid.: 3). Whether Taiwan is representative of the so-called third world we will postpone discussing, but was the choice of Taichung an apt one to represent Taiwan itself? To select an urban site for an analysis of a population more than half of which was rural, in any case, tipped the scale toward a sector possibly more receptive to birth control than the average. Even in the cities the official climate was still rather hostile to birth control, and one reason for selecting Taichung was that "it was far enough from Taipei [the capital] to escape some of the political problems that might be expected in that international center" (ibid.: 12–13). It is perhaps typical of community studies that they are unrepresentative: the Lynds, who as Marxists were looking for a two-class society in some "Middletown," found in Muncie one of the very few cities of its size completely dominated by a single firm; the declining textile town of Newburyport was ideal to illustrate the deterioration of the culture that the authors of "Yankee City" wanted to demonstrate. It would not seem that the choice of Taichung was entirely free from this kind of unconscious bias.

The Chinese population of Taiwan (that is, all except the small minority of Formosans, who are of a different race) is divided into two sectors: the Taiwanese, who lived on the island when it was a Japanese colony, and the Mainlanders, who retreated to this bastion when the Nationalists were defeated by Communist armies. A differential analysis based on this distinction can be made, of course, only by someone aware of it, and in their first reports the Michigan team made no mention of it. In various other studies of Taiwan (S. H. Chen et al. 1963; Eberhard and Eberhard 1967), Mainlander women were found to be much more likely to use contraceptives, presumably because of their better education and higher status. In Taichung, however, the Michigan team did not analyze Mainlanders as a separate category because their proportion was "relatively small." In fact, according to a sample survey by the research team, 25 percent of the husbands and 13 percent of the wives in Taichung were Mainlanders, compared with only about one-tenth of the island's whole population (Freedman and Takeshita 1969: 37, 453). By ignoring this factor, the authors reduced the representativeness of Taichung somewhat more.

The most important section of the work we are examining (ibid.: chap. 6) constitutes an attempt to distinguish the effects of the family-planning program from all other factors. The team allocated four "treatments" randomly among Taichung's approximately 2,400 neighborhood units (or *lin*): (1) no special efforts to reach couples directly; (2) a series of letters and pamphlets mailed to couples with specified characteristics on methods of contraception, the location of clinics, and the like; (3) these mailings supplemented by neighborhood meetings mixing entertainment with information and by personal visits of health workers to speak with the women; and (4) the same stimuli, except that the health workers spoke to both wives and husbands. Those *lin* in which home visits were made were divided further according to whether the mail stimulus was light, medium, or heavy. In all, the health workers made nearly 12,000 first home visits, and some 500 neighborhood meetings were organized. Family-planning services and supplies were offered at ten clinics in various parts of the city.

Several of the experimental variations made no difference in the observed results. Mailed appeals had no special effect, and visiting both husband and wife no greater effect than visiting the wife alone. The three-way differentiation according to the strength of the stimulus broke down into a dichotomy between heavy and medium-light. With both a heavy dosage of mailed propaganda and home visits by health workers, the percentage of women accepting contraceptives services increased from 15 to 28. The utility of these stimuli to family-planning programs seemed to have been demonstrated.

In fact, however, the experiment had a number of faults that cast doubt on this conclusion. The details highlight the difficulty of conducting simultaneously an action program and an experiment to test its effectiveness. Some 50,000 copies of sixteen posters were placed in prominent locations throughout the city, irrespective of *lin* boundaries; these presented the idea of family planning in a simple, attractive form and invited the reader to visit the nearest health station for further information. Since each *lin* was very small, with an average of only twenty households and twelve married women aged 20-39, there is no reason in any case to postulate that no leakage took place among them. Of the women who either had an IUD fitted or received supplies or instructions on other methods, "presumably with intent to use them," more than 15 percent came from outside the city and thus outside the presumed experimental population. In contrast, only 2 percent of those receiving brochures acted on the suggestion that they write to invite a home visit by a health worker. Acceptances were "especially high among couples who had once used contraception but had given it up—that is, among motivated but unsatisfied couples" (ibid.: 130).

On the basis of the success that the Taichung experiment seemed to have, the Taiwan Provincial Health Department started a more extensive program to bring family-planning services to the whole of the island. It began slowly in 1964, and by the end of 1967 there were 380,000 insertions or reinsertions of IUDs. Counting each as an original insertion, this would have represented protection for about 22 percent of the married women of childbearing age, but this percentage has to be deflated—as we have noted earlier—by the considerable proportion who either were not completely fecund or were getting loops for the second or third time (ibid.: 314).

Whatever doubts one may have about the seeming success of the program in Taichung are reinforced when one compares the total fertility rates (that is, the sums of age-specific fertility rates) of Taichung and other portions of the population. From 1962 to 1970, while this rate fell by an annual average of 182 units in all of Taiwan, by 211 units in small towns, and by 156 in all major cities, in Taichung it fell by only 154 units—less than in any of the other categories! One need not conclude that the special effort in Taichung inhibited the decline that was going on "naturally," but one can hardly ascribe to it any reinforcement of that downward trend. The same conclusion comes from a temporal analysis: not only did the downward trend in fertility begin well before the program got under way but it continued at precisely the same slope (Li 1973).

The main reason for the decline in Taiwan's birth rate was its extraordinarily buoyant economy and the consequent opportunities for rapid upward mobility, associated with the probable dissemination of modernist views and aspirations. Family size was cut in part through a higher age at marriage, only in part through a wider use of contraceptives. No evidence suggests that the widely publicized campaign to promote the limitation of births had any success, even in this exceptionally favorable environment.

Like Taiwan, the other places where efforts to reduce fertility have attained at least the appearance of success—Puerto Rico, Jamaica, Singapore, South Korea, Thailand—have a number of characteristics in common. They are relatively small, stable, and generally well administered, so that the substantial financial grants from advanced countries could be put to good use, affording new opportunities to those equipped to take advantage of them. A realistic prognosis for the populations of all underdeveloped countries must be based on the fact that in many (e.g., in Africa and Latin America) government programs to cut natality have barely started, and in others (e.g., the larger countries of Asia) the official efforts have had no discernible effect on their birth rates. In size, in complexity, in receptivity to any modernizing influence, Taiwan is not India, Puerto Rico is not Mexico.

Family-Planning Projects in India

The Indian government's efforts to reduce fertility were initially opposed, as we have seen, by Gandhi, Nehru, and his Minister of Health, but eventually the family-planning program became the most important, with the possible exception of China, in a sizable underdeveloped country. It evolved slowly. In the progress reports on the First Five-Year Plan (1951–56) the program was described as of "supreme" importance, but as late as 1955 the Deputy Minister of Health, when asked whether it would be accelerated, replied, "The question is still under consideration." With the Rs. 6.5 million allocated, 147 clinics were established in all of India, 126 in cities and 21 in rural areas (Samuel 1966). The allotment in the Second Plan (1956–61) was also small, and a large part was not spent. Three months after the start of the plan period, Nehru asserted that family planning was being assisted "not in a major way but in experimentation." The emphasis was medical, to promote the "health and happiness" of the family. A bureaucratic structure was set up both in the federal government and in each of the states, and by the end of the Second Plan the government had established over 4,000 clinics, where contraceptives were issued at subsidized rates or gratis. After three years, of the 75 to 80 million families in India contact had been made with 7 million, and of these only 1.4 million had been given advice. "It is evident that the pace of progress is slow" (Gopalaswami 1962).

One reason for this fact was that, in imitation of private planned-parenthood associations, the work was organized through clinics, which by their very nature reached only a fraction of the population. For the first year the only contraceptives available were those conventionally distributed through such agencies. These required the couple to exercise regular and responsible control each time they had intercourse; to clean and store the pessary in a home with no running water and little privacy; to return periodically to the clinic for new supplies (Israel 1966). An acceptable contraceptive method, Chand had stated (1956: 98), should be fully effective, completely harmless, cheap, suited to the conditions of the particular community, and esthetically satisfactory; he concluded that "a contraceptive meeting these requirements and adapted to the needs of India does not exist at present." At the end of the Second Plan, "India has not achieved any reduction of its birth rate, . . . and there is no sign that a downturn will occur in the next few years. . . . So far we have been engaged only on what may be regarded as pilot experimentation" (Gopalaswami 1962).

The year 1961, according to one analyst, marked "the beginning of the policy of population control" (Samuel 1966). An additional impetus was the result of the 1961 census, after which the government evinced a greater concern with population increase and its economic and social consequences. In the Third Plan (1962–67) the family-planning program was decentralized, with federal allocations spent through state projects, and a greater effort was made to evaluate the results. The search for an appropriate means of contraception continued. The so-called natural methods (rhythm and *coitus interruptus*) were still advocated by some on moral grounds, by others (e.g., Gopalaswami 1962) because of the low cost to the government. Diaphragm and spermicide were inappropriate for the reasons already cited. Oral contraceptives have never become popular in India. "Twenty pills a month for months on end is expensive. And, expense apart, there will always be women who will forget to take their daily dose" (Chandrasekhar 1967a).

With any method of contraception, a prime factor in determining its success is the strength of the people's motivation, and in India some efforts have been made to generate this. In one of the volumes of the 1951 census, Gopalaswami, writing officially as the Registrar General, defined all childbirths above the third order as "improvident maternity." The incidence of improvident maternity, between 40 and 45 percent in 1951, had to be reduced to under 5 percent within 15 years. Whether such appeals, however reasonable, have any effect on the fertility of potential parents can be doubted. Even those who become aware of the argument and accept it in overall terms may not apply it to themselves. Among a sample of rural high-school teachers, 60 percent believed that India

The men who are learning how a pessary works (*Peter Schmid—PIX*) seem to be more interested, or less apprehensive, than the woman being introduced to an IUD (*World Health Organization*).

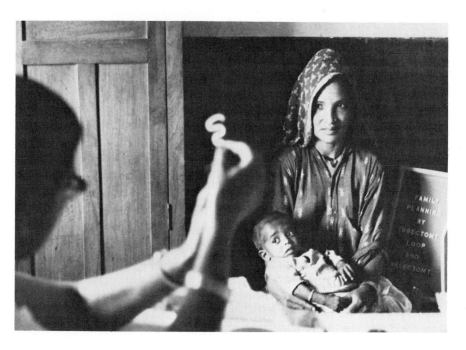

Table 16-8. Failure Rates of Intra-uterine Devices According to Various Studies, India, 1960s

Place of Study	Sample	Rates per 100 IUD users			
		EXPULSIONS	REMOVALS	PREG-NANCIES	TOTAL FAILURES
Ajmer	1,850	3.5	14.4	0.6	18.5
Ambala (1)	144	11.1	34.0	0.7	45.8
Ambala (2)	100	8.0	24.0	0	32.0
Bareilly	1,581	4.3	14.3	0.9	19.5
Bombay[a]	775	10.9	21.9	0.9	34.0
Hooghly	200	4.5	7.0	0.5	12.0
Poona	265	3.7	18.5	0.4	22.6
Trivandrun (1)	86	6.0	6.0	0	12.0
Trivandrun (2)	80	—	—	—	37.5

[a] Based on life-table method.
SOURCE: S. N. Agarwala, "The Progress of IUCD in India," in International Union for the Scientific Study of Population, *Proceedings, 1967* (Sydney, 1967), pp. 424–430.

is overpopulated, more than 40 percent were opposed in principle to birth control, and three-quarters did not practice it themselves (Reeder and Krishnamurty 1964).

Some saw intra-uterine devices as the ideal means, but the experience in India has not warranted this confidence (Table 16-8). Very few of the women who retained the IUD—according to a number of Indian studies, less than 1 percent—became pregnant, but as many as one-tenth of the users automatically expelled the device and as many as one-third removed it because of excessive bleeding, pain or discomfort, or the fear generated by the bleeding of others. Failure rates were higher among young women and among those above the lowest income bracket. During the first year (1965–66), after a slow start, 800,000 IUDs were inserted, but in the following year only about 790,000, or 19 percent of the target of 6 million (Murty 1967).

In 1967, Sripati Chandrasekhar became Minister of Health and Family Planning. A world-renowned demographer, he had spent much of his professional life advocating that India control her population growth. With his appointment, there came a new emphasis on sterilization, "of all the methods tried so far the only [one that] has yielded significant results" (Chandrasekhar 1967a). As early as 1957, Madras State (of whose Family-Planning Board Gopalaswami was a prominent member) had started a program of subsidized sterilization. Subsequently three other states—Mysore, Kerala, and Maharashtra—instituted similar projects. A federal program was started on a small scale in 1958, and from 1966 on New Delhi reimbursed state governments at the rate of Rs. 11

for each IUD insertion, Rs. 30 for each vasectomy, and Rs. 40 for each salpingectomy. The enthusiasm for sterilization was great (1 rupee = approximately U.S. 20¢).

Effective, inexpensive and entirely harmless methods are already available, by which every married couple can stop their career of childbearing at that stage of their married life when they decide they have had enough children. What is required to be done immediately is for the leaders of the people to acquire the conviction that this is so and to transmit that conviction to the people. The next step is for every State Government to organize the provision of necessary surgical facilities free of all expense to the people. There is no doubt whatever that India's birth rate can be halved if such facilities are organized and used on a scale sufficient to perform five operations every year in every local community of one thousand people. The solution of the population problem of India, which seems so intractable today, is really as simple as that [Gopalaswami 1959].

The calculation has been cited often, but it is somewhat misleading. The laws under which doctors perform the operation, whether vasectomy or salpingectomy, vary from one Indian state to another; but they all prescribe a written agreement from both spouses, a minimum number of living children, a minimum age of the patient (e.g., Gopalaswami 1962). The consequence—which is of course reinforced by the usual characteristics of those who volunteer to undergo a generally irreversible end to fecundity—was that only the top of India's excess fertility could thus be removed. According to a study of vasectomy in Maharashtra, the average age of the 3,465 men sterilized was 39 to 40 (the ages of 102 of the patients ranged from 53 to 68+), and they were fathers of an average of 5.33 living children. "There appears ... to be no possibility of vasectomy camps having a significant effect on the birth rate, ... [but] they have no doubt helped to create a climate favorable for popularizing family planning" (Dandekar 1963; cf. Kurup and Mathen 1966).

Since a decline in fertility in underdeveloped countries would help accelerate economic growth, it would be worthwhile for these nations to invest in nonbirths (Simmons 1971). The American economist Stephen Enke calculated in 1960 that in India the value of permanently preventing a birth was roughly $125, and that a considerable percentage of this sum might advantageously be offered as a bonus to young, married, fecund men who offered to have themselves sterilized (Enke 1960; cf. Enke 1963: 377–384; Krueger and Sjaastad, with reply by Enke, 1962). A partial approach to this rationale has been in operation in certain areas of India. As Madras State set it up in mid-1958, the allowance was limited to lower civil servants in Madras City; fathers who underwent an operation were paid Rs. 14 and mothers Rs. 25. A year and a half later, the scheme was extended to include the 35 million people of Madras State, and the bonus was increased to Rs. 30. In Maharashtra a sterilization campaign was started on "All-India Family-Planning Day," December 18, 1950, and during the next three weeks the more than 7,000 men who underwent a vasectomy were

A street scene in India (*Baldev—PIX*).

each paid Rs. 20 for their loss of working time. As a member of Parliament, Chandrasekhar suggested that India request permission of the U.S. Government to use counterpart funds accumulated in India to pay a cash bonus of, say, Rs. 100 to each man undergoing a vasectomy. That would still be only about $20 rather than the $125 Enke proposed, but for nine-tenths of the sample studied in Maharashtra it would have been more than a month's income (Dandekar 1963). However, nothing came of the proposal: "both governments are extremely sensitive in this area" (Chandrasekhar 1967a).

If . . . calculations are made on the basis of the projected population as given by the Expert Committee on Population, it is found that 28 million operations performed in ten years will bring down the birth rate by only 5.5 points [from an estimated 42 per thousand]. . . . If the birth rate is to be reduced from 40 to 25 in a period of ten years, roughly 6 million sterilization operations will have to be performed each year [Agarwala 1966a].

The total number of operations actually performed from 1956 to March 1967 was 2.27 million (Murty 1967), or about 3.5 percent of the annual rate required according to this calculation.

In a few small areas of India where an intensive effort to reduce fertility was made, the estimated birth rates fell appreciably up to the mid-1960s. But "it is doubtful if the national birth rate has shown any decline" (Murty 1967; cf. Chandrasekhar, 1967a). According to twenty-seven studies of family-planning practices in India, not more than 2 percent of currently married rural females of reproductive ages were practicing birth control of any kind (Agarwala 1966b).

During the first quarter of 1969 a U.N. Advisory Mission (1970), appointed by the agency at the request of the Government of India, studied the family-planning program and made recommendations for its improvement. Its report is rather dismal. From Rs. 1.4 million in 1951 to Rs. 370 million in 1968–69, the expenditures had risen in a logarithmic curve. At the latter date the number of regular employees numbered some 70,000, including physicians, "extension educators," "lady health visitors," and "auxiliary nurse midwives." More than a fifth of the total budget went for "compensation money," payments to sterilization or IUD clients, "motivators," doctors, and paramedical staff. A public enterprise, Hindustan Latex Ltd., had been built to manufacture condoms, and about a tenth of the budget was used to distribute these free. About 12 percent of the Rs. 370 million was spent on "education" and "research." The decline in the number of sterilizations had been by about 10 percent during the prior year, and "it seem[ed] clear that increased acceptance of sterilization will depend upon intensified motivational efforts." Over the past 2 years, the number of IUD insertions had declined by well over half, and "all efforts should be made to rehabilitate the IUD program." The number of condoms distributed increased to either 50.6 or 89 million in 1968–69 (the report gives both figures, with no explanation). "Scarcely anything is known, however, concerning the regularity of use and the use–effectiveness of condoms, and studies of these aspects are much needed." At the time abortion was illegal except in order to save the life of the mother; it was legalized in 1971. About the impact of these rising expenditures and declining services on India's fertility the Advisory Mission was reluctant to speculate. "Until some system is put into effect to monitor the completeness of reporting in the Sample Registration Scheme, the use of its estimates in family-planning evaluation is limited."

According to the 1971 census, India's population totaled some 547.4 million, representing an increase during the intercensal decade by 108.2 million, or just under one-fourth. The crude birth and death rates during the decade, estimated from a dozen sample surveys, averaged 40 and 18, respectively. The overall increase, thus, was by 2.2 percent per year, but in so large a country this national figure does not indicate the concentration in the areas growing most rapidly. Nizard (1972) included a map giving the rates of increase between 1951 and 1971 of the various states and territories; these ranged from hardly more than a third up to 60 to 85 percent in both western and eastern coastal regions. In 1971 only 13.2 percent of females were reported as economically active, down from 28.0 percent a decade earlier. Whatever effect work outside the home might have on family size was being dispensed with, together with much of the family-planning program.

When the 1973–74 budget was announced, the allocation for birth-control programs was cut drastically. Rather than the $104 million allocated the year before, R. K. Khadilkar, the Minister of Health and Family Planning, had requested $81.1 million; he got $75.1 million. The decision had been made at the highest levels: because of the unplanned expenditures made necessary by drought relief, wage increases for government employees, and inflation, cuts had to be

According to the advertisement of a sexologist in the old section of Delhi, he can either control births or increase fertility. Note that one regimen is for the birth specifically of a son (*Baldev—PIX*).

made in "nonessentials." "Senior health officials publicly deny that the budget cuts will seriously curtail family-planning programs." Later, in response to sharp criticism both at home and abroad, a portion of the cut was restored. "We are hoping to devise new strategies," Mr. Khadilkar reported (*New York Times*, August 6 and November 11, 1973).

SUMMARY

So far as we can tell from various types of data, none of them fully adequate, the crude birth rates of the major underdeveloped countries are around 40, sometimes lower but also sometimes higher. Combined with death rates sometimes as low as around 10—or if substantially higher still falling—this natality results in a population growth so rapid that plans to modernize the economy are endangered. It is not feasible to wait for the decline in average family size that will presumably accompany full social–economic development, for during the period of transition it would seem that fertility is as likely to rise as to fall. In an era when no other element of the society operates according to laissez-faire principles, the "natural" functioning of reproduction can result in disaster.

The conflict between traditional ideologies and modernizing movements, a conventional framework for studying trends in underdeveloped countries, is a misleading guide to the analysis of their fertility. The major religions of the non-Western world, it is true, reinforce the family and prescribe parental responsibilities, but their stands on such a key question as the legitimacy of contraception are generally ambivalent or self-contradictory. The weight of left-wing nationalism, on the contrary, has usually been to stress the moral, economic, and military worth of a large and rapidly growing population and thus, until the pressure becomes acute, to oppose family planning. And the planned-parenthood movement, whatever its value in the West, is almost irrelevant to problems on the massive new scale of present-day Asia, Africa, and Latin America.

Government programs to reduce the birth rate have had a certain success in a number of small, stable countries, typically transitional to a developed economy rather than truly "underdeveloped." But "there have as yet been no examples of populations in less developed countries that have managed to *initiate* a reduction in fertility by means of a family-planning program" (Hauser 1973). And in the large, populous countries (apart from Communist China, which is discussed in the following chapter), official efforts have barely begun or, as in India, have not succeeded in reducing the country's fertility at all. One reason is the erroneous premise that people want small families and that their numerous progeny results from ignorance and loosely based attitudes, both of which can be changed by propaganda. Actually, polls in various countries give the average number of children desired as four. "Current programs will not enable a government to control population size. . . . The unthinking identification of family planning with population control is an ostrich-like approach in that it permits people to hide from themselves the enormity and unconventionality of the task" (Davis 1967).

Modernization takes place not by any regular, precise process, but by a complex interaction among a typical range of key institutions in a manner that reflects both the interrelation among them (e.g., modern industry demands a literate population; literacy opens up new potentials in culture and politics) and the tie of each culture to its specific past. Those analysts in each social discipline who have attempted to transgress the bounds of a single case have very often erred on the side of too facile generalization, and repeatedly we have been put to the task of freeing our thoughts from one or another monistic bond—in earlier generations racial or geographic determinism and, more recently, their economic or demographic analogues. How much of a guide is the past development of advanced countries for mapping the future modernization of presently backward areas? In some overall sense, obviously, the world is becoming more homogeneous, and it is just this metamorphosis that we mean by modernization. But to assume that details of the process must follow a known course, or that the homogenization must eventually eliminate all fundamental differences, is to commit the egregious error of comparative analysis.

CITED REFERENCES AND SUGGESTIONS FOR FURTHER READING

Writings on the population of the underdeveloped countries have increased at a rate that almost matches that of their subject matter. This pouring forth of print reflects the importance of the issue but also, unfortunately, a mounting dissensus. Even if the more extremist statements on either side are ignored, within the range of professional commentators differences have sharpened on a number of questions. The conventional view of the proponents of family planning, represented in such a work as the volume edited by Berelson *et al.* (1966a), continues in both similar compendia (e.g., Revelle *et al.* 1971) and periodic surveys of activities the world over (e.g., Nortman 1972). This point of view has been increasingly challenged in several ways. Most fundamental is the criticism of scholars like Ester Boserup (1965), who has analyzed the positive effect of population growth on the rural economy, or Mamdani (1972), who shows why, within the framework of traditional agricultural institutions, each peasant needs a numerous progeny. Other critics have pointed to the failures of birth-control efforts (e.g., Davis 1967; Li 1973) or have stressed the importance of factors other than propaganda (e.g., May and Heer 1968; Raulet 1970; Chandrasekhar 1972).

The crucial facts are that modernization is a less simple process than it was once pictured and, in particular, that its effect on fertility is complex and ambivalent. Good analyses on this key theme have been offered by Robinson (1961), Abu-Lughod (1964, 1965), Heer (1966), and Zarate (1967a), among others.

Excellent guidance to further reading is given in Driver's 1,280-page annotated bibliography (1971), which covers the whole world but is organized by country.

*ABU-LUGHOD, JANET. 1964. "Urban-Rural Differences as a Function of the Demographic Transition: Egyptian Data and an Analytical Model," *American Journal of Sociology*, **69**, 476–490.

———. 1965. "The Emergence of Differential Fertility in Urban Egypt," *Milbank Memorial Fund Quarterly*, **43**, 235–253.

AGARWALA, S. N. 1966a. "The Arithmetic of Sterilization in India," *Eugenics Quarterly*, **13**, 209–213.

———. 1966b. *Some Problems of India's Population*. Bombay: Vora.

AHMED, MOHIUDDIN. 1966. "Rates and Levels of Mortality and Fertility in Pakistan," *Population Review*, **10**, 44–60.

ARCINIEGAS, GERMÁN. 1967. *Latin America: A Cultural History*. New York: Knopf.

BERELSON, BERNARD, *et al.*, editors. 1966a. *Family Planning and Population Programs: A Review of World Developments*. Chicago: University of Chicago Press.

———. 1966b. "KAP Studies on Fertility," in Berelson 1966a.

BLACKER, C. P. 1955. "The Rhythm Method: Two Indian Experiments," *Eugenics Review*, **47**, 93–105 and 163–172.

BLACKER, J. G. C. 1959. "Fertility Trends of the Asian Population of Tanganyika," *Population Studies*, **13**, 46–60.

*BLAKE, JUDITH. 1965. "Demographic Science and the Redirection of Population Policy," in Sheps and Ridley 1965.

BOGUE, DONALD J. 1964. "The Demographic Breakthrough: From Projection to Control," *Population Index*, **30**, 449–454.

———. 1967. "The End of the Population Explosion," *Public Interest*, no. 7, pp. 11–20.

BOSERUP, ESTER. 1965. *The Conditions of Agricultural Growth: The Agrarian Change under Population Pressure*. Chicago: Aldine.

BOURCIER DE CARBON, PHILIPPE. 1973. "Projections de la population algérienne jusqu'en 2001," *Population*, **28**, 291–334.

BURNIGHT, ROBERT G., NATHAN L. WHETTEN, and BRUCE D. WAXMAN. 1956. "Differential Rural-Urban Fertility in Mexico," *American Sociological Review*, **21**, 3–8.

CALDWELL, J. C. 1967. "Fertility Differentials as Evidence of Incipient Fertility Decline in a Developing Country," *Population Studies*, **21**, 5–21.

CHAND, GYAN. 1956. *Some Aspects of the Population Problem of India*. Bihar, India: Patna University Press.

CHANDRASEKHAR, S. 1960. "A Note on Demographic Statistics in India," *Population Review*, **4**, 40–45.

———. 1967a. "India's Population: Fact, Problem and Policy," in Chandrasekhar 1967b.

———, editor. 1967b. *Asia's Population Problems*. London: Allen & Unwin.

———. 1972. *Infant Mortality, Population Growth and Family Planning in India*. Chapel Hill: University of North Carolina Press.

CHEN SHAO-HSING, YAO-TUNG WANG, and FREDERIC J. FOLEY. 1963. "Pattern of Fertility in Taiwan," *Journal of Social Science* (Taipei), **13**, 209–294.

CHOLDIN, HARVEY M., A. MAJEED KAHN, and B. HOSNE ARA. 1967. "Cultural Complications in Fertility Interviewing," *Demography*, **4**, 244–252.

COALE, ANSLEY J. 1963. "Estimates of Various Demographic Measures Through the Quasi-Stable Age Distribution," in Milbank Memorial Fund, *Emerging Techniques in Population Research*. New York.

*———, and EDGAR M. HOOVER. 1958. *Population Growth and Economic Development in Low-Income Countries: A Case Study of India's Prospects*. Princeton, N.J.: Princeton University Press.

———, and FRANK LORIMER. 1968. "Summary of Estimates of Fertility and Mortality," in William Brass *et al.*, editors, *The Demography of Tropical Africa*. Princeton, N.J.: Princeton University Press.

COLLVER, O. ANDREW. 1965. *Birth Rates in Latin America: New Estimates of Historical Trends and Fluctuations*. Berkeley: Institute of International Studies, University of California.

COOKE, DOROTHY S. 1969. "Population Growth Estimation Experiment in Pakistan," *Statistical Reporter*, no. 69–11.

DANDEKAR, KUMUDINI. 1963. "Vasectomy Camps in Maharashtra," *Population Studies*, **17**, 147–154.

DAS GUPTA, AJIT. 1958. "Determination of Fertility Level and Trend in Defective Registration Areas," *Bulletin de l'Institut International de Statistique*, **36**, 127–136.

*DAVIS, KINGSLEY. 1951. *The Population of India and Pakistan*. Princeton, N.J.: Princeton University Press.

DAVIS, KINGSLEY. 1964. "The Place of Latin America in World Demographic History," *Milbank Memorial Fund Quarterly*, **42**, 19–47.

*———. 1967. "Population Policy: Will Current Programs Succeed?" *Science*, **158**, 730–739.

DELGADO GARCÍA, RAMIRO. 1966. "Perspectives of Family Planning Programs in Latin America," in Stycos and Arias 1966.

DEMENY, PAUL. 1965. "Estimation of Vital Rates for Populations in the Process of Destabilization," *Demography*, **2**, 516–530.

*DRIVER, EDWIN D. 1971. *World Population Policy: An Annotated Bibliography*. Lexington, Mass.: Lexington Books.

*———. 1972. *Essays on Population Policy*. Lexington, Mass.: Lexington Books.

*EBERHARD, WOLFRAM, and ALIDE EBERHARD. 1967. "Family Planning in a Taiwan Town," in Wolfram Eberhard, *Settlement and Social Change in Asia*. Hong Kong: Hong Kong University Press.

EL-BADRY, M. A. 1956. "Some Aspects of Fertility in Egypt," *Milbank Memorial Fund Quarterly*, **34**, 22–43.

———. 1965. "Trends in the Components of Population Growth in the Arab Countries of the Middle East: A Survey of Present Information," *Demography*, **2**, 140–186.

———. 1971. "Latin American Population Prospects in the Next Fifteen Years: A Brief Analysis," *Population Studies*, **25**, 183–192.

*ENKE, STEPHEN. 1960. "Government Bonuses for Smaller Families," *Population Review*, **4**, 47–50.

———. 1962. "Some Misconconceptions of Krueger and Sjaastad Regarding the Vasectomy-Bonus Plan to Reduce Births in Overpopulated and Poor Countries," *Economic Development and Cultural Change*, **10**, 427–431.

———. 1963. *Economics for Development*. Englewood Cliffs, N.J.: Prentice-Hall.

FINNIGAN, O. D., and S. M. KEENY. 1971. "Taiwan 1970: Report on the National Family Planning Programs," *Studies in Family Planning*, **2**, 63–69.

FISCHER, LOUIS. 1942. *A Week with Gandhi*. New York: Duell.

FREEDMAN, RONALD. 1963. "Norms for Family Size in Underdeveloped Areas," *Proceedings of the Royal Society*, B, **159**, 220–245.

———, ALBERT HERMALIN, and T. H. SUN. 1972. "Fertility Trends in Taiwan: 1961–1970," *Population Index*, **38**, 141–166.

———, and JOHN Y. TAKESHITA. 1969. *Family Planning in Taiwan: An Experiment in Social Change*. Princeton, N.J.: Princeton University Press.

GAETE-DARBÓ, ADOLFO. 1964. "Appraisal of Vital Statistics in Latin America," *Milbank Memorial Fund Quarterly*, **42**, 86–103.

GANDHI, M. K. 1959. *Birth-Control: The Right Way and the Wrong Way*. Ahmedabad: Navajivan.

GILLESPIE, ROBERT W. 1965. *Family Planning on Taiwan, 1964–1965*. Taichung: Population Council.

GOPALASWAMI, R. A. 1959. "How Japan Halved Her Birth Rate in Ten Years: The Lessons for India," *Population Review*, **3**, 52–57.

———. 1962. "Family Planning: Outlook for Government Action in India," in Kiser 1962.

HAUSER, PHILIP M. 1973. "Population Criteria in Foreign Aid Programs," Population Reference Bureau, Selection no. 42.

HAWKINS, EVERETT. 1967. "Indonesia's Population Problems," in Chandrasekhar 1967b.

*HEER, DAVID M. 1966. "Economic Development and Fertility," *Demography*, 3, 423–444.

HENIN, R. A. 1968. "Fertility Differentials in the Sudan," *Population Studies*, 22, 147–164.

HERMALIN, ALBERT I., and LIEN-PIN CHOW. 1971. "Motivational Factors in IUD Termination: Data from the Second Taiwan IUD Follow-up Survey," *Journal of Biosocial Sciences*, 3, 351–375.

HUTCHINSON, BERTRAM. 1961. "Fertility, Social Mobility, and Urban Migration in Brazil," *Population Studies*, 14, 182–189.

*HYRENIUS, HANNES, and ULLA ÅHS. 1968. *The Sweden–Ceylon Family Planning Pilot Project*. Göteborg, Sweden: Demographic Institute, University of Göteborg.

ISRAEL, SARAH. 1966. "Contraceptive Testing in India," *Population Review*, 10, 51–60.

KHALIFA, ATEF M. 1973. "A Proposed Explanation of the Fertility Gap Differentials by Socio-economic Status and Modernity: The Case of Egypt," *Population Studies*, 27, 431–442.

KINCH, ARNE. 1962. "A Preliminary Report from the Sweden–Ceylon Family Planning Pilot Project," in Kiser 1962.

*KISER, CLYDE V., editor. 1962. *Research in Family Planning*. Princeton: N.J.: Princeton University Press.

KRUEGER, ANNE O., and LARRY A. SJAASTAD. 1962. "Some Limitations of Enke's Economics of Population," *Economic Development and Cultural Change*, 10, 423–426.

KUCZYNSKI, ROBERT R. 1948–53. *Demographic Survey of the British Colonial Empire*, 3 vol. New York: Oxford University Press.

KURUP, R. S., and T. K. MATHEN. 1966. "Sterilization as a Method of Family Limitation in Kerala State," *Population Review*, 10, 61–68.

LEE SHU-CHING. 1953. "China's Traditional Family, Its Characteristics and Disintegration," *American Sociological Review*, 18, 272–280.

*LI, WEN L. 1973. "Temporal and Spatial Analysis of Fertility Decline in Taiwan," *Population Studies*, 27, 97–104.

LIU, P. T., and L. P. CHOW. 1971. "A Stochastic Approach to the Estimation of the Prevalence of IUD: Example of Taiwan, Republic of China," *Demography*, 8, 341–352.

LORIMER, FRANK, et al. 1954. *Culture and Human Fertility: A Study of the Relation of Cultural Conditions to Fertility in Non-Industrial and Transitional Societies*. Zurich: Unesco.

*MAMDANI, MAHMOOD. 1972. *The Myth of Population Control: Family, Caste, and Class in an Indian Village*. New York: Monthly Review Press.

MATHEN, K. K. 1962. "Preliminary Lessons Learned from the Rural Population Control Study of Singur," in Kiser 1962.

*MAULDIN, W. PARKER. 1965. "Application of Survey Techniques to Fertility Studies," in Sheps and Ridley 1965.

MAY, DAVID A., and DAVID M. HEER. 1968. "Son Survivorship and Family Size in India: A Computer Simulation," *Population Studies*, 32, 199–210.

MAYER, PHILIP. 1961. *Townsmen or Tribesmen*. Cape Town: Oxford University Press.

MILBANK MEMORIAL FUND. 1952. *Approaches to Problems of High Fertility in Agrarian Societies*. New York.

MIRÓ, CARMEN A. 1964. "The Population of Latin America," *Demography*, 1, 15–41.

*MORTARA, GIORGIO. 1964. "Appraisal of Census Data for Latin America," *Milbank Memorial Fund Quarterly*, 42, 57–71.

*MURAMATSU, MINORU, and PAUL A. HARPER, editors. 1965. *Population Dynamics: International Action and Training Programs*. Baltimore: Johns Hopkins Press.

MURTY, D. V. R. 1967. "Evaluation of Family Planning Programme in India," in International Union for the Scientific Study of Population, *Proceedings, 1967*. Sydney.

NARAGHI, EHSAN. 1960. *L'étude des populations dans les pays à statistique incomplète*. Paris: Mouton.

NIZARD, ALFRED. 1972. "La population de l'Inde: Premiers résultats du recensement de 1971," *Population*, 27, 1102–1117.

NORTMAN, DOROTHY. 1972. "Population and Family Planning Programs: A Factbook," *Reports on Population/Family Planning*, no. 2.

PANIKKAR, K. M. n.d. *Asia and Western Dominance*. New York: Day.

PATAI, RAPHAEL. 1959. *Sex and Family in the Bible and the Middle East*. Garden City, N.Y.: Doubleday.

PÉREZ RAMÍREZ, GUSTAVO. 1966. "The Catholic Church and Family Planning— Current Perspectives," in Stycos and Arias 1966.

PETERSEN, WILLIAM. 1967. "Taiwan's Population Problem," in Chandrasekhar 1967b.

*POTI, S. J., B. CHAKRABORTI, and C. R. MALAKAR. 1962. "Reliability of Data Relating to Contraceptive Practices," in Kiser 1962.

QUERISHI, ANWAR IQBAL. 1967. "Pakistan's Population Problem," in Chandrasekhar 1967b.

RADHAKRISHNAN, S., editor. 1953. *The Principal Upanishads*. New York: Harper.

RAULET, HARRY M. 1970. "Family Planning and Population Control in Developing Countries," *Demography*, 7, 211–234.

REEDER, LEO G., and GOTETI B. KRISHNAMURTY. 1964. "Family Planning in Rural India: A Problem in Social Change," *Social Problems*, 12, 212–223.

*RELE, J. R. 1963. "Fertility Differentials in India: Evidence from a Rural Background," *Milbank Memorial Fund Quarterly*, 41, 183–199.

————. 1967. *Fertility Analysis through Extension of Stable Population Concepts*. Berkeley: University of California.

REVELLE, ROGER, et al., editors. 1971. *Rapid Population Growth: Consequences and Policy Implications*. Baltimore: Johns Hopkins Press.

RICHARDS, AUDREY I., and PRISCILLA REINING. 1954. "Report on Fertility Surveys in Buganda and Buhaya, 1952," in Lorimer 1954.

RIDLEY, JEANNE CLARE. 1965. "Recent Natality Trends in Underdeveloped Countries," in Sheps and Ridley 1965.

ROBERTS, D. F., and R. E. S. TANNER. 1959. "A Demographic Study in an Area of Low Fertility in North-East Tanganyika," *Population Studies*, 13, 61–80.

ROBERTS, GEORGE W. 1967. "Reproductive Performance and Reproductive Capacity in Less Industrialized Societies," *Annals of the American Academy of Political and Social Science*, 369, 37–47.

*ROBINSON, WARREN C. 1961. "Urban–Rural Differences in Indian Fertility," *Population Studies*, **14**, 218–234.

―――――. 1963. "Urbanization and Fertility: The Non-Western Experience," *Milbank Memorial Fund Quarterly*, **41**, 291–308.

ROMANIUK, A. 1967. "Estimation of the Birth Rate for the Congo through Non-conventional Techniques," *Demography*, **4**, 688–709.

RYAN, BRYCE. 1954. "Hinayana Buddhism and Family Planning in Ceylon," in Milbank Memorial Fund, *The Interrelations of Demographic, Economic, and Social Problems in Selected Underdeveloped Areas.* New York.

SABAGH, GEORGES, and CHRISTOPHER SCOTT. 1967. "A Comparison of Different Survey Techniques for Obtaining Vital Data in a Developing Country," *Demography*, **4**, 759–772.

*SAMUEL, T. J. 1966. "The Development of India's Policy of Population Control," *Milbank Memorial Fund Quarterly*, **44**, 49–67.

SCHIEFFELIN, OLIVIA, editor. 1967. *Muslim Attitudes Toward Family Planning.* New York: Population Council.

SCHULTZ, T. PAUL. 1969. "The Effectiveness of Family Planning in Taiwan: A Proposal for a New Evaluation Methodology" (mimeographed). Santa Monica, Calif.: Rand Corporation.

SHAH, LELAL M. 1961. "Sex Life in India and Pakistan," in Albert Ellis and Albert Abarnel, editors, *The Encyclopedia of Sexual Behavior.* New York: Hawthorn.

*SHEPS, MINDEL C., and JEANNE CLARE RIDLEY, editors. 1965. *Public Health and Population Change: Current Research Issues.* Pittsburgh: University of Pittsburgh Press.

SIMMONS, GEORGE B. 1971. *The Indian Investment in Family Planning.* New York: Population Council.

SMITH, T. E. 1963. "A General Survey of Current Population Trends in the Commonwealth Countries of Tropical Africa," in T. E. Smith and J. G. C. Blacker, editors, *Population Characteristics of the Commonwealth Countries of Tropical Africa.* London: Athlone Press.

SMITH, T. LYNN. 1958. "The Reproduction Rate in Latin America: Levels, Differentials and Trends," *Population Studies*, **12**, 4–16.

SOVANI, N. V. 1952. "The Problems of Fertility Control in India: Cultural Factors and Development of Policy," in Milbank Memorial Fund 1952.

STONE, ABRAHAM. 1953. "Fertility Problems in India," *Fertility and Sterility*, **4**, 210–217.

STYCOS, J. MAYONE. 1962. "A Critique of the Traditional Planned Parenthood Approach in Underdeveloped Areas," in Kiser 1962.

―――――. 1963. "Obstacles to Programs of Population Control—Facts and Fancies," *Marriage and Family Living*, **25**, 5–13.

*―――――. 1965. "Opinions of Latin-American Intellectuals on Population Problems and Birth Control," *Annals of the American Academy of Political and Social Science*, **360**, 11–26.

―――――. 1966. "Demography and the Study of Population Problems in Latin America," in Stycos and Arias 1966.

―――――, and JORGE ARIAS, editors. 1966. *Population Dilemma in Latin America.* American Assembly. Washington, D.C.: Potomac Books.

TUAN CHI-HSIEN. 1958. "Reproductive Histories of Chinese Women in Rural Taiwan," *Population Studies*, **12**, 40–50.

UDRY, J. RICHARD, KARL A. BAUMAN, and CHARLES L. CHASE. 1973. "Population Growth Rates in Perfect Contraceptive Populations," *Population Studies*, **27**, 365–371.

U.N. ADVISORY MISSION. 1970. "An Evaluation of the Family Planning Programme of the Government of India" (excerpted), *Studies in Family Planning*, no. 56, pp. 4–18.

WOLFERS, D. 1969. "The Demographic Effects of a Contraceptive Programme," *Population Studies*, **23**, 111–140.

WYON, JOHN B., and JOHN E. GORDON. 1971. *The Khanna Study: Population Problems in the Rural Punjab*. Cambridge, Mass.: Harvard University Press.

YAUKEY, DAVID. 1961. *Fertility Differences in a Modernizing Country: A Survey of Lebanese Couples*. Princeton, N.J.: Princeton University Press.

*ZARATE, ALVAN O. 1967a. "Differential Fertility in Monterrey, Mexico: Prelude to Transition?" *Milbank Memorial Fund Quarterly*, **45**, 93–108.

———. 1967b. "Some Factors Associated with Urban–Rural Fertility Differentials in Mexico," *Population Studies*, **21**, 283–293.

THE POPULATION OF TOTALITARIAN SOCIETIES

17

The distinction between democracy and totalitarianism is the most important one of 20th-century life, and it is necessary to make it precisely. In a simplistic view, all societies that are not "democratic" are "totalitarian," and vice versa. As I use the term, a totalitarian society is one dominated by a single minority Party, which, in order to realize its particular vision of a perfect community, attempts to achieve total control over the major workings of all significant institutions. The several components of the definition are all essential. Rule by a minority over a country with important loci of competing power is not totalitarian; in the Ghana of Nkrumah, for instance, the rule of his supporters could be challenged by traditionalist chiefs, the urban middle class, and the army; in Spain the Falangists must compete with the army, the Church, and the monarchist clique. And even if a group holds complete political power, it is not totalitarian (but "authoritarian" or "autocratic") if it does not also penetrate the social institutions in order to move them toward its utopian goal; the military dictatorship of a Latin American country or of a province of pre-Communist China is not totalitarian. No society, indeed, is completely totalitarian (just as none is completely democratic). The three that come closest to the pure type are the Soviet Union, Nazi Germany, and Communist China, and this chapter has a section on each.

These three countries differ in much more than the national cultures, diverse as they are. Yet whatever the context, totalitarian population phenomena vary systematically from those in a nontotalitarian country. In order to specify this contrast in concrete terms, to discuss the type of controls that totalitarian states impose on fertility, mortality, and migration and the effect of these controls on population structure and composition, we shall focus on the Soviet Union. The reasons for this choice are that (as contrasted with Communist China) there are enough data to analyze over several decades and that (as contrasted with Nazi Germany) the Soviet system is of more than historical interest. The following, less exhaustive analyses of China and Germany help lay a basis for generalizing about population in the whole class of totalitarian societies.

THE SOVIET UNION:
POLITICAL–ECONOMIC BACKGROUND

In this discussion of the almost six decades since the 1917 revolution, greater emphasis will be laid on three—from the death of Lenin in 1924 to that of Stalin in 1953—during which the latter was either in ascendancy or in full control. For the Stalinist phenomenon, of considerable historical importance in itself, is also a key to understanding a wider range of political, economic, and population trends. And no one can yet be certain whether the post-Stalin revisions, however significant in some respects, are indications of a continuing democratization or merely "within-system changes" (as Bertram Wolfe termed them) that leave the totalitarian essence intact.

Sources of Information

Soviet statistics differ from those available for any Western nation first of all in sheer quantity. If an economy can be planned, it must be done by relating a record of past production to future goals; and as in principle virtually everything in the society is planned, a huge, complex system of reporting, record keeping, and accounting embraces almost every activity and every person in the country. Whether even primary data are accurate, however, is often dubious. A statistical count is likely to be most accurate if it is independent of any other administrative function, but in a planned economy *all* data are compiled as one element of State control. A person asked a question by the representative of a totalitarian regime may answer falsely either because of fear or, on the contrary, as a mild form of sabotage. How often hospital clerks and registration officers tamper with the original compilations of births and deaths, for example, we do not know, but there used to be "many reports of such cases in the Soviet press and in the pages of *Vestnik Statistiki*, the organ of the Central Statistical Administration of the USSR" (Gordon 1957; cf. Schattman 1956).

Whatever the accuracy of the data, only some of them are made available outside the country, and those that Westerners can work with are often the least reliable. In 1956 the Soviet government issued an official statistical *Handbook*, translated a year later into English (USSR Council of Ministers, Central Statistical Board, *National Economy of the USSR: Statistical Returns*, Moscow: Foreign Language Publishing House, 1957). This was reviewed by Naum Jasny, an outstanding Western sovietologist. His criticisms of this particular volume apply to Soviet statistics generally, and represent an excellent introduction to this difficult terrain. Many important data, which we know from other sources are collected in the Soviet Union, were omitted from the *Handbook*—for instance, all statistics on family budgets or the consumption of various goods. As in this case, the reason for the concealment is usually patent.

The figures available abroad are full of traps for nonspecialists. For example, the territory of the Soviet Union is appreciably larger than before World War II, but time series have in general not been redone to take this difference into account. Some series are calculated as percentages of the figures for 1940, a year when several territorial changes occurred, without informing the reader which area is taken as the base. Or, as another example, the crop "yields" reported until 1954 were estimates made in the field, before harvesting; for the years 1950–53 these "biological" crops ranged between 121 and 131 million tons, while the actual annual yields as now officially reported for these same years were between 76 and 89 million tons (Jasny 1957: 94–95). In short, "Soviet statistics are an amalgam of elements varying from trustworthy data (mostly pertaining to physical units or details) through ambiguities to obviously distorted estimates (mostly data for aggregates)" (ibid.: 14).

Specifically, those responsible for compiling demographic statistics know that these reflect in part the welfare that the economy affords the common man, and that the discrepancy between Soviet propaganda on this subject and Soviet reality has been great. The vital statistics issued to the public, for instance, were grossly incomplete.

Publishing the statistics only for favorable factors or periods is certainly very much akin to falsification. For example, the birth rate in 1938 was made known in due time (38.3 per 1,000), but not for 1939 and 1940. Western analysts realized that, due to the change in age composition and other factors, the birth rate in 1940 must have been lower than in 1938, but nobody seems to have thought of as low a figure as 31.7 per 1,000, now, after all these years, disclosed in the *Handbook* [ibid.: 13].

Our main source of Soviet population data is the censuses, but these also are not very satisfactory. The first census taken under Soviet auspices was in 1920, only three years after the Bolsheviks took power and while their rule was still being fought in parts of the country. Scores of enumerators were beaten up as representatives of the government, and thirty-three were murdered by the people they were attempting to count. The 1920 census is not regarded as accurate.

The next Soviet census was taken in 1926, after the country had been pacified. In order to ensure an accurate return, special directives were issued to the public promising, on the one hand, to treat all information received as confidential and, on the other hand, threatening with reprisals and indictments those who gave false information. No enumerators were killed, but the response of the people in many areas was not friendly (Selegen and Petrov 1959). In spite of these limitations, the 1926 count was relatively good.

Censuses were ordered in 1933 and 1935, but they did not take place (Holubnychy 1958). A census was taken in 1937, but the results were suppressed in their entirety because, according to the official report, inaccuracies and ideological errors were discovered in the formulation of questions and the development of the data (Lorimer 1946: 222n.). The actual reason, it can be surmised, is that the population figure would have suggested how many millions had been killed in the enforced collectivization of agriculture during the First Five-Year Plan.

The next attempt was made two years later, in 1939. Both "unconscientious" respondents and irresponsible enumerators were threatened with official reprisals (Selegen and Petrov 1959). Only a small portion of the data collected in this census was published in the original volume. Some of the unpublished parts were found in German-occupied areas during the war, and these formed the basis for an unofficial analysis of population during the 1930s (Martschenko 1953). Two decades later, as part of the 1959 census, a substantial portion of the 1939 data was finally issued by the Soviet government.

According to rumors, a sample survey of the population was taken shortly after World War II, but the number of survivors indicated such devastating losses that the data were suppressed (Gordon 1957).

Two postwar censuses were completed, one in 1959 (cf. Perevedentsev 1967) and the most recent in 1970 (cf. Feshbach 1972). In contrast to the long series of aborted counts, thus, information on the Soviet population depends essentially on the portions that have been published of the censuses of 1926, 1959, and 1970.

In summary, Soviet statistics available abroad include distortions and inaccuracies of a number of types, apart from the errors that result simply from human fallibility or inefficiency. (1) The pressure to maintain production norms is so great that the response to it sometimes is to tamper with one's reports. Original data include deliberate falsifications in a literal sense; a manager of a factory or a collective farm changes 5,000 to 6,000. Whether adulteration of this kind takes place at the level of the Central Statistical Administration is a moot point among Western sovietologists. (2) A more appropriate term to describe the usual practices of the Moscow bureaus is contextual distortion. For example, two percentages are compared without informing the reader that they were calculated on different bases, or a standard word like *harvest* is used in a very special sense. The intent is to give the foreign public a wrong impression, but this intent can sometimes be defeated (as it cannot be with falsification of the first type) by the application of careful and informed scholarship. (3) The omission of crucial data can be considered another type of distortion. For example, figures are published for good years, none for poor years. Or statistical aggregates are calculated with no hint as to which of several alternative formulas was used.

There has been a considerable improvement in the amount and somewhat less in the quality of the data available during the most recent years. Important gaps still persist, however, and any discussion of trends must be based in part on earlier, less reliable statistics.

Communist Ideology and Population Theory

Why should Communists, whose first principle is a planned society, have for so long objected to family planning? This hostility continues the dispute that

Malthus started in his attack on utopians like Condorcet and Godwin. In Marx's writings "the contemptible Malthus" is rejected as a "plagiarist," "a shameless sycophant of the ruling classes," who perpetrated a "sin against science," "this libel on the human race." Apart from such vituperations, Marx's (1906, vol. 1: 693) main objection to the principle of population can be stated in a single sentence: "Every special historic mode of production has its own special laws of population, historically valid within its limits alone." Marx himself, however, had nothing to say about what governed growth of numbers in primitive, feudal, or socialist societies; and he took the rapid population increase of 19th-century Europe as a permanent feature and built his system around it, without even so imperfect a theory as Malthus's principle to account for it. If the population declined at the same rate at which machines displaced workers (a contingency that many demographers of the 1930s considered not only possible but even likely), then there would be no industrial reserve army, no "immiseration," no Marxian model altogether. Marx could reject Malthus only by taking vulgar Malthusianism for granted.

Both socialism and neo-Malthusianism sometimes appealed to the same rebellious individuals, but the usual pattern, and the all but invariable one for organizations rather than individuals, was contravention. Socialists and neo-Malthusians dealt in competing utopias. For the "Malthusian" true believer, the one social problem was population; to solve that was to solve all. An orthodox Marxist, on the contrary, believed that when the capitalist system was supplanted by a planned economy, population pressure would disappear, and that before such a fundamental transformation took place, the limitation of family size could not improve matters substantially.

The variation on this theme in the Soviet Union can be exemplified by a typical attack on Malthusianism, "the man-hating ideology of imperialists" (Popov 1953). It began with the basic Marxist dictum that each type of society—slave-owning, feudal, capitalist, socialist—has its own law of population. But under all circumstances population growth is good. "There is no absolute overpopulation under any social order. Even under capitalism, the level of productive forces is entirely adequate to feed the people." Indeed, a population increase in a country that has not yet achieved socialism is progressive in that it can help the transition from one stage to the next higher. "For example, the considerable population growth in the United States during the 19th century (due primarily to immigration) undoubtedly contributed to the rapid development of its capitalist economy." At any stage before the final one, it is true, society may suffer from a "relative" surplus of population, or unemployment. "Socialism [however] does not know crises, poverty, and unemployment. Relative overpopulation, therefore, does not exist and cannot exist under socialism. The growth of population accelerates the development of a socialist society, increases its power and strength." By the standards of Communist orthodoxy, the advantages derived from a growing population have no limit. In 1947, the Soviet delegate to the U.N. Population Commission, speaking to its first meeting, stated the dogma with a breathtaking abandon: "I would consider it barbaric for the Commission to contemplate a limitation of marriages or of legitimate births, and this for any country whatsoever, at any period whatsoever. With an adequate social organization it is possible to face any increase in population" (quoted by Sauvy 1952, vol. 1: 174). In subsequent sessions, although continuing to reject the concept of an optimum population even as a theoretical abstraction, the Soviet delegates to the Commission eventually accepted, "reluctantly," one of an optimum *rate* of population growth, thus compromising their utopian stand very little, for even in a socialist society a population can hardly grow at an infinite rate (Sauvy 1948; cf. Minc 1955; Ryabushkin 1955).

The population doctrine of the Stalinist period, thus, consisted of a number of theses:

1. The Party is omnipotent. It can cope with any increase in population. The idea that the resources at the command of society are not only unlimited but "clearly" so, that man's ability to shape his environment to his needs is manifestly infinite, is the fundamental faith. "The notion of optimum is bourgeois because it sets a limit" (Sauvy 1948). In this sense, totalitarian rulers are the direct descendants of pre-Marxian socialists like Godwin and Condorcet. For both, the only limitations on man's control over nature are those imposed artificially, and thus remediably, by his inadequate institutions. The early utopians were idealists in both senses of the word: they based their acts on a humanitarian ideal of the future, and they refused to accept the limitations of the material world. As they remained ineffectual, they are remembered for their humanitarian values, but when their view of the world is combined with state power, it leads directly to mass terror. For one of man's principal limitations is his own physical nature, and in a state where human frailties are not admitted, weakness must be defined as malingering and error as sabotage. For a totalitarian state to grant that any task is physically impossible would be to forgo the total control over its people to which it aspires. To the Party, nothing is impossible: "there is no fortress," said Stalin, "that Bolsheviks cannot take by storm."

2. Population theory has the same purpose as any other science: to bolster the power of the Party within Soviet society, and that of the Soviet State in the international arena.

3. Control of fertility is associated with neo-Malthusianism and is thus anathema. "Raving fascists," "bestial imperialists," "lackeys of American monopolies who openly advocate cannibalism," "racist lynchers in Himmler's footsteps"—these are some of the designations of planned-parenthood advocates culled from the Soviet press of the 1950s (Petersen 1970: 103–124).

4. The welfare of the proletariat can be enhanced, however, by improving maternal health through birth-control measures that are ruled out on social–political grounds.

In one branch of international socialism, the utopianism of Marx and Engels was eventually relinquished: the Revisionists in Germany, the labor parties elsewhere, became more reasonable—that is, both more moderate and more rational. In the Soviet Union such Revisionist views began to be expressed openly only in the mid-1960s, mainly in a series of articles in *Literaturnaya Gazeta* (Brackett 1968). Within a few weeks at the end of 1965, several junior economists moved from a cautious recognition of population pressure elsewhere, to an admission that it exists also in the Soviet Union, to a proposed change in Marxist dogma. Orthodoxy was defended by, among others, Strumilin, who suggested that the spread of socialism may cause birth rates to fall so much as to cause underpopulation.[1] The final voice in this dialogue up to the time was an article by the demographer, E. Arab-Ogly (1966). This was a well rounded statement of the new rationale.

The capital investment which any society can afford every year is not arbitrary; the amount is limited by annual accumulations. Every accumulation is a deduction from current consumption. Depending upon how they are earmarked, these capital investments can in turn be directed toward . . . doubling the prosperity of a constant population, say every twenty years, or doubling the population while maintaining the same level of living in approximately the same period. One and the same pudding cannot be eaten twice under two different names. . . . The state, of course, is not entitled to decide for people who should have children and how many. But it can, on the basis of the current and long-term demands of society as well as of a judicious combination of personal and social interests, bring to light the optimal rate of population growth. And it is entitled to influence the wishes of people to have more or less children, to help free them from prejudices in order to realize their objective interests, as well as to place at their disposal the most perfected and harmless means by which the actual number of children in the family may be made to correspond to the number desired. . . .

Malthus's notorious geometric progression should not make us despair, but the formula establishing the inverse correlation of birth rate and prosperity is a highly problematic basis for optimism. Genuine optimism stems from confidence that mankind is able to prevail over spontaneous social processes, including demographic ones, and that in the last analysis it will be able, as Engels noted, "to control the production of people just as it will by that time control the production of things."

Only a few symbols of orthodoxy remained—the attack on Malthus, the respectful quotation from Engels. In the main, this statement differed remarkably little from what non-Catholic Western demographers had been arguing for years. Those aberrant Soviet voices are like the Catholic ones that have challenged the Church's stand on birth control. In both cases it was a new departure that the attack was made openly and without immediate and overt punishment for

---

[1] Compare the proposal (p. 520, n.1) that the way to bring population growth under control is to foster the spread of Catholicism. Stanislav G. Strumilin spoke with the greatest authority among the older generation of Soviet economists and statisticians. Born in 1877, he had professional and revolutionary careers well under way by 1917, and through all the subsequent shifts of policy he stayed in some post of authority and high honor. One is reminded of Abbé Sieyès, who, when asked what he had done in monarchist, revolutionary, Napoleonic, and republican France, replied, "I survived."

the dissidents. But in neither instance can we expect the institution, the Soviet State or the Catholic Church, to divest itself completely of its considerable investment in traditional dogma. Although those arguing for a new position try to base themselves on new interpretations of sacred texts, it is not possible in either context to disguise the fact that what they want resembles very closely, in fact, what has heretofore been condemned as the kernel of heterodox thinking.

In the early 1970s there were some indications of a shift back from the position that Arab-Ogly represented. The heritage of what is termed "Marxist–Leninist demography" had persisted (e.g., Khalatbari 1971), ready whenever needed. After the Soviet birth rate fell enough to cause official worry, a doctrinal indifference to rapid population growth became more timely, though a full revival of the absurdities of the Stalin period did not seem likely.

War and Revolution

Thus far we have reviewed the sources of information on the Soviet population available to Western scholars and the Communist theories that, at least in the abstract, guide the demographic policies of the Soviet State. How in fact have these theories worked out, so far as one can tell from the partial and deficient record?

Under the new regime that the Bolsheviks established in November 1917, the sale or purchase of commodities was prohibited in principle, but the alternative system of rationing could not be made to work (e.g., Chamberlin 1965: chap. 25). Industry was disorganized, the transportation system damaged and worn out, the government administration disrupted by widespread strikes. Cities could be fed only by sending armies out into the countryside to confiscate the peasants' food. The state printing presses deprived paper rubles of all value: from 1913 to 1917, prices increased by three times, but by 1921 they were some 16,800 times the 1913 figure (Vernadsky 1961: 316). A serious strike wave in Petrograd, which quickly developed from economic to political goals, was broken with lockouts and military force.

The 7 years of war, aggravated by tsarist and Bolshevik bureaucratic inefficiency, had a fearful impact on the population. Thousands were killed by terror and counterterror, hundreds of thousands in the civil strife, but these were by far not the major component of the extraordinary mortality. With the constant movement of hungry hordes, epidemics spread through the country. Typhus alone killed more than 1.5 million in 1919–20. In the winter of 1921–22. after years of food shortages and a serious drought, Russia suffered a devastating famine (Fisher 1927).

The depletion in the population during this whole period is not at all easy to calculate. Tsarist Russia's only census had been in 1897, and, as we have noted, the first reliable Soviet census was in 1926. Over this interval, adjusting for changes in Russia's territory, the population increased from 106 to 147 million, or by 38.6 percent in slightly less than 30 years. The losses between 1914 and

1923 can be estimated if we postulate that the "normal" rate of natural increase was constant from 1897 on. Such an assumption would seem to be reasonable. In the thirty-nine provinces of European Russia that remained Russian after the revolution, the average birth rate is estimated to have fallen from 50.4 in 1899–1901 to 47.6 in 1911–13, and the average death rate from 33.1 to 29.6. The rate of natural increase varied, thus, only between 17.3 and 18.0 per thousand. If, to be conservative, we take 17.15 as the average annual increase per thousand from 1897 on, this would have resulted in a population of 175 million in 1926. The actual census count was 28 million short of this (or 16 percent); and this difference can be taken as the total deficit (Lorimer 1946: chap. 3). The factors responsible for this population loss from 1914 to 1926, as estimated by Lorimer from various more or less satisfactory data, are as follows:

Military deaths	2 million
Civilian deaths	14
Net emigration	2
Birth deficit[2]	10
TOTAL	28 million

These figures are not precise, of course, but they are probably correct to the nearest million, as shown. "During the years 1915–23 the Russian people underwent the most cataclysmic changes since the Mongol invasion in the early 13th century" (ibid.: 42).

The Bolshevik revolution was a *political* coup; its main purpose was to take power. The Bolshevik *social* revolution began on October 1, 1928, when the First Five-Year Plan went into effect. The principal purpose of the planned economy as a whole has been to develop heavy industry, but in the first plan the emphasis was on the collectivization of agriculture, which could be realized only through mass terror. This momentous process not only converted the peasantry into a landless proletariat, peons of the State, but also shaped every element of Soviet society. In particular, it had a tremendous effect on the population both directly by the millions who were killed and indirectly by the fact that the Soviet Union has to this day not been able to establish an efficient agriculture.

The Russian peasantry was essentially a single class, unified by both its way of life and its hostility to the regime. In Soviet law and in Party practice, however, the class was divided into three: the "wealthy" kulaks, the "middle" peasants, and the "poor" peasants. The word *kulak* means "fist"; the implication is a greedy, grasping person who closes his hand around anything he can get hold of. The Party's program of "dekulakization" was to be achieved, if

[2] That is, the difference between the actual number of births and the number that would have occurred if the "normal" fertility had continued during this period.

possible, by engaging the poor and middle peasants against the kulaks. In Stalin's words (1942: 145–164):

We have recently passed from the policy of *restricting* the exploiting proclivities of the kulaks to the policy of *eliminating the kulaks as a class.* . . . The expropriation of the kulaks is an integral part of the formation and development of the collective farms. That is why it is ridiculous and fatuous to expatiate today on the expropriation of the kulaks. You do not lament the loss of the hair of one who has been beheaded.

There is another question which seems no less ridiculous: whether the kulak should be permitted to join the collective farms. Of course not, for he is a sworn enemy of the collective farm movement. Clear, one would think.[3]

As the collectivization proceeded, the legal criteria defining kulaks were changed repeatedly; the precise boundary became more and more elusive as the Party approached its goal. Eventually all those who tried to fight the Party programs were defined as kulaks or, if this was too preposterous, as kulak-followers (*podkulachniki*).[4]

By reinforcing the jealousies and hatreds in the village, by recreating the mood of the civil war, the tiny Party was able to manipulate the overwhelming majority of the population and expropriate the peasants' property *in toto* almost before they knew what was happening. At first some of the "middle" and "poor" peasants probably really believed that the Party organizer had intervened in their interest. All through the year 1929 collectivization was pushed forward with quasi-legal methods—through extra tax levies, quotas, attachments, auctions, trials before special traveling courts, and so on. As a consequence, "a million families suddenly found themselves pariahs, without any rights which need be respected, and without any knowledge as to what they might do to be saved" (Strong 1931: 81). This newly created class of outcasts was expropriated of its means of subsistence, disfranchised, deprived of ration cards and of the right to purchase in the cooperative stores; their children were expelled from school, and their sick were excluded from medical treatment. By the beginning of 1930, when still less than a quarter of the peasant households were collectivized, the Party dropped its pretense that it was intervening to support the poor peasants against their class enemies and opened up a mass offensive against the Soviet peoples. The world was justifiably horrified when the Nazis punished the activities of the Czech underground by completely destroying one village, Lidice; but we have no record of how many Russian Lidices were obliterated by their own State police. For example,

Sixteen villages in the Ukraine failed to produce the grain required from them, and their failure was attributed by the authorities to deliberate sabotage. A decree was published in the local papers announcing that all grain hoarded in the offending

---

[3] Compare Hitler on Jews: "One must not show mercy to people who fate has determined will perish" (Hilberg 1967: 662).

[4] See pp. 735–737 on the ambiguities in the Nazis' definition of *Jews*.

Street scenes in Kharkov, USSR, in the summer of 1933. [Ewald Ammende, *Human Life in Russia* (London: Allen & Unwin, 1936).]

Above: Familiarity breeds indifference; pedestrians pass by several who had died of hunger with hardly a glance.

Below: Collecting corpses for burial.

villages was to be confiscated, the cooperative stores in the villages were to be closed, and no State distributing authority was to arrange to send food to them—in other words, sixteen villages were condemned to starve or secretly flee from their homes [Monkhouse 1934: 207].

With such methods, Stalin's "solid collectivization" developed rapidly. From January 20 to March 1, 1930, the number of peasant homesteads collectivized increased from 4.4 to 14.3 million, or from 21.6 to 55.0 percent of the total (Baykov 1946: 196). After these forty days of terror, Stalin condemned the "feverish pursuit of inflated collectivization figures" he had previously decreed. His famous speech, "Dizziness from Success," was promptly published and distributed by the millions. "The Bolsheviks had pursued their typical tactics—they had driven through with greater strength than needed, and could retire to consolidate position" (Strong 1931: 93).

The collectives formed by these methods were hardly model farms. Rather than deliver their property to the State, the peasants burned the seed grain and killed the livestock. Two-fifths of the cattle disappeared, two-thirds of the sheep and goats, more than half the swine and the horses (Lorimer 1946: 109). In 1930 all Russia had only 72,000 tractors, and this was the mechanical base of the collectivization. And on such a base a large farm without draft animals was a contradiction in terms. There was a comparable depletion in human labor power. After the most skillful and diligent peasants had been ousted, their place as rural leaders was taken by 25,000 city men and youths,[5] anxious only for the Party career they could establish by successfully corraling the peasant mass.

The chaos in agriculture had as its inevitable consequence an increasing food shortage, culminating in another famine. In the number of deaths it brought about, this was comparable to the one 12 years before, but the regime's attitude was different. In 1921–22, the Soviet Union had appealed for and received substantial aid from abroad; in 1932–33, the government denied the very fact of the famine. Dr. Ewald Ammende, who had worked in Russia a decade earlier as a representative of the Red Cross, in 1933 became secretary of another international relief organization; but he was not permitted to do more than send in a few food parcels, some of which were returned (Ammende 1936; cf. Chamberlin 1934).

In general, city dwellers fared better, but their life was not easy. Housing was incredibly poor, and for a period got worse. To enforce labor discipline, the government reintroduced from tsarist days the internal passport and instituted a wide range of measures designed to quicken the country's industrialization. Food cards were abolished, and class distinctions were established in the amount of food given out.

[5] See the report of Kaganovich to the 16th Party Congress, "Organizational Report of the Central Committee," *International Press Correspondence*, 10 (July 25, 1930), 638–649.

Political–Economic Terror and Forced Labor

A few weeks after they took power, the Bolsheviks had established the Cheka, or the Extraordinary Commission for Combating Counterrevolution, Sabotage, and Speculation. Over the years, the designation of the security police has been changed repeatedly—from Cheka to GPU (State Political Administration) to OGPU (United GPU) to NKVD to MVD (the People's Commissariat—or, later, Ministry—of Internal Affairs)—reflecting a continual enlargement of its function, reorganization based on Party–State jealousies, and possibly the attempt to keep some of its activities secret. As the NKVD or MVD, it became an outlandish combination of routine civil administration and terror apparatus. Its duties ranged from tasks like the registration of vital events or fire-fighting to the resettlement of populations and the control of forced-labor camps and other penal institutions.[6] Under the conditions generated or aggravated by the collectivization of agriculture, control of the population was possible only by a considerable increase in the size and power of the terror apparatus.

Forced labor was of several types, ranging from lesser to greater severity:

1. Work performed by those detained in ordinary prisons. This differs from the system in other countries mainly in that under a planned economy there is no pressure from trade unions or private entrepreneurs to restrict the unfair competition of prison labor.

2. "Corrective" labor performed by a person at his usual place of work, usually as a punishment for a minor infraction of labor discipline.

3. The corvée, or the sixth day's work without pay, required of all able-bodied male and female members of collective farms.

4. Forced resettlement, or deportation to a prescribed place of exile where persons lived in the general community but under Chekists' supervision.

5. "Labor colonies," which combined deportation, forced labor during working hours, and residence outside camps.

6. Forced labor *per se*, under which persons were sent to forced-labor camps where they worked and lived entirely under control of the NKVD.

Which elements constitute characteristic features of a totalitarian regime—where in this list to draw the line—is to some degree a matter of opinion. This discussion is restricted mainly to the last type, the ultimate degradation of laborers to the status of industrial slaves. By now we have hundreds of detailed descriptions of Soviet forced labor. From such accounts—by former inmates, by NKVD officials who defected, by Western analyses of the half-hidden

---

[6] In 1941, a portion of the NKVD was separated off as the NKGB (People's Commissariat of State Security), and it was this unit that carried out the postwar purges. Its successor, the MGB, was transformed after Stalin's death into the KGB (Committee of State Security), headed initially by General Ivan A. Serov, a veteran of the system who had been responsible for some of its greatest terror. The partial continuity throughout the term of the Soviet regime is suggested by the fact that members of the security police have always retained their original designation—"Chekists."

information in official records—we know how many camps there were, where they were situated, and what camp life was like. The one point on which there is substantial disagreement among Western scholars is also one of the most important—what was the slave-labor population?

Up until 1928 the figures were relatively negligible; at the beginning of that year there were 30,000 men detained in the camps. Thereafter the figure rose to many millions, but how many? The variation in estimates is due in part, of course, to the inherent blocks to interpreting the incomplete and defective data. But a portion of the range reflects the cyclical growth in the total camp population from one period to another. To borrow the terminology of the economists, slave labor was a commodity with a rapid turnover, so that it is important to distinguish between stock and flow.

The death rate in the camps was extremely high. Many of them were situated in the far North, where even under the best conditions life is dangerous. A camp inmate worked ten to fourteen hours a day at heavy, exhausting labor—removing earth, felling and chopping trees, mining, fishing. He was driven to work hard both by guards and by a differential food ration, which ranged from grossly inadequate for those who completed their quota of work to a starvation diet for those who did not. The clothing of the prisoners was unsuitable, and when they took sick they had to depend on a poorly staffed dispensary that lacked essential equipment and drugs. According to one estimate, during a six-month period 30 percent of the inmates of one camp died; and something like this rate must have been typical until the middle-aged and less sturdy portions of a new group of prisoners were killed off. The general mortality of the camp population, estimated at about 10 percent in 1933, probably rose to about 20 percent by 1938 (Swianiewicz 1965: 17).

Therefore the number of slaves, whatever it was at any time, could hardly have been maintained by the routine terror of normal Stalinism. It must have depended on the extraordinary spurts that recurred every several years. We can distinguish three periods of major recruitment: (1) 1929–32, when the principal source of slaves was the disaffected peasantry; (2) 1936–38, when Yezhov, starting in the Party and its periphery, was eventually able to uncover "traitors" in every sector of the society; and (3) 1941–45, when the camp population was renewed from substantial percentages of conquered nations, Soviet ethnic minorities, enemy prisoners of war, and the like. At the height of these drives the total was at a maximum, and during the intervening periods of relaxed terror, at a minimum. Depending on where in this cycle estimates happened to fall, they could be quite precise and yet vary by a factor, say, of 1 to 3.

1. During the transformation of the Soviet countryside, 70 to 80 percent of the labor-camp population—or some 3.5 million persons—were peasants. Perhaps as many were deported to forced settlements, where limits in the type of work usually available generally also meant a shift out of agriculture, and as many again died from privation or were executed. The surplus agricultural population, which had resulted in the underemployment of peasants and their families, was thus reduced by some 10 million—the figure that, according to Churchill's memoirs, Stalin gave him as the number of peasants processed during the 4-year collectivization campaign.

2. Once the rational economic purpose of the terror had been achieved, a sizable number of the Party were for a relaxation. The leading advocate of this position was Sergei M. Kirov, whose murder started a new and greater cycle of terror.[7] In 1936 Nikolai I. Yezhov, who had been Stalin's liaison between the Politburo and the security police, was appointed chief of the NKVD. During the 2 years he held the post he administered a wave of terror that has been named after its director—the Yezhovshchina. The first victims were those in the Party and its affiliates who had opposed Stalin, and from these nuclei the purge spread throughout Soviet society.

The vicious practice was condoned of having the NKVD prepare lists of persons whose cases were under the jurisdiction of the Military Collegium and whose sentences were prepared in advance. Yezhov would send these lists to Stalin personally for his approval of the proposed punishment. In 1937–38, 383 such lists containing the names of many thousands of Party, Soviet, Komsomol, Army, and economic workers were sent to Stalin. He approved these lists [Khrushchev 1956: 32].

The number of forced laborers on the eve of World War II, consisting of the survivors of dissident peasants and the victims of Yezhov's policy, was probably some 6.9 million (Swianiewicz 1965: 31; cf. Lorimer 1946: 229).

After summarizing evidence from the NKVD's labor demands listed in a captured plan for economic development, various prisoners' reports, a number of oddities in published Soviet statistics, and statements by the NKVD itself, Conquest (1971: 706–709) pointed out that the several types of data converged on the following running estimates of the camp population, specifically excluding criminals of the ordinary sort:

In prison or camp, January 1937		c. 5 million
Arrested January 1937–December 1938		c. 7
		c. 12 million
Of whom, executed	c. 1 million	
died in camp, 1937–38	c. 2	
In captivity, late 1938		c. 9 million
Of whom, in prison	c. 1 million	
Camp population		c. 8 million

[7] His assassin was one Leonid Nikolayev, a former member of the Komsomol (Communist Youth) and of the Cheka. From the very beginning it was rumored that the person behind the murder was Stalin, whose imminent defeat in the Party dispute was thus averted. Evidence has since accumulated to make this supposition a virtual certainty; see the masterful summary by Conquest (1971: chap. 2).

3. During the war and its aftermath, non-Russians comprised the new stock from which forced laborers were selected. In addition to the ethnic minorities expunged from Russia's polyglot empire (see pp. 685–690), these new sources were occupied Poland; the roughly 23 million persons inhabiting annexed territories (Table 17-1); some 5 million prisoners of war; former Soviet prisoners of war and so-called *Ostarbeiter* (Slavs sent from German-occupied territories to forced labor in Germany), both of whom were regarded as suspect. Out of the total new stock of some 14.7 million (Table 17-2), the proportion subjected to forced labor or forced settlement differed among the various categories— virtually all of the 400,000 Volga Germans or 200,000 Crimean Tatars, a relatively small percentage of the returned Soviet prisoners of war. "The total war-time influx of compulsory labor from [non-Russian] external and internal sources . . . was probably between 7 and 8 million, not counting the Poles released

Table 17-1.   Annexations to the USSR, 1939–45

Date	Region	Size (sq. km.)	Population (–000)
November, 1939	Polish provinces (excluding Vilna)	194,800	12,500[a]
March, 1940	Finnish provinces	35,100	420[a]
August, 1940	Rumanian provinces (Bessarabia and North Bukovina)	50,400	3,700
August, 1940	Lithuania (including Vilna)	59,800	2,925
August, 1940	Latvia	65,800	1,951
August, 1940	Estonia	47,500	1,122
September, 1944	Petchenga Raion (Murmansk)	10,480	5
September, 1944	Tuva Autonomous Oblast	150,000	70
October, 1944	Memel territory	2,850	150
August, 1945	Kaliningrad Oblast (Königsberg area)	9,000	400
August, 1945	Byalistock-Suwalki and Przemysl areas—lost to Poland	– 14,200	– 850
September, 1945	Transcarpathian area	12,620	800
September, 1945	Karafuto (South Sakhalin)	36,090	420
September, 1945	Kurile Islands	10,100	5
NET GAIN, November, 1939–September, 1945		670,340	23,618

[a] The cited figures do not take into account concomitant losses. Following the partition of Poland, an exchange of populations between Germany and the USSR resulted in a net loss of 260,000 persons from the Soviet-annexed Polish provinces; similarly, from the Soviet-incorporated Finnish areas some 415,000 Karelians were evacuated to Finland.

SOURCE: Abram Bergson and Hans Heymann, Jr., *Soviet National Income and Product, 1940–48* (New York: Columbia University Press, 1954), Table 1. Copyright 1954, The RAND Corporation.

Table 17-2. Estimated Numbers Deported to the Soviet Union from Annexed or Occupied Territories, Including Soviet Minorities Transported within the USSR, 1939 to c. 1948

Alien Deportees		2,044,000
Polish	880,000[a]	
Lithuanian	38,000	
Latvian	34,000	
Estonian	97,000	
German and Volksdeutsche[b]	700,000	
Hungarian	295,000	
Rumanian	?	
Prisoners of War		4,889,000
German	3,740,000	
Japanese	594,000	
Hungarian	325,000	
Rumanian	230,000	
Italian, Spanish, French, Finnish, Slovak	?	
Soviet Subjects Returned to the USSR		4,500,000
Prisoners of War	2,000,000	
Civilians	2,500,000	
Soviet "Unpeoples"[c]		3,261,000
Germans	1,424,000[d]	
Kirghiz	884,000	
Chechens	408,000	
Crimean Tatars	200,000	
Ingushi	92,000	
Balkars	43,000	
Karachay	76,000	
Kalmyks	134,000	
TOTAL		14,694,000

[a] This may be too conservative an estimate. According to figures compiled by the Polish Embassy in Moscow from the testimony of some 18,000 witnesses, from September 17, 1939, to June 14, 1941 (that is, during the period of the Soviet-Nazi Friendship Pact), 1,692,000 Poles, Jews, Ukrainians, and Byelorussians, including 160,000 children and adolescents, were forcibly taken from their homes and deported to the Soviet Union. Included were 230,000 soldiers and officers of the Polish Army; 990,000 civilians with a "nationalistic bourgeois background"; 25,000 "class enemies"; 210,000 Poles conscripted into the Red Army and then sent deep into the Soviet Union; and 12,000 other Poles gathered from the Baltic area. See Rozek 1958: 46, 66n.

[b] The "Volksdeutsche" were persons of German stock and culture living in German-speaking enclaves in various East European countries.

[c] The figures are the totals in the 1939 census.

[d] The Volga Germans, those most immediately affected, numbered about 400,000. However, persons of German culture living in other parts of the Soviet Union were probably also subject to deportation (cf. Barghoorn 1956: 80).

SOURCE: Various estimates, as compiled in S. Swianiewicz, *Forced Labour and Economic Development: An Enquiry into the Experience of Soviet Industrialisation* (London: Oxford University Press, 1965), pp. 42–45.

in 1941–42" (Swianiewicz 1965: 43). The estimate of 6.9 million in 1941 included about a million alien deportees; and if this overlap is excluded and mortality during the period is ignored, the postwar total comes to some 13 million. In 1948 the British Government concluded that the number of forced laborers was more than 10 million (ibid.: 44), and this is perhaps as good a guess as one can make of the total when the post-Stalin relaxation got under way.

Recent data on forced-labor camps come partly from former prisoners, as reported often in the *samizdat* underground press. However biased, this is considerably more accurate on such matters than the only alternative source, official Soviet documents. According to a compilation of these materials (Reddaway *et al.* 1973), the reduction in the camp population following Stalin's death in 1953 continued up to about 1957, after which the trend was reversed. The report includes a map showing the location of many of the camps, estimated to number about 1,000 in all.

In making fairly precise estimates, we have benefited from a close analysis of the available camp addresses, and especially their serial numbers. Camp 10 in Mordovia, for example, has the address: Mordovian Autonomous Republic, Leplei Station, Post Box ZhKh-385/10. Here the "ZhKh-385" is the code number for the Mordovian camp administration (*uchrezhdenie*) of the Ministry of Internal Affairs (MVD), while the serial number 10 indicates the particular camp situated near Leplei Station. The Mordovian serial numbers (all of which we know) run from 1 to 19, with a few gaps representing camps which have been closed down, leaving 15 camps in all which are operative [ibid.].

The number of prisoners per camp varies from a few hundred to several thousand, with an average estimated at 1,200. This would give a total of 1.2 million, which to be conservative can be cut to 1 million, of whom "not less than a five-figure number" were political prisoners narrowly defined. Article 36 of the new Fundamental Principles of Corrective Labor Legislation, introduced in 1969, openly provided for the use of punitive food rations in penal institutions, and the most consistent complaint from the camps was that their inmates were starving.

NATIONALITIES OF THE USSR

That ethnic minorities contributed so substantially to the camp population represented a recent phase of the traditional hostility between Great Russians and the peoples they had conquered. Between the end of the 15th century and the end of the 19th, the Russian empire expanded at an estimated 50 square miles per day. In 1897, at the time of the only pre-Soviet census, non-Russians made up more than 55 percent of the population (or actually, since the criterion was language rather than ethnicity and since many had assimilated to the Russian-language elite, the proportion was probably closer to 60 percent). There were, for example, almost 11 million Turks, fully as many as in the Ottoman Empire. There were Lithuanians and Latvians, Germans and Jews, Georgians and Armenians, as well as a hundred smaller peoples, many of them nomads. And there were the three subordinate Slav peoples: almost 18 million Ukrainians, more than 6 million Poles, and not quite 5 million Byelorussians (Pipes 1964: chap. 1).

In the 20th century, when all other imperial powers were forced to divest themselves of their colonies, the Soviet Union has continued to expand. The fate of the diverse units of the Soviet population (and, with the extension of its influence, of Eastern Europe) has been based on three doctrines: (1) the Marxist and particularly Bolshevik opposition to nationalism, (2) the Communist slogan of national self-determination, and (3) the growth of Russian patriotism from the First Five-Year Plan on. National self-determination has been consistently followed only at the propagandistic level of folk dancing and the like. With respect to more significant elements of minority cultures, the Party has vacillated, sometimes encouraging minority-language schools, newspapers, and theaters, sometimes banning them (cf. Kucera 1954).

Over the whole period of Soviet rule the dominant trend has been toward russification. For example, the program adopted at the 22nd Party Congress (1961) called for the "voluntary" adoption of the Russian language as "the common medium of intercourse and cooperation" (Vardys 1965). Another policy, an internal manifestation of the Pan-Slav movement, has been to treat "the Russians as first-class citizens, the Ukrainians as second-class, and the remainder as third-class" (Conquest 1960: 125–126). The increase in Slav, as contrasted with Russian, control can be shown most graphically by comparing the proportions of various nationalities in the population with those in the Party and particularly its leadership. Under Stalin a number of Caucasian nationalities had been favored, especially Georgians (Stalin and Beria were both of Georgian stock) and Armenians. From 1939 to 1961, while the Russians remained the dominant group in the Party's Central Committee, the percentages of both full and alternate members changed as follows: Georgians, 4.3 to 0.7; Armenians, 3.6 to 1.7; Jews, 10.8 to 0.3; Ukrainians, 7.9 to 18.5; Byelorussians, 0.7 to 3.4 (Bialer 1964).

Party policy is ubiquitous. Even the simplest statistical fact—how many ethnic groups exist—has marked political overtones. National self-determination of a kind has been encouraged for small minorities, in order to prevent them from coalescing into more meaningful but also more powerful units. The Bashkir Republic is one instance of this policy of divide and rule: "the task of Bashkir nationalism from the Soviet point of view was to render impossible the emergence of a Moslem State on the borders of Europe and Asia, which might have covered over 150,000 square miles with a population of over 5 million" (Kolarz 1955: 41). The 180 nationalities often cited in Soviet statistics are double the number of peoples with even a minimum cultural or linguistic self-expression; only 30 to 45 nationalities are generally represented in formal institutions.

The Soviet population has been classified by nationality in each of the four major censuses, as shown in Table 17-3. These figures are difficult to interpret,

Table 17-3. Nationalities of the USSR, Census Dates

Nationality	Population (−000)				Percent Change		
	1926	1939	1959	1970	1926–39	1939–59	1959–70
USSR	147,028	170,467	208,827	241,720	+16	+23	+15.8
Major Nationalities[a]							
Russian	77,791	99,020	114,114	129,015	+27	+15	+13.1
Ukrainian	31,195	28,070	37,253[b]	40,753	−10	+33[b]	+9.4
Uzbek	3,955	4,844	6,015	9,195	+22	+24	+52.9
Byelorussian	4,739	5,267	7,913[b]	9,052	+11	+50[b]	+14.4
Tatar	3,478	4,300	4,968	5,931	+24	+16	+19.4
Kazakh	3,968	3,099	3,622	5,299	−22	+17	+46.3
Azerbaidzhanian	1,707	2,275	2,940	4,380	+33	+29	+49.0
Armenian	1,568	2,152	2,787	3,559	+37	+30	+27.7
Georgian	1,821	2,249	2,692	3,245	+24	+20	+20.5
Moldavian	279	260	2,214[b]	2,698	−7	[b]	+21.9
Lithuanian	43	32	2,326[b]	2,665	−26	[b]	+14.6
Jewish	2,672	3,020	2,268	2,151	+13	−25	−5.2
Displaced nationalities							
German	1,247	1,424	1,620	1,846	+14	+14	+14.0
Chechen	319	408	419	613	+28	+3	+46.3
Ingush	74	92	106	158	+24	+15	+49.1
Kalmyk	129	134	106	137	+4	−21	+29.2
Karachay	55	76	81	113	+38	+7	+39.5
Balkar	33	43	42	60	+30	−2	+42.9

[a] Those nationalities of more than 2 million in 1970, in order of size at that date.
[b] Increase due to annexation of new territory.
SOURCES: Frank Lorimer, *The Population of the Soviet Union: History and Prospects* (Princeton, N.J.: Princeton University Press, 1946), Table 55; Roman Szporluk, "The Nations of the USSR in 1970," *Survey*, **17** (1971), 68–100.

however, for a recorded intercensal growth or decline can be the consequence of any of three factors:

1. Statistical Reclassification.   The counts in the censuses, it must be emphasized, are not wholly comparable. Even the Russian word translated as "nationality" was different (*narodnost* in 1926, *natsionalnost* in 1939 and 1959), and the returns in 1939 and 1959 were far less complete than in 1926 and 1970. Supposedly, some of these adjustments were made to disguise the size of the depletion of the peoples that had suffered especially from one or another policy.

2. Assimilation.   Between 1926 and 1939, there was an absolute decrease in most of the minorities not then identified with a USSR republic or district—Poles, Estonians, Latvians, Lithuanians, Bulgarians, Kurds, Iranians and Chinese—presumably because these scattered groups assimilated to one of the major Soviet nationalities, particularly the Russian. Although in previous censuses persons were required to prove their nationality from their internal passports, in 1959 they were permitted to state the nationality with which they chose to be identified. This was an opportunity for members of ethnic minorities to "pass" as Russians, and some took advantage of it. Thus, the number of enumerated Ukrainians living outside the Ukraine fell from 8.0 million in 1926 to 5.1 million in 1959; and most of this loss may have been through a change in self-identification.

3. Differential Growth.   Since the Ukraine bore the brunt of the enforced collectivization of agriculture and the consequent famine, another portion of the decline in the number of Ukrainians represents the price they paid for the social transformation. The demographic effect of the parallel policy of forcing nomads to settle on the land, similarly, can probably be measured by the figures given for some of the nomadic peoples. The reported number of Kazakhs, for instance, decreased by 869,000 between 1926 and 1939; since this is a group whose age structure and social norms favored rapid procreation, we should have expected an *increase* at least at the average rate for the whole country, or by 635,000 persons. Thus, some 1.5 million out of 4.0 million disappeared during the enforced "denomadization," when the Kazakhs' herds were depleted by about four-fifths. The virtually stationary Kalmyk population presumably reflects the somewhat less devastating effects of the policy on *this* nomadic people. The nationalities subjected to special terror during the 1930s, in short, included those at both ends of the cultural spectrum—large minorities with a cultural level comparable to the Russians', such as the Ukrainians and the ethnic Germans, and the more primitive, smaller peoples.

During and immediately following World War II, the government dissolved four Autonomous Republics of the USSR and expunged four major and several minor peoples from the ethnographic list, banishing their populations *en masse* (see Table 17-3). In his speech in 1956 to the 20th Party Congress, Khrushchev (1956: 44–45) characterized these deportations as "monstrous." The policy of the Soviet government, in his words, had been "to make whole nations responsible for inimical activity, including women, children, old people,

Communists and Komsomol; to use mass repression against them; and to expose them to misery and suffering for the hostile acts of individual persons or groups of persons." In 1957, a dozen years after the banishment, the list of "autonomous" republics and territories was expanded to include again some of those who had been expunged, and some of the deported people—of those who had survived—were permitted to return. The re-established Chechen-Ingush Republic does not have the old boundaries: some of the Ingush territory was not regained, and in its place the inhabitants were compensated with an area marked "sand" on an official map (Conquest 1960: 173). In recent years a considerable amount of new information has become available about these mass deportations, and the matter is important enough to warrant giving details about three or four particular nationalities.

The strangest case is that of the "Meskhetians," various peoples listed in the censuses as Turkish or Azerbaidzhanian who were welded into a new people by their common fate. Since their land was never occupied by the German army, the removal was not punitive; rather, reflecting Soviet ambitions for Turkish territory, officials thought it better to move Turkic peoples from the border region and transport them to Central Asia and Kazakhstan. All told, they numbered some 200,000, of whom perhaps as many as 30,000 to 50,000 died from hunger and cold. Since no charge was ever made against them, they could not be rehabilitated. The world learned of their removal only in 1968, when they were given the right—on paper—to return home; but the very decree noted that they had "taken root" where they were. From the listing in the 1970 census it would seem that many "Meskhetians" have reverted to the designation "Turks," and in 1970 and 1971 a number of attempts were made to obtain permission to emigrate to Turkey, with no success. Several leaders who addressed an appeal to the United Nations succeeded only in getting themselves sentenced to prison terms (Sheehy 1973: 31–34).

The Soviet Germans comprise various sectors; many had forebears who were invited by Peter or Catherine to immigrate to Imperial Russia and settle there. Most of those living in European Russia were deported in 1941–42, as a precautionary measure. It was only against the Volga Germans that a mass accusation of disloyalty was made. In 1964, when Khrushchev was trying to establish better relations with West Germany, the Volga Germans were rehabilitated; but they learned of this from reading the decree in the East German publication *Neues Deutschland*. Only after their protest was the decree so much as published in the Soviet gazette, and the formal permission to return home was once again linked to an assertion that the Soviet Germans had "taken firm root in their new places of residence." The following year a delegation succeeded in meeting with A. I. Mikoyan, vice-chairman of the Council of Ministers. Presumably because of Germany's interest in the issue, Mikoyan expressed sympathy, but he explained that German labor power was badly needed in the "virgin-land" agriculture of Kazakhstan and the Karaganda coal mines. Since no resolution was possible in the Soviet context, Germans also tried to get permission to leave.

There has been a marked correlation between Moscow's desire to win favor in Bonn and the number allowed to emigrate, most of whom, however, had been born in Germany or Eastern Europe and deported eastward at the end of the war. From 1959 through 1972, a total of only 7,321 native-born Soviet Germans were permitted to emigrate, compared with 30,000 on file waiting to rejoin members of their families plus a much larger number who would get out if they could (ibid.: 22–30).

The greatest amount of discussion and agitation in the Soviet Union has been in support of the Crimean Tatars, who may have been treated the worst. They are counted in the censuses together with the more numerous Volga Tatars, and their precise numbers are not known. Their deportation was described in an "Open Letter from the Russian Friends of the Crimean Tatars," written in 1968 or 1969 and distributed illegally in the Soviet Union:

> It was a journey of lingering death in cattle trucks crammed with people, like mobile gas chambers. The journey lasted three to four weeks and took them across the scorching summer steppes of Kazakhstan. . . . Men were fighting at the front, but deportation awaited them at the end of the war. In the meantime women and children constituted the vast majority. . . . On the long stages the corpses decomposed in the huddle of the trucks, and at the short halts, where water and food were handed out, the people were not allowed to bury their dead.

Perhaps a quarter of a million were deported several thousand miles to the east. On the basis of a census that they administered in 1966, the Crimean Tatars claim that 46 percent, or some 110,000 persons, died either en route or within eighteen months of reaching their destination. Soviet authorities dispute the figure: a mere 22 percent, or some 33,000 persons, of those who arrived died within that period, they say, while neglecting altogether the mortality on the cattle trains.

The rehabilitation decree, issued in 1967, noted that the "indiscriminate accusations against all citizens of Tatar nationality resident in the Crimea ought to be lifted, the more so since a new generation of people has embarked on its working and political life." "The Tatars formerly resident in the Crimea," the decree went on to note, had "taken root" in the Uzbek and other eastern regions. Formally, they had the right thereafter to live anywhere in the Soviet Union, requiring only the usual residence permit, which now is normally granted as soon as evidence of available accommodations is furnished. In fact, of the 6,000 or so who managed to get back to Crimea up to the end of 1967, only three single men and two families succeeded in getting registered. The others were deported or, when their funds gave out, had to leave of their own accord. Tatars who managed to get jobs in the Crimea were dismissed as soon as their nationality was discovered. According to a protest addressed to the U.N. Human Rights Commission, members of eleven families who had been refused registration were seized in the middle of the night, put on trains leaving the Caucasus, and dumped at railroad stations, destitute except for a handful of possessions they were able to carry with them. They were all reduced to begging in order to keep alive. This incident took place not under Stalin but in 1969. Because of the publicity given to it and to similar brutalities, Crimean Tatars are now barred from Moscow hotels, in order to cut their communication with those who can be reached in the capital (ibid.: 7–21).

Soviet policy toward the Jews deserves special examination for, from the 1917 revolution on, propaganda has contrasted it with tsarist or Nazi pogroms. Actually, Soviet policy has never been entirely free of anti-Semitism. Many Jews of tsarist Russia were socialists, but few were Bolsheviks. The Bolshevik victory meant that Jews were persecuted as members of a religious faith, as businessmen, as nationalists, and as socialists, but for a time the pogroms that had been endemic in tsarist Russia disappeared. Specific opposition to Jews as Jews developed during the 1930s, was strongly reinforced by the Nazi–Soviet Friendship Pact of 1939–41, and survived the German invasion of Russia. In the postwar period, in both Russia and its East European satellites, the campaign against Jews developed from opposition to "cosmopolitans" or "Zionist bourgeois nationalists" to virulent, undisguised persecution of Jews.[8]

Some of the major events or trends have been:

The "Doctors' Plot" (1953). Nine Jewish physicians were to be unmasked as agents of an American–Zionist conspiracy, allegedly masterminded by the Joint Distribution Committee (a relief agency active in Eastern Europe but not in the Soviet Union). Only Stalin's death saved them and—considering the fate of other minorities—perhaps the entire Jewish community.

Judaism as a religion is subjected to far greater hostility than other religions. Prayerbooks, hymnals, and other sacred works are available to all other denominations; no Hebrew Bible has been published since 1917. The study of Hebrew was long banned. Until after Stalin's death the Soviet Union had no yeshiva (rabbinical seminary); up to 1963, the one established in 1957 graduated two men, neither of whom functioned as a synagogue leader. In 1970 it was

---

[8] Among the most informative accounts of the 1950s and 1960s are a number of articles in *Commentary*, published by the American Jewish Committee—for example, Peter Meyer, "Soviet Anti-Semitism in High Gear," February 1953, pp. 115–120; Franz Borkenau, "Was Malenkov Behind the Anti-Semitic Plot?," May 1953, pp. 438–466; Walter Z. Laqueur, "Soviet Policy and Jewish Fate," October 1956, pp. 303–312; A. Wiseman and O. Pick, "Soviet Jews under Khrushchev," February 1959, pp. 127–132; Maurice Friedberg, "The State of Soviet Jewry," January 1965, pp. 38–43. See also, as among the best of a sizable literature, Schwarz 1951; Erich Goldhagen, "Communism and Anti-Semitism," *Problems of Communism*, 9 (1960), 35–42; Decter 1963; Moshe Decter, "Silence and Yearning," the whole of a special issue of *Congress Bi-Weekly*, December 5, 1966; Maurice Friedberg, "On Reading Recent Soviet Judaica," *Survey* (London), no. 62 (1967), 167–178. In England a regular periodical was established to report on "events affecting Jews in the Soviet bloc": *Jews in Eastern Europe* (London). Patterns of anti-Semitism in satellite countries are variations on the Russian theme; for a detailed account up to the death of Stalin, see Peter Meyer et al., *The Jews in the Soviet Satellites* (Syracuse, N.Y.: Syracuse University Press, 1953).

estimated that the whole country had only thirty-five to forty active rabbis (Gerstenmaier 1970).

Yiddish culture has been all but obliterated. In 1932 (the high point since 1917) 668 Yiddish books were published; in 1940, still 359; from 1949 to 1958, none; from 1959 to 1966, a total of eleven, mostly classics by authors no longer living. There is one periodical, *Sovietish Heimland* (Soviet Fatherland), a bimonthly founded in 1961; among probably all the world's Jewish periodicals, it had the dubious distinction of being the only one to ignore *Babii Yar*, Yevgenii Yevtushenko's poem indicting Soviet anti-Semitism.

Official anti-Semitism, especially virulent in the provincial press, uses all of the conventional Russian stereotypes—Jews as money worshippers, drunks, cosmopolitans who are potentially or actually subversive, and so on. In 1963 the Ukrainian Academy of Sciences officially sponsored a book, *Judaism without Embellishment*, by Trofim K. Kichko, illustrated by caricatures hauntingly reminiscent of Julius Streicher's *Der Stürmer*, the most vicious of the Nazis' anti-Jewish publications. One cartoon, for example, shows a hook-nosed man bowing obsequiously to an enormous boot emblazened with a swastika; the caption reads, "During the years of the Hitlerite occupation, the Zionist leaders served the Fascists" (cf. *New Leader*, March 16, 1964; Decter 1967). After much protest abroad, especially from non-Russian Communists, Kichko's book was withdrawn. It was replaced by another, *Beware, Zionism!* by Yu. Ivanov (Moscow, 1968; 2nd ed. 1970), which has been compared with the notorious "Protocols of the Elders of Zion" (Gerstenmaier 1970).

Jews are barred from social advancement. The two principal roads, upper positions in the Party and university study, once had as many Jews as one would expect from their concentration in urban centers and their frequent professional qualifications for administrative posts. The percentage of Jews in the student bodies of "higher education" (which includes normal schools, music conservatories, and journalism institutes) fell from 13.5 in 1935 to 3.1 in 1962; in universities alone, the decline was even sharper. The increasing dominance of Slavic peoples in the leading ranks of the Party (see p. 685) has reduced the status especially of the Jews (cf. Altschuler 1973).

Jews as embezzlers and speculators have been featured in the campaign against economic crimes. During the first two years after a 1961 law establishing the death penalty for such acts, thirty-six trials were reported in twenty-six different cities. Not only were there forty-two Jews among the seventy condemned to death, but they were so identified and depicted as typical of a cunning and unscrupulous people.

In sum, Soviet policy places the Jews in an inextricable vise. They are allowed neither to assimilate, nor live a full Jewish life, nor to emigrate (as many would wish) to Israel or any other place where they might live freely as Jews [Decter 1963].

By mid-1970, after a certain relaxation of the last of these charges, several thousand Jews had been permitted to emigrate. The number seeking exit permits was rising sharply, and the Soviet government imposed what was in effect a ransom, disguised as recompense for the cost of schooling but demanded also of elderly men whose years of service had long since compensated the economy many times over. In order to get permission to leave, persons had to furnish amounts ranging up to $25,000 paid either by themselves or, better, by friends or relatives abroad who could provide foreign currency. The new levy was kept secret, but under these conditions not for long; when its existence became known, the Soviet authorities busied themselves making headlines about all the exemptions they were granting. A propaganda film was produced to demonstrate that exit visas are as easy to acquire as postage stamps, but forty Jews who had been denied permission to emigrate issued a joint public denunciation of the sham. The trade concessions that the Soviet Union was seeking from the United States were endangered; some 76 Senators and 270 Representatives backed Senator Henry Jackson's efforts to block giving Russia the status of "most favored nation." In the spring of 1973 the levy was suspended, and at least for the time being more Jews were allowed to leave without paying for the privilege. (In the worldwide denunciation of Soviet anti-Semitism, it was not noted that by Soviet standards Jews were especially favored: some of them were getting exit visas.)

In the several years before the 1970 census, it was freely predicted in the Soviet press that the almost 2.3 million Jews enumerated in 1959 would have increased to 3 million, partly because of natural increase, partly because of a readier willingness to identify oneself as Jewish (cf. Friedberg 1970). The actual decline in the number of Jews enumerated in 1970—by 117,000 or 5.2 percent—is many times larger than the total emigration. That some Jews have openly affiliated with Zionism (Teller 1972) has helped revivify the endemic anti-Semitism of the Soviet Union, and it would seem that fewer were willing to identify themselves as *Untermenschen* than had been supposed.

INTERNAL MIGRATION AND URBANIZATION

In a free economy one factor determining the location of industry is an available supply of workers; but if not enough are in the area to start with, an effort is made to attract more with higher wages. Soviet industry has been developed mainly in areas chosen by national or specifically military criteria, and the system by which consumer goods are supplied and distributed has never been efficient enough to afford attractions to in-migrants. In the post-Stalin period, public-opinion surveys have been taken over from the United States in the hope that, by pinpointing the main reasons for dissatisfaction, the State will be able to achieve labor's compliance as cheaply as possible. However, according to a large manpower survey conducted by a Novosibirsk institute, higher wages would not be enough to get people to settle in Siberia, for the main discontent was with inadequate housing and public services. During the Seven-Year Plan (1959–65), probably more people left Siberia than could be induced to come to it (*New York Times*, October 31, 1967). In any case, the continued push to disperse the Soviet population could be effected by a differential income only to the degree that the supply of commodities permits. Agriculture has remained the prime headache of the economy, but after decades of a narrow concentration on capital accumulation, the recurrent crisis in food production is only one block to the repeatedly proclaimed intention to shift to a greater stress on consumer goods. Each manager in charge of manufacturing them knows that his professional reputation and income depend on whether he meets or overfulfills the factory's output quota, as defined in terms of weight or price or, in plants operating under the newly implemented Liberman system, profit—but hardly ever quality (cf. Shaffer 1963). Soviet distribution services are notoriously inefficient: in each shop each customer must stand in line three times, once to price the merchandise, once to pay for it, and once to pick it up.

Apart from the quality of the goods and the consumer's convenience, how much can he acquire? This is not a question easy to answer, for the mountains of data collected contain little that can be used to estimate real purchasing power. Medical services are free in the Soviet Union and rent is cheap, but the costs of other consumer goods and services are much higher than in the West (e.g., Chapman 1964). The relative costs of various consumer goods in hours of working time indicate how much the Soviet consumer in 1966 lagged behind his American counterpart (Table 17-4). Wages were the averages earned by workers in manufacturing, 0.60 rubles per hour in Moscow and $2.70 per hour in New York. Moscow prices were those in State stores, and since these are lower than those in private trade, the indicated purchasing power of Soviet workers may be somewhat inflated. No similar comparison is available for a later date, but an analysis by Bronson and Severin (1973) lends substance to the general impression that there was a substantial improvement over the next period. The lack of data makes it difficult even to estimate the inflation rate in the Soviet Union, but by a reasonable guess the real disposable money income per capita rose by more than half from 1965 to 1972.

The manifest dissatisfaction of the Soviet consumer affected his productivity enough to stimulate some modifications. The Eighth Five-Year Plan (1966–70) brought into being two policy innovations introduced by Khrushchev's successors, Brezhnev's agricultural program and Kosygin's economic reform. As always, the report on the plan declared that goals had been reached in every respect. Among a list of thirty-nine commodities on which data were available, however, the fulfillment of the 1970 output targets ranged from 117.5 percent for automation equipment down to 43 percent for passenger cars, with a median of 83.3 percent. The claim that economic performance improved from the first to the second half of the 1960s can hardly be substantiated except in two very important sectors: agricultural production and personal consumption. Weather conditions were exceptionally favorable, and the often announced shift to consumer production was realized to some degree. The "main task" of the Ninth Five-Year Plan ostensibly was also to raise "the material and cultural level of life

Table 17-4. Approximate Work Time Required to Buy Selected Commodities in Moscow and New York City, January 15, 1966

Commodity	Moscow	New York	Moscow as Percent of New York
Food			
White bread (half kilogram)	28 min.	6.6 min.	400
Potatoes (kilogram)	10 min.	3.3 min.	300
Rib roast (kilogram)	160 min.	44 min.	350
Salted butter (kilogram)[a]	360 min.	37 min.	1,000
Sugar (kilogram)	104 min.	6 min.	1,500
Milk (liter)	30 min.	6.2 min.	500
Eggs (per 10)[b]	90 min.	11.7 min.	800
Tea (50 grams)	38 min.	3.2 min.	1,200
Clothing			
Men's cotton shirt, low-priced (each)	13 hrs.	1.7 hr.	750
Men's suit, wool, single-breasted, medium-priced (each)	183 hrs.	23.6 hrs.	800
Men's leather shoes (pair)	41 hrs.	6.6 hrs.	600
Women's street dress, rayon (each)	49 hrs.	5 hrs.	1,000
Women's leather shoes, medium-priced (pair)	38 hrs.	5.5 hrs.	700
Nylon stockings (pair)	5 hrs.	0.51 hr.	1,000
Other			
Toilet soap (100-gram cake)	21 min.	2.7 min.	800
Cigarettes (package of 20)	20 min.	8 min.	250
Vodka (half liter)	5 hrs.	1.25 hr.	400

[a] First quality in New York; quality not specified in Moscow.
[b] Large, Grade A, in New York; second grade in Moscow, though eggs at this price were usually not available.
SOURCE: Edmund Nash, "Recent Changes in Labor Controls in the Soviet Union," in Congress of the United States, Joint Economic Committee, *New Directions in the Soviet Economy*, Part III: *The Human Resources* (Washington, D.C.: U.S. Government Printing Office, 1966).

of the people," a formulation much emphasized in the major speeches (Grossman 1971).

During the first years of the Ninth Five-Year Plan (1971–75), however, several setbacks made a mockery of these guidelines. The 1972 crop, blighted by what Soviet sources called the worst weather in a century, was estimated at about 160 million tons, compared to a goal of 190 million and an actual harvest the previous year of 181 million. Only the massive shipment of $1 billion of wheat from the capitalist United States averted a disaster. The reasons for the food shortage are not only unfavorable weather; the peasant has been fully demoralized by the consequences of enforced collectivization and oppressive taxation (in the form of low fixed prices for agricultural goods), not to say the incredible dreariness of Soviet rural life. The prospects for Soviet agriculture are not good (Laird 1971). Nor indeed are those for Soviet industry. One of the worst shortages, and the one most relevant in this context, is of laborers. By 1970, 92.4 percent of the able-bodied population (compared with only 76.4 percent in the United States) was either gainfully employed or studying full time. With a population one-fifth larger than that of the United States, the Soviet Union had a work force 45 percent larger. During the Ninth Plan the size of the labor force was projected to increase by only 1.3 percent annually, or by roughly the expected growth in the population (Meyer 1973). There is an acute and growing labor shortage, and one can understand why in economic terms the Soviet State looks with disfavor on the ethnic minorities' hopes of emigrating. Since the economy cannot furnish sufficient means to stimulate the redistribution of population called for in plans, this is effected also through a number of programs, which are briefly described in the following paragraphs, beginning with the most voluntarist and ending with current examples of forced migrations.

1. **The family-resettlement program,** intended mainly to facilitate the migration of peasants to thinly populated rural areas, operates as a truly voluntary system. Under certain conditions, the head of a family is permitted to investigate the proposed resettlement site and to return home before making his decision. Inducements to move may include, in addition to assurance of work in the new place, exemption from taxation for a specified period, financial assistance in building a home and getting settled, free transportation of the whole family and in some cases also of household possessions and personally owned livestock (Roof 1960).

2. **"Volunteer" programs,** ordinarily organized through the Komsomol, are designed mainly to recruit young people for unskilled construction or agricultural work. Recent graduates from the 10-year general school, who often have difficulties in finding a job, sometimes welcome a chance to work elsewhere, but local youth organizations may be assigned "quotas," or may "pledge" a certain number of "volunteers" in advance of any solicitation. Volunteers have the theoretical right to return home if they so choose, but they must accumulate their own return fare by saving a portion of their meager pay. Those who cooperate willingly are publicly commended as "patriots" and given various honorific insignia. In short, the program is a kind of labor draft mitigated by voluntarist features (ibid.).

3. **Graduates of institutions of higher learning** are dispersed according to the type of school. Assignments to universities and technical schools are sought after. In order to ensure a sufficient supply of semiskilled workers, the State used to draft from each collective farm a quota of lower-class boys and girls

aged 14 to 18 to be sent to labor-reserve schools; in 1955 this recruitment was put on a voluntary basis. Graduates of labor-reserve schools are assigned to a specific job for 4 years and those of the other institutions for 3 years. As many of the schools are in European Russia and most of the vacancies for trained personnel are in the trans-Urals region, the assignment often involves a removal from a large or middle-sized city with temperate seasons to a raw provincial area with a harsh climate. Graduates sometimes connive with administrative officials to be excused from their 3 or 4 years of service, or to be assigned to a large city even if in a post not requiring their skill (ibid.).

4. Organized recruitment of labor was instituted in 1931, and from 1932 to 1940 some 2.5 million workers were drafted annually. The system was set up to settle workers permanently in the new areas, and under a 1940 decree they were bound to the job all their life. This industrial serfdom lapsed after the war and was formally abolished in 1956. Presently workers and employees are required to sign contracts for a number of years (varying according to the type of work, location, etc.), and if they then leave their jobs, they forfeit the substantial monetary benefits and social security that can accrue with seniority. Allocation of laborers is based on local needs as specified by the economic councils. Only about one-third of the recruits begin with definite vocational skills, and most of even these undergo retraining when at their new place of work. According to one Soviet report, "almost four-fifths" of those drafted under the system had been fired from previous jobs, some of them because of "infractions of labor discipline" (M. Y. Sonin, cited in ibid.). When skilled workers are recruited into the system, administrators have the right to use them in any job, irrespective of their training and qualifications.

5. By 1957, according to Soviet sources, 70 percent of the inmates of **forced-labor camps** had been released (Roof and Leedy 1959). At the 21st Party Congress in 1959, Khrushchev declared categorically that there were "no political prisoners in our country's prisons at present." The reform, while significant, was less wholesale than this assertion implies. It is not clear, first of all, what proportion were permitted to return home and how many became forced settlers, still restricted to the general region of the camps. "In important respects, the freedom . . . to migrate internally has not improved. A forced-labor 'colony' system has replaced the former forced-labor 'camps'" (Roof 1960). And for the general rubric "political prisoners" there has been substituted such more specific designations as "enemies of the state," "traitors," "saboteurs," "counterrevolutionaries," all as defined anew in the 1958 criminal code (Gsovski 1959). Two Soviet studies published in 1960—one a manual for law students, the other a study on "the purpose of the corrective-labor law"—added much to what is known about this change of policy.

6. Forced labor, moreover, has been replenished through the operation of the **"anti-parasites decrees"** of most of the Soviet republics. "Parasites," variously defined, are subject to arrest, exile, and forced labor for various periods. According to "the shortest, mildest, and least comprehensive" version, decreed in Georgia in September 1960, adult, able-bodied, urban citizens who avoid "socially useful" work and lead an "antisocial and parasitic life" may be deported for six months to two years, with forced labor at the place of exile. In the Ukrainian decree the definition of "parasites" includes alcoholics, those who "manifestly live beyond their earned income," "persons with an unconscientious attitude toward their work," and those who accept employment "only to divert attention" from their parasitism. Both in the Ukraine and in the Russian Republic, "parasites" are subject to punishment either by People's Courts or by vigilante meetings of workers or collective farmers (Beermann 1961; cf. Nash 1966). As with the traditional forced labor of the 1930s, such decrees apparently are intended to serve a double purpose: to transfer "antisocial" types to areas where they must produce for the socialist economy, and to frighten the rest of the population into working harder.

The redistribution of the population denoted in the censuses does not, of course, suggest any of these means of bringing it about. The long-term trend from west to east continued: the population east of the Urals—a total of 45.5 million, or 21.8 percent, in 1959—increased to 58.2 million, or 24.1 percent, in 1970. In the Uzbek, Kazakh, Kirgiz, Tadzhik, and Turkmen Republics, the intercensal increases were all by more than 40 percent, compared with the national average of 15.8 percent. In mid-1973 a new rural-resettlement decree, in part a codification of regulations going back to the 1930s, upped the benefits available to those who settled in disputed areas on the Chinese border. Migrants going to build up the Soviet population there were eligible for larger lump-sum payments,

Table 17-5.   Total Net Migration (–000) During the Intercensal Period, by Republic, USSR, 1959–70

Republics Losing Population	Net Out-migration	Republics Gaining Population	Net In-migration
RSFSR (Russian)	1,745	Kazakh SSR	703
Byelorussian SSR	319	Ukrainian SSR	429
Georgian SSR	93	Uzbek SSR	364
Azerbaidzhan SSR	44	Kirgiz SSR	134
		Tadzhik SSR	129
		Armenian SSR	124
		Latvian SSR	122
		Estonian SSR	72
		Moldavian SSR	63
		Lithuanian SSR	41
		Turkmen SSR	20

SOURCE: Frederick A. Leedy "Demographic Trends in the U.S.S.R.," in U.S. Congress, Joint Economic Committee, *Soviet Economic Prospects for the Seventies* (Washington, D.C.: U.S. Government Printing Office, 1973).

homebuilding loans with one-third of the financing paid by the government, loans for livestock, and even vacations with travel expenses paid (*New York Times*, August 5, 1973).

From the two census counts and the republics' natural increase, as estimated from their vital statistics, Leedy calculated the implied migration totals shown in Table 17-5. Apart from the movement to the Far East already noted, these estimates showed a continuing flow of migrants to some labor-surplus areas (e.g., the North Caucasus, southern Ukraine)—a matter of considerable concern to Soviet officialdom.

Urban Growth

In most countries of the world the population is becoming increasingly urban, for people are moving from the periphery to the centers of national culture. In the Soviet Union the urban growth taking place under State auspices has meant, on the contrary, a predominant shift from the center to the periphery.

The tsarist government tried repeatedly to entice a larger portion of the Russian population across the Urals into Siberia, but these efforts were unsuccessful. In even the most inhospitable areas the Soviet government has been able to establish large cities—in the sense of population settlements of a certain minimum size. Between the 1926 and the 1939 censuses, net in-migration to towns and cities totaled some 23 million. Urban growth was still at a relatively low rate in 1927–28, but from 1929 on, with deportations getting under way, it rose rapidly. 1931 marks the high point of both dekulakization and urban growth, with a net in-migration to cities of 4.1 million persons in that year (Lorimer 1946: 150). The impression given by this chronology is reinforced when we look at the new urban sites. Lorimer lists forty-nine "boom cities"—that is, those with 50,000 or more inhabitants in 1939 that had increased by three times or more during the intercensal period. The one heading the list, which did not exist in 1926 and in 1939 had a population of 166,000, was Karaganda (ibid.: 148), the center of a particularly notorious forced-labor complex. A number of other Soviet cities grew in the same way. These figures, it should be noted, did not comprise the camp populations but presumably only the administrative staffs, plus possibly the exiles compelled to reside in these areas. Similarly, among the country's regions Karelo-Murmansk underwent the largest intercensal urban increase— by 5.6 times; and this growth was concentrated in the extreme northern districts, the site of a number of large forced-labor mining complexes. The intercensal increase in urban population in Central Siberia was by 3.1 times, in East Siberia by 3.8 times, in the Soviet Far East by 3.3 times (ibid.: 152). In large part these figures reflect mining, logging, and construction camps, all peopled by forced laborers. After 1938–40, when the Soviet Union instituted the controls already mentioned (internal passports, labor books and labor conscription for youths of 14 to 19), migration was "almost totally an expression of government plans and programs" (Shimkin 1960). Between 1939 and 1959 in-migrants to the cities totaled between 24 and 25 million.

The stream of reports announcing new industrial cities being built in the Soviet wilderness are highly reminiscent of the socialist State's earlier conquests of hostile nature. "In the new heart of the taiga," the swampy forest south of Lake Baikal, the new city of Baikalsk was constructed, the site of a cellulose plant scheduled to go into operation in 1965, conveniently close to the timber camps (*Pravda*, April 25, 1961). New cities are springing up in the mining areas of West Siberia; "some of them already have names, such as Nikitinsky" (*Trud*, January 25, 1962)—presumably after Khrushchev. In "Far Siberia," the new town of Shelekhov was being built as the center of the aluminum industry (*Pravda*, February 16, 1962). Mirny, the "diamond center of the country," was "hewn out of wilderness" in temperatures of 50 to 60 degrees below zero; the first in-migrants lived in tents while building "a beautiful and modern city" (*Pravda*, December 29, 1961).

A regional Party secretary, V. Uvachan, could write in *Kommunist*, No. 14, 1967: "The North contains virtually all the diamond resources of the country, nearly half the gold and tin, and a large part of the nickel, mica, and apatites." This alone justifies . . . the construction of many towns: Norilsk (over 120,000 in 1964), Vorkuta (200,000, with its neighbors in the coalfield, in 1965), Kirovsk (40,000 in 1959), Apatity (20,000 in 1959), Mirny (20,000 in 1965), and numbers of smaller places [Armstrong 1968; cf. Ways 1968].

Resistance to the State plans for dispersing the population has also affected migration patterns considerably. Persistent efforts to limit the growth of Moscow and some of the other large cities of European Russia are successfully circumvented by both industry and in-migrants. According to a Soviet city planner, "measures to stem the flow—restrictions on residence registration, the drawing of hard city boundaries, and the creation of such barriers as green belts—have proved futile" (*New York Times*, November 13, 1966). "Tens of thousands of skilled specialists for whose knowledge and experience Moscow has no use . . . do not leave Moscow because this would mean they would not return" (*Literaturnaya Gazeta*, March 10, 1966).

Between 1959 and 1970, while the rural population declined by 2.9 percent, the urban one grew by 36 percent. Of the 36 million more persons living in towns and cities, 14.6 represented the surplus of births over deaths, 5 million resulted from a redesignation of formerly rural places, and the balance of some 16.4 million was the total net migration into the urban sector. Cities with more than a million inhabitants, only three in 1959 (Moscow, Leningrad, and Kiev), numbered ten in 1970. Both Moscow and Leningrad grew faster than the national average, indicating a continuing failure of the policy to limit their expansion. In general, however, the regional distribution of the new urbanization followed the pattern of population growth, with highest rates in the Caucasus and Central Asia (Leedy 1973).

DEMOGRAPHIC EFFECTS OF
SOVIET TOTALITARIANISM

Soviet policies and practices have affected fertility and mortality, age structure, population distribution and composition. Although it is not possible to specify any of these effects in precise quantitative terms, the data afford the basis for some reasonable estimates. It so happens that the dates of three of the censuses fall almost exactly where they should to separate internal terror from international war. In 1926 War Communism was long over and, 2 years later, the 5-year plans would start. In 1939, when the drive to collectivize agriculture was over and that to purge Soviet society of its "treasonable" elements was interrupted, it was only 2 years before Russia was to enter the war. The losses from the war were so stupendous that for a period demographic facts were guarded as State secrets, but from the count of age brackets in 1959 we can estimate the size of that enormous blood-letting and thus of postwar purges.

A male deficit in a census count roughly measures the cost in lives of some of the special risks that Soviet men incurred during the prior period, not only war and civil war but also forced labor (the camp population was overwhelmingly male), terror, and miscellaneous manifestations of the regime's ill will. Not all types of extraordinary mortality, one should emphasize, are reflected in a distorted sex ratio. Famine, for example, generally affects the two sexes equally, and in each of the two famines the Soviet regime brought about (1921–22 and 1933–34), millions died of hunger or accompanying diseases. Some of the other acts against whole populations, such as the deportation of minorities, also must have killed off males and females in more or less equal proportion. The female surplus, thus, can be taken as an index of the minimum cost of wars and the Bolshevik regime.

The male deficit in the Soviet Union grew steadily up to 1959 (Table 17-6). In prerevolutionary Russia there was a slight female surplus, probably due more

Table 17-6. Population by Sex, Soviet Union at Each Census, 1897–1970

Date	Millions of Persons			Males per 100 Females
	MALE	FEMALE	FEMALE EXCESS	
1897 (Russia)	62.5	63.2	0.7	98.9
1926	71.0	76.0	5.0	93.4
1939	81.7	88.8	7.1	92.0
1959	94.0	114.8	20.8	81.9
1970	111.4	130.3	18.9	85.5

SOURCES: Yury P. Miromenko, "The Ratio Between Men and Women in the Population of the USSR," *Analysis of Current Developments in the Soviet Union* (Munich: Institute for the Study of the USSR, 1959); Frederick A. Leedy, "Demographic Trends in the U.S.S.R.," in U.S. Congress, Joint Economic Committee, *Soviet Economic Prospects for the Seventies* (Washington, D.C.: U.S. Government Printing Office, 1973).

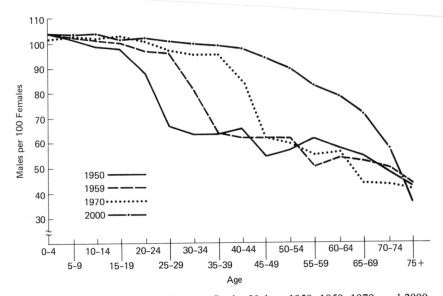

Figure 17-1.   Sex Ratios by Age, Soviet Union, 1950, 1959, 1970, and 2000

SOURCE: Frederick A. Leedy, "Demographic Trends in the U.S.S.R.," in U.S. Congress, Joint Economic Committee, *Soviet Economic Prospects for the Seventies* (Washington, D.C.: U.S. Government Printing Office, 1973).

to emigration than to differential rates of natural increase. In 1926 the excess of females amounted to 5 million. As we have noted (p. 675), military deaths for this period are estimated at about 2 million; thus, the remaining male deficit of about 3 million must be ascribed to extraordinary mortality among the civilian males. During the more than 12 years between the censuses, the imbalance should have been reduced by the twelve new cohorts, each with a sex ratio starting at approximately 104. The excess of females, on the contrary, amounted to 2.1 million more in 1939 than in 1926; one can estimate that during this period this many more males than females died. By 1959 the depletion of males amounted to 20.8 million, the population of a middle-sized country.

From this datum alone it is not yet possible to distinguish between the portion due to military casualties and that resulting from other elements of Stalinism. With the age structure as well as the sex ratio, however, one can estimate the timing of losses more precisely.[9] The population structure in 1959, used already in Figure 3-3 (p. 81) to exemplify an irregular pyramid, is compared with that of several other years in Figure 17-1. The near parity between the sexes held only up to age 17 in 1950; by 1970, with the aging of the cohorts that carried

[9] This may be why publication of these data for the 1939 census was held up so long. Lorimer's analysis in 1946 had to be based on a fitting together of fragments from scattered sources, and an article published 10 years later still lacked a full schedule of age categories (Kulischer and Roof 1956). This basic information became available only in 1957, 18 years after the census count (Roof 1957; Biraben 1960).

Table 17-7 Basis for Analyzing Extraordinary Male Mortality in the Soviet Union, 1917–70

Born in —	Age in Designated Year					
	1917[a]	1921[b]	1928[c]	1941[d]	1959[e]	1970[e]
(1) 1900 or before	17+	21+	28+	41+	59+	70+
(2) 1901–04	13–16	17–20	24–27	37–40	55–58	66–69
(3) 1905–24	12 or under	16 or under	4–23	17–36	35–54	46–65
(4) 1925–29	—	—	3 or under	12–16	30–34	41–45
(5) 1930–39	—	—	—	2–11	20–29	31–40
(6) 1940–59	—	—	—	1	0–19	11–30

[a] End of World War I, beginning of civil war.
[b] End of War Communism, beginning of NEP.
[c] End of NEP, beginning of First Five-Year Plan.
[d] The Soviet Union became a belligerent in World War II.
[e] Dates of last Soviet censuses.

the evidence of mass terror, this normal ratio held up to about age 37. Only at the end of the century does the whole curve begin to approach the standard shape, with the greater longevity of females reflected from age 50 and above.

In Table 17-7 the ages of the successive cohorts are linked to the dates of key events in Russian history, so that one can mark at least approximately the impact of each. The following list refers to successive rows of that table.

1. Males born in 1900 or before were old enough to be soldiers in World War I and to die from any of the later social catastrophes, including World War II for a portion of the cohort. If we ignore the effect of females' naturally greater longevity, this age bracket suffered the largest losses, with only one male surviving to 1959 for every two females. By 1970, when all in the cohort were old men, the extraordinary depletion of males had been compounded by the naturally shorter life of males from age 50 onward.

2. However, the males just too young to be soldiers in World War I, whose extraordinary mortality thus began with the period of War Communism, had no relative advantage. In fact, those aged 55–58 in 1959 had a sex ratio slightly lower than those 5 or 10 years older. The human losses in World War I, great as they were, were less than those in the establishment of Bolshevik power.

3. Persons aged 35–54 in 1959 had a sex ratio of 62 to 64. These had been children during the founding of the Soviet Union, and they grew up during a low point in the terror cycle. Only a portion of the males were old enough at the beginning of forced collectivization to suffer differentially from that. All of this age category were of military age during World War II, and it can be regarded as the prime source of the army's manpower. Remarkably, its sex ratio, though low enough by normal standards, was yet significantly higher than the cohorts that suffered more of the prewar terror. The number of men reported to have served in the Soviet army during the war was about 20 million. If we assume that half were killed (even considering conditions on the eastern front, this is probably an overestimate, and hence conservative for our argument), this still leaves an unexplained deficit of males of almost 11 million in 1959 (Eason 1959). The reason cannot have been the bombing of cities or other civilian hardships, for deaths from such causes, just because of the concentration of males at the front, would have had a higher incidence among females, if there was any difference by sex at all. By 1970 this cohort was aged 46–65 and thus was just beginning to retire. In the years following 1970, thus, the effects of the terror and wars on the population structure would gradually disappear from all except the very old.

4. Persons born in 1925–29 were still children when World War II started, and most of the males of these cohorts who fought as soldiers started after the bloodiest battles were past. Probably the male deficit of 1.8 million in 1959 was mainly the consequence of the postwar terror, from 1945 to after Stalin's death in 1953.

5. The interpretation that the postwar terror killed some millions is reinforced when we look at those born too late to serve in the army during the war but who were aged 14–23 when Stalin died. The male deficit of something over half a million in 1959 is suggestive.

6. Only among those born in 1940 or after, all of whom were children during the postwar terror, is the sex ratio normal.

From the male deficit of 20.8 million in 1959, then, we should subtract the 12 million military casualties in the two world wars, leaving a balance of some 9 million. These nonmilitary male deaths, to repeat, represent only those elements of extraordinary mortality to which males were especially susceptible. And in order to get the full demographic effect of the periodic social cataclysms, we must add extraordinary deaths of both sexes and the birth deficit; the latter is estimated at 10 million for World War I and the civil war (cf. p. 675) and, including extraordinary infant mortality, at 20 million for the 1940–50 decade (Eason 1959). The total depletion during the whole of the Bolshevik era has been 80 million, probably correct to the nearest 10 million—about 25 million extraordinary deaths and nonbirths during the civil war and the establishment of the Communist dictatorship, at least 10 million during the social revolution of the 1930s, and some 45 million during and immediately after World War II.

However correct these assertions are about the past, the distortion of the population structure revealed in the postwar censuses will affect Soviet life for as long as the depleted cohorts live. The U.S. Bureau of the Census has projected the future growth assuming constant fertility and found that the abnormal structure will persist well into the next century. In 1980 there will be a male deficit of 14 million, in 1990 one of 9.4 million, in 2000 still one of 5.2 million. Not until the year 2020 will the sex ratio again be over 100 (Brackett and DePauw 1966).

The depletions in the population structure have affected the economy most

Table 17-8.   Soviet Labor Force, Estimated and Projected, 1900–75

Date	Labor Force (–000)						Percent Female of Total Labor Force
	TOTAL	AVERAGE ANNUAL INCREMENT	MALES	AVERAGE ANNUAL INCREMENT	FEMALES	AVERAGE ANNUAL INCREMENT	
1900	64,400	—	35,400	—	29,000	—	45.0
1930	88,500	803.3	47,400	400	41,100	403.3	46.4
1940	105,300	1,680	58,400	1,100	46,900	580	44.5
1950	105,300	—	51,900	−650	53,400	650	50.7
1955	111,600	1,260	58,000	1,220	53,600	40	48.0
1960	114,800	640	62,100	820	52,700	−180	45.9
1965	117,100	460	65,800	740	51,300	−280	43.8
1970	123,100	1,200	72,000	1,240	51,100	−40	41.5
1975	130,600	1,500	79,400	1,480	51,200	20	39.2

SOURCE: Warren W. Eason, "Comparisons of the United States and Soviet Economies: The Labor Force," in U.S. Congress, Joint Economic Committee, *Comparisons of the United States and Soviet Economies* (Washington, D.C.: U.S. Government Printing Office, 1959).

directly through the shrunken and malformed labor force. Young people in the Soviet Union generally start work at age 16, and 16 years after each major disaster there is a shortage in the number of workers to be recruited into the work force. Up to 1920, according to an estimate by Strumilin (1961), the male labor potential was cut by more than a tenth, and for both sexes by almost 15 percent. From admittedly poor data, Eason estimated the size of the Soviet labor force from 1930 through 1975 (Table 17-8). Whether the figures are precise or not, the trend is accurate, reflecting the end of the collectivization and famine in the mid-1930s, the relative prosperity of the late 1930s, the war beginning in 1941 and quickly developing into a national calamity, and the postwar terror and subsequent relaxation.

Normal Mortality

The demographic feature most distinctive of a totalitarian regime is the massive extraordinary mortality it inflicts on the population. These deaths are generally not included in the standard statistics, which measure the types of mortality registered in any country. The contrast in normal mortality between totalitarian and other types of states, while of course much smaller than in other characteristics, is yet significant. To the primary goals of the Soviet regime—collectivization of agriculture, rapid industrialization, and military prowess—all other purposes were subordinated, including specifically the welfare of the population. Allocation of resources to medicine and public health, thus, were "the minimum consistent with a certain level of functioning of the system as defined by the regime" (Mark Field 1957: 12). In the most recent period this minimum has been raised considerably, in line with the attempt to improve consumer goods, but there has been no change in the State's rationale.

The doctor's role, similarly, is to balance his professional duties with his job as a State official. "The Soviet physician often saw his best efforts frustrated by political and economic organs, with disastrous results in morbidity and accident rates," for which the physician himself was often held responsible (ibid.: 22). Medical services are available according to one's place in the class hierarchy. In what Field terms the "closed network," reserved to members of the Party and associated elites, everything from care to food is superior. The "open network" available to the general population differs greatly among various regions of the country and especially between cities and rural areas. An American medical team that visited the Soviet Union in 1970 noted that the ratio of physicians to middle paramedical workers was 1:2 in Leningrad, compared to 1:3.5 for the whole country. "This reflects," as they noted, "the world-wide problem of physicians preferring big cities," and it is interesting to find it manifested also in a socialist economy. In a Soviet cartoon (*Krokodil*, August 1968), a rural physician examines the throat of one patient while he tries to listen to the heart of another; in an urban clinic, meanwhile, three physicians and two helpers concentrate on a single patient (Steinfeld *et al.* 1972: 10–11). For a physician as for most specialists, "an assignment to the countryside is regarded as a kind of exile from the urban cultural amenities, to be avoided if at all possible." Many rural areas are serviced only by *feldshers*, ostensibly semiprofessional physicians' assistants but in fact often the dispensers of second-class medicine (Mark Field 1966). In addition to the 645,000 physicians serving the Soviet population in 1970 (thus, 2.66 per 1,000 population), there were 2,043,000 paramedical workers, ranging from "dental doctors" (with a special training, after a 10-year general schooling, of 2 years and 10 months) through *feldshers* and midwives (2 years and 6 months), to nurses, dental and laboratory technicians, and pharmacists (1 year and 10 months). "Feldshers . . . are not considered physician assistants or surrogate physicians except under very special circumstances. . . . They continue to play their historic role in rural areas where physicians are in short supply, and serve at 'forward health stations' in the transport and shop system" (Steinfeld *et al.* 1972: 30).

Crude death rates often used to be lower in the Soviet Union than, for example, in the United States, and Soviet publicists were not receptive to the comment that one reason (as in underdeveloped countries) was the relative paucity of elderly persons. According to the first Soviet life table published in several decades, in 1958–59 the average life expectancy at birth was 64.4 years (male) and 71.2 (female), or only slightly less than in advanced Western countries (Pressat 1963b; Myers 1964). Is this an accurate measure of Soviet mortality; and, if so, does it reflect, as Soviet propaganda assures us that it does, the superiority of the Communist social system?

That something is wrong with the record is suggested by the schedule of age-specific death rates in 1958–59, which compared with that for most countries

Table 17-9. Age-Specific Death Rates, the Soviet Union, 1958–59 and 1970–71, and the United States, 1959 and 1971

Age Bracket	Soviet Union 1958–59	United States 1959	Soviet Union as Percent of United States	Soviet Union 1970–71	United States 1971	Soviet Union as Percent of United States
All ages	7.4	9.4	78.7	8.2	9.3	88.2
Under 1 year	40.6	29.5	137.6	} 6.7	} 18.5	
1–4 years	4.0	1.1	363.6		0.8	
5–9	1.1	0.5	220.0	0.7	0.4	175.0
10–14	0.8	0.5	160.0	0.5	0.4	125.0
15–19	1.3	0.9	144.4	1.0	1.1	90.9
20–24	1.8	1.1	163.6	1.6	1.5	106.7
25–29	2.2	1.2	183.3	2.2	1.4	157.1
30–34	2.6	1.7	152.9	2.8	1.7	164.7
35–39	3.1	2.2	140.9	3.8	2.4	158.3
40–44	4.0	3.6	111.1	4.7	3.7	127.0
45–49	5.4	5.7	94.7	6.0	5.6	107.1
50–54	7.9	9.2	85.9	8.7	8.7	100.0
55–59	11.2	14.0	80.0	11.8	13.1	90.1
60–64	17.1	20.8	82.2	17.9	20.1	89.1
65–69	25.2	33.3	75.7	26.9	29.1	92.4
70 years and over	63.8	80.8	79.0	74.9	73.8	101.5
75 years and over	87.0	105.1	82.8		95.8	

SOURCES: James W. Brackett, "Demographic Trends and Population Policy in the Soviet Union," in U.S. Congress, Joint Economic Committee, *Dimensions of Soviet Economic Power* (Washington, D.C., 1962); Frederick A. Leedy, "Demographic Trends in the U.S.S.R.," in U.S. Congress, Joint Economic Committee, *Soviet Economic Prospects for the Seventies* (Washington, D.C., 1973); National Center for Health Statistics, *Monthly Vital Statistics Report*, **22** (1973), no. 9, Supplement.

(the United States is used as an example) was relatively high for ages up to 44 and relatively low thereafter (Table 17-9). The reasons for this anomaly that Soviet demographers suggested include the high incidence of pneumonia as a cause of death (but there is no reason why only in the Soviet Union the elderly should not be susceptible to this disease) and the high mortality of the weak during an earlier period of war and famine, leaving many who are resistant to all infections (but the effect of social disasters has always been to kill off some of the population and weaken most of the rest). That the aberration was not due to conditions affecting Soviet mortality is indicated by the fact that it did not persist to the later date (note the last column of Table 17-9). Two seemingly valid explanations for the low death rates at advanced ages apply especially to 1958–59, though some vestigial effect may be reflected also in the 1970–71 rates. (1) As longevity is especially prized in both Russian folk culture and Soviet medicine, one can assume that once past the middle years more persons exaggerate their age than elsewhere. The consequence would be artificially low age-specific death rates for the elderly. (2) According to the supposition of some Soviet statisticians, "the lower death rates are the results of defects in the registration." Underregistration is admittedly greater in rural areas, which have a greater proportion of older persons, and throughout the country among those not presently part of the work force, including especially those who have retired (Brackett 1962).

It may be that not only at higher but at all ages there used to be a considerable underregistration. Age-standardized death rates, computed from officially registered crude death rates for 1960 and the 1959 age distribution, are lowest in Central Asia, the part of the USSR where medical facilities are at their poorest (Heer 1968). If the interpretation is correct that the lower rates for ages 45 and over are spurious, then the higher rates at ages 0–44 denote something closer to the overall mortality. If all age-specific rates are understated, then in 1958–59 the Soviet Union's mortality was higher than that of the United States or Western Europe.

Family and Fertility

In any society the family has three main functions: to perpetuate the population, to maintain cultural continuity from one generation to the next, and to determine the place of each newborn infant in the social structure. The family policy of totalitarian societies often reflects a conflict among these functions. On the one hand, the State denies the legitimacy of the society it has supplanted, and it cannot tolerate the strong emotional bond between the old and the new inherent in the father–son relation. Nor can such a regime accept the principle that the son shall inherit, even as a base from which to rise, his father's place in society, for ultimately each person's status must be determined solely by his relation to the Party. On the other hand, a totalitarian regime finds the family something of a necessary evil, for the State's expansionist aims demand a rapidly growing population. The only way out of this contradiction would be to devise an alternative procreative institution, but all attempts to do this have failed.

In the Soviet Union the Party has responded to the dilemma by a gradual shift of emphasis in its family policy. During the first decade and a half of Soviet rule a generally consistent and complete policy was gradually developed (Schlesinger 1949: 33–41). All legal inequalities between the sexes were abolished. Bigamy, adultery, even incest were dropped from the statutory list of crimes. Religious marriage was no longer recognized by law, and even a civil ceremony was legally unnecessary and socially unimportant. There were perhaps a quarter-million "nonregistered marriages" by 1936, when the law was changed. Divorce could be had simply and cheaply at the wish of either partner, and at least among the small minority directly influenced by the Party line, it was frequent. That these early decrees were predominantly negative reflects their principal purpose: to hasten the disintegration of the patriarchal family of tsarist Russia, the most pervasive and therefore, perhaps, the most powerful brake on the forward course of the revolution. This early phase is now often passed over lightly in Communist accounts, which propagate the myth that "concern for children and mothers and for strengthening the family has always been a major task of the Soviet State" (*Pravda*, May 10, 1959).

And in spite of another assiduously propagated legend to the contrary, the right of parents to decide for themselves the spacing and number of their children was not a Soviet norm. Opinion on the matter within the Party was divided, and policy therefore ambivalent, but in the dominant official view "birth control [was] . . . a bourgeois panacea for social ills which could have no place in a socialist society" (Smith 1928: 186). As contraceptives were not generally available, even in the cities, abortion was the usual means for limiting family size. The official policy toward abortions was unambiguously hostile: they were legalized only in order to facilitate their rigid control. A woman desiring an operation was required to go before an official committee, which tried to convince her that it was her duty to society to give birth to her child. In cases of first pregnancy, requests were denied except when supported by urgent medical considerations (Alice Field 1932: 89). According to the official in charge of Moscow's clinics, the Soviet Union of this period was "the country in which abortion is least practiced" (Halle 1934: 144). This was hardly the case in Moscow itself during the worst years of the dekulakization and famine. The rate in that city is not known for the early 1930s, but in 1934 there were 2.71 recorded abortions for every birth (Lorimer 1946: 127).

While combating the traditional family, the State also tried to institute various alternatives to it. During the middle 1920s an attempt was made in Party circles to develop "socialist" marriage and other family ceremonies, and the regime also began to establish State-run nurseries and kindergartens as substitutes for the parents. Progress was slow, however, in translating these visions into actuality, and all these early efforts to make over the family were more important as indications of future Soviet policy than for their immediate effect.

Beginning in the mid-1930s the line shifted toward tightening family bonds again. Marriages were stimulated by an official approval of romantic love of the old-fashioned bourgeois variety. Divorce was discouraged by a succession of increasingly restrictive measures, which ultimately removed all but political reasons as absolute grounds. These changes in policy culminated in a decree issued in 1944 (Schlesinger 1949: 367 ff.), which re-established the distinction between civil and unregistered marriages, and hence between legitimate and illegitimate children. The restrictions on abortion were replaced by a flat prohibition except when it was necessary to save the woman's life. Unmarried persons and parents of only one or two children were subjected to special taxes, while especially fertile mothers received progressively larger subsidies according to their procreation. A woman who had borne and raised ten or more children was entitled to the highest award—the title of "Heroine Mother," carrying a lump payment of 5,000 rubles plus 300 rubles monthly for 4 years.

The Soviet Union was not, of course, the only state to pay family subsidies (see pp. 549–550). The political range of countries that have instituted such a policy suggests that various ends can be sought by this means, and it is necessary to estimate their purpose if family endowments are to be judged accurately. The most succinct way of doing this is to ask, *cui bono*—the individual, the family, or the state? In the Soviet Union the device of progressive premiums was, as Schlesinger has pointed out, primarily intended as "an incentive to the production of enormous numbers of children." By his estimate, a mother of six or more children, but not of a smaller number, could acquire an income sufficient to live modestly during her childbearing years (ibid.: 368, 372, 397; cf. Heer and Bryden 1966).

The usual explanation of the shift in Soviet family policy after the early 1930s has been that "conservatism, in the sense of respect for the acceptable heritage of the past as well as for the fruitful achievements of the present, was edging radicalism out of the picture" (Hindus 1949; cf. Timasheff 1946). But this explanation seems somewhat wide of the mark. While it is difficult to find a single adjective to describe the Soviet society of the Stalinist period, "conservative" scarcely characterizes the stupendous goals of the 5-year plans, the collectivization of the peasants at the rate of a million a day (with 5 or 6 million discards), the Moscow show-trials, the *Gleichschaltung* of the arts and sciences, the territorial expansion in Europe and Asia.

Two factors underlay the decision to revitalize the family. The first was the huge population loss resulting from the collectivization program, the Yezhovshchina, and World War II. The second was the need to restore stability to Soviet society, which the social revolution of the first two 5-year plans had broken down into a dangerously fluid mass.[10] In both phases the Soviet

[10] The trend in Soviet education policy was parallel. The first period was dominated by a calculated chaos, instituted consciously and purposely in order to eliminate the power of the old school and undermine the domination of the pre-Revolution intellectuals. Then, when the system had been reduced to a malleable pulp, it was restructured as a prop to Soviet authority.

family was different from its Western counterpart. When the policy was ostensibly "liberal," individuals were not given the right freely to determine what size family they would have. When it became "conservative," religious and other traditional norms did not set the pattern of family life. During the whole of the Stalinist regime, that is to say, the Party set family policy by what it interpreted the State's interests to be. In the post-Stalin period the two earlier, partly contradictory policies have both persisted. The fundamental thesis of the earlier years—that the prime purpose of the family is to serve the State—is retained, but the Party is now not sure about precisely what it wants or how to achieve it.

In spite of pronatalist measures, the crude birth rate fell from 31.3 in 1940 to 25–27 in the 1950s to 17.0 in 1969, rising slightly in 1970–71 (Table 17-10).

Table 17-10.   Rates of Birth, Death, and Natural Increase per 1,000 Population, Soviet Union, 1950–71

Year	Birth			Death	Natural Increase
	TOTAL	URBAN	RURAL		
1950	26.7	26.0	27.1	9.7	17.0
1955	25.7	23.5	27.4	8.2	17.5
1960	24.9	21.9	27.8	7.1	17.8
1961	23.8	21.1	26.5	7.2	16.6
1962	22.4	19.9	24.9	7.5	14.9
1963	21.1	18.5	24.0	7.2	13.9
1964	19.5	17.3	22.1	6.9	12.6
1965	18.4	16.1	21.1	7.3	11.1
1966	18.2	16.0	20.8	7.3	10.9
1967	17.3	15.4	19.8	7.6	9.7
1968	17.2	15.3	19.5	7.7	9.5
1969	17.0	15.6	18.7	8.1	8.9
1970	17.4	16.4	18.7	8.2	9.2
1971	17.8	16.9	19.2	8.2	9.6

SOURCE: Frederick A. Leedy, "Demographic Trends in the U.S.S.R.," in U.S. Congress, Joint Economic Committee, *Soviet Economic Prospects for the Seventies* (Washington, D.C.: U.S. Government Printing Office, 1973).

Until the mid-1960s the age structure and changes in marital status favored a high fertility; thereafter, when these demographic factors were no longer operative, the antinatalist consequences of several social policies became noticeable (Heer 1972). By the early 1970s they became the central issue of demographic research. Most Soviet economists and demographers have viewed the declining rate of growth with apprehension, if not alarm (e.g., Perevedentsev

1972); and from their point of view, it is even worse when analyzed differentially. As the downward trend accelerated, the difference increased between urban and rural (Pressat 1963a), between the irreligious and the Moslems (Mazur 1967), and between the Russians and some of the non-Slavic subnations (see Table 17-3, p. 686). To some degree these are three ways of expressing the same contrast, but it is the last that Soviet leaders probably find most disturbing. As one would expect, those national minorities least assimilated to the Russian culture (as measured by the proportion fluent in the Russian language) were also generally the ones with the greatest population growth (Figure 17-2). The principal exceptions to this generalization, nationalities with high growth rates even though fluent in Russian, were mainly those deported *en masse* under

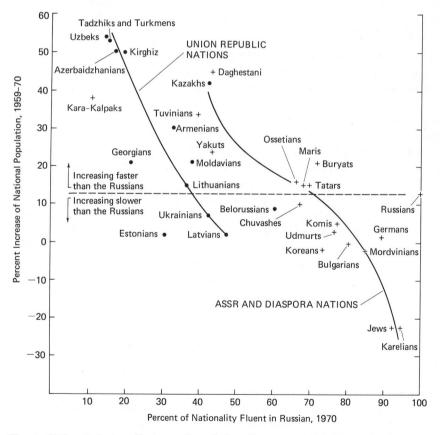

Figure 17-2. Relation Between Population Increase, 1959–70, and Fluency in Russian in 1970, Ethnic Minorities of the USSR

SOURCE: Rein Taagepera, "The 1970 Soviet Census: Fusion or Crystallization of Nationalities," *Soviet Studies*, **23** (1971), 216–221.

Stalin. Their forced contact with the language of the center hardly made them more receptive to Slavic dominance than other non-Slavs.

The discussion of population policy, by which one now means the discussion of how to raise the birth rate, can be broken down into a number of dilemmas:

Family Allowances.   As instituted in 1944, family allowances provided munificent sums relative to the average wage. In 1947, with all the strains of postwar reconstruction, the size of the subsidy was cut in half, and subsequently its value relative to the average wage fell steadily. To raise the allowance to its earlier level in real terms, however, would not only be extremely costly; it would also benefit mostly the nationalities with a currently high fertility.

The most frequently heard policy position is that the Soviet Union should seek to raise its birth rate but do so primarily by increasing the birth rate in the low-fertility areas. ... D. I. Valentey of Moscow University [for instance] ... suggests that the family allowance might vary regionally according to variations in fertility levels [Heer 1972].

But to institute such a policy, whether or not it raises the Russian birth rate, would certainly aggravate interethnic hostilities.

Abortions.   In 1955, after nearly two decades of restrictive laws, the Soviet Union permitted abortions at the woman's request unless there were medical contra-indications. According to Heer's estimate (1965), by the late 1950s there must have been more abortions than live births. From 1954 to 1966, according to a study that he cites (Heer 1972), the number of both legal and illegal abortions increased 4.2 times. No more recent official data have been published. E. A. Sadvokasova's monograph, *Social–Hygienic Aspects of the Regulation of Family Size* (Moscow: Meditsina, 1969), was based on a doctoral dissertation accepted by Moscow State University in 1965, and the principal analysis is of prior data. In her well based opinion, the prohibition of abortions (except those medically required) in 1936 had been ill advised, since it merely shifted the operation from legal to illegal facilities. There was a short-term rise in fertility until the new pattern became established, but no significant effect on family size. During the 1960s the Ministry of Public Health issued a series of booklets and even several films warning of the dangers of abortion. But except for condoms, which are generally available but also of very poor quality, alternative means of controlling fertility were lacking, and even knowledge about contraception was seemingly slight among educated women.

Working Women.   In 1967 precisely half of the work force was female, with far higher proportions in the lower-level sectors, with relatively poorer pay, than in the upper ranks. An associate of the State Committee on the Utilization of Labor Resources put the issue squarely: "In the USSR, the fertility of working women is half that of the housewife. It is very difficult for women to both work and raise children. And often, if the choice is between working and raising children, women choose work" (quoted in Lennon 1971). But with the drastic shortage of labor power, a shift of females out of the work force is hardly feasible. The alternative might be to induce more of them to take on the double role of worker–mother. But this double role, even without adding the care of small children, is onerous in a country lacking most of the household conveniences and services that have become routine in Western countries. Although the number of places available in state-run nurseries more than doubled from 1960 to 1970, at the latter date they still could accommodate only about a quarter of the children aged 1 to 6, and far fewer than that in rural areas. Moreover, as some of the husbands and wives reported in surveys, they disapproved of the "social upbringing" that their children would get in State nurseries (ibid.).

Housing.   According to an urban survey cited by Heer (1972), the lack of an adequate home was the chief factor cited for not having another child. Among working-class women aged 25–29, more than half gave this as one reason; among white-collar workers aged 18–24, some 88.3 percent. In their campaign to encourage larger families, Soviet newspapers often mention the long wait of couples for an apartment of their own as a serious deterrent. "The ideal of one family to an apartment is now being viewed as a goal for the end of this decade"—that is, by 1980 (*New York Times*, December 12, 1972). But with an economy that is palpably squeezed, this seemingly modest target may not be realized. In any case, the shift to the production of consumer goods, including housing, has also had the effect of raising the people's level of expectation; whether even a utopian improvement in residential construction would induce potential parents to have more children is an open question.

In sum, in the words of Warren Eason (1973), there is a Soviet population crisis. The crisis has three elements: the maldistribution of labor by both region and economic sector; the slow population growth, with the net reproduction rates of the key Slavic peoples below unity; and the expectation that by the 1980s the decline in fertility will be reflected in a falling off not only of the new entrants to the work force but even of its total size. The way to ameliorate the crisis, in the view of most Soviet officials and scholars, is to bring about an increase in the birth rate. But each of the roads to this goal involves costs that seem to be unmanageable.

THE POPULATION OF COMMUNIST CHINA

No one familiar with the development of social–economic policy in the Soviet Union can overlook the parallels in Communist China. As in Russia, so also in China, the Party came to power in part because the peasantry was won over by a land reform, which some years later was obliterated in a mass collectivization of agriculture. The forced-labor camps, the Yezhovshchina, the manmade famines, and so on through the list of Soviet terror—all have their Chinese counterparts. It is an oversimplification, however, to assume that Communism in China is a replica of the other version, or even that it is Russian totalitarianism filtered through the remnants of traditional Chinese culture and society. One quite important difference is in the economic level from which the two regimes started. Another is in scale. In 1967, when the Soviet Union celebrated the fiftieth anniversary of the 1917 revolution, Communist China had been in existence only 18 years. Crowding a half-century into two decades, Mao was both Lenin and Stalin.[11] China's rulers, even if they no more than reproduced the Soviet pattern, would have wreaked a far greater havoc on the fifth of the world's population under their control, and their demand for a yet speedier pace of social transformation multiplied the toll in human suffering and life.

Periods of Political–Economic Development

Since all of the demographic topics to be discussed—measurement, number of people, population policy—followed the violent shifts in the economic line, it is useful to begin with a brief review of China's overall development. The swing of the pendulum from maximum terror to relative relaxation is more clearly marked there than in the Soviet Union. Six periods are quite precisely delineated: 1949–52, 1953–57, 1958–60, 1961–65, 1966–69, and 1970 and after (Ashbrook 1967).

Establishment of Power (1949–52). In about 3 years from the taking of power, the Party extended its rule over the whole country, restored the rail system and irrigation dikes, established nationwide tax and rationing systems, and generally laid a basis for continued rule and economic advance. A portion of China's 5 million soldiers fought in the Korean War (1950–53), with casualties estimated as high as a million men. Far larger numbers of "bandits," "landlords," "warlords," "reactionaries," "counterrevolutionaries," and other "enemies of the people" lost their lives.

According to an official figure, the number of landlords executed for "various crimes" was about 2.5 million. And in 1951 Lo Jui-ch'ing, then Minister for Public Security, claimed that his Ministry alone had "liquidated 15 million counterrevolutionaries," although it was not made clear what the term "liquidation" in this context meant. In 1952 Po I-p'o, then Minister for Finance, publicly admitted that the People's Government had liquidated 2 million "bandits" in the preceding three years. The term "bandit" was not defined [apart from the fact that] the regime applies the word to anyone who is against the present Communist government [Chandrasekhar 1959a: 58].

"The objectives of this period—the establishment of economic law and order, the seizure of the commanding heights of the economy, and the restoration of existing productive facilities—were all achieved" (Ashbrook 1967).

---

[11] Mao Tse-tung, born in 1893 to a "middle" peasant of Hunan province, joined the Party when it was founded in 1921. After some years spent organizing the peasants of his native province, he broke with Marxist orthodoxy and declared that the peasantry, rather than the urban proletariat, constituted China's revolutionary potential. In 1933, after the Communist–Nationalist alliance had changed into civil war, Mao led the hard-pressed Party cadres on the legendary 6,000-mile march to a new base in Yenan. Some 15 years later the regrouped Communists emerged from this remote retreat and took power, with Mao as Party Chairman.

First Five-Year Plan (1953–57). Under a series of agreements, the Soviet Union committed itself to transfer to China over the next 15 years (1953–67) some 300 industrial plants worth a total of $3 billion, plus the cost of training and equipment needed for further advance. This enormous assistance laid the base for the notable progress in industrialization. From very small starts, the production of major industrial materials increased several fold, and some thousands of workers acquired industrial skills (Li 1960).

More than a decade passed from the distribution of land to Russian peasants to the reversal; in China it was less than half that time. Collectivization began in 1953, reached a high tide after the 1955 harvest, and according to official reports was successfully completed by the end of the following year. In a nationwide "liquidation of counterrevolutionaries," huge numbers of "upper" or "middle" peasants were executed or shipped to labor camps. The consequence was a rapid deterioration in agriculture. "Slaughter of farm animals and destruction of farm implements were widespread" (ibid.). "As late as the end of 1957, official statements admitted that agricultural production could be increased by 20 or 30 percent if the collectives could raise their yield to the level of the remaining individual peasants" (Lindsay 1960). The increase in agricultural production over the 5 years was far less than the population growth.

The Great Leap Forward (1958–60). Sweeping aside the targets sketched out for a Second Five-Year Plan (1958–62), the Party greatly quickened the hyperrapid pace it had set. The theories underlying the "Great Leap Forward" were three:

1. China's vast population was an economic asset; "man should be viewed as a producer rather than a consumer" (Liu Shao-chi, at the 8th Party Congress, 1958; quoted in Ashbrook 1967).

2. Chinese agriculture was dragged down by a vast, wasteful underemployment, since for much of the year no farm work was possible (actually the peasants used these intervals for all the other activities necessary to sustain the almost self-sufficient village economy).

3. Material incentives could be dispensed with; the whole population could be imbued with the same fervor that had inspired the Party during its struggle for power. Production was at a frenzied rate, with little regard for the reduction in quality, the exhaustion of workers, or the depletion of machinery and other capital stock.

Agricultural collectives were converted into "people's communes." Each comprised some 25,000 people rather than the several hundred in the largest of the collectives. All remaining private property was taken over by the State; and the peasant, no longer entitled to a share of the crop, was paid a wage of usually 100 yuan (or $40) *per year*, half in money and half in kind (the figure is from an article by Finance Minister Li Hsien-nien, quoted in Rousset 1959). The commune was not merely an agricultural unit but a general work force: labor armies sowed and harvested in season, and during unproductive periods they were shuttled about the country digging canals and wells, dragging rivers, draining swamps, building levees, carrying fertile soil onto naked rock, reforesting. After a slight pause to consolidate the Party's gains, a new leap was taken—communes in the cities. According to official claims, by the spring of 1960 communal living had been imposed on not only 400 million Chinese peasants but also 20 million town dwellers, a majority of those living in the three populous northern provinces of Heilungkiang, Honan, and Hopei.

The commune was intended as a complete substitute for the home. In order to "emancipate" women from domestic chores so that they could also produce for the State, communes established great mess halls, nurseries and kindergartens, and tailor shops. According to the description of one commune in a nationally distributed Party magazine, "The frames of individual families which had existed for thousands of years have been completely smashed."

In the more advanced communes, children see their parents twice a month. [During the day] wives see their husbands only at mealtimes, which are given only half to eating and half to participating in discussion in vast communal mess halls—unless, of course, their husbands are "camping out" at work projects from 60 to 100 miles away from their commune base. Grandparents are isolated in "Happiness Homes" where they will serve the "big family" by tilling communal vegetable plots, weaving communal baskets or feeding communal chickens. . . . A group of Young Pioneers (7- to 14-year olds) in Canton recently smelted their first heat of medium-carbon steel [Rich 1959].

The commune was controlled by naked terror. Part of what Rousset terms China's "universalization of forced labor" was the creation, also in August 1958, of a new "people's militia." These were armed units of young activists, both male and female, organized as integral parts of the labor armies.

As in Russia, the transformation of the countryside was carried out by young men anxious for a Party career. Following a decision at the highest level, they insisted that furrows be dug 6 feet deep rather than 1, that rice seedlings be planted 2 inches apart rather than the traditional 5 to 6 inches. Triumphantly the regime announced an increase in the crop from 185 million tons in 1957 to 375 million in 1958; plans for 1959 reduced the acreage of food crops. But this "harvest," estimated while the rice was still growing, proved to be a mirage. The stalks grew, but the heads were mostly empty. This momentous error, when compounded by the drought and floods two years running, developed into what was finally admitted to be the worst famine in a century. But the Party was too thoroughly inculpated to be able to react quickly. Still in 1959 more than $1 billion in exports, mostly agricultural products, were shipped out, and even in 1961 the regime rejected an offer of help from the International Red Cross. Three emergency measures were taken:

1. "Bad elements" in the State bureaucracy, estimated at one-tenth of the total, were blamed for the catastrophe and purged.

2. Members of communes were permitted to have small private plots and to work them two to four days a month. Since twice before the Party had sanctioned such a modest return to private ownership and then commandeered the produce, the peasants may well have been mistrustful.

3. Food, too little and too late, was purchased from the capitalist world. Each year from 1961 on, China paid $300 million to $400 million out of its meager stock of foreign exchange to import 5–6 million tons of grain (Ashbrook 1967).

As part of its manic euphoria, China mounted an increasingly acerbic attack on Russia, which it claimed had not moved as far toward full Communism as Mao's State. In the mid-1960s the Soviet technicians were summarily withdrawn, and those plants built with Russian aid, lacking expert managers and spare parts, sometimes could not continue operating. Much of the capital stock built up with 8 years of iron rations suddenly became useless. "A revolution," as we know from one of Chairman Mao's famous aphorisms, "is not an invitation to a banquet."

The Great Retreat (1961–65).   The famine of 1959–61 was manmade, and the name of the man was Mao Tse-tung. In 1961, Po I-p'o, then chairman of the National Economic Council, warned that there had to be a slowdown in industrial production, so that not only all surplus manpower but millions of factory workers could be diverted to agriculture. Even two of the most publicized achievements of the earlier period, the Wuhan steel works and the Anshan industrial complex, were cut back. Only the chemical industry, manufacturing fertilizers and insecticides to foster food production, was exempted from the overall industrial retreat. Peasants were once again encouraged to tend tiny private plots, and private enterprise was permitted to reappear in the form of petty traders and craftsmen.

In the only significant advance during this period, China set off its first nuclear device.

Proletarian Cultural Revolution (1966–69).   In 5 years some—certainly not all—of the damage incurred in the Great Leap was repaired, and the Party shifted again to reckless activism. The country's children and youth were organized into Red Guards, who attacked, verbally and physically, all who deviated from absolute adherence to absolute orthodoxy. All schools were dismissed in order to fill the ranks of these frenetic guardians of revolutionary purity. By the autumn of 1966, 10 million were engaged in a struggle against "bourgeois" and "revisionist" elements in the Party and affiliated elites. Some 30 percent of the country's transport was placed at their disposal, and they swarmed like locusts on the meager resources of the overcrowded cities.[12]

[12] "Hundreds of cesspools have been dug in the central streets as temporary toilets. They are screened off from the crowds only by strips of canvas on which are traced in huge red hieroglyphs the words: 'Raise higher the banner of Chairman Mao's ideas'" (Andronov 1966).

Children at the age of 3 years began their training in blind loyalty to Chairman Mao, canonized as the font of all wisdom, the inspiration that solves all problems. In fact, the struggle was over who would succeed Mao, aged 73 in 1966. Of all sectors of the Chinese population, none was less capable of understanding than those disseminating ideological cant through the Red Guards' wall posters. Clearly they were being used: their seemingly anarchic antics were directed by the army; until mid-1962 they had their headquarters in the Peking public-security building; during their mass demonstrations, they traveled in army trucks, with two or three soldiers in each. And the heir apparent to Mao became Lin Piao, Minister of Defense (cf. Ravenholt 1967), who was later killed by the rival faction of the Party.

How much damage this new manic phase inflicted on the economy cannot be assessed precisely. Any hope of a Soviet–Chinese rapprochement, and thus of a renewal of Soviet aid, was quashed.[13] With the revived emphasis on "spiritual" incentives, those who would pay for efficient and conscientious work with good wages were guilty of "economism."

The Second Great Retreat (1970–?). The most remarkable elements of the new turnabout were diplomatic—the rapprochement with the United States, the admission to the United Nations. The best summary of the economy is the title of an excellent report: "I Have Seen China—and They Work" (Kraar 1972): "At every level, China mobilizes its abundant resources of labor—from a population that amounts to nearly a quarter of mankind—to compensate for a scarcity of capital." Bonuses and overtime were eliminated, so that everyone could work as "a contribution to the socialist revolution." The earnings of industry constituted a major source of government revenue. Backyard steel furnaces had been abandoned, but communes were much in evidence. Their operation was illustrated by the Kwangchow Heavy Machine Tool Plant:

At the entrance a billboard proclaims in bold red letters, "Unite to win even greater victories." Within the huge, fenced compound, 5,000 employees work in three shifts turning out equipment for mining, petroleum refineries, chemical plants, and sugar mills. Along with keeping industrial production going around the clock, the factory maintains agricultural plots for raising pigs and growing vegetables, dormitories for unmarried workers, eating facilities, and an array of anti-aircraft guns discreetly shrouded in canvas. And it serves as a center for subtle group dynamics and political action—directed toward motivating workers to increase output [ibid.].

The wages at the plant averaged $26.80 a month, tax free. Medical services cost nothing; rent for a worker's dwelling averaged perhaps $2 a month, food about

[13] Virtually the whole of the April 1967 issue of *Survey* is devoted to translations from a variety of Soviet periodicals on China. The articles typically display a detailed knowledge of the manifestations that they condemn. Some of these have an unconscious humor. Thus, *Komsomolskaya Pravda* (September 27, 1966) finds it "amazing" that "in the seventeenth year of the Chinese People's Republic's existence" laconic accusations against "counter-revolutionary, rightist elements" are heard everywhere. The seventeenth year of the Soviet Union's existence was the winter of 1934–35.

The Red Guards use a truck to convey "counterrevolutionaries" in dunce caps through the streets of Peking (*Wide World Photos*).

$6. In spite of the egalitarian and nonmaterial verbiage, however, the range in pay in this plant was from $16 to $59.60 per month. Peasants, some 85 percent of the population, got cash incomes as low as one-sixth of the average factory wage.

Sources of Information

With the cycle of manic-depressive politics, there was a fluctuation also in the amount and accuracy of the quantitative data available. In preparation for the First Five-Year Plan, a State Statistical Bureau was established in 1952, and by the middle of that period data were as reliable as at any time during the Communist regime. With the Great Leap into wishful thinking, all realistic appraisals of actual achievements were dispensed with. The "harvest" of 1958, already noted, is but one example of recurrent exaggeration or falsification. For example, as proof of the allegation that the level of living increased from 1950 to 1955, the regime cited the rise in retail sales in State-operated stores (which merely took over the business previously done by private merchants). With the debacle came an end even to such misleading figures as had been available.

The overwhelming problem that faces all students of the contemporary Chinese economic scene is the blackout of economic statistics imposed by the Chinese authorities in 1960, and continued [up to the date of his paper]. . . . The Chinese have gone far beyond the Russians. . . . Visitors have been given an odd figure or two, but there is nothing of a systematic character, not even plan figures [Galenson 1967].

A crucial misrepresentation was in agricultural statistics. The National Agricultural Research Bureau of the Republic of China had estimated the production on about three-quarters of the cultivated land. For the base figure from which they started in 1949, the Communists took this estimated production and divided it by the *total* number of cultivated acres. Beginning from too low a figure in 1949, they exaggerated each year's increase up to 1958, the year of the paper harvest (Buck 1966: 48). According to the best analysis possible from the available data, the calories per capita from all food, adjusted for imports or exports of food grains, decreased from an average of 2,410 in 1929–33 to 2,017 in 1949–58—what are termed "the great ten years" (ibid.: 11). "After seventeen years of Communist rule, the economy of Mainland China . . . does not yet provide a tolerable living standard for the exploding population, let alone a margin necessary for sustained growth" (Larsen 1967).

The demographic data are no better than any other. For more than a century before the Communists took power, we have only unreliable estimates of the total population. The new regime also has not collected much information, and a portion of that has not been released. The one important exception is the 1953 census–registration, which constitutes the only relatively firm set of data.

According to that count, the population of Mainland China in mid-1953 was almost 583 million. Understandably, the first reaction in the West to this stupendous figure was disbelief. Previously even the Communists themselves had generally estimated the population of the country at about 100 million less than this. The jubilant tone of the announcement, the fact that it was used to make political capital (cf. Kirby 1958), also argued against accepting it. And the further statement that a check on the enumeration had uncovered a net undercount of only 0.116 percent, thus making this the most accurate large-scale census in world history, was "both preposterous and foolish" (Aird 1967b). Western scholars, however, soon began to accept as a fact the claim that China represents one-fifth to one-quarter of the human race. The census administrators had expert Soviet advisors, who probably kept the census's faults within limits. According to the most comprehensive Western analyses of the enumeration and processing, the claimed total may even have reflected a considerable undercount (Krader and Aird 1959; Aird 1960; U.S. Bureau of the Census 1961).

For the period since 1953, the further growth of population was supposedly recorded through a continuous registration. In fact, this was not begun for several years, and then it was conducted as a police check on the population. According to Party newspapers, the household registration was used to lay the basis for grain expropriations and to expose "counterrevolutionaries and other bad elements," who "assume false identities, fake evidence, and make false reports to the registration authorities." The records so collected are two or three times removed from their source when they reach the county (*hsien*) administrative center where they are compiled (Orleans 1965; 1972: chaps. 1–2). "With the appearance late in 1959 of the registration figure of 647 million for year-end 1957, publication of official population totals came to an end" (Aird 1967a).

For a half-dozen years the announced population of China remained static at 650 million, and by all indications the country's leaders had no better data themselves.[14] The full 1953 schedule of ages by sex was never released to the public, and the partial schedule only through papers of individual Chinese demographers (Ch'en 1958). The sex ratio was high, 107.7 males per 100 females, presumably reflecting the female infanticide. Various other anomalies in the population structure—in particular, the lack of a male deficit in the cohorts most affected by war casualties—cannot be explained without better primary data.

From the wide range of estimated populations following the 1953 census–registration (Table 17-11), one must conclude that very little can be said about numerical trends of any kind. For in any statistical series the total population figures are the simplest and thus usually the most accurate. In the following discussion of internal migration, rural–urban residence, fertility, mortality, and other fundamental characteristics, some figures are given to illustrate the argument, but none should be taken literally.

Mortality

How many have been killed in China by terror and manmade famine we have no way of estimating, though the figure is certainly in the tens of millions. The Party was more reckless with its human charges than in Russia, and a depletion by even the same proportion would have meant a considerably greater mortality.

Nor is there any reliable basis for gauging the rate of normal mortality,[15]

[14] There was a distinct reluctance to admit the existence of a larger number. The official estimate of grain requirements of 220 million tons, divided by the conventional standard of 300 kilograms per capita, indicated a population of 733 million at the end of 1964. When Edgar Snow cited these figures, Mao responded that, as deaths were concealed in rural areas in order to augment the grain rations, the registration data were inflated (Jones 1967). It is a telling commentary on Asian socialism, whether or not Mao was lying. In 1966, however, Mao himself referred to "the 700 million Chinese people."

[15] According to a survey conducted by the Ministry of the Interior in 1953, for a sizable sample of the population the birth rate was 37, the death rate 17 (Chen 1967: 6). The information given to Chandrasekhar (1959a: 50) was that by 1957 these rates had fallen to 34 and 11, respectively. No subsequent figures are available, even as implausible as these. Salaff (1973) has made a valiant effort from scanty data to validate official claims both that mortality fell precipitously and that this was due to "the unique organization of Chinese public health practices."

Table 17-11. Estimates or Projections of the Population (millions), Mainland China, 1953–71

Year	Beginning of Year					Midyear	
	OFFICIAL ESTIMATES[a]	VICTOR-BOSTRUM FUND[f]	AIRD[g] LOW ESTIMATE	AIRD[g] HIGH ESTIMATE	ORLEANS[h]	OFFICIAL ESTIMATES[i]	UNITED NATIONS ESTIMATES[n]
1953	575.0[b]		576.0	578.0	582.6		561.6–582.6[o]
1954	588.0	588.0	588.0	589.0	587.0		571.9
1955	602.0	602.0	599.0	603.0	596.4		582.3
1956	615.0	615.0	611.0	619.0	606.5		592.8
1957	628.0	630.0	624.0	634.0	617.4	640.0[j]	603.4
1958	647.0[c]	645.0	637.0	650.0	629.2		614.1
1959		659.0	650.0	667.0	641.7	669.0[k]	624.9
1960		669.0	662.0	682.0	655.2	659.0[l]	636.0
1961		676.0	673.0	696.0		646.5[c]	647.2
1962		680.0	682.0	706.0			658.7
1963		687.0	691.0	715.0		646.5[c]	670.6
1964	700.0[d]	697.0	702.0	728.0			682.6–868.0
1965		712.0	715.0	743.0			695.0–700.0
1966		728.0	728.0	760.0			707.6–710.0
1967		742.0	741.0	777.0			720.4
1968	750.0[e]	757.0	754.0	793.0		730.0[m]	733.4
1969		776.0					746.5
1970		795.0					759.6
1971		815.0					

[a] Robert Michael Field, "A Note on the Population of Communist China," *China Quarterly*, no. 38 (April–June, 1969), p. 159.

[b] 1953–57: "Data on China's Population from 1949 to 1956," *T'ung-chi kung-tso* [Statistical Work], no. 11 (1957), p. 24.

[c] State Statistical Bureau, *Ten Great Years* (Peking, 1960), p. 11. The population of Taiwan was excluded.

[d] *Jen-min jih-pao* [The People's Daily], June 19, 1966.

[e] Radio Kansu, February 11, 1968.

[f] Victor-Bostrum Fund and the Population Crisis Committee, "Balancing Population and Food," *Population and Family Planning in the People's Republic of China*, Spring, 1971.

[g] John S. Aird, "Estimates and Projections of the Population of Mainland China: 1953–1986," U.S. Bureau of the Census, *Current Population Reports*, Series P-91, no. 17, 1968. Washington, D.C.

[h] Leo A. Orleans, *Professional Manpower and Education in Communist China*, Washington, D.C.: National Science Foundation, 1960.

[i] *Population Index*, vols. 24–36, 38.

[j] *Jen-min jih-pao* [The People's Daily], as reported by United Nations.

[k] Mean of estimates by Ministry of Health, Peking, 1959, and the New China News Agency, February 4, 1959, as reported by United Nations.

[l] Mean of estimates by Ministry of Health, Peking, and the New China News Agency, less the estimated population of Taiwan (erroneously included in former estimates), as reported by United Nations.

[m] Chinese Revolutionary Committee, reported by Mainichi, Tokyo.

[n] United Nations, *Demographic Yearbook, 1970* (New York, 1971), Table 4.

[o] U.N. Economic Commission for Asia and the Far East.

though some intimations are available from the changes in medical institutions. The slight base from which the Communist State started is suggested by a single datum: the number of physicians in the whole country in 1950 was 41,000, increased to 70,500 by 1955 (Davidoff 1957). Whether the quality remained constant, however, is doubtful. In 1956, when Mao invited criticism with his famous speech, "A Hundred Flowers Must Bloom and One Hundred Schools of Thought Contend," intellectuals—with doctors among them—denounced the rigid Party control that had hampered their professional work. The following year a "rectification movement" was initiated to rid the country of these nonconformists. Modern medicine had derived from the West, very often by way of Christian missionaries, and physicians were more suspect than members of some other professions. Those professors of medical schools who were Christians were denounced in student–faculty assemblies, and with the depleted training staffs the course of medical study was cut from 7 to 5 years.

Nevertheless during the First Five-Year Plan much was accomplished in a vigorous all-out attack on China's major epidemic diseases. The experiences of a young parasitologist, who fled to Hong Kong in 1962 after having worked as a physician in six different provinces, are indicative. He practiced in Fukien province, for example, where the director of public health was an energetic woman who had been a nurse with the Communist forces in Yenan. Under the system that she set up, a hospital was established in each of the sixty-odd *hsien*, usually staffed by two doctors and ten "assistant doctors." "This entire health organization was energized by vigorous support and ample funds from above, such as had never been available during the pre-Communist era. . . . Vaccines [were] available in abundance from the new factories established for their production." The effort concentrated on eliminating major epidemic diseases. Peasants were vaccinated against cholera, forcibly if necessary; school children were required to kill flies and to deliver a daily quota of dead rats to their teachers. The incidence of cholera and the plague, as well as of smallpox and typhoid, was brought under substantial control, and there was some success in the attack on other diseases (Ravenholt 1962).

With the chronic malnutrition brought on by the Great Leap Forward, much of this progress was negated. For example, in 1962 Fukien's per-capita ration of bean curd, the country's protein staple, was one small block per month. The refugee doctor estimated that 40 percent of the province suffered from nutritional hepatitis; there and elsewhere in China, edema, another disease of malnutrition, was common (ibid.).

The extended working hours, long political indoctrination sessions, and lack of sleep and rest that were so characteristic of the frantic production drive during the Great Leap made millions of workers more susceptible to sickness and disease. Furthermore, of particular significance in terms of health were the conditions at numerous construction projects, which engaged scores of millions of people and in which many of the most basic sanitary measures were absent [Orleans 1972: 53].

As Chinese Communism became increasingly xenophobic, the Party laid greater emphasis on traditional Chinese medical lore. There used to be "a far-reaching and interlocking relationship of the practices of medicine with superstition and religious practices, magic, divination, sorcery, astrology, alchemy, palmistry, geomancy, physiognomy, necromancy, spiritism, demonology, fortune-telling, etc." (Morse 1934: 117). How much of this is still appended to Chung-i, or Chinese medicine and pharmacy, is difficult to tell. In this system much diagnosis is by a complicated procedure for feeling the pulse. A 16th-century herbal, with 1,892 remedies and 10,000 prescriptions, lays the basis for the present pharmacopeia, which includes such exotic items as crickets, deer musk, toad tears, tiger bones, and the preserved Adam's apple of an elderly monkey. Some of these products are being imported into the United States, where the Food and Drug Administration finds the claims contrary to American law. "Pantocrin," for instance, is ground deer antlers, with which it is asserted that one can ameliorate or cure nervous exhaustion, heart failure, impotence, loss of memory, poor appetite, or malnutrition. A large shipment of White Flower Embrocation, as another example, was seized because of the claim on the label that it is "particularly for colds, influenza, headache, stomache [stet] ache, cholera, coughs, rheumatism, toothache and children's stomach trouble" and that it "stops itching, kills germs, heals burns and scalds, stops bleeding and pains, cures swelling and blood poisoning, pimples and sea sickness" (*Wall Street Journal*, March 29, 1974).

Apart from such dubious drugs, the best known treatment is acupuncture, the insertion of needles some distance into various portions of the body. For acute appendicitis, for example, a needle is inserted into the right leg. Remarkably, the main symbol of the new China fad (which spread in Western democracies far more quickly than the comparable Soviet fad of the 1920s) has been acupuncture, which has been credited with virtually miraculous powers. According to the visitor to China most competent to judge its effectiveness in anesthesia, Dr. John F. Bonica, chief of anesthesiology at the University of Washington, the Chinese use Western-style anesthetics in 85 percent of their surgery. They are getting irritated, Dr. Bonica reported, at Americans' exaggerations of the genuine but slight effect of the technique.[16]

In 1959 the Central Committee ordered all geographical units of the country to establish special curricula through which Western-style physicians could learn Chung-i. In six-month cram courses thousands of practitioners of this ancient lore are trained in, among other places, the former Peiping Union Medical College, American-founded and once American-supported, and in the

---

[16] According to William S. Kroger, author of a work titled *Clinical and Experimental Hypnosis*, acupuncture is analogous to the methods he uses in "numerous painless major and minor surgical procedures." The method is not new: in the first decades of the 19th century James Esdaile performed "many formidable surgical procedures in India," using what was then called "mesmeric anesthesia" but has since become "needleism" (letter to *Science*, **180** (1973), 1002).

pre-Communist era famous throughout Asia (Durdin 1960; cf. Orleans 1969a). Mao noted several grave defects in the system of delivering health care: too much pure research, insufficient attention to preventive care, disorganization of the communal health-care system, the slighting of traditional Chinese medicine, and the "coziness" of the Party and the medical profession. The consequent shift was drastic in a number of respects. Up to the beginning of 1966 the contents of the Chinese medical journal reported research, mainly "pure" and partly applied; thereafter 85 percent of the journal consisted of political exhortation (Lampton 1972).

By the end of 1968, Tachai (a famous commune in northwest China) became a model in health care by establishing a school to train barefoot doctors. Each barefoot doctor is recruited from his [or her] own commune or brigade, after 3 years of experience in manual labor, and is chosen by his peers to go to the hsien hospital to study for 3 months, or to be trained by a mobile medical team [ibid.].

One can agree that the health-care system particularly of a country at China's economic level is rendered more effective by supplementing fully trained physicians with a hierarchy of paramedical personnel. But is it really "a pragmatic approach to medicine," as one American physician (Geiger 1973) termed it, to sacrifice modern medicine to the medieval superstitions of native lore, to use people of high school age with three months of "training" as the equivalent of *feldshers*, to permit the rarer nurses to extend their role as far as brain surgery (*New York Times*, November 10, 1968)? For all its organizational competence, the system also recalls the backyard smelters.

Fertility and Family Policy

During the first years of the Communist regime, the policy was to encourage China's traditionally high fertility. Not only infanticide but also birth control were condemned, the latter as "a means of killing off the Chinese people without shedding blood" (quoted in Kirby 1958). The Party repeatedly boasted of the high rate of population growth, which reflected, it claimed, the improved living conditions. Its "hundreds of millions of people" were constantly referred to as China's most treasured asset. By this view, "overpopulation is not the cause of China's impoverishment, but merely a reflection of that deterioration in Chinese society which began under the rule of the alien Manchus." With the new Communist regime, this deterioration had been reversed and all difficulties now would vanish as though by magic (Chang 1949; Barclay 1950).

A convincing argument for the position that the 1953 census was either correct or an undercount is that the Chinese Communists themselves reacted to it. After the census the naive approbation of large numbers disappeared, to be replaced by what might be called a "soft" and a "hard" population policy. The soft line has been to reduce fertility, the hard one to risk measures demanding a sizable increase in mortality in a frenetic Leap Forward. The two have

丰 收 的 果 实

One of the hundreds of thousands
of New Year's cards inculcating
the Party line of the moment—in
this case, a bumper crop of both
agricultural produce and children
(*New York Times Magazine*).

run parallel courses, but over the following two decades the effort to reduce
fertility became dominant.

In 1953, it would seem, some tentative plans for controlling population
existed, and in August of that year the Ministry of Health was quietly instructed
to foster both abortion and contraception (Tien 1963). Two years later *Study*,
the Party's principal ideological journal, came out for the new line—to retain
Marx, repudiate Malthus, hurl invectives at neo-Malthusians, and advocate the
limitation of births. According to this article, no "conceivable" rates of population growth could approach the increase in production envisioned in the First
Five-Year Plan. The advocacy of family planning was in the interest not of
society but only of individual families (Taeuber 1956).

A somewhat more direct support of family planning was made by Ma Yin-chu,
an economist trained at Yale and Columbia and at the time president of Peking
University. Although subjected to a widespread and virulent attack, he was
permitted to voice his still deviant position, perhaps because of his age (he
was in his 70s), more likely because of the protection of someone high in the
Party. His "New Principle of Population," made public in 1957, offered the
following argument. China's population growth, which he believed to be higher
than the assumed 2 percent per year, impedes the economic development.
Of her low national income, 79 percent must be used for current consumption

(compared with 75 in the Soviet Union). "Our population is too large; it drags down the speed of industrialization" (quoted in Chandrasekhar 1959b).

A no less direct connection between population increase and economic difficulties was made by Premier Chou En-lai[17] in an official report to the National People's Congress in 1957: 10 to 15 percent of China's population—that is, some 60 to 90 million persons—"are short of food and clothes and need aid from the State or the agricultural producers' cooperatives" (quoted in Sarker 1958). Another speaker, without mentioning Malthus by name, repeated the essence of his principle: "The proverb, 'Two in the first generation means a thousand in ten generations' (1, 2, 4, 8, 16, 32, 64, 128, 256, 512, 1024), is not without foundation" (quoted in Tien 1963). During the term of the First Five-Year Plan, thus, the Party's hostility to family planning was opposed at first indirectly and finally in open recognition of the social–economic consequences of rapid increase in numbers. "Maternal health" became "population control."

All methods of birth control were considerd. The first was to encourage the delay of marriages (Tien 1970). Abortion specifically for medical reasons was legalized in 1954, and in the following years the conditions were liberalized. The first severe restrictions on sterilization were gradually eased. The main emphasis throughout the campaign, however, was on contraception. The Minister of Health was reportedly collecting the centuries-old Chung-i formulas as part of a search for contraceptives. One herbalist seriously offered the following prescription to a National People's Congress:

Fresh tadpoles coming out in the spring should be washed clean in cold well water, and swallowed whole three or four days after menstruation. If a woman swallows fourteen live tadpoles on the first day and ten more on the following day, she will not conceive for five years. If contraception is still required after that, she can repeat the formula twice, and be forever sterile. . . . This formula is good in that it is effective, safe, and not expensive. The defect is that it can be used only in the spring [quoted in Taeuber 1956].

When he was in China at the end of 1958, Chandrasekhar (1959b) was permitted to visit two contraceptive factories, a small one in Shanghai manufacturing 500,000 diaphragms and 5 million condoms annually, and a larger one in Canton, only 2 years old, with a productive capacity of 120 million condoms but an actual output in that year (after the propaganda for family planning had ceased) of only half that. Condoms cost 4 cents to produce and were sold in the villages for 2 cents. During the height of the campaign, from 1955 to 1958, birth control was advertised in newspapers, magazines, and special pamphlets; with posters and billboards; at exhibitions and meetings, with lantern slides and

[17] Chou En-lai, born in Huaian, Kiangsu, in 1898 of an old Mandarin family, was educated in Chinese universities and in Japan and France. He joined the Communist movement while in France and became a founding member of the Chinese Party in 1921. For three years, 1928–31, he was trained in Moscow. After serving in several local Party posts, he participated in the Long March to Yenan, acted as the chief liaison officer between the Communist Party and the Nationalist Government.

lectures. At a Birth Control Exhibition in Peking, "the authorities were not leaving anything to chance. Even the most illiterate peasant and the least intelligent worker went away from the exhibition knowing exactly what to do to prevent conception."

With the Great Leap Forward, the line on birth control changed abruptly; part of the manic phase was the certainty that economic development would be fast enough to absorb any growth in numbers (but see Aird 1962). Six persons who had been members of the State Council when it initiated the new policy in 1953 were accused of being "anti-Party, anti-people, anti-socialist, and anti-democratic dictatorship, and of harboring political ambitions" (Tien 1963). Several who had earlier advocated population control saved themselves by joining in the denunciations.

In the bitter aftermath of the Great Retreat, contraception again became the Party line. In the spring of 1962 an exhibition in Canton, a counterpart to the earlier one in Peking, displayed charts, models, and specimens. Contraceptives were imported duty-free. The principal Party newspaper advertised publications like *China's Women* in which methods of birth control were described and advocated. "A vigorous birth-control program has been waged in the cities since early 1963, employing rather stringent social pressures and evidently achieving significant results. Its extension to the rural areas is as yet limited, and possibly experimental, and few successes have been noted. However, a recent hardening of pressures in some rural areas, such as denying rations to fourth and subsequent births, may be effective" (Jones 1967). If everything up to a revival of China's traditional infanticide has been implemented, one can say the effort to reduce fertility is a serious one.

There have been a number of competent reviews of China's family policy (e.g., Orleans 1969b; Chen 1970; Meijer 1971; Salaff 1972; Tien 1972), but of course no one has discovered a means of testing to what degree the policies have worked. Salaff cites two studies of IUD insertions, one by parity and the other by age; but the samples are tiny relative to China's population and the significance of such compilations, as we have noted, is at best somewhat ambivalent. She also cites a survey among sixty refugees in Hong Kong, but this kind of information is barely indicative. Orleans (1969b) offers a "surmise" that the birth-control program, "after many years of trying" (but interrupted periodically by policy reversals, one should note), has probably had some success. The population is more literate; the public-health system has expanded; there are suggestions that the IUD (rather than tadpoles?) is becoming the dominant means. Only such a blatant propagandist as Han Suyin (*New York Times*, September 1, 1973) states categorically that the birth rate has fallen.

Internal Migration and Urban Growth

China is a vast land (Figure 17-3), but a large proportion of its 3.7 million square miles is economically useless and hardly habitable. About 60 percent of the

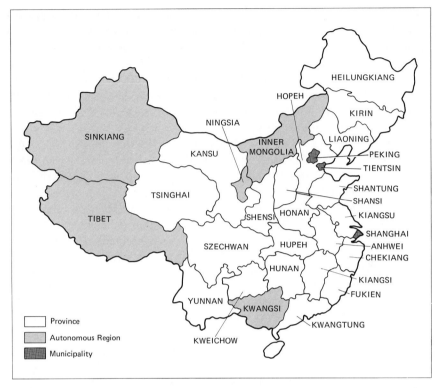

Figure 17-3.   Map of Communist China, Showing Provinces, Autonomous Regions, and Municipalities as of the Early 1970s

SOURCE: U.S. Central Intelligence Agency, *People's Republic of China: Atlas* (Washington, D.C.: U.S. Government Printing Office, 1971).

country is a mile or more above sea level, the greater part of the Tibetan high-lands more than two miles. "Over about eight-ninths of China, the terrain limits or completely excludes human endeavors" (Pearcy 1966). The present territory is the same as that traditionally known as Greater China, except that the former Outer Mongolia is now the People's Republic of Mongolia. Greater China comprised five major regions—China Proper, Manchuria, Mongolia, Sinkiang, and Tibet—and the main drift of migrations over all of history was from the periphery to the first of these, in the southeast corner. Beginning in the 17th century the Manchus raided China for laborers, who were used to develop their land; by 1850 Chinese colonization, first forced and later surreptitious, had virtually obliterated the indigenous culture of Manchuria, now China's north-east province.

The consequence of China's geography and migratory streams is a great concentration of population in the East and extremely low densities inland. A straight line drawn from Ai-hui on the border of Manchuria and Soviet

Siberia to T'eng-chung near the border of Burma divides the country into two unequal parts—to the east 40 percent of the land with 96 percent of the population in 1953 and to the west the remaining 4 percent scattered over 60 percent of the land (Orleans 1960). The densities in the settled areas are among the highest in the world. In 1967 the number of persons per square mile of cultivated land was about 1,100 in India, 1,400 in Pakistan, and 1,800 to 2,200 in China, depending on what assumptions are made concerning the size of China's population (Aird 1967b).

Until very recently geographers believed that China's interior was as empty of resources as of people. According to present estimates, "China is one of the richest coal nations in the world"; its iron ore totals between a conservative 12 billion and a probably too extravagant 100 billion tons; sizable deposits exist of other industrial metals and of petroleum (Pearcy 1966; cf. Wang 1967). Some of these finds were on the border of the settled area, others as far away as Urumchi, deep in the Asian heartland. Rail lines have been built to outlying areas, but a rail network exists only in the eastern region, and even there no highway system exists for fast vehicles. Travel that used to be reckoned in weeks or months sometimes can be completed now in days, or in hours if an airline has been established (Pearcy 1966).

Migration since 1949 has been on the same scale as the country's size and population. The millions moving or being moved in various directions can be classified into three main types:

1. The Soviet policy of fostering a population movement eastward into the Siberian steppes has had a Chinese counterpart. The exploitation of the new mineral discoveries; the construction of factories, transportation lines, cities, dams, and hydro-electric plants—all this demanded new reserves of labor. A program for the reclamation of wasteland was cast on even more ambitious dimensions. According to government estimates, the 1.6 billion mou (1 mou = 0.1647 acre) under cultivation, amounting to only slightly more than a tenth of China's total area, could be matched by another 1.5 billion mou of potentially arable land, almost a third of which was reported to be of good quality. During the First Five-Year Plan some 40 million mou were to be reclaimed; and if one assumes an average of 3 mou per settler, or slightly more than the average in China Proper, some 13 million persons could be established per 5-year period, or about one-fifth of the estimated natural increase (Tien 1964). Between 1953 and 1959 the estimated population of Urumchi (Sinkiang) increased from 140,700 to 700,000, that of Pao-t'ou (Inner Mongolia) from 149,000 to 800,000, that of Lan-chou (Kansu) from 397,400 to 1 million, that of Hsi-ning (Tsinghai) from 93,000 to 400,000; and many smaller towns grew at an even faster rate (Orleans 1972: 83).

2. Spontaneous migrations, what official reports term "blind" movements, continued the shift from west to east and especially from countryside to cities. If one postulates that the rural population of some 500 million increased at

2 percent per year and that only half of this increment left, the demand for new urban jobs and homes would be at the rate of 5 million annually. In fact, once collectivization got under way and hunger was reinforced by terror, in many areas the proportion fleeing the land was undoubtedly much greater. In the first years the regime exulted in the large rural–urban migration as a sign of industrial progress, but from 1952 on this was seen as excessive.

The ten most populous cities are all in the East, including several ports. With a comparable list for the United States, they were the following:

China, 1957 Estimate (–000,000)		United States, 1970 Census (–000,000)	
Shanghai	6.9	New York	7.9
Peking	4.0	Chicago	3.4
Tientsin	3.2	Los Angeles	2.8
Shen-yang (Mukden)	2.4	Philadelphia	1.9
Wu-han	2.1	Detroit	1.5
Ch'ung-ch'ing	2.1	Houston	1.2
Canton	1.8	Baltimore	0.9
Ha-erh-pin (Harbin)	1.6	Dallas	0.8
Lü-ta	1.5	Washington, D.C.	0.8
Nan-ching (Nanking)	1.4	Cleveland	0.8

3. The government not only restricted movement to cities but organized return migrations from the cities. The numbers involved, according to Aird's compilation of the few official data, were large but, considering the fact that many did not stay put, far too small to relieve urban population pressure or that on the densely settled agricultural land. By 1957, after 5 years of effort to control the movement, a survey of fifteen cities showed that 60 percent of their inhabitants were "nonproductive," that is, mostly in-migrants unable to find work. In that year the planned redistribution of population was extended to sectors of the established urban population. By a decentralization of government and Party offices, some 1.3 million administrative personnel were moved from urban centers in a single year, and many graduates of primary and middle schools were assigned to rural or frontier areas. When the Five-Year Plan ended in 1958, the official record showed an increase in urban population of 8 million, aggravated each year by a natural increment of some 2 million. During the Great Leap, the peasants being herded into communes fled when and where they could: over the 3 years, some 20 million additional in-migrants went to the cities or mining areas. The Leap failed not only in its central purpose but also in such corollary goals as preventing the unproductive growth of China's cities (Aird 1967b).

Each year during the late 1960s and early 1970s several million graduates of middle schools were sent off to work the land. In reporting a cut in this figure, the *New York Times* (November 26, 1972) headlined the story: "PEKING

The Cultural Revolution: Red Guards hold up their sayings of Mao (*PIX*).

REDUCING EXODUS TO FARMS, Only 400,000 Young People Sent from Cities in '72." It is a salutary reminder of the impact of the Chinese policies when a labor draft affecting 400,000 teen-agers is introduced by "only." According to various estimates, the total number rusticated from 1968 to 1973 ranged between more than 7 million (official statement) and 15 million (*New York Times*, November 7, 1973).

The so-called May 7th schools, set up following a directive in 1968 to train Party cadres, often have urban and rural sectors, and the schools have become an integral part of the whole administrative system. Every office sees up to a third of its employees disappear for three months to a year, shipped off to barren sites in the countryside to build themselves dormitories and to create farms out of sandy or water-logged soil.

The Chinese insist that there is no punitive element in the process; it is merely a way of converting age-old barriers between city and countryside and between mental and manual labor. Still, there was an ironic wink as the official from Peking's health and sanitation bureau was introduced in her new place of work—the pigsty [*Economist*, November 25, 1972].

Presumably this is the answer to the puzzle that the *Times* reporter posed: the reason for the apparent reduction in the exodus to the countryside was, in that striking phrase of David Rousset, the universalization of forced labor. The "educated youth," as they are designated, are hardly made welcome.

According to frank reports in the Chinese press, there is a systematic discrimination against the urbanites in pay, housing, and admission to the Communist Youth League, the *sine qua non* for any future advancement (*New York Times*, November 7, 1973).

A NOTE ON NAZI GERMANY

Nazi (that is, National Socialist) Germany lasted only a dozen years, from the taking of power in 1933 to the final defeat in 1945, and during half of that period the country was at war. In many cases, thus, totalitarian institutions either were never fully developed or were linked to the military machine. Some parallels with the Soviet Union or Communist China are nevertheless manifest— the ubiquitous control by the Party, the deaths imposed by the terror apparatus, the forced labor and forced migrations. Many of the data from Nazi Germany are far more accurate—though not, of course, the record of specifically totalitarian practices. The excellence of "normal" statistics, moreover, can be regarded as a probably temporary residue from the pre-Nazi period; if the regime had persisted long enough, its corrupting influence would undoubtedly have spread to economic and demographic records, for every administrator responsible for collecting, collating, and publishing data had to see that they reinforced the officially sponsored faith in the social system's superiority.

Two topics only are discussed here—the partial and preliminary attempts to make over the family, and the annihilation of Jews.

Like Soviet and Chinese officials, those in Nazi Germany tried to break down the family, and more than in the other two states they wanted to increase fertility. One avowed purpose of the Hitler Youth, for instance, was to reduce parental influence, whereas on the other hand such anti-feminist slogans as *Kinder, Kirche, Küche* (Children, Church, Kitchen) were given substance by decrees granting subsidies to parents of large families. One of Heinrich Himmler's titles was Reich Commissar for Strengthening German Folkdom. His main function, of course, was to head the *Schutzstaffel*, or SS ("Security Guard"), but in fact Himmler was more important than any formal designation would suggest: he was the main liaison between Party and State (cf. Hilberg 1967: 134). He and his assistants proposed a number of means of improving—from the Nazi point of view—Europe's racial composition (Koehl 1957). SS-men were given weekend leaves in order to impregnate women that the Party had selected for their racial characteristics, and this effort to bypass the family, though not successful, is important as an indication of the regime's intent. In the words of Martin Bormann, second only to Hitler in the Party structure, "After the war, those women who have lost husbands, or who do not get husbands, should enter a marriage-like relationship with preferably one man, from which should result as many children as possible." The stipulation "after the war" was made, of course, only to prevent a drastic decline in morale: if the plan had been made public at once, "not every soldier forthwith would desire that

in the event of his death his wife or his betrothed should beget children with another man" (Hale 1957). The whole of Bormann's memorandum is a fascinating
admixture of Nazi ideology, opportunist checks on its immediate application,
and such progressive ideas as, for instance, that the legal distinction between
legitimate and illegitimate births must be abolished.

The most notorious expression of the Nazis' demographic policies was their
campaign to exterminate the Jews. In what ways was this specific, in what ways
part of the general totalitarian pattern?

That anti-Semitism was not restricted to National Socialism everyone
knows,[18] and the conventional attacks on Jews, which in the 1920s the Party
had used to rouse revolutionary passions, were rationalized very soon after the
Nazis came to power. There were to be "no more beerhouse brawling and indiscriminate parading of uniforms and banners" (Reitlinger 1953: 7). As late
as 1938, Hermann Göring (Deputy to Hitler and Commander of the Air Force)
was protesting that random demonstrations against Jewish businessmen
"don't harm the Jew, but me, because I am responsible for the coordination
of the German economy" (Hilberg 1967: 26). Nazism was distinguished from
other versions of anti-Semitism, in short, by the Party's insistence that Jews
be degraded in an orderly fashion, and that this degradation be carried to the
"final solution" of organized mass murder.

The first step in this process was **to define** Jews.[19] In the Reichstag of the 1890s
the anti-Semitic faction had been unable to identify the group they wanted to
attack precisely enough to write discriminatory laws. The Nazis found a way
to link the long Christian tradition against Judaism with an attack on Jews who
had become irreligious or been converted to Christianity. By the original proposal, all persons with at least one (religiously) Jewish grandparent would
be categorized as a (racial) Jew. But this was not sufficient to draw a rigorous
line between "Aryan" and "non-Aryan."[20] Party experts and the Ministry of
the Interior disagreed on how to differentiate the two castes being established

[18] Hilberg (1967: chap. 1) gives in parallel columns items from the canon law of the
Catholic Church or from the secular laws of pre-Nazi Germany and those decreed under
Hitler. The overlap in many instances is startling.

[19] According to one school of thought this was not only unnecessary, but silly. Karl
Lueger, an anti-Semitic mayor of 19th-century Vienna, was famous for his aphorism,
"Wer Jude ist, bestimme ich!" (*I* decide who is a Jew). And later Himmler wrote to one of
his underlings, "Do not publish the decree defining Jews. Such foolish precision ties our
hands."

[20] In Sanskrit, *Aryan* meant "noble" or "a nobleman"; thus, like many of the locutions
that people use to designate themselves, it had overtones of greatness or superiority. Properly used, *Aryan* now refers to the Indo-European group of languages or to the language
from which they all hypothetically derived; but long before Hitler, many believed the racially
heterogeneous peoples who spoke these related languages to be biologically one. As the
great 19th-century linguist Max Müller put it, "To me an ethnologist who speaks of Aryan
race, Aryan blood, Aryan eyes and hair, is as great a sinner as a linguist who speaks of a
dolichocephalic dictionary or a brachycephalic grammar."

In Nazi-occupied Holland, Jews begin their journey to concentration camps, and beyond (*left*), and (*below*) slave laborers are gathered in the streets of Amsterdam (*Netherlands Government Information Bureau*).

(Hilberg 1967: 46), and the problem was not wholly solved by the Nuremberg decree that in 1935 set suitable relations between Jews and Gentiles. (1) Those Jewish by "race" but Christian by religion were repeatedly granted certain concessions; as one example out of many, when their deportation from Holland was postponed, some few were saved from destruction (ibid.: 375). (2) The "*Mischlinge,*" of part Jewish and part non-Jewish family background, were categorized by the proportion of Jewish "blood," their religion, the "race" of their spouse, etc. Still in 1941 the *Mischlinge* were "unfinished business." The Party wanted to exterminate them, the State ministries to sterilize them, and the civil service to leave them alone (ibid.: 269). In the Nazi-occupied countries with their own tradition of anti-Semitism, the confusion was compounded (e.g., on Hungary, ibid.: 513).

Until the outbreak of the war, the denigration of Jews was by legal or quasi-legal methods—ousting them from the civil service, professions, and business; subjecting them to special taxes, wage regulations, and rationing; fining them a billion marks to pay for the damage in anti-Semitic riots. All of these Hilberg classifies as the second stage—**expropriation.**

Various attempts were made to free Germany of Jews through forcible **emigration**—for example, by inducing Western powers to ransom Jews and to assist them to move to Madagascar or some other equivalent of Siberia. When this plan failed, "the most fanatical" of the racists, as Reitlinger terms Reinhardt Heydrich (Chief of the Reichssicherheitshauptamt, which controlled both the Criminal Police and the Secret State Police, or Gestapo), believed that small nations might be used as compulsory dumping grounds for German Jews, and this policy continued for the first year and a half of the war. Some thousands of Jews were bundled into freight trains and transported to Vichy France; many more were pushed into Poland, to join there the 2 million Jews who had fallen into the Gestapo's hands when the Nazi–Soviet Friendship Pact was signed. Subsequently thousands more were shipped still farther east, particularly to the area of Riga and Minsk.

Preparatory to these moves, both German and Polish Jews were **concentrated** into ghettos. In the fall of 1940 authorities closed off the Warsaw ghetto, for example; 360,000 Jews were congregated in an area that normally housed 160,000 people. It was left to the Jewish welfare organization to provide food, mainly a weak brew. "By the end of 1941 there were 100,000 people living on this soup, which had sometimes to be made of hay" (Reitlinger 1953: 58–59). The conditions were murderous, and many died. When the deaths in the Warsaw ghetto hovered around 5,000 per month, a government official reported laconically, "The first case of hunger-cannibalism was recorded" (Hilberg 1967: 172).

But was this mass murder in the full sense? "It does not seem," in Reitlinger's opinion (p. 59), "that at this period systematic extermination of the Jews was considered" (cf. Poliakov 1954: 2). Indeed, in 1939 two SS-men had been court-martialed for murdering fifty Jews and sentenced to 9 and 3 years of imprisonment, respectively (Reitlinger 1953: 33). Seemingly, the Nazis' *Endlösung*—final solution—of the Jewish problem meant total emigration until July 31, 1941. This was some six weeks after the Nazi invasion of the Soviet Union had started, and shortly before the United States and Japan entered the war. In brief, around the time that the European combat developed into World War II, "a new policy of annihilation was inaugurated" (Hilberg 1967: 262). However, in none of the subsequent voluminous correspondence directing the

Door to a gas chamber at the Dachau concentration camp. The words under the skull read: "Caution, gas. Mortal danger. Do not open." The sign above gives the time when the door may be safely opened again (*Documentation Française*).

slaughter was the policy openly stated. Killing centers were referred to collectively as "the East," individually as "labor camps," "concentration camps," "PW camps," even "transit camps"; killing was usually called by the same term used in the Soviet Union, "special treatment" (ibid.: 619). In the West these efforts to conceal the operation were aided by the fact that rumors about killing centers were mixed with false statements borrowed from propaganda that the Allies had used against Germany in World War I, for instance, that humans were boiled down to make soap (ibid.: 624).

As the German armies moved east into Russia, they were followed by four *Einsatzgruppen*, or Action Groups, which operated in the field. Action Group A was assigned to the Baltic countries, up to the outskirts of Leningrad; Action Group B to the area of White Russia between Warsaw and Moscow; Action Group C to the major portion of the Ukraine, including Kiev and Kharkov; and Action Group D to the Crimea and the Caucasus. Their function was to check the conduct of German military commanders, and to supervise the murder of Jews, Gypsies, and Communist commissars.

Basically, the procedure of "Resettlement" was the same everywhere. Jews who could produce no sort of protection certificate were collected in market places or large buildings, herded into trains, buses, lorries, or sledge carts and taken to the woods or moors, where the burial pits had been prepared. . . . A Semitic appearance or a neighborly denunciation was enough. Thus numerous Tatars, Gypsies, and people of Oriental appearance were often included [Reitlinger 1953: 203–204].

The main death camp was 4 kilometers from Auschwitz (in Polish, Oświęcim), a small town in Upper Silesia. It was adjacent to several rail lines, close to forced-labor camps, and yet in a relatively isolated site. Its director, Rudolf Höss, a former convict, told the Allied judges at the Nuremberg trial that under his administration 2.5 million persons were killed at the camp. According to the estimates of both Hilberg and Reitlinger, the actual total of those killed was about a million. It is significant that Höss, the ambitious Nazi bureaucrat, chose a higher figure. His SS service file commended him as "a true pioneer in this field." At the railroad siding, two SS-physicians divided newcomers between able-bodied workers and victims by pointing their canes right or left. Their rule of thumb depended mostly on age and sex, and the percentage denoted

British troops clearing the Belsen concentration camp (*Imperial War Museum, London*).

fit for labor varied greatly from one shipment to another. Höss used hydrogen cyanide crystals for killing his charges, rather than the less efficient carbon monoxide from internal-combustion engines. He initiated a routine deception that saved time and trouble: candidates for gassing were informed that they were to take a shower, so that they undressed themselves and walked into the gas chamber. The conditions of the forced laborers at Auschwitz, on the other hand, were no different from those in other Nazi camps.

How many Jews *did* the Nazis kill? In the Nuremberg indictment in 1945 the figure 5,721,800 was given, and in most subsequent accounts this has been rounded up to 6 million. This total was derived by subtracting the number of survivors from the prewar Jewish population, which for many countries is highly conjectural. The difficulty in establishing a more precise figure derives not only from the paucity of accurate data but from the ambiguity of the question. As we have noted, the delimitation of "Jews" caused the German authorities almost as much trouble as that of "kulaks" or "saboteurs" to the Soviet officials. And what is meant by "kill"? At Theresienstadt, the relatively indulgent concentration camp set up especially for the elderly and for severely wounded war veterans, a quarter of the inmates (about 33,000 out of 140,000) died from the conditions they were subjected to (Hilberg 1967: 283). More generally, "that prisoners should be cheated of their food and forced to 'organize' in order to live, that they should be beaten to death at their work in order to give their guards exercise, that they should drop from exhaustion at evening *Appell* because of the inability of these guards to count, were inevitable things, given the nature of their masters" (Reitlinger 1953: 121). The process of destruction in the labor camps and ghettos differed from that in the killing centers, but genocide, as defined by the United Nations, includes both. If we are to use the term at all precisely, we cannot define it broadly with respect to Nazi operations but narrowly with respect to counterparts in other totalitarian states.

From SS records, which he believes are fairly accurate and err, if at all, in exaggerating the extraordinary mortality, Reitlinger estimated the total number of Jews killed between 4,194,200 and 4,581,200 (p. 501). More than a third of the missing European Jews, and of German Jews perhaps as many as four-fifths, died from overwork, disease, hunger, and neglect. Two-thirds, or roughly 3 million, were exterminated directly. Hilberg also gives 3 million as the number annihilated in the killing centers, and to this he adds 1.4 million persons by the operations of the *Einsatzgruppen* (900,000 authenticated plus a more approximate 500,000 not tabulated) and 700,000 "aggravated deaths" in ghettos and elsewhere. His total, thus, is 5.1 million. Even these figures, monstrous as they are, understate the number of Nazi victims, as both pertain only to Jews, who constituted the major component. The total is considerably larger, for it includes also other "inferior" "races" (Gypsies, Slavs, Soviet ethnic minorities), political opponents (democrats, socialists, Catholics, Communists), and bystanders.

SUMMARY

Ever since Yugoslavia broke with Moscow in 1948, more and more of the conflicts within the Communist world, which Stalin half-succeeded in suppressing or at least hiding, have come out into the open. Western observers, many of whom once overstressed the oneness of the Communist "monolith," have sometimes swung over to an exaggeration of the multiplicity of Communism. To insist on the fact that there are important differences between the Soviet Union and China, or between East Germany and Rumania, or between all of them and Nazi Germany, should not mean that we overlook the common characteristics that distinguish these societies from all others. Even between Nazism and Communism, distinct species of the totalitarian genus, the differences are less striking than the parallels.

With respect specifically to population, we have noted similarities in family and migration policies and practices. But the key point is mortality, the demographic feature that most clearly distinguishes totalitarianism. Just as the death rates of the great civilizations of Asia contained, in Mallory's words, "a constant famine factor," so the vital statistics of totalitarian states include a constant terror factor. For not only has the population been depleted periodically by mass purges, but these have a marked effect on the age structure and sex ratio, and thus on the birth and death rates during the whole of the subsequent generation. Causes of death have included not only diseases, accidents, and old age, but also war and civil war, purges, forced labor, and man-made famines. These are not accidental features but reflect the essence of totalitarian systems, the "constant balance between oppression and relaxation" (Brzezinski 1956: 168).

The total population deficit up to 1959 from both extraordinary deaths and nonbirths is of the order of 80 million or more in the Soviet Union: 25 million during the taking of power and the wrecking of the capitalist economy; another 10 million during the collectivization, denomadization, purge of the Party, and russification of the 1930s; and 45 million during World War II and its aftermath. In this category political rather than economic or social factors have dominated.

These depletions in the population have not been randomly distributed in any sense. The totalitarian system has been a decisive factor in determining the population composition by nationality, by religion, by social class, by rural or urban residence. Among cohorts aged 32 and over in 1959, there were only six males to every ten females, and the consequences for postwar marital and fertility patterns hardly need to be specified. Efforts to encourage a high birth rate, though they undoubtedly have had some influence, have not been successful. One reason is the Party's initial hostility to the family, but more important is the fact, as Martin Bormann put it concerning Nazi Germany, that the Party "cannot order the women and girls to beget children." The effort to increase family size was frustrated also by the necessity of bringing as many females as possible into the Soviet labor force. Males had been killed off in monstrous numbers, and the new cohorts that were to replace them were initially extremely small. In 1955, by Eason's estimate, more than half of the labor force was female, and more than two-thirds of women aged 16 and over were gainfully employed. But in the 1960s, when the larger cohorts born in the postwar years began to seek jobs, the economy suffered from what is esoterically termed a relative surplus population—or, more prosaically, mass unemployment. In the 1970s and especially, by projection, the 1980s, the problem again is the shortage of labor; the population crisis on which Soviet officialdom has concentrated is how, without undue sacrifice of other goals, to raise the birth rate and produce a sufficiency of workers in the next generation.

In short, the population trends of a totalitarian state, like all other social phenomena, are shaped by the Party's drive for total power. The word *shaped* is used advisedly: most social events are in response to policy decisions, but not necessarily the response that the Party planned. Yet the terror has also been functional, as some sociologists would say, in maintaining the regime, and not merely in the obvious sense that actual or potential oppositionists were obliterated. If we accept an estimate of 50 million as the total of more or less forced out-migration plus the extraordinary mortality in the rural sector during the Soviet Union's mass collectivization of agriculture, what effect did this have on the economy?

With 50 (or 40, or 30) million more people in the villages after the war, could the rate of extraction of agricultural "surplus" have been as high as it was? If not: Could recovery in urban living standards from the postwar low in 1946 have been as fast as it was? Could there have been as large an urban population, and hence as rapid reconstruction and further economic growth, as there was in the late 1940s and the 1950s? ...

If both the total and the rural population of the USSR were now, say, 50 million larger than they are, the urban population would comprise not about 45 percent of the total population as it does [48 percent in the 1959 census], but about 35 percent [Grossman, 1958].

The period since the mid-1950s constitutes a new era in the Soviet Union, but the new was linked to the old by the continuity of the country's institutions. Should one stress that the forced-labor population is much smaller than at its postwar peak—or that forced labor continues as one element of the economic–punitive system; that the Chechen and Ingush have been permitted to return to their homelands—or that the Volga Germans and Crimean Tatars have not; that the rule of the Party is less harsh—or that it remains the implacable rule of a tiny minority? Since the early 1920s Western statesmen, experts, and intellectuals have seen each turn in Soviet policy as a mellowing, and their prognoses were usually wrong (cf. Wolfe 1963). In a demographic analysis, moreover, the continuity is inescapable: even if Stalin had been succeeded by a democrat, the trends in the economy and the society would still have been determined in part by the gaps he had made in the population.

The differences and parallels between the extraordinary mortality under Nazi and Communist auspices can be summed up as follows:

1. The Nazis lost the war. Their own statements, their own records, were used to make a legal case against them at Nuremberg. Otherwise we would have had to depend mainly on the testimony of former camp inmates, the often biased source on which we must rely for much of our information about labor camps in Communist countries. Until almost the end of the war, a false death certificate was in principle prepared for each person the Nazis exterminated, and this fabrication might have withstood any but minute scrutiny. For even when the evidence became overwhelming, the ordinary man in the West found it difficult to believe that death-camps were part of the world he thought he knew.

2. The Nazi ideology was *racist*; the Communists oppose *class* enemies.[21] The difference is important but not fundamental, for a person is no more responsible for his "class origin" than for his blood type. Moreover, terror generates a momentum of its own. Both the Nazis and the Communists have used hardened criminals under the supervision of self-hardened zealots, and under these circumstances the careful discrimination between the "guilty"— however defined—and the innocent is impossible. The slaughter begins in different sectors of the population and is concentrated there, but in both cases spreads to the whole society.

3. The Soviet terror is more rational, or less rational, than the Nazi. Both points have been made by various writers, and both have an element of truth. The Soviet regime never erected gas chambers and crematoriums, but it has not hesitated to exterminate large numbers of persons by other means. The massacre of some 14,000 Polish army officers in Katyn Woods is a well known example (see Rozek 1958: chaps. 4–5). Moreover, large areas of the Soviet Union constitute, under the conditions of life imposed on camp dwellers, natural killing centers. Forced labor was apparently more important in Soviet than in Nazi camps (Reitlinger 1953: 115). The Soviet rationalization of forced labor is that it "reforges" the criminals, whereas the dominant purpose of Nazi camps was to punish. Nazi prisoners were poorly fed, but until shortages developed throughout Germany, probably the food was better than in Soviet camps, where differential hunger was used as a spur to harder work. A number of persons, in particular Margarete Buber (1949), survived both Nazi and Soviet

---

[21] However, the tendency toward xenophobia in the Marxist tradition is greater than most persons realize. Frederick Engels wrote two pamphlets on the national question so devoid of what is ordinarily taken to be socialist feeling that many believed they had been composed by a Prussian general; and Marx, his good friend and collaborator, wrote to congratulate him on his "exceedingly clever" analysis. The key point was to classify European nationalities into two types—one, Germany, Poland, and Hungary, which are destined to triumph, and the other comprising "ruins of peoples, leftovers . . . subject to the nation which had become the bearer of historical development" (see Wolfe 1965: chap. 2). The Russian nationalism of Soviet Communism and the Han nationalism of Chinese derive from one important element of the Marxist tradition.

camps and have written interesting comparative reports. Mrs. Buber, a German oppositionist Communist, was arrested in Moscow in 1938 and sent to Siberia. During the Nazi–Soviet Friendship Pact, she and a number of other former German Communists were handed over to the Gestapo, and she spent another period in the Ravensbrück camp.

How Chinese forced labor compares with its two counterparts we do not know in detail. At least in intention, as manifested during the Great Leap Forward, China goes beyond the prior dimensions of terror, with forced labor generalized to virtually the whole of the population. Especially in China the manic–depressive cycle has constituted the opposite of rational planning: what is accomplished in one phase is ruthlessly destroyed in the next.

Totalitarian ideology is based on what in German is called a *Stufenlehre*, a doctrine of stages. All analysis, all planning, begins not from the empirical present but from the inevitable, perfect future. This last stage in mankind's forward development is typically not clearly depicted, except that it is homogenized into a "classless" (or *Judenfrei*, "Jewless") sameness, with rural–urban and other structural distinctions reduced to the minimum. The road to this inescapable paradise is clearly seen only by the Party, whose function it is to move the rest of the population toward its destiny. The drive for industrialization, as Barrington Moore (1954: 71) remarked of the Soviet Union, thus "comes almost wholly from the top," which must substitute its impetus for "the adventurous spirit that has built the great industrial and financial empires of the Western world." A built-in stagnation lies just beneath the surface, and whenever the elite's drive is slackened, the apathy of the population becomes apparent. In all totalitarian countries the problem of squaring military–economic advance with political cohesion continually invites a terrorist solution, and this generic feature overrides the specifics of this or that example.

The final difference between Communism and Nazism is the picture that Western democrats have of them. Indeed, all of the terms to designate the horrors of the 20th century—*totalitarianism, genocide*, and so on—have been vulgarized and lost some of their initial impact. *Communist* and *fascist*, similarly, have been used as mere epithets to designate one's political opponents. But Western scholars and academics, most of whom are left of center, view Nazism with total loathing but Communism, in many instances, as an aberrant version of their own political belief. The designations *Right* and *Left*, used originally to indicate the seating pattern of 19th-century parliaments, have been dragged into another era in order to characterize Communism and fascism as polar opposites. They are based, it is said, on the support of different social classes. Too often one forgets that the NSDAP, the National Socialist German Workers Party, had distinct elements of socialism and laborism (see Kele 1972) as well as German nationalism, or that the socialist ideology of Communism was similarly amalgamated with Russian (or Chinese, or whatever) nationalist fervor. Workers have fared equally ill under either type of regime. The confusion is crucial, for it blurs the genuine distinction of 20th-century politics, between totalitarianism and democracy.

CITED REFERENCES AND
SUGGESTIONS FOR FURTHER READINGS

Elsewhere I have collaborated with a political scientist in compiling a general bibliography on Communism (Petersen and Zinner 1963), and some of the works listed there are still worthy of study. The Soviet and Nazi terror machines have been analyzed with superb scholarship by, respectively, Conquest (1971) and Hilberg (1967), but there is not yet any general work on China. Lorimer's excellent analysis (1946) is the standard work on the Soviet population up to World War II; it has no counterpart for the most recent period, but the detailed paper by Leedy (1973) comes closest to full coverage. For lack of data, most of the papers and even books on China's population concern policy rather than trends; the one important exception is Orleans's effort (1972) to break through the barrier of poor statistics. The enormous literature on various elements of these populations is well represented in this list, and the marked items indicate the best route to a deeper understanding.

AIRD, JOHN S. 1960. "The Present and Prospective Population of Mainland China," in Milbank Memorial Fund 1960.
———. 1962. "Population Policy in Mainland China," *Population Studies*, **16**, 38–57.
———. 1967a. "Estimating China's Population," *Annals of the American Academy of Political and Social Science*, **369**, 61–72.
*———. 1967b. "Population Growth and Distribution in Mainland China," in U.S. Congress 1967.
ALTSCHULER, MORDECHAI. 1973. "Some Statistical Data on the Jews among the Scientific Elite of the Soviet Union," *Jewish Journal of Sociology*, **15**, 45–55.
AMMENDE, EWALD. 1936. *Human Life in Russia*. London: Allen & Unwin.
ANDRONOV, L. 1966. "China This Autumn," *New Times* (Moscow), November 30 and December 14.
ARAB-OGLY, E. 1966. "Scientific Calculation or Reliance on Spontaneity?" *Literaturnaya Gazeta*, June 11, translated in *Atlas*, September, pp. 24–26.
ARMSTRONG, TERENCE. 1968. "The Soviet North," *Survey*, no. 67, pp. 116–121.
*ASHBROOK, ARTHUR G., JR. 1967. "Main Lines of Communist Economic Policy," in U.S. Congress 1967.
BARCLAY, GEORGE W. 1950. "China's Population Problem: A Closer View," *Pacific Affairs*, **23**, 184–192.
BARGHOORN, FREDERICK C. 1956. *Soviet Russian Nationalism*. New York: Oxford University Press.
BAYKOV, ALEXANDER. 1946. *The Development of the Soviet Economic System*. Cambridge, England: Cambridge University Press.
BEERMANN, R. 1961. "The Parasites Law," *Soviet Studies*, **13**, 191–205.
BIALER, SEWERYN. 1964. "How Russians Rule Russia," *Problems of Communism*, **13** (September–October), 45–52.
B[IRABEN], J[EAN-] N[OEL]. 1960. "La structure par âge de la population de l'U.R.S.S.," *Population*, **15**, 894–898.

BRACKETT, JAMES W. 1962. "Demographic Trends and Population Policy in the Soviet Union," in U.S. Congress, Joint Economic Committee, *Dimensions of Soviet Economic Power*, Part VII. Washington, D.C.

*_____. 1968. "The Evolution of Marxist Theories on Population: Marxism Recognizes the Population Problem," *Demography*, **5**, 158–173.

_____, and JOHN W. DePAUW. 1966. "Population Policy and Demographic Trends in the Soviet Union," in U.S. Congress 1966.

BRONSON, DAVID W., and BARBARA S. SEVERIN. 1973. "Soviet Consumer Welfare: The Brezhnev Era," in U.S. Congress 1973.

BRZEZINSKI, ZBIGNIEW K. 1956. *The Permanent Purge: Politics in Soviet Totalitarianism*. Cambridge, Mass.: Harvard University Press.

BUBER, MARGARETE. 1949. *Under Two Dictators*. London: Gollancz.

BUCK, JOHN LOSSING. 1966. "Food Grain Production in Mainland China Before and During the Communist Regime," in Buck, Owen L. Dawson, and Yuan-li Wu, *Food and Agriculture in Communist China*. Hoover Institution on War, Revolution, and Peace. New York: Praeger.

*CHAMBERLIN, WILLIAM HENRY. 1934. *Russia's Iron Age*. Boston: Little, Brown.

*_____. 1965. *The Russian Revolution, 1917–1921*, 2 vol. New York: Grosset & Dunlap.

CHANDRASEKHAR, S. 1959a. *China's Population: Census and Vital Statistics*. Hong Kong: Hong Kong University Press.

_____. 1959b. "China's Population Problems: A Report," *Population Review*, **3**, 17–38.

CHANG CHIH-YI. 1949. "China's Population Problem—A Chinese View," *Pacific Affairs*, **22**, 339–356.

CHAPMAN, JANET. 1964. "The Minimum Wage in the USSR," *Problems of Communism*, **13** (September–October), 76–79.

CHEN NAI-RUENN. 1967. *Chinese Economic Statistics: A Handbook for Mainland China*. Chicago: Aldine.

CHEN PI-CHAO. 1970. "China's Birth Control Action Programme, 1956–1964," *Population Studies*, **24**, 141–158.

CH'EN TA. 1958. "New China's Population Census of 1953 and Its Relations to National Reconstruction and Demographic Research," *Bulletin de l'Institut International de Statistique*, **36**, 255–271.

*CONQUEST, ROBERT. 1960. *The Soviet Deportation of Nationalities*. London: Macmillan.

_____. 1971. *The Great Terror: Stalin's Purge of the Thirties*. Harmondsworth, England: Penguin Books.

DAVIDOFF, GEORGES. 1957. "De la médecine et de la sécurité sociale en Chine," *Population*, **12**, 679–694.

*DECTER, MOSHE. 1963. "The Status of the Jews in the Soviet Union," *Foreign Affairs*, **41**, 420–430.

_____, editor. 1967. *Israel and the Jews in the Soviet Mirror: Soviet Cartoons on the Middle East Crisis*. New York: Conference on the Status of Soviet Jews.

DURDIN, PEGGY. 1960. "Medicine in China: A Revealing Story," *New York Times Magazine*, February 28.

EASON, WARREN W. 1959. "The Soviet Population Today: An Analysis of the First Results of the 1959 Census," *Foreign Affairs*, **37**, 598–606.

EASON, WARREN. 1973. "The Soviet Population Crisis." Paper presented at a symposium on The Soviet Population Crisis, Ohio State University.

FESHBACH, MURRAY. 1972. "Observations on the Soviet Census," in William Petersen, editor, *Readings in Population*. New York: Macmillan.

FIELD, ALICE W. 1932. *Protection of Women and Children in Soviet Russia*. New York: Dutton.

*FIELD, MARK G. 1957. *Doctor and Patient in Soviet Russia*. Cambridge, Mass.: Harvard University Press.

————. 1966. "Health Personnel in the Soviet Union: Achievements and Problems," *American Journal of Public Health*, **56**, 1904–1920.

FISHER, H. H. 1927. *The Famine in Soviet Russia, 1919–1923*. New York: Macmillan.

FRIEDBERG, MAURICE. 1970. "The Plight of Soviet Jews," *Problems of Communism*, **19** (November–December), 17–26.

*GALENSON, WALTER. 1967. "The Current State of Chinese Economic Studies," in U.S. Congress 1967.

GEIGER, H. JACK. 1973. "Putting China's Medicine in Perspective," *Medical World News*, **14** (May), 43–49; (June), 22–28.

GERSTENMAIER, CORNELIA. 1970. "The Jews as a Religious Minority," in Michael Bourdeaux, editor, *Religious Minorities in the Soviet Union (1960–70)*, London: Minority Rights Group.

GORDON, MYRON K. 1957. "Notes on Recent Soviet Population Statistics and Research," *Population Index*, **23**, 2–16.

*GROSSMAN, GREGORY. 1958. "Thirty Years of Soviet Industrialization," *Soviet Survey*, no. 26, 15–21.

————. 1971. "From the Eighth to the Ninth Five-Year Plan," in Norton T. Dodge, editor, *Analysis of the USSR's 24th Party Congress and 9th Five-Year Plan*. Mechanicsville, Md.: Cremona Foundation.

GSOVSKI, VLADIMIR. 1959. "The Soviet Union's Revised Criminal Code," *New Leader*, April 27, pp. 10–13.

HALE, ORON J. 1957. "Adolf Hitler and the Post-War German Birthrate: An Unpublished Memorandum," *Journal of Central European Affairs*, **17**, 166–173.

HALLE, FANNINA W. 1934. *Woman in Soviet Russia*. London: Routledge.

*HEER, DAVID M. 1965. "Abortion, Contraception, and Population Policy in the Soviet Union," *Demography*, **2**, 531–539.

————. 1968. "The Demographic Transition in the Russian Empire and the Soviet Union," *Journal of Social History*, **1**, 193–240.

*————. 1972. "Recent Developments in Soviet Population Policy," *Studies in Family Planning*, **3**, 257–264.

————, and JUDITH G. BRYDEN. 1966. "Family Allowances and Fertility in the Soviet Union," *Soviet Studies*, **18**, 152–163.

*HILBERG, RAUL. 1967. *The Destruction of the European Jews*. Chicago: Quadrangle Paperbacks.

HINDUS, MAURICE. 1949. "The Family in Russia," in Ruth Nanda Anshen, editor, *The Family: Its Function and Destiny*. New York: Harper.

HOLUBNYCHY, VSEVOLOD. 1958. "Organization of Statistical Observation in the U.S.S.R.," *American Statistician*, **12**, 13–17.

JASNY, NAUM. 1957. *The Soviet 1956 Statistical Handbook: A Commentary*. East Lansing: Michigan State University Press.

JONES, EDWIN F. 1967. "The Emerging Pattern of China's Economic Revolution," in U.S. Congress 1967.

KELE, MAX H. 1972. *Nazis and Workers: National Socialist Appeals to German Labor, 1919–1933*. Chapel Hill: University of North Carolina Press.

KHALATBARI, PARVIZ. 1971. "Zu einigen Grundfragen der Marxistisch-Leninistischen Demographie," *Jahrbuch für Wirtschaftsgeschichte*, Part 2, pp. 245–253.

*KHRUSHCHEV, NIKITA S. 1956. "The Crimes of the Stalin Era: Special Report to the 20th Congress of the Communist Party of the Soviet Union, Closed Session, February 24–25, 1956," *New Leader*, Section 2, July 16.

KIRBY, E. STUART. 1958. "Peiping's Growing Dilemma—Population," *Problems of Communism*, 7 (March–April), 36–41.

KOEHL, ROBERT L. 1957. *RKFDV: German Resettlement and Population Policy, 1939–1945*. Cambridge, Mass.: Harvard University Press.

*KOLARZ, WALTER. 1955. *Russia and Her Colonies*, 3rd ed. New York: Praeger.

KRAAR, LOUIS. 1972. "I Have Seen China—and They Work," *Fortune* (August), pp. 111 ff.

KRADER, LAWRENCE, and JOHN AIRD. 1959. "Sources of Demographic Data on Mainland China," *American Sociological Review*, 24, 623–630.

KUCERA, JINDRICH. 1954. "Soviet Nationality Policy: The Linguistic Controversy," *Problems of Communism*, 3 (March–April), 24–29.

KULISCHER, EUGENE M., and MICHAEL K. ROOF. 1956. "A New Look at the Soviet Population Structure of 1939," *American Sociological Review*, 21, 280–290.

LAIRD, ROY D. 1971. "Prospects for Soviet Agriculture," *Problems of Communism*, 20 (September–October), 31–40.

*LAMPTON, DAVID M. 1972. "Public Health and Politics in China's Past Two Decades," *Health Services Reports*, 87, 895–904.

LARSEN, MARION R. 1967. "China's Agriculture Under Communism," in U.S. Congress 1967.

*LEEDY, FREDERICK A. 1973. "Demographic Trends in the U.S.S.R.," in U.S. Congress 1973.

LENNON, LOTTA. 1971. "Women in the USSR," *Problems of Communism*, 20 (July–August), 47–58.

LI CHOH-MING. 1960. "Economic Development," *China Quarterly*, no. 1, pp. 35–50.

LINDSAY, MICHAEL. 1960. "Agrarian Policy and Communist Motivation," *China Quarterly*, no. 1, pp. 15–17.

*LORIMER, FRANK. 1946. *The Population of the Soviet Union: History and Prospects*. League of Nations. Princeton, N.J.: Princeton University Press.

MARTSCHENKO, BASILIUS. 1953. "Soviet Population Trends, 1926–1939" (in Russian with an English summary). New York: Research Program on the USSR.

MARX, KARL. 1906. *Capital*, 2 vol. Chicago: Kerr.

MAZUR, D. PETER. 1967. "Fertility Among Ethnic Groups in the USSR," *Demography*, 4, 172–195.

MEIJER, M. J. 1971. *Marriage Law and Policy in the Chinese People's Republic*. Hong Kong: Hong Kong University Press.

MEYER, HERBERT E. 1973. "Why the Russians Are Shopping in the U.S.," *Fortune* (February), pp. 66 ff.

MILBANK MEMORIAL FUND. 1960. *Population Trends in Eastern Europe, the USSR and Mainland China*. New York.

MINC, BRONISLAW. 1955. Statement for the Soviet delegation to the Rome population congress. U.N. Population Commission, "World Population Conference," E/CN.9/115, pp. 33–34. New York.

*MONKHOUSE, ALLAN. 1934. *Moscow, 1911–1933*. Boston: Little, Brown.

MOORE, BARRINGTON, JR. 1954. *Terror and Progress—U.S.S.R.* Cambridge, Mass.: Harvard University Press.

MORSE, WILLIAM R. 1934. *Chinese Medicine*. New York: Hoeber.

MYERS, ROBERT J. 1964. "Analysis of Mortality in the Soviet Union According to 1958–59 Life Tables," *Transactions of the Society of Actuaries*, **16**, 309–317.

NASH, EDMUND. 1966. "Recent Changes in Labor Controls in the Soviet Union," in U.S. Congress 1966.

*ORLEANS, LEO A. 1960. "Population Redistribution in Communist China," in Milbank Memorial Fund 1960.

———. 1965. "Population Statistics: An Illusion," *China Quarterly*, no. 21, pp. 168–178.

———. 1969a. "Medical Education and Manpower in Communist China," *Comparative Education Review*, **13**, 20–42.

———. 1969b. "Evidence from Chinese Medical Journals on Current Population Policy," *China Quarterly*, no. 40, pp. 137–146.

*———. 1972. *Every Fifth Child: The Population of China*. Stanford, Calif,: Stanford University Press.

*PEARCY, G. ETZEL. 1966. "Mainland China: Geographic Strengths and Weaknesses," *U.S. Department of State Bulletin*, **55**, 294–303.

PEREVEDENTSEV, V. 1967. "Controversy about the Census," *Literaturnaya Gazeta*, January 11; translated in *Current Digest of the Soviet Press*, **19** (February 1), 15–16.

———. 1972. "New Demographic Literature," *Problems of Economics*, **14**, 69–86.

PETERSEN, WILLIAM. 1970. *The Politics of Population*. Gloucester, Mass.: Peter Smith.

———, and PAUL E. ZINNER. 1963. "World Communism: A Reading List for Nonspecialists," in William Petersen, editor, *The Realities of World Communism*. Englewood Cliffs, N.J.: Prentice-Hall.

*PIPES, RICHARD. 1964. *The Formation of the Soviet Union: Communism and Nationalism, 1917–1923*, rev. ed. Cambridge, Mass.: Harvard University Press.

POLIAKOV, LÉON. 1954. *Harvest of Hate: The Nazi Program for the Destruction of the Jews of Europe*. Syracuse, N.Y.: Syracuse University Press.

POPOV, A. Y. 1953. *Sovremennoe Mal'tusianstvo—Chelovekonenavistnichevskaya ideologiia imperialistov*. Moscow: Gosudarstvennoe Izdatel'stvo Politicheskoe Literatur.

PRESSAT, ROLAND. 1963a. "La natalité et la nuptialité en Union Soviétique," *Population*, **18**, 777–786.

———. 1963b. "Les premières tables de mortalité de l'Union Soviétique, 1958–1959," *Population*, **18**, 65–92.

RAVENHOLT, ALBERT. 1962. "The Human Price of China's Disastrous Food Shortage: A Refugee Doctor Describes His Patients," in American Universities Field Staff, *Reports*, East Asia Series, **10**, no. 4.

———. 1967. "The Red Guards," in American Universities Field Staff, *Reports*, East Asia Series, **14**, no. 3.

REDDAWAY, PETER, *et al.* 1973. "The Forced Labour Camps in the U.S.S.R. Today:

An Unrecognized Example of Modern Inhumanity" (mimeographed). Brussels: International Committee for the Defence of Human Rights in the U.S.S.R.

REITLINGER, GERALD. 1953. *The Final Solution: The Attempt to Exterminate the Jews of Europe, 1939–1945.* New York: Beechhurst.

RICH, STANLEY. 1959. "The Communes—Mao's 'Big Family,'" *Problems of Communism*, 8 (January–February), 1–5.

ROOF, MICHAEL F. 1957. "Supplementary Note Concerning the Soviet Population Structure of 1939," *American Sociological Review*, 22, 581–582.

*———. 1960. "Recent Trends in Soviet Internal Migration Policies," Research Group for European Migration Problems, *Bulletin*, 8, 1–18.

———, and FREDERICK A. LEEDY. 1959. "Population Redistribution in the Soviet Union, 1939–1956," *Geographical Review*, 49, 208–221.

*ROUSSET, DAVID. 1959. "The New Tyranny in the Countryside," *Problems of Communism*, 8 (January–February), 5–13.

ROZEK, EDWARD J. 1958. *Allied Wartime Diplomacy: A Pattern in Poland.* New York: Wiley.

RYABUSHKIN, T. 1955. "On the World Population Conferences" (translated in full from *Vestnik Statistiki*, no. 1, 1955), *Soviet Studies*, 7, 220–230.

SALAFF, JANET W. 1972. "Institutionalized Motivation for Fertility Limitation in China," *Population Studies*, 26, 233–262.

———. 1973. "Mortality Decline in the People's Republic of China and the United States," *Population Studies*, 27, 551–576.

SARKER, SUBHASH CHANDRA. 1958. "Population Planning in China," *Population Review*, 2, 49–58.

*SAUVY, ALFRED. 1948. "Doctrine soviétique en matière de population," *Rivista Italiana di Demografia e Statistica*, 2, 475–484.

———. 1952. *Théorie générale de la population*, 2 vol. Paris: Presses Universitaires de France.

SCHATTMAN, STEPHAN E. 1956. "Dogma vs. Science in Soviet Statistics," *Problems of Communism*, 5 (January–February), 30–36.

SCHLESINGER, RUDOLF. 1949. *Changing Attitudes in Soviet Russia: The Family in the U.S.S.R.* London: Routledge & Kegan Paul.

SCHWARZ, SOLOMON M. 1951. *The Jews in the Soviet Union.* Syracuse, N.Y.: Syracuse University Press.

SELEGEN, GALINA V., and VICTOR P. PETROV. 1959. "Soviet People Versus Population Census," *American Statistician*, 13, 14–15.

SHAFFER, HARRY G. 1963. "A New Incentive for Soviet Managers," *Russian Review*, 22, 410–416.

*SHEEHY, ANN. 1973. *The Crimean Tatars, Volga Germans and Meskhetians: Soviet Treatment of Some National Minorities*, 2nd ed. London: Minority Rights Group.

*SHIMKIN, DEMITRI B. 1960. "Demographic Changes and Socio-Economic Forces within the Soviet Union, 1939–59," in Milbank Memorial Fund 1960.

SMITH, JESSICA. 1928. *Woman in Soviet Russia.* New York: Vanguard.

STALIN, JOSEPH. 1942. *Leninism: Selected Writings.* New York: International Publishers.

STEINFELD, JESSE L., et al. 1972. *Medical Care in the USSR: Report of the U.S. Delegation on Health Care Services and Planning.* Washington, D.C.: U.S. Public Health Service.

*STRONG, ANNA LOUISE. 1931. *The Soviets Conquer Wheat: The Drama of Collective Farming.* New York: Holt.

STRUMILIN, STANISLAV G. 1961. "Nos ressources de main-d'oeuvre et les perspectives: Une étude d'un économiste soviétique en 1922," *Population*, 16, 249–258.

*SWIANIEWICZ, S. 1965. *Forced Labour and Economic Development: An Enquiry into the Experience of Soviet Industrialisation.* Royal Institute of International Affairs. London: Oxford University Press.

TAEUBER, IRENE B. 1956. "Population Policies in Communist China," *Population Index*, 22, 261–274.

TELLER, JUDD L. 1972. "Portrait of a Soviet Zionist," *Commentary* (July), pp. 56–61.

*TIEN, H. YUAN. 1963. "Birth Control in Mainland China: Ideology and Politics," *Milbank Memorial Fund Quarterly*, 41, 269–290.

———. 1964. "The Demographic Significance of Organized Population Transfers in Communist China," *Demography*, 1, 220–226.

———. 1970. "Marital Moratorium and Fertility Control in China," *Population Studies*, 24, 311–323.

———. 1972. *China's Population Struggle: Demographic Decisions of the People's Republic, 1949–1969.* Columbus: Ohio State University Press.

TIMASHEFF, NICHOLAS S. 1946. *The Great Retreat: The Growth and Decline of Communism in Russia.* New York: Dutton.

U.S. BUREAU OF THE CENSUS. 1961. "The Size, Composition, and Growth of the Population of Mainland China," *International Population Statistics Report*, Series P-90, no. 15. Washington, D.C.

*U.S. CONGRESS. JOINT ECONOMIC COMMITTEE. 1966. *New Directions in the Soviet Economy.* Part III: *The Human Resources.* 89th Congress, 2nd Session. Washington, D.C.

*———. ———. 1967. *An Economic Profile of Mainland China,* 2 vol. Washington, D.C.

*———. ———. 1973. *Soviet Economic Prospects for the Seventies.* 93d Congress, 1st Session. Washington, D.C.

VARDYS, V. STANLEY. 1965. "Soviet Nationality Policy Since the XXII Party Congress," *Russian Review*, 24, 323–340.

*VERNADSKY, GEORGE. 1961. *A History of Russia,* 5th rev. ed. New Haven, Conn.: Yale University Press.

WANG, K. P. 1967. "The Mineral Resource Base of Communist China," in U.S. Congress 1967.

WAYS, MAX. 1968. "The 'House of the Dead' Is Now the Liveliest Part of the U.S.S.R.," *Fortune* (August), pp. 112 ff.

WOLFE, BERTRAM D. 1963. "Communist Ideology and Soviet Foreign Policy," in William Petersen, editor, *The Realities of World Communism.* Englewood Cliffs, N.J.: Prentice-Hall.

*———. 1965. *Marxism: One Hundred Years in the Life of a Doctrine.* New York: Dial Press.

Index